STUDIES IN

CONTRACT LAW

SIXTH EDITION

by

RICHARD E. SPEIDEL
Beatrice Kuhn Professor of Law Emeritus,
Northwestern University School of Law; Distinguished Visiting Professor,
University of San Diego School of Law

IAN AYRES
William K. Townsend Professor of Law
Yale Law School

FOUNDATION PRESS

NEW YORK, NEW YORK

2003

Foundation Press, a division of West Group, has created this publication to provide you with accurate and authoritative information concerning the subject matter covered. However, this publication was not necessarily prepared by persons licensed to practice law in a particular jurisdiction. Foundation Press is not engaged in rendering legal or other professional advice, and this publication is not a substitute for the advice of an attorney. If you require legal or other expert advice, you should seek the services of a competent attorney or other professional.

 TEXT IS PRINTED ON 10% POST CONSUMER RECYCLED PAPER

To Elizabeth and Jennifer.

*

PREFACE

"Contract law has deep roots in the past, and much of its present structure is shaped by historical precedents. But as is true in all vital fields of law, familiar concepts are being reexamined and new patterns are emerging."

Thus began the preface to the first edition of *Studies in Contract Law* (1970). Over the intervening decades, through five additional editions, we have sought to chronicle these developments in a way that assists teacher and student in exploring this wonderful world of contract law.

For we remain convinced, as remarked in the preface to the third edition (1984), that contract law should continue to be the "centerpiece of the first-year law school curriculum."

The basic purpose, however, is to assist in the *study* of law. This involves not only familiarizing oneself with certain data, but reflecting upon that data in a way that helps to form a first-rate professional competence. A great legal scholar whom we quoted in previous editions, John Henry Wigmore, put it this way: "Every institute and principle of law has a philosophy—as every object in the sunlight has its attendant shadow. In the quest for the rule we must insist on including its reasons, and on lifting them out into the open."

RICHARD E. SPEIDEL
IAN AYRES

May, 2003

*

ACKNOWLEDGMENTS

The authors acknowledge, with gratitude, the kind permission to reprint copyrighted materials of the following authors and publishers: American Law Institute, Professor Ian Ayres; Professor Randy Barnett; Professor Jennifer Gerada Brown; Cambridge Law Review; Columbia Law Review; Cornell Law Review; Down Jones & Company, Inc.; Professor Melvin A. Eisenberg; Professor Daniel Fischel; Professor Eric Green; Iowa Law Review; Journal of Law and Commerce; Journal of Legal Education; Professor Lewis Kornhauser; Professor Charles L. Knapp; Professor Andrew Kull; Law Book Co. of Australasia Pty. Ltd.; Michigan Law Review; Minnesota Law Review; Fred B. Rothman & Co.; New York University Law Review; Northwestern University Law Review; Sir David Hughes Parry; Professor Walter F. Pratt, Jr.; Professor Richard E. Speidel; Professor Robert S. Summers; Professor G. H. Treitel; United Features Syndicate; Universal Press Syndicate; University of Chicago Law Review; University of Colorado Law Review; University of Southern California Law Review; South Carolina Law Review; Professor Lea S. VanderVelde; Wall Street Journal; West Publishing Company; Professor James J. White; William & Mary Law Review; Professor Glanville Williams; The Honourable Sir Victor Windeyer; Wisconsin Law Review; Yale Law Journal; Professor Eval Zamir.

Professor Speidel is indebted to Ms. Shirley Scott of Northwestern University School of Law and Ms. Justine Phillips of the University of San Diego School of Law for administrative support on the Sixth Edition. Sydney Foster, Kevin Reed, Nasser Zakariaya, and Yair Listokin provided research assistance to Professor Ayres. The authors also thank Professor Michael Asimow of U.C.L.A. for his helpful suggestions about the Fifth Edition, many of which are incorporated in the Sixth Edition.

*

SUMMARY OF CONTENTS

*

TABLE OF CONTENTS

TABLE OF CASES

Principal cases are in bold type. Non-principal cases are in roman type. References are to Pages.

TABLE OF UNIFORM COMMERCIAL CODE CODE CITATIONS

*

STUDIES IN

CONTRACT LAW

*

CHAPTER ONE

THE IMPORTANCE OF PROMISE

SECTION 1. INTRODUCTION

Contract as Binding Promise. This course of study will deal primarily with the legal implications of promise making. For every issue respecting the legal enforcement of a promise is broadly a contracts issue. An authoritative and acceptable working definition is that of Restatement (Second) of Contracts: "A contract is a promise or set of promises for the breach of which the law gives a remedy, or the performance of which the law in some way recognizes as a duty."[1]

The focus upon promise is useful, since a common element in all contracts is promise, defined in the first Restatement as "an undertaking, however expressed, either that something shall happen, or that something shall not happen, in the future."[2] Yet the result of a contract is the creation of a *legal relationship* involving rights and duties of persons.[3] Thus, it may be better to emphasize the result of the promise rather than the promise itself. To an extent the Uniform Commercial Code does this: " 'Contract' means the total legal obligation which results from the parties' agreement as affected by this Act and any other applicable rules of law."[4]

Contract law thus concerns the promises we make, and it takes but a moment's reflection to be impressed by the broad scope of the subject. Instances are legion in which we repose confidence in the promises of others. Limited to the commercial area alone, every employment agreement, sales contract, promissory note or check, rental or lease agreement,

---

1. Restatement (Second), Contracts § 1 (1981).

2. Restatement, Contracts § 2 (1932). "A promise is a manifestation of intention to act or refrain from acting in a specified way, so made as to justify a promisee in understanding that a commitment has been made," Restatement (Second), Contracts § 2.

3. A useful discussion of terms, emphasizing legal relations arising from contract and prior negotiations, is Goble, *A Redefinition of Basic Legal Terms,* 35 Colum.L.Rev. 535 (1935). See also Sharp, *Promissory Liability,* 7 U.Chi.L.Rev. 1 (1939).

4. Uniform Commercial Code § 1–201(11). [Rev. 1–201(12)] Similarly, in defining agreement as the "bargain of the parties in fact," UCC 1–201(3), [Rev. 1–201(3)] the UCC moves even farther away from promise as an indispensable foundation word. For example, the word "promise" is used several times in the UCC Article 2, Sales, see, e.g., UCC 2–206(1)(b), 2–210(4) and 2–313(1)(a), but defined only in Article 3, Commercial Paper, as "an undertaking to pay" and "more than an acknowledgment." UCC 13–102(1)(c). The definition of agreement as a "bargain" without defining the word "bargain," however, suggests that the ordinary usages of that term may be employed. In Restatement (Second) § 4, bargain is defined as "an agreement to exchange promises or to exchange a promise for a performance or to exchange performances."

and so on, embodies a promise or contractual undertaking. And lest one conclude too hastily that humankind is totally unregenerate consider that in the vast majority of these cases, people keep these promises. They do what they say they will do. Goods are ordered, delivered, and paid for. Work is performed; wages are paid. Funds are deposited and returned with interest. And so on, through a myriad of economic transactions.

Why Keep Promises? Why do people ordinarily fulfill their contractual obligations? Why the high rate of contract performance? No doubt the fear of legal sanction helps to deter breach. But the matter surely goes beyond mere fear of the law. Indeed, the fear of officially imposed sanction (e.g., a judgment for damages) may be a relatively minor deterrent in many situations. One thinks, for example, of the great Law Merchant tradition of the late medieval period, out of which much of our modern commercial law developed.[5] The merchants themselves administered a remarkably effective system which did not depend upon state enforcement mechanisms or procedures, but relied upon private sanctions such as refusal to deal or boycott.

Obviously, it is often in one's self-interest to keep promises. If one is to have credibility for the future, one must perform one's promises today. Finally, most people believe that promises ought to be kept because it is the right thing to do. It is a part of the way an honest person behaves.

It is not surprising that there emerged in our legal tradition the notion of "sanctity of contract." One writer summarized the prevalence of this attitude as follows:

> [Throughout the development of the English common law] the giving of a promise or the conclusion of an agreement involved a solemn undertaking the breach of which amounted in the eyes of the Church to a sin and in the eyes of the general body of contemporary lawyers to an immoral or unethical act. With the special emphasis placed by the nineteenth-century philosophers and jurists on the importance of freedom and the manifestation and extension of an individual's freedom through contract, it was not surprising that contracts developed a juristic blessedness or halo and were so often regarded as sacred.[6]

In contrast to this unqualified duty to perform, Oliver W. Holmes argued that "the duty to keep a contract at common law means a prediction that you must pay damages if you do not keep it—and nothing else."[7] For Holmes, a contractual promise was merely a promise to perform or pay damages.

Why Should Promises Be Legally Enforced? Although there is no record of a legal system that has undertaken to enforce all promises, there is yet to appear an organized society which has repudiated altogether the

---

5. See, generally, W. Mitchell, An Essay on the Early History of the Law Merchant (1904); L. Trakman, The Law Merchant: The Evolution of Commercial Law (1983).

6. D. Parry, The Sanctity of Contract 17–18 (1959).

7. Oliver W. Holmes, *The Path of the Law*, 10 Harv. L. Rev. 457, 462 (1897) (stating that "nowhere is the confusion between legal and moral ideas more manifest than in the law of contract").

concept of binding promise or contract. To be sure, criteria of enforcement have varied. Moreover, the sanction imposed for nonperformance has at times been merely social, or religious, rather than an official court command to perform the promise (specific performance) or a judgment awarding monetary damages. Still, the modern who insists "you gave me your word" or "a bargain's a bargain" is not advancing novel doctrine. The Roman Law maxim *pacta sunt servanda* (agreements are to be kept) reflects a characteristic human attitude.[8] In this respect, the ancient Code of Hammurabi, the celebrated Code of Justinian, and the contemporary Uniform Commercial Code are quite alike in fundamental orientation.[9]

The economic importance of promise making and promise keeping can hardly be exaggerated. Dean Roscoe Pound put it this way: "In a developed economic order the claim to promised advantages is one of the most important of the individual interests that press for recognition. * * * Credit is a principal form of wealth. It is a presupposition of the whole economic order that promises will be kept. Indeed, the matter goes deeper. The social order rests upon stability and predictability of conduct, of which keeping promises is a large item."[10]

With good reason, Sir Frederick Pollock, the English legal historian, could maintain: "Enforcement of good faith in matters of bargain and promise is among the most important functions of legal justice. It might not be too much to say that, next after keeping the peace and securing property against violence and fraud so that business may be possible, it is the most important."[11]

In his book *The Promises Men Live By,* Harry Scherman, an economist, makes this bold assertion: "I do not think there is any single fact more important for men to recognize, with all its implications, than this simple

8. See Wehberg, *Pacta Sunt Servanda,* 53 Am.J.Int'l L. 795 (1959). Professor Harry W. Jones has stressed "the deeply ingrained power that the idea of contract has had, throughout recorded history, on the minds of men and women; the centrality of contract as a basic institution of contemporary society; and the significance of freedom of contract as one of the great 'constitutional' devices for the dispersion of power in a society fearful, as ours has always and rightly been, of too much power in too few hands." Jones, *The Jurisprudence of Contracts,* 44 U.Cin.L.Rev. 43, 44 (1975).

9. See, generally, C. Fried, Contract as Promise: A Theory of Contractual Obligation (1981); Farnsworth, *The Past of Promise: An Historical Introduction to Contract,* 69 Colum.L.Rev. 576 (1969). Hannah Arendt has noted: "[T]he power of stabilization inherent in the faculty of making promises has been known throughout our tradition. We may

trace it back to the Roman legal system, the inviolability of agreements and treaties (*pacta sunt servanda*); or we may see its discoverer in Abraham, the man from Ur, whose whole story, as the Bible tells it, shows such a passionate drive toward making covenants that it is as though he departed from his country for no other reason than to try out the power of mutual promise in the wilderness of the world, until eventually God himself agreed to make a Covenant with him. At any rate, the great variety of contract theories since the Romans attests to the fact that the power of making promises has occupied the center of political thought over the centuries." H. Arendt, The Human Condition 243–44 (1958).

10. 3 Pound, Jurisprudence 162–63 (1959).

11. 7 Encyclopedia Britannica 35 (11th ed. 1910).

one—*that their individual well-being, as well as that of the whole society, is determined by the volume of exchanges going on in the whole society.*"[12]

The facilitation of economic exchange is a basic policy of commercial law in general and contract law in particular. Enforcing contracts facilitates trade by promoting present reliance on future promise. When the exchanged promises are to be performed at different times, legal enforcement can assure the person who has promised to perform first that she can rely on the subsequent performance by the other side to the agreement. By encouraging a high volume of private exchange and the economic growth and development that results therefrom, the law contributes to both the welfare of the individual participants and the nation as a whole. If legal impediments to voluntary exchange are kept to a minimum, the law plays a market-supporting role by providing a general framework within which private planners can rationally allocate resources. And this, it is believed, is an essential ingredient of a dynamic economic order.

Beyond Economics. One cannot gainsay the importance of freedom of contract to a market economy and the relative superiority of such a system to unproductive command economies which are, seemingly, in decline throughout the world today. But there are more than economic advantages; there are political advantages as well:

> Freedom of contract, together with the right to own property, were core elements in the American vision of personal liberty. * * * The American constitutional scheme places contract liberty well above common law status; it is a guaranteed personal right. Liberty of contract is recognized not as power delegated by the sovereign, but as power originating in and guaranteed to the people.[13]

Private contract is a powerful tool for diffusing power in a society, for dividing decision-making and opportunities between the state on the one hand and private persons on the other.[14] In a sense, contracting parties are lawmakers. By entering into a binding contract, they make law for themselves.[15] They incur obligations which are enforceable by public authority, the courts. As indicated, the amount of legal obligation of this type is staggering. Any analysis of the real government of the people must take note of this extensive network of contractual obligations.

But even as one acknowledges these enormous practical advantages, one feels the need to press beyond social considerations. The matter goes beyond economics and politics. It touches on the very nature of a human person.[16] In her book *The Human Condition,* Hannah Arendt relates the

12. H. Scherman, The Promises Men Live By 393 (1983) (emphasis in original).

13. Blum and Wellman, *Participation, Assent and Liberty in Contract Formation,* 1982 Ariz.St.L.J. 901, 907–8.

14. Jones, supra note 8 at 50.

15. Id. at 53.

16. Contracts can be used by individuals to escape from disadvantaged status and to protect their lifestyles through wills and trusts, cohabitation agreements and quasi-marriage contracts. See Testy, *An Unlikely Resurrection*, 90 Nw. U. L. Rev. 219 (1995); Amy Kastely, *Cogs or Cyborgs?: Blasphemy* power to promise to the power to forgive, the one (forgiveness) providing a remedy for a painful past and the other (promise) a remedy for an uncertain future. She explains: "The possible redemption from the predicament of irreversibility—of being unable to undo what one has done * * * is the faculty of forgiving. The remedy for unpredictability, for the uncertainty of the future, is contained in the faculty to make and keep promises. The two faculties belong together in so far as one of them, forgiving, serves to undo the deeds of the past, whose 'sins' hang like Damocles' sword over every new generation; and the other, binding oneself through promises, serves to set up in the ocean of uncertainty, which the future is by definition, islands of security without which not even continuity, let alone durability of any kind, would be possible in the relationships between men."[17]

Only persons forgive; only persons promise. Indeed, Charles Fried insists that "if we decline to take seriously the assumption of an obligation * * *, to that extent we do not take [the promisor] seriously as a person."[18] There are many, of course, who view these awesome powers as conferred by the Creator who both forgives and promises and commands that we do likewise. According to scripture, God has always dealt with people in terms of covenant and covenantal law.

Sources of Contract Law: The Common Law Tradition. The mainstream of our law is that which evolved within the English common law tradition, encompassing mainly the decisions of common law courts, but also, in the larger sense, those of the separate and in many ways competing Chancery Court.[19] As the royal courts expanded and a law common to the entire realm came to be administered, a significant portion of the judicial precedents thus amassed dealt with what we would regard today as the law of contracts. But this is not how these cases were regarded initially. The common lawyer viewed law in terms of remedies available (*viz.*, "writs" which would be granted to redress wrongs) rather than as a body of substantive doctrine or legal principles. There was no law of contracts, as such, but certain actions were available to enforce rights which, in retrospect at least, we see as "contractual" in nature. The development and expansion of the writ system to meet the exigencies of the times account for the remarkable continuity and durability of the common law. Contracts developed principally from the writ of assumpsit, itself an offshoot of trespass on the case, a "tort" remedy.[20]

and Irony in Contract Theories, 90 Nw. U. L. Rev. 132 (1995).

17. H. Arendt, supra note 9 at 237.

18. Fried, supra note 9 at 20–21.

19. See Newman, Equity and Law: a Comparative Study 11–49 (1961).

20. See also Professor Simpson's exceptional work, A.W.B. Simpson, A History of the Common Law of Contract: The Rise of the Action of Assumpsit (1975). In a book with a provocative title, "The Death of Contract," Professor Grant Gilmore insists that recent "contract" trends manifest a return to "tort" roots, so much so that traditional emphasis upon "bargained-for exchange" as the prototypical contractual transaction is obsolete, having been largely superseded by theory allowing recovery for "unbargained-for" reliance. For a critical review, see Speidel, *An Essay on the Reported Death and Continued*

While common law judges proceeded modestly on a case by case basis, adjudicating individual controversies brought before them, they did not act in a strictly *ad hoc* manner or without guidelines of any sort. They adhered to a principle of *stare decisis* as regards their own past and were also influenced by other bodies of legal learning, especially Roman Law, Canon Law and the Law Merchant.[21] Of particular interest here is the influence of the Law Merchant, aptly called "the private international [commercial] law of the Middle Ages."[22] Based upon the customs of merchants, and strongly impressed by an international character, the Law Merchant existed as a body of rules and principles pertaining to merchants and mercantile transactions, distinct from the ordinary law of the land. A characteristic of the mercantile courts, which regularly functioned at fairs and markets, was the dispatch with which disputes were settled. Moreover, it is said that this law, eminently practical and adapted to the requirements of commerce, "was characterized by the spirit of equity."[23] By the 16th century, all the great principles that mark the commercial law of modern times had evolved. "By that time every great country in Europe had recognized in commercial cases the principles of representation, the negotiability of bills of exchange, the liability of the real property of the debtor for his debts, the validity, to a certain extent at least, of formless contracts, the necessity of speedy justice, the importance of the principles of equity and the claims of the bona fide possessor to the protection of the law. The legal relations of partners to one another and to the outside world had, in almost every important point, been definitely settled, and a new commercial contract, insurance, had been evolved and the legal principles that were to govern its development clearly marked."[24]

Until well into the eighteenth century a large part of Anglo–American law pertaining to the sale of goods (and indeed commercial law generally) remained that which was fashioned and administered by the merchants themselves. But gradually this mercantile practice was brought within the common law tradition. One of the chief instruments of the assimilation was a very remarkable jurist, Lord Mansfield, who became Lord Chief Justice of the King's Bench in 1756. Holdsworth called him the "greatest lawyer of the century."[25] Mansfield was a master at adapting the common law to the needs of the age.[26] This was done by both a careful scrutiny of the work of his predecessors and the use of principles developed in other legal systems. He did not always succeed in his efforts, as we shall see, but his accom-

---

Vitality of Contract, 27 Stan.L.Rev. 1161 (1975).

21. See Phillip Hamburger, *The Development of the Nineteenth–Century Consensus Theory of Contract* 241, Law & Hist.Rev. (1989).

22. Maitland, Select Pleas in Manorial Courts 133.

23. Mitchell, supra note 5 at 16.

24. Id. at 156–8.

25. Holdsworth, Some Makers of the English Law 161 (1938).

26. Edmund Burke, a contemporary, said of him: "His ideas go to the growing melioration of the law, by making its liberality keep pace with the demands of justice, and actual concerns of the world; not restricting the infinitely diversified occasions of men and the rules of natural justice, but conforming our jurisprudence to the growth of our commerce and of our empire." Id. at 169.

plishments are impressive. It is interesting to note that one of the tools which he used was a jury of merchants, men who gave him advice on commercial matters. Because of this, some complained that Lombard Street (the merchants) was dictating to Westminster (the judges). In part, of course, this was true. But how fortunate for the common law, especially in view of the fact that during this period the great expansion of trade and commerce made it imperative that the law keep better pace with changing times.

Legislative Codification. Just prior to the turn of this century there began, in England, the legislative codification of large segments of commercial law. One of the early statutes was the English Sale of Goods Act, drafted by Mackenzie D. Chalmers and enacted in 1893. Lord Chalmers admirably executed his mandate from Parliament to "reproduce exactly as possible the existing law," thereby preserving continuity with case precedent. Codification of sales law in the United States began in 1902,[27] when the National Conference of Commissioners on Uniform State Laws entrusted the task of drafting a statute to Professor Samuel Williston. The result was the Uniform Sales Act, approved by the Commissioners in 1906 and recommended to the various State legislatures. The response was highly favorable, with over thirty States adopting it. In the main Professor Williston followed the English statute, often copying verbatim Chalmers' language. In treating of contracts for the sale of goods, each statute touched on matters of general contractual import. But since, as noted, a determined effort was made to preserve a continuity with the common law, the basic structure of contract law was not changed.

In 1923 the American Law Institute, whose activities have had a profound effect upon American law and practice, was founded "to promote the clarification and simplification of the law and its better administration of justice and to encourage and carry on scholarly and scientific work."[28] Among the Institute's accomplishments was the preparation of the Restatement of Contracts, a respected work to which frequent reference will be made in this book. As the title implies, a restatement purports to be a systematic statement of prevailing law, both decisional and statutory. Work on the Contracts Restatement (and on those covering Torts, Conflict of Laws and Agency) began in 1923, with Professor Williston serving as Reporter. He was a most logical choice for this position, since his monumental treatise on contracts had just recently been published and he was recognized as the leading authority in the United States.[29] Among Williston's advisers on the project was Professor Arthur L. Corbin, himself a renowned authority on contract law and later the author of a major treatise

---

27. For an interesting history of earlier and largely unsuccessful efforts to codify American law, see John Honnold, The Life of the Law 100–145 (1964).

28. Restatement, Contracts viii (1932).

29. The original edition of Williston on Contracts was published in 1920. The text was revised by Professor Williston, in collaboration with Professor George Thompson, in 1936–38. The third edition was revised by Professor Walter H.E. Jaeger and the fourth edition, by Richard A. Lord, was completed in 2001.

on the subject.[30] The final draft was approved in May, 1932, and it has been a very influential document. A measure of judicial acceptance can be seen in the fact that it has been cited thousands of times by appellate courts.[31] Williston stated that "the endeavor in the Restatement is to restate the law as it is, not as new law."[32] However, the end product had a strong normative aspect as well; many provisions had only marginal case support and were quite obviously advanced as improvements upon prevailing doctrine.

In the early 1960's, the American Law Institute began work on the Second Restatement of Contracts with Professor Robert Braucher as reporter. He served in that capacity until 1971 when he was appointed to the Supreme Judicial Court of Massachusetts. He was succeeded by Professor Allan Farnsworth. Each year from 1963, a new tentative draft of the Second Restatement was produced, sixteen in all, until 1979 when the American Law Institute adopted the entire Restatement (Second). After some final editing, the Restatement was published in 1981. Like the first Restatement, the second Restatement's primary thrust was to restate the law as it is, not as it should be. Nevertheless, it does contain some outright innovations, the most significant of which is the increased recognition of reliance as a basis of liability.[33]

By far the most significant recent event in the development of contract law has been the appearance of the **Uniform Commercial Code (UCC)**, a comprehensive statute dealing with a wide range of commercial transactions. Work on the Code began in the early 1940's, under joint sponsorship of the National Conference of Commissioners on Uniform State Laws and the American Law Institute. The first edition was approved in 1952. A revised edition, known as the 1958 Official Text with Comments, was published in 1958, followed four years later by the 1962 Official Text, ten years after that by the 1972 Official Text, six years later by the 1978 version, and then by a seemingly endless stream of official texts. Forty-nine States, plus the District of Columbia and the Virgin Islands, have enacted the UCC. In addition, Louisiana has adopted Articles 1, 3, 4 and 5. At this writing every article of the UCC has been or will be revised. The twenty-first century could herald a new age of codification for domestic and transnational contract law.[34]

---

30. Professor Arthur Corbin's multivolume treatise was published in 1950–1, and Corbin continued to update it with Pocket Supplements. After his death in 1967, the supplements have been updated initially by Professor Colin Kelly Kaufman and more recently by Lawrence Cunningham and Arthur Jacobson. The entire treatise is currently being revised under the general editorship of Professor Joseph Perillo.

31. Goodrich and Wolkin, The Story of the American Law Institute 39 (1961).

32. 3 ALI Proceedings 159 (1925).

33. See Farnsworth, *Ingredients in the Redaction of the Restatement (Second) of Contracts*, 81 Colum.L.Rev. 1 (1981).

34. On January 1, 1988, the Convention for the International Sale of Goods (CISG) became effective in the United States. The convention applies to contracts for the sale of goods between businesses having a place of business in countries that are parties to the convention (so long as the parties do not expressly specify that a particular jurisdiction's law should apply).

The primary architect of the Code was the late Professor Karl Llewellyn,[35] assisted by many others from the ranks of the judiciary, the practicing bar, the law schools and business. Unlike Chalmers and Williston, Llewellyn and colleagues did not feel a special need or obligation to follow previously charted courses.

As the Sixth Edition goes to press, a revision of Article 2, Sales of the Uniform Commercial Code is approaching completion. Final approval to the draft was given by the National Conference of Commissioners on Uniform State Law in July, 2002 and the American Law Institute, the co-sponsor, is expected to give their approval in May, 2003. At that point, the revision will be ready for enactment by the states. The proposed changes will be noted, where relevant, throughout this book. An excellent discussion of the uniform laws revisions process, with particular attention paid to problems in revising Article 2, can be found in Symposium, *Perspectives on the Uniform Laws Revision Process*, 52 Hastings L. J. 603 (2001). The experience of one of your co-authors as Reporter to the Article 2 revision is recounted in Richard E. Speidel, *Revising UCC Article 2: A View From the Trenches*, 52 Hastings L. J. 607 (2001).

Throughout this book, we will study, primarily, Article 2 of the UCC (which governs the sale of goods) as a source of more modern ideas about contract and examine the not so subtle impact of the Code upon the development of Restatement (Second).

International developments. Two developments in international commerce will be noted here and referred to throughout the book.

First, the United Nations Convention on Contracts for the International Sale of Goods (CISG) has been ratified by 65 countries, including the NAFTA trading partners, Canada, Mexico, and the United States. Japan, Brazil, and the United Kingdom have not ratified the Convention. CISG applies to contracts for the sale of goods between parties who do business in different countries when both countries have ratified the Convention. Art. I(1)(a). When applicable, it preempts the domestic law of sales which, in the United States, is Article 2 of the UCC.[36]

Second, in 1994 the International Institute for the Unification of Private Law finalized the UNIDROIT Principles of International Commercial Contracts. It is trite but accurate to call the document a restatement of international contract principles. They are not law but purport to respond to international needs and practices and could be adopted by the parties as the "law" of the contract.[37]

35. For an interesting study of Llewellyn, his life, times, ideas and role in UCC drafting, see William. Twining, Karl Llewellyn and the Realist Movement (1973).

36. Materials on CISG can be accessed through a website maintained by Pace University School of Law. http://www.cisg.law.pace.edu. A leading treatise is John Honnold, Uniform Law for International Sales under the 1980 U.N. Convention (3d ed. 2000).

37. For an overview see Joseph Perillo, The UNIDROIT Principles of International Contracts: A Black Letter Text and a Review, 63 Fordham L. Rev. 281 (1994).

Default vs. Immutable Rules. Most of the rules that you will study in this course can be altered by the private agreements of the parties. Such rules that the parties can contract around are often called "default" or "gap-filling" rules. Just as computer word processing software establishes a *default* left-hand margin of 1 inch (which individual users can alter by affirmatively reformatting a document), contract law provides default rules about what is sufficient to reach an agreement[38] and about what the parties' obligations are under an agreement.[39] Default rules govern when the parties have remained silent—i.e. in the absence of agreements to the contrary.

Not every contract rule, however, can be contracted around. Some rules are mandatory or "immutable." This distinction between default and immutable rules is emphasized in the very first section of the UCC: "The effect of provisions of this Act may be varied by agreement, except as otherwise provided in this Act and except that the obligations of good faith . . . may not be disclaimed by agreement."[40] Thus, in learning the rules of contract it is essential to identify (i) *whether* particular rules can be contracted around and (ii) *how* private parties might opt for alternative provisions. Indeed, a worthwhile exercise after reading each case is to consider what contractual provisions would be sufficient to reverse the court's decision. If there is no language that could reverse the decision, then the court has in effect created an immutable rule.

Immutable rules are established by both courts and legislatures. The common law (i.e., law made by judges) established immutable limitations on the maximum amount of damages that parties can contract for (restrictions on so-called liquidated damages) and limitations on the maximum length of "covenants not to compete." In the last 60 years, legislative (and administrative) bodies have promulgated a host of immutable rules that restrict freedom of contract. Many matters, e.g., insurance and labor, have in a sense been removed from the free market and many other commercial activities are limited in scope by such things as the antitrust laws.[41] For

---

38. For example, UCC § 2–206 provides that "unless otherwise unambiguously indicated by the language or circumstances" an offer to buy goods invites acceptance by either a prompt promise to ship or by shipment of the goods itself. The offeror, however, as master of the offer, can alter this rule by "unambiguously indicating" that only a particular type of acceptance will be effective.

39. For example, if an agreement fails to specify a price, the UCC fills this gap by establishing the buyer's obligation to pay "a reasonable price." UCC § 2–305(1).

40. UCC § 1–102(2). [Rev. 1–302] Karl Llewellyn referred to default and mandatory rules, respectively as "iron" and "yielding" rules. See Alan Schwartz, *Karl Llewellyn and the Origins of Contract Theory*, The Jurispru-

dential Foundations of Corporate and Commercial Law 12, 14–17 (2000).

41. Some commentators have suggested that the preemption of common-law rules by market-specific statutes and/or by the encroachment of tort has rendered contract law "dead" or transformed it into a residual category. See G. Gilmore, The Death of Contract (1974); L. Friedman, Contract Law in America (1965); Symposium, *The Relevance of Contract Theory*, 1967 Wis.L.Rev. 803–839. Others focusing on the default nature of law have characterized contract law as imperialistic theory swallowing large segments of the legal landscape. See, e.g., John Langbein, *The Contractarian Basis of the Law of Trusts*, 105 Yale L.J. 625, 630 (1995) ("Contract has become the dominant doctrinal current in mod-example, since 1964, employers have had an immutable duty not to discriminate on the basis of race or gender in making employment decisions. Even the relatively simple construction of a private home is awash with immutable regulatory duties.[42]

As a normative matter, there is "surprising consensus among academics at an abstract level on two normative bases for immutability. Put most simply immutable rules are justifiable if society wants to protect (1) parties within the contract, or (2) parties outside the contract. The former justification turns on parentalism; the latter on externalities. Immutable rules displace freedom of contract. Immutability is justified only if unregulated contracting would be socially deleterious because parties internal or external to the contract cannot adequately protect themselves."[43]

However, even when contract law chooses not to restrict contractual freedom, it must still decide which default rule will govern when the parties are silent and what manifestations are sufficient and/or necessary to displace the default rule. At times, it might be useful to establish defaults which penalize one or both parties to encourage more explicit contracting— as the parties act to contract around the penalty default. For example, the UCC refuses to enforce contracts that omit the quantity to be sold—which effectively establishes a default quantity of zero.[44] In stark contrast to the "reasonable price" default, this "zero quantity" default is likely to induce private parties to provide better information about the terms of their agreement.[45]

Appreciating the default nature of much of contract law suggests that contract law is not just created by courts and legislatures, but, perhaps most importantly, by private parties themselves. Indeed, people in their daily interactions may contract around immutable rules as well as default rules by largely ignoring what contract law ordains to be a legally mandatory obligation.[46] Important parts of the way parties actually exchange and resolve promissory obligations may be beyond the shadow of the law.[47] "If,

---

ern American law. In fields ranging from corporations and partnership to landlord and tenant to servitudes to the law of marriage, scholars have come to understand our legal rules as resting mainly on imputed bargains that are susceptible to alteration by actual bargains.").

42. An increasing amount of this regulatory activity has as its avowed purpose the protection of consumers. See, e.g., Macaulay, *Bambi Meets Godzilla: Reflections on Contracts Scholarship and Teaching vs. State Unfair and Deceptive Trade Practices and Consumer Protection Statutes*, 26 Hous. L.Rev. 575 (1989).

43. Ian Ayres & Robert Gertner, *Filling Gaps in Incomplete Contracts: An Economic Theory of Default Rules*, 99 Yale L.J. 87, 88 (1989).

44. UCC § 2–201(1) ("a contract . . . is not enforceable under this [provision] beyond the quantity of goods shown").

45. See Ayres & Gertner, supra note 43 (arguing that "penalty defaults" by inducing explicit contracting might produce valuable information for parties to the agreement or third parties—such as courts). See also Ayres & Gertner, *Majoritarian v. Minoritarian Defaults*, 51 Stan. L. Rev. 1591 (1999).

46. See Stewart Macaulay, *Non-Contractual Relations in Business: A Preliminary Study*, 28 Am.Soc.Rev. 55 (1963); Ellickson, Order Without Law (1991).

47. See Edward Rubin, *The Nonjudicial Life of Contract: Beyond the Shadow of the Law*, 90 Nw.U.L.Rev. 107, 109 (1995).

because of the high cost of litigation, the increased use of alternative dispute resolution techniques, and the limitations of adjudication, more behavior occurs outside of the 'shadow of the law,' the impact of contract law is reduced, and theories based upon assumptions that people are influenced by the law are weakened.''[48]

In sum, contract operates on two levels. The first is the vast area of agreement in fact, where bargains are performed and disputes settled without resort to public agencies of decision. This level may be likened to that large part of the iceberg which is under water. The second level is that of litigated disputes ultimately resolved by courts or other agencies and the results published in reported opinions. This is the "visible" law of contracts, which emerges as courts resolve disputes between private bargainers. This is the body of doctrine which, in theory, influences rational pretransaction planning and provides standards for the settlement of disputes. A primary thrust of our study of contract law will be to determine how courts allocate resources through bargain and exchange. But since the "visible" law of contracts has been carefully selected, classified and truncated for insertion into your casebook, you should realize that you are studying the top of the iceberg.

Recurring Questions. As you begin to study the multiple problems of contract law and to draw on both legal materials and your own experience and training, several recurring questions should be kept firmly in mind.

1.   Which promises will be enforced?

2.   When enforceable, what is the scope and content of promissory obligations?

3.   How will these promises be enforced?

4.   Which of the foregoing answers can the parties contract around (and how)?[49]

SECTION 2.   WHAT IS A PROMISE

Bailey v. West (wins)

Supreme Court of Rhode Island, 1969.
105 R.I. 61, 249 A.2d 414.

■ PAOLINO, JUSTICE. This is a civil action wherein the plaintiff alleges that the defendant is indebted to him for the reasonable value of his services

---

48. Richard E. Speidel, *The Shifting Domain of Contract*, 90 Nw.U.L.Rev. 254, 257 (1995).

49. The following abbreviations will be used in subsequent references: UCC—Uniform Commercial Code, 2002 Official Text; Restatement—Restatement, (First) Contracts (1932); Restatement (Second)—Restatement (Second), Contracts (1981); Corbin—Corbin on Contracts (Rev. Ed.); Williston—Williston on Contracts (Lord ed.); Farnsworth—Allan Farnsworth, Contracts (3d ed. 1999); Calamari and Perillo—John Calamari and Joseph Perillo, Contracts (4th ed. 1998); Murray—John Murray, Murray on Contracts (4th ed. 2001).

rendered in connection with the feeding, care and maintenance of a certain race horse named "Bascom's Folly" from May 3, 1962 through July 3, 1966. The case was tried before a justice of the superior court sitting without a jury, and resulted in a decision for the plaintiff for his cost of boarding the horse for the five months immediately subsequent to May 3, 1962, and for certain expenses incurred by him in trimming its hoofs. The cause is now before us on the plaintiff's appeal and defendant's cross appeal from the judgment entered pursuant to such decision.

The facts material to a resolution of the precise issues raised herein are as follows. In late April 1962, defendant, accompanied by his horse trainer, went to Belmont Park in New York to buy race horses. On April 27, 1962, defendant purchased "Bascom's Folly" from a Dr. Strauss and arranged to have the horse shipped to Suffolk Downs in East Boston, Massachusetts. Upon its arrival defendant's trainer discovered that the horse was lame, and so notified defendant, who ordered him to reship the horse by van to the seller at Belmont Park. The seller refused to accept delivery at Belmont on May 3, 1962, and thereupon, the van driver, one Kelly, called defendant's trainer and asked for further instructions. Although the trial testimony is in conflict as to what the trainer told him, it is not disputed that on the same day Kelly brought "Bascom's Folly" to plaintiff's farm where the horse remained until July 3, 1966, when it was sold by plaintiff to a third party.

While "Bascom's Folly" was residing at his horse farm, plaintiff sent bills for its feed and board to defendant at regular intervals. According to testimony elicited from defendant at the trial, the first such bill was received by him some two or three months after "Bascom's Folly" was placed on plaintiff's farm. He also stated that he immediately returned the bill to plaintiff with the notation that he was not the owner of the horse nor was it sent to plaintiff's farm at his request. The plaintiff testified that he sent bills monthly to defendant and that the first notice he received from him disclaiming ownership was " * * * maybe after a month or two or so" subsequent to the time when the horse was left in plaintiff's care.

In his decision the trial judge found that defendant's trainer had informed Kelly during their telephone conversation of May 3, 1962, that " * * * he would have to do whatever he wanted to do with the horse, that he wouldn't be on any farm at the defendant's expense * * *." He also found, however, that when "Bascom's Folly" was brought to his farm, plaintiff was not aware of the telephone conversation between Kelly and defendant's trainer, and hence, even though he knew there was a controversy surrounding the ownership of the horse, he was entitled to assume that " * * * there is an implication here that, 'I am to take care of this horse.'" Continuing his decision, the trial justice stated that in view of the result reached by this court in a recent opinion wherein we held that the instant defendant was liable to the original seller, Dr. Strauss, for the purchase price of this horse,* there was a contract "implied in fact"

---

* [See Strauss v. West, 100 R.I. 388, 216 A.2d 366 (1966). The court held that Bascom's Folly was "sound" at the time delivery was tendered by Strauss, that title had passed to West and that West was liable to Strauss for the purchase price of $1,800. Ed.].

between the plaintiff and defendant to board "Bascom's Folly" and that this contract continued until plaintiff received notification from defendant that he would not be responsible for the horse's board. The trial justice further stated that " * * * I think there was notice given at least at the end of the four months, and I think we must add another month on there for a reasonable disposition of his property."

In view of the conclusion we reach with respect to defendant's first two contentions, we shall confine ourselves solely to a discussion and resolution of the issues necessarily implicit therein, and shall not examine other subsidiary arguments advanced by plaintiff and defendant.

I

The defendant alleges in his brief and oral argument that the trial judge erred in finding a contract "implied in fact" between the parties. We agree.

* * *

The source of the obligation in a contract "implied in fact," as in express contracts, is in the intention of the parties. We hold that there was no mutual agreement and "intent to promise" between the plaintiff and defendant so as to establish a contract "implied in fact" for defendant to pay plaintiff for the maintenance of this horse. From the time Kelly delivered the horse to him plaintiff knew there was a dispute as to its ownership, and his subsequent actions indicated he did not know with whom, if anyone, he had a contract. After he had accepted the horse, he made inquiries as to its ownership and, initially, and for some time thereafter, sent his bills to both defendant and Dr. Strauss, the original seller.

There is also uncontroverted testimony in the record that prior to the assertion of the claim which is the subject of this suit neither defendant nor his trainer had ever had any business transactions with plaintiff, and had never used his farm to board horses. Additionally, there is uncontradicted evidence that this horse, when found to be lame, was shipped by defendant's trainer not to plaintiff's farm, but back to the seller at Belmont Park. What is most important, the trial justice expressly stated that he believed the testimony of defendant's trainer that he had instructed Kelly that defendant would not be responsible for boarding the horse on any farm.

From our examination of the record we are constrained to conclude that the trial justice overlooked and misconceived material evidence which establishes beyond question that there never existed between the parties an element essential to the formulation of any true contract, namely, an "intent to contract." Compare Morrissey v. Piette, R.I., 241 A.2d 302, 303.

II

The defendant's second contention is that, even assuming the trial justice was in essence predicating defendant's liability upon a quasi-contractual theory, his decision is still unsupported by competent evidence and is clearly erroneous.

The following discussion of quasi-contracts appears in 12 Am.Jur., Contracts, § 6 (1938) at pp. 503 to 504:

" * * * A quasi contract has no reference to the intentions or expressions of the parties. The obligation is imposed despite, and frequently in frustration of, their intention. For a quasi contract neither promise nor privity, real or imagined, is necessary. In quasi contracts the obligation arises, not from consent of the parties, as in the case of contracts, express or implied in fact, but from the law of natural immutable justice and equity. The act, or acts, from which the law implies the contract must, however, be voluntary. Where a case shows that it is the duty of the defendant to pay, the law imputes to him a promise to fulfil that obligation. The duty, which thus forms the foundation of a quasi-contractual obligation, is frequently based on the doctrine of unjust enrichment. * * *

unjust enrichment

" * * * The law will not imply a promise against the express declaration of the party to be charged, made at the time of the supposed undertaking, unless such party is under legal obligation paramount to his will to perform some duty, and he is not under such legal obligation unless there is a demand in equity and good conscience that he should perform the duty."

Therefore, the essential elements of a quasi-contract are a benefit conferred upon defendant by plaintiff, appreciation by defendant of such benefit, and acceptance and retention by defendant of such benefit under such circumstances that it would be inequitable to retain the benefit without payment of the value thereof. . . .

✳ Quasi K R 86

The key question raised by this appeal with respect to the establishment of a quasi-contract is whether or not plaintiff was acting as a "volunteer" at the time he accepted the horse for boarding at his farm. There is a long line of authority which has clearly enunciated the general rule that " * * * if a performance is rendered by one person without any request by another, it is very unlikely that this person will be under a legal duty to pay compensation." 1 A Corbin, Contracts § 234.

Thought he was helping? ✳ ✳

The Restatement of Restitution, § 2 (1937) provides: "A person who officiously confers a benefit upon another is not entitled to restitution therefor." Comment *a* in the above-mentioned section states in part as follows:

" * * * Policy ordinarily requires that a person who has conferred a benefit * * * by way of giving another services * * * should not be permitted to require the other to pay therefor, unless the one conferring the benefit had a valid reason for so doing. A person is not required to deal with another unless he so desires and, ordinarily, a person should not be required to become an obligor unless he so desires."

✳

Applying those principles to the facts in the case at bar it is clear that plaintiff cannot recover. The plaintiff's testimony on cross-examination is the only evidence in the record relating to what transpired between Kelly and him at the time the horse was accepted for boarding. The defendant's attorney asked plaintiff if he had any conversation with Kelly at that time, and plaintiff answered in substance that he had noticed that the horse was very lame and that Kelly had told him: "That's why they wouldn't accept him at Belmont Track." The plaintiff also testified that he had inquired of Kelly as to the ownership of "Bascom's Folly," and had been told that "Dr. Strauss made a deal and that's all I know." It further appears from the record that plaintiff acknowledged receipt of the horse by signing a uniform livestock bill of lading, which clearly indicated on its face that the horse in question had been consigned by defendant's trainer not to plaintiff, but to Dr. Strauss's trainer at Belmont Park. Knowing at the time he accepted the horse for boarding that a controversy surrounded its ownership, plaintiff could not reasonably expect remuneration from defendant, nor can it be said that defendant acquiesced in the conferment of a benefit upon him. The undisputed testimony was that defendant, upon receipt of plaintiff's first bill, immediately notified him that he was not the owner of "Bascom's Folly" and would not be responsible for its keep.

It is our judgment that the plaintiff was a mere volunteer who boarded and maintained "Bascom's Folly" at his own risk and with full knowledge that he might not be reimbursed for expenses he incurred incident thereto.

The plaintiff's appeal is denied and dismissed, the defendant's cross appeal is sustained, and the cause is remanded to the superior court for entry of judgment for the defendant.

NOTES

(1) What are plaintiff's theories of recovery? How do they differ?

(2) Suppose West personally delivered "Bascom's Folly" to Bailey's farm, but nothing was said specifically about Bailey's caring for the horse or West's paying for that care. Would West be liable? If so, on what theory?

As one court put it:

An implied-in-fact contract has the same legal effect as an express contract. . . . The only difference between them is the means by which the parties manifest their agreement. In an express contract, the parties manifest their agreement by the words, whether written or spoken . . . In an implied-in-fact contract, the parties' agreement is inferred, in whole or in part, from their conduct. [Nevertheless] an implied contract must still have discernable terms * * * For such a situation to exist, the parties must exhibit mutual expressions of agreement.

Novak v. Seiko Corp., 37 Fed.Appx. 239, 2002 WL 1011580, *3 (9th Cir.2002) (unpublished).

(3) What if Bailey found "Bascom's Folly" collapsed alongside the highway, took him in and cared for him, and thereafter sought out West. Would the latter be responsible to Bailey for the care given the horse? If so, on what

theory? See, generally, John Wade, *Restitution for Benefits Conferred Without Request,* 19 Vand.L.Rev. 1183 (1966). "One who, without intent to act gratuitously, confers a measurable benefit upon another, is entitled to restitution, if he affords the other an opportunity to decline the benefit or else has as reasonable excuse for failing to do so. If the other refuses to receive the benefit, he is not required to make restitution unless the actor justifiably performs for the other a duty imposed upon him by law." Id. at 1212.

(4) Promise: Toward a Working Definition. Contract is a theory of promissory liability. Without a promise, express or implied, there can be no contract. See Restatement (Second) § 1. But what is a promise? Consider the following attempts at a definition.

Restatement (First) § 1: "A promise is an undertaking, however expressed, either that something shall happen, or that something shall not happen, in the future."

Sharp, *Promissory Liability,* 7 U.Chi.L.Rev. 1, 4–5 (1939): "What then is a promise? * * * As a matter of every day experience and common usage, a promise has something reliable about it. * * * It may be suggested that a promise is the maker's statement about his future conduct so made that the maker should expect the person to whom it is made mentally to rely on it as dependable. It will be observed that the maker's actual intention is not regarded as important and this is true at least in the courts. * * * Thus we say that the maker of a promise is one who ought to expect another to rely on his statement. * * * The person who says he has relied on another's work has a kind of burden of showing that the other was in the wrong. * * * He has to give affirmative reasons for deciding that the other has not acted in accordance with ordinary standards of business communication, in making his statement."

Restatement (Second) § 2(1): "A promise is a manifestation of intention to act or refrain from acting in a specified way, so made as to justify a promisee in understanding that a commitment has been made."

See also Charles Fried, Contract as Promise 9–14 (1981), who argues that a promise invokes a commitment to a future course of conduct that "absent our commitment is morally neutral." The force of a promise, then, is in the commitment, not in what reliance it may induce.

Unlike the restatement, the U.C.C. avoids a definition of promise and instead focuses on "agreement" as the touchstone for enforceability. See UCC § 1–201(3) (" 'Agreement' means the bargain of the parties in fact * * * ").

(5) According to Judge Richard Posner:

Promises are usually forward-looking; one promises to do something, necessarily in the future. The promise that All–Tech stresses as the basis for its claim of promissory estoppel—that Amway had thoroughly researched the TeleCharge program before offering it to distributors—is not of that character. It warrants existing conditions rather than committing to some future action and is more precisely described as a warranty rather than a promise. UCC 2–313(1)(a)... . But a warranty is a type of promise—in this case a promise by Amway to pay for the consequences should the research that went into the development of TeleCharge not have been thorough after all. Metropolitan Coal Co. v. Howard, 155 F.2d 780, 784 (2d

Cir.1946) (L. Hand, J.) (a warrant "amounts to a promise to indemnify the promisee for any loss if the fact warranted proves untrue, for obviously the promisor cannot control what is already in the past");.... cf. Oliver Wendell Holmes, Jr., The Common Law 298–301 (1881). Since a warranty can induce reasonable reliance, its breach can be the basis for a claim of promissory estoppel....

All–Tech Telecom, Inc. v. Amway Corp., 174 F.3d 862, 868–69 (7th Cir.1999).

Bolin Farms v. American Cotton Shippers Association

U.S. District Court, Western District of Louisiana, 1974.
370 F.Supp. 1353.

■ EDWIN F. HUNTER, JR., CHIEF JUDGE: This litigation arises out of the attempts by eleven (11) cotton farmers to test the contracts by which they concededly obligated themselves to sell and deliver their cotton. In essence, defendants agreed to purchase whatever was planted by these farmers on specific acreage at a price agreed upon between January and March of 1973, irrespective of what the price might be at harvest time. Meanwhile, the price of cotton unexpectedly skyrocketed to at least double the price agreed upon. The complaints seek a declaration that the contracts are null and void, so that plaintiffs may achieve a better price than they bargained for. The fundamental question in each action involves the enforceability *vel non* of contracts for the advance or forward sale of cotton grown for the 1973 crop.

* * *

The record is a morass of pleadings which can best be unraveled by proceeding to the very core of the case—that is, the validity and enforceability of a contract for the purchase and sale of cotton, entered into between a willing buyer and a willing seller, both adult (experienced cotton farmers on the one hand and experienced cotton buyers on the other hand) on an open and competitive market. The case on summary judgment presents two facets:

(1) The prayer of plaintiffs for a declaratory judgment annulling the cotton sales contracts, and

(2) The prayer of defendants that the contracts be adjudged lawful and valid.

* * *

It is a matter of public record and public knowledge that as a result of the sudden and spectacular rise in the price of cotton in the latter part of 1973, literally scores of suits have been filed, either to enforce or rescind these advance or forward contracts. Defendants have cited thirteen (13) cases that arose between September 18 and November 9, 1973. In each, the validity of the contracts has been upheld by either summary judgment,

declaratory judgment, preliminary injunction, and/or permanent injunction.
. . .

* * *

Jurisdiction is pegged on diversity. We are governed by Louisiana law.

The contracts are in evidence. They speak for themselves. No useful purpose would be served by detailing each provision. They were entered into between January 9, 1973 and March 29, 1973. In each, plaintiffs obligated themselves to sell and deliver to the defendant cotton buyers all of the cotton raised and harvested on designated acreage. The price ranged from 29 to 41 cents per pound. The actual cotton produced was physically to be delivered to the buyers, to be by them physically received and paid for on delivery. These contracts were negotiated prior to planting. We call them "forward" sales contracts. Each plaintiff cotton farmer was experienced, having been a cotton producer for several years, and each was familiar with the forward sale contract procedure.

The depositions reveal that during the period of time from January 9th through March 29, 1973, the competitive open market range ran from 28 to 32 cents per pound. On the basis of the record it would be difficult to quarrel with the proposition that the sales were for a fair market price at the time they were made, and as a matter of law we conclude that the price and circumstances prevailing at the time are determinative.

From April through September, the cotton market rose spectacularly. The price of 29 or 30 cents a pound, which looked so good to the farmers in February, no longer looked so good against 80 cents in September.

These farmers certainly have every right to contest the validity of their contracts. Likewise, the buyer has every right to assert the validity of their bargain. To quote the Honorable Wilbur D. Owens, Jr., U.S. District Judge, Middle District of Georgia (see Mitchell–Huntley Cotton Co. v. Fulton Benson, Civil Action 2902):

> "Ladies and Gentlemen, this case illustrates about as well as any case that will ever be in a court room that life is a two way street, that when we make bargains that turn out to be good for us that we keep them and then when we make bargains that turn out to be bad for us that we also keep them. That seems to be the essence of what this case is about.

> "The defendants, naturally, don't want to sell cotton because the price has gone up and if I were one of those defendants I would feel the same way. I would be sick as an old hound dog who ate a rotten skunk, but unfortunately—well, not unfortunately—fortunately we all abide by contracts and that (is) the foundation of which all of the business that you have heard about here today is done."

What caused the upward price spiral of April to September? There were many causes. We are unable to pin down any one. Be that as it may, the cause has no relevance to the validity of the contracts. Some of the deponents point to such factors as large export shipments to China, high water and flood conditions in the cotton belt; late plantings forced by heavy rains, and the devaluation of the dollar. These elements and others are reasonable causes, but whatever causes the market to go up and down after the date of a contract has no relevancy to its validity. One facet of plaintiffs' attack is that the cotton buyers had inside information at the time they contracted with plaintiffs, and that these factors would coincide and drive the price of cotton to the level that it had never before reached. The record does not reveal this to be true. The record will reveal that Dallas Thomason sold his cotton at 30 cents, Frank Jones, Jr., Executive Vice-President of Cook Industries, Inc., sold his cotton at 30 cents, Conner Morscheimer, cotton buyer for W.K. Kennedy Co., Inc., sold his cotton at 29½ cents.

Plaintiffs emphasize that the cotton farmer has always been at the mercy of the weather and the boll weevil. This may be true, but by firm forward selling, the farmer shifts many of his risks to the buyer. The farmer guarantees neither quality nor quantity. He obligates himself to sell and the buyer obligates himself to buy all the cotton the farmer harvests from identifiable acreage. He sells it at a price at which he figures at the time of the contract he can make a profit in relation to his expectable costs. Against that firm contract he can arrange his crop financing. The depositions reveal the system used, and there can be no argument that it does give the grower a very real limitation of risk.

* * *

Moving quickly to validity, we appreciate that the 13 cases cited are not controlling, but we do find it extremely persuasive that in 13 recent cases attacking the validity, in federal and state courts, all upheld the contracts. * * *

Attached are formal judgments in each case.

NOTES

(1) *Excuse by Reason of Changed Circumstances.* When, if ever, should a promisor be excused because of supervening events which make performance impossible or impracticable? Even if it is still possible for the promisor to perform and performance has not become impracticable, should a frustration of purpose or objective which the promisor sought to achieve from the contract be grounds for excusing non-performance? These are among the most difficult and challenging questions that must be addressed in any legal system. What, for example, of dramatic market price increases or decreases brought on by external events (e.g., war, rationing, embargoes)? In the early cases, common law judges had an emphatic answer: no excuse. Absent an explicit qualification of duty in the contract itself, the promisor was obligated to perform regardless of supervening events. *Pacta sunt servanda!* As stated in a seventeenth-century English case, "when the party by his own contract creates a duty or charge upon himself, he is bound to make it good, if he may, notwithstanding any accident by inevitable necessity, because he might have provided against it by his contract." Paradine v. Jane, Aleyn 26, 27, 82 Eng.Rep. 897 (K.B.1647). Later cases provided a degree of mitigation of this strict rule, and UCC 2–615

recognizes excuse by failure of presupposed conditions as follows: "Except so far as a seller may have assumed a greater obligation * * * (a) Delay in delivery or non-delivery in whole or in part by a seller * * * is not a breach of his duty under a contract for sale if performance as agreed has been made impracticable by the occurrence of a contingency the non-occurrence of which was a basic assumption on which the contract was made or by compliance in good faith with any applicable foreign or domestic governmental regulation or order whether or not it later proves to be invalid. * * * " This subject is treated at length in Chapter Six, Section 4, infra.

SECTION 3. THEORIES OF PROMISSORY LIABILITY

What promises ought to be legally binding? In this section we explore the bases of promissory liability, and the reasons for enforcing a promise, any promise. To start, consider Professor Randy Barnett's assessment of some current theories of contractual obligations. We will study each of these theories in Chapter Two.

Comment: Professor Barnett's Assessment of Current Theories of Contractual Obligation

"Five theories—the will, reliance, efficiency, fairness, and bargain theories—are most commonly offered to explain which commitments merit enforcement and which do not. These theories of contractual obligation actually exemplify three types of contract theories. Will and reliance theories are *party-based*. Efficiency and fairness theories are *standards-based*. The bargain theory is *process-based*. At least some of each theory's weaknesses are characteristics of its type. For this reason, each type of theory shall be separately considered here.

* * *

Will, reliance, efficiency, fairness, and bargain are best understood as core concerns of contract law. A theory of contractual obligation is needed to provide a framework that specifies when one of these concerns should give way to another. Their proper relationship cannot be explained by a theory based solely on any one concern or on some unspecified combination.

* * *

A. *Party-Based Theories*

Theories described here as party-based are those that focus on protecting one particular party to a transaction. A more accurate (though more awkward) label is "one-sided party-based." Will theories are primarily concerned with protecting the promisor. Reliance theories are primarily concerned with protecting the promisee. The undue emphasis that the will and reliance theories each place on one specific party creates insoluble problems for each approach.

1. *Will Theories.* Will theories maintain that commitments are enforceable because the promisor has "willed" or chosen to be bound by his commitment. "According to the classical view, the law of contract gives expression to and protects the will of the parties, for the will is something inherently worthy of respect."[7] In this approach, the use of force against a reneging promisor is morally justified because the promisor herself has warranted the use of force by her prior exercise of will. A promisor cannot complain about force being used against her, since she intended that such force could be used when she made the commitment.[8]

Will theories depend for their moral force upon the notion that contractual duties are binding because they are freely assumed by those who are required to discharge them. Consequently, enforcement is not morally justified without a genuine commitment by the person who is to be subjected to a legal sanction. This position leads quite naturally to an inquiry as to the promisor's actual state of mind at the time of agreement— the so-called "subjective" viewpoint. After all, the theory can hardly be based on *will* if the obligation was *not* chosen by the individual but instead was imposed by law.

It has long been recognized that a system of contractual enforcement would be unworkable if it adhered to a will theory requiring a subjective inquiry into the putative promisor's intent. Where we cannot discern the actual subjective intent or will of the parties, there is no practical problem, since we assume it corresponds to objectively manifested intentions. But where subjective intent can somehow be proved and is contrary to objectively manifested behavior, subjective intent should prevail if the moral integrity and logic of a will theory are to be preserved.

Of course, any legal preference for the promisor's subjective intent would disappoint a promisee who has acted in reliance on the appearance of legally binding intent. Permitting a subjective inquiry into the promisor's intent could also enable a promisor to fraudulently undermine otherwise perfectly clear agreements by generating and preserving extrinsic evidence of ambiguous or conflicting intentions. Such a strategy might create a de facto option in the promisor. The promisor could insist on enforcement if the contract continued to be in her interest, but if it were no longer advantageous, she could avoid the contract, by producing evidence of a differing subjective intent.

---

7. Cohen, The Basis of Contract, 46 Harv.L.Rev. 553, 575 (1933).

8. See Charles Fried, Contract as Promise 16 (1981) ("An individual is morally bound to keep his promises because he has *intentionally* invoked a convention whose function it is to give grounds—moral grounds—for another to expect the promised performance.") (emphasis added); see also Burrows, Contract, Tort and Restitution—A Satisfactory Division or Not?, 99 Law Q.Rev.

217, 258 (1983) ("It is the acceptance of an obligation that is vital; it is not enough to have represented that facts are true or to have merely declared that one is intending to do something, for in such situations, the will has not committed itself to do anything."). Anthony T. Kronman also categorizes Professor Fried as a "will theorist." See Kronman, A New Champion for the Will Theory (Book Review), 91 Yale L.J. 404, 404 (1981).

Because the subjective approach relies on evidence inaccessible to the promisee, much less to third parties, an inquiry into subjective intent would undermine the security of transactions by greatly reducing the reliability of contractual commitments. Not surprisingly, and notwithstanding the logic of obligation based on "will," the objective approach has largely prevailed. The subjectivist moral component, on which a will theory focuses to justify legal enforcement, conflicts unavoidably with the practical need for a system of rules based to a large extent on objectively manifested states of mind. While a person's objective manifestations generally reflect subjective intentions, a will theorist must explain the enforcement of the objective agreement where it can be shown that the subjective understanding of a party differs from her objectively manifested behavior.

Some will theorists uneasily resolve this conflict by acknowledging that other "interests"—for example, reliance—may take priority over the will. By permitting individuals to be bound by promises never intended by them to be enforceable, such a concession deprives a will theory of much of its force. Requiring the promisor's subjective will to yield always, or almost always, to the promisee's reliance on the promisor's objective manifestation of assent undermines the claim that contractual obligation is grounded in the individual's will and bolsters the view that contractual obligations may be imposed rightfully on unwilling parties. The inability of will theories to explain adequately the enforcement of objective manifestations of intention also accounts in part for the continued interest in reliance-based theories of contractual obligation.

2. *Reliance Theories.* Theories that explain contractual obligation as an effort to protect a promisee's reliance on the promises of others have the apparent virtue of explaining why persons may be bound by the common meaning of their words regardless of their intentions. Thus, it has become increasingly fashionable to assert that contractual obligation is created by reliance on a promise.[17] A reliance theory is based upon the intuition that we ought to be liable in contract law for our assertive behavior when it creates "foreseeable" or "justifiable" reliance in others, in much the same way that we are held liable in tort law for harmful consequences of other acts.

Reliance theories have nonetheless faced a seemingly insuperable difficulty. As Morris Cohen wrote as early as 1933: "Clearly, not all cases of injury resulting from reliance on the word or act of another are actionable,

---

17. While the literature is replete with suggestions about "the reliance principle," a comprehensive reliance theory of contract has never been systematically presented. Such an approach clearly underlies Gilmore's seminal work, *The Death of Contract.* See, e.g., G. Gilmore, The Death of Contract 71–72, 88 (1974). Atiyah appears to call for a reliance theory, although he also acknowledges that "the voluntary creation and extinction of rights and liabilities" should re-main one of the "basic pillars of the law of obligations." note 16, at 779; see also Feinman, Promissory Estoppel and Judicial Method, 97 Harv.L.Rev. 678, 716–17 (1984) ("reliance principle" undermines "classical" contract law doctrines); Henderson, Promissory Estoppel and Traditional Contract Doctrine, 78 Yale L.J. 343, 344 (1969) (rules of promissory estoppel create a contract grounded on effects of reliance).

and the theory before us offers no clue as to what distinguishes those which are." This deficiency has led necessarily to the employment of such phrases as "justifiable" reliance or "reasonable" reliance. These adjectives, however, depend on (usually vague) standards of evaluation that are unrelated to reliance itself, because, whether justified or unjustified, reasonable or unreasonable, reliance is present in any event.

Furthermore, whether a person has "reasonably" relied on a promise depends on what most people would (or ought to) do. We cannot make this assessment independently of the legal rule in effect in the relevant community, because what many people would do in reliance on a promise is crucially affected by their perception of whether or not the promise is enforceable. A reliance theory, therefore, ultimately does no more than pose the crucial question that it is supposed to answer: is this a promise that should be enforced?

The analysis is no different if we ask whether the promisor knew or had reason to know the promise would induce others to act in reliance,[21] even though this formulation lessens a reliance theory's preference for the promisee's interests. Unlike the subject of the prediction required by foreseeability analysis in tort law—the physical consequences that follow from physical actions—the subject of the prediction required by foreseeability analysis in contract law is the actions of a self-conscious person. A prediction that a promise can reasonably be expected to induce reliance by a promisee or third party will unavoidably depend upon whether the promisee or third party believes that reliance will be legally protected. The legal rule itself cannot be formulated based on such a prediction, however, without introducing a practical circularity into the analysis.

Furthermore, if a promise is defined, as in the Restatement (Second) of Contracts, as "a manifestation of intention to act or refrain from acting in a specified way, so made as to justify a promisee in understanding that a commitment has been made,"[23] then it would seem that *every* promisor should reasonably expect to induce reliance. If so, "The real issue is not whether the promisor should have expected the promisee to rely, but whether the extent of the promisee's reliance was reasonable." But this returns us once again to the difficulties of discerning "reasonable" reliance.

By providing an overly expansive criterion of contractual obligation, any theory that bases obligation on detrimental reliance begs the basic question to be resolved by contract theory: which *potentially* reliance-

---

21. See, e.g., Restatement (Second) of Contracts § 90(1) (1979). Section 90 qualifies reliance-based recoveries at the level of formation, by requiring both a "reasonable" expectation of reliance and the imposition of sanctions only if "injustice" cannot otherwise be avoided, and, at the level of remedies, by limiting the remedy "as justice requires." Id. Traditionally, however, the legal method employs doctrinal and theoretical analysis (that is consistent with underlying notions of jus-

tice) *to discover* where justice resides in a particular case. See Barnett, Why We Need Legal Philosophy, 8 Harv.J.L. & Pub.Pol. 6–10 (1985). Section 90 obviously begs this question. While it may have been the victim of overly cautious draftsmanship, no more precise formulations have been offered to take its place.

23. Restatement (Second) of Contracts § 2 (1979). * * *

inducing actions entail legal consequences and which do not? A person's actions in reliance on a commitment are not justified—and therefore legally protected—simply *because* she has relied. Rather, reliance on the words of others is legally protected because of some as yet undefined circumstances.

In short, a person, rather than being entitled to legal enforcement because reliance is justified, is justified in relying on those commitments that will be legally enforced. Reliance theories therefore must appeal to a criterion other than reliance to distinguish justified acts of reliance. Such a criterion has yet to be identified. It is suggested below that a consent theory provides such a criterion.

3. *The Problem With Party-Based Theories.* These difficulties reveal that reliance theories have much in common with will theories. Both sets of theories must resort to definitions of contractual enforcement that do not follow from either will or reliance, but are based on more fundamental principles that are left unarticulated. By failing to distinguish adequately between those commitments that are worthy of legal protection and those that are not, both the will and reliance theories have failed in their basic mission. Consequently, actual contract cases must be resolved ad hoc using vague concepts such as "reasonableness" or "public policy," or by employing clearer but formalistic criteria such as "consideration."

* * *

B. *Standards–Based Theories*

Standards-based theories are those which evaluate *the substance* of a contractual transaction to see if it conforms to a standard of evaluation that the theory specifies as primary. Economic efficiency and substantive fairness are two such standards that have received wide attention.

1. *Efficiency Theories.* One of the most familiar standards-based legal theories is the efficiency approach associated with the "law and economics" school. Economic efficiency is viewed by some in this school as the maximization of some concept of social wealth or welfare: "the term *efficiency* will refer to the relationship between the aggregate benefits of a situation and the aggregate costs of the situation.... In other words, efficiency corresponds to 'the size of the pie.' "[28] According to this view, legal rules and practices are assessed to see whether they will expand or contract the size of this pie.

In its least assertive variation, an economic assessment of law does not constitute a distinct theory of contractual obligation. Rather, economic analysis of legal rules is simply viewed as a "value-free" scientific inquiry that is confined to accounting for or explaining the consequences that result from particular legal rules or schemes. So viewed, economic analysis

---

28. A. Polinsky, An Introduction to Law and Economics 7 (1983); cf. Cooter & Eisenberg, Damages for Breach of Contract, 73 Calif.L.Rev. 1432, 1460 (1985) ("Econo- mists say that a contract is efficient if its terms maximize the value that can be created by the contemplated exchange.").

is not a competing theory of contractual obligation, but only one of many yardsticks for assessing competing legal theories.

Economic analysis may also be viewed as a normative theory of law—that is, economic efficiency is seen as providing the best or only yardstick of law. However, because standard economic analysis begins by assuming that some agreements are enforceable,[33] normative efficiency theories fail to provide a distinction between enforceable and unenforceable commitments. In a world of no transaction costs, it is asserted, individual economizing behavior would—by means of mutually advantageous exchanges of entitlements—ensure that legal entitlements are freely transferred to their highest value use. Because such a hypothetical world presupposes enforceable exchanges of legal entitlements, it cannot (without much more) tell us why or when some promises are enforceable while others are not.

In a world of positive transaction costs, economists who employ a model of "perfect competition" wish to assess the extent to which such costs block the movement of resources to their highest value use and the ways that legal rules and remedies—including those defining the background set of entitlements—can be altered to minimize such "inefficiency." Such an analysis, based on detecting deviations from the background efficiency "norm" of initial entitlements and cost-free exchanges, must ultimately rest on no more than an assumption that such voluntary economizing exchanges are to some extent enforceable. Typically, then, efficiency analyses focus on the real world problems of forced exchanges (tort law) in an effort to make legal solutions to these nonmarket transactions approximate market solutions as closely as possible. Efficiency analyses of voluntary exchanges (contract law) typically focus on issues other than the source of contractual obligation itself, such as appropriate remedies and other enforcement mechanisms, and assume, rather than demonstrate, the enforceability of all voluntary commitments. How we recognize voluntary commitments that ought to be enforced, as opposed to mere social promises that are not enforceable, is not generally discussed.

Moreover, some normative efficiency theories generate additional problems. If we are to enforce only those real world agreements that increase the overall wealth of society, then it must be either claimed or assumed that a neutral observer (for example, an economist-judge) has access to this information—that is, knows *which* agreements increase wealth and which do not. Two problems arise from this assumption or claim. The first concerns its truth. Can observers ever have information about value-

33. What these economists sometimes refer to as "market transactions," see, e.g., Coase, The Problem of Social Cost, 3 J.L. & Econ. 1, 15 (1960) ("The argument has proceeded up to this point on the assumption . . . that there were no costs involved *in carrying out market transactions.*" (emphasis added)), are in fact contracts. See Cheung, Transaction Costs, Risk Aversion, and the Choice of Contractual Arrangements, 12 J.L. & Econ. 23 (1969) ("Every transaction involves a contract."); Furubotn & Pejovich, Property Rights and Economic Theory: A Survey of Recent Literature, 10 J.Econ.Literature 1137, 1141 (1972) ("[T]he standard competitive model envisions a special system where one particular set of private property rights governs the use of *all* resources, and where the exchange, policing and enforcement costs of contractual activities are *zero.*").

enhancing exchanges independent of the demonstrated preferences of the market participants? More importantly, can a legal system practically base its decisions on such information? It has been persuasively argued that such knowledge is simply not available independently of the production of information by real markets. If it is not available, then it cannot provide workable criteria to distinguish enforceable from unenforceable promises.

Assuming, however, that such knowledge is available, if we have direct access to information sufficient to know whether particular exchanges are value enhancing or not, why bother with contract law at all? Why not simply have a central authority use this knowledge to transfer entitlements independently of the parties' agreement, particularly given the fact that the need to reach agreements creates transaction costs? Or, why not let judges use this knowledge to ratify "efficient thefts"—that is, give thieves the option of obtaining title to property that they have taken from others without their consent, provided only that the thief pays court-assessed damages equal to the value to the victim of her property? Normative economists are barred by their assumption about available information from responding that we need the market to provide such information.

Observations provided by economic theory about the effects of certain contract rules or principles on the efficient allocation of resources may rightly influence our normative assessment of those rules or principles, particularly when these effects are considered along with the effects such rules and principles would have on private autonomy, or "will," and on reliance. Most notably, the efficient allocation of resources may require a market composed of consensual exchanges that reveal and convey other-wise unobtainable information about personal preferences and economic opportunities. Economic analysis may, therefore, suggest that demonstrat-ed consent plays an important role in the law of contract, provided that efficient allocation of resources is a social activity that should be facilitated by a legal system. From this perspective, the "transaction costs" created by a requirement of consent are no worse from an efficiency standpoint than any other cost of production. The costs of negotiating to obtain the consent of another may be resources well-spent because such negotiations serve to reveal valuable information.

Where the negotiating costs of obtaining consent become so high as to bar exchanges thought to be desirable by observers, at least three conclu-sions are possible. Each, however, argues against enforcing involuntary transfers. First, in the absence of a consensual demonstration of prefer-ences, we do not really know if the exchange is worthwhile—value enhanc-ing—or not. Second, the inefficiency of government legal institutions that needlessly raise transaction costs may be principally responsible for making these consensual transactions prohibitively expensive. If so, then "govern-ment failure" and not "market failure" may be responsible for preventing the exchange and the appropriate response is to eliminate the true source of the inefficiency. Finally, when negotiation costs make consensual agree-ments too expensive a means of obtaining the vital information about value, several alternative ways exist to generate this information without negotiation—for example, by forming a new company or "firm," by merging one company with another, or by combining products into a single package.

In this analysis, demonstrated consent can be seen as playing an important role in any effort to achieve economic or allocative efficiency. Efficiency notions alone, however, cannot completely explain why certain commitments *should* be enforced unless it is further shown that economic efficiency is the exclusive goal of a legal order. The attempt to provide such a normative theory of wealth maximization, in the area of contract law at least, is fundamentally flawed. * * *

2. *Substantive Fairness Theories.* Another standards-based school of thought attempts to evaluate the substance of a transaction to see if it is "fair." Substantive fairness theories have a long tradition dating back at least to the Christian "just price" theorists of the Middle Ages and perhaps even to Aristotle. Their modern incarnation in contract law can be found in nineteenth century discussions of the "adequacy of consideration" and, more recently, in some treatments of "unconscionability."[58]

A substantive fairness theory assumes that a standard of value can be found by which the substance of any agreement can be objectively evaluated.[59] Such a criterion has yet to be articulated and defended. Without such a criterion, substantive fairness theories fall back on one or both of two incomplete approaches. On the one hand, such theories tend to focus all their attention on a small fraction of commitments—those that are thought to be so "extreme" as to "shock the conscience" of the courts. Most real world agreements are considered to be presumptively enforceable. On the other hand, such theories tend to become process based—looking for either information asymmetries or what is called "unequal bargaining power."

The first of these responses attempts to find extreme instances of violations of a standard that cannot be articulated—or at least cannot be articulated for most transactions, while the latter represents a retreat from the substantive fairness position altogether. Therefore, at best a substantive fairness approach attempts to deal with a qualitative issue by making either a quantitative or a procedural assessment, but *what* is being measured—the nature of the unfairness—is not disclosed.

---

58. See, e.g., Restatement (Second) of Contracts § 208 comment c (1979) ("Theoretically it is possible for a contract to be oppressive taken as a whole, even though there is no weakness in the bargaining process....").

59. Cohen noted this problem with what he called "the equivalent theory" of contract. See Cohen, supra note 7, at 581 (Due to problems of measurement, modern law "professes to abandon the effort of more primitive systems to enforce material fairness within the contract. The parties to the contract must themselves determine what is fair."). As a purely descriptive matter, the idea that exchange occurs because goods are of "equivalent" or equal value captivated economists for centuries, see supra notes 55–56 and accompanying text, until it was shown to be quite false. In fact, exchange occurs because both parties ex ante perceive the value of the goods to be exchanged as unequal. Each subjectively perceives the good or service offered by the other to be of greater value (to an unknowable extent) than what they are willing to trade for it. See C. Menger, Principles of Economics 180 (J. Dingwall & B. Hoselitz trans. 1981).

Most importantly for this discussion, however, the substantive fairness approach fails to address squarely the most central and common problem of contract theory: which *conscionable* agreements should be enforced and which should not? This after all, is, or ought to be, the starting point of a useful theory of contractual obligation that purports to discern which commitments merit legal enforcement. In sum, the substantive fairness approach provides neither meaningful standards nor predictable results. Both the extreme indeterminacy and the focus on aberrant cases inherent in a principle of substantive fairness prevent it from providing the over-arching account of contractual obligation that contract theory requires.

3. *The Problem With Standards-Based Theories.* All standards-based theories face two problems, one that is obvious and another that is more subtle. The obvious problem, which has already been discussed, is identifying and defending the appropriate standard by which enforceable commitments can be distinguished from those that should be unenforceable. The more subtle problem arises from the fact that standards-based contract theories are types of what Robert Nozick has called "patterned" principles of distributive justice:

> [A] principle of distribution [is] *patterned* if it specifies that a distribution is to vary along with some natural dimension, weighted sum of natural dimensions, or lexicographic ordering of natural dimensions....
>
> Almost every suggested principle of distributive justice is patterned: to each according to his moral merit, or needs, or marginal product, or how hard he tries, or the weighted sum of the foregoing, and so on.[67]

The problem created by such patterned theories of justice—including theories based on some notion of efficiency—is that they require constant interferences with individual preferences. "Render possessions ever so equal, man's different degrees of art, care, and industry will immediately break that equality." The maintenance of a pattern, therefore, requires either that persons be stopped from entering the contracts they desire, or that those in power "continually (or periodically) interfere to take from some persons resources that others for some reason chose to transfer to them."

Such interferences are at least presumptively suspect. They may sometimes even be objectionable according to the particular standard that is being used to justify the intervention. For example, inefficiency might be shown to be the ultimate result of interventions to achieve "efficiency" that thwart individual preferences in this way. And a system in which judges may, in the absence of fraud, duress, or some other demonstrable defect in the formation process, second-guess the wisdom of the parties may create more substantive unfairness than it cures. More fundamentally, a theory of rights might support the conclusion that such interferences are unjust and wrong.

----

67. R. Nozick, Anarchy, State and Utopia 156–57 (1974).

C. *Process-Based Theories*

Process-based theories shift the focus of the inquiry from the contract parties and from the substance of the parties' agreement to the manner in which the parties reached their agreement. Such theories posit appropriate procedures for establishing enforceable obligations and then assess any given transaction to see if these procedures were followed. The best known theory of this sort is the bargain theory of consideration.

1. *The Bargain Theory of Consideration.* The origin of the modern doctrine of consideration can be traced to the rise of the action of assumpsit. When the voluntary assumption of obligation came to be viewed as the basis of contractual enforcement, no one seriously suggested that *every* demonstrable agreement could or should be legally enforced. The number of agreements made every day are so numerous that for reasons of both practice and principle some distinction, apart from that made by purely evidentiary requirements, must be made between enforceable and unenforceable agreements.

The doctrine of consideration was devised to provide this distinction. Where consideration is present, an agreement ordinarily will be enforced. And, most significantly, where there is no consideration, even if the commitment is clear and unambiguous, enforcement is supposed to be unavailable. In the nineteenth century, the "bargain theory of consideration" was promoted by some, most notably Holmes and Langdell, as a way of answering the problem of which commitments merit legal protection. Today it is probably the predominant theory of consideration and is embodied in section 71 of the Restatement (Second) of Contracts:

(1) To constitute consideration, a performance or a return promise must be bargained for.

(2) A performance or return promise is bargained for if it is sought by the promisor in exchange for his promise and is given by the promisee in exchange for that promise.

This approach attempts to discern "mutuality" of inducement from the motives and acts of both parties to the transaction. It is not *what* is bargained for that is important; what solely matters is that each person's promise or performance is induced by the other's.

The difficulties presented by the doctrine of consideration depend on which way the concept is viewed. If the doctrine is interpreted restrictively, then whole classes of "serious" agreements will be thought to be lacking consideration. In his recent discussion of consideration, Charles Fried lists four kinds of cases—promises to keep an offer open, to release a debt, to modify an obligation, and to pay for past favors—where promisees have traditionally had considerable difficulty obtaining legal relief for nonperformance because bargained-for consideration is lacking, although it is generally conceded that the parties may have intended to be legally bound and that enforcement should therefore be available. To these may be added unbargained-for promises to assume the obligations of another, to convey land, to give to charities, and those made by bailees and within the family.

In each of these types of cases, a promise is made and then broken. The promisee then seeks to base his cause of action on the promise. In many of these cases, the promise is a serious and unambiguous one. In each situation, however, there is no "bargain" and therefore no consideration for the promise.

Such cases as these invite attempts by judges and others to expand the concept of consideration beyond the bargain requirement. Any such attempt to capture these and other types of cases will, however, run afoul of an opposing difficulty. If the web of consideration doctrine is woven too loosely, it will increasingly capture "social" agreements where legal enforcement is not contemplated—for example, promises of financial assistance between family members. Thus, any expanded concept of consideration threatens to undermine the doctrine's traditional function: distinguishing enforceable from unenforceable agreements in a predictable fashion to allow for private planning and to prevent the weight of legal coercion from falling upon those informal or "social" arrangements where the parties have not contemplated legal sanctions for breach.

Each strategy to deal with the problems generated by a doctrine of consideration, therefore, wreaks havoc in its own way with a coherent theory of contractual obligation. With a restrictive definition like that of bargain, serious promises which merit enforcement are left unenforced. With an expansive formulation, informal promises that are thought to be properly outside the province of legal coercion will be made the subject of legal sanctions. The most recognized problem with the bargain theory is that it appears to have erred too far in the direction of under-enforcement. However, the bargain theory suffers in a more fundamental way from its purely process-based character.

2. *The Problem With Process-Based Theories.* The problem with process-based theories is not simply that they must strike a balance between over—and under—enforcement. Such trade-offs cannot be completely avoided in any system that bases decision-making on rules and principles of general application. The real problem with process-based theories like the bargain theory of consideration is that they place insurmountable obstacles in the way of minimizing such difficulties of enforcement.

First, a process-based theory's *exclusive* focus on the process that justifies contractual enforcement conceals the substantive values that must support any choice of process. By obscuring these values, process-based theories come to treat their favored procedural devices as ends, rather than as means. Then, when the adopted procedures inevitably give rise to problems of fit between means and ends, a process-based theory that is divorced from ends cannot say why this has occurred or what is to be done about it. This inherent weakness of process-based theories has plagued the bargain theory of consideration.

The bargain theory, which was devised to limit the applicability of assumpsit, fails to ensure the enforcement of certain reasonably well-defined categories of unbargained-for, but "serious" commitments. Then, when courts are moved to enforce such commitments, the principal theory of consideration to which they adhere cannot account for these "exceptions" to the normal requirement of a bargain without appealing to concepts more fundamental than bargaining. Ironically, the rise of assumpsit—the source of the need for the consideration doctrine—was itself due to the inability of the then existing process-based writ system to accommodate enforcement of informal, but serious promises.

Second, an exclusively process-based theory cannot itself explain why certain *kinds* of commitments are not and should not be enforceable. For example, it is widely recognized that agreements to perform illegal acts should not be enforceable. Similarly, slavery contracts are also thought to be unenforceable per se. If, however, agreements of these types were reached in conformity with all "rules of the game," a theory that looks only to the rules of the game to decide issues of enforceability cannot say why such an otherwise "proper" agreement should be unenforceable.

These two types of problems, however, are not confined to process-based theories. As was seen above, party-based theories based on will and reliance are also plagued by an inability to account for and explain certain "exceptional" agreements that are enforceable without recourse to their animating principles. And theories based on principles of will, reliance, or efficiency have as hard a time as process-based theories explaining why certain agreements are unenforceable due to so-called "public policy" exceptions to their respective norms of contractual obligation.

Notwithstanding the weaknesses inherent in process-based theories, such theories offer significant advantages over both party-based and standards-based theories. By employing a neutral criterion for determining contractual enforcement, a process-based theory can better protect both the contractual intent and the reliance of both parties than one-sided party-based theories, provided it identifies features of the contractual process that normally correspond to the presence of contractual intent and substantial reliance. By identifying judicially workable criteria of enforcement, process-based theories can avoid the difficulties of extreme indeterminacy that were seen to plague standards-based theories. They can, in short, better provide the traditionally acknowledged advantages of a system of generally applicable laws, such as facilitating private planning and helping to ensure equal treatment of similarly situated persons. Perhaps it is these advantages that have permitted a process-based theory like the bargain theory to survive its frequent detractors.

The significant administrative advantages of process-based theories suggest that the best approach to contractual obligation is one that preserves a procedural aspect of contract law, while recognizing that such procedures are *dependent* for their ultimate justification on more fundamental, substantive principles of right that occasionally affect procedural analysis in two ways. First, these principles might suggest specific improvements in procedures governing contract formation that are appropriate in the event that previously adopted procedures have created well-defined problems of under-enforcement. Second, these principles might serve to deprive certain procedurally immaculate agreements of their normal moral significance, thereby ameliorating identifiable problems of over-enforcement.''

Randy Barnett, *A Consent Theory of Contract*, 86 Colum.L.Rev. 269, 271–291 (1986). [Copyright © 1986 by Directors of the Columbia Law Review Association, Inc. All Rights Reserved. Reprinted by permission.]

NOTES

(1) To what extent are the fives theories *normative*—providing an account of what promises *should* be enforced? To what extent are the fives theories *positive*—providing a descriptive account of what promises *are* (or tend to be) enforced? Notice that Barnett at times conflates the normative and the positive, saying that a particular theory is not a successful normative theory because it does not explain what enforcement practices currently are.

(2) "Unfortunately, contract, like most of the basic terms constituting the intellectual tools of law, is conventionally defined in a circular fashion. By the most common definition, a contract is a promise or set of promises for the breach of which the law gives a remedy or the performance of which the law recognizes as a duty. This amounts to saying that a contract is a legally enforceable promise. But a promise is legally enforceable only if it is a contract. Thus nothing less than the whole body of applicable precedents suffices to define the term 'contract.'

Although the definition of contract does not help much in determining what expressions shall be held to impose legal obligations, it does direct attention to a promise as the starting point of inquiry. Both in popular and legal usage, a promise is an assurance, in whatever form of expression given, that a thing will or will not be done. While we must take care to distinguish between statements meant to express merely present intention and those meant to give an assurance as to a future event, this involves no more than the common difficulty of seeking precise meaning in the usually imprecise, and often careless, expressions of ordinary colloquy.

* * *

However, the fact that a promise was given does not necessarily mean that a contract was made. It is clear that not every promise is legally enforceable. Much of the vast body of law in the field of contracts is concerned with determining which promises should be legally enforced. On the one hand, in a civilized community men must be able to assume that those with whom they deal will carry out their undertakings according to reasonable expectations. On the other hand, it is neither practical nor reasonable to expect full performance of every assurance given, whether it be thoughtless, casual and gratuitous, or deliberately and seriously made.

The test that has been developed by the common law for determining the enforceability of promises is the doctrine of consideration. This is a crude and not altogether successful attempt to generalize the conditions under which promises will be legally enforced. Consideration requires that a contractual promise be the product of a bargain. However, in this usage, 'bargain' does not mean an exchange of things of equivalent, or any, value. It means a negotiation resulting in the voluntary assumption of an obligation by one party upon condition of an act or forbearance by the other. Consideration thus insures that the promise enforced as a contract is not accidental, casual, or gratuitous, but has been uttered intentionally as a result of some deliberation, manifested by reciprocal bargaining or negotiation. In this view, the requirement of consideration is no mere technicality, historical anachronism, or arbitrary formality. It is an attempt to be as reasonable as we can in deciding which promises constitute contracts. Although the doctrine has been criticized, no satisfactory substitute has been suggested. It is noteworthy that the civil law has a corresponding doctrine of 'causa' which, to the eye of a common-law lawyer, is not much different than consideration.

Consideration, as essential evidence of the parties' intent to create a legal obligation, must be something adopted and regarded by the parties as such. Thus, the same thing may be consideration or not, as it is dealt with by the parties. In substance, a contractual promise must be of the logical form: 'If . . . (consideration is given) . . . then I promise that. . . .' Of course, the substance may be expressed in any form of words, but essentially this is the logical structure of those promises enforced by the law as contracts."

Loevinger, J. in Baehr v. Penn–O–Tex Oil Corporation, 258 Minn. 533, 104 N.W.2d 661, 664–66 (1960).

(3) *Economic Functions of Contract Law.* In the view of Professor (now Judge) Richard A. Posner, the law of contracts performs three economic functions: first, it furnishes "incentives for value-maximizing conduct in the future," i.e., conduct that exploits economic resources in such a way that human satisfaction as measured by aggregate consumer willingness to pay for goods and services is maximized; second, it reduces the "complexity and hence cost of transactions by supplying a set of normal terms which, in the absence of a law of contracts, the parties would have to negotiate expressly"; and third, it furnishes "prospective transacting parties with information concerning the many contingencies that may defeat an exchange, and hence to assist them in planning their exchange sensibly." These economic functions are supported by the doctrine of consideration, which is used to "deny liability for breach of a promise . . . where there is no exchange and where, therefore, enforcement of the promise would not advance the economic purpose of the law of contracts which is to facilitate exchange. A truly gratuitous, nonreciprocal promise to confer a benefit is not a part of the process by which resources are moved, through a series of exchanges, into successively more valuable uses." R. Posner, Economic Analysis of Law 68–71 (2d ed. 1977). [Although this influential book is now in its 5th edition (1998), we retain the text from the 2d edition.]

(4) *Contract as a Basic Social Institution.* After discussing the "emotive and symbolic power" of the idea of contract and the "moral imperative" that clusters about the phrase *"pacta sunt servanda,"* that "obligations freely agreed to are to be honored and performed," Professor Harry W. Jones has this to say about contract as a "basic social institution, one comparable in importance to such other pervading social institutions as property, the family, even the institution of representative government":

In a society like ours, people live not by birds in the hand but by promises: for example, anyone's job is an exchange of promises, by him to work and by his employer to pay agreed or understood wages. Investments are essentially promises by corporate powerholders to manage a business in proper ways and to pay dividends as earned. A bank account is a promise to hold and return money deposited; even money is a promise, though rather less reliable than in earlier days, by government to pay something on due presentation.... John Kenneth Galbraith may or may not have been right to characterize our national community as *The Affluent Society;* he would have said something unquestionably true, and perhaps of even greater economic significance, if he had called us the *promissory* society. A promissory society, by definition, is one energized and bound together by the institution of contract.... The law of contract—and "law of contract" here includes what we elsewhere break up into such segments as commercial transactions, partnerships, corporations, labor law and many more—has as its ultimate purpose the security of those reasonable expectations that arise from agreement between seller and buyer, borrower and depositor, stockholder and corporation, employer and organized employees.

Harry W. Jones, *The Jurisprudence of Contracts*, 44 U.Cin.L.Rev. 43, 47–48 (1975).

CHAPTER TWO

THE BASES OF CONTRACT LIABILITY

Contemporary American law recognizes four types of enforceable promises or contracts, each involving a transaction where something is added to the promise so as to make it legally binding. They are: promise plus consideration (Section 1); promise plus antecedent benefit (Section 2); promise plus unbargained-for reliance (Section 3); and promise plus form (Section 4).

SECTION 1. THE CONSIDERATION REQUIREMENT

Comment: An Historical and Definitional Note

(1) *Consideration as Either Benefit to Promisor or Detriment to Promisee:* According to the New York Court of Appeals:

During the early phases of the development of English common law, an action on an obligation other than one embodied in a sealed instrument was maintainable only through a writ to recover on a debt. The availability of such writs, however, was limited to those narrow situations in which one of the parties withheld payment of a fixed, bargained for sum of money after the other party had performed his part of the bargain by making a loan or delivering goods or services. The underlying theory of the action was that the parties had made a bargain or had agreed upon a *quid pro quo* exchange and the promisor or debtor was now wrongfully withholding the property of the promisee by refusing to make payment after receiving that which he had bargained for. It was from this concept of a bargained for *quid pro quo* that the notion of consideration as a benefit flowing to the promisor was derived (see 1 Corbin, Contracts, § 121; Morgan, Introduction to the Study of Law [2d ed.], pp. 92–93; 1 Williston, Contracts [Jaeger 3d ed.], § 99; Holmes, Early English Equity, 1 L.Q.Rev. 162, 171).

The action on a debt, however, proved unsatisfactory for a variety of reasons, not the least of which was its limited scope. Litigants, as a consequence, turned with increasing frequency to the vehicle of assumpsit, which was originally a simple variant of trespass on the case, the forerunner of our modern tort cause of action (see Ames, History of Assumpsit, 2 Harv.L.Rev. 1). Although assumpsit ultimately evolved into a separate and distinct form of action, its earliest uses were confined to claims based upon malfeasance or faulty performance of an assumed duty (see Williston, at p. 384). Consistent with its origins in trespass on the case, the gist of the action in assumpsit remained the injury to the promisee resulting from the promisor's misconduct in improperly performing his obligation. It was apparently not until 1588 that assumpsit was definitively expanded to encompass actions for nonfeasance or simple failure to perform a contractual duty. In that year, it was held that 'a promise against a promise will maintain an action upon the case [in assumpsit], as in consideration that you do give me £10 on such a day, I promise to give you £10 such a day after' (Strangborough and Warner's Case, 4 Leon 3, 74 Eng.Rep. 686 [QB]). With this expansion in the availability of assumpsit, the original requirement of an injury resulting from misfeasance was broadened, and an action in assumpsit could thereafter be maintained upon a showing of any detriment, loss or disadvantage to the promisee arising from the bargain (see, generally, Holdsworth, Debt, Assumpsit and Consideration, 11 Mich. L.Rev. 347).

The final critical development in the law of assumpsit occurred in 1602 with the decision in Slade's Case (4 Coke 91a, 92b, 76 Eng.Rep. 1072, 1074 [KB]). That decision paved the way for litigants to sue in assumpsit on claims for fixed sums of money previously maintainable only in the older form of an action based on a *quid pro quo* to recover a debt (see Moses v. Macferlan, 2 Burr. 1005, 1008, 97 Eng.Rep. 676 [KB]). As a result of this development, assumpsit became the primary vehicle for litigation on contractual obligations, and the notion of 'consideration' became a term of art encompassing both a benefit to the promisor, the equivalent of the former *quid pro quo,* and a detriment to the promisee, the equivalent of the former requirement of injury in actions sounding in assumpsit (see Williston, at pp. 368–369).

This dual notion of consideration as either a benefit to the promisor *or* a detriment to the promisee has persisted to the present day and has become an integral part of our modern approach to the enforceability of contracts. Thus, it has repeatedly been stated that '[a] valuable consideration may consist of some right, interest, profit or benefit accruing to one party, or some forbearance, detriment, loss or responsibility given, suffered or undertaken by the other' (Rector of St. Mark's Church v. Teed, 120 N.Y. 583, 586). Indeed, we have expressly held that a promisee who has incurred a specific, bargained for legal detriment may enforce a promise against the promisor, notwithstanding the fact that the latter may have realized no concrete benefit as a result of the bargain." Holt v. Feigenbaum, 52 N.Y.2d 291, 296–299, 437 N.Y.S.2d 654, 419 N.E.2d 332 (1981).

(2) *Consideration as Bargained-For Exchange:*

Restatement (Second) § 71 defines consideration as follows:

(1) To constitute consideration, a performance or a return promise must be bargained for.

(2) A performance or return promise is bargained for if it is sought by the promisor in exchange for his promise and is given by the promisee in exchange for that promise.

(3) The performance may consist of: (a) an act other than a promise, or (b) a forbearance, or (c) the creation, modification, or destruction of a legal relation.

(4) The performance or return promise may be given to the promisor or to some other person. It may be given by the promisee or by some other person.

This formulation, which has changed little from the first Restatement, has been described by Professor Patterson as including both "a thing (promise or performance) that the promisor bargains for * * * [and] the process of bargaining for it. * * * Consideration * * * implies that something happened, a bargain or exchange." Edwin W. Patterson, *An Apology for Consideration*, 58 Colum.L.Rev. 929, 932–933 (1958). There is not much doubt—in this country at least—"that the bargain theory is the 'generally accepted idea of consideration.' " Williston § 100.

But what are the historical origins of the bargain requirement? In his stimulating book, The Death of Contract, Professor Grant Gilmore argued that the bargain requirement miraculously arose from the pages of O.W. Holmes' classic, The Common Law. Between the merger of debt and assumpsit at the beginning of the 17th century (see infra at 109–112) and 1880, the date of The Common Law, consideration for a promise had come to be defined as either a detriment to the plaintiff or a benefit to the defendant. According to Gilmore, Holmes, with hardly any support from the precedents or historical materials, promoted the definition to something bargained for and given in exchange for the promise.

Holmes said, the "root of the whole matter is the relationship of conventional inducement, each for the other, between consideration and promise." Holmes, The Common Law 230 (M. Howe ed. 1963). This "revolutionary doctrine" was then elaborated by Williston and others as the exclusive basis for enforcing promises and began to infect the entire life history of contracts. Promises on the periphery of the market, options, requirements contracts, modifications and discharges, all felt the influence of bargain and its attendant slogans, such as "mutuality of obligation." Thus, according to Gilmore, the miraculous birth and spectacular promotion of the new child as the exclusive basis for promissory liability narrowed the scope of contract, unrealistically sharpened the differences between contract and tort and left in limbo the question of liability for unbargained-for benefits voluntarily conferred (moral obligation) and for induced but not bargained-for reliance (promissory estoppel). See G. Gilmore, The Death of Contract 5–53 (1974).

Professor Speidel has noted: "The bargain idea has enjoyed a striking persistence in American contract law. This is partially explained, no doubt, by its strong congruence with basic human behavior. * * * [I]n retrospect, the bargain theory appears to be a very natural adaptation of prevailing economic attitudes to serve important legal needs. As an operating principle, the 'bargain' theory of consideration (1) provided a natural formality to channel human conduct and insure deliberation; (2) protected and structured the important market transaction; (3) expanded legal protection by supporting the executory exchange—a promise for a promise—and shielding the creative or idiosyncratic bargainer from later claims that the agreed exchange was disproportionate; and (4) it permitted a fuller development of remedies that protected the plaintiff's expectation interest, that is, the value to the plaintiff of the agreed exchange." Richard E. Speidel, *An Essay on the Reported Death and Continued Vitality of Contract*, 27 Stan.L.Rev. 1161, 1168–1170 (1975).

See also Farnsworth §§ 2.1–2.20; Calamari and Perillo §§ 4–1 to 4–15, 5–11 to 5–20; Murray §§ 54–65; C. Fried, Contract as Promise (1981); Val D. Ricks, *The Sophisticated Doctrine of Consideration*, 9 G. Mason L. Rev. 99 (2000).

(A) BARGAINED FOR AND GIVEN IN EXCHANGE

Kirksey v. Kirksey

Supreme Court of Alabama, 1845.
8 Ala. 131.

Error to the Circuit Court of Talladega.

Assumpsit by the defendant, against the plaintiff in error. The question is presented in this Court, upon a case agreed, which shows the following facts:

The plaintiff was the wife of defendant's brother, but had for some time been a widow, and had several children. In 1840, the plaintiff resided on public land, under a contract of lease, she had held over, and was comfortably settled, and would have attempted to secure the land she lived on. The defendant resided in Talladega county, some sixty, or seventy miles off. On the 10th of October, 1840, he wrote to her the following letter:

"Dear sister Antillico—Much to my mortification, I heard, that brother Henry was dead, and one of his children. I know that your situation is one of grief, and difficulty. You had a bad chance before, but a great deal worse now. I should like to come and see you, but cannot with convenience at present. * * * I do not know whether you have a preference on the place you live on, or not. If you had, I would advise you to obtain your preference, and sell the land and quit the country, as I understand it is very unhealthy, and I know society is very bad. If you will come down and see me, I will let you have a place to raise your family, and I have more open land than I can tend; and on the account of your situation, and that of your family, I feel like I want you and the children to do well."

Within a month or two after the receipt of this letter, the plaintiff abandoned her possession, without disposing of it, and removed with her family, to the residence of the defendant, who put her in comfortable houses, and gave her land to cultivate for two years, at the end of which time he notified her to remove, and put her in a house, not comfortable, in the woods, which he afterwards required her to leave.

A verdict being found for the plaintiff, for two hundred dollars, the above facts were agreed, and if they will sustain the action, the judgment is to be affirmed, otherwise it is to be reversed.

ORMOND, J. The inclination of my mind, is, that the loss and inconvenience, which the plaintiff sustained in breaking up and moving to the defendant's, a distance of sixty miles, is a sufficient consideration to support the promise, to furnish her with a house, and land to cultivate, until she could raise her family. My brothers, however, think that the promise on the part of the defendant, was a mere gratuity, and that an action will not lie for its breach. The judgment of the Court below must therefore be reversed, pursuant to the agreement of the parties.

NOTES

(1) Does it appear from *Kirksey* that a promise, simply because it is a promise, is presumptively enforceable?

(2) Assuming that the defendant's promise in *Kirksey* was, as characterized by the court, "a mere gratuity," should that, of itself, preclude relief for the plaintiff? Is it a policy of the law to discourage gratuities? Why might a court hesitate, however, to enforce a Kirksey-like promise? For example, what remedy should be given for breach of contract? See James Gordley, *Enforcing Promises*, 83 Cal.L.Rev. 541, 579–582 (1985), who notes that even though the case was decided before the rise of so-called promissory estoppel, Sister Antillico would not be a sympathetic figure if she "herself suspected that the promise might be indeliberate, defeasible for a host of reasons, and not intended to confer a right of action."

(3) The legend of Sister Antillico lives on. See Carol Weisbrod, *An Uncertain Trumpet: A Gloss on Kirksey v. Kirksey*, 32 Conn. L. Rev. 1699 (2000), who speculates on the role of dissent in American case law and the unique function performed by Judge Ormond, who "wrote for the court and was thus majority and dissent, authority and critic at the same time."

Hamer v. Sidway

Court of Appeals of New York, 1891.
124 N.Y. 538, 27 N.E. 256.

Appeal from an order of the general term of the supreme court in the fourth judicial department, reversing a judgment entered on the decision of the court at special term in the county clerk's office of Chemung county on the 1st day of October, 1889. The plaintiff presented a claim to the executor of William E. Story, Sr., for $5,000 and interest from the 6th day of February, 1875. She acquired it through several mesne assignments from William E. Story, 2d. The claim being rejected by the executor, this action was brought. It appears that William E. Story, Sr., was the uncle of William E. Story, 2d; that at the celebration of the golden wedding of Samuel Story and wife, father and mother of William E. Story, Sr., on the 20th day of March, 1869, in the presence of the family and invited guests, he promised his nephew that if he would refrain from drinking, using tobacco, swearing, and playing cards or billiards for money until he became 21 years of age, he would pay him the sum of $5,000. The nephew assented thereto, and fully performed the conditions inducing the promise. When the nephew arrived at the age of 21 years, and on the 31st day of January, 1875, he wrote to his uncle, informing him that he had performed his part of the agreement, and had thereby become entitled to the sum of $5,000. The uncle received the letter, and a few days later, on the 6th day of February, he wrote and mailed to his nephew the following letter: "Buffalo, Feb. 6, 1875. W.E. Story, Jr.—Dear Nephew: Your letter of the 31st ult. came to hand all right, saying that you had lived up to the promise made to me several years ago. I have no doubt but you have, for which you shall have five thousand dollars, as I promised you. I had the money in the bank the day you was twenty-one years old that I intend for you, and you shall have the money certain. Now, Willie, I do not intend to interfere with this money in any way till I think you are capable of taking care of it, and the sooner that time comes the better it will please me. I would hate very much to have you start out in some adventure that you thought all right and lose this money in one year. The first five thousand dollars that I got together cost me a heap of hard work. You would hardly believe me when I tell you that to obtain this I shoved a jack-plane many a day, butchered three or four years, then came to this city, and, after three months' perseverance, I obtained a situation in a grocery store. I opened this store early, closed late, slept in the fourth story of a building in a room 30 by 40 feet, and not a human being in the building but myself. All this I done to live as cheap as I could to save something. I don't want you to take up with this kind of fare. I was here in the cholera season of '49 and '52, and the deaths averaged 80 to 125 daily, and plenty of small-pox. I wanted to go home, but Mr. Fisk, the gentleman I was working for, told me, if I left them, after it got healthy he probably would not want me. I stayed. All the money I have saved I know just how I got it. It did not come to me in any mysterious way, and the reason I speak of this is that money got in this way stops longer with a fellow that gets it with hard knocks than it does when he finds it. Willie, you are twenty-one, and you have many a thing to learn yet. This money you have earned much easier than I did, besides acquiring good habits at the same time, and you are quite welcome to the money. Hope you will make good use of it. I was ten long years getting this together after I was your age. Now, hoping this will be satisfactory, I stop. * * * Truly yours, W.E. Story. P.S. You can consider this money on interest." The nephew received the letter, and thereafter consented that the money should remain with his uncle in accordance with the terms and conditions of the letter. The uncle died on the 29th day of January, 1887, without having paid over to his nephew any portion of the said $5,000 and interest.

■ PARKER, J. The question which provoked the most discussion by counsel on this appeal, and which lies at the foundation of plaintiff's asserted right of recovery, is whether by virtue of a contract defendant's testator, William E. Story, became indebted to his nephew, William E. Story, 2d, on his twenty-first birthday in the sum of $5,000. The trial court found as a fact that "on the 20th day of March, 1869, * * * William E. Story agreed to and with William E. Story, 2d, that if he would refrain from drinking liquor, using tobacco, swearing, and playing cards or billiards for money until he should become twenty-one years of age, then he, the said William E. Story, would at that time pay him, the said William E. Story, 2d, the sum of $5,000 for such refraining, to which the said William E. Story, 2d, agreed," and that he "in all things fully performed his part of said agreement." The defendant contends that the contract was without consideration to support it, and therefore invalid. He asserts that the promisee, by refraining from the use of liquor and tobacco, was not harmed, but benefited; that that which he did was best for him to do, independently of his uncle's promise,—and insists that it follows that, unless the promisor was benefited, the contract was without consideration,—a contention which, if well founded, would seem to leave open for controversy in many cases whether that which the promisee did or omitted to do was in fact of such benefit to him as to leave no consideration to support the enforcement of the promisor's agreement. Such a rule could not be tolerated, and is without foundation in the law. The exchequer chamber in 1875 defined "consideration" as follows: "A valuable consideration, in the sense of the law, may consist either in some right, interest, profit, or benefit accruing to the one party, or some forbearance, detriment, loss, or responsibility given, suffered, or undertaken by the other." Courts "will not ask whether the thing which forms the consideration does in fact benefit the promisee or a third party, or is of any substantial value to any one. It is enough that something is promised, done, forborne, or suffered by the party to whom the promise is made as consideration for the promise made to him." Anson, Cont. 63. "In general a waiver of any legal right at the request of another party is a sufficient consideration for a promise." Pars. Cont. *444. "Any damage, or suspension, or forbearance of a right will be sufficient to sustain a promise." 2 Kent, Comm. (12th Ed.) *465. Pollock in his work on Contracts, (page 166,) after citing the definition given by the exchequer chamber, already quoted, says: "The second branch of this judicial description is really the most important one. 'Consideration' means not so much that one party is profiting as that the other abandons some legal right in the present, or limits his legal freedom of action in the future, as an inducement for the promise of the first." Now, applying this rule to the facts before us, the promisee used tobacco, occasionally drank liquor, and he had a legal right to do so. That right he abandoned for a period of years upon the strength of the promise of the testator that for such forbearance he would give him $5,000. We need not speculate on the effort which may have been required to give up the use of those stimulants. It is sufficient that he restricted his lawful freedom of action within certain prescribed limits upon the faith of his uncle's agreement, and now, having fully performed the conditions imposed, it is of no moment whether such performance actually proved a benefit to the promisor, and the court will not inquire into it; but, were it a proper subject of inquiry, we see nothing in this record that would permit a determination that the uncle was not benefited in a legal sense. Few cases have been found which may be said to be precisely in point, but such as have been, support the position we have taken. In Shadwell v. Shadwell, 9 C.B. (N.S.) 159, an uncle wrote to his nephew as follows: "My dear Lancey: I am so glad to hear of your intended marriage with Ellen Nicholl, and, as I promised to assist you at starting, I am happy to tell you that I will pay you 150 pounds yearly during my life and until your annual income derived from your profession of a chancery barrister shall amount to 600 guineas, of which your own admission will be the only evidence that I shall receive or require. Your affectionate uncle, Charles Shadwell." It was held that the promise was binding, and made upon good consideration. * * * In Talbott v. Stemmons, 12 S.W.Rep. 297, (a Kentucky case, not yet officially reported,) the step-grandmother of the plaintiff made with him the following agreement: "I do promise and bind myself to give my grandson Albert R. Talbott $500 at my death if he will never take another chew of tobacco or smoke another cigar during my life, from this date up to my death; and if he breaks this pledge he is to refund double the amount to his mother." The executor of Mrs. Stemmons demurred to the complaint on the ground that the agreement was not based on a sufficient consideration. The demurrer was sustained, and an appeal taken therefrom to the court of appeals, where the decision of the court below was reversed. In the opinion of the court it is said that "the right to use and enjoy the use of tobacco was a right that belonged to the plaintiff, and not forbidden by law. The abandonment of its use may have saved him money, or contributed to his health; nevertheless, the surrender of that right caused the promise, and, having the right to contract with reference to the subject-matter, the abandonment of the use was a sufficient consideration to uphold the promise." * * * The order appealed from should be reversed, and the judgment of the special term affirmed, with costs payable out of the estate. All concur.

NOTES

(1) Was there equivalency of exchange in *Hamer?* Did the promisor gain a pecuniary advantage? Did he derive any "benefit" from the transaction at all, or is enforcement predicated solely upon "detriment" to the promisee? In what way was plaintiff's conduct detrimental?

Langer v. Superior Steel Corp.

Superior Court of Pennsylvania, 1932.
105 Pa.Super. 579, 161 A. 571.

BALDRIGE, J. This in an action of assumpsit to recover damages for breach of a contract. The court below sustained questions of law raised by defendant, and entered judgment in its favor.

The plaintiff alleges that he is entitled to recover certain monthly payments provided for in the following letter:

"August 31, 1927.

"Mr. Wm. F. Langer,

"Dear Sir:

"As you are retiring from active duty with this company, as superintendent of the annealing department, on August 31st, we hope that it will give you some pleasure to receive this official letter of commendation for your long and faithful service with the Superior Steel Corporation.

"The directors have decided that you will receive a pension of $100 per month as long as you live and preserve your present attitude of loyalty to the company and its officers and are not employed in any competitive occupation. We sincerely hope that you will live long to enjoy it and that this and the other evidences of the esteem in which you are held by your fellow employees and which you will today receive with this letter, will please you as much as it does us to bestow them.

> "Cordially yours,
> "(Signed) Frank R. Frost,
> "President."

The defendant paid the sum of $100 a month for approximately four years when the plaintiff was notified that the company no longer intended to continue the payments.

The issue raised by the affidavit of defense is whether the letter created a gratuitous promise or an enforceable contract. It is frequently a matter of great difficulty to differentiate between promises creating legal obligations and mere gratuitous agreements. Each case depends to a degree upon its peculiar facts and circumstances. Was this promise supported by a sufficient consideration, or was it but a condition attached to a gift? If a contract was created, it was based on a consideration, and must have been the result of an agreement bargained for in exchange for a promise: ... It was held in Presbyterian Board of Foreign Missions v. Smith, 209 Pa. 361, 363, that "a test of good consideration is whether the promisee, at the instance of the promisor, has done, forborne or undertaken to do anything real, or whether he has suffered any detriment or whether in return for the promise he has done something that he was not bound to do or has promised to do some act or has abstained from doing something." Mr. Justice Sadler pointed out in York M. & Alloys Co. v. Cyclops S. Co., 280 Pa. 585, that a good consideration exists if one refrains from doing anything that he has a right to do, "whether there is any actual loss or detriment to him or actual benefit to the promisor or not."

* * *

The plaintiff, in his statement, which must be admitted as true in considering the statutory demurrer filed by defendant, alleges that he refrained from seeking employment with any competitive company, and that he complied with the terms of the agreement. By so doing, has he sustained any detriment? Was his forbearance sufficient to support a good consideration? Professor Williston, in his treatise on Contracts, sec. 112, states: "It is often difficult to determine whether words of condition in a promise indicate a request for consideration or state a mere condition in a gratuitous promise. An aid, though not a conclusive test in determining which construction of the promise is more reasonable is an inquiry whether the happening of the condition will be a benefit to the promisor. If so, it is a fair inference that the happening was requested as a consideration. . . . In case of doubt where the promisee has incurred a detriment on the faith of the promise, courts will naturally be loath to regard the promise as a mere gratuity, and the detriment incurred as merely a condition.''

It is reasonable to conclude that it is to the advantage of the defendant if the plaintiff, who had been employed for a long period of time as its superintendent in the annealing department, and who, undoubtedly, had knowledge of the methods used by the employer, is not employed by a competitive company; otherwise, such a stipulation would have been unnecessary. That must have been the inducing reason for inserting that provision. There is nothing appearing of record, except the condition imposed by the defendant, that would have prevented this man of skill and experience from seeking employment elsewhere. By receiving the monthly payments, he impliedly accepted the conditions imposed and was thus restrained from doing that which he had a right to do. This was a sufficient consideration to support a contract.

The appellee refers to **Kirksey v. Kirksey**, 8 Ala. 131, which is also cited by Professor Williston in his work on Contracts, sec. 112, note 51, as a leading case on this subject under discussion. The defendant wrote his sister-in-law, the plaintiff: "If you will come down and see me, I will let you have a place to raise your family and I have more open land than I can tend; and on the account of your situation and that of your family, I feel like I want you and the children to do well." The plaintiff left her home and moved her family a distance of 67 miles to the residence of the defendant, who gave her the house and land, and after a period of two years, requested her to leave. The court held that the promise was a mere gratuity. In that case, as well as in Richards's Exr. v. Richards, 46 Pa. 78, there was no benefit to be derived by the promisor, as in the case at bar, and, therefore, a good consideration was lacking.

In this view, this contract is enforceable also on the theory of promissory estoppel. This principle has been stated by the American Law Institute in section 90 of the Restatement of the Law of Contracts, as follows: "A promise which the promisor should reasonably expect to induce action or forbearance of a definite and substantial character on the part of the promisee and which does induce such action or forbearance is binding if injustice can be avoided only by enforcement of the promise." As we have already observed, the plaintiff was induced by the promises made to refrain from seeking other employment. A promissory estoppel differs from the equitable estoppel, as it rests upon a promise to do something in the future, while the latter rests upon a statement of a present fact. We have an example of the former in Ricketts v. Scothorn, 57 Neb. 51, 77 N.W. 365, where a grandfather handed his granddaughter a note for $2,000 saying, "I have fixed out something that you have not got to work any more. None of my grandchildren work and you don't have to." The grandfather did not ask his granddaughter to give up her employment, but merely promised that she would not have to work unless she wanted to. She stopped working, relying upon getting $2,000. The court admitted that there was no consideration, but enforced the promise because it had misled the promisee in such a way that it would be unfair to her to do otherwise; thereby invoking the principle of promissory estoppel. We do not mean to state that in all cases where a gratuitous promise is made, and one relies upon it, the promisee can recover, but, if a detriment of a definite and substantial character has been incurred by the promisee, then the court may enforce the promise.

Judgment is reversed, and the defendant is hereby given permission to file an affidavit of defense to the merits of the plaintiff's claims.*

NOTES

(1) How does the court in *Langer* purport to distinguish *Kirksey?* If the *Langer* court had decided *Kirksey* would the result likely have been the same?

(2) The "first" Restatement defined consideration in § 75(1): "Consideration for a promise is

(a) an act other than a promise, or

(b) a forbearance, or

(c) the creation, modification or destruction of a legal relation, or

(d) a return promise,

bargained for and given in exchange for the promise." How does this compare with the Restatement (Second) definition, see supra at 37–38?

(3) For a general perspective, see E. Allan Farnsworth, *The Past of Promise: An Historical Introduction to Contract,* 69 Colum.L.Rev. 576 (1969). In this article the author quotes the following excerpt from Adam Smith's The Wealth of Nations:

> [M]an has almost constant occasion for the help of his brethren, and it is vain for him to expect it from their benevolences only. He will be more likely to prevail if he can interest their self-love in his favour, and shew them that it is for their own advantage to do for him what he requires of them. Whoever offers to another a bargain of any kind, proposes to do this. Give me that which I want, and you shall have this which you want, is the meaning of every such offer; and it is in this manner that we obtain from one another the far greater part of those good offices which we stand in need of. We address ourselves, not to their humanity but to their self-love, and never talk to them of our own necessities but of their advantages. Nobody but a beggar chooses to depend chiefly upon the benevolence of his fellow citizens.

69 Colum.L.Rev. at 576–77.

---

* [Upon remand, the plaintiff obtained a jury verdict. But plaintiff's judgment was reversed on appeal. Langer v. Superior Steel Co., 318 Pa. 490, 178 A. 490 (1935). Reversal was not based on lack of consideration, however, but resulted from a finding that the president lacked authority to bind the corporation. Ed.]

Bogigian v. Bogigian

Court of Appeals of Indiana, Second District, 1990.
551 N.E.2d 1149, rehearing denied, 559 N.E.2d 1199.

■ BUCHANAN, JUDGE.

CASE SUMMARY

Respondent-appellant David Bogigian (David) appeals from the reinstatement of a judgment in favor of Hazel Bogigian (Hazel), claiming the trial court erred when it determined Hazel's release of her judgment was not supported by consideration.

We affirm.

FACTS

The facts most favorable to the trial court's judgment reveal that on January 31, 1986, David's marriage to Hazel was dissolved, and Hazel was given the following judgment:

"Wife shall receive a judgment on the family home in the amount of Ten Thousand Three Hundred Dollars ($10,300) ... Said judgment is to be paid when the parties' youngest child is emancipated, when Husband remarries, or if a woman is living in the residence in a married situation, *or when the Husband sells the real estate,* or if the children or the Husband cease to reside in the residence, whichever occurs first."

Record at 32 (emphasis supplied).

The residence was sold by David on February 20, 1987, and Hazel attended the closing with David. At the closing, Hazel executed several documents to effectuate the sale of the house. Among the documents executed was a quit claim deed and the release of her judgment against David. The release provided:

"Comes now HAZEL BOGIGIAN, this 20TH day of FEBRUARY, 1987, being first duly sworn upon oath, who deposes and says:

That a certain judgment rendered JANUARY 31, 1986, as Cause number #S385–126, against DAVID J. BOGIGIAN in favor of HAZEL BOGIGIAN, is hereby satisfied and released."

Record at 67.

Because David had no equity in the residence, the sale did not provide any funds from which to satisfy Hazel's judgment. Several months after the closing, David paid Hazel five dollars as her share of the sale's proceeds.

On June 30, 1988, Hazel initiated proceedings supplemental to satisfy her judgment. On January 1, 1989, David filed the release of judgment signed by Hazel during the closing. After a hearing on February 22, 1989, the trial court concluded that the release executed by Hazel was voidable for lack of consideration. The trial court reinstated Hazel's judgment on May 4, 1989.

ISSUE

David raises several issues on review which we consolidate and restate as:

Whether the trial court erred when it reinstated Hazel's judgment?

DECISION

PARTIES' CONTENTIONS—David contends that because Hazel received a benefit, as she was released from her obligations on the mortgage, her release was supported by consideration and therefore the trial court erred when it reinstated her judgment. In the alternative, David argues that Hazel should be equitably estopped from executing the judgment because he relied to his detriment on her release. Hazel responds that there was no consideration supporting her release because she did not realize the release she signed was a release of her judgment against David.

CONCLUSION—The trial court did not err when it reinstated Hazel's judgment because her release was not supported by consideration.

* * *

A release, to be valid, must be supported by consideration.... Consideration consists of *bargained-for exchange*....

The evidence adequately supports the trial court's factual finding and legal conclusion that Hazel received no consideration for the release. The record demonstrates that Hazel and David did not *bargain* for the release in exchange for any benefits flowing to Hazel for detriments incurred by David. Both Hazel and David admitted that no representations concerning the release were made. *Record* at 136–37, 155. Hazel testified she thought she was signing the release of the mortgage so the house could be sold. *Record* at 165. Any benefit received by Hazel, or any detriment suffered by David, therefore, cannot be consideration for the release because David and Hazel did not *agree* the benefit or detriment would be consideration ...

The United States Supreme Court, almost one hundred years ago, recognized:

> "The mere presence of some incident to a contract which might, under certain circumstances, be upheld as a consideration for a promise, does not necessarily make it the consideration for the promise in that contract. To give it that effect, it must have been offered by one party, and accepted by the other, as one element of the contract."

Fire Ins. Assoc., Ltd. v. Wickham (1891), 141 U.S. 564, 579. That consideration must actually be bargained-for is a long recognized and fundamental common law principle, ...; 1 Williston, Contracts 100 (3rd Ed.1957); Restatement, Contracts 75 Comment b (1932), a principle which frequently is seen in the cases as part of the definition of consideration: "Consideration consists of bargained-for exchange." ...

Because David and Hazel did not bargain for the release, the evidence most favorable to the trial court's judgment supports its finding and conclusion that Hazel received no consideration for the release. * * *

Because David and Hazel did not bargain for the release, and because no representations concerning the release were made, David has failed to establish that the release was made with the intent that David act upon it; thus David has failed to establish Hazel should be equitably estopped from having her judgment reinstated. . . .

Judgment affirmed.

■ STATON, J. concurs.

■ SULLIVAN, J., dissents with opinion.

■ SULLIVAN, JUDGE, dissenting.

The adage that "hard cases make bad law"[1] might be applied to the case before us. But assuming that the law enunciated is not "bad," the decision nevertheless represents a dramatic change in the law of contracts—more particularly with regard to consideration.

The majority opinion states that consideration must consist of a "bargained-for exchange." In order to meet this test, it is not necessary that the benefit or detriment be negotiated, agreed upon by both parties and reflected by specific language in the instruments. It is sufficient that the detriment or benefit to the particular party flows from the bargain. The transaction of which the release was a part must be considered in its entirety. The consideration for the release need not be found in the release itself. It may be found in contemporaneous aspects of the transaction. . . .

It is not necessary that the consideration flow between the promisor and the promisee. So long as the promisor obtains a benefit, the benefit may flow from a third party, e.g., the mortgagee here. . . .

It is clear that the benefit to Hazel was bargained for. The mortgagee's release of her upon the obligation was clearly and specifically a part of the bargain. Hazel's judgment constituted a lien against the real estate in David's name. Therefore it had to be released before the mortgage could be satisfied, taxes paid and clear title delivered. Therefore Hazel did benefit by the liability avoidance. That specific benefit was, by Hazel's own testimony, specifically contemplated as a consequence of her execution of the documents. That this bargained-for consideration was not specifically stated as the *quid pro quo* for the unambiguous release is not determinative. As noted in 17 C.J.S., Contracts Sec. 74, p. 763, cited by the majority, consideration exists

> "if it is present anywhere in the entire transaction surrounding the agreement, regardless of whether any label has been put on it, and regardless of whether it was spelled out in the writing."

There were absolutely no representations or misrepresentations made by David nor by the mortgagee to Hazel with regard to the release. There

1. Holmes, J. in Northern Securities Co. v. United States 193 U.S. 197 (1904).

was no hint of undue influence. The release executed was clear, unequivo-cal and unambiguous. That Hazel perhaps did not avail herself of the full and fair opportunity to read the release does not relieve her from the consequences of that clear and unambiguous instrument ... The release therefore must be given its full legal effect. * * *

Though in retrospect Hazel may have made a bad bargain, such does not diminish the effect of her execution of the release. As set forth in Rutter v. Excel Industries, Inc. (1982) 3d Dist. Ind.App., 438 N.E.2d 1030, 1031:

"The freedom to contract includes the freedom to contract improvi-dently, and in the absence of countervailing policy considerations, private reservations or mistake will not avoid the results of apparent consent.

"If, whatever a man's real intention may be, he so conducts himself that a reasonable man would believe he was assenting to the terms proposed by the other party, and that the other party upon that belief enters into the contract with him, the man thus conducting himself would be equally bound as if he had intended to agree to the other party's terms." Smith v. Hughes (Eng.1871), L.R. 6 Q.B. 597.

That the amount of Hazel's mortgage and tax liability avoidance may have been of a substantially lesser amount than the $10,300 judgment released is not a basis for the trial court's judgment. Inadequate consider-ation, as opposed to failure of consideration is not a basis for setting the release aside....

A compassionate motivation to relieve Hazel from the consequences of her arguably bad bargain is understandable. Absent fraud, undue influence, incapacity or some other cognizable grounds for relief, however, I am unable to discern any legal basis for the holding today. The fact remains that Hazel signed the release which clearly stated its tenor and effect. In doing so she gave up the hope or possibility of recovering her $10,300 judgment against David, who at the time was virtually bankrupt and without any assets either in Indiana or Florida. In return she avoided having a judgment against her for an amount in excess of the $41,000 mortgage balance due at the time of closing. In light of David's relatively precarious financial position, it is not unlikely that Hazel would have felt the major impact of that mortgage liability. In this light, the bargain from Hazel's perspective may not have been all that unwise.

In any event I am constrained to dissent. I would reverse the judgment and direct the court to give full force and effect to the release.

[In denying David's petition for rehearing, Judge Buchanan added brief elaboration to his opinion that Hazel's release was not supported by consideration. See 559 N.E.2d 1199 (Ind.App.1990).]

NOTES

(1) In *Bogigian,* what was the asserted consideration for Hazel's agree-ment to discharge the lien? Why was this insufficient? Is this, as suggested by

the dissenting judge, an instance of a hard case making bad law? If so, what, precisely, is the "bad" law that is made?

(2) To satisfy the "bargain" requirement, should it be necessary that the consideration flow from the promisee? From whom did the consideration flow to Hazel?

(3) Could you have drafted the documents in *Bogigian* so as to obviate the objections of the court majority? How much actual bargaining must occur before consideration can be found?

(4) *The Case of the Injured Mechanic.* Ray Dehn, a skilled mechanic and traveling representative of Transit Bus Sales Company of St. Louis, was sent to Knoxville to repair a bus which Ross Palmer had purchased from the company. Dehn inspected the bus and told Palmer a belt was too loose. Palmer's driver went away and got the belt tightened. When the driver returned with the tightened belt, the three of them discussed the matter at length. Dehn then attempted to show Palmer how tight it should be when the driver started the motor cutting off two of Dehn's fingers. Dehn thought all the time that the driver was out of the bus and that no one was inside who could start the motor. Palmer immediately rushed Dehn to a local hospital. On the way, Palmer said: "I am awful sorry this happened, but don't worry a minute. I will see you are compensated for loss of your finger, take care of your expenses for the loss of your finger, and all." On these facts, what theories of liability would you expect Dehn to advance? Was there consideration for Palmer's promise? Is there any basis for promissory liability? See Palmer v. Dehn, 29 Tenn.App. 597, 198 S.W.2d 827 (1946).

(5) *The Case of the Proud Grandfather.* A baby boy was born to Mr. and Mrs. Lanfier on December 17. Two days later they named the boy "August Dwayne." He was named "August" after his maternal grandfather, August Schultz. A week later the grandfather promised the parents that if they named the baby "August" he would give them a certain painting, valued at $5,000. They agreed. Was there a binding contract? Cf. Lanfier v. Lanfier, 227 Iowa 258, 288 N.W. 104 (1939). Would all doubt concerning enforceability have been removed if, in addition, Schultz had prescribed and received a $1 payment from the Lanfiers? See materials which follow.

PROBLEM: THE CASE OF THE LESSEE'S WELL

Stone leased land to Oil Company for ten years. Oil Company was to operate a service station and had an option to purchase the land at any time for $20,000. The lease provided that Stone was to supply water to Oil Company from an existing well but "in case Lessor's well fails to supply ample water, they are not responsible, and the Lessee will be required to make their own arrangements for securing water." The well failed after 18 months and the parties, after negotiations, agreed to have a new well drilled and to split the cost. A written agreement was prepared and signed by both parties. Shortly after drilling commenced, Stone visited the site and talked with a company representative, Mr. Brinson. Stone asked "What happens to my investment in the well if you exercise the option and buy the land" and Brinson promptly answered (in front of witnesses) "Don't worry about that, you'll get your money." The well was completed at a cost of $4,000 and the parties each paid the well driller $2,000. Six months later, Oil Company exercised the option but at the closing refused to reimburse Stone for his well drilling expenses. Oil Company argued that Brinson's oral promise, if made, was unenforceable because there was no consideration. Is this argument correct? See Stonestreet v. Southern Oil Co., 226 N.C. 261, 37 S.E.2d 676 (1946).

(B) MIXED MOTIVES AND NOMINAL CONSIDERATION

Thomas v. Thomas

Queen's Bench, 1842.
2 Q.B. 851, 114 Eng.Rep. 330.

Assumpsit. The declaration stated an agreement between plaintiff and defendant that the defendant should, when thereto required by the plaintiff, by all necessary deeds, conveyances, assignments, or other assurances, grants, etc., or otherwise, assure a certain dwelling house and premises, in the county of Glamorgan, unto plaintiff for her life * * *.

At the trial, before Coltman, J., at the Glamorganshire Lent Assizes, 1841, it appeared that John Thomas, the deceased husband of the plaintiff, at the time of his death, in 1837, was possessed of a row of seven dwelling houses in Merthyr Tidvil, in one of which, being the dwelling house in question, he was himself residing; and that by his will he appointed his brother Samuel Thomas (since deceased) and the defendant executors thereof, to take possession of all his houses, etc., subject to certain payments in the will mentioned, among which were certain charges in money for the benefit of the plaintiff. In the evening before the day of his death he expressed orally a wish to make some further provision for his wife; and on the following morning he declared orally, in the presence of two witnesses, that it was his will that his wife should have either the house in which he lived and all that it contained, or an additional sum of £100 instead thereof.

This declaration being shortly afterward brought to the knowledge of Samuel Thomas and the defendant, the executors and residuary legatees, they consented to carry the intentions of the testator so expressed into effect; and, after the lapse of a few days, they and the plaintiff executed the agreement declared upon; which, after stating the parties, and briefly reciting the will, proceeded as follows:

"And, whereas the said testator, shortly before his death, declared in the presence of several witnesses, that he was desirous his said wife should have and enjoy during her life, or so long as she continue his widow, all and singular the dwelling house," etc., "or £100 out of his personal estate," in addition to the respective legacies and bequests given her in and by his said will; "but such declaration and desire was not reduced to writing in the lifetime of the said John Thomas and read over to him; but the said Samuel Thomas and Benjamin Thomas are fully convinced and satisfied that such was the desire of the said testator, and are willing and desirous that such intention should be carried into full effect. Now these presents witness, and it is hereby agreed and declared by and between the parties, that, in consideration of such desire and of the premises," the executors would convey the dwelling house, etc., to the plaintiff and her assigns during her life, or for so long a time as she should continue a widow and unmarried: "provided nevertheless, and it is hereby further agreed and declared, that the said Eleanor Thomas, or her assigns, shall and will, at all times during which she shall have possession of the said dwelling house, etc., pay to the said Samuel Thomas and Benjamin Thomas, their executors, etc., the sum of £1 yearly toward the ground rent payable in respect of the said dwelling house and other premises thereto adjoining, and shall keep the said dwelling house and premises in good and tenantable repair"; with other provisions not affecting the questions in this case.

The plaintiff was left in possession of the dwelling house and premises for some time; but the defendant, after the death of his coexecutor, refused to execute a conveyance tendered to him for execution pursuant to the agreement, and, shortly before the trial, brought an ejectment, under which he turned the plaintiff out of possession. It was objected for the defendant that, a part of the consideration proved being omitted in the declaration, there was a fatal variance. The learned judge overruled the objection, reserving leave to move to enter a non-suit. Ultimately a verdict was found for the plaintiff on all the issues; and, in Easter Term last, a rule nisi was obtained pursuant to the leave reserved.

* * *

■ LORD DENMAN, C.J. There is nothing in this case but a great deal of ingenuity, and a little wilful blindness to the actual terms of the instrument itself. There is nothing whatever to show that the ground rent was payable to a superior landlord; and the stipulation for the payment of it is not a mere proviso, but an express agreement. * * * This is in terms an express agreement, and shows a sufficient legal consideration quite independent of the moral feeling which disposed the executors to enter into such a contract. * * *

■ PATTESON, J. * * * Motive is not the same thing with consideration. Consideration means something which is of some value in the eye of the law, moving from the plaintiff; it may be some benefit to the plaintiff [defendant], or some detriment to the defendant [plaintiff]; but at all events it must be moving from the plaintiff. Now that which is suggested as the consideration here, a pious respect for the wishes of the testator, does not in any way move from the plaintiff; it moves from the testator; therefore, legally speaking, it forms no part of the consideration. Then it is said that, if that be so, there is no consideration at all, it is a mere voluntary gift; but when we look at the agreement we find that this is not a mere proviso that the donee shall take the gift with the burthens; but it is an express agreement to pay what seems to be a fresh apportionment of a ground rent, and which is made payable not to a superior landlord, but to the executors. So that this rent is clearly not something incident to the assignment of the house, for in that case, instead of being payable to the executors, it would have been payable to the landlord. Then as to the repairs, these houses may very possibly be held under a lease containing covenants to repair; but we know nothing about it, for anything that appears the liability to repair is first created by this instrument. The proviso certainly struck me at first * * * that the rent and repairs were merely attached to the gift by the donors; and, had the instrument been executed by the donors only, there might have been some ground for that construction; but the fact is not so. * * *

■ COLERIDGE, J. The concessions made in the course of the argument have, in fact, disposed of the case. It is conceded that mere motive need not be stated, and we are not obliged to look for the legal consideration in any particular part of the instrument, merely because the consideration is usually stated in some particular part; ut res magis valeat, we may look to any part. In this instrument, in the part where it is usual to state the consideration, nothing certainly is expressed but a wish to fulfil the intentions of the testator, but in another part we find an express agreement to pay an annual sum for a particular purpose, and also a distinct agreement to repair. If these had occurred in the first part of the instrument, it could hardly have been argued that the declaration was not well drawn and supported by the evidence. As to the suggestion of this being a voluntary conveyance, my impression is that this payment of £1 annually is more than a good consideration, it is a valuable consideration, it is clearly a thing newly created and not part of the old ground rent.

Rule discharged.

Comment: Mixed Motives, Nominal Consideration, and the Relevance of Form

Mixed Motives. The case of *Thomas v. Thomas*, just considered, introduces the problem of mixed motives into the consideration mix. An important motive behind the executors' promise was a desire to honor the deathbed wishes of their brother, John Thomas. That desire was expressed in the writing. Another motive expressed in the writing was to obtain from the spouse a promise to pay to the executors a stated annual ground rent and to keep the premises in good repair. There is no evidence of any bargaining between the executors and Eleanor Thomas but the court, based upon the last part of the writing, concluded that the promised performance was a newly created and "valuable consideration" running to the executors. That was enough, despite the other motives, to enforce the promise.

With the *Thomas* case apparently in mind, Restatement (Second) 81(1) states that the "fact that what is bargained for does not of itself induce the making of the promise does not prevent it from being consideration for the promise." Subsection 81(2) makes the same points about the motives of the promisee. The parties may have more than one motive, even in a commercial exchange. But this supposes, does it not, that the performance was bargained for. As comment (b) puts it: "Unless both parties know that the purported consideration is mere pretense, it is immaterial that the promisor's desire for the consideration is incidental to other objectives and even that the other party knows this to be so."

Nominal Consideration. The mixed motive case sits uneasily between the paradigm bargain contract, such as the agreed exchange of goods for a price, and the "gift" promise which, without more, is not enforceable under American law. In the absence of an authorized formality, such as a seal or legislation, a "gift" promise, even though written, signed, and containing language that the promisor intends to assume a legal obligation is not enforceable. Attempts to dress up the gift promise by false recitals of consideration, such as a recitation in the writing that the "consideration for a promise to deliver 1,000 shares of IBM stock is $1, the receipt of which is hereby acknowledged" are likely to be dismissed as a "pretense of bargain." Restatement (Second), 71, comment b.

Decline of the Seal. Throughout history various formalities have been observed by contracting parties, either as a matter of custom or of official requirement.

Formalities of an almost limitless variety have been used in the making of contracts. Both Homer and Herodotus describe a ceremonial libation which accompanied solemn agreements.[1] Contracting parties will today, as they have presumably from time immemorial, "shake hands on it," as if the added form imported special obligation. Professor Corbin has observed that "[t]he small boys of today no doubt feel the weight of an awful sanction when they say 'I cross my heart [hope] to die.' " Thus, even though, as he puts it, "[t]he keeping of promises is in the folkways and mores of mankind" and "in the vast majority of cases they are kept and performed without the thought of breach or necessity of enforcement," not all promises are enforceable, or ever have been. And one of the factors traditionally employed in determining enforceability has been the form in which the promise is made or expressed. See Corbin § 240 (original Treatise).

A notable example of a promise cast in a formal mode, and thereby recognized as legally binding, was the famous *stipulatio* or stipulation of the Roman law. Briefly, this was a method whereby one might secure, through a process of interrogation and response, the enforceable promise of another. A would ask of B if he would promise to do such and such, and B's promise to do so would bind him in law. This formality has both ancient and modern counterparts. Today in civil law countries the promise in a notarial deed (executed before a notary, a governmental official) is binding precisely because of the method employed in making it.

---

1. The biblical account of God's "covenant" with Abraham describes an elaborate form: "And now God said to him, I am the Lord, who brought thee out of Ur of the Chaldees, to give thee possession of this land instead. And when he asked, Lord God, what assurance may I have that it is mine? the Lord answered, Bring me a three-year-old heifer, a three-year-old she-goat, and a three-year-old ram, and a turtle-dove, and a pigeon. All these he brought to him, and cut them in half, laying the two halves of each on opposite sides, except the dove and the pigeon; he did not divide these.... So the sun went down, and when the darkness of night came on, a smoking furnace was seen, a torch of fire that passed between the pieces of flesh. And the Lord, that day, made a covenant with Abram." Genesis 15:7–10, 17–18.

At common law the form *par excellence* was the seal, at first a wax substance attached to the document. Later, writing the word "seal" or "L.S." (*locus sigilli,* place of the seal) was more common. A sealed promise was enforceable centuries before the evolution of the doctrine of consideration. Enforceability did not derive from bargain or exchange, but precisely because of the formal mode in which the promise was cast.

It has been contended that consideration itself is merely a form. This was Holmes' position: "In one sense, everything is form which the law requires in order to make a promise binding over and above the mere expression of the promisor's will. Consideration is a form as much as a seal. The only difference is, that the one form is of modern introduction, and has a foundation in good sense, or at least falls in with our common habits of thought, so that we do not notice it, whereas the other is a survival from an older condition of the law, and is less manifestly sensible, or less familiar." Holmes, The Common Law 273 (1881). Is this a valid evaluation of consideration? An excellent review, at this point, would be to take another look at the consideration materials with a view of discerning instances where consideration seems to be employed as a kind of form or formality. See Lon L. Fuller, *Consideration and Form,* 41 Colum.L.Rev. 799 (1941).

By decision and statute, the seal has lost virtually all of its former efficacy. A UCC section "makes it clear that every effect of the seal which relates to 'sealed instruments' as such is wiped out insofar as contracts for sale are concerned." UCC 2–203, comment 1.

In view of this decline of the seal, one is surprised to find a Restatement (Second) provision which can be read as proposing a general revival. Section 95(1) reads: "In the absence of statute a promise is binding without consideration if (a) it is in writing and sealed; and (b) the document containing the promise is delivered; and (c) the promisor and promisee are named in the document or so described as to be capable of identification when it is delivered."

Model Written Obligations Act. The general abolition of the seal did not prove an unmixed blessing. Many regarded the seal as a useful legal device, if for no other reason than providing a convenient method for making binding gratuitous promises. It was inevitable that attention would be given to filling the vacuum, and it was most natural to turn to that most common of contemporary "forms," the signed writing. In 1925, largely at the instigation of Professor Williston, the National Conference of Commissioners on Uniform State Laws approved the draft of the Uniform Written Obligations Act. This recommended statute provides as follows:

"A written release or promise made and signed by the person releasing or promising shall not be invalid or unenforceable for lack of consideration, if the writing also contains an additional express statement in any form of language that the signer intends to be legally bound."

The proposal met with a singular, and somewhat surprising, lack of success. Only Pennsylvania has adopted and retained the Act, and in 1943 it was redesignated, quite appropriately, the Model Written Obligations

Act. For a discussion of the Act, see Reeve, *Uniform Written Obligations Act,* 76 U.Pa.L.Rev. 580 (1928).

In addition, there are a few statutes which accord some extraordinary legal effect to a signed writing. But with the exception of New York, the practical significance of this legislation seems to have been minimal. See New York General Obligations Law §§ 5–1101—5–1115.

Uniform Commercial Code. Some resurgence of "contract form" has been ushered in by the Uniform Commercial Code. In two instances the Code uses a signed writing as a substitute for consideration. The text of these provisions is set out below:

UCC 1–107 [Rev. 1–307]. *Waiver or Renunciation of Claim or Right After Breach.* Any claim or right arising out of an alleged breach can be discharged in whole or in part without consideration by a written waiver or renunciation signed and delivered by the aggrieved party.

UCC 2–205. *Firm Offers.* An offer by a merchant to buy or sell goods in a signed writing which by its terms gives assurance that it will be held open is not revocable, for lack of consideration, during the time stated or if no time is stated for a reasonable time, but in no event may such period of irrevocability exceed three months; but any such term of assurance on a form supplied by the offeree must be separately signed by the offeror.

In addition, UCC 2–209(1), relating to modification, rescission and waiver, states: "An agreement modifying a contract within this Article needs no consideration to be binding." In effect, this is added emphasis upon form, since the requirements of the Statute of Frauds section of Article 2 (UCC 2–201) must be satisfied if the contract as modified is within its provisions. UCC 2–209(3).

The reach of the foregoing sections, even if confined to the strict letter, is substantial. But there is the possibility that by analogous application the impact will be even more far-reaching, resulting in a considerable reorientation of contract theory. For example, if "firm offer" is recognized in an offer to sell goods situation, why not in an offer to perform a service? And if Sears, Roebuck and Co. makes a firm offer by the requisite assurance, why not John Sears, non-merchant? Or if a sales contract can be modified without consideration, why not a construction contract? And so on.

Can law rescue Peanuts?

© 1964 United Feature Syndicate, Inc.

Should gift promises be enforced? Should a promise to make a gift be enforced even though there is no "real" consideration?

Professor Melvin A. Eisenberg has this to say about this question.

Given that unrelied-upon donative promises are normally unenforceable, the question arises whether the law should recognize some special form through which a promisor with the specific intent to be legally bound could achieve that objective. "It is something," said Williston, "that a person ought to be able ... if he wishes to do it ... to create a legal obligation to make a gift. Why not? ... I don't see why a man should not be able to make himself liable if he wishes to do so."

At early common law the seal served this purpose. In modern times, most state legislatures have either abolished the distinction between sealed and unsealed promises, abolished the use of a seal in contracts, or otherwise limited the seal's effect. * * *

Should the law then recognize some new formality to play the role once played by the seal? An obvious candidate is nominal consideration— that is, the form of a bargain—because it can be safely assumed that parties who falsely cast a nonbargain promise as a bargain do so for the express purpose of making the promise legally enforceable. A rule that promises in this form were enforceable would have obvious substantive advantages, but would also involve serious difficulties of administration. As a practical matter, such a form would be primarily employed to render donative promises enforceable. Both morally and legally, however, an obligation created by a donative promise should normally be excused either by acts of the promisee amounting to ingratitude, or by personal circumstances of the promisor that render it improvident to keep the promise. If Uncle promises to give Nephew $20,000 in two years, and Nephew later wrecks Uncle's living room in an angry rage, Uncle should not remain obliged. The same result should ordinarily follow if Uncle suffers a serious financial setback and is barely able to take care of the needs of his immediate family, or if Uncle's wealth remains constant but his personal obligations significantly increase in an unexpected manner, as through illness or the birth of children.

Form alone cannot meet these problems. Thus the French and German Civil Codes, while providing special forms that enable a donative promise to be rendered legally enforceable, also provide extensive treatment of improvidence and ingratitude as defenses. For example, under article 519(1) of the German Civil Code, a promisor may refuse to keep a donative promise "insofar as, having regard to his other obligations, he is not in a position to fulfill the promise without endangering his own reasonable maintenance or the fulfillment of obligations imposed upon him by law to furnish maintenance to others." Under article 530(1), a donative promise may be revoked "if the donee, by any serious misconduct towards the donor or a close relative of the donor shows himself guilty of gross ingratitude." Similarly, under articles 960–966 of the French Civil Code, a donative promise made by a person with no living descendants is normally revoked by operation of law upon the birth of a child. Under articles 953 and 955, a donative promise can be revoked on the ground of ingratitude that involves serious cruelty, wrongs, or injuries.

As these rules suggest, the common law could not appropriately make donative promises enforceable solely on the basis of a form unless our courts were also prepared to develop and administer a body of rules dealing with the problems of improvidence and ingratitude. Certainly such an enterprise is possible. It may be questioned, however, whether the game would be worth the candle. An inquiry into improvidence involves the measurement of wealth, lifestyle, dependents' needs, and even personal utilities. An inquiry into ingratitude involves the measurement of a maelstrom, because many or most donative promises arise in an intimate context in which emotions, motives, and cues are invariably complex and highly interrelated. Perhaps the civil-law style of adjudication is suited to wrestling with these kinds of inquiries, but they have held little appeal for common-law courts, which traditionally have been oriented toward inquiry into acts rather than into personal characteristics. The question is whether the social and economic benefits of a facility for making donative promises enforceable would be worth its social and economic costs. The answer is that benefits and costs are in rough balance, so that nonrecognition of such a facility is at least as supportable as recognition would be.

Melvin A. Eisenberg, *The Principles of Consideration*, 67 Cornell L.Rev. 640, 659–62 (1982).

See also E. Allan Farnsworth, Changing Your Mind: The Law of Regretted Decisions 82–89 (1998) (advocating that gift promises should be enforceable if the promisor has expressed an intention to assume a legal obligation).

PROBLEM: MIXED MOTIVES AND AGREED EXCHANGE

Your client, Pauline, is a second-year student at Yale Law School. Pauline's Uncle Fred, a Harvard law graduate, owns a first edition of Langdell's "Cases on Contracts", published in 1871. The value of the book is $5,000. Pauline expressed an interest in the book (to add to a growing collection) and, at Thanksgiving, Uncle Fred made a statement at the dinner table that he would give the book to her for Christmas. The next day Uncle Fred was shown Pauline's coin collection and discovered that she had two 1909s-VDB pennies, one in very fine condition (valued at $1,000) and one in fine condition (valued at $500). Fred confessed that he needed such a penny to round out his collection of Lincoln pennies and Pauline stated that she would give him the penny in "fine" condition for Christmas.

Shortly after the first of the year, Pauline visited your office and presented a writing, dated December 1, 2003, which stated: "In consideration of one penny, receipt of which is hereby acknowledged, I promise to give my niece Pauline my first edition of Langdell on Christmas day, 2003." The writing, which had been mailed to Pauline, was signed by Fred. She further said that on Christmas Day she tendered the "fine" 1909s-VDB penny to Fred and he took it. Fred, however, refused to tender the Langdell, saying he was a bit short of cash and that he had sold it to the Harvard Law Library for $7,500. He did thank Pauline for her "wonderful gift."

Advise Pauline of her rights.

(C) LIMITS OF THE CONSIDERATION DOCTRINE

(1) ADEQUACY OF VALUES EXCHANGED

Reread the case of *Hamer v. Sidway*, supra at 40. What definition of consideration did the court use, the "bargained for" concept or the "either-

or'' concept? If "bargained for" was used, was there equivalency of exchange? Did the promisor gain a pecuniary advantage? Did he derive any "benefit" from the transaction at all, or is enforcement predicated solely upon "detriment" to the promisee? In what way was plaintiff's conduct detrimental? Note who the plaintiff was. Is the fact that she purchased nephew's rights under the alleged contract for value relevant to the case?

Haigh v. Brooks

Q.B. 1839; Exch.Ch. 1840.
113 Eng.Rep. 119.

[Haigh sold goods to Lees on credit. Brooks, who was interested in Lee's affairs, signed a writing purporting to guaranty Lees debts to Haigh in the amount of 10,000 pounds. The problem was that the guaranty, to be enforceable under the statute of frauds, had to show in the writing that consideration was given for the promise to answer for the debt of another and the particular writing said "in consideration of your being in advance" to Lees in the sum of 10,000 pounds for the purchase of cotton "I do hereby give you my guarantee for that amount." For reasons not clear from the record, Brooks induced Haigh to surrender the writing in exchange for a promise to pay three drafts accepted by Lees in total of 9,666 pounds when they came due. Lees failed to pay at that time, Haigh sued on the promise and Brooks demurred on the ground that there was no consideration.

A final judgment was entered for the plaintiff.] * * *

Lord Denman, C.J.[1], delivered the judgment of the Queen's Bench:

It was argued for the defendant that this guarantee is of no force, because the fact of the plaintiffs being already in advance to Lees could form no consideration for the defendant's promise to guarantee to the plaintiffs the payment of Lees's acceptances. In the first place, this is by no means clear. That "being in advance" must necessarily mean to assert that he was in advance at the time of giving the guarantee, is an assertion open to argument. It may possibly have been intended as prospective. If the phrase had been "in consideration of your becoming in advance," or "on condition of your being in advance," such would have been the clear import. As it is, nobody can doubt that the defendant took a great interest in the affairs of Messrs. Lees, or believe that the plaintiffs had not come under the advance mentioned at the defendant's request. Here is then sufficient doubt to make it worth the defendant's while to possess himself of the guarantee; and, if that be so, we have no concern with the adequacy or inadequacy of the price paid or promised for it.

But we are by no means prepared to say that any circumstances short of the imputation of fraud in fact could entitle us to hold that a party was

---

1. Thomas Denman (1779–1854) became Chief Justice of the Queen's Bench in 1832 and was made a Baron in 1834. We first encountered him in the case of *Thomas v.* *Thomas*, supra at 52. It was said that he was not taken with legal theory but was a skilled practitioner and politician.

not bound by a promise made upon any consideration which could be valuable; while of its being so the promise by which it was obtained from the holder of it must always afford some proof.

Here, whether or not the guarantee could have been available within the doctrine of Wain v. Warlters, 5 East, 10, the plaintiffs were induced by the defendant's promise to part with something which they might have kept, and the defendant obtained what he desired by means of that promise. Both being free and able to judge for themselves, how can the defendant be justified in breaking this promise, and discovering afterwards that the thing in consideration of which he gave it did not possess that value which he supposed to belong to it? It cannot be ascertained that that value was what he most regarded. He may have had other objects and motives; and of their weight he was the only judge. We therefore think the plea bad: and the demurrer must prevail.

Judgment for the plaintiffs.''

[The judgment was affirmed on appeal to Exchequer. LORD ABINGER, C.B., delivered the judgment of the Exchequer Chamber.]

In the case of Brooks v. Haigh the judgment of the Court is to affirm the judgment of the Court of Queen's Bench.

It is the opinion of all the Court that there was in the guaranty an ambiguity that might be explained by evidence, so as to make it a valid contract; and therefore this was a sufficient consideration for the promise declared upon.

It is also the opinion of all the Court, with the exception of my brother Maule, who entertained some doubt on the question, that the words both of the declaration and the plea import that the paper on which the guaranty was written was given up; and that the actual surrender of the possession of the paper to the defendant was a sufficient consideration without reference to its contents.

Judgment affirmed.

Apfel v. Prudential–Bache Securities, Inc.

Court of Appeals of New York, 1993.
81 N.Y.2d 470, 600 N.Y.S.2d 433, 616 N.E.2d 1095.

■ SIMONS, JUDGE.

Defendant, an investment bank, seeks to avoid an agreement to purchase plaintiffs' idea for issuing and selling municipal bonds. Its principal contention is that plaintiffs had no property right in the idea because it was not novel and, therefore, consideration for the contract was lacking. For reasons which follow, we conclude that a showing of novelty is not required to validate the contract. The decisive question is whether the idea had value, not whether it was novel.

I

In 1982, plaintiffs, an investment banker and a lawyer, approached defendant's predecessor with a proposal for issuing municipal securities through a system that eliminated paper certificates and allowed bonds to be sold, traded, and held exclusively by means of computerized "book entries". Initially, the parties signed a confidentiality agreement that allowed defendant to review the techniques as detailed in a 99–page summary. Nearly a month of negotiations followed before the parties entered into a sale agreement under which plaintiffs conveyed their rights to the techniques and certain trade names and defendant agreed to pay a stipulated rate based on its use of the techniques for a term from October 1982 to January 1988. Under the provisions of the contract, defendant's obligation to pay was to remain even if the techniques became public knowledge or standard practice in the industry and applications for patents and trademarks were denied. Plaintiffs asserted that they had not previously disclosed the techniques to anyone and they agreed to maintain them in confidence until they became public.

From 1982 until 1985, defendant implemented the contract, although the parties dispute whether amounts due were fully paid. Defendant actively encouraged bond issuers to use the computerized "book entry" system and, for at least the first year, was the sole underwriter in the industry employing such a system. However, in 1985, following a change in personnel, defendant refused to make any further payments. It maintained that the ideas conveyed by plaintiffs had been in the public domain at the time of the sale agreement and that what plaintiffs sold had never been theirs to sell. Defendant's attempts to patent the techniques proved unsuccessful. By 1985, investment banks were increasingly using computerized systems, and by 1990 such systems were handling 60% of the dollar volume of all new issues of municipal securities.

Plaintiffs commenced this litigation seeking $45 million in compensatory and punitive damages. They asserted 17 causes of action based on theories of breach of contract, breach of a fiduciary duty, fraud, various torts arising from defendant's failure to obtain patents, and unjust enrichment. Defendant's answer interposed defenses and counterclaims for breach of contract, breach of warranty, waiver, fraud, estoppel, laches, mutual mistake, rescission, and a lack of consideration. Plaintiffs then moved for partial summary judgment, defendant cross-moved for summary judgment dismissing the complaint, and plaintiffs responded with a motion seeking dismissal of the affirmative defenses.

Supreme Court concluded that triable issues existed on the questions of whether defendant breached the contract by refusing to make payments and whether plaintiffs committed a breach by allegedly disclosing the techniques to another company. The court also found defendant had raised a triable issue on whether plaintiffs had partially waived their right to payment by forgoing certain claims to compensation. The remainder of the pleadings were found to be legally insufficient. Accordingly, the court dismissed all the causes of action except the first, which alleges breach of contract, and struck all defendant's defenses and counterclaims except those relating to breach of contract and the partial defense of waiver. The Appellate Division modified the order by reinstating defendant's claim that the sale agreement lacked consideration, 183 A.D.2d 439, 583 N.Y.S.2d 386. It held that novelty was required before an idea could be valid consideration but concluded that the question was one of fact to be decided at trial. It also reinstated the cause of action for unjust enrichment, holding that the presence of an express contract did not foreclose recovery on a theory of quasi contract.

On this appeal, defendant's principal contention is that no contract existed between the parties because the sale agreement lacked consideration. Underlying that argument is its assertion that an idea cannot be legally sufficient consideration unless it is novel. . . . Plaintiffs insist that their system was indeed novel, but contend that, in any event, novelty is not required to validate the contract at issue here.

II

Defendant's cross motion for summary judgment insofar as it sought to dismiss the first cause of action alleging breach of contract was properly denied. Additionally, plaintiffs' motion to dismiss the lack of consideration defenses and counterclaims should be granted.

Under the traditional principles of contract law, the parties to a contract are free to make their bargain, even if the consideration exchanged is grossly unequal or of dubious value . . . It is enough that something of "real value in the eye of the law" was exchanged. . . . The fact that the sellers may not have had a property right in what they sold does not, by itself, render the contract void for lack of consideration. . . .

Manifestly, defendant received something of value here; its own conduct establishes that. After signing the confidentiality agreement, defendant thoroughly reviewed plaintiffs' system before buying it. Having done so, it was in the best position to know whether the idea had value. It decided to enter into the sale agreement and aggressively market the system to potential bond issuers. For at least a year, it was the only underwriter to use plaintiffs' "book entry" system for municipal bonds, and it handled millions of such bond transactions during that time. Having obtained full disclosure of the system, used it in advance of competitors, and received the associated benefits of precluding its disclosure to others, defendant can hardly claim now the idea had no value to its municipal securities business. Indeed, defendant acknowledges it made payments to plaintiffs under the sale agreement for more than two years, conduct that would belie any claim it might make that the idea was lacking in value or that it had actually been obtained from some other source before plaintiffs' disclosure.

Thus, defendant has failed to demonstrate on this record that the contract was void or to raise a triable issue of fact on lack of consideration.

III

[The court, after reviewing the New York cases, held that novelty of the idea was not required. Rather, it was sufficient to prove that the party to whom the idea was disclosed was not aware of the idea.]

* * *

These decisions do not support defendant's contention that novelty is required in all cases involving disclosure of ideas. Indeed, we have explicitly held that it is not ... [The] decisions involve a distinct factual pattern: the buyer and seller contract for disclosure of the idea with payment based on use, but no separate postdisclosure contract for use of the idea has been made. Thus, they present the issue of whether the idea the buyer was using, was, in fact, the seller's.

Such transactions pose two problems for the courts. On the one hand, how can sellers prove that the buyer obtained the idea from them, and nowhere else, and that the buyer's use of it thus constitutes misappropriation of property? Unlike tangible property, an idea lacks title and boundaries and cannot be rendered exclusive by the acts of the one who first thinks it. On the other hand, there is no equity in enforcing a seemingly valid contract when, in fact, it turns out upon disclosure that the buyer already possessed the idea. In such instances, the disclosure, though freely bargained for, is manifestly without value. A showing of novelty, at least novelty as to the buyer, addresses these two concerns. Novelty can then serve to establish both the attributes of ownership necessary for a property-based claim and the value of the consideration—the disclosure—necessary for contract-based claims.

There are no such concerns in a transaction such as the one before us. Defendant does not claim that it was aware of the idea before plaintiffs disclosed it but, rather, concedes that the idea came from them. When a seller's claim arises from a contract to use an idea entered into after the disclosure of the idea, the question is not whether the buyer misappropriated property from the seller, but whether the idea had value to the buyer and thus constitutes valid consideration. In such a case, the buyer knows what he or she is buying and has agreed that the idea has value, and the Court will not ordinarily go behind that determination. The lack of novelty, in and of itself, does not demonstrate a lack of value ... To the contrary, the buyer may reap benefits from such a contract in a number of ways—for instance, by not having to expend resources pursuing the idea through other channels or by having a profit-making idea implemented sooner rather than later. The law of contracts would have to be substantially rewritten were we to allow buyers of fully disclosed ideas to disregard their obligation to pay simply because an idea could have been obtained from some other source or in some other way.

* * *

Accordingly, the order of the Appellate Division should be modified, without costs, in accordance with this opinion, and, as so modified, affirmed, and the certified question answered in the negative.

Comment: The Peppercorn Theory of Consideration and the Doctrine of Fair Exchange in Contract Law

The following comment was written by an anonymous student in 1935. What do you think?

Pervading the complex field of fine-spun theories of consideration are two inconsistent ideas. On the one hand, consideration is said to be only a form; on the other, it assures a fair exchange. In substantiation of the first view and in virtually absolute negation of the second stands the age-old formula that mere inadequacy of consideration is never a bar to enforcement of a contract. Although frequently subject to evasion this general formula has gone virtually unchallenged by the courts and has met with only occasional criticism by the writers.

Justification for this purported refusal to supervise the ethics of the market place is sought in doctrines of *laissez–faire*. Aside from the somewhat anachronistic character of the argument in a period of rising recognition of the social interest in "private business," it is clear that there has been constant judicial delimitation, in the law of fraud and duress, of the permissible pressures to be used in the bargaining process. In general, the freedom from regulation postulated by *laissez–faire* adherents is demonstrably non-existent and virtually inconceivable. Bargaining power exists only because of government protection of the property rights bargained, and is properly subject to government control. Undaunted, the courts urge that their inability to compare values justifies the inadequacy rule. While the complexity of the exchange process renders a precise standard utopian, the total inability is belied in practice. Enforcement has been denied to contracts involving unfair disparity. Even more refined comparison is attempted by those jurisdictions which recognize "inadequacy" as a bar to specific performance but will decree cancellation only for "gross inadequacy." Valid logical or practical opposition to judicial enforcement of fair exchange has thus not been offered. Further, however, the weight of the mass of pronouncements supporting the rule that inadequacy is immaterial is substantially weakened by an examination of the cases. A classification of the fact situations reveals frequent unnecessary citation of the rule in cases where a fair exchange actually did exist, or where other ethical factors upheld the decision.

The non-commercial, non-bargain situation offers little difficulty. Obviously, it is not unfair to enforce a disparate promise when the promisor both knew and *desired* such disparity. As a matter of fact, it is at least arguable that there is no disparity, since the promisor has "bargained" for a psychological satisfaction not measurable in pecuniary terms. Judicial refusal to recognize such bargain equivalence is reflected in the unenforceability of executory gifts in the absence of a formal consideration. On the other hand, it is nonetheless true that enforcement of such gifts where the formal requirements are satisfied is needlessly buttressed by reference to the immateriality of inadequacy. In a similar category fall cases enforcing against a promisor's heir agreements to pay a substantial sum for a small service or for the privilege of naming a new-born child. Hardly distinguishable are transactions motivated by loyalty rather than profit, such as family settlements or payment of the debt of one member of the family by another acting under a sense of moral obligation.

The commercial bargain situation threatens greater difficulty. Men in economic transactions do not *desire* disparity; here if anywhere its disregard will conflict with the notion of fair exchange. However, in cases presenting the bargain situation and relying on the immateriality of inadequacy, difference in value is often only apparent since significant elements of the whole transaction have been overlooked. Thus, the apparent disparity in the grant of a valuable option for only one dollar diminishes in the light of the realization that the option is only preliminary to a sale. And when the inequality in the option is sufficient to render the whole transaction patently unfair, enforcement may be denied.

Frequently an element of risk renders the disparity illusory, the value of the bargain being contingent on an event the occurrence of which is independent of the will of either party. Typical instances are the promise to care for a person for life, the purchase of a going concern or of a speculative commodity, a loan for the purpose of speculative investment, compromise of an uncertain legal claim. In virtually all, reference to inadequacy is unnecessary.

Indeed, undesired disparity in a transaction would seem possible only where one party erred as to the market values of the products exchanged or where the parties were unequal in bargaining power. If the benefited party was ignorant of his advantage, the problem involves a resolution of a conflict between the enforcement of a fair exchange and the satisfaction of just expectations. Expectations based on a known error are, of course, scarcely "just," so relief is normally granted to the injured party. Disparities resulting from inequalities of bargaining power, however, can scarcely be eliminated in a capitalist economy which must enforce the inequality of property rights that produces those results. Nevertheless economic anarchy does not exist. In addition to the outlawing of fraud and duress as bargaining pressures the courts have refused enforcement of advantages gained by exercise of a power resulting from fortuitous circumstances not within the ethical range of accepted economic practice. The disadvantageous sale of a legacy by an impecunious legatee is a typical instance. Unfair exactions resulting from the creditor-debtor relationship have been subjected to a control which is facilitated by the usury analogy, but the courts have, in addition, recognized the inferior bargaining power of debtors as a class. The employer-employee relationship suggests itself as one calling for similar treatment. Legislative recognition of the individual laborer's bargaining weakness has been forced time and again. Typical judicial legalism, however, unhampered by realistic analysis, has resulted in some indications that employment at will is regarded as sufficient consideration for release by the employee of a personal injury claim against his employer. On the other hand, the rule is subject to evasion and, further, employment at will has been held an insufficient return for other exactions.

Constant reiteration of the immateriality of inadequacy has obscured the notion of fair exchange in contract law. But the rule, while prominent in dictum, is only occasionally the true basis of decision. Conscious judicial regard for the ethical norms necessarily operative in any event must dwarf, if not destroy, the peppercorn theory of consideration.

Note, 35 Colum.L.Rev. 1090 (1935).

Jones v. Star Credit Corp.

Supreme Court of New York, 1969.
59 Misc.2d 189, 298 N.Y.S.2d 264.

■ WACHTLER, J. On August 31, 1965, the plaintiffs, who are welfare recipients, agreed to purchase a home freezer unit for $900 as the result of a visit from a salesman representing Your Shop At Home Service, Inc. With the addition of the time credit charges, credit life insurance, credit property insurance, and sales tax, the purchase price totaled $1,234.80. Thus far the plaintiffs have paid $619.88 toward their purchase. The defendant claims that with various added credit charges paid for an extension of time there is a balance of $819.81 still due from the plaintiffs. The uncontroverted proof at the trial established that the freezer unit, when purchased, had a maximum retail value of approximately $300. The question is whether this transaction and the resulting contract could be considered unconscionable within the meaning of § 2–302 of the Uniform Commercial Code which provides * * *:

"(1) If the court as a matter of law finds the contract or any clause of the contract to have been unconscionable at the time it was made the court may refuse to enforce the contract, or it may enforce the remainder of the contract without the unconscionable clause, or it may so limit the application of any unconscionable clause as to avoid any unconscionable result.

"(2) When it is claimed or appears to the court that the contract or any clause thereof may be unconscionable the parties shall be afforded a reasonable opportunity to present evidence as to its commercial setting, purpose and effect to aid the court in making the determination" (L.1962, chap. 553, eff. Sept. 27, 1964).

There was a time when the shield of "caveat emptor" would protect the most unscrupulous in the marketplace—a time when the law, in granting parties unbridled latitude to make their own contracts, allowed exploitive and callous practices which shocked the conscience of both legislative bodies and the courts.

The effort to eliminate these practices has continued to pose a difficult problem. On the one hand it is necessary to recognize the importance of preserving the integrity of agreements and the fundamental right of parties to deal, trade, bargain, and contract. On the other hand there is the concern for the uneducated and often illiterate individual who is the victim of gross inequality of bargaining power, usually the poorest members of the community.

Concern for the protection of these consumers against overreaching by the small but hardy breed of merchants who would prey on them is not novel. The dangers of inequality of bargaining power were vaguely recognized in the early English common law when Lord Hardwicke wrote of a fraud, "which may be apparent from the intrinsic nature and subject of the bargain itself; such as no man in his senses and not under delusion would make." The English authorities on this subject were discussed in Hume v. United States (132 U.S. 406, 10 S.Ct. 134 [1889]), where the United States Supreme Court characterized these as "cases in which one party took advantage of the other's ignorance of arithmetic to impose upon him, and the fraud was apparent from the face of the contracts."

The law is beginning to fight back against those who once took advantage of the poor and illiterate without risk of either exposure or interference. From the common law doctrine of intrinsic fraud we have, over the years, developed common and statutory law which tells not only the buyer but also the seller to beware. This body of laws recognizes the importance of a free enterprise system but at the same time will provide the legal armor to protect and safeguard the prospective victim from the harshness of an unconscionable contract.

Section 2–302 of the Uniform Commercial Code enacts the moral sense of the community into the law of commercial transactions. It authorizes the court to find, as a matter of law, that a contract or a clause of a contract was "unconscionable at the time it was made," and upon so finding the court may refuse to enforce the contract, excise the objectionable clause or limit the application of the clause to avoid an unconscionable result. "The principle," states the Official Comment to this section, "is one of the prevention of oppression and unfair surprise." It permits a court to accomplish directly what heretofore was often accomplished by construction of language, manipulations of fluid rules of contract law and determinations based upon a presumed public policy.

There is no reason to doubt, moreover, that this section is intended to encompass the price term of the agreement. In addition to the fact that it has already been so ..., the statutory language itself makes it clear that not only a clause of the contract, but the contract in toto, may be found unconscionable as a matter of law. Indeed, no other provision of an agreement more intimately touches upon the question of unconscionability than does the term regarding prices.

Fraud, in the instant case, is not present; nor is it necessary under the statute. The question which presents itself is whether or not, under the circumstances of this case, the sale of a freezer unit having a retail value of $300 for $900 ($1,439.69 including credit charges and $18 sales tax) is unconscionable as a matter of law. The court believes it is.

Concededly, deciding the issue is substantially easier than explaining it. No doubt, the mathematical disparity between $300, which presumably includes a reasonable profit margin, and $900, which is exorbitant on its face, carries the greatest weight. Credit charges alone exceed by more than $100 the retail value of the freezer. These alone, may be sufficient to sustain the decision. Yet, a caveat is warranted lest we reduce the import of § 2–302 solely to a mathematical ratio formula. It may, at times, be that; yet it may also be much more. The very limited financial resources of the purchaser, known to the sellers at the time of the sale, is entitled to weight in the balance. Indeed, the value disparity itself leads inevitably to the felt conclusion that knowing advantage was taken of the plaintiffs. In addition, the meaningfulness of choice essential to the making of a contract can be negated by a gross inequality of bargaining power (Williams v. Walker–Thomas Furniture Co., 121 U.S.App.D.C. 315, 350 F.2d 445).

There is no question about the necessity and even the desirability of installment sales and the extension of credit. Indeed, there are many, including welfare recipients, who would be deprived of even the most basic conveniences without the use of these devices. Similarly, the retail merchant selling on installment or extending credit is expected to establish a pricing factor which will afford a degree of protection commensurate with the risk of selling to those who might be default prone. However, neither of these accepted premises can clothe the sale of this freezer with respectability.

Support for the court's conclusion will be found in a number of other cases already decided. In American Home Imp., Inc. v. MacIver [201 A.2d 886], the Supreme Court of New Hampshire held that a contract to install windows, a door and paint, for the price of $2,568.60, of which $809.60 constituted interest and carrying charges and $800 was a salesman's commission was unconscionable as a matter of law. In State by Lefkowitz v. ITM, Inc. [275 N.Y.S.2s 303], a deceptive and fraudulent scheme was involved, but standing alone, the court held that the sale of a vacuum cleaner, among other things, costing the defendant $140 and sold by it for $749 cash or $920.52 on time purchase was unconscionable as a matter of law. Finally, in Frosti–Fresh Corp. v. Reynoso [281 N.Y.S.2s 964], the sale of a refrigerator costing the seller $348 for $900 plus credit charges of $245.88 was unconscionable as a matter of law.

* * *

Having already [been] paid more than $600 toward the purchase of this $300 freezer unit, it is apparent that the defendant has already been amply compensated. In accordance with the statute, the application of the payment provision should be limited to amounts already paid by the plaintiffs and the contract be reformed and amended by changing the payments called for therein to equal the amount of payment actually so paid by the plaintiffs.

Submit judgment on notice.

NOTES

(1) Upon what grounds was the price term found to be unconscionable? Although the facts reveal that the plaintiff was on welfare and that the sale was probably made at home, there is no other evidence on the relative bargaining capacities (e.g., education, language skills, health, intelligence) of the parties. Does this support the "felt conclusion that knowing advantage was taken of the plaintiff?" If the contract price was disclosed and the plaintiff could have obtained a comparable freezer from another seller for $300, is judicial review of the adequacy of the exchange justified? What else do you need to know before that question can be answered?

(2) According to Frank P. Darr, there are three interrelated questions at work in price unconscionability cases: (1) Is there a community norm as to price, i.e., a range of reasonableness, (2) What was the quality of the bargaining process in the particular case, and (3) If the market has not set a competitive price, what is the likelihood of a market correction over time. See Frank P. Darr, *Unconscionability and Price Fairness*, 30 Hous.L.Rev. 1819 (1994). For example, in *Jones v. Star Credit*, the problem appears to be deficiencies in the bargaining process rather than the absence of a community norm or a market failure. But what defects? We return to the unconscionability problem in Chapter Five, Section 2D, *infra*.

Comment: Adequacy of Consideration

By now it should be clear that if there is consideration the courts will resist a request to inquire into the adequacy of the agreed exchange. This has been regarded as a corollary of freedom of contract, buttressed by laissez–faire economics. Reflecting this approach, the first Restatement states flatly that "the relative values of a promise and the consideration for it, do not affect the sufficiency of consideration." (§ 81). Similarly, the revised Restatement provides that there is no requirement of "equivalence in the values exchanged." Restatement (Second) § 79(b). This general respect for private autonomy, encompassing a broad recognition of the power of contracting parties to determine their own obligations, can be discerned in contemporary contract law. See Robert Braucher, *Freedom of Contract and the Second Restatement,* 78 Yale L.J. 598 (1969).

Even so, how should courts protect contracting parties from "bad bargains," i.e. agreed exchanges which in retrospect involve materially disparate values?

One approach is to find that the exchange was not bargained for because the promisor was not aware of the disparity and did not in fact bargain for it. If there is no consideration the insulation of "adequacy" from judicial review does not arise. This appears to be the approach of the majority opinion in *Bogigian v. Bogigian*, supra at 47.

If there was a bargained for exchange, another approach is to examine the quality of the bargaining process that preceded the agreement. Was the promisor's access to information or choice impaired by fraud or duress by the other party or by mistake? These are process-based exceptions to the adequacy principle and will be considered later in the course. Similarly, the doctrine of unconscionability is concerned with process where there is no fraud, duress, or mistake. As noted in *Jones v. Star Credit*, the hallmarks of unconscionability are "unfair surprise" and "oppression." We will return to see how this plays out in other cases, typically so-called "contracts of adhesion," i.e., form "contracts" drafted exclusively by one party and offered to the other on a "take-it-or-leave-it" basis, later in the course.

Another approach is to refuse enforcement where the outcome of the exchange shocks the conscience without explicitly examining the process. This was the general medieval attitude, influenced in part by Roman law antecedents, which sought to insure equivalency of value in all exchanges. Concepts of "just price," for example, were formulated to inhibit unfair advantage in bargaining, even where the disadvantage arose from inadvertence, inexperience, carelessness, or the like. See Alphonse Squillante, *The Doctrine of Just Price—Its Origin and Development,* 74 Com.L.J. 333 (1969). By the doctrine of *laesio enormis* a vendor could rescind a transaction where the price received was less than one-half its value. This was limited to real estate transactions under Roman law, but extended to others by the canonists. There are some vestiges of the lesion doctrine in civil law countries, but the trend has been in the other direction. See, e.g., Amos and Walton, Introduction to French Law 163–5 (2d ed. 1963)

In re Greene

United States District Court, Southern District of New York, 1930.
45 F.2d 428.

■ WOOLSEY, DISTRICT JUDGE. The petition for review is granted, and the order of the referee is reversed.

I.   The claimant, a woman, filed proof of claim in the sum of $375,700, based on an alleged contract, against this bankrupt's estate. The trustee in bankruptcy objected to the claim.

A hearing was held before the referee in bankruptcy and testimony taken.

The referee held the claim valid and dismissed the objections. The correctness of this ruling is raised by the trustee's petition to review and the referee's certificate.

II.   For several years prior to April 28, 1926, the bankrupt, a married man, had apparently lived in adultery with the claimant. He gave her substantial sums of money. He also paid $70,000 for a house on Long Island acquired by her, which she still owns.

Throughout their relations the bankrupt was a married man, and the claimant knew it. The claimant was well over thirty years of age when the connection began. She testified that the bankrupt had promised to marry her as soon as his wife should get a divorce from him; this the bankrupt denied.

The relations of intimacy between them were discontinued in April, 1926, and they then executed a written instrument under seal which is alleged to be a binding contract and which is the foundation of the claim under consideration.

In this instrument, which was made in New York, the bankrupt undertook (1) to pay to the claimant $1,000 a month during their joint lives; (2) to assign to her a $100,000 life insurance policy on his life and to keep up the premiums on it for life, the bankrupt to pay $100,000 to the claimant in case the policy should lapse for nonpayment of premiums; and (3) to pay the rent for four years on an apartment which she had leased.

It was declared in the instrument that the bankrupt had no interest in the Long Island house or in its contents, and that he should no longer be liable for mortgage interest, taxes, and other charges on this property.

The claimant on her part released the bankrupt from all claims which she had against him.

The preamble to the instrument recites as consideration the payment of $1 by the claimant to the bankrupt, "and other good and valuable considerations."

✗ What?

The bankrupt kept up the several payments called for by the instrument until August, 1928, but failed to make payments thereafter.

* * *

In view of my conclusion that the entire claim is void, however, the matter of damages is of no present importance.

* * *

The problem in the present case * * * is one of consideration, not of illegality, and it is clear that the past illicit intercourse is not consideration.

* * *

V. The question, therefore, is whether there was any consideration for the bankrupt's promises, apart from the past cohabitation. It seems plain that no such consideration can be found, but I will review the following points emphasized by the claimant as showing consideration:

(1) The $1 consideration recited in the paper is nominal. It cannot seriously be urged that $1, recited but not even shown to have been paid, will support an executory promise to pay hundreds of thousands of dollars.

(2) "Other good and valuable considerations" are generalities that sound plausible, but the words cannot serve as consideration where the facts show that nothing good or valuable was actually given at the time the contract was made.

(3) It is said that the release of claims furnishes the necessary consideration. So it would if the claimant had had any claims to release. But the evidence shows no vestige of any lawful claim. Release from imaginary claims is not valuable consideration for a promise. In this connection, apparently, the claimant testified that the bankrupt had promised to marry her as soon as he was divorced. Assuming that he did—though he denies it—the illegality of any such promise, made while the bankrupt was still married, is so obvious that no claim could possibly arise from it, and the release of such claim could not possibly be lawful consideration.

(4) The claimant also urges that by the agreement the bankrupt obtained immunity from liability for taxes and other charges on the Long Island house. The fact is that he was never chargeable for these expenses. He doubtless had been in the habit of paying them, just as he had paid many other expenses for the claimant; but such payments were either gratuitous or were the contemporaneous price of the continuance of his illicit intercourse with the claimant.

It is absurd to suppose that, when a donor gives a valuable house to a donee, the fact that the donor need pay no taxes or upkeep thereafter on the property converts the gift into a contract upon consideration. The present case is even stronger, for the bankrupt had never owned the house and had never been liable for the taxes. He furnished the purchase price, but the conveyance was from the seller direct to the claimant.

(5) Finally, it is said that the parties intended to make a valid agreement. It is a non sequitur to say that therefore the agreement is valid.

A man may promise to make a gift to another, and may put the promise in the most solemn and formal document possible; but, barring exceptional cases, such, perhaps, as charitable subscriptions, the promise will not be enforced. The parties may shout consideration to the housetops, yet unless consideration is actually present, there is not a legally enforceable contract.

What the bankrupt obviously intended in this case was an agreement to make financial contribution to the claimant because of his past cohabitation with her, and, as already pointed out, such an agreement lacks consideration.

V.   The presence of the seal would have been decisive in the claimant's favor a hundred years ago. Then an instrument under seal required no consideration, or, to keep to the language of the cases, the seal was conclusive evidence of consideration. In New York, however, a seal is now only presumptive evidence of consideration on an executory instrument. Civil Practice Act, § 342; Harris v. Shorall, 230 N.Y. 343, 348, 130 N.E. 572; Alexander v. Equitable Life Assurance Society, 233 N.Y. 300, 307, 135 N.E. 509. This presumption was amply rebutted in this case, for the proof clearly shows, I think, that there was not in fact any consideration for the bankrupt's promise contained in the executory instrument signed by him and the claimant.

An order in accordance with this opinion may be submitted for settlement on two days' notice.

Fiege v. Boehm

Court of Appeals of Maryland, 1956.
210 Md. 352, 123 A.2d 316.

■ DELAPLAINE, JUDGE. This suit was brought in the Superior Court of Baltimore City by Hilda Louise Boehm against Louis Gail Fiege to recover for breach of a contract to pay the expenses incident to the birth of his bastard child and to provide for its support upon condition that she would refrain from prosecuting him for bastardy.

Plaintiff alleged in her declaration substantially as follows: (1) that early in 1951 defendant had sexual intercourse with her although she was unmarried, and as a result thereof she became pregnant, and defendant acknowledged that he was responsible for her pregnancy; (2) that on September 29, 1951, she gave birth to a female child; that defendant is the father of the child; and that he acknowledged on many occasions that he is its father; (3) that before the child was born, defendant agreed to pay all her medical and miscellaneous expenses and to compensate her for the loss of her salary caused by the child's birth, and also to pay her ten dollars per week for its support until it reached the age of 21, upon condition that she would not institute bastardy proceedings against him as long as he made the payments in accordance with the agreement; (4) that she placed the child for adoption on July 13, 1954, and she claimed the following sums: Union Memorial Hospital, $110; Florence Crittenton Home, $100; Dr. George Merrill, her physician, $50; medicines $70.35; miscellaneous expenses, $20.45; loss of earnings for 26 weeks, $1,105; support of the child, $1,440; total, $2,895.80; and (5) that defendant paid her only $480, and she demanded that he pay her the further sum of $2,415.80, the balance due under the agreement, but he failed and refused to pay the same.

Defendant demurred to the declaration on the ground that it failed to allege that in September, 1953, plaintiff instituted bastardy proceedings against him in the Criminal Court of Baltimore, but since it had been found from blood tests that he could not have been the father of the child, he was acquitted of bastardy. The Court sustained the demurrer with leave to amend.

Plaintiff then filed an amended declaration, which contained the additional allegation that, after the breach of the agreement by defendant, she filed a charge with the State's Attorney that defendant was the father of her bastard child; and that on October 8, 1953, the Criminal Court found defendant not guilty solely on a physician's testimony that "on the basis of certain blood tests made, the defendant can be excluded as the father of the said child, which testimony is not conclusive upon a jury in a trial court."

Defendant also demurred to the amended declaration, but the Court overruled that demurrer.

Plaintiff, a typist, now over 35 years old, who has been employed by the Government in Washington and Baltimore for over thirteen years, testified in the Court below that she had never been married, but that at about midnight on January 21, 1951, defendant, after taking her to a moving picture theater on York Road and then to a restaurant, had sexual intercourse with her in his automobile. She further testified that he agreed to pay all her medical and hospital expenses, to compensate her for loss of salary caused by the pregnancy and birth, and to pay her ten dollars per week for the support of the child upon condition that she would refrain from instituting bastardy proceedings against him. She further testified that between September 17, 1951, and May, 1953, defendant paid her a total of $480.

Defendant admitted that he had taken plaintiff to restaurants, had danced with her several times, had taken her to Washington, and had brought her home in the country; but he asserted that he had never had sexual intercourse with her. He also claimed that he did not enter into any agreement with her. He admitted, however, that he had paid her a total of $480. His father also testified that he stated "that he did not want his mother to know, and if it were just kept quiet, kept principally away from his mother and the public and the courts, that he would take care of it."

Defendant further testified that in May, 1953, he went to see plaintiff's physician to make inquiry about blood tests to show the paternity of the child; and that those tests were made and they indicated that it was not possible that he could have been the child's father. He then stopped making payments. Plaintiff thereupon filed a charge of bastardy with the State's Attorney.

The testimony which was given in the Criminal Court by Dr. Milton Sachs, hematologist at the University Hospital, was read to the jury in the Superior Court. In recent years the blood-grouping test has been employed in criminology, in the selection of donors for blood transfusions, and as evidence in paternity cases. The Landsteiner blood-grouping test is based on the medical theory that the red corpuscles in human blood contain two affirmative agglutinating substances, and that every individual's blood falls into one of the four classes and remains the same throughout life. According to Mendel's law of inheritance, this blood individuality is an hereditary characteristic which passes from parent to child, and no agglutinating substance can appear in the blood of a child which is not present in the blood of one of its parents. The four Landsteiner blood groups, designated as AB, A, B, and O, into which human blood is divided on the basis of the compatibility of the corpuscles and serum with the corpuscles and serum of other persons, are characterized by different combinations of two agglutinogens in the red blood cells and two agglutinins in the serum. Dr. Sachs reported that Fiege's blood group was Type O. Miss Boehm's was Type B, and the infant's was Type A. He further testified that on the basis of these tests, Fiege could not have been the father of the child, as it is impossible for a mating of Type O and Type B to result in a child of Type A.

Although defendant was acquitted by the Criminal Court, the Superior Court overruled his motion for a directed verdict. In the charge to the jury the Court instructed them that defendant's acquittal in the Criminal Court was not binding upon them. The jury found a verdict in favor of plaintiff for $2,415.80, the full amount of her claim.

Defendant filed a motion for judgment n.o.v. or a new trial. The Court overruled that motion also, and entered judgment on the verdict of the jury. Defendant appealed from that judgment.

Defendant contends that, even if he did enter into the contract as alleged, it was not enforceable, because plaintiff's forbearance to prosecute was not based on a valid claim, and hence the contract was without consideration. He, therefore, asserts that the Court erred in overruling (1) his demurrer to the amended declaration, (2) his motion for a directed verdict, and (3) his motion for judgment n.o.v. or a new trial.

It was originally held at common law that a child born out of wedlock is *filius nullius*, and a putative father is not under any legal liability to contribute to the support of his illegitimate child, and his promise to do so is unenforceable because it is based on purely a moral obligation. Some of the courts in this country have held that, in the absence of any statutory obligation on the father to aid in the support of his bastard child, his promise to the child's mother to pay her for its maintenance, resting solely on his natural affection for it and his moral obligation to provide for it, is a promise which the law cannot enforce because of lack of sufficient consideration. . . . On the contrary, a few courts have stated that the natural affection of a father for his child and the moral obligation upon him to support it and to aid the woman he has wronged furnish sufficient consideration for his promise to the mother to pay for the support of the child to make the agreement enforceable at law. . . .

However, where statutes are in force to compel the father of a bastard to contribute to its support, the courts have invariably held that a contract by the putative father with the mother of his bastard child to provide for the support of the child upon the agreement of the mother to refrain from invoking the bastardy statute against the father, or to abandon proceedings already commenced, is supported by sufficient consideration. . . .

In Maryland it is now provided by statute what whenever a person is found guilty of bastardy, the court shall issue an order directing such person (1) to pay for the maintenance and support of the child until it reaches the age of eighteen years, such sum as may be agreed upon, if consent proceedings be had, or in the absence of agreement, such sum as the court may fix, with due regard to the circumstances of the accused person; and (2) to give bond to the State of Maryland in such penalty as the court may fix, with good and sufficient securities, conditioned on making the payments required by the court's order, or any amendments thereof. Failure to give such bond shall be punished by commitment to the jail or the House of Correction until bond is given but not exceeding two years. Code Supp.1955, art. 12, § 8.

Prosecutions for bastardy are treated in Maryland as criminal proceedings, but they are actually civil in purpose.... While the prime object of the Maryland Bastardy Act is to protect the public from the burden of maintaining illegitimate children, it is so distinctly in the interest of the mother that she becomes the beneficiary of it. Accordingly a contract by the putative father of an illegitimate child to provide for its support upon condition that bastardy proceedings will not be instituted is a compromise of civil injuries resulting from a criminal act, and not a contract to compound a criminal prosecution, and if it is fair and reasonable, it is in accord with the Bastardy Act and the public policy of the State.

Of course, a contract of a putative father to provide for the support of his illegitimate child must be based, like any other contract, upon sufficient consideration. The early English law made no distinction in regard to the sufficiency of a claim which the claimant promised to forbear to prosecute, as the consideration of a promise, other than the broad distinction between good claims and bad claims. No promise to forbear to prosecute an unfounded claim was sufficient consideration. In the early part of the Nineteenth Century, an advance was made from the criterion of the early authorities when it was held that forbearance to prosecute a suit which had already been instituted was sufficient consideration, without inquiring whether the suit would have been successful or not. . . .

In 1867 the Maryland Court of Appeals, in the opinion delivered by Judge Bartol in Hartle v. Stahl, 27 Md. 157, 172, held: (1) that forbearance to assert a claim before institution of suit, if not in fact a legal claim, is not of itself sufficient consideration to support a promise; but (2) that a compromise of a doubtful claim or a relinquishment of a pending suit is good consideration for a promise; and (3) that in order to support a compromise, it is sufficient that the parties entering into it thought at the time that there was a *bona fide* question between them, although it may eventually be found that there was in fact no such question.

We have thus adopted the rule that the surrender of, or forbearance to assert, an invalid claim by one who has not an honest and reasonable belief in its possible validity is not sufficient consideration for a contract. 1 Restatement, Contracts, sec. 76(b). We combine the subjective requisite that the claim be *bona fide* with the objective requisite that it must have a reasonable basis of support. Accordingly a promise not to prosecute a claim which is not founded in good faith does not of itself give a right of action on an agreement to pay for refraining from so acting, because a release from mere annoyance and unfounded litigation does not furnish valuable consideration.

Professor Williston was not entirely certain whether the test of reasonableness is based upon the intelligence of the claimant himself, who may be an ignorant person with no knowledge of law and little sense as to facts; but he seemed inclined to favor the view that "the claim forborne must be neither absurd in fact from the standpoint of a reasonable man in the position of the claimant, nor, obviously unfounded in law to one who has an elementary knowledge of legal principles." 1 Williston on Contracts, Rev.

Ed., sec. 135. We agree that while stress is placed upon the honesty and good faith of the claimant, forbearance to prosecute a claim is insufficient consideration if the claim forborne is so lacking in foundation as to make its assertion incompatible with honesty and a reasonable degree of intelligence. Thus, if the mother of a bastard knows that there is no foundation, either in law or fact, for a charge against a certain man that he is the father of the child, but that man promises to pay her in order to prevent bastardy proceedings against him, the forbearance to institute proceedings is not sufficient consideration.

On the other hand, forbearance to sue for a lawful claim or demand is sufficient consideration for a promise to pay for the forbearance if the party forbearing had an honest intention to prosecute litigation which is not frivolous, vexatious, or unlawful, and which he believed to be well founded.... Thus the promise of a woman who is expecting an illegitimate child that she will not institute bastardy proceedings against a certain man is sufficient consideration for his promise to pay for the child's support, even though it may not be certain whether the man is the father or whether the prosecution would be successful, if she makes the charge in good faith. The fact that a man accused of bastardy is forced to enter into a contract to pay for the support of his bastard child from fear of exposure and the shame that might be cast upon him as a result, as well as a sense of justice to render some compensation for the injury he inflicted upon the mother, does not lessen the merit of the contract, but greatly increases it....

* * *

In the case at bar there was no proof of fraud or unfairness. Assuming that the hemotologists were accurate in their laboratory tests and findings, nevertheless plaintiff gave testimony which indicated that she made the charge of bastardy against defendant in good faith. For these reasons the Court acted properly in overruling the demurrer to the amended declaration and the motion for a directed verdict.

* * *

Judgment affirmed, with costs.

NOTES

(1) In either case was there a legal obligation which the promisee agreed to relinquish? Should the existence of such a legal obligation be a necessary prerequisite to enforcement of the other's promise?

(2) Are *Greene* and *Fiege* inconsistent? In terms of the apparent rationale of consideration, should courts establish a general policy of favoring compromise agreements of the kind discussed?

(3) Should the requirement be that the claimant have both an honest *and* a reasonable belief in the validity of a claim, as in Restatement § 76, or should honest belief ("the forbearing or surrendering party believes that the claim or defense may be fairly determined to be valid") or good faith alone suffice, as under Restatement (Second) § 74(1)(b)? Can the two standards be sharply

delineated? Might not the absence of a reasonable belief itself be some evidence of bad faith? See Corbin § 140. A Missouri appellate court candidly addressed the problem as follows:

"The law favors compromise of doubtful claims, and forbearance may be a sufficient consideration for such compromise, even though the claim upon which it is based should develop to be ill-founded. The fact that, had the parties proceeded to litigate the claim, one of them would certainly have won, does not destroy the consideration for the compromise, for the consideration is said to be the settlement of the dispute.

"But there are certain essentials to the validity of such consideration. For one thing, and by all authority, the claim upon which the settlement is based must be one made in good faith.... Secondly, the claim must have *some* foundation. As to this second consideration we find the courts using varying language. The claim cannot be 'utterly baseless.' It has been said that it must have a 'tenable ground' or a 'reasonable, tenable ground.' It must be based on a 'colorable right,' or on some 'legal foundation.' It must have at least an appearance of right sufficient to raise a 'possible doubt' in favor of the party asserting it. . . .

"It is difficult to reconcile the antinomous rules and statements which are applied to the 'doubtful claims' and to find the words which will exactly draw the line between the compromise (on the one hand) of an honestly disputed claim which has some fair element of doubt and is therefore to be regarded as consideration and (on the other hand) a claim, though honestly made, which is so lacking in substance and virility as to be entirely baseless. The Missouri courts have struggled and not yet found apt language. We think we had best leave definitions alone, confident that, as applied to each individual case, the facts will make the thing apparent. But if we should make further effort to distinguish we would say that if the claimant, *in good faith*, makes a mountain out of a mole hill the claim is 'doubtful.' But if there is no discernible mole hill in the beginning, then the claim has no substance." Duncan v. Black, 324 S.W.2d 483, 486–8 (Mo.App.1959).

Was there a "mole hill" in *In re Greene*? In *Fiege v. Boehm?*

(2) PRE–EXISTING DUTY RULE

In our legal tradition, an agreement to discharge an existing obligation and an agreement to modify an existing contract may have consideration implications because of the so-called pre-existing duty rule. The rule is that the performance or the promise to perform a pre-existing duty does not constitute consideration. Perhaps no common law rule has been subjected to more critical evaluation than this staple of contract law. Courts have exercised considerable ingenuity in fashioning "exceptions," and there is a significant reorientation of the matter in the Uniform Commercial Code. See UCC 1–107 [Rev. 1–306], 2–209(1).

The rule emerged in cases involving the discharge of obligations. To illustrate: Debtor owes Creditor $1,000. The parties agree that Creditor will accept $500 in full settlement. Debtor pays the agreed $500; Creditor sues for the remaining $500. Creditor wins.

Based upon the previous cases in this chapter, is this a predictable result? Is it a good result? What additional facts might influence your judgment as to the proper outcome?

As the rule developed it was also applied to the modification of an existing contract in which one party undertook to do something additional and the other performed (or promised to perform) that which he or she had already agreed to perform. For example, Contractor agrees to build a garage, and Owner promises to pay $5,000. Contractor refuses to perform unless Owner agrees to pay an additional $1,000. Owner promises to pay the additional amount. Is this promise enforceable? The traditional answer is no. There is no consideration for Owner's promise to pay the $1,000, because Contractor did no more than that which it was already obliged to do.

Is a result favorable to Owner the logical outcome under the concept of consideration as elaborated in the preceding cases? Is it a fair result? Again, what additional factual data would be helpful?

Reflection upon these questions and a study of the materials which follow in this section will indicate that the problems in these types of cases go beyond the scope normally reached by consideration theory. Moreover, there are policy considerations which are simply not dealt with adequately under the rubric of consideration. For this reason, we return later in the book to aspects of both discharge and modification of contractual obligations. Collateral reading: Farnsworth §§ 4.21–4.25; Calamari and Perillo §§ 4–9 – 4–11; Murray § 64.

Levine v. Blumenthal

Supreme Court of New Jersey, 1936.
117 N.J.L. 23, 186 A. 457.

■ HEHER, J. By an indenture dated April 16th, 1931, plaintiff leased to defendants, for the retail merchandising of women's wearing apparel, store premises situate in the principal business district of the city of Paterson. The term was two years, to commence on May 1st next ensuing, with an option of renewal for the further period of three years, and the rent reserved was $2,100 for the first year, and $2,400 for the second year, payable in equal monthly installments in advance.

The state of the case settled by the District Court judge sets forth that defendants adduced evidence tending to show that, in the month of April, 1932, before the expiration of the first year of the term, they advised plaintiff that "it was absolutely impossible for them to pay any increase in rent; that their business had so fallen down that they had great difficulty in meeting the present rent of $175 per month; that if the plaintiff insisted upon the increase called for in the lease, they would be forced to remove from the premises or perhaps go out of business altogether;" and that plaintiff "agreed to allow them to remain under the same rental 'until business improved.' " While conceding that defendants informed him that "they could not pay the increase called for in the lease because of adverse business conditions," plaintiff, on the other hand, testified that he "agreed to accept the payment of $175 each month, on account" For eleven months of the second year of the term rent was paid by defendants, and accepted by plaintiff, at the rate of $175 per month. The option of renewal was not exercised; and defendants surrendered the premises at the expiration of the term leaving the last month's rent unpaid. This action was brought to recover the unpaid balance of the rent reserved by the lease for the second year—$25 per month for eleven months, and $200 for the last month.

The District Court judge found, as a fact, that "a subsequent oral agreement had been made to change and alter the terms of the written lease, with respect to the rent paid," but that it was not supported by "a lawful consideration," and therefore was wholly ineffective.

The insistence is that the current trade depression had disabled the lessees in respect of the payment of the full rent reserved, and a consideration sufficient to support the secondary agreement arose out of these special circumstances; and that, in any event, the execution of the substituted performance therein provided is a defense at law, notwithstanding the want of consideration.... It is said also that, "in so far as the oral agreement has become executed as to the payments which had fallen due and had been paid and accepted in full as per the oral agreement," the remission of the balance of the rent is sustainable on the theory of gift, if not of accord and satisfaction....

It is not suggested that the primary contract under consideration was of a class which may not lawfully be modified by parol, except to the extent that the substituted performance has been actually and fully executed and accepted; and we are not therefore called upon to consider that question. ... The point made by respondent is that the subsequent oral agreement to reduce the rent is *nudum pactum*, and therefore created no binding obligation.

It is elementary that the subsequent agreement, to impose the obligation of a contract, must rest upon a new and independent consideration. The rule was laid down in very early times that even though a part of a matured liquidated debt or demand has been given and received in full satisfaction thereof, the creditor may yet recover the remainder. The payment of a part was not regarded in law as a satisfaction of the whole, unless it was in virtue of an agreement supported by a consideration. ... The principle is firmly imbedded in our jurisprudence that a promise to do what the promisor is already legally bound to do is an unreal consideration. ... It has been criticised [sic], at least in some of its special applications as "mediaeval" and wholly artificial—one that operates to defeat the "reasonable bargains of business men." See Professor Ames' Treatise, tit. *"Two Theories of Consideration,"* in 12 Harvard Law Review 515, 521; ... But these strictures are not well grounded. They reject the basic principle that a consideration, to support a contract, consists either of a benefit to the promisor or a detriment to the promisee—a doctrine that has always been fundamental in our conception of consideration. It is a principle, almost universally accepted, that an act or forbearance required by a legal duty owing to the promisor that is neither doubtful nor the subject of honest and reasonable dispute is not a sufficient consideration....

Yet any consideration for the new undertaking, however insignificant, satisfies this rule.... For instance, an undertaking to pay part of the debt before maturity, or at a place other than where the obligor was legally bound to pay, or to pay in property, regardless of its value, or to effect a composition with creditors by the payment of less than the sum due, has been held to constitute a consideration sufficient in law. The test is whether there is an additional consideration adequate to support an ordinary contract, and consists of something which the debtor was not legally bound to do or give. ...

And there is authority for the view that, where there is no illegal preference, a payment of part of a debt, "accompanied by an agreement of the debtor to refrain from voluntary bankruptcy," is a sufficient consideration for the creditor's promise to remit the balance of the debt. But the mere fact that the creditor "fears that the debtor will go into bankruptcy, and that the debtor contemplates bankruptcy proceedings," is not enough; that alone does not prove that the creditor requested the debtor to refrain from such proceedings....

The cases to the contrary either create arbitrary exceptions to the rule, or profess to find a consideration in the form of a new undertaking which in essence was not a tangible new obligation or a duty not imposed by the lease, or, in any event, was not the price "bargained for as the exchange for the promise" (see *Coast National Bank v. Bloom,* supra), and therefore do violence to the fundamental principle. They exhibit the modern tendency, especially in the matter of rent reductions, to depart from the strictness of the basic common law rule and give effect to what has been termed a "reasonable" modification of the primary contract. ...

So tested, the secondary agreement at issue is not supported by a valid consideration; and it therefore created no legal obligation. General economic adversity, however disastrous it may be in its individual consequences, is never a warrant for judicial abrogation of this primary principle of the law of contracts.

It remains to consider the second contention that, in so far as the agreement has been executed by the payment and acceptance of rent at the reduced rate, the substituted performance stands, regardless of the want of consideration. This is likewise untenable. Ordinarily, the actual performance of that which one is legally bound to do stands on the same footing as his promise to do that which he is legally compellable to do.... Anson on Contracts (Turck Ed.) 234; Williston on Contracts (Rev.Ed.), §§ 130, 130a. This is a corollary of the basic principle. Of course, a different rule prevails where *bona fide* disputes have arisen respecting the relative rights and duties of the parties to a contract, or the debt or demand is unliquidated, or the contract is wholly executory on both sides.... Anson on Contracts (Turck Ed.) 240, 241.

It is settled in this jurisdiction that, as in the case of other contracts, a consideration is essential to the validity of an accord and satisfaction. . . . On reason and principle, it could not be otherwise. This is the general rule. . . . It results that the issue was correctly determined.

Judgment affirmed, with costs.

Alaska Packers' Association v. Domenico

United States Court of Appeals, Ninth Circuit, 1902.
54 C.C.A. 485, 117 Fed. 99.

[On March 26, 1900, appellees entered into a written contract with appellant in San Francisco under which they agreed to sail on a vessel provided by appellant to Pyramid Harbor, Alaska for the 1900 fishing season and then to return. Appellant had a salmon cannery at that location in which they had invested $150,000. They agreed, as sailor and fishermen, to do "regular ship's duty, both up and down, discharging and loading: and to do any other work whatsoever when requested to do so by the captain or agent of the Alaska Packer's Association." For this work, some appellees were to be paid $50 and others $60 for the season and all were to be paid "two cents for each red salmon in the catching of which he took part."

The appellees arrived at Pyramid Harbor in April, 1900 and began to unload the ship and fit up the cannery. On May 19, however, they "stopped work in a body, and demanded of the company's superintendent there in charge $100 for services in operating the vessel to and from Pyramid Harbor, instead of the sums stipulated for in the contracts; stating that unless they were paid this additional wage they would stop work entirely, and return to San Francisco." The evidence showed that the superintendent stated that he had no authority to modify the contract and was unable to induce the appellees to continue working. Because of the remoteness of the location and the shortness of the season, he was also unable to obtain replacements. On May 22, the superintendent "yielded to their demands" and substituted $100 for the previously agreed seasonal rates in a document that was signed by the appellees before a shipping commissioner who had been brought in for the occasion. After completing the season and returning to San Francisco, the appellees were informed by appellant that they would be paid only the amounts agreed to in March. Some of the appelles sued to enforce the agreed modification and received a judgment in the district court.]

■ Ross, Circuit Judge.

The real questions in the case as brought here are questions of law, and, in the view that we take of the case, it will be necessary to consider but one of those. Assuming that the appellant's superintendent at Pyramid Harbor was authorized to make the alleged contract of May 22d, and that he executed it on behalf of the appellant, was it supported by a sufficient consideration? From the foregoing statement of the case, it will have been seen that the libelants agreed in writing, for certain stated compensation, to render their services to the appellant in remote waters where the season for conducting fishing operations is extremely short, and in which enterprise the appellant had a large amount of money invested; and, after having entered upon the discharge of their contract, and at a time when it was impossible for the appellant to secure other men in their places, the libelants, without any valid cause, absolutely refused to continue the services they were under contract to perform unless the appellant would consent to pay them more money. Consent to such a demand, under such circumstances, if given, was, in our opinion, without consideration, for the reason that it was based solely upon the libelants' agreement to render the exact services, and none other, that they were already under contract to render. The case shows that they willfully and arbitrarily broke that obligation. As a matter of course, they were liable to the appellant in damages, and it is quite probable, as suggested by the court below in its opinion, that they may have been unable to respond in damages. But we are unable to agree with the conclusions there drawn, from these facts, in these words:

"Under such circumstances, it would be strange, indeed, if the law would not permit the defendant to waive the damages caused by the libelants' breach, and enter into the contract sued upon,—a contract mutually beneficial to all the parties thereto, in that it gave to the libelants reasonable compensation for their labor, and enabled the defendant to employ to advantage the large capital it had invested in its canning and fishing plant."

Certainly, it cannot be justly held, upon the record in this case, that there was any voluntary waiver on the part of the appellant of the breach of the original contract. The company itself knew nothing of such breach until the expedition returned to San Francisco, and the testimony is uncontradicted that its superintendent at Pyramid Harbor, who, it is claimed made on its behalf the contract sued on, distinctly informed the libelants that he had no power to alter the original or to make a new contract; and it would, of course, follow that if he had no power to change the original, he would have no authority to waive any rights thereunder. The circumstances of the present case bring it, we think, directly within the sound and just observations of the supreme court of Minnesota in the case of King v. Railway Co., 61 Minn. 482, 63 N.W. 1105:

"No astute reasoning can change the plain fact that the party who refuses to perform, and thereby coerces a promise from the other party to the contract to pay him an increased compensation for doing that which he is legally bound to do, takes an unjustifiable advantage of the necessities of the other party. Surely it would be a travesty on justice to hold that the party so making the promise for extra pay was estopped from asserting that the promise was without consideration. A party cannot lay the foundation of an estoppel by his own wrong, where the promise is simply a repetition of a subsisting legal promise. There can be no consideration for the promise of the other party, and there is no warrant for inferring that the parties have voluntarily rescinded or modified their contract. The promise cannot be legally enforced, although the other party has completed his contract in reliance upon it."

In Lingenfelder v. Brewing Co., 103 Mo. 578, 15 S.W. 844, the court, in holding void a contract by which the owner of a building agreed to pay its architect an additional sum because of his refusal to otherwise proceed with the contract, said:

"It is urged upon us by respondents that this was a new contract. New in what? Jungenfeld was bound by his contract to design and supervise this building. Under the new promise, he was not to do anything more or anything different. What benefit was to accrue to Wainwright? He was to receive the same service from Jungenfeld under the new, that Jungenfeld was bound to tender under the original, contract. What loss, trouble, or inconvenience could result to Jungenfeld that he had not already assumed? No amount of metaphysical reasoning can change the plain fact that Jungenfeld took advantage of Wainwright's necessities, and extorted the promise of five per cent. on the refrigerator plant as the condition of his complying with his contract already entered into. Nor had he even the flimsy pretext that Wainwright had violated any of the conditions of the contract on his part. Jungenfeld himself put it upon the simple proposition that 'if he, as an architect, put up the brewery, and another company put up the refrigerating machinery, it would be a detriment to the Empire Refrigerating Company,' of which Jungenfeld was president. To permit plaintiff to recover under such circumstances would be to offer a premium upon bad faith, and invite men to violate their most sacred contracts that they may profit by their own wrong. That a promise to pay a man for doing that which he is already under contract to do is without consideration is conceded by respondents. The rule has been so long imbedded in the common law and decisions of the highest courts of the various states that nothing but the most cogent reasons ought to shake it. [Citing a long list of authorities.] But it is 'carrying coals to Newcastle' to add authorities on a proposition so universally accepted, and so inherently just and right in itself. The learned counsel for respondents do not controvert the general proposition. Their contention is, and the circuit court agreed with them, that, when Jungenfeld declined to go further on his contract, the defendant then had the right to sue for damages, and not having elected to sue Jungenfeld, but having acceded to his demand for the additional compensation, defendant cannot now be heard to say his promise is without consideration. While it is true Jungenfeld became liable in damages for the obvious breach of his contract, we do not think it follows that defendant is estopped from showing its promise was made without consideration. * * *"

It results from the views above expressed that the judgment must be reversed, and the cause remanded, with directions to the court below to enter judgment for the respondent, with costs. It is so ordered.

NOTES

(1) Consideration is normally regarded as something which is bargained for and given in exchange for a promise. Was not the bargain requirement

satisfied in *Levine?* Why, then, does the court reject the defendants' position? Would the decision have been different were it clearly established that the lessor importuned the lessees to stay on under the new arrangement?

(2) Is there a reasonable basis for distinguishing *Levine* and *Alaska Packers* on consideration theory? Assuming the consideration argument were unavailing in *Alaska Packers*, could you argue persuasively for a similar result predicated on other grounds?

(3) *It's the nets, stupid.* In *Alaska Packers*, the fishermen tried to prove that the nets furnished to them were not serviceable because they permitted the smaller salmon to slip through. The district court concluded that the contention was not proven (a finding affirmed in the full opinion of the Ninth Circuit), reasoning in part that Alaska Packers had every incentive to supply nets adequate to the task. Nevertheless, the district court held that an executory contract could be validly modified by substituting the modifying agreement for the original contract (a novation) and that there was no duress to prevent enforcement. On appeal, the Ninth Circuit rejected the novation theory, holding that new consideration was required to validate the modification. Moreover, the court of appeals appears to conclude that the modification was extracted under duress—by an unlawful threat to breach the contract, leaving the Packers without any viable alternatives and some very uncertain damage remedies.

For an interesting context study of this case that completes the record and develops some alternative stories about what likely occurred, see Deborah L. Threedy, *A Fish Story: Alaska Packers' Association v. Domenico,* 2000 Utah L. Rev. 185 (2000). For example, she suggests that the fishermen, because of differences in language and experience, might have misunderstood that the nets were serviceable. While this would not justify a strike, it tends to neutralize the claim of duress. 2000 Utah L. Rev. at 205–07. She also suggests that nets which appear unserviceable to those hoping to catch more fish (the fishermen) would be perfect for the Packers who were concerned about catching too many fish or, perhaps, cutting corners on equipment.

Angel v. Murray

Supreme Court of Rhode Island, 1974.
113 R.I. 482, 322 A.2d 630.

■ ROBERTS, CHIEF JUSTICE. This is a civil action brought by Alfred L. Angel and others against John E. Murray, Jr., Director of Finance of the City of Newport, the city of Newport, and James L. Maher, alleging that Maher had illegally been paid the sum of $20,000 by the Director of Finance and praying that the defendant Maher be ordered to repay the city such sum. The case was heard by a justice of the Superior Court, sitting without a jury, who entered a judgment ordering Maher to repay the sum of $20,000 to the city of Newport. Maher is now before this court prosecuting an appeal.

The record discloses that Maher has provided the city of Newport with a refuse-collection service under a series of five-year contracts beginning in 1946. On March 12, 1964, Maher and the city entered into another such contract for a period of five years commencing on July 1, 1964, and terminating on June 30, 1969. The contract provided, among other things, that Maher would receive $137,000 per year in return for collecting and removing all combustible and noncombustible waste materials generated within the city.

In June of 1967 Maher requested an additional $10,000 per year from the city council because there had been a substantial increase in the cost of collection due to an unexpected and unanticipated increase of 400 new dwelling units. Maher's testimony, which is uncontradicted, indicates the 1964 contract had been predicated on the fact that since 1946 there had been an average increase of 20 to 25 new dwelling units per year. After a public meeting of the city council where Maher explained in detail the reasons for his request and was questioned by members of the city council, the city council agreed to pay him an additional $10,000 for the year ending on June 30, 1968. Maher made a similar request again in June of 1968 for the same reasons, and the city council again agreed to pay an additional $10,000 for the year ending on June 30, 1969.

The trial justice found that each such $10,000 payment was made in violation of law. His decision, as we understand it, is premised on two independent grounds. First, he found that the additional payments were unlawful because they had not been recommended in writing to the city council by the city manager. Second, he found that Maher was not entitled to extra compensation because the original contract already required him to collect all refuse generated within the city and, therefore, included the 400 additional units. The trial justice further found that these 400 additional units were within the contemplation of the parties when they entered into the contract. It appears that he based this portion of the decision upon the rule that Maher had a preexisting duty to collect the refuse generated by the 400 additional units, and thus there was no consideration for the two additional payments.

* * *

[The court concluded that the charter provision did not preclude the city council from acting without the city manager's recommendation in altering the written contract.]

* * *

Having found that the city council had the power to modify the 1964 contract without the written recommendation of the city manager, we are still confronted with the question of whether the additional payments were illegal because they were not supported by consideration.

* * *

It is generally held that a modification of a contract is itself a contract, which is unenforceable unless supported by consideration. See Simpson, supra, § 93. In Rose v. Daniels, 8 R.I. 381 (1866), this court held that an agreement by a debtor with a creditor to discharge a debt for a sum of money less than the amount due is unenforceable because it was not supported by consideration.

Rose is a perfect example of the preexisting duty rule. Under this rule an agreement modifying a contract is not supported by consideration if one of the parties to the agreement does or promises to do something that he is legally obligated to do or refrains or promises to refrain from doing something he is not legally privileged to do. . . . In *Rose* there was no consideration for the new agreement because the debtor was already legally obligated to repay the full amount of the debt.

Although the preexisting duty rule is followed by most jurisdictions, a small minority of jurisdictions, Massachusetts, for example, find that there is consideration for a promise to perform what one is already legally obligated to do because the new promise is given in place of an action for damages to secure performance. See Swartz v. Lieberman, 323 Mass. 109, 80 N.E.2d 5 (1948); Munroe v. Perkins, 26 Mass. (9 Pick.) 298 (1830). *Swartz* is premised on the theory that a promisor's forbearance of the power to breach his original agreement and be sued in an action for damages is consideration for a subsequent agreement by the promisee to pay extra compensation. This rule, however, has been widely criticized as an anomaly. . . .

The primary purpose of the preexisting duty rule is to prevent what has been referred to as the "hold-up game." See 1A Corbin, supra, § 171. A classic example of the "hold-up game" is found in Alaska Packers' Ass'n v. Domenico, 117 F. 99 (9th Cir.1902). . . .

* * *

Another example of the "hold-up game" is found in the area of construction contracts. Frequently, a contractor will refuse to complete work under an unprofitable contract unless he is awarded additional compensation. The courts have generally held that a subsequent agreement to award additional compensation is unenforceable if the contractor is only performing work which would have been required of him under the original contract. . . .

These examples clearly illustrate that the courts will not enforce an agreement that has been procured by coercion or duress and will hold the parties to their original contract regardless of whether it is profitable or unprofitable. However, the courts have been reluctant to apply the preexisting duty rule when a party to a contract encounters unanticipated difficulties and the other party, not influenced by coercion or duress, voluntarily agrees to pay additional compensation for work already required to be performed under the contract. For example, the courts have found that the original contract was rescinded, Linz v. Schuck, 106 Md. 220, 67 A. 286 (1907); abandoned, Connelly v. Devoe, 37 Conn. 570 (1871), or waived, Michaud v. MacGregor, 61 Minn. 198, 63 N.W. 479 (1895).

Although the preexisting duty rule has served a useful purpose insofar as it deters parties from using coercion and duress to obtain additional compensation, it has been widely criticized as a general rule of law. With regard to the preexisting duty rule, one legal scholar has stated: "There has been a growing doubt as to the soundness of this doctrine as a matter of social policy. * * * In certain classes of cases, this doubt has influenced courts to refuse to apply the rule, or to ignore it, in their actual decisions. Like other legal rules, this rule is in process of growth and change, the process being more active here than in most instances. The result of this is that a court should no longer accept this rule as fully established. It should never use it as the major premise of a decision, at least without giving careful thought to the circumstances of the particular case, to the moral deserts of the parties, and to the social feelings and interests that are involved. It is certain that the rule, stated in general and all-inclusive terms, is no longer so well-settled that a court must apply it though the heavens fall." 1A Corbin, supra, § 171; see also Calamari & Perillo, supra, § 61.

The modern trend appears to recognize the necessity that courts should enforce agreements modifying contracts when unexpected or unanticipated difficulties arise during the course of the performance of a contract, even though there is no consideration for the modification, as long as the parties agree voluntarily.

Under the Uniform Commercial Code, § 2–209(1), which has been adopted by 49 states, "[a]n agreement modifying a contract [for the sale of goods] needs no consideration to be binding." See G.L.1956 (1969 Reenactment) § 6A–2–209(1). Although at first blush this section appears to validate modifications obtained by coercion and duress, the comments to this section indicate that a modification under this section must meet the test of good faith imposed by the Code, and a modification obtained by extortion without a legitimate commercial reason is unenforceable.

The modern trend away from a rigid application of the preexisting duty rule is reflected by § 89D(a) [Section 89(a) in the final draft] of the American Law Institute's Restatement Second of the Law of Contracts,[1] which provides: "A promise modifying a duty under a contract not fully performed on either side is binding (a) if the modification is fair and equitable in view of circumstances not anticipated by the parties when the contract was made * * *."

We believe that § 89D(a) is the proper rule of law and find it applicable to the facts of this case.[2] It not only prohibits modifications obtained by

---

1. The first nine chapters of the Restatement Second of the Law of Contracts were given tentative approval by the American Law Institute at successive meetings from 1964 to 1972. These chapters, which include §§ 1–255, were published by the Institute in 1973 in a hard-cover edition. Herbert Wechsler, Director of the Institute, in a foreword to this edition indicates that although these sections are still tentative and await final approval, it is unlikely that any further changes will be made.

2. The fact that these additional payments were made by a municipal corporation rather than a private individual does not in our opinion affect the outcome of this case. Unlike many other jurisdictions, there is no constitutional or statutory restriction in this state limiting the power of a city or town to award extra compensation to a private contractor. See, e.g., McGovern v. City of New York, 234 N.Y. 377 (1923); Annot., 25 A.L.R. 1450 (1923), supplemented by Annot., 55

coercion, duress, or extortion but also fulfills society's expectation that agreements entered into voluntarily will be enforced by the courts.[3] See generally Horwitz, The Historical Foundations of Modern Contract Law, 87 Harv.L.Rev. 917 (1974). Section 89D(a), of course, does not compel a modification of an unprofitable or unfair contract; it only enforces a modification if the parties voluntarily agree and if (1) the promise modifying the original contract was made before the contract was fully performed on either side, (2) the underlying circumstances which prompted the modification were unanticipated by the parties, and (3) the modification is fair and equitable.

The evidence, which is uncontradicted, reveals that in June of 1968 Maher requested the city council to pay him an additional $10,000 for the year beginning on July 1,1968, and ending on June 30, 1969. This request was made at a public meeting of the city council, where Maher explained in detail his reasons for making the request. Thereafter, the city council voted to authorize the Mayor to sign an amendment to the 1964 contract which provided that Maher would receive an additional $10,000 per year for the

A.L.R. 1333 (1928), and Annot., 138 A.L.R. 136 (1942). Absent such limitation, a city or town may modify an existing contract in precisely the same manner as a private individual as long as the modification is reasonable and proper. See Arnold v. Mayor of Pawtucket, 21 R.I. 15, 19 (1898).

3. The drafters of § 89D(a) of the Restatement Second of the Law of Contracts use the following illustrations in comment (b) as examples of how this rule is applied to certain transactions:

"1. By a written contract A agrees to excavate a cellar for B for a stated price. Solid rock is unexpectedly encountered and A so notifies B. A and B then orally agree that A will remove the rock at a unit price which is reasonable but nine times that used in computing the original price, and A completes the job. B is bound to pay the increased amount.

"2. A contracts with B to supply for $300 a laundry chute for a building B has contracted to build for the Government for $150,000. Later A discovers that he made an error as to the type of material to be used and should have bid $1,200. A offers to supply the chute for $1,000, eliminating overhead and profit. After ascertaining that other suppliers would charge more, B agrees. The new agreement is binding.

"3. A is employed by B as a designer of coats at $90 a week for a year beginning November 1 under a written con-

tract executed September 1. A is offered $115 a week by another employer and so informs B. A and B then agree that A will be paid $100 a week and in October execute a new written contract to that effect simultaneously tearing up the prior contract. The new contract is binding.

"4. A contracts to manufacture and sell to B 2,000 steel roofs for corn cribs at $60. Before A begins manufacture a threat of a nationwide steel strike raises the cost of steel about $10 per roof, and A and B agree orally to increase the price to $70 per roof. A thereafter manufactures and delivers 1,700 of the roofs, and B pays for 1,500 of them at the increased price without protest, increasing the selling price of the corn cribs by $10. The new agreement is binding.

"5. A contracts to manufacture and sell to B 100,000 castings for lawn mowers at 50 cents each. After partial delivery and after B has contracted to sell a substantial number of lawn mowers at a fixed price, A notifies B that increased metal costs require that the price be increased to 75 cents. Substitute castings are available at 55 cents, but only after several months delay. B protests but is forced to agree to the new price to keep its plant in operation. The modification is not binding."

duration of the contract. Under such circumstances we have no doubt that the city voluntarily agreed to modify the 1964 contract.

Having determined the voluntariness of this agreement, we turn our attention to the three criteria delineated above. First, the modification was made in June of 1968 at a time when the five-year contract which was made in 1964 had not been fully performed by either party. Second, although the 1964 contract provided that Maher collect all refuse generated within the city, it appears this contract was premised on Maher's past experience that the number of refuse-generating units would increase at a rate of 20 to 25 per year. Furthermore, the evidence is uncontradicted that the 1967–1968 increase of 400 units "went beyond any previous expectation." Clearly, the circumstances which prompted the city council to modify the 1964 contract were unanticipated.[4] Third, although the evidence does not indicate what proportion of the total this increase comprised, the evidence does indicate that it was a "substantial" increase. In light of this, we cannot say that the council's agreement to pay Maher the $10,000 increase was not fair and equitable in the circumstances.

The judgment appealed from is reversed, and the cause is remanded to the Superior Court for entry of judgment for the defendants.

NOTES

(1) Is the "unexpected or unanticipated difficulties" exception referred to in the instant case a mere technical evasion? Or is there a sound basis in policy for upholding modifications under such circumstances?

(2) *Modification under the Uniform Commercial Code.* Section 2–209(1) of the Code provides: "An agreement modifying a contract within this Article

4. The trial justice found that sec. 2(a) of the 1964 contract precluded Maher from recovering extra compensation for the 400 additional units. Section 2(a) provided: *"The Contractor, having made his proposal after his own examinations and estimates, shall take all responsibility for, and bear, any losses resulting to him in carrying out the contract;* and shall assume the defence of, and hold the City, its agents and employees harmless from all suits and claims arising from the use of any invention, patent, or patent rights, material, labor or implement, by or from any act, omission or neglect of, the Contractor, his agents or employees, in carrying out the contract." (Emphasis added). The trial justice, quoting the italicized portion of sec. 2(a), found that this section required that any losses incurred in the performance of the contract were Maher's responsibility. In our opinion, however, the trial justice overlooked the thrust of sec. 2(a) when read in its entirety.

It is clearly a contractual provision requiring the contractor to hold the city harmless and to defend it in any litigation arising out of the performance of his obligations under the contract, whether a result of affirmative action or some omission or neglect on the part of Maher or his agents or employees. We are persuaded that the portion of sec. 2(a) specifically referred to by the court refers to losses resulting to Maher from some action or omission on the part of his own agents or employees. It cannot be disputed, however, that any losses that resulted from an increase in the cost of collecting from the increased number of units generating refuse in no way resulted from any action on the part of either Maher or his employees. Rather, whatever losses he did entail by reason of the requirement of such extra collection resulted from actions completely beyond his control and thus unanticipated.

needs no consideration to be binding." The drafters appended the following commentary:

> Subsection (1) provides that an agreement modifying a sales contract needs no consideration to be binding.

> However, modifications made thereunder must meet the test of good faith imposed by this Act. The effective use of bad faith to escape performance on the original contract terms is barred, and the extortion of a "modification" without legitimate commercial reason is ineffective as a violation of the duty of good faith. Nor can a mere technical consideration support a modification made in bad faith.

> The test of "good faith" between merchants or as against merchants includes "observance of reasonable commercial standards of fair dealing in the trade" (Section 2–103), and may in some situations require an objectively demonstrable reason for seeking a modification. But such matters as a market shift which makes performance come to involve a loss may provide such a reason even though there is no such unforeseen difficulty as would make out a legal excuse from performance under Sections 2–615 and 2–616.

UCC 2–209(1) of the Code is obviously a departure from the common law and, as elaborated in the comments, basically reorients the subject. The emphasis is no longer upon consideration, but upon good faith. For example, it is noted that a "mere technical consideration" cannot support a "modification made in bad faith." To what extent should the Code apply in analogous transactions, as for example, construction contracts or employment contracts? Would the Code furnish a superior method of approach in these cases, or would the more traditional view(s) appear more conducive to the attainment of satisfactory results?

PROBLEM: THE CASE OF THE DISSATISFIED ENTERTAINER

(You are a justice of a state appellate court, and the following is the beginning of an opinion which you are to complete for submission to your colleagues.)

This is an appeal from a judgment entered in the Circuit Court, after a jury trial in which the plaintiff, Oliver Ajax, received a verdict for $35,000 in a breach of contract action against the defendant, James Bond.

On February 15, Ajax and Bond entered into a written contract whereby the former, a professional entertainer, was to perform at Bond's resort hotel for the week of July 1–7 for $20,000. In late spring, Ajax had a hit record which virtually overnight made him a star who could command at least $50,000 for a one-week engagement. In early June he contacted Bond to renegotiate their contract, demanding $50,000 for the July 1–7 period. Initially, Bond refused to renegotiate, but when Ajax said he would not appear, Bond relented. After discussion Bond dictated a new contract to his stenographer, in the exact words of the first contract and running for the same period with the compensation changed to $35,000. As they signed the new contract they tore up the old one. Thereafter, Ajax kept the engagement, but Bond refused to pay more than $20,000. Whereupon Ajax filed the instant suit for $35,000.

Over defendant's objection, the trial judge instructed the jury as follows: "If you find that the '$20,000 contract' was prior to or at the time of the execution of the '$35,000 contract' cancelled and revoked by the parties by their mutual consent, then it is your duty to find that there was consideration for the making of the contract in suit and, in that event, the plaintiff is entitled to your verdict in the amount of $35,000." On this appeal, the defendant contends that the giving of this instruction constituted reversible error.

(✱) PROBLEM: THE CASE OF THE SUBCONTRACTOR'S ADDED INDUCEMENT

Edward Woodward is the owner of a laundry establishment in Metropolis. On August 7, Woodward entered into a written contract with Peter Rogers, a general contractor, for the construction of an additional power plant.

On August 14, Rogers entered into a written subcontract with John Newman for the erection of all structural steel work required for the power plant. For the purpose of performing his work, Newman rented certain equipment for use until the job was completed. The work continued until October 7, when a strike occurred among the employees of Newman, and work was discontinued for a period of approximately nine weeks. During this time Newman was obliged to pay rent for the equipment and other sums to insure its safekeeping.

A meeting was called to adjust differences. In attendance were Newman, Rogers, Woodward and a representative of the union of the strikers. As a result of lengthy discussion the strike was called off. However, Newman refused to continue performance unless he was paid for the rentals and charges accruing during the time of the strike. ~~Woodward~~ *Rogers* then promised to pay this amount so that the work could proceed.

The work was completed under the contracts, but ~~Woodward~~ *Rogers* refused to pay the rentals and charges. Newman consults you. Advise him.

(3) MUTUALITY OF OBLIGATION

Within our legal tradition, a contractual obligation is not easily imposed upon an unwilling party. One may refuse to negotiate altogether, or explicitly state that one will not agree to any bargain unless the other party agrees to a particular term or, in the final agreement, expressly state that one will have no duty of performance unless a specified event first occurs. In the last situation, it is assumed that an enforceable contract subject to an express condition has been created. When that event is beyond the control of the promisor and, upon the failure of it to occur, he or she acts promptly to call the deal off, the courts normally will protect a privilege to withdraw without liability.

The problem becomes more complicated, however, when the final agreement of the parties or some rule of law permits one of them to withdraw sometime after performance begins for reasons totally or partially within his or her control. From one point of view, the problem is complicated by the view that consideration for a promise is a return promise, bargained for and given in exchange for the promise. Thus, if

Anne promises to appear on Friday to paint Paul's house and Paul agrees to pay $1,000 when the job is completed "if I feel like it," if Anne fails to show and Paul sues for breach, Anne can defend on the ground that Paul gave no consideration for her promise. Paul's assent was illusory. Or, to put the matter more traditionally, in the attempted bilateral contract there was no mutuality of obligation ... no consideration! But suppose Anne appeared and painted the house in a proper manner. If Paul refused to pay, could Anne recover the agreed price? The reasonable value of her services? Paul will argue that he made no promise to pay and that Anne, therefore, assumed the risk. Will that argument succeed? Or will the court imply or impose some limitation upon Paul's discretion, such as a duty to act in good faith, in order to protect Anne's investment?

The following materials will touch upon these questions in several types of exchange relationships, and the subject will be developed, in a broader context, later in the book. Collateral reading: Farnsworth § 2.13–2.15; Calamari and Perillo §§ 4–12—4–13; Murray § 65.

Rehm–Zeiher Co. v. F.G. Walker Co.

Court of Appeals of Kentucky, 1913.
156 Ky. 6, 160 S.W. 777.

Appeal from Circuit Court, Jefferson County, Common Pleas Branch, Fourth Division.

Action by the Rehm–Zeiher Company against the F.G. Walker Company. Judgment for defendant, and plaintiff appeals. Affirmed.

■ CARROLL, J. The appellant, a corporation, in the years 1908, 1909, 1910, 1911, and 1912, and prior thereto, was engaged in the business of selling whisky; that is to say, it purchased from distillers certain brands and quantities of whisky, and then sold the whisky so bought to the trade. The appellee, during the years named, and prior thereto, owned and operated a distillery. In 1908 the parties entered into the following contract:

"This contract made and entered into this November 17, 1908, by and between the F.G. Walker Company, of Bardstown, Nelson county, Kentucky, a corporation, party of the first part, and the Rehm–Zeiher Company, of Louisville, Jefferson county, Kentucky, party of the second part. The party of the first part has this day sold to the party of the second part 2,000 cases of old Walker whisky put up under a private brand, to be delivered during the years 1909, 3,000 cases to be delivered during the year 1910, 4,000 cases to be delivered during the year 1911, and 5,000 cases to be delivered during the year 1912, at the following prices: Quarts bottled in bond, $6.70; pints bottled in bond, $7.20; half pints bottled in bond, $7.70. Should the party of the first part lose by fire the whisky with which this bottling is to be done or the bottling room during the life of this contract, then they are to be held excusable for not filling same. If for any unforeseen reason the party of the second part find that they cannot use the full amount of the above-named goods, the party of the first part agrees to release them from the contract for the amount desired by party of the second part.''

In 1912 the appellant brought this suit against the appellee to recover damages for its failure to furnish 2,596 cases of the 4,000 cases of whisky it was provided in the contract should be furnished in 1911. The petition averred that during the year 1911 the appellant demanded that the appellee furnish to it 4,000 cases of old Walker whisky, but that in violation of its contract the appellee only furnished 1,044 cases, and refused to furnish the remainder, to its damage in the sum of $6,798, which sum it averred was the loss it sustained by the failure of the appellee to furnish the 2,596 cases it failed and refused to furnish.

After a demurrer had been overruled, an answer was filed setting up various defenses, which were controverted by a reply, and the parties went to trial before a jury. After the evidence for the appellant had been concluded, the lower court directed a verdict in favor of the appellee, upon the ground that the contract was lacking in mutuality, and therefore could not be made the subject of an action for its breach by either party. On this appeal the only question we need concern ourselves with is the one upon which the trial judge rested his opinion that the appellant could not recover.

It appears without contradiction that in 1909 the appellant only ordered and received 786 cases of the 2,000 called for by the contract, and that in 1910 it only ordered and received 1,200 cases of the 3,000 cases called for by the contract, and that the appellee did not demand or request that it should take in either of these years the full number of cases specified in the contract or any greater number than it did take. It further appears that in the early part of 1911 whisky advanced in price, and the appellee refused to deliver to the appellant whisky it ordered. After this, however, the appellee, upon request, furnished to the appellant 1,044 cases of the 1911 whisky; but in September, 1911, it peremptorily refused to furnish any more, and thereupon this suit was brought.

* * *

There is a line of cases holding that, where, for example, A. and B. enter into a contract by which A. agrees to furnish to B. all the coal that B. will require in the operation of an established factory, the contract is not lacking in mutuality, as B. may require A. to furnish him all the coal he needs to operate his factory, and A. may insist that B. shall take from him all the coal he needs for this purpose.

An illustration of this class of cases is Crane v. Crane, 105 Fed. 869, 45 C.C.A. 96, where the court said: ''It is within legal competency for one to bind himself to furnish another with such supplies as may be needed during some certain period for some certain business or manufacture, or with such commodities as the purchaser has already bound himself to furnish another. Reasonable provision in business requires that such contracts, though more or less indefinite, should be upheld. Thus a foundry may purchase all the coal needed for the season, or a furnace company its

requirements in the way of iron, or a hotel its necessary supply of ice. * * *
So, too, a dealer in coal in any given locality may contract for such coal as
he may need to fulfill his existing contracts, regardless of whether delivery
by him to his customers is to be immediate or in the future. * * * In all
these cases contracts looking towards the future, and embodying subject-
matter necessarily indefinite in quantity, have been upheld; but it will be
observed that, although the quantity under contract is not measured by
any certain standard, it is capable of an approximately accurate forecast.
The capacity of the furnace, the needs of the railroad, or the requirements
of the hotel are, within certain limits, ascertainable by the vendor.''

* * *

If the contract had specified that the Rehm–Zeiher Company was only
obliged to take so much of the whisky as it "desired to take," or as it
"pleased to take," it would not any more certainly have given the company
the right to exercise its pleasure as to how much whisky it would take than
do the words "unforeseen reason." The unforeseen reason that would
excuse the company from only taking so much of the whisky as it desired to
take, if any, left the amount it should take entirely to its discretion. The
contract places no limitation whatever upon the meaning of the words
"unforeseen reason," so that any reason that the company might assign for
not taking the whisky would relieve it of any obligation to do so. It was not
necessary that the reason should be a good reason or a reasonable reason.

If the Walker Company had sought by a suit to compel the Rehm–
Zeiher Company to take in any of the years the amount of whisky specified
in the contract, or any part of it, it is clear that the Rehm–Zeiher Company
could have defeated this suit by pleading that some unforeseen reason had
arisen that justified them in not taking any of the whisky, and therefore
they were not obliged to do so. If, as we think, the contract was nonenforceable by the Walker Company, either in whole or in part, it was certainly
lacking in such mutuality of obligation as rendered it nonenforceable by the
Rehm–Zeiher Company.

* * *

Some importance seems to be attached to the circumstance that the
Walker Company furnished in 1909, 1910, and 1911 a part of the whisky
mentioned in the contract, for which the Rehm–Zeiher Company paid the
prices agreed upon. We do not think, however, that this circumstance is
entitled to any controlling weight in determining the rights of the parties in
the present litigation. The Walker Company was not obligated to furnish
any whisky in the years named, nor was the Rehm–Zeiher Company obliged
to take any, and the mere fact that the Walker Company voluntarily chose
to furnish some of the whisky did not deny to it the privilege of refusing at
its election to furnish the remainder of the whisky. In other words, its
conduct in furnishing part of the whisky did not affect in any manner the
rights of the parties to the contract, or amount to an election on the part of
the Rehm–Zeiher Company, to accept unconditionally the terms of the
contract. In short, the obstacle in the way of the Rehm–Zeiher Company in

this case is that they are seeking to enforce a contract that was never at any time binding upon them. Their acceptance of a part of the whisky provided for in the contract in the years 1909 and 1910 did not oblige them to take any of it in the subsequent years.

* * *

Upon the whole case our conclusion is that the judgment of the lower court was correct, and it is affirmed.

NOTES

Frequently, parties do business for an extended period of time under an arrangement where some of the terms are agreed but neither party makes a promise to the other. Here there is no contract until one party offers to sell or to buy and the other accepts that proposal. Under these arrangements, either party can refuse to deal without risk of liability. For such a case, see Mid–South Packers v. Shoney's, Inc., 761 F.2d 1117 (5th Cir.1985). Is *Rehm–Zeiher* such a case? Suppose the market price had dropped and the seller had demanded that the buyer take and pay for the 4,000 cases. Could the buyer defend on the ground that the seller had made no promise—that seller's unexercised decision to declare "unforeseen reasons" made the purported promise illusory? The answer depends upon how the phrase "unforeseen reason" is interpreted by the court. Does the phrase give the seller unfettered discretion (a "free way out") or is that discretion limited by what is foreseen and what is not? And what is unforeseen in this business context, a rise in liquor prices? Hardly. In the words of an unknown economist, "on a clear day you can foresee forever."

McMichael v. Price

Supreme Court of Oklahoma, 1936.
177 Okl. 186, 58 P.2d 549.

■ OSBORN, VICE CHIEF JUSTICE. This action was instituted in the district court of Tulsa county by Harley T. Price, doing business as Sooner Sand Company, hereinafter referred to as plaintiff, against W.M. McMichael, hereinafter referred to as defendant, as an action to recover damages for the breach of a contract. The cause was tried to a jury and a verdict returned in favor of plaintiff for $7,512.51. The trial court ordered a remittitur of $2,500, which was duly filed. Thereafter the trial court rendered judgment upon the verdict for $5,012.51, from which judgment defendant has appealed.

The pertinent provisions of the contract, which is the basis of this action, are as follows:

* * *

"In consideration of the mutual promises herein contained, first party agrees to purchase and accept from second party all of the sand of various grades and quality which the said first party can sell, for shipment to various and sundry points outside of the City of Tulsa, Oklahoma, provided that the sand so agreed to be furnished and loaded by the said second party shall at least be equal to in quality and comparable with the sand of various grades sold by other sand companies in the City of Tulsa, Oklahoma, or vicinity. First party agrees to pay and the second party agrees to accept as payment and compensation for said sand so furnished and loaded, a sum per ton which represents sixty percent (60%) of the current market price per ton of concrete sand at the place of destination of said shipment. It is agreed that statements are to be rendered by second party to first party every thirty days; the account is payable monthly by first party with a discount to be allowed by second party of four cents per ton for payment within ten days after shipment of any quantity of sand. * * *

"This contract and agreement shall cover a period of ten years from the date hereof, . . ."

* * *

Defendant contends that the contract between the parties was a mere revocable offer and is not a valid and binding contract of purchase and sale for want of mutuality. The general rule is that in construing a contract where the consideration on the one side is an offer or an agreement to sell, and on the other side an offer or agreement to buy, the obligation of the parties to sell and buy must be mutual, to render the contract binding on either party, or, as it is sometimes stated, if one of the parties, not having suffered any previous detriment, can escape future liability under the contract, that party may be said to have a "free way out" and the contract lacks mutuality. Consolidated Pipe Line Co. v. British American Oil Co., 163 Okl. 171, 21 P.(2d) 762. Attention is directed to the specific language used in the contract binding the defendant to "furnish all of the sand of various grades and qualities which the first party can sell" and whereby plaintiff is bound "to purchase and accept from second party all of the sand of various grades and qualities which the said first party (plaintiff) can sell." It is urged that plaintiff had no established business and was not bound to sell any sand whatever and might escape all liability under the terms of the contract by a mere failure or refusal to sell sand. In this connection it is to be noted that the contract recites that plaintiff is "engaged in the business of selling and shipping sand from Tulsa, Oklahoma, to various points." The parties based their contract on this agreed predicate.

* * *

At the time the contract involved herein was executed, plaintiff was not the owner of an established sand business. The evidence shows, however, that he was an experienced salesman of sand, which fact was well known to defendant, and that it was anticipated by both parties that on account of the experience, acquaintances, and connections of plaintiff, he would be able to sell a substantial amount of sand to the mutual profit of the contracting parties. The record discloses that for the nine months immediately following the execution of the contract plaintiff's average net profit per month was $516.88.

By the terms of the contract the price to be paid for sand was definitely fixed. Plaintiff was bound by a solemn covenant of the contract to purchase all the sand he was able to sell from defendant and for a breach of such covenant could have been made to respond in damages. The argument of defendant that the plaintiff could escape liability under the contract by going out of the sand business is without force in view of our determination, in line with the authorities hereinabove cited, that it was the intent of the parties to enter into a contract which would be mutually binding.

* * *

The judgment is affirmed.

NOTES

(1) Should any degree of limitation upon freedom of action be sufficient to insulate an agreement against a defense based on lack of mutuality? For instance, what if Price had not been an experienced sand dealer, but merely contemplated entering the business?

(2) Seller agrees with Buyer for the sale of a certain boat then owned by a third party. It was stipulated in the written contract of purchase that Seller's obligation was contingent upon his acquiring the boat from said third party. Thereafter, Seller did purchase the boat, but refuses to abide by his commitment to Buyer. He insists that the contract lacks mutuality of obligation; therefore, neither party is bound. Do you agree? Cf. *Scott v. Moragues Lumber Co.*, 202 Ala. 312, 80 So. 394 (1918).

(3) *Requirements and Output Contracts.* As will be discussed later, infra at Chapter Five, Section 4(C), the Uniform Commercial Code is quite sympathetic to the use of "open price" terms. Section 2–305. Similarly, the code promotes an additional measure of "certainty with flexibility" regarding quantity terms in its treatment of requirements and output contracts. UCC 2–306(1) provides: "A term which measures the quantity by the output of the seller or the requirements of the buyer means such actual output or requirements as may occur in good faith, except that no quantity unreasonably disproportionate to any stated estimate or in the absence of a stated estimate to any normal or otherwise comparable prior output or requirements may be tendered or demanded." Is *McMichael v. Price* an "output" contract? For a discussion of the commercial utility of these contract types, see John Weistart, *Requirements and Output Contracts: Quantity Variations under the UCC*, 1973 Duke L.J. 599.

Wood v. Lucy, Lady Duff–Gordon

Court of Appeals of New York, 1917.
222 N.Y. 88, 118 N.E. 214.

■ CARDOZO, J. The defendant styles herself "a creator of fashions." Her favor helps a sale. Manufacturers of dresses, millinery and like articles are glad to pay for a certificate of her approval. The things which she designs, fabrics, parasols, and what not, have a new value in the public mind when issued in her name. She employed the plaintiff to help her to turn this vogue into money. He was to have the exclusive right, subject always to her approval, to place her indorsements on the designs of others. He was also to have the exclusive right to place her own designs on sale, or to license others to market them. In return, she was to have one-half of "all profits and revenues" derived from any contracts he might make. The exclusive right was to last at least one year from April 1, 1915, and thereafter from year to year unless terminated by notice of ninety days. The plaintiff says that he kept the contract on his part, and that the defendant broke it. She placed her indorsement on fabrics, dresses and millinery without his knowledge, and withheld the profits. He sues her for the damages, and the case comes here on demurrer.

The agreement of employment is signed by both parties. It has a wealth of recitals. The defendant insists, however, that it lacks the elements of a contract. She says that the plaintiff does not bind himself to anything. It is true that he does not promise in so many words that he will use reasonable efforts to place the defendant's indorsements and market her designs. We think, however, that such a promise is fairly to be implied. The law has outgrown its primitive stage of formalism when the precise word was the sovereign talisman, and every slip was fatal. It takes a broader view today. A promise may be lacking, and yet the whole writing may be "instinct with an obligation," imperfectly expressed (SCOTT, J., in McCall Co. v. Wright, 133 App.Div. 62). If that is so, there is a contract.

The implication of a promise here finds support in many circumstances. The defendant gave an *exclusive* privilege. She was to have no right for at least a year to place her own indorsements or market her own designs except through the agency of the plaintiff. The acceptance of the exclusive agency was an assumption of its duties. . . . We are not to suppose that one party was to be placed at the mercy of the other. . . . Many other terms of the agreement point the same way. We are told at the outset by way of recital that "the said Otis F. Wood possesses a business organization adapted to the placing of such indorsements as the said Lucy, Lady Duff–Gordon has approved." The implication is that the plaintiff's business organization will be used for the purpose for which it is adapted. But the terms of the defendant's compensation are even more significant. Her sole compensation for the grant of an exclusive agency is to be one-half of all the profits resulting from the plaintiff's efforts. Unless he gave his efforts, she could never get anything. Without an implied promise, the transaction cannot have such business "efficacy as both parties must have intended that at all events it should have" (BOWEN, L.J., in the Moorcock, 14 P.D. 64, 68). But the contract does not stop there. The plaintiff goes on to promise that he will account monthly for all moneys received by him, and that he will take out all such patents and copyrights and trademarks as may in his judgment be necessary to protect the rights and articles affected by the agreement. It is true, of course, as the Appellate Division has said, that if he was under no duty to try to market designs or to place certificates of indorsement, his promise to account for profits or take out copyrights would be valueless. But in determining the intention of the parties, the promise *has* a value. It helps to enforce the conclusion that the plaintiff *had* some duties. His promise to pay the defendant one-half of the profits and revenues resulting from the exclusive agency and to render accounts monthly, was a promise to use reasonable efforts to bring profits and revenues into existence. For this conclusion, the authorities are ample. ...

The judgment of the Appellate Division should be reversed, and the order of the Special Term affirmed, with costs in the Appellate Division and in this court.

■ CUDDEBACK, MCLAUGHLIN and ANDREWS, JJ., concur; HISCOCK, CH.J., CHASE and CRANE, JJ., dissent.

Judgment reversed, etc.

NOTES

(1) *You Picked a Fine Time to Leave Me, Lucile.* In *Lucy*, what did each party expressly promise? Why were not these express commitments sufficient, of themselves, to satisfy the demands of mutuality? Does the finding of implied promise do violence to the expressed understanding of the parties? See UCC 2–306(2).

According to Professor Lawrence A. Cunningham, the *Lucy* opinion exhibits Judge Benjamin Cardozo's concerns about the "risks of interparty exploitation and the judicial need to balance freedom of contract with other social values." Further, Cunningham suggests than the implication of a promise to use best efforts "now seems so intuitive as to be commonplace, yet at the time, the opinion amounted to an extraordinary innovation." In short, Judge Cardozo's approach was an "attempt to keep law congruent with commercial reality" and the "finding of consideration" was just a "kernel of the opinion and just one illustration of [his] wider ability to work within the received doctrine and to achieve a richer balance of both fairness and the efficiency of consensual exchange." Lawrence A. Cunningham, *Cardozo and Posner: A Study in Contracts*, 36 Wm. & Mary L. Rev. 1379, 1395–98 (1995). For a splendid biography of Judge Cardozo, see Andrew L. Kaufman, Cardozo (1998).

(2) *Lucy, Lady Duff–Gordon: A Creator of Fashions.* Lucy, Lady Duff–Gordon led a charmed life. She and her husband, Sir Cosmos Duff–Gordon, booked separate first class cabins on the maiden voyage of Titanic. After Titanic hit the iceberg, she and her husband managed to board a life-boat and survive. Although Sir Cosmos never quite overcame the stigma of being a male survivor in a half-full life boat, Lucy (as the following description by Walter Pratt reveals) continued her innovative ways.

"As she did with the general development of the period, Lucy personified the particular changes in the economy and in contract practice. Very much independent, Lucy renounced the traditions of her generation when she began her own business, designing women's clothing. Like many of the entrepreneurs of the period, Lucy started with little capital. Nevertheless, after overcoming early difficulties, she established herself by 1900 as one of the pre-eminent designers of fashion for women. In a manner typical of the personal style of the American economy during the Reconstruction era, Lucy at first designed only for individual women for specific grand occasions such as coronations and state funerals. Because her designs were created for one woman to wear on a particular occasion, they became known as 'personality' dresses.

"As the times changed, so did Lucy. First, she became a company, with the name 'Lucile.' Later, in 1910, she opened a branch office in New York City where she continued to embody the economic changes by depersonalizing her services. In common with much of the production in the United States, Lucy no longer personally designed each dress for each customer. Instead, she hired others to design and sew; she even began to produce more than one dress of each design. With the change in style and the concentration of population in urban areas, Lucy could now profit from marketing multiple copies of the same design. In addition, Lucy hired a manager for her branch office, further increasing the distance between herself and her customers; she would no longer be able to devote personal attention to each client for each occasion.

"Lucy also came to appreciate that something as ephemeral as her name could be of value in the emerging consumer society of the United States. As seller after seller saw production overtake demand in the last years of the nineteenth century, advertising became increasingly important both to inform buyers of products and to persuade customers to buy. To take advantage of that new demand, Lucy turned to an advertising agent, yet another intermediary between herself and her clients.

* * *

"[Lucy] brought Wood's lawsuit upon herself when, in one of the more innovative decisions of her career, she arranged with Sears, Roebuck and Company to sell her dresses through its catalogues. Sears published the first catalogue (which it called a 'portfolio') of Lucy's designs for the fall and winter of 1916–1917. That Lucy was once again at the forefront of commercial practice was evident from a comment in the trade journal *Printer's Ink,* which reported that the announcement of the agreement threw 'a bomb into the camp of rival mail-order houses.' The announcement, the journal further explained, was 'by far the most spectacular bid for prestige which this daring advertiser [Sears] has made since it first announced the new handy edition of the Encyclopedia Britannica.' " Walter Pratt, *American Contract Law at the Turn of the Century,* 39 S.Car.L.Rev. 415, 429–432, 439 (1988).

(3) UCC 2–306(2): "A lawful agreement by either the seller or buyer for exclusive dealing in the kind of goods concerned imposes unless otherwise agreed an obligation by the seller to use best efforts to supply the goods and by the buyer to use best efforts to promote their sale."

Omni Group, Inc. v. Seattle–First National Bank

Court of Appeals of Washington, 1982.
32 Wash.App. 22, 645 P.2d 727.

■ JAMES, JUDGE.

Plaintiff Omni Group, Inc. (Omni), a real estate development corporation, appeals entry of a judgment in favor of John B. Clark, individually, and as executor of the estate of his late wife, in Omni's action to enforce an earnest money agreement for the purchase of realty owned by the Clarks. We reverse.

In December 1977, Mr. and Mrs. Clark executed an exclusive agency listing agreement with the Royal Realty Company of Bellevue (Royal) for the sale of approximately 59 acres of property. The list price was $3,000 per acre.

In early May, Royal offered the Clark property to Omni. On May 17, following conversations with a Royal broker, Omni signed an earnest money agreement offering $2,000 per acre. Two Royal brokers delivered the earnest money agreement to the Clarks. The Clarks signed the agreement dated May 19, but directed the brokers to obtain further consideration in the nature of Omni's agreement to make certain improvements on adjacent land not being offered for sale. Neither broker communicated these additional terms to Omni.

In pertinent part, the earnest money agreement provides:

> This transaction is subject to purchaser receiving an engineer's and architect's feasibility report prepared by an engineer and architect of the purchaser's choice. Purchaser agrees to pay all costs of said report. If said report is satisfactory to purchaser, purchaser shall so notify seller in writing within fifteen (15) days of seller's acceptance of this offer. If no such notice is sent to seller, this transaction shall be considered null and void.

Exhibit A, ¶ 6. Omni's purpose was to determine, prior to actual purchase, if the property was suitable for development.

On June 2, an Omni employee personally delivered to the Clarks a letter advising that Omni had decided to forgo a feasibility study. They were further advised that a survey had revealed that the property consisted of only 50.3 acres. The Clarks agreed that if such were the case, they would accept Omni's offer of $2,000 per acre but with a minimum of 52 acres ($104,000). At this meeting, the Clarks' other terms (which had not been disclosed by Royal nor included in the earnest money agreement signed by the Clarks) were discussed. By a letter of June 8, Omni agreed to accept each of the Clarks' additional terms. The Clarks, however, refused to proceed with the sale after consulting an attorney.

The Clarks argued and the trial judge agreed, that by making its obligations subject to a satisfactory "engineer's and architect's feasibility report" in paragraph 6, Omni rendered its promise to buy the property illusory. Omni responds that paragraph 6 created only a condition precedent to Omni's duty to buy, and because the condition was for its benefit, Omni could waive the condition and enforce the agreement as written. We conclude Omni's promise was not illusory.

A promise for a promise is sufficient consideration to support a contract. E.g., Cook v. Johnson, 37 Wash.2d 19, 221 P.2d 525 (1950). If, however, a promise is illusory, there is no consideration and therefore no enforceable contract between the parties. Interchange Associates v. Interchange, Inc., 16 Wash.App. 359, 557 P.2d 357 (1976). Consequently, a party cannot create an enforceable contract by waiving the condition which renders his promise illusory. But that a promise given for a promise is dependent upon a condition does not necessarily render it illusory or affect its validity as consideration.... Furthermore,

> a contractor can, by the use of clear and appropriate words, make his own duty expressly conditional upon his own personal satisfaction with the quality of the performance for which he has bargained and in return for which his promise is given. Such a limitation on his own duty does not invalidate the contract as long as the limitation is not so great as to make his own promise illusory.

3A A. Corbin, Contracts § 644 at 78–79 (1960).

Paragraph 6 may be analyzed as creating two conditions precedent to Omni's duty to buy the Clarks' property. First, Omni must receive an "engineer's and architect's feasibility report." Undisputed evidence was presented to show that such "feasibility reports" are common in the real estate development field and pertain to the physical suitability of the property for development purposes. Such a condition is analogous to a requirement that a purchaser of real property obtain financing, which imposes upon the purchaser a duty to make a good faith effort to secure financing.... In essence, this initial language requires Omni to attempt, in good faith, to obtain an "engineer's and architect's feasibility report" of a type recognized in the real estate trade.

1st Cond. Precedent

The second condition precedent to Omni's duty to buy the Clarks' property is that the feasibility report must be "satisfactory" to Omni. A condition precedent to the promisor's duty that the promisor be "satisfied" may require performance personally satisfactory to the promisor or it may require performance acceptable to a reasonable person. Whether the promisor was actually satisfied or should reasonably have been satisfied is a question of fact. In neither case is the promisor's promise rendered illusory. 3A A. Corbin, Contracts § 644 (1960).

2ND Cond. Precedent

In *Mattei v. Hopper*, 51 Cal.2d 119 (1958), plaintiff real estate developer contracted to buy property for a shopping center "[s]ubject to Coldwell Banker & Company obtaining leases satisfactory to the purchaser." Plaintiff had 120 days to consummate the purchase, including arrangement of satisfactory leases for shopping center buildings, before he was committed to purchase the property. The trial judge found the agreement "illusory." The California Supreme Court reversed. The court's language is apposite:

> [I]t would seem that the factors involved in determining whether a lease is satisfactory to the lessor are too numerous and varied to permit the application of a reasonable man standard as envisioned by this line of cases. Illustrative of some of the factors which would have to be considered in this case are the duration of the leases, their provisions for renewal options, if any, their covenants and restrictions, the amounts of the rentals, the financial responsibility of the lessees, and the character of the lessees' businesses.

Comparable factors doubtless determine whether an "engineer's and architect's feasibility report" is satisfactory. But

> [t]his *multiplicity* of factors which must be considered in evaluating a lease shows that this case more appropriately falls within the second line of authorities dealing with "satisfaction" clauses, being those involving fancy, taste, or judgment. Where the question is one of judgment, the promisor's determination that he is not satisfied, when made in good faith, has been held to be a defense to an action on the contract.... Although these decisions do not expressly discuss the issues of mutuality of obligation or illusory promises, they necessarily imply that the promisor's duty to exercise his judgment in good faith is an adequate consideration to support the contract. None of these cases voided the contracts on the ground that they were illusory or lacking in mutuality of obligation. Defendant's attempts to distinguish these cases are unavailing, since they are predicated upon the assumption that the deposit receipt was not a contract making plaintiff's performance conditional on his satisfaction. As seen above, this was the precise nature of the agreement.

Further,

> [e]ven though the "satisfaction" clauses discussed in the above-cited cases dealt with performances to be received as parts of the agreed exchanges, the fact that the leases here which determined plaintiff's satisfaction were not part of the performance to be rendered is not material. The standard of evaluating plaintiff's satisfaction—good faith—applies with equal vigor to this type of condition and prevents it from nullifying the consideration otherwise present in the promises exchanged.

Mattei v. Hopper, supra at 123–24. Thus, even the fact that "[i]t was satisfaction with the leases that [the purchaser] was himself to obtain" was immaterial. 3A A. Corbin, Contracts § 644 at 84.... We conclude that the condition precedent to Omni's duty to buy requiring receipt of a "satisfactory" feasibility report does not render Omni's promise to buy the property illusory.

Paragraph 6 further provides, "If said report is satisfactory to purchaser, purchaser shall so notify seller in writing within fifteen (15) days of seller's acceptance of this offer"; otherwise, the transaction "shall be considered null and void." We read this language to mean that Omni is required ("shall") to notify the Clarks of its acceptance if the feasibility report was "satisfactory." As we have stated, this determination is not a matter within Omni's unfettered discretion.

Omni has, by the quoted language, reserved to itself a power to cancel or terminate the contract.... Such provisions are valid and do not render the promisor's promise illusory, where the option can be exercised upon the occurrence of specified conditions.... Here, Omni can cancel by failing to give notice only if the feasibility report is not "satisfactory." Otherwise, Omni is bound to give notice and purchase the property. Accordingly, we conclude paragraph 6 does not render Omni's promise illusory. The earnest money agreement was supported by consideration.

The judgment is reversed and remanded with instructions to enter a decree ordering specific performance of the earnest money agreement.

■ CALLOW and DURHAM, JJ., concur.

NOTES

(1) In *Omni,* the court observes that a "personal satisfaction" clause does not render a promise illusory, even if the satisfaction required is that of the promisor (subjective) rather than what would be acceptable to a reasonable person (objective). But does not the subjective measure provide the promisor with, to use the *McMichael* court standard (supra at 98), a "free way out?"

(2) "When it is a condition of an obligor's duty that he be satisfied with respect to the obligee's performance or with respect to something else, and it is practicable to determine whether a reasonable person in the position of the obligor would be satisfied, an interpretation is preferred under which the condition occurs if such a reasonable person in the position of the obligor would be satisfied." Restatement (Second) § 228.

(3) *Mutuality of Obligation and UCC 2–204.* In seeking to salvage an obligation counsel must frequently press beyond the words of the written agreement. For example, in Warrick Beverage Corp. v. Miller Brewing Co., 170 Ind.App. 114, 352 N.E.2d 496 (1976), the court considered an "arrangement" between a brewery and a beer distributor. A letter from the brewery to the distributor provided, in part, as follows: "Our relationship is that of seller and buyer and in no other respect is any relationship established between us. You are not required to place orders, nor are we required to accept orders for beer. As is the custom in our industry, these sales are made on a shipment-to-shipment basis only, and either of us can terminate this relationship at any time without incurring liability to the other." Upon being "terminated" by the brewer the distributor sought the advantage of an Indiana statute which made it unlawful to "cancel or terminate an agreement or contract between a beer wholesaler and a brewer for the sale of beer, unfairly and without due regard for the equities of the other party." In rejecting the brewer's mutuality of obligation argument, the court referred to conduct after the execution of the writing which, in effect, recognized the existence of some type of contractual obligation. Principal reliance was upon UCC 2–204(1): "A contract for sale of goods may be made in any manner sufficient to show agreement, including conduct by both parties which recognizes the existence of such a contract."

(4) *The Inadequacy of Mutuality Criteria.* It is commonplace for agreements to provide a "way out" for one or both of the parties. It may be provided that performance is conditional upon the purchaser obtaining satisfactory leases, securing suitable financing, etc. Or there may be a reserved power of termination, exercisable by one or both of the parties. Cases of this type have traditionally been addressed in terms of mutuality of obligation. If, in the words of one court, a party is "free to perform or to withdraw from the agreement at his own unrestricted pleasure, the promise is deemed illusory and it provides no consideration." Mattei v. Hopper, 51 Cal.2d 119, 122, 330 P.2d 625, 626 (1958),

cited in *Omni Group, Inc. v. Seattle–First National Bank,* supra at 103. The standard does not on its face seem difficult to apply, but cases of this type have given courts a great deal of trouble. There has been an accumulation of confusing and conflicting precedents, few of which contain convincing reasons or any analysis of the deeper problems involved.

There is here the same undercurrent of conflict that characterizes the cases elaborating a so-called "peppercorn" theory of consideration. For it is easy enough to locate the requisite "peppercorn" if one is intent upon doing so. One can usually find that a promisor's discretion is limited in *some* respect. Any circumscription of freedom of action would enable one to say there is no "*free* way out," to use the language of *McMichael v. Price,* supra at 98. As illustrated by *Omni,* a frequently employed technique, especially in the later cases, has been to imply an obligation of "good faith." This may be productive of satisfactory results, but then again it may not. The establishment of a minimal bargain may not remove doubts as to ultimate lack of fairness. All sorts of factors may have a bearing on the proper resolution of the case, including, most importantly, reliance by the parties. A bargain might be viewed as requiring some measure of "regulation," emanating from the courts or the legislature. The Code treatment of requirements and output contracts is one example; the implied obligation to use "best efforts" in an exclusive dealer arrangement is another. A contemporary focus is upon powers of cancellation or termination contained in franchise agreements. See, e.g., O.M. Droney Beverage Co. v. Miller Brewing Co., 365 F.Supp. 1067 (D.Minn.1973); Zapatha v. Dairy Mart, Inc., infra at 564. See, generally, Gillian Hadfield, *Problematic Relations: Franchising and the Law of Incomplete Contracts*, 42 Stan.L.Rev. 927 (1990). This general topic is developed further in Chapter 5, Section 4(E).

See Val D. Ricks, *In Defense of Mutuality of Obligation: Why "Both Should be Bound, or Neither,"* 78 Neb.L.Rev. 491 (1999).

PROBLEM: THE CASE OF THE ILLUSORY BONUS

John was an agent for Super Life, an insurance company, and was paid a salary and commissions for writing life insurance policies. In early February, 1997, Super Life issued a bulletin addressed to all agents. The Bulletin was titled "Extra Earnings Agreement" and stated that "you will receive at the end of each 12 month period a bonus" in accordance with a formula based upon the percentage of policies that you are able to renew after lapse. The lower the lapse ratio the higher the bonus. Thus, if an agent's lapse ratio was between 0 and 10% the bonus would be 150% of the average monthly premiums in force but if the lapse ratio were, say, between 40 and 50% the bonus would only be 60% of the premiums. If the lapse ratio was over 70% there would be no bonus. In paragraph 7 (there were 12 paragraphs in all) the following term appeared in the same type size as the rest of the bulletin:

> This renewal bonus is a *voluntary* contribution on the part of Super Life. It is agreed by you and by us that it may be with-held, increased, decreased or discontinued, individually or collectively, with or without actual notice. Further, this Renewal Bonus is contingent upon you actually writing business for this Company as a licensed agent at the time such Bonus is paid.

The agents were exhorted to give their "best efforts" and requested to sign and return the "enclosed copy of this agreement." John complied.

In February, 1998 John reported that his lapse ratio over the last twelve months was between 20 and 30% and that, under the schedule, he was entitled to a bonus or 100% of the average monthly premiums in force, some $10,000. Without giving any notice or reasons, however, Super Life discontinued the bonus plan on February 15, 1998 without paying any bonuses.

John, and other agents, sued for the bonuses. Super Life filed a motion to dismiss and argued: (1) No promise was made, since the "voluntary" contribution clause reserved complete and unfettered discretion to the company; (2) The plain and ordinary language of the clause, which the agents as "White Collar" workers should reasonably understand, should be implemented; and (3) Even if a promise was made, there was no consideration since the Agents were already obligated to sell and renew life insurance policies.

In opposing the motion to dismiss, John's attorney made the following argument. "Your honor, we think that a literal interpretation of the bonus plan language should be avoided, especially where extra efforts were expended by the agents. Super Life is subject to a duty of good faith in the performance of the contract and that duty should be imposed upon the exercise of the reserved discretion to terminate the plan unless both parties intended Super Life to have unfettered discretion. The question is whether this interpretation was within the fair contemplation of the parties and the answer is not found in the 'four corners' of the writing and the 'plain meaning' of language. If no such intention is found, the next question is whether Super Life acted in bad faith and this, at a minimum, requires an examination of Super Life's reasons for withdrawing the plan. Thus, factual questions over intention and bad faith are presented and the motion to dismiss should be dismissed." John's brief cited Nolan v. Control Data Corp., 243 N.J.Super. 420, 579 A.2d 1252 (App.Div.1990) to support this argument.

How would you rule?

SECTION 2.   MORAL OBLIGATION: PROMISE PLUS ANTECEDENT BENEFIT

(A) RESTITUTION AND THE SCOPE OF QUASI-CONTRACT

Return with us now to the plight of "Bascom's Folly," the ill-fated horse without an owner in *Bailey v. West,* supra at 12. It seems clear that Bailey could have recovered the reasonable value of his services if West had, by words or conduct, requested those services in exchange for a promise to pay. The benefit conferred on West's property would have been part of an agreed exchange. His promise to pay, whether express or implied, would have been supported by consideration.

The general problem with which this section is concerned, however, begins with the conclusion in *Bailey v. West* that the benefit conferred was not requested—that Bailey was not justified under the circumstances in believing that he was invited to render the service and could expect compensation from West. Without an express or implied-in-fact contract, is there any way that Bailey can obtain compensation? The obvious answer is yes, *if* the conditions for an implied-in-law or quasi-contract are met. The fact that they were not in *Bailey v. West* only stimulates a closer inquiry into quasi-contract and the claim of unjust enrichment. But first, let us take a brief look at the concept of restitution as it relates to the law of contracts.

As an initial matter it is necessary to distinguish between restitution as a basis for liability and restitution as a measure of damage for breach of contract. In this section, we are concerned with restitution as a basis for liability (i.e. a potential cause of action) and the related concepts of quasi-contract (or contract implied in law), quantum meruit and unjust enrichment. Chapter 7, *infra* at Section 2B, will take up the restitution measure of damages for breach of contract.

Restitution, in general, is a broad-gauged and independent basis of liability designed to prevent "unjust" enrichment. A person "who is unjustly enriched at the expense of another is liable in restitution to the other." Restatement (Third) Restitution and Unjust Enrichment § 1 (Disc. Draft, March 2000). As Professor Palmer put it, "unjust enrichment is an indefinable idea in the same way that justice is indefinable." 1 G. Palmer, Law of Restitution § 1.1 (1978).

The prevention of unjust enrichment is an important objective in and around the law of contracts. But "every transaction giving rise to a liability in restitution has a benefit [that] has been conferred or obtained *outside the consensual framework* that would ordinarily govern both the transfer and any claim for compensation." Restatement (Third) Restitution, § 2, Comment. As one court put it:

> [A] contract implied in law [or quasi-contract] is not a contract at all, but an obligation imposed by law for the purpose of bringing about justice and equity without reference to the intent or the agreement of the parties and, in some cases, in spite of an agreement between the parties.... It is a non-contractual obligation that is to be treated procedurally as if it were a contract, and is often referred to as quasi contract, unjust enrichment, implied in law contract or restitution. * * * [T]he essence of a contract implied in law lies in the fact that the defendant has received a benefit which it would be inequitable for him to retain.

Continental Forest Products, Inc. v. Chandler Supply Co., 95 Idaho 739, 743, 518 P.2d 1201 (1974).

When, then, is it "inequitable" for Party B to retain a benefit conferred by Party A without Party B's request? To put the matter more concretely, why, in *Bailey v. West,* was Bailey denied recovery for the benefit conferred on West's horse? There are at least two necessary elements in this inquiry.

First, did Party A confer a measurable benefit on Party B with the expectation of compensation? In *Bailey,* the answer to the benefit question was yes and no. Bailey conferred a measurable benefit on West's horse by feeding and caring for it for over four months. But after West knew of the benefit, he refused to receive it by abandoning the horse. In cases of this sort, West was not required to make restitution unless Bailey had justifiably performed a duty imposed upon West by law, e.g., the duty of a parent to provide necessary medical care to a dependent child. See State, Division of Family Services v. Hollis, 639 S.W.2d 389 (Mo.App.1982). West clearly had no legal duty to provide necessaries to his horse, dependent or not.

Second, if Party B retained the benefit after knowing that it had been conferred and A expected compensation, did A give B an opportunity to decline the benefit before it was conferred? If so, and B did not object, we have taken a big step toward liability based upon a theory of consent. If not, A cannot recover in quasi-contract unless there is a reasonable excuse for failing to do so:

> There is no liability in restitution in respect of a benefit intentionally conferred by the claimant on the recipient, unless the circumstances of the transaction are such as to excuse the claimant from the necessity of basing a claim to payment on a contract with the recipient. Restatement (Third) Restitution, § 2(4).

An excuse may exist when initial "contracting was impracticable." *Id.* Thus, a classic illustration of where restitution liability would lie concerns a medical exigency, say where aid is given to an unconscious patient who could not have consented to contract.

In *Bailey v. West* those circumstances did not exist. The life or well being of the horse was not in jeopardy, and Bailey could easily have contacted West before performing services. Thus, Bailey's intervention was "officious" and West's enrichment, to the extent it existed, was not unjust.

Instead of the aphorism "would of, could of, should of," restitution liability often results from a finding of "would of, but couldn't of." The court believes that the parties would have been interested in contracting (a real benefit was conferred), but simultaneously believes that the parties did not have an opportunity to contract. In these situations, contracts implied in law substitute for the contracts that parties "would of" liked to make, but "couldn't of."

What is the measure of recovery if restitution is justified? The typical answer is Quantum Meruit. As one court put it:

> Confusion surrounds the use and application of *quantum meruit,* * * * because courts have used the terms *quantum meruit,* contract implied in fact, contract implied in law, quasi-contract, unjust enrichment, and/or restitution without analytical precision. * * * *Quantum meruit* has two distinct branches. Both branches, however, are rooted in "justice," * * * to prevent the defendant's enrichment at the plaintiff's expense. * * * Contract implied in law, also known as quasi-contract or unjust enrichment, is one branch of *quantum meruit.* A quasi-contract is not a contract at all, but rather is a legal action in restitution. * * * The elements of a quasi-contract, or a contract

implied in law, are: (1) the defendant received a benefit; (2) an appreciation or knowledge by the defendant of the benefit; (3) under circumstances that would make it unjust for the defendant to retain the benefit without paying for it. * * * The measure of recovery under quasi-contract, or contract implied in law, is the value of the benefit conferred on the defendant (the defendant's gain) and not the detriment incurred by the plaintiff, * * * or necessarily the reasonable value of the plaintiff's services. A contract implied in fact is the second branch of *quantum meruit*. A contract implied in fact is a "contract" established by conduct. * * * The elements of a contract implied in fact are: (1) the defendant requested the plaintiff to perform work; (2) the plaintiff expected the defendant to compensate him or her for those services; and (3) the defendant knew or should have known that the plaintiff expected compensation. * * * "Technically, recovery in contract implied in fact is the amount the parties intended as the contract price. If that amount is unexpressed, courts will infer that the parties intended the amount to be the reasonable market value of the plaintiff's services." Kovacic, *A Proposal to Simplify Quantum Meruit Litigation*, 35 Am.U.L.Rev. 547, 556 (1986).

Davies v. Olson, 746 P.2d 264, 268–69 (Utah App.1987). For a fascinating overview of this complex area, see Peter Linzer, *Rough Justice: A Theory of Restitution and Reliance, Contracts and Torts*, 2001 Wis. L. Rev. 695.

(B) MORAL OBLIGATION

With this bit of essential background behind us, we can turn to the specific problem with which this section is concerned, moral obligation. The pattern is as follows. In the past, A has conferred a measurable benefit on B. On the one extreme, the benefit may have been intended by A to be a gift. On the other extreme, the benefit may give rise to a legal obligation to pay on the part of B, either in contract or quasi-contract. Or, the transaction may be in the fuzzy middle ground—neither clearly gift nor contract but with some elements from both extremes. Motivated by the past, B then promises to pay A for the benefit conferred. Is that promise enforceable? If so, when and why? In confronting these questions, consider first Justice Windeyer's summary of legal developments in England and then the following cases and problems.

By his readiness to enlarge the scope of assumpsit and indebitatus assumpsit, Mansfield greatly assisted the development of the law of contract, which is the basis of all commercial law. But he failed to gain acceptance for a theory of consideration which, if it had been adopted, would have entirely altered the English law of contract. The established principle of English law today is that a merely gratuitous promise is not legally binding, except it be under seal. To make an enforceable agreement, otherwise than by deed, it is necessary that the promise should be given for some valuable consideration. It is not necessary that the consideration should be adequate, but it must be certain and of some value in the eye of the law. 'A valuable consideration in the sense of the law, may consist either in some right, interest, profit or benefit accruing to one party, or some forbearance, detriment, loss or responsibility given, suffered or undertaken by the other'. The origin of the doctrine of consideration is not free from doubt. ... Probably it owes something to the notion of *quid pro quo*, an element in the old action of debt which, as we have seen, was superseded by indebitatus assumpsit. Certainly it was chiefly developed as the result of the technicalities of the action of assumpsit in which the plaintiff was required to allege the consideration for the defendant's promise. The canon law too may have made an indirect contribution, for it had, by a singular adaptation of Roman law principles, reached the conclusion that promises were enforceable when supported by *causa*. The meaning of *causa* was not indisputedly defined. 'The general meaning on which all were agreed was the necessity of a purpose to be attained. There was *causa*, if the promisor had in view a definite result, either some definite legal act or something more comprehensive, such as peace.' The Court of Chancery in the sixteenth century was working out a theory of contract with, as its basis, the canonists' theory of *causa*, which it translated as 'consideration'. Promises were enforceable if made for a sufficient consideration. A material consideration was not necessary; a good motive, a moral obligation or natural love and affection towards the promisee was enough.

The common law courts never accepted the Chancery Court's doctrine of consideration. The Chancery theory ultimately perished. It was the common law theory of contract and the common law doctrine of valuable consideration which became the accepted principles of English law. Some criterion of the enforceability of agreements was considered necessary as the action of assumpsit developed. The breach of every promise was not to be permitted to give rise to an action of assumpsit. How then could the agreements in respect of which assumpsit would lie be determined? The common lawyers adopted the Roman principle that *ex nudo pacto non oritur actio*. But they understood this maxim in a sense different from that which it bore in Roman law. Roman law had no generalised theory of consideration. For the common law, a *nudum pactum* was a promise not supported by consideration. A mere naked promise could have no assistance from the common law; but if clothed with a consideration, however scanty, it was received with little less respect than the covenant in its sealed vestment.

By the eighteenth century it seemed clearly established that consideration was an essential condition of an action of assumpsit. But the scope of the doctrine was still unsettled. Mansfield cared little for procedural rules, but much for good faith and honest dealing. He was eager to break down some of the barriers between law and equity and to apply equitable principles in the administration of the common law. He confidently asserted that any moral obligation arising from the dictates of good conscience was a sufficient consideration to make a promise actionable. He went even further and denied that consideration was essential to the validity of a contract. In his view consideration had only an evidentiary value. If a promise was supported by consideration, it showed that the parties had intended their engagement to be legally binding. But this might be evidenced in other ways, for example an agreement which was reduced to writing in obedience to the Statute of Frauds or as the result of commercial custom was, in Mansfield's opinion, binding without consideration. 'A *nudum pactum*,' he said 'does not exist in the usage and law of merchants.' This doctrine, which he put forward in Pillans v. Van Mierop (3 Burr. 1663), would have made all written agreements enforceable, though they were not under seal. But the traditions of the common law were here too strong even for Mansfield's great prestige. Thirteen years later the House of Lords in Rann v. Hughes (7 T.R. 350), after consulting the judges, overruled his opinion and established the need for consideration in all contracts other than those embodied in a deed. 'All contracts', the judges declared, 'are by the laws of England distinguished into agreements by specialty and agreements by parol; nor is there any such third class as . . . contracts in writing. If they be merely written and not specialties, they are parol and a consideration must be proved.'

But, although Mansfield's doctrine that no consideration at all was required to support a written agreement was soon overthrown, his opinion that a merely moral obligation was sufficient to constitute a consideration received general assent throughout the eighteenth century. It was not finally displaced until 1840, when Lord Denman pointed out in Eastwood v. Kenyon (11 Ad. & E. 438) that it would "annihilate the necessity for any consideration at all, inasmuch as the mere fact of giving of promise creates a moral obligation to perform it."

Windeyer, Lectures on Legal History 237–40 (2d ed. rev. 1957).

Mills v. Wyman

Supreme Judicial Court of Massachusetts, 1825.
20 Mass. (3 Pick.) 207.

This was an action of assumpsit brought to recover a compensation for the board, nursing, & c., of Levi Wyman, son of the defendant, from the 5th to the 20th of February, 1821. The plaintiff then lived at Hartford, in Connecticut; the defendant, at Shrewsbury, in this county. Levi Wyman, at the time when the services were rendered, was about 25 years of age, and had long ceased to be a member of his father's family. He was on his return from a voyage at sea, and being suddenly taken sick at Hartford, and being poor and in distress, was relieved by the plaintiff in the manner and to the extent above stated. On the 24th of February, after all the expenses had been incurred, the defendant wrote a letter to the plaintiff, promising to pay him such expenses. There was no consideration for this promise, except what grew out of the relation which subsisted between Levi Wyman and the defendant, and Howe, J., before whom the cause was tried in the Court of Common Pleas, thinking this not sufficient to support the action, directed a nonsuit. To this direction the plaintiff filed exceptions.

■ PARKER, C.J. General rules of law established for the protection and security of honest and fair-minded men, who may inconsiderately make promises without any equivalent, will sometimes screen men of a different character from engagements which they are bound in *foro conscientiae* to perform. This is a defect inherent in all human systems of legislation. The rule that a mere verbal promise, without any consideration, cannot be enforced by action, is universal in its application, and cannot be departed from to suit particular cases in which a refusal to perform such a promise may be disgraceful.

The promise declared on in this case appears to have been made without any legal consideration. The kindness and services towards the sick son of the defendant were not bestowed at his request. The son was in no respect under the care of the defendant. He was twenty-five years old, and had long left his father's family. On his return from a foreign country, he fell sick among strangers, and the plaintiff acted the part of the good Samaritan, giving him shelter and comfort until he died. The defendant, his father, on being informed of this event influenced by a transient feeling of gratitude, promises in writing to pay the plaintiff for the expenses he had incurred. But he has determined to break this promise, and is willing to have his case appear on record as a strong example of particular injustice sometimes necessarily resulting from the operation of general rules.

It is said a moral obligation is a sufficient consideration to support an express promise; and some authorities lay down the rule thus broadly; but upon examination of the cases we are satisfied that the universality of the rule cannot be supported, and that there must have been some preexisting obligation, which has become inoperative by positive law, to form a basis for an effective promise. The cases of debts barred by the statute of limitations, of debts incurred by infants, of debts of bankrupts, are generally put for illustration of the rule. Express promises founded on such preexisting equitable obligations may be enforced; there is a good consideration for them; they merely remove an impediment created by law to the recovery of debts honestly due, but which public policy protects the debtors from being compelled to pay. In all these cases there was originally a *quid pro quo;* and according to the principles of natural justice the party receiving ought to pay; but the legislature has said he shall not be coerced; then comes the promise to pay the debt that is barred, the promise of the man to pay the debt of the infant, of the discharged bankrupt to restore to his creditor what by the law he had lost. In all these cases there is a moral obligation founded upon an antecedent valuable consideration. These promises therefore have a sound legal basis. They are not promises to pay something for nothing; not naked pacts; but the voluntary revival or creation of obligation which before existed in natural law, but which had been dispensed with, not for the benefit of the party obliged solely, but principally for the public convenience. If moral obligation, in its fullest sense, is a good substratum for an express promise, it is not easy to perceive why it is not equally good to support an implied promise. What a man ought to do, generally he ought to be made to do, whether he promise or refuse. But the law of society has left most of such obligations to the *interior* forum, as the tribunal of conscience has been aptly called. Is there not a moral obligation upon every son who has become affluent by means of the education and advantages bestowed upon him by his father, to relieve that father from pecuniary embarrassment, to promote his comfort and happiness, and even to share with him his riches, if thereby he will be made happy? And yet such a son may, with impunity, leave such a father in any degree of penury above that which will expose the community in which he dwells, to the danger of being obliged to preserve him from absolute want. Is not a wealthy father under strong moral obligation to advance the interest of an obedient, well disposed son, to furnish him with the means of acquiring and maintaining a becoming rank in life, to rescue him from the horrors of debt incurred by misfortune? Yet the law will uphold him in any degree of parsimony, short of that which would reduce his son to the necessity of seeking public charity.

Without doubt there are great interests of society which justify withholding the coercive arm of the law from these duties of imperfect obligation, as they are called; imperfect, not because they are less binding upon the conscience than those which are called perfect, but because the wisdom of the social law does not impose sanctions upon them.

A deliberate promise, in writing, made freely and without any mistake, one which may lead the party to whom it is made into contracts and expenses, cannot be broken without a violation of moral duty. But if there was nothing paid or promised for it, the law, perhaps wisely, leaves the execution of it to the conscience of him who makes it. It is only when the party making the promise gains something, or he to whom it is made loses something, that the law gives the promise validity. . . .

* * *

For the foregoing reasons we are all of opinion that the nonsuit directed by the Court of Common Pleas was right, and that judgment be entered thereon for costs for the defendant.

NOTES

(1) Professor Geoffrey R. Watson concluded that the facts stated in *Mills v. Wyman* were "falsely rendered" and that the opinion was "misguided." His research shows that Levi Wyman did not die (as the court stated) from his illness, but recovered and lived for many years. Also, the letter from Seth Wyman to Mills (who expected to be paid) appeared to promise to pay for continued care of Levi not just for completed services. The jury, however, found that only past services were involved and this finding was not overturned. According to Watson, the opinion was misguided because Judge Parker missed an opportunity to promote the approach to consideration espoused by Lord Mansfield in the late 18th Century (see supra at 112–114) and ignored an earlier opinion written by him (Judge Parker) that might have justified

liability. See Geoffrey R. Watson, *In the Tribunal of Conscience: Mills v. Wyman Reconsidered*, 71 Tul. L. Rev. 1749 (1997).

(2) Under what circumstances, if any, should a promise not supported by consideration but motivated by a past benefit conferred be enforceable as a contract? Restatement (Second) § 86 provides: "(1) A promise made in recognition of a benefit previously received by the promisor from the promisee is binding to the extent necessary to prevent injustice. (2) A promise is not binding under Subsection (1), (a) if the promisee conferred the benefit as a gift or for other reasons the promisor has not been unjustly enriched; or (b) to the extent that its value is disproportionate to the benefit." Would *Mills* be decided differently under this section? Suppose it is clear that Mills did not intend to confer a gift on Wyman's son.

(3) Are you persuaded by Judge Parker's distinction between legal and moral obligations in the making of promises? If, as Posner argues, the doctrine of consideration supports economic efficiency in exchange, what arguments can be made for enforcing promises where there is no bargain and exchange? See C. Fried, Contract as Promise 14–17 (1981).

Manwill v. Oyler

Supreme Court of Utah, 1961.
11 Utah 2d 433, 361 P.2d 177.

■ CROCKETT, JUSTICE. Defendants petitioned and obtained leave to bring this interlocutory appeal to challenge the denial of their motion to dismiss the plaintiff's complaint. The only issue presented is whether it states a cause of action against them.

Plaintiff alleged that during the years 1950, 1951, 1952 and 1953 he made payments on defendants' behalf aggregating $5,506.20 on a farm now occupied by the defendants; and that in the year 1954 he transferred to defendants a grazing permit worth $1,800 and 18 head of cattle worth $3,000. It is conceded that any action on those transactions would be barred by the statute of limitations. But the plaintiff further alleged that in July or August, 1956, the defendants orally agreed to pay said sums to him. After defendants filed a motion to dismiss, he amended to state that the oral promise to pay him $5,506.20 occurred in October, 1957. The motion to dismiss was considered as directed to the complaint as amended. It was denied and they were given 15 days in which to answer. Instead of doing so, they petitioned this court for an interlocutory appeal under Rule 72, U.R.C.P.

* * *

The position the plaintiff essays is that the earlier payments he claims to have made for the defendants' benefit placed them under moral obligation to repay him, and that this constitutes valid consideration to make their 1957 oral promise a binding contract. The rule quite generally recognized is that a moral obligation by itself will not do so. Although some authorities appear to be otherwise, it will usually be found that there are special circumstances bolstering what is termed the moral obligation.

The difficulty we see with the doctrine is that if a mere moral, as distinguished from a legal, obligation were recognized as valid consideration for a contract, that would practically erode to the vanishing point the necessity for finding a consideration. This is so, first because in nearly all circumstances where a promise is made there is some moral aspect of the situation which provides the motivation for making the promise even if it is to make an outright gift. And second, if we are dealing with moral concepts, the making of a promise itself creates a moral obligation to perform it. It seems obvious that if a contract to be legally enforceable need be anything other than a naked promise, something more than mere moral consideration is necessary. The principle that in order for a contract to be valid and binding, each party must be bound to give some legal consideration to the other by conferring a benefit upon him or suffering a legal detriment at his request is firmly implanted in the roots of our law.

In urging that the moral consideration here present makes a binding contract, plaintiff places reliance on what is termed the "material benefit rule" as reflecting the trend of modern authority. The substance of that rule is that where the promisors (defendants) have received something from the promisee (plaintiff) of value in the form of money or other material benefits under such circumstances as to create a moral obligation to pay for what they received, and later promise to do so there is consideration for such promise. But even the authorities standing for that rule affirm that there must be something beyond a bare promise, as of an offered gift or gratuity. The circumstances must be such that it is reasonably to be supposed that that promisee (plaintiff) expected to be compensated in some way therefor.

Accepting that proposition for the sake of argument, the plaintiff has not set forth any of the facts surrounding the original transactions to show that there was any expectation that he would be compensated in this case. This may have been done advisedly because of the difficulty which would confront him: if the circumstances were such that the parties reasonably expected he was to be paid, there may have been an implied contract, which is now outlawed. Insofar as the statements in his complaint disclose, any benefits conferred on defendants would have been donative. Therefore, at the time of the alleged 1957 promise there could have existed nothing but a bare moral obligation to support the defendants' claimed oral promise to repay him. This alone would not constitute valid consideration to make a binding contract.

The conclusion we have reached finds support in the fact that by our statute the time in which an action may be brought is extended by an acknowledgement or promise to pay the same but it "must be in writing and signed by the party to be charged thereby." This affirmative provision, which has the effect of permitting an outlawed obligation to be renewed by a promise in writing, indicates an awareness and recognition of the well-established principle that an oral promise will not revive such an obligation.

Since the plaintiff has not alleged facts sufficient to make the alleged oral promise of 1957 a binding contract, it was error to deny the defendants' motion to dismiss.

Reversed with directions to dismiss the action. Costs to defendants (appellants).

NOTES

(1) *Promise to Pay Antecedent Indebtedness.* The implicit assumptions in *Manwill* unfold in two stages.

First, "a promise to pay all or part of an antecedent contractual or quasi-contractual indebtedness owed by the promisor is binding if the indebtedness is still enforceable. ..." Restatement (Second) § 82(1). Was the plaintiff successful in establishing that there ever was any obligation by the promisor to pay? See Realty Assoc. v. Valley National Bank, 153 Ariz. 514, 738 P.2d 1121, 1124–1125 (Ariz.App.1986)(written promise to pay broker after service rendered enforced).

Second, there is a "well settled" general rule "that a moral obligation arising from or connected with what was once a legal liability, which has since become suspended or barred by operation of a positive rule of law or statute, will furnish consideration for a subsequent executory promise." Osborn v. Old National Bank of Washington, 10 Wash.App. 169, 516 P.2d 795, 797 (1973). Where the insulating event is the statute of limitations, the litigation frequently involves whether the defendant made the requisite promise, see Restatement (Second) § 82(2), and, if so, whether it met any formality requirements imposed by other legislation. Assuming, in *Manwill,* that defendant had an earlier implied contractual obligation which was barred by the statute of limitations, why was the alleged second promise not enforceable?

Assuming an antecedent contractual or quasi-contractual obligation which has not been barred, what reasons seem to justify enforcement of a second promise without new consideration to pay the earlier obligation? Professor Sullivan has suggested some historical reasons, in that enforcement was the "first step in the development of assumpsit as a functional substitute for debt.... [I]f a plaintiff could show a second promise to pay, subsequent to the creation of the obligation sought to be enforced, his action in assumpsit would be free of the disabling procedural impediments of debt ...," e.g., the wager of law requirement. The reasons for this development have long since disappeared, but, again, the melody lingers on. See Sullivan, *The Concept of Benefit in the Law of Quasi–Contract*, 64 Geo.L.J. 1, 2–4 (1975).

(2) *Promise to Pay Debt Discharged in Bankruptcy: Effect of Bankruptcy Reform Act of 1978.* Traditionally, one's promise to pay a debt discharged in bankruptcy was enforceable. This "reaffirmation" rule was altered significantly by Congress in 1978. See 11 U.S.C.A. § 524(c), (d). These sections, together with amendments enacted in 1984, place stringent restrictions upon the enforcement of such "reaffirmation" agreements. The agreement must have been made prior to the debtor's discharge, and it must contain a statement advising the debtor of a right to rescind at any time before discharge or within sixty days after the agreement is filed with the court, whichever is later. Moreover, if

the debtor was not represented by an attorney during the negotiation of the "reaffirmation" agreement, court approval is required. The court must be convinced that the agreement does not impose an undue hardship on the debtor (or a dependent) and is in his or her best interest.

(3) Without an antecedent debt, barred or otherwise, would enforcement of a promise based upon prior benefit conferred require judicial enforcement of all such promises? Would, as Austin maintained, a judge be able "to enforce just whatever he pleases?" Austin, Jurisprudence 224 (3d ed. 1869). Or, as contended by Professor Fuller, could not the scope of the moral obligation principle be "tamed" by a process of judicial inclusion and exclusion? See Fuller, *Consideration and Form*, 41 Colum.L.Rev. 799, 821–22 (1941).

(4) *The Case of Jack Tallas' Estate.* In Dementas v. Estate of Tallas, 764 P.2d 628 (Utah App.1988), Dementas filed a claim against the estate of Jack Tallas based on the following memorandum (originally in Greek but translated into English, revised, and notarized by Tallas shortly before his death):

PETER K. DEMENTAS, is my best frient (sic) I have in this country and since he came to the United States he treats me like a father and I think of him as my own son.

I visit his house and have dinner with his family twice a week. He takes me in his car grocery shopping. He drives me to the doctor and has also takes me every week to Bingham to pick up my mail, collect the rents and manage my properties.

For all the services Peter hos (sic) given me all these years, for the use of his automobile, for the money he spent on gasoline and his time, I owe to him the amount of $50,000 (Fifty Thousand Dollars.) I have already mentioned Peter in my will for all the services and love he has offered me during all these years and I will shortly change my will to include him as my heir. [The memo was signed by Tallas and notarized.]

Tallas died with a sizeable estate but without changing his will. Dementas filed a timely claim for $50,000 against the estate which was denied. Dementas sued and after a trial (apparently without a jury), the trial court dismissed the suit deciding, in essence, that the memo was at best an expression of Tallas' appreciation for "services gratuitously performed by Dementas" and an unenforceable promise to make a will that was executed before death. On appeal, the judgment was affirmed.

The appellate court conceded that Dementas performed some services for Tallas but could find no evidence that they were bargained for. The court stated that "past consideration" was the "legal equivalent of no consideration." [The trial judge had remarked that if "Tallas thought it was worth 50,000 bucks to get one ride to Bingham, that's Tallas's decision.... The only thing you can't do is take it with you."]

What about moral obligation? The court, citing *Manwill v. Oyler*, stated that the so-called "moral obligation doctrine" had not been embraced in Utah. Manwill v. Oyler involved a case where a promise was made to pay for earlier services rendered under an implied in fact contract where the claim was barred by the statute of limitations. The court noted the "logical flaw" in the doctrine, identified in Manwill v. Oyler, but stated that even if the moral obligation doctrine was recognized Dementas would not prevail: the "services rendered by

Dementas to Tallas were not rendered with the expectation of being compensated, but were rendered gratuitously." 765 P.2d at 633.

Webb v. McGowin

Court of Appeals of Alabama, 1935.
27 Ala.App. 82, 168 So. 196.

■ BRICKEN, PRESIDING JUDGE. This action is in assumpsit. The complaint as originally filed was amended. The demurrers to the complaint as amended were sustained, and because of this adverse ruling by the court the plaintiff took a nonsuit, and the assignment of errors on this appeal are predicated upon said action or ruling of the court.

A fair statement of the case presenting the questions for decision is set out in appellant's brief, which we adopt.

"On the 3d day of August, 1925, appellant while in the employ of W.T. Smith Lumber Company, a corporation, and acting within the scope of his employment, was engaged in clearing the upper floor of mill No. 2 of the company. While so engaged he was in the act of dropping a pine block from the upper floor of the mill to the ground below; this being the usual and ordinary way of clearing the floor, and it being the duty of the plaintiff in the course of his employment to so drop it. The block weighed about 75 pounds.

"As appellant was in the act of dropping the block to the ground below, he was on the edge of the upper floor of the mill. As he started to turn the block loose so that it would drop to the ground, he saw J. Greeley McGowin, testator of the defendants, on the ground below and directly under where the block would have fallen had appellant turned it loose. Had he turned it loose it would have struck McGowin with such force as to have caused him serious bodily harm or death. Appellant could have remained safely on the upper floor of the mill by turning the block loose and allowing it to drop, but had he done this the block would have fallen on McGowin and caused him serious injuries or death. The only safe and reasonable way to prevent this was for appellant to hold to the block and divert its direction in falling from the place where McGowin was standing and the only safe way to divert it so as to prevent its coming into contact with McGowin was for appellant to fall with it to the ground below. Appellant did this, and by holding to the block and falling with it to the ground below, he diverted the course of its fall in such way that McGowin was not injured. In thus preventing the injuries to McGowin appellant himself received serious bodily injuries, resulting in his right leg being broken, the heel of his right foot torn off and his right arm broken. He was badly crippled for life and rendered unable to do physical or mental labor.

"On September 1, 1925, in consideration of appellant having prevented him from sustaining death or serious bodily harm and in consideration of the injuries appellant had received, McGowin agreed with him to care for and maintain him for the remainder of appellant's life at the rate of $15 every two weeks from the time he sustained his injuries to and during the remainder of appellant's life; it being agreed that McGowin would pay this sum to appellant for his maintenance. Under the agreement McGowin paid or caused to be paid to appellant the sum so agreed on up until McGowin's death on January 1, 1934. After his death the payments were continued to and including January 27, 1934, at which time they were discontinued. Thereupon plaintiff brought suit to recover the unpaid installments accruing up to the time of the bringing of the suit.

* * *

1.   The averments of the complaint show that appellant saved McGowin from death or grievous bodily harm. This was a material benefit to him of infinitely more value than any financial aid he could have received. Receiving this benefit, McGowin became morally bound to compensate appellant for the services rendered. Recognizing his moral obligation, he expressly agreed to pay appellant as alleged in the complaint and complied with this agreement up to the time of his death; a period of more than 8 years.

Had McGowin been accidentally poisoned and a physician, without his knowledge or request, had administered an antidote, thus saving his life, a subsequent promise by McGowin to pay the physician would have been valid. Likewise, McGowin's agreement as disclosed by the complaint to compensate appellant for saving him from death or grievous bodily injury is valid and enforceable.

Where the promisee cares for, improves, and preserves the property of the promisor, though done without his request, it is sufficient consideration for the promisor's subsequent agreement to pay for the service, because of the material benefit received. . . .

In Boothe v. Fitzpatrick, 36 Vt. 681, the court held that a promise by defendant to pay for the past keeping of a bull which had escaped from defendant's premises and been cared for by plaintiff was valid, although there was no previous request, because the subsequent promise obviated that objection; it being equivalent to a previous request. On the same principle, had the promisee saved the promisor's life or his body from grievous harm, his subsequent promise to pay for the services rendered would have been valid. Such service would have been far more material than caring for his bull. Any holding that saving a man from death or grievous bodily harm is not a material benefit sufficient to uphold a subsequent promise to pay for the service, necessarily rests on the assumption that saving life and preservation of the body from harm have only a sentimental value. The converse of this is true. Life and preservation of the body have material, pecuniary values, measurable in dollars and cents. Because of this, physicians practice their profession charging for services rendered in saving life and curing the body of its ills, and surgeons perform operations. The same is true as to the law of negligence, authorizing the assessment of damages in personal injury cases based upon the extent of the injuries, earnings, and life expectancies of those injured.

In the business of life insurance, the value of a man's life is measured in dollars and cents according to his expectancy, the soundness of his body, and his ability to pay premiums. The same is true as to health and accident insurance.

It follows that if, as alleged in the complaint, appellant saved J. Greeley McGowin from death or grievous bodily harm, and McGowin subsequently agreed to pay him for the service rendered, it became a valid and enforceable contract.

2. It is well settled that a moral obligation is a sufficient consideration to support a subsequent promise to pay where the promisor has received a material benefit, although there was no original duty or liability resting on the promisor. . . . State ex rel. Bayer v. Funk, 105 Or. 134, 199 P. 592, 209 P. 113, 25 A.L.R. 625, 634. . . . In the case of State ex rel. Bayer v. Funk, supra, the court held that a moral obligation is a sufficient consideration to support an executory promise where the promisor has received an actual pecuniary or material benefit for which he subsequently expressly promised to pay.

The case at bar is clearly distinguishable from that class of cases where the consideration is a mere moral obligation or conscientious duty unconnected with receipt by promisor of benefits of a material or pecuniary nature. . . . Here the promisor received a material benefit constituting a valid consideration for his promise.

3. Some authorities hold that, for a moral obligation to support a subsequent promise to pay, there must have existed a prior legal or equitable obligation, which for some reason had become unenforceable, but for which the promisor was still morally bound. This rule, however, is subject to qualification in those cases where the promisor, having received a material benefit from the promisee, is morally bound to compensate him for the services rendered and in consideration of this obligation promises to pay. In such cases the subsequent promise to pay is an affirmance or ratification of the services rendered carrying with it the presumption that a previous request for the service was made. . . .

Under the decisions above cited, McGowin's express promise to pay appellant for the services rendered was an affirmance or ratification of what appellant had done raising the presumption that the services had been rendered at McGowin's request.

4. The averments of the complaint show that in saving McGowin from death or grievous bodily harm, appellant was crippled for life. This was part of the consideration of the contract declared on. McGowin was benefited. Appellant was injured. Benefit to the promisor or injury to the promisee is a sufficient legal consideration for the promisor's agreement to pay. . . .

5. Under the averments of the complaint the services rendered by appellant were not gratuitous. The agreement of McGowin to pay and the acceptance of payment by appellant conclusively shows the contrary.

* * *

From what has been said, we are of the opinion that the court below erred in the ruling complained of; that is to say, in sustaining the demurrer, and for this error the case is reversed and remanded.

Reversed and remanded.

■ SAMFORD, JUDGE (concurring). The questions involved in this case are not free from doubt, and perhaps the strict letter of the rule, as stated by judges, though not always in accord, would bar a recovery by plaintiff, but following the principle announced by Chief Justice Marshall in Hoffman v. Porter, Fed.Cas. No. 6,577, 2 Brock. 156, 159, where he says "I do not think that law ought to be separated from justice, where it is at most doubtful," I concur in the conclusions reached by the court.*

Harrington v. Taylor

Supreme Court of North Carolina, 1945.
225 N.C. 690, 36 S.E.2d 227.

■ PER CURIAM. The plaintiff in this case sought to recover of the defendant upon a promise made by him under the following peculiar circumstances:

The defendant had assaulted his wife, who took refuge in plaintiff's house. The next day the defendant gained access to the house and began another assault upon his wife. The defendant's wife knocked him down with an axe, and was on the point of cutting his head open or decapitating him while he was laying on the floor, and the plaintiff intervened, caught the axe as it was descending, and the blow intended for defendant fell upon her hand, mutilating it badly, but saving defendant's life.

Subsequently, defendant orally promised to pay the plaintiff her damages; but after paying a small sum, failed to pay anything more. So, substantially, states the complaint.

The defendant demurred to the complaint as not stating a cause of action, and the demurrer was sustained. Plaintiff appealed.

The question presented is whether there was a consideration recognized by our law as sufficient to support the promise. The Court is of the opinion that, however much the defendant should be impelled by common gratitude to alleviate the plaintiff's misfortune, a humanitarian act of this kind, voluntarily performed, is not such consideration as would entitle her to recover at law.

The judgment sustaining the demurrer is

Affirmed.

NOTES

(1) Is *Webb v. McGowin* an example of the old saw that "hard cases make bad law?" Can the decision be reconciled with *Mills v. Wyman,* supra at 114?

---

* [Certiorari denied by Alabama Supreme Court, 232 Ala. 374, (1936)].

(2) Taking Dean Wade's summary of the bases for quasi-contract, supra at 16–17, can quasi-contract liability be found in either *Mills or Webb*? What about *Harrington*? If so, the subsequent promise would be enforceable, would it not? If not, where is the deficiency? Can it be argued that the defendant's subsequent decision to make a promise, being an exercise of choice, neutralizes the deficiency in quasi-contract and, therefore, supports enforcement?

(3) The California experience is of particular interest, since there are statutes of long standing which appear to provide alternatives to consideration. Section 1550 of the California Civil Code provides that there must be either "a sufficient cause or consideration." "Cause," or *causa,* is a concept employed in civil law countries, notably in Europe and South America. See Lorenzen, *Causa and Consideration in the Law of Contracts,* 28 Yale L.J. 621 (1919). Moreover, § 1606 of the California code states: "An existing legal obligation resting upon the promisor, *or a moral obligation originating in some benefit conferred upon the promisor, or prejudice suffered by the promisee,* is * * * good consideration for a promise, to an extent corresponding with the extent of the obligation, but no further or otherwise." (Emphasis added). For a discussion of the California decisions, set against a broad historical background, see Keyes, *Cause and Consideration in California—A Re–Appraisal,* 47 Calif.L.Rev. 74 (1959). See also Grosse, *Moral Obligation as Consideration in Contracts,* 17 Vill.L.Rev. 1 (1971).

(4) Section 5–1105 of the New York General Obligations Law provides:

A promise in writing and signed by the promisor or by his agent shall not be denied effect as a valid contractual obligation on the ground that consideration for the promise is past or executed, if the consideration is expressed in the writing and is proved to have been given or performed and would be a valid consideration but for the time when it was given or performed.

See Dick v. Dick, 167 Conn. 210, 355 A.2d 110 (1974), where it was held that the above quoted statute required proof that any consideration stated in the writing was actually paid.

Comment: Restatement (Second) § 86 and the Future of "Moral Obligation"

The first Restatement dealt with the problem of "past" consideration or "moral" obligation under the umbrella of the bargain theory, set forth in Section 75. Provision was made for the limited enforcement of "second" promises made to pay antecedent debts, whether or not barred by the statute of limitations or discharged in bankruptcy. But beyond this, forays into the realm of *Webb v. McGowin* were met by the "bargained for and given in exchange" requirement. The revised Restatement, however, contains a new Section 86, entitled "Promise for Benefit Received":

(1) A promise made in recognition of a benefit previously received by the promisor from the promisee is binding to the extent necessary to prevent injustice.

(2) A promise is not binding under Subsection (1)

(a) if the promisee conferred the benefit as a gift or for other reasons the promisor has not been unjustly enriched; or

(b) to the extent that its value is disproportionate to the benefit.

This section eschews such terminology as "past consideration" and "moral obligation," preferring to explain it as an effort to preclude an unjust enrichment that might have occurred if the courts were limited to traditional principles of quasi-contract.

In speaking of cases such as *Webb v. McGowin,* the first Reporter, Professor Braucher, observed: "What you have, really, is a line of distinction between essentially gratuitous transactions and cases which are on the borderline of quasi-contracts, where promise removes the difficulty which otherwise would bar quasi-contractual relief." He conceded that the section "bristles with nonspecific concepts," but insisted that it captured the principle that can be sustained by the cases. 42 ALI Proceedings 273–74 (1965). Be this as it may, Professor Gilmore has noted that Section 89A, as numbered in the tentative draft, "gives overt recognition to an important principle whose existence *Restatement* ignored and, by implication denied." He suggested, wistfully perhaps, that "by the time we get to Restatement (Third) it may well be that § 89A will have flowered like Jack's bean-stalk in the same way that § 90 did between *Restatement* and *Restatement (Second)*." G. Gilmore, The Death of Contract 76 (1974). See also Henderson, *Promises Grounded in the Past: The Idea of Unjust Enrichment and the Law of Contracts,* 57 Va.L.Rev. 1115 (1971), an article that repays careful study. A search for recent cases finds nothing to suggest that this prophecy will be fulfilled. See First Nat. Bankshares of Beloit, Inc. v. Geisel, 853 F.Supp. 1344, 1356–1357 (D.Kan.1994)("material benefit" rule not applicable on facts); Steven Thel & Edward Yorio, *The Promissory Basis of Past Consideration*, 78 Va. L. Rev. 1045 (1992). See also, Jean Fleming Powers, *Rethinking Moral Obligation as a Basis for Contract Recovery*, 54 Me. L. Rev. 1 (2002); Kevin M. Teeven, The Advent of Recovery on Market Transactions in the Absence of a Bargain, 39 Am. Bus. L.J. 289 (1998).

With the foregoing cases, statutes and materials in mind, how would you resolve the following problems?

PROBLEM: THE CASE OF THE BROKERAGE RENEWAL

Joe Broker, a Metropolis realtor, was contacted by Tom Owner relative to finding a buyer for certain commercial property in the city. On July 1, they executed a "listing agreement," which provided, among other things: "You [Broker] are hereby appointed exclusive agent to secure a purchaser for [here a description of the property and the price were inserted] for 90 days. In case of sale by the undersigned owner before expiration of this agreement you are to receive full cash commission." The stated commission for finding someone willing and able to buy was 7% of the selling price.

Despite strenuous efforts during the late summer and early fall, Broker was unable to locate any real prospect. He had virtually given up hope when he happened to run into Paula Purchaser at a football tailgater (November 4). He learned from Paula of her interest in finding commercial property in Metropolis. Knowing that Paula and Tom were friends, he suggested that Paula give Tom a call. Paula did so, and in a matter of days the two of them had put together a deal at the listed price. Deed and payment were exchanged on November 22.

On November 24, Broker, after learning that Owner and Purchaser had closed the deal, called Owner to his office and had Owner sign a new listing agreement, which was, in effect, a renewal of the old agreement for an additional ninety days.

A problem has come up. Owner died on December 1, and an associate in the office has warned Broker that he may not be able to collect the commission. Broker consults you. Analyze his legal position and advise him as to whether or not he has a valid claim against Owner's estate. See Realty Associates of Sedona v. Valley National Bank of Arizona, 153 Ariz. 514, 738 P.2d 1121 (App.1986).

PROBLEM: THE CASE OF THE KINDLY NEIGHBOR

Barlow, a widower aged 78, moved into a small house on Blossom Avenue next door to Anna, a married woman of 60. Shortly thereafter, Barlow fell and sprained his ankle. Anna saw the accident, took Barlow to the doctor and rendered assistance during his period of recuperation at home. Anna and her husband liked Barlow and felt sorry for him. During the next three years the three of them became fast friends. Anna did household chores for Barlow, took him shopping, fixed innumerable meals and had him for dinner at least once a week. Barlow, who lived alone and had no close relatives, was extremely appreciative. He repeatedly assured Anna that she would be well paid for her kind attention. On Christmas day almost three years after they first met, Barlow delivered to Anna a signed writing which promised to pay Anna "$25,000 from my estate upon death for services rendered." Two weeks later, Barlow was dead of a stroke, leaving an estate of $75,000 and no will. The executor refused to honor the written promise to pay $25,000, and Anna brought suit against the estate. It is stipulated that the reasonable value for services rendered by Anna over a three-year period is $4,500. What result? Cf. In re Gerke's Estate, 271 Wis. 297, 73 N.W.2d 506 (1955); In re Hatten's Estate, 233 Wis. 199, 288 N.W. 278 (1939). See also Restatement (Second) § 86, Illus. 12, 13; McMurry v. Magnusson, 849 S.W.2d 619, 622–623 (Mo.App.1993)(implied promise to pay for nursing and other services rendered in a non-family relationship).

PROBLEM: THE CASE OF THE GRATEFUL MERCHANT

Marley was a wealthy merchant with a small child. Marley hired Cratchet to serve as a bodyguard for the child to reduce the threat of kidnapping for ransom. Cratchet received a reasonable salary [$50,000 per annum] and fringes which included a life insurance policy with a death benefit of $250,000 payable to his wife and three children.

One sad afternoon when Cratchet was picking up the Marley child after school, Moriarty attempted to kidnap the child. Cratchet responded to this threat with total disregard for his own safety. He dispatched Moriarty, but was severely wounded during the incident. Ironically, it had been Cratchet's day off [his first in three months], but he knew that there had been talk of a plot to kidnap the Marley child, so he canceled his cricket match in order to safeguard the child.

As Cratchet lay dying, Marley told him: "Fear not for your family; I shall care for them." Whereupon Cratchet expired.

At Cratchet's funeral, Marley gave the bereaved widow Cratchet a signed memorandum which stated: "In consideration of the extraordinary services of your dearly departed husband, I will pay to you the sum of $500 per month for the rest of your natural life."

Damp and chilly weather prevailed at Cratchet's funeral. Marley took ill, and shortly thereafter, he died.

Mrs. Cratchet received the insurance policy proceeds, but Scrooge, as the Executor of Marley's estate, denied any liability to Mrs. Cratchet for the $500 per month payment. Mrs. Cratchet brought an action against the estate, and now has appealed the dismissal of her complaint by the trial court.

You are a law clerk for a justice on the Supreme Court of the State of Dickens, which state follows the common law of contracts, but this is a case of first impression. Your Justice has advised you that he is leaning toward Mrs. Cratchet's position. He wants an analysis of the theory or theories that he might advance to win the votes of a majority of the Supreme Court Justices. (Ignore any probate issues in your answer.)

SECTION 3. PROMISSORY ESTOPPEL: PROMISE PLUS UNBARGAINED-FOR RELIANCE

Comment: The Evolution of Promissory Estoppel

"Nemo potest mutare consilium suum in alterius injuriam. No one can change his purpose to the injury of another." Justinian's Digest, 50, 17, 75.

"Equitable estoppel * * * arises from the *conduct* of a party, using that word in its broadest meaning as including his spoken or written words, his positive acts, and his silence or negative omission to do anything. Its foundation is justice and good conscience. Its object is to prevent the unconscientious and inequitable assertion or enforcement of claims or rights which might have existed or been enforceable by other rules of law, unless prevented by the estoppel; and its practical effect is, from motives of equity and fair dealing, to create and vest opposing rights in the party who obtains the benefit of the estoppel."

3 Pomeroy, A Treatise on Equity Jurisprudence 180 (5th ed. 1941).

"The vital principle [of equitable estoppel] is that he who by his language or conduct leads another to do what he would not otherwise have done, shall not subject such person to loss or injury by disappointing the expectations upon which he acted."

Dickerson v. Colgrove, 100 U.S. (10 Otto) 578, 580, 25 L.Ed. 618 (1879).

"A promise which the promisor should reasonably expect to induce action or forbearance on the part of the promisee or a third person and which does induce such action or forbearance is binding if injustice can be avoided only by enforcement of the promise. The remedy granted for breach may be limited as justice requires."

Restatement (Second) § 90.

Our inquiry concerning legally enforceable promises has involved mainly an extended look at the doctrine of consideration, the traditional Anglo–American theory of contract. To be sure, for centuries a promise under seal was enforceable (and still may be in a few jurisdictions), and there is still some vitality to the idea, promoted particularly by Lord Mansfield, that "moral obligation" is a sufficient basis for enforcement of a promise. Supra at 109–112. But in the main the common law courts have enforced bargains; something (either of benefit to the promisor or detrimental to the promisee) has to be bargained for and given in exchange for the promise.

There have always, however, been discernible traces of uneasiness respecting this orthodox doctrine. Much of the present day dissatisfaction (and consequent activity) relates to transactions where there is substantial *unbargained-for* reliance upon the promise. For instance, if as in *Ricketts v. Scothorn,* the next case, one quits a job in reliance upon her grandfather's promise to pay her $2,000, is there a sound basis for binding the promisor to some sort of legal obligation? If so, what kind? Contract? Tort? The Nebraska court, in holding there was "an equitable estoppel which ought to preclude the defendant from alleging that the note in controversy is lacking in one of the essential elements of a valid contract," stated as follows: "Having intentionally influenced the plaintiff to alter her position for the worse on the faith of the note being paid when due, it would be grossly inequitable to permit the maker or his executor, to resist payment on the ground that the promise was given without consideration." Judgment for the full amount was affirmed by the Court.

That one might be "estopped" (apparently derived from the Old French *estopper,* to stop, bar) by conduct which leads another to act in reasonable reliance was hardly unprecedented. It has long been recognized that a defendant's conduct may estop or preclude one from raising an otherwise available defense or contesting the accuracy of a representation of fact. As the California Supreme Court put it:

The doctrine of equitable estoppel is founded on concepts of equity and fair dealing. It provides that a person may not deny the existence of a state of facts if he intentionally led another to believe a particular circumstance to be true and to rely upon such belief to his detriment. The elements of the doctrine are that (1) the party to be estopped must be apprised of the facts; (2) he must intend that his conduct shall be acted upon, or must so act that the party asserting the estoppel has a right to believe it was so intended; (3) the other party must be ignorant of the true state of facts; and (4) he must rely upon the conduct to his injury.

Strong v. County of Santa Cruz, 15 Cal.3d 720, 725, 125 Cal.Rptr. 896, 898, 543 P.2d 264, 266 (1975). See Griswold v. Haven, 25 N.Y. 595 (1862). But the use of estoppel in the *Ricketts* context was unusual since there was an extreme reluctance on the part of courts to extend equitable estoppel to statements concerning "future facts." Still less was there recognition of *promissory estoppel* as an alternative or substitute for consideration. On the contrary, the first use of that term seems to have been by Professor Williston in the original edition of his treatise, published in 1920. See Boyer, *Promissory Estoppel: Requirements and Limitations of the Doctrine,* 98 U.Pa.L.Rev. 459 (1950). And the appearance of Restatement § 90, quoted above, which formulated general doctrine without using the term "promissory estoppel" undoubtedly caught many by surprise.

Professor Grant Gilmore has boldly suggested that the famous Section 90, the "unwanted stepchild of *Restatement (First),*" has, in Restatement (Second), "swallowed up the bargain principle of § 75." G. Gilmore, The Death of Contract 72 (1974). Professor Gilmore's claim, however, is overstated. Liability based on contract (good old promise plus consideration) has different and at times more easily proven elements. Moreover, contract damages may exceed those of promissory estoppel which are "limited as justice requires."

In the cases that follow, the reliance idea seems to serve both as a device to achieve "justice" in particular transactions and to effect a transition to principles of liability based upon policies somewhat beyond either consideration or promissory estoppel. See Shattuck, *Gratuitous Promises—A New Writ,* 35 Mich.L.Rev. 908 (1938). Finally, the question of remedy is constantly posed—should loss be measured by the value of the promised performance or the actual reliance?

Ricketts v. Scothorn

Supreme Court of Nebraska, 1898.
57 Neb. 51, 77 N.W. 365.

■ SULLIVAN, J. In the district court of Lancaster county the plaintiff Katie Scothorn recovered judgment against the defendant Andrew D. Ricketts, as executor of the last will and testament of John C. Ricketts, deceased. The action was based upon a promissory note, of which the following is a copy:

"May the first, 1891. I promise to pay to Katie Scothorn on demand, $2,000, to be at 6 per cent per annum. J.C. Ricketts."

In the petition the plaintiff alleges that the consideration for the execution of the note was that she should surrender her employment as bookkeeper for Mayor Bros. and cease to work for a living. She also alleges that the note was given to induce her to abandon her occupation, and that, relying on it, and on the annual interest, as a means of support, she gave up the employment in which she was then engaged. These allegations of the petition are denied by the executor. The material facts are undisputed. They are as follows: John C. Ricketts, the maker of the note, was the grandfather of the plaintiff. Early in May,—presumably on the day the note bears date,—he called on her at the store where she was working. What transpired between them is thus described by Mr. Flodene, one of the plaintiff's witnesses:

A. Well the old gentleman came in there one morning about 9 o'clock,—probably a little before or a little after, but early in the morning,—and he unbuttoned his vest and took out a piece of paper in the shape of a note; that is the way it looked to me; and he says to Miss Scothorn, "I have fixed out something that you have not got to work any more." He says, "None of my grandchildren work and you don't have to."

Q. Where was she?

A. She took the piece of paper and kissed him; and kissed the old gentleman and commenced to cry.

It seems Miss Scothorn immediately notified her employer of her intention to quit work and that she did soon after abandon her occupation. The mother of the plaintiff was a witness and testified that she had a conversation with her father, Mr. Ricketts, shortly after the note was executed in which he informed her that he had given the note to the plaintiff to enable her to quit work; that none of his grandchildren worked and he did not think she ought to. For something more than a year the plaintiff was without an occupation; but in September, 1892, with the consent of her grandfather, and by his assistance, she secured a position as bookkeeper with Messrs. Funke & Ogden. On June 8, 1894, Mr. Ricketts died. He had paid one year's interest on the note, and a short time before his death expressed regret that he had not been able to pay the balance. In the summer or fall of 1892 he stated to his daughter, Mrs. Scothorn, that if he could sell his farm in Ohio he would pay the note out of the proceeds. He at no time repudiated the obligation. We quite agree with counsel for the defendant that upon this evidence there was nothing to submit to the jury, and that a verdict should have been directed peremptorily for one of the parties. The testimony of Flodene and Mrs. Scothorn, taken together, conclusively establishes the fact that the note was not given in consideration of the plaintiff pursuing, or agreeing to pursue, any particular line of conduct. There was no promise on the part of the plaintiff to do or refrain from doing anything. Her right to the money promised in the note was not made to depend upon an abandonment of her employment with Mayer Bros. and future abstention from like service. Mr. Ricketts made no condition, requirement, or request. He exacted no *quid pro quo*. He gave the note as a gratuity and looked for nothing in return. So far as the evidence discloses, it was his purpose to place the plaintiff in a position of independence where she could work or remain idle as she might choose. The abandonment by Miss Scothorn of her position as bookkeeper was altogether voluntary. It was not an act done in fulfillment of any contract obligation assumed when she accepted the note. The instrument in suit being given without any valuable consideration, was nothing more than a promise to make a gift in the future of the sum of money therein named. Ordinarily, such promises are not enforceable even when put in the form of a promissory note. . . . But it has often been held that an action on a note given to a church, college, or other like institution, upon the faith of which money has been expended or obligations incurred, could not be successfully defended on the ground of a want of consideration. . . . In this class of cases the note in suit is nearly always spoken of as a gift or donation, but the decision is generally put on the ground that the expenditure of money or assumption of liability by the donee, on the faith of the promise, constitutes a valuable and sufficient consideration. It seems to us that the true reason is the preclusion of the defendant, under the doctrine of estoppel, to deny the consideration. Such seems to be the view of the matter taken by the supreme court of Iowa in the case of Simpson Centenary College v. Tuttle, 71 Ia. 596, where Rothrock, J., speaking for the court, said: "Where a note, however, is based on a promise to give for the support of the objects referred to, it may still be open to this defense [want of consideration], unless it shall appear that the donee has, prior to any revocation, entered into engagements or made expenditures based on such promise, so that he must suffer loss or injury if the note is not paid. This is based on the equitable principle that, after allowing the donee to incur obligations on the faith that the note would be paid, the donor would be estopped from pleading want of consideration." And in the case of Reimensnyder v. Gans, 110 Pa.St. 17, 2 Atl.Rep. 425, which was an action on a note given as a donation to a charitable object, the court said: "The fact is that, as we may see from the case of Ryerss v. Trustees, 33 Pa.St. 114, a contract of the kind here involved is enforceable rather by way of estoppel than on the ground of consideration in the original undertaking." It has been held that a note given in expectation of the payee performing certain services, but without any contract binding him to serve, will not support an action. . . . But when the payee changes his position to his disadvantage, in reliance on the promise, a right of action does arise. . . .

Under the circumstances of this case is there an equitable estoppel which ought to preclude the defendant from alleging that the note in controversy is lacking in one of the essential elements of a valid contract? We think there is. An estoppel *in pais* is defined to be "a right arising from acts, admissions, or conduct which have induced a change of position in accordance with the real or apparent intention of the party against whom they are alleged." Mr. Pomeroy has formulated the following definition: "Equitable estoppel is the effect of the voluntary conduct of a party whereby he is absolutely precluded, both at law and in equity, from asserting rights which might perhaps have otherwise existed, either of property, or contract, or of remedy, as against another person who in good faith relied upon such conduct, and has been led thereby to change his position for the worse, and who on his part acquires some corresponding right either of property, of contract, or of remedy." (2 Pomeroy, Equity Jurisprudence 804.) According to the undisputed proof, as shown by the record before us, the plaintiff was a working girl, holding a position in which she earned a salary of $10 per week. Her grandfather, desiring to put her in a position of independence, gave her the note, accompanying it with the remark that his other grandchildren did not work, and that she would not be obliged to work any longer. In effect he suggested that she might abandon her employment and rely in the future upon the bounty which he promised. He, doubtless, desired that she should give up her occupation, but whether he did or not, it is entirely certain that he contemplated such action on her part as a reasonable and probable consequence of his gift. Having intentionally influenced the plaintiff to alter her position for the worse on the faith of the note being paid when due, it would be grossly inequitable to permit the maker, or his executor, to resist payment on the ground that the promise was given without consideration. The petition charges the elements of an equitable estoppel, and the evidence conclusively establishes them. If errors intervened at the trial they could not have been prejudicial. A verdict for the defendant would be unwarranted. The judgment is right and is

Affirmed.

NOTES

(1) How would *Ricketts* be decided under Section 90 of the Restatement (Second)?

(2) Was there "agreement" here? Can there ever be contractual obligation without an agreement?

(3) In *Ricketts v. Scothorn,* there was no consideration for the grandfather's promise. Katie's act of quitting her job was not bargained for and given in exchange for the written promise to pay $2,000 plus interest. The court, however, concluded that grandfather's executor was estopped or precluded from raising the defense of "no consideration." Why? Because grandfather's promise induced reliance by Katie that made it inequitable for the executor later to claim that there was no consideration. As a result, the promise was enforced in full as if there was consideration.

There are two difficulties with this analysis. First the analysis tends to confuse two types of estoppel, "equitable" and "promissory." As one court put it: "Equitable estoppel ... is based upon a representation of existing or past facts, while promissory estoppel requires the existence of a promise.... Equitable estoppel ... is available only as a 'shield' or defense, while promissory estoppel can be used as a 'sword' in a cause of action for damages." Klinke v. Famous Recipe Fried Chicken, Inc., 94 Wash.2d 255, 616 P.2d 644, 646 (1980). Second, the consequence of the confusion is that some courts have treated reliance induced by a promise as a reason to foreclose an attack on the enforceability of the promise and to limit the remedy to the loss suffered in reliance. See, e.g., Wheeler v. White, 398 S.W.2d 93 (Tex.1965). A more affirmative statement of "promissory" estoppel appears in Section 90 of Restatement (Second):

(1) A promise which the promisor should reasonably expect to induce action or forbearance on the part of the promisee or a third person and which does induce such action or forbearance is binding if injustice can be avoided only by enforcement of the promise. The remedy granted for breach may be limited as justice requires.

Allegheny College v. National Chautauqua County Bank of Jamestown

Court of Appeals of New York, 1927.
246 N.Y. 369, 159 N.E. 173.

■ CARDOZO, CH.J. The plaintiff, Allegheny College, is an institution of liberal learning at Meadville, Pennsylvania. In June 1921, a "drive" was in progress to secure for it an additional endowment of $1,250,000. An appeal to contribute to this fund was made to Mary Yates Johnston of Jamestown, New York. In response thereto, she signed and delivered on June 15, 1921, the following writing:

"Estate Pledge,

"Allegheny College Second Century Endowment

"Jamestown, N.Y., June 15, 1921.

"In consideration of my interest in Christian Education, and in consideration of others subscribing, I hereby subscribe and will pay to the order of the Treasurer of Allegheny College, Meadville, Pennsylvania, the sum of Five Thousand Dollars; $5,000.

"This obligation shall become due thirty days after my death, and I hereby instruct my Executor, or Administrator, to pay the same out of my estate. This pledge shall bear interest at the rate of _____ per cent per annum, payable annually, from _____ till paid. The proceeds of this obligation shall be added to the Endowment of said Institution, or expended in accordance with instructions on reverse side of this pledge.

"Name   MARY YATES JOHNSTON,
"Address   306 East 6th Street,
                                               "Jamestown N.Y.

"Dayton E. McClain   Witness
"T.R. Courtis   Witness
              "to authentic signature."

On the reverse side of the writing is the following indorsement: "In loving memory this gift shall be known as the Mary Yates Johnston Memorial Fund, the proceeds from which shall be used to educate students preparing for the Ministry, either in the United States or in the Foreign Field.

"This pledge shall be valid only on the condition that the provisions of my Will, now extant, shall be first met.

"MARY YATES JOHNSTON."

The subscription was not payable by its terms until thirty days after the death of the promisor. The sum of $1,000 was paid, however, upon account in December, 1923, while the promisor was alive. The college set the money aside to be held as a scholarship fund for the benefit of students preparing for the ministry. Later, in July, 1924, the promisor gave notice to the college that she repudiated the promise. Upon the expiration of thirty days following her death, this action was brought against the executor of her will to recover the unpaid balance.

The law of charitable subscriptions has been a prolific source of controversy in this State and elsewhere. We have held that a promise of that order is unenforceable like any other if made without consideration. . . . On the other hand, though professing to apply to such subscriptions the general law of contract, we have found consideration present where the general law of contract, at least as then declared, would have said that it was absent. . . .

A classic form of statement identifies consideration with detriment to the promisee sustained by virtue of the promise (Hamer v. Sidway, 124 N.Y. 538; Anson, Contracts [Corbin's ed.], p. 116; 8 Holdsworth, History of English Law, 10). So compendious a formula is little more than a half truth. There is need of many a supplementary gloss before the outline can be so filled in as to depict the classic doctrine. "The promise and the consideration must purport to be the motive each for the other, in whole or at least in part. It is not enough that the promise induces the detriment or that the detriment induces the promise if the other half is wanting" (Wisc. & Mich. Ry. Co. v. Powers, 191 U.S. 379, 386; McGovern v. City of N.Y., 234 N.Y. 377, 389; Walton Water Co. v. Village of Walton, 238 N.Y. 46, 51; 1 Williston, Contracts, § 139; Langdell, Summary of the Law of Contracts, pp. 82–88). If A promises B to make him a gift, consideration may be lacking, though B has renounced other opportunities for betterment in the faith that the promise will be kept.

The half truths of one generation tend at times to perpetuate themselves in the law as the whole truths of another, when constant repetition brings it about that qualifications, taken once for granted, are disregarded or forgotten. The doctrine of consideration has not escaped the common lot. As far back as 1881, Judge Holmes in his lectures on the Common Law (p. 292), separated the detriment which is merely a consequence of the promise from the detriment which is in truth the motive or inducement, and yet added that the courts "have gone far in obliterating this distinction." The tendency toward effacement has not lessened with the years. On the contrary, there has grown up of recent days a doctrine that a substitute for consideration or an exception to its ordinary requirements can be found in what is styled "a promissory estoppel" (Williston, Contracts, §§ 139, 116). Whether the exception has made its way in this State to such an extent as to permit us to say that the general law of consideration has been modified accordingly, we do not now attempt to say. Cases such as Siegel v. Spear & Co. (234 N.Y. 479) and DeCicco v. Schweizer (221 N.Y. 431) may be signposts on the road. Certain, at least it is that we have adopted the doctrine of promissory estoppel as the equivalent of consideration in connection with our law of charitable subscriptions. So long as those decisions stand, the question is not merely whether the enforcement of a charitable subscription can be squared with the doctrine of consideration in all its ancient rigor. The question may also be whether it can be squared with the doctrine of consideration as qualified by the doctrine of promissory estoppel.

We have said that the cases in this State have recognized this exception, if exception it is thought to be. Thus, in Barnes v. Perine (12 N.Y. 18) the subscription was made without request, express or implied, that the church do anything on the faith of it. Later, the church did incur expense to the knowledge of the promisor, and in the reasonable belief that the promise would be kept. We held the promise binding, though consideration there was none except upon the theory of a promissory estoppel. In Presbyterian Society v. Beach (74 N.Y. 72) a situation substantially the same became the basis for a like ruling. So in Roberts v. Cobb (103 N.Y. 600) and Keuka College v. Ray (167 N.Y. 96) the moulds of consideration as fixed by the old doctrine were subjected to a like expansion. Very likely, conceptions of public policy have shaped, more or less subconsciously, the rulings thus made. Judges have been affected by the thought that "defences of that character" are "breaches of faith toward the public, and especially toward those engaged in the same enterprise, and an unwarrantable disappointment of the reasonable expectations of those interested." (W.F. Allen, J., in Barnes v. Perine, supra, page 24; and cf. Eastern States League v. Vail, 97 Vt. 495, 505, and cases there cited). The result speaks for itself irrespective of the motive. Decisions which have stood so long, and which are supported by so many considerations of public policy and reason, will not be overruled to save the symmetry of a concept which itself came into our law, not so much from any reasoned conviction of its justice, as from historical accidents of practice and procedure (8 Holdsworth, History of English Law, 7 et seq.). The concept survives as one of the distinctive features of our legal system. We have no thought to suggest that it is obsolete or on the way to be abandoned. As in the case of other concepts, however, the pressure of exceptions has led to irregularities of form.

It is in this background of precedent that we are to view the problem now before us. The background helps to an understanding of the implications inherent in subscription and acceptance. This is so though we may find in the end that without recourse to the innovation of promissory estoppel the transaction can be fitted within the mould of consideration as established by tradition.

The promisor wished to have a memorial to perpetuate her name. She imposed a condition that the "gift" should "be known as the Mary Yates Johnston Memorial Fund." The moment that the college accepted $1,000 as a payment on account, there was an assumption of a duty to do whatever acts were customary or reasonably necessary to maintain the memorial fairly and justly in the spirit of its creation. The college could not accept the money, and hold itself free thereafter from personal responsibility to give effect to the condition. ... More is involved in the receipt of such a fund than a mere acceptance of money to be held to a corporate use. ... The purpose of the founder would be unfairly thwarted or at least inadequately served if the college failed to communicate to the world, or in any event to applicants for the scholarship, the title of the memorial. By implication it undertook, when it accepted a portion of the "gift" that in its circulars of information and in other customary ways, when making announcement of this scholarship, it would couple with the announcement the name of the donor. The donor was not at liberty to gain the benefit of such an undertaking upon the payment of a part and disappoint the expectation that there would be payment of the residue. If the college had stated after receiving $1,000 upon account of the subscription that it would apply the money to the prescribed use, but that in its circulars of information and when responding to prospective applicants it would deal with the fund as an anonymous donation, there is little doubt that the subscriber would have been at liberty to treat this statement as the repudiation of a duty impliedly assumed, a repudiation justifying a refusal to make payments in the future. Obligation in such circumstances is correlative and mutual. * * * We do not need to measure the extent either of benefit to the promisor or of detriment to the promisee implicit in this duty. "If a person chooses to make an extravagant promise for an inadequate consideration it is his own affair" (8 Holdsworth, History of English Law, p. 17). It was long ago said that "when a thing is to be done by the plaintiff, be it ever so small, this is a sufficient consideration to ground an action" (Sturlyn v. Albany, 1587, Cro.Eliz. 67, quoted by Holdsworth, supra; cf. Walton Water Co. v. Village of Walton, 238 N.Y. 46, 51). The longing for posthumous remembrance is an emotion not so weak as to justify us in saying that its gratification is a negligible good.

We think the duty assumed by the plaintiff to perpetuate the name of the founder of the memorial is sufficient in itself to give validity to the subscription within the rules that define consideration for a promise of that order. When the promisee subjected itself to such a duty at the implied request of the promisor, the result was the creation of a bilateral agreement. . . . There was a promise on the one side and on the other a return promise, made it is true, by implication, but expressing an obligation that had been exacted as a condition of the payment. A bilateral agreement may exist though one of the mutual promises be a promise "implied in fact," an inference from conduct as opposed to an inference from words (Williston, Contracts, §§ 90, 22–a; Pettibone v. Moore, 75 Hun, 461, 464). We think the fair inference to be drawn from the acceptance of a payment on account of the subscription is a promise by the college to do what may be necessary on its part to make the scholarship effective. The plan conceived by the subscriber will be mutilated and distorted unless the sum to be accepted is adequate to the end in view. Moreover, the time to affix her name to the memorial will not arrive until the entire fund has been collected. The college may thus thwart the purpose of the payment on account if at liberty to reject a tender of the residue. It is no answer to say that a duty would then arise to make restitution of the money. If such a duty may be imposed, the only reason for its existence must be that there is then a failure of "consideration." To say that there is a failure of consideration is to concede that a consideration has been promised since otherwise it could not fail. No doubt there are times and situations in which limitations laid upon a promisee in connection with the use of what is paid by a subscriber lacks the quality of a consideration, and are to be classed merely as conditions (Williston, Contracts, § 112; Page, Contracts, § 523). "It is often difficult to determine whether words of condition in a promise indicate a request for consideration or state a mere condition in a gratuitous promise. An aid, though not a conclusive test in determining which construction of the promise is more reasonable is an inquiry whether the happening of the condition will be a benefit to the promisor. If so, it is a fair inference that the happening was requested as a consideration" (Williston, supra, § 112). Such must be the meaning of this transaction unless we are prepared to hold that the college may keep the payment on account, and thereafter nullify the scholarship which is to preserve the memory of the subscriber. The fair implication to be gathered from the whole transaction is assent to the condition and the assumption of a duty to go forward with performance. . . . The subscriber does not say: I hand you $1,000, and you make up your mind later, after my death, whether you will undertake to commemorate my name. What she says in effect is this: I hand you $1,000, and if you are unwilling to commemorate me, the time to speak is now.

The conclusion thus reached makes it needless to consider whether, aside from the feature of a memorial, a promissory estoppel may result from the assumption of a duty to apply the fund, so far as already paid, to special purposes not mandatory under the provisions of the college charter (the support and education of students preparing for the ministry), an assumption induced by the belief that other payments sufficient in amount to make the scholarship effective would be added to the fund thereafter upon the death of the subscriber (Ladies Collegiate Inst. v. French, 16 Gray, 196; Barnes v. Perine, 12 N.Y. 18, and cases there cited).

The judgment of the Appellate Division and that of the Trial Term should be reversed, and judgment ordered for the plaintiff as prayed for in the complaint, with costs in all courts.

■ Kellogg, J. (dissenting). The Chief Judge finds in the expression, "In loving memory this gift shall be known as the Mary Yates Johnston Memorial Fund" an offer on the part of Mary Yates Johnston to contract with Allegheny College. The expression makes no such appeal to me. Allegheny College was not requested to perform any act through which the sum offered might bear the title by which the offeror states that it shall be known. The sum offered was termed a "gift" by the offeror. Consequently, I can see no reason why we should strain ourselves to make it, not a gift, but a trade. Moreover, since the donor specified that the gift was made "In consideration of my interest in Christian education, and in consideration of others subscribing," considerations not adequate in law, I can see no excuse for asserting that it was otherwise made in consideration of an act or promise on the part of the donee, constituting a sufficient *quid quo pro* to convert the gift into a contract obligation. To me the words used merely expressed an expectation or wish on the part of the donor and failed to exact the return of an adequate consideration. But if an offer indeed was present, then clearly it was an offer to enter into a unilateral contract. The offeror was to be bound provided the offeree performed such acts as might be necessary to make the gift offered become known under the proposed name. This is evidently the thought of the Chief Judge, for he says: "She imposed a condition that the 'gift' should be known as the Mary Yates Johnston Memorial Fund." In other words, she proposed to exchange her offer of a donation in return for acts to be performed. Even so there was never any acceptance of the offer and, therefore, no contract, for the acts requested have never been performed. The gift has never been made known as demanded. Indeed, the requested acts, under the very terms of the assumed offer, could never have been performed at a time to convert the offer into a promise. This is so for the reason that the donation was not to take effect until after the death of the donor, and by her death her offer was withdrawn. (Williston on Contracts, sec. 62.) Clearly, although a promise of the college to make the gift known, as requested, may be implied, that promise was not the acceptance of an offer which gave rise to a contract. The donor stipulated for acts, not promises. "In order to make a bargain it is necessary that the acceptor shall give in return for the offer or the promise exactly the consideration which the offeror requests. If an act is requested, that very act and no other must be given. If a promise is requested, that promise must be made absolutely and unqualifiedly." (Williston on Contracts, sec. 73.) "It does not follow that an offer becomes a promise because it is accepted; it may be and frequently is, conditional, and then it does not become a promise until the conditions are satisfied; and in case of offers for a consideration, the performance of the consideration is always deemed a condition." (Langdell, Summary of the Law of Contracts, sec. 4). It seems clear to me that there was here no offer, no acceptance of an offer, and no contract. Neither do I agree with the Chief Judge that this court "found consideration present where the general law of contract, at least as then declared, would have said it was absent" in the cases of Barnes v. Perine (12 N.Y. 18), Presbyterian Society v. Beach (74 N.Y. 72) and Keuka College v. Ray (167 N.Y. 96). * * * However, even if the basis of the decisions be a so-called "promissory estoppel," nevertheless they initiated no new doctrine. A so-called "promissory estoppel," although not so termed, was held sufficient by Lord Mansfield and his fellow judges as far back as the year 1765. (Pillans v. Van Mierop, 3 Burr. 1663.) Such a doctrine may be an anomaly; it is not a novelty. Therefore, I can see no ground for the suggestion that the ancient rule which makes consideration necessary to the formation of every contract is in danger of effacement through any decisions of this court. To me that is a cause for gratulation rather than regret. However, the discussion may be beside the mark, for I do not understand that the holding about to be made in this case is other than a holding that consideration was given to convert the offer into a promise. With that result I cannot agree and, accordingly, must dissent.

■ POUND, CRANE, LEHMAN and O'BRIEN, JJ., concur with CARDOZO, CH. J.; KELLOGG, J. dissents in opinion, in which ANDREWS, J., concurs.

Judgment accordingly.

NOTES

(1) Does Judge Cardozo in *Allegheny College* purport to find consideration for the promise being sued upon? Is the conclusion that Mrs. Johnston

bargained for and received a promise by the college, implied from the conduct of accepting the $1,000 payment and putting it aside, to set up and publicize the fund when the final payment was made convincing? For a line-by-line analysis of *Allegheny College*, see Alfred Konefsky, *How to Read, Or at Least Not Misread, Cardozo in the Allegheny College Case*, 36 Buff.L.Rev. 645 (1989).

(2) "It would seem * * * that the framers of section 90 recognized the fact that there is a class of cases where gratuitous promises should be enforced for compelling reasons of justice, where the promisee incurs a substantial detriment on the faith of such promises, and this, whether the promisor intended the detriment or not. The test seems to be whether the promisor could reasonably have expected the detriment to be incurred on the strength of the promise. If the detriment is incurred, and there is no other way of avoiding injustice, the promise is enforceable. Of course, as pointed out by Judge Baldrige, in Langer v. Superior Steel Corp. . . . and also by Professor Williston in his work on 'Contracts' not every gratuitous promise and reliance thereon is enforceable. The doctrine must be limited in its application to that group of cases where the reliance on the promise brought about such a substantial, changed condition on the part of the promisee that enforcement of the promise is the only way to avoid injustice. What constitutes injustice has not been defined; that, it would seem, must be determined from all the surrounding circumstances of each case. Professor Williston hints that injustice does not necessarily mean pecuniary loss. As he points out, the meaning is 'purposely left somewhat indefinite,' which means that the equities of each case must point the way to its solution under this doctrine of promissory estoppel." Trexler's Estate, 27 Pa.D. & C. 4, 13 (Orphans' Court of Lehigh County, Pennsylvania, 1936).

(3) *Charitable Subscriptions.* Cases enforcing promises to charities on the basis of unbargained-for reliance can be counted among the historical antecedents of modern promissory estoppel theory. See B. Boyer, *Promissory Estoppel: Principle from Precedents,* 50 Mich.L.Rev 639, 873 (1952). There are references to some of these decisions in *Ricketts* and *Allegheny College*. Hence, even if a court is unwilling to stretch to find consideration, as Judge Cardozo did in *Allegheny College,* there may be an alternative basis of recovery. However, this alternative basis requires a showing of reliance on the part of the promisee, and it may be impossible to establish any specific reliance. See, e.g., Mount Sinai Hospital of Greater Miami, Inc. v. Jordan, 290 So.2d 484 (Fla.1974); Congregation Kadimah Toras–Moshe v. DeLeo, 405 Mass. 365, 540 N.E.2d 691 (1989) ("The inclusion of the promised $25,000 in the budget, by itself, merely reduced to writing the Congregation's expectation that it would have additional funds. A hope or expectation, even though well founded, is not equivalent to either legal detriment or reliance." 540 N.E.2d at 693).

To obviate this difficulty, the drafters of Restatement (Second) propose to dispense with the necessity of proving reliance. Subsection (2) of Section 90 provides: "A charitable subscription * * * is binding * * * without proof that the promise induced action or forbearance." For a case adopting the Restatement position, see Salsbury v. Northwestern Bell Telephone Co., 221 N.W.2d 609 (Iowa 1974). The Iowa Supreme Court commented as follows: "We believe public policy supports this view. It is more logical to bind charitable subscriptions without requiring a showing of consideration or detrimental reliance.

Charitable subscriptions often serve the public interest by making possible projects which otherwise could never come about. * * * [W]here a subscription is unequivocal the pledgor should be made to keep his word." 221 N.W.2d at 613. But see King v. Trustees of Boston University, 420 Mass. 52, 647 N.E.2d 1196, 1200 (1995), where the Restatement standard for charitable gifts was rejected.

(4) *Promissory Estoppel In New York.* The development of promissory estoppel in New York was traced in Cyberchron Corp. v. Calldata Systems Development, Inc., 47 F.3d 39, 44–46 (2d Cir.1995). According to the federal court, prior to 1980 New York courts limited promissory estoppel as a "substitute for consideration" to limited contexts, such as charitable subscriptions and bailments and to disputes over the statute of frauds. After 1980, some lower courts embraced the more general principle but imposed higher standards than those expressed in Section 90 of the Second Restatement. Thus, the promise must be "clear and unambiguous," reliance must be foreseeable to the promisor and reasonable by the promisee and the resulting injury must be "unconscionable." Some have argued that Judge Cardozo impeded the development of promissory estoppel in New York by his decision in *Allegheny College.* Do you agree? See Phuong N. Pham (Comment), *The Waning of Promissory Estoppel,* 79 Cornell L. Rev. 1263 (1994).

Feinberg v. Pfeiffer Co.

St. Louis Court of Appeals, Missouri, 1959.
322 S.W.2d 163.

■ DOERNER, COMMISSIONER. This is a suit brought in the Circuit Court of the City of St. Louis by plaintiff a former employee of the defendant corporation on an alleged contract whereby defendant agreed to pay plaintiff the sum of $200 per month for life upon her retirement. A jury being waived, the case was tried by the court alone. Judgment below was for plaintiff for $5,100, the amount of the pension claimed to be due as of the date of the trial together with interest thereon, and defendant duly appealed.

The parties are in substantial agreement on the essential facts. Plaintiff began working for the defendant, a manufacturer of pharmaceuticals, in 1910, when she was but 17 years of age. By 1947 she had attained the position of bookkeeper, office manager, and assistant treasurer of the defendant, and owned 70 shares of its stock out of a total of 6,503 shares issued and outstanding. Twenty shares had been given to her by the defendant or its then president, she had purchased 20, and the remaining 30 she had acquired by a stock split or stock dividend. Over the years she received substantial dividends on the stock she owned, as did all of the other stockholders. Also, in addition to her salary, plaintiff from 1937 to 1949, inclusive, received each year a bonus varying in amount from $300 in the beginning to $2,000 in the later years.

On December 27, 1947, the annual meeting of the defendant's Board of Directors was held at the Company's offices in St. Louis, presided over by Max Lippman, its then president and largest individual stockholder. The other directors present were George L. Marcus, Sidney Harris, Sol Flammer, and Walter Weinstock, who, with Max Lippman, owned 5,007 of the 6,503 shares then issued and outstanding. At that meeting the Board of Directors adopted the following resolution, which, because it is the crux of the case, we quote in full:

"The Chairman thereupon pointed out that the Assistant Treasurer, Mrs. Anna Sacks Feinberg, has given the corporation many years of long and faithful service. Not only has she served the corporation devotedly, but with exceptional ability and skill. The President pointed out that although all of the officers and directors sincerely hoped and desired that Mrs. Feinberg would continue in her present position for as long as she felt able, nevertheless, in view of the length of service which she has contributed provision should be made to afford her retirement privileges and benefits which should become a firm obligation of the corporation to be available to her whenever she should see fit to retire from active duty, however many years in the future such retirement may become effective. It was, accordingly, proposed that Mrs. Feinberg's salary which is presently $350.00 per month, be increased to $400.00 per month, and that Mrs. Feinberg would be given the privilege of retiring from active duty at any time she may elect to see fit so to do upon a retirement pay of $200.00 per month for life, with the distinct understanding that the retirement plan is merely being adopted at the present time in order to afford Mrs. Feinberg security for the future and in the hope that her active services will continue with the corporation for many years to come. After due discussion and consideration, and upon motion duly made and seconded, it was—

"Resolved that the salary of Anna Sacks Feinberg be increased from $350.00 to $400.00 per month and that she be afforded the privilege of retiring from active duty in the corporation at any time she may elect to see fit so to do upon retirement pay of $200.00 per month, for the remainder of her life."

At the request of Mr. Lippman his sons-in-law, Messrs. Harris and Flammer, called upon the plaintiff at her apartment on the same day to advise her of the passage of the resolution. Plaintiff testified on cross-examination that she had no prior information that such a pension plan was contemplated, that it came as a surprise to her, and that she would have continued in her employment whether or not such a resolution had been adopted. It is clear from the evidence that there was no contract, oral or written, as to plaintiff's length of employment, and that she was free to quit, and the defendant to discharge her, at any time.

Plaintiff did continue to work for the defendant through June 30, 1949, on which date she retired. In accordance with the foregoing resolution, the defendant began paying her the sum of $200 on the first of each month. Mr. Lippman died on November 18, 1949, and was succeeded as president of the company by his widow. Because of an illness, she retired from that office and was succeeded in October, 1953, by her son-in-law, Sidney M. Harris. Mr. Harris testified that while Mrs. Lippman had been president she signed the monthly pension check paid plaintiff, but fussed about doing so, and considered the payments as gifts. After his election, he stated, a new accounting firm employed by the defendant questioned the validity of the payments to plaintiff on several occasions, and in the Spring of 1956, upon its recommendation, he consulted the Company's then attorney, Mr. Ralph Kalish. Harris testified that both Ernst and Ernst, the accounting firm, and Kalish told him there was no need of giving plaintiff the money. He also stated that he had concurred in the view that the payments to plaintiff were mere gratuities rather than amounts due under a contractual obligation, and that following his discussion with the Company's attorney plaintiff was sent a check for $100 on April 1, 1956. Plaintiff declined to accept the reduced amount, and this action followed. Additional facts will be referred to later in this opinion.

* * *

It is defendant's contention, in essence, that the resolution adopted by its Board of Directors was a mere promise to make a gift, and that no contract resulted either thereby, or when plaintiff retired, because there was no consideration given or paid by the plaintiff. It urges that a promise to make a gift is not binding unless supported by a legal consideration; that the only apparent consideration for the adoption of the foregoing resolution was the "many years of long and faithful service" expressed therein; and that past services are not a valid consideration for a promise. Defendant argues further that there is nothing in the resolution which made its effectiveness conditional upon plaintiff's continued employment, that she was not under contract to work for any length of time but was free to quit whenever she wished, and that she had no contractual right to her position and could have been discharged at any time.

Plaintiff concedes that a promise based upon past services would be without consideration, but contends that there were two other elements which supplied the required element: First, the continuation by plaintiff in the employ of the defendant for the period from December 27, 1947, the date when the resolution was adopted, until the date of her retirement on June 30, 1949. And, second, her change of position, i.e., her retirement, and the abandonment by her of her opportunity to continue in gainful employment, made in reliance on defendant's promise to pay her $200 per month for life.

We must agree with the defendant that the evidence does not support the first of these contentions. There is no language in the resolution predicating plaintiff's right to a pension upon her continued employment. She was not required to work for the defendant for any period of time as a condition to gaining such retirement benefits. She was told that she could quit the day upon which the resolution was adopted, as she herself testified, and it is clear from her own testimony that she made no promise or agreement to continue in the employ of the defendant in return for its promise to pay her a pension. Hence there was lacking that mutuality of obligation which is essential to the validity of a contract. . . .

But as to the second of these contentions we must agree with plaintiff. By the terms of the resolution defendant promised to pay plaintiff the sum of $200 a month upon her retirement. Consideration for a promise has been defined in the Restatement of the Law of Contracts, Section 75, as:

"(1) Consideration for a promise is

(a) an act other than a promise, or

(b) a forbearance, or

(c) the creation, modification or destruction of a legal relation, or

(d) a return promise,

bargained for and given in exchange for the promise."

As the parties agree, the consideration sufficient to support a contract may be either a benefit to the promisor or a loss or detriment to the promisee. . . .

Section 90 of the Restatement of the Law of Contracts states that: "A promise which the promisor should reasonably expect to induce action or forbearance of a definite and substantial character on the part of the promisee and which does induce such action or forbearance is binding if injustice can be avoided only by enforcement of the promise." This doctrine has been described as that of "promissory estoppel," as distinguished from that of equitable estoppel or estoppel in pais, the reason for the differentiation being stated as follows:

"It is generally true that one who has led another to act in reasonable reliance on his representations of fact cannot afterwards in litigation between the two deny the truth of the representations, and some courts have sought to apply this principle to the formation of contracts, where, relying on a gratuitous promise, the promisee has suffered detriment. It is to be noticed, however, that such a case does not come within the ordinary definition of estoppel. If there is any representation of an existing fact, it is only that the promisor at the time of making the promise intends to fulfill it. As to such intention there is usually no misrepresentation and if there is, it is not that which has injured the promisee. In other words, he relies on a promise and not on a misstatement of fact; and the term 'promissory' estoppel or something equivalent should be used to make the distinction." Williston on Contracts, Rev.Ed., Sec. 139, Vol. 1.

In speaking of this doctrine, Judge Learned Hand said in Porter v. Commissioner of Internal Revenue, 2 Cir., 60 F.2d 673, 675, that " * * * 'promissory estoppel' is now a recognized species of consideration."

* * *

Was there such an act on the part of plaintiff, in reliance upon the promise contained in the resolution, as will estop the defendant, and therefore create an enforceable contract under the doctrine of promissory estoppel? We think there was. One of the illustrations cited under Section 90 of the Restatement is: "2. A promises B to pay him an annuity during B's life. B thereupon resigns a profitable employment, as A expected that he might. B receives the annuity for some years, in the meantime becoming disqualified from again obtaining good employment. A's promise is binding." This illustration is objected to by defendant as not being applicable to the case at hand. The reason advanced by it is that in the illustration B became "disqualified" from obtaining other employment *before* A discontinued the payments, whereas in this case the plaintiff did not discover that she had cancer and thereby became unemployable until *after* the defendant had discontinued the payments of $200 per month. We think the distinction is immaterial. The only reason for the reference in the illustration to the disqualification of A is in connection with that part of Section 90 regarding the prevention of injustice. The injustice would occur regardless of when the disability occurred. Would defendant contend that the contract would be enforceable if the plaintiff's illness had been discovered on March 31, 1956, the day before it discontinued the payment of the $200 a month, but not if it occurred on April 2nd, the day after? Furthermore, there are more ways to become disqualified for work, or unemployable, than as the result of illness. At the time she retired plaintiff was 57 years of age. At the time the payments were discontinued she was over 63 years of age. It is a matter of common knowledge that it is virtually impossible for a woman of that age to find satisfactory employment, much less a position comparable to that which plaintiff enjoyed at the time of her retirement.

The fact of the matter is that plaintiff's subsequent illness was not the "action or forbearance" which was induced by the promise contained in the resolution. As the trial court correctly decided, such action on plaintiff's part was her retirement from a lucrative position in reliance upon defendant's promise to pay her an annuity or pension. In a very similar case, Ricketts v. Scothorn, 57 Neb. 51, 77 N.W. 365, 367, 42 L.R.A. 794, the Supreme Court of Nebraska said:

"* * * According to the undisputed proof, as shown by the record before us, the plaintiff was a working girl, holding a position in which she earned a salary of $10 per week. Her grandfather, desiring to put her in a position of independence, gave her the note accompanying it with the remark that his other grandchildren did not work, and that she would not be obliged to work any longer. In effect, he suggested that she might abandon her employment, and rely in the future upon the bounty which he promised. He doubtless desired that she should give up her occupation, but, whether he did or not, it is entirely certain that he contemplated such action on her part as a reasonable and probable consequence of his gift. Having intentionally influenced the plaintiff to alter her position for the worse on the faith of the note being paid when due, it would be grossly inequitable to permit the maker, or his executor, to resist payment on the ground that the promise was given without consideration."

The Commissioner therefore recommends, for the reasons stated, that the judgment be affirmed.

■ PER CURIAM.

The foregoing opinion by DOERNER, C., is adopted as the opinion of the court. The judgment is, accordingly, affirmed.

NOTES

(1) Did the defendant, in *Feinberg,* bargain for Mrs. Feinberg's early retirement? For cases finding consideration to support a promise to pay a pension or similar benefit in either the promisor's desire to induce early retirement or restrict the plaintiff's post-retirement conduct, see Osborne v. Locke Steel Chain Co., 153 Conn. 527, 218 A.2d 526 (1966) (retired officer to be available for consultation and to refrain from competition with former employer); Lowndes Cooperative Association v. Lipsey, 240 Miss. 71, 126 So.2d 276 (1961) (promise conditioned on early retirement and post-retirement cooperation); Specht v. Eastwood–Nealley Corp., 34 N.J.Super. 156, 111 A.2d 781 (1955) (promise conditioned upon non-disclosure of trade secrets, non-competition, etc.). For cases enforcing the promise on the grounds of either consideration or promissory estoppel, see Hessler, Inc. v. Farrell, 226 A.2d 708 (Del. 1967) (employee induced to forego other offers and remain with company); Wickstrom v. Vern E. Alden Co., 99 Ill.App.2d 254, 240 N.E.2d 401 (1968) (employee induced to retire early). If there was no legitimate basis for inferring a bargain in *Feinberg,* did the court stretch unduly to enforce the promise under Section 90? For a reaffirmation of *Feinberg* in Missouri, see Katz v. Danny Dare, Inc., 610 S.W.2d 121 (Mo.App.1980). Cf. Hayes v. Plantations Steel Co., 438 A.2d 1091 (R.I.1982) (*Feinberg* distinguished; court found that promise of pension in no way induced employee to retire).

(2) *Contemporary Pension Plans.* It is common practice for employers to establish private pension plans for the benefit of their employees. Prior to the passage of The Employee Retirement Income Security Act of 1974 (ERISA), vesting provisions for many of these plans were often harsh and incapable of attainment. ERISA was enacted to improve and strengthen the protection for the majority of the participants of contemporary plans by providing statutory protection for participants in both private employee benefit plans and welfare benefit plans. ERISA's statutory protection and enforcement procedures in this area preempt state law which enforced vesting on theories of bargain contract or promissory estoppel. However, these theories still apply to unfunded plans and other types of plans exempt from ERISA coverage. For a discussion of ERISA's effect, see M. Canan, Qualified Retirement and Other Employer Benefit Plans (1990). See also, Schonholz v. Long Island Jewish Medical Center, 87 F.3d 72, 78 (2d Cir.1996)(promissory estoppel applies in ERISA cases under extraordinary circumstances).

(3) *Enforcing Gratuitous Promises in Tort, Agency and Bailment.* The problem of gratuitous promises or undertakings arises in several conceptual contexts; *viz.,* liability in tort, obligations of agents and bailees, the existence of contract and more. Some of them are unexpected. For example, in King v. Riveland, 125 Wash.2d 500, 886 P.2d 160, 168–169 (1994), prisoners convicted of sex offenses were induced, in part, to enter a state run sex offender treatment program by a promise that whatever was divulged in the program would be confidential. The prisoners sought an injunction against a threatened disclosure, which the court granted on a contract theory. Although there was no consideration, the promise did induce reliance and justice required its enforcement. The court relied upon Section 90.

In Abresch v. Northwestern Bell Telephone Co., 246 Minn. 408, 75 N.W.2d 206 (1956), the plaintiff sought damages he suffered when a building which he owned was destroyed by fire. Upon discovering the fire, he phoned the tele-phone operator, requesting her to call the fire department. The court noted that "while the telephone company is under no duty to assume responsibility of delivering messages in cases of emergency, if it does voluntarily assume such responsibility and thereby leads others to rely on such assumption of duty and to refrain from taking other and more direct action to protect themselves, the company is required to exercise reasonable care in performing the duty so assumed for a failure of which it may become liable in a tort action." 75 N.W.2d at 211–12. "It is ancient learning that one who assumes to act, even though gratuitously, may thereby become subject to the duty of acting carefully, if he acts at all." Glanzer v. Shepard, 233 N.Y. 236, 239, 135 N.E. 275, 276 (1922). See Restatement (Second) of Torts § 323.

Litigants have sought to enhance prospects of recovery by attempting to show that the defendant was or undertook to become an agent or bailee of the plaintiff. Certain obligations adhere to the principal-agent and bailor-bailee relationships by operation of law quite apart from the explicit agreement or understanding of the parties. See, for example, Lester v. Marshall, 143 Colo. 189, 352 P.2d 786 (1960), where a real estate broker engaged by the plaintiffs to find a home for them also gratuitously undertook to "take care of every-thing" prior to and after closing, assuring plaintiffs they would get title free of encumbrances. The court relied upon the revised Restatement of Agency, which in section 378 provides as follows: "One who, by a gratuitous promise or other conduct which he should realize will cause another reasonably to rely upon the performance of definite acts of service by him as the other's agent, causes the other to refrain from having such acts done by other available means is subject to a duty to use care to perform such service or, while other means are available, to give notice that he will not perform." Restatement of Agency (Second) § 378.

While still a relatively undeveloped area, there is some possibility of liability for malfeasance (the negligent performance of a promised act) as well as for misfeasance (the non-performance of a promised act). For it is recognized that the underlying basis of liability is the reasonable reliance, which clearly can follow a negligent performance of a promised act (as well as a failure to perform the promised act altogether). See Restatement (Second) of Torts § 323, comment d.

(4) *Promissory Estoppel in England.* No unitary principle of promissory estoppel has emerged in English and Commonwealth contract law. One rather suspects that the reliance interest has been (or could be) protected under the flexible definition of consideration as either a benefit to the promisor or a detriment to the promisee. The bargain rhetoric does not dominate discussions of consideration in English law. See G. Treitel, The Law of Contract, Chapter 3 (10th ed. 1999). For a more general argument about the relationship of consideration and freedom of contract in England, see Patrick S. Atiyah, The Rise and Fall of Freedom of Contracts (1979).

Grouse v. Group Health Plan, Inc.

Supreme Court of Minnesota, 1981.
306 N.W.2d 114.

■ OTIS, JUSTICE.

Plaintiff John Grouse appeals from a judgment in favor of Group Health Plan, Inc., in this action for damages resulting from repudiation of an employment offer. The narrow issue raised is whether the trial court erred by concluding that Grouse's complaint fails to state a claim upon which relief can be granted. In our view, the doctrine of promissory estoppel entitles Grouse to recover and we, therefore, reverse and remand for a new trial on the issue of damages.

The facts relevant to this appeal are essentially undisputed. Grouse, a 1974 graduate of the University of Minnesota School of Pharmacy, was employed in 1975 as a retail pharmacist at Richter Drug in Minneapolis. He worked approximately 41 hours per week earning $7 per hour. Grouse desired employment in a hospital or clinical setting, however, because of the work environment and the increased compensation and benefits. In the summer of 1975 he was advised by the Health Sciences Placement office at the University that Group Health was seeking a pharmacist.

Grouse called Group Health and was told to come in and fill out an application. He did so in September and was, at that time, interviewed by Cyrus Elliott, Group Health's Chief Pharmacist. Approximately 2 weeks later Elliott contacted Grouse and asked him to come in for an interview with Donald Shoberg, Group Health's General Manager. Shoberg explained company policies and procedures as well as salary and benefits. Following this meeting Grouse again spoke with Elliott who told him to be patient, that it was necessary to interview recent graduates before making an offer.

On December 4, 1975, Elliott telephoned Grouse at Richter Drug and offered him a position as a pharmacist at Group Health's St. Louis Park Clinic. Grouse accepted but informed Elliott that 2 week's notice to Richter Drug would be necessary. That afternoon Grouse received an offer from a Veteran's Administration Hospital in Virginia which he declined because of Group Health's offer. Elliott called back to confirm that Grouse had resigned.

Sometime in the next few days Elliott mentioned to Shoberg that he had hired, or was thinking of hiring, Grouse. Shoberg told him that company hiring requirements included a favorable written reference, a background check, and approval of the general manager. Elliott contacted two faculty members at the School of Pharmacy who declined to give references. He also contacted an internship employer and several pharmacies where Grouse had done relief work. Their responses were that they had not had enough exposure to Grouse's work to form a judgment as to his capabilities. Elliott did not contact Richter because Grouse's application requested that he not be contacted. Because Elliott was unable to supply a favorable reference for Grouse, Shoberg hired another person to fill the position.

On December 15, 1975 Grouse called Group Health and reported that he was free to begin work. Elliott informed Grouse that someone else had been hired. Grouse complained to the director of Group Health who apologized but took no other action. Grouse experienced difficulty regaining full time employment and suffered wage loss as a result. He commenced this suit to recover damages; the trial judge found that he had not stated an actionable claim.

In our view the principle of contract law applicable here is promissory estoppel. Its effect is to imply a contract in law where none exists in fact.... On these facts no contract exists because due to the bilateral power of termination neither party is committed to performance and the promises are, therefore, illusory. The elements of promissory estoppel are stated in *Restatement of Contracts* § 90 (1932):

> A promise which the promisor should reasonably expect to induce action or forbearance * * * on the part of the promisee and which does induce such action or forbearance is binding if injustice can be avoided only by enforcement of the promise.

Group Health knew that to accept its offer Grouse would have to resign his employment at Richter Drug. Grouse promptly gave notice to Richter Drug and informed Group Health that he had done so when specifically asked by Elliott. Under these circumstances it would be unjust not to hold Group Health to its promise.

The parties focus their arguments on whether an employment contract which is terminable at will can give rise to an action for damages if anticipatorily repudiated.... Group Health contends that recognition of a cause of action on these facts would result in the anomalous rule that an employee who is told not to report to work the day before he is scheduled to begin has a remedy while an employee who is discharged after the first day does not. We cannot agree since under appropriate circumstances we believe section 90 would apply even after employment has begun.

When a promise is enforced pursuant to section 90 "[t]he remedy granted for breach may be limited as justice requires." Relief may be limited to damages measured by the promisee's reliance.

The conclusion we reach does not imply that an employer will be liable whenever he discharges an employee whose term of employment is at will. What we do hold is that under the facts of this case the appellant had a right to assume he would be given a good faith opportunity to perform his duties to the satisfaction of respondent once he was on the job. He was not only denied that opportunity but resigned the position he already held in reliance on the firm offer which respondent tendered him. Since, as respondent points out, the prospective employment might have been terminated at any time, the measure of damages is not so much what he would have earned from respondent as what he lost in quitting the job he held and in declining at least one other offer of employment elsewhere.

Reversed and remanded for a new trial on the issue of damages.

NOTES

(1) In *Grouse,* the court observed that "no contract exists because due to the bilateral power of termination neither party is committed to performance and the promises are, therefore, illusory." Do you agree? Is *Grouse* an instance

of one being justified in relying upon an "illusory" promise? What promise did the court enforce? See, generally, Metzger and Phillips, *Promissory Estoppel and Reliance on Illusory Promises,* 44 Sw.L.J. 841 (1990). For a case in accord with *Grouse* in which liability also extended to a third person, the wife of the promisee, see Ravelo v. County of Hawaii, 66 Hawaii 194, 658 P.2d 883 (1983).

(2) How did the court measure damages in *Grouse?* Suppose Grouse had been permitted to work for a week and then terminated? Suppose Grouse worked for a year before termination? Is there any point at which the court should have measured damages by the value to Grouse of the promised employment?

(3) *The Case of the Disappointed Mortgagee.* Brad wanted to buy some land from Harold and build a new home. Harold was willing to sell 3 acres in his subdivision for $6,000. Company, in another state, was willing to sell Brad a prefabricated home for $40,000, to be delivered to the site and set up by Brad. Bank agreed to loan Brad $6,000 to pay Harold for the land and created a first mortgage in the property. Company was willing to sell the home to Brad for $3,000 down with a promise to pay the balance in installments but Company, knowing of Bank's involvement, wanted a second mortgage in the land. Company reasoned that the land with a home would be valuable and that even if Brad defaulted, the proceeds from any foreclosure sale would exceed the amount of Bank's loan. The second mortgage was executed, but before shipping the home to Brad Company obtained a written promise from Bank that if Brad was seriously in default to Bank, Bank would promptly notify Company. Company shipped the home, which Brad attempted to set up. Before the work was done, Brad was seriously in default to Bank. Bank, however, did not notify company. Rather, Bank sold Brad's note and the first mortgage to Harold for $5,500, the amount due under the loan. Harold then foreclosed the mortgage and, at the foreclosure sale, bid on the property and purchased it for $6,000. Harold then completed construction of the home for $10,000 and sold the lot and completed home to Frank for $30,000.

Company has been advised that it cannot upset the foreclosure sale to Frank (it had notice of the sale but did not attend) and accepts that advice. However, it wants to sue Bank for the failure to give notice of Brad's default. Is Bank's promise enforceable? If so, what damages should Company recover? See Miles Homes Division of Insilco Corp. v. First State Bank of Joplin, 782 S.W.2d 798 (Mo.App.1990).

(4) *The Case of Friendly Ford's Loaner Vehicle.* Richard Keller purchased a new Taurus station wagon from Friendly Ford, Inc. which he returned to the dealer and for which he sought a refund "because obviously it was a lemon." Thereafter, he needed a car to drive his daughter to college in another state, and Friendly Ford's sales manager assured him on the phone that he could "have a loaner vehicle" for the journey. But when he came to pick up the "loaner," the company president refused to supply the car. At that point Keller said he had no choice but to drive the Taurus "and hope and pray it didn't break down on the trip." But break down it did, causing Keller considerable inconvenience and expense (e.g., rental of a van to complete the trip). Keller's efforts to recover for these expenses were unsuccessful. Keller v. Friendly Ford, Inc., 782 S.W.2d 170 (Mo.App.1990). The court said that while Keller might recover for the expense in driving to the dealership to pick up the car, in going

ahead in the Taurus he was not acting in reliance on the promise of a free automobile. The court noted: "Had plaintiff, a week before the journey, been told by defendant's employees that no free automobile would be supplied, and had plaintiff, faced with that knowledge, commenced the journey in the Taurus instead of renting a more dependable vehicle or utilizing public transportation, it is manifest plaintiff could not have recovered from defendant the cost of the rental vehicles plaintiff was obliged to use * * * unless, of course, there was some clause in the warranty on the Taurus or some independent contractual obligation imposing such liability on defendant. No such showing was made at the trial * * *." 782 S.W.2d at 174.

(5) *Promissory Estoppel and Entertainment Contracts: The Ohio Players and "Funky Worm"; Aretha Franklin and "Mahalia."* After The Ohio Players struck it big with their hit record "Funky Worm," they sought to back out of the recording agreement they had with Westbound Records, Inc. alleging a lack of consideration. They maintained that although they were bound to record exclusively for Westbound, the latter was not, by the express terms of the agreement, obliged to make any records using the group. But the Appellate Court of Illinois found consideration in a $4,000 advance against royalties and prescinded from any inquiry into adequacy. Bonner v. Westbound Records, Inc., 76 Ill.App.3d 736, 31 Ill.Dec. 926, 394 N.E.2d 1303 (1979). Moreover, the court met an objection based on lack of mutuality of obligation by implying an obligation by Westbound to act in good faith, and, following *Wood v. Lucy, Lady Duff–Gordon,* supra at 100, a duty to use its best efforts. Finally, the court found that liability could be predicated upon promissory estoppel "as a substitute for consideration." In reliance upon the recording agreement, Westbound undertook a substantial business risk, incurring more than $80,000 in expenses which it could recoup only if the recordings were successful. The court explained: "The Ohio Players now seek to deny Westbound the sole reward of its success. Their aim is to keep for themselves the fame and money which, judging by their past experience, they could not have acquired without Westbound's aid, by asserting that Westbound did not originally promise to do what it has already actually done. This the plaintiffs are estopped to do; even if the agreements were not originally supported by consideration, they became enforceable when Westbound performed in reliance on the promises of The Ohio Players, and indeed advanced additional monies not called for by the contract, to protect its investment." 394 N.E.2d at 1312.

A musical producer sought to produce a Broadway musical based on the life of Mahalia Jackson and wanted Aretha Franklin for the title role. The latter was very receptive. They negotiated over a period of several months, working out many details (including a handsome compensation package). The parties circulated drafts of a proposed agreement, but never executed a final draft. Meanwhile, the producer, on the basis of Franklin's assurance, went ahead with making arrangements, incurring substantial expense. After negotiations broke down, the producer sued. The court found that the parties were not to be bound contractually until the draft agreement was signed, but proceeded to base recovery on promissory estoppel. Elvin Associates v. Franklin, 735 F.Supp. 1177 (S.D.N.Y.1990). The court stated: "It is difficult to imagine a more fitting case for applying [promissory estoppel]. Although for her own business purposes Franklin insisted that the formal contract be with the corporate entity through which her services were to be 'furnished,' in the real world the agreement was with her, and we find that she had unequivocally and intentionally committed herself to appear in the production long before the day on which it was intended that the finished agreement with her corporation would be signed. * * * [U]nder the circumstances * * * it would be unconscionable not to compensate [plaintiff] for the losses he incurred through his entirely justified reliance on Franklin's oral promises." 735 F.Supp. at 1182–1183.

(6) *Promissory estoppel and corporate relocation.* In recent years, corporations who decided to close or move business operations have been sued by employees, a union or a local government unit on a promissory estoppel theory. The claim was that the plaintiff had relied upon a corporate promise to remain or to stay open and that injustice could be prevented only by giving an appropriate remedy, whether damages or an injunction. These claims have all foundered because a clear and definite promise by the corporation could not be proved. See, e.g., Abbington v. Dayton Malleable, Inc., 738 F.2d 438 (6th Cir.1984); Local 1330, United Steel Workers v. United States Steel Corp., 631 F.2d 1264 (6th Cir.1980); Marine Transport Lines, Inc. v. International Organization of Masters, Mates & Pilots, 636 F.Supp. 384 (S.D.N.Y.1986). See also, Charter Twp. of Ypsilanti v. General Motors Corp., 201 Mich.App. 128, 506 N.W.2d 556 (1993), appeal denied, 443 Mich. 882, 509 N.W.2d 152 (1993). The assumption in these cases is, however, that if the requisite promise and reliance were established, the court would inquire into the "injustice" question. Should a court do this? See the next case.

Cohen v. Cowles Media Co.

Supreme Court of Minnesota, 1992.
479 N.W.2d 387.

■ SIMONETT, JUSTICE. This case comes to us on remand from the United States Supreme Court. We previously held that plaintiff's verdict of $200,000 could not be sustained on a theory of breach of contract. On remand, we now conclude the verdict is sustainable on the theory of promissory estoppel and affirm the jury's award of damages.

The facts are set out in *Cohen v. Cowles Media Co.*, 457 N.W.2d 199, 200–02 (Minn.1990),* and will be only briefly restated here. On October 28, 1982, the Minneapolis Star and Tribune (now the Star Tribune) and the St. Paul Pioneer Press each published a story on the gubernatorial election campaign, reporting that Marlene Johnson, the DFL nominee for lieutenant governor, had been charged in 1969 for three counts of unlawful assembly and in 1970 had been convicted of shoplifting. Both newspapers revealed that Dan Cohen had supplied this information to them. The Star Tribune identified Cohen as a political associate of the Independent–Republican gubernatorial candidate and named the advertising firm where Cohen was employed.

Cohen then commenced this lawsuit against defendants Cowles Media Company, publisher of the Minneapolis Star Tribune, and Northwest Publications, Inc., publisher of the St. Paul Pioneer Press Dispatch. It was

_____

* Reprinted infra at 241 [Ed].

undisputed that Cohen had given the information about Marlene Johnson's arrests and conviction to a reporter for each of the newspapers in return for the reporters' promises that Cohen's identity be kept confidential. The newspapers' editors overruled these promises. The disparaging information about the candidate leaked in the closing days of the election campaign was such, decided the editors, that the identity of the source of the information was as important, as newsworthy, as the information itself. Put another way, the real news story was one of political intrigue, and the information about the particular candidate was only a part, an incomplete part, of that story. Moreover, not to reveal the source, felt the editors, would be misleading, as it would cast suspicion on others; and, in any event, it was likely only a matter or time before competing news media would uncover Cohen's identity. Finally, the Star Tribune had endorsed the Perpich–Johnson ticket in its opinion section, and thus to withhold Cohen's identity might be construed as an effort by the newspaper to protect its favored candidates. On the same day as the newspaper stories were published, Cohen was fired.

The case was submitted to the jury on theories of breach of contract and fraudulent misrepresentation. The jury found liability on both theories and awarded $200,000 compensatory damages against the two defendants, jointly and severally. The jury also awarded $250,000 punitive damages against each newspaper on the misrepresentation claim. The court of appeals set aside recovery on the basis of fraudulent misrepresentation (and with it the punitive damages award), but affirmed recovery of the compensatory damages on the basis of a breach of contract. *Cohen v. Cowles Media Co.*, 445 N.W.2d 248, 262 (Minn.App.1989).

We affirmed denial of recovery for fraudulent misrepresentation but also held that there could be no recovery for breach of contract. While the newspapers may have had a moral and ethical commitment to keep their source anonymous, we said this was not a situation where the parties were thinking in terms of a legally binding contract. Cohen I, 457 N.W.2d at 203. "To impose a contract theory on this arrangement," we said, "puts an unwarranted legal rigidity on a special ethical relationship, precluding necessary consideration of factors underlying that ethical relationship." Id. * * * We observed that when applying a contract analysis in this context "the focus was more on whether a binding promise was intended and breached, not so much on the contents of that promise or the nature of the information exchanged for the promise." Id. at 204. We concluded that a contract theory, which looks only to whether there was a promise and an acceptance, does not fit a situation where the essential concern is with the intrinsic nature of the overall transaction.

We went on in *Cohen I* to consider enforcement of a confidentiality promise under the doctrine of promissory estoppel. Under this theory, the court would consider all aspects of the transaction's substance in determining whether enforcement was necessary to prevent an injustice. We found this approach, which differed from the neutral approach of the classic contract analysis, best fit the kind of confidential commitments that news media in newsgathering made. There was, however, a problem. To shed the neutrality of a contract analysis for an inquiry into the editorial process of deciding whether the identity of the news source was needed for a proper reporting of a news story constituted, we concluded, an impermissible intrusion into the newspaper's First Amendment free press rights. Consequently, we held plaintiff Cohen's verdict was not sustainable. 457 N.W.2d at 205.

The United States Supreme Court granted certiorari and held that the doctrine of promissory estoppel does not implicate the First Amendment. The doctrine is one of general application, said the Court, and its employment to enforce confidentiality promises has only "incidental effects" on news gathering and reporting, so that the First Amendment is not offended. *Cohen v. Cowles Media Co.*, 501 U.S. 663, 111 S.Ct. 2513, 2518–19, 115 L.Ed.2d 586 (1991). The Court refused to reinstate the jury verdict for $200,000 in compensatory damages, stating this was a matter for our consideration, and remanded the case.

On remand, we must address four issues: (1) Does Cohen's failure to plead promissory estoppel bar him from pursuing that theory now; (2) does our state constitutional guarantee of a free press bar use of promissory estoppel to enforce promises of confidentiality; (3) does public policy bar Cohen from enforcing the newspapers' promises of confidentiality; and (4) if Cohen may proceed under promissory estoppel, should the case be remanded for retrial or should the jury's award of compensatory damages be reinstated?

* * *

What we have here is a novel legal issue of first impression where this court has adopted an approach closely akin to the theory on which the case was originally pled and tried; under these unique circumstances we conclude it is not unfair to the defendants to allow the case to be decided under principles of promissory estoppel.

* * *

III

What, then, should be the appropriate disposition of this case? We conclude a retrial is unnecessary.

Under promissory estoppel, a promise which is expected to induce definite action by the promisee, and does induce the action, is binding if injustice can be avoided only by enforcing the promise. *Cohen I*, 457 N.W.2d at 204; Restatement (Second) of Contracts § 90(1) (1981). First of all, the promise must be clear and definite. As a matter of law, such a promise was given here. *Cohen I*, 457 N.W.2d at 204 ("[W]e have, without dispute, the reporters' unambiguous promise to treat Cohen as an anonymous source."). Secondly, the promisor must have intended to induce reliance on the part of the promisee, and such reliance must have occurred to the promisee's detriment. Here again, these facts appear as a matter of law. In reliance on the promise of anonymity, Cohen turned over the court records and, when the promises to keep his name confidential were broken, he lost his job. *Id.*

This leads to the third step in a promissory estoppel analysis: Must the promise be enforced to prevent an injustice? As the Wisconsin Supreme Court has held, this is a legal question for the court, as it involves a policy decision. *Hoffman v. Red Owl Stores, Inc.,* 26 Wis.2d 683, 698 (1965); *see also ... Grouse v. Group Health Plan, Inc.,* 306 N.W.2d 114, 116 (Minn. 1981) (this court on appeal found all three elements of promissory estoppel were present).

It is perhaps worth noting that the test is not whether the promise should be enforced to do justice, but whether enforcement is required to prevent an injustice. As has been observed elsewhere, it is easier to recognize an unjust result than a just one, particularly in a morally ambiguous situation. Cf. Edmond Cahn, *The Sense of Injustice* (1964). The newspapers argue it is unjust to be penalized for publishing the whole truth, but it is not clear this would result in an injustice in this case. For example, it would seem veiling Cohen's identity by publishing the source as someone close to the opposing gubernatorial ticket would have sufficed as a sufficient reporting of the "whole truth."

Cohen, on the other hand, argues that it would be unjust for the law to countenance, at least in this instance, the breaking of a promise. We agree that denying Cohen any recourse would be unjust. What is significant in this case is that the record shows the defendant newspapers themselves believed that they generally must keep promises of confidentiality given a news source. The reporters who actually gave the promises adamantly testified that their promises should have been honored. The editors who countermanded the promises conceded that never before or since have they reneged on a promise of confidentiality. A former Minneapolis Star managing editor testified that the newspapers had "hung Mr. Cohen out to dry because they didn't regard him very highly as a source." The Pioneer Press Dispatch editor stated nothing like this had happened in her 27 years in journalism. The Star Tribune's editor testified that protection of sources was "extremely important." Other experts, too, stressed the ethical importance, except on rare occasions, of keeping promises of confidentiality. It was this long-standing journalistic tradition that Cohen, who has worked in journalism, relied upon in asking for and receiving a promise of anonymity.

Neither side in this case clearly holds the higher moral ground, but in view of the defendants' concurrence in the importance of honoring promises of confidentiality, and absent the showing of any compelling need in this case to break that promise, we conclude that the resultant harm to Cohen requires a remedy here to avoid an injustice. In short, defendants are liable in damages to plaintiff for their broken promise.

This leaves, then, the issue of damages. For promissory estoppel, "[t]he remedy granted for breach may be limited as justice requires." Restatement (Second) of Contracts § 90(1)(1981). *See generally Midamar Corp. v. National–Ben Franklin Ins. Co.,* 898 F.2d 1333, 1338–39 (8th Cir.1990);

Hoffman v. Red Owl Stores, Inc., 26 Wis.2d at 701 In this case the jury was instructed:

> A party is entitled to recover for a breach of contract only those damages which: (a) arise directly and naturally in the usual course of things from the breach itself; or (b) are the consequences of special circumstances known to or reasonably supposed to have been contemplated by the parties when the contract was made.

This instruction, we think, provided an appropriate damages remedy for the defendants' broken promise, whether considered under a breach of contract or a promissory estoppel theory. There was evidence to support the jury's award of $200,000, and we see no reason to remand this case for a new trial on damages alone.

Our prior reversal of the verdict having been vacated, we now affirm the court of appeals' decision, but on promissory estoppel grounds. We affirm, therefore, plaintiff's verdict and judgment for $200,000 compensatory damages.

Affirmed on remand on different grounds.

NOTES

(1) If Cohen bargained for a promise of confidentiality, if the information was published in exchange for delivering the documents, and Cowles bargained for the documents in exchange for the promise, why wasn't there consideration? Is it possible to have a bargained for exchange of a promise for a performance that is not enforceable as a contract? If so (and the promise is important), why? What can the parties do to signal that they intend to assume legal obligations?

(2) Upon remand from the Supreme Court, the court reaffirms its decision on the consideration issue and then enforces the oral promise of confidentiality on a "promissory estoppel" theory. If the parties did not intend to assume legal obligations, how can Cowles be liable for induced reliance? Does Section 90, which the court purports to apply, depend upon the intention of the parties? If not, how would you characterize the theory? Does the court's approach deviate from Section 90?

(3) *Can A Newspaper Contract Around New York Times v. Sullivan?* In Cohen, the court found that parties did not intend their promises to be legally enforceable. But imagine a newspaper, the *Servanda*, that on the front page of each issue (i) expressly promises to compensate any individual that it mentions who is injured by the newspaper's negligent misrepresentation and (ii) expressly represents that it intends this promise to be legally enforceable. Like the Carbolic Smoke Ball Co., *infra* at 296, *Servanda* believes that it can sell more newspapers if it warrants the quality of its product. Putting aside consideration problems, would it be constitutional to enforce the contract? Is New York Times v. Sullivan, 376 U.S. 254, 84 S.Ct. 710, 11 L.Ed.2d 686 (1964) (requiring actual malice for libel liability), merely a default rule? If so, could the legislature flip the default and require newspapers who didn't want to stand behind

the truthfulness of their statements to opt out of liability by including a short disclaimer somewhere in the publication?

(4) *Impact of Cowles*. In an interesting empirical study, conducted after *Cowles* through extensive interviews with newspaper publishers and others, Daniel Levin and Ellen Rupert concluded that the damage award had not had any substantial effect on confidentiality policy. Of those publishers who had policies on confidentiality (e.g., the authority of reporters to promise confidentiality without prior permission or the power of publishers to override earlier promises), one-third were aware of the *Cowles* decision and roughly 50% of those had reviewed their policies within the last five years. Only one publisher had made changes in light of *Cowles* and there was no evidence of a trend toward greater supervision of reporters. In fact, around 70% of the group which was aware accepted the *Cowles* result as "fair and not a particularly serious infringement on editor's rights." Levin & Blumberg, *Promises of Confidentiality to News Sources after Cohen v. Cowles Media Company: A Survey of Newspaper Editors,* 24 Golden Gate U.L.Rev. 423, 460–461 (1994).

(5) *Recent Scholarly Opinion*. A slew of empirical studies have disputed (i) the extent and importance of promissory estoppel, and (ii) whether courts actually in the name of promissory estoppel are willing to find liability in the absence of actual detrimental reliance. A recent article summarizing and adding to the debate is Juliet P. Kostritsky, *The Rise and Fall of Promissory Estoppel or Is Promissory Estoppel Really as Unsuccessful As Scholars Say it Is: A New Look at the Data,* 37 Wake Forest L. Rev. 531 (2002) (finding some life in the old doctrine after all). For a magnificent overview, see Charles L. Knapp, *Rescuing Reliance: The Perils of Promissory Estoppel,* 49 Hastings L.J. 1191 (1998).

All–Tech Telecom, Inc. v. Amway Corporation

United States Court of Appeals, Seventh Circuit, 1999.
174 F.3d 862.

■ POSNER, CHIEF JUDGE.

A disappointed plaintiff, All–Tech Telecom, appeals from the district court's grant of summary judgment to the defendant, Amway, on All–Tech's claims of intentional and negligent misrepresentation and promissory estoppel. All–Tech was allowed to get to the jury on claims of breach of warranty, and the jury found a breach but awarded no damages. There is no challenge to the jury's verdict, only to the grant of summary judgment on the other claims. The basis of federal jurisdiction is diversity of citizenship, and the parties agree that the substantive issues are governed by Wisconsin law. * * *

[The court's detailed statement of the facts is omitted.]

The district court threw out All–Tech's claims of misrepresentation on the basis of the "economic loss" doctrine of the common law. Originally this doctrine was merely a limitation on who could bring a tort suit for the consequences of a personal injury or damage to property: only the injured person himself, or the owner of the damaged property himself, and not also persons having commercial links to the owner, such as employees or suppliers of a merchant whose store was burned down as a result of the negligence of a third party, the tort defendant.... Since damage to property and even to person is a real cost and hence "economic," the doctrine would be better named the "commercial loss" doctrine....

One explanation for it is that a tort may have indirect consequences that are beneficial—in the example just given, to competitors of the burned-down store—as well as harmful, and since the tortfeasor is not entitled to sue for the benefits, neither should he have to pay for the losses.... Another and less esoteric explanation is the desirability of confining remedies for contract-type losses to contract law. Suppliers injured in their pocketbook because of a fire at the shop of a retailer who buys and distributes their goods sustain the kind of purely business loss familiarly encountered in contract law, rather than the physical harm, whether to person or to property, with which tort law is centrally concerned. These suppliers can protect themselves from the loss caused them by the fire by buying business-loss insurance, by charging a higher price, or by including in their contract with the retailer a requirement that he buy a minimum quantity of goods from the supplier, regardless. The suppliers thus don't need a tort remedy....

This point has implications for commercial fraud as well as for business losses that are secondary to physical harms to person or property. Where there are well-developed contractual remedies, such as the remedies that the Uniform Commercial Code (in force in all U.S. states) provides for breach of warranty of the quality, fitness, or specifications of goods, there is no need to provide tort remedies for misrepresentation. The tort remedies would duplicate the contract remedies, adding unnecessary complexity to the law. Worse, the provision of these duplicative tort remedies would undermine contract law. That law has been shaped by a tension between a policy of making the jury the normal body for resolving factual disputes and the desire of parties to contracts to be able to rely on the written word and not be exposed to the unpredictable reactions of lay factfinders to witnesses who testify that the contract means something different from what it says. Many doctrines of contract law, such as the parol evidence and "four corners" rules, are designed to limit the scope of jury trial of contract disputes (another example is the statute of frauds). Tort law does not have these screens against the vagaries of the jury. In recognition of this omission, the "economic loss" doctrine in the form invoked by the district judge in this case on the authority of a growing body of case law forbids commercial contracting parties (as distinct from consumers, and other individuals not engaged in business) to escalate their contract dispute into a charge of tortious misrepresentation if they could easily have protected themselves from the misrepresentation of which they now complain. * * *

The function of the economic-loss doctrine in confining contract parties to their contractual remedies is particularly well illustrated by cases involving product warranties,.... If the seller makes an oral representation that is important to the buyer, the latter has only to insist that the seller embody that representation in a written warranty. The warranty will protect the buyer, who will have an adequate remedy under the Uniform Commercial Code if the seller reneges. To allow him to use tort law in effect to enforce an oral warranty would unsettle contracts by exposing sellers to the risk of being held liable by a jury on the basis of self-interested oral testimony and perhaps made to pay punitive as well as compensatory damages. This menace is averted by channeling disputes into warranty (contract) law, where oral warranties can be expressly disclaimed, or extinguished by operation of the parol evidence rule. UCC §§ 2–202, 2–316(1) and comment 2; 1 James J. White & Robert S. Summers, *Uniform Commercial Code*, § 12–4 (3d ed. 1988). It is true that, in principle, the cheapest way to prevent fraud is to punish the fraudfeasor; but in practice, owing to the ever-present possibility of legal error, the really cheapest way in some cases may be to place a burden of taking precautions on the potential victim. Cf. Alon Harel, "Efficiency and Fairness in Criminal Law: The Case for a Criminal Law Principle of Comparative Fault," 82 *Calif. L. Rev.* 1181 (1994).

* * *

[The court discussed and doubted whether the economic loss doctrine abolished the tort of fraudulent or deliberate misrepresentation.]

But the representations challenged in this case do not press against the boundaries of the economic-loss doctrine. For they are in the nature of warranties (remember that the plaintiff made warranty claims, which the judge sent to the jury), and we cannot think of a reason why the fact that the "product" warranted was a hybrid of a product and a service should affect the application of the doctrine. A genuine stumbling block to affirming on its basis, however, is the fact that its application to cases of *intentional* misrepresentation is uncertain.

* * *

[The court found that All–Tech had failed to present any evidence of actionable misrepresentation. Moreover, some of the alleged misrepresentations were made by independent contractors, not Amway, and others were "pure puffing" on which no reasonable person would rely. There were, in short, no actionable misrepresentations.]

All–Tech's alternative claim is promissory estoppel. The doctrine of promissory estoppel provides an alternative basis to consideration for treating a promise as a contractual undertaking. When applicable, which to say when the promise is definite enough to induce a reasonable person to rely, ... the doctrine makes the promise enforceable.

Promises are usually forward-looking; one promises to do something, necessarily in the future. The promise that All–Tech stresses as the basis for its claim of promissory estoppel—that Amway had thoroughly researched the TeleCharge program before offering it to distributors—is not of that character. It warrants a past or existing condition rather than committing to some future action and is thus more precisely described as a warranty than as a promise. UCC § 2–313(1)(a); *Restatement (Second) of Contracts* § 2 comment d (1981); ... But a warranty is a type of promise—in this case a promise by Amway to pay for the consequences should the research that went into the development of TeleCharge not have been thorough after all. *Metropolitan Coal Co. v. Howard*, 155 F.2d 780, 784 (2d Cir.1946) (L. Hand, J.) (a warranty "amounts to a promise to indemnify the promisee for any loss if the fact warranted proves untrue, for obviously the promisor cannot control what is already in the past"); *Restatement of Contracts* § 2 (1932); cf. Oliver Wendell Holmes, Jr., *The Common Law* 298–301 (1881).

Since a warranty can induce reasonable reliance, its breach can be the basis for a claim of promissory estoppel. But only in limited circumstances. A promisee cannot be permitted to use the doctrine to do an end run around the rule that puffing is not actionable as misrepresentation, or around the parol evidence rule.... That rule is as applicable to a suit on an oral warranty as to a suit on any other oral promise. The Uniform Commercial Code is explicit about this. UCC § 2–316(1) and comment 2; ...

The objections to All–Tech's claim of promissory estoppel are related to our earlier point that the economic-loss doctrine serves to protect contract doctrines and to prevent the piling on of duplicative remedies. Promissory estoppel is meant for cases in which a promise, not being supported by consideration, would be unenforceable under conventional principles of contract law. When there is an express contract governing the relationship out of which the promise emerged, and no issue of consideration, there is no gap in the remedial system for promissory estoppel to fill.... To allow it to be invoked becomes in those circumstances gratuitous duplication or, worse, circumvention of carefully designed rules of contract law. In our case the parties had a contract covering the relationship in the course and within the scope of which the alleged warranty of thorough research was made. This either was one of the warranties of the contract or it was not (by virtue of disclaimer, the puffing exemption, or the parol evidence rule). If it was not (and it was not), we cannot think of any reason for using the doctrine of promissory estoppel to resuscitate it. "Promissory estoppel is not a doctrine designed to give a party ... a second bite at the apple in the event it fails to prove a breach of contract." *Walker v. KFC Corp.*, 728 F.2d 1215, 1220 (9th Cir.1984). * * *

NOTES

(1) Under UCC 2–313(1), express warranties include promises and affirmations made by the seller to the buyer about the goods which become "part of the basis of the bargain." There is no explicit requirement that the buyer rely on the promise or affirmation, but the alleged express warranty will not become part of the bargain if the seller proves that the buyer, in fact, did not rely.

(2) There are at least three consequences that flow from Judge Posner's analysis.

First, despite the tort-like rhetoric in *Cohen v. Cowles Media Co., supra,* an action on a promissory estoppel theory must be in contract rather than in tort where the induced reliance results only in economic loss. Thus, even though the promisor promised intending to induce reliance and even though there is no consent by the promisee, the law of torts does not apply.

Second, there is no place for promissory estoppel where the claimed actionable reliance was in fact bargained for by the promisor. Thus, in *Cohen v. Cowles Media,* if the agreed exchange of Cohen's disclosure for Cowles's promise of confidentiality created a legal obligation, the presence of consideration would foreclose the use of promissory estoppel. As we shall see, however, there may be promises made within the bargain that induce unbargained-for reliance. A claim in promissory estoppel is proper in these cases. See *infra* at Chapter Four, Section 2.

Third, a party who makes a representation (warranty) that becomes part of a bargain also (according to the court) promises to pay damages if the warranty is not satisfied. For this proposition, Judge Posner relies on language from an opinion by Judge Learned Hand and cites the famous book by Oliver Wendell Holmes, Jr., The Common Law. Put differently, the performer has a choice to satisfy the warranty or to pay damages. But note that this is not a genuine case of promised alternative performances. Arguably, the so-called promise to pay damages on breach is fictional and reflects the view that it is efficient and not immoral to breach a contract and pay damages. Support for this oft criticized view is found (by some at least) in Holmes's "bad man" theory of law. See Robert Henry, *The Values of Oliver Wendell Holmes,* 5 Green Bag 105 (2001).

Comment: Promissory Estoppel and the Choice of Remedies

From one point of view, distinctly Willistonian, the full range of contract remedies should be available to enforce promises which are contracts, whether the reason for enforcement is consideration or reliance. A contract is a contract is a contract. Thus, Grandfather's promise to pay Katie Scothorn $2,000, the employer's promise to pay retirement benefits and the donor's promise to make a charitable subscription should be performed in full even though the promisee's detriment was induced rather than bargained for and, if quantified and valued, would be worth less than the value of the promised performance. Section 90 of the first Restatement was silent on this point, stating only that a promise which induces foreseeable reliance "of a definite and substantial character * * * is binding if injustice can be avoided only by enforcement of the promise." However, the total structure of the Restatement, with its definition of contract as "a promise * * * for the breach of which the law gives a remedy," (§ 1), and its expectation oriented approach to remedies (§§ 326–384), along with the comments of its Reporter, Professor Williston, see 4 A.L.I. Proceedings 97–106 (1926), support the conclusion that expectation damages were intended to be the rule rather than the exception. See G. Gilmore, The Death of Contract 59–65 (1974).

From another and less doctrinal point of view, recovery could be limited to the amount of Plaintiff's reliance, whether this be measured in terms of "out of pocket" expenditures, foregone opportunities or both. In its historical setting, the doctrine of estoppel was defensive in that the representor was estopped to deny the accuracy of what had been stated. When the representation was by promise, *Ricketts v. Scothorn,* supra at 130, concluded that the promisor was estopped to deny the absence of consideration, and Wheeler v. White, 398 S.W.2d 93 (Tex.1965), concluded that "promissory estoppel acts defensively so as to prevent an attack upon the enforceability of a contract." The *Wheeler* court stated: "Under this theory, losses of expected profits will not be allowed even if expected profits are provable with certainty." According to Professor (now Judge) Posner, the historical limitations are consistent with the theory of economic efficiency in contract law. For example, Posner asserts that it "obscures analysis to equate reliance with consideration in circumstances where no exchange is contemplated" and suggests that a "better approach would be to treat the breach of promise likely to induce reliance as a form of actionable negligence under tort law." R. Posner, Economic Analysis of Law 70 (2d ed. 1977). The few cases on this point accord with *Wheeler v. White* even though the transaction in which the promise was made contemplated the exchange of resources. See, e.g., Hoffman v. Red Owl Stores, Inc., infra at 468.

Recognizing this other point of view, Restatement (Second) § 90 eliminates the first Restatement requirement that the reliance be "definite and substantial" and provides that the "remedy granted for breach may be limited as justice requires." Thus, the promise "is binding if injustice can be avoided only by enforcement" and the remedy may be limited "as justice requires." The assumption is that one starts from a position of full-scale enforcement, but that the "same factors which bear on whether any relief should be granted also bear on the extent and character of the remedy." This recovery might "sometimes be limited to restitution or to damages or specific relief measured by the extent of the promisee's reliance rather than by the terms of the promise." Comment d. See 1A Corbin § 205. Factors which should be relevant in the decision include policies implicit in the transaction type, (i.e., charitable subscriptions, retirement promises, family relations), the reason for the non-performance, (financial reverses might suggest a lesser while dishonest conduct might support a greater remedy), the degree of disproportion associated with enforcement of the promise, (e.g., the promise to obtain insurance), and any historical patterns of enforcement associated with the transaction type, (e.g., the bailment).

Nevertheless, Professor Melvin Eisenberg, among others, has argued that if the reason for enforcing the promise is reliance rather than bargain, then the scope of remedial protection should be limited by the reliance interest. As he put it, it is a "nice question how much difference there is between a rule that donative promises are unenforceable unless reasonably relied upon, and a rule that donative promises are enforceable but only to the extent reasonably relied upon." Eisenberg, *Donative Promises,* 47 U.Chi.L.Rev. 1, 33 (1979). This argument is part of a broader assertion that the primary reason for protecting the expectation interest in bargain contracts is to insure that "hidden" reliance, frequently in the form of hard to measure and prove opportunity costs, is fully compensated. In short, protecting the expectation interest is a surrogate for protecting reliance in the bargain contract. Thus, in a non-bargain contract, the assumption should be that the court will protect the reliance interest, with expectation damages awarded only when necessary to insure that "hidden" reliance is fully compensated. See Eisenberg, *The Bargain Principle and its Limits,* 95 Harv.L.Rev. 741, 785–98 (1982); *The Principles of Consideration,* 67 Cornell L.Rev. 640, 656–59 (1982).

A decision supporting Professor Eisenberg's thesis is Walters v. Marathon Oil Co., 642 F.2d 1098 (7th Cir.1981). Relying on defendant's promise to supply gasoline and "continuing negotiations," plaintiff purchased and made improvements on a vacant service station site. After the negotiations were completed, however, defendant refused to sign the dealership agreement because of a newly announced moratorium on dealerships. The trial court found for plaintiff on the theory of promissory estoppel and awarded damages based upon the profits that plaintiff would have made on the sale of gasoline during the first year under the promised dealership. On appeal, defendant argued that plaintiff's damages should be measured by its reliance on the promise, namely, the investment in and improvements on the service station. As such, defendant claimed, there should be no recovery because the fair market value of the improved service station exceeded plaintiff's out-of-pocket expenditure. The court of appeals, however, affirmed the trial court. The court noted that the plaintiff had suffered "a loss of profits as a direct result of their reliance ... and the amount of the lost profits was ascertained with reasonable certainty." Moreover, "in reliance upon appellant's promise, they had foregone the opportunity to make the investment elsewhere." Characterizing promissory estoppel as "an equitable matter," the court concluded that the award of lost profits was necessary to "secure complete justice." As the court put it: "An equity court possesses some discretionary power to award damages in order to do complete justice. ... Furthermore, since it is the historic purpose of equity to secure complete justice, the courts are able to adjust the remedies so as to grant the necessary relief, ... and a district court sitting in equity may even devise a remedy which extends or exceeds the terms of a prior agreement between the parties, if it is necessary to make the injured party whole." 642 F.2d at 1000. But see Walser v. Toyota Motor Sales, U.S.A., Inc., 43 F.3d 396, 400–402 (8th Cir.1994) (damages for breach of promise to grant dealership properly limited to out of pocket expenditures).

Assuming that damage should be measured by the reliance interest, the proper measure is still a matter of some debate. See, for example, Cyberchron Corp. v. Calldata Systems Development, Inc., 47 F.3d 39 (2d Cir.1995)(plaintiff recovers expenditures incurred in part performance of proposed but never finalized contract plus "shut down" costs and overhead). See generally, Kevin M. Teeven, *The Advent of Recovery on Market Transactions in the Absence of a Bargain,* 39 Am. Bus. L.J. 289 (2002).

PROBLEM: THE CASE OF THE INDEPENDENT CAB DRIVER

During a lull in the proceedings of a Legion convention a few of the participants made their way to a nearby bar for refreshments and conversation.

One of the men, Marty Lawless, began bemoaning the lot of a cab driver. Since his discharge from the Army, Marty had been driving a cab in a metropolitan area for a large company. "If I could only lay my hands on twenty thousand bucks," he remarked, "I could really make out. I could get a cab and license of my own and start working for myself, instead of the other guy."

In the group was Jim Craven, who had attended law school after his discharge and had built up a lucrative personal injury practice. After questioning Marty a bit more regarding what the latter could do with a cab of his own, Jim said to him: "I'll loan you the money. Pay it back when you want, up to ten years. And it won't cost you a thing. I owe you a lot more than that, heaven knows." (This last remark referred to the fact that Jim credits Marty with saving his life in battle.)

But Marty was hesitant. He didn't want any "charity." He answered: "I appreciate your offer, Jim. I really do. But I couldn't take it. I think a bank will loan me the money."

"Aw, Lawless, you're crazy to pass up a deal like that," said John Coburn, another member of the group.

Jim spoke up: "Now hold on. It's not charity, if that's what you're thinking. We'll make it carry one percent interest. How's that?"

This was too good to pass up, thought Marty. And, after all, Craven could afford it. So he replied: "Thanks a lot, Jim. It will sure give me a boost. And don't worry, you'll be repaid."

Jim then raised a glass and said to everyone present: "All right, everybody. Let's drink to the world's newest independent cab driver!" Everyone complied.

Upon returning home, one of Marty's first stops was to the office of his employer, where he resigned his job.

But a few days later he received a letter from Craven in which he said he had a "big deal" come up and didn't have the money to loan now. He expressed his regrets and said he hoped they "can get together real soon."

Lawless has hastened to your office and now awaits your advice. Advise him.

SECTION 4.   FORMAL REQUIREMENTS: THE STATUTE OF FRAUDS

Earlier (supra, Chapter Two, Section 1) we considered whether a formal writing could be *sufficient* for legal enforcement of a promise (as a substitute for consideration). Here we consider under what conditions a formal writing is *necessary* for legal enforcement of a promise (in addition to the consideration requirement).

(A) GENERAL SCOPE AND EFFECT

Historical origins. Samuel Goldwyn reportedly said that an oral contract is not worth the paper it is written on. One can hardly gainsay the desirability of reducing a contract to writing, but such has never been, in Anglo–American law, a general requisite of legal enforceability. In 1677, however, Parliament did enact legislation requiring that certain contracts be in writing, "signed by the party to be charged," and our state legislatures followed this lead. The English law, called the Statute of Frauds, was a comprehensive "Act for Prevention of Frauds and Perjuries" and applied to a wide range of transactions. Sections 4 and 17, set out below, pertained to contracts.

Section 4: [N]o action shall be brought

(1) whereby to charge any executor or administrator upon any special promise, to answer for damages out of his own estate;

(2) or whereby to charge the defendant upon any special promise to answer for the debt, default or miscarriage of another person;

(3) or to charge any person upon any agreement made upon consideration of marriage;

(4) or upon any contract or sale of lands, tenements or hereditaments, or any interest in or concerning them;

(5) or upon any agreement that is not to be performed within the space of one year from the making thereof;

unless the agreement upon which such action shall be brought, or some memorandum or note thereof, shall be in writing, and signed by the party to be charged therewith or some other person thereunto by him lawfully authorized.

Section 17: And be it further enacted [that] no contract for the sale of any goods, wares and merchandizes, for the price of ten pounds sterling or upwards, shall be allowed to be good, except the buyer shall accept part of the goods so sold, and actually receive the same, or give something in earnest to bind the bargain, or in part of payment, or that some note or memorandum in writing of the said bargain be made and signed by the parties to be charged by such contract, or their agents thereunto lawfully authorized.

Section 4 was widely followed in this country, although the language was altered in some cases and other transactions (e.g., contract to make a will or to pay a commission to a real estate agent) were sometimes added. An American counterpart of section 17 was section 4 of the Uniform Sales Act, which provided as follows:

(1) A contract to sell or a sale of any goods or choses in action of the value of five hundred dollars or upwards shall not be enforceable by action unless the buyer shall accept part of the goods or choses in action so contracted to be sold or sold, and actually receive the same, or give something in earnest to bind the contract or in part payment, or

unless some note or memorandum in writing of the contract or sale be signed by the party to be charged or his agent in that behalf.

(2) The provisions of this section apply to every such contract or sale notwithstanding that the goods may be intended to be delivered at some future time or may not at the time of such contract or sale be actually made, procured, or provided, or fit, or ready for delivery, or some act may be requisite for the making or completing thereof, or rendering the same fit for delivery; but if the goods are to be manufactured by the seller especially for the buyer and are not suitable for sale to others in the ordinary course of the seller's business, the provisions of this section shall not apply.

(3) There is an acceptance of goods within the meaning of this section when the buyer, either before or after delivery of the goods, expresses by words or conduct his assent to becoming the owner of those specific goods.

Section 4 of the Uniform Sales Act has now been replaced by Section 2–201 of the Uniform Commercial Code, which recently has been revised. We will look at the specifics of Section 2–201 later on in the Section.

Should the statute be repealed? An enormous amount of litigation has arisen respecting the Statute of Frauds. Indicative is the fact that nearly one-sixth of Professor Corbin's major treatise is devoted to this subject. The judicial treatment has mirrored divergent convictions concerning the utility of such legislation. Controversy in this regard arose at an early date and continues unabated to this time. A commission of the Lord Chancellor gave this brief sketch of English opinion:

Lord Kenyon's verdict: "One of the wisest laws in our Statute Book" (Chaplin v. Rogers, 1800, 1 East at p. 194), and, "I lament extremely that exceptions were ever introduced in construing the Statute" (Chester v. Beckett, 7 T.R. at p. 204) contrasts with that pronounced by Wilmot J., and concurred in by Lord Mansfield (in Simon v. Metivier, 1766, 1 Bl.W. at p. 601): "Had the Statute of Frauds been always carried into execution according to the letter, it would have done ten times more mischief than it has done good, by protecting, rather than by preventing, frauds."

Law Revision Committee, Sixth Interim Report 6 (1937).

The repeated claim that the statute's writing requirement may as Lord Cambell argued "promote more fraud than it prevents" is a claim about two different types of fraud. A plaintiff can falsely assert the existence of a promise (where the defendant in fact had not promised). Or a defendant can falsely deny the existence of a contract (where in fact she had previously made an oral promise). The writing requirement reduces fraudulent assertions of promise, but it can exacerbate the fraudulent denials of promise—as oral promisors learn that the writing requirement grants them a degree of freedom to disclaim their promise without legal penalty.

It would seem accordingly that as a theoretical matter lawmakers should be agnostic about whether a writing requirement would cause or prevent fraud—the presence or the absence of a writing requirement would exacerbate one of the two types of fraud. But in the shadow of a writing requirement, a potential plaintiff/promisee can protect herself from a oral promissor's false denial by simply demanding that the oral promise be reduced to writing before relying on it. In sharp contrast, without a legal writing requirement, a potential defendant cannot effectively prove that she never promised the plaintiff who falsely asserts that a promise was made. It's theoretically easier for potential victims of false denials to protect themselves than for potential victims of false assertions. The problem comes when promisees—notwithstanding the writing requirement—fail to demand a writing and nonetheless rely.*

American opinion has also been divided. For example, Professor Llewellyn gave this salute: "That statute is an amazing product. In it de Leon might have found his secret of perpetual youth. After two centuries and a half the statute stands, in essence better adapted to our need than when it first was passed." Karl N. Llewellyn, *What Price Contract?—An Essay in Perspective*, 40 Yale L.J. 104, 747 (1931). On the other hand, Professor Willis, condemning the contract clauses of the Statute of Frauds as anachronistic, arguing that:

> The original reasons for a Statute of Frauds—to prevent men from being held by means of perjury on promises they had never made— were first the uncontrolled discretion of the jury, second, the rule as to competency of witnesses, and, third, the immaturity of contract law in the seventeenth century.
>
> While the process of the evolution of the jury, from a tribunal where the jurors were witnesses and decided the facts in cases on their own knowledge, to a tribunal where the jurors were judges of the facts and decided cases on evidence given in open court, was just about completed, the modern control of the court over the jury, in the matter of limits and elements of injury, the rules by which compensation for pecuniary injuries shall be ascertained, and in cases of passion and prejudice, was only just beginning. It was therefore a wise precaution at this time to require certain kinds of evidence as proof of certain contracts in order to place a limitation upon the uncontrolled power of the jury, which would be exercised only in this way * * *.
>
> At the time of the enactment of the original Statute of Frauds neither the parties to the action, nor any person who had any interest in the result of the litigation, were competent witnesses * * *. Such a state of the law of evidence was a temptation to plaintiffs to procure perjured testimony, and exposed defendants to outrageous liabilities; and it probably was in this state of the law a wise precaution to require

---

* The parol evidence rule, discussed infra in chapter 6, raises parallel issues. There the core question is not whether a contract exists but rather whether a particular oral promise adding additional terms was part of the contract. Again, there are two types of fraud— false assertions and false denials. The presence or absence of a writing requirement (now with regard to the asserted additional term) will reduce one type of fraud and exacerbate another. Finally, potential victims of false denials can protect themselves by demanding that oral promises be reduced to writing.

for such liability, either writing or other adequate evidence, at least where it was feasible to do so as in the case of contracts. * * *

Willis, *The Statute of Frauds—A Legal Anachronism*, 3 Ind.L.J. 427, 429–31 (1928).

It has been suggested, however, that even if the original reasons are no longer persuasive, there are additional grounds for insisting upon a writing in some situations. This was Professor Llewellyn's view and no doubt partly accounts for the retention of a Statute of Frauds provision, albeit in a significantly modified form, in the Uniform Commercial Code:

> The statute serves a useful purpose in so far as it contributes to the business habit of requiring a writing. The lay tradition, often encountered, that a writing signed by the party must be had to make a contract binding probably is to a certain extent derived from the statute of frauds. Not only is a writing useful to prevent fraud by deliberate overreaching regarding the terms of the bargain, but the presence of a writing prevents to a large extent otherwise possible innocent misunderstanding of what actually were the terms of the bargain. It also preserves the exact wording of the terms, rather than leaving them to the recollection of their general purport preserved in the elusive and treacherous memory of interested parties.

Vold, *The Application of the Statute of Frauds under the Uniform Sales Act*, 15 Minn.L.Rev. 391, 393–95 (1931).

Proponents of abolition scored a victory in England in 1954, when Parliament repealed all but the sections relating to promises to answer for the debts of another (suretyship clause) and contracts for the sale of land. Law Reform (Enforcement of Contracts) Act, 1954, 2 & 3 Eliz. II, c. 34. There does not seem a likelihood of general repeal in this country, at least not in the near future. Rather, as noted by one authority, "a cautious approach to the Statute of Frauds seems to be in harmony with American professional opinion." Braucher, *The Commission and the Law of Contracts*, 40 Cornell L.Q. 696, 705 (1955). It is likely that "erosion" will continue through judicial interpretations restricting statutory coverage, easing the requirements for statutory compliance, and making assertion of the statutory defense more difficult.

In a bold move, the July, 1996 Draft of revised Article 2, Sales, proposed the repeal of the statute of frauds, including the "one year" clause, for contracts for the sale of goods. This followed the English repeal, discussed above, and Article 11 of the United Nations Convention on Contracts for the International Sale of Goods (CISG), which provides: "A contract for sale need not be concluded in or evidenced by writing and is not subject to any other requirement as to form." Not surprisingly, the proposal was controversial and prompted strong objection from some quarters. See, e.g., Morris G. Shanker, *In Defense of the Sales Statute of Frauds and Parole Evidence Rule: A Fair Price of Admission to the Courts*, 100 Commercial L.J. 259 (1995). The 2003 proposed draft generally retains the writing requirement for contracts where the price is greater than $5000 but eliminates the "one year" clause.

(B) "WITHIN THE STATUTE"

(1) THE "ONE YEAR" CLAUSE

A typical statute in most states provides: "No action shall be brought ... upon any agreement that is not to be performed within the space of one year from the making thereof ... unless the agreement upon which such action shall be brought, or some memorandum or note thereof, shall be in writing, and signed by the party to be charged therewith or some other person thereunto by him lawfully authorized."

The courts' reluctance to require a writing is shown in the extremely narrow interpretation given to this "one year" provision. One court explained: "[Courts] have observed the exact words of this provision and have interpreted them literally and very narrowly. The words are 'agreement that is not to be performed.' They are not 'agreement that is not in fact performed' or 'agreement that may not be performed' or 'agreement that is not at all likely to be performed.' To fall within the words of the provision, therefore, the agreement must be one of which it can truly be said at the very moment that it is made, 'This agreement is not to be performed within one year'; in general, the cases indicate that there must not be the slightest possibility that it can be fully performed within one year." Goodwin v. Southtex Land Sales, 243 S.W.2d 721, 725 (Tex.Civ.App.1951). See also C.R. Klewin, Inc. v. Flagship Properties, Inc., 220 Conn. 569, 600 A.2d 772 (1991) (oral agreement must say in express terms that performance is to have a specific duration beyond one year).

North Shore Bottling Co. v. C. Schmidt & Sons, Inc.

Court of Appeals of New York, 1968.
22 N.Y.2d 171, 292 N.Y.S.2d 86, 239 N.E.2d 189.

■ FULD, CHIEF JUDGE. This appeal, here by permission of the Appellate Division on a certified question, calls upon us to determine the validity, under the one-year provision of the Statute of Frauds, of an oral agreement which entitled the defendant to terminate its contractual arrangement with the plaintiff within one year of its making.

* * *

The Statute of Frauds requires an agreement to be in writing if "[b]y its terms [it] is not to be performed within one year from the making thereof" (General Obligations Law, § 5–701, subd. 1 [formerly Personal Property Law, § 31, subd. 1]). According to the complaint before us, the plaintiff and the defendant Schmidt "entered into an agreement whereby plaintiff became the exclusive wholesale distributor in Queens County of Schmidt beer * * * for as long as Schmidt sold beer in the New York metropolitan area", and the question presented is whether the defendant's power under the agreement itself to put an end to it within the year—by discontinuing its sales of beer in the New York area—took the agreement out of the operation of the statute.

It was long ago stated, and frequently repeated, that "[i]t is not the meaning of the statute that the contract must be performed within a year. * * * if the obligation of the contract is not, by its very terms or necessary construction, to endure for a longer period than one year, it is a valid agreement, although it may be capable of an indefinite continuance." (Trustees of First Baptist Church v. Brooklyn Fire Ins. Co., 19 N.Y. 305, 307); ... In other words, as another court expressed the matter, "the statute only applies to agreements which are, by expressed stipulation, not to be performed within a year. It does not apply to an agreement which appears by its terms to be capable of performance within the year; nor to cases in which the performance of the agreement depends upon a contingency which may or may not happen within the year." (Dresser v. Dresser, 35 Barb. 573, 577, supra.) And in Blake v. Voigt (134 N.Y. 69, 31 N.E. 256, supra), in which the plaintiff promised "to cause to be consigned all the goods that I could influence to" the defendant, with an option in either party to give notice of termination after seven months, this court wrote: "The ultimate question, therefore, is whether a contract, which by the terms applicable to the leading subject thereof is not to be performed within a year, is taken out of the statute by the fact that it was a part of such contract that either party might rightfully terminate it within the year. It is contended that termination is not performance, but rather the destruction of the contract, and this is true where there is no provision authorizing either of the parties to terminate as a matter of right. Performance, however, is simply carrying out the contract by doing what it requires or permits."

* * *

Applying, these principles to the present case, it is clear that the agreement asserted by the plaintiff does not fall within the ban of the Statute of Frauds. Although the parties may have expected the agreement to last over a long period, they contemplated its possible termination by action—unquestionably within the defendant's power to take at any time—discontinuing its beer sales in the New York area. That being so, the agreement did not, by its terms, "of necessity extend beyond one year from the time of its making." (Nat Nal Serv. Stas. v. Wolf, 304 N.Y. 332, 336, 107 N.E.2d 473, 475, supra.) It is hardly necessary to say that since envisaged by its terms, such an occurrence would amount to a performance permitted by the contract. As the court declared in Blake v. Voigt (134 N.Y. 69, 72–73, 31 N.E. 256, 257, supra), it "would be executed in a way that the parties agreed that it might be executed. The contingency did not defeat the contract, but simply advanced the period of fulfillment." To state this in slightly different fashion, the parties contemplated two possibilities—a long term distributorship in the plaintiff or a termination should the defendant decide to discontinue beer sales in the New York area. The first contingency is not, in the ordinary course, performable within a year, the second is. The existence of one of two contingencies performable within a year is sufficient to take the case out of the statute. (See, e.g., 2 Corbin, Contracts [1950], § 446; 3 Williston, Contracts [3d ed., 1960], §§ 495, 498, 498B.)

* * *

Accordingly, since the present agreement was susceptible of performance within a year, it falls outside the bar of the Statute of Frauds. It follows, therefore, that the first cause of action may not be dismissed.

* * *

NOTES

(1) Suppose that E and R orally agreed that if E terminated their employment contract at any time, E would not compete with R within a 20 mile radius for five years but if E did compete E would pay R a liquidated damage sum of $10,000 per year until the five year period expired. After two years, E started to compete with R. Six months later E was killed by lightning on a golf course. Alleging the oral agreement, R sued E's estate for $25,000, the liquidated amount due for the balance of the five year period. E's executor moved to dismiss, arguing that the alleged oral agreement was within the "one year" provision. R then argued that death fully performed a contract not to compete, citing *Young v. Ward*, 917 S.W.2d 506 (Tex.App.1996), and since death could have occurred within one year of the alleged agreement the "one year" provision did not apply. Moreover, the agreement to pay liquidated damages could not possibly be performed within one year. E responded that R's argument failed to distinguish between performance of the contract and an excuse for non-performance. Death fell into the latter category. E cited Frantz v. Parke, 111 Idaho 1005, 729 P.2d 1068, 1071 (App.1986), where the court stated: "[T]he great weight of authority holds that a contract not to compete would be 'terminated,' not fully performed, by death of the promisor . . . . Indeed, if the unstated but omnipresent possibility of death could take an agreement for a definite time outside the statute of frauds, it would eviscerate the statute in virtually all contracts for definite terms between mortals." Assuming that the covenant not to compete and the liquidated damage provision are otherwise enforceable, how should the statute of frauds defense be decided?

(2) *One Side Rule.* Restatement § 198: "Where any of the promises in a bilateral contract cannot be fully performed within a year from the time of the formation of the contract, all promises in the contract are within [the one-year clause of the Statute of Frauds], unless and until one party to such a contract completely performs what he has promised. When there has been such complete performance, none of the promises in the contract is [within such provision]." Restatement (Second) § 130 is in accord. As one court put it: "Why, in the present case, should not a plaintiff be entitled to recover upon a contract which he has completely performed? The defendant has received the full benefit—not of an implied contract, but of an express one. He has received everything that the express contract stipulated that he should receive and nothing remains to be done on his part but the payment of money. Nor do we see any substance in

the minority rule. In almost every case where a recovery on the contract has been refused it has been suggested that a recovery could be had under quantum meruit or quantum valebant counts." Emerson v. Universal Products Co., 35 Del. 277, 162 A. 779, 781 (1932).

(3) *Cumulative Effect of Statute of Frauds Provisions.* In Freedman v. Chemical Construction Corporation, 43 N.Y.2d 260, 401 N.Y.S.2d 176, 372 N.E.2d 12 (1977), the plaintiff, "a self-described retired industrialist," sued on an alleged oral agreement to pay him a 5% fee ($2,500,000) for his participation in the obtaining by the defendant of a $41,000,000 contract to build a plant in Saudi Arabia. Payment was to be made upon completion of the plant. Plaintiff's services extended over a three-year period, and it took another six years to build the plant. Nonetheless, the alleged contract was not within the "one year" clause, for "[i]t matters not * * * that it was unlikely or improbable that a $41 million plant would be constructed within one year." 372 N.E.2d at 15. However, the court held that the action was barred by another Statute of Frauds provision covering "a contract to pay compensation for services rendered in negotiating a loan, or in negotiating the purchase, sale, exchange, renting or leasing of any real estate or interest therein, *or of a business opportunity,* business, its good will, inventory, fixtures or an interest therein. * * *" (Emphasis added) Statute of Frauds provisions are "cumulative." It takes but one provision to bar enforcement. For a consideration of the possibility of restitutionary relief for one who performs pursuant to an alleged oral agreement within the Statute of Frauds, see infra at 190.

There is, however, support for the view that if an oral contract for the sale of goods meets the requirements of UCC 2–201 it is enforceable despite the fact that it might be unenforceable under another general statute of frauds provision. See, e.g., Roth Steel Products v. Sharon Steel Corp., 705 F.2d 134 (6th Cir.1983); H & W Industries, Inc. v. Formosa Plastics Corp., USA, 860 F.2d 172 (5th Cir.1988). This view is reinforced by Revised 2–201(4), which provides that a "contract that is enforceable under this section is not rendered unenforceable merely because it is not capable of being performed within one year or any other applicable period after its making."

PROBLEM: THE CASE OF JANE FONDA'S ATTORNEY

In 1968, Jane Fonda retained the services of a New York law firm to represent her in general business matters, orally agreeing to pay five percent of her earnings as compensation for the firm's services. Richard Rosenthal, a member of the firm, assumed responsibility for a large share of the firm's activities on Fonda's behalf.

In 1971, the law firm dissolved and in 1972, Rosenthal began to represent her as an independent private practitioner. In April of 1972, he and Fonda entered into an oral contract whereby he agreed to continue performing a variety of services for her and she, in turn, agreed to pay him ten percent of all gross professional income derived from the projects that were initiated during his tenure.

Rosenthal continued to represent Fonda from his New York office. But in 1978, he and his family moved to California, at Fonda's request, so that he could represent her more effectively.

Approximately two years later, on May 30, 1980, Fonda discharged Rosenthal. Rosenthal sued to recover commissions on projects that were initiated during his tenure and produced or continued to produce income after his termination. What result? See *Rosenthal v. Fonda*, 862 F.2d 1398 (9th Cir. 1988).

(2) CONTRACTS FOR THE SALE OF GOODS

Section 2–201 provides a statute of frauds for contracts for the sale of goods. The pre-revision version of 2–201 provided:

(1) Except as otherwise provided in this section a contract for the sale of goods for the price of $500 or more is not enforceable by way of action or defense unless there is some writing sufficient to indicate that a contract for sale has been made between the parties and signed by the party against whom enforcement is sought or by his authorized agent or broker. A writing is not insufficient because it omits or incorrectly states a term agreed upon but the contract is not enforceable under this paragraph beyond the quantity of goods shown in such writing.

(2) Between merchants if within a reasonable time a writing in confirmation of the contract and sufficient against the sender is received and the party receiving it has reason to know its contents, it satisfies the requirements of subsection (1) against such party unless written notice of objection to its contents is given within ten days after it is received.

(3) A contract which does not satisfy the requirements of subsection (1) but which is valid in other respects is enforceable

(a) if the goods are to be specially manufactured for the buyer and are not suitable for sale to others in the ordinary course of the seller's business and the seller, before notice of repudiation is received and under circumstances which reasonably indicate that the goods are for the buyer, has made either a substantial beginning of their manufacture or commitments for their procurement; or

(b) if the party against whom enforcement is sought admits in his pleading, testimony or otherwise in court that a contract for sale was made, but the contract is not enforceable under this provision beyond the quantity of goods admitted; or

(c) with respect to goods for which payment has been made and accepted or which have been received and accepted (Sec. 2–606).

Revised UCC 2–201 makes several changes.

First, the word "record," which means "information that is inscribed on a tangible medium or that is stored in an electronic or other medium and is retrievable in perceivable form," Rev. UCC 2–103(1)(*l*), replaces the word "writing" through UCC 2–201 (and elsewhere in Revised Article 2 as well).

Second, the price must be $5,000 or more before the statute of frauds applies.

Third, Rev. 2–201(1) is revised to clarify that "the record must contain a quantity term" and that the contract is not enforceable beyond the quantity of goods shown in the record.

Fourth, Rev. 2–201(3)(b) is revised to clarify that the admission which takes the case out of the statute may be in the "party's pleading, or in the party's testimony or otherwise under oath. . . ."

Finally, Rev. 2–201(4) makes it clear that a contract enforceable under this section is "not rendered unenforceable merely because it is not capable of being performed within one year or any other applicable period after its making."

What are "goods" within the phrase "contract for the sale of goods" in UCC 2–201(1)? Problems of classification have arisen most often in differentiating goods and land (e.g., what of the sale of standing timber?) and goods and services (e.g., what of the sale of false teeth made specially for the buyer?). The Code provides specific guidance.

Section 2–105(1) defines goods as follows:

> "Goods" means all things (including specially manufactured goods) which are movable at the time of identification to the contract for sale other than the money in which the price is to be paid, investment securities (Article 8) and things in action. "Goods" also includes the unborn young of animals and growing crops and other identified things attached to realty as described in the section on goods to be severed from realty (Section 2–107).

UCC 2–107(1) and (2) treat goods to be severed from realty as follows:

> (1) A contract for the sale of minerals or the like (including oil and gas) or a structure or its materials to be removed from realty is a contract for the sale of goods within this Article if they are to be severed by the seller but until severance a purported present sale thereof which is not effective as a transfer of an interest in land is effective only as a contract to sell.

> (2) A contract for the sale apart from the land of growing crops or other things attached to realty and capable of severance without material harm thereto but not described in subsection (1) or of timber to be cut is a contract for the sale of goods within this Article whether the subject matter is to be severed by the buyer or by the seller even though it forms part of the realty at the time of contracting, and the parties can by identification effect a present sale before severance.

As indicated in the extensive interpretive caselaw, the basic character of the performance due will determine whether the contract is for goods or services. A leading case on the Code's applicability to "mixed" contracts which involve both goods and services is Bonebrake v. Cox, 499 F.2d 951

(8th Cir.1974). The court held that a contract for the sale and installation of bowling equipment was a contract for the sale of goods under the UCC. "The test for inclusion or exclusion is not whether they are mixed, but, granting that they are mixed, whether their predominant factor, their thrust, their purpose, reasonably stated, is the rendition of service, with goods incidentally involved (e.g., contract with artist for painting) or is a transaction of sale, with labor incidentally involved (e.g., installation of a water heater in a bathroom)." 499 F.2d at 960. Accord: Colorado Carpet Installation, Inc. v. Palermo, 668 P.2d 1384 (Colo.1983) (sale and installation of carpeting and other flooring materials).

The UCC offers additional guidance in determining Statute of Frauds coverage where specially manufactured or custom made goods are involved. See UCC 2–201(3)(a). Goods specially manufactured *for* the buyer (even if not manufactured *by* the seller) are *not* within UCC 2–201 if (1) they are not suitable for sale to others in the ordinary course of the seller's business and (2) the seller, before notice of repudiation is received and under circumstances which indicate that the goods are for the buyer, has made either a substantial beginning of their manufacture or commitments for their procurement. A contract for the sale of standard white shirts would be covered by the goods section of the Statute of Frauds. Not so if the seller, under the contract, added the buyer's business name and logo to the shirts. See e.g., Smith–Scharff Paper Co. v. P. N. Hirsch & Co. Stores, Inc., 754 S.W.2d 928 (Mo.App.1988) (paper bags imprinted with buyer's logo); Flowers Baking Co. of Lynchburg, Inc. v. R–P Packaging, Inc., 229 Va. 370, 329 S.E.2d 462 (1985) (cellophane wrapping material manufactured to size required by buyer's containers and imprinted with buyer's name and unique artwork). Cf. Mel–Tex Valve, Inc. v. Rio Supply Co., 710 S.W.2d 184 (Tex.App.1986). What if the seller is in the business of manufacturing custom designed goods, and the goods, with some alteration, could be marketed? Should the seller be able to claim the advantage of the specially manufactured goods exception? See Impossible Electronic Techniques, Inc. v. Wackenhut Protective Systems, Inc., 669 F.2d 1026 (5th Cir.1982) (sale of electronic closed-circuit cameras). See, generally, Annot., *Sales: "Specially Manufactured Goods" Statute of Frauds Exception in UCC § 2–201(3)(a)*, 45 A.L.R.4th 1126 (1986).

Section 2–201 is not the only Statute of Frauds provision in the Code. UCC 2A–201 governs leases of goods. In addition, there are sections which, although not ordinarily referred to as Statute of Frauds provisions, do prescribe a writing as a formal requisite of liability. Examples are negotiable instruments (UCC 3–104(a)), letters of credit (UCC 5–104), and security agreements (Rev. 9–203(b)). Beyond this there are numerous statutory provisions of a regulatory nature which not only insist upon a signed writing as a *sine qua non* of legal obligation, but prescribe, often in considerable detail, the content of the writing. Examples are statutes dealing with insurance, small loans and retail installment sales.

Note, however, that the residual statute of frauds, UCC 1–206, formerly found in Article 1, has been repealed in Revised Article 1, as has the statute of frauds provision in earlier versions of Article 8. UCC 8–113.

PROBLEMS: APPLICATION OF UCC 2–201

(1) The quantity term causes problems.

What is the effect of a signed record without a quantity term?

Suppose the writing stated 20 units and the buyer claimed that the agreement was for 200 units. What effect?

Suppose the writing stated that the deal was for the seller's output. Is the statute satisfied?

Suppose that the seller is able to get the buyer to admit in a deposition under oath that there was an oral agreement but not what the quantity term was. Is the statute satisfied?

(2) On February 1, S, a farmer, and B, a grain dealer, agree over the telephone that S will sell its output of corn to B for $3 per bushel, delivery on October 1. B immediately resells S's corn to C, a cereal maker, for $3.50 per bushel. B then sends to S a written, signed memorial of the transaction, stating in effect "this is to confirm our deal for the output of your farm at $3.00 per bushel." S receives the memo, but does not read it (and in fact throws it away). Later the market moves to $4 per bushel and S sells the output to D. B sues S for breach of contract and S raises the statute of frauds defense. What result? See UCC 2–201(1), (2).

(3) Suppose, in (2) above, that B had resold the output to C, S knew it, but B did not send a confirmatory memo. Does the statute of frauds apply?

(3) INTERESTS IN REALTY

All versions of the statute of frauds purport to cover oral agreements to convey an interest in land. According to Section 125(1) of the Restatement, Second, a "promise to transfer to any person any interest in land is within the statute of frauds." "Interest in land" is defined as "any right, privilege, power or immunity, or combination thereof, which is an interest in land under the law of property and is not 'goods' within the Uniform Commercial Code." Section 127. Although the scope of this section and the memo required to satisfy the statute cause difficulties, most courts recognize that action in reliance on an oral promise to transfer an interest in land may take the case "out of the statute." See Restatement, Second, Section 129, which requires reasonable reliance on the contract, the "continuing assent of the party against whom enforcement is sought," and a sufficient change of position so that "injustice can be avoided only by specific performance." See Farnsworth, Section 6.5; Murray, Section 71.

(C) COMPLIANCE WITH THE STATUTE

Once an oral agreement is found to be "within" an applicable provision of the statute of frauds, the fun begins. Have the requirements of the statute been satisfied? If so, there are no formal barriers to enforcement. If not, the agreement is not enforceable (even though other requisites have been satisfied) unless other grounds, e.g., waiver, an admission or estoppel, can be established. See subsection (D), infra.

What, then, does it take to comply with the statute?

Crabtree v. Elizabeth Arden Sales Corp.

Court of Appeals of New York, 1953.
305 N.Y. 48, 110 N.E.2d 551.

■ FULD, JUDGE. In September of 1947, Nate Crabtree entered into preliminary negotiations with Elizabeth Arden Sales Corporation, manufacturers and sellers of cosmetics, looking toward his employment as sales manager. Interviewed on September 26th, by Robert P. Johns, executive vice-president and general manager of the corporation, who had apprised him of the possible opening, Crabtree requested a three-year contract at $25,000 a year. Explaining that he would be giving up a secure well-paying job to take a position in an entirely new field of endeavor—which he believed would take him some years to master—he insisted upon an agreement for a definite term. And he repeated his desire for a contract for three years to Miss Elizabeth Arden, the corporation's president. When Miss Arden finally indicated that she was prepared to offer a two-year contract, based on an annual salary of $20,000 for the first six months, $25,000 for the second six months and $30,000 for the second year, plus expenses of $5,000 a year for each of those years, Crabtree replied that that offer was "interesting". Miss Arden thereupon had her personal secretary make this memorandum on a telephone order blank that happened to be at hand:

"EMPLOYMENT AGREEMENT WITH

NATE CRABTREE At 681—5th Ave	Date Sept. 26–1947 6:PM

* * *

Begin	20000.
6 months	25000.
6 "	30000.

5000.—per year
Expense Money
[2 years to make good]

Arrangement with Mr. Crabtree

By Miss Arden

Present

 Miss Arden

 Mr. John

 Mr. Crabtree

 Miss O'Leary"

A few days later, Crabtree phoned Mr. Johns and telegraphed Miss Arden; he accepted the "invitation to join the Arden organization", and Miss Arden wired back her "welcome". When he reported for work, a "payroll change" card was made up and initialed by Mr. Johns, and then forwarded to the payroll department. Reciting that it was prepared on

September 30, 1947, and was to be effective as of October 22d, it specified the names of the parties, Crabtree's "Job Classification" and, in addition, contained the notation that "This employee is to paid as follows:

"First six months of employment	$20,000.	per annum
Next six months of employment	25,000.	" "
After one year of employment	30,000.	" "

Approved by,   RPJ   [initialed]"

After six months of employment, Crabtree received the scheduled increase from $20,000 to $25,000, but the further specified increase at the end of the year was not paid. Both Mr. Johns and the comptroller of the corporation, Mr. Carstens, told Crabtree that they would attempt to straighten out the matter with Miss Arden, and, with that in mind, the comptroller prepared another "pay-roll change" card, to which his signature is appended, noting that there was to be a "Salary increase" from $25,000 to $30,000 a year, "per contractual arrangements with Miss Arden". The latter, however, refused to approve the increase and, after further fruitless discussion, plaintiff left defendant's employ and commenced this action for breach of contract.

At the ensuing trial, defendant denied the existence of any agreement to employ plaintiff for two years, and further contended, that, even if one had been made, the statute of frauds barred its enforcement. The trial court found against defendant on both issues and awarded plaintiff damages of about $14,000, and the Appellate Division, two justices dissenting, affirmed. Since the contract relied upon was not to be performed within a year, the primary question for decision is whether there was a memorandum of its terms, subscribed by defendant, to satisfy the statute of frauds, Personal Property Law, § 31.

Each of the two payroll cards—the one initialed by defendant's general manager, the other signed by its comptroller—unquestionably constitutes a memorandum under the statute. That they were not prepared or signed with the intention of evidencing the contract, or that they came into existence subsequent to its execution, is of no consequence, ...; it is enough, to meet the statute's demands, that they were signed with intent to authenticate the information contained therein, and that such information does evidence the terms of the contract. ... Those two writings contain all of the essential terms of the contract—the parties to it, the position that plaintiff was to assume, the salary that he was to receive— except that relating to the duration of plaintiff's employment. Accordingly, we must consider whether that item, the length of the contract, may be supplied by reference to the earlier unsigned office memorandum, and, if so, whether its notation, "2 years to make good", sufficiently designates a period of employment.

The statute of frauds does not require the "memorandum * * * to be in one document." It may be pieced together out of separate writings, connected with one another either expressly or by the internal evidence of subject-matter and occasion." Marks v. Cowdin, supra, 226 N.Y. 138, 145, see, also, 2 Williston, op. ct., p. 1671; Restatement, Contracts, § 208, subd. [a]. Where each of the separate writings has been subscribed by the party to be charged, little if any difficulty is encountered. See, e.g., Marks v. Cowdin, supra, 226 N.Y. 138, 144–145. Where, however, some writings have been signed, and others have not—as in the case before us—there is basic disagreement as to what constitutes a sufficient connection permitting the unsigned papers to be considered as part of the statutory memorandum. The courts of some jurisdictions insist that there be a reference, of varying degrees of specificity, in the signed writing to that unsigned, and, if there is no such reference, they refuse to permit consideration of the latter in determining whether the memorandum satisfies the statute.... That conclusion is based upon a construction of the statute which requires that the connection between the writings and defendant's acknowledgment of the one not subscribed, appear from examination of the papers alone, without the aid of parol evidence. The other position—which has gained increasing support over the years—is that a sufficient connection between the papers is established simply by a reference in them to the same subject matter or transaction.... The statute is not pressed "to the extreme of a literal and rigid logic", Marks v. Cowdin, supra, 226 N.Y. 138, 144, 123 N.E. 139, 141, and oral testimony is admitted to show the connection between the documents and to establish the acquiescence, of the party to be charged, to the contents of the one unsigned. ...

The view last expressed impresses us as the more sound, and, indeed—although several of our cases appear to have gone the other way, ... this court has on a number of occasions approved the rule, and we now definitively adopt it, permitting the signed and unsigned writings to be read together, provided that they clearly refer to the same subject matter or transaction. ...

The language of the statute—"Every agreement * * * is void, unless * * * some note or memorandum thereof be in writing, and subscribed by the party to be charged", Personal Property Law, § 31 does not impose the requirement that the signed acknowledgment of the contract must appear from the writings alone, unaided by oral testimony. The danger of fraud and perjury, generally attendant upon the admission of parol evidence, is at a minimum in a case such as this. None of the terms of the contract are supplied by parol. All of them must be set out in the various writings presented to the court, and at least one writing, the one establishing a contractual relationship between the parties, must bear the signature of the party to be charged, while the unsigned document must on its face refer to the same transaction as that set forth in the one that was signed. Parol evidence—to portray the circumstances surrounding the making of the memorandum—serves only to connect the separate documents and to show that there was assent, by the party to be charged, to the contents of the one unsigned. If that testimony does not convincingly connect the papers, or does not show assent to the unsigned paper, it is within the province of the judge to conclude, as a matter of law, that the statute has not been satisfied. True, the possibility still remains that, by fraud or perjury, an agreement never in fact made may occasionally be enforced under the subject matter or transaction test. It is better to run that risk, though, than to deny enforcement to all agreements, merely because the signed document made nonspecific mention of the unsigned writing. As the United States Supreme Court declared, in sanctioning the admission of parol evidence to establish the connection between the signed and unsigned writings, "There may be cases in which it would be a violation of reason and common sense to ignore a reference which derives its significance from such [parol] proof. If there is ground for any doubt in the matter, the general rule should be enforced. But where there is no ground for doubt, its enforcement would aid, instead of discouraging, fraud." * * *

Turning to the writings in the case before us—the unsigned office memo, the payroll change form initialed by the general manager Johns, and the paper signed by the comptroller Carstens—it is apparent, and most patently, that all three refer on their face to the same transaction. The parties, the position to be filled by plaintiff, the salary to be paid him, are all identically set forth; it is hardly possible that such detailed information could refer to another or a different agreement. Even more, the card signed by Carstens notes that it was prepared for the purpose of a "Salary increase per contractual arrangements with Miss Arden". That certainly constitutes a reference of sorts to a more comprehensive "arrangement," and parol is permissible to furnish the explanation.

The corroborative evidence of defendant's assent to the contents of the unsigned office memorandum is also convincing. Prepared by defendant's agent, Miss Arden's personal secretary, there is little likelihood that that paper was fraudulently manufactured or that defendant had not assented to its contents. Furthermore, the evidence as to the conduct of the parties at the time it was prepared persuasively demonstrates defendant's assent to its terms. Under such circumstances, the courts below were fully justified in finding that the three papers constituted the "memorandum" of their agreement within the meaning of the statute.

Nor can there be any doubt that the memorandum contains all of the essential terms of the contract.... Only one term, the length of the employment, is in dispute. The September 26th office memorandum contains the notation, "2 years to make good". What purpose, other than to denote the length of the contract term, such a notation could have, is hard to imagine. Without it, the employment would be at will, ... and its inclusion may not be treated as meaningless or purposeless. Quite obviously, as the courts below decided, the phrase signifies that the parties agreed to a term, a certain and definite term, of two years, after which, if plaintiff did not "make good", he would be subject to discharge. And examination of other parts of the memorandum supports that construction. Throughout the writings, a scale of wages, increasing plaintiff's salary periodically, is set out; that type of arrangement is hardly consistent with the hypothesis that the employment was meant to be at will. The most that may be argued from defendant's standpoint is that "2 years to make good", is a cryptic and ambiguous statement. But, in such a case, parol evidence is admissible to explain its meaning.... Having in mind the relations of the parties, the

[handwritten margin note: Only length of Employ is in dispute]

course of the negotiations and plaintiff's insistence upon security of employment, the purpose of the phrase—or so the trier of the facts was warranted in finding—was to grant plaintiff the tenure he desired.

The judgment should be affirmed, with costs.

NOTES

(1) What writings constituted the requisite memorandum? To what extent was parol evidence needed to show actual connection?

(2) The first Restatement, § 208, stated: "The memorandum may consist of several writings, (a) if each writing is signed by the party to be charged and the writings indicate that they relate to the same transaction, or (b) though one writing only is signed if (i) the signed writing is physically annexed to the other writing by the party to be charged, or (ii) the signed writing refers to the unsigned writing, or (iii) it appears from examination of all the writings that the signed writing was signed with reference to the unsigned writings." Did *Crabtree* go beyond the limits set in the Restatement? Should it have?

Restatement (Second) § 132, influenced by *Crabtree,* provides: "The memorandum may consist of several writings if one of the writings is signed and the writings in the circumstances clearly indicate that they relate to the same transaction."

(3) *Satisfying UCC 2–201.* UCC 2–201(1) requires "some writing sufficient to indicate that a contract for sale has been made between the parties and signed by the party against whom enforcement is sought or his authorized agent or broker." Further: "A writing is not insufficient because it omits or incorrectly states a term agreed upon but the contract is not enforceable under this paragraph beyond the quantity of goods shown in such writing." The drafters added the following commentary: "The required writing need not contain all the material terms of the contract and such material terms as are stated need not be precisely stated. All that is required is that the writing afford a basis for believing that the offered oral evidence rests on a real transaction. . . . It need not indicate which party is buyer and which the seller. The only term which must appear is the quantity term which need not be accurately stated. The price, time and place of payment or delivery, the general quality of the goods, or any particular warranty may all be omitted." UCC 2–201, Comment 1. Courts have tended to be strict respecting the need for a statement of quantity in the writing. See, e.g., Thomas J. Kline, Inc. v. Lorillard, Inc., 878 F.2d 791 (4th Cir.1989). For a powerful critique, see Bruckel, *The Weed and the Web: Section 2–201's Corruption of the UCC's Substantive Provisions—the Quantity Problem,* U.Ill.L.Rev. 811 (1983). What would be the effect of a statutory revision that deleted all reference to quantity in UCC 2–201?

(4) Consider the following problem. Farmer and Dealer have done business together for over 10 years. In 1997, their transaction followed the usual pattern. In March, Farmer telephoned Dealer and offered to sell 5,000 bushels of #1 Yellow Corn for $3.00 per bushel, October delivery. After some discussion, there was an oral agreement to sell at $2.80 per bushel. As Farmer knew it would, Dealer immediately resold the corn to a cereal producer for $3.80 per

bushel, November, 1997 delivery. Dealer also mailed to Farmer a written, signed memorandum stating simply: "This is to confirm our agreement to sell and buy your output of corn for October, 1997 delivery." Farmer received the memo and did not respond. In September, 1997 Farmer harvested 6,000 bushels from the farm and tendered 1,000 bushels to Dealer, which dealer accepted. Because of bad weather elsewhere, the market price of #1 Yellow Corn had risen to $5.00 per bushel. Farmer then sold the balance of the crop on the open market for $5.00 per bushel and refused to deliver any more to Dealer. Farmer's attorney argued that the alleged oral agreement, if any, was unenforceable under UCC 2–201. You represent Farmer. Review Section 2–201 very carefully. Make a list of the issues that must be resolved before Farmer can prevail. What do you think?

PROBLEM: THE CASE OF THE UNANSWERED PURCHASE ORDER

Karen Fedorko, representing Mast Industries, and Tuvia Feldman, representing Bazak International, negotiated an oral agreement for the sale by Mast of certain textiles to Bazak for $103,330. One week later Feldman sent a "purchase order" to the Mast office. It contained a description of the goods, the price and other essential terms. It also contained the handwritten words: "As presented by Karen Fedorko," and was signed by an authorized representative of Bazak.

Mast received the order and made no objections to its content. However, it refuses to deliver the goods, and Bazak contemplates suit. If litigation ensues, how would you expect a court to rule? See Bazak International Corp. v. Mast Industries, Inc., 73 N.Y.2d 113, 538 N.Y.S.2d 503, 535 N.E.2d 633 (1989).

Comment: Electronic "Writings" and the Statute of Frauds

Various provisions of Article 2 of the Uniform Commercial Code have traditionally required a "writing" for transactional recognition or enforcement; notably, Section 2–201. A "writing" included "printing, typewriting or any other intentional reduction to tangible form." UCC 1–201(46).

But with advent of the Internet and massive shift toward electronic business, it became imperative for the law to create certainty about the validity of electronically formed contracts. Both state and federal law makers have responded.

In 1999, the National Conference of Commissioners on Uniform State Law approved the Uniform Electronic Transactions Act (UETA) which has been adopted by 41 states. In 2000, President Clinton signed the Electronic Signatures in Global and National Commerce Act ("E–Sign"), 114 Stat. 473 (2000). Both UETA and E–Sign make clear that a contract may not be denied legal effect solely because it is in electronic form or because an electronic signature or electronic record was used in its formation.

The UCC is following suit. The requirement of a "writing" is being replaced in proposed Section 2–201 now with a requirement of a "record" sufficient to indicate that a contract has been made. Proposed Section 2–212 clarifies that clicking on an icon (take note Amazon.com one-click users) can be sufficient to create a legally binding contract "if the record was created by or the authentication was the act of the person or the person's electronic agent." Moreover, the word "sign" has been defined to include intention to adopt a record by an "electronic sound, symbol, or process." Rev. 2–103(1)(*o*). See the new definitions in Rev. 2–103(1) and review Rev. 2–204(4) and 2–111 through 2–113.

See generally Margaret Jane Radin, *Online Standardization and the Integrating of Text and Machine,* 70 Fordham L. Rev. 1125 (2002).

(D) EFFECT OF NON-COMPLIANCE

An oral contract which is within and does not satisfy the Statute of Frauds is not a complete nullity. Rather, the vast majority of the cases have held that such a contract is "not void in the strict sense that no contract has come into being at all, but [is] merely unenforceable at the option of the party against whom enforcement is sought." Borchardt v. Kulick, 234 Minn. 308, 319, 48 N.W.2d 318, 325 (1951). For example, "a contract that cannot be performed within one year, though described as 'void' by the statute and by courts on occasion ... is actually voidable or unenforceable." Keenan v. Artintype, Inc., 145 Misc.2d 90, 546 N.Y.S.2d 741, 743 (1989). This means that the defense may be waived. In addition, if there has been complete performance there is no cause to "undo" the transaction.

Although waivable, the defense has traditionally been relatively easy to raise. One has been able, for example, to admit *arguendo* the existence of an oral agreement while insisting upon its nonenforceability. One has not been obliged to deny the existence of the alleged oral contract before being permitted to assert the statutory defense. The ethical propriety of this procedure has been questioned. See, e.g., Stevens, *Ethics and the Statute of Frauds,* 37 Cornell L.Rev. 355 (1952). Moreover, the issue has become more prominent, particularly with respect to contracts for the sale of goods, by reason of UCC 2–201(3)(b), which provides that a contract not satisfying the requirements of subsection (1) but valid in other respects *is* enforceable "if the party against whom enforcement is sought admits in his pleading, testimony or otherwise in court that a contract for sale was made, but the contract is not enforceable under this provision beyond the quantity of goods admitted."

Judicial opinion and scholarly comment would indicate that this provision is likely to have a significant impact, perhaps, as one writer put it, eventually removing "all remaining vestiges of the bar of the statute of frauds where a valid oral contract existed, save for the party willing to commit perjury by denying the existence of the contract in his pleading, testimony, or otherwise in court." Cunningham, *A Proposal to Repeal Section 2–201: The Statute of Frauds Section of Article 2,* 85 Com.L.J. 361, 363 (1980). Although the judicial returns are not all in, and there are conflicting precedents, the clear direction is toward permitting full discovery and a trial on the merits in order to afford the plaintiff an opportunity to elicit an admission from the defendant.

These are issues which are being litigated:

First, may the defendant demur or move to dismiss on the ground that the agreement as alleged is unenforceable?

Second, may the defendant move for summary judgment on the basis that the pleadings and supporting affidavits show an unenforceable oral agreement?

Third, when may the plaintiff "compel" admissions, either in a deposition or by cross-examination in open court, and thereby render the contract enforceable?

Fourth, must the admission conclusively prove the existence of the contract? Or is it sufficient if it merely evidences the contract?*

Fifth, to what extent can the defense be avoided on grounds of estoppel, either equitable or promissory?

Finally, a plaintiff who is unsuccessful in removing the bar of the statute as such may seek restitution for benefits conferred. This is treated in the concluding problem, infra at 190.

DF Activities Corporation v. Brown

United States Court of Appeals, Seventh Circuit, 1988.
851 F.2d 920.

■ POSNER, CIRCUIT JUDGE.

This appeal in a diversity breach of contract case raises an interesting question concerning the statute of frauds, in the context of a dispute over a chair of more than ordinary value. The plaintiff, DF Activities Corporation (owner of the Domino's pizza chain), is controlled by a passionate enthusiast for the work of Frank Lloyd Wright. The defendant, Dorothy Brown, a resident of Lake Forest (a suburb of Chicago) lived for many years in a house designed by Frank Lloyd Wright—the Willits House—and became the owner of a chair that Wright had designed, the Willits Chair. This is a stark, high-backed, uncomfortable-looking chair of distinguished design that DF wanted to add to its art collection. In September and October 1986, Sarah–Ann Briggs, DF's art director, negotiated with Dorothy Brown to buy the Willits Chair. DF contends—and Mrs. Brown denies—that she agreed in a phone conversation with Briggs on November 26 to sell the chair to DF for $60,000, payable in two equal installments, the first due on December 31 and the second on March 26. On December 3 Briggs wrote Brown a letter confirming the agreement, followed shortly by a check for $30,000. Two weeks later Brown returned the letter and the check with the following handwritten note at the bottom of the letter: "Since I did not hear from you until December and I spoke with you the middle of November, I have made other arrangements for the chair. It is no longer

---

* California did not adopt Section 2–201(3)(b). For reasons supporting the omission, see California State Bar Committee Commercial Code, 37 Calif.St.B.J. 141–42 (1962).

available for sale to you." Sometime later Brown sold the chair for $198,000, precipitating this suit for the difference between the price at which the chair was sold and the contract price of $60,000. Brown moved under Fed.R.Civ.P. 12(b)(6) to dismiss the suit as barred by the statute of frauds in the Uniform Commercial Code. See UCC § 2–201. (The Code is, of course, in force in Illinois, and the substantive issues in this case are, all agree, governed by Illinois law.) Attached to the motion was Brown's affidavit that she had never agreed to sell the chair to DF or its representative, Briggs. The affidavit also denied any recollection of a conversation with Briggs on November 26, and was accompanied by both a letter from Brown to Briggs dated September 20 withdrawing an offer to sell the chair and a letter from Briggs to Brown dated October 29 withdrawing DF's offer to buy the chair.

The district judge granted the motion to dismiss and dismissed the suit. DF appeals, contending that although a contract for a sale of goods at a price of $500 or more is subject to the statute of frauds, the (alleged) oral contract made on November 26 may be within the statutory exception for cases where "the party against whom enforcement is sought admits in his pleading, testimony or otherwise in court that a contract for sale was made." UCC § 2–201(3)(b). DF does not argue that Brown's handwritten note at the bottom of Briggs' letter is sufficient acknowledgment of a contract to bring the case within the exemption in section 2–201(1).

At first glance DF's case may seem quite hopeless. Far from admitting in her pleading, testimony, or otherwise in court that a contract for sale was made, Mrs. Brown denied under oath that a contract had been made. DF argues, however, that if it could depose her, maybe she would admit in her deposition that the affidavit was in error, that she had talked to Briggs on November 26, and that they had agreed to the sale of the chair on the terms contained in Briggs' letter of confirmation to her.

There is remarkably little authority on the precise question raised by this appeal—whether a sworn denial ends the case or the plaintiff may press on, and insist on discovery. In fact we have found no authority at the appellate level, state or federal. Many cases hold, it is true, that the defendant in a suit on an oral contract apparently made unenforceable by the statute of frauds cannot block discovery aimed at extracting an admission that the contract was made, simply by moving to dismiss the suit on the basis of the statute of frauds or by denying in the answer to the complaint that a contract had been made.... The clash of views is well discussed in Triangle Marketing, Inc. v. Action Industries, Inc., 630 F.Supp. 1578, 1581–83 (N.D.Ill.1986), which, in default of any guidance from Illinois courts, adopted the Boylan position. We need not take sides on the conflict. When there is a bare motion to dismiss, or an answer, with no evidentiary materials, the possibility remains a live one that, if asked under oath whether a contract had been made, the defendant would admit it had been. The only way to test the proposition is for the plaintiff to take the defendant's deposition, or, if there is no discovery, to call the defendant as an adverse witness at trial. But where as in this case the defendant swears in an affidavit that there was no contract, we see no point in keeping the lawsuit alive. Of course the defendant may blurt out an admission in a deposition, but this is hardly likely, especially since by doing so he may be admitting to having perjured himself in his affidavit. Stranger things have happened, but remote possibilities do not warrant subjecting the parties and the judiciary to proceedings almost certain to be futile.

A plaintiff cannot withstand summary judgment by arguing that although in pretrial discovery he has gathered no evidence of the defendant's liability, his luck may improve at trial. . . . The statement in a leading commercial law text that a defense based on the statute of fraud must always be determined at trial because the defendant might in cross-examination admit the making of the contract, see White & Summers, Handbook of the Law Under the Uniform Commercial Code 67 (1980), reflects a misunderstanding of the role of summary judgment; for the statement implies, contrary to modern practice, that a party unable to generate a genuine issue of fact at the summary judgment stage, because he has no evidence with which to contest an affidavit of his adversary, see Fed.R.Civ.P. 56(e), may nevertheless obtain a trial of the issue. He may not. By the same token, a plaintiff in a suit on a contract within the statute of frauds should not be allowed to resist a motion to dismiss, backed by an affidavit that the defendant denies the contract was made, by arguing that his luck may improve in discovery. Just as summary judgment proceedings differ from trials, so the conditions of a deposition differ from the conditions in which an affidavit is prepared; affidavits in litigation are prepared by lawyers, and merely signed by affiants. Yet to allow an affiant to be deposed by opposing counsel would be to invite the unedifying form of discovery in which the examining lawyer tries to put words in the witness's mouth and construe them as admissions.

The history of the judicial-admission exception to the statute of frauds, well told in Stevens, *Ethics and the Statute of Frauds,* 37 Cornell L.Q. 355 (1952), reinforces our conclusion. The exception began with common-sense recognition that if the defendant admitted in a pleading that he had made a contract with the plaintiff, the purpose of the statute of frauds—protection against fraudulent or otherwise false contractual claims—was fulfilled. (The situation would be quite otherwise, of course, with an oral admission, for a plaintiff willing to testify falsely to the existence of a contract would be equally willing to testify falsely to the defendant's having admitted the existence of the contract.) Toward the end of the eighteenth century the courts began to reject the exception, fearing that it was an invitation to the defendant to perjure himself. Later the pendulum swung again, and the exception is now firmly established. The concern with perjury that caused the courts in the middle period to reject the exception supports the position taken by Mrs. Brown in this case. She has sworn under oath that she did not agree to sell the Willits Chair to DF. DF wants an opportunity to depose her in the hope that she can be induced to change her testimony. But if she changes her testimony this will be virtually an admission that she perjured herself in her affidavit (for it is hardly likely that her denial was based simply on a faulty recollection). She is not likely to do this. What is possible is that her testimony will be sufficiently ambiguous to enable DF to argue that there should be still further factual investigation—perhaps a full-fledged trial at which Mrs. Brown will be questioned again about the existence of the contract.

With such possibilities for protraction, the statute of frauds becomes a defense of meager value. And yet it seems to us as it did to the framers of the Uniform Commercial Code that the statute of frauds serves an important purpose in a system such as ours that does not require that all contracts be in writing in order to be enforceable and that allows juries of lay persons to decide commercial cases. The methods of judicial factfinding do not distinguish unerringly between true and false testimony, and are in any event very expensive. People deserve some protection against the risks and costs of being hauled into court and accused of owing money on the basis of an unacknowledged promise. And being deposed is scarcely less unpleasant than being cross-examined—indeed, often it is more unpleasant, because the examining lawyer is not inhibited by the presence of a judge or jury who might resent hectoring tactics. The transcripts of depositions are often very ugly documents.

Some courts still allow the judicial-admission exception to be defeated by the defendant's simple denial, in a pleading, that there was a contract; this is the position well articulated in Judge Shadur's opinion in the *Triangle Marketing* case. To make the defendant repeat the denial under oath is already to erode the exception (as well as to create the invitation to perjury that so concerned the courts that rejected the judicial-admission exception altogether), for there is always the possibility, though a very small one, that the defendant might be charged with perjury. But, in any event, once the defendant has denied the contract under oath, the safety valve of section 2–201(3)(b) is closed. The chance that at a deposition the defendant might be badgered into withdrawing his denial is too remote to justify prolonging an effort to enforce an oral contract in the teeth of the statute of frauds. If Dorothy Brown did agree on November 27 to sell the chair to DF at a bargain price, it behooved Briggs to get Brown's signature on the dotted line, posthaste.

AFFIRMED.

■ FLAUM, CIRCUIT JUDGE, dissenting.

Because I disagree with the majority's holding that additional discovery is prohibited whenever a defendant raises a statute of frauds defense and submits a sworn denial that he or she formed an oral contract with the plaintiff, I respectfully dissent. Neither would I hold, however, that a plaintiff is automatically entitled to additional discovery in the face of a defendant's sworn denial that an agreement was reached. Rather, in my view district courts should have the authority to exercise their discretion to determine the limits of permissible discovery in these cases. This flexibility is particularly important where, as here, the defendant's affidavit does not contain a conclusive denial of contract formation. While district courts have broad discretion in discovery matters, I believe the district court abused that discretion in the present case.

* * *

Because in my view the district court abused its discretion when it prohibited further discovery, I would remand this case to the district court with instructions to permit discovery to continue at least to the point where DF is given an opportunity to depose Brown. If Brown then denies under oath during her deposition that any oral contract was made, summary judgment might well be appropriate at that time.

NOTES

(1) *To Demur or Not to Demur?* Judge Posner notes that the court did not have to take sides as to whether a defendant in a suit on an oral contract can block discovery aimed at extracting an admission by moving to dismiss. But (alas), you do, at least for classroom purposes. Before deciding, consider these examples of the "clash of views" to which Judge Posner alludes:

(a) "The admission exception now included in the Statute of Frauds governing sales would be meaningless were the defendant permitted by the simple expedient of a motion to dismiss to deprive plaintiff of the opportunity to obtain from defendant either an admission 'in his pleading, testimony or otherwise in court' or a sworn denial of the existence of a contract.... If a prepleading motion to dismiss is permitted to defeat a cause of action on an oral sales contract before plaintiff has had an opportunity to elicit from defendant a statement in court of any kind, only malpractice by defendant's attorney would subject the defendant to the statute's ameliorative purpose. The Legislature in adopting the Uniform Commercial Code and the drafters of the Code cannot reasonably be thought to have intended that the exception have such limited application." Meyer, J., dissenting in Boylan v. G.L. Morrow Co., 63 N.Y.2d 616, 623, 479 N.Y.S.2d 499, 503, 468 N.E.2d 681, 684–85 (1984).

(b) "But those 'admissions' are not really admissions in the factual sense at all. Parties who move to dismiss do not truly say: 'I admit the things you allege are true fact, but I am entitled to judgment on the law.' They rather say something more like: 'Even if your allegations were true, I am entitled to judgment on the law.' Thus a motion to dismiss 'admits' the complaint's allegations only in a 'technical' sense inadequate to meet Section 2–201(3)(b)'s admission requirement...." Shadur, J. in Triangle Marketing, Inc. v. Action Industries, Inc., 630 F.Supp. 1578, 1583–1584 (N.D.Ill.1986).

(2) If the defense is provided by statute, should there not be a convenient procedure by which to raise the defense? If so, what should it be?

Comment: The Statute of Frauds and Estoppel

Assume that Farmer and Dealer made an oral contract in March to sell 5,000 bushels of #1 Yellow Corn for $2.80 per bushel, delivery in October. Relying on Farmer's oral promise, Dealer promptly resold the corn to a third person for $3.50 per bushel. Farmer, based upon their prior course of dealing, knew that this resale would probably occur. When the market price rose to $5.00 per bushel in September, Farmer refused to deliver. Dealer, alleging the oral contract and the resale, claims damages. Farmer moves to dismiss on the ground of the statute of frauds. UCC 2–201. Dealer argues that the statute of frauds should be avoided because of reliance upon Farmer's oral promise to deliver. Should this argument be accepted?

The question has created difficulty because an affirmative answer appears to be in direct conflict with the purpose and policy of the statute. There are no misrepresentations of fact by Farmer here and no representation that Farmer will not will not insist upon a writing. Rather, it is the oral promise that should have been in writing that induced the reliance by Dealer. According to one Court: "[T]he moral wrong of refusing to be bound by an agreement because it does not comply with the Statute of Frauds, does not of itself authorize the application of the doctrine of estoppel, for the breach of a promise which the law does not regard as binding is not a fraud. . . . To hold otherwise would be to render the statute entirely nugatory." Ozier v. Haines, 411 Ill. 160, 103 N.E.2d 485 (1952).

Reflecting the sparsity of case law in which a plaintiff has successfully employed estoppel in a Statute of Frauds case, the drafters of the first Restatement did not include a specific section on the subject. They did, however, append the following comment: "Though there has been no satisfaction of the Statute, an estoppel may preclude objection on that ground in the same way that objection to the non-existence of other facts essential for the establishment of a right or a defense may be precluded. A misrepresentation that there has been such satisfaction if substantial action is taken in reliance on the representation, precludes proof by the party who made the representation that it was false; and a promise to make a memorandum, if similarly relied on, may give rise to an effective promissory estoppel if the Statute would otherwise operate to defraud." Restatement § 178, Comment f.

By contrast, the revised Restatement includes a separate section on "enforcement by virtue of action in reliance." Restatement (Second) § 139. It provides as follows:

(1) A promise which the promisor should reasonably expect to induce action or forbearance on the part of the promisee or a third person and which does induce the action or forbearance is enforceable notwithstanding the Statute of Frauds if injustice can be avoided only by enforcement of the promise. The remedy granted for breach is to be limited as justice requires.

(2) In determining whether injustice can be avoided only by enforcement of the promise, the following circumstances are significant: (a) the availability and adequacy of other remedies, particularly cancellation and restitution; (b) the definite and substantial character of the action or forbearance in relation to the remedy sought; (c) the extent to which the action or forbearance corroborates evidence of the making and terms of the promise, or the making and terms are otherwise established by clear and convincing evidence; (d) the reasonableness of the action or forbearance; (e) the extent to which the action or forbearance was foreseeable by the promisor.

Section 139 complements Section 90 of the revised Restatement, and, like that section, states a "flexible" principle. However, it is acknowledged that "the requirement of consideration is more easily displaced than the requirement of a writing." Restatement (Second) § 139, Comment b.

Section 139 should give Dealer hope, especially if subsection 2(c) can be satisfied. Despite this embrace of the general principal, there is disagreement over whether promissory estoppel is available to save an oral contract for sale under UCC 2–201. The legislative history, the language, and the structure of Section 2–201 show that promissory estoppel was not to be used to evade the rather simple requirements of the section. Gibson, *Promissory Estoppel, Article 2 of the U.C.C., and the Restatement (Third) of Contracts,* 73 Iowa L.Rev. 659, 695 (1988). Given that the opening words of UCC 2–201 are that "[e]xcept as otherwise provided in this section" an oral contract for $500 or more is not enforceable, there is no warrant for engrafting an additional promissory estoppel "exception" to UCC 2–201.

Professor Gibson documents the split of authority. Some courts refuse to use promissory estoppel in this area; some apply it whenever fraud or unconscionability is present; still others, like the Seventh Circuit in *R.S. Bennett & Co. v. Economy Mechanical Industries, Inc., 606 F.2d 182 (7th Cir.1979),* will evidently apply it whenever the ordinary elements of promissory estoppel are present. See generally Comment, *Jeffrey Kagan, The Indelibility of Invisible Ink: A Critical Survey of The Enforcement of Oral Contracts Without the Statute of Frauds under the Uniform Commercial Code,* 19 Whittier L. Rev. 423 (1997).

Thesis: In view of the erosion of UCC 2–201, through "admissions" and "estoppel" exceptions, the provision no longer serves a useful purpose and should be repealed. Agree or disagree?

PROBLEM: THE CASE OF THE LAKE WOBEGON LOT PURCHASE

For years Paula Purchaser has sought to buy a lot on Lake Wobegon owned by Vincent Vendor. Last week Paula made yet another attempt to purchase the land, a one acre lot with lake frontage and the only property owned by Vince, and this time the latter was agreeable. While discussing the matter at Vince's house, they agreed upon all of the essential terms, including the cash price of $10,000. After "shaking on it," Paula wrote a check for $1,000, down payment on the purchase. The check was made out to Vincent Vendor and contained the following legend: "$1,000 down on lot on Lake Wobegon, balance due $9,000." The following week, however, Vince changed his mind about selling and tendered the check back to Paula. Does Paula have legal recourse? What if Paula, in the meantime, had made a commitment to a bank to borrow funds to complete the purchase?

Assume, instead, that after agreeing upon the essential terms, including the cash price of $10,000, Paula wrote out the $1,000 check as down payment (but without the legend, as above) and gave it to Vince. Vince immediately cashed the check. Thereafter, Paula determined not to go through with the deal and wants her down payment returned. Vince, however, is willing to complete the transaction whenever agreeable to Paula. Is Paula entitled to a return of the $1,000?

CHAPTER THREE

AN INTRODUCTION TO CONTRACT REMEDIES

SECTION 1. BASIC POLICIES

We have just examined the various bases of promissory liability, that is, the grounds for creating a contractual obligation. This Chapter provides an introduction to the remedies available for breach of contract. A fuller treatment of remedies is provided in Chapter Seven.

As you will see in Chapter Seven, Section (1), the types of breach that trigger remedies fall into three categories: (1) A failure without justification to perform a contractual promise or bargain at the time agreed; (2) A repudiation of the promise or bargain; and (3) bad faith in the form of preventing or hindering the other party's performance or failing to cooperate. We assume here that an actionable breach has occurred.

Here are some basic remedial policies.

First, a contractual duty is usually conditioned on the other side not breaching its own promises. Accordingly, a material breach by one party gives the non-breaching party the option to suspend its performance or to cancel the contract and sue for damages. A non-material breach does not give the option to cancel, but the aggrieved party is entitled to recover damages for breach. Suspension or cancellation, when available, are self-help remedies: they do not depend on a court judgment.

Second, Anglo–American law has exhibited a preference for monetary damages (compensation) instead of specific performance (a judicial order to perform or go to jail for contempt). Specific performance is normally given only if the subject matter of the contract is unique or monetary damages are inadequate. But there are some scholars who believe that specific performance should be the rule rather than the exception. These remedies, damages or specific performance, do depend upon a court judgment.

Third, although there are several ways to measure in dollars the loss caused by a breach, a basic assumption (in bargain transactions at least) is that the aggrieved party should recover both net gains prevented by the breach (expectation) and any other uncompensated losses resulting from the breach. Thus, a primary purpose of damages for breach of a bargain contract is to put the aggrieved party in the position that it would have been in if the defendant had fully performed. But note, the plaintiff may assert claims based upon restitution or reliance either in addition to or in lieu of expectation. How the courts treat these claim is a matter of importance.

Fourth, as a corollary, it is stated that the primary purpose of contract remedies however measured is to compensate the aggrieved party for losses suffered rather than to punish the contract breacher. Unlike the law of crimes or torts, deterrence is almost never an objective in contract remedies. Thus, punitive damages for breach of contract are rarely awarded.

As one court put it:

[O]ur system of contract remedies rejects, for the most part, compulsion of the promisor as a goal. It does not impose criminal penalties on one who refuses to perform his promise, nor does it generally require him to pay punitive damages. Our system of contract remedies is not directed at *compulsion* of *promisors* to *prevent* breach; it is aimed, instead, at *relief* to *promisees* to *redress* breach. Its preoccupation is not with the question: how can promisors be made to keep their promises? Its concern is with a different question: how can people be encouraged to deal with those who make promises? . . .

Frankenmuth Mutual Insurance Company v. Keeley, 433 Mich. 525, 558 n. 23, 447 N.W.2d 691 (1989) (dissent. op.).

One reason for this is economic: it is, perhaps, more efficient to say to the breacher: "You may breach this contract and move your resources to higher levels of utility if you are prepared to compensate the aggrieved party for the losses thereby caused. Thus, as you decide whether to breach, you need consider only the probability that a judgment for compensatory damages will be imposed, not the risk of an additional amount for punishment." This, in a nutshell, is one version of the doctrine of "efficient breach."

Fifth, there are several explicit policies that permeate the process of translating losses caused by the breach into dollars:

(a) The plaintiff must prove that (1) the breach was the substantial cause of the loss complained of, and (2) the amount of the loss caused with reasonable certainty. Proof problems are more important than causation problems in the law of contracts.

(b) The provable losses caused by the breach must have been reasonably foreseeable to the defendant at the time of contracting. If not, these consequential damages are not recoverable. This is the famous rule of *Hadley v. Baxendale*, infra at 206.

(c) The plaintiff has a "duty" after the breach to make all reasonable efforts to avoid the consequences of the breach. If the defendant, who has the burden of proof, establishes a failure to "mitigate damages," this item of recovery, even if caused, certain and foreseeable, may not be recovered.

Sixth, the parties have power through agreement to expand or narrow the remedies normally available for breach of contract. In addition, they may substitute arbitration or some other dispute resolving mechanism for the judicial process.

Seventh, in addition to compensatory damages, the victorious party may also recover interest on sums of money withheld and, in the discretion of the court, the costs associated with the litigation. But attorney fees are not awarded to the victor in the absence of agreement, statute or, perhaps, a vexatious and unfounded suit brought by the plaintiff. More pointedly, there is no way to compensate either party for what we might call imperfections or inefficiencies in the process of adjudication, such as delay. These transaction costs clearly influence the plaintiff's choice on when to seek judicial remedies and how far to go before considering a settlement.

Now let's see how these policies play out in some cases.

SECTION 2.   MEASURING AND COMPENSATING LOSS RESULTING FROM A BREACH

Sullivan v. O'Connor

Supreme Judicial Court of Massachusetts, 1973.
363 Mass. 579, 296 N.E.2d 183.

■ KAPLAN, JUSTICE. The plaintiff patient secured a jury verdict of $13,500 against the defendant surgeon for breach of contract in respect to an operation upon the plaintiff's nose. The substituted consolidated bill of exceptions presents questions about the correctness of the judge's instructions on the issue of damages.

The declaration was in two counts. In the first count, the plaintiff alleged that she, as patient, entered into a contract with the defendant, a surgeon, wherein the defendant promised to perform plastic surgery on her nose and thereby to enhance her beauty and improve her appearance; that he performed the surgery but failed to achieve the promised result; rather the result of the surgery was to disfigure and deform her nose, to cause her pain in body and mind, and to subject her to other damage and expense. The second count, based on the same transaction, was in the conventional form for malpractice, charging that the defendant had been guilty of negligence in performing the surgery. Answering, the defendant entered a general denial.

On the plaintiff's demand, the case was tried by jury. At the close of the evidence, the judge put to the jury, as special questions, the issues of liability under the two counts, and instructed them accordingly. The jury returned a verdict for the plaintiff on the contract count, and for the defendant on the negligence count. The judge then instructed the jury on the issue of damages.

As background to the instructions and the parties' exceptions, we mention certain facts as the jury could find them. The plaintiff was a professional entertainer, and this was known to the defendant. The agreement was as alleged in the declaration. More particularly, judging from exhibits, the plaintiff's nose had been straight, but long and prominent; the defendant undertook by two operations to reduce its prominence and somewhat to shorten it, thus making it more pleasing in relation to the plaintiff's other features. Actually the plaintiff was obliged to undergo three operations, and her appearance was worsened. Her nose now had a concave line to about the midpoint, at which it became bulbous; viewed frontally, the nose from bridge to midpoint was flattened and broadened, and the two sides of the tip had lost symmetry. This configuration evidently could not be improved by further surgery. The plaintiff did not demonstrate, however, that her change of appearance had resulted in loss of employment. Payments by the plaintiff covering the defendant's fee and hospital expenses were stipulated at $622.65.

The judge instructed the jury, first, that the plaintiff was entitled to recover her out-of-pocket expenses incident to the operations. Second, she could recover the damages flowing directly, naturally, proximately, and foreseeably from the defendant's breach of promise. These would comprehend damages for any disfigurement of the plaintiff's nose—that is, any change of appearance for the worse—including the effects of the consciousness of such disfigurement on the plaintiff's mind, and in this connection the jury should consider the nature of the plaintiff's profession. Also consequent upon the defendant's breach, and compensable, were the pain and suffering involved in the third operation, but not in the first two. As there was no proof that any loss of earnings by the plaintiff resulted from the breach, that element should not enter into the calculation of damages.

By his exceptions the defendant contends that the judge erred in allowing the jury to take into account anything but the plaintiff's out-of-pocket expenses (presumably at the stipulated amount). The defendant excepted to the judge's refusal of his request for a general charge to that effect, and, more specifically, to the judge's refusal of a charge that the plaintiff could not recover for pain and suffering connected with the third operation or for impairment of the plaintiff's appearance and associated mental distress.

The plaintiff on her part excepted to the judge's refusal of a request to charge that the plaintiff could recover the difference in value between the nose as promised and the nose as it appeared after the operations. However, the plaintiff in her brief expressly waives this exception and others made by her in case this court overrides the defendant's exceptions; thus she would be content to hold the jury's verdict in her favor.

We conclude that the defendant's exceptions should be overruled.

It has been suggested on occasion that agreements between patients and physicians by which the physician undertakes to effect a cure or to bring about a given result should be declared unenforceable on grounds of public policy.... But there are many decisions recognizing and enforcing such contracts, see annotation, 43 A.L.R.3d 1221, 1225, 1229–1233, and the law of Massachusetts has treated them as valid, although we have had no decision meeting head on the contention that they should be denied legal sanction. ... These causes of action are, however, considered a little suspect, and thus we find courts straining sometimes to read the pleadings as sounding only in tort for negligence, and not in contract for breach of promise, despite sedulous efforts by the pleaders to pursue the latter theory. ...

It is not hard to see why the courts should be unenthusiastic or skeptical about the contract theory. Considering the uncertainties of medical science and the variations in the physical and psychological conditions of individual patients, doctors can seldom in good faith promise specific results. Therefore it is unlikely that physicians of even average integrity will in fact make such promises. Statements of opinion by the physician with some optimistic coloring are a different thing, and may indeed have therapeutic value. But patients may transform such statements into firm promises in their own minds, especially when they have been disappointed in the event, and testify in that sense to sympathetic juries.[2] If actions for breach of promise can be readily maintained, doctors, so it is said, will be frightened into practicing "defensive medicine." On the other hand, if these actions were outlawed, leaving only the possibility of suits for malpractice, there is fear that the public might be exposed to the enticements of charlatans, and confidence in the profession might ultimately be shaken. See Miller, The Contractual Liability of Physicians and Surgeons, 1953 Wash.L.Q. 413, 416–423. The law has taken the middle of the road position of allowing actions based on alleged contract, but insisting on clear proof. Instructions to the jury may well stress this requirement and point to tests of truth, such as the complexity or difficulty of an operation as bearing on the probability that a given result was promised . . . .

If an action on the basis of contract is allowed, we have next the question of the measure of damages to be applied where liability is found. Some cases have taken the simple view that the promise by the physician is to be treated like an ordinary commercial promise, and accordingly that the successful plaintiff is entitled to a standard measure of recovery for breach of contract—"compensatory" ("expectancy") damages, an amount intended to put the plaintiff in the position he would be in if the contract had been performed, or, presumably, at the plaintiff's election, "restitution" damages, an amount corresponding to any benefit conferred by the plaintiff upon the defendant in the performance of the contract disrupted by the defendant's breach. See Restatement: Contracts § 329 and comment a, §§ 347, 384(1). Thus in Hawkins v. McGee, 84 N.H. 114, the defendant doctor was taken to have promised the plaintiff to convert his damaged hand by means of an operation into a good or perfect hand, but the doctor so operated as to damage the hand still further. The court, following the usual expectancy formula, would have asked the jury to estimate and award to the plaintiff the difference between the value of a good or perfect hand, as promised, and the value of the hand after the operation. (The same formula would apply, although the dollar result would be less, if the operation had neither worsened nor improved the condition of the hand.) If the plaintiff had not yet paid the doctor his fee, that amount would be

---

2. Judicial skepticism about whether a promise was in fact made derives also from the possibility that the truth has been tortured to give the plaintiff the advantage of the longer period of limitations sometimes available for actions on contract as distinguished from those in tort or for malpractice. See Lillich, The Malpractice Statute of Limitations in New York and Other Jurisdictions, 47 Cornell L.Q. 339; annotation, 80 A.L.R.2d 368.

deducted from the recovery. There could be no recovery for the pain and suffering of the operation, since that detriment would have been incurred even if the operation had been successful; one can say that this detriment was not "caused" by the breach. But where the plaintiff by reason of the operation was put to more pain than he would have had to endure, had the doctor performed as promised, he should be compensated for that difference as a proper part of his expectancy recovery. It may be noted that on an alternative count for malpractice the plaintiff in the *Hawkins* case had been nonsuited; but on ordinary principles this could not affect the contract claim, for it is hardly a defense to a breach of contract that the promisor acted innocently and without negligence. The New Hampshire court further refined the *Hawkins* analysis in McQuaid v. Michou, 85 N.H. 299, 157 A. 881, all in the direction of treating the patient-physician cases on the ordinary footing of expectancy. See McGee v. United States Fid. & Guar. Co., 53 F.2d 953 (1st Cir.) (later development in the *Hawkins* case); ...

Other cases, including a number in New York, without distinctly repudiating the *Hawkins* type of analysis, have indicated that a different and generally more lenient measure of damages is to be applied in patient-physician actions based on breach of alleged special agreements to effect a cure, attain a stated result, or employ a given medical method. This measure is expressed in somewhat variant ways, but the substance is that the plaintiff is to recover any expenditures made by him and for other detriment (usually not specifically described in the opinions) following proximately and foreseeably upon the defendant's failure to carry out his promise.... This, be it noted, is not a "restitution" measure, for it is not limited to restoration of the benefit conferred on the defendant (the fee paid) but includes other expenditures, for example, amounts paid for medicine and nurses; so also it would seem according to its logic to take in damages for any worsening of the plaintiff's condition due to the breach. Nor is it an "expectancy" measure, for it does not appear to contemplate recovery of the whole difference in value between the condition as promised and the condition actually resulting from the treatment. Rather the tendency of the formulation is to put the plaintiff back in the position he occupied just before the parties entered upon the agreement, to compensate him for the detriments he suffered in reliance upon the agreement. This kind of intermediate pattern of recovery for breach of contract is discussed in the suggestive article by Fuller and Perdue, The Reliance Interest in Contract Damages, 46 Yale L.J. 52, 373, where the authors show that, although not attaining the currency of the standard measures, a "reliance" measure has for special reasons been applied by the courts in a variety of settings, including noncommercial settings. See 46 Yale L.J. at 396–401.[4]

For breach of the patient-physician agreements under consideration, a recovery limited to restitution seems plainly too meager, if the agreements

---

4. Some of the exceptional situations mentioned where reliance may be preferred to expectancy are those in which the latter measure would be hard to apply or would impose too great a burden; performance was interfered with by external circumstances; the contract was indefinite. See 46 Yale L.J. at 373–386; 394–396.

are to be enforced at all. On the other hand, an expectancy recovery may well be excessive. The factors, already mentioned, which have made the cause of action somewhat suspect, also suggest moderation as to the breadth of the recovery that should be permitted. Where, as in the case at bar and in a number of the reported cases the doctor has been absolved of negligence by the trier, an expectancy measure may be thought harsh. We should recall here that the fee paid by the patient to the doctor for the alleged promise would usually be quite disproportionate to the putative expectancy recovery. To attempt, moreover, to put a value on the condition that would or might have resulted, had the treatment succeeded as promised, may sometimes put an exceptional strain on the imagination of the fact finder. As a general consideration, Fuller and Perdue argue that the reasons for granting damages for broken promises to the extent of the expectancy are at their strongest when the promises are made in a business context, when they have to do with the production or distribution of goods or the allocation of functions in the market place; they become weaker as the context shifts from a commercial to a noncommercial field. 46 Yale L.J. at 60–63.

There is much to be said, then, for applying a reliance measure to the present facts, and we have only to add that our cases are not unreceptive to the use of that formula in special situations. We have, however, had no previous occasion to apply it to patient-physician cases.[5]

The question of recovery on a reliance basis for pain and suffering or mental distress requires further attention. We find expressions in the decisions that pain and suffering (or the like) are simply not compensable in actions for breach of contract. The defendant seemingly espouses this proposition in the present case. True, if the buyer under a contract for the purchase of a lot of merchandise, in suing for the seller's breach, should

5. In Mt. Pleasant Stable Co. v. Steinberg, 238 Mass. 567, the plaintiff company agreed to supply teams of horses at agreed rates as required from day to day by the defendant for his business. To prepare itself to fulfill the contract and in reliance on it, the plaintiff bought two "Cliest" horses at a certain price. When the defendant repudiated the contract, the plaintiff sold the horses at a loss and in its action for breach claimed the loss as an element of damages. The court properly held that the plaintiff was not entitled to this item as it was also claiming (and recovering) its lost profits (expectancy) on the contract as a whole. Cf. Noble v. Ames Mfg. Co. (The loss on sale of the horses is analogous to the pain and suffering for which the patient would be disallowed a recovery in Hawkins v. McGee, 84 N.H. 114, because he was claiming and recovering expectancy damages.) The court in the *Mt. Pleasant* case referred, however, to Pond v. Harris, 113 Mass. 114, as a contrasting situation where the expectancy could not be fairly determined. There the defendant had wrongfully revoked an agreement to arbitrate a dispute with the plaintiff (this was before such agreements were made specifically enforceable). In an action for the breach, the plaintiff was held entitled to recover for his preparations for the arbitration which had been rendered useless and a waste, including the plaintiff's time and trouble and his expenditures for counsel and witnesses. The context apparently was commercial but reliance elements were held compensable when there was no fair way of estimating an expectancy. See, generally, annotation, 17 A.L.R.2d 1300. A noncommercial example is Smith v. Sherman, 4 Cush. 408, 413–414, suggesting that a conventional recovery for breach of promise of marriage included a recompense for various efforts and expenditures by the plaintiff preparatory to the promised wedding. . . .

claim damages for mental anguish caused by his disappointment in the transaction, he would not succeed; he would be told, perhaps, that the asserted psychological injury was not fairly foreseeable by the defendant as a probable consequence of the breach of such a business contract. See Restatement: Contracts, § 341, and comment a. But there is no general rule barring such items of damage in actions for breach of contract. It is all a question of the subject matter and background of the contract, and when the contract calls for an operation on the person of the plaintiff, psychological as well as physical injury may be expected to figure somewhere in the recovery, depending on the particular circumstances. The point is explained in Stewart v. Rudner, 349 Mich. 459, 469.... Again, it is said in a few of the New York cases, concerned with the classification of actions for statute of limitations purposes, that the absence of allegations demanding recovery for pain and suffering is characteristic of a contract claim by a patient against a physician, that such allegations rather belong in a claim for malpractice.... These remarks seem unduly sweeping.

Suffering or distress resulting from the breach going beyond that which was envisaged by the treatment as agreed, should be compensable on the same ground as the worsening of the patient's condition because of the breach. Indeed it can be argued that the very suffering or distress "contracted for"—that which would have been incurred if the treatment achieved the promised result—should also be compensable on the theory underlying the New York cases. For that suffering is "wasted" if the treatment fails. Otherwise stated, compensation for this waste is arguably required in order to complete the restoration of the status quo ante.[6]

In the light of the foregoing discussion, all the defendant's exceptions fail; the plaintiff was not confined to the recovery of her out-of-pocket expenditures; she was entitled to recover also for the worsening of her condition,[7] and for the pain and suffering and mental distress involved in the third operation. These items were compensable on either an expectancy or a reliance view. We might have been required to elect between the two

---

6. Recovery on a reliance basis for breach of the physician's promise tends to equate with the usual recovery for malpractice, since the latter also looks in general to restoration of the condition before the injury. But this is not paradoxical, especially when it is noted that the origins of contract lie in tort. See Farnsworth, The Past of Promise: An Historical Introduction to Contract, 69 Col.L.Rev. 576, 594–596; Breitel, J. in Stella Flour & Feed Corp. v. National City Bank, 285 App.Div. 182, 189, 136 N.Y.S.2d 139 (dissenting opinion). A few cases have considered possible recovery for breach by a physician of a promise to sterilize a patient, resulting in birth of a child to the patient and spouse. If such an action is held maintainable, the reliance and expectancy measures would, we think, tend to equate, because the promised condition was preservation of the family status quo....

It would, however, be a mistake to think in terms of strict "formulas." For example, a jurisdiction which would apply a reliance measure to the present facts might impose a more severe damage sanction for the wilful use by the physician of a method of operation that he undertook not to employ.

7. That condition involves a mental element and appraisal of it properly called for consideration of the fact that the plaintiff was an entertainer. Cf. McQuaid v. Michou, 85 N.H. 299, 303–304 (discussion of continuing condition resulting from physician's breach).

views if the pain and suffering connected with the first two operations contemplated by the agreement, or the whole difference in value between the present and the promised conditions, were being claimed as elements of damage. But the plaintiff waives her possible claim to the former element, and to so much of the latter as represents the difference in value between the promised condition and the condition before the operations.

Plaintiff's exceptions waived.

Defendant's exceptions overruled.

NOTES

(1) *Protected interests of the promisee.* Comment (a) to Section 329 of the first Restatement stated simply: "In awarding compensatory damages, the effort is made to put the injured party in as good a position as that in which he would have been put by full performance of the contract, at the least cost to the defendant and without charging him with harms that he had no sufficient reason to foresee when he made the contract." Compare UCC 1–106(1) [Rev. 1–305(a)].

Section 344 of Restatement (Second) states the "purposes" of contract remedies as follows:

Judicial remedies under the rules stated in this Restatement serve to protect one or more of the following interests of a promisee:

(a) his "expectation interest," which is his interest in having the benefit of his bargain by being put in as good a position as he would have been in had the contract been performed,

(b) his "reliance interest," which is his interest in being reimbursed for loss caused by reliance on the contract by being put in as good a position as he would have been in had the contract not been made, or

(c) his "restitution interest," which is his interest in having restored to him any benefit that he has conferred on the other party.

The court in *Sullivan* identified these three interests of the promisee that might be protected upon breach by the promisor: expectation, reliance and restitution. Why did the court refuse to protect Ms. Sullivan's "expectation" interest? What expenditures of Ms. Sullivan fit into her "restitution" interest? Her "reliance" interest? How would you classify a claim for pain and suffering or mental anguish caused by the breach?

(2) As the court indicates, promises by doctors and other providers of professional services to achieve a particular result are rare indeed. But are they against public policy? If not, should they be treated like any other promise?

In the absence of an enforceable promise to achieve a particular result, to what standard is the doctor held in performing the surgery? In general, the law requires the exercise of that skill and judgment which can be reasonably expected from similarly situated professionals, not perfect results. See Note, *Contorts: Patrolling the Borderland of Contract and Tort in Legal Malpractice Actions,* 22 B.C.L.Rev. 545 (1981).

(3) *Why Protect The Expectation Interest?* Why should contract remedies protect the expectation interest? Why not limit recovery to reliance or restitution?

One set of reasons involves the perceived need to support "efficient" exchange in competitive markets. Protecting expectations (1) rewards risk taking in market transactions and, therefore, contributes to allocative efficiency, and (2) deters the inefficient breach, i.e., a breach where the value derived when the breaching party re-employs resources committed to the contract is equaled or exceeded by the loss to the promisee. Put affirmatively, when contract law clearly protects the expectation interest, the parties can plan more effectively at the time of contracting and the breacher can better assess at the time of breach when the gains through breach will exceed the cost of compensating the aggrieved party. See Charles Goetz & Robert Scott, *Enforcing Promises: An Examination of the Basis of Contract,* 89 Yale L.J. 1261 (1980). The assumption here is that the efficient breach is a good thing, so long as the expectation interest of the aggrieved party is fully protected. There are, of course, skeptics. See, e.g., David Friedman, *The Efficient Breach Fallacy,* 18 J.Leg.Stud. 1 (1989); Ian R. Macneil, *Efficient Breach of Contract: Circles in the Sky,* 68 Va.L.Rev. 947 (1982).

Another set of reasons involves the asserted need to protect the reliance interest. The argument is that reliance is the primary interest to be protected but that proof of reliance, whether by action or forbearance, is costly and uncertain. There is a real risk that reliance that is "hidden" in opportunities foregone by the promisee will not be compensated. The solution is to award expectation damages, when provable with reasonable certainty, as a "surrogate" for accurate measurement of reliance. Thus, expectation recovery is viewed as an outer limit of recovery for actual but unprovable costs incurred and opportunities foregone in reliance on the promise. See Melvin A. Eisenberg, *The Bargain Principle and Its Limits,* 95 Harv.L.Rev. 741, 785–98 (1982). In the latter view, the importance of protecting expectations has more to do with fairness in the particular transaction than overall market efficiency. See Mark Pettit, *Private Advantage and Public Power: Reexamining the Expectation and Reliance Interests in Contract Damages,* 38 Hast.L.J. 417 (1987). Compare C. Fried, Contract as Promise: A Theory of Contractual Obligation 17–21 (1981), where both expectation and reliance are rejected as the basis of a theory of moral obligation.

Are these reasons persuasive? Can you think of any more reasons?

Curtice Brothers Co. v. Catts

Court of Chancery of New Jersey, 1907.
72 N.J.Eq. 831, 66 A. 935.

Complainant is engaged in the business of canning tomatoes and seeks the specific performance of a contract wherein defendant agreed to sell to complainant the entire product of certain land planted with tomatoes. Defendant contests the power of this court to grant equitable relief.

■ LEAMING, V.C. The fundamental principles which guide a court of equity in decreeing the specific performance of contracts are essentially the same whether the contracts relate to realty or to personalty. By reason of the fact that damages for the breach of contract for the sale of personalty are, in most cases, easily ascertainable and recoverable at law, courts of equity, in such cases withhold equitable relief. Touching contracts for the sale of land the reverse is the case. But no inherent difference between real estate and personal property controls the exercise of the jurisdiction. Where no adequate remedy at law exists specific performance of a contract touching the sale of personal property will be decreed with the same freedom as in the case of a contract for the sale of land. Professor Pomeroy, in referring to the distinction, says:

"In applying these principles, taking into account the discretionary nature of the jurisdiction, an agreement for the sale of land is *prima facie* presumed to come within their operation so as to be subject to specific performance, but a contrary presumption exists in regard to agreements concerning chattels." Pom. on Const. § 11.

Judge Story urges that there is no reasonable objection to allowing the party who is injured by the breach of any contract for the sale of chattels to have an election either to take damages at law or to have a specific performance in equity. 2 Story Eq.Jur. (13th Ed.) § 717a. While it is probable that the development of this branch of equitable remedies is decidedly toward the logical solution suggested by Judge Story, it is entirely clear that his view can not at this time be freely adopted without violence to what has long been regarded as accepted principles controlling the discretion of a court of equity in this class of cases. The United States Supreme Court has probably most nearly approached the view suggested by Judge Story. In Mechanics Bank of Alexandria v. Seton, 1 Pet. (U.S.) 299, 305, Mr. Justice Thompson, delivering the opinion of that court, says: "But notwithstanding this distinction between personal contracts for goods and contracts for lands is to be found laid down in the books as a general rule, yet there are many cases to be found where specific performance of contracts relating to personalty have been enforced in chancery, and courts will only view with greater nicety contracts of this description than such as relate to land." See also, Barr v. Lapsley, 1 Wheat. (U.S.) 151. In our own state contracts for the sale of chattels have been frequently enforced and the inadequacy of the remedy at law, based on the characteristic features of the contract or peculiar situation and needs of the parties, have been the principal grounds of relief. ...

I think it clear that the present case falls well within the principles defined by the cases already cited from our own state. Complainant's factory has a capacity of about one million cans of tomatoes. The season for packing lasts about six weeks. The preparations made for this six weeks of active work must be carried out in all features to enable the business to succeed. These preparations are primarily based upon the capacity of the plant. Cans and other necessary equipments, including labor, must be provided and secured in advance with reference to the capacity of the plant during the packing period. With this known capacity and an estimated average yield of tomatoes per acre the acreage of land necessary to supply the plant is calculated. To that end the contract now in question was made, with other like contracts, covering a sufficient acreage to insure the essential pack. It seems immaterial whether the entire acreage is contracted for to insure the full pack, or whether a more limited acreage is contracted for and an estimated available open market depended upon for the balance of the pack; in either case a refusal of the parties who contract to supply a given acreage to comply with their contracts leaves the factory helpless except to whatever extent an uncertain market may perchance supply the deficiency. The condition which arises from the breach of the contracts is not merely a question of the factory being compelled to pay a higher price for the product; losses sustained in that manner could, with some degree of accuracy, be estimated. The condition which occasions the irreparable injury by reason of the breaches of the contracts is the inability to procure at any price at the time needed and of the quality needed the necessary tomatoes to insure the successful operation of the plant. If it should be assumed as a fact that upon the breach of contracts of this nature other tomatoes of like quality and quantity could be procured in the open market without serious interference with the economic arrangements of the plant, a court of equity would hesitate to assume to interfere, but the very existence of such contracts proclaims their necessity to the economic management of the factory. The aspect of the situation bears no resemblance to that of an ordinary contract for the sale of merchandise in the course of an ordinary business. The business and its needs are extraordinary in that the maintenance of all of the conditions prearranged to secure the pack are a necessity to insure the successful operation of the plant. The breach of the contract by one planter differs but in degree from a breach by all.

Conditions were set + Known

The objection that to specifically perform the contract personal services are required will not divest the court of its powers to preserve the benefits of the contract. Defendant may be restrained from selling the crop to others, and if necessary, a receiver can be appointed to harvest the crop.

A decree may be devised pursuant to the prayer of the bill. By reason of the manner in which the facts on which the opinion is based were stipulated, no costs will be taxed.

NOTES

(1) This case, decided in 1907, involved a contract for the sale of goods. How would it be decided under Section 2–716(1) of the UCC, which provides: "Specific performance may be decreed where the goods are unique or in other proper circumstances?"

(2) Suppose, in *Sullivan v. O'Connor*, supra, the doctor had refused to perform the promised operation and no other surgeon would agree to perform the surgery. Could the plaintiff get a specific performance decree against the doctor?

(3) In Kessler v. Tortoise Development, Inc., 134 Idaho 264, 1 P.3d 292 (2000), the court affirmed the trial court's decision to condition an award of

specific performance upon the plaintiff/purchaser paying some of the costs incurred by the vendor in paying its unexpected cost of performance, i.e., paying off questionable liens before closing. The court said:

> There is no legal right to specific performance ... Specific performance is an extraordinary remedy that can provide relief when legal remedies are inadequate ... The inadequacy of remedies at law is presumed in an action for breach of a real estate purchase and sale agreement due to the perceived uniqueness of land ... But, specific performance is an equitable remedy and should not be granted when it would be unjust, oppressive, or unconscionable ... * * * The decision to grant specific performance is a matter within the district court's discretion ... When making its decision the court must balance the equities between the parties to determine whether specific performance is appropriate ... * * * We hold that the district court had the discretion to enter a conditional decree of specific performance in order to properly balance the equities of the case. 1 P.3d at 298.

(4) Rule 4 lives! The *Kessler* decision represents an unusual application of a "compensated injunction." Cf. Spur Indus., Inc. v. Del E. Webb Dev. Co., 108 Ariz. 178, 494 P.2d 700, 708 (1972)(plaintiff developer of retirement home forced to compensate defendant for injunction blocking operation of defendant's hog operation).

Comment on Calabresi and Melamed's Cathedral

In an immensely important article, Guido Calabresi (now a second circuit judge) and Doug Melamed (former head of the Justice Department's antitrust division) pointed out that legal entitlements tend to be protected in one of two distinctive ways.* Some entitlements are protected by strong "property rules" which attempt to deter third-parties from non-consensually taking the entitlement. Property rule protections are punitive in nature—often involving the threat of jail or supra-compensatory, punitive fines. In contrast, other entitlements are protected by weaker "liability rules" which attempt to compensate an entitlement holder for the loss of an entitlement that is non-consensually taken. Property rules are motivated by deterrence (of potential takers); liability rules are motivated by compensation (of potential takees). Intentionally take my car and the criminal law sends you to jail, but if you negligently destroy my car, the law of torts says you merely have to compensate me.

Calabresi and Melamed went on to suggest that property rule protections were likely to be more efficient when "transaction costs" were low and that liability rules were more likely to be efficient when transaction costs were high. If parties can easily contract (agree to consensually transfer an entitlement), we should protect the entitlement with a strong property rule to induce them to expressly contract. But liability rules make more sense when the parties don't have an opportunity to contract—for

* Guido Calabresi & A. Douglas Melamed, Property Rules, Liability Rules, and Inalienability: One View of the Cathedral, 85 Harv.L.Rev. 1089 (1972).

example, in the tort setting where it would be infeasible to contract with the myriad people who might hit your car.

Curiously, however, Calabresi and Melamed, who surveyed vast portions of law, did not analyze how contractual entitlements should be protected. If Calabresi contracts to sing at Melamed's wedding, Melamed has a contractual entitlement to Calabresi's performance. How should Melamed's entitlement be protected?

Calabresi and Melamed's theory might suggest that contractual entitlements should be protected by property rules—such as court orders of specific performance (perform or go to jail). After all, the parties were able to contract initially. Calabresi should be able to *renegotiate* if he doesn't want to perform. Calabresi could buy Melamed's contractual entitlement to hear Calabresi sing. But as emphasized above, contract law normally does not protect contractual entitlements with specific performance. Instead, the normal remedy is a liability-rule protection: expectation damages.*

Still there are several instances where contractual entitlements are protected by property rules. The exceptional cases where breach gives rise to punitive damages are an obvious example. But also stiffer remedies that might deter a promissor from breaching in the first place have a property rule quality. For example, a court that measures expectation damages by how much the promissor would have to pay to perform the promise (the so called "cost of performance" measure) will tend to deter the promissor from breaching (why breach if it doesn't save you any money).

Comment on Coase

The second central contribution of law and economics to contractual analysis is Ronald Coase's *The Problem of Social Cost*, 3 J. Law & Econ. 1 (1960) (the most cited article in legal academics!). The "Coase Theorem" says that in a world with no transaction costs, the choice of legal rules would not affect efficiency—because private parties would always bargain their way to optimal behavior.** This suggests that if renegotiation were costless, property rules and liability rule protections would be equally efficient.

Oliver Wendell Holmes famously reoriented contract law toward a dyadic conception of contractual duties. For Holmes, a contractual promise was not a sacred duty that simply had to be performed. Rather a contractual promise was merely the duty to perform or to pay (compensatory) damages. [Or in Calabresian terminology, the promisee's entitlement is only protected by a liability rule.]

* Maybe this is because it's easier to contract initially (when there are many potential singers and weddings) then to renegotiate (when there is only one potential buyer and seller).

** The Coase theorem has generated a huge literature—showing inter alia that the predicted effect will only hold true if the potential bargainers have sufficient information and wealth to bargain their way to the optimum.

But the Coase theorem invites a "triadic" conception of promise. For Coase a promise is a duty to (i) perform; (ii) pay damages; or (iii) renegotiate your way out of performance.

Imagine, for example, we're in a bizarre jurisdiction that imposed "property rule" damages that are twenty times the contract price. If Ayres has promised to paint Speidel's picture by the end of the year for $1,000, and Farnsworth comes along and offers Ayres $10,000 to paint Farnsworth's picture instead, the prospect of huge damages would normally deter Ayres from breaching the initial contract. But the Coase theorem suggests that Ayres will have an incentive to approach Speidel and try to buy his way out of the contract. The Coase theorem suggests that we don't have to worry about too few breaches when damages are high, because promissors will bribe their way out of having to perform.*

Comment: Restitution as a Remedy for Breach of Contract

As *Sullivan v. O'Connor* recognized, the plaintiff's payment to the doctor—the price paid to obtain the promised surgery—was an essential part of the agreed exchange. But the plaintiff did not choose to recover that payment alone. Rather, the plaintiff claimed and recovered both the payment made and other out-of-pocket costs as reliance expenditures.

Could the plaintiff choose to recover restitution of the price paid as the only remedy for breach of contract? According to Section 373 of the Restatement (Second), the answer is yes: the plaintiff is "entitled to restitution for any benefit he has conferred" on a party who commits a "total" breach "by way of part performance or reliance." This principle was embraced by the United States Supreme Court in Mobil Oil Exploration v. U.S., 530 U.S. 604, 607–639, 120 S.Ct. 2423, 147 L.Ed.2d 528 (2000). In *Mobil Oil*, the plaintiff had paid the United States $156 million in return for leases giving them the right to explore for and develop oil on public lands off the North Carolina coast. When the United States repudiated those leases (the main issue in the case), the plaintiff was entitled to recover the money paid as restitution. The Court concluded that the United States as a contracting party is "governed generally by the law applicable to contracts between private individuals" and endorsed the Restatement as a reflection "of the principles of contract law that are applicable to this case."

So far so good. But here are some questions, to be considered later in Chapter 7.

First, suppose the plaintiff would have lost money if the contract had been fully performed. Suppose, for example, that the plaintiff in *Mobil Oil* would have spent millions in exploration and never found any oil. Should the restitution recovery be adjusted for those losses and, if so, in what proportion and who has the burden of proof? Is it fair that a plaintiff might be made better off by the defendant's breach?

---

* Similarly, we don't have to worry about too much breach when damages are low, be- cause promisees will bribe promissors not to breach.

Second, in cases where the payment of money is not involved, what is the measure of the benefit conferred on the defendant? Is it the reasonable value of the services measured in market terms or the value to the defendant of what was received, or something else? This question has arisen in the aftermath of United States v. Winstar Corp., 518 U.S. 839, 116 S.Ct. 2432, 135 L.Ed.2d 964 (1996), which held the United States liable for breach of promises made to certain savings and loan companies who agreed to take over and operate failed thrifts. A hint of the complexity of that question in the particular context is revealed in California Federal Bank, FSB v. United States, 245 F.3d 1342 (Fed.Cir.2001) (en banc).

Third, it is important to distinguish "restitution" as a measure of damages for breach of contract from "restitution" as a separate cause of action for "receipt of an economic benefit under circumstances such that its retention without payment would result in the unjust enrichment." Restatement (Third) of Restitution § 1 Comment (2002). The latter, liability in restitution is "the law of nonconsensual or nonbargained benefits in the sense that torts is the law of nonconsensual and nonlicensed harms." Id. at § 2. Liability in restitution is related to liability in quasi-contract (discussed in *Bailey v. West* supra at 12.

Finally, how does restitution as a remedy for breach of contract relate to restitution as a pervasive remedy to prevent unjust enrichment? We will return to this question in Chapter Seven, Section 2(B), *infra*.

Hadley v. Baxendale

Court of Exchequer, 1854.
9 Exch. 341, 156 Eng.Rep. 145.

The plaintiffs carried on an extensive business as millers at Gloucester on the 11th of May, their mill was stopped by a breakage of the crank shaft by which the mill was worked. The steam-engine was manufactured by Messrs. Joyce & Co., the engineers, at Greenwich, and it became necessary to send the shaft as a pattern for a new one to Greenwich. The fracture was discovered on the 12th, and on the 13th the plaintiffs sent one of their servants to the office of the defendants, who are the well-known carriers trading under the name of Pickford & Co., for the purpose of having the shaft carried to Greenwich. [The plaintiffs' servant *did not* tell the carrier that the mill was stopped and that the shaft must be sent immediately. Ed.] In answer to the inquiry when the shaft would be taken, the answer was, that if it was sent up by twelve o'clock any day, it would be delivered at Greenwich on the following day. On the following day the shaft was taken by the defendants, before noon, for the purpose of being conveyed to Greenwich, and the sum of £2, 4s. was paid for its carriage for the whole distance; at the same time the defendants' clerk was told that a special entry, if required, should be made to hasten its delivery. The delivery of the shaft at Greenwich was delayed by some neglect; and the consequence was, that the plaintiffs did not receive the new shaft for several days after they would otherwise have done, and the working of their mill was thereby delayed, and they thereby lost the profits they would otherwise have received.

On the part of the defendants, it was objected that these damages were too remote, and that the defendants were not liable with respect to them. The learned Judge left the case generally to the jury, who found a verdict with £25 damages beyond the amount paid into Court.

Whateley, in last Michaelmas Term, obtained a rule nisi for a new trial on the ground of misdirection.

* * *

■ ALDERSON, B. We think that there ought to be a new trial in this case; but, in so doing, we deem it to be expedient and necessary to state explicitly the rule which the Judge, at the next trial, ought, in our opinion, to direct the jury to be governed by when they estimate the damages.

It is, indeed, of the last importance that we should do this; for, if the jury are left without any definite rule to guide them, it will in such cases as these, manifestly lead to the greatest injustice. . . .

* * *

Now we think the proper rule in such a case as the present is this: — Where two parties have made a contract which one of them has broken, the damages which the other party ought to receive in respect of such breach of contract should be such as may fairly and reasonably be considered either arising naturally, i.e., according to the usual course of things, from such breach of contract itself, or such as may reasonably be supposed to have been in the contemplation of both parties, at the time they made the contract, as the probable result of the breach of it. Now, if the special circumstances under which the contract was actually made were communicated by the plaintiffs to the defendants, and thus known to both parties, the damages resulting from the breach of such a contract, which they would reasonably contemplate, would be the amount of injury which would ordinarily follow from a breach of contract under these special circumstances so known and communicated. But, on the other hand, if these special circumstances were wholly unknown to the party breaking the contract, he, at the most, could only be supposed to have had in his contemplation the amount of injury which would arise generally, and in the great multitude of cases not affected by any special circumstances, from such a breach of contract. For, had the special circumstances been known, the parties might have specially provided for the breach of contract by special terms as to the damages in that case; and of this advantage it would be very unjust to deprive them. Now the above principles are those by which we think the jury ought to be guided in estimating the damages arising out of any breach of contract. It is said, that other cases such as breaches of contract in the non-payment of money, or in the not making a good title to land, are to be treated as exceptions from this, and as governed by a conventional rule. But as, in such cases, both parties must be supposed to be cognizant of that well-known rule, these cases may, we think, be more properly classed under the rule above enunciated as to cases under known special circumstances, because there both parties may reasonably be presumed to contemplate the estimation of the amount of damages according to the conventional rule. Now, in the present case, if we are to apply the principles above laid down, we find that the only circumstances here communicated by the plaintiffs to the defendants at the time the contract was made, were, that the article to be carried was the broken shaft of a mill, and that the plaintiffs were the millers of that mill. But how do these circumstances shew reasonably that the profits of the mill must be stopped by an unreasonable delay in the delivery of the broken shaft by the carrier to the third person? Suppose the plaintiffs had another shaft in their possession put up or putting up at the time, and that they only wished to send back the broken shaft to the engineer who made it; it is clear that this would be quite consistent with the above circumstances, and yet the unreasonable delay in the delivery would have no effect upon the intermediate profits of the mill. Or, again, suppose that, at the time of the delivery to the carrier, the machinery of the mill had been in other respects defective, then, also the same results would follow. Here it is true that the shaft was actually sent back to serve as a model for a new one, and that the want of a new one was the only cause of the stoppage of the mill, and that the loss of profits really arose from not sending down the new shaft in proper time, and that this arose from the delay in delivering the broken one to serve as a model. But it is obvious that, in the great multitude of cases of millers sending off broken shafts to third persons by a carrier under ordinary circumstances, such consequences would not, in all probability, have occurred; and these special circumstances were here never communicated by the plaintiffs to the defendants. It follows, therefore, that the loss of profits here cannot reasonably be considered such a consequence of the breach of contract as could have been fairly and reasonably contemplated by both the parties when they made this contract. For such loss would neither have flowed naturally from the breach of this contract in the great multitude of such cases occurring under ordinary circumstances, nor were the special circumstances, which, perhaps, would have made it a reasonable and natural consequence of such breach of contract, communicated to or known by the defendants. The Judge ought, therefore, to have told the jury, that, upon the facts then before them, they ought not to take the loss of profits into consideration at all in estimating the damages. There must therefore be a new trial in this case.

Rule absolute.

NOTES

(1) The losses claimed in *Hadley v. Baxendale* are thought to be consequential because they result from the inability to use the defendant's promised performance, i.e., the timely return of the mill shaft. Why did the court deny recovery? Suppose that the loss could be proved with reasonable certainty, resulted from the breach, and that the defendant made every reasonable effort to mitigate the loss by finding a spare shaft. Same result?

(2) *Hadley v. Baxendale and the English Courts.* Since *Hadley v. Baxendale,* the English courts have invested considerable energy in fine-tuning the test of foreseeability that limits liability for consequential damages. See, e.g., Johnson v. Gore Wood & Co., 2 Q.B. (Ch) 776 (2002); Victoria Laundry (Windsor) Limited v. Newman Industries Limited, 2 K.B. 528 (1949); The Heron II (Koufos v. C. Czarnikow, Limited), 3 All E.R. 686 (House of Lords 1967). For example, in Parsons Limited v. Uttley Ingham & Co. (C.A.), 1 Q.B. 791, 802 (1977), Lord Denning summarized the results of that effort when the breach caused lost profits or "economic" loss.

> [T]he defaulting party is only liable for the consequences if they are such as, at the time of the contract, he ought reasonably to have contemplated as a serious possibility or a real danger. You must assume that, at the time of the contract, he had the very kind of breach in mind—such a breach as afterwards happened, as for instance, delay in transit—and you must ask: ought he reasonably to have contemplated that there was a serious possibility that such a breach would involve the plaintiff in a loss of profit. If yes, the contractor is liable for the loss unless he has taken care to exempt himself from it by a condition in the contract—as, of course, he is able to do if it was the sort of thing which he could reasonably contemplate.

In *Parsons*, however, the plaintiff's pigs died after eating moldy nuts stored in a bulk food storage hopper supplied by the defendant. The cause of the mold was an improperly installed ventilator. The judge below gave judgment for the plaintiff even though concluding that at the time of contracting the parties could not have reasonably contemplated that there would be a serious possibility of moldy pignuts causing serious illness in the pigs. The appeal was denied by the Court of Appeal. Lord Denning distinguished the case where breach of contract caused lost profits from that where it caused physical injury. In the latter case, "the defaulting party is liable for any loss or expense which he ought to have foreseen at the time of the breach as a possible consequence, even if it was only a slight possibility. You must assume that he was aware of his breach, and then you must ask: ought he reasonably to have foreseen, at the time of the breach, that something of this kind might happen in consequence of it?" 1 Q.B. at 803.

(3) *American Tests of Foreseeability.* Two American statements of the "foreseeability" test in *Hadley v. Baxendale* are UCC 2–715(2) (1995) and Restatement (Second) § 351.

UCC 2–715(2) provides:

Consequential damages resulting from the seller's breach include (a) any loss resulting from general or particular requirements and needs of which the seller at the time of contracting had reason to know and which could not reasonably be prevented by cover or otherwise; and (b) injury to person or property proximately resulting from any breach of warranty.

Restatement (Second) § 351 provides:

(1) Damages are not recoverable for loss that the party in breach did not have reason to foresee as the probable result of the breach when the contract was made.

(2) Loss may be foreseeable as a probable result of a breach because it follows from the breach (a) in the ordinary course of events, or (b) as a

result of special circumstances, beyond the ordinary course of events, that the party in breach had reason to know.

(3) A court may limit damages for foreseeable loss by excluding recovery for loss of profits, by allowing recovery only for loss incurred in reliance, or otherwise if it concludes that in the circumstances justice so requires in order to avoid disproportionate compensation.

Here are some questions to consider:

(1) How does the American test of "foreseeability" differ from the English? Is there an American distinction between "economic" loss and physical damage to property? See UCC 2–715(2)(b).

(2) How does Restatement (Second) § 351 differ from UCC 2–715(2), i.e., is it easier or harder to get consequential damages under Restatement (Second)?

(3) How should subsection (3) of Section 351 be applied? See Margaret Kniffen, *A Newly Identified Contract Unconscionability: Unconscionability of Remedy,* 63 Notre Dame L.Rev. 247 (1988); Burnett Harvey, *Discretionary Justice Under the Restatement (Second) of Contracts,* 67 Cornell L.Rev. 666 (1982). In the early 90's a number of courts were unwilling to use subsection (3) to limit damages, see e.g., Perini Corp. v. Greate Bay Hotel & Casino, 129 N.J. 479, 610 A.2d 364 (1992), but increasingly the subsection has been used to limit plaintiff claims for lost profit damages. See Alaska Tae Woong Venture v. Westward Seafoods, 963 P.2d 1055 (Alaska 1998).

PROBLEM: THE CASE OF THE RECALCITRANT MANUFACTURER

Smirgo, Inc., a manufacturer of bakery equipment, specializes in custom made ovens. Bisko, Inc. operates a medium sized bakery in a highly competitive market and sells primarily to restaurants, hotels and other institutional buyers.

On May 15, Bisko's research people informed the president that a new bread had been developed for the institutional trade. It was described as "revolutionary" and "likely to sell like hotcakes." A business decision was then made by the board of directors to purchase two new custom ovens and make a concerted effort to expand the business. At this time Bisko policymakers knew that Caraway Co., a competitor, was working on the development of a similar bread but had no idea what progress had been made.

On June 1, Smirgo and Bisko entered a written contract for the manufacture and sale of custom-made ovens to bake the new bread. The basic design was supplied by Bisko engineers. The agreed price was $30,000, to be paid in full 90 days after Smirgo had delivered both ovens to Bisko on the promised delivery date, November 1. While Smirgo and Bisko had done business before, this was the first contract for custom made ovens. At the time the contract was signed, the president of Smirgo was informed that the "ovens will be used in a business expansion," "prompt delivery is critical," and "we have a new product coming out." After the contract was signed, Bisko spent $7,500 in readying its plant for the new ovens.

A.   On November 1, Smirgo loaded the two ovens on a company truck and drove to Bisko's bakery. After Smirgo arrived, Bisko informed it that it would not accept the ovens. The bread market was depressed and Bisko no longer wanted to expand the business. Smirgo comes to you for advice. Can Smirgo recover the contract price from Bisko under Article 2 of the UCC? If not, what other remedies are available? Study the remedy options in UCC 2–703 and explore the possibilities in Sections 2–704 through 2–710.

B. Suppose, instead, that on November 1, the time agreed for delivery, Smirgo informed Bisko that while the new ovens were completed they would not be delivered unless Bisko paid $30,000 cash. There was no justification for this demand; it was clearly a breach of contract since a 90 day credit term had been agreed. On November 2 Bisko discovered that there were three concerns within a hundred mile radius that would manufacture the custom made ovens at an average price of $29,500. The estimated time of delivery was six months, however, and no business concern had the type of oven needed by Bisko in stock. On November 3, Caraway Co. announced that it was marketing an institutional bread almost identical to that developed by Bisko. The next day, the Bisko sales manager informed the president that unless the ovens were obtained within ten days, Bisko would lose an estimated $20,000 in profits on six long-term contracts already made and an estimated $100,000 in profits on contracts under negotiation but not yet signed. During the past 5 years, Bisko's net profits have averaged $100,000 per year.

On the afternoon of November 4, the president of Bisko came to you for legal advice. Assume that Smirgo is in breach of contract and that the Uniform Commercial Code governs this case. Based upon an analysis of UCC Article 2, Part 7, Sections 2–711 through 2–717, and the business situation, what would you advise Bisko to do? Go as far as you can with the relevant statutory provisions.

SECTION 3.   MENTAL ANGUISH AND PUNITIVE DAMAGES

In *Sullivan v. O'Connor*, supra, the plaintiff recovered mental anguish resulting from the defendant's breach but did not claim punitive damages. Under what circumstances are these damages proper in an action for breach of contract?

Bohac v. Department of Agriculture

United States Court of Appeals, Federal Circuit. 2001.
239 F.3d 1334.

■ Dyk, Circuit Judge.

This case presents the issue whether non-pecuniary damages—here recovery for alleged pain and suffering, injury to reputation, and injury to family life—are recoverable under section 1221 of the Whistleblower Protection Act. 5 U.S.C. § 1221(g)(1)(A)(ii). We hold that non-pecuniary damages are not recoverable and that the government has not waived its sovereign immunity with respect to such claims. Accordingly, we affirm the decision of the Merit Systems Protection Board ("Board").

I

In 1998, Janice Bohac ("petitioner") successfully appealed her removal from her research geneticist position with the United States Department of

Agriculture ("agency") on the ground that her removal violated the Whistleblower Protection Act. On July 14, 1998, Ms. Bohac filed a motion for damages, requesting an award of $14,021.32 for pecuniary losses, and $150,000 for non-pecuniary damages. The non-pecuniary damages sought by Ms. Bohac included damages for physical and emotional suffering, damage to her personal and professional reputation, and damages for various injuries to her family life. In an October 26, 1998, initial decision an administrative judge for the Board awarded Ms. Bohac pecuniary damages in the amount requested, but denied her claim for non-pecuniary damages. The administrative judge held that non-pecuniary damages do not constitute "consequential damages" allowable under the Whistleblower Protection Act. Ms. Bohac petitioned for review of the initial decision to the full Board.

On April 21, 1999, the Board denied Ms. Bohac's petition for review. . . .

II

We have jurisdiction over this petition for review pursuant to 28 U.S.C. § 1295(a)(9). Our review of the Board's decision requires statutory interpretation which is a question of law. . . . We review questions of law *de novo*. . . .

III

Congress passed the Whistleblower Protection Act of 1989, Pub.L. No. 101–12, 103 Stat. 16 (codified in scattered sections of 5 U.S.C.) ("WPA"), to protect "government employees from being punished for disclosing potentially embarrassing information about the operation of government." *Weber v. Dep't of the Army,* 9 F.3d 97, 101 (Fed.Cir.1993). In the WPA, Congress expressed its intention to strengthen the protections available to Federal whistleblowers from reprisals for protected disclosures of information. . . . Congress created, *inter alia,* an individual right of action under 5 U.S.C. § 1221(a) to complement the relief previously available through the Office of Special Counsel ("OSC"), and expanded other rights for protected whistleblowers . . .

Pursuant to 5 U.S.C. § 1221(a), an employee affected by personnel actions alleged to have been in retaliation for whistleblowing must first seek corrective action from the OSC under section 1214 of title 5. 5 U.S.C. §§ 1214(a)(3), 1221(a); . . . If the employee is unsuccessful before the OSC, the employee may then file an individual right of action ("IRA") seeking corrective action from the Board. 5 U.S.C. § 1214(a)(3); . . .

Under the WPA of 1989, a prevailing employee, in addition to the corrective action, could recover only "reasonable attorney's fees and any other reasonable costs incurred." 5 U.S.C. §§ 1221(g)(1)–(2) (1988 & Supp. V 1993). In the 1994 amendments to the WPA, Congress also provided additional rights and remedies for protected whistleblowers. Specifically, the 1994 amendments, Pub.L. 103–424, § 8(b)(2), 108 Stat. 4361, 4365, amended section 1221(g) by inserting new paragraph (1)(A) providing that "corrective action" by the Board may include:

(i) that the individual be placed, as nearly as possible, in the position the individual would have been in had the prohibited personnel practice not occurred; and

(ii) back pay and related benefits, medical costs incurred, travel expenses, and *any other reasonable and foreseeable consequential changes.*

5 U.S.C. § 1221(g)(1)(A) (emphasis added). * * *

The issue before us is the meaning of the phrase "any other reasonable and foreseeable consequential changes" in section 1221(g) of the current statute.

IV

* * *

[The court first held that although the statute allows recovery for "consequential changes," a drafting error had occurred. It was obvious that Congress intended "consequential damages" and the court so interpreted the statute.]

V

As might be expected, the parties urge opposite positions with respect to the interpretation of the phrase "consequential damages." Petitioner suggests that Congress intended to incorporate the contract law concept of consequential damages, meaning foreseeable damages, as most famously announced in *Hadley v. Baxendale,* 9 Ex. 341, 156 Eng. Rep. 145 (1854), and that non-pecuniary damages are recoverable. The government, on the other hand, urges that the term refers to pecuniary damages by which it means reimbursement of out-of-pocket costs. While the issue is not free from doubt, we conclude that the government is correct.

[The conclusion that the phrase "consequential damages" was limited to pecuniary damages meant that the United States had not waived its sovereign immunity to a law suit claiming non-pecuniary damages.] * * *

First, the term "consequential damages" does not have a well-established common law meaning that includes non-pecuniary damages. In interpreting a Congressional statute using common law terminology, there is a presumption that Congress intended the common law meaning. * * * It is therefore a "settled principle of statutory construction that, absent contrary indications, Congress intends to adopt the common law definition of statutory terms." *United States v. Shabani,* 513 U.S. 10, 13 115 S.Ct. 382, 130 L.Ed.2d 225 (1994); . . .

Many of the authorities discussing the term "consequential damages" cited by the parties here do not reflect common law usage at all. Instead they reflect casual use by courts to describe particular types of damages or use of the term in a variety of other statutory contexts. The usage in those contexts varies considerably, and the authorities are essentially unhelpful.

More pertinently, petitioner urges us to apply the common law contract law concept of "consequential damages," including the foreseeability test of *Hadley v. Baxendale*. Even if we were to assume, as petitioner urges, that Congress intended to incorporate the meaning of the phrase "consequential damages" from contract law, this does not suggest the result that petitioner seeks. The concept of "consequential damages" in contract law relates to the concept of foreseeability at the time the contract is executed, not, as the petitioner would have it, foreseeability at the time of the breach ... In general, this has led the courts to limit recovery to pecuniary damages, which are most likely to be foreseeable at the time of contracting, as opposed to non-pecuniary damages, which are more dependent on the circumstances of the individual plaintiff at the time of the breach....

The cases have focused particularly on damages for emotional distress. Under the traditional contract law approach, "[i]t is well established that, as a general rule, no damages will be awarded for the mental distress or emotional trauma that may be caused by a breach of contract." John D. Calamari & Joseph M. Perillo, *The Law of Contracts* § 14.5(b), at 549 (4th ed.1998); *see also* Williston, *Williston on Contracts* §§ 1338, 1341, at 200, 214; Restatement (Second) of Contracts § 353. To be sure there are exceptions, such as contracts of carriers and innkeepers with passengers and guests, contracts for the carriage or proper disposition of dead bodies, and contracts for the delivery of messages concerning death.... In these cases, however, breach of the contract is particularly likely to cause serious emotional disturbance. Restatement (Second) of Contracts § 353, cmt. a. Moreover, with the limited exception of contracts for the delivery of messages concerning death, damages for mental suffering are usually refused absent wanton and willful misconduct.... Ordinary negligence does not suffice....

This case clearly does not fit into any of these categories of cases for which awards of mental suffering were awarded for breach of contract at common law. Indeed, a whistleblowing claim seems most closely akin to a claim for wrongful discharge and, historically, at common law only traditional contract damages were recoverable for such claims. *See* 2 Mark A. Rothstein et al., *Employment Law* § 8.21, at 315–16 (1999).

Petitioner cites a number of wrongful discharge cases beginning in the 1980s ... which have allowed emotional distress damages. Such wrongful discharge claims are sometimes based in contract and sometimes in tort.... Some courts ... have upheld awards of emotional distress damages for wrongful discharge where public policy concerns are implicated. Others have refused to award emotional distress damages for wrongful discharge, thereby limiting damages to ordinary contract damages.... Thus, while the common law limits on wrongful discharge damages may have changed in at least some states, it is clear that historically there was no uniform common law rule in this area allowing recovery of non-pecuniary damages, much less an established common law meaning of the term "consequential damages" that would include non-pecuniary damages in the context of contract law. We have also been unable to determine that the term "consequential damages" has any well-defined common law meaning in the tort context, and neither party urges that it does.

Second, if Congress had intended to allow broad recovery for non-pecuniary damages, it seems likely that it would have used the well-understood term "compensatory damages." " 'Compensatory damages' are the damages awarded to a person as compensation, indemnity or restitution for harm sustained by him." Restatement (Second) of Torts § 903 (1979). Compensatory damages are divided into two categories: pecuniary and non-pecuniary. *Id.* at §§ 905 and 906. Non-pecuniary compensatory damages include compensation for bodily harm and emotional distress, and are awarded without proof of pecuniary loss. *Id.* at § 905. It is well-understood that the term "compensatory damages" includes non-pecuniary damages such as pain and suffering. * * *

[The court considered other aids in statutory interpretation, including the legislative history, and found no persuasive evidence that Congress intended the phrase "consequential changes," interpreted to mean "consequential damages" to include non-pecuniary loss.]

NOTES

(1) Claims for mental anguish or emotional distress damages are on the borderline between contract and tort. The emotional disturbance results from a breach of contract (a wrongful termination) but the injury is to what might be called a "tort" rather than a "contract" interest. In addition to losing the value of the bargain, the plaintiff is worse off physically than before the contract. See W. Prosser & P. Keeton, The Law of Torts § 12 (5th ed. 1984).

How is this borderline straddled in Restatement (Second) Section 353, which provides:

Recovery for emotional disturbance will be excluded unless the breach also caused bodily harm or the contract or the breach is of such a kind that serious emotional disturbance was a particularly likely result.

How well did the court in *Bohac* deal with the line between contract and tort?

(2) *In Gaglidari v. Denny's Restaurants, Inc.,* 117 Wash.2d 426, 815 P.2d 1362 (1991), the court concluded that emotional distress damages were not available for breach of an employment contract. The court emphasized that an employment contract did not have "elements of personality" and that the parties had not agreed to protect those losses. According to the court, the type of contract involved rather than the nature of the breach or whether the loss was foreseeable was the critical issue.

This appears to be the prevailing view. See Francis v. Lee Enterprises, Inc., 89 Hawai'i 234, 971 P.2d 707, 708 (1999), where the court rejected prior cases awarding damages for "tortious breach of contract" because "such a rule unnecessarily blurs the distinction between—and undermines the discrete theories of recovery relevant to—tort and contract."

We now hold that Hawai'i law will not allow tort recovery in the absence of conduct that (1) violates a duty that is independently recognized by principles of tort law and (2) transcends the breach of the contract.

Consistent with this rule, emotional distress damages will only be recoverable where the parties specifically provide for them in the contract or where the nature of the contract or where the nature of the breach clearly indicates that such damages were within the contemplation of the parties.

See, generally, Douglas Whaley, *Paying for the Agony: The Recovery of Emotional Distress Damages in Contract Actions*, 26 Suffolk U.L. Rev. 935 (1992). See also Erlich v. Menezes, 21 Cal.4th 543, 87 Cal.Rptr.2d 886, 981 P.2d 978 (1999) (damages for emotional distress not available for negligent breach of contract to construct a home).

PROBLEM: THE CASE OF THE DISTRESSED NEWLYWEDS

Fred and Joyce were engaged in January and set the wedding date for June 21. Among other things, the couple entered a written agreement, dated February 21, with a local band, the High Flyers, to play at the wedding reception. The couple paid $300 down and agreed to pay $700 more after the reception. The agreement said nothing about the consequences of a breach. Since the High Flyers were in great demand, Joyce called on June 1 to confirm the engagement and was told by the leader, "Hey man, no problem." The High Flyers, however, did not show up at the reception. On June 14, they took another job for the big evening (the fee was $2,000) and neglected to notify either Fred or Joyce. After an hour of no music, Fred induced his younger brother to rig up a stereo system and play disc jockey for the rest of the evening. Fred paid brother $75 for the job.

The couple consulted their attorney, claiming that the quality of the substitute music was inferior to that promised by the High Flyers and that they both suffered extreme anxiety and distress resulting from the deliberate breach of the type of contract where mental distress was foreseeable.

(1) How much, if anything, should Fred and Joyce recover from the High Flyers? If the High Flyers offered $375 to settle the case, would you recommend that the newlyweds accept?

(2) Can Fred and Joyce recover punitive damages? See the next cases.

Acquista v. New York Life Insurance Company

Appellate Division of New York, 2001.
285 A.D.2d 73, 730 N.Y.S.2d 272.

■ SAXE, J.

This appeal considers plaintiff's entitlement to insurance benefits under three disability insurance policies purchased through defendant insurance agents Jenny Kho and Helen Kho, and issued by defendant New York Life Insurance Company.

In November 1995, plaintiff, a physician with specialities in internal and pulmonary medicine, initially became ill. While an exact diagnosis turned out to be difficult, he underwent numerous bone marrow aspirates, biopsies, and cytogenetic examinations, including blood tests, which revealed abnormalities and the presence of a blood disorder. Dr. Acquista was ultimately informed of a possible diagnosis of myelodysplasia, a disease that might convert into leukemia. His treating physicians have instructed him to avoid exposure to radiation. Presently, he suffers generally from easy fatigue, headaches, and diffuse muscle and joint pain.

However, his application for disability benefits under the three disability insurance policies was rejected by the defendant insurer, on the ground that he can still perform some of "the substantial and material duties" of his regular job or jobs and therefore is not "totally disabled." This lawsuit followed, in which plaintiff brought claims for breach of contract, bad faith and unfair practices, fraud and fraudulent misrepresentation, and negligent infliction of emotional distress.

Upon defendants' motion under CPLR 3211, the Supreme Court granted dismissal of all plaintiff's causes of action except the one based upon the policy provision for residual and partial disability benefits. We now modify the order so as to reinstate a number of the dismissed causes of action.

The Breach of Contract Claims

* * *

[The court held that the question whether the plaintiff could perform "the substantial and material duties" was factual and the trial court's determination that he could was, on the record, unwarranted. The dismissal of the breach of contract claims, therefore, was error.]

The question therefore becomes whether those tasks that plaintiff is still demonstrably able to handle, such as seeing a limited number of patients who can make office visits, are substantial enough to amount to the ability to perform "the substantial and material duties" of his regular job or jobs as they existed prior to the onset of his illness. We consider this question to involve a factual determination, precluding dismissal of plaintiff's first, second and third causes of action at this juncture.

Bad Faith Conduct

Plaintiff's fifth and sixth causes of action allege a pattern of bad faith conduct and unfair practices on the part of defendant insurer, and claim resulting emotional distress as well as economic and non-economic injury. The claim that defendant insurance company acted in bad faith is founded upon allegations that it undertook a conscious campaign calculated to delay and avoid payment on his claims, while having determined at the outset that it would deny coverage. He sets forth defendant's ongoing pattern of avoiding the claim, by which it would make multiple requests for additional documentation, upon receipt of which further documents would be demanded, after which plaintiff's claims file would then be transferred to a new examiner, who in turn would make more requests. Plaintiff adds that defendant waited more than two years to request or schedule an independent medical examination.

In seeking dismissal of the bad faith claim, defendant asserts that New York law does not recognize an independent tort cause of action for an insurer's alleged failure to perform its contractual obligations under an insurance policy. . . .

It is correct that, to date, this State has maintained the traditional view that an insurer's failure to make payments or provide benefits in accordance with a policy of insurance constitutes merely a breach of contract, which is remedied by contract damages. Yet, for some time, courts and commentators around the country have increasingly acknowledged that a fundamental injustice may result when a traditional contract analysis is applied to circumstances where insurance claims were denied despite the insurers' lack of a reasonable basis to deny them (*see generally ...*, Note, *First Party Bad Faith: The Search for a Uniform Standard of Culpability,* 52 Hastings LJ 181, 187–189 [2000]).

Under the traditional analysis, because insurance policies are viewed as contracts for the payment of money only, the damages available for an insurer's failure to pay or provide benefits has been limited to the amount of the policy plus interest. . . . Yet, an award, at the conclusion of litigation, of money damages equal to what the insurer should have paid in the first place, may not actually achieve the goal of contract damages, which is to place the plaintiff in the position he would have been in had the contract been performed. . . .

Among other things, this concept of damages presumes that a plaintiff has access to an alternative source of funds from which to pay that which the insurer refuses to pay. This is frequently an inaccurate assumption. Additionally, an insured's inability to pay that which the insurer should be covering may result in further damages to the insured. Of course, limiting the potential damages to the policy amount also fails to address the potential for emotional distress or even further physical injury that may result where a plaintiff under the strain of serious medical problems is forced to also undertake the stress of extended litigation. What is more, if statutory interest is lower than that which the insurer can earn on the sums payable, the insurer has a financial incentive to decline to cover or pay on a claim. . . .

In view of the inadequacy of contract remedies where an insurer purposefully declines or avoids a claim without a reasonable basis for doing so, a majority of states have responded to this need for a more suitable remedy by adopting a tort cause of action applicable to circumstances where an insurer has used bad faith in handling a policyholder's claim. . . .

This cause of action is generally stated as a breach of the insurer's duty of good faith. Under this approach, where an insured demonstrates more than merely a denial of benefits promised under a policy of insurance, but instead, that the insurer's denial of the claim was deliberately made in bad faith, with knowledge of the lack of a reasonable basis for the denial, the insured may be entitled to compensatory tort damages.

Other states, troubled by imposing upon insurance companies a tort duty in such circumstances, have instead expanded the scope of contract remedies to encompass more than just the policy limits. These courts have instead held that the contract damages available, where an insurer fails to pay benefits to which the insured was entitled, may include foreseeable money damages beyond the policy limit. . . . While some states would exclude compensation for mental or emotional distress unrelated to physical injury, caused by the denial of a payment others include the possibility of consequential damages for mental distress or aggravation. . . . Of course, such non-economic losses would be compensable only in circumstances where they were a foreseeable result of a breach at the time the policy was entered into.

We are unwilling to adopt the widely-accepted tort cause of action for "bad faith" in the context of a first-party claim, because we recognize that to do so would constitute an extreme change in the law of this State. Essentially, we accept the more conservative approach adopted by the minority of jurisdictions that "the duties and obligations of the parties [to an insurance policy] are contractual rather than fiduciary. . . ." However, as this Court has recently acknowledged, "an insured should have an adequate remedy to redress an insurer's bad faith refusal of benefits under its policy. . . ." Providing such a remedy cannot be accomplished where a policyholder who makes out a claim of bad faith avoidance of a valid insurance claim may only obtain a judgment for the face amount of the policy.

Therefore, in order to ensure the availability of an appropriate and sufficient remedy, we [conclude] that there is no reason to limit damages recoverable for breach of a duty to investigate, bargain, and settle claims in good faith to the amount specified in the insurance policy. Nothing inherent in the contract law approach mandates this narrow definition of recoverable damages. Although the policy limits define the amount for which the insurer may be held responsible in performing the contract, they do not define the amount for which it may be liable upon a breach.

We consider the need for this form of damages to be apparent. The problem of dilatory tactics by insurance companies seeking to delay and avoid payment of proper claims has apparently become widespread enough to prompt most states to respond with some sort of remedy for aggrieved policyholders. To term such a claim "unique to these parties" as the dissent does, and therefore not warranting a remedy beyond that traditionally available for an insurer's failure to pay on a claim, is to utterly ignore this fact.

As to the dissent's suggestion that the claim of bad faith is undermined by our finding that an issue of fact exists as to whether plaintiff is entitled to coverage at all, we must recall that we have before us a dismissal motion under CPLR 3211. Just as it may ultimately be found that plaintiff was entitled to coverage, it may also be found, as he alleges, that the insurer's delay, avoidance and ultimate rejection of the claim was based not upon a reasonable assessment of the situation but rather, solely upon its own financial self-interest. For this Court to say, in the context of a motion under CPLR 3211, that the denial of benefits was reasonable as a matter of law, is to reject out of hand plaintiff's factual assertions and to accept the facts as defendant insurer alleges them to be.

* * *

■ ANDRIAS, J. (dissenting in part)

[Judge Andrias agreed that on the breach of contract claims "there are questions of fact presented, which cannot be determined as a matter of law on this dismissal motion, as to whether plaintiff was 'totally disabled' within the meaning of the three subject insurance policies...." The dissent was that the remaining claims sounding in tort, including bad faith, should have been dismissed.]

Plaintiff's tort claims are based upon his allegations that, even though he provided all requested documentation, New York Life continued to delay in determining his claim; that he made a reasonable settlement demand, which New York Life wrongfully and unjustifiably refused to accept; and, that New York Life's dilatory tactics in delaying processing of his claim included shuffling plaintiff from employee to employee. Such allegations, however, describe what "is essentially a 'private' contract dispute over policy coverage and the processing of a claim which is unique to these parties, not conduct which affects the consuming public at large.... Militating against any causes of action based upon New York Life's alleged bad faith in processing and denying plaintiff's claim is our finding that there are issues of fact as to whether plaintiff's ailments qualify him for coverage under the subject policies. The majority questions the validity of the foregoing statement in the context of a motion to dismiss. However, such finding is significant in that it undermines his claim of bad faith denial of benefits by demonstrating that despite defendant's thorough investigation and evaluation of plaintiff's claim there is still uncertainty as to its merits. As noted ... encouraging premature settlement of claims would contravene an insurer's "contractual right and obligation of thorough investigation." * * *

[The dissent relied upon New York precedents that a "claim based on an alleged breach of the implied covenant of good faith and fair dealing should be dismissed as duplicative of a cause of action for breach of contract." Moreover, allegations of a conscious campaign to delay a decision on claims are insufficient to establish that the insurer's conduct "constituted a 'gross disregard' of the insured's interest—that is, a deliberate or reckless failure to place on equal footing the interests of its insured with its own interests when considering a settlement offer.... In other words, a bad-faith plaintiff must establish that the defendant insurer engaged in a pattern of behavior evincing a conscious or knowing indifference to the probability that an insured would be held personally accountable for a large judgment if a settlement offer within the policy limits were not accepted...." In order to meet this standard, a plaintiff would have to allege and ultimately prove that the insurer unreasonably "failed to carry out an investigation", failed to "evaluate" the feasibility of settlement (in this case plaintiff's claim) or, failed to offer the policy limits (in this case pay plaintiff's claim), after the merits of the claim were "clearly and fully assessed". Here, on the other hand, plaintiff's complaint is really the opposite: that defendant took too much time in investigating and evaluating his claim before denying it, after its merits were "clearly and fully assessed".]

NOTES

(1) In Harris v. Provident Life & Accident Ins. Co., 310 F.3d 73 (2d Cir.2002), the court ruled that New York does not recognize a "separate cause of action for breach of the implied covenant of good faith and fair dealing when a breach of contract claim based on the same facts is also pled." 310 F.3d at 81. The court also noted that there is a disagreement over whether the *Acquista* case, *supra*, was correct in holding that the plaintiff was entitled to consequential damages for an alleged bad faith breach of an insurance contract. 310 F.3d at 80, n. 3.

Boise Dodge, Inc. v. Clark

Supreme Court of Idaho, 1969.
92 Idaho 902, 453 P.2d 551.

[Clark purchased an automobile from Boise Dodge with 165 miles showing on the odometer and described by a salesman as "new." In fact, the car was a "demonstrator" and the general manager knew that the odometer had been set back from 6,968 miles. Clark traded in a car valued at $1,100 and issued checks for $500 and $1,562 for the balance of the purchase price. Payment was stopped when Clark discovered that the car was "used." Boise sued on the checks and Clark counterclaimed for damages for breach of contract and deceit as well as punitive damages. The court, after trial, instructed the jury that it might find damages for breach of contract (the difference between the car's value as represented and its actual value) or for deceit (the difference between the price paid for the car and its actual value). On the theory that the contract had been affirmed rather than rescinded, the jury found for Boise in the amount of the checks, some $2,062, and for Clark in the amount of $350, the difference between the value of the car as represented, $2,400, and its actual value, $2,050. This award was not contested on appeal. The court also instructed the jury that it could award punitive damages if it found Boise's actions to have been willful, wanton, gross or outrageous but that the punitive damages must bear a reasonable relation to any actual damages found. The jury awarded punitive damages to Clark in the amount of $12,500. On appeal, respondent Boise presented a single ultimate issue: whether or not the award of punitive damages was proper. The Court affirmed the judgment, holding first that the plaintiff was entitled to an award of some punitive damages.]

■ McQUADE, JUSTICE.

* * *

Appellant complains mainly about the amount of punitive damages awarded. The court gave its Instruction No. 18 as follows:

"There is no fixed or mathematical proportion, ratio, or relation between amount of actual damages and amount of exemplary or punitive damages, which in a proper case may be awarded, but such an award must not be so disproportionate to actual damages sustained as to be result of passion or prejudice rather than reason, and such an award must bear some reasonable relation or proportion to actual damages, and exemplary damages must bear some relation to damages complained of and cause thereof." (Tr. 104).

This instruction also correctly stated the law relevant to the determination of an amount of punitive damages in an action at law. The question thus becomes whether the jury can be said as a matter of law to have exceeded the bounds of its discretion in making the award of damages.

We note preliminarily that, under the instructions of the court on the measure of actual damages sustained by respondent Clark, the jury apparently applied the standard for breach of contract rather than that for the tort of deceit. We do not view that course of action by the jury as indicating a negation of the elements of misrepresentation, fraud or deceit present in the case. In any event, from the legal point of view of the imposition of punitive damages in this case, it does not matter whether respondent's counterclaim technically sounded in contract or tort. The rule established in Idaho is that punitive damages may be assessed in contract actions where there is fraud, malice, oppression or other sufficient reason for doing so. This rule recognizes that in certain cases elements of tort, for which punitive damages have always been recoverable upon a showing of malice, may be inextricably mixed with elements of contract, in which punitive damages generally are not recoverable. In such cases, punitive damages are allowed according to the substance of a showing of willful fraud.

The assessment of punitive damages, like the assessment of all damages, is in the first instance for the discretion of the jury. Though the existence of punitive damages has been denounced as anomalous in the law, "[d]espite such denunciations the great majority of states retain the doctrine of exemplary damages in full force." The criticism that punitive damages are superfluous in view of the criminal law fallaciously assumes complete identity of criminal and civil punishment. The existence of such a remedy serves useful, if limited, functions in the law as a means of punishing conduct which consciously disregards the rights of others and as a means of deterring tortious conduct generally.

Various jurisdictions, including Idaho, have limited the discretion of juries in imposing punitive damages by declaring that the amount of punitive damages must bear a "reasonable relation" to the amount of actual damages. It is never made clear precisely upon what basis an amount of punitive damages will be declared "reasonable" or "unreasonable" in relation to the amount of actual damages, especially in view of the often-repeated statement that no strict mathematical ratio is to be applied. Of course, the ratios of punitive to actual damages which may be gleaned from the cases have little precedential value when excised from their respective factual settings. This is true because the culpability of a defendant's conduct and the sociological significance of damages as a deterrent vary from case to case. Thus, the true basis for an award of one amount of punitive damages as opposed to another amount lies in an overall appraisal of the circumstances of the case.

The amount of actual damages sustained by a plaintiff is one indication of the culpability of the defendant's acts, but it cannot be the sole criterion for the assessment of punitive damages. Also relevant is the prospective deterrent effect of such an award upon persons situated similarly to the defendant, the motives actuating the defendant's conduct, the degree of calculation involved in the defendant's conduct, and the extent of the defendant's disregard of the rights of others. These are legitimate concerns of the law, and the application of any fixed arithmetic ratio to all cases in which punitive damages are assessed would be arbitrary. It therefore must be recognized that the requirement of a "reasonable relation" between actual and punitive damages serves as a rough device available to trial and appellate courts for the purpose of paring down plainly extreme awards of punitive damages.

Applying these principles to the case at bar, we are satisfied that the jury's award of $12,500 punitive damages against Boise Dodge, Inc., was justified, and [the] court below did not commit error in refusing to set aside that verdict. This is a case of calculated commercial fraud in broad disregard of the rights not only of respondent Clark but the consuming public generally. It occurs in an area of sales in which consumers are unable to gain accurate information about the product. On this basis we find particularly appropriate the reasoning used in the case of Walker v. Sheldon, [179 N.E.2d 497 (1961),] in which the New York Court of Appeals determined that punitive damages would be allowed in fraud and deceit actions. That case involved the fraudulent commercial activities of Comet Press which were characterized as a "virtually larcenous scheme to trap generally the unwary." That court, in a thoughtful opinion by Judge Fuld, stated:

> "Exemplary damages are more likely to serve their desired purpose of deterring similar conduct in a fraud case, such as that before us, than in any other area of tort. One who acts out of anger or hate, for instance, in committing assault or libel, is not likely to be deterred by the fear of punitive damages. On the other hand, those who deliberately and coolly engage in a far-flung fraudulent scheme, systematically conducted for profit, are very much more likely to pause and consider the consequences if they have to pay more than the actual loss suffered by an individual plaintiff. An occasional award of compensatory damages against such parties would have little deterrent effect. A judgment simply for compensatory damages would require the offender to do no more than return the money which he had taken from the plaintiff. In the calculation of his expected profits, the wrongdoer is likely to allow for a certain amount of money which will have to be returned to those victims who object too vigorously, and he will be perfectly content to bear the additional cost of litigation as the price for continuing his

illicit business. It stands to reason that the chances of deterring him are materially increased by subjecting him to the payment of punitive damages.''

Those considerations are fully applicable to the case at bar.

* * *

The judgment of the court below is affirmed. Costs to respondent.

NOTES

(1) *Punitive Damages for Breach of Contract?* The traditional rule was that "punitive damages are not recoverable for breach of contract." Restatement (First) § 342. Section 355 of Restatement (Second) has opened the door just a crack: "Punitive damages are not recoverable for a breach of contract unless the conduct constituting the breach is also a tort for which punitive damages are recoverable." A common statement of the "rule" is that the breach must constitute an "independent and wilful tort accompanied by fraud, malice, wantonness or oppression." McIntosh v. Magna Systems, Inc., 539 F.Supp. 1185, 1190 (N.D.Ill.1982). See Miller Brewing Co. v. Best Beers of Bloomington, Inc., 608 N.E.2d 975, 982 (Ind.1993)(punitive damages not available in contract actions unless plaintiff establishes "each element of a recognized tort for which Indiana law would permit the recovery of punitive damages"). See also, Alfred Hill, *Breach of Contract as a Tort,* 74 Colum.L.Rev. 40 (1974).

(2) The purposes of punitive damages may involve punishment, deterrence and, to a lesser extent, compensation.

> Often, the function of punitive damages * * * is to legitimate the jury's giving vent to a sense of outrage at the conduct of the defendant and to relieve it of the sometimes difficult task of quantifying the degree to which the plaintiff has literally been harmed. Further, punitive damages are assessed to deter conduct of a serious antisocial or irresponsible nature.

Madisons Chevrolet, Inc. v. Donald, 109 Ariz. 100, 505 P.2d 1039, 1042–43 (1973). In commercial transactions, however, the courts have resisted imposing punitive damages even though the breach was "knowing and wilful." As one court put it, compensatory damages are sufficient for the plaintiff "without the necessity of assuaging his feelings or allaying community outrage" and that the award of punitive damages for a "pure" breach of contract would "seriously jeopardize the stability and predictability of commercial transactions, so vital to the smooth and efficient operation of the modern American economy." General Motors Corp. v. Piskor, 281 Md. 627, 381 A.2d 16, 20–23 (1977). Accord: Pogge v. Fullerton Lumber Co., 277 N.W.2d 916, 918–20 (Iowa 1979) (award of punitive damages creates uncertainty and confusion in commercial transactions); J.G.S., Inc. v. Lifetime Cutlery Corp., 87 A.D.2d 810, 448 N.Y.S.2d 780 (1982).

For a recent call on expanded use of punitive damages in contracting to punish and deter opportunistic breaches, see Steve Dodge, *The Case for Punitive Damages in Contracts*, 48 Duke L. J. 629 (1999).

(3) The reluctance of courts to award punitive damages for breach of contract parallels recent attacks upon the power of courts to award punitive

damages in tort law. In BMW of North America, Inc. v. Gore, 517 U.S. 559, 116 S.Ct. 1589, 134 L.Ed.2d 809 (1996), the Supreme Court held that the 14th Amendment prohibits a state protecting its legitimate interests from imposing "grossly excessive" punitive damages on a tortfeasor. The discretion of state courts to award punitive damages is limited by the state interest to be protected and the reprehensibility of the defendant's conduct. Assuming a legitimate state interest, the award of punitive damages must not be grossly out of proportion to the severity of the offense.

Comment: The Rise and Fall of Punitive Damages for Breach of Non–Insurance Contracts in California

California, like many states, recognizes that every contract is subject to an implied covenant of good faith and fair dealing. The question is when, if ever, a breach of the implied covenant may constitute a tort for which punitive damages may be awarded. California courts have held that in contracts for insurance, the insurer's refusal to settle within the terms of an insurance policy or to pay an undisputed claim of an insured may be a bad faith tort, for which the insured can recover damages for mental anguish and punitive damages. The bases for such a tort consist of the following "special circumstances":

> (1) One of the parties to the contract enjoys a superior bargaining position to the extent that it is able to dictate the terms of the contract; (2) the purpose of the weaker party in entering into the contract is not primarily to profit but rather to secure an essential service or produce financial security or peace of mind; (3) the relationship of the parties is such that the weaker party places trust and confidence in the larger entity; and (4) there is conduct on the part of the defendant indicating an intent to frustrate the weaker party's enjoyment of the contract rights.

Louderback & Jurika, *Standards for Expanding the Tort of Bad Faith Breach of Contract*, 16 U.San.F.L.Rev. 187, 227 (1982).

The question whether tort liability for a "bad faith breach" would be extended beyond insurance or other contracts where "special circumstances" exist was presented in Seaman's Direct Buying Service, Inc. v. Standard Oil of California, Inc., 36 Cal.3d 752, 206 Cal.Rptr. 354, 686 P.2d 1158 (1984). The answer was a qualified yes.

> For the purposes of this case it is * * * sufficient to recognize that a party to a contract may incur tort remedies when, in addition to breaching the contract, it seeks to shield itself from liability by denying, in bad faith and without probable cause, that the contract exists.

> It has been held that a party to a contract may be subject to tort liability, including punitive damages, if he coerces the other party to pay more than is due under the contract terms through the threat of a lawsuit, made "without probable cause and with no belief in the existence of the cause of action." (Adams v. Crater Well Drilling, Inc. (1976) 276 Or. 789, 556 P.2d 679, 681.) There is little difference, in

principle, between a contracting party obtaining excess payment in such manner, and a contracting party seeking to avoid all liability on a meritorious contract claim by adopting a "stonewall" position ("see you in court") without probable cause and with no belief in the existence of a defense. Such conduct goes beyond the mere breach of contract. It offends accepted notions of business ethics.... Acceptance of tort remedies in such a situation is not likely to intrude upon the bargaining relationship or upset reasonable expectations of the contracting parties.

206 Cal.Rptr. at 363, 686 P.2d at 1167.

In the aftermath of critical reactions to *Seaman's* the California Supreme Court initiated a retreat in Foley v. Interactive Data Corp., 47 Cal.3d 654, 254 Cal.Rptr. 211, 765 P.2d 373 (1988) that culminated in the overruling of *Seaman's* in Freeman & Mills, Inc. v. Belcher Oil Co., 11 Cal.4th 85, 44 Cal.Rptr.2d 420, 900 P.2d 669, 679 (1995) "in favor of a general rule precluding tort recovery for noninsurance contract breach, at least in the absence of violation of 'an independent duty arising from principles of tort law' ... other than the bad faith denial of the existence of, or liability under, the breached contract."

Seaman's had been sharply criticized and its overruling urged by Judge Alexander Kozinski, concurring in Oki America, Inc. v. Microtech Intern., Inc., 872 F.2d 312, 314–317 (9th Cir.1989).

Nowhere but in the Cloud Cuckooland of modern tort theory could a case like this have been concocted. One large corporation is complaining that another obstinately refused to acknowledge they had a contract. For this shocking misconduct it is demanding millions of dollars in punitive damages. I suppose we will next be seeing lawsuits seeking punitive damages for maliciously refusing to return telephone calls or adopting a condescending tone in interoffice memos. Not every slight, nor even every wrong, ought to have a tort remedy. The intrusion of courts into every aspect of life, and particularly into every type of business relationship, generates serious costs and uncertainties, trivializes the law, and denies individuals and businesses the autonomy of adjusting mutual rights and responsibilities through voluntary contractual agreement.

* * *

The eagerness of judges to expand the horizons of tort liability is symptomatic of a more insidious disease: the novel belief that any problem can be ameliorated if only a court gets involved. Not so. Courts are slow, clumsy, heavy-handed institutions, ill-suited to oversee the negotiations between corporations, to determine what compromises a manufacturer and a retailer should make in closing a mutually profitable deal, or to evaluate whether an export-import consortium is developing new markets in accordance with the standards of the business community. See generally Snyderman, *What's So Good About*

Good Faith? The Good Faith Performance Obligation in Commercial Lending, 55 U.Chi.L.Rev. 1335, 1361 (1988).

Moreover, because litigation is costly, time consuming and risky, judicial meddling in many business deals imposes onerous burdens. It wasn't so long ago that being sued (or suing) was an unthinkable event for many small and medium-sized businesses. Today, legal expenses are a standard and often uncontrollable item in every business's budget, diverting resources from more productive areas of entrepreneurship. Nor can commercial enterprises be expected to flourish in a legal atmosphere where every move, every innovation, every business decision must be hedged against the risk of exotic new causes of action and incalculable damages. See generally P. Huber, Liability: *The Legal Revolution and Its Consequences* 153–71 (1988).

Perhaps most troubling, the willingness of courts to subordinate voluntary contractual arrangements to their own sense of public policy and proper business decorum deprives individuals of an important measure of freedom. The right to enter into contracts—to adjust one's legal relationships by mutual agreement with other free individuals—was unknown through much of history and is unknown even today in many parts of the world. Like other aspects of personal autonomy, it is too easily smothered by government officials eager to tell us what's best for us. The recent tendency of judges to insinuate tort causes of action into relationships traditionally governed by contract is just such overreaching. It must be viewed with no less suspicion because the government officials in question happen to wear robes.

What do you think?

Comment: Enforcement of Money Judgments

The successful plaintiff in a breach of contract action will normally obtain a money judgment against the defendant. That judgment will evidence a right to compensatory damages for breach of contract plus interest and costs. Except where a confession of judgment is authorized, or the defendant fails to answer the complaint, judgment will be entered after litigation resolves disputes arising out of a variety of transactions, involving both professional business people and consumers. What must the plaintiff do to secure what the late Professor Garrard Glenn called the "first principle of creditor's rights," a "satisfied" judgment? Glenn, Cases on Creditor's Rights 4 (1940).

A judgment does not order the defendant to pay any particular sum. Rather it orders that the plaintiff shall recover "of the defendant" the stated sum and have "execution" therefor. If the defendant pays, the matter is settled. If the defendant does not pay, the plaintiff must proceed by the process of execution to obtain satisfaction from the defendant's real and personal property.

[Why don't courts order defendants to pay the money owed (or else go to jail)? The answer probably lies in our antipathy toward debtors' prisons (and possibly the penumbral impact of the 13th Amendment). But why don't courts at least order defendants who have the wherewithal to pay or face prison?]

Execution involves a number of steps and procedures, the details of which vary from state to state. The basic objectives are to impose by attachment, levy, garnishment or docketing of the judgment, i.e., by operation of law, a lien upon the defendant's non-exempt property and, through the sheriff or other public official, to conduct a public sale the proceeds of which are used to satisfy the judgment. If the proceeds are sufficient, the judgment is discharged and any excess paid to the defendant. However, there is many a slip between the docketing and satisfaction of a judgment. For example, the defendant may not have any property in the jurisdiction, the sheriff may not be able to find that which is there, other creditors may have liens with priority, the proceeds from the public sale may be insufficient or bankruptcy may intervene. Further, the concern for consumer protection has produced further pressure to limit the traditional rights enjoyed by creditors. Nevertheless, unless the claim reduced to judgment is discharged in bankruptcy, the plaintiff normally has a 20–year renewable period to obtain satisfaction.

Suppose, then, that a seller has tendered and a buyer has accepted goods on credit. If the buyer fails to pay on time the seller is entitled to a judgment for the agreed price. UCC 2–709(1). (In the absence of an agreement on security, however, the seller is rarely able upon breach to take possession of the goods sold. But see UCC 2–702.) Further, "self help" to other of the buyer's property is not permitted. Finally, even with a judgment, satisfaction is not automatic. The various risks in the enforcement procedure, therefore, may help to explain some of the doctrines of contract law and the practices of professional business people. For example, one way to avoid the need for enforcement is to demand payment before the goods are delivered. Constructive "concurrent" conditions of exchange implement this non-credit transaction in the absence of agreement to the contrary. Similarly, many business people will extend unsecured credit only if convinced that the buyer is willing and able to pay on time. If substantial doubts exist, credit is not extended or security is demanded.

A brief word on the secured transaction might here be in order. Under Article 9 of the UCC, sellers of goods on credit or other lenders may easily create by agreement with the buyer or borrower a security interest in personal property and "perfect" it by filing a financing statement in the appropriate public office. Security interest means an "interest in personal property * * * which secures payment or performance of an obligation." UCC 1–201(37). The written agreement creating the security interest (called a security agreement) is often accompanied by a negotiable promissory note which evidences the debtor's obligation to pay in a lump sum or installments. See UCC 3–104.

Upon default by the debtor either on the note or as defined in the security agreement, the secured party—without suing, obtaining judgement or hiring a sheriff—may privately take possession of the property subject to the security interest if no breach of the peace is involved. The ability to privately take possession or "repossessing" (or "repoing") without delay or legal expense is the key benefit of a secured interest.

Subject to a limited right of redemption and the possible claims of other lien or secured creditors, the property will usually be sold by the secured creditor at a public or private sale. The proceeds of this sale will be used to reimburse the secured creditor for expenses incurred in repossessing, to satisfy the underlying obligation and to satisfy the security interests of those subordinate to the repossessing creditor. If a surplus exists, it is paid to the debtor. If an inadequate sum is produced, the secured party is entitled to seek a deficiency judgment for the balance due and, in effect, becomes unsecured. The entire process, which can occur without the need for direct intervention by a court or sheriff, is closely regulated by Article 9. For example, any public or private sale must be accomplished in a commercially reasonable manner; basic debtor rights cannot be eroded by agreement with the creditor; the debtor is given extensive private remedies if the creditor fails to comply with Article 9. Even so, many feel that this protection is inadequate for the consumer. Efforts for reform are manifested in the 1997 revision of Article 9 (which has been adopted by every state) and legislation such as the Uniform Consumer Credit Code (which has not been widely adopted). A more extensive treatment of financing patterns and problems where personal property or real estate is involved (whether by mortgage or installment sales contract) must be reserved for another time and another course.

CHAPTER FOUR

THE BARGAIN RELATIONSHIP

SECTION 1. THE AGREEMENT PROCESS: MANIFESTATION OF MUTUAL ASSENT

In the bargain relationship, the two primary objectives of the parties are to reach agreement on a proposed exchange of economic or other resources and then satisfactorily to complete the exchange. Depending upon the situation of the parties, the transaction and other market or legal constraints, a certain amount of negotiation over terms may precede the final expression of agreement. Put another way, whenever the options of the parties are subject to their own choice rather than predetermined by law or circumstances, negotiation (or bargaining) is likely to occur. See J. Cross, The Economics of Bargaining 3–15 (1969). Thus, in any given transaction the parties may negotiate over such items as willingness to deal one with the other, the description, quality and quantity of what it is that one party is proposing to provide, the price and method of payment, the time and method of performance, which party bears what risks, the duration of the relationship and so forth. An assumption here is that individual bargainers will define their wants in a rational way and seek to satisfy them through a process of voluntary exchange. Similarly, if there is adequate information and sufficient choice, another assumption is that both parties will gain from the completed exchange, that is, that both parties will conclude that the transaction has increased if not maximized their satisfactions.

The two objectives of the bargain relationship (agreement and performance) are consistent with the concept of consideration, examined in Chapter Two, and an exchange completed to the satisfaction of both parties satisfies a standard of efficiency. Further, to the extent that our legal system permits these transactions to occur and supports them through adequate remedies whenever disputes erupt, it promotes the exercise of individual freedom through private ordering, supports the development of a market economy and encourages a system of decentralized power which Professor Harry W. Jones has called the "institution of contract." Harry W. Jones, *The Jurisprudence of Contract*, 44 U.Cin.L.Rev. 43, 50–54 (1975).

Against this general background, the purpose of this section is to explore the legal consequences of breakdowns in the first objective of the bargain relationship, the effort to reach agreement on the proposed exchange. In a typical dispute, after negotiations have commenced and sometimes before any performance of the proposed exchange has occurred, one party will withdraw from the relationship. The other will assert that agreement had reached a point where a contract was formed and that the withdrawal is a breach of contract. How the withdrawing party responds to this and the extent to which the law of contracts supports these responses at various stages of the agreement process is the central problem to be considered. At stake is the general issue of freedom "from" contract. In most situations an individual in our society can refuse to deal or to negotiate with another without liability. But once negotiations have commenced, to what extent is one party privileged to withdraw for any reason without liability? What is the scope of mobility once the bargaining begins?

(A) Ascertainment of Assent: The "Objective" Test

What is the overall approach that a court should take to ascertaining whether the parties have assented to a bargain and what their relevant intentions were in the process? The traditional answer and some of the problems associated with it are suggested in the following two cases and notes.

Embry v. Hargadine, McKittrick Dry Goods Co.

St. Louis Court of Appeals, Missouri, 1907.
127 Mo.App. 383, 105 S.W. 777.

[Appellant's written employment contract with Appellee expired on December 15, 1903. He had been unsuccessful in obtaining a meeting with Appellee's president before the expiration date. On December 23, during peak season, Appellant met with the president, Mr. McKittrick, and, according to his testimony, stated that unless he had another contract for the next year he would "quit" then and there. According to Appellant, the president replied: "Go ahead, you're all right; get your men out and don't let that worry you." Appellant thought that the contract had been renewed and made no further effort to find employment. When his employment was terminated on March 1, 1904, Appellant sued for breach of contract. At the trial, the president denied making the "you're all right statement" and testified that he was pressed to prepare for a board meeting, did not intend at that point to renew the contract and had deferred the renewal issue until a later date.]

■ GOODE, J.

* * *

It is assigned for error that the court required the jury, in order to return a verdict for appellant, not only to find the conversation occurred as appellant swore, but that both parties intended by such conversation to contract with each other for plaintiff's employment for the year from December, 1903, at a salary of $2,000. * * * [I]t remains to determine whether or not this part of the instruction was a correct statement of the law in regard to what was necessary to constitute a contract between the parties; that is to say, whether the formation of a contract by what, according to Embry, was said, depended on the intention of both Embry and McKittrick. Or, to put the question more precisely, did what was said constitute a contract of re-employment on the previous terms irrespective of the intention or purpose of McKittrick?

Judicial opinion and elementary treatises abound in statements of the rule that to constitute a contract there must be a meeting of the minds of the parties, and both must agree to the same thing in the same sense. Generally speaking, this may be true; but it is not literally or universally true. That is to say, the inner intention of parties to a conversation subsequently alleged to create a contract cannot either make a contract of what transpired, or prevent one from arising, if the words used were sufficient to constitute a contract. In so far as their intention is an influential element, it is only such intention as the words or acts of the parties indicate; not one secretly cherished which is inconsistent with those words or acts. The rule is thus stated by a text-writer, and many decisions are cited in support of his text: "The primary object of construction in contract law is to discover the intention of the parties. This intention in express contracts is, in the first instance, embodied in the words which the parties have used and is to be deduced therefrom. This rule applies to oral contracts, as well as to contracts in writing, and is the rule recognized by courts of equity." 2 Page, Contracts, § 1104. So it is said in another work: "Now this measure of the contents of the promise will be found to coincide, in the usual dealings of men of good faith and ordinary competence, both with the actual intention of the promisor and with the actual expectation of the promisee. But this is not a constant or a necessary coincidence. In exceptional cases, a promisor may be bound to perform something which he did not intend to promise, or a promisee may not be entitled to require that performance which he understood to be promised to him." Walds–Pollock, Contracts (3d Ed.) 309. In Brewington v. Mesker, 51 Mo.App. 348, 356, it is said that the meeting of minds, which is essential to the formation of a contract, is not determined by the secret intention of the parties, but by their expressed intention, which may be wholly at variance with the former. * * *

In view of those authorities, we hold that, though McKittrick may not have intended to employ Embry by what transpired between them according to the latter's testimony, yet if what McKittrick said would have been taken by a reasonable man to be an employment, and Embry so understood it, it constituted a valid contract of employment for the ensuing year.

The next question is whether or not the language used was of that character, namely, was such that Embry, as a reasonable man, might consider he was re-employed for the ensuing year on the previous terms, and act accordingly. * * * Embry was demanding a renewal of his contract, saying he had been put off from time to time, and that he had only a few days before the end of the year in which to seek employment from other houses, and that he would quit then and there unless he was re-employed. McKittrick inquired how he was getting along with the department, and Embry said they (i.e., the employees of the department) were very busy getting out salesmen; whereupon McKittrick said: "Go ahead, you are all right; get your men out and do not let that worry you." We think no reasonable man would construe that answer to Embry's demand that he be employed for another year, otherwise than as an assent to the demand, and that Embry had the right to rely on it as an assent. The natural inference is, though we do not find it testified to, that Embry was at work getting samples ready for the salesmen to use during the ensuing season. Now, when he was complaining of the worry and mental distress he was under because of his uncertainty about the future, and his urgent need, either of an immediate contract with respondent, or a refusal by it to make one, leaving him free to seek employment elsewhere, McKittrick must have answered as he did for the purpose of assuring appellant that any apprehension was needless, as appellant's services would be retained by the respondent. The answer was unambiguous, and we rule that if the conversation was according to appellant's version, and he understood he was employed, it constituted in law a valid contract of re-employment, and the court erred in making the formation of a contract depend on a finding that both parties intended to make one. It was only necessary that Embry, as a reasonable man, had a right to and did so understand.

Some other rulings are assigned for error by the appellant, but we will not discuss them because we think they are devoid of merit.

The judgment is reversed, and the cause remanded. All concur.

Lucy v. Zehmer

Supreme Court of Appeals of Virginia, 1954.
196 Va. 493, 84 S.E.2d 516.

■ BUCHANAN, JUSTICE. This suit was instituted by W.O. Lucy and J.C. Lucy, complainants, against A.H. Zehmer and Ida S. Zehmer, his wife, defendants, to have specific performance of a contract by which it was alleged the Zehmers had sold to W.O. Lucy a tract of land owned by A.H. Zehmer in Dinwiddie county containing 471.6 acres, more or less, known as the Ferguson farm, for $50,000. J.C. Lucy, the other complainant, is a brother of W.O. Lucy, to whom W.O. Lucy transferred a half interest in his alleged purchase.

The instrument sought to be enforced was written by A.H. Zehmer on December 20, 1952, in these words: "We hereby agree to sell to W.O. Lucy the Ferguson Farm complete for $50,000.00, title satisfactory to buyer," and signed by the defendants, A.H. Zehmer and Ida S. Zehmer.

The answer of A.H. Zehmer admitted that at the time mentioned W.O. Lucy offered him $50,000 cash for the farm, but that he, Zehmer, considered that the offer was made in jest; that so thinking, and both he and Lucy having had several drinks, he wrote out "the memorandum" quoted above and induced his wife to sign it; that he did not deliver the memorandum to Lucy, but that Lucy picked it up, read it, put it in his pocket, attempted to offer Zehmer $5 to bind the bargain, which Zehmer refused to accept, and realizing for the first time that Lucy was serious, Zehmer assured him that he had no intention of selling the farm and that the whole matter was a joke. Lucy left the premises insisting that he had purchased the farm.

Depositions were taken and the decree appealed from was entered holding that the complainants had failed to establish their right to specific performance, and dismissing their bill. The assignment of error is to this action of the court.

[At the trial, Lucy testified that he was a farmer and had known Zehmer for 15 to 20 years. He stated that he knew the farm well and, seven years earlier, Zehmer had rejected his offer to purchase it for $20,000. Lucy claimed that he wanted to try again to buy the farm and said to Zehmer, "bet you won't take $50,000." Zehmer responded, "yes, but you wouldn't give it" and expressed doubt that Lucy could raise the money. Lucy then told Zehmer to write an agreement and, after 30–40 minutes of discussion and modification, all of the parties, including Mrs. Zehmer, signed. Zehmer then refused Lucy's tender of $5 to seal the bargain. Lucy conceded that there was a bottle on the table between them and that they had had a "couple of drinks." He also testified that the next day, in order to raise the $50,000, he persuaded his brother to put up half of the money. He also had the title examined. Upon stating that he was ready to proceed, Zehmer told him that there was no contract.

[Zehmer's testimony was that he had purchased the farm eleven years ago for $11,000 and had refused many offers to buy it. It was just before Christmas, there was "lots of drinking," and he was "high as a Georgia pine." When Lucy approached him about selling the farm, Zehmer doubted that Lucy had $50,000. He claimed he was just "needling" and stated that after the writing was signed he told Lucy that it was just "liquor talking" and that he would not sell. Zehmer's wife testified that she would not sign the writing until told it was a joke, that both men were "tight" and that the husband told Lucy before he left that there was no sale. This latter fact was corroborated by a waitress, who witnessed the transaction.]

* * *

The defendants insist that the evidence was ample to support their contention that the writing sought to be enforced was prepared as a bluff or dare to force Lucy to admit that he did not have $50,000; that the whole matter was a joke; that the writing was not delivered to Lucy and no binding contract was ever made between the parties.

It is an unusual, if not bizarre, defense. When made to the writing admittedly prepared by one of the defendants and signed by both, clear evidence is required to sustain it.

In his testimony Zehmer claimed that he "was high as a Georgia pine," and that the transaction "was just a bunch of two doggoned drunks bluffing to see who could talk the biggest and say the most." That claim is inconsistent with his attempt to testify in great detail as to what was said and what was done. It is contradicted by other evidence as to the condition of both parties, and rendered of no weight by the testimony of his wife that when Lucy left the restaurant she suggested that Zehmer drive him home. The record is convincing that Zehmer was not intoxicated to the extent of being unable to comprehend the nature and consequences of the instrument he executed, and hence that instrument is not to be invalidated on that ground.... It was in fact conceded by defendants' counsel in oral argument that under the evidence Zehmer was not too drunk to make a valid contract.

The evidence is convincing also that Zehmer wrote two agreements, the first one beginning "I hereby agree to sell." Zehmer first said he could not remember about that, then that "I don't think I wrote but one out." Mrs. Zehmer said that what he wrote was "I hereby agree," but that the "I" was changed to "We" after that night. The agreement that was written and signed is in the record and indicates no such change. Neither are the mistakes in spelling that Zehmer sought to point out readily apparent.

The appearance of the contract, the fact that it was under discussion for forty minutes or more before it was signed; Lucy's objection to the first draft because it was written in the singular, and he wanted Mrs. Zehmer to sign it also; the rewriting to meet that objection and the signing by Mrs. Zehmer; the discussion of what was to be included in the sale, the provision for the examination of the title, the completeness of the instrument that was executed, the taking possession of it by Lucy with no request or suggestion by either of the defendants that he give it back, are facts which furnish persuasive evidence that the execution of the contract was a serious business transaction rather than a casual, jesting matter as defendants now contend.

* * *

If it be assumed, contrary to what we think the evidence shows, that Zehmer was jesting about selling his farm to Lucy and that the transaction was intended by him to be a joke, nevertheless the evidence shows that Lucy did not so understand it but considered it to be a serious business transaction and the contract to be binding on the Zehmers as well as on himself. The very next day he arranged with his brother to put up half the money and take a half interest in the land. The day after that he employed an attorney to examine the title. The next night, Tuesday, he was back at Zehmer's place and there Zehmer told him for the first time, Lucy said, that he wasn't going to sell and he told Zehmer, "You know you sold that place fair and square." After receiving the report from his attorney that the title was good he wrote to Zehmer that he was ready to close the deal.

Not only did Lucy actually believe, but the evidence shows he was warranted in believing, that the contract represented a serious business transaction and a good faith sale and purchase of the farm.

In the field of contracts, as generally elsewhere, "We must look to the outward expression of a person as manifesting his intention rather than to his secret and unexpressed intention. 'The law imputes to a person an

intention corresponding to the reasonable meaning of his words and acts.' "
First Nat. Exchange Bank of Roanoke v. Roanoke Oil Co., 169 Va. 99, 114.

* * *

The mental assent of the parties is not requisite for the formation of a contract. If the words or other acts of one of the parties have but one reasonable meaning, his undisclosed intention is immaterial except when an unreasonable meaning which he attaches to his manifestations is known to the other party. Restatement of the Law of Contracts, Vol. I, § 71, p. 74.

" * * * The law, therefore, judges of an agreement between two persons exclusively from those expressions of their intentions which are communicated between them. * * *." Clark on Contracts, 4 ed., § 3, p. 4.

An agreement or mutual assent is of course essential to a valid contract but the law imputes to a person an intention corresponding to the reasonable meaning of his words and acts. If his words and acts, judged by a reasonable standard, manifest an intention to agree, it is immaterial what may be the real but unexpressed state of his mind....

So a person cannot set up that he was merely jesting when his conduct and words would warrant a reasonable person in believing that he intended a real agreement....

Whether the writing signed by the defendants and now sought to be enforced by the complainants was the result of a serious offer by Lucy and a serious acceptance by the defendants, or was a serious offer by Lucy and an acceptance in secret jest by the defendants, in either event it constituted a binding contract of sale between the parties.

* * *

The complainants are entitled to have specific performance of the contract sued on. The decree appealed from is therefore reversed and the cause is remanded for the entry of a proper decree requiring the defendants to perform the contract in accordance with the prayer of the bill.

Reversed and remanded.

NOTES

(1) *Some History.* At one time common law judges, along with their counterparts in civil law countries, strictly adhered to the subjective theory, requiring, as they were fond of saying, a "meeting of minds." For example, if A made an offer to B, allowing the offeree until later in the afternoon to accept or reject, B's assent to the proposal within that period would be ineffective if A could establish he or she was not then of a mind to contract. An offeror need not communicate a withdrawal (revocation) of the offer; one need only prove one no longer intended to contract when the other party undertook to accept. See Cook v. Oxley, 3 Term.R. 653, 100 Eng.Rep. 785 (1790). Secret, unmanifested intention could defeat what outwardly was an expression of assent. For if actual assent was the decisive factor, the outward manifestation was not controlling.

It must not be supposed, however, that even under the subjective theory the outward expression is of no consequence. One would obviously have some explaining to do if it were maintained in court that when one said "I promise to pay $5,000," one actually meant to say "I promise to pay $4,000." Just as in other fields of law where the central inquiry is the ascertainment of actual intent, circumstances may be very persuasive.

There has been a notable shift in the common law decisions, especially since the turn of the century, toward a greater acceptance of the objective theory. The avowed reason has been to protect the stability of contractual relationships by enabling one to act upon reasonable appearance. There is then no assumption of the risk that what was said was different from what was meant. The break with the subjective theory was cautious at first, but eventually courts began to express themselves in this uncompromising fashion: "While ordinarily present, it is not the meeting of minds of the parties, but the expression of their mutual assent that * * * is the culmination of the contract-making process * * *. It is not the subjective thing known as meeting of the minds, but the objective thing, manifestation of mutual assent, which is essential." Field–Martin Company v. Fruen Milling Company, 210 Minn. 388, 298 N.W. 574, 575 (1941).

(2) *Tests for Objectivity*.

The following statement by Justice Learned Hand is recognized as a classic statement of the objective theory of contracts:

> A contract has, strictly speaking, nothing to do with the personal, or individual, intent of the parties. A contract is an obligation attached by mere force of law to certain acts of the parties, usually words, which ordinarily accompany and represent a known intent. If, however, it were proved by twenty bishops that either party, when he used the words, intended something else than the usual meaning which the law imposes upon them, he would still be held, unless there were some mutual mistake or something else of the sort.

Hotchkiss v. National City Bank of New York, 200 Fed. 287, 293 (S.D.N.Y. 1911).

A contemporary judge, Frank Easterbrook, put it this way:

> * * * Walters stoutly maintains that he subjectively intended to be bound and he wants to invite a jury to infer the same about Telstar. * * * Yet "intent" does not invite a tour through Walters's cranium, with Walters as the guide. * * * 'The intent of the parties [to be bound] must necessarily be derived from a consideration of their words, written and oral, and their actions.' * * * Secret hopes and wishes count for nothing. The status of a document as a contract depends on what the parties express to each other and to the world, not on what they keep to themselves. * * * The objective approach is an essential ingredient to allowing the parties jointly to control the effect of their document. If unilateral or secret intentions could bind, parties would become wary, and the written word would lose some of its power. The ability to fix the consequences with certainty is especially important in commercial transactions that are planned with care in

advance." Easterbrook, J., in Skycom Corporation v. Telstar Corporation, 813 F.2d 810, 814–5 (7th Cir.1987).

There is, however, as one prominent writer observed, "a 'subjective' as well as an 'objective' side" to the law of contracts, and "although the 'objective' theory has now become fashionable," it is "erroneous to regard it as a complete statement of the law." Williams, *Mistake as to Party in the Law of Contract*, 23 Can.B.Rev. 271, 380, 387 (1945). Consider the following statement:

> Whether the parties are merely negotiating a contract or entering into a present contract is purely a question of intention. ... [I]n construing contracts, courts must look not only to the specific language employed but also to the subject matter contracted about, the relationship of the parties, the circumstances surrounding the transaction, or in other words place themselves in the same position the parties occupied when the contract was entered into and view the terms and intent of the agreement in the same light in which the parties did when the same was formulated and accepted.

Cohen v. Johnson, 91 F.Supp. 231, 235 (M.D.Pa.1950).

How does this test of objectivity differ from that used by Judge Learned Hand? Suppose it was clear that the trial court used the *Cohen v. Johnson* test in *Lucy v. Zehmer*. What test of objectivity did the Supreme Court of Appeals apply? Would differences in the test explain the different results?

Suppose that despite everything that was said and done in the bar Lucy knew that Zehmer was joking—that he and his wife did not intend to sell. Should the objective test trump Lucy's actual knowledge? See Article 8(1) of CISG, which provides: "For purposes of this Convention, statements made by and other conduct of a party are to be interpreted according to his intent where the other party knew or could not have been unaware what that intent was."

(3) *Consequences of "Objective" Approach*. What is at stake in the choice between a "subjective" and an "objective" approach to contract? One consequence is revealed in the two cases just considered. If Mr. McKittrick did not intend to renew Mr. Embry's contract and Mr. Zehmer did not intend to sell the land to Mr. Lucy and both acted honestly, the objective test excludes as irrelevant what they actually intended. It protects the plaintiff's reasonable understanding based upon what was said and done rather than what was thought. Put another way, if the court and jury find that the plaintiff's expectations based upon what was said or done were reasonable and the other requisites for contract formation are present, those expectations are protected. Thus, in *Embry*, Mr. Embry reasonably thought that his contract had been renewed. He remained on the job, thereby foregoing other opportunities, and was not informed about Mr. McKittrick's real intention until over two months later.

But are the facts so compelling in *Lucy?* At what point was Mr. Lucy first clearly informed that Mr. Zehmer did not intend to sell? Had Mr. Lucy changed his position in any substantial way at that time? Should that make any difference? See Malcolm P. Sharp, "Contracts" in *Mr. Justice Holmes: Some Modern Views,* 31 U.Chi.L.Rev. 268, 272–74 (1964), where it is argued that in light of the costs to individual freedom, the objective test should be employed only where the defendant has carelessly used language which induced actual and justified reliance by the plaintiff.

A broader consequence is that the "objective" test affords the courts an opportunity to control or regulate individual exchange behavior through use of that great "collectivist," the "reasonable" person. As Professor J. Willard Hurst has put it, the test satisfied a "particular need" in a market society "to create and maintain a framework of reasonably well defined and assured expectations as to the likely official and nonofficial consequences of private venture and decision." J.W. Hurst, Law and the Conditions of Freedom in Nineteenth Century America 21–22 (1956).

Professor Gilmore, a bit more critical, has noted that the objective test represents a move toward absolute liability and, under the guidance of O.W. Holmes, Jr. and Williston, it became the "great metaphysical solvent—the critical test for distinguishing between the false and the true." G. Gilmore, The Death of Contract 42–43 (1974). And, finally, Professor Horwitz has suggested that the development in the nineteenth century of an objective approach based on the external manifestation of mutual assent was a pro-commercial market attack on the theory of intrinsic value which lay at the base of the eighteenth century equity idea of contract. It expressed a market ideology, downplayed justice and gave courts an opportunity to prefer certain groups and interests as more reasonable than others. Morton Horwitz, *The Historical Foundations of Modern Contract Law*, 87 Harv.L.Rev. 917 (1974).

A final and more practical consequence concerns the problem of proof. As we shall see in the following materials, the focus is upon what was said and done rather than what was thought, and the question is what the plaintiff could reasonably understand or, in some cases, what the defendant knew or should have known that the plaintiff understood. Throughout, a question concerning the range of "objective" evidence relevant to the question of what the parties knew or should have known becomes critical. Also, who should make the critical determination of reasonableness, the court or the jury? Would you conclude, for example, that it would be sounder to limit extrinsic evidence to the words, written or spoken, of the parties and let the court decide who is reasonable or have a more expansive concept of relevance with the jury as the ultimate arbiter of reasonableness?

(4) *A Lawyer's Alice.*

At that moment Alice's attention was distracted by the entry of a fluffy white figure. It was the White Rabbit, and a hum of conversation broke out from the gathering as he entered. He was dressed in immaculate morning dress, with a white camellia in the buttonhole, and immediately went up to where the little Lizard was sitting.

Alice suddenly realised the reason for the whole proceeding. The White Rabbit was to be married to the Lizard. That was why he had been so agitated about the time. "Of course," Alice said aloud to herself when she made this discovery.

"My dear, then I am so happy," said the Tortoise.

"Happy about what?" asked Alice.

"Happy that you will marry me," said the Tortoise.

"I will do nothing of the kind," replied Alice with dignity.

"But you just said so. I asked you to marry me and you replied 'Of course.' "

"I didn't hear you asking me to marry you, and I was talking to myself."

"Oh, Oh," cried the Tortoise, weeping bitterly. "I didn't know that. You couldn't expect me to." He sighed gustily, and looked up at Alice with a face all smeary with tears.

"Still," he added, brightening, "you have promised to marry me, you know."

"I have done nothing of the sort," said Alice.

"Yes you have," replied the Tortoise. "I thought you promised, therefore you did promise."

"How could I make you a promise," asked Alice, "when I was not speaking to you?"

"Anyway," said the Tortoise, "promise or not, I thought you were promising, and it was quite natural that I should think so. So you really ought to marry me."

Alice had never before considered marrying a Tortoise, but she had once kept one in her garden and had thought it quite a nice creature.

She did not feel at all certain what was the right thing to do in the circumstances, but the easiest thing seemed to be to do as the Tortoise wanted, and to see what would happen. Accordingly she replied, "Oh, all right," which made the Tortoise look contented.

Glanville Williams, *A Lawyer's Alice*, 9 Camb.L.J. 171, 172 (1945).

PROBLEM: THE CASE OF THE HOLE–IN–ONE

Amos was playing in the East End Open Golf Tournament on the Fairview Golf Course. Fairview was a popular public course and hosted several corporate outings a month. When Amos arrived at the ninth tee, a 185 yard par three playing into the wind, he saw a new Chevrolet Beretta with signs posted reading as follows: "HOLE–IN–ONE Wins this 2003 Chevrolet Beretta GT Courtesy of Tiger Buick Chevy Pontiac $49 OVER FACTORY INVOICE." There were no observers on either the tee or at the green. Cobaugh aced the hole (with a solid three iron) and claimed the automobile as his prize. Tiger refused. It had offered the car as a prize for a charity golf tournament sponsored by the local Sertoma Club two days earlier and had neglected to remove the car and signs. Amos sues. What result?

Cohen v. Cowles Media Company

Supreme Court of Minnesota, 1990.
457 N.W.2d 199, *reversed*, 501 U.S. 663, 111 S.Ct. 2513, 115 L.Ed.2d 586 (1991), opinion on remand, 479 N.W.2d 387 (1992).

[The facts are stated *supra* at 152, where the Supreme Court of Minnesota, after remand from the United States Supreme Court, affirmed its earlier conclusion that the promise of confidentiality was not enforceable on a bargain theory but, nevertheless, enforced the promise on a reliance theory.]

■ SIMONETT, JUSTICE.

I.

First of all, we agree with the court of appeals that the trial court erred in not granting defendants' post-trial motions for judgment notwithstanding the verdict on the misrepresentation claim.

For fraud there must be a misrepresentation of a past or present fact. A representation as to future acts does not support an action for fraud merely because the represented act did not happen, unless the promisor did not intend to perform at the time the promise was made. *Vandeputte v. Soderholm*, 298 Minn. 505, 508, 216 N.W.2d 144, 147 (1974). Cohen admits that the reporters intended to keep their promises, as, indeed, they testified and as their conduct confirmed. Moreover, the record shows that the editors had no intention to reveal Cohen's identity until later when more information was received and the matter was discussed with other editors. These facts do not support a fraud claim. For this reason and for the other reasons cited by the court of appeals, we affirm the court of appeals' ruling. Because the punitive damages award hinges on the tort claim of misrepresentation, it, too, must be set aside as the court of appeals ruled.

II.

A contract, it is said, consists of an offer, an acceptance, and consideration. Here, we seemingly have all three, plus a breach. We think, however, the matter is not this simple.

Unquestionably, the promises given in this case were intended by the promisors to be kept. The record is replete with the unanimous testimony of reporters, editors, and journalism experts that protecting a confidential source of a news story is a sacred trust, a matter of "honor," of "morality," and required by professional ethics. Only in dire circumstances might a promise of confidentiality possibly be ethically broken, and instances were cited where a reporter has gone to jail rather than reveal a source. The keeping of promises is professionally important for at least two reasons. First, to break a promise of confidentiality which has induced a source to give information is dishonorable. Secondly, if it is known that promises will not be kept, sources may dry up. The media depend on confidential sources for much of their news; significantly, at least up to now, it appears that journalistic ethics have adequately protected confidential sources.

The question before us, however, is not whether keeping a confidential promise is ethically required but whether it is legally enforceable; whether, in other words, the law should superimpose a legal obligation on a moral and ethical obligation. The two obligations are not always coextensive.

The newspapers argue that the reporter's promise should not be contractually binding because these promises are usually given clandestinely and orally, hence they are often vague, subject to misunderstanding, and a fertile breeding ground for lawsuits. See Ruzicka v. Conde Nast Publications, Inc., 733 F.Supp. 1289, 1300–01 (D.Minn.1990) (a promise not to make a source identifiable found too vague to be enforceable). Perhaps so, and this may be a factor to weigh in the balance; but this objection goes only to problems of proof, rather than to the merits of having such a cause of action at all. Moreover, in this case at least, we have a clear-cut promise.

The law, however, does not create a contract where the parties intended none. . . . Nor does the law consider binding every exchange of promises. See, e.g., Minn.Stat. ch. 553 (1988) (abolishing breaches of contract to marry); see also Restatement (Second) of Contracts §§ 189–91 (1981) (promises impairing family relations are unenforceable). We are not persuaded that in the special milieu of media newsgathering a source and a reporter ordinarily believe they are engaged in making a legally binding contract. They are not thinking in terms of offers and acceptances in any commercial or business sense. * * *

In other words, contract law seems here an ill fit for a promise of news source confidentiality. To impose a contract theory on this arrangement puts an unwarranted legal rigidity on a special ethical relationship, precluding necessary consideration of factors underlying that ethical relationship. We conclude that a contract cause of action is inappropriate for these particular circumstances. * * *

[The dissents of Justices Yetka and Kelly and some footnotes are omitted.]

NOTES

(1) The court recognizes that there was, seemingly, an offer, an acceptance, and consideration. Why, then, was there not a contract?

(2) *Intention to Be Bound as a Requisite of Contractual Obligation.* Refusing to superimpose "a legal obligation on a moral and ethical obligation," the court insists that the law "does not create a contract where the parties intended none." Based upon your studies to this point, do you agree? Is it necessary that there be an intent to assume a legal obligation (subjective) or a manifestation of intent to assume such an obligation (objective)? See Restatement (Second) § 21: "Neither the real nor apparent intention that a promise be legally binding is essential to the formation of a contract. . . ." In the typical contract, it may be wondered whether the parties ever consciously consider the legal consequences of their agreement. The question evidently did not come up

during the negotiations here. If they had thought about the matter, do you believe the parties would have considered their agreement to be legally binding?

Professor Randy Barnett disagrees with the Restatement position, arguing for a general theory of contract which relies heavily upon determining whether there is "a manifestation of intention to be legally bound," see Randy Barnett, *A Consent Theory of Contract*, 86 Colum.L.Rev. 269 (1986). More concretely:

> A consent theory of contract specifies that an enforceable contract requires the satisfaction of at least two conditions. First, the *subject* of the contract must be a morally cognizable right possessed by the transferor that is interpersonally transferable, or "alienable." Second, the holder of the right must *consent* to its transfer. Thus, commitments will generally be enforced only if they manifest to the promisee the promisor's assent to transfer rights.

Randy Barnett, *Contract Remedies and Inalienable Rights*, 4 Soc.Phil. & Pol. 179, 184 (1986).

(3) *Manifested Intention Not to Be Bound.* The objective theory, by considering the impression on the hearer rather than the intent of the speaker, obviously makes it possible for one to be held to a contract without any real intention to assume a legal obligation. For no protest of intention differing from the outward manifestation is recognized. Should the converse be true as well? That is, if the outward expression clearly negates contractual intent, should that manifestation be controlling?

In Rose & Frank Company v. JR Crompton & Brothers, Ltd., a 1923 decision of the English Court of Appeal ([1923] 2 K.B. 261), there was an elaborate document executed by the parties pertaining to the sale of paper by British companies to an American corporation, appointing the latter exclusive selling agent in the United States for a three-year period. One clause of the document read as follows:

> This agreement is not entered into, nor is this memorandum written, as a formal or legal agreement, and shall not be subject to legal jurisdiction in the Law Courts either of the United States or England, but it is only a definite expression and record of the purpose and intention of the three parties concerned to which they each honourably pledge themselves with the fullest confidence, based on past business with each other, that it will be carried through by each of the three parties with mutual loyalty and friendly cooperation.

The court refused to recognize the document as evidencing a contract. In his opinion, Lord Justice Scrutton observed:

> Now it is quite possible for parties to come to an agreement by accepting a proposal with the result that the agreement concluded does not give rise to legal relations. The reason for this is that the parties do not intend that their agreement shall give rise to legal relations. This intention may be implied from the subject matter of the agreement, but it may also be expressed by the parties. In social and family relations such an intention is readily implied, while in business matters the opposite result would ordinarily follow. But I see no reason why, even in business matters, the parties should not intend to rely on each other's good faith and honour,

and to exclude all idea of settling disputes by any outside intervention, with the accompanying necessity of expressing themselves so precisely that outsiders may have no difficulty in understanding what they mean. If they clearly express such an intention I can see no reason in public policy why effect should not be given to their intention.

For other cases in accord, see Kind v. Clark, 161 F.2d 36, 46 (2d Cir.1947); I.H. Rubenstein & Son, Inc. v. Sperry & Hutchinson Co., 222 So.2d 329 (La.App. 1969); Smith v. MacDonald, 37 Cal.App. 503, 174 P. 80 (1918). See also Pappas v. Hauser, 197 N.W.2d 607 (Iowa 1972) (explicit agreement that charitable pledge was not intended to be binding).

(4) *Social Engagements*. Ordinarily, social engagements are not thought to be legally binding, and cases of this type rarely reach the courts. That there are exceptions is attested by the following New York Times article of May 23, 1973, dateline San Francisco:

> It had to happen in this litigious nation. A San Francisco woman has been sued in Small Claims Court here by a San Jose area man for breaking a date.
>
> Tom Horsley of Campbell is asking Alyn Chesselet for $38 as a matter of principle, because she broke an "oral contract" to have dinner and see a show with him early this year.
>
> Miss Chesselet said Mr. Horsley is "nuts" to think she will pay.
>
> Mr. Horsley wants to be paid for two hours spent driving to and from San Francisco at his minimum rate as a certified public accountant of $8.50 an hour and 17 cents a mile in auto expenses for the 100–mile distance. His claim is for $34 plus $2 filing fee and $2 to serve court papers.
>
> "She had 10 days to call me and cancel the date," Mr. Horsley said in a telephone interview. "And she promised to pay."
>
> Miss Chesselet said that she had had to cancel her date with Mr. Horsley at the last moment because of a sudden change in her work schedule as a waitress and that she had made every attempt to let him know. "So I told him I'd pay his expenses or to sue me, but I was just kidding," she said.
>
> The case is tentatively scheduled to be heard in July. In the words of his lawyer ... in one letter, Mr. Horsley is "not the type of man to take standing up lying down."

Judge Judy, call your answering service!

Were Tom to press the matter in court, how might Alyn respond? She might argue that although there was some sort of bargain, the context suggests to a reasonable person that she did not intend to assume legal obligations. The social setting is as effective to convey this intention as the explicit "not legally binding" clause in a commercial agreement. See *Rose & Frank Company v. JR Crompton & Brothers, Ltd.*, supra note 3. As Professor Corbin put it: "If the subject matter and terms are not such as customarily have affected legal relations, the transaction is not legally operative unless the expressions of the party indicate an intention to make it so." Corbin § 34.

What do you think of the following statement by the late Professor Grover Grismore:

> The fact is that, in most cases, when people make offers and acceptances they give no thought whatever to the question as to whether the undertakings shall be legally obligatory. When agreements are made it is normally assumed that they will be performed without regard to the law. The thought of legal sanction does not enter in, since serious agreements are made to be performed not to be broken. Of course, we might say the intent to contract will be presumed in the absence of affirmative evidence of a contrary intent, on the assumption that if the parties had thought about the matter at all they would have intended that their agreement should be legally obligatory. However, if we do say this we are in reality saying that no such intent is essential. Unless we take some such view as this, it would be almost impossible to find the existence of contract in most cases; since, as has already been indicated, when parties make agreements they seldom address their minds to the question of legal obligation, and seldom have any intent in regard to it. It is believed that the views here set forth are in accord with what is actually decided by the courts. The cases which have been thought to go counter to this view are those involving social engagements and family agreements. Thus, it said that, if A invites B to dinner and B accepts, no binding obligations exist. This is probably true. But it is true, not because an intent to have a contract is essential to contractual obligation, and no such intent can be shown here; but because in such a case it is fair to say that had the parties thought about the matter at all, it is quite clear they would have regarded such an engagement as binding only in honor.

Grover Grismore, Contracts § 19 (1st ed. 1947). For Professor John Murray's elaboration of this basic point, see Murray on Contracts § 31D (4th ed. 2001).

Alyn might further maintain that even if the circumstances remove the usual assumptions about social agreements, there are strong policy arguments against enforcement. First, it would be wrong for the court to regulate these transactions through the imposition of liability. These agreements are on the periphery of the market where "talk is cheap," mobility is important and certain non-legal sanctions, such as social stigma, are more effective than contract remedies. Second, unless the parties have clearly indicated the importance to them of a non-economic transaction, the cost to society of enforcing these promises far outweighs any conceivable benefits. Third, the losses to Tom are insignificant. Alyn has not been unjustly enriched, and Tom's reliance has not produced any substantial losses. Intervention here would create a dangerous precedent.

(B) OFFER: CREATION OF POWER OF ACCEPTANCE

Lonergan v. Scolnick

Court of Appeals of California, 1954.
129 Cal.App.2d 179, 276 P.2d 8.

■ BARNARD, PRESIDING JUSTICE. This is an action for specific performance or for damages in the event specific performance was impossible.

The complaint alleged that on April 15, 1952, the parties entered into a contract whereby the defendant agreed to sell, and plaintiff agreed to buy a 40–acre tract of land for $2,500; that this was a fair, just and reasonable value of the property; that on April 28, 1952, the defendant repudiated the contract and refused to deliver a deed; that on April 28, 1952, the property was worth $6,081; and that plaintiff has been damaged in the amount of $3,581. The answer denied that any contract had been entered into, or that anything was due to the plaintiff.

By stipulation, the issue of whether or not a contract was entered into between the parties was first tried, reserving the other issues for a further trial if that became necessary. The issue as to the existence of a contract was submitted upon an agreed statement, including certain letters between the parties, without the introduction of other evidence.

The stipulated facts are as follows: During March, 1952, the defendant placed an ad in a Los Angeles paper reading, so far as material here, "Joshua Tree vic. 40 acres, * * * need cash, will sacrifice." In response to an inquiry resulting from this ad the defendant, who lived in New York, wrote a letter to the plaintiff dated March 26, briefly describing the property, giving directions as to how to get there, stating that his rock-bottom price was $2,500 cash, and further stating that "This is a form letter." On April 7, the plaintiff wrote a letter to the defendant saying that he was not sure he had found the property, asking for its legal description, asking whether the land was all level or whether it included certain jutting rock hills, and suggesting a certain bank as escrow agent "should I desire to purchase the land." On April 8, the defendant wrote to the plaintiff saying "From your description you have found the property"; that this bank "is O.K. for escrow agent"; that the land was fairly level; giving the legal description; and then saying, "If you are really interested, you will have to decide fast, as I expect to have a buyer in the next week or so." On April 12, the defendant sold the property to a third party for $2,500. The plaintiff received defendant's letter of April 8, on April 14. On April 15 he wrote to the defendant thanking him for his letter "confirming that I was on the right land", stating that he would immediately proceed to have the escrow opened and would deposit $2,500 therein "in conformity with your offer", and asking the defendant to forward a deed with his instructions to the escrow agent. On April 17, 1952, the plaintiff started an escrow and placed in the hands of the escrow agent $100, agreeing to furnish an additional $2,400 at an unspecified time, with the provision that if the escrow was not closed by May 15, 1952, it should be completed as soon thereafter as possible unless a written demand for a return of the money or instruments was made by either party after that date. It was further stipulated that the plaintiff was ready and willing at all times to deposit the $2,400.

The matter was submitted on June 11, 1953. On July 10, 1953, the judge filed a memorandum opinion stating that it was his opinion that the letter of April 8, 1952, when considered with the previous correspondence, constituted an offer of sale which offer was, however, qualified and conditioned upon prompt acceptance by the plaintiff; that in spite of the condition thus imposed, the plaintiff delayed more than a week before notifying the defendant of his acceptance; and that since the plaintiff was aware of the necessity of promptly communicating his acceptance to the defendant his delay was not the prompt action required by the terms of the offer. Findings of fact were filed on October 2, 1953, finding that each and all of the statements in the agreed statement are true, and that all allegations to the contrary in the complaint are untrue. As conclusions of law, it was found that the plaintiff and defendant did not enter into a contract as alleged in the complaint or otherwise, and that the defendant is entitled to judgment against the plaintiff. Judgment was entered according-ly, from which the plaintiff has appealed.

The appellant contends that the judgment is contrary to the evidence and to the law since the facts, as found, do not support the conclusions of law upon which the judgment is based. It is argued that there is no conflict in the evidence, and this court is not bound by the trial court's construction of the written instruments involved; that the evidence conclusively shows that an offer was made to the plaintiff by the defendant, which offer was accepted by the mailing of plaintiff's letter of April 15; that upon receipt of defendant's letter of April 8th plaintiff had a reasonable time within which to accept the offer that had been made; that by his letter of April 15 and his starting of an escrow the plaintiff accepted said offer; and that the agreed statement of facts establishes that a valid contract was entered into between the parties. In his briefs the appellant assumes that an offer was made by the defendant, and confined his argument to contending that the evidence shows that he accepted that offer within a reasonable time.

There can be no contract unless the minds of the parties have met and mutually agreed upon some specific thing. This is usually evidenced by one party making an offer which is accepted by the other party. Section 25 of the Restatement of the Law on Contracts reads:

"If from a promise, or manifestation of intention, or from the circum-stances existing at the time, the person to whom the promise or manifesta-tion is addressed knows or has reason to know that the person making it does not intend it as an expression of his fixed purpose until he has given a further expression of assent, he has not made an offer."

The language used in Niles v. Hancock, 140 Cal. 157, 73 P. 840, 842, "It is also clear from the correspondence that it was the intention of the defendant that the negotiations between him and the plaintiff were to be purely preliminary," is applicable here. The correspondence here indicates an intention on the part of the defendant to find out whether the plaintiff was interested, rather than an intention to make a definite offer to the plaintiff. The language used by the defendant in his letters of March 26 and April 8 rather clearly discloses that they were not intended as an expres-sion of fixed purpose to make a definite offer, and was sufficient to advise the plaintiff that some further expression of assent on the part of the defendant was necessary.

The advertisement in the paper was a mere request for an offer. The letter of March 26 contains no definite offer, and clearly states that it is a form letter. It merely gives further particulars, in clarification of the advertisement, and tells the plaintiff how to locate the property if he was interested in looking into the matter. The letter of April 8 added nothing in the way of a definite offer. It merely answered some questions asked by the plaintiff, and stated that if the plaintiff was really interested he would have to act fast. The statement that he expected to have a buyer in the next week or so indicated that the defendant intended to sell to the first-comer, and was reserving the right to do so. From this statement, alone, the plaintiff knew or should have known that he was not being given time in which to accept an offer that was being made, but that some further assent on the part of the defendant was required. Under the language used the plaintiff was not being given a right to act within a reasonable time after receiving the letter; he was plainly told that the defendant intended to sell to another, if possible, and warned that he would have to act fast if he was interested in buying the land.

Regardless of any opinion previously expressed, the court found that no contract had been entered into between these parties, and we are in accord with the court's conclusion on that controlling issue. The court's construction of the letters involved was a reasonable one, and we think the most reasonable one, even if it be assumed that another construction was possible.

The judgment is affirmed.

NOTES

(1) How does the analysis of the appellate court differ from that of the trial court?

(2) Would the result likely have been different if the March 26th letter had not contained the sentence "This is a form letter"? Or, if the concluding sentence of the April 8th letter ("If you are really interested ... ") had been omitted?

(3) *What is an offer?* Section 25 of the First Restatement, quoted in *Lonergan*, formulates what may be called the "fixed purpose" test. Is the focus upon the intention of the one who makes the manifestation, or is it upon the reasonable impression created in the mind of the other? The corresponding provision of Restatement (Second) § 26 reads as follows: "A manifestation of willingness to enter into a bargain is not an offer if the person to whom it is addressed knows or has reason to know that the person making it does not intend to conclude a bargain until he has made a further manifestation of assent." More affirmatively, Section 24 of the Restatement defines an offer as "the manifestation of willingness to enter into a bargain, so made as to justify another person in understanding that his assent to that bargain is invited and will conclude it."

(4) An offer has an immediate and significant legal effect. It enables or empowers the offeree to accept and thereby place the parties in a contractual

relationship. Thus, an offer is said to confer upon the offeree a "power of acceptance." See Corbin § 11 (original edition). Cases and other materials in this section consider the existence and attributes of this power; that is, how it is created (Subsection B), how it is exercised (Subsection C), how it is terminated (Subsection D), and how it may be made indestructible (Subsection E).

Lefkowitz v. Great Minneapolis Surplus Store

Supreme Court of Minnesota, 1957.
251 Minn. 188, 86 N.W.2d 689.

■ MURPHY, JUSTICE. This is an appeal from an order of the Municipal Court of Minneapolis denying the motion of the defendant for amended findings of fact, or, in the alternative, for a new trial. The order for judgment awarded the plaintiff the sum of $138.50 as damages for breach of contract.

This case grows out of the alleged refusal of the defendant to sell to the plaintiff a certain fur piece which it had offered for sale in a newspaper advertisement. It appears from the record that on April 6, 1956, the defendant published the following advertisement in a Minneapolis newspaper:

"Saturday 9 A.M. Sharp
3 Brand New
Fur
Coats
Worth to $100.00
First Come
First Served
$1 Each"

On April 13, the defendant again published an advertisement in the same newspaper as follows:

"Saturday 9 A.M.
2 Brand New Pastel
Mink 3–Skin Scarfs
Selling for $89.50
Out they go
Saturday. Each ... $1.00
1 Black Lapin Stole
Beautiful,
worth $139.50 ... $1.00
First Come
First Served"

The record supports the findings of the court that on each of the Saturdays following the publication of the above-described ads the plaintiff was the first to present himself at the appropriate counter in the defendant's store and on each occasion demanded the coat and the stole so advertised and indicated his readiness to pay the sale price of $1. On both occasions, the defendant refused to sell the merchandise to the plaintiff, stating on the first occasion that by a "house rule" the offer was intended for women only and sales would not be made to men, and on the second visit that plaintiff knew defendant's house rules.

The trial court properly disallowed plaintiff's claim for the value of the fur coats since the value of these articles was speculative and uncertain. The only evidence of value was the advertisement itself to the effect that the coats were "Worth to $100.00," how much less being speculative especially in view of the price for which they were offered for sale. With reference to the offer of the defendant on April 13, 1956, to sell the "1 Black Lapin Stole * * * worth $139.50 * * *" the trial court held that the value of this article was established and granted judgment in favor of the plaintiff for that amount less the $1 quoted purchase price.

1. The defendant contends that a newspaper advertisement offering items of merchandise for sale at a named price is a "unilateral offer" which may be withdrawn without notice. He relies upon authorities which hold that, where an advertiser publishes in a newspaper that he has a certain quantity or quality of goods which he wants to dispose of at certain prices and on certain terms, such advertisements are not offers which become contracts as soon as any person to whose notice they may come signifies his acceptance by notifying the other that he will take a certain quantity of them. Such advertisements have been construed as an invitation for an offer of sale on the terms stated, which offer, when received, may be accepted or rejected and which therefore does not become a contract of sale until accepted by the seller; and until a contract has been so made, the seller may modify or revoke such prices or terms. ... Craft v. Elder & Johnston Co., 34 Ohio L.A. 603; Annotation, 157 A.L.R. 746.

The defendant relies principally on Craft v. Elder & Johnston Co. supra. In that case, the court discussed the legal effect of an advertisement offering for sale, as a one-day special, an electric sewing machine at a named price. The view was expressed that the advertisement was (34 Ohio L.A. 605) "not an offer made to any specific person but was made to the public generally. Thereby it would be properly designated as a unilateral offer and not being supported by any consideration could be withdrawn at will and without notice." It is true that such an offer may be withdrawn before acceptance. Since all offers are by their nature unilateral because they are necessarily made by one party or on one side in the negotiation of a contract, the distinction made in that decision between a unilateral offer and a unilateral contract is not clear. On the facts before us we are concerned with whether the advertisement constituted an offer, and, if so, whether the plaintiff's conduct constituted an acceptance.

There are numerous authorities which hold that a particular advertisement in a newspaper or circular letter relating to a sale of articles may be construed by the court as constituting an offer, acceptance of which would complete a contract. ...

The test of whether a binding obligation may originate in advertisements addressed to the general public is "whether the facts show that some performance was promised in positive terms in return for something requested." 1 Williston Contracts (Rev. ed.) § 27.

The authorities above cited emphasize that, where the offer is clear, definite, and explicit, and leaves nothing open for negotiation, it constitutes an offer, acceptance of which will complete the contract. The most recent case on the subject is Johnson v. Capital City Ford Co., La.App., 85 So.2d 75, in which the court pointed out that a newspaper advertisement relating to the purchase and sale of automobiles may constitute an offer, acceptance of which will consummate a contract and create an obligation in the offeror to perform according to the terms of the published offer.

Whether in any individual instance a newspaper advertisement is an offer rather than an invitation to make an offer depends on the legal intention of the parties and the surrounding circumstances. ... We are of the view on the facts before us that the offer by the defendant of the sale of the Lapin fur was clear, definite, and explicit, and left nothing open for negotiation. The plaintiff having successfully managed to be the first one to appear at the seller's place of business to be served, as requested by the advertisement, and having offered the stated purchase price of the article, he was entitled to performance on the part of the defendant. We think the trial court was correct in holding that there was in the conduct of the parties a sufficient mutuality of obligation to constitute a contract of sale.

2.   The defendant contends that the offer was modified by a "house rule" to the effect that only women were qualified to receive the bargains advertised. The advertisement contained no such restriction. This objection may be disposed of briefly by stating that, while an advertiser has the right at any time before acceptance to modify his offer, he does not have the right, after acceptance, to impose new or arbitrary conditions not contained in the published offer. ...

Affirmed.

NOTES

(1) *Advertisement: Making an Offer or Inviting an Offer?* Does the ordinary advertisement indicate a "fixed purpose" by the advertiser to be bound without a further expression of assent? In the view of most courts, the answer is no unless there are exceptional circumstances and the words are "plain and clear." Thus, in O'Keefe v. Lee Calan Imports, Inc., 128 Ill.App.2d 410, 262 N.E.2d 758 (1970), the court held that the presumption against an offer was not overcome where a dealer's newspaper ad to sell a used car contained an error in the price (the intended price was $1,795; the advertised price was $1,095), the error was not the fault of the dealer, and there was "no reference to several material matters relating to the purchase of an automobile, such as equipment to be furnished or warranties to be offered by defendant. Indeed the terms were so incomplete and so indefinite that they could not be regarded as a valid offer."

On the other hand, in Donovan v. RRL Corporation, 26 Cal.4th 261, 109 Cal.Rptr.2d 807, 27 P.3d 702 (2001) the court held that a proposal by a car dealer in a newspaper ad to sell a 1995 Jaguar XJ6 Vanden Plas for a stated price was an offer even though it did not request performance of a specific act (such as "first come first serve") to conclude the bargain. But the court interpreted the ad with provisions of the California Vehicle Code which regulated the content of dealer advertising. As the court put it, "legislation can affect consumer expectations and cause reasonable individuals to regard certain retail advertisements for the sale of goods as offers to complete a bargain." 27 P.3d at 711. But since the ad mistakenly understated the intended price by $12,000, the court permitted the dealer to avoid the contract for mistake.

(2) Did the fact that the plaintiff had been told of the "house" rule have any bearing on the outcome of *Lefkowitz?* Should it have? Did the court regard the advertisement as legally objectionable? In the *O'Keefe* case, supra note 1, *Lefkowitz* was distinguished on the ground that the defendant "deliberately used misleading advertising." States have statutes, modeled generally upon Section 5 of the Federal Trade Commission Act, prohibiting "unfair" and "deceptive" trade practices or acts. A few outlaw false advertising in general terms, while others specify types of prohibited advertising in a "laundry list" of per se violations. See, generally, J. Sheldon, Unfair and Deceptive Acts and Practices (4th Ed. 2000). For more on these UDAP statutes, see infra at 500–517.

(3) *Bait and Switch.* If, in *Lefkowitz,* the advertisement was not used as a bona fide device to make or solicit offers but, rather, as a means of obtaining leads, we have an illustration of so-called "bait advertising." This practice can also be evidenced by a seller's refusal to show the advertised product, a demonstration of a defective product, a failure to have available for sale a sufficient quantity of the advertised product to meet reasonably anticipated demands, or a sales or compensation plan which has the effect of discouraging sales personnel from selling the advertised product. The Federal Trade Commission's Guides Against Bait Advertising, 16 C.F.R. § 238, define the practice as follows: "Bait advertising is an alluring but insincere offer to sell a product or service which the advertiser in truth does not intend or want to sell. Its purpose is to switch consumers from buying the advertised merchandise, in order to sell something else, usually at a higher price or on a basis more advantageous to the advertiser. The primary aim of a bait advertisement is to obtain leads as to persons interested in buying merchandise of the type so advertised." Neither the law of contracts nor ordinary judicial remedies have been of great help to the unwary consumer who is persuaded to make the switch. Some state legislatures have declared bait advertising to be a misdemeanor, subjecting the violator to criminal sanctions. Others have defined the practice as within their consumer protection statutes and thus made relief available to private parties harmed by the proscribed activity. The Federal Trade Commission, however, has been responsible for most of the litigation and activity in this area. It issues cease and desist orders and frequently seeks injunctive relief. See, J. Sheldon, Unfair and Deceptive Acts and Practices § 4.6.1 (4th ed. 2000); Annot., *Validity, Construction, and Effect of State Legislation Regulating or Controlling "Bait-and-Switch" or Disparagement Advertising or Sales Practices,* 50 A.L.R.3d 1008 (1973).

PROBLEM: THE CASE OF THE STATUE OF LIBERTY COMMEMORATIVE COINS

In 1985, Congress authorized the sale of a limited number of specially-minted commemorative coins "to restore and renovate the Statue of Liberty and the facilities used for immigration at Ellis Island." Pursuant to this authorization, the U.S. Mint mailed certain advertising materials to previous customers/coin collectors. The materials, which included an order form, represented that if the Mint received "your reservation by December 31, 1985, you will enjoy a favorable Pre–Issue Discount saving you up to 16% on your coins." Payment could be made either by check, money order, or credit card.

Demand for the five-dollar gold coins far exceeded the 500,000 supply. News of the sell-out caused keen disappointment to would-be purchasers, especially in view of the fact that the gold coins had increased in value by approximately 200% within the first few months of 1986.

Mary and Anthony Mesaros were among the many disappointed parties. They had forwarded an order to the Mint on November 26, 1985, but the order was not filled, ostensibly because of an inability to process their credit card but really because of the deluge of orders. Mr. and Mrs. Mesaros filed a class action lawsuit against the government. Based on *Lefkowitz,* what are the prospects of recovery? See Mesaros v. United States, 845 F.2d 1576 (Fed.Cir.1988).

PROBLEM: THE CASE OF THE "HIS AND HERS" MERCEDES

In 1993, Nationwide Insurance announced a contest to create a theme or a slogan for the 1994 South Central Regional Offices claims convention. Employees were urged to submit a slogan limited to not more than eight words. Prizes were involved:

> Here's what you could win: His and Hers Mercedes. An all expense paid trip for two around the world. Additional prizes to be announced. (All prizes subject to availability).

Mears submitted the slogan "At the top and still climbing," and shortly thereafter left the employ of Nationwide. Later he was informed that he had won the contest and (according to Mears) was told that he had won two Mercedes–Benz automobiles. Still later, he was told that he might not receive the autos because the theme might change before the Convention, he was no longer employed by Nationwide, and the contest was a joke. Nationwide, however, did use the theme (it dominated the convention) but refused to deliver the cars. Rather, they offered Mears a restaurant gift.

Mears, claiming that he had accepted an offer, sued for breach of contract, claiming either the autos themselves or damages. What result? See Mears v. Nationwide Insurance Co., 91 F.3d 1118 (8th Cir.1996).

Leonard v. Pepsico, Inc.

United States District Court, Southern District of New York, 1999.
88 F.Supp.2d 116, aff'd, 210 F.3d 88 (2d Cir.2000).

■ KIMBA M. WOOD, DISTRICT JUDGE.

Plaintiff brought this action seeking, among other things, specific performance of an alleged offer of a Harrier Jet, featured in a television advertisement for defendant's "Pepsi Stuff" promotion. Defendant has moved for summary judgment pursuant to Federal Rule of Civil Procedure 56. For the reasons stated below, defendant's motion is granted.

I. Background

This case arises out of a promotional campaign conducted by defendant, the producer and distributor of the soft drinks Pepsi and Diet Pepsi. The promotion, entitled "Pepsi Stuff," encouraged consumers to collect "Pepsi Points" from specially marked packages of Pepsi or Diet Pepsi and redeem these points for merchandise featuring the Pepsi logo.... While living in Seattle, plaintiff saw the Pepsi Stuff commercial that he contends constituted an offer of a Harrier Jet.

A. The Alleged Offer

Because whether the television commercial constituted an offer is the central question in this case, the Court will describe the commercial in detail. The commercial opens upon an idyllic, suburban morning, where the chirping of birds in sun-dappled trees welcomes a paperboy on his morning route. As the newspaper hits the stoop of a conventional two-story house, the tattoo of a military drum introduces the subtitle, "MONDAY 7:58 AM." The stirring strains of a martial air mark the appearance of a well-coiffed teenager preparing to leave for school, dressed in a shirt emblazoned with the Pepsi logo, a red-white-and-blue ball. While the teenager confidently preens, the military drumroll again sounds as the subtitle "T–SHIRT 75 PEPSI POINTS" scrolls across the screen. Bursting from his room, the teenager strides down the hallway wearing a leather jacket. The drumroll sounds again, as the subtitle "LEATHER JACKET 1450 PEPSI POINTS" appears. The teenager opens the door of his house and, unfazed by the glare of the early morning sunshine, puts on a pair of sunglasses. The drumroll then accompanies the subtitle "SHADES 175 PEPSI POINTS." A voiceover then intones, "Introducing the new PepsiStuff catalog," as the camera focuses on the cover of the catalog.*

The scene then shifts to three young boys sitting in front of a high school building. The boy in the middle is intent on his Pepsi Stuff Catalog, while the boys on either side are each drinking Pepsi. The three boys gaze in awe at an object rushing overhead, as the military march builds to a crescendo. The Harrier Jet is not yet visible, but the observer senses the presence of a mighty plane as the extreme winds generated by its flight create a paper maelstrom in a classroom devoted to an otherwise dull physics lesson. Finally, the Harrier Jet swings into view and lands by the side of the school building, next to a bicycle rack. Several students run for cover, and the velocity of the wind strips one hapless faculty member down to his underwear. While the faculty member is being deprived of his dignity, the voiceover announces: "Now the more Pepsi you drink, the more great stuff you're gonna get."

The teenager opens the cockpit of the fighter and can be seen, helmetless, holding a Pepsi. "[L]ooking very pleased with himself," (Pl. Mem. at 3,) the teenager exclaims, "Sure beats the bus," and chortles. The military drumroll sounds a final time, as the following words appear:

---

*At this point, the following message appears at the bottom of the screen: "Offer not available in all areas. See details on specially marked packages."

"HARRIER FIGHTER 7,000,000 PEPSI POINTS." A few seconds later, the following appears in more stylized script: "Drink Pepsi—Get Stuff." With that message, the music and the commercial end with a triumphant flourish.

Inspired by this commercial, plaintiff set out to obtain a Harrier Jet. Plaintiff explains that he is "typical of the 'Pepsi Generation' ... he is young, has an adventurous spirit, and the notion of obtaining a Harrier Jet appealed to him enormously." Plaintiff consulted the Pepsi Stuff Catalog. The Catalog features youths dressed in Pepsi Stuff regalia or enjoying Pepsi Stuff accessories, such as "Blue Shades" ("As if you need another reason to look forward to sunny days."), "Pepsi Tees" ("Live in 'em. Laugh in 'em. Get in 'em."), "Bag of Balls" ("Three balls. One bag. No rules."), and "Pepsi Phone Card" ("Call your mom!"). The Catalog specifies the number of Pepsi Points required to obtain promotional merchandise. The Catalog includes an Order Form which lists, on one side, fifty-three items of Pepsi Stuff merchandise redeemable for Pepsi Points (see id. (the "Order Form")). Conspicuously absent from the Order Form is any entry or description of a Harrier Jet. The amount of Pepsi Points required to obtain the listed merchandise ranges from 15 (for a "Jacket Tattoo" ("Sew 'em on your jacket, not your arm.")) to 3300 (for a "Fila Mountain Bike" ("Rugged. All-terrain. Exclusively for Pepsi.")). It should be noted that plaintiff objects to the implication that because an item was not shown in the Catalog, it was unavailable.

The rear foldout pages of the Catalog contain directions for redeeming Pepsi Points for merchandise. These directions note that merchandise may be ordered "only" with the original Order Form. The Catalog notes that in the event that a consumer lacks enough Pepsi Points to obtain a desired item, additional Pepsi Points may be purchased for ten cents each; however, at least fifteen original Pepsi Points must accompany each order.

Although plaintiff initially set out to collect 7,000,000 Pepsi Points by consuming Pepsi products, it soon became clear to him that he "would not be able to buy (let alone drink) enough Pepsi to collect the necessary Pepsi Points fast enough." Reevaluating his strategy, plaintiff "focused for the first time on the packaging materials in the Pepsi Stuff promotion," and realized that buying PepsiPoints would be a more promising option. Through acquaintances, plaintiff ultimately raised about $700,000.

B. Plaintiff's Efforts to Redeem the Alleged Offer

On or about March 27, 1996, plaintiff submitted an Order Form, fifteen original Pepsi Points, and a check for $700,008.50. Plaintiff appears to have been represented by counsel at the time he mailed his check; the check is drawn on an account of plaintiff's first set of attorneys. At the bottom of the Order Form, plaintiff wrote in "1 Harrier Jet" in the "Item" column and "7,000,000" in the "Total Points" column. In a letter accompanying his submission, plaintiff stated that the check was to purchase additional Pepsi Points "expressly for obtaining a new Harrier jet as advertised in your Pepsi Stuff commercial."

On or about May 7, 1996, defendant's fulfillment house rejected plaintiff's submission and returned the check, explaining that:

> The item that you have requested is not part of the Pepsi Stuff collection. It is not included in the catalogue or on the order form, and only catalogue merchandise can be redeemed under this program. The Harrier jet in the Pepsi commercial is fanciful and is simply included to create a humorous and entertaining ad. We apologize for any misunderstanding or confusion that you may have experienced and are enclosing some free product coupons for your use.

Plaintiff's previous counsel responded on or about May 14, 1996, as follows:

> Your letter of May 7, 1996 is totally unacceptable. We have reviewed the video tape of the Pepsi Stuff commercial . . . and it clearly offers the new Harrier jet for 7,000,000 Pepsi Points. Our client followed your rules explicitly. . . . This is a formal demand that you honor your commitment and make immediate arrangements to transfer the new Harrier jet to our client. If we do not receive transfer instructions within ten (10) business days of the date of this letter you will leave us no choice but to file an appropriate action against Pepsi. . . .

This letter was apparently sent onward to the advertising company responsible for the actual commercial, BBDO New York ("BBDO"). In a letter dated May 30, 1996, BBDO Vice President Raymond E. McGovern, Jr., explained to plaintiff that:

> I find it hard to believe that you are of the opinion that the Pepsi Stuff commercial ("Commercial") really offers a new Harrier Jet. The use of the Jet was clearly a joke that was meant to make the Commercial more humorous and entertaining. In my opinion, no reasonable person would agree with your analysis of the Commercial. * * *

Litigation of this case initially involved two lawsuits, the first a declaratory judgment action brought by PepsiCo in this district (the "declaratory judgment action"), and the second an action brought by Leonard in Florida state court (the "Florida action"). PepsiCo brought suit in this Court on July 18, 1996, seeking a declaratory judgment stating that it had no obligation to furnish plaintiff with a Harrier Jet. * * * The Florida suit was transferred to this Court. * * *

The question of whether or not a contract was formed is appropriate for resolution on summary judgment. As the Second Circuit has recently noted, "Summary judgment is proper when the 'words and actions that allegedly formed a contract [are] so clear themselves that reasonable people could not differ over their meaning.' " Krumme v. Westpoint Stevens, Inc., 143 F.3d 71, 83 (2d Cir.1998). . . . Summary judgment is appropriate in such cases because there is "sometimes no genuine issue as to whether the parties' conduct implied a 'contractual understanding.' . . . In such cases, 'the judge must decide the issue himself, just as he decides any factual issue in respect to which reasonable people cannot differ.' " Bourque, 42 F.3d at 708.

2.   Choice of Law

[Under Florida's choice of law principles, whether New York or Florida law applied could not be determined until it was determined whether defendant's advertisement was an offer.]

* * *

B.   Defendant's Advertisement Was Not an Offer

1.   Advertisements as Offers

The general rule is that an advertisement does not constitute an offer. The Restatement (Second) of Contracts explains that: Advertisements of goods by display, sign, handbill, newspaper, radio or television are not ordinarily intended or understood as offers to sell. The same is true of catalogues, price lists and circulars, even though the terms of suggested bargains may be stated in some detail. It is of course possible to make an offer by an advertisement directed to the general public, but there must ordinarily be some language of commitment or some invitation to take action without further communication. Restatement (Second) of Contracts § 26 cmt. b (1979). Similarly, a leading treatise notes that: It is quite possible to make a definite and operative offer to buy or sell goods by advertisement, in a newspaper, by a handbill, a catalog or circular or on a placard in a store window. It is not customary to do this, however; and the presumption is the other way. ... Such advertisements are understood to be mere requests to consider and examine and negotiate; and no one can reasonably regard them as otherwise unless the circumstances are exceptional and the words used are very plain and clear. 1 Arthur Linton Corbin & Joseph M. Perillo, Corbin on Contracts § 2.4, at 116–17 (rev. ed.1993) (emphasis added).

An advertisement is not transformed into an enforceable offer merely by a potential offeree's expression of willingness to accept the offer through, among other means, completion of an order form. In Mesaros v. United States, 845 F.2d 1576 (Fed.Cir.1988), for example, the plaintiffs sued the United States Mint for failure to deliver a number of Statue of Liberty commemorative coins that they had ordered. When demand for the coins proved unexpectedly robust, a number of individuals who had sent in their orders in a timely fashion were left empty-handed. The court began by noting the "well-established" rule that advertisements and order forms are "mere notices and solicitations for offers which create no power of acceptance in the recipient." Restatement(Second) of Contracts § 26 ("A manifestation of willingness to enter a bargain is not an offer if the person to whom it is addressed knows or has reason to know that the person making it does not intend to conclude a bargain until he has made a further manifestation of assent."). The spurned coin collectors could not maintain a breach of contract action because no contract would be formed until the advertiser accepted the order form and processed payment. See also Alligood v. Procter & Gamble, 72 Ohio App.3d 309 (1991)(finding that no offer was made in promotional campaign for baby diapers, in which consumers were to redeem teddy bear proof-of-purchase symbols for catalog merchandise). Under these principles, plaintiff's letter of March 27, 1996, with the Order Form and the appropriate number of Pepsi Points, constituted the offer. There would be no enforceable contract until defendant accepted the Order Form and cashed the check.

The exception to the rule that advertisements do not create any power of acceptance in potential affairs is where the advertisement is "clear, definite, and explicit, and leaves nothing open for negotiation," in that circumstance, "it constitutes an offer, acceptance of which will complete the contract." Lefkowitz v. Great Minneapolis Surplus Store, 251 Minn. 188, (1957). * * * [The court discussed the *Lefkowitz* case, supra.]

The present case is distinguishable from Lefkowitz. First, the commercial cannot be regarded in itself as sufficiently definite, because it specifically reserved the details of the offer to a separate writing, the Catalog. The commercial itself made no mention of the steps a potential offeree would be required to take to accept the alleged offer of a Harrier Jet. The advertisement in Lefkowitz, in contrast, "identified the person who could accept." Second, even if the Catalog had included a Harrier Jet among the items that could be obtained by redemption of Pepsi Points, the advertisement of a Harrier Jet by both television commercial and catalog would still not constitute an offer. As the Mesaros court explained, the absence of any words of limitation such as "first come, first served," renders the alleged offer sufficiently indefinite that no contract could be formed. See Mesaros, 845 F.2d at 1581. "A customer would not usually have reason to believe that the shopkeeper intended exposure to the risk of a multitude of acceptances resulting in a number of contracts exceeding the shopkeeper's inventory." Farnsworth, supra, at 242. There was no such danger in Lefkowitz, owing to the limitation "first come, first served."

The Court finds, in sum, that the Harrier Jet commercial was merely an advertisement. The Court now turns to the line of cases upon which plaintiff rests much of his argument.

2. Rewards as Offers

In opposing the present motion, plaintiff largely relies on a different species of unilateral offer, involving public offers of a reward for performance of a specified act. Because these cases generally involve public declarations regarding the efficacy or trustworthiness of specific products, one court has aptly characterized these authorities as "prove me wrong" cases. See Rosenthal v. Al Packer Ford, 36 Md.App. 349 (1977). The most venerable of these precedents is the case of Carlill v. Carbolic Smoke Ball Co., 1 Q.B. 256 (Court of Appeal, 1892), a quote from which heads plaintiff's memorandum of law: "[I]f a person chooses to make extravagant promises ... he probably does so because it pays him to make them, and, if he has made them, the extravagance of the promises is no reason in law why he should not be bound by them." Carbolic Smoke Ball, 1 Q.B. at 268 (Bowen, L.J.).

Long a staple of law school curricula, Carbolic Smoke Ball owes its fame not merely to "the comic and slightly mysterious object involved," A.W. Brian Simpson. Quackery and Contract Law: Carlill v. Carbolic

Smoke Ball Company (1893), in Leading Cases in the Common Law 259, 281 (1995), but also to its role in developing the law of unilateral offers. The case arose during the London influenza epidemic of the 1890s. Among other advertisements of the time, for Clarke's World Famous Blood Mixture, Towle's Pennyroyal and Steel Pills for Females, Sequah's Prairie Flower, and Epp's Glycerine Jube–Jubes, see Simpson, supra, at 267, appeared solicitations for the Carbolic Smoke Ball. The specific advertisement that Mrs. Carlill saw, and relied upon, read as follows: 100 £ reward will be paid by the Carbolic Smoke Ball Company to any person who contracts the increasing epidemic influenza, colds, or any diseases caused by taking cold, after having used the ball three times daily for two weeks according to the printed directions supplied with each ball. 1000 £ is deposited with the Alliance Bank, Regent Street, showing our sincerity in the matter. During the last epidemic of influenza many thousand carbolic smoke balls were sold as preventives against this disease, and in no ascertained case was the disease contracted by those using the carbolic smoke ball. Carbolic Smoke Ball, 1 Q.B. at 256–57. "On the faith of this advertisement," id. at 257, Mrs. Carlill purchased the smoke ball and used it as directed, but contracted influenza nevertheless.* The lower court held that she was entitled to recover the promised reward.

Affirming the lower court's decision, Lord Justice Lindley began by noting that the advertisement was an express promise to pay £ 100 in the event that a consumer of the Carbolic Smoke Ball was stricken with influenza. See id. at 261. The advertisement was construed as offering a reward because it sought to induce performance, unlike an invitation to negotiate, which seeks a reciprocal promise. As Lord Justice Lindley explained, "advertisements offering rewards ... are offers to anybody who performs the conditions named in the advertisement, and anybody who does perform the condition accepts the offer."** Because Mrs. Carlill had complied with the terms of the offer, yet contracted influenza, she was entitled to £ 100.

Like Carbolic Smoke Ball, the decisions relied upon by plaintiff involve offers of reward. * * * [The court discussed several cases.]

Other "reward" cases underscore the distinction between typical advertisements, in which the alleged offer is merely an invitation to negotiate

---

* Although the Court of Appeals's opinion is silent as to exactly what a carbolic smoke ball was, the historical record reveals it to have been a compressible hollow ball, about the size of an apple or orange, with a small opening covered by some porous material such as silk or gauze. The ball was partially filled with carbolic acid in powder form. When the ball was squeezed, the powder would be forced through the opening as a small cloud of smoke. At the time, carbolic acid was considered fatal if consumed in more than small amounts.

** Carbolic Smoke Ball includes a classic formulation of this principle: "If I advertise to the world that my dog is lost, and that anybody who brings the dog to a particular place will be paid some money, are all the police or other persons whose business it is to find lost dogs to be expected to sit down and write a note saying that they have accepted my proposal?" Carbolic Smoke Ball, 1 Q.B. at 270 (Bowen, L.J.).

for purchase of commercial goods, and promises of reward, in which the alleged offer is intended to induce a potential offeree to perform a specific action, often for noncommercial reasons. In Newman v. Schiff, 778 F.2d 460 (8th Cir.1985), for example, the Fifth Circuit held that a tax protestor's assertion that, "If anybody calls this show ... and cites any section of the code that says an individual is required to file a tax return, I'll pay them $100,000," would have been an enforceable offer had the plaintiff called the television show to claim the reward while the tax protestor was appearing.... The court noted that, like Carbolic Smoke Ball, the case "concerns a special type of offer: an offer for a reward." James v. Turilli, 473 S.W.2d 757 (Mo.Ct.App.1971), arose from a boast by defendant that the "notorious Missouri desperado" Jesse James had not been killed in 1882, as portrayed in song and legend, but had lived under the alias "J. Frank Dalton" at the "Jesse James Museum" operated by none other than defendant. Defendant offered $10,000 "to anyone who could prove me wrong." The widow of the outlaw's son demonstrated, at trial, that the outlaw had in fact been killed in 1882. On appeal, the court held that defendant should be liable to pay the amount offered.

In the present case, the Harrier Jet commercial did not direct that anyone who appeared at Pepsi headquarters with 7,000,000 Pepsi Points on the Fourth of July would receive a Harrier Jet. Instead, the commercial urged consumers to accumulate Pepsi Points and to refer to the Catalog to determine how they could redeem their Pepsi Points. The commercial sought a reciprocal promise, expressed through acceptance of, and compliance with, the terms of the Order Form. As noted previously, the Catalog contains no mention of the Harrier Jet. Plaintiff states that he "noted that the Harrier Jet was not among the items described in the catalog, but this did not affect [his] understanding of the offer." It should have.*

* * *

C. An Objective, Reasonable Person Would Not Have Considered the Commercial an Offer

Plaintiff's understanding of the commercial as an offer must also be rejected because the Court finds that no objective person could reasonably have concluded that the commercial actually offered consumers a Harrier Jet.

1. Objective Reasonable Person Standard

In evaluating the commercial, the Court must not consider defendant's subjective intent in making the commercial, or plaintiff's subjective view of what the commercial offered, but what an objective, reasonable person would have understood the commercial to convey. * * *

---

* In his affidavit, plaintiff places great emphasis on a press release written by defendant, which characterizes the Harrier Jet as "the ultimate Pepsi Stuff award." Plaintiff simply ignores the remainder of the release, which makes no mention of the Harrier Jet even as it sets forth in detail the number of points needed to redeem other merchandise.

If it is clear that an offer was not serious, then no offer has been made: What kind of act creates a power of acceptance and is therefore an offer? It must be an expression of will or intention. It must be an act that leads the offeree reasonably to conclude that a power to create a contract is conferred. * * *

2. Necessity of a Jury Determination

Plaintiff also contends that summary judgment is improper because the question of whether the commercial conveyed a sincere offer can be answered only by a jury. Relying on dictum from Gallagher v. Delaney, 139 F.3d 338 (2d Cir.1998), plaintiff argues that a federal judge comes from a "narrow segment of the enormously broad American socio-economic spectrum," and, thus, that the question whether the commercial constituted a serious offer must be decided by a jury composed of, inter alia, members of the "Pepsi Generation," who are, as plaintiff puts it, "young, open to adventure, willing to do the unconventional." Plaintiff essentially argues that a federal judge would view his claim differently than fellow members of the "Pepsi Generation."

Plaintiff's argument that his claim must be put to a jury is without merit. Gallagher involved a claim of sexual harassment in which the defendant allegedly invited plaintiff to sit on his lap, gave her inappropriate Valentine's Day gifts, told her that "she brought out feelings that he had not had since he was sixteen," and "invited her to help him feed the ducks in the pond, since he was 'a bachelor for the evening.' " Gallagher, 139 F.3d at 344. The court concluded that a jury determination was particularly appropriate because a federal judge lacked "the current real-life experience required in interpreting subtle sexual dynamics of the workplace based on nuances, subtle perceptions, and implicit communications." Id. at 342. This case, in contrast, presents a question of whether there was an offer to enter into a contract, requiring the Court to determine how a reasonable, objective person would have understood defendant's commercial. Such an inquiry is commonly performed by courts on a motion for summary judgment.

3. Whether the Commercial Was "Evidently Done In Jest"

Plaintiff's insistence that the commercial appears to be a serious offer requires the Court to explain why the commercial is funny. Explaining why a joke is funny is a daunting task; as the essayist E.B. White has remarked, "Humor can be dissected, as a frog can, but the thing dies in the process. . . ." The commercial is the embodiment of what defendant appropriately characterizes as "zany humor." * * *

First, the . . . implication of the commercial is that Pepsi Stuff merchandise will inject drama and moment into hitherto unexceptional lives. . . . A reasonable viewer would understand such advertisements as mere puffery, not as statements of fact, see, e.g., Hubbard v. General Motors Corp., 95 Civ. 4362 (S.D.N.Y. May 22, 1996) (advertisement describing automobile as "Like a Rock," was mere puffery, not a warranty of quality); and refrain from interpreting the promises of the commercial as being literally true.

Second, the callow youth featured in the commercial is a highly improbable pilot . . .

Third, the notion of traveling to school in a Harrier Jet is an exaggerated adolescent fantasy. . . .

Fourth, . . . [i]n light of the Harrier Jet's well-documented function in attacking and destroying surface and air targets, armed reconnaissance and air interdiction, and offensive and defensive anti-aircraft warfare, depiction of such a jet as a way to get to school in the morning is clearly not serious even if, as plaintiff contends, the jet is capable of being acquired "in a form that eliminates [its] potential for military use."

Fifth, the number of Pepsi Points the commercial mentions as required to "purchase" the jet is 7,000,000. To amass that number of points, one would have to drink 7,000,000 Pepsis (or roughly 190 Pepsis a day for the next hundred years—an unlikely possibility), or one would have to purchase approximately $700,000 worth of Pepsi Points. The cost of a Harrier Jet is roughly $23 million dollars, a fact of which plaintiff was aware when he set out to gather the amount he believed necessary to accept the alleged offer. Even if an objective, reasonable person were not aware of this fact, he would conclude that purchasing a fighter plane for $700,000 is a deal too good to be true.

Plaintiff argues that a reasonable, objective person would have understood the commercial to make a serious offer of a Harrier Jet because there was "absolutely no distinction in the manner" in which the items in the commercial were presented. Plaintiff also relies upon a press release highlighting the promotional campaign, issued by defendant, in which "[n]o mention is made by [defendant] of humor, or anything of the sort." * * * In light of the obvious absurdity of the commercial, the Court rejects plaintiff's argument that the commercial was not clearly in jest.

* * * Finally, plaintiff's assertion that he should be afforded an opportunity to determine whether other individuals also tried to accumulate enough Pepsi Points to "purchase" a Harrier Jet is unavailing. The possibility that there were other people who interpreted the commercial as an "offer" of a Harrier Jet does not render that belief any more or less reasonable. The alleged offer must be evaluated on its own terms. Having made the evaluation, the Court concludes that summary judgment is appropriate on the ground that no reasonable, objective person would have understood the commercial to be an offer. * * *

In sum, there are three reasons why plaintiff's demand cannot prevail as a matter of law. First, the commercial was merely an advertisement, not a unilateral offer. Second, the tongue-in-cheek attitude of the commercial would not cause a reasonable person to conclude that a soft drink company would be giving away fighter planes as part of a promotion. Third, there is no writing between the parties sufficient to satisfy the Statute of Frauds.

NOTES

(1) The opinion of the district court was affirmed by the Second Circuit, per curiam, for "substantially the reasons stated in Judge Wood's opinion." 210 F.3d 88 (2d Cir.2000).

(2) What relevance should be the commercial's characterization of *"Offer not available in all areas"*?

(3) Another "Prove Me Wrong" Case. In December 1995, the Republican National Committee ran full page advertisements in *USA Today* and *Roll Call* which showed a picture of RNC Chair Haley Barbour holding an oversized $1 million check. The copy of the ad read in part: "Heard the one about Republicans 'cutting' Medicare? The fact is Republicans are increasing Medicare spending by more than half. I'm Haley Barbour, and I'm so sure of that fact I'm willing to give you this check for a million dollars if you can prove me wrong." In another portion of the add enclosed with the filigree of a legal form, entitled "Million Dollar Medicare Challenge," the advertisement said:

> The Republican National Committee will present a cashier's check for $1 million to the first American who can prove the following statement is false: "In November 1995, the U.S. House and Senate passed a balanced budget bill. It increases total federal spending on Medicare by more than 50% from 1995 to 2002 pursuant to Congressional Budget Office standards.

More than 80 people sent in responses claiming the prize. Douglas Frymire, a 70–year old from Idaho claimed the statement was false because Congress cannot guarantee budget numbers for more than one year. Leslie Kee, a 42–year old high school teacher from Wyoming argued that if you compare the Republican plan with what would already have been allocated to Medicare under existing law, the GOP proposal would actually *reduce* spending. Charles Resor argued that a bill doesn't actually increase anything until it becomes law. Representative Gene Taylor argued the statement was false because the "balanced budget bill" did not actually balance the budget. The RNC refused to pay and one of the claimants, Bob Shireman, an analyst at the U.S. Office of Management and Budget filed a breach-of-contract suit against Barbour and the RNC in Washington, D.C. Superior Court. The RNC responded in 1997 by filing a declaratory judgement action against all 80 claimants in Jackson, Mississippi. The suit argues that the advertisement was a "mere puff." If the statement were shown to be false, should the RNC and Barbour be liable for $1 million? See John Solomon, Prize Fight, The New Republic 23 (Nov. 15, 1999).

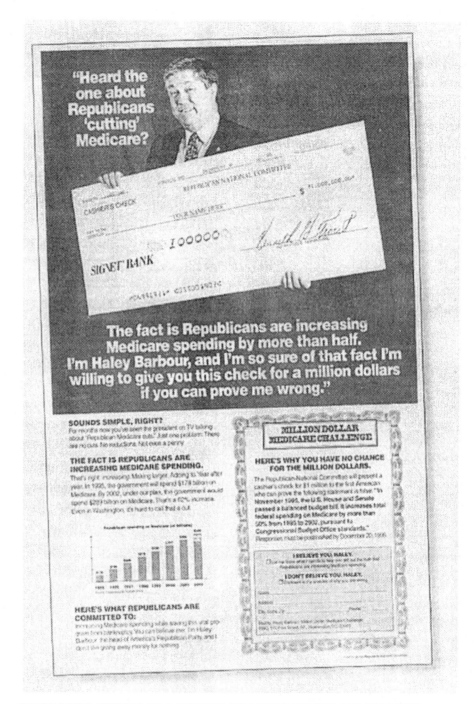

PROBLEM: WHEN IS A PRICE SOLICITATION AN OFFER?

On September 21, 2002, Defendant, a grain dealer in Oregon, mailed a sample of clover seed to numerous parties, including Plaintiff, a grain wholesaler in Wisconsin. The following language appeared on the face of the envelope containing the seed: "Red clover. 50,000 lbs. like sample. I am asking 24 cents per pound, f.o.b. Amity, Oregon." Plaintiff acknowledged receipt of the sample and advised Defendant that it had accumulated quite a stock of clover seed and preferred to wait a while before "operating further."

After rains created unfavorable hulling conditions, Defendant, on October 4, contacted Plaintiff again and Plaintiff responded: "Special delivery sample received. Your price is too high. Wire firm offer, naming absolutely lowest f.o.b." On October 8, Defendant telegraphed Plaintiff as follows: "I am asking 23 cents per pound for the car of red clover seed from which your sample was taken. No. 1 seed, practically no plantain whatever. Have an offer 22¾ per pound, f.o.b. Amity."

Plaintiff promptly telegraphed "We accept your offer" and gave shipment instructions. Plaintiff also resold the clover seed to a third party at a profit. Defendant, however, sold the carload to another buyer and refused to deliver.

Plaintiff sued Defendant for damages. The court held that Defendant had made no offer and dismissed the petition. In essence, the trial court concluded that from the language "am asking" in the telegram of October 8 Defendant should have known that Plaintiff was still soliciting offers to buy rather than making an offer to sell. Even though all other material terms were stated, the implication was that Defendant must say "I will sell to you" before any offer to sell was made.

The case is now on appeal to the appellate court. The partner has asked you, her associate, to help develop a theory to reverse the trial court. She has given you a Memo to get you going:

Memo:

1. This case is governed by Article 2 of the UCC, but the code does not define offer. See UCC 2–204, 2–205, 2–206, 2–207. How do we decide what is an offer in a purported contract to sell goods? My impression is that if Article 2 does not displace the common law, common law concepts apply under UCC 1–103 [Rev. 1–103(b).] If that is correct, what definition would apply, that in Section 24 of the Restatement, Second? This result finds support in Cannavino & Shea, Inc. v. Water Works Supply Corp., 361 Mass. 363, 280 N.E.2d 147 (1972) and, more recently, in *Architectural Metal Systems, Inc. v. Consolidated Systems, Inc.*, 58 F.3d 1227 (7th Cir.1995)(Illinois law).

2. The trial court's decision is somewhat rigid. Is there any way to persuade the appellate court that the reasonable meaning of language used early in the negotiations, i.e., "am asking," may change as the discussions proceed? Here's what I've found.

In Fairmount Glass Works v. Grunden–Martin Woodenware Co., 106 Ky. 659, 51 S.W. 196, 197–98 (1899), the appellee-buyer asked the appellant-seller to "advise us the lowest price you can make" on certain goods. The latter obliged with a price quotation which was stated to be "for immediate acceptance." The court held this to be an offer and gave the following reasons:

> [E]ach case must turn largely upon the language used. In this case we think there was more than a quotation of prices, although appellant's letter uses the word "quote" in stating the prices given. The true meaning of the correspondence must be determined by reading it as a whole. Appellee's

letter ... which began the transaction, did not ask for a quotation of prices. It reads: "Please advise us the lowest price you can make us on our order for ten carloads of Mason green jars. ... State terms and cash discount." From this appellant could not fail to understand that appellee wanted to know at what price it would sell ten car loads of these jars; so when, in answer, it wrote: "We quote you Mason fruit jars ... pints $4.50, quarts $5.00, half gallons $6.50, per gross, ... "—it must be deemed as intending to give appellee the information it asked for. We can hardly understand what is meant by the words "for immediate acceptance," unless the latter was intended as a proposition to sell at these prices if accepted immediately. In construing every contract, the aim of the court is to arrive at the intention of the parties. ... The expression in appellant's letter, "for immediate acceptance," taken in connection with appellee's letter, in effect, at what price it would sell it the goods, is, it seems to us, much stronger evidence of a present offer, which, when accepted immediately, closed the contract. Appellee's letter was plainly an inquiry for the price and terms on which appellant would sell it the goods, and appellant's answer to it was not a quotation of prices, but a definite offer to sell on the terms indicated, and could not be withdrawn after the terms had been accepted.

There is also an excerpt, somewhat dated, from an article by Professor Malcolm P. Sharp [Malcolm P. Sharp, *Promissory Liability*, 7 U.Chi.L.Rev. 1, 3–4 (1939)]:

It is the offer which may start the trouble. * * * After negotiations in which the word "quote" appears, together with a price list for flour and bran "subject to change without notice" and a boast that the prospective seller will "meet all competition in prices," the buyer inquires about a price for bran. He names a price at which he can buy at his place of business, and adds "If you will sell us at the same price wire us this A.M. as we have an order to fill." The same day the seller replies by letter, "cannot sell bran for less than" a named price. There is no reference to quantity. The next day, on receipt of the letter, the buyer wires ordering fifty tons, a not unreasonable quantity. It has been held that there is an offer, which has been accepted, and so a contract. [College Mill Co. v. Fidler, 58 S.W. 382 (Tenn.App.1899).]

* * *

What is it that a sensible business man is looking for in such a series of communications? We say an offer, as distinguished from a mere statement of intention or invitation to deal, and we find that when we examine the matter further, we begin to talk naturally about promises. The offer which may be significant in these situations is also a promise.

What then is a promise? * * * As a matter of everyday experience and common usage, a promise has something reliable about it. In the bran case, in spite of the ambiguity of the words used and vagueness about the terms, a striking circumstance is that the buyer has told the seller that he has an order to fill. He has almost, if not quite, said he is going to count on the reply to his inquiry. The reply must be read in relation to the inquiry. The seller seems to be saying you can rely on this proposal, first in your thinking and then in the conduct of your affairs. * * *

It may be suggested that a promise is the maker's statement about his future conduct so made that the maker should expect the person to whom it is made mentally to rely on it as dependable. [Compare Section 2(1) of the Restatement, Second of Contracts. Ed.]

3. And what about the next case, does that help?

Prepare a memo for your partner.

Southworth v. Oliver

Supreme Court of Oregon, 1978.
284 Or. 361, 587 P.2d 994.

[The defendant first approached the plaintiff, who was a neighbor, to determine his possible interest in purchasing grazing land identified on a map. The plaintiff was definitely interested, but price, other terms, and the treatment of certain grazing permits in which a neighbor was interested were not determined. Subsequently, the plaintiff telephoned the defendant to inquire how things were going and to renew his interest in the land and confirm that he had the money ready for a purchase. The defendant stated that he was making progress and would soon have information to establish the land value.

Several days later plaintiff received from defendants a letter dated June 17, 1976, which stated:

"Enclosed please find the information about the ranch sales that I had discussed with you previously.

"These prices are the market value according to the records of the Grant County Assessor.

"Please contact me if there are any questions."

There were two enclosures with that letter. The first was as follows:

"JOSEPH C. and ARLENE G. OLIVER

"200 Ford Road

"John Day, OR 97845

"Selling approximately 2933 Acres in Grant County in T. 16 S., R. 31 E., W.M. near Seneca, Oregon at the assessed market value of:

"LAND	$306,409
"IMPROVEMENTS	18,010
" Total	$324,419

"Terms available—29% down—balance over 5 years at 8% interest. Negotiate sale date for December 1, 1976 or January 1, 1977.

"Available after hay is harvested and arrangements made for removal of hay, equipment and supplies.

"ALSO: Selling

"Little Bear Creek allotment permit . . . 100 head @ $225

"Big Bear Creek allotment permit . . . . 200 head @ $250"

The second enclosure related to "selling approximately 6365 acres" in Grant County near John Day—another ranch owned by the Oliver family.

Defendant Joseph Oliver testified that this letter and enclosures were "drafted" by his wife, defendant Arlene Oliver; that he then read and signed it; that he sent it not only to plaintiff, but also to Clyde Holliday and two other neighbors; that it was sent because "I told them I would send them all this information and we would go from there," that it was not made as an offer, and that it was his intention that the "property" and "permits" be transferred "together."

Upon receiving that letter and enclosures, plaintiff immediately responded by letter addressed to both defendants, dated June 21, 1976, as follows:

"Re the land in Bear Valley near Seneca, Oregon that you have offered to sell; I accept your offer."

Thereafter, confusion and misunderstanding broke out. On June 24 (apparently after consulting an attorney), the defendant mailed the following letter to the plaintiff:

We received your letter of June 21, 1976. You have misconstrued our prior negotiations and written summaries of the lands which we and J.C. wish to sell. That was not made as or intended to be a firm offer of sale, and especially was not an offer of sale of any portion of the lands and permits described to any one person separately from the rest of the lands and permits described.

The memorandum of ours was for informational purposes only and as a starting point for further negotiation between us and you and the others also interested in the properties.

It is also impossible to tell from the attachment to our letter of June 17, 1976, as to the legal description of the lands to be sold, and would not in any event constitute an enforceable contract.

We are open to further negotiation with you and other interested parties, but do not consider that we at this point have any binding enforceable contract with you."

This lawsuit then followed.

The court held that the defendant's letter of June 17 was an offer to sell the land which the plaintiff accepted and affirmed the trial court's decree of specific performance. Here are some excerpts from that opinion:]

In Kitzke v. Turnidge, 209 Or. 563, 573, 307 P.2d 522, 527 (1957), this court quoted with approval the following rule as stated in 1 Williston on Contracts 49–50, § 22A (1957):

" ' * * * In the early law of assumpsit stress was laid on the necessity of a promise in terms, but the modern law rightly construes both acts and words as having the meaning which a reasonable person present would put upon them in view of the surrounding circumstances. Even where words are used, "a contract includes not only what the parties said, but also what is necessarily to be implied from what they said." And it may be said broadly that any conduct of one party, from which the other may reasonably draw the inference of a promise, is effective in law as such.' "

* * *

As also stated in 1 Restatement of Contracts § 25, Comment (a) (1932) as quoted by this court with approval in Metropolitan Life Ins. Co. v. Kimball, 163 Or. 31, 58, 94 P.2d 1101, 1111 (1939):

> It is often difficult to draw an exact line between offers and negotiations preliminary thereto. It is common for one who wishes to make a bargain to try to induce the other party to the intended transaction to make the definite offer, he himself suggesting with more or less definiteness the nature of the contract he is willing to enter into. Besides any direct language indicating an intent to defer the formation of a contract, the definiteness or indefiniteness of the words used in opening the negotiation must be considered, as well as the usages of business, and indeed all accompanying circumstances."

The difficulty in determining whether an offer has been made is particularly acute in cases involving price quotations, as in this case. It is recognized that although a price quotation, standing alone, is not an offer, there may be circumstances under which a price quotation, when considered together with facts and circumstances, may constitute an offer which, if accepted, will result in a binding contract. It is also recognized that such an offer may be made to more than one person. Thus, the fact that a price quotation is sent to more than one person does not, of itself, require a holding that such a price quotation is not an offer.

We agree with the analysis of this problem as stated in Murray on Contracts 37–40, § 24 (1977), as follows:

> If *A* says to *B*, "I am going to sell my car for $500," and *B* replies, "All right, here is $500, I will take it," no contract results, assuming that *A's* statement is taken at its face value. *A's* statement does not involve any promise, commitment or undertaking; it is at most a statement of *A's present intention*. * * *

> * * * However, a price quotation or advertisement may contain sufficient indication of willingness to enter a bargain so that the party to whom it is addressed would be justified in believing that his assent would conclude the bargain. * * *

The basic problem is found in the expressions of the parties. People very seldom express themselves either accurately or in complete detail. Thus, difficulty is encountered in determining the correct interpretation of the expression in question. Over the years, some more or less trustworthy guides to interpretation have been developed.

The first and strongest guide is that the particular expression is to be judged on the basis of what a reasonable man in the position of the offeree has been led to believe. This requires an analysis of what the offeree should have understood under all of the surrounding circumstances, with all of his opportunities for comprehending the intention of the offeror, rather than what the offeror, in fact, intended. This guide may be regarded as simply another manifestation of the objective test. Beyond this universally accepted guide to interpretation, there are other guides which are found in the case law involving factors that tend to recur. The most important of the remaining guides is the language used. If there are no words of promise, undertaking or commitment, the tendency is to construe the expression to be an invitation for an offer or mere preliminary negotiations in the absence of strong, countervailing circumstances. Another guide which has been widely accepted is the determination of the party or parties to whom the purported offer has been addressed. If the expression definitely names a party or parties, it is more likely to be construed as an offer. If the addressee is an indefinite group, it is less likely to be an offer. The fact that this is simply a guide rather than a definite rule is illustrated by the exceptional cases which must be noted. The guide operates effectively in relation to such expressions as advertisements or circular letters. The addressee is indefinite, and, therefore, the expression is probably not an offer. However, in reward cases, the addressee is equally indefinite and, yet, the expression is an offer. Finally, the definiteness of the proposal itself may have a bearing on whether it constitutes an offer. In general, the more definite the proposal, the more reasonable it is to treat the proposal as involving a commitment. * * * "

Upon application of these tests to the facts of this case we are of of the opinion that defendants' letter to plaintiff dated June 17, 1976, was an offer to sell the ranch lands. We believe that the "surrounding circumstances" under which this letter was prepared by defendants and sent by them to plaintiff were such as to have led a reasonable person to believe that defendants were making an offer to sell to plaintiff the lands described in the letter's enclosure and upon the terms as there stated.

That letter did not come to plaintiff "out of the blue," as in some of the cases involving advertisements or price quotations. Neither was this a price quotation resulting from an inquiry by plaintiff. According to what we believe to be the most credible testimony, defendants decided to sell the lands in question and defendant Joseph Oliver then sought out the plaintiff who owned adjacent lands. Defendant Oliver told plaintiff that defendants were interested in selling that land, inquired whether plaintiff was interested, and was told by plaintiff that he was "very interested in the land," after which they discussed the particular lands to be sold. That conversation was terminated with the understanding that Mr. Oliver would "determine" the value and price of that land, i.e., "what he wanted for the land," and that plaintiff would undertake to arrange financing for the purchase of that land. In addition to that initial conversation, there was a further telephone conversation in which plaintiff called Mr. Oliver "to ask him if his plans for selling * * * continued to be in force" and was told "yes"; that there had been some delay in getting information from the assessor, as needed to establish the value of the land; and that plaintiff then told Mr. Oliver that "everything was in order" and that "he had the money available and everything was ready to go."

Under these facts and circumstances, we agree with the finding and conclusion by the trial court, in its written opinion, that when plaintiff received the letter of June 17th, with enclosures, which stated a price of $324,419 for the 2,933 acres in T 16 S, R 31 E., W.M., as previously identified by the parties with reference to a map, and stating "terms" of 29 percent down—balance over five years at eight percent interest—with a "sale date" of either December 1, 1976, or January 1, 1977, a reasonable person in the position of the plaintiff would have believed that defendants were making an offer to sell those lands to him.

This conclusion is further strengthened by "the definiteness of the proposal," not only with respect to price, but terms, and by the fact that "the addressee was not an indefinite group." *See* Murray, supra at 40.

As previously noted, defendants contend that they "obviously did not intend [the letter] as an offer." While it may be proper to consider evidence of defendants' subjective intent under the "objective test" to which this court is committed, it is the manifestation of a previous intention that is controlling, rather than a "person's actual intent." We do not agree with defendants' contention that it was "obvious" to a reasonable person, under the facts and circumstances of this case that the letter of January 17th was not intended to be an offer to sell the ranch lands to plaintiff.

We recognize, as contended by defendants, that the failure to use the word "offer," the fact that the letter included the "information" previously discussed between the parties, and the fact that plaintiff knew that the same information was to be sent to others, were important facts to be considered in deciding whether plaintiff, as a reasonable person, would have been led to believe that this letter was an "offer." See also Murray, supra, at 40. We disagree, however, with defendants' contention that these and other factors relied upon by defendants "preponderate" so as to require a holding that the letter of January 17th was not an offer.

The failure to add the word "offer" and the use of the word "information" are also not controlling, and, as previously noted, an offer may be made to more than one person. The question is whether, under all of the facts and circumstances existing at the time that this letter was received, a reasonable person in the position of the plaintiff would have understood the letter to be an offer by defendants to sell the land to him.

Defendants also contend that "plaintiff knew of the custom of transferring [Forest Service grazing] permits with the land and had no knowledge from the writing or previous talk that defendants were selling any cattle" (so as to provide such a basis for a transfer of the permits). Plaintiff testified, however, that at the time of the initial conversation, Mr. Oliver told plaintiff that he thought plaintiff "would be interested in the land and that Clyde would be interested in the permits." In addition, defendant Joseph Oliver, in response to questions by the trial judge, although denying that at that time he told plaintiff that he was "going to offer the permits to Mr. Holliday," admitted that he "knew Mr. Holliday was interested in the permits" and "could have" told plaintiff that he was "going to talk to Mr. Holliday about him purchasing the permits."

On this record we believe that plaintiff's knowledge of the facts noted by defendants relating to the transfer of such permits did not require a holding that, as a reasonable man, he did not understand or should not have understood that defendants' letter of June 17th was an offer to sell the ranch lands to him.

* * *

[The Court concluded that the plaintiff's letter of June 21, 1976, was an acceptance of defendants' offer to sell the ranch lands; that the resulting agreement was sufficiently definite for enforcement by specific performance; and that the Statute of Frauds was no bar to the action.]

For all of these reasons, the decree of the trial court [granting specific performance] is affirmed.

Bretz v. Portland General Electric Co.

United States Court of Appeals, Ninth Circuit, 1999.
882 F.2d 411.

■ KOZINSKI, CIRCUIT JUDGE:

We consider again the validity of Sam Goldwyn's aphorism that an oral contract isn't worth the paper it's written on. L.R. Bretz, a Montana resident, brought a diversity suit against Portland General Electric (PGE), an Oregon corporation, for breach of a contract for the sale of PGE's stock in its wholly-owned subsidiary, the Beartooth Coal Company. The district court granted PGE's motion for summary judgment, holding that the exchange of letters between Bretz and PGE did not satisfy Montana's statute of frauds. We review the district court's grant of summary judgment de novo....

Facts

In the late summer of 1983, Bretz, identifying himself as special agent in Montana for Western States Energy Ventures, wrote PGE and Beartooth offering to buy the Beartooth stock for $2 million. Bretz sought a variety of representations from PGE concerning the Beartooth securities, their sole ownership by PGE, the nature and assignability of Beartooth's holdings, and so forth. The letter also detailed an elaborate procedure for PGE's acceptance of the offer and for the completion of the transaction.* PGE

* Bretz's August 1, 1983, letter stated: It is to be understood that the exact procedure from point of your receipt of this offer will be as follows:

responded on August 5, 1983, by sending Bretz a revised version of his offering letter, along with a request that Bretz "resubmit[] the letter as an offer so that it can be considered by Portland General Electric Company's officers." PGE's August 5 letter also included a disclaimer: "Although we have reworked the terms and conditions [of your offer], we have not discussed the same nor the amount of your offer with Company management. They may request other or different terms or additional compensation."

On August 10, 1983, Bretz replied, noting that "[y]ou have redrafted my offer and it appears that we are coming to a meeting of the minds." Bretz incorporated PGE's suggestions and added some "slight" revisions of his own. As in the first offer, Bretz's August 10 communication spelled out a detailed and precise means for PGE to indicate its acceptance. In its August 23, 1983, response to Bretz's August 10 letter, PGE stated:

Dear Mr. Bretz:

Thank you for your offer of August 10, 1983 to purchase the stock of Beartooth Coal Company. Two issues have caused problems.

Your offer of $2,000,000 cash is not commensurate with the outstanding commitment we have for purchase of the stock. Financing arrangements have caused two delays in closing this commitment. *Consequently we would be receptive to an offer of $2,750,000 from you and your associates provided the matter could be closed in a timely manner as proposed in your letter of August 10, 1983.*

The warranty of quantity and quality referenced in your letter would have to be based on the best information available to PGE....

I would appreciate you resubmitting your offer on the above basis.

On August 29, 1983, Bretz wrote PGE an amended version of his reworked offer. The amendment, captioned "Acceptance of Offer," and signed by Bretz, stated that the "Foregoing Offer is amended to state a purchase price of $2,750,000.00. *The joint venture accepts your counter-offer which includes our terms as set forth in letter, as above. We consider that a contract for sale exists.*" The following day, Bretz, allegedly under the impression that he had a contract to purchase PGE's interest in Beartooth, executed an agreement with a third party for the sale of coal from the

I. You will advise by telegraphic communication as follows:

"YOUR OFFER AS PER LETTER OF AUGUST 1, 1983 IS ACCEPTED"

II. I will immediately thereafter send you a draft to hold in the amount of $500,000.00 pending:

a) Receipt of all documentation needed to verify your offering data;

b) Receipt of all of your proposed transferring papers; and

c) Receipt of copy of current Mining Permit and confirmation of transferability.

III. Upon completion of Steps II(a)(b)(c) I will come to Portland, Oregon, pickup all closing papers, as required, and, if all are in order, I will execute same on behalf of jv and pay over to you, or your order, the balance of $1,500,000.00.

Time and confidentiality are of the essence at all times in this transaction.

Beartooth property. On September 7, 1983, Tom Owens of Beartooth telegraphed Bretz that "It is urgent that you contact me immediately re your offer for Beartooth Coal Co." Bretz alleges that on or about that day PGE breached its contract for the sale of Beartooth.

Bretz then filed this lawsuit, claiming breach of contract and seeking over $25 million in damages. PGE filed a motion for summary judgment, arguing that the exchange of letters did not create an enforceable contract because they did not comply with Montana's statute of frauds. Magistrate Dale agreed, holding that the letters reflected only unconcluded negotiations, not a consummated contract. He further held that parol evidence could not be used to bring the writings into compliance with the statute. The magistrate also rejected Bretz's equitable estoppel argument, finding "no evidence that defendant's conduct caused Bretz to change his position to his detriment." ER 16. The district court adopted the magistrate's findings and recommendations and granted PGE's motion for summary judgment.

Discussion

A.   Bretz first contends that PGE's August 23 letter, when considered in conjunction with prior conversations and correspondence, was a counter-offer by PGE which, when accepted by Bretz, matured into a contract. At the very least, he argues, the documents paint an ambiguous picture which he should be allowed to fill in with parol evidence.

The parties agree that PGE's sale of Beartooth stock is covered by Montana's statute of frauds. Mont.Code Ann. § 30–8–319 (1987). Although the writing required by the statute of frauds need not be contained in a single document. . . . the writings together must contain all the essential elements of a contract, including evidence of the parties' assent to be bound to the terms of the agreement. . . . While parol evidence may not be used to supply an essential contract term, . . . such evidence is admissible to explain ambiguities . . .

In Montana, as in most other jurisdictions, "[t]he mutual assent essential to the formation of a contract . . . must be gathered from the outward objective manifestations of the parties and not by the subjective undisclosed intent of one of the parties." *Miller v. Walter,* 165 Mont. 221, (1974); . . . * Whether a party has made a firm offer therefore turns on the

---

* This was not always the case. As Professor Farnsworth has observed, whether a court's determination of a party's assent to an agreement should turn on the party's actual or apparent intent "provoked one of the most significant doctrinal struggles in the development of contract law, that between the subjective and objective theories." E.A. Farnsworth, *Contracts* § 3.6 at 113 (1982). The dispute was resolved in favor of the objective theory of assent, *id.* at 114, which, as Professor Randy Barnett has pointed out, promotes greater "reliability of contractual commitments": Permitting a subjective inquiry into the promisor's intent could . . . enable a promisor to fraudulently undermine otherwise perfectly clear agreements by generating and preserving extrinsic evidence of ambiguous or conflicting intentions. Such a strategy might create a de facto option in the promisor. The promisor could insist on enforcement if the contract continued to be in her interest, but if it were no longer advantageous, she could avoid the contract, by pro-

facts and circumstances of each situation, as well as on what the other party might reasonably have inferred from the statements and behavior of the first. The classic statement of this objective theory of assent was offered by Williston:

The modern law rightly construes both acts and words as having the meaning which a reasonable person present would put upon them in view of the surrounding circumstances. Even where words are used, "a contract includes not only what the parties said, but also what is necessarily to be implied from what they said." And it may be said broadly that any conduct of one party, from which the other may reasonably draw the inference of a promise, is effective in law as such. 1 S. Williston, *A Treatise on the Law of Contracts* § 22A, at 49–50 (3d ed. 1957). In making this inquiry, courts must ask whether the document at issue, in light of prior negotiations and the expectations of both parties, reasonably led its recipient to believe it was within his power to close the deal by acceptance.

The key question here is whether PGE's August 23 letter could reasonably be construed as an offer, or whether it was merely an invitation to Bretz to renew his offer to PGE. An examination of the letter and the surrounding circumstances lead to only one reasonable conclusion: PGE's August 23 letter was merely an invitation to continue negotiations. The letter plainly states that PGE remained "receptive to an offer" from Bretz, and suggests terms that might make the offer more acceptable to PGE.* The letter also refers to another commitment PGE had for the sale of the stock, implying that PGE would have to free itself from that commitment before undertaking another. PGE's letter also specifies the manner in which the deal would be closed: "as proposed in [Bretz's] letter of August 10, 1983," which, in turn, provided an elaborate mechanism for closing the deal. . . . Finally, PGE's letter concludes, not with an offer to close the deal, but with an invitation that Bretz "resubmit [his] offer on the above basis."

The August 23 letter quite clearly evidences PGE's intent *not* to make an offer. Under Montana law, "when the instrument itself negates the existence of a contract," it may not be relied on for purposes of satisfying the statute of frauds. . . . Neither PGE's August 23 letter alone, nor the letter considered in concert with the remaining documents and communications, establishes the existence of a written contract that would satisfy Montana's statute of frauds. The district court therefore did not err in concluding that the parties had failed to enter into an enforceable contract for the sale of the Beartooth stock and granting summary judgment on that issue.

ducing evidence of a differing subjective intent. Barnett, *A Consent Theory of Contract*, 86 Colum.L.Rev. 269, 273 (1986).

   * "The dissent argues that Bretz could reasonably have read 'receptive to an offer' " to mean that PGE would accept Bretz's indication of agreement. We fail to understand how this helps Bretz. Reading the August 23 letter as the dissent suggests makes it even clearer that the letter was not an offer. By indicating that PGE retains the final power of acceptance, the letter establishes that it was not within Bretz's power to close the deal unilaterally.

B.   [The court held that PGE was not equitably estopped to raise the statute of frauds defense.]

* * *

We have already held that the writings in this case were insufficient to create a contract. The only other relevant evidence Bretz presents is a phone conversation between himself and a PGE representative on August 25. Bretz submits a copy of what he claims is a contemporaneous memorandum of the conversation:

> LRB [Bretz] now asks "Warren is this deal done now—so I know where I stand?"

> Hastings [PGE's representative] says "Yes"—"Send over something in writing—put it with your letter of August 10—*when we have it*—you have the mine on deal we have made"

According to Bretz's own memorandum, PGE conditioned formation of the contract on PGE's receipt of Bretz's letter.

Bretz did not mail the August 29 letter until the afternoon or evening of August 30. He entered into the third party contract for the sale of coal on August 30, *the same day* that he mailed the letter to PGE. Even if we accept Bretz's contention that the writings together with the phone call could constitute a contract, the contract was not formed until PGE received the August 29 letter, several days after Bretz allegedly sold the coal. Thus, construing the evidence most favorably to Bretz, there was no contract between Bretz and PGE at the time he made his contract for the sale of the coal. Bretz therefore cannot invoke equitable estoppel to override PGE's statute of frauds defense.... Bretz could not reasonably have relied on the existence of a contract between himself and PGE on August 30, when, by his own evidence, the contract would not be formed until sometime later when PGE received his letter.

Bretz did not reasonably rely on any representations from PGE; he simply jumped the gun and he has no one but himself to blame for losses he may have suffered as a consequence. His attempt to shift his losses to PGE was properly rejected by the district court.

AFFIRMED.

■ BOOCHEVER, CIRCUIT JUDGE, dissenting:

Because I believe that extraneous evidence was admissible and that there are genuine issues of fact to be resolved whether the parties entered an enforceable contract, and concerning Bretz' estoppel claim, I respectfully dissent. * * *

Equitable Life Assurance Society of the United States v. First National Bank

Supreme Court of South Dakota, 1999.
602 N.W.2d 291.

■ GILBERTSON, JUSTICE.

[The Olsons owned ranch land subject to two mortgages, the first mortgage in the amount of $1,250,000 to Equitable, and the second mortgage in the amount of $870,000 to First National Bank (FNB). When the Olsons defaulted on both notes, Equitable obtained a foreclosure judgment and the principal balance of $1,212,500 was adjudged to be the superior lien. The court ordered the property to be sold at a public auction, stating the time and place and the notice required under South Dakota law.] * * *

On October 14, 1998, the day before the sale, Equitable and FNB entered into an agreement under which FNB would purchase Equitable's interest in the mortgage for approximately $1,300,000. Later that afternoon, FNB wired funds to Equitable in order to pay off the debt. Prior to receiving notice of confirmation of receipt of the funds, Equitable's attorney, Brian Hagg (Hagg), contacted the Jones County Deputy Sheriff and informed him that he was 95% sure the judgment would be paid and the sale would be called off. Hagg also testified at trial he told the deputy that the sheriff should cancel the sale. Hagg further told the deputy, Hagg would either personally appear or call prior to the time set for the sale. Hagg did not receive confirmation of the funds until the morning of October 15. Hagg testified he attempted to call the Jones County Sheriff's Office between 10:00 and 10:30 a.m. that morning, but received a busy signal and could not get through. Just before 11:00 a.m., the sheriff checked with the clerk of courts to see if there was any indication the sale was going to be cancelled. The clerk told the sheriff no such messages had been received. The sheriff's sale commenced at 11:05 a.m. CDT.

Hagg again called the sheriff's office and this time did reach the deputy at 11:15 a.m. CDT. The attorney was advised the sale had already commenced. Hagg advised the deputy the sale should be canceled as Equitable had been paid and judgment assigned to FNB. The deputy interrupted the sale with the bidding at $1,800,000 and at about 11:30 a.m. the sheriff spoke directly to Hagg.

Despite this notice and clear confusion about the legal status of the auction, the sheriff, at the request of two bidders, continued the auction and completed the sale by accepting a bid of $1,810,000 by Carl Mathews, the highest bidder. Upon a petition from Hagg, the circuit court issued order holding all proceedings in abeyance until a hearing could be held. At the hearing the court confirmed the auction sale, concluding as a matter of law that the requirements for a public auction had been satisfied.

Equitable, FNB and Olsons appeal, raising the following issue for our consideration:

Whether a sheriff's sale of real property conducted pursuant to a Judgment of Foreclosure can be canceled by the mortgagee after the bidding commences. * * *

The trial court's Judgment of Foreclosure and Sale ordered "that the mortgaged premises ... shall be sold at public auction ... in the manner as provided by the laws of the State of South Dakota for foreclosure and sale of real property...." SDCL 21–47–14 provides, in pertinent part:

> All sales of mortgaged premises under an order and decree of foreclosure must be made by a referee, sheriff, or his deputy, of the county where the court in which the judgment is rendered is held, or other person appointed by the court for that purpose, and must be made in the county where the premises, or some part of them, are situated, and shall be made upon like notice and in the same manner as provided by law for the sale of real property upon execution.

The law for the sale of real property upon execution is contained in SDCL ch. 15–19. This was an execution sale for real property pursuant to SDCL 15–19–8 and was to be made at "public auction, to the highest bidder, for cash." SDCL 15–19–13. Equitable argues as the mortgagee in this case, it alone, and not the sheriff, had the power and authority to decide whether or not to cancel the sale. We agree. This Court stated in *State v. Ruden*, 60 S.D. 521, (1932), the power of sale in its broader sense is in the person to whom the mortgagor gives it; that is, the mortgagee. "It is for the mortgagee to determine when the power of sale will be exercised, and to give notice of the sale. It is the duty of the mortgagee to know what goes on at the sale, and to direct and supervise the same ..." *Id.* While the actual sale is conducted by the sheriff, the exercise of power is in the mortgagee....

Equitable claims the circuit court erred in holding as a matter of law a sheriff's execution sale is a sale "without reserve." Whether the owner of property to be sold at auction may withdraw such property prior to the acceptance of a bid depends largely upon whether the auction is "with reserve" or "without reserve."

> In an auction with reserve the auctioneer may withdraw the goods at any time until he announces completion of the sale. In an auction without reserve, after the auctioneer calls for bids on an article or lot, that article or lot cannot be withdrawn unless no bid is made within a reasonable time.

SDCL 57A–2–328(3); *see also* 7 Am.Jur.2d *Auctions and Auctioneers* § 17 (1980).

Because no fact suggests the sale was advertised as one "without reserve," the sheriff's sale should be presumed to be a sale with reserve. The Olsons, as mortgagors, retained the right of redemption pursuant to SDCL 21–52–1 and 21–52–2. Second, in the absence of a sale declared to be "without reserve," the general rule is that:

> a seller of property at auction or the auctioneer may withdraw the property from sale at any time before the acceptance of a bid, on the theory that a bid constitutes a mere offer for a contract and until it is accepted there is no contract between the parties.... The offer to sell the property was rightfully withdrawn by Equitable, and the sheriff advised the bidders he was to cancel the sale. Bidder Mathews was put

on notice before the "fall of the hammer" the offer to sell was to be withdrawn. Thus, there was no offer to accept.

Since the Judgment for Foreclosure and Sale ordered the mortgaged premises to be sold at public auction, the sheriff's role was that of an auctioneer. Generally, an auctioneer is the agent of the person whose property the auctioneer sells.... The auctioneer must act in good faith and in the interest of the principal, and make the sale in accordance with the instructions of the principal. *Id.* This concept is supported by SDCL 59–8–1 which states: "[a]n auctioneer in the absence of special authorization or usage to the contrary, *has authority from the seller* ... " (emphasis added). Also, a sale at auction, like every other sale, must have the assent, express or implied, of both seller and buyer.... Since a sheriff conducting the public auction obtains his authority from the mortgagee, it logically follows the mortgagee can strip the sheriff's authority for conducting the sale. "[T]he right, under appropriate circumstances, to order a delay in making an execution sale, has been recognized on the ground that an execution is the process of the judgment creditor and is under his control." 30 Am. Jur.2d *Executions* § 475 (1994).

It is undisputed the sheriff was notified he was to cancel the sale *prior* to the hammer falling. Equitable, as mortgagee, not the sheriff, had the power of sale. We find it was Equitable, who, through its attorney, had the legal authority and right to direct the sheriff to cancel the sale. * * *

We reverse the circuit court's order confirming the sale and order the parties be returned to their positions as if the sale had been canceled on October 15, 1998.

NOTES

(1) *Auctions.* An auction is a contracting technique invoked most frequently by sellers of goods or land to stimulate price competition. The seller, by soliciting bids from a group of prospective buyers, seeks to develop a market whose prices are determined by on-the-spot competitive bidding. Auctions dispose of real estate, livestock, household goods, antiques, wine, and works of art. In addition to owners, they are used by repossessing creditors, public officials, such as the sheriff, and executors of decedents' estates. The terms and procedures of an auction are usually determined by the advertisement, trade usage or practice and statutes. The terms of the sale are normally set out in advertisements and other writings before the auction is conducted. See, e.g., Dulman v. Martin Fein & Co., Inc., 66 A.D.2d 809, 411 N.Y.S.2d 358 (1978); Restatement (Second) § 28(2). Often, auction disputes involve a combination of advertisement, trade usage and statutory controls and raise issues of agency law (the auctioneer is agent for a principal who may be undisclosed) and property ownership (sometimes stolen goods are sold by auction).

In most auctions the only important term left for agreement is price. The prospective buyer should understand that the function of an auction is to generate price competition and that there is, therefore, some risk that the property will be withdrawn before being sold. The law supports the seller: the consistent legal conclusion has been that, in the absence of agreement to the contrary, an advertisement describing property to be sold to the highest bidder at a stated time and place is not an offer, even though the power to withdraw the goods is *not* expressly reserved. The advertisement merely solicits offers which the seller is privileged to accept or reject. See UCC 2–328(3); Restatement (Second) § 28(1)(a); Weinstein v. Green, 347 Mass. 580, 199 N.E.2d 310 (1964). Unless otherwise agreed, the offer is accepted when the auctioneer "so announces by the fall of the hammer or in other customary manner." UCC 2–328(2).

On the other hand, if the sale is announced to be "without reserve" then the sale must be made to the highest bidder. In the language of UCC 2–328(3): "In an auction without reserve, after the auctioneer calls for bids on an article or lot, that article or lot cannot be withdrawn unless no bid is made within a reasonable time." Accord: Pitchfork Ranch Co. v. Bar TL, 615 P.2d 541 (Wyo.1980); Zuhak v. Rose, 264 Wis. 286, 58 N.W.2d 693 (1953) (high bidder gets specific performance after dissatisfied owner of land discharges auctioneer). Moreover, in an auction without reserve the seller cannot bid. See Pyles v. Goller, 109 Md.App. 71, 674 A.2d 35 (1996).

Does this mean that the advertisement is converted into an offer which is accepted by the bidder, subject to discharge if a higher bid is made? Or, has the high bidder simply made an offer which the auctioneer has a legal duty to accept? One court has stated that the best explanation is "that the owner, by making such an announcement, enters into a collateral contract with all persons bidding at the auction that he will not withdraw the property for sale, regardless of how low the highest bid may be." Drew v. John Deere Company of Syracuse, 19 A.D.2d 308, 241 N.Y.S.2d 267, 269 (N.Y.A.D.1963). But to further complicate matters, UCC 2–328(3) provides that the high bidder "may retract this bid until the auctioneer's announcement of completion of the sale" and that the retraction does not revive any previous bids which have lapsed upon the making of a higher bid. Accord: Restatement (Second) § 28(1)(c). Thus, if it is a "collateral" contract it binds the auctioneer but not the high bidder—at least until the hammer falls.

At first blush these rules appear to be anomalous deviations from normal contract formation procedures. But they serve a useful purpose in auctions. The "without reserve" language informs prospective bidders that the owner is dispensing with a broad power to withdraw goods once they are put up for sale—that he or she is willing to take the highest bid produced by competition. This information may induce greater reliance on the part of individual bidders in attending the auction. The bidder's withdrawal privilege affords some measure of protection from a hasty bid made in the heat of competition. There is some time to reflect and repent before the hammer falls. In view of this, is the fact that bidders have more mobility than sellers in "without reserve" auctions disturbing? Anomalous? For additional discussion, see Corbin § 108; Williston §§ 29–30.

A bid in a sealed auction of "*X* dollars over the highest bid" is commonly referred to as a "sharp" bid, and the practice has been soundly condemned. Such a bid is said to be unfair to other bidders, by allowing the "sharp" bidder to appropriate the judgment of the other bidders, as well as unfair to the seller, in that, if allowed, it would discourage and drive off sum-certain bidders. Webster v. French, 11 Ill. 254 (1849) (contrary to public policy and void); Casey

v. Independence County, 109 Ark. 11, 159 S.W. 24 (1913) ("no bid at all," being both unfair and incomplete). Sharp bidding is clearly a fraudulent practice, and with respect to a public sale, such a bid is void from its inception. It is illegal *per se.* In case of a private sale, it has been held that while concealed sharp bidding taints a resulting contract with fraud, it is not void but voidable at the election of the defrauded parties. Ordinarily, the defrauded parties would be the seller and the highest sum-certain bidder. See Short v. Sun Newspapers, Inc., 300 N.W.2d 781 (Minn.1980).

(2) *Public contracting.* Government entities at all levels employ competitive procedures in procuring supplies and services. The Competition in Contracting Act, enacted by Congress in 1984, is designed to further encourage competitive practice by the federal government. Title VII of Division B of the Deficit Reduction Act of 1984, P.L. 98–369, 98 Stat. 494. Under the Act, "sealed bidding" must be utilized (1) if time permits the solicitation, submission, and evaluation of sealed bids, (2) the award will be made on the basis of price and other price-related factors, (3) it is not necessary to conduct discussion with the responding sources about their bids, and (4) there is a reasonable expectation of receiving more than one sealed bid. Otherwise, the contract is negotiated through the solicitation of competitive proposals from private contractors.

A variation of the auction technique, sealed bidding unfolds in a series of distinct steps. First, contracting officials prepare an invitation for bids (IFB) which describes the government's needs, states the basic terms and conditions (quantity, time and place of delivery, method of payments, etc.), and incorporates by reference applicable standard forms of the government. Second, the IFB is distributed or otherwise publicized to a sufficient number of prospects so as to insure adequate competition. Third, bidders prepare and submit their bids. This bid is the offer. To be eligible for acceptance, it must be submitted on time and conform in every material respect to the IFB. That is, the bidder must submit a responsive bid. Fourth, the bids are opened and evaluated by the government. After bid opening, the bidder cannot change the bid or withdraw the offer unless a mistake has been made and some rather rigid conditions are satisfied. Unlike the private auction, the offeror may not withdraw after bids are opened, but the offeree may reject all bids if there is a "compelling" reason for doing so; e.g., supplies or services contracted for are no longer required; bids indicate that the needs of the government can be satisfied by a less expensive article differing from that for which the bids were invited. Federal Acquisitions Regulation 14.404. Fifth, if everything is in order, an award is made, either by written notice of award or by furnishing the successful bidder with an executed award document. FAR 14.407. The award is, of course, the acceptance, a matter to be examined a "little bid later."

Sealed bidding minimizes the questions as to whether an offer was made and, if so, by whom. This highly structured process is designed to produce full and complete agreement on all material terms without negotiation and clearly designates the bidder as offeror. Litigation over traditional questions of offer and acceptance in government contracts is rare.

(3) *Interpretation Against Party Soliciting Competitive Offers.* An interesting twist is found in Jenkins Towel Service, Inc. v. Fidelity–Philadelphia Trust Co., 400 Pa. 98, 161 A.2d 334 (1960). Because of an acute cash shortage, the defendant trustees decided to sell certain real estate which was part of the

trust. After an initial offering at a public auction was withdrawn because of low bids, the trustees negotiated with several parties, including the plaintiff, without success for the next three years. At the end of this period, Defendant offered to sell the property to Plaintiff for $85,000, but Plaintiff's counter-offer of $82,500 was declined. Defendant then decided to cease negotiations and to sell the property to the party who submitted the highest acceptable cash bid in excess of $92,000. A letter was mailed to Plaintiff and others, which read as follows:

"June 18, 1959

"Jenkins Towel Service, Inc.

"Attention: Mr. James E. Mitchell Vice President

"Dear Mr. Mitchell:

"We wish to acknowledge your letter of recent date submitting an offer for the purchase of the group of properties situate and known as '241–47 North 11th Street, 1030–32 Vine Street, and 1018–22 Vine Street', Philadelphia, Pa.

"As you already know, several offers have been submitted for the purchase of these properties which offers are approximately of the same amount and on the same terms and conditions. The Fidelity–Philadelphia Trust Company is acting in a fiduciary capacity in the management of these properties and is, of course, obligated to recommend the offer which it believes most advantageous to its Estate.

"In order to give each and every prospect a fair and equal chance and in order to secure the highest and best price for the Estate which it represents it has been decided to ask for sealed bids from all interested parties. It is suggested, therefore, that you forward to this office on or before Wednesday, June 24, 1959, your highest offer for the properties. At that time the bids will be opened and an Agreement of Sale tendered to the highest acceptable bidder provided the offer is in excess of $92,000. cash, free and clear of any and all brokerage commissions. All offers must be on an all cash basis and must be accompanied by a check to the order of the Fidelity–Philadelphia Trust Company, Trustee, in the amount of at least 10% of the offer. The Agreement of Sale will provide for the equal division of all Realty Transfer Taxes between buyer and seller. The Agreement of sale shall also contain a provision that the Vendee or purchaser has not been interested in the property through any real estate broker or attorney and that no commission is therefore due by the Vendor to anyone. Further, that if any claim is filed for a commission by any broker or attorney, the Vendee or purchaser is to assume full responsibility therefor. The Trustees, of course, reserve the right to approve or disapprove of any and all offers, or to withdraw the properties from the market.

"In submitting your bid please note on the envelope containing the bid and check 'Sealed bid—June 24, 1959' and direct the bid to the undersigned.

"If you desire any further information or if we can be of any assistance please do not hesitate to call upon us.

> "Very truly yours,
> "George Butterworth, Jr.
> "Assistant Vice President."

Plaintiff's response manifested unequivocal assent to Defendant's letter, and the only other "bidder" submitted a conditional response. Defendant, however, asserted that its letter of June 18 merely solicited offers and refused to convey the property to Plaintiff. Over a strong dissent, the court found Defendant's letter of June 18 to be ambiguous and, therefore, to be interpreted "most strongly against the Fidelity, which drew it." It held that the lower court erred in sustaining Defendant's preliminary objections and dismissing Plaintiff's amended complaint.

If, as defendants contend, Fidelity's letter of June 18 was merely an invitation to prospective purchasers who had been negotiating unsuccessfully for several years to submit a higher bid or offer which it could accept or reject in its sole and arbitrary discretion, why did Fidelity ask for "sealed bids" from all interested parties on or before June 24, 1959, and further state "at that time the bids will be opened and an Agreement of Sale tendered to the highest acceptable bidder, provided the offer is in excess of $92,000.00 cash, free and clear of all brokerage commissions," and then specify in detail the other provisions which were to be incorporated in the agreement of sale? On its face, and especially in the light of the prior negotiations, the surrounding circumstances and the objects which the parties apparently had in view, the contention of defendants that this was merely an invitation to bid, which Fidelity could reject in its unfettered discretion, is unreasonable.

In an attempt to support Fidelity's construction and position, defendants have overlooked not only the law as to the interpretation of a contract which must be considered in its entirety, but also the most important provision, viz. that after the bids are opened it will tender to the highest acceptable bidder an agreement of sale, the details of which are set forth in Fidelity's letter of June 18.

Defendants rely upon the statement in Fidelity's letter that "it was acting as fiduciary and was obligated to recommend the offer which it believed most advantageous to its estate." This contention is devoid of merit. Plaintiff unconditionally and unqualifiedly accepted all the terms and conditions of Fidelity's offer, and no other party did; and there was no higher or more advantageous offer. Defendants also rely upon the following sentence—"The Trustees, of course, reserve the right to approve or disapprove of any and all offers, or to withdraw the properties from the market." This sentence standing alone is what creates a possible ambiguity. This sentence must be interpreted, we repeat, by considering the surrounding circumstances, the objects Fidelity apparently had in view, and the contract in its entirety, and if there is any ambiguity which is reasonably susceptible of two interpretations, the ambiguity must be resolved against the Fidelity which drew the letter-offer. So interpreted, we believe the sentence means that Fidelity can withdraw the properties from the market at any time before the opening of the sealed bids, and can approve or disapprove any offer which does not fully comply with all the conditions set forth by the Fidelity, or which complies but adds unsatisfactory terms.

Jenkins Towel is unique because the interpretation technique was used to determine the *existence* rather than the *meaning* of a contract. Other courts are reluctant to go down that path.

> Because of strict rules governing offer and acceptance, which require that an acceptance be in terms of the offer, we are reluctant to follow by analogy rules laid down with respect to contracts already formed. In passing upon questions of offer and acceptance, courts may wisely require greater exactitude than when they are trying to salvage an existing contract. Where no contract has been completed and neither party has acted to his detriment, there is no compulsion on a court to guess at what the parties intended. Henry Simons Lumber Co. v. Simons, 232 Minn. 187, 44 N.W.2d 726, 730 (1950).

See also United States v. Braunstein, 75 F.Supp. 137 (S.D.N.Y.1947), appeal dismissed, 168 F.2d 749 (2d Cir.1948); Fenstermacher v. Philadelphia National Bank, 493 F.2d 333, 341–43 (3d Cir.1974) (absence of special circumstances and ambiguity in writing supports application of ordinary rule that notices soliciting competitive bids for the sale of stock invite offers not acceptances).

(C) ACCEPTANCE: EXERCISE OF POWER OF ACCEPTANCE

(1) ACCEPTANCE BY PROMISE

La Salle National Bank v. Vega

Appellate Court of Illinois, Second District, 1988.
167 Ill.App.3d 154, 117 Ill.Dec. 778, 520 N.E.2d 1129.

■ Presiding JUSTICE LINDBERG delivered the opinion of the court:

* * *

Plaintiff's first amended complaint alleged the existence of a contract for the sale of real estate between it and Mel [Vega] and sought specific performance of the alleged contract and damages from defendants for willfully and intentionally breaching it. Borg was permitted to intervene and filed a counterclaim naming plaintiff and defendants as counterdefendants. As finally amended, the counterclaim sought specific performance of a different contract for sale of the same real estate to Borg; a judgment declaring the alleged contract between Mel and plaintiff void and holding it for naught; and, if the alleged contract with plaintiff was "held to be a valid and enforceable contract," damages from defendants for fraud for failure to disclose the contract with plaintiff to Borg.

Borg moved for partial summary judgment (Ill.Rev.Stat.1985, ch. 110, par. 2–1005(d)) requesting a determination by the court that the alleged contract between plaintiff and Mel was unenforceable because it was not "signed in accordance with its terms and provisions" and because plaintiff abandoned it. The trial court granted partial summary judgment on the basis of the first ground argued by Borg.

In its verified first amended complaint, plaintiff alleged, *inter alia:*

"The Defendant, MEL VEGA, on March 12, 1985, in his own behalf and in behalf of all the owners of record, entered into a Real Estate Sale Contract (herein 'Contract') with the Plaintiff, a true and correct copy of said Contract is attached hereto and incorporated herein as Exhibit A."

Exhibit A is a document, drafted by counsel for plaintiff, entitled "Real Estate Sale Contract." On the first page of this document appears the date March 12, 1985, and the statement that "Attached Rider is part of this Contract." One of the Rider's provisions states:

"This contract has been executed and presented by an authorized agent for the purchaser, the beneficiaries of the La Salle National Bank, under Trust No. 109529, as Trustee aforesaid for the benefit of the Trust only and not personally. Upon execution of this contract by the Seller, this contract shall be presented to the trust for full execution. Upon the trust's execution, this contract will then be in full force and a copy of a fully executed contract along with evidence of the earnest money deposit will be delivered back to Seller."

The document was signed by Bernard Ruekberg as the purchaser's purchasing agent and by Mel Vega (on March 19, 1985, according to the date by his signature on the Rider) as the seller but not by the trustee for the purchaser.

* * *

It has long been settled that a contract is " 'an agreement between competent parties, upon a consideration sufficient in law, to do or not to do a particular thing.' " (Steinberg v. Chicago Medical School (1977), 69 Ill.2d 320, 329, quoting People v. Dummer (1916), 274 Ill. 637, 640.) The formation of a contract requires an offer, an acceptance, and consideration.... The trial court held that there was no genuine issue of material fact that no contract was formed because the offer was made by Mel, the offer could only be accepted by execution of the document at issue by the trust, and the document was not executed by the trust. * * *

Whether a contract was formed without execution of the document by the trust may now be considered. This requires first an analysis of the events which occurred with respect to the document in terms of offer and acceptance.

The pertinent provision of the document stated:

[The court quoted the attached rider, supra.]

Thus, a specific order of events was contemplated, after which the contract would be in full force. Ruekberg (the purchasing agent) was to execute the document and present it to Mel (the seller). Then Mel was to execute it. After Mel executed it, the document was to be presented to the trust for execution. Finally, "upon the trust's execution," the contract would be in full force.

An offer is an act on the part of one person giving another person the legal power of creating the obligation called a contract. . . . From the provisions contained in the document at bar, particularly the language quoted, it is apparent that there was to be no contract (i.e., the "contract" was not to be in full force) until it was executed by the trust. Thus, Ruekberg's presentation of the document he had executed to Mel was not an offer because it did not give Mel the power to make a contract by accepting it. On the other hand, when Mel executed the document and gave it back to Ruekberg he made an offer which could be accepted by execution of the document by the trust.

An offeror has complete control over an offer and may condition acceptance to the terms of the offer. . . . The language of an offer may moreover govern the mode of acceptance required, and, where an offer requires a written acceptance, no other mode may be used. . . . In the case at bar, the document at issue stated clearly that the contract would be in full force upon the trust's execution. This indicates that the only mode by which Mel's offer could be accepted was execution of the document by the trust. The trust not having executed the document, there was no acceptance of the offer, and so there was no contract. . . .

* * *

The judgment of the circuit court of Du Page County is accordingly affirmed.

Affirmed.

Hendricks v. Behee

Missouri Court of Appeals, Southern District, 1990.
786 S.W.2d 610.

■ FLANIGAN, PRESIDING JUDGE.

Plaintiff Steve L. Hendricks, d/b/a Hendricks Abstract & Title Co., instituted this interpleader action, Rule 52.07, V.A.M.R., against defendants Eugene Behee, Artice Smith, and Pearl Smith. Plaintiff was the escrowee of $5,000 which had been paid by defendant Behee as a deposit accompanying Behee's offer to purchase real estate owned by defendants Artice Smith and Pearl Smith, husband and wife, in Stockton, Missouri. A dispute between Behee and the Smiths as to whether their dealings resulted in a binding contract prompted the interpleader action. Behee filed a cross-claim against the Smiths.

After a nonjury trial, the trial court awarded plaintiff $997.50 to be paid out of the $5,000 deposit. None of the parties challenges that award. The trial court awarded the balance of $4,002.50 to defendant Behee. Defendants Smith appeal.

In essence the Smiths contend that the dealings between them and Behee ripened into a contract and entitled the Smiths to the balance of $4,002.50, and that the trial court erred in ruling otherwise.

After Behee, as prospective buyer, and the Smiths, as prospective sellers, had engaged in unproductive negotiations, Behee, on March 2, 1987, made a written offer of $42,500 for the real estate and $250 for a dinner bell and flower pots. On March 3 that offer was mailed to the Smiths, who lived in Mississippi, by their real estate agent. There were two real estate agents involved. The trial court found that both were the agents of the Smiths, and that finding has not been disputed by the Smiths in this appeal. For simplicity, the two agents will be considered in this opinion as one agent who acted on behalf of the Smiths.

On March 4 the Smiths signed the proposed agreement in Mississippi. Before Behee was notified that the Smiths had accepted the offer, Behee withdrew the offer by notifying the real estate agent of the withdrawal. That paramount fact is conceded by this statement in the Smiths' brief: "On either March 5, 6 or 7, 1987, Behee contacted [the Smiths' real estate agent] and advised her that he desired to withdraw his offer to purchase the real estate. Prior to this communication, Behee had received no notice that his offer had been accepted by the Smiths."

There is no contract until acceptance of an offer is communicated to the offeror....

An uncommunicated intention to accept an offer is not an acceptance.... When an offer calls for a promise, as distinguished from an act, on the part of the offeree, notice of acceptance is always essential.... A mere private act of the offeree does not constitute an acceptance.... Communication of acceptance of a contract to an agent of the offeree is not sufficient and does not bind the offeror....

Unless the offer is supported by consideration, ... an offeror may withdraw his offer at any time "before acceptance and communication of that fact to him." ... To be effective, revocation of an offer must be communicated to the offeree before he has accepted....

Notice to the agent, within the scope of the agent's authority, is notice to the principal, and the agent's knowledge is binding on the principal....

Before Behee was notified that the Smiths had accepted his offer, Behee notified the agent of the Smiths that Behee was withdrawing the offer. The notice to the agent, being within the scope of her authority, was binding upon the Smiths. Behee's offer was not supported by consideration and his withdrawal of it was proper. * * *

The judgment is affirmed.

NOTES

(1) *Offeror's Mastery of Offer*. The offeror is master of the offer. It is recognized that the offeror may stipulate the terms upon which he or she is willing to bargain, and, also, prescribe the method by which the offeree may accept. The offeror fashions the power of acceptance which is conferred upon the offeree and can expressly limit the ways in which that power may be exercised. Hence, it follows that an examination of the terms of the offer is a first step in determining the validity of an alleged acceptance.

Consider the *La Salle Bank* and the *Hendricks* cases and answer the following questions: (a) What did the offeror indicate as to the permissible manner of acceptance? Was that manner invited or required? (b) Did the offeree accept in either case? Why not? (c) Suppose in *La Salle Bank* that the bank had executed the written offer by signature before Vega revoked it. Would there then be a contract or would, as in *Hendricks*, notice to Vega of the signature be required?

(2) A signature, if invited or required as a method of acceptance, constitutes assent to the proposed bargain, including a promise to perform the agreement. A signature is not part performance of the proposed exchange. But is the signature alone enough? Consider this quote from an earlier treatise on contracts. See also, Restatement (Second), Contracts Sections 50–56.

> If we are to proceed on an objective theory of mutual assent, it would seem to be too clear for argument that the offeree's assent should be communicated or manifested to the offeror before a contract can come into being. This is so because, it is what the one party has caused the other to believe he intends, that is important, rather than what he actually intends or what he has caused the world at large to believe he intends. Moreover, where the offer is one that calls for the making of a promise as the requested return, there is an additional reason for reaching this conclusion. The very idea of promise involves communication. In other words, a promise is a communicated undertaking.

Grismore, Contracts § 45 (1st ed. 1947). [Professor John E. Murray, Jr., took over the Grismore treatise, and has produced an excellent treatise on contracts, now in its 4th edition. See Murray on Contracts § 46 (4th ed. 2001).

Ever–Tite Roofing Corp. v. Green

Court of Appeal of Louisiana, 1955.
83 So.2d 449.

■ AYRES, JUDGE. This is an action for damages allegedly sustained by plaintiff as the result of the breach by the defendants of a written contract for the re-roofing of defendants' residence. Defendants denied that their written proposal or offer was ever accepted by plaintiff in the manner stipulated therein for its acceptance, and hence contended no contract was ever entered into. The trial court sustained defendants' defense and rejected plaintiff's demands and dismissed its suit at its costs. From the judgment thus rendered and signed, plaintiff appealed.

Defendants executed and signed an instrument June 10, 1953, for the purpose of obtaining the services of plaintiff in re-roofing their residence situated in Webster Parish, Louisiana. The document set out in detail the work to be done and the price therefor to be paid in monthly installments. This instrument was likewise signed by plaintiff's sale representative, who, however, was without authority to accept the contract for and on behalf of the plaintiff. This alleged contract contained these provisions:

"This agreement shall become binding only upon written acceptance hereof, by the principal or authorized officer of the Contractor, *or upon commencing performance of the work.* This contract is Not Subject to Cancellation. . . . " (Emphasis supplied.)

Inasmuch as this work was to be performed entirely on credit, it was necessary for plaintiff to obtain credit reports and approval from the lending institution which was to finance said contract. With this procedure defendants were more or less familiar and knew their credit rating would have to be checked and a report made. On receipt of the proposed contract in plaintiff's office on the day following its execution, plaintiff requested a credit report, which was made after investigation and which was received in due course and submitted by plaintiff to the lending agency. Additional information was requested by this institution, which was likewise in due course transmitted to the institution, which then gave its approval.

The day immediately following this approval, which was either June 18 or 19, 1953, plaintiff engaged its workmen and two trucks, loaded the trucks with the necessary roofing materials and proceeded from Shreveport to defendants' residence for the purpose of doing the work and performing the services allegedly contracted for the defendants. Upon their arrival at defendants' residence, the workmen found others in the performance of the work which plaintiff had contracted to do. Defendants notified plaintiff's workmen that the work had been contracted to other parties two days before and forbade them to do the work.

Formal acceptance of the contract was not made under the signature and approval of an agent of plaintiff. It was, however, the intention of plaintiff to accept the contract by commencing the work, which was one of the ways provided for in the instrument for acceptance, as will be shown by reference to the extract from the contract quoted hereinabove. Prior to this time, however, defendants had determined on a course of abrogating the agreement and engaged other workmen without notice thereof to plaintiff.

The basis of the judgment appealed was that defendants had timely notified plaintiff before "commencing performance of work". The trial court held that notice to plaintiff's workmen upon their arrival with the materials that defendants did not desire them to commence the actual work was sufficient and timely to signify their intention to withdraw from the contract. With this conclusion we find ourselves unable to agree.

Defendants' attempt to justify their delay in thus notifying plaintiff for the reason they did not know where or how to contact plaintiff is without merit. The contract itself, a copy of which was left with them, conspicuously displayed plaintiff's name, address and telephone number. Be that as it may, defendants at no time, from June 10, 1953, until plaintiff's workmen arrived for the purpose of commencing the work, notified or attempted to notify plaintiff of their intention to abrogate, terminate or cancel the contract.

Defendants evidently knew this work was to be processed through plaintiff's Shreveport office. The record discloses no unreasonable delay on plaintiff's part in receiving, processing or accepting the contract or in commencing the work contracted to be done. No time limit was specified in the contract within which it was to be accepted or within which the work was to be begun. It was nevertheless understood between the parties that some delay would ensue before the acceptance of the contract and the commencement of the work, due to the necessity of compliance with the requirements relative to financing the job through a lending agency. The evidence as referred to hereinabove shows that plaintiff proceeded with due diligence.

The general rule of law is that an offer proposed may be withdrawn before its acceptance and that no obligation is incurred thereby. This is, however, not without exceptions. For instance, Restatement of the Law of Contracts stated:

"(1) The power to create a contract by acceptance of an offer terminates at the time specified in the offer, or, if no time is specified, at the end of a reasonable time.

"What is a reasonable time is a question of fact depending on the nature of the contract proposed, the usages of business and other circumstances of the case which the offeree at the time of his acceptance either knows or has reason to know."

* * *

Therefore, since the contract did not specify the time within which it was to be accepted or within which the work was to have been commenced, a reasonable time must be allowed therefor in accordance with the facts and circumstances and the evident intention of the parties. A reasonable time is contemplated where no time is expressed. What is a reasonable time depends more or less upon the circumstances surrounding each particular case. The delays to process defendants' application were not unusual. The contract was accepted by plaintiff by commencement of the performance of the work contracted to be done. This commencement began with the loading of the trucks with the necessary materials in Shreveport and transporting such materials and the workmen to defendants' residence. Actual commencement or performance of the work therefore began before any notice of dissent by defendants was given plaintiff. The proposition and its acceptance thus became a completed contract.

By their aforesaid acts defendants breached the contract. They employed others to do the work contracted to be done by plaintiff and forbade plaintiff's workmen to engage upon that undertaking. By this breach defendants are legally bound to respond to plaintiff in damages. . . .

* * *

Plaintiff expended the sum of $85.37 in loading the trucks in Shreveport with materials and in transporting them to the site of defendants' residence in Webster Parish and in unloading them on their return, and for wages for the workmen for the time consumed. Plaintiff's Shreveport manager testified that the expected profit on this job was $226. None of this evidence is controverted or contradicted in any manner.

* * *

For the reasons assigned, the judgment appealed is annulled, avoided, reversed and set aside and there is now judgment in favor of plaintiff, Ever–Tite Roofing Corporation, against the defendants, G.T. Green and Mrs. Jessie Fay Green, for the full sum of $311.37, with 5 per cent per annum interest thereon from judicial demand until paid, and for all costs.

Reversed and rendered.

NOTES

(1) In legal contemplation what did "commencement of performance" signify in *Ever-Tite*? Was it a promise to perform the work? If so, should it have been communicated to the offeror before the contract was concluded? See Restatement (Second), Contracts secs. 53 & 54.

(2) Granted that an acceptance by "commencement of performance" was invited in *Ever-Tite,* was there, on the facts stated, such a commencement? At what point could one say the work commenced? With the loading of the trucks? When the trip to Webster Parish began? Note that the offer (by the homeowner) was made on a form prepared by the offeree. How should this fact affect the analysis?

(3) Homeowner submitted an order to Manufacturer on a form prepared by Manufacturers for the purchase of aluminum storm doors and windows. The order contained the following stipulation: "This contract is not binding on manufacturer until accepted by signature of authorized agent at the home office. It shall then be a binding contract as to all parties, and is not, thereafter, subject to cancellation." When the order was received at the home office, Manufacturer checked Homeowner's credit and found it satisfactory. Whereupon, it began fabricating the doors and windows. At no time, however, was the order signed by Manufacturer, nor did the latter notify Homeowner that work had commenced. Homeowner telephoned Manufacturer that he had changed his mind and wanted to cancel the order. Was his revocation timely? See Venters v. Stewart, 261 S.W.2d 444 (Ky.1953). Would your answer be the same if Homeowner had been aware that work had begun?

Corinthian Pharmaceutical Systems, Inc. v. Lederle Laboratories

United States District Court, Southern District, Indiana, 1989.
724 F.Supp. 605.

■ MCKINNEY, DISTRICT JUDGE.

* * *

Defendant Lederle Laboratories is a pharmaceutical manufacturer and distributor that makes a number of drugs, including the DTP vaccine. Plaintiff Corinthian Pharmaceutical is a distributor of drugs that purchases supplies from manufacturers such as Lederle Labs and then resells the product to physicians and other providers. One of the products that Corinthian buys and distributes with some regularity is the DTP vaccine.

In 1984, Corinthian and Lederle became entangled in litigation when Corinthian ordered more than 6,000 vials of DTP and Lederle refused to fill the order. That lawsuit was settled by written agreement whereby Lederle agreed to sell a specified amount of vaccine to Corinthian at specified times. Lederle fully performed under the 1984 settlement agreement, and that prior dispute is not at issue. One of the conditions of the settlement was that Corinthian "may order additional vials of [vaccine] from Lederle at the market price and under the terms and conditions of sale in effect as of the date of the order."

After that litigation was settled Lederle continued to manufacture and sell the vaccine, and Corinthian continued to buy it from Lederle and other sources. Lederle periodically issued a price list to its customers for all of its products. Each price list stated that all orders were subject to acceptance by Lederle at its home office, and indicated that the prices shown "were in effect at the time of publication but are submitted without offer and are subject to change without notice." The price list further stated that changes in price "take immediate effect and unfilled current orders and back orders will be invoiced at the price in effect at the time shipment is made."

From 1985 through early 1986, Corinthian made a number of purchases of the vaccine from Lederle Labs. During this period of time, the largest single order ever placed by Corinthian with Lederle was for 100 vials. When Lederle Labs filled an order it sent an invoice to Corinthian.

* * *

During this period of time, product liability lawsuits concerning DTP increased, and insurance became more difficult to procure. As a result, Lederle decided in early 1986 to self-insure against such risks. In order to cover the costs of self-insurance, Lederle concluded that a substantial increase in the price of the vaccine would be necessary.

In order to communicate the price change to its own sales people, Lederle's Price Manager prepared "PRICE LETTER NO. E–48." This document was dated May 19, 1986, and indicated that effective May 20, 1986, the price of the DTP vaccine would be raised from $51.00 to $171.00 per vial. Price letters such as these were routinely sent to Lederle's sales force, but did not go to customers. Corinthian Pharmaceutical did not know of the existence of this internal price letter until a Lederle representative presented it to Corinthian several weeks after May 20, 1986.

Additionally, Lederle Labs also wrote a letter dated May 20, 1986, to its customers announcing the price increase and explaining the liability and insurance problems that brought about the change. Corinthian somehow gained knowledge of this letter on May 19, 1986, the date before the price increase was to take effect. In response to the knowledge of the impending price increase, Corinthian immediately ordered 1000 vials of DTP vaccine from Lederle. Corinthian placed its order on May 19, 1986, by calling Lederle's "Telgo" system. The Telgo system is a telephone computer ordering system that allows customers to place orders over the phone by communicating with a computer. After Corinthian placed its order with the Telgo system, the computer gave Corinthian a tracking number for its order. On the same date, Corinthian sent Lederle two written confirmations of its order. On each form Corinthian stated that this "order is to receive the $64.32 per vial price."

On June 3, 1986, Lederle sent invoice 1771 to Corinthian for 50 vials of DTP vaccine priced at $64.32 per vial. The invoice contained the standard Lederle conditions noted above. The 50 vials were sent to Corinthian and were accepted. At the same time, Lederle sent its customers, including Corinthian, a letter regarding DTP vaccine pricing and orders. This letter stated that the "enclosed represents a partial shipment of the order for DTP vaccine, which you placed with Lederle on May 19, 1986." The letter stated that under Lederle's standard terms and conditions of sale the normal policy would be to invoice the order at the price when shipment was made. However, in light of the magnitude of the price increase, Lederle had decided to make an exception to its terms and conditions and ship a portion of the order at the lower price. The letter further stated that the balance would be priced at $171.00, and that shipment would be made during the week of June 16. The letter closed, "If for any reason you wish to cancel the balance of your order, please contact [us] . . . on or before June 13."

Based on these facts, plaintiff Corinthian Pharmaceutical brings this action seeking specific performance for the 950 vials of DTP vaccine that Lederle Labs chose not to deliver. In support of its summary judgment motion, Lederle urges a number of alternative grounds for disposing of this claim, including that no contract for the sale of 1000 vials was formed, that if one was formed, it was governed by Lederle's terms and conditions, and that the 50 vials sent to Corinthian were merely an accommodation.

* * *

[T]his is a straightforward sale of goods problem resembling those found in a contracts or sales casebook. The fundamental question is whether Lederle Labs agreed to sell Corinthian Pharmaceuticals 1,000 vials of DTP vaccine at $64.32 per vial. As shown below, the undisputed material facts mandate the conclusion as a matter of law that no such agreement was ever formed.

* * *

The starting point in this analysis is where did the first offer originate. An offer is "the manifestation of willingness to enter into a bargain, so made as to justify another person in understanding that his assent to that bargain is invited and will conclude it." H. Greenberg, *Rights and Remedies Under U.C.C. Article 2* § 5.2 at 50 (1987) [*hereinafter* "Greenberg,

U.C.C. Article 2"], (*quoting* 1 *Restatement (Second), Contracts* § 4 (1981)). The only possible conclusion in this case is that Corinthian's "order" of May 19, 1986, for 1,000 vials at $64.32 was the first offer. Nothing that the seller had done prior to this point can be interpreted as an offer.

* * *

Thus, as a matter of law, the first offer was made by Corinthian when it phoned in and subsequently confirmed its order for 1,000 vials at the lower price. The next question, then, is whether Lederle ever accepted that offer.

Under the Code, an acceptance need not be the mirror-image of the offer. U.C.C. § 2–207. However, the offeree must still do some act that manifests the intention to accept the offer and make a contract. Under § 2–206, an offer to make a contract shall be construed as inviting acceptance in any manner and by any medium reasonable in the circumstances. The first question regarding acceptance, therefore, is whether Lederle accepted the offer prior to sending the 50 vials of vaccine.

The record is clear that Lederle did not communicate or do any act prior to shipping the 50 vials that could support the finding of an acceptance. When Corinthian placed its order, it merely received a tracking number from the Telgo computer. Such an automated, ministerial act cannot constitute an acceptance. . . . Thus, there was no acceptance of Corinthian's offer prior to the deliver of 50 vials.

The next question, then, is what is to be made of the shipment of 50 vials and the accompanying letter. Section 2–206(b) of the Code speaks to this issue:

> [A]n order or other offer to buy goods for prompt or current shipment shall be construed as inviting acceptance either by a prompt promise to ship or by the prompt or current shipment of conforming or non-conforming goods, *but such a shipment of non-conforming goods does not constitute an acceptance if the seller seasonably notifies the buyer that the shipment is offered only as an accommodation to the buyer.*

§ 2–206 (emphasis added). Thus, under the Code a seller accepts the offer by shipping goods, whether they are conforming or not, but if the seller ships non-conforming goods and seasonably notifies the buyer that the shipment is a mere accommodation, then the seller has not, in fact, accepted the buyer's offer. See Greenberg, *U.C.C. Article 2* § 5.5 at 53.

In this case, the offer made by Corinthian was for 1,000 vials at $64.32. In response, Lederle Labs shipped only 50 vials at $64.32 per vial, and wrote Corinthian indicating that the balance of the order would be priced at $171.00 per vial and would be shipped during the week of June 16. The letter further indicated that the buyer could cancel its order by calling Lederle Labs. Clearly, Lederle's shipment was non-conforming, . . . The narrow issue, then, is whether Lederle's response to the offer was a shipment of non-conforming goods not constituting an acceptance because it was offered only as an accommodation under § 2–206.

An accommodation is an arrangement or engagement made as a favor to another. *Black's Law Dictionary* (5th ed. 1979). The term implies no consideration. *Id.* In this case, then, even taking all inferences favorably for the buyer, the only possible conclusion is that Lederle Labs' shipment of 50 vials was offered merely as an accommodation; that is to say, Lederle had no obligation to make the partial shipment, and did so only as a favor to the buyer. The accommodation letter, which Corinthian is sure it received, clearly stated that the 50 vials were being sent at the lower price as an exception to Lederle's general policy, and that the balance of the offer would be invoiced at the higher price. The letter further indicated that Lederle's proposal to ship the balance of the order at the higher price could be rejected by the buyer. Moreover, the standard terms of Lederle's invoice stated that acceptance of the order was expressly conditioned upon buyer's assent to the seller's terms.

Under these undisputed facts, § 2–206(1)(b) was satisfied. Where, as here, the notification is properly made, the shipment of nonconforming goods is treated as a counteroffer just as at common law, and the buyer may accept or reject the counteroffer under normal contract rules. 2 W. Hawkland, *Uniform Commercial Code Series* § 2–206:04 (1987).

Thus, the end result of this analysis is that Lederle Lab's price quotations were mere invitations to make an offer, that by placing its order Corinthian made an offer to buy 1,000 vials at the low price, that by shipping 50 vials at the low price Lederle's response was non-conforming, but the non-conforming response was a mere accommodation and thus constituted a counteroffer. Accordingly, there being no genuine issues of material fact on these issues and the law being in favor of the seller, summary judgment must be granted for Lederle Labs.

* * *

For all these reasons, the defendant's motion for summary judgment is granted.

IT IS SO ORDERED.

NOTES

(1) Read UCC 2–206 carefully. What are the different ways that an offer can be accepted under this section? Had Lederle Labs not given notice to Corinthian that the 50 vials were shipped as an accommodation, what would have been the legal effect of such shipment? Is it possible, under UCC 2–206, to have an "acceptance" which is also a "breach"?

(2) Read UCC 2–204 carefully. How does this section relate to UCC 2–206? Does it recognize that a contract for sale may be formed by offer and acceptance? By what other ways can a contract be formed?

(3) If the offeror specifies that "the signed acceptance of this proposal shall constitute a contract," the requisite signature would seem to conclude a

contract whether or not the offeror knew the action had been taken and despite the lack of any attempt by the offeree to so inform the offeror. For the offeror's mastery of the offer enables one to prescribe how the power of acceptance can be exercised, and one may, if one sees fit, agree to be bound at the moment of signing. By necessary inference the offeror appears to dispense with the necessity of communication of the offeree's assent, and one can be placed in a contractual relationship without knowing it. But what if the offeror does not expressly indicate when the acceptance is to become operative? Are we to assume, then, that there must be a communication, just as there would seem to be no operative offer until it is communicated?

PROBLEM: THE CASE OF THE LASER SALE

Swift Ray is a manufacturer of industrial lasers. After extended negotiations with Swift Ray, Brice Electronics mailed, on October 7, a written detailed offer to Swift Ray which concluded as follows: "If you will agree to manufacture the lasers according to the above stated terms, we will pay the stipulated contract price upon delivery next January." When Swift Ray received the offer on October 9, the president told his purchasing agent: "It's a good deal. Buy the necessary materials to fill the order." The order to suppliers was placed the next day. Similarly, the sales manager prepared and signed an acknowledgment. However, on October 12, before the acknowledgment was mailed, the purchasing agent from Brice Electronics telephoned Swift Ray and cancelled the order. An unexpected cutback in business was given as the justification.

Swift Ray sued Brice for damages whereupon Brice filed a motion to dismiss the complaint for failure to state a cause of action. At the hearing on the motion, Brice argued that the written offer clearly invited acceptance by a promise to perform. As such, the offeree failed to complete every act essential to the making of the promise before the revocation was received, i.e., the offeree did not actually notify or exercise reasonable diligence to notify the offeror of his agreement. Swift Ray argued that the written offer did not unambiguously narrow the method and manner of acceptance to that asserted by Brice. Rather, the offer should be interpreted as inviting the offeree to accept either by promise or by rendering part of the performance. Since the offer did not request notification, no notification of acceptance by performance was required unless the offeree had reason to know that the offeror had no adequate way of learning of the acceptance and then failed to exercise due diligence in notification.

offeror - Brice
offeree - Swift

1.   What result under UCC 2–206?

2.   Suppose that Swift Ray mailed the acknowledgment on October 9. Thereafter but before the acknowledgment arrived, Brice telephoned Swift Ray and canceled the deal. Is there a contract? See UCC 2–206(1).

(2) ACCEPTANCE BY PERFORMANCE NOT BY PROMISE

Carlill v. Carbolic Smoke Ball Co.

Court of Appeals, 1893.
[1893]   1 Q.B. 256.

The defendants, who were the proprietors and vendors of a medical preparation called "The Carbolic Smoke Ball," inserted in the *Pall Mall*

Gazette of November 13, 1891, and in other newspapers, the following advertisement: "100£. reward will be paid by the Carbolic Smoke Ball Company to any person who contracts the increasing epidemic influenza, colds, or any disease caused by taking cold, after having used the ball three times daily for two weeks according to the printed directions supplied with each ball. 1000£. is deposited with the Alliance Bank, Regent Street, shewing our sincerity in the matter.

JAN. 23, 1892 THE ILLUSTRATED LONDON NEWS 113

CARBOLIC SMOKE BALL

WILL POSITIVELY CURE

COUGHS	CATARRH	HOARSENESS	THROAT DEAFNESS	INFLUENZA	CROUP
Cured in 1 week	Cured in 1 to 3 months.	Cured in 12 hours	Cured in 1 to 3 mon'hs.	Cured in 24 hours.	Relieved in 5 minutes.
COLD IN THE HEAD	ASTHMA	LOSS OF VOICE	SNORING	HAY FEVER	WHOOPING COUGH
Cured in 12 hours.	Relieved in 10 minutes.	Fully restored.	Cured in 1 week	Cured in every case.	Relieved the first application.
COLD ON THE CHEST	BRONCHITIS	SORE THROAT	SORE EYES	HEADACHE	NEURALGIA
Cured in 12 hours.	Cured in every case.	Cured in 12 hours.	Cured in 2 weeks.	Cured in 10 minutes.	Cured in 10 minutes.

As all the Diseases mentioned above proceed from one cause, they can be Cured by this Remedy

£100 REWARD

WILL BE PAID BY THE

CARBOLIC SMOKE BALL CO.

to any Person who contracts the Increasing Epidemic.

INFLUENZA,

Colds, or any Diseases caused by taking Cold, after having used the **CARBOLIC SMOKE BALL** according to the printed directions supplied with each Ball.

Free Trials at our Consulting Room.

For Inhalation Only.

Free Trials at our Consulting Room.

For Inhalation Only.

£1000 IS DEPOSITED

with the ALLIANCE BANK, Regent Street, showing our sincerity in the matter

During the last epidemic of **INFLUENZA** many thousand **CARBOLIC SMOKE BALLS** were sold as preventives against this disease, and in no ascertained case was the disease contracted by those using the **CARBOLIC SMOKE BALL.**

THE CARBOLIC SMOKE BALL,

TESTIMONIALS.

The DUKE OF PORTLAND writes: "I am much obliged for the Carbolic Smoke Ball which you have sent me, and which I find most efficacious."

SIR FREDERICK MILNER, Bart., M.P., writes from Nice, March 1, 1890 : "Lady Milner and my children have derived much benefit from the Carbolic Smoke Ball."

Lady MOSTYN writes from Carshalton, Cary Crescent, Torquay, Jan. 10, 1890 : "Lady Mostyn believes the Carbolic Smoke Ball to be a certain check and a cure for a cold, and will have great pleasure in recommending it to her friends. Lady Mostyn hopes the Carbolic Smoke Ball will have all the success its merits deserve."

Lady ERSKINE writes from Spratton Hall, Northampton, Jan. 1, 1890 : "Lady Erskine is pleased to say that the Carbolic Smoke Ball has given every satisfaction; she considers it a very good invention."

Mrs. GLADSTONE writes : "She finds the Carbolic Smoke Ball has done her a great deal of good."

Madame ADELINA PATTI writes: "Madame Patti has found the Carbolic Smoke Ball very beneficial, and the only thing that would enable her to rest well at night when having a severe cold."

AS PRESCRIBED BY
SIR MORELL MACKENZIE, M.D.,
HAS BEEN SUPPLIED TO
H.I.M. THE GERMAN EMPRESS.

H.R.H. The Duke of Edinburgh, K.G.
H.R.H. The Duke of Connaught, K.G.
The Duke of Fife, K.T.
The Marquis of Salisbury, K.G.
The Duke of Argyll, K.T.
The Duke of Westminster, K.G.
The Duke of Richmond and Gordon, K.G.
The Duke of Manchester.
The Duke of Newcastle.
The Duke of Norfolk.
The Duke of Rutland, K.G.
The Duke of Wellington
The Marquis of Ripon, K.G.
The Earl of Derby, K.G
Earl Spencer, K.G.
The Lord Chancellor.
The Lord Chief Justice.
Lord Tennyson.

TESTIMONIALS.

The BISHOP OF LONDON writes: "The Carbolic Smoke Ball has benefited me greatly."

The MARCHIONESS DE SALIS writes from Padworth House, Reading, Jan. 13, 1890 : "The Marchioness de Salis has daily used the Smoke Ball since the commencement of the epidemic of Influenza, and has not taken the Influenza, although surrounded by those suffering from it."

Dr. J. RUSSELL HARRIS M.D. writes from 6, Adam Street, Adelphi, Sept. 21, 1891 : "Many obstinate cases of post-nasal catarrh, which have resisted other treatment, have yielded to your Carbolic Smoke Ball."

A. GINNERS, Esq., Editor of the *Lady's Pictorial*, writes from 172, Strand, W.C., Feb 14, 1890 : "During a recent sharp attack of the prevailing epidemic I had none of the unpleasant and dangerous catarrh and bronchial symptoms. I attribute this entirely to the use of the Carbolic Smoke Ball."

The Rev. Dr. CHICHESTER A. W. READE, LL.D., D.C.L., writes from Banstead Downs, Surrey, May 1890. : "My duties in a large public institution have brought me daily during the recent epidemic of influenza, in close contact with the disease. I have been perfectly free from any symptoms by having the Smoke Ball always handy. It has also wonderfully improved my voice for speaking and singing."

The Originals of these Testimonials may be seen at our Consulting Rooms, with hundreds of others.

One **CARBOLIC SMOKE BALL** will last a family several months, making it the cheapest remedy in the world at the price 10s., post free.

The **CARBOLIC SMOKE BALL** can be refilled, when empty, at a cost of 5s., post free. Address:

CARBOLIC SMOKE BALL CO., 27, PRINCES ST., HANOVER SQ., LONDON, W.

[B4345]

"During the last epidemic of influenza many thousand carbolic smoke balls were sold as preventives against this disease, and in no ascertained case was the disease contracted by those using the carbolic smoke ball.

"One carbolic smoke ball will last a family several months, making it the cheapest remedy in the world at the price, 10s., post free. The ball can be refilled at a cost of 5s. Address, Carbolic Smoke Ball Company, 27 Princes Street, Hanover Square, London."

The plaintiff [Lilli Carlill], a lady, on the faith of this advertisement, bought one of the balls at a chemist's, and used it as directed, three times a day, from November 20, 1891, to January 17, 1892, when she was attacked by influenza. Hawkins, J., held that she was entitled to recover the 100£. The defendants appealed.

■ LINDLEY, L.J.

* * * The first observation I will make is that we are not dealing with any inference of fact. We are dealing with an express promise to pay 100£. in certain events. Read the advertisement how you will, and twist it about as you will, here is a distinct promise expressed in language which is perfectly unmistakable—"100£. reward will be paid by the Carbolic Smoke Ball Company to any person who contracts the influenza after having used the ball three times daily for two weeks according to the printed directions supplied with each ball."

We must first consider whether this was intended to be a promise at all, or whether it was a mere puff which meant nothing. Was it a mere puff? My answer to that question is No, and I base my answer upon this passage: "1000£. is deposited with the Alliance Bank, shewing our sincerity in the matter." Now, for what was that money deposited or that statement made except to negative the suggestion that this was a mere puff and meant nothing at all? The deposit is called in aid by the advertiser as proof of his sincerity in the matter—that is, the sincerity of his promise to pay this 100£. in the event which he has specified. I say this for the purpose of giving point to the observation that we are not inferring a promise; there is the promise, as plain as words can make it.

Then it is contended that it is not binding. In the first place, it is said that it is not made with anybody in particular. Now that point is common to the words of this advertisement and to the words of all other advertisements offering rewards. They are offers to anybody who performs the conditions named in the advertisement, and anybody who does perform the condition accepts the offer. In point of law this advertisement is an offer to pay 100£. to anybody who will perform these conditions, and the performance of the conditions is the acceptance of the offer.

* * *

We, therefore, find here all the elements which are necessary to form a binding contract enforceable in point of law, subject to two observations. First of all it is said that this advertisement is so vague that you cannot really construe it as a promise—that the vagueness of the language shews that a legal promise was never intended or contemplated. The language is vague and uncertain in some respects, and particularly in this, that the 100£. is to be paid to any person who contracts the increasing epidemic after having used the balls three times daily for two weeks. It is said, When are they to be used? According to the language of the advertisement no time is fixed, and, construing the offer most strongly against the person who has made it, one might infer that any time was meant. I do not think that was meant, and to hold the contrary would be pushing too far the doctrine of taking language most strongly against the person using it. I do not think that business people or reasonable people would understand the words as meaning that if you took a smoke ball and used it three times daily for two weeks you were to be guaranteed against influenza for the rest of your life, and I think it would be pushing the language of the advertisement too far to construe it as meaning that. But if it does not mean that, what does it mean? It is for the defendants to shew what it does mean; and it strikes me that there are two, and possibly three, reasonable constructions to be put on this advertisement, any one of which will answer the purpose of the plaintiff. Possibly it may be limited to persons catching the "increasing epidemic" (that is, the then prevailing epidemic), or any colds or diseases caused by taking cold, during the prevalence of the increasing epidemic. That is one suggestion; but it does not commend itself to me. Another suggested meaning is that you are warranted free from catching this epidemic, or colds or other diseases caused by taking cold, whilst you are using this remedy after using it for two weeks. If that is the meaning, the plaintiff is right, for she used the remedy for two weeks and went on using it till she got the epidemic. Another meaning, and the one which I rather prefer, is that the reward is offered to any person who contracts the epidemic or other disease within a reasonable time after having used the smoke ball. Then it is asked, What is a reasonable time? It has been suggested that there is no standard of reasonableness; that it depends upon the reasonable time for a germ to develop! I do not feel pressed by that. It strikes me that a reasonable time may be ascertained in a business sense and in a sense satisfactory to a lawyer, in this way; find out from a chemist what the ingredients are; find out from a skilled physician how long the effect of such ingredients on the system could be reasonably expected to endure so as to protect a person from an epidemic or cold, and in that way you will get a standard to be laid before a jury, or a judge without a jury, by which they might exercise their judgment as to what a reasonable time would be. It strikes me, I confess, that the true construction of this advertisement is that 100£. will be paid to anybody who uses this smoke ball three times daily for two weeks according to the printed directions, and who gets the influenza or cold or other diseases caused by taking cold within a reasonable time after so using it; and if that is the true construction, it is enough for the plaintiff. . . .

It appears to me, therefore, that the defendants must perform their promise, and, if they have been so unwary as to expose themselves to a great many actions, so much the worse for them.

■ BOWEN, L.J. I am of the same opinion.

* * * One cannot doubt that, as an ordinary rule of law, an acceptance of an offer made ought to be notified to the person who makes the offer, in order that the two minds may come together. Unless this is done the two minds may be apart, and there is not that consensus which is necessary according to the English law—I say nothing about the laws of other countries—to make a contract. But there is this clear gloss to be made upon the doctrine, that as notification of acceptance is required for the benefit of the person who makes the offer, the person who makes the offer may dispense with notice to himself if he thinks it desirable to do so and I suppose there can be no doubt that where a person in an offer made by him to another person, expressly or impliedly intimates a particular mode of acceptance as sufficient to make the bargain binding, it is only necessary for the other person to whom such offer is made to follow the indicated method of acceptance; and if the person making the offer, expressly or impliedly intimates in his offer that it will be sufficient to act on the proposal without communicating acceptance of it to himself, performance of the condition is a sufficient acceptance without notification.

* * *

Now, if that is the law, how are we to find out whether the person who makes the offer does intimate that notification of acceptance will not be necessary in order to constitute a binding bargain? In many cases you look to the offer itself. In many cases you extract from the character of the transaction that notification is not required, and in the advertisement cases it seems to me to follow as an inference to be drawn from the transaction itself that a person is not to notify his acceptance of the offer before he performs the condition, but that if he performs the condition notification is dispensed with. It seems to me that from the point of view of common sense no other idea could be entertained. If I advertise to the world that my dog is lost, and that anybody who brings the dog to a particular place will be paid some money, are all the police or other persons whose business it is to find lost dogs to be expected to sit down and write me a note saying that they have accepted my proposal? Why, of course, they at once look after the dog, and as soon as they find the dog they have performed the condition. The essence of the transaction is that the dog should be found, and it is not necessary under such circumstances, as it seems to me, that in order to make the contract binding there should be any notification of acceptance. It follows from the nature of the thing that the performance of the condition is sufficient acceptance without the notification of it, and a person who makes an offer in an advertisement of that kind makes an offer which must be read by the light of that common sense reflection. He does, therefore, in his offer impliedly indicate that he does not require notification of the acceptance of the offer.

A further argument for the defendants was that this was a nudum pactum—that there was no consideration for the promise—that taking the influenza was only a condition, and that the using the smoke ball was only a condition, and that there was no consideration at all; in fact that there was no request, express or implied, to use the smoke ball. * * * Can it be said here that if the person who reads this advertisement applies thrice daily, for such time as may seem to him tolerable, the carbolic smoke ball to his nostrils for a whole fortnight, he is doing nothing at all—that it is a mere act which is not to count towards consideration to support a promise (for the law does not require us to measure the adequacy of the consideration). Inconvenience sustained by one party at the request of the other is enough to create a consideration. I think, therefore, that it is consideration enough that the plaintiff took the trouble of using the smoke ball. But I think also that the defendants received a benefit from this user, for the use of the smoke ball was contemplated by the defendants as being indirectly a benefit to them, because the use of the smoke balls would promote their sale.

* * *

* * * I cannot picture to myself the view of the law on which the contrary could be held when you have once found who are the contracting parties. If I say to a person, "If you use such and such a medicine for a week I will give you 5£.," and he uses it, there is ample consideration for the promise.

■ A.L. SMITH, L.J.

* * *

[I]t was argued, that if the advertisement constituted an offer which might culminate in a contract if it was accepted, and its conditions performed, yet it was not accepted by the plaintiff in the manner contemplated, and that the offer contemplated was such that notice of the acceptance had to be given by the party using the carbolic ball to the defendants before user, so that the defendants might be at liberty to superintend the experiment. All I can say is, that there is no such clause in the advertisement, and that, in my judgment, no such clause can be read into it; and I entirely agree with what has fallen from my Brothers, that this is one of those cases in which a performance of the condition by using these smoke balls for two weeks three times a day is an acceptance of the offer.

* * *

Lastly, it was said that there was no consideration, and that it was nudum pactum. There are two considerations here. One is the consideration of the inconvenience of having to use this carbolic smoke ball for two weeks three times a day; and the other more important consideration is the money gain likely to accrue to the defendants by the enhanced sale of the smoke balls, by reason of the plaintiff's user of them. There is ample consideration to support this promise. I have only to add that as regards the policy and the wagering points, in my judgment, there is nothing in either of them.

Appeal dismissed.

NOTES

(1) Review Judge Wood's discussion of rewards as offers in general and the Carbolic Smoke Ball in particular in Leonard v. Pepsico, supra at 253.

(2) What manner of acceptance was invited by the offer? Could a member of the public, for example, create a contract by promising to buy and use the Smoke ball? At what point did a contract come into existence? Was notification of the offeror a requisite of contractual obligation?

Glover v. Jewish War Veterans of United States

Municipal Court of Appeals for the District of Columbia, 1949.
68 A.2d 233.

■ CLAGETT, ASSOCIATE JUDGE. The issue determinative of this appeal is whether a person giving information leading to the arrest of a murderer without any knowledge that a reward has been offered for such information by a non-governmental organization is entitled to collect the reward. The trial court decided the question in the negative and instructed the jury to return a verdict for defendant. Claimant appeals from the judgment on such instructed verdict.

The controversy grows out of the murder on June 5, 1946, of Maurice L. Bernstein, a local pharmacist. The following day, June 6, Post No. 58, Jewish War Veterans of the United States, communicated to the newspapers an offer of a reward of $500 "to the person or persons furnishing information resulting in the apprehension and conviction of the persons guilty of the murder of Maurice L. Bernstein." Notice of the reward was published in the newspaper June 7. A day or so later Jesse James Patton, one of the men suspected of the crime, was arrested and the police received information that the other murderer was Reginald Wheeler and that Wheeler was the "boy friend" of a daughter of Mary Glover, plaintiff and claimant in the present case. On the evening of June 11 the police visited Mary Glover, who in answer to questions informed them that her daughter and Wheeler had left the city on June 5. She told the officers she didn't know exactly where the couple had gone, whereupon the officers asked for names of relatives whom the daughter might be visiting. In response to such questions she gave the names and addresses of several relatives, including one at Ridge Spring, South Carolina, which was the first place visited by the officers and where Wheeler was arrested in company with plaintiff's daughter on June 13. Wheeler and Patton were subsequently convicted of the crime.

Claimant's most significant testimony, in the view that we take of the case, was that she first learned that a reward had been offered on June 12, the day after she had given the police officers the information which enabled them to find Wheeler. Claimant's husband, who was present during the interview with the police officers, also testified that at the time of the interview he didn't know that any reward had been offered for Wheeler's arrest, that nothing was said by the police officers about a reward and that he didn't know about it "until we looked into the paper about two or three days after that."

We have concluded that the trial court correctly instructed the jury to return a verdict for defendant. While there is some conflict in the decided cases on the subject of rewards, most of such conflict has to do with rewards offered by governmental officers and agencies. So far as rewards offered by private individuals and organizations are concerned, there is little conflict on the rule that questions regarding such rewards are to be based upon the law of contracts.

Since it is clear that the question is one of contract law, it follows that, at least so far as private rewards are concerned, there can be no contract unless the claimant when giving the desired information knew of the offer of the reward and acted with the intention of accepting such offer; otherwise the claimant gives the information not in the expectation of receiving a reward but rather out of a sense of public duty or other motive unconnected with the reward. "In the nature of the case," according to Professor Williston, "it is impossible for an offeree actually to assent to an offer unless he knows of its existence." After stating that courts in some jurisdictions have decided to the contrary, Williston adds, "It is impossible, however, to find in such a case [that is, in a case holding to the contrary] the elements generally held in England and America necessary for the formation of a contract. If it is clear the offeror intended to pay for the service, it is equally certain that the person rendering the service performed it voluntarily and not in return for a promise to pay. If one person expects to buy, and the other to give, there can hardly be found mutual assent. These views are supported by the great weight of authority, and in most jurisdictions a plaintiff in the sort of case under discussion is denied recovery."

The American Law Institute in its Restatement of the Law of Contracts follows the same rule, thus: "It is impossible that there should be an acceptance unless the offeree knows of the existence of the offer." The Restatement gives the following illustration of the rule just stated: "A offers a reward for information leading to the arrest and conviction of a criminal. B, in ignorance of the offer, gives information leading to his arrest and later, with knowledge of the offer and intent to accept it, gives other information necessary for conviction. There is no contract."

We have considered the reasoning in state decisions following the contrary rule. Mostly, as we have said, they involve rewards offered by governmental bodies and in general are based upon the theory that the government is benefited equally whether or not the claimant gives the information with knowledge of the reward and that therefore the government should pay in any event. We believe that the rule adopted by Professor Williston and the Restatement and in the majority of the cases is the better reasoned rule and therefore we adopt it. We believe furthermore that this rule is particularly applicable in the present case since the claimant did not herself contact the authorities and volunteer information but gave the information only upon questioning by the police officers and did not claim any knowledge of the guilt or innocence of the criminal but only knew where he probably could be located.

Affirmed.

NOTES

(1) "The liability for a reward of this kind must be created, if at all, by contract. There is no rule of law which imposes it except that which enforces contracts voluntarily entered into. A mere offer or promise to pay does not give rise to a contract. That requires the assent or meeting of two minds, and therefore is not complete until the offer is accepted. Such an offer as that alleged may be accepted by any one who performs the service called for when the acceptor knows that it has been made and acts in performance of it, but not otherwise. He may do such things as are specified in the offer, but, in so doing, does not act in performance of it, and therefore does not accept it, when he is ignorant of its having been made. There is no such mutual agreement of minds as is essential to a contract. The offer is made to any one who will accept it by performing the specified acts, and it only becomes binding when another mind has embraced and accepted it. The mere doing of the specified things without reference to the offer is not the consideration for which it calls. This is the theory of the authorities which we regard as sound." Broadnax v. Ledbetter, 100 Tex. 375, 99 S.W. 1111–12 (1907).

(2) "If the offer was made in good faith, why should the defendant inquire whether the plaintiff knew that it had been made? Would the benefit to him be diminished by the discovery that the plaintiff, instead of acting from mercenary motives, has been impelled solely by the desire to prevent the larceny from being profitable to the person who had committed it?" Dawkins v. Sappington, 26 Ind. 199, 201 (1866).

(3) Do you think the result would have been different in *Glover* if the reward had been offered by a public authority, as, for example, the District of Columbia? This problem came before the court two years later. See Glover v. District of Columbia, 77 A.2d 788 (Mun.Ct.D.C.1951).

(4) Assume Mary Glover knew of the reward, but when she furnished the information she did so reluctantly and with no desire to assist apprehension. Would she be entitled to the reward?

(5) Again, assuming Mary Glover knew of the reward, but it was her information combined with information from another person that led to the apprehension. What, if anything, should she recover? See Reynolds v. Charbeneau, 744 S.W.2d 365 (Tex.App.1988).

(6) Assume that the reward claimant was a District police officer, who furnished the information in the course of his usual employment. Would he be eligible for the reward? Would your answer be the same if it were established that he had not been assigned to the Bernstein murder case, nor had he participated in the official investigation thereof, but had worked on the matter, with the hope of obtaining the reward, during off-duty hours? See Maryland Casualty Co. v. Mathews, 209 F.Supp. 822 (S.D.W.Va.1962). *Cf.* Denney v. Reppert, 432 S.W.2d 647 (Ky.1968) (Deputy sheriff who assisted in arrest outside of his jurisdiction held entitled to reward.)

(7) *A Unilateral Contract Sampler.* Although not used in the Restatement (Second), the phrase "unilateral contract" refers to an offer which invites acceptance by performance of the bargained for exchange and does not invite acceptance by a promise. See Section 53(3). Unilateral contract analysis has been utilized in resolving an important employment contract issue. See e.g., Pine River State Bank v. Mettille, 333 N.W.2d 622 (Minn.1983) (whether terms of employee handbook become part of contract). But even if a unilateral contract case lacks real importance, it is seldom lacking in human interest. E.g.:

Barnes v. Treece, 15 Wash.App. 437, 549 P.2d 1152 (1976) (Offer by punch board distributor to pay $100,000 to anyone who found a "crooked" punchboard.)

Las Vegas Hacienda, Inc. v. Gibson, 77 Nev. 25, 359 P.2d 85 (1961) (Offer by owner of golf course to pay $5,000 to anyone shooting a hole-in-one.)

James v. Turilli, 473 S.W.2d 757 (Mo.App.1971) (Offer by owner of "Jesse James Museum" in Stanton, Missouri, to pay $10,000 to anyone who could disprove his claim that the man shot and buried in 1882 as Jesse James was an impostor, and that the real Jesse James, under the name of J. Frank Dalton, lived at the offeror's museum for many years.)

Newman v. Schiff, 778 F.2d 460 (8th Cir.1985) (Offer on CBS Nightwatch program to pay $100,000 to anyone who called the show and cited any section of the Internal Revenue Code "that says an individual is required to file a tax return.")

Harris v. Time, Inc., 191 Cal.App.3d 449, 237 Cal.Rptr. 584 (1987) (Offer to give a calculator watch free "just for opening this envelope" was accepted by opening envelope, but plaintiff failed to give defendant notice of acceptance within a reasonable time).

See also Leonard v. Pepsico, Inc., 88 F.Supp.2d 116 (S.D.N.Y.1999), supra at 253.

All of this and Carbolic Smoke Balls too!

Industrial America, Inc. v. Fulton Industries, Inc.

Supreme Court of Delaware, 1971.
285 A.2d 412.

[The plaintiff, "Industrial America," Inc., was a broker specializing in the sale or merger of businesses. Bush Hog, Inc. (B–H) was a farm machinery company which had informed several brokers, including the plaintiff, of its desire to consummate a merger. With B–H's authorization, and armed with documentary data furnished by it, the plaintiff's president, Millard B. Deutsch, first approached the Borg Warner Corporation with the B–H merger possibility; but nothing came of that effort. Next, again with B–H's authorization and updated material, Deutsch attempted to interest the Wickes Corporation in the merger possibility. After negotiations were carried on for several months between the two corporations, Deutsch participating actively therein, the talks ceased in early 1965. During the Wickes discussions, Deutsch outlined to B–H the commission arrangement he would expect if the merger were consummated. After the Wickes negotiations ended, according to B–H, it decided not to deal further with Deutsch or any other broker; but this decision was never communicated to Deutsch.

In the fall of 1965, while eating lunch with an accountant friend, Deutsch learned that Fulton Industries, Inc., (and its successor, Allied Products Corporation), the defendant herein, was an "acquisition minded" company. Deutsch forthwith took from his own office files a copy of the following ad in the *Wall Street Journal:*

> WANTED—PRODUCT LINES! Heavy or Medium Machinery of Industrial Products. One of Fulton Industries' divisions desires additional products to manufacture. Its modern manufacturing facility of more than 250,000 sq. ft. includes grey iron foundry, heavy and light machining, sheet metal forming, and capable engineering, sales and service staffs.
>
> Fulton will buy outright, or acquire by merger, active product line with annual sales of $2 million or more. Will take over manufacture, sales, service and key people. Brokers fully protected.

On October 7, 1965, Deutsch wrote to Fulton, describing but not naming B–H as a prospective acquisition; the response, dated October 14, was a request for financial data. On October 19, Deutsch replied by naming B–H as the prospect and transmitting financial data supplied to him by B–H. By letter dated October 22, Fulton stated it was "very much interested," and requested Deutsch to arrange a visit by the Fulton people to the B–H plant. By letter of October 26, with copy to Fulton, Deutsch advised B–H of Fulton's interest and suggestion for a visit. At some time after October 26 and prior to November 2, Fulton's executive vice president telephoned B–H's president directly and arranged a meeting for November 4. Deutsch first learned of this when, on November 3, he inquired of B–H regarding its failure to reply to his letter of October 26. Despite his repeated efforts and offers to assist, neither B–H nor Fulton dealt further with Deutsch; they both ignored his inquiries except for B–H's promise to keep him informed. Negotiations between B–H and Fulton continued until March 11, 1966, when a merger agreement between them was consummated.

After a series of hearings and appeals, the plaintiff was successful in getting a judgment for his broker's commission against B–H ($125,000) on the grounds that it was the procuring cause. The plaintiff, however, was unsuccessful in recovering judgment against Fulton; through special interrogatories, the trial court found that the plaintiff had never accepted Fulton's "offer."]

■ HERRMANN, JUSTICE.

* * *

The basic question for decision in this appeal, in our view, is whether the plaintiff had the burden of proving a subjective intent on the part of

Deutsch to accept the offer of guaranty which had been made in the advertisement by Fulton under the jury's findings.

We are of the opinion that Deutsch's subjective intent was not a relevant issue; that, rather, the relevant issues were (1) whether Fulton's offer of guaranty invited acceptance by performance; (2) whether Deutsch knew of the offer; and (3) whether Deutsch's course of action constituted a performance amounting to an acceptance.

It is basic that overt manifestation of assent—not subjective intent—controls the formation of a contract; that the "only intent of the parties to a contract which is essential is an intent to say the words or do the acts which constitute their manifestation of assent"; that "the intention to accept is unimportant except as manifested." Restatement of Contracts, § 20; . . .

Where an offeror requests an act in return for his promise and the act is performed, the act performed becomes the requisite overt manifestation of assent if the act is done intentionally; i.e., if there is a "conscious will" to do it. Restatement of Contracts, § 20; 1 Williston on Contracts (3d Ed.) § 68. But "it is not material what induces the will," Restatement of the Law of Contracts, § 20, Comment (a). Otherwise stated, motive in the manifestation of assent is immaterial. There may be primary and secondary reasons or motives for a performance constituting manifestation of assent to an offer inviting acceptance by performance; and the "chief reason" or the prevailing motive need not necessarily be the offer itself. A unilateral contract may be enforceable when the promisor has received the desired service even though the service was primarily motivated by a reason other than the offer. The "motivating causes of human action are always complex and are frequently not clearly thought out or expressed by the actor himself. This being true, it is desirable that not much weight should be given to the motives of an offeree and that no dogmatic requirement should be embodied in a stated rule of law." 1 Corbin on Contracts, § 58, p. 244, § 59, p. 246. It follows that a unilateral contract may arise even though at the time of performance the offeree did not "rely" subjectively upon, i.e., was not primarily motivated by, the offer. See Simmons v. United States (4 Cir.) 308 F.2d 160 (1962); Eagle v. Smith (Del.) 4 Houst. 293 (1871); Carlill v. Carbolic Smoke Ball Co. [1893] Q.B. 256; Restatement of Contracts, § 55, Comment b (1932): " * * * contracts may exist where if the offer is in any sense a cause of the acceptor's action it is so slight a factor that a statement that the acceptance is caused by the offer is misleading."

The clear trend and development of the law in this connection is demonstrated by a proposed change in the status of Section 55 of the Restatement of Contracts (1932).[2] The development of this facet of the law

---

2. Section 55 provided:

"ACCEPTANCE OF OFFER FOR UNILATERAL CONTRACT; NECESSITY OF INTENT TO ACCEPT

"If an act or forbearance is requested by the offeror as the consideration for a unilateral contract, the act or forbearance must be given with the intent of accepting the offer."

of contracts became apparent in Section 55 of the 1964 Tentative Draft of Restatement of Contracts (Second).[3] A comparison of the 1932 and the 1964 versions of Section 55 indicates that under the currently developing rule of law, an offer that invites an acceptance by performance will be deemed accepted by such performance unless there is a manifestation of intention to the contrary. See 1 Williston on Contracts (3d Ed.) § 67. Thus, in the establishment of a contractual obligation, the favored rule shifts the emphasis away from a manifestation of intent to accept to a manifestation of intent not to accept; thereby establishing, it would appear, a rebuttable presumption of acceptance arising from performance when the offer invites acceptance by performance. See Braucher, Offer and Acceptance in Second Restatement, 74 Yale L.J. 302, 308 (1964). The law thus rightfully imputes to a person an intention corresponding to the reasonable meaning of his words and deeds.

The defendants contend that, because an offer of guaranty is here involved, the issue is whether the plaintiff gave to Fulton the necessary notice of acceptance of the offer, citing 1 Williston on Contracts (3d Ed.) § 69AA, p. 223. The position is untenable in the light of the following portion of the *Williston* statement upon which the defendants rely:

> "Ordinarily there is no occasion to notify the offeror of the acceptance of such an offer, if the doing of the act is sufficient acceptance, and the promisor knows that he is bound when he sees that action has been taken on the faith of his offer. * * *."

See also Restatement of Contracts, § 56 (1932); 1 Corbin on Contracts, § 68, f. n. 91. The facts of this case meet the test. In this connection, the Trial Judge ruled that Fulton's knowledge of the plaintiff's submission of B–H's name to it was notice to Fulton of an act constituting acceptance of its offer. We concur in that ruling.

Applying the law we find applicable to the facts of this case: we conclude that the Trial Court erred in submitting the issue of subjective reliance to the jury under Interrogatory No. 4. We hold that there was no relevant issue of fact as to the plaintiff's subjective reliance upon Fulton's offer. As a matter of law, it appears unquestionable that Fulton's offer invited acceptance by performance; it is uncontroverted that Deutsch knew of the offer at the time of performance; by the jury's finding of procuring cause, it has been established that the plaintiff did in fact and in law perform. It follows as a matter of law, in the absence of any manifestation of intention to the contrary, that the plaintiff's performance constituted an

---

3. The Draft contains the following:

"ACCEPTANCE BY PERFORMANCE; MANIFESTATION OF INTENTION NOT TO ACCEPT

"(1) An offer may be accepted by the rendering of a performance only if the offer invites such an acceptance. (2) Except as stated in § 72, the rendering of a performance does not constitute an acceptance if within a reasonable time the offeree exercises reasonable diligence to notify the offeror of nonacceptance. (3) Where an offer of a promise invites acceptance by performance and does not invite a promissory acceptance, the rendering of the invited performance does not constitute an acceptance if before the offeror performs his promise the offeree manifests an intention not to accept." [This is § 53 in the final draft. Ed.]

acceptance of the offer of Fulton which was found by the jury to be an offer of guaranty outstanding and viable at the time of the performance.

The necessary result of the foregoing chain is that the plaintiff is entitled to judgments against Fulton and Allied as a matter of law upon the basis of the judgment against B–H, unless there is validity in any of the grounds of the defendants' appeals herein.

* * *

Accordingly, upon the bases of the jury's answers to the special interrogatories and of the conclusions we have reached herein, we conclude that as a matter of law the plaintiff is entitled to judgments against Fulton and Allied as well as against B–H upon the verdict of $125,000. The cause is remanded for further proceedings consistent herewith.

NOTES

To understand this case, note that there were two possible offers that the plaintiff could have accepted by finding the buyer that resulted in the sale. Try to identify the two offers. Next, consider which offer the plaintiff intended to accept by its conduct of full performance. The defendant argued that the plaintiff intended to accept the other offer, not its ad in the Wall Street Journal. How does the court deal with this argument?

PROBLEM: THE CASE OF THE LITTLE LEAGUE SPONSORS

Charley, a public spirited citizen, placed an advertisement in the Suburbia *Press,* stating that he would give $1,000 to anyone who sponsored a little league baseball club in the area for the ensuing season.

Baker, unaware of the advertisement, sponsored a little league club that year in Suburbia. He did not learn of the ad until the season was over, but at the instigation of his son, a first-year law student, brought suit against Charley for the $1,000. Any recovery? Assume, instead, that Baker had seen the advertisement before the season began but did not give it another thought until the season was concluded. Would he then be entitled to claim the $1,000?

Abel, owner of a Suburbia restaurant, sponsored a local club that season, the same as he had in previous years. He did not learn of the advertisement until midseason, at which time he determined to claim the $1,000. At the end of the season he filed suit against Charley. What result?

Comment: Acceptance by Performance Under Restatement (Second)

In the first Restatement, a sharp dichotomy between bilateral and unilateral contracts was maintained. Although Section 31 established a presumption in favor of the bilateral contract, it was supposed that every offer invited acceptance by either a promise or by full performance. This view was criticized by Karl Llewellyn, see Llewellyn, *Our Case Law of Contract—Offer and Acceptance,* 48 Yale L.J. 779, 786 (1939), and was explicitly rejected by UCC 2–206(1)(a), which provides that "unless otherwise unambiguously indicated," an offer "shall be construed as inviting acceptance in any manner and by any medium reasonable in the circumstances." [See UCC 2–205(a)(1) (1997)]. Thus, if a buyer offers to purchase goods for "prompt or current shipment," and the language or circumstances do not unambiguously indicate that acceptance by shipment is required, the offer "shall be construed as inviting acceptance either by a prompt promise to ship or by the prompt or current shipment" of goods. UCC 2–206(1)(b). [UCC 2–205(a)(2)]. The rule of construction operates to give an offeree a choice among reasonable methods of acceptance and by expanding the power to create a contract protects the offeree's reasonable reliance.

Restatement (Second) has followed this lead by abolishing the labels "bilateral" and "unilateral" and by charting a middle ground for acceptance between assent expressed by words of promise and assent expressed by completing a performance that the offeror required exclusively for acceptance. For a critical view of this development, see Mark Pettit, *Modern Unilateral Contracts*, 63 B.U.L.Rev. 551 (1983). This middle ground emerges in a case where acceptance by "rendering a performance" is invited or required by the offer but where the offeree also has power to accept by making a promise. To accept the offer, the offeree must at least perform or tender part of the performance invited. Section 50(2). More importantly, this tender or beginning of performance is an acceptance which "operates as a promise to render complete performance." Section 62(2). It does not create an option contract, à la Section 45. Rather, it creates a full-blown reciprocal commitment, which used to be called a "bilateral" contract. Finally, "no notification is necessary to make such an acceptance effective unless the offer requests" it. Section 54(1). The contractual duties may be discharged if the offeree "has reason to know that the offeror has no adequate means of learning of the performance with reasonable promptness" and fails to exercise "reasonable diligence to notify the offeror of acceptance." Section 54(2)(a). But the contract, under these circumstances, is formed by the conduct of part performance or tender, not the giving or the effort to give notice to the offeror.

The intricate Restatement (Second) maze can be illustrated by three examples.

1. A, who lives in the city, owns 100 acres of farm land some 100 miles away. In the past, B, a farmer, has plowed the field for A in the Spring. On Monday, A telephoned B and said: "If you will agree by 4 PM tomorrow to plow my field, I will pay you $500 when the job is done." B said he would "consider it." The next day, B started to plow the field at 3 PM but had not notified A by 4 PM and, in fact, did not inform A until the next morning. There is no contract if the court accepts the following version of the case. The offer invited or required B's acceptance to be made "by an affirmative answer in words" and did not invite acceptance by performance. Section 30. Put another way, the language and circumstances clearly limited the manner of acceptance to an affirmative promise in words. See Section 32. As such, B did not "complete every act essential to the making of the promise," Section 50(3), or exercise "reasonable diligence to notify the offeror of acceptance," Section 56, before the offer lapsed at 4 PM. What about B's reliance (and A's enrichment, to the extent the field was plowed)?

In theory, at least, if B knew that the only way to accept was to "say yes" before 4 PM and failed to do so, he plowed at his own peril.

2.   Suppose, in Example #1, that A had telephoned B and said: "When and only when you plow my 100 acres by 4 PM next Monday, I will pay you $500." B replied: "I'll do it. You can count on it." A responded: "I want a plowed field not a promise. Plow it or we have no deal." B started to plow the field on Friday, completing 20% by sunset. The next day, A telephoned before 7 AM and revoked the offer. B ignored A and completed the plowing before 4 PM on Monday. There is a contract if the court accepts the following version of the case. A's offer required acceptance by rendering a completed performance but did not invite acceptance by promise. These limitations were clear and unambiguous. As such, B's commencing performance does not operate as a "promise to render complete performance." See Section 62. But it did create an option contract under Section 45 when B began the invited performance. And, under Section 45(2), B properly completed the performance "in accordance with the terms of the offer," thus imposing on A the duty to pay $500. Note that Section 45 applies only where the offer "invites an offeree to accept by rendering a performance and does *not* invite a promissory acceptance."

3.   Suppose, in Example #1, that A had telephoned B and said: "If you will plow my field by 4 PM next Monday I will pay you $500." B replied: "I'll consider it." The next day, B started to plow the field and was 20% completed when, in the evening, A called to revoke the offer. There is a contract if the court accepts the following version of the case. The offer empowered B to make a choice between acceptance by promise (he could have said yes over the telephone) and acceptance by performance. Section 30. There are no language or circumstances clearly to the contrary and Section 32 provides that "in case of doubt an offer is interpreted as inviting the offeree to accept either by promising to perform what the offer requests or by rendering the performance, as the offeree chooses." Thus, the offer was accepted when part-performance occurred, Section 50(2), and the acceptance by performance operated as a promise to complete the plowing. Section 62(2). Notice of acceptance to A was not required, Section 54(1), and, anyway, A learned of the performance when he telephoned to revoke the offer. Note that where the offer invites a choice between a performance and a promise, the reliance in part performance creates a promise to complete (yes, a "bilateral" contract) rather than an option under Section 45.

(3) ACCEPTANCE BY CONDUCT OR SILENCE

Russell v. Texas Co.

United States Court of Appeals, Ninth Circuit, 1956.
238 F.2d 636.

■ HALBERT, DISTRICT JUDGE. Plaintiff-appellant, Russell, claims title to certain real property, which will be referred to in this opinion as section 23.

Russell's predecessors in interest acquired their interest in this property from the Northern Pacific Railway Company, defendant-appellee herein, through a contract followed by a warranty deed executed in 1918. In both the contract and the deed was a reservation of mineral rights by the grantor. The Texas Company, defendant-appellee and cross-appellant herein, has been conducting extensive operations on section 23 since 1952 under an oil and gas lease granted by Northern Pacific Railway Company. The Texas Company has also made use of the surface of section 23 in connection with operations carried on by it on lands other than section 23.

Russell, as plaintiff, instituted this action seeking relief under three causes of action. * * * By the second and third causes of action, Russell seeks to recover damages from The Texas Company for its use of the surface of section 23 in connection with its operations on section 23 and on adjacent lands.

* * *

Second and Third Causes of Action. The damages which Russell seeks to recover from The Texas Company in his second and third causes of action are based on the following:

* * *

(B) The sums alleged to be due under a revocable license commencing on October 30, 1952, which obligated The Texas Company to pay Russell $150.00 a day for the continued use of section 23 in connection with its operations on adjacent lands, a use admittedly in excess of the easement flowing from the mineral reservation in the original deed.

The evidence shows that The Texas Company received on October 30, 1952, an offer from Russell for a revocable license to cover the use of section 23 in connection with operations on adjacent lands for the sum of $150.00 a day, which offer contained the express proviso that, "your continued use of the roadway, water and/or materials will constitute your acceptance of this revocable permit." The evidence further shows that The Texas Company did so continue to use section 23 until November 22, 1952, and it was not until sometime in December of that year that Russell finally received a communication from the Company to the effect that the offer was rejected. Neither party depends in any material respect on this purported rejection.

* * *

Judgment was entered in favor of Russell and against The Texas Company in the amount of $3,837.60, which consisted of $3,600.00 due under the revocable license and $237.60 due for the use of the land under the terms of the mineral reservation.

The Texas Company appeals from that portion of the judgment which awarded Russell $3,600.00 as the amount due under the terms of the revocable license, contending that the court erred as a matter of law in finding that the offer for the said license was accepted.

Russell appeals from that portion of the judgment against The Texas Company which awarded him $237.60, claiming that the court, in arriving at the measure of compensation, applied the wrong rule of damages. * * *

The Texas Company argues that the revocable license, which Russell offered to it in connection with its wrongful use of section 23, was never accepted, because the Company had no intention of accepting it. Appellant presents for our consideration numerous passages from the Restatement of Contracts and Williston on Contracts dealing with the necessity of the offeree's intent to accept where an ambiguous act is selected by the offeror to signify acceptance, or where silence and inaction can be considered an acceptance. None of these citations deal with the precise question that we are confronted with in this case. The question here is whether an offeree may vitiate a contract by a claim of lack of intention to accept an offer when he accepts and retains the benefits offered to him by the offeror, with a positive and affirmative proviso by the offeror that such acceptance of the benefits will, in and of itself, be deemed by the offeror to be an acceptance. To put the problem in homely terms, may an offeree accept all of the benefits of a contract and then declare that he cannot be held liable for the burdens because he secretly had said, "King's Ex"? We think not. A rule with such effect would be unconscionable and is not in line with either fairness or justice. The correct rule, we believe, is found in § 72(2) of the Restatement of Contracts, wherein it is stated:

"Where the offeree exercises dominion over things which are offered to him, such exercise of dominion in the absence of other circumstances showing a contrary intention is an acceptance. *If circumstances indicate that the exercise of dominion is tortious the offeror may at his option treat it as an acceptance, though the offeree manifests an intention not to accept.*" (Emphasis added).

Russell's offer of the license in clear and unambiguous terms stated that the continued use of section 23 in connection with activities and operations on other lands would constitute an acceptance of the offer of the license. The trial court found on the evidence that The Texas Company did so continue to use section 23, and hence unequivocally came within the terms specified for acceptance. It is a well established principle of property law that the right to use the surface of land as an incident of the ownership of mineral rights in the land, does not carry with it the right to use the surface in aid of mining or drilling operations on other lands. . . . That such use by The Texas Company was tortious admits of no doubt. But even in the absence of a tortious use, the true test would be whether or not the offeror was reasonably led to believe that the act of the offeree was an acceptance, and upon the facts of this case it seems evident that even this test is met.

* * *

The conclusion reached by the trial court on this phase of the case was correct.

* * *

The judgment is affirmed as to both appellants. [The Court's discussion of issues raised by Russell's appeal is omitted.]

NOTES

(1) The court refers to authority dealing with "the necessity of the offeree's intent to accept where an ambiguous act is selected by the offeror to signify acceptance." Is the decision in *"Industrial America"*, supra at 305, inconsistent with this view?

(2) Was there a "meeting of minds" in *Russell?* Was there a manifestation of mutual assent?

(3) *Waiver of Tort and Suit in Assumpsit.* Offeror offers goods to Offeree upon specified terms. Offeree, without responding expressly to the offer, proceeds to exercise dominion over the goods, as, for example, by using them. What legal recourse is available to Offeror? Offeror might sue Offeree for the tort of conversion and recover damages. Might Offeror, however, sue for breach of contract? Prevailing authority indicates that this option might be available. Restatement (Second) § 69 provides: "An offeree who does any act inconsistent with the offeror's ownership of offered property is bound in accordance with the offered terms unless they are manifestly unreasonable. But if the act is wrongful as against the offeror it is an acceptance only if ratified by him." The use of the goods, albeit a wrongful use, can be construed as an implied acceptance of the offer. In effect, Offeror can treat Offeree as either a tortfeasor or a contract breaker.

The foregoing option grew out of a common law procedural alternative called "waiver of tort and suit in assumpsit." This process encompassed not only "implied acceptance" situations, but also those in which there was no outstanding offer. For instance, A steals goods belonging to B and sells them to C. It came to be recognized that B could "waive" the tort and sue in "assumpsit" under the fictitious assumption that A promised to restore to B benefits received from C. The remedy was essentially restitutionary in nature, designed to prevent A's unjust enrichment. Since the objective was the disgorgement of A's benefit, the amount of recovery might, if A made an advantageous sale to C, exceed the market value of the goods, the tort measure of recovery. Problems in this area are taken up in other law school courses.

(4) "We have not been cited to a case in this state involving the liability of a person who, though not having subscribed for a newspaper, continues to accept it by receiving it through the mail. There are, however, certain well-understood principles in the law of contracts that ought to solve the question. It is certain that one cannot be forced into contractual relations with another and that therefore he cannot, against his will, be made the debtor of a newspaper publisher. But it is equally certain that he may cause contractual relations to arise by necessary implication from his conduct. The law in respect of contractual indebtedness for a newspaper is not different from that relating to other things which have not been made the subject of an express agreement. Thus one may not have ordered supplies for his table, or other household necessities, yet if he continue to receive and use them, under circumstances where he had no right to suppose they were a gratuity, he will be held to have agreed, by implication, to pay their value. In this case defendant admits that,

notwithstanding he ordered the paper discontinued at the time when he paid a bill for it, yet plaintiff continued to send it, and he continued to take it from the post office to his home. This was an acceptance and use of the property, and, there being no pretense that a gratuity was intended, an obligation arose to pay for it." Austin v. Burge, 156 Mo.App. 286, 137 S.W. 618 (1911).

(5) *The Problem of Unordered Merchandise.* The widespread practice of sending unordered merchandise to prospective purchasers has elicited legislative responses at both the state and federal levels. As with the problem of "bait advertising," discussed supra at 252, general contract law has not operated as an effective control of the abusive practice. The Federal Trade Commission has become increasingly active in the area through issuance of cease and desist orders. These are based on findings that the methods employed constitute unfair and deceptive acts and practices in violation of Section 5 of the Federal Trade Commission Act. In addition, there is now a federal statute covering the shipment of unsolicited merchandise through the mails. It provides as follows:

(a) Except for (1) free samples clearly and conspicuously marked as such, and (2) merchandise mailed by a charitable organization soliciting contributions, the mailing of unordered merchandise or of communications prohibited by subsection (c) of this section constitutes an unfair method of competition and an unfair trade practice in violation of section 45(a)(1) of title 15 [§ 5 of Federal Trade Commission Act].

(b) Any merchandise mailed in violation of subsection (a) of this section, or within the exceptions contained therein, may be treated as a gift by the recipient, who shall have the right to retain, use, discard, or dispose of it in any manner he sees fit without any obligation whatsoever to the sender. All such merchandise shall have attached to it a clear and conspicuous statement informing the recipient that he may treat the merchandise as a gift to him and has the right to retain, use, discard, or dispose of it in any manner he sees fit without any obligation whatsoever to the sender.

(c) No mailer of any merchandise mailed in violation of subsection (a) of this section, or within the exceptions contained therein, shall mail to any recipient of such merchandise a bill for such merchandise or any dunning communications.

(d) For the purposes of this section, "unordered merchandise" means merchandise mailed without the prior expressed request or consent of the recipient. 39 U.S.C.A. § 3009. See Annot., *Validity, Construction, and Application of 39 U.S.C.A. § 3009, Making It an Unfair Trade Practice to Mail Unordered Merchandise*, 39 A.L.R.Fed. 674 (1978).

State authorities have also been responsive to this problem. An Illinois statute, for instance, reads as follows: "Unless otherwise agreed, where unsolicited goods are delivered to a person, he has a right to refuse to accept delivery of the goods and is not bound to return such goods to the sender. If such unsolicited goods are either addressed to or intended for the recipient, they shall be deemed a gift to the recipient, who may use them or dispose of them in any manner without any obligation to the sender." Smith–Hurd Ill.Ann.Stat. ch. 121½, § 351. See, generally, Comment, *Unsolicited Merchandise: State and Federal Remedies for a Consumer Problem*, 1970 Duke L.J. 991; J. Sheldon, Unfair and Deceptive Acts and Practices § 5.8.4 (2d ed.1988).

Ammons v. Wilson & Co.

Supreme Court of Mississippi, 1936.
176 Miss. 645, 170 So. 227.

■ ANDERSON, JUSTICE. Appellant brought this action in the circuit court of Bolivar county against appellee, a Delaware corporation engaged in the meat packing business with its principal office at Kansas City, Kansas, to recover the sum of six hundred and fifty-eight dollars and seventy-four cents—damages claimed by appellant and alleged to have been caused by appellee's breach of contract to ship appellant nine hundred and forty-two cases of shortening. Appellant testified in his own behalf, and was the only witness who testified in the case. At the conclusion of the evidence, on appellee's motion, the court excluded it and directed a verdict and judgment for appellee which were accordingly entered. From that judgment appellant prosecutes this appeal.

Appellant was engaged in the wholesale grocery business at Beulah in Bolivar county. Appellee, as stated, was engaged in the business of meat packing, part of which was the manufacture and sale of shortening. Appellant made the following case by his evidence: Appellee had one Tweedy as its traveling salesman in the territory including Bolivar county. On or about the 9th, 10th or 11th of August, 1934 (appellant could not make it more definite in his testimony), Tweedy "booked" him for sixty thousand pounds of shortening at seven and one-half cents per pound tierce basis. The booking meant nothing more than the appellee was willing to receive orders from appellant for shortening up to that amount at seven and one-half cents per pound tierce basis, such orders subject to acceptance by appellee, and that by the booking appellant was not bound to order all or any part of the sixty thousand pounds, nor was appellee bound to accept orders for all or any part thereof. In other words, the evidence showed that the booking neither constituted a contract nor an absolute offer to contract—it was merely tentative. On the 23rd and 24th of August appellant, through appellee's traveling salesman Tweedy, ordered for prompt shipment nine hundred and forty-two cases of shortening, aggregating forty-three thousand, nine hundred and sixteen pounds. These orders were sent in by Tweedy. Appellant heard nothing from them until the 4th of September following, when he was advised by appellee, in response to his inquiry as to when the shipment would be made, that the orders had been declined. At that time the price of shortening was nine cents instead of seven and one-half cents a pound. In other words, appellee waited twelve days from the time the orders were given before declining to accept them. Tweedy had represented appellee in that territory for six or eight months and during that time he had taken several orders from appellant for certain of appellee's products, which orders in every case had been accepted and shipped not later than one week from the time they were given.

The orders here involved, as well as prior ones, were in writing and contained this provision: "This order taken subject to acceptance by seller's authorized agent at point of shipment." Under this stipulation the orders constituted mere offers to purchase on appellant's part and were not binding on appellee until received and accepted. It is also true, as contended by appellee, that its traveling salesman Tweedy was without authority to make a binding contract for it. The extent of his authority was to solicit and transmit orders to his principal for approval. . . .

The question in the case is whether or not, under the law, appellee should be charged with an implied acceptance of the orders by its silence. As above stated, all of appellant's previous orders had been accepted and the goods shipped not later than a week from the giving of such orders, while appellee was silent for twelve days after the giving of the orders here involved, and then refused to accept them in response to appellant's request for shipment. We think the sound governing principles are laid down in Restatement, Contracts, subsection 1(c) of section 72, the applicable part of which is as follows:

"(1) Where an offeree fails to reply to an offer, his silence and inaction operate as an acceptance in the following cases and in no others: * * *

"(c) Where because of previous dealings or otherwise, the offeree has given the offeror reason to understand that the silence of [or] inaction is intended by the offeree as a manifestation of assent, and the offeror does so understand."

"Illustration of Subsection (1, c): 5. A, through salesmen, has frequently solicited orders for goods from B, the orders to be subject to A's personal approval. In every case A has shipped the goods ordered within a week and without other notification to B than billing the goods to him. A's salesman solicits and receives another order from B. A receives the order and remains silent. B relies on the order and forbears to buy elsewhere for a week. A is bound to fill the order."

We are not aware of any decisions of our court in conflict with these principles; certainly those relied on by appellee are not.

We are of the opinion that it was a question for the jury whether or not appellee's delay of twelve days before rejecting the orders, in view of the past history of such transactions between the parties, including the booking, constituted an implied acceptance. The evidence was rather uncertain as to the damages suffered by appellant on account of the alleged breach of contract. If there was a breach, appellant was entitled to at least nominal damages. If there were actual damages, it devolves on appellant to trace them directly to the breach of the contract and make them definite enough to comply with the governing rules of law.

Reversed and remanded.

NOTES

(1) *Silence as Assent.* If *A* offers to sell *B* a certain book for $5, and the latter remains silent, is the silence indicative of assent? Not necessarily. *B* may be weighing the proposal, mentally determining whether to accept or reject, or may be thinking about something else altogether. Hence, there is the general refusal of courts to regard silence, standing alone, as constituting acceptance.

But what if *A* adds: "If you say nothing I will know you accept." What objection is there then to holding *B* to a contract? Should the offeree be obliged to reply in order to prevent a contract? Finally, would there be any reason for objection to contract if *B*, taking *A* at his or her word, remained silent with the intention of accepting the offer?

(2) If it be conceded that an offeror, acting reasonably, should not ordinarily interpret silence to mean assent, what additional factors might alter the reasonable impression?

(3) Would the result in *Ammons* have been the same even if there had been no previous dealings? Most likely there would have been no contract. What, then, was the effect of the prior course of dealing? The court in *Ammons* held that the jury should decide whether there was an implied acceptance. How does the Restatement (Second) change that analysis? See Section 69, quoted in the next note.

(4) Restatement (Second) § 69, pertaining to acceptance by silence or exercise of dominion, provides as follows:

(1) Where an offeree fails to reply to an offer, his silence and inaction operate as an acceptance in the following cases only:

(a) Where an offeree takes the benefit of offered services with reasonable opportunity to reject them and reason to know that they were offered with the expectation of compensation.

(b) Where the offeror has stated or given the offeree reason to understand that assent may be manifested by silence or inaction, and the offeree in remaining silent and inactive intends to accept the offer.

(c) Where because of previous dealings or otherwise, it is reasonable that the offeree should notify the offeror if he does not intend to accept.

(2) An offeree who does any act inconsistent with the offeror's ownership of offered property is bound in accordance with the offered terms unless they are manifestly unreasonable. But if the act is wrongful as against the offeror it is an acceptance only if ratified by him.

(5) What is the difference between an express contract and a so-called implied-in-fact contract? In what sense might all contracts be regarded as "express"? Is there a sense in which all contracts are "implied"?

(6) *An Agent's Authority.* In *Ammons*, Tweedy, the traveling salesman, was an agent of Wilson & Co., but did not have the authority to bind the latter contractually. When does an agent have such authority? In brief, when the principal confers the authority (actual) or holds the agent out as having the authority (apparent).

As defined by the Restatement of Agency, authority is "the power of the agent to affect the legal relations of the principal by acts done in accordance with the principal's manifestations of consent to him." Restatement (Second) of Agency § 7 (1958). This actual authority may be express (i.e., spelled out by the principal in directions to the agent) or implied (i.e., inferred from directions to the agent, customs of trade, etc.)

Whereas actual authority, express or implied, derives from what the principal tells the agent, apparent authority results from the principal's manifestations to third persons. "To bind the principal * * * the one dealing with the agent must prove that the principal was responsible for the appearance of authority by doing something or permitting the agent to do something which reasonably led others, including the plaintiff, to believe that the agent had the authority he purported to have. If this is proved, the principal should have realized that his conduct would cause others to believe that the agent was authorized, and the principal and the other party are bound by the ordinary rules of contract, unless the other has notice that the agent was unauthorized." Seavey, Handbook of the Law of Agency 13 (1964). Obviously, the objective theory of contracts and the agency doctrine of apparent authority are compatible ideas.

Comment: The Role of Conduct in UCC Article 2

UCC 1–201(3) defines "agreement" as the "bargain of the parties in fact as found in their language or by implication from other circumstances including course of dealing or usage of trade or course of performance as provided in this Act (Sections 1–205, 2–208, ...). 'Contract' is defined as the 'total legal obligation which results from the parties' agreement as affected by this Act and any other applicable rules of law.' UCC 1–201(11). Where a claimed sale of goods or a lease of goods are involved, whether an agreement as defined in Article 1 is a contract depends upon the application of Article 2 or Article 2A of the UCC. In answering the formation question in a 'code covered' transaction, e.g., an alleged sale of goods, Article 1 and Article 2 may be read together.

Consider again the facts in *Ammons v. Wilson & Co.*, supra. The seller's agent, Tweedy, solicited an order of a specific quantity of goods at a fixed price from Ammons for "prompt shipment." This order was treated as an offer.

Under UCC 2–206(1)(a), the offer could be accepted by a "prompt promise to ship" or by the "prompt or current shipment of conforming goods ... " Thus, an invited method of acceptance is the conduct of shipment. Moreover, the "beginning of a requested performance", if reasonable, may also create a contract. UCC 2–206(2). This, however, is not the *Ammons* case.

To vary the facts a bit more, suppose the offer was for 942 cases of shortening and the seller responded by telephone that it could ship only 800 cases. At this point there is no contract but the seller has made a counteroffer to ship 800 cases which the seller can accept or reject. Suppose the buyer initially says no to the counteroffer but the seller, nevertheless, ships 800 cases and the buyer accepts them without objection. Is there a contract? See UCC 2–204(1). If so, what are the terms? More pointedly, what is the agreement upon which the contract rests? Clearly, it is at a minimum an agreement to buy 800 cases.

Return to *Ammons* where the offer was to buy 942 cases at 7 ½ cents per pound. Since Wilson neither shipped nor promised to ship (and in fact ultimately rejected the offer), is the failure to reject within a reasonable time an acceptance under Article 2? The answer depends on whether the seller has agreed to the buyer's proposed bargain and this turns on how one uses the prior course of dealing between the parties. Read UCC 1–205(1) & (3). Is that course of dealing "other circumstances" from which the seller's agreement to accept orders by silence unless a prompt rejection is given can be implied? If not, may the buyer turn to the protective arm of Section 69(1)(c) of the Restatement (Second)? We think that the answer to the first question is "probably not" but that the answer to the second question is yes.

(4) TIME WHEN ACCEPTANCE IS EFFECTIVE

Adams v. Lindsell

Court of King's Bench, 1818.
1 Barn. & Ald. 681, 106 Eng.Rep. 250.

Action for non-delivery of wool according to agreement. At the trial at the last Lent Assizes for the county of Worcester, before Burrough, J., it appeared that the defendants, who were dealers in wool, at St. Ives, in the county of Huntingdon, had, on Tuesday the 2d of September 1817, written the following letter to the plaintiffs, who were woolen manufacturers residing in Bromsgrove, Worcestershire. "We now offer you eight hundred tods of weather fleeces, of a good fair quality of our country wool, at 35s. 6d. per tod, to be delivered at Leicester, and to be paid for by two months' bill in two months, and to be weighed up by your agent within fourteen days, receiving your answer in course of post."

This letter was misdirected by the defendants, to Bromsgrove, Leicestershire, in consequence of which it was not received by the plaintiffs in Worcestershire till 7 P.M. on Friday, September 5th. On that evening the plaintiffs wrote an answer, agreeing to accept the wool on the terms proposed. The course of the post between St. Ives and Bromsgrove is through London, and consequently this answer was not received by the defendants till Tuesday, September 9th. On the Monday September 8th, the defendants not having, as they expected, received an answer on Sunday September 7th, (which in case their letter had not been misdirected, would have been in the usual course of post,) sold the wool in question to another person. Under these circumstances, the learned Judge held, that the delay having been occasioned by the neglect of the defendants, the jury must take it, that the answer did come back in due course of post; and that then the defendants were liable for the loss that had been sustained; and the plaintiffs accordingly recovered a verdict.

Jervis having in Easter term obtained a rule nisi for a new trial, on the ground that there was no binding contract between the parties.

Dauncey, Puller, and Richardson, showed cause. They contended, that at the moment of the acceptance of the offer of the defendants by the plaintiffs, the former became bound. And that was on the Friday evening, when there had been no change of circumstances. They were then stopped by the Court, who called upon Jervis and Campbell in support of the rule. They relied on Payne v. Cave (3 T.R. 148), and more particularly on Cooke

v. Oxley (Ibid. 653). In that case, Oxley, who had proposed to sell goods to Cooke, and given him a certain time at his request, to determine whether he would buy them or not, was held not liable to the performance of the contract, even though Cooke, within the specified time, had determined to buy them, and given Oxley notice to that effect. So here the defendants who have proposed by letter to sell this wool, are not to be held liable, even though it be now admitted that the answer did come back in due course of post. Till the plaintiffs' answer was actually received, there could be no binding contract between the parties; and before then, the defendants had retracted their offer, by selling the wool to other persons. But—

The Court said, that if that were so, no contract could ever be completed by the post. For if the defendants were not bound by their offer when accepted by the plaintiffs till the answer was received, then the plaintiffs ought not to be bound till after they had received notification that the defendants had received their answer and assented to it. And so it might go on ad infinitum. The defendants must be considered in law as making, during every instant of the time their letter was travelling, the same identical offer to the plaintiffs; and then the contract is completed by the acceptance of it by the latter. Then as to the delay in notifying the acceptance, that arises entirely from the mistake of the defendants, and it therefore must be taken as against them, that the plaintiffs' answer was received in course of post.

Rule discharged.

NOTES

(1) Exactly what did *Adams v. Lindsell* hold, that the contract was formed when the letter of acceptance was posted or something else?

A justification for forming the contract at the time of posting was attempted by an English court in 1879:

> There is no doubt that the implication of a complete, final, and absolutely binding contract being formed, as soon as the acceptance of an offer is posted, may in some cases lead to inconvenience and hardship. But such there must be at times in every view of the law. It is impossible in transactions which pass between parties at a distance, and have to be carried on through the medium of correspondence, to adjust conflicting rights between innocent parties, so as to make the consequences of mistake on the part of a mutual agent fall equally upon the shoulders of both. At the same time I am not prepared to admit that the implication in question will lead to any great or general inconvenience or hardship. An offeror, if he chooses, may always make the formation of the contract which he proposes dependent upon the actual communication to himself of the acceptance. If he trusts to the post he trusts to a means of communication which, as a rule, does not fail, and if no answer to his offer is received by him, and the matter is of importance to him, he can make inquiries of the person to whom his offer was addressed. On the other hand, if the contract is not finally concluded, except in the event of the acceptance actually reaching the offerer, the door would be opened to the perpetration of much

fraud, and, putting aside this consideration, considerable delay in commercial transactions, in which despatch, is as a rule, of the greatest consequence, would be occasioned; for the acceptor would never be entirely safe in acting upon his acceptance until he had received notice that his letter of acceptance had reached its destination.

Household Fire & Carriage Accident Insurance Co., Ltd. v. Grant (1879) 4 Ex.D. 216, 223–24. Is this persuasive? See G.H. Treitel, The Law of Contracts 23–29 (10th ed.1999) (describing the rule as arbitrary but workable).

(2) *Justifications for and Scope of the Mailbox Rule.* The so-called "mailbox" rule, derived from the landmark case of *Adams v. Lindsell* and others which followed, has gained almost universal acceptance in common law jurisdictions.

Restatement (Second) § 63(a) provides: "Unless the offer provides otherwise, (a) an acceptance made in a manner and by a medium invited by an offer is operative and completes the manifestation of mutual assent as soon as put out of the offeree's possession, without regard to whether it ever reaches the offeror; * * *."

A frontal attack upon the rule by the Court of Claims has apparently failed. In Rhode Island Tool Co. v. United States, 130 Ct.Cl. 698, 128 F.Supp. 417 (1955), the offeror, who had made a mistake in bid, communicated a withdrawal of the offer to the contracting officer after written notice of award was mailed but before it was received. The court, in holding that no contract was created, relied substantially upon revised postal regulations which gave the sender control over a letter up to delivery: "The acceptance, therefore, is not final until the letter reaches destination, since the sender has the absolute right of withdrawal from the post office, and even the right to have the postmaster at the delivery point return the letter at any time before actual delivery." Is this reasoning persuasive?

The mail-box rule, of course, is a default rule and the offeror can always require communication before the contract is formed. For a recent example of stipulation in an offer for receipt of acceptance, precluding application of "mailbox" rule, see Crane v. Timberbrook Village, Ltd., 774 P.2d 3 (Utah App.1989). Even so, what is the justification for ever holding an offeror to a bilateral contract before he or she knows of the acceptance? Perhaps a justification can be found in the fact that the rule is a default that can be contracted around by the offeror herself. The mail-box rule is a default that disadvantages the offeror, but the offeror to free opt out of this rule and condition acceptance on receipt.

Another problem of formation concerns the optimal number of confirmations. As recognized in Crook v. Cowan, 64 N.C. 743 (1870), the last person to confirm will always be at at an informational disadvantage because she will not know whether her confirmation got through:

> [I]f an offer and acceptance—an unconditional and specific order, and an exact fulfillment, as in this case, does not complete the contract, how would it be possible to complete a contract by mail? A sends an unconditional order to B, and instead of B's filling the order, he writes back that he accepts the order and will fill it, but in the meantime, A may have changed his mind, and lest he has, he must write back to B and so on, for ever....

[If we were to require such serial re-confirmations], no contract could ever be completed by post. For if the defendant was not bound by his offer, when accepted by the plaintiff, until the answer was received, then the plaintiff ought not to be bound until after he had received the notification that the defendant had received his answer and assented to it. And so it might go on *ad infinitum*.

Id. At 746. Another rationale for limiting the number of confirmations necessary to form a contract is that these confirmations do not reduce the chance of mistake, they merely shift it to the other side and waste social resources to boot. See Eric Talley, *Interdisciplinary Gap Filling*, 22 L. & Soc. Inquiry 1055 (1997).

The mailbox issue also arises with regard to counteroffers and revocations. But here the common law makes these communications effective when received instead of when sent. Restatement (Second) of Contract §§ 40, 42. Why? [Maybe because these rules are also defaults that are set against the person who has a unilateral power to opt out.]

If there is some justification, to what methods of communication and to what kind of facts should the "mailbox" rule be limited? For example, if an offer is sent by telegraph is a contract formed when an acceptance is mailed? Sent by carrier pigeon? Spoken into a telephone receiver? See UCC 2–206(1).

Similarly, should the "mailbox" rule apply to all of the following fact situations: offeree mails acceptance, offeror communicates revocation of offer before acceptance received; offeree mails acceptance which is lost and never received by offeror; offeree mails acceptance, changes mind and communicates rejection before offeror receives acceptance; offeree, in State A, mails an acceptance which is received by offeror in State B—offeree claims that law of State A governs because that is where the contract was formed? These problems are well discussed in Ian Macneil, *Time of Acceptance: Too Many Problems for a Single Rule,* 112 U.Pa.L.Rev. 947 (1964).

§ 40 of the Restatement of Contracts creates a limited exception to the mail box rule when sending of acceptance is preceded by previous sending of counteroffer or revocation. See the "Acceptance Race" Problem, *infra* at p. 366.

(3) *Electronic Communication and the Demise of the "Mailbox" Rule?* As time goes on, more and more contracting will be by electronic transmission where communication is virtually instantaneous. Under such circumstances, there is good reason for holding that an acceptance is effective when received, not when transmitted. The authors of an influential study observed that an important premise upon which the "mailbox" rule is predicated is the notion that delayed media, such as mailed writings, do not provide either party the ability to verify in a timely fashion that receipt of a message has occurred and that the message as received is without error. Hence, they maintain that electronic transmission should be governed by the same rules that apply when parties are in the presence of each other and the acceptance should be deemed effective when received. See *The Commercial Use of Electronic Data Interchange—A Report and Model Trading Partner Agreement,* 45 Bus.Law. 1645, 1666–67 (1990).

The "effective when received" rule is implicit in the treatment of contracting by computer in Rev. 2–204(4), which is derived from Section 14 of the Uniform Electronic Transactions Act. See also Rev. 2–211 through 2–213.

(4) *Civil Law and International Law Treatment.* While generalization is risky, it seems that other legal systems, particularly the civil law, are more willing to enforce an offeror's statement that the offer is "irrevocable" without the presence of formality, bargain or reliance than the common law. See 1 Rudolph Schlesinger, Formation of Contracts: A Study of the Common Core of Legal Systems 109–11, 747–91 (1968).

There is clearly some correlation between the irrevocability of an offer and the willingness of a particular legal system to hold that a contract is created when the acceptance is mailed. Thus, in Austria and Germany where offers are normally irrevocable, a contract is not formed until the acceptance is received by the offeror since there is "no necessity for fixing an earlier moment for the acceptance in order to protect the offeree against possible speculations of the offeror." Schlesinger, supra at 159. As we shall see, the common law starts from the premise that an offer stated to be "irrevocable" is nevertheless revocable unless accompanied by authorized formality, consideration or reliance.

Could it be that the "mailbox" rule evolved as a common law substitute for the civil law doctrine of irrevocability? Put another way, does the "mailbox" rule make the most sense when employed to protect the offeree's opportunity to make a sound decision against an unexpected revocation? If so, should it be extended to fact patterns where no threat of revocation is involved? If, as we shall see, the doctrine of promissory estoppel is increasingly invoked to protect the relying offeree against precipitous revocation, is there any real need for a "mailbox" rule?

Articles 16(2) and 18(2) of the Convention on Contracts for the International Sale of Goods (CISG) are more consistent with the civil law. Note that while Article 18(2) states that an acceptance is not effective until it "reaches" the offeror, Article 16(2) states that an offer cannot be revoked after the offeree has "dispatched" the acceptance. The UNIDROIT Principles of International Commercial Contracts are in accord. See Artices 2.4(2) and 2.6(2).

(5) Assume that upon receipt of a written "Offer and Acceptance" signed by Purchaser, Vendor signed as seller and deposited the writing in the mail, properly addressed to Purchaser. Before the letter arrived Vendor telephoned Purchaser that he had decided not to sell. Was there a binding contract? Cf. Morrison v. Thoelke, 155 So.2d 889 (Fla.App.1963).

PROBLEM: ACCEPTANCE OF RESIGNATION BY MAIL

In July, 1990 Carol was hired as a special education teacher by the Huron School District for the 1990–91 school year. On August 15, 1990, Carol handed to Ed, her supervisor, a letter of resignation effective on August 17, 1990. In the letter she requested that her final check be mailed to an address some fifty miles away (her parents home). Ed gave the letter to Mary, the superintendent with authority to hire and fire, on August 20. That same day, Mary prepared and mailed a letter properly addressed to Carol at her parents accepting the resignation. The next day Carol hand delivered a letter to Mary withdrawing her resignation. Mary told Carol that the resignation had been accepted and handed her a copy of the letter mailed the day before. That letter did not reach Carol's parents' home until August 24. Carol claims that the resignation had been withdrawn in time because the acceptance letter should have been handed to her.

(1) What are the strongest arguments for the School District? How should the court decide? See Cantu v. Central Education Agency, 884 S.W.2d 565 (Tex.App.1994).

(2) Suppose Carol had sent a telegram of resignation from her parents' home and Mary had mailed a letter of acceptance to that address. Before the letter arrived, Carol revoked the resignation by e-mail.

(3) Suppose Carol had telephoned Mary but when Mary was "not available to take your call," Carol left the resignation on Mary's voice mail. How should Mary accept the resignation on these facts? Suppose the resignation came by facsimile? See Equity Fire & Casualty Co. v. Traver, 330 Ark. 102, 953 S.W.2d 565 (1997) (where offer by Fax stated that acceptance must be received, mailing an acceptance did not create a contract).

(5) NATURE AND EFFECT OF COUNTER–OFFER

Minneapolis & St. Louis Railway Co. v. Columbus Rolling–Mill Co.

Supreme Court of the United States, 1886.
119 U.S. 149, 7 S.Ct. 168, 30 L.Ed. 376.

This was an action by a railroad corporation established at Minneapolis in the State of Minnesota against a manufacturing corporation established at Columbus in the State of Ohio. The petition alleged that on December 19, 1879, the parties made a contract by which the plaintiff agreed to buy of the defendant, and the defendant sold to the plaintiff, two thousand tons of iron rails of the weight of fifty pounds per yard, at the price of fifty-four dollars per ton gross, to be delivered free on board cars at the defendant's rolling mill in the month of March, 1880, and to be paid for by the plaintiff in cash when so delivered. The answer denied the making of the contract. It was admitted at the trial that the following letters and telegrams were sent at their dates, and were received in due course, by the parties, through their agents.

December 5, 1879. Letter from plaintiff to defendant: "Please quote me prices for 500 to 3000 tons 50 lb. steel rails, and for 2000 to 5000 tons 50 lb. iron rails, March 1880 delivery."

December 8, 1879. Letter from defendant to plaintiff: "Your favor of the 5th inst. at hand. We do not make steel rails. For iron rails, we will sell 2000 to 5000 tons of 50 lb. rails for fifty-four ($54.00) dollars per gross ton for spot cash, F.O.B. cars at our mill, March delivery, subject as follows: In case of strike among our workmen, destruction of or serious damage to our works by fire or the elements, or any causes of delay beyond our control, we shall not be held accountable in damages. If our offer is accepted, shall expect to be notified of same prior to Dec. 20th, 1879."

December 16, 1879. Telegram from plaintiff to defendant: "Please enter our order for twelve hundred tons rails, March delivery, as per your favor of the eighth. Please reply."

December 16, 1879. Letter from plaintiff to defendant: "Yours of the 8th came duly to hand. I telegraphed you to-day to enter our order for twelve hundred (1200) tons 50 lb. iron rails for next March delivery, at fifty-four dollars ($54.00) F.O.B. cars at your mill. Please send contract. Also please send me templet of your 50 lb. rail. Do you make splices? If so, give me prices for splices for this lot of iron."

December 18, 1879. Telegram from defendant to plaintiff received same day: "We cannot book your order at present at that price."

December 19, 1879. Telegram from plaintiff to defendant: "Please enter an order for two thousand tons rails, as per your letter of the sixth. Please forward written contract. Reply." (The word "sixth" was admitted to be a mistake for "eighth.")

December 22, 1879. Telegram from plaintiff to defendant: "Did you enter my order for two thousand tons rails, as per my telegram of December nineteenth? Answer."

After repeated similar inquiries by the plaintiff, the defendant, on January 19, 1880, denied the existence of any contract between the parties.

The jury returned a verdict for the defendant, under instructions which need not be particularly stated; and the plaintiff alleged exceptions, and sued out this writ of error.

Mr. Justice Gray, after making the foregoing statement of the case, delivered the opinion of the court.

The rules of law which govern this case are well settled. As no contract is complete without the mutual assent of the parties, an offer to sell imposes no obligation until it is accepted according to its terms. So long as the offer has been neither accepted nor rejected, the negotiation remains open, and imposes no obligation upon either party; the one may decline to accept, or the other may withdraw his offer; and either rejection or withdrawal leaves the matter as if no offer had ever been made. A proposal to accept, or an acceptance, upon terms varying from those offered, is a rejection of the offer, and puts an end to the negotiation, unless the party who made the original offer renews it, or assents to the modification suggested. The other party, having once rejected the offer, cannot afterwards revive it by tendering an acceptance of it. ... If the offer does not limit the time for its acceptance, it must be accepted within a reasonable time. If it does, it may, at any time within the limit and so long as it remains open, be accepted or rejected by the party to whom, or be withdrawn by the party by whom, it was made. ...

The defendant, by the letter of December 8, offered to sell to the plaintiff two thousand to five thousand tons of iron rails on certain terms specified, and added that if the offer was accepted the defendant would expect to be notified prior to December 20. This offer, while it remained open, without having been rejected by the plaintiff or revoked by the defendant, would authorize the plaintiff to take at his election any number of tons not less than two thousand nor more than five thousand, on the terms specified. The offer, while unrevoked, might be accepted, or rejected by the plaintiff at any time before December 20. Instead of accepting the offer made, the plaintiff, on December 16, by telegram and letter, referring to the defendant's letter of December 8, directed the defendant to enter an order for twelve hundred tons on the same terms. The mention, in both telegram and letter, of the date and the terms of the defendant's original offer, shows that the plaintiff's order was not an independent proposal, but an answer to the defendant's offer, a qualified acceptance of that offer, varying the number of tons, and therefore in law a rejection of the offer. On December 18, the defendant by telegram declined to fulfil the plaintiff's order. The negotiation between the parties was thus closed, and the plaintiff could not afterwards fall back on the defendant's original offer. The plaintiff's attempt to do so, by the telegram of December 19, was therefore ineffectual and created no rights against the defendant.

Such being the legal effect of what passed in writing between the parties, it is unnecessary to consider whether, upon a fair interpretation of the instructions of the court, the question whether the plaintiff's telegram and letter of December 16 constituted a rejection of the defendant's offer of December 8 was ruled in favor of the defendant as a matter of law, or was submitted to the jury as a question of fact. The submission of a question of law to the jury is no ground of exception if they decide it aright....

Judgment affirmed.

NOTES

(1) *Common Law Mirror Image Rule.* "When the plaintiffs submitted this offer in their letter of April 4th to the defendant, only one of two courses of action was open to the defendant. It could accept the offer made and thus manifest that assent which was essential to the creation of a contract, or it could reject the offer. There was no middle course. * * * A proposal to accept the offer it modified or an acceptance subject to other terms and conditions was equivalent to an absolute rejection of the offer made by the plaintiffs." Poel v. Brunswick–Balke–Collender Co., 216 N.Y. 310, 110 N.E. 619, 622 (1915). In so speaking the New York Court of Appeals was simply reaffirming settled doctrine that for a valid bargain contract there must be an offer and an acceptance, with the acceptance expressing unconditional assent to the terms of the offer. An offeree cannot pick and choose from among the terms, agreeing here and disagreeing there, and then assert the existence of an operative acceptance. If the terms are varied or changed, there is a counter-offer. No contract can arise until agreement is reached as to those changes; i.e., until the counter-offer has itself been accepted. Traditionally, courts have insisted upon total congruence between offer and acceptance, the latter required to be the "mirror image" of the former. Even a non-material variation is fatal. See Minar v. Skoog, 235 Minn. 262, 50 N.W.2d 300, 302 (1951) (valid acceptance must

embrace terms of offer with exactitude and unequivocally express an intent to create without more a contract).

(2) *Effect of requests or suggestions.* Although a reply which purports to be an acceptance but which adds qualifications or requires performance of conditions is not an acceptance, but a counter-offer, Restatement (Second) § 59, an acceptance which *requests* a change or addition to the terms of the offer is not invalidated unless the acceptance is made to depend on an assent to the changed or added terms. Restatement (Second) § 61. There is a considerable body of law differentiating a so-called "conditional" acceptance, which is really no acceptance at all, from a genuine acceptance accompanied by mere "inquiries," "requests," or "suggestions" of the offeree. See, e.g., Valashinas v. Koniuto, 308 N.Y. 233, 124 N.E.2d 300 (1954). Finally, it must be borne in mind that an added term or qualifier in the acceptance may be no more than a repetition of what is already contained, expressly or impliedly, in the offer. United States v. National Optical Stores Co., 407 F.2d 759 (7th Cir.1969) is illustrative. The federal government's notice of acceptance was made subject to approval of credit and antitrust clearance by the Department of Justice. But these two conditions were found to be incorporated in the bid itself. The court concluded: "Since defendant's bid promise included the credit data and antitrust conditions and was accepted by the Government, both parties then became bound in accordance with the mutual assent they had expressed. * * * The Government's letter * * * imposed no additional or different terms from those offered and was therefore not a counter-offer." 407 F.2d at 761.

(3) *Whose Default?* Like many of the formation rules, the idea that a counteroffer terminates an offeree's power of acceptance is a default rule which can be contracted around unilaterally by *either* the offeror or offeree:. "An offeree's power of acceptance is terminated by his making of a counter-offer, unless the offeror has manifested a contrary intention or unless the counter-offer manifests a contrary intention of the offeree." Restatement (Second) of Contracts § 39(2). But what happens if the original offer explicitly states that any counteroffer terminates the offer, but the offeree nonetheless counteroffers expressly manifesting an intention to retain her power of acceptance?

(4) *The "Grumbling" Acceptance.* In Panhandle Eastern Pipe Line Co. v. Smith, 637 P.2d 1020 (Wyo.1981), an employer (Panhandle) fired an employee (Smith). The latter, following the grievance procedure of a collective bargaining agreement, unsuccessfully challenged the dismissal. However, Mr. Smith's union representative requested Panhandle to reconsider, and the latter responded with a letter to Smith in which it offered to withdraw the discharge if he would comply with certain terms and conditions. Smith signed under the typewritten words, "Understood, Agreed to and Accepted," added some handwritten notations, and again signed his name. The notations contained a request by Smith to see his personnel file and to contest any mistakes he found there. Panhandle contended that Smith, by adding the request to see his personnel file and to contest mistakes, made a counter-offer. The Wyoming Supreme Court disagreed. There was testimony that all Panhandle employees had a right to see their personnel files, and while the court acknowledged that the acceptance was what Corbin once referred to as a "grumbling" acceptance, it was an acceptance nonetheless.

(5) *The Battle of Forms, Mirror Image and UCC 2–207.* In *Minneapolis & St. Louis Railway Co*, supra, the parties, who were at a distance, exchanged letters and telegrams. The terms of these writings were read and responded to. But the contract failed because of a disagreement over a material, negotiated term, the quantity of steel to be sold.

In many transactions, the writings of the parties may be a bit more complex. The buyer's purchase order and the seller's acknowledgment may be standard forms that contain terms that are not read or negotiated over by the other party. Put differently, these terms are in the pre-printed "boiler plate" and are drafted by one party in their own interest. Sometimes these terms add to terms in the offer of the other party or to an agreement previously reached. Sometimes these terms contradict other terms. In all cases, however, the party drafting the terms will claim that they are part of the agreement.

In resolving disputes of this sort, keep your eye on three questions: (1) Was any contract formed between the parties; (2) If so, what are its terms; and (3) What commercial policies explain (or should explain) UCC 2–207? Consider the words of one court:

> The problem underlying any "battle of the forms" is that parties engaged in commerce have failed to incorporate into one formal, signed contract the terms of their contractual relationship. Instead, each has been content to rely upon standard terms which each has included in its purchase orders or acknowledgments, terms which often conflict with those in the other party's documents. Usually, these standard terms mean little, for a contract looks to its fulfillment and rarely anticipates its breach. Hope springs eternal in the commercial world and expectations are usually, but not always, realized. It is only when the good faith expectations of the parties are frustrated that the legal obligations and rights of the parties must be precisely determined. This case presents a situation typical in any battle of the forms: it is not that the parties' forms have said too little, but rather that they have said too much yet have expressly agreed upon too little.

McJunkin Corporation v. Mechanicals, Inc., 888 F.2d 481, 482 (6th Cir. 1989).

Leonard Pevar Company v. Evans Products Co.

United States District Court, D. Delaware, 1981.
524 F.Supp. 546.

■ LATCHUM, CHIEF JUDGE.

This is a diversity action by the Leonard Pevar Company ("Pevar") against the Evans Products Company ("Evans") for an alleged breach of express and implied warranties in Evans' sale to Pevar of medium density overlay plywood. Defendant denies liability, claiming that it expressly disclaimed warranties and limited its liability in its contract with Pevar. The parties agree that their respective rights and liabilities in this action are governed by the Uniform Commercial Code. The parties have filed cross motions for summary judgment pursuant to Rule 56, F.R.Civ.P. This Court will deny both motions because it finds material facts that are in genuine dispute.

* * *

In the fall of 1977, Pevar began obtaining price quotations for the purchase of medium density overlay plywood to be used in the construction of certain buildings for the State of Pennsylvania. As part of this process, Pevar's contract administrator, Marc Pevar, contacted various manufacturers of this product. Evans was one of the manufacturers contacted and was the supplier that quoted the lowest price for this material.

On October 12, 1977, Marc Pevar had a telephone conversation with Kenneth Kruger of Evans to obtain this price quotation. It is at this juncture that a material fact appears in dispute that precludes this Court from granting summary judgment. Pevar claims that on October 14 it again called Evans, ordered plywood, and entered into an oral contract of sale. Evans admits that Pevar called Evans, but denies that Evans accepted that order.

After the October 14th telephone conversation, Pevar sent a written purchase order to Evans for the plywood. In the purchase order, Pevar did not make any reference to warranties or remedies, but simply ordered the lumber specifying the price, quantity and shipping instructions. On October 19, 1979, Evans sent an acknowledgment to Pevar stating, on the reverse side of the acknowledgment and in boilerplate fashion, that the contract of sale would be expressly contingent upon Pevar's acceptance of all terms contained in the document.[12] One of these terms disclaimed most warranties and another limited the "buyer's remedy" by restricting liability if the plywood proved to be defective.[13]

* * *

Turning now to Section 2–207, it provides:

(1) A definite and seasonable expression of acceptance or a written confirmation which is sent within a reasonable time operates as an acceptance even though it states terms additional to or different from

---

12. Paragraph 1 of the Acknowledgment provided:

> Any acceptance by Seller contained herein is expressly made conditional on Buyer's assent to the additional or different terms contained herein. Any acceptance by Buyer contained herein is expressly limited to the terms herein.

See D.I. 4, Exhibit B.

13. Both of these terms were in boldface type:

> Unless seller delivers to buyer a separate written warranty with respect to goods, to the extent legally permissible the sale of all goods is "as is" and there is hereby

excluded and seller hereby disclaims any express or implied warranty, including, without limiting the generality of the foregoing, any implied warranty of merchantability or any implied warranty of fitness for any particular use or purpose; provided, however, there is not hereby excluded or disclaimed any implied warranty that seller owns goods or any implied warranty that goods are free from any security interest or other lien or encumbrance of which buyer has no knowledge at the time of contracting to buy such goods.

those offered or agreed upon, unless acceptance is expressly made conditional on assent to the additional or different terms.

(2) The additional terms are to be construed as proposals for addition to the contract. Between merchants such terms become part of the contract unless:

   (a) the offer expressly limits acceptance to the terms of the offer;

   (b) they materially alter it; or

   (c) notification of objection to them has already been given or is given within a reasonable time after notice of them is received.

(3) Conduct by both parties which recognizes the existence of a contract is sufficient to establish a contract for sale although the writings of the parties do not otherwise establish a contract. In such case the terms of the particular contract consists of those terms on which the writings of the parties agree, together with any supplementary terms incorporated under any other provisions of this Act.

Section 2–207 was intended to eliminate the "ribbon matching" or "mirror" rule of common law, under which the terms of an acceptance or confirmation were required to be identical to the terms of the offer or oral agreement, respectively ... The drafters of the Code intended to preserve an agreement, as it was originally conceived by the parties, in the face of additional material terms included in standard forms exchanged by merchants in the normal course of dealings. ... Section 2–207 recognizes that a buyer and seller can enter into a contract by one of three methods. First, the parties may agree orally and thereafter send confirmatory memoranda. § 2–207(1). Second, the parties, without oral agreement, may exchange writings which do not contain identical terms, but nevertheless constitute a seasonable acceptance. § 2–207(1). Third, the conduct of the parties may recognize the existence of a contract, despite the previous failure to agree orally or in writing. § 2–207(3).

A.   *Oral agreement followed by confirmation.*

Section 2–207(1) applies to those situations where an "oral agreement has been reached ... followed by one or both of the parties sending formal memoranda embodying the terms so far as agreed upon and adding terms not discussed." Uniform Commercial Code, Comment 1 to § 2–207. These additional terms are treated as proposals under 2–207(2) and will become part of the agreement unless they materially alter it.

In the present case, paragraphs 9 and 12 of Evans' acknowledgment, which disclaimed warranties and limited liability,[18] may include terms not in the original agreement. Generally, these types of clauses "materially alter" the agreement. Uniform Commercial Code, Comment 4 to § 2–207. Nevertheless, the question of a material alteration rests upon the facts of each case.[19] *See Dorton,* supra, 453 F.2d at 1169 n. 8; Medical Development

Material Alteration

---

18.   *See* note 13 *supra.*

19.   Therefore, even if there were no dispute that the oral agreement existed, the

Corp. v. Industrial Molding Corp., 479 F.2d 345, 348 (C.A.10, 1973); *Ebasco Services Inc. v. Pennsylvania Power & Light Co.*, 402 F.Supp. 421, 442 (E.D.Pa.1975). If the trier of fact determines that the acknowledgment includes additional terms which do not materially alter the oral agreement, then the terms will be incorporated into the agreement. If they materially alter it, however, the terms will not be included in the agreement, and the standardized "gap filler" provisions of Article Two will provide the terms of the contract. If the facts reveal that no oral agreement was created, then § 2–207(1) may still apply, but in a different manner.

Gap Filler provisions

B. *Written documents not containing identical terms.*

The second situation in which § 2–207(1) may apply is where the parties have not entered into an oral agreement but have exchanged writings which do not contain identical terms. If the Court determines that Pevar and Evans did not orally agree prior to the exchange of documents, then this second situation may apply. In such a case, both Pevar and Evans agree that Pevar's purchase order constituted an offer to purchase. The parties, however, disagree with the characterization of Evans' acknowledgment and Pevar's acceptance of and payment for the shipped goods. Evans contends that the terms disclaiming warranties and limiting liability in the acknowledgment should control because the acknowledgment constituted a counteroffer which Pevar accepted by receiving and paying for the goods. Evans argues that by inserting the "unless" proviso[20] in the terms and conditions of acceptance of the acknowledgment, it effectively rejected and terminated Pevar's offer, and initiated a counteroffer; and when Pevar received and paid for the goods, it accepted the terms of the counteroffer.

Evans relies upon *Roto–Lith, Ltd. v. F.P. Bartlett & Co.*, 297 F.2d 497 (C.A.1, 1962) for the proposition that a buyer accepts the terms of the seller's counteroffer merely by receiving and paying for shipped goods. In *Roto–Lith*, the buyer of goods sent a written purchase order to the seller. The seller thereafter sent an acknowledgment, accepting the purchase order in part, but also added terms which disclaimed warranties and limited liabilities. The buyer received the goods but did not object to the seller's terms. The court found that the seller's acceptance (acknowledgment) was expressly conditional on assent to the additional terms and, therefore, a counteroffer. It held that the buyer accepted the terms of the counteroffer when it received and paid for the goods.

Roto–Lith has been widely criticized because it does not reflect the underlying principles of the Code. Rather, it reflects the orthodox common law reasoning—that the terms of the counteroffer control if the goods are accepted unless the counter-offeree specifically objects to those terms. The drafters of the Code, however, intended to change the common law in an attempt to conform contract law to modern day business transactions. They

question of materiality would preclude the Court from granting summary judgment.

20. Section 2–207(1) "unless" proviso provides: "unless acceptance is expressly made conditional on assent to the additional or different terms." Evans followed this language in its acknowledgment.

believed that businessmen rarely read the terms on the back of standardized forms and that the common law, therefore, unduly rewarded the party who sent the last form prior to the shipping of the goods. The Code disfavors any attempt by one party to impose unilaterally conditions that would create hardship on another party. Thus, before a counteroffer is accepted, the counter-offeree must expressly assent to the new terms.

When CO made, new terms MUST be accepted

This Court joins those courts that have rejected the *Roto–Lith* analysis.... "It finds that [t]he consequence of a clause conditioning acceptance on assent to the additional or different terms is that *as of the exchanged writings there is no contract.* Either party may at this point in their dealing walk away from the transaction" or reach an express assent. *Itoh,* at 1236, *quoting Duesenberg & King, Sales & Bulk Transfer* (Bender) § 3.06(3) at 73. Without the express assent by the parties no contract is created pursuant to § 2–207(1).[21] Nevertheless, the parties' conduct may create a contract pursuant to § 2–207(3).

C.   *Conduct establishing the existence of a contract.*

Section 2–207(3) is the third method by which parties may enter into a contract. This section applies when the parties have not entered into an oral or written contract. Section 2–207(3) provides that "[c]onduct by both parties which recognizes the existence of a contract is sufficient to establish a contract for sale although the writing of the parties do not otherwise establish a contract." As *Dorton,* supra, 453 F.2d at 1166 noted:

> When no contract is recognized under Subsection 2–207(1) ... the entire transaction aborts at this point. If, however, the subsequent conduct of the parties—particularly, performance by both parties under what they apparently believe to be a contract—recognizes the existence of a contract, under Subsection 2–207(3), such conduct by both parties is sufficient to establish a contract, notwithstanding the fact that no contract would have been recognized on the basis of their writings alone.

> Section 2–207(3) also provides that where a contract has been consummated by the conduct of the parties, "the terms of the particular contract consist of those terms in which the writings of the parties agree, together with any supplementary terms incorporated under any other provisions of this Act."

---

21. Pevar and Evans had conversations subsequent to the shipping of the goods where Pevar did not object to the terms of Evans' acknowledgment. Evans, relying upon *Construction Aggregates,* supra, contends that Pevar's failure to object to the acknowledgment during these subsequent conversations constitutes an implicit acceptance of those terms. The facts in *Construction Aggregates* are readily distinguishable from the facts in this case. In that case, the buyer specifically objected to some terms of the acknowledgment, while remaining silent on the others. The court found that the purchaser thereby agreed to those terms in which it remained silent. Contrasting *Construction Aggregates,* Pevar and Evans did not specifically discuss Evans' acknowledgment. Thus, there is no basis to hold that Pevar consented to those terms.

In this case, the parties' conduct indicates that they recognized the existence of a contract. If this Court finds after trial that Pevar and Evans did not enter into an oral agreement, Section 2–207(3) will apply. The terms of the contract will include those terms in which Pevar's purchase order and Evans' acknowledgment agree. For those terms where the writings do not agree, the standardized "gap filler" provisions of Article Two will provide the terms of the contract. *Itoh*, supra, 552 F.2d at 1237.[22]

An Order will be entered in accordance with this Memorandum Opinion.

NOTES

(1) Although disputes like that in *Pevar* are frequently called a "battle of the forms," UCC 2–207 neither defines "standard forms" nor limits its application to standard form contracts. Does this mean that UCC 2–207 applies to disputes like that in *Minneapolis & St. Louis Ry. Co.*, supra? If so, how would the dispute in that case be resolved under UCC 2–207? Can there ever be a "definite acceptance" when the purported acceptance materially varies the quantity or price terms?

(2) *Routes to contract formation.* There are at least three routes to contract formation in UCC 2–207, the first before the comma in subsection (1) and the second in subsection (3). The first varies the common law "mirror image" rule but the second is consistent with prior law. See UCC 2–204(1).

The third route opens after the comma in subsection (1). Suppose that the offeree sends a response with additional or different terms and states clearly "this acceptance is conditioned upon the offeror agreeing to the additional or different terms." This is a counteroffer, right? See UCC 2–207(1), after the comma. How can it be accepted? If the goods are not shipped to and accepted by the buyer, acceptance of the counteroffer would be by words of assent. Silence would not do it. See *Textile Unlimited v. A..BMH & Co.*, infra at 336.

Suppose, however, the offeree, a seller, ships the goods and the buyer accepts them. Does the buyer's conduct accept the counteroffer? Or is this a case for the application of UCC 2–207(3)? Although early decisions interpreting UCC 2–207 held that the counteroffer was accepted by conduct, the preferred view is that UCC 2–207(3) controls in all cases where no contract is formed under subsection (1) and the seller ships and the buyer accepts the goods. See JOM, Inc. v. Adell Plastics, Inc., 193 F.3d 47, 52–59 (1st Cir.1999).

(3) It has been said that UCC 2–207(1) is "unusually poorly drafted as it applies to written confirmations." Utz, *More on the Battle of the Forms: The Treatment of "Different" Terms Under the Uniform Commercial Code*, 16 U.C.C.L.J. 103, 105, n. 5 (1983). The written confirmation is said to operate as an acceptance even though it states terms at variance with those agreed upon. But if the parties reached a prior agreement, was there not a prior acceptance? Note that a written confirmation may salvage an oral agreement otherwise within the statute of frauds. UCC 2–201(2).

---

22. See e.g., §§ 2–314, 315 & 715.

(4) What is the rationale for concluding that a seller's acknowledgment might operate as an acceptance even if it contains variant terms; e.g., disclaimer of warranty? How might a seller make certain that the response is not so interpreted? Should language such as that contained in Evans' acknowledgment suffice? On the need for explicit language of condition, see Idaho Power Co. v. Westinghouse Electric Corp., 596 F.2d 924 (9th Cir.1979); Dorton v. Collins & Aikman Corp., 453 F.2d 1161 (6th Cir.1972).

(5) *What are the terms of the contract?* In most cases under UCC 2–207 a contract has been formed and the dispute is over what terms are part of the contract. What are the terms of the following contracts:

(a) B makes an offer to buy goods on a purchase order which, on the back in smaller type, provides that seller shall pay "liquidated damages" in the amount of $500 for each day of delayed delivery. Assume that clause, if agreed to, would be enforceable. See UCC 2–718(1). S responds by telegram and "accepts" the offer. There are no additional or different terms. S breaches the contract by a 20 day delay in delivery.

(b) B makes an offer to buy goods on a purchase order. S sends an acknowledgment which accepts the offer and contains a form clause on the back that purports to exclude all liability for consequential damages resulting from the delay. Assume that the clause, if agreed to, would be enforceable. See UCC 2–719(3). S ships the goods and B accepts and uses them. Due to nonconformities, B suffers consequential losses of $50,000. Is the "excluder" term part of the contract? Should the question be answered under UCC 2–207(2) or 2–207(3)? What is the difference?

(c) Suppose B makes an offer to buy goods. On the back of the purchase order is a form clause that S shall pay $500 per day for consequential damages caused by delay in delivery. S responds by an acknowledgment that accepts the offer, but the acknowledgment provides (on the back in a form term) that the seller shall not be liable for consequential damages caused by any delay in delivery. S is 20 days late in delivery and B, invoking its liquidated damage clause, sues for $10,000. Should the question be answered under UCC 2–207(2) or (3)? What is the difference?

It is to be noted that UCC 2–207(1) uses the phrase "terms additional to or different from" but that subsection (2) refers to "additional" terms. It is generally assumed that both types of variant terms should be disposed of in accordance with the rules of subsection (2). However, the omission of "different" from subsection (2) has influenced some courts to apply a so-called "knock out" doctrine, whereby even if a contract is formed under subsection (1), the terms of the contract are not those contained in the "offer" plus whatever terms are added by reason of subsection (2), but those upon which the "forms" agree. That is, the differing terms cancel each other. See, e.g., Northrop Corp. v. Litronic Industries, 29 F.3d 1173 (7th Cir.1994); Daitom, Inc. v. Pennwalt Corp., 741 F.2d 1569 (10th Cir.1984). Where is the statutory basis for this? If the "different" terms in the "acceptance" are not handled under subsection (2), they should drop out altogether.

(6) The *Pevar* court says that even if an oral agreement existed, the question of materiality would preclude the court from granting summary judgment. Why? Because of doubt as to whether the terms were material?

There has been extensive litigation as to whether particular terms (e.g., disclaimer of warranty, arbitration clauses) constitute a material alteration, resulting in a bewildering array of precedent.

(7) *International Contracts and Sales.* Despite the fact that form contracts and terms are used by both seller and buyer in international sales, CISG rejected the approach of UCC 2–207. Thus, Article 19(1) provides:

A reply to an offer which purports to be an acceptance but contains additions, limitations or other modifications is a rejection of the offer and constitutes a counter-offer.

Article 19(2) states that a contract may be created if a purported acceptance "contains additional or different terms which do not materially alter the terms of the offer," and Article 19(3) attempts to state the terms that are considered to alter the terms of an offer materially. A notable inclusion is terms relating to the settlement of disputes, such as arbitration provisions.

Article 2.11 of the Unidroit Principles of International Commercial Contracts follows CISG Art. 19 up to a point. Special rules, however, are applicable to contracting under standard terms. See Art. 2.19 through 2.22. Article 2.22 deals specifically with the "battle of the forms:"

Where both parties use standard terms [defined in Art. 2.19(2)] and reach agreement except on those terms, a contract is concluded on the basis of the agreed terms and of any standard terms which are common in substance unless one party clearly indicates in advance, or later and without undue delay informs the other party, that it does not intend to be bound by such a contract. To the extent that there is no agreement, the disputed standard terms are "knocked out."

Textile Unlimited, Inc. v. A .. BMH and Company, Inc.

United States Court of Appeals, Ninth Circuit, 2001.
240 F.3d 781.

■ THOMAS, CIRCUIT JUDGE:

In this appeal, we consider, *inter alia,* the proper venue for a suit to enjoin an arbitration. Under the circumstances presented by this case, we conclude that the Federal Arbitration Act does not require venue in the contractually-designated arbitration locale.

I

Textile Unlimited, Inc. ("Textile") claims that A .. BMH and Company, Inc. ("A .. BMH") is, in the parlance of the industry, spinning a yarn by contending that the two companies had agreed to settle contract disputes by binding arbitration in Georgia. A .. BMH counters that Textile is warping the facts.

Over the course of ten months of this tangled affair, Textile bought goods from A .. BMH in approximately thirty-eight transactions. Each followed a similar pattern. Textile would send a purchase order to a broker in California containing the date, item number, item description, quantity ordered, and price. A .. BMH would respond with an invoice, followed by shipment of the yarn and an order acknowledgment. Both the invoice and the order acknowledgment contained a twist: additional terms tucked into the back of the invoice and the face of the acknowledgment, terms that had not adorned Textile's purchase order. Specifically, the A .. BMH documents provided:

> *Terms.* All sales of yarn by A .. BMH & Co., Inc. ("Seller") are governed by the terms and conditions below. Seller's willingness to sell yarn to you is conditioned on your acceptance of these Terms of Sale. If you do not accept these terms, you must notify Seller in writing within 24 hours of receiving Seller's Order Confirmation. If you accept delivery of Seller's yarn, you will be deemed to have accepted these Terms of Sale in full. You expressly agree that these Terms of Sale supersede any different terms and conditions contained in your purchase order or in any other agreement.

. . .

> *Arbitration.* All disputes arising in connection with this agreement shall be settled in Atlanta, Georgia by binding arbitration conducted under the Commercial Arbitration Rules of the American Arbitration Association. The arbitrator will not be permitted to award punitive damages with respect to any dispute. Judgment upon the award rendered may be entered, and enforcement sought, in any court having jurisdiction. The total costs of arbitration, including attorneys' fees, will be paid by the losing party.

> *Governing Law and Venue.* This transaction shall be governed by and construed in accordance with the laws of the State of Georgia. If any court action is brought to enforce the provisions of this agreement, venue shall lie exclusively in the Superior Court of Fulton County, Georgia. You expressly consent to personal jurisdiction in the Superior Court of Fulton County, Georgia, and waive the right to bring action in any other state or federal court.

Textile did not request any alterations. However, after receiving a shipment in September 1998, Textile refused to pay, alleging that the yarn was defective. A .. BMH submitted the matter to arbitration in Atlanta, Georgia. The American Arbitration Association ("AAA") notified both parties on January 10, 2000, that it had received the arbitration request. Textile did not object to the arbitration within the time provided by AAA rules. Textile eventually protested, contending that the arbitration clause had not been woven into the contract. Textile also argued that the objection period should have been lengthened because the initial notice had been sent to an attorney no longer with its law firm. Textile reserved the right to challenge the jurisdiction of the AAA, and indicated that nothing in the letter should be deemed a waiver.

With arbitration looming, Textile filed an action on April 10, 2000 in the United States District Court for the Central District of California to enjoin the arbitration. Unruffled, the AAA Arbitrator found on May 5, 2000 that the case was arbitrable. On June 26, 2000, Textile moved for a stay of the arbitration pending in Georgia. On July 17, 2000, the district court preliminarily enjoined both the pending arbitration and A .. BMH from any further action regarding arbitration of the dispute in question. A .. BMH timely appealed the district court's order.

II

The district court correctly concluded that venue was proper in the Central District of California under 28 U.S.C. § 1391. Contrary to A .. BMH's arguments, nothing in the Federal Arbitration Act ("FAA" or "the Act"), 9 U.S.C. § 1 *et seq.*, requires that Textile's action to enjoin arbitration be brought in the district where the contract designated the arbitration to occur. [The court reviewed the judicial decisions interpreting the venue provisions of the Federal Arbitration Act.] * * *

In sum, the district court correctly determined that venue was proper in the Central District of California. * * * This result is consistent with the underpinnings of arbitration theory. One of the threads running through federal arbitration jurisprudence is the notion that "arbitration is a matter of contract and a party cannot be required to submit to arbitration any dispute which he has not agreed so to submit." *AT & T Techs., Inc. v. Communications Workers,* 475 U.S. 643, 648 (1986) (quoting *United Steelworkers v. Warrior and Gulf Navigation Co.,* 363 U.S. 574, 582 (1960)). Requiring a party to contest the very existence of an arbitration agreement in a forum dictated by the disputed arbitration clause would run counter to that fundamental principle.

III

The district court did not abuse its discretion in granting the preliminary injunction. . . . * * *

The district court found that Textile would suffer irreparable harm if the arbitration were not stayed, that the balance of hardships tipped in Textile's favor and that it was in the public interest to stay arbitration. These findings were not clearly erroneous, and A .. BMH does not contest them on appeal.

Thus, to obtain a preliminary injunction, Textile needed only to show that serious questions were raised. The district court determined that not only were serious questions raised, but that Textile had shown a probability of success on the merits. The district court did not err in that assessment.

A

Section 2207 of the California Commercial Code controls contract interpretation when the parties have exchanged conflicting forms. . . . It provides:

[The court quoted UCC 2–207 in full.] * * *

Under § 2207(1), an acceptance will operate to create a contract even if additional or different terms are stated *unless* the acceptance is expressly conditioned on assent to the new terms. If a contract is created under § 2207(1), then § 2207(2) defines the terms of the contract.... However, if the acceptance is expressly conditioned on the offeror's assent to the new terms, the acceptance operates as a counteroffer. If the counteroffer is accepted, a contract exists and the additional terms become part of the contract.... To qualify as an acceptance under § 2207(1), an offeror must "give specific and unequivocal assent" to the supplemental terms. [The court relied upon Diamond Fruit Growers, Inc. v. Krack Corp., 797 F.2d 1440 (9th Cir. 1986), interpreting the Oregon enactment of UCC 2–207.] If the new provisos are not accepted, then no contract is formed. However, even when the parties' written expressions do not establish a binding agreement under § 2207(1), a contract may arise based upon their subsequent conduct pursuant to § 2207(3). *Id.*

A .. BMH argues that a contract including the arbitration clause was formed pursuant to § 2207(1) because the fine print provided that Textile was "deemed to have accepted these terms in full" if Textile did not respond in 24 hours. This contention is foreclosed ... because Textile did not "give specific and unequivocal assent" to the supplemental conditions. Thus, a contract containing the new terms that A .. BMH attempted to pin on Textile was not formed under § 2207(1).

Part of ... the rationale [in *Diamond Fruit Growers*, supra] was to avoid a rule which would allow one party to obtain "all of its terms simply because it fired the last shot in the exchange of forms." *Id.* at 1444. In short, modern commercial transactions conducted under the U.C.C. are not a game of tag or musical chairs. Rather, if the parties exchange incompatible forms, "all of the terms on which the parties' forms do not agree drop out, and the U.C.C. supplies the missing terms."

A .. BMH also claims that a contract formed under § 2207(1) because its acceptance was not expressly made conditional on Textile's assent to the additional or different terms. Thus, A .. BMH reasons, a contract was formed under § 2207(1) and we must turn to § 2207(2) to ascertain the contract terms. However, A .. BMH's assertion is belied by the plain words of its documents which provide that "Seller's willingness to sell yarn to you is conditioned on your acceptance of these Terms of Sale." Thus, A .. BMH's claim is unavailing.

No Orac K

B

Because no contract was formed under § 2207(1), our interpretation of the agreement must be guided by § 2207(3) which examines the conduct of the parties to determine whether a contract for sale has been established and the terms thereof. The parties do not dispute that through their actions, they formed a contract under § 2207(3).

Actions Result = K

The terms of an agreement formed pursuant to § 2207(3) are those terms upon which the parties expressly agreed, coupled with the standard "gap-filler" provisions of Article Two. The U.C.C. does not contain a "gap-filler" provision providing for arbitration. ...

Under § 2207(3), the disputed additional items on which the parties do not agree simply "drop out" and are trimmed from the contract.... Thus, the supplemental terms proposed by A .. BMH, including the arbitration clause, do not festoon the contract between the parties.

C

[The court held that Textile did not waive its right to object to arbitration.]

* * *

IV

In sum, this action was properly venued in the Central District of California. The district court did not abuse its discretion in granting the preliminary injunction. To the contrary, the district court's reasoning was correct in all respects.

AFFIRMED.

NOTES

(1) The court concludes that no contract to arbitrate was made under UCC 2–207(1) and that the seller made a counteroffer. If the buyer accepted the goods without objection, isn't that an acceptance of the counteroffer with the arbitration clause? How did the court interpret UCC 2–207 to avoid this result? Do you see any support for that interpretation in the text or the comments?

(2) The parties had an extensive prior course of dealing, some 38 transactions. Is that relevant to deciding cases under UCC 2–207? In Deer Stags, Inc. v. Garrison Indus., 2000 WL 1800491 (S.D.N.Y.2000), the seller's definite acceptance under UCC 2–207(1) contained an additional term, an arbitration clause. The buyer accepted the goods without objection. The court held that under UCC 2–207(2), the arbitration clause was not material and became part of the contract. The court reasoned that since the parties had engaged in more than 50 transactions in the past with the same terms, there was no unfair surprise or hardship to the buyer to include the term. Is this a proper reading of the statute?

(3) Commentary upon UCC 2–207 is voluminous, much of it critical. See e.g. Daniel Keating, *Exploring the Battle of Forms in Action*, 98 Mich. L. Rev. 2678 (2000), and other articles in this Symposium. What do you think?

Comment: Arbitration Terms and the Battle of the Forms

In arbitration, the parties agree in writing to submit defined disputes, either existing or future, to independent third persons (arbitrators) for a final decision on the merits. The parties control what disputes are submitted, the selection of the arbitrators, and the procedures to be followed and are entitled to a fair hearing on the merits. Once the award is made, however, judicial review is limited: an award cannot be vacated because the arbitrators made errors of fact or law.

In the United States, there are three layers of arbitration law. The first is international arbitration, which is governed by the United Nations Convention on the Recognition and Enforcement of Foreign Awards (The New York Convention), as implemented by Chapter 2 of the Federal Arbitration Act, 9 U.S.C. sec. 201–208. The second is interstate arbitration, which is governed by Chapter 1 of the FAA, 9 U.S.C. sec. 1–16. The third is intrastate arbitration law, which is governed by the applicable state arbitration act (frequently the Uniform Arbitration Act, which has recently been revised).

All three layers of arbitration law require, at a minimum, that the arbitration agreement be in a writing assented to (but not necessarily signed) by both parties. In the *Textile Unlimited* case, just considered, Chapter 1 of the FAA applied. Section 2 provides:

> A written provision in any ... contract evidencing a transaction involving commerce to settle by arbitration a controversy thereafter arising out of such contract or controversy, or the refusal to perform the whole or any part thereof, or an agreement in writing to submit to arbitration an existing controversy arising out of such a contract, transaction, or refusal, shall be valid, irrevocable, and enforceable, save upon such grounds as exist at law or in equity for the revocation of any contract.

Because the FAA provides little guidance on when a "written provision" is contained in a contract or agreed to by the parties, resort to state law is necessary. In contracts for the sale of goods, that state law is UCC Article 2 and, in transactions like that in *Textile Unlimited*, the specific provision is UCC 2–207. Since the court held that the seller's written arbitration term was not included in the contract for sale, the conditions of FAA Section 2 were not satisfied and the buyer was entitled to an injunction against arbitration. If the written term were included in the contract, i.e., the buyer had expressly agreed to the arbitration term in the seller's form, the buyer would be bound to arbitrate and the seller could get both an order compelling arbitration under FAA sec. 4 and an order staying any litigation commenced by the buyer pending arbitration, FAA sec. 3.

Suppose the same facts except that the seller's place of business was Toronto, Canada and the buyer's place of business was in California. Two things change here: First, the international contract for sale is governed by CISG, see Article 1(1)(a); and Second, the question whether the seller's arbitration term is enforceable is governed by Article II of the New York Convention. At the risk of over-simplification, in this international transaction the arbitration clause would be enforceable. Why? Under Article 19 of CISG, the seller's response with an arbitration clause would be a counteroffer [a material alteration of the offer] which the buyer would accept by the conduct of accepting the goods. CISG Art. 18(1). CISG does not include a section like UCC 2–207 and is not concerned with such issues like whether the buyer was unfairly surprised by the form. This, in turn, would satisfy the requirement of NYC Article II(1) that the arbitration agreement be in writing because it is contained "in an exchange of letters or telegrams."

Art. II(1). Put differently, the exchange of letters was the seller's offer and the buyer's counteroffer to which the buyer assented by conduct. In this case, there is no requirement that the written agreement be signed.

Comment: Revised Section 2–207: Some History

The latest revision of UCC 2–207 provides:

If (i) conduct by both parties recognizes the existence of a contract although their records do not otherwise establish a contract, (ii) a contract is formed by an offer or acceptance, or (iii) a contract formed in any manner confirmed by a record that contains terms additional to or different from those in the contract being confirmed, the terms of the contract, subject to Section 2–202, are:

(a) terms that appear in the records of both parties;

(b) terms, whether in a record or not, to which both parties agree; and

(c) terms supplied or incorporated under any provision of this Act.

Revised Section 2–206(3) provides that a "definite and seasonable expression of acceptance in a record operates as an acceptance even if it contains terms additional to or different from the offer."

The current revision evolved from the November, 1996 Draft of revised Article 2, which, following the lead of the Unidroit Principles, dealt specifically with problems created by the use of standard forms and standard terms in contract formation. This approach was ultimately rejected by the Drafting Committee for the simple "knock out" rule approach of the revision. Now there is no distinction between standard terms and negotiated terms in the statute. Nor is any distinction drawn between exactly how the contract was formed, i.e., by offer and acceptance or by conduct.

Hill v. Gateway 2000

United States Court of Appeals, Seventh Circuit 1997.
105 F.3d 1147, cert. denied, 522 U.S. 808, 118 S.Ct. 47, 139 L.Ed.2d 13 (1997).

■ EASTERBROOK, JUDGE. A customer picks up the phone, orders a computer, and gives a credit card number. Presently a box arrives, containing the computer and a list of terms, said to govern unless the customer returns the computer within 30 days. Are these terms effective as the parties' contract, or is the contract term-free because the order-taker did not read any terms over the phone and elicit the customer's assent?

One of the terms in the box containing a Gateway 2000 system was an arbitration clause. Rich and Enza Hill, the customers, kept the computer more than 30 days before complaining about its components and performance. They filed suit in federal court arguing, among other things, that the product's shortcomings make Gateway a racketeer (mail and wire fraud are said to be the predicate offenses), leading to treble damages under

RICO for the Hills and a class of all other purchasers. Gateway asked the district court to enforce the arbitration clause; the judge refused, writing that "[t]he present record is insufficient to support a finding of a valid arbitration agreement between the parties or that the plaintiffs were given adequate notice of the arbitration clause." Gateway [appealed].

The Hills say that the arbitration clause did not stand out: they concede noticing the statement of terms but deny reading it closely enough to discover the agreement to arbitrate, and they ask us to conclude that they therefore may go to court. Yet an agreement to arbitrate must be enforced "save upon such grounds as exist at law or in equity for the revocation of any contract." 9 U.S.C. § 2. *Doctor's Associates, Inc. v. Casarotto,* 517 U.S. 681, 116 S.Ct. 1652 (1996), holds that this provision of the Federal Arbitration Act is inconsistent with any requirement that an arbitration clause be prominent. A contract need not be read to be effective; people who accept take the risk that the unread terms may in retrospect prove unwelcome. Terms inside Gateway's box stand or fall together. If they constitute the parties' contract because the Hills had an opportunity to return the computer after reading them, then all must be enforced.

ProCD, Inc. v. Zeidenberg, 86 F.3d 1447 (7th Cir.1996), holds that terms inside a box of software bind consumers who use the software after an opportunity to read the terms and to reject them by returning the product. Likewise, *Carnival Cruise Lines, Inc. v. Shute,* 499 U.S. 585 (1991), enforces a forum-selection clause that was included among three pages of terms attached to a cruise ship ticket. *ProCD* and *Carnival Cruise Lines* exemplify the many commercial transactions in which people pay for products with terms to follow. The district court concluded in *ProCD* that the contract is formed when the consumer pays for the software; as a result, the court held, only terms known to the consumer at that moment are part of the contract, and provisos inside the box do not count. Although this is one way a contract could be formed, it is not the only way: "A vendor, as master of the offer, may invite acceptance by conduct, and may propose limitations on the kind of conduct that constitutes acceptance. A buyer may accept by performing the acts the vendor proposes to treat as acceptance." *Id.* at 1452. Gateway shipped computers with the same sort of accept-or-return offer ProCD made to users of its software. *ProCD* relied on the Uniform Commercial Code rather than any peculiarities of Wisconsin law; both Illinois and South Dakota, the two states whose law might govern relations between Gateway and the Hills, have adopted the UCC; neither side has pointed us to any atypical doctrines in those states that might be pertinent; *ProCD* therefore applies to this dispute.

Plaintiffs ask us to limit *ProCD* to software, but where's the sense in that? *ProCD* is about the law of contract, not the law of software. Payment preceding the revelation of full terms is common for air transportation, insurance, and many other endeavors. Practical considerations support allowing vendors to enclose the full legal terms with their products. Cashiers cannot be expected to read legal documents to customers before ringing up sales. If the staff at the other end of the phone for direct-sales operations such as Gateway's had to read the four-page statement of terms before taking the buyer's credit card number, the droning voice would anesthetize rather than enlighten many potential buyers. Others would hang up in a rage over the waste of their time. And oral recitation would not avoid customers' assertions (whether true or feigned) that the clerk did not read term X to them, or that they did not remember or understand it. Writing provides benefits for both sides of commercial transactions. Customers as a group are better off when vendors skip costly and ineffectual steps such as telephonic recitation, and use instead a simple approve-or-return device. Competent adults are bound by such documents, read or unread. For what little it is worth, we add that the box from Gateway was crammed with software. The computer came with an operating system, without which it was useful only as a boat anchor. Gateway also included many application programs. So the Hills' effort to limit *ProCD* to software would not avail them factually, even if it were sound legally—which it is not.

For their second sally, the Hills contend that *ProCD* should be limited to executory contracts (to licenses in particular), and therefore does not apply because both parties' performance of this contract was complete when the box arrived at their home. This is legally and factually wrong: legally because the question at hand concerns the *formation* of the contract rather than its *performance*, and factually because both contracts were incompletely performed. ... One element of the transaction was the warranty, which obliges sellers to fix defects in their products. The Hills have invoked Gateway's warranty and are not satisfied with its response, so they are not well positioned to say that Gateway's obligations were fulfilled when the motor carrier unloaded the box.

Next the Hills insist that *ProCD* is irrelevant because Zeidenberg was a "merchant" and they are not. Section 2–207(2) of the UCC, the infamous battle-of-the-forms section, states that "additional terms [following acceptance of an offer] are to be construed as proposals for addition to a contract. Between merchants such terms become part of the contract unless ... ". Plaintiffs tell us that *ProCD* came out as it did only because Zeidenberg was a "merchant" and the terms inside ProCD's box were not excluded by the "unless" clause. This argument pays scant attention to the opinion in *ProCD*, which concluded that, when there is only one form, "sec. 2–207 is irrelevant." 86 F.3d at 1452. The question in *ProCD* was not whether terms were added to a contract after its formation, but how and when the contract was formed—in particular, whether a vendor may propose that a contract of sale be formed, not in the store (or over the phone) with the payment of money or a general "send me the product," but after the customer has had a chance to inspect both the item and the terms. *ProCD* answers "yes," for merchants and consumers alike....

Perhaps the Hills would have had a better argument if they were first alerted to the bundling of hardware and legal-ware after opening the box and wanted to return the computer in order to avoid disagreeable terms, but were dissuaded by the expense of shipping.

What the remedy would be in such a case—could it exceed the shipping charges?—is an interesting question, but one that need not detain us because the Hills knew before they ordered the computer that the carton would include *some* important terms, and they did not seek to discover these in advance. Gateway's ads state that their products come with limited warranties and lifetime support. How limited was the warranty—30 days, with service contingent on shipping the computer back, or five years, with free onsite service? What sort of support was offered? Shoppers have three principal ways to discover these things. First, they can ask the vendor to send a copy before deciding whether to buy. The Magnuson–Moss Warranty Act requires firms to distribute their warranty terms on request, 15 U.S.C. § 2302(b)(1)(A); the Hills do not contend that Gateway would have refused to enclose the remaining terms too. Concealment would be bad for business, scaring some customers away and leading to excess returns from others. Second, shoppers can consult public sources (computer magazines, the Web sites of vendors) that may contain this information. Third, they may inspect the documents after the product's delivery. Like Zeidenberg, the Hills took the third option. By keeping the computer beyond 30 days, the Hills accepted Gateway's offer, including the arbitration clause.

The decision of the district court is vacated, and this case is remanded with instructions to compel the Hills to submit their dispute to arbitration.

Klocek v. Gateway

United States District Court, D. Kansas, 2000.
104 F.Supp.2d 1332, order vacated for lack of subject matter jurisdiction, 2000 WL 1372886 (D.Kan.2000), aff'd, 2001 WL 1568346 (D.Kan.2001).

* * *

The Uniform Commercial Code ("UCC") governs the parties' transaction under both Kansas and Missouri law ... Regardless whether plaintiff purchased the computer in person or placed an order and received shipment of the computer, the parties agree that plaintiff paid for and received a computer from Gateway. This conduct clearly demonstrates a contract for the sale of a computer. ... Thus the issue is whether the contract of sale includes the Standard Terms as part of the agreement.

State courts in Kansas and Missouri apparently have not decided whether terms received with a product become part of the parties' agreement. Authority from other courts is split ... It appears that at least in part, the cases turn on whether the court finds that the parties formed their contract *before* or *after* the vendor communicated its terms to the purchaser. ...

Gateway urges the Court to follow the Seventh Circuit decision in *Hill* [Hill v. Gateway, supra]. That case involved the shipment of a Gateway computer with terms similar to the Standard Terms in this case, except that Gateway gave the customer 30 days—instead of 5 days—to return the computer. In enforcing the arbitration clause, the Seventh Circuit relied on its decision in ProCD, where it enforced a software license which was contained inside a product box.... In *ProCD*, the Seventh Circuit noted that the exchange of money frequently precedes the communication of detailed terms in a commercial transaction. Citing UCC § 2–204, the court reasoned that by including the license with the software, the vendor proposed a contract that the buyer could accept by using the software after having an opportunity to read the license ... Specifically, the court stated:

> A vendor, as master of the offer, may invite acceptance by conduct, and may propose limitations on the kind of conduct that constitutes acceptance. A buyer may accept by performing the acts the vendor proposes to treat as acceptance....

The *Hill* court followed the *ProCD* analysis, noting that "[p]ractical considerations support allowing vendors to enclose the full legal terms with their products." *Hill,* 105 F.3d at 1149....*

The Court is not persuaded that Kansas or Missouri courts would follow the Seventh Circuit reasoning in *Hill* and *ProCD*. In each case the Seventh Circuit concluded without support that UCC § 2–207 was irrelevant because the cases involved only one written form.... This conclusion is not supported by the statute or by Kansas or Missouri law. Disputes under § 2–207 often arise in the context of a "battle of forms," ... but nothing in its language precludes application in a case which involves only one form. The statute provides: [The court quoted UCC 2–207] * * *

By its terms, § 2–207 applies to an acceptance or written confirmation. It states nothing which requires another form before the provision becomes effective. In fact, the official comment to the section specifically provides that §§ 2–207(1) and (2) apply "where an agreement has been reached orally ... and is followed by one or both of the parties sending formal memoranda embodying the terms so far agreed and adding terms not discussed." Official Comment 1 of UCC § 2–207. Kansas and Missouri courts have followed this analysis.... Thus, the Court concludes that Kansas and Missouri courts would apply § 2–207 to the facts in this case....

---

* Legal scholars have criticized the reasoning of the Seventh Circuit *See, e.g.,* Jean R. Sternlight, *Gateway Widens Doorway to Imposing Unfair Binding Arbitration on Consumers,* Fla. Bar J., Nov. 1997, at 8, 10–12 (outcome in *Gateway* is questionable on federal statutory, common law and constitutional grounds and as a matter of contract law and is unwise as a matter of policy because it unreasonably shifts to consumers search cost of ascertaining existence of arbitration clause and return cost to avoid such clause); Thomas J. McCarthy et al., *Survey: Uniform Commercial Code,* 53 Bus. Law. 1461, 1465–66 (Seventh Circuit finding that UCC § 2–207 did not apply is inconsistent with official comment); Batya Goodman, *Honey, I Shrink–Wrapped the Consumer: the Shrinkwrap Agreement as an Adhesion Contract,* 21 Cardozo L.Rev. 319, 344–352 (Seventh Circuit failed to consider principles of adhesion contracts); Jeremy Senderowicz, *Consumer Arbitration and Freedom of Contract: A Proposal to Facilitate Consumers' Informed Consent to Arbitration Clauses in Form Contracts,* 32 Colum. J.L. & Soc. Probs. 275, 296–299 (judiciary (in multiple decisions, including *Hill*) has ignored issue of consumer consent to an arbitration clause) [The court cited several cases that have followed *Hill.*]

In addition, the Seventh Circuit provided no explanation for its conclusion that "the vendor is the master of the offer...." In typical consumer transactions, the purchaser is the offeror, and the vendor is the offeree.... While it is possible for the vendor to be the offeror, ... Gateway provides no factual evidence which would support such a finding in this case. The Court therefore assumes for purposes of the motion to dismiss that plaintiff offered to purchase the computer (either in person or through catalog order) and that Gateway accepted plaintiff's offer (either by completing the sales transaction in person or by agreeing to ship and/or shipping the computer to plaintiff)....

Under § 2–207, the Standard Terms constitute either an expression of acceptance or written confirmation. As an expression of acceptance, the Standard Terms would constitute a counter-offer only if Gateway expressly made its acceptance conditional on plaintiff's assent to the additional or different terms.... Gateway provides no evidence that at the time of the sales transaction, it informed plaintiff that the transaction was conditioned on plaintiff's acceptance of the Standard Terms. Moreover, the mere fact that Gateway shipped the goods with the terms attached did not communicate to plaintiff any unwillingness to proceed without plaintiff's agreement to the Standard Terms....

Because plaintiff is not a merchant, additional or different terms contained in the Standard Terms did not become part of the parties' agreement unless plaintiff expressly agreed to them. *See* K.S.A. § 84–2–207, Kansas Comment 2 (if either party is not a merchant, additional terms are proposals for addition to the contract that do not become part of the contract unless the original offeror expressly agrees).* Gateway argues that plaintiff demonstrated acceptance of the arbitration provision by keeping the computer more than five days after the date of delivery. Although the Standard Terms purport to work that result, Gateway has not presented evidence that plaintiff expressly agreed to those Standard Terms. Gateway states only that it enclosed the Standard Terms inside the computer box for plaintiff to read afterwards. It provides no evidence that it informed plaintiff of the five-day review-and-return period as a condition of the sales transaction, or that the parties contemplated additional terms to the agreement.... The Court finds that the act of keeping the computer past five days was not sufficient to demonstrate that plaintiff expressly agreed to the Standard Terms.... Thus, because Gateway has not provided evidence sufficient to support a finding under Kansas or Missouri law that plaintiff agreed to the arbitration provision contained in Gateway's Standard Terms, the Court overrules Gateway's motion to dismiss.**

* * *

---

* The Court's decision would be the same if it considered the Standard Terms as a proposed modification under UCC § 2–209....

** The Court is mindful of the practical considerations which are involved in commercial transactions, but it is not unreasonable for a vendor to clearly communicate to a buyer—at the time of sale—either the com-

PROBLEMS: STANDARD TERMS IN CONTRACT FORMATION; "SHRINK WRAP" LICENSES

(1) After negotiations without an agreement, Buyer in California sends Seller in New York an offer to buy described factory machinery. On the back of the offer a standard term provided that "all disputes arising out of or relating to this contract shall be arbitrated in Los Angeles under the Rules of the American Arbitration Association." Seller sends Buyer an acknowledgment of the order and ships the goods by carrier. On the back of the acknowledgment, which Buyer received, there was a standard term that provided "all disputes relating to the conformity of the described goods to the contract shall be arbitrated in New York City under the rules of the International Chamber of Commerce." The goods were destroyed by fire in transit and a dispute arose over who had the risk of loss. Seller filed suit against Buyer in Los Angeles to recover the price. Buyer sought an order staying the litigation pending arbitration and an order compelling arbitration in Los Angeles.

(A) How would this come out under current UCC 2–207?

(B) How would this come out under Revised UCC 2–207?

(C) If Seller's place of business was in Toronto, Canada, how would this come out under CISG?

(2) Malcolm, a CPA who worked at home, needed a new computer. He saw a trade journal advertisement by DellWay Computer, stating "Build Your Own Computer" and urging those interested to check the DellWay Website for the components with which to work. Malcolm visited the Website, made a list of components that he needed, and then faxed an order to DellWay. The next day, DellWay called to confirm that such a computer could be built and quoted to Malcolm a price, including delivery, of $2,500. Malcolm agreed and, at Dell-Way's request, gave his credit card number in payment. The charge was promptly processed and approved. Five days later, Malcolm received the computer by U.P.S. In the box taped to the computer was an enveloped containing three pages of standard terms in 10 point print. A term on page two excluded DellWay from any and all liability for consequential damages. A term on page three obligated DellWay and Malcolm to arbitrate any and all disputes in New York City under the arbitration rules of the International Chamber of Commerce. At the bottom of page three, the following appeared in BOLD PRINT: PLEASE READ THESE TERMS. IF YOU DO NOT ACCEPT THEM, YOU MAY RETURN THE COMPUTER TO US AT OUR EXPENSE. USE OF THE COMPUTER WITHOUT OBJECTION WILL CONSTITUTE ACCEPTANCE OF THE TERMS.

Malcolm did not read the terms and used the computer. Later a non-conformity appeared causing Malcolm to lose important work he was doing for a client. Malcolm complained to DellWay and was told about the excluder and arbitration clauses which he "agreed to" by using the computer. Are those terms part of the contract?

plete terms of the sale or the fact that the vendor will propose additional terms as a   condition of sale, if that be the case.

(D) ASSENT IN ELECTRONIC COMMERCE

In the past few years, we have heard much about buying goods on the internet or downloading software, either for a fee or for free. In these electronic transactions, the purchaser accesses the website of the seller through its computer and internet server and initiates the process. An order is placed, payment is made by credit card, and the goods are sent to the purchaser or the software is downloaded.

If a dispute arises, however, three questions are likely to be raised: (1) What about the validity of electronic contracts, which may be concluded between computers without the presence of a human being and involve electronic signatures and records, (2) If valid, when is a contract formed in electronic commerce, and (3) If a contract is formed, what are its terms? The second and third of these questions are confronted in the important case that follows.

The first question, however, has been answered by recent legislation on the federal and state level. The federal legislation is the Electronic Signatures in Global and National Commerce Act (E–SIGN), 15 U.S.C. secs. 7001–7031, effective on October 1, 2001, and the Uniform Electronic Transactions Act (UETA), which as of July, 2003, had been enacted in every state. According to Professor Jane K. Winn:

> The core provisions of these statutes were designed to end discussion over the validity of electronic contracting in general without changing any underlying doctrine of contract law and without mandating the use of any particular technology.

Jane K. Winn, *Electronic Commerce: 2001 Developments*, 57 Bus. Lawyer 541 (2001). Although these statutes are too complicated to summarize here, the gist of the solution can be quickly grasped by studying the definitions in Section 2 of UETA and then reading the text of the statute.

What about the second and third questions? The answers depend upon what substantive law applies to the electronic transaction and whether that law is influenced by the manner in which the deal is concluded.

Specht v. Netscape Communications Corporation

United States Court of Appeals, Second Circuit, 2002.
306 F.3d 17.

■ SOTOMAYOR, CIRCUIT JUDGE.

This is an appeal from a judgment of the Southern District of New York denying a motion by defendants-appellants Netscape Communications Corporation and its corporate parent, America Online, Inc. (collectively, "defendants" or "Netscape"), to compel arbitration and to stay court proceedings. In order to resolve the central question of arbitrability presented here, we must address issues of contract formation in cyberspace. Principally, we are asked to determine whether plaintiffs-appellees ("plaintiffs"), by acting upon defendants' invitation to download free software made available on defendants' webpage, agreed to be bound by the software's license terms (which included the arbitration clause at issue), even though plaintiffs could not have learned of the existence of those terms unless, prior to executing the download, they had scrolled down the webpage to a screen located below the download button. We agree with the district court that a reasonably prudent Internet user in circumstances such as these would not have known or learned of the existence of the license terms before responding to defendants' invitation to download the free software, and that defendants therefore did not provide reasonable notice of the license terms. In consequence, plaintiffs' bare act of downloading the software did not unambiguously manifest assent to the arbitration provision contained in the license terms.

We also agree with the district court that plaintiffs' claims relating to the software at issue—a "plug-in" program entitled SmartDownload ("SmartDownload" or "the plug-in program"), offered by Netscape to enhance the functioning of the separate browser program called Netscape Communicator ("Communicator" or "the browser program")—are not subject to an arbitration agreement contained in the license terms governing the use of Communicator. * * *

We therefore affirm the district court's denial of defendants' motion to compel arbitration and to stay court proceedings.

BACKGROUND

I. Facts

In three related putative class actions, plaintiffs alleged that, unknown to them, their use of SmartDownload transmitted to defendants private information about plaintiffs' downloading of files from the Internet, thereby effecting an electronic surveillance of their online activities in violation of two federal statutes, the Electronic Communications Privacy Act, 18 U.S.C. §§ 2510 *et seq.*, and the Computer Fraud and Abuse Act, 18 U.S.C. § 1030.

Specifically, plaintiffs alleged that when they first used Netscape's Communicator—a software program that permits Internet browsing—the program created and stored on each of their computer hard drives a small text file known as a "cookie" that functioned "as a kind of electronic identification tag for future communications" between their computers and Netscape. Plaintiffs further alleged that when they installed SmartDownload—a separate software "plug-in" that served to enhance Communicator's browsing capabilities—SmartDownload created and stored on their computer hard drives another string of characters, known as a "Key," which similarly functioned as an identification tag in future communications with Netscape. According to the complaints in this case, each time a computer user employed Communicator to download a file from the Internet, SmartDownload "assume[d] from Communicator the task of downloading" the file and transmitted to Netscape the address of the file being downloaded together with the cookie created by Communicator and the Key created by SmartDownload. These processes, plaintiffs claim, constituted unlawful "eavesdropping" on users of Netscape's software products as well as on Internet websites from which users employing SmartDownload downloaded files.

In the time period relevant to this litigation, Netscape offered on its website various software programs, including Communicator and Smart-Download, which visitors to the site were invited to obtain free of charge. It is undisputed that five of the six named plaintiffs—Michael Fagan, John Gibson, Mark Gruber, Sean Kelly, and Sherry Weindorf—downloaded Communicator from the Netscape website. These plaintiffs acknowledge that when they proceeded to initiate installation of Communicator, they were automatically shown a scrollable text of that program's license agreement and were not permitted to complete the installation until they had clicked on a "Yes" button to indicate that they accepted all the license terms.* If a user attempted to install Communicator without clicking "Yes," the installation would be aborted. All five named user plaintiffs expressly agreed to Communicator's license terms by clicking "Yes." The Communicator license agreement that these plaintiffs saw made no mention of SmartDownload or other plug-in programs, and stated that "[t]hese terms apply to Netscape Communicator and Netscape Navigator" and that "all disputes relating to this Agreement (excepting any dispute relating to intellectual property rights)" are subject to "binding arbitration in Santa Clara County, California."

Although Communicator could be obtained independently of Smart-Download, all the named user plaintiffs, except Fagan, downloaded and installed Communicator in connection with downloading SmartDownload. Each of these plaintiffs allegedly arrived at a Netscape webpage captioned "SmartDownload Communicator" that urged them to "Download With Confidence Using SmartDownload!" At or near the bottom of the screen facing plaintiffs was the prompt "Start Download" and a tinted button labeled "Download." By clicking on the button, plaintiffs initiated the download of SmartDownload. Once that process was complete, SmartDownload, as its first plug-in task, permitted plaintiffs to proceed with downloading and installing Communicator, an operation that was accompanied by the clickwrap display of Communicator's license terms described above.

---

* This kind of online software license agreement has come to be known as "click-wrap" (by analogy to "shrinkwrap," used in the licensing of tangible forms of software sold in packages) because it "presents the user with a message on his or her computer screen, requiring that the user manifest his or her assent to the terms of the license agreement by clicking on an icon. The product cannot be obtained or used unless and until the icon is clicked." *Specht*, 150 F.Supp.2d at 593–94. Just as breaking the shrinkwrap seal and using the enclosed computer program after encountering notice of the existence of governing license terms has been deemed by some courts to constitute assent to those terms in the context of tangible software, *see, e.g., ProCD, Inc. v. Zeidenberg*, 86 F.3d 1447, 1451 (7th Cir.1996), so clicking on a webpage's clickwrap button after receiving notice of the existence of license terms has been held by some courts to manifest an Internet user's assent to terms governing the use of downloadable intangible software, . . . "

The signal difference between downloading Communicator and down-loading SmartDownload was that no clickwrap presentation accompanied the latter operation. Instead, once plaintiffs Gibson, Gruber, Kelly, and Weindorf had clicked on the "Download" button located at or near the bottom of their screen, and the downloading of SmartDownload was complete, these plaintiffs encountered no further information about the plug-in program or the existence of license terms governing its use. The sole reference to SmartDownload's license terms on the "SmartDownload Communicator" webpage was located in text that would have become visible to plaintiffs only if they had scrolled down to the next screen.

Had plaintiffs scrolled down instead of acting on defendants' invitation to click on the "Download" button, they would have encountered the following invitation: "Please review and agree to the terms of the *Netscape SmartDownload software license agreement* before downloading and using the software." Plaintiffs Gibson, Gruber, Kelly, and Weindorf averred in their affidavits that they never saw this reference to the SmartDownload license agreement when they clicked on the "Download" button. They also testified during depositions that they saw no reference to license terms when they clicked to download SmartDownload, although under question-ing by defendants' counsel, some plaintiffs added that they could not "remember" or be "sure" whether the screen shots of the SmartDownload page attached to their affidavits reflected precisely what they had seen on their computer screens when they downloaded SmartDownload.

In sum, plaintiffs Gibson, Gruber, Kelly, and Weindorf allege that the process of obtaining SmartDownload contrasted sharply with that of ob-taining Communicator. Having selected SmartDownload, they were re-quired neither to express unambiguous assent to that program's license agreement nor even to view the license terms or become aware of their existence before proceeding with the invited download of the free plug-in program. Moreover, once these plaintiffs had initiated the download, the existence of SmartDownload's license terms was not mentioned while the software was running or at any later point in plaintiffs' experience of the product.

Even for a user who, unlike plaintiffs, did happen to scroll down past the download button, SmartDownload's license terms would not have been immediately displayed in the manner of Communicator's clickwrapped terms. Instead, if such a user had seen the notice of SmartDownload's terms and then clicked on the underlined invitation to review and agree to the terms, a hypertext link would have taken the user to a separate webpage entitled "License & Support Agreements." The first paragraph on this page read, in pertinent part:

> The use of each Netscape software product is governed by a license agreement. You must read and agree to the license agreement terms BEFORE acquiring a product. Please click on the appropriate link below to review the current license agreement for the product of interest to you before acquisition. For products available for download, you must read and agree to the license agreement terms BEFORE you

install the software. If you do not agree to the license terms, do not download, install or use the software.

Below this paragraph appeared a list of license agreements, the first of which was *"License Agreement for Netscape Navigator and Netscape Communicator Product Family* (Netscape Navigator, Netscape Communicator and Netscape SmartDownload)." If the user clicked on that link, he or she would be taken to yet another webpage that contained the full text of a license agreement that was identical in every respect to the Communicator license agreement except that it stated that its "terms apply to Netscape Communicator, Netscape Navigator, and Netscape SmartDownload." The license agreement granted the user a nonexclusive license to use and reproduce the software, subject to certain terms:

> BY CLICKING THE ACCEPTANCE BUTTON OR INSTALLING OR USING NETSCAPE COMMUNICATOR, NETSCAPE NAVIGATOR, OR NETSCAPE SMARTDOWNLOAD SOFTWARE (THE "PRODUCT"), THE INDIVIDUAL OR ENTITY LICENSING THE PRODUCT ("LICENSEE") IS CONSENTING TO BE BOUND BY AND IS BECOMING A PARTY TO THIS AGREEMENT. IF LICENSEE DOES NOT AGREE TO ALL OF THE TERMS OF THIS AGREEMENT, THE BUTTON INDICATING NON–ACCEPTANCE MUST BE SELECTED, AND LICENSEE MUST NOT INSTALL OR USE THE SOFTWARE.

Among the license terms was a provision requiring virtually all disputes relating to the agreement to be submitted to arbitration:

> Unless otherwise agreed in writing, all disputes relating to this Agreement (excepting any dispute relating to intellectual property rights) shall be subject to final and binding arbitration in Santa Clara County, California, under the auspices of JAMS/EndDispute, with the losing party paying all costs of arbitration.

Unlike the four named user plaintiffs who downloaded SmartDownload from the Netscape website, the fifth named plaintiff, Michael Fagan, claims to have downloaded the plug-in program from a "shareware" website operated by ZDNet, an entity unrelated to Netscape. Shareware sites are websites, maintained by companies or individuals, that contain libraries of free, publicly available software. The pages that a user would have seen while downloading SmartDownload from ZDNet differed from those that he or she would have encountered while downloading SmartDownload from the Netscape website. Notably, instead of any kind of notice of the SmartDownload license agreement, the ZDNet pages offered only a hypertext link to "more information" about SmartDownload, which, if clicked on, took the user to a Netscape webpage that, in turn, contained a link to the license agreement. Thus, a visitor to the ZDNet website could have obtained SmartDownload, as Fagan avers he did, without ever seeing a reference to that program's license terms, even if he or she had scrolled through all of ZDNet's webpages.

The sixth named plaintiff, Christopher Specht, never obtained or used SmartDownload, but instead operated a website from which visitors could download certain electronic files that permitted them to create an account with an internet service provider called WhyWeb. Specht alleges that every time a user who had previously installed SmartDownload visited his website and downloaded WhyWeb-related files, defendants intercepted this information. Defendants allege that Specht would receive a representative's commission from WhyWeb every time a user who obtained a WhyWeb file from his website subsequently subscribed to the WhyWeb service. Thus, argue defendants, because the "Netscape license agreement . . . conferred on each user the right to download and use both Communicator and SmartDownload software," Specht received a benefit under that license agreement in that SmartDownload "assisted in obtaining the WhyWeb file and increased the likelihood of success in the download process." This benefit, defendants claim, was direct enough to require Specht to arbitrate his claims pursuant to Netscape's license terms. Specht, however, maintains that he never received any commissions based on the WhyWeb files available on his website.

II.   Proceedings Below

[The court discussed the opinion below, written by Judge Alvin K. Hellerstein, which held that the plaintiffs had not agreed in writing to arbitrate.]

* * *

Defendants took this timely appeal pursuant to 9 U.S.C. § 16, and the district court stayed all proceedings in the underlying cases pending resolution of the appeal. This Court has jurisdiction pursuant to § 16(a)(1)(B), as this is an appeal from an order denying defendants' motion to compel arbitration under the FAA.

DISCUSSION

I.   Standard of Review and Applicable Law

A district court's denial of a motion to compel arbitration is reviewed *de novo*. . . . The determination of whether parties have contractually bound themselves to arbitrate a dispute—a determination involving interpretation of state law—is a legal conclusion also subject to *de novo* review. . . . The findings upon which that conclusion is based, however, are factual and thus may not be overturned unless clearly erroneous. . . .

If a court finds that the parties agreed to arbitrate, it should then consider whether the dispute falls within the scope of the arbitration agreement. . . . A district court's determination of the scope of an arbitration agreement is reviewed *de novo*. . . . In addition, whether a party may be compelled to arbitrate as a result of direct benefits that he or she allegedly received under a contract entered into by others is an issue of arbitrability that is reviewed *de novo*. . . .

The FAA provides that a "written provision in any . . . contract evidencing a transaction involving commerce to settle by arbitration a controversy thereafter arising out of such contract or transaction . . . shall be valid, irrevocable, and enforceable, save upon such grounds as exist at law or in equity for the revocation of any contract.'' 9 U.S.C. § 2. It is well settled that a court may not compel arbitration until it has resolved ''the question of the very existence'' of the contract embodying the arbitration clause . . . Unless the parties clearly provide otherwise, ''the question of arbitrability—whether a[n] . . . agreement creates a duty for the parties to arbitrate the particular grievance—is undeniably an issue for judicial determination.''

The district court properly concluded that in deciding whether parties agreed to arbitrate a certain matter, a court should generally apply state-law principles to the issue of contract formation. . . . Therefore, state law governs the question of whether the parties in the present case entered into an agreement to arbitrate disputes relating to the SmartDownload license agreement. The district court further held that California law governs the question of contract formation here; the parties do not appeal that determination. * * *

[The court held that the district court properly decided the question of reasonable notice and objective manifestation of assent as a matter of law on the record before it, and declined defendants' request to remand for a full trial on that question.]

III.   Whether the User Plaintiffs Had Reasonable Notice of and Manifested Assent to the SmartDownload License Agreement

Whether governed by the common law or by Article 2 of the Uniform Commercial Code (''UCC''), a transaction, in order to be a contract, requires a manifestation of agreement between the parties. . . .* Mutual manifestation of assent, whether by written or spoken word or by conduct, is the touchstone of contract. . . . Although an onlooker observing the disputed transactions in this case would have seen each of the user plaintiffs click on the SmartDownload ''Download'' button . . . a consumer's clicking on a download button does not communicate assent to contractual terms if the offer did not make clear to the consumer that clicking on the download button would signify assent to those terms. . . . California's common law is clear that ''an offeree, regardless of apparent manifestation of his consent, is not bound by inconspicuous contractual provisions of which he is unaware, contained in a document whose contractual nature is not obvious.'' . . .

---

* The district court concluded that the SmartDownload transactions here should be governed by ''California law as it relates to the sale of goods, including the Uniform Commercial Code in effect in California.'' *Specht,* 150 F.Supp.2d at 591. It is not obvious, however, that UCC Article 2 (''sales of goods'') applies to the licensing of software that is downloadable from the Internet . . . * * *

We need not decide today whether UCC Article 2 applies to Internet transactions in downloadable products. The district court's analysis and the parties' arguments on appeal show that, for present purposes, there is no essential difference between UCC Article 2 and the common law of contracts. We therefore apply the common law, with exceptions as noted.

Arbitration agreements are no exception to the requirement of manifestation of assent. "This principle of knowing consent applies with particular force to provisions for arbitration...." Clarity and conspicuousness of arbitration terms are important in securing informed assent. "If a party wishes to bind in writing another to an agreement to arbitrate future disputes, such purpose should be accomplished in a way that each party to the arrangement will fully and clearly comprehend that the agreement to arbitrate exists and binds the parties thereto.... Thus, California contract law measures assent by an objective standard that takes into account both what the offeree said, wrote, or did and the transactional context in which the offeree verbalized or acted.

A. The Reasonably Prudent Offeree of Downloadable Software

Defendants argue that plaintiffs must be held to a standard of reasonable prudence and that, because notice of the existence of SmartDownload license terms was on the next scrollable screen, plaintiffs were on "inquiry notice" of those terms. We disagree with the proposition that a reasonably prudent offeree in plaintiffs' position would necessarily have known or learned of the existence of the SmartDownload license agreement prior to acting, so that plaintiffs may be held to have assented to that agreement with constructive notice of its terms.... But courts are quick to add: "An exception to this general rule exists when the writing does not appear to be a contract and the terms are not called to the attention of the recipient. In such a case, no contract is formed with respect to the undisclosed term."

. . .

Most of the cases cited by defendants in support of their inquiry-notice argument are drawn from the world of paper contracting....

As the foregoing cases suggest, receipt of a physical document containing contract terms or notice thereof is frequently deemed, in the world of paper transactions, a sufficient circumstance to place the offeree on inquiry notice of those terms. "Every person who has actual notice of circumstances sufficient to put a prudent man upon inquiry as to a particular fact, has constructive notice of the fact itself in all cases in which, by prosecuting such inquiry, he might have learned such fact." Cal. Civ.Code § 19. These principles apply equally to the emergent world of online product delivery, pop-up screens, hyperlinked pages, clickwrap licensing, scrollable documents, and urgent admonitions to "Download Now!". What plaintiffs saw when they were being invited by defendants to download this fast, free plug-in called SmartDownload was a screen containing praise for the product and, at the very bottom of the screen, a "Download" button. Defendants argue that under the principles set forth in the cases cited above, a "fair and prudent person using ordinary care" would have been on inquiry notice of SmartDownload's license terms....

We are not persuaded that a reasonably prudent offeree in these circumstances would have known of the existence of license terms. Plaintiffs were responding to an offer that did not carry an immediately visible notice of the existence of license terms or require unambiguous manifestation of assent to those terms. Thus, plaintiffs' "apparent manifestation of . . . consent" was to terms "contained in a document whose contractual nature [was] not obvious. . . ." Moreover, the fact that, given the position of the scroll bar on their computer screens, plaintiffs may have been aware that an unexplored portion of the Netscape webpage remained below the download button does not mean that they reasonably should have concluded that this portion contained a notice of license terms. In their deposition testimony, plaintiffs variously stated that they used the scroll bar "[o]nly if there is something that I feel I need to see that is on—that is off the page," or that the elevated position of the scroll bar suggested the presence of "mere [ ] formalities, standard lower banner links" or "that the page is bigger than what I can see." Plaintiffs testified, and defendants did not refute, that plaintiffs were in fact unaware that defendants intended to attach license terms to the use of SmartDownload.

We conclude that in circumstances such as these, where consumers are urged to download free software at the immediate click of a button, a reference to the existence of license terms on a submerged screen is not sufficient to place consumers on inquiry or constructive notice of those terms. The SmartDownload webpage screen was "printed in such a manner that it tended to conceal the fact that it was an express acceptance of [Netscape's] rules and regulations." Internet users may have, as defendants put it, "as much time as they need[ ]" to scroll through multiple screens on a webpage, but there is no reason to assume that viewers will scroll down to subsequent screens simply because screens are there. When products are "free" and users are invited to download them in the absence of reasonably conspicuous notice that they are about to bind themselves to contract terms, the transactional circumstances cannot be fully analogized to those in the paper world of arm's-length bargaining. * * *

B.   Shrinkwrap Licensing and Related Practices

Defendants cite certain well-known cases involving shrinkwrap licensing and related commercial practices in support of their contention that plaintiffs became bound by the SmartDownload license terms by virtue of inquiry notice. * * * [The court cited and discussed several cases.] These cases do not help defendants. To the extent that they hold that the purchaser of a computer or tangible software is contractually bound after failing to object to printed license terms provided with the product, [they] do not differ markedly from the cases involving traditional paper contracting discussed in the previous section. * * * In sum, the foregoing cases [because the purchaser was clearly aware of the terms at issue before using the computer] are clearly distinguishable from the facts of the present action.

C.   Online Transactions

Cases in which courts have found contracts arising from Internet use do not assist defendants, because in those circumstances there was much clearer notice than in the present case that a user's act would manifest assent to contract terms....*

After reviewing the California common law and other relevant legal authority, we conclude that under the circumstances here, plaintiffs' downloading of SmartDownload did not constitute acceptance of defendants' license terms. Reasonably conspicuous notice of the existence of contract terms and unambiguous manifestation of assent to those terms by consumers are essential if electronic bargaining is to have integrity and credibility. We hold that a reasonably prudent offeree in plaintiffs' position would not have known or learned, prior to acting on the invitation to download, of the reference to SmartDownload's license terms hidden below the "Download" button on the next screen. We affirm the district court's conclusion that the user plaintiffs, including Fagan, are not bound by the arbitration clause contained in those terms. * * *

[The court held that other claims were beyond the scope of the arbitration clause to which the plaintiff assented and that Specht could not be required to arbitrate as a non-party beneficiary.]

CONCLUSION

For the foregoing reasons, we affirm the district court's denial of defendants' motion to compel arbitration and to stay court proceedings.

NOTES

(1) *Applicable law.* The question of applicable law will continue to plague the internet transaction. If the contract was for the sale of goods, UCC Article 2

---

* The district court concluded that the SmartDownload transactions here should be governed by "California law as it relates to the sale of goods, including the Uniform Commercial Code in effect in California." *Specht*, 150 F.Supp.2d at 591. It is not obvious, however, that UCC Article 2 ("sales of goods") applies to the licensing of software that is downloadable from the Internet. *Cf. Advent Sys. Ltd. v. Unisys Corp.*, 925 F.2d 670, 675 (3d Cir.1991) ("The increasing frequency of computer products as subjects of commercial litigation has led to controversy over whether software is a 'good' or intellectual property. The [UCC] does not specifically mention software."); Lorin Brennan, *Why Article 2 Cannot Apply to Software Transactions*, PLI Patents, Copyrights, Trademarks, & Literary Property Course Handbook Series (Feb.-Mar.2001) (demonstrating the trend in case law away from application of UCC provisions to software sales and licensing and toward application of intellectual property principles). There is no doubt that a sale of tangible goods over the Internet is governed by Article 2 of the UCC. *See, e.g., Butler v. Beer Across Am.*, 83 F.Supp.2d 1261, 1263–64 & n. 6 (N.D.Ala.2000) (applying Article 2 to an Internet sale of bottles of beer). Some courts have also applied Article 2, occasionally with misgivings, to sales of off-the-shelf software in tangible, packaged formats. *See, e.g., ProCD*, 86 F.3d at 1450 ("[W]e treat the [database] licenses as ordinary contracts accompanying the sale of products, and therefore as governed by the common law of contracts and the Uniform Commercial Code. Whether there are legal differences between 'contracts' and 'licenses' (which may matter under the copyright doctrine of first sale) is a subject for another day."); *i.LAN Sys., Inc. v. NetScout Serv. Level Corp.*, 183 F.Supp.2d 328, 332 (D.Mass.2002) (stating, in the context of a dispute between business parties, that "Article 2 technically does not, and certainly will not in the future, govern software licenses, but for the time being, the Court will assume that it does"). * * *

will apply even if the contract was concluded electronically. But what are goods? For example, should there be any difference between a CD boxed and sold in a store and the content of that CD downloaded from a website? And what about so-called "smart goods," like a Palm Pilot, that in a real sense contain computers and are operated by software?

Revised Article 2 did not answer these questions, and, except for excluding an undefined term "information," retains the traditional definition of goods. See Rev. 2–103(1)(k). The reason for silence here appears to be a disagreement with the sponsors of the Uniform Computer Information Transactions Act (UCITA), which deals with transactions in "computer information," see UCITA 102(a)(10), which would bring both the license of a boxed CD and the sale of "smart goods" within its scope. For now, at least, this important scope problem is left to courts like the Second Circuit. What contract law did the court apply in the *Specht* case? Here's what the court said about UCITA.

> Downloadable software, however, is scarcely a "tangible" good, and, in part because software may be obtained, copied, or transferred effortlessly at the stroke of a computer key, licensing of such Internet products has assumed a vast importance in recent years. Recognizing that "a body of law based on images of the sale of manufactured goods ill fits licenses and other transactions in computer information," the National Conference of Commissioners on Uniform State Laws has promulgated the Uniform Computer Information Transactions Act ("UCITA"), a code resembling UCC Article 2 in many respects but drafted to reflect emergent practices in the sale and licensing of computer information. UCITA, prefatory note (rev. ed. Aug.23, 2001) (available at www.ucitaonline.com/ucita.html). UCITA—originally intended as a new Article 2B to supplement Articles 2 and 2A of the UCC but later proposed as an independent code—has been adopted by two states, Maryland and Virginia. *See* Md.Code Ann. Com. Law §§ 22–101 *et seq.;* Va.Code Ann. §§ 59.1–501.1 *et seq.* * * *

> In addition, the model code, UCITA, discussed above, generally recognizes the importance of conspicuous notice and unambiguous manifestation of assent in online sales and licensing of computer information. For example, § 112, which addresses manifestation of assent, provides that a user's opportunity to review online contract terms exists if a "record" (or electronic writing) of the contract terms is "made available in a manner that ought to call it to the attention of a reasonable person and permit review." UCITA, § 112(e)(1) (rev. ed. Aug.23, 2001) (available at www.ucitaonline.com/ucita.html).

(2) How did Revised Article 2 adapt to legislation about electronic commerce, such as UETA? Consider the following Sections: Rev. 2–103(1)(b),(1)(f),(1)(g),(1)(h),(1)(m),(1)(p), 2–108(4), 2–204(4), 2–210, 2–212, 2–213.

(3) See Robert Hillman and Jeffrey J. Rachlinski, *Standard-Form Contracting in the Electronic Age*, 77 N.Y.U. L. Rev. 429 (2002), who argue that while an individual's opportunity to protect herself against one-sided standard forms is arguably greater when contracting by computer than when contracting through written forms, the "cognitive perspective that consumers tend to adopt with respect to contractual risks makes it unlikely that many will take advantage of these new [electronic] tools ... [and] the electronic environment gives businesses new opportunities to exploit consumers." Id. at 495. In short,

almost no one reads the terms of the "click wrap" license before assenting to the program. Should they? How can the law take into account the fact that they will not read?

(E) TERMINATION OF OFFER: DESTRUCTION OF POWER OF ACCEPTANCE

By now a few patterns should be apparent. In the bargaining relationship, an offer, however defined, must be communicated to be effective. Once communicated, the offer creates in the offeree a power of acceptance, the duration of which may be limited by either the terms of the offer or some concept of reasonable time. Up to now, we have examined the efforts by offerees to accept the offer before the power of acceptance was terminated. The focus has been upon what an acceptance is and by what method or manner assent should be manifested. And we have seen that when something called a counter-offer is actually communicated to the offeror, the power of acceptance is terminated, much like a specific rejection, by conduct of the offeree. See *Minneapolis & St. Louis Railway Co. v. Columbus Rolling–Mill Co.,* supra at 325. But in the fuzzy background of these cases, it is apparent that there is a race between the proper exercise of the power of acceptance by the offeree and, perhaps, lapse of time, a change of mind by the offeror or some other terminating event. This "race" is vividly demonstrated in the so-called "mailbox" rule, where the contract is created if the letter of acceptance is posted before the offeror's revocation is actually received by the offeree.

In this subsection, we will briefly explore some other aspects of this "race," emphasizing the overlaps with problems previously discussed and the underlying policies. In the next subsection, we will survey the basic varieties of option contracts, with emphasis upon the methods of creation, effect upon the power of acceptance and overlap with materials previously covered.

Hendricks v. Behee

Missouri Court of Appeals, Southern District, 1990.
Supra at 286.

Dickinson v. Dodds

Court of Appeal, Chancery Division, 1876.
2 Ch.D. 463.

On Wednesday, the 10th of June, 1874, the Defendant John Dodds signed and delivered to the Plaintiff, George Dickinson, a memorandum, of which the material part was as follows:—

"I hereby agree to sell to Mr. George Dickinson the whole of the dwelling-houses, garden ground, stabling, and outbuildings thereto belonging, situate at Croft, belonging to me, for the sum of 800. As witness my hand this tenth day of June, 1874.

"£800.(Signed) John Dodds."

"P.S.—This offer to be left over until Friday, 9 o'clock, A.M. J.D. (the twelfth), 12th June, 1874.

"(Signed) J. Dodds."

The bill alleged that Dodds understood and intended that the Plaintiff should have until Friday 9 A.M. within which to determine whether he would or would not purchase, and that he should absolutely have until that time the refusal of the property at the price of £800, and that the Plaintiff in fact determined to accept the offer on the morning of Thursday, the 11th of June, but did not at once signify his acceptance to Dodds, believing that he had the power to accept it until 9 A.M. on the Friday.

In the afternoon of the Thursday the Plaintiff was informed by a Mr. Berry that Dodds had been offering or agreeing to sell the property to Thomas Allan, the other Defendant. Thereupon the Plaintiff, at about half-past seven in the evening, went to the house of Mrs. Burgess, the mother-in-law of Dodds, where he was then staying, and left with her a formal acceptance in writing of the offer to sell the property. According to the evidence of Mrs. Burgess this document never in fact reached Dodds, she having forgotten to give it to him.

On the following (Friday) morning, at about seven o'clock, Berry, who was acting as agent for Dickinson, found Dodds at the Darlington railway station, and handed to him a duplicate of the acceptance by Dickinson, and explained to Dodds its purport. He replied that it was too late, as he had sold the property. A few minutes later Dickinson himself found Dodds entering a railway carriage, and handed him another duplicate of the notice of acceptance, but Dodds declined to receive it, saying, "You are too late. I have sold the property."

It appeared that on the day before, Thursday, the 11th of June, Dodds had signed a formal contract for the sale of the property to the Defendant Allan for £800, and had received from him a deposit of £40.

The bill in this suit prayed that the Defendant Dodds might be decreed specifically to perform the contract of the 10th of June, 1874; that he might be restrained from conveying the property to Allan; that Allan might be restrained from taking any such conveyance; that, if any such conveyance had been or should be made, Allan might be declared a trustee of the property for, and might be directed to convey the property to, the Plaintiff; and for damages.

The cause came on for hearing before Vice–Chancellor Bacon on the 25th of January, 1876.

[A decree for specific performance was entered, and the Defendants appealed.]

■ JAMES, L.J., after referring to the document of the 10th of June, 1874, continued:—

The document, though beginning "I hereby agree to sell," was nothing but an offer, and was only intended to be an offer, for the Plaintiff himself tells us that he required time to consider whether he would enter into an agreement or not. Unless both parties had then agreed there was no concluded agreement then made; it was in effect and substance only an offer to sell. The Plaintiff, being minded not to complete the bargain at that time, added this memorandum—"This offer to be left over until Friday, 9 o'clock A.M., 12th June, 1874." That shews it was only an offer. There was no consideration given for the undertaking or promise, to whatever extent it may be considered binding, to keep the property unsold until 9 o'clock on Friday morning; but apparently Dickinson was of opinion, and probably Dodds was of the same opinion, that he (Dodds) was bound by that promise, and could not in any way withdraw from it, or retract it, until 9 o'clock on Friday morning, and this probably explains a good deal of what afterwards took place. But it is clear settled law, on one of the clearest principles of law, that this promise, being a mere nudum pactum, was not binding, and that at any moment before a complete acceptance by Dickinson of the offer, Dodds was as free as Dickinson himself. Well, that being the state of things, it is said that the only mode in which Dodds could assert that freedom was by actually and distinctly saying to Dickinson, "Now I withdraw my offer." It appears to me that there is neither principle nor authority for the proposition that there must be an express and actual withdrawal of the offer, or what is called a retraction. It must, to constitute a contract, appear that the two minds were at one, at the same moment of time, that is, that there was an offer continuing up to the time of the acceptance. If there was not such a continuing offer, then the acceptance comes to nothing. Of course it may well be that the one man is bound in some way or other to let the other man know that his mind with regard to the offer has been changed; but in this case, beyond all question, the Plaintiff knew that Dodds was no longer minded to sell the property to him as plainly and clearly as if Dodds had told him in so many words, "I withdraw the offer." This is evident from the Plaintiff's own statements in the bill.

The Plaintiff says in effect that, having heard and knowing that Dodds was no longer minded to sell to him, and that he was selling or had sold to some one else, thinking that he could not in point of law withdraw his offer, meaning to fix him to it, and endeavouring to bind him, "I went to the house where he was lodging, and saw his mother-in-law, and left with her an acceptance of the offer, knowing all the while that he had entirely changed his mind. I got an agent to watch for him at 7 o'clock the next morning, and I went to the train just before 9 o'clock, in order that I might catch him and give him my notice of acceptance just before 9 o'clock, and when that occurred he told my agent, and he told me, you are too late, and he then threw back the paper." It is to my mind quite clear that before there was any attempt at acceptance by the Plaintiff, he was perfectly well aware that Dodds had changed his mind, and that he had in fact agreed to sell the property to Allan. It is impossible, therefore, to say there was ever that existence of the same mind between the two parties which is essential in point of law to the making of an agreement. I am of opinion, therefore, that the Plaintiff has failed to prove that there was any binding contract between Dodds and himself.

■ MELLISH, L.J.:—

I am of the same opinion. The first question is, whether this document of the 10th of June, 1874, which was signed by Dodds, was an agreement to sell, or only an offer to sell, the property therein mentioned to Dickinson; and I am clearly of opinion that it was only an offer, although it is in the first part of it, independently of the postscript, worded as an agreement. I apprehend that, until acceptance, so that both parties are bound, even though an instrument is so worded as to express that both parties agree, it is in point of law only an offer, and, until both parties are bound, neither party is bound. It is not necessary that both parties should be bound within the Statute of Frauds, for, if one party makes an offer in writing, and the other accepts it verbally, that will be sufficient to bind the person who has signed the written document. But, if there be no agreement, either verbally or in writing, then, until acceptance, it is in point of law an offer only, although worded as if it were an agreement. But it is hardly necessary to resort to that doctrine in the present case, because the postscript calls it an offer, and says, "This offer to be left over until Friday, 9 o'clock A.M." Well, then, this being only an offer, the law says—and it is a perfectly clear rule of law—that, although it is said that the offer is to be left open until Friday morning at 9 o'clock, that did not bind Dodds. He was not in point of law bound to hold the offer over until 9 o'clock on Friday morning. He was not so bound either in law or in equity. Well, that being so, when on the next day he made an agreement with Allan to sell the property to him, I am not aware of any ground on which it can be said that that contract with Allan was not as good and binding a contract as ever was made. Assuming Allan to have known (there is some dispute about it, and Allan does not admit that he knew of it, but I will assume that he did) that Dodds had made the offer to Dickinson, and had given him till Friday morning at 9 o'clock to accept it, still in point of law that could not prevent Allan from making a more favourable offer than Dickinson, and entering at once into a binding agreement with Dodds.

Then Dickinson is informed by Berry that the property has been sold by Dodds to Allan. Berry does not tell us from whom he heard it, but he says that he did hear it, that he knew it, and that he informed Dickinson of it. Now, stopping there, the question which arises is this—If an offer has been made for the sale of property, and before that offer is accepted, the person who has made the offer enters into a binding agreement to sell the property to somebody else, and the person to whom the offer was first made receives notice in some way that the property has been sold to another person, can he after that make a binding contract by the acceptance of the offer? I am of opinion that he cannot. The law may be right or wrong in saying that a person who has given to another a certain time within which to accept an offer is not bound by his promise to give that time; but, if he is not bound by that promise, and may still sell the property to some one else, and if it be the law that, in order to make a contract, the two minds must be in agreement at some one time, that is, at the time of the acceptance, how is it possible that when the person to whom the offer has been made knows that the person who has made the offer has sold the property to someone else, and that, in fact, he has not remained in the same mind to sell it to him, he can be at liberty to accept the offer and thereby make a binding contract? It seems to me that would be simply absurd. If a man makes an offer to sell a particular horse in his stable, and says, "I will give you until the day after to-morrow to accept the offer," and the next day goes and sells the horse to somebody else, and receives the purchase-money from him, can the person to whom the offer was originally made then come and say, "I accept," so as to make a binding contract, and so as to be entitled to recover damages for the non-delivery of the horse? If the rule of law is that a mere offer to sell property, which can be withdrawn at any time, and which is made dependent on the acceptance of the person to whom it is made, is a mere nudum pactum, how is it possible that the person to whom the offer has been made can by acceptance make a binding contract after he knows that the person who has made the offer has sold the property to some one else? It is admitted law that, if a man who makes an offer dies, the offer cannot be accepted after he is dead, and parting with the property has very much the same effect as the death of the owner, for it makes the performance of the offer impossible. I am clearly of opinion that, just as when a man who has made an offer dies before it is accepted it is impossible that it can then be accepted, so when once the person to whom the offer was made knows that the property has been sold to some one else, it is too late for him to accept the offer, and on that ground I am clearly of opinion that there was no binding contract for the sale of this property by Dodds to Dickinson, and even if there had been, it seems to me that the sale of the property to Allan was first in point of time. However, it is not necessary to consider, if there had been two binding contracts, which of them would be entitled to priority in equity, because there is no binding contract between Dodds and Dickinson.

NOTES

(1) Restatement (Second) § 36: "(1) An offeree's power of acceptance may be terminated by (a) rejection or counter-offer by the offeree, or (b) lapse of time, or (c) revocation by the offeror, or (d) death or incapacity of the offeror or offeree. (2) In addition, an offeree's power of acceptance is terminated by the non-occurrence of any condition of acceptance under the terms of the offer."

(2) Since under the doctrine of *Adams v. Lindsell* an acceptance may be effective upon dispatch, a decided advantage to the offeree, would it not be fair to accord a similar benefit to the offeror by making a revocation effective upon the sending of the message?

(3) "It seems to us a reasonable requirement that, to disable the plaintiffs from accepting their offer, the defendants should bring home to them actual notice that it has been revoked. By their choice and act they brought about a relation between themselves and the plaintiffs, which the plaintiffs could turn

into a contract by an act on their part, and authorized the plaintiffs to understand and to assume that that relation existed. When the plaintiffs acted in good faith on the assumption, the defendants could not complain. Knowingly to lead a person reasonably to suppose that you offer, and to offer, are the same thing. ... The offer must be made before the acceptance, and it does not matter whether it is made a longer or shorter time before, if, by its express or implied terms, it is outstanding at the time of the acceptance. Whether much or little time has intervened, it reaches forward to the moment of the acceptance, and speaks then. It would be monstrous to allow an inconsistent act of the offeror, not known or brought to the notice of the offeree, to affect the making of the contract; for instance, a sale by an agent elsewhere one minute after the principal personally has offered goods which are accepted within five minutes by the person to whom he is speaking. The principle is the same when the time is longer, and the act relied on a step looking to, but not yet giving notice." Holmes, J. in Brauer v. Shaw, 168 Mass. 198, 46 N.E. 617–18 (1897).

(4) Why was not the offer, in *Dickinson,* irrevocable in view of the postscript that "this offer to be left over until Friday ... 12th June, 1874"?

(5) Do the opinions clearly disclose whether Berry told Dickinson that Dodds had actually contracted to sell to another or had merely made an offer to sell? Would the result likely be the same in either case?

(6) Is *Dickinson* consistent with the objective theory of contracts? See G. Gilmore, The Death of Contract 28–34 (1974).

(7) Restatement § 42, following *Dickinson,* states: "Where an offer is for the sale of an interest in land or in other things, if the offeror, after making the offer, sells or contracts to sell the interest to another person, and the offeree acquires reliable information of that fact, before he has exercised his power of creating a contract by acceptance of the offer, the offer is revoked." Should this rule of "indirect revocation" be limited to cases involving "the sale of an interest in land or in other things"? The drafters of the revised Restatement have extended the scope of this section as follows: "An offeree's power of acceptance is terminated when the offeror takes definite action inconsistent with an intention to enter into the proposed contract and the offeree acquires reliable information to that effect." Restatement (Second) § 43.

(8) Suppose, in *Dickinson,* that Dodds learned from a reliable third person that Dickinson was no longer interested in the offer and had agreed to purchase other property instead. Could Dickinson, assuming he had not spoken with Dodds about the matter, change his mind and accept the offer of Dodds?

(9) *Rewards.* Additional considerations are involved in determining how a general offer may be revoked. If, for example, the offeror in *Glover v. Jewish War Veterans* (supra at 302) had decided to withdraw its offer, how could it have done so? It would scarcely be feasible to notify directly all offerees, nor would "indirect revocation" reach the vast majority of those who had read the advertisements. The authorities favor a practical rule which, in general, obliges the offeror to give the notice of revocation publicity equal to that given the offer. See Restatement (Second) § 46; Corbin § 41; Williston §§ 59–59A.

(10) *Lapse of Offer.* An offer "lapses" of its own terms after the expiration of the time stipulated in the offer or upon the occurrence of a stipulated event, or if there is no such stipulation, after a reasonable period of time. See

Restatement (Second) § 41. What is reasonable will depend upon the circumstances. For example, one would expect an offer to sell securities which are subject to rapid price fluctuations to lapse after a shorter period of time than an offer to sell unimproved real estate. Where the offer stipulates that it will be open for a stated period (e.g., ten days), generally the period will begin when the offer is received, not when it is dispatched. Caldwell v. Cline, 109 W.Va. 553, 156 S.E. 55 (1930). Finally, an offer made by one to another in face to face conversation is ordinarily deemed to continue only to the close of their conversation, and cannot be accepted thereafter. Akers v. J.B. Sedberry, Inc., 39 Tenn.App. 633, 286 S.W.2d 617 (1955). See also Newman v. Schiff, 778 F.2d 460 (8th Cir.1985) (Schiff's statement on the live CBS Nightwatch program that he would pay $100,000 to anyone who called the show and cited any section of the Internal Revenue Code "that says an individual is required to file a tax return" constituted an offer, but it did not extend beyond the time of the program).

PROBLEM: THE CASE OF THE REJECTION, REVOCATION AND ACCEPTANCE RACE

On July 4, A mailed to B a written offer to sell ten shares of an unlisted stock at $60.00 per share. B was given four days from the date of the letter to accept. The offer was received on July 6, at 2 PM. At 3 PM on July 6, B mailed a letter to A which stated, in part: "will purchase ten shares at $55.00 per share. ..." At 11 AM on July 6, however, A had sold the ten shares to C for $65.00 and at 1 PM of the same day had mailed a letter to B revoking the offer. B, who was blissfully unaware of A's activity, learned at 4 PM on July 6 that the market price of the shares might increase and, at 5 PM on the same day, telegraphed A to "disregard letter ... will take offered stock for $60.00 per share." B's telegram of July 6 was received by A at 9 AM on July 7. B's letter of July 6 was received by A at 2 PM on July 8. A's letter of July 6 was received by B at 2 PM on July 8.

(1) B claims that he has a contract with A for the purchase of the stock. Is this contention correct?

(2) Suppose at 3 PM on July 6 that B mailed a letter to A which "accepted your offer." Shortly thereafter the market for the shares of stock dropped sharply and, at 5 PM, B telegraphed A to "disregard" my prior letter, I have "decided not to buy." The telegram was received by A on July 7 at 9 AM, whereupon A sold the shares to C. B's letter of acceptance was received on July 8 at 2 PM. Is there a contract? What are A's options?

(3) Draft a new section for the proposed Restatement (Third) Contracts that would resolve this question.

See Restatement (Second) of Contracts §§ 40, 42.

PROBLEM: THE CASE OF THE DEAD GUARANTOR

You are an Associate Justice of the Supreme Court of Nowhere. The case of *Millcreek Corporation v. Simmons, Executor,* is now under advisement. Set out below are draft opinions by our colleagues. You are the "swing" vote in the case. Prepare a short opinion in which you either affirm or reverse the courts below and give reasons for your decision.

The facts of the case are simple. Beginning in 1989 the plaintiff, a wholesaler of building supplies, sold a number of items to Bishop, a house painter. The sales were on credit, and although all of the bills were finally paid, Bishop was slow in paying and appeared to be in some financial difficulty. Early in 1990, Millcreek refused to sell paint and other supplies to Bishop unless he paid cash or provided suitable security. Bishop then contacted his father, a retired building contractor of some wealth who lived some 300 miles away, and the father agreed to "guarantee" Bishop's debts to Millcreek. Later, Bishop presented for Millcreek's approval a written guaranty agreement, dated February 1, 1990, in which his father promised that if, in the next six months, Millcreek extended credit to Bishop in an amount not to exceed $8,000, he (the father) would pay Bishop's obligation to Millcreek if Bishop failed to do so when the obligation was due. After calling the elder Bishop's attorney to verify the signature, Millcreek accepted the guaranty as appropriate security.

From February 5 through March 13, Millcreek made five separate credit sales to Bishop. Three of these sales occurred after March 8, when, unknown to Millcreek (but clearly known to Bishop), the elder Bishop had died. The amount involved in these three transactions was $5,000. On March 13, Millcreek received a letter from the elder Bishop's executor, informing it of the death and requesting a surrender of the guaranty. Later, after Bishop failed to pay the $5,000 obligations due to insolvency, Millcreek brought suit against Simmons, the executor, to recover on the guaranty contract. The trial court, at the conclusion of the evidence, granted Simmons' motion for a judgment on the ground that the guaranty constituted an offer for a series of separate contracts and that the death of the offeror on March 8 automatically terminated the offer with regard to sales made thereafter. This judgment was affirmed in the appellate court and the plaintiff, Millcreek, has appealed.

Altman, J. I am of the opinion that the judgment below should be affirmed. The law is clear. An offer is terminated by the death of the offeror before an acceptance occurs, even if the offeree is unaware of that death. This rule finds consistent support in the precedents of this and other states and in the Restatement of Contracts of the American Law Institute. See, e.g., Restatement (First) § 48; Jordan v. Dobbins, 122 Mass. 168 (1877); New Headley Tobacco Warehouse Co. v. Gentry's Ex'r, 307 Ky. 857, 212 S.W.2d 325 (1948). As one court put it: "This rule has been criticized on the ground that under the modern view of the formation of contracts, it is not the actual meeting of minds of the contracting parties that is the determining fact, but rather the apparent state of mind of the parties embodied in an expression of mutual consent; so that the acceptance by an offeree of an offer, which is apparently still open, should result in an enforceable contract notwithstanding the prior death of the offeror unknown to the offeree. On the other hand, it has been forcibly suggested that ordinarily the condition is implied in an offer that the offeror will survive to supervise the performance if his offer is accepted, and therefore an acceptance after death is ineffective even though the acceptor be ignorant of the offeror's death. ... These conflicting views, however, were given consideration in the preparation of the Restatement, and the rule announced was adopted as representing the weight of authority and professional opinion." Chain v. Wilhelm, 84 F.2d 138, 140 (4th Cir.1936). Accord: Restatement (Second) § 48: A. Farnsworth, Contracts § 3.18 (3d ed.1999). See also In re

Severtson's Estate, 1998 WL 88253 (Minn.App.1998); Biggins v. Shore, 523 Pa. 148, 565 A.2d 737 (1989).

The guaranty, properly interpreted, was an offer looking forward to a series of separate acceptances. No contract was formed until Millcreek had actually extended credit to Bishop within the limits of the guaranty. Although the decedent agreed that the guaranty should last for six months, Millcreek gave no consideration to support this promise. As such, the agreement to keep the offer of guaranty open for six months was not enforceable.

From these rules it logically follows that the offer to guarantee Bishop's debts was terminated by the offeror's death on March 8, and the judgment below is affirmed.

Oliver, J., concurring. I concur in the majority opinion written by Justice Altman, but for different reasons. Surely we can agree that a sound judicial decision cannot be made from logic and logic alone. As Justice Holmes said, "the life of the law has been experience, not logic." I feel strongly that law in general and contract law in particular exists to serve human needs and that the rules of contract must constantly be adjusted and adapted to the human conditions which produce the disputes. But there is no evidence of those "human conditions" in this case and the court has no way of knowing what impact the rather clear rule that death terminates an unaccepted offer has had upon the planning and other relevant behavior of contracting parties. Do the parties take this rule into account when they negotiate guaranty contracts? What would be the impact upon business practices if the rule were overturned? There are no answers to these questions contained in the record before us. Since the rule has a long history of acceptance in the law and since the effect of its alteration by this court is uncertain, I am hesitant to intervene at this time and change the law. The risk of death is well known to all and surely the plaintiff in this case is just as capable as the decedent to make provision in the agreement or otherwise against the risk of death. If change is needed it should come from the legislature, not the court.

Roscoe, J. dissenting. I dissent. It is obviously unfair to leave the risk of death upon the plaintiff in this case. The plaintiff relied in good faith upon a written promise of guaranty without actual knowledge that the guarantor had died. The plaintiff had no reason to know of the death—the guarantor lived 300 miles away and no method of quick notice was available. A basic policy of the law of contracts is to protect the reasonable expectations of parties to whom promises have been made. See Corbin § 54. Application of the old rule in this case would impair this policy and produce an unfair result in this case. Neither result would, in my mind, be sound.

But we do not have to change the law in this case. A realistic construction of the writing signed by the decedent persuades me that an offer looking forward to a bilateral contract accepted by the first extension of credit was made. Thus, when the plaintiff made the first extension of credit on February 5, he impliedly promised that during the life of the guaranty he would extend credit up to the $8,000 limit to Bishop. See Restatement (Second) §§ 53(1), 54(1) and 62. Thus, the decedent died during the performance of an existing bilateral contract, not before an outstanding offer had been accepted. Or, if the bilateral contract analysis is unsound, the court should, after the first extension of credit is made, imply a promise to hold the guaranty open for six months.

Restatement (Second) § 87(2). See § 88. In either case, thus, the question is whether obligations to pay money incurred after death but when the plaintiff had no knowledge of the death are enforceable against the Estate. The answer is "yes." See Restatement (Second) § 262. Although death of one contracting party may discharge some contracts, when the other party has fully performed and the obligation is to pay money alone, the obligation will not be discharged. In my view, the court below erroneously construed the guaranty writing and committed other material errors of law. The judgment below should be reversed and a final judgment entered for the plaintiff.

Earl, J., dissenting. The rule of law in dispute here is of ancient vintage and, presumably, served some legitimate purpose in a time when contracts were more personal and a "subjective" theory of relationships seemed to dominate. But in this day of impersonal, complicated and widespread commerce, the old rule is anachronistic. It is but another example of "slow moving" law getting out of joint with ever changing life. At the same time, the rule seems to provide a rather arbitrary protection to promisors who die without considering the interests of promisees—those who rely on promises. Assuming that both parties have legitimate interests to protect, if they have not provided for the risk of death clearly in the agreement, the question is whether the current rule provides a fair allocation of risk in the circumstances.

The question is not without difficulty. If we limit, as we must, the problem to contracts of guaranty (and not try to over-generalize), we find almost no evidence in the record about business practices and methods of risk allocation in this particular setting. Perhaps it is enough to say that the burden is on the plaintiff to show clearly that the old rule produces disruptive and unfair results when applied to guaranty contracts, especially when the decedent was not compensated for the risk he assumed. As the defendant Executor forcefully argued, why should the estate make payments to the detriment of lawful heirs for credit extensions which occurred after death and for which the estate received no valuable exchange? This makes the point of Justice Oliver in a slightly different manner.

Even so, it seems clear that in the absence of clear agreement by the parties allocating the risk and other compelling social policies, the general purpose to be achieved by these rules of offer and acceptance should be to facilitate and promote ongoing commercial transactions. Without a strained construction of the writing, the parties contemplated a six-month period where the plaintiff probably would be extending credit to Bishop. They were at a distance, and it is unrealistic to expect the plaintiff to telephone the decedent or check the obituary column in the newspaper before every extension of credit. The plaintiff honestly and without reason to know of death, did precisely what the written guaranty permitted—extended credit to Bishop in reliance upon the decedent's promise. In this context, at least, where both parties were equally capable of providing against the risk in the contract, there seems to be no reason for the arbitrary preference given to the decedent. The broader policy concern for smooth, dependable commercial activity supports the plaintiff's contention that the rule should be changed, and we would so hold. In guaranty contracts, at least, where death occurs before the extension of credit but the promisee acts in good faith and without reason to know, the estate must pay these obligations. This rule is realistically attuned to the needs and problems of

rejects mechanical applications of the old and strained construc-
to put the law more solidly into the life around it. The result is
fficient unless the plaintiff was the "least cost" risk avoider. See
ntracts 124–25 (4th ed. 2001) (a relic of the obsolete view that
es a "meeting of the minds").

ABLE OFFER: OPTION CONTRACTS

& Refining Co. v. Westside Investment Corp.

Supreme Court of Texas, 1968.
428 S.W.2d 92.

■ SMITH, JUSTICE. Petitioner, Humble Oil & Refining Company, filed this suit on February 10, 1965, against Westside Investment Corporation seeking a judgment commanding specific performance based on a written option and contract for the sale of real estate. Petitioner, Marvin H. Mann, a realtor, as a third-party plaintiff, filed a plea in intervention, seeking a judgment for $1260.00 against Westside as brokerage charges in connection with the transaction. Westside, Humble and Mann each filed a motion for summary judgment. The court granted Westside's motion, and overruled the motions of Humble and Mann. The court of civil appeals affirmed, 419 S.W.2d 448. We reverse the judgments of the courts below. We hold that Humble is entitled to specific performance of the option contract and render judgment for Humble. We hold that a material issue of fact exists as to whether Mann is entitled to a brokerage commission and remand that portion of the case to the district court for trial.

The facts, most of which are either stipulated or established by affidavits, are these:

On April 5, 1963, Westside as seller and Humble as buyer agreed and entered into a written contract whereby Westside gave and granted to Humble an exclusive and irrevocable option to purchase for a consideration of $35,000.00 a tract of land situated outside of the city limits of San Antonio, Bexar County, Texas, being all of lots 19, 20, 21, 22 and 23 of Block 2, Lackland Heights Subdivision.

The option contract was supported by a consideration. The contract provided that Humble might exercise the option by giving notice at any time prior to 9:00 p.m. on the 4th day of June, 1963, and by paying to Westside at the time of such notice or within ten (10) days following such notice the sum of $1750.00 as earnest money. This sum of money, together with the sum of Fifty Dollars ($50.00) as consideration paid at the time of the execution of the option contract, made a total of $1800.00 paid by Humble, leaving a balance of $33,200.00 yet to be paid as purchase money in accordance with the option contract.

On May 14, 1963, within the time period provided for in the option contract, Humble paid the above mentioned sum of $1750.00 to the designated escrow agent, Commercial Abstract & Title Company.

Westside admits in its pleadings that it entered into the option contract with Humble, but contends that the option agreement was "rejected, repudiated, and terminated by Humble." Westside contends that summary judgment proof of rejection of the option contract is contained in letters written by Humble to Westside on May 2, 1963, and May 14, 1963. The pertinent portion of the May 2nd letter reads:

"Humble Oil & Refining Company hereby exercises its option to purchase Lots 19, 20, 21, 22 and 23, Block 2, Lackland Heights Subdivision, in or near the City of San Antonio, Bexar County, Texas, granted in Option and Purchase Contract dated April 5, 1963. As additional inducement for Humble to exercise its option to purchase, you have agreed that all utilities (gas, water, sewer and electricity) will be extended to the property prior to the closing of the transaction. The contract of sale is hereby amended to provide that Seller shall extend all utility lines to the property before the date of closing.

"Please sign and return one copy of this letter in the space indicated below to signify your agreement to the amendment to the purchase contract."

The May 14th communication provided, in part, as follows:

"Humble * * * hereby notifies you of its intention to exercise the option granted in option and purchase contract dated April 5, 1963, covering Lots 19, 20, 21, 22 and 23, Block 2, Lackland Heights Subdivision in or near the City of San Antonio, Bexar County, Texas. *The exercise of said option is not qualified and you may disregard the proposed amendment to the contract suggested in letter of May 2, 1963.* * * * " (Emphasis added.)

We conclude from this record that the parties are in agreement that Humble's letter of May 14, 1963, and the payment of earnest money within 10 days thereof was in law a timely exercise of the option to purchase *unless* Humble's letter of May 2, 1963, terminated and rendered unenforceable the option contract. The narrow question to be determined is whether or not the letter of May 2, 1963, constitutes a rejection of the option contract. If it does, the trial court properly granted Westside's motion for summary judgment and the court of civil appeals correctly affirmed such judgment.

Westside contends that Humble's letter of May 2nd was a conditional acceptance which amounted in law to a rejection of the option contract. Westside argues that the letter of May 2nd "clearly evidences Humble's intent to accept the offer *only if* Westside would agree to an amendment to the terms of its original offer." (Emphasis added.) It further argues that Humble's letter of May 14, 1963, reflects that Humble itself understood that its letter of May 2, 1963, contained a qualified acceptance, and did not form a contract. The basis for this conclusion is the sentence in the May 14 letter which reads: "The exercise of said option is not qualified and you may disregard the proposed amendment to the contract suggested in letter dated May 2, 1963, from the undersigned. * * * " We cannot agree with Westside's contentions.

' mere fact that the parties may choose to negotiate before accept-
ption does not mean that the option contract is repudiated. As
'ames on Option Contracts § 838:

'aid down in the law of offers that a qualified or conditional
.nce is a rejection of the offer. It is clearly established by the
.ecisions that a qualified or conditional acceptance of an offer does not
raise a contract because the minds of the parties do not meet in agreement
upon the same terms. It is said that such an acceptance is a counterproposal for a new contract, to give legal life to which requires the assent
or acceptance of the other party. It is in this sense that a qualified or
conditional acceptance is a rejection of the offer first made because the
original negotiations are dropped and negotiations for a new and different
contract begun.

"An option is a contract, the negotiations for the making of which are
concluded by the execution and delivery of the option. The minds of the
parties have met in agreement, the distinctive feature of which is that the
optionor, for a consideration, binds himself to keep the option open for
election by the optionee, for and during the time stipulated, or implied by
law.

"Under an option, the act necessary to raise a binding promise to sell,
is not, therefore, an acceptance of the offer, but rather the performance of
the condition of the option contract. If this is true, then the rule peculiar to
offers to the effect that a conditional acceptance is, in itself, in every case, a
rejection of the offer, is not applicable to an option contract, supported by a
consideration and fixing a time limit for election."

* * *

We hold that Humble's letter of May 2, 1963, did not terminate the
option contract. Humble, for a valuable consideration, purchased the right
to keep the option contract open for the time specified, and the right to
create a contract of purchase. Although Humble did have the right to *accept*
or *reject* the option in the sense that it was free to take the action required
to close the transaction, Humble was not foreclosed from negotiating
relative to the contract of sale as distinguished from the option. The option,
considered as an independent completed agreement, gave the optionee the
right to purchase the property within the time specified. The option
contract bound Humble to do nothing but granted it the right to accept or
reject the option in accordance with its terms within the time and in the
manner specified in the option. Westside was bound to keep the option
open and could not act in derogation of the terms of the option. By the
letter of May 2, 1963, Humble did not surrender or reject the option. The
option to purchase was still a binding obligation between the parties when
Humble exercised it on May 14, 1963. . . .

Our holding falls within the rule stated in 1 Corbin on Contracts § 91.
According to Corbin:

"If the original offer is an irrevocable offer, creating in the offeree a
'binding option,' the rule that a counter offer terminates the power of

acceptance does not apply. Even if it is reasonable to hold that it terminates a revocable power, it should not be held to terminate rights and powers created by a contract. A 'binding option' is such a contract (usually unilateral); and an offer in writing, that allows a time for acceptance (either definite or reasonable) and that is irrevocable by virtue of a statute, is itself a unilateral contract. A counter offer by such an offeree, or other negotiation not resulting in a contract, does not terminate the power of acceptance."

* * *

NOTES

(1) Critically evaluate the following statement from Langdell, Law of Contracts § 178 (2d ed. 1880): "An offer is merely one of the elements of a contract; and it is indispensable to the making of a contract that the wills of the contracting parties do, in legal contemplation, concur at the moment of making it. An offer, therefore, which the party making it has no power to revoke, is a legal impossibility."

(2) "While it may seem at first blush a legal paradox that a contract for the sale of land, mutual and enforceable, can be made when at the time it is claimed to have been made one party to it is openly protesting that he will make no such contract, and while reasons may be advanced to support the proposition that the option holder should be in such a case remitted to an action for damages for refusal to hold the offer open for the stipulated time, there is reason and precedent for holding that the offer to sell, if paid for, may not be withdrawn during the stipulated time, being, in law, a continuing offer to sell." Ostrander, J., concurring in Solomon Mier Co. v. Hadden, 148 Mich. 488, 111 N.W. 1040, 1043 (1907).

(3) *Effect of Rejection by Optionee.* "Where an offer is supported by a binding contract that the offeree's power of acceptance shall continue for a stated time, will a communicated rejection terminate the offeree's power to accept within the time? On principle, there is no reason why it should. The offeree has a contract right to accept within the time. At most rejection is a waiver of this right, but waiver not supported by consideration or an estoppel by change of position can have no effect upon subsequent assertion of the right. So an option holder may complete a contract by communicating his acceptance despite the fact that he has previously rejected the offer. Where, however, before the acceptance the offeror has materially changed his position in reliance on the communicated rejection, as by selling or contracting to sell the subject matter of the offer elsewhere, the subsequent acceptance will be inoperative. Here the rejection is a waiver of the offeree's contract right to accept the offer, binding the offeree by estoppel, so his power to accept is gone." Simpson on Contracts, 2d ed., § 23, quoted in Ryder v. Wescoat, 535 S.W.2d 269, 270 (Mo.App.1976). See also Restatement (Second) § 37: "[T]he power of acceptance under an option contract is not terminated by rejection or counter-offer, by revocation, or by death or incapacity of the offeror, unless the requirements are met for the discharge of a contractual duty." For a criticism of the majority view that rejection or counter-offer by offeree-optionee should not, of itself,

terminate the latter's power of acceptance, see Cozzillio, *The Option Contract: Irrevocable Not Irrejectable,* 39 Cath.U.L.Rev. 491 (1990).

(4) *Option Varieties.* Restatement (Second) § 25 defines an "option contract" as follows: "An option contract is a promise which meets the requirements for the formation of a contract and limits the promisor's power to revoke an offer." This may take the form of a collateral contract not to revoke an existing offer. ("In consideration of $1, I promise not to revoke for thirty days my offer to sell Blackacre for $10,000....") Another method is a contract between the parties whereby, for a consideration (usually a nominal payment), the owner promises to sell and convey the property for a stated price on condition of either notice of acceptance or actual payment within a specified time. ("In consideration of $1, I promise to convey Blackacre, if within thirty days you pay me $10,000. ...") This type of "option contract" is actually a conditional contract to sell; it does not take the form of an offer accompanied by an enforceable promise not to revoke. By prevailing law the practical effect is the same in both cases; *viz.,* the offeror has no power to revoke, and any attempt to do so is ineffectual. See Corbin § 262. An option may also appear as part of a larger transaction, as, for example, a renewal option in a lease. See, e.g., 1020 Park Ave., Inc. v. Raynor, 97 Misc.2d 288, 411 N.Y.S.2d 172 (1978).

(5) *Recital of Consideration as Implied Promise to Pay.* "The majority of cases from other jurisdictions hold that the offeror may prove that the consideration had not been paid and that no other consideration had taken its place. Bard v. Kent, 19 Cal.2d 449 (1942); Calamari & Perillo, Law of Contracts, § 58 (1970). However, the minority rule, and what we consider to be the best view, is that even if it is shown that the dollar was not paid it does not void the contract. We have held many times that the recital of the one dollar consideration gives rise to an implied promise to pay which can be enforced by the other party." Smith v. Wheeler, 233 Ga. 166, 210 S.E.2d 702, 703–4 (1974). Contra: Board of Control of Eastern Michigan University v. Burgess, 45 Mich.App. 183, 206 N.W.2d 256 (1973)(recited consideration of $1 must be paid or tendered).

Restatement (Second) § 87(1)(a) provides: "An offer is binding as an option contract if it (a) is in writing and signed by the offeror, recites a purported consideration for the making of the offer, and proposes an exchange on fair terms within a reasonable time. ..."

(6) *Irrevocability by Statute.* Certain offers are made irrevocable by statute. For example, UCC 2–205 provides: "An offer by a merchant to buy or sell goods in a signed writing which by its terms gives assurance that it will be held open is not revocable, for lack of consideration, during the time stated or if no time is stated for a reasonable time, but in no event may such period of irrevocability exceed three months; but any such term of assurance on a form supplied by the offeree must be separately signed by the offeror." See also Article 16 of the United Nations Convention on Contracts for the International Sale of Goods: "(1) Until a contract is concluded an offer may be revoked if the revocation reaches the offeree before he has dispatched an acceptance. (2) However, an offer cannot be revoked: (a) if it indicates, whether by stating a fixed time limit or otherwise, that it is irrevocable; or (b) if it was reasonable for the offeree to rely on the offer as being irrevocable and the offeree has acted in reliance on the offer."

(7) *The "Mailbox" Rule and Acceptance under an Option Contract.* As you will recall, under the "mailbox" rule, supra at 320, a dispatched but uncommunicated acceptance may preclude revocation of the offer, for the acceptance is effective upon dispatch. Should the rule apply as well in the option contract context, as, for example, where optionee must "notify" optionor before a stipulated date? Most courts have said no, the position adopted by the Restatement of Contracts. See Restatement (Second) § 63. In the view of the drafters, since the option contract provides for irrevocability of the offer, the primary reason for the rule of *Adams v. Lindsell* and its progeny is absent. Professor Corbin has commented: "If in an option contract the duty of the promisor is conditional on notice within 30 days, does this mean notice received or notice properly mailed? It is believed that, in the absence of an expression of contrary intention, it should be held that the notice must be received. As above explained, the notice is in one respect a notice of acceptance of an offer; but in another aspect it is a condition of the promisor's already existing conditional duty. It is more likely to be regarded in this latter aspect by the parties themselves. The rule that an acceptance by post is operative on mailing was itself subjected to severe criticism; and, even though it may now be regarded as settled, it should not be extended to notice of acceptance in already binding option contracts." Corbin § 264. See Romain v. A. Howard Wholesale Co., 506 N.E.2d 1124 (Ind.App.1987). Not all courts follow this powerful tandem, however. See, e.g., Worms v. Burgess, 620 P.2d 455 (Okl.App.1980). See also Jameson v. Foster, 646 P.2d 955 (Colo.App.1982) (Exercise of option effective upon mailing where the option clause provided: "The lessees have an option to purchase said property * * * should the option be exercised on or before Jan. 1, 1980."); APC Operating Partnership v. Mackey, 841 F.2d 1031 (10th Cir.1988) (option to renew lease properly exercised).

(8) *Options in International Sales.* Suppose Seller in Canada faxes an offer to Buyer in Chicago that states, in part, you have five days to accept. The five day period begins to run from the time the offer reaches Buyer. CISG Art.15, 24. During that time, Seller cannot revoke the offer because it indicates, whether by stating a fixed time for acceptance, or otherwise, that it is irrevocable." Art. 16(2)(a). This result does not depend upon the form in which the offer was made, see UCC 2–205, or the presence of consideration. Even if the requirements of Art. 16(2)(b) are not satisfied, the offer is not revocable if it "was reasonable for the offeree to rely on the offer as being irrevocable and the offeree has acted in reliance on the offer."

Under Article 15(1), an offer, whether revocable or not, is not effective until it "reaches" the offeror. But suppose that the offeree has dispatched the acceptance and the offeror communicates a revocation before the acceptance reaches the offeror. According to Art. 16(1), dispatching the acceptance prevents revocation even though an option is not created under Article 16. This protects the offeree against the normal CISG rule that an acceptance is not effective until it reaches the offeror. Art. 18(2).

How does the "mail box" rule differ from CISG?

PROBLEM: EFFECT OF FIRST REFUSAL

Defendant owned a tract of land containing three lots, all of which were zoned commercial. In June, 1989, Defendant sold two of the lots to Plaintiff for

$400,000. As part of the transaction, Defendant granted Plaintiff a "first refusal" on the third lot for a period to end on July 1, 1991. In June, 1991, Defendant, without informing Plaintiff, solicited offers on the third lot from third parties. A written offer to buy for $175,000 cash was made by a third party. Plaintiff learned of the offer and, on June 25, 1991, informed Defendant that it intended to exercise the right of "first refusal" and tendered a certified check for $175,000. Defendant rejected both the third party offer and Plaintiff's tender and did not sell the property.

It is now July 10, 1991. The property has not been sold. Plaintiff claims that it exercised its right of "first refusal" before July 1, 1991 and that it is entitled to specific performance for the third lot. As authority, it cites *Humble Oil,* supra, and other authorities on option contracts. What result?

PROBLEM: CREATION OF RELIANCE OPTIONS

Peter owned real estate in New York City worth $100,000. Patrick held an installment promissory note in the amount of $50,000 upon which Peter was the maker. The note was secured by a first mortgage on the property. Peter had paid $40,000 on the note, plus interest and the balance was due in 12 months, on October 1, 2003. On July 1, 2003, Patrick telephoned Peter and said he would be willing to cancel the note and the mortgage if Peter would pay him $8,500 in cash within 7 days. Peter said he was a bit short of cash and would have to think about it. Patrick then said "if you pay me $8,500 cash by 4 PM on July 8, I will cancel the note and release the mortgage." Peter hung up after thanking Patrick and saying he would try to raise the money.

On July 7, Peter was able to sell his valuable coin collection to a dealer for $10,000. On the morning of July 8, Peter agreed in writing to sell his New York property to Priscilla free of any mortgage for $100,000. With the cash in his brief case, Peter began to look for Patrick. He was not in his office and could not be found at his favorite pub. The bar tender, however, said that Patrick had gone to his home in the Bronx and that some deal was brewing with Paul about some mortgage. Peter then took a taxi to the Bronx, arriving at Patrick's home about 3:45 PM. As he walked up the driveway, he saw Patrick at the open window, waved his briefcase and yelled: "Good news, I've got the money to pay off the mortgage." Patrick responded that you are too late, I sold the note and the mortgage to Paul this morning. Patrick then closed the window and refused to open the door.

Crestfallen, Peter consults you for advice. Consider the materials we have studied so far and those to come in the balance of this section, what is the strongest argument for Peter? Will it be successful?

Marchiondo v. Scheck

Supreme Court of New Mexico, 1967.
78 N.M. 440, 432 P.2d 405.

■ WOOD, JUDGE, Court of Appeals.

The issue is whether the offeror had a right to revoke his offer to enter a unilateral contract.

Defendant, in writing, offered to sell real estate to a specified prospective buyer and agreed to pay a percentage of the sales price as a commission to the broker. The offer fixed a six-day time limit for acceptance. Defendant, in writing, revoked the offer. The revocation was received by the broker on the morning of the sixth day. Later that day, the broker obtained the offeree's acceptance.

Plaintiff, the broker, claiming breach of contract, sued defendant for the commission stated in the offer. On the above facts, the trial court dismissed the complaint.

We are not concerned with the revocation of the offer as between the offeror and the prospective purchaser. With certain exceptions ... , the right of a broker to the agreed compensation, or damages measured thereby, is not defeated by the refusal of the principal to complete or consummate a transaction. . . .

Plaintiff's appeal concerns the revocation of his agency. As to that revocation, the issue between the offeror and his agent is not whether defendant had the power to revoke; rather, it is whether he had the right to revoke. . . .

When defendant made his offer to pay a commission upon sale of the property, he offered to enter a unilateral contract; the offer was for an act to be performed, a sale. 1 Williston on Contracts, § 13 at 23 (3rd ed. 1957); Hutchinson v. Dobson–Bainbridge Realty Co., 31 Tenn.App. 490 (1946).

Many courts hold that the principal has the right to revoke the broker's agency at any time before the broker has actually procured a purchaser. See Hutchinson v. Dobson–Bainbridge Realty Co., supra, and cases therein cited. The reason given is that until there is performance, the offeror has not received that contemplated by his offer, and there is no contract. Further, the offeror may never receive the requested performance because the offeree is not obligated to perform. Until the offeror receives the requested performance, no consideration has passed from the offeree to the offeror. Thus, until the performance is received, the offeror may withdraw the offer. Williston, supra, § 60; Hutchinson v. Dobson–Bainbridge Realty Co., supra.

Defendant asserts that the trial court was correct in applying this rule. However, plaintiff contends that the rule is not applicable where there has been part performance of the offer.

Hutchinson v. Dobson–Bainbridge Realty Co., supra, states:

"A greater number of courts, however, hold that part performance of the consideration may make such an offer irrevocable and that where the offeree or broker manifests his assent to the offer by entering upon performance and spending time and money in his efforts to perform, then the offer becomes irrevocable during the time stated and binding upon the principal according to its terms. * * * "

Defendant contends that the decisions giving effect to a part performance are distinguishable. He asserts that in these cases the offer was of an exclusive right to sell or of an exclusive agency. Because neither factor is present here, he asserts that the "part performance" decisions are not applicable.

Many of the decisions do seem to emphasize the exclusive aspects of the offer. . . .

Such emphasis reaches its extreme conclusion in Tetrick v. Sloan, 170 Cal.App.2d 540, 339 P.2d 613 (1959), where no effect was given to the part performance because there was neither an exclusive agency, nor an exclusive right to sell.

Defendant's offer did not specifically state that it was exclusive. Under § 70–1–43, N.M.S.A.1953, it was not an exclusive agreement. It is not the exclusiveness of the offer that deprives the offeror of the right to revoke. It is the action taken by the offeree which deprives the offeror of that right. Until there is action by the offeree—a partial performance pursuant to the offer—the offeror may revoke even if his offer is of an exclusive agency or an exclusive right to sell. . . .

Once partial performance is begun pursuant to the offer made, a contract results. This contract has been termed a contract with conditions or an option contract. This terminology is illustrated as follows:

"If an offer for a unilateral contract is made, and part of the consideration requested in the offer is given or tendered by the offeree in response thereto, the offeror is bound by a contract, the duty of immediate performance of which is conditional on the full consideration being given or tendered within the time stated in the offer, or, if no time is stated therein, within a reasonable time." Restatement of Contracts, § 45 (1932).

Restatement (Second) Contracts § 45, Tent.Draft No. 1, (approved 1964, Tent.Draft No. 2, p. vii) states:

"(1) Where an offer invites an offeree to accept by rendering a performance and does not invite a promissory acceptance, an option contract is created when the offeree begins the invited performance or tenders part of it.*

"(2) The offeror's duty of performance under any option contract so created is conditional on completion or tender of the invited performance in accordance with the terms of the offer."

Restatement (Second) Contracts § 45, Tent.Draft No. 1, comment (g), says:

"This Section frequently applies to agency arrangements, particularly offers made to real estate brokers. * * * "

See Restatement (Second) Agency § 446, comment (b).

The reason for finding such a contract is stated in Hutchinson v. Dobson–Bainbridge Realty Co., supra, as follows:

---

* [The final draft replaces the final three   Ed.]
words, "part of it," with "a beginning of it."

"This rule avoids hardship to the offeree, and yet does not hold the offeror beyond the terms of his promise. It is true by such terms he was to be bound only if the requested act was done; but this implies that he will let it be done, that he will keep his offer open till the offeree who has begun can finish doing it. At least this is so where the doing of it will necessarily require time and expense. In such a case it is but just to hold that the offeree's part performance furnishes the 'acceptance' and the 'consideration' for a binding subsidiary promise not to revoke the offer, or turns the offer into a presently binding contract conditional upon the offeree's full performance."

We hold that part performance by the offeree of an offer of a unilateral contract results in a contract with a condition. The condition is full performance by the offeree. Here, if plaintiff-offeree partially performed prior to receipt of defendant's revocation, such a contract was formed. Thereafter, upon performance being completed by plaintiff, upon defendant's failure to recognize the contract, liability for breach of contract would arise. Thus, defendant's right to revoke his offer depends upon whether plaintiff had partially performed before he received defendant's revocation. * * *

What constitutes partial performance will vary from case to case since what can be done toward performance is limited by what is authorized to be done. Whether plaintiff partially performed is a question of fact to be determined by the trial court.

The trial court denied plaintiff's requested finding concerning his partial performance. It did so on the theory that partial performance was not material. In this the trial court erred. * * *

The cause is remanded for findings on the issue of plaintiff's partial performance of the offer prior to its revocation, and for further proceedings consistent with this opinion and the findings so made.

It is so ordered.

NOTES

(1) In *Marchiondo*, the offer looked forward to a performance (finding a ready, able and willing buyer) as the only method of acceptance. A promise would not do. That buyer was not found before the agency was terminated. Do the facts support the court's theory?

(2) It will be noted the first Restatement does not state that the offer becomes irrevocable after part performance, but that the offeror is "bound by a contract," etc. The formulation of the rule in this manner by Professor Williston, principal author of the Restatement, was challenged at a discussion of the tentative draft. The following colloquy took place:

JUDGE CARDOZO: Are there any suggestions as to * * * Section 45? * * *

MR. WILLIS: I wonder if there is not an inaccuracy in Section 45 in lines 22, 23 and 24 as follows: "the offeror is bound by a contract, liability upon which is conditional on the completion by the offeree of the requested performance within the time stated in the offer, etc." Under such circumstances as we find in Section 45, we do not have a contract of course. The statement in line 23 does not say that we have a contract, and yet it says the offeror is bound by a contract. I wonder if that is not misleading. The actual fact is that in our most recent cases and the modern development of the law the power of revocation on the part of the offeror is destroyed, and therefore the offeree has the power to go on if he wants to and complete his acceptance. If he does we finally get a contract, but if he does not go on and perform the rest of the work of course there is no contract. * * *

MR. WILLISTON: I call an irrevocable offer a contract. The offeror has promised to do something and he is liable if he does not do it.

MR. WILLIS: I beg your pardon, you do not want to call this an irrevocable offer, do you?

MR. WILLISTON: That is what you called it, did you not?

MR. WILLIS: Oh, no.

MR. WILLISTON: You stated the power to revoke is destroyed.

MR. WILLIS: It becomes irrevocable—

MR. WILLISTON: All right. When it becomes irrevocable it is an irrevocable offer.

MR. WILLIS: But it does not seem to me that that is so; it seems to me that a contract is one thing and an irrevocable offer is another.

MR. WILLISTON: We are apart on that. An irrevocable [offer] is not *the* contract which the offer proposes, but being a binding promise, it is a contract.

3 ALI Proceedings 204–5 (1925).

(3) The drafters of the first Restatement appended the following commentary to § 45: "The main offer includes as a subsidiary promise, necessarily implied, that if part of the requested performance is given, the offeror will not revoke his offer, and that if tender is made it will be accepted. Part performance or tender may thus furnish consideration for the subsidiary promises. Moreover, merely acting in justifiable reliance on an offer may in some cases serve as sufficient reason for making a promise binding (see § 90)." Is this comment consistent with the "black letter" of Section 45?

PROBLEM: THE CASE OF PROFESSOR FUZZY'S WELL

The well of Professor Fuzzy's suburban homesite ran dry during an extended drought period. He hastened to make arrangements for the drilling of a new one, contacting among others the Retaw Drilling Company. He told of his plight, but a company representative said they were so committed they could not assist him. Fuzzy countered by saying he was desperate and would give them $1,000 if they would drill a well for him, a sum about double the estimated cost. The drilling company agent said, "Well, we can't guarantee you anything, but if we can pull a rig off another job, we'll try to help you out."

It happened the following day that a rig did become available, and the company, at considerable expense, moved drilling equipment onto Professor Fuzzy's property.

Meanwhile, however, the professor's neighbor informed him that a connection could be made to the municipal water supply system and it was a waste of money to drill a new well. Fuzzy verified the fact that he was eligible to so purchase water from the city and decided this was his best course. Accordingly, he told the company not to drill. The company transferred its equipment to another location, but sent him a bill. The latter asserted he "did not owe a cent." The Retaw Drilling Company sues for damages. Any recovery?

Assume, instead, that after transfer of the equipment to Fuzzy's property, circumstances arose which prompted the drilling company to claim the absence of obligation to proceed. (E.g., a more profitable job came along.) Would Fuzzy have any legal recourse?

James Baird Co. v. Gimbel Brothers, Inc.

United States Court of Appeals, Second Circuit, 1933.
64 F.2d 344.

■ L. HAND, CIRCUIT JUDGE. The plaintiff sued the defendant for breach of a contract to deliver linoleum under a contract of sale; the defendant denied the making of the contract; the parties tried the case to the judge under a written stipulation and he directed judgment for the defendant. The facts as found, bearing on the making of the contract, the only issue necessary to discuss, were as follows: The defendant, a New York merchant, knew that the Department of Highways in Pennsylvania had asked for bids for the construction of a public building. It sent an employee to the office of a contractor in Philadelphia, who had possession of the specifications, and the employee there computed the amount of the linoleum which would be required on the job, underestimating the total yardage by about one-half the proper amount. In ignorance of this mistake, on December twenty-fourth the defendant sent to some twenty or thirty contractors, likely to bid on the job, an offer to supply all the linoleum required by the specifications at two different lump sums, depending upon the quality used. These offers concluded as follows: "If successful in being awarded this contract, it will be absolutely guaranteed, * * * and * * * we are offering these prices for reasonable" (sic), "prompt acceptance after the general contract has been awarded." The plaintiff, a contractor in Washington, got one of these on the twenty-eighth, and on the same day the defendant learned its mistake and telegraphed all the contractors to whom it had sent the offer, that it withdrew it and would substitute a new one at about double the amount of the old. This withdrawal reached the plaintiff at Washington on the afternoon of the same day, but not until after it had put in a bid at Harrisburg at a lump sum, based as to linoleum upon the prices quoted by the defendant. The public authorities accepted the plaintiff's bid on December thirtieth, the defendant having meanwhile written a letter of confirmation of its withdrawal, received on the thirty-first. The plaintiff formally accepted the offer on January second, and, as the defendant persisted in declining to recognize the existence of a contract, sued it for damages on a breach.

Unless there are circumstances to take it out of the ordinary doctrine, since the offer was withdrawn before it was accepted, the acceptance was too late. Restatement of Contracts, § 35. To meet this the plaintiff argues as follows: It was a reasonable implication from the defendant's offer that it should be irrevocable in case the plaintiff acted upon it, that is to say, used the prices quoted in making its bid, thus putting itself in a position from which it could not withdraw without great loss. While it might have withdrawn its bid after receiving the revocation, the time had passed to submit another, and as the item of linoleum was a very trifling part of the cost of the whole building, it would have been an unreasonable hardship to expect it to lose the contract on that account, and probably forfeit its deposit. While it is true that the plaintiff might in advance have secured a contract conditional upon the success of its bid, this was not what the defendant suggested. It understood that the contractors would use its offer in their bids, and would thus in fact commit themselves to supplying the linoleum at the proposed prices. The inevitable implication from all this was that when the contractors acted upon it, they accepted the offer and promised to pay for the linoleum, in case their bid were accepted.

It was of course possible for the parties to make such a contract, and the question is merely as to what they meant; that is, what is to be imputed to the words they used. Whatever plausibility there is in the argument, is in the fact that the defendant must have known the predicament in which the contractors would be put if it withdrew its offer after the bids went in. However, it seems entirely clear that the contractors did not suppose that they accepted the offer merely by putting in their bids. If, for example, the successful one had repudiated the contract with the public authorities after it had been awarded to him, certainly the defendant could not have sued him for a breach. If he had become bankrupt, the defendant could not prove against his estate. It seems plain therefore that there was no contract between them. And if there be any doubt as to this, the language of the offer sets it at rest. The phrase, "if successful in being awarded this contract," is scarcely met by the mere use of the prices in the bids. Surely such a use was not an "award" of the contract to the defendant. Again the phrase, "we are offering these prices for * * * prompt acceptance after the general contract has been awarded," looks to the usual communication of an acceptance, and precludes the idea that the use of the offer in the bidding shall be the equivalent. It may indeed be argued that this last language contemplated no more than an early notice that the offer had been accepted, the actual acceptance being the bid, but that would wrench its natural meaning too far, especially in the light of the preceding phrase. The contractors had a ready escape from their difficulty by insisting upon a contract before they used the figures; and in commercial transactions it does not in the end promote justice to seek strained interpretations in aid of those who do not protect themselves.

But the plaintiff says that even though no bilateral contract was made, the defendant should be held under the doctrine of "promissory estoppel." This is to be chiefly found in those cases where persons subscribe to a venture, usually charitable, and are held to their promises after it has been completed. It has been applied much more broadly, however, and has now been generalized in section 90, of the Restatement of Contracts. We may arguendo accept it as it there reads, for it does not apply to the case at bar. Offers are ordinarily made in exchange for a consideration, either a counter-promise or some other act which the promisor wishes to secure. In such cases they propose bargains; they presuppose that each promise or performance is an inducement to the other.... But a man may make a promise without expecting an equivalent; a donative promise, conditional or absolute. The common law provided for such by sealed instruments, and it is unfortunate that these are no longer generally available. The doctrine of "promissory estoppel" is to avoid harsh results of allowing the promisor in such a case to repudiate, when the promisee has acted in reliance upon the promise.... But an offer for an exchange is not meant to become a promise until a consideration has been received, either a counterpromise or whatever else is stipulated. To extend it would be to hold the offeror regardless of the stipulated condition of his offer. In the case at bar the defendant offered to deliver the linoleum in exchange for the plaintiff's acceptance, not for its bid, which was a matter of indifference to it. That offer could become a promise to deliver only when the equivalent was received; that is, when the plaintiff promised to take and pay for it. There is no room in such a situation for the doctrine of "promissory estoppel."

Nor can the offer be regarded as of an option, giving the plaintiff the right seasonably to accept the linoleum at the quoted prices if its bid was accepted, but not binding it to take and pay, if it could get a better bargain elsewhere. There is not the least reason to suppose that the defendant meant to subject itself to such a one-sided obligation. True, if so construed, the doctrine of "promissory estoppel" might apply, the plaintiff having acted in reliance upon it, though, so far as we have found, the decisions are otherwise.... As to that, however, we need not declare ourselves.

Judgment affirmed.

Drennan v. Star Paving Co.

Supreme Court of California, 1958.
51 Cal.2d 409, 333 P.2d 757.

■ TRAYNOR, JUSTICE. Defendant appeals from a judgment for plaintiff in an action to recover damages caused by defendant's refusal to perform certain paving work according to a bid it submitted to plaintiff.

On July 28, 1955, plaintiff, a licensed general contractor, was preparing a bid on the "Monte Vista School Job" in the Lancaster school district. Bids had to be submitted before 8:00 p.m. Plaintiff testified that it was customary in that area for general contractors to receive the bids of subcontractors by telephone on the day set for bidding and to rely on them in computing their own bids. Thus on that day plaintiff's secretary, Mrs. Johnson, received by telephone between fifty and seventy-five subcontractors' bids for various parts of the school job. As each bid came in, she wrote it on a special form, which she brought into plaintiff's office. He then posted it on a master cost sheet setting forth the names and bids of all subcontractors. His own bid had to include the names of subcontractors who were to perform one-half of one percent or more of the construction work, and he had also to provide a bidder's bond of ten percent of his total bid of $317,385 as a guarantee that he would enter the contract if awarded the work.

Late in the afternoon, Mrs. Johnson had a telephone conversation with Kenneth R. Hoon, an estimator for defendant. He gave his name and telephone number and stated that he was bidding for defendant for the paving work at the Monte Vista School according to plans and specifications and that his bid was $7,131.60. At Mrs. Johnson's request he repeated his bid. Plaintiff listened to the bid over an extension telephone in his office and posted it on the master sheet after receiving the bid form from Mrs. Johnson. Defendant's was the lowest bid for the paving. Plaintiff computed his own bid accordingly and submitted it with the name of defendant as the subcontractor for the paving. When the bids were opened on July 28th, plaintiff's proved to be the lowest, and he was awarded the contract.

On his way to Los Angeles the next morning plaintiff stopped at defendant's office. The first person he met was defendant's construction engineer, Mr. Oppenheimer. Plaintiff testified: "I introduced myself and he immediately told me that they had made a mistake in their bid to me the night before, they couldn't do it for the price they had bid, and I told him I would expect him to carry through with their original bid because I had used it in compiling my bid and the job was being awarded them. And I would have to go and do the job according to my bid and I would expect them to do the same."

Defendant refused to do the paving work for less than $15,000. Plaintiff testified that he "got figures from other people" and after trying for several months to get as low a bid as possible engaged L & H Paving Company, a firm in Lancaster, to do the work for $10,948.60.

The trial court found on substantial evidence that defendant made a definite offer to do the paving on the Monte Vista job according to the plans and specifications for $7,131.60, and that plaintiff relied on defendant's bid in computing his own bid for the school job and naming defendant therein as the subcontractor for the paving work. Accordingly, it entered judgment for plaintiff in the amount of $3,817.00 (the difference between defendant's bid and the cost of the paving to plaintiff) plus costs.

Defendant contends that there was no enforceable contract between the parties on the ground that it made a revocable offer and revoked it before plaintiff communicated his acceptance to defendant.

There is no evidence that defendant offered to make its bid irrevocable in exchange for plaintiff's use of its figures in computing his bid. Nor is there evidence that would warrant interpreting plaintiff's use of defendant's bid as the acceptance thereof, binding plaintiff, on condition he received the main contract, to award the subcontract to defendant. In sum, there was neither an option supported by consideration nor a bilateral contract binding on both parties.

Plaintiff contends, however, that he relied to his detriment on defendant's offer and that defendant must therefore answer in damages for its refusal to perform. Thus the question is squarely presented: Did plaintiff's reliance make defendant's offer irrevocable?

Section 90 of the Restatement of Contracts states: "A promise which the promisor should reasonably expect to induce action or forbearance of a definite and substantial character on the part of the promisee and which does induce such action or forbearance is binding if injustice can be avoided only by enforcement of the promise." This rule applies in this state. . . .

Defendant's offer constituted a promise to perform on such conditions as were stated expressly or by implication therein or annexed thereto by operation of law. . . . Defendant had reason to expect that if its bid proved the lowest it would be used by plaintiff. It induced "action * * * of a definite and substantial character on the part of the promisee."

Had defendant's bid expressly stated or clearly implied that it was revocable at any time before acceptance we would treat it accordingly. It was silent on revocation, however, and we must therefore determine whether there are conditions to the right of revocation imposed by law or reasonably inferable in fact. In the analogous problem of an offer for a unilateral contract, the theory is now obsolete that the offer is revocable at any time before complete performance. Thus section 45 of the Restatement of Contracts provides: "If an offer for a unilateral contract is made, and part of the consideration requested in the offer is given or tendered by the offeree in response thereto, the offeror is bound by a contract, the duty of immediate performance of which is conditional on the full consideration being given or tendered within the time stated in the offer, or, if no time is stated therein, within a reasonable time." In explanation, comment *b* states that the "main offer includes as a subsidiary promise, necessarily implied, that if part of the requested performance is given, the offeror will not revoke his offer, and that if tender is made it will be accepted. Part performance or tender may thus furnish consideration for the subsidiary promise. Moreover, merely acting in justifiable reliance on an offer may in some cases serve as sufficient reason for making a promise binding (see § 90)."

Whether implied in fact or law, the subsidiary promise serves to preclude the injustice that would result if the offer could be revoked after the offeree had acted in detrimental reliance thereon. Reasonable reliance resulting in a foreseeable prejudicial change in position affords a compelling basis also for implying a subsidiary promise not to revoke an offer for a bilateral contract.

The absence of consideration is not fatal to the enforcement of such a promise. It is true that in the case of unilateral contracts the Restatement finds consideration for the implied subsidiary promise in the part performance of the bargained-for exchange, but its reference to section 90 makes clear that consideration for such a promise is not always necessary. The very purpose of section 90 is to make a promise binding even though there was no consideration "in the sense of something that is bargained for and given in exchange." (See 1 Corbin, Contracts 634 et seq.) Reasonable reliance serves to hold the offeror in lieu of the consideration ordinarily required to make the offer binding. In a case involving similar facts the Supreme Court of South Dakota stated that "we believe that reason and justice demand that the doctrine [of section 90] be applied to the present facts. We cannot believe that by accepting this doctrine as controlling in the state of facts before us we will abolish the requirement of a consideration in contract cases, in any different sense than an ordinary estoppel abolishes some legal requirement in its application. We are of the opinion, therefore, that the defendants in executing the agreement [which was not supported by consideration] made a promise which they should have reasonably expected would induce the plaintiff to submit a bid based thereon to the Government, that such promise did induce this action, and that injustice can be avoided only by enforcement of the promise." Northwestern Engineering Co. v. Ellerman, 69 S.D. 397, 408, 10 N.W.2d 879, 884; see also, Robert Gordon, Inc., v. Ingersoll–Rand Co., 7 Cir., 117 F.2d 654, 661; cf. James Baird Co. v. Gimbel Bros., 2 Cir., 64 F.2d 344.

When plaintiff used defendant's offer in computing his own bid, he bound himself to perform in reliance on defendant's terms. Though defendant did not bargain for this use of its bid neither did defendant make it idly, indifferent to whether it would be used or not. On the contrary it is reasonable to suppose that defendant submitted its bid to obtain the subcontract. It was bound to realize the substantial possibility that its bid would be the lowest, and that it would be included by plaintiff in his bid. It was to its own interest that the contractor be awarded the general contract; the lower the subcontract bid, the lower the general contractor's bid was likely to be and the greater its chance of acceptance and hence the greater defendant's chance of getting the paving subcontract. Defendant had reason not only to expect plaintiff to rely on its bid but to want him to. Clearly defendant had a stake in plaintiff's reliance on its bid. Given this interest and the fact that plaintiff is bound by his own bid, it is only fair that plaintiff should have at least an opportunity to accept defendant's bid after the general contract has been awarded to him.

It bears noting that a general contractor is not free to delay acceptance after he has been awarded the general contract in the hope of getting a better price. Nor can he reopen bargaining with the subcontractor and at the same time claim a continuing right to accept the original offer.... In the present case plaintiff promptly informed defendant that plaintiff was being awarded the job and that the subcontract was being awarded to defendant.

Defendant contends, however, that its bid was the result of mistake and that it was therefore entitled to revoke it. * * * Plaintiff, however, had no reason to know that defendant had made a mistake in submitting its bid, since there was usually a variance of 160 per cent between the highest and lowest bids for paving in the desert around Lancaster. He committed himself to performing the main contract in reliance on defendant's figures. Under these circumstances defendant's mistake, far from relieving it of its obligation, constitutes an additional reason for enforcing it, for it misled plaintiff as to the cost of doing the paving. Even had it been clearly understood that defendant's offer was revocable until accepted, it would not necessarily follow that defendant had no duty to exercise reasonable care in preparing its bid. It presented its bid with knowledge of the substantial possibility that it would be used by plaintiff; it could foresee the harm that would ensue from an erroneous underestimate of the cost. Moreover, it was motivated by its own business interest. Whether or not these considerations alone would justify recovery for negligence had the case been tried on that theory (see Biakanja v. Irving, 49 Cal.2d 647, 650, 320 P.2d 16), they are persuasive that defendant's mistake should not defeat recovery under the rule of section 90 of the Restatement of Contracts. As between the subcontractor who made the bid and the general contractor who reasonably relied on it, the loss resulting from the mistake should fall on the party who caused it.

* * *

The judgment is affirmed.

NOTES

(1) In *Drennan,* Judge Traynor observes that "there was neither an option supported by consideration nor a bilateral contract binding on both parties." He then proceeds to create an option under promissory estoppel doctrine. How does he avoid Judge Hand's reasoning in *Baird*? For what reasons and by what methodology is the option created? What is the scope of the protection afforded the general contractor by the option?

(2) Did the general contractor, in *Drennan,* know or have reason to know that a mistake had been made? Would such knowledge affect the outcome?

(3) The position adopted by Judge Traynor has come to predominate. See Pavel v. A.S. Johnson, 342 Md. 143, 674 A.2d 521, 526–530 (1996); Bishop, *The Subcontractor's Bid: An Option Contract Arising through Promissory Estoppel,* 34 Emory L.J. 42 (1985). The revised Restatement appears not only to follow *Drennan,* but to extend it. Section 87(2) provides: "An offer which the offeror should reasonably expect to induce action or forbearance of a substantial character by the offeree before acceptance and which does induce such action or forbearance is binding as an option contract to the extent necessary to avoid injustice." But what is the likely impact of limiting the binding effect of the option "to the extent necessary to avoid injustice"? Cf. Loranger Construction Corp. v. E.F. Hauserman Co., 376 Mass. 757, 384 N.E.2d 176 (1978). In an opinion by Judge Braucher, first Reporter of Restatement (Second), the court eschews promissory estoppel analysis ("it tends to confusion rather than clarity"), preferring to base liability on a "typical bargain."

(4) Oil Lease Owner offered to enter a "farmout agreement" with Oil Driller. The offer stated that it was irrevocable for a period of 120 days, plus a 30 day extension. Driller, who was to accept the offer by drilling on a designated parcel, paid nothing for the option. Before acceptance, Driller in reliance on the option drilled a test well on another parcel. Data from this drilling would help to evaluate whether to accept the offer. Before acceptance, however, Owner attempted to change the terms of the offer. Held: Under Section 90 of the Restatement (Second), Driller's reliance upon the written option promise made the offer irrevocable and Driller could create a contract on the original terms of the offer. Strata Production v. Mercury Exploration, 121 N.M. 622, 916 P.2d 822, 827–830 (1996).

(5) *Protection for the Subcontractor?* Under *Drennan,* a general contractor, armed with an award of the overall project, can solicit a new round of subcontractor bids. Subcontractors thus anxious about the prospect of obtaining certain subcontracts for the project are susceptible to pressures to lower their bids. Since the overall project contract has already been awarded at this point, only the general contractor, not the project owner, will profit from this "bid shopping." How can a subcontractor protect itself from bid shopping by the general contractor?

Recognizing a potential for abuse, in 1963 the California legislature adopted the Subletting and Subcontracting Fair Practices Act, West's Ann.Cal. Gov.Code §§ 4100–08. This statute provides that a general contractor bidding on "any public work or improvement" must disclose in its bid the name of any subcontractor whose bid is incorporated into and exceeds ½ of 1% of the price of the general contractor's bid. The statute further provides that a general contractor whose bid on a public project is accepted shall not replace a subcontractor listed in his bid with another subcontractor, except where a listed subcontractor refuses to execute or perform a written contract for the work, becomes insolvent, or fails to satisfy bonding requirements. In addition, replacement of a listed subcontractor under any of these circumstances requires the awarding authority's consent. In Southern California Acoustics Co. v. C.V. Holder, Inc., 71 Cal.2d 719, 79 Cal.Rptr. 319, 456 P.2d 975 (1969), the California Supreme Court held that public authorities have a duty to listed subcontractors under the Act not to consent to wrongful substitutions. See also W.J. Lewis Corp. v. C. Harper Construction Co., Inc., 116 Cal.App.3d 27, 171 Cal.Rptr. 806 (1981). Florida has enacted similar legislation. See West's Fla. Stat.Ann. § 286.27. See E.M. Watkins Co. v. Board of Regents, 414 So.2d 583 (Fla.Dist.Ct.App.1982).

(6) "Generally, the mere use of a subcontractor's bid by a general contractor bidding on a prime contract does not constitute acceptance of the subcontractor's bid and imposes no obligation upon the prime contractor to accept the subcontractor's bid. . . . Moreover, ECM concedes that the mere solicitation of bids by a general contractor is not an offer and does not impose any obligations upon the general contractor. But ECM points out that even if it were obligated not to revoke its bid, it was not obligated to bid in the first place. ECM alleged in its complaint that it initially refused Maeda's solicitation to bid and only subsequently bid because Maeda promised that if ECM undertook the time and expense to prepare and submit an electrical subcontractor's bid, Maeda would award ECM the subcontract if its bid were the lowest. While this is an issue of

first impression, we believe that where a subcontractor allegedly agreed to bid only after receiving the general contractor's promise to accept the bid if it were the low bid and if the general contractor were awarded the prime contract, there is consideration for the general contractor's promise. The consideration for Maeda's promise was ECM's submission of a bid—an act for which Maeda bargained and that ECM was not under a legal duty to perform. See Restatement (Second) of Contracts §§ 71–73 (any bargained for performance other than the performance of a legal duty owed to the promisor is consideration for a promise)...." Electrical Construction & Maintenance Co. v. Maeda Pacific Corp., 764 F.2d 619 (9th Cir.1985).

SKB Industries, Inc. v. Insite

Court of Appeals of Georgia, 2001.
250 Ga.App. 574, 551 S.E.2d 380.

■ ANDREWS, PRESIDING JUDGE.

* * *

1. SKB contends the trial court erred by allowing Insite to pursue its claim based on promissory estoppel.

This claim was based on evidence that Beers Construction Company, a general contractor, was accepting bids for work to build the Georgia International Plaza in preparation for the 1996 Summer Olympic Games in Atlanta. The project comprised two elements: building large structural concrete planting containers across the top of an existing parking deck (hardscaping), and placing soil, plants, and drainage features in the containers to create a landscaped plaza on top of the deck (landscaping). Insite, a hardscaping contractor, was preparing to submit a bid to Beers to do both the hardscaping and landscaping work on the project. For the purpose of submitting a bid for the whole project, Insite received a bid from SKB, a landscaping subcontractor, to do the landscaping portion of the work for $1,085,222.50. Insite included SKB's bid in its bid to Beers to do the whole project for $3,161,411.

Insite's bid was significantly lower than the next lowest bid on the project, and Beers suspected that the landscaping portion of the bid from SKB may not have been based on materials specified by the contract documents for the project. When this concern was brought to SKB's attention, SKB confirmed to Beers and Insite that it had received all the documents containing the project specifications and that its bid to Insite was based on all the required materials. However, SKB subsequently informed Insite that its bid was not based on the required materials, but rather included lower priced materials not approved in the project specifications. Subsequently, SKB sent Insite a revised bid to do the landscaping work with the required materials for a higher price. Ultimately, a change in the project specifications was negotiated by Beers to allow SKB to use materials less expensive than those originally required, and SKB assured Insite that it would do the landscaping work using these materials. After SKB made these assurances, Beers accepted Insite's bid, and Insite became contractually obligated to perform the hardscaping and landscaping work on the project for the amount of its bid to Beers.

Insite sent SKB a written subcontract showing a new price for the landscaping portion of the work in the amount of $1,112,222.50 based on the use of the newly approved materials. After receiving the subcontract, SKB sent Insite a notice to contract and requested an initial payment for work making reference to the subcontract amount of $1,112,222.50. However, SKB never signed the subcontract and ultimately refused to do a substantial portion of the landscaping work included in its bid. Because of SKB's refusal to perform all the work included in its bid and the time constraints of the project, Insite was forced to perform landscaping work in which it had no expertise, and which cost it substantially more to do than the price for this work included in SKB's bid. Although SKB refused to fully perform the work in its bid, it later entered into a written subcontract with Insite to perform a small portion of the work included in its bid. SKB claimed it refused to perform because of disputes over language in the first subcontract sent to it by Insite, but there was also evidence from which the jury could have concluded that, after SKB assured Insite it would do the bid work, SKB refused to perform because it realized it had mistakenly bid too low on portions of the landscape work.

Even though there was no binding contract between Insite and SKB for the portion of the landscape work at issue, there was evidence supporting Insite's promissory estoppel claim for the difference between the cost it incurred in performing the landscape work SKB refused to do and the price for this work submitted by SKB in its bid, as revised for the new materials. Insite's promissory estoppel claim required proof that: (1) SKB made a promise to do the landscape work in the bid it submitted to Insite; (2) SKB should have expected that Insite would rely on the promise; (3) Insite did rely on the promise to its detriment; and (4) injustice can be avoided only by enforcement of the promise.... SKB clearly expected Insite to rely on its bid because it was submitted to Insite for the express purpose of allowing Insite to include it in the bid made by Insite to Beers for the whole project. It was also foreseeable to SKB that Insite would suffer damage if SKB refused to perform the bid work after Insite relied on SKB's bid as a basis for Insite's bid to Beers. There was no evidence that SKB's bid was intended to be revocable at any time before acceptance. Under these circumstances, Insite's reliance on SKB's bid provided consideration sufficient under the principle of promissory estoppel to imply an enforceable promise by SKB to keep its bid offer to Insite open for a reasonable period of time to allow Insite to accept the bid after Beers awarded Insite the project. *Loy's Office Supplies v. Steelcase, Inc.*, 174 Ga.App. 701, 702 (1985); see *Drennan v. Star Paving Co.*, 51 Cal.2d 409 (1958). After Insite was awarded the project, it promptly notified SKB that its bid was accepted and tendered SKB the landscape work at the bid price as revised by the parties.

We find no merit in SKB's contention that the written subcontract it subsequently entered into with Insite to perform a portion of the landscape work represented the entire agreement between the parties for all the landscape work and rendered promissory estoppel inapplicable. Certainly, if Insite and SKB had reached a subsequent agreement covering all the landscaping work in the bid, then Insite could not claim it detrimentally relied. . . . However, the subcontract expressly states that the landscaping work which SKB refused to perform was excluded from the subcontract. We decline to accept SKB's contention that the work expressly excluded should be deemed included because the subcontract contains a clause excluding it. Even if there was some ambiguity in the subcontract as to whether Insite intended to release SKB from its bid, evidence admissible under the parol evidence rule which explained the ambiguity was presented showing that Insite and SKB had no such intention . . . . * * *

Judgment affirmed

PROBLEM: THE CASE OF THE BID–SHOPPING CONTRACTOR

School Corporation decided to build an annex to its senior high school. Plans and specifications were prepared, and various building firms were invited to submit bids. Among those contacted was Contractor. The latter, in turn, determined to submit a bid and proceeded to contact potential subcontractors relative to various components of the project.

Subcontractor A telephoned a bid for the excavating work. Since this was the low bid of the responding excavating subcontractors, Contractor used A's figure in computing his bid to School Corporation. Subcontractor B submitted a bid in writing for the electrical work, which Contractor also used in computing the general bid since B's price was the lowest of the electrical subcontractors. Subcontractor C's bid was low for the plumbing component, and it, too, was used by Contractor in preparing the prime bid.

At the bid opening on March 18, Contractor was found to be low bidder, and two days later was awarded the contract. Armed with this award, Contractor immediately sought out other excavating subcontractors in an effort to get a lower figure, but he was unsuccessful. On March 22 he wired an acceptance to A. He fared better, however, with respect to the electrical work. He secured, on March 23, the agreement of subcontractor D to do the work for $15,000 less than specified by B. He took no further action regarding B's bid.

At the bid opening Contractor mentioned to another general contractor that he thought C's bid on the plumbing work was too high and that he could do much better elsewhere. Two days later the other contractor told C of this conversation, and the latter, thinking Contractor would not want him to do the work, accepted an outstanding offer from another. However, Contractor did not seek out other plumbing subcontractors, and on March 24 undertook to accept C's offer.

Contractor is now beset with problems. A and C refuse to perform; B insists he has a binding contract for the electrical work. Contractor consults you. Advise him both as to his present difficulties and as to how he should proceed in future post-award negotiations.

SECTION 2. INSUFFICIENT AGREEMENT: INDEFINITE, INCOMPLETE, AND DEFERRED TERMS

In the foregoing materials on the agreement process, we have considered the nature and effect of "offer" and "acceptance" and the circumstances under which negotiations can be terminated without liability to either party. We now turn to a closely related problem. If, after the negotiations have produced some agreement on the proposed exchange, one party withdraws because certain material terms were not agreed, or were agreed in an indefinite way or were explicitly left for future agreement, when, if ever, will that withdrawal result in liability for damages caused? If the withdrawing party has explicitly conditioned a willingness to deal upon the other party's clear agreement to material terms and the other has failed or refused to agree, no liability should attach. See Fairway Center Corp. v. U.I.P. Corp., 502 F.2d 1135 (8th Cir.1974). But suppose there is no explicit condition. Should contract law provide that there can be no contract until clear and complete agreement to all material terms is reached? If so, why? Or, should contract law permit the parties, if they so intend, to conclude bargains without clear agreement on all material terms? If so, why? How should lack of complete agreement or indefiniteness affect the enforcement of these bargains? What if the parties "agree to agree" on a term and do not? Are there any duties to negotiate or to bargain in good faith? These are some of the questions to be considered in this section.

Before seeking answers to these questions, it should be noted that you will observe a shift from a strict view that no contract can be formed until clear and complete agreement is reached on material terms to a more flexible standard, such as those announced in UCC 2–204 and Sections 33 and 34 of Restatement (Second). There are several explanations for this shift from "rules to standards." See Speidel, *Restatement Second: Omitted Terms and Contract Method,* 67 Cornell L.Rev. 785, 786–92 (1982). According to Professor Ian Macneil, a possible reason is a different perception of the nature of contractual relationships. The assumption underlying the so-called "strict" view was that the parties could and should "presentiate," that is, express all of the material elements of the future exchange in the present agreement. In its extreme form, the transaction model was the "one shot deal" involving the sale of Dobbin or Blackacre. See Macneil, *Restatement (Second) of Contracts and Presentiation,* 60 Va.L.Rev. 589, 592–94 (1974). But the assumptions underlying the traditional theory of mutual assent are hardly consistent with such long-term relationships that exist between professor and university, husband and wife, union and corporation, supplier and middleman, government and aircraft manufacturer, franchisor and franchisee or, even, two state-owned enterprises in a socialist economy. These parties may wish to have the protection of contract but be unwilling or unable to articulate all terms of the future exchange in an initial agreement. But if that protection is extended to them, new techniques must be developed to manage the inevitable disputes that will arise as the parties attempt to perform and to adjust these open-ended relationships. See also Ian R. Macneil, *The Many Futures of Contracts,* 47 S.Cal.L.Rev. 691 (1974); Macneil, *A Primer of Contract Planning,* 48 S.Cal.L.Rev. 627 (1975).

(A) DEFECTIVE FORMULATION AND EXPRESSION OF AGREEMENT

We now consider a series of problems associated with attempts to withdraw from the bargaining relationship. These problems derive from the "objective" test, introduced supra at 231, and focus upon one party's assertion that certain "defects" in the process of either formulating or expressing an agreement justify withdrawal or avoidance without liability, even though that agreement otherwise satisfies the requisites for a contract.

Your task in this section will be to develop a feel for the conditions that must exist before relief will be granted, the nature of that relief, and the policies implicit in the undertaking. Also, you should be aware that although these problems appear to be analytically distinct, there are clear overlaps with other areas. For example, although the theory of avoidance is not fraud or misrepresentation by one party (we will consider this infra in Chapter Five, Section 1(B)), a relevant factor may be whether one party has taken unfair advantage of a mistake by the other. Similarly, although the law of torts is not explicitly involved, an underlying purpose of the objective test is to protect the reasonable expectations or reliance of one party against the careless or negligent errors of another. Look carefully for themes premised upon fault in these materials. Further, even though the manifested agreement is supported by consideration, the defect in the process of formulation or expression may produce such disproportion as to make enforcement of the agreement unfair.

Raffles v. Wichelhaus

Court of Exchequer, 1864.
2 H. & C. 906, 159 Eng.Rep. 375.

Declaration. For that it was agreed between the plaintiff and the defendants, to wit, at Liverpool, that the plaintiff should sell to the defendants, and the defendants buy of the plaintiff, certain goods, to wit, 125 bales of Surat cotton, guaranteed middling fair merchant's Dhollorah, to arrive ex "Peerless" from Bombay; and that the cotton should be taken from the quay, and that the defendants would pay the plaintiff for the same at a certain rate, to wit, at the rate of 17¼d. per pound, within a certain time then agreed upon after the arrival of said goods in England. Averments: that the said goods did arrive by the said ship from Bombay in England, to wit, at Liverpool, and the plaintiff was then and there ready and willing and offered to deliver the said goods to the defendants, & c. Breach: that the defendants refused to accept the said goods or pay the plaintiff for them.

Plea. That the said ship mentioned in the said agreement was meant and intended by the defendants to be the ship called the "Peerless," which sailed from Bombay, to wit, in October; and that the plaintiff was not ready and willing, and did not offer to deliver to the defendants any bales of cotton which arrived by the last-mentioned ship, but instead thereof was only ready and willing, and offered to deliver to the defendants 125 bales of Surat cotton which arrived by another and different ship, which was also called the "Peerless," and which sailed from Bombay, to wit, in December.

Demurrer, and joinder therein.

Milward, in support of the demurrer. The contract was for the sale of a number of bales of cotton of a particular description, which the plaintiff was ready to deliver. It is immaterial by what ship the cotton was to arrive, so that it was a ship called the "Peerless." The words "to arrive ex 'Peerless,'" only mean that if the vessel is lost on the voyage, the contract is to be at an end. [Pollock, C.B. It would be a question for the jury whether both parties meant the same ship called the "Peerless."] That would be so if the contract was for the sale of a ship called the "Peerless"; but it is for the sale of cotton on board a ship of that name. [Pollock, C.B. The defendant only bought that cotton which was to arrive by a particular ship. It may as well be said, that if there is a contract for the purchase of certain goods in warehouse A., that is satisfied by the delivery of goods of the same description in warehouse B.] In that case there would be goods in both warehouses; here it does not appear that the plaintiff had any goods on board the other "Peerless." [Martin, B. It is imposing on the defendant a contract different from that which he entered into. Pollock, C.B. It is like a contract for the purchase of wine coming from a particular estate in France or Spain, where there are two estates of that name.] The defendant has no right to contradict by parol evidence a written contract good upon the face of it. He does not impute misrepresentation or fraud, but only says that he fancied the ship was a different one. Intention is of no avail, unless stated at the time of the contract. [Pollock, C.B. One vessel sailed in October and the other in December.] The time of sailing is no part of the contract.

Mellish (Cohen with him), in support of the plea. There is nothing on the face of the contract to shew that any particular ship called the "Peerless" was meant; but the moment it appears that two ships called the "Peerless" were about to sail from Bombay there is a latent ambiguity, and parol evidence may be given for the purpose of shewing that the defendant meant one "Peerless," and the plaintiff another. That being so, there was no consensus ad idem, and therefore no binding contract. He was then stopped by the Court.

■ PER CURIAM. There must be judgment for the defendants.

Judgment for the defendants.

NOTES

(1) Professor Corbin stated that the subject of mistake is "one of the most difficult in the law * * * because men make so many mistakes, of so many different kinds, with so many varying effects." Corbin § 103. Was *Raffles v. Wichelhaus,* commonly referred to as the *Peerless Case,* a mistake case? If so, what kind of mistake was involved? If both parties manifested assent to "Peerless" (and this term was to determine the time for delivery), why did not the court apply the objective test and enforce the contract?

(2) *Gilmore on the Peerless Case.* Professor Grant Gilmore, in the course of tracing the development of the objective test, suggests that a break in the price of cotton on the Liverpool market between the arrival dates of the two ships Peerless may explain why the buyer rejected the goods and that the court, despite the probing of plaintiff's counsel Milward, remained unshaken in its conclusion that "Peerless" was a material term in the bargain in that it manifested the time for delivery of the goods.

In any event it does not necessarily follow that a ship sailing from Bombay in October would have made port in Liverpool before a ship sailing in December. Either Peerless may have been a sailing vessel, subject to the vagaries of wind and weather—or both of them may have been—and either one (or both) may have called at intermediate ports. Since the buyer did not in his plea raise any issue about the time of the seller's tender in Liverpool, we may, I think, safely assume that there was no such issue to be raised. Furthermore, as Milward * * * correctly pointed out, there was no provision in the contract relating to the time of sailing from Bombay. * * * None of the judges thought of asking Mellish what would seem to be obvious questions. Would a reasonably well-informed cotton merchant in Liverpool have known that there were two ships called Peerless? Ought this buyer to have known? If in fact the October Peerless had arrived in Liverpool first, had the buyer protested the seller's failure to tender the cotton?

The failure to probe Mellish with the same zeal exhibited toward Milward suggests to Gilmore that the court was "entirely content to let the case go off on the purely subjective failure of the minds to meet at the time the contract was entered into." G. Gilmore, The Death of Contract 35–39 (1974).

(3) *Holmes on the Peerless Case.*

"It is commonly said that such a contract is void, because of mutual mistake as to the subject matter, and because therefore the parties did not consent to the same thing. But this way of putting it seems to me misleading. The law has nothing to do with the actual state of the parties' minds. In contract, as elsewhere, it must go by externals, and judge parties by their conduct. If there had been but one 'Peerless,' and the defendant had said 'Peerless' by mistake, meaning 'Peri,' he would have been bound. The true ground of the decision was not that each party meant a different thing from the other, as is implied by the explanation which has been mentioned, but that each said a different thing. The plaintiff offered one thing, the defendant expressed his assent to another." O. W. Holmes, The Common Law 242 (Howe ed. 1963).

(4) *Gilmore on Holmes on the Peerless Case.*

"Even for Holmes this was an extraordinary tour de force. * * * The magician who could 'objectify' *Raffles v. Wichelhaus* could, the need arising, objectify anything." G. Gilmore, The Death of Contract 41 (1974). See Birmingham, *Holmes on "Peerless": Raffles v. Wichelhaus and the Objective Theory of Contract*, 47 U.Pitt.L.Rev. 183 (1985).

(5) *Simpson on Gilmore on the Peerless Case.*

What of Grant Gilmore's discussion of the case in *The Death of Contract* ? His speculations as to the background are inevitably misconceived, being unrelated to evidence. But his principal point was that the judges in the case foolishly failed to grasp, in spite of Clement Milward's attempts to put the point to them, that in terms of commercial understanding the identity of the carrying ship was immaterial. Its only relevance was to the risk of loss. He backs this claim up with a classic statement of the ahistorical attitude to legal sources: "In commercial understanding, that is exactly what the terms mean today and there is no reason to believe that they meant anything else a hundred years ago." And to be sure, Gilmore is correct in saying that there is no reason if we pay no attention whatever to the historical context in which the dispute arose. But from what I have said, it is perfectly plain that in arrival contracts where ship and port were named, the identity of the carrying vessel was of central importance. It was the identity of the carrying vessel that fixed the time of arrival and delivery. In the volatile cotton market, that time was critical to the success or failure of the speculation. The reason why time was not specified directly was technological, and as the technology changed, "shipments" were to be superseded by a new form of contract, "deliveries," which did directly specify time. Out of transactions involving this newer form of arrival contract was to develop the practice of futures trading, but that is another story. Simpson, *Contracts for Cotton to Arrive: The Case of the Two Ships Peerless*, 11 Cardozo L.Rev. 287, 324 (1989).

(6) *Restatement (Second) on the Peerless Case.*

Effect of Misunderstanding.

(1) There is no manifestation of mutual assent to an exchange if the parties attach materially different meanings to their manifestations and (a) neither party knows or has reason to know the meaning attached by the other; or (b) each party knows or each party has reason to know the meaning attached by the other.

(2) The manifestations of the parties are operative in accordance with the meaning attached to them by one of the parties if (a) that party does not know of any different meaning attached by the other, and the other knows the meaning attached by the first party; or (b) that party has no reason to know of any different meaning attached by the other, and the other has reason to know the meaning attached by the first party.

Restatement (Second) § 20.

Translation, please! See also, William Young, *Equivocation in the Making of Agreements*, 64 Colum.L.Rev. 619 (1964); George Palmer, *The Effect of Misunderstanding on Contract Formation and Reformation under the Restatement of Contracts, Second*, 65 Mich.L.Rev. 33, 33–51, 56–58 (1966); E. Allan Farnsworth, *"Meaning" in the Law of Contracts*, 76 Yale L.J. 939 (1967).

Konic International Corporation v. Spokane Computer Services, Inc.

Court of Appeals of Idaho, 1985.
109 Idaho 527, 708 P.2d 932.

■ WALTERS, CHIEF JUDGE.

Konic International Corporation sued Spokane Computer Services, Inc., to collect the price of an electrical device allegedly sold by Konic to

Spokane Computer. The suit was tried before a magistrate sitting without a jury. The magistrate entered judgment for Spokane Computer, concluding there was no contract between the parties because of lack of apparent authority of an employee of Spokane Computer to purchase the device from Konic. The district court, on appeal, upheld the magistrate's judgment. On further appeal by Konic, we also affirm the magistrate's judgment but base our result on reasoning different from that of the lower court.

The magistrate found the following facts. David Young, an employee of Spokane Computer, was instructed by his employer to investigate the possibility of purchasing a surge protector, a device which protects computers from damaging surges of electrical current. Young's investigation turned up several units priced from $50 to $200, none of which, however, were appropriate for his employer's needs. Young then contacted Konic. After discussing Spokane Computer's needs with a Konic engineer, Young was referred to one of Konic's salesmen. Later, after deciding on a certain unit, Young inquired as to the price of the selected item. The salesman responded, "fifty-six twenty." The salesman meant $5,620. Young in turn thought $56.20.

The salesman for Konic asked about Young's authority to order the equipment and was told that Young would have to get approval from one of his superiors. Young in turn prepared a purchase order for $56.20 and had it approved by the appropriate authority. Young telephoned the order and purchase order number to Konic who then shipped the equipment to Spokane Computer. However, because of internal processing procedures of both parties the discrepancy in prices was not discovered immediately. Spokane Computer received the surge protector and installed it in its office. The receipt and installation of the equipment occurred while the president of Spokane Computer was on vacation. Although the president's father, who was also chairman of the board of Spokane Computer, knew of the installation, he only inquired as to what the item was and who had ordered it. The president came back from vacation the day after the surge protector had been installed and placed in operation and was told of the purchase. He immediately ordered that power to the equipment be turned off because he realized that the equipment contained parts which alone were worth more than $56 in value. Although the president then told Young to verify the price of the surge protector, Young failed to do so. Two weeks later, when Spokane Computer was processing its purchase order and Konic's invoice, the discrepancy between the amount on the invoice and the amount on the purchase order was discovered. The president of Spokane Computer then contacted Konic, told Konic that Young had no authority to order such equipment, that Spokane Computer did not want the equipment, and that Konic should remove it. Konic responded that Spokane Computer now owned the equipment and if the equipment was not paid for, Konic would sue for the price. Spokane Computer refused to pay and this litigation ensued.

Following trial, the magistrate found that Young had no actual, implied, or apparent authority to enter into the transaction and, therefore, Spokane Computer did not owe Konic for the equipment.[1] In reaching its decision, the magistrate also noted that when Spokane Computer acquired full knowledge of the facts, it took prompt action to disaffirm Young's purchase.

We agree with the magistrate's result. However, rather than base our decision on the agency principle of apparent authority, as did the trial court, we believe that more basic principles of contract are determinative in this case. "When the result reached by the trial court is correct, but entered on a different theory, we will affirm it on the correct theory." Goodwin v. Nationwide Insurance Co., 104 Idaho 74, 83 (Ct.App.1982).

Basically what is involved here is a failure of communication between the parties. A similar failure to communicate arose over 100 years ago in the celebrated case of Raffles v. Wichelhaus, 2 Hurl. 906, 159 Eng.Rep. 375 (1864) which has become better known as the case of the good ship "Peerless". In *Peerless*, the parties agreed on a sale of cotton which was to be delivered from Bombay by the ship "Peerless". In fact, there were two ships named "Peerless" and each party, in agreeing to the sale, was referring to a different ship. Because the sailing time of the two ships was materially different, neither party was willing to agree to shipment by the "other" Peerless. The court ruled that, because each party had a different ship in mind at the time of the contract, there was in fact no binding contract. The *Peerless* rule later was incorporated into section 71 of the RESTATEMENT OF CONTRACTS and has now evolved into section 20 of RESTATEMENT (SECOND) OF CONTRACTS (1981). Section 20 states in part:

(1) There is no manifestation of mutual assent to an exchange if the parties attach materially different meanings to their manifestations and

(a) neither knows or has reason to know the meaning attached by the other.

Comment (c) to section 20 further explains that "even though the parties manifest mutual assent to the same words of agreement, there may be no contract because of a material difference of understanding as to the terms of the exchange." Another authority, Williston, discussing situations where a mistake will prevent formation of a contract, agrees that "where a phrase of contract ... is reasonably capable of different interpretations ... there is no contract." 1 S. WILLISTON, CONTRACTS § 95 (3d ed. 1957).

One commentator on the *Peerless* case, maintaining that the doctrine should be cautiously applied, indicates three principles about the case doctrine that are generally in agreement: (1) "the doctrine applies only when the parties have different understandings of their expression of

---

1. Although the trial court's decision was not explicit about possession of the equipment, the district court, on appeal, determined that Konic was entitled to possession of the equipment.

agreement"; (2) the doctrine does not apply when one party's understanding, because of that party's fault, is less reasonable than the other party's understanding; and (3) parol evidence is admissible to establish the facts necessary to apply the rule. Young, *Equivocation in the Making of Agreements*, 64 COLUM.L.REV. 619 (1964).

The second principle indicates that the doctrine may be applicable to this case because, arguably, both parties' understandings were reasonable. Also, as pointed out by the district court, both parties were equally at fault in contributing to the resulting problems. The third principle is not relevant to the present case.

* * *

In the present case, both parties attributed different meanings to the same term, "fifty-six twenty." Thus, there was no meeting of the minds of the parties. With a hundred fold difference in the two prices, obviously price was a material term. Because the "fifty-six twenty" designation was a material term expressed in an ambiguous form to which two meanings were obviously applied, we conclude that no contract between the parties was ever formed. Accordingly, we do not reach the issue of whether Young had authority to order the equipment.

[Judgment affirmed.]

NOTES

(1) *The key question*: when the parties to a bargain assert materially different understandings of the same words or conduct, how is the court to determine which understanding to prefer? The *"Peerless"* result, as reflected in *Konic,* means that no contract was formed and that any reliance by either party on the arrangement will be protected only if the other party has received and retained a measurable benefit. The risk of unreimbursed reliance and the fortuity of which party is left with the difficult burden of proving the existence of a contract has led some courts to express a preference for avoiding the *Peerless* result "if there is any reasonable means to giving effect to the contract at issue." Consumers Ice Company v. United States, 201 Ct.Cl. 116, 475 F.2d 1161, 1165 (1973). One such reasonable means is through expansive principles of contract interpretation, which deem a wide range of context evidence relevant to the question of which party's understanding is the more reasonable. See, e.g., Frigaliment Importing Co. v. B.N.S. International Sales Corp., 190 F.Supp. 116 (S.D.N.Y.1960) (What is "chicken?" Does the term include "stewing" chickens as well as broilers?), infra at 648. See also Shrum v. Zeltwanger, 559 P.2d 1384 (Wyo.1977) (What is a "cow"? Does the term include a "heifer" which has not had a calf?) If this process of interpretation is inconclusive, the court may, as a last resort, prefer the understanding "which operates against the party who supplies the words or from whom a writing otherwise proceeds." Restatement (Second) § 206. In effect, the basis for preference here is the failure of one party responsible for supplying key language to be clear enough. But if the process of interpretation fully extended is inconclusive, it may be possible to show that one party, from particularized information, knew or had

reason to know that the other party had a materially different understanding. Put another way, although a reasonable person placed in the negotiations would not from objective factors in language or circumstances know that the seller had the "December" Peerless in mind, the particular buyer, from a prior course of dealing or even from a luncheon conversation, might know what the seller intended. If the buyer fails to clarify the situation, does this mean that there is a contract on the seller's understanding? If so, on what theory? See Restatement (Second) §§ 20, 201. On the basis of the foregoing, was *Konic* decided correctly?

(2) *The Case of the "Ambiguous" Legal Description.* Vendor owned land containing three contiguous tracts. Vendor listed the middle and northern tracts with a broker. Purchaser offered to buy these tracts, but Vendor made a counter-offer. In this proposal, which Purchaser accepted, the land to be sold was identified by detailed legal description alone and described the middle and *southern* tracts. After Vendor's refusal to perform, Purchaser seeks specific performance. Assuming that extrinsic evidence shows that Vendor intended to sell the middle and northern tracts and the Purchaser intended to buy the middle and southern tracts, what result? See Hill–Shafer Partnership v. Chilson Family Trust, 165 Ariz. 469, 799 P.2d 810 (1990).

(B) INDEFINITE AGREEMENTS

Varney v. Ditmars

Court of Appeals of New York, 1916.
217 N.Y. 223, 111 N.E. 822.

■ CHASE J. This is an action brought for an alleged wrongful discharge of an employee. The defendant is an architect employing engineers, draftsmen, and other assistants. The plaintiff is an architect and draftsman. In October, 1910, he applied to the defendant for employment and when asked what wages he wanted, replied that he would start for $40 per week. He was employed at $35 per week. A short time thereafter he informed the defendant that he had another position offered to him, and the defendant said that if he would remain with him and help him through the work in his office he thought he could offer him a better future than anybody else. He continued in the employ of the defendant and became acquainted with a designer in the office, and said designer and the plaintiff from time to time prior to the 1st of February, 1911, talked with the defendant about the work in his office. On that day by arrangement the two remained with the defendant after the regular office hours, and the defendant said: "I am going to give you $5 more a week; if you boys will go on and continue the way you have been and get me out of this trouble and get these jobs started that were in the office three years, on the 1st of next January I will close my books and give you a fair share of my profits." That was the result of the conversation. That was all of that conversation.

The plaintiff was given charge of the drafting. Thereafter suggestions were made by the plaintiff and said designer about discharging many of the defendant's employees and employing new men, and such suggestions were carried out and the two worked in the defendant's office overtime and many Sundays and holidays. At least one piece of work that the defendant said had been in his office for three years was completed. The plaintiff on his cross-examination told the story of the employment of himself and said designer as follows: "And he says at that time, 'I am going to give you $5 more a week starting this week.' This was about Thursday. He says, 'You boys go on and continue the work you are doing and the first of January next year I will close my books and give you a fair share of my profits.' Those were his exact words."

Thereafter the plaintiff was paid $40 a week. On November 6, 1911, the night before the general election in this state, the defendant requested that all of his employees that could do so, should work on election day. The plaintiff told the defendant that he wanted to remain at home to attend an election in the village where he lived. About 4 o'clock in the afternoon of election day he was taken ill and remained at his house ill until a time that as nearly as can be stated from the evidence was subsequent to December 1, 1911. On Saturday, November 11th, the defendant caused to be delivered to the plaintiff a letter in which he said: "I am sending you herewith your pay for one day's work of seven hours, performed on Monday, the 6th inst. On Monday night, I made it my special duty to inform you that the office would be open all day Election Day and that I expected you and all the men to report for work. Much to my surprise and indignation, on Tuesday you made no appearance and all of the men remained away, in obedience of your instructions to them of the previous evening. An act of this kind I consider one of extreme disloyalty and insubordination and I therefore am obliged to dispense with your services."

After the plaintiff had recovered from his illness and was able to do so he went to the defendant's office (the date does not appear) and told him that he was ready, willing, and able to continue his services under the agreement. The defendant denied that he had any agreement with him, and refused to permit him to continue in his service. Thereafter and prior to January 1, 1912, the plaintiff received for special work about $50.

The plaintiff seeks to recover in this action for services from November 7, 1911, to December 31, 1911, inclusive, at $40 per week and for a fair and reasonable percentage of the net profits of the defendant's business from February 1, 1911, to January 1, 1912, and demands judgment for $1,680.

At the trial he was the only witness sworn as to the alleged contract, and at the close of his case the complaint was dismissed.

The statement alleged to have been made by the defendant about giving the plaintiff and said designer a fair share of his profits is vague, indefinite, and uncertain, and the amount cannot be computed from anything that was said by the parties or by reference to any document, paper, or other transaction. The minds of the parties never met upon any particular share of the defendant's profits to be given the employees or upon any plan by which such share could be computed or determined. The contract so far as it related to the special promise or inducement was never consummated. It was left subject to the will of the defendant or for further negotiation. It is urged that the defendant by use of the word "fair," in referring to a share of his profits, was as certain and definite as people are in the purchase and sale of a chattel when the price is not expressly agreed upon, and that if the agreement in question is declared to be too indefinite and uncertain to be enforced, a similar conclusion must be reached in every case where a chattel is sold without expressly fixing the price therefor.

The question whether the words "fair" and "reasonable" have a definite and enforceable meaning when used in business transactions is dependent upon the intention of the parties in the use of such words and upon the subject-matter to which they refer. In cases of merchandising and in the purchase and sale of chattels the parties may use the words "fair and reasonable value" as synonymous with "market value." A promise to pay the fair market value of goods may be inferred from what is expressly agreed by the parties. The fair, reasonable, or market value of goods can be shown by direct testimony of those competent to give such testimony. The competency to speak grows out of experience and knowledge. The testimony of such witnesses does not rest upon conjecture. The opinion of this court in United Press v. N.Y. Press Co., 164 N.Y. 406, 58 N.E. 527, 53 L.R.A. 288, was not intended to assert that a contract of sale is unenforceable, unless the price is expressly mentioned and determined.

In the case of a contract for the sale of goods or for hire without a fixed price or consideration being named it will be presumed that a reasonable price or consideration is intended, and the person who enters into such a contract for goods or service is liable therefor as on an implied contract. Such contracts are common, and when there is nothing therein to limit or prevent an implication as to the price they are, so far as the terms of the contract are concerned, binding obligations.

The contract in question, so far as it relates to a share of the defendant's profits, is not only uncertain, but it is necessarily affected by so many other facts that are in themselves indefinite and uncertain that the intention of the parties is pure conjecture. A fair share of the defendant's profits may be any amount from a nominal sum to a material part according to the particular views of the person whose guess is considered. Such an executory contract must rest for performance upon the honor and good faith of the parties making it. The courts cannot aid parties in such a case when they are unable or unwilling to agree upon the terms of their own proposed contract.

It is elementary in the law that, for the validity of a contract, the promise, or the agreement, of the parties to it must be certain and explicit, and that their full intention may be ascertained to a reasonable degree of certainty. Their agreement must be neither vague nor indefinite, and, if thus defective, parol proof cannot be resorted to. *United Press v. N.Y. Press Co.*, supra, and cases cited; Ruling Case Law, vol. 6, 644.

The courts in this state, in reliance upon and approval of the rule as stated in the United Press Case, have decided many cases involving the same rule. Thus, in Mackintosh v. Thompson, 58 App.Div. 25, 68 N.Y.Supp. 492, and again in Mackintosh v. Kimball, 101 App.Div. 494, 92 N.Y.Supp. 132, the plaintiff sought to recover compensation in addition to a stated salary which he had received and which additional amount rested upon a claim by him that while he was employed by the defendants he informed them that he intended to leave their employ, unless he was given an increase in salary, and that one of the defendants said to him that they would make it worth his while if he would stay on, and would increase his salary, and that his idea was to give him an interest in the profits on certain buildings that they were then erecting. The plaintiff further alleges that he asked what would be the amount of the increase and was told, "You can depend upon me; I will see that you get a satisfactory amount." The court held that the arrangement was too indefinite to form the basis of any obligation on the part of the defendant.

* * *

The rule stated from the United Press Case does not prevent a recovery upon quantum meruit in case one party to an alleged contract has performed in reliance upon the terms thereof, vague, indefinite, and uncertain though they are. In such case the law will presume a promise to pay the reasonable value of the services. Judge Gray, who wrote the opinion in the United Press Case, said therein: "I entertain no doubt that, where work has been done, or articles have been furnished, a recovery may be based upon quantum meruit, or quantum valebant; but, where a contract is of an executory character and requires performance over a future period of time, as here, and it is silent as to the price which is to be paid to the plaintiff during its term, I do not think that it possesses binding force. As the parties had omitted to make the price a subject of covenant, in the nature of things, it would have to be the subject of future agreement, or stipulation." Page 412 of 164 N.Y., page 529 of 58 N.E. (53 L.R.A. 288).

In Petze v. Morse Dry Dock & Repair Co., 125 App.Div. 267, 109 N.Y.S. 328, 331, the court said: "There is no contract so long as any essential element is open to negotiation." In that case a contract was made by which an employee in addition to certain specified compensation was to receive 5 per cent. of the net distributable profits of a business, and it was further provided: "That 'the method of accounting to determine the net distributable profits is to be agreed upon later when the company's accounts have developed for a better understanding.' "

The parties never agreed as to the method of determining the net profits and the plaintiff was discharged before the expiration of the term. The court in the opinion say: "That 'the plaintiff could recover for what he had done on a quantum meruit, and the employment must be deemed to have commenced with a full understanding on the part of both parties that that was the situation.' "

The judgment of the Appellate Division was unanimously affirmed without opinion in this court. 195 N.Y. 584, 89 N.E. 1110.

So, in this case, while I do not think that the plaintiff can recover anything as extra work, yet if the work actually performed as stated was worth more than $40 per week he, having performed until November 7,

1910, could, on a proper complaint, recover its value less the amount received. . . .

* * *

The judgment should be affirmed, with costs.

■ CARDOZO, J., (dissenting). I do not think it is true that a promise is always and of necessity too vague to be enforced. . . . The promise must, of course, appear to have been made with contractual intent. . . . But if that intent is present, it cannot be said from the mere form of the promise that the estimate of the reward is inherently impossible. The data essential to measurement may be lacking in the particular instance, and yet they may conceivably be supplied. It is possible, for example, that in some occupations an employee would be able to prove a percentage regulated by custom. The difficulty in this case is not so much in the contract as in the evidence. Even if the data required for computation might conceivably have been supplied, the plaintiff did not supply them. He would not have supplied them if all the evidence which he offered and which the court excluded had been received. He has not failed because the nature of the contract is such that damages are of necessity incapable of proof. He has failed because he did not prove them.

There is nothing inconsistent with this view in United Press v. N.Y. Press Co., 164 N.Y. 406, 58 N.E. 527, 53 L.R.A. 288. The case is often cited as authority for the proposition that an agreement to buy merchandise at a fair and reasonable price is so indefinite that an action may not be maintained for its breach in so far as it is still executory. Nothing of the kind was decided, or with reason could have been. What the court did was to construe a particular agreement, and to hold that the parties intended to reserve the price for future adjustment. If instead of reserving the price for future adjustment, they had manifested an intent on the one hand to pay and on the other to accept a fair price, the case is far from holding that a jury could not determine what such a price would be and assess the damages accordingly. Such an intent, moreover, might be manifested not only through express words, but also through reasonable implication. It was because there was neither an express statement nor a reasonable implication of such an intent that the court held the agreement void to the extent that it had not been executed.

On the ground that the plaintiff failed to supply the data essential to computation, I concur in the conclusion that profits were not to be included as an element of damages. I do not concur, however, in the conclusion that he failed to make out a case of damage to the extent of his loss of salary. The amount may be small, but none the less it belongs to him. The hiring was not at will. . . . The plain implication was that it should continue until the end of the year when the books were to be closed. The evidence would permit the jury to find that the plaintiff was discharged without cause, and he is entitled to damages measured by his salary for the unexpired term.

The judgment should be reversed, and a new trial granted, with costs to abide the event.

Judgment affirmed.

Lefkowitz v. Great Minneapolis Surplus Store

Supreme Court of Minnesota, 1957.
Supra at 249.

NOTES

(1) If the majority opinion in *Varney* represents the traditional approach to judging definiteness in contracting, how would you characterize that approach? What is the difference between the majority and the dissent of Judge Cardozo?

(2) In Community Design Corporation v. Antonell, 459 So.2d 343 (Fla.App. 1984), an employer promised a specific bonus if an architect completed an indefinite amount of work. The court held the contract to be sufficiently definite to allow a jury to give reasonable meaning to ambiguous terms. The court in *Community* distinguished *Varney* because a particular amount was offered. Is this a sufficient reason for enforcement?

(3) Should a different rule govern indefinite offers than covers indefinite contracts? Consider Ian Ayres and Robert Gertner, *Filling Gaps in Incomplete Contracts: An Economic Theory of Default Rules*, 99 Yale L.J. 87, 106 (1989):

> In applying the common-law standard that indefinite contracts are unenforceable, the [Lefkowitz] court ignored the likely market response to the non-enforceability default. [N]on-enforceability can be viewed as a penalty default that encourages both parties to come forward and fill in the gap; that is, refusing to enforce indefinite contracts drives out indefinite contracts. In Lefkowitz, however, the court's refusal to enforce the indefinite offer leads to exactly the opposite result. Ask yourself the simple question: What kind of ad is the Great Minneapolis Surplus Store going to run the week following the court's decision? By lending its imprimatur to the indefinite ad, the court allows retailers to induce inefficient consumer reliance with impunity. The Lefkowitz case dramatically illustrates that only by enforcing indefinite offers against the offeror can one drive out indefinite offers.

(4) In Schade v. Diethrich, 158 Ariz. 1, 760 P.2d 1050 (1988), an employer offered, in consideration of the employee's resignation, "a very generous and fair separation agreement that reflects the contributions that you have made to this organization, to the Institute, and to me over this 10 year period." Reluctant to resign, and doubtful of the employer's ability to be fair under the circumstances, the employee voiced his doubts to the employer's attorney. The latter proposed the appointment of a committee to recommend an appropriate severance package. The employee agreed to this. The committee recommended the payment of one year's salary as separation pay, plus compensation for untaken vacation time over the past two years. After the employer refused to abide by this recommendation, the employee sued. The Supreme Court of Arizona upheld the employee's claim. Finding that the parties clearly manifested an intention to be bound, any requirement of "reasonable certainty" is satisfied if the agreement provides "a basis for determining the existence of a

breach and for giving an appropriate remedy.'' Restatement (Second) § 33(2). The court noted that the task here was made easier because it had the opinion of experts mutually selected by the parties.

(5) If a court is convinced that the parties have manifested an intention to be bound, should it, despite indefiniteness of expression, strive to resolve all questions of doubt on the basis of what seems fair and reasonable? Or would this amount to the court "making the contract for the parties"? Influenced by the Uniform Commercial Code and reflecting some modern precedent, Restatement (Second) § 33 sets forth the following standards for judging the impact of indefiniteness and open terms:

> "(1) Even though a manifestation of intention is intended to be understood as an offer, it cannot be accepted so as to form a contract unless the terms of the contract are reasonably certain. (2) The terms of a contract are reasonably certain if they provide a basis for determining the existence of a breach and for giving an appropriate remedy. (3) The fact that one or more terms of a proposed bargain are left open or uncertain may show that a manifestation of intention is not intended to be understood as an offer or as an acceptance."

(6) *Varieties of Indefiniteness.* There is never a shortage of litigation contesting contractual validity on the basis of alleged indefiniteness of terms. Each term must, of course, be considered contextually, as Judge Cardozo insisted in *Varney*. But even when so considered, many fail to pass muster. For a sampling of contemporary litigation, see Union State Bank v. Woell, 434 N.W.2d 712 (N.D.1989) (promise of bank to provide future financing if borrower could market a particular product nationally); Roy v. Danis, 553 A.2d 663 (Me.1989) (promise of purchaser of transmission business to employ the seller for life to do "anything [purchaser] asked," such as "putting [seller] on the road * * * running errands"; promise of purchaser to seller that if latter started another shop, purchaser would "send him some work"); Trimmer v. Van Bomel, 107 Misc.2d 201, 434 N.Y.S.2d 82 (1980) (promise of wealthy widow to her former companion and paid escort to pay latter an amount sufficient to cover "costs and expenses for sumptuous living and maintenance for the remainder of his life"); Champaign National Bank v. Landers Seed Co., Inc., 165 Ill.App.3d 1090, 116 Ill.Dec. 742, 519 N.E.2d 957 (1988) (promise of bank not to collect on note "as long as [debtor] make[s] progress toward profitability"); University National Bank v. Ernst & Whinney, 773 S.W.2d 707 (Tex.App. 1989) (promise of accounting firm to provide "loan supervision information" for bank); Cobble Hill Nursing Home, Inc. v. Henry and Warren, 74 N.Y.2d 475, 548 N.Y.S.2d 920, 548 N.E.2d 203 (1989) (promise of nursing home owner to sell property to New York Department of Health "at a price to be determined by the Department in accordance with the Public Health Law and all applicable rules and regulations of the Department"); Kane v. McDermott, 191 Ill.App.3d 212, 138 Ill.Dec. 541, 547 N.E.2d 708 (1989) (promise in option to sell property "at the appraised bid as established by three disinterested persons").

(7) In Hall v. Busst, a 1960 decision of the High Court of Australia (34 A.L.J.R. 332), the court considered the following "price term" of an option contained in a contract for the sale of an island off the coast of Queensland:

> "The purchase price relating to such option shall be [13,157 4s.] to which shall be added the value of all additions and improvements to the said property

since date of purchase by the Grantor (such value to be taken as at date of exercise of this option) and from which shall be subtracted the value of all deficiencies of chattel property and a reasonable sum to cover depreciation of all buildings and other property on the land." The majority found this to be too uncertain to be the basis of an enforceable contract. Dixon, C.J., observed:

"There could be no external standard of value of additions and improvements to the island: no standard yielding a figure reasonably fixed or ascertainable. Still less would it be possible to find an external standard for the reasonable sum to cover depreciation even if one knew what "other property" is referred to. And indeed the value of deficiencies is another uncertain element in the ascertainment of the price. It is said that "value" or "fair value" is to be found objectively by a jury. But here we are dealing with substantive rights, not the procedure by which they are to be enforced. Can it be supposed that men contract to pay a price if and when fixed by a jury in a law suit?" (34 A.L.J.R. at 334–5).

■ WINDEYER, J., dissenting, disagreed:

"An offer to sell at a fair value might, of course, be no more than an offer to negotiate as to a price. But, if parties, intending to make a concluded contract of sale, agree that the sale shall be at a fair valuation of the property sold, they have fixed the price by reference to an ascertainable fact—the fair value. The value of any property, except commodities commonly bought and sold and having a current market price, may, in one sense, be always a matter of opinion unless there be some fixed or standard price; so that subjective considerations necessarily intrude into questions of value. Yet the law regards value as an ascertainable fact, and land no less than other forms of property as susceptible of valuation. The valuation of land and improvements upon land is, in fact, commonly undertaken for a variety of purposes, for example, for rating, or to determine compensation on a compulsory acquisition, or for trustees proposing to invest funds upon mortgage. I do not find any logical difficulty in the idea of a reasonable price for land in a system of law that by statute asserts that there is a reasonable price for goods of all kinds—for a picture, a race-horse, or an ancient vase, for examples, just as much as for a loaf of bread or a pound of tea." (34 A.L.J.R. at 344).

For a thorough and critical study of English and Commonwealth materials, see Ellinghaus, *Agreements Which Defer "Essential" Terms*, 45 Austr.L.J. 4–20, 72–82 (1971).

(C) INCOMPLETE AND DEFERRED AGREEMENT

Metro–Goldwyn–Mayer, Inc. v. Scheider

Court of Appeals of New York, 1976.
40 N.Y.2d 1069, 392 N.Y.S.2d 252, 360 N.E.2d 930.

■ PER CURIAM.

Following a nonjury trial and confronted with sometimes conflicting evidence, the court found that the parties had entered into an oral contract by which appellant had agreed to be principal actor in a pilot film and in the television series which might develop therefrom. After performing in the pilot and being fully compensated therefor, appellant refused to perform in the subsequent television series.

The core issue on this appeal is whether the determination that there was a complete contract between the parties is to be upheld. The negotiations of the parties extended over many weeks. Initially the broad outlines of the contract and its financial dimensions were agreed to in September, 1971, with explicit expectations that further agreements were to follow. Additional important provisions were negotiated over the following weeks. It was during this period that appellant went to Europe for the filming of the pilot. All culminated in supplemental agreements concluded in February, 1972. The only essential term as to which there was no finding of articulated understanding was the starting date for filming the television series. This term was supplied by a finding of the trial court based on proof of established custom and practice in the industry, of which both parties were found to be aware, set in the context of the other understandings reached by them. As Mr. Justice Arnold L. Fein wrote at Trial Term (75 Misc.2d 418, 422, 347 N.Y.S.2d 755, 761): "[W]here the parties have completed their negotiations of what they regard as essential elements, and performance has begun on the good faith understanding that agreement on the unsettled matters will follow, the court will find and enforce a contract even though the parties have expressly left these other elements for future negotiation and agreement, if some objective method of determination is available, independent of either party's mere wish or desire. Such objective criteria may be found in the agreement itself, commercial practice or other usage and custom. If the contract can be rendered certain and complete, by reference to something certain, the court will fill in the gaps" (see Restatement 2d, Contracts, § 230, esp. Comment *d*; § 247; Corbin, Contracts, § 95, pp. 401–404; cf. May Metropolitan Corp. v. May Oil Burner Corp., 290 N.Y. 260, 49 N.E.2d 13).

The findings of fact by the trial court were expressly approved and adopted at the Appellate Division. In this procedural posture such findings, supported as they are by evidence in this record, are now beyond the scope of our review.

Noting that the defense predicated in the courts below on the Statute of Frauds has been abandoned on the appeal to us, we have examined appellant's objection to the Appellate Division's remand for a second trial on the issue of damages and his other contentions and find them to be without merit.

Accordingly, the judgment of Supreme Court should be affirmed.

Joseph Martin, Jr., Delicatessen, Inc. v. Schumacher

Court of Appeals of New York, 1981.
52 N.Y.2d 105, 436 N.Y.S.2d 247, 417 N.E.2d 541.

■ FUCHSBERG, JUDGE.

This case raises an issue fundamental to the law of contracts. It calls upon us to review a decision of the Appellate Division, 70 A.D.2d 1, 419

N.Y.S.2d 558 which held that a realty lease's provision that the rent for a renewal period was "to be agreed upon" may be enforceable.

The pertinent factual and procedural contexts in which the case reaches this court are uncomplicated. In 1973, the appellant, as landlord, leased a retail store to the respondent for a five-year term at a rent graduated upwards from $500 per month for the first year to $650 for the fifth. The renewal clause stated that "[t]he Tenant may renew this lease for an additional period of five years at annual rentals to be agreed upon; Tenant shall give Landlord thirty (30) days written notice, to be mailed certified mail, return receipt requested, of the intention to exercise such right". It is not disputed that the tenant gave timely notice of its desire to renew or that, once the landlord made it clear that he would do so only at a rental starting at $900 a month, the tenant engaged an appraiser who opined that a fair market rental value would be $545.41.

The tenant thereupon commenced an action for specific performance in Supreme Court, Suffolk County, to compel the landlord to extend the lease for the additional term at the appraiser's figure or such other sum as the court would decide was reasonable. For his part, the landlord in due course brought a holdover proceeding in the local District Court to evict the tenant. On the landlord's motion for summary judgment, the Supreme Court, holding that a bald agreement to agree on a future rental was unenforceable for uncertainty as a matter of law, dismissed the tenant's complaint. Concordantly, it denied as moot the tenant's motion to remove the District Court case to the Supreme Court and to consolidate the two suits.

It was on appeal by the tenant from these orders that the Appellate Division, expressly overruling an established line of cases in the process, reinstated the tenant's complaint and granted consolidation. In so doing, it reasoned that "a renewal clause in a lease providing for future agreement on the rent to be paid during the renewal term is enforceable if it is established that the parties' intent was not to terminate in the event of a failure to agree." It went on to provide that, if the tenant met that burden, the trial court could proceed to set a "reasonable rent." One of the Justices, concurring, would have eliminated the first step and required the trial court to proceed directly to the fixation of the rent. Each party now appeals by leave of the Appellate Division pursuant to CPLR 5602 (subd. [b], par. 1). The tenant seeks only a modification adopting the concurrer's position. The question formally certified to us by the Appellate Division is simply whether its order was properly made. Since we conclude that the disposition at the Supreme Court was the correct one, our answer must be in the negative.

We begin our analysis with the basic observation that, unless otherwise mandated by law (e.g., residential emergency rent control statutes), a contract is a private "ordering" in which a party binds himself to do, or not to do, a particular thing (Fletcher v. Peck, 6 Cranch [10 U.S.] 87, 136; 3

L.Ed. 162. Hart and Sachs, Legal Process, 147–148 [1958]). This liberty is no right at all if it is not accompanied by freedom not to contract. The corollary is that, before one may secure redress in our courts because another has failed to honor a promise, it must appear that the promisee assented to the obligation in question.

It also follows that, before the power of law can be invoked to enforce a promise, it must be sufficiently certain and specific so that what was promised can be ascertained. Otherwise, a court, in intervening, would be imposing its own conception of what the parties should or might have undertaken, rather than confining itself to the implementation of a bargain to which they have mutually committed themselves. Thus, definiteness as to material matters is of the very essence in contract law. Impenetrable vagueness and uncertainty will not do * * *.

Dictated by these principles, it is rightfully well settled in the common law of contracts in this State that a mere agreement to agree, in which a material term is left for future negotiations, is unenforceable ... This is especially true of the amount to be paid for the sale or lease of real property * * *. The rule applies all the more, and not the less, when, as here, the extraordinary remedy of specific performance is sought * * *.

This is not to say that the requirement for definiteness in the case before us now could only have been met by explicit expression of the rent to be paid. The concern is with substance, not form. It certainly would have sufficed, for instance, if a methodology for determining the rent was to be found within the four corners of the lease, for a rent so arrived at would have been the end product of agreement between the parties themselves. Nor would the agreement have failed for indefiniteness because it invited recourse to an objective extrinsic event, condition or standard on which the amount was made to depend. All of these, *inter alia,* would have come within the embrace of the maxim that what can be made certain is certain (9 Coke, 47a). * * *

But the renewal clause here in fact contains no such ingredients. Its unrevealing, unamplified language speaks to no more than "annual rentals to be agreed upon." Its simple words leave no room for legal construction or resolution of ambiguity. Neither tenant nor landlord is bound to any formula. There is not so much as a hint at a commitment to be bound by the "fair market rental value" which the tenant's expert reported or the "reasonable rent" the Appellate Division would impose, much less any definition of either. Nowhere is there an inkling that either of the parties directly or indirectly assented, upon accepting the clause, to subordinate the figure on which it ultimately would insist, to one fixed judicially, as the Appellate Division decreed be done, or, for that matter, by an arbitrator or other third party.

Finally in this context, we note that the tenant's reliance on May Metropolitan Corp. v. May Oil Burner Corp., 290 N.Y. 260, 49 N.E.2d 13 is misplaced. There the parties had executed a franchise agreement for the sale of oil burners. The contract provided for annual renewal, at which time each year's sales quota was "to be mutually agreed upon". In holding that the defendant's motion for summary judgment should have been denied, the court indicated that the plaintiff should be given an opportunity to establish that a series of annual renewals had ripened into a course of dealing from which it might be possible to give meaning to an otherwise uncertain term. This decision, in the more fluid sales setting in which it occurred, may be seen as a precursor to the subsequently enacted Uniform Commercial Code's treatment of open terms in contracts for the sale of goods (see Uniform Commercial Code, § 1–205, subd. [1]; § 2–204, subd. [3]; see, also, Restatement, Contracts 2d, § 249). As the tenant candidly concedes, the code, by its very terms, is limited to the sale of goods. The *May* case is therefore not applicable to real estate contracts. Stability is a hallmark of the law controlling such transactions * * *.

For all these reasons, the order of the Appellate Division should be reversed, with costs, and the orders of the Supreme Court, Suffolk County, reinstated. The certified question, therefore, should be answered in the negative. As to the plaintiff's appeal, since that party was not aggrieved by the order of the Appellate Division, the appeal should be dismissed (CPLR 5511), without costs.

■ MEYER, JUDGE (concurring).

While I concur in the result because the facts of this case do not fit the rule of May Metropolitan Corp. v. May Oil Burner Corp., 290 N.Y. 260, 49 N.E.2d 13, I cannot concur in the majority's rejection of that case as necessarily inapplicable to litigation concerning leases. That the setting of that case was commercial and that its principle is now incorporated in a statute (the Uniform Commercial Code) which by its terms is not applicable to real estate is irrelevant to the question whether the principle can be applied in real estate cases.

As we recognized in Farrell Lines v. City of New York, 30 N.Y.2d 76, 82, 330 N.Y.S.2d 358, 281 N.E.2d 162, quoting from A.Z.A. Realty Corp. v. Harrigan's Cafe, 113 Misc. 141, 147, 185 N.Y.S. 212: "An agreement of lease possesses no peculiar sanctity requiring the application of rules of construction different from those applicable to an ordinary contract." To the extent that the majority opinion can be read as holding that no course of dealing between the parties to a lease could make a clause providing for renewal at a rental "to be agreed upon" enforceable I do not concur.

■ JASEN, JUDGE (dissenting in part).

While I recognize that the traditional rule is that a provision for renewal of a lease must be "certain" in order to render it binding and enforceable, in my view the better rule would be that if the tenant can establish its entitlement to renewal under the lease, the mere presence of a provision calling for renewal at "rentals to be agreed upon" should not prevent judicial intervention to fix rent at a reasonable rate in order to avoid a forfeiture. Therefore, I would affirm the order of the Appellate Division for the reasons stated in the opinion of Justice Leon D. Lazer at the Appellate Division.

On defendant's appeal: Order reversed, with costs, the orders of Supreme Court, Suffolk County, reinstated and the question certified answered in the negative.

On plaintiff's appeal: Appeal dismissed, without costs.

NOTES

(1) *Agreement to Negotiate in Good Faith.* In Channel Home Centers, Division of Grace Retail Corporation v. Grossman, 795 F.2d 291 (3d Cir.1986), a retailer negotiated with a mall developer for a lease. The parties executed a detailed "letter of intent," containing a commitment by the developer "to withdraw the Store from the rental market, and only negotiate the above described leasing transaction to completion." The letter of intent specified, however, that execution of the lease was expressly subject to approval by the retailer's parent corporation. Negotiations were cut off after the developer made a deal with a competitor of the retailer at a substantially higher rental than that contemplated in the letter of intent. In concluding that there was sufficient evidence to support a finding that the parties intended to enter into "a binding agreement to negotiate in good faith," the court stated:

> It is hornbook law that evidence of preliminary negotiations or an agreement to enter into a binding contract in the future does not alone constitute a contract. * * * [Developer believes] that this doctrine settles this case, but, in so arguing, [developer misconstrues retailer's] contract claim. [Retailer] does not contend that the letter of intent is binding as a lease or an agreement to enter into a lease. Rather, it is [retailer's] position that this document is enforceable as a mutually binding obligation *to negotiate in good faith.* By unilaterally terminating negotiations with [retailer] and precipitously entering into a lease agreement with Mr. Good Buys, [retailer] argues, [developer] acted in bad faith and breached his promise to "withdraw the Store from the rental market and only negotiate the above-described leasing transaction to completion." * * *

> Under Pennsylvania law, the test for enforceability of an agreement is whether both parties have manifested an intention to be bound by its terms and whether the terms are sufficiently definite to be specifically enforced. * * * Additionally, of course, there must be consideration on both sides. * * *

> Although no Pennsylvania court has considered whether an agreement to negotiate in good faith may meet these conditions, the jurisdictions that have considered the issue have held that such an agreement, if otherwise meeting the requisites of a contract is an enforceable contract. See, e.g., *Thompson v. Liquichimica of America, Inc.,* 481 F.Supp. 365, 366 (S.D.N.Y. 1979); ("Unlike an agreement to agree, which does not constitute a closed proposition, an agreement to use best efforts [or to negotiate in good faith] is a closed proposition, discrete and actionable."); . . . see generally Kessler and Fine, *Culpa in Contrahendo, Bargaining in Good Faith, and Freedom of Contract, a Comparative Study,* 77 Harv.L.Rev. 401 (1984). We are satisfied that Pennsylvania would follow this rule. . . .

(2) *Contract to Bargain.* Professor Charles Knapp has analyzed transactions where final agreement has been delayed either to await the occurrence of future events which control future agreement (agreement to agree). He argues that in cases like these where the parties have reached agreement to such a degree that they regard themselves as bound to each other, neither can withdraw for an "unjustified" reason yet neither can be compelled to perform if, after good faith bargaining, actual agreement cannot be reached. Thus is created a "contract to bargain" which stresses that unjustified withdrawals will give rise to appropriate contract remedies but that essential obligations are met by bargaining in good faith for as long as may reasonably be required under the circumstances. See Charles L. Knapp, *Enforcing the Contract to Bargain*, 44 N.Y.U.L.Rev. 673 (1969).

(3) *Written Contract Intended.* Suppose it is clear that both parties to a negotiation contemplate that their final agreement will be reduced to writing and signed by both of them. Suppose, further, that the parties reach sufficient agreement to conclude a contract but that one of them withdraws from the relationship before the writing is signed. Is there a contract? If the parties have explicitly stated that they do not intend to be bound until the writing is signed, the answer is no. The writing clearly is a condition precedent to liability. Even without an explicit condition, the question is still whether parties who contemplate a written memorial of the agreement intend that event to occur before a contract is formed. See, e.g., Asbestos Products, Inc. v. Healy Mechanical Contractors, 306 Minn. 74, 235 N.W.2d 807 (1975); Pennsylvania Co. v. Wilmington Trust Co., 39 Del.Ch. 453, 166 A.2d 726 (1960); Smith v. Onyx Oil and Chemical Co., 218 F.2d 104 (3d Cir.1955); Knapp, *Enforcing the Contract to Bargain*, 44 N.Y.U.L.Rev. 673, 716–719 (1969). But how is this intention to be ascertained? A Second Circuit case, applying New York law, gives the following criteria: "We have articulated several factors that help determine whether the parties intended to be bound in the absence of a document executed by both sides. The court is to consider (1) whether there has been an express reservation of the right not to be bound in the absence of a writing; (2) whether there has been partial performance of the contract; (3) whether all of the terms of the alleged contract have been agreed upon; and (4) whether the agreement at issue is the type of contract that is usually committed to writing." Winston v. Mediafare Entertainment Corporation, 777 F.2d 78, 80 (2d Cir.1985).

Oglebay Norton Company v. Armco, Inc.

Supreme Court of Ohio, 1990.
52 Ohio St.3d 232, 556 N.E.2d 515.

On January 9, 1957, Armco Steel Corporation, n.k.a. Armco, Inc., appellant, entered into a long-term contract with Columbia Transportation Company, which later became a division of Oglebay Norton Company, appellee. The principal term of this contract required Oglebay to have adequate shipping capacity available and Armco to utilize such shipping capacity if Armco wished to transport iron ore on the Great Lakes from mines in the Lake Superior district to Armco's plants in the lower Great Lakes region.

In the 1957 contract, Armco and Oglebay established a primary and a secondary price rate mechanism which stated:

"*Armco agrees to pay* * * * for all iron ore transported hereunder *the regular net contract rates for the season* in which the ore is transported, *as recognized by the leading iron ore shippers* in such season for the transportation of iron ore* * * *. If,* in any season of navigation hereunder, *there is no regular net contract rate recognized by the leading iron ore shippers* for such transportation, *the parties shall mutually agree upon a rate* for such transportation, *taking into consideration the contract rate being charged for similar transportation* by the leading independent vessel operators engaged in transportation of iron ore from The Lake Superior District." (Emphasis added.)

During the next twenty-three years, Armco and Oglebay modified the 1957 contract four times. With each modification Armco agreed to extend the time span of the contracts beyond the original date. Both parties acknowledged that the ever-increasing requirements capacity Armco sought from Oglebay would require a substantial capital investment from Oglebay to maintain, upgrade, and purchase iron ore carrier vessels.

The fourth amendment, signed in 1980, required Oglebay to modify and upgrade its fleet to give each Oglebay vessel that Armco utilized a self-unloading capability.[1] It is undisputed that Oglebay began a $95 million capital improvement program at least in part to accommodate Armco's new shipping needs. For its part, Armco agreed to pay an additional twenty-five cents per ton for ore shipped in Oglebay's self-unloading vessels[2] and agreed to extend the running of the contract until December 31, 2010.

During trial, the court recognized Armco's and Oglebay's close and long-standing business relationship, which included a seat for Armco on Oglebay's Board of Directors, Armco's owning Oglebay Norton stock, and a partnership in another venture. In fact, one of Oglebay's vessels was named "The Armco."

This relationship is perhaps best characterized by the language contained in the 1962 amendment, wherein the parties provided:

" * * * Armco has a vital and unique interest in the continued dedication of * * * [Oglebay's] bulk vessel fleet * * * since such service is a necessary prerequisite to Armco's operation as a major steel producer. * * * Armco's right to require the dedication of * * * [Oglebay's] bulk vessels to Armco's service * * * is the essence of this Agreement[.] * * *." The amendment also granted to Armco the right to seek a court order for specific performance of the terms of the contract.

---

1. A self-unloading vessel has the capability to unload without the assistance of cranes and crews standing by on dockside. This capability somewhat lessens cargo capacity but allows the vessel more freedom from docking restraints.

2. The twenty-five cents per gross ton differential was a standard rate charged by Columbia and Oglebay Norton to its shipping customers for use of its self-unloading vessels.

From 1957 through 1983 the parties established the contract shipping rate that Oglebay charged Armco by referring to a specified rate published in "Skillings Mining Review," in accordance with the 1957 contract's primary price mechanism. The published rate usually represented the price that Innerlake Steamship Company, a leading independent iron ore shipper, charged its customers for a similar service. Oglebay would quote this rate to Armco, which would then pay it to Oglebay.

Unfortunately, in 1983 the iron and steel industry suffered a serious downturn in business. Thus, in late 1983, when Oglebay quoted Armco the shipping rate for the 1984 season, Armco challenged that rate. Due to its weakened economic position, Armco requested that Oglebay reduce the rate Oglebay was going to charge Armco. The parties then negotiated a mutually satisfactory rate for the 1984 season.

In late 1984 the parties were unable to establish a mutually satisfactory shipping rate for the 1985 season. Oglebay billed Armco $7.66 ($.25 self-unloading vessel surcharge included) per gross ton, and Armco reduced the invoice amount to $5 per gross ton. Armco then paid the $5 per ton figure, indicating payment in full language on the check to Oglebay, and explaining its position in an accompanying letter. In late 1985, the parties again attempted to negotiate a rate, this time for the 1986 season. Again they failed to reach a mutually satisfactory rate.

On April 11, 1986, Oglebay filed a declaratory judgment action requesting the court to declare the rate set forth in the contract to be the correct rate, or in the absence of such a rate, to declare a reasonable rate for Oglebay's services. Armco's answer denied that the $7.41 rate sought by Oglebay was the "contract rate," and denied that the trial court had jurisdiction to declare this rate of its own accord, as a "reasonable rate" or otherwise.

During the 1986 season, Oglebay continued to ship iron ore for Armco. Armco paid Oglebay $4.22 per gross ton for ore shipped prior to August 1, 1986 and $3.85 per gross ton for ore shipped after August 1, 1986.

On August 12, 1987, Armco filed a supplemental counterclaim[3] seeking a declaration that the contract was no longer enforceable, because the contract had failed of its purpose due to the complete breakdown of the rate pricing mechanisms.

After a lengthy bench trial, the trial court on November 20, 1987 issued its declaratory judgment, which made four basic findings of fact and law. First, the court held that it was apparent from the evidence presented that Oglebay and Armco intended to be bound by the 1957 contract, even though the rate or price provisions in the contract were not settled.

Second, the court held that where the parties intended to be bound, but where a service contract pricing mechanism based upon the mutual

---

3. According to the trial court, Armco withdrew its first counterclaim in open court   at trial.

agreement of the parties fails, " * * * then the price shall be the price that is 'reasonable' under all the circumstances at the time the service is rendered."

Third, the trial court held that the parties must continue to comply with the alternative pricing provision contained within paragraph two of the 1957 contract. That alternative pricing provision mandates that the parties consider rates charged for similar services by leading independent iron ore vessel operators.

Fourth, the trial court held that if the parties were unable to agree upon a rate for the upcoming seasons, then the parties must notify the court immediately. Upon such notification, the court, through its equitable jurisdiction, would appoint a mediator and require the parties' chief executive officers " * * * to meet for the purpose of mediating and determining the rate for such season, i.e., that they 'mutually agree upon a rate.' "

The court of appeals affirmed the judgment of the trial court.

The cause is now before the court upon the allowance of a motion to certify the record.

■ PER CURIAM.

This case presents three mixed questions of fact and law. First, did the parties intend to be bound by the terms of this contract despite the failure of its primary and secondary pricing mechanisms? Second, if the parties did intend to be bound, may the trial court establish $6.25 per gross ton as a reasonable rate for Armco to pay Oglebay for shipping Armco ore during the 1986 shipping season? Third, may the trial court continue to exercise its equitable jurisdiction over the parties, and may it order the parties to utilize a mediator if they are unable to mutually agree on a shipping rate for each annual shipping season? We answer each of these questions in the affirmative and for the reasons set forth below affirm the decision of the court of appeals.

I

Appellant Armco argues that the complete breakdown of the primary and secondary contract pricing mechanisms renders the 1957 contract unenforceable, because the parties never manifested an intent to be bound in the event of the breakdown of the primary and secondary pricing mechanisms. Armco asserts that it became impossible after 1985 to utilize the first pricing mechanism in the 1957 contract, i.e., examining the published rate for a leading shipper in the "Skillings Mining Review," because after 1985 a new rate was no longer published. Armco asserts as well that it also became impossible to obtain the information necessary to determine and take into consideration the rates charged by leading independent vessel operators in accordance with the secondary pricing mechanism. This is because that information was no longer publicly available after 1985 and because the trial court granted the motions to quash of nonparties, who were subpoenaed to obtain this specific information.[4] Armco argues that since the parties never consented to be bound by a contract whose specific pricing mechanisms had failed, the trial court should have declared the contract to be void and unenforceable.

The trial court recognized the failure of the 1957 contract pricing mechanisms. Yet the trial court had competent, credible evidence before it to conclude that the parties intended to be bound despite the failure of the pricing mechanisms. The evidence demonstrated the long-standing and close business relationship of the parties, including joint ventures, interlocking directorates and Armco's ownership of Oglebay stock. As the trial court pointed out, the parties themselves contractually recognized Armco's vital and unique interest in the combined dedication of Oglebay's bulk vessel fleet, and the parties recognized that Oglebay could be required to ship up to 7.1 million gross tons of Armco iron ore per year.

Whether the parties intended to be bound, even upon the failure of the pricing mechanisms, is a question of fact properly resolved by the trier of fact. Normandy Place Assoc. v. Beyer (1982), 2 Ohio St.3d 102, 106, 2 OBR 653, 656, 443 N.E.2d 161, 164. Since the trial court had ample evidence before it to conclude that the parties did so intend, the court of appeals correctly affirmed the trial court regarding the parties' intent. We thus affirm the court of appeals on this question.

II

Armco also argues that the trial court lacked jurisdiction to impose a shipping rate of $6.25 per gross ton when that rate did not conform to the 1957 contract pricing mechanisms. The trial court held that it had the authority to determine a reasonable rate for Oglebay's services, even though the price mechanism of the contract had failed, since the parties intended to be bound by the contract. The court cited 1 Restatement of the Law 2d, Contracts (1981) 92, Section 33, and its relevant comments to support this proposition. Comment *e* to Section 33 explains in part:

" * * * Where * * * [the parties] * * * intend to conclude a contract for the sale of goods * * * and the price is not settled, the price is a reasonable price at the time of delivery if * * * (c) the price is to be fixed in terms of some agreed market or other standard as set or recorded by a third person or agency and it is not so set or recorded. Uniform Commercial Code § 2–305(1)." Id. at 94–95.

---

4. Oglebay Norton sought subpoenas from independent vessel operators and captive fleets to obtain information about rates those carriers were charging for the transportation of iron ore to lower lake ports. The other carriers resisted the subpoenas, requesting that the court quash the subpoenas or issue a protective order. The subpoenas were quashed prior to trial. The trial court's reasons for sustaining the motion to quash rather than issuing a protective order are unclear. It would appear that such information taken pursuant to a protective order under Civ.R. 26(C) might have been appropriate, given the dearth of reliable information concerning past and future controversies regarding rates.

As the trial court noted, Section 33 was cited with approval by the Court of Appeals for Cuyahoga County in Mr. Mark Corp. v. Rush, Inc. (1983), 11 Ohio App.3d 167, 11 OBR 259, 464 N.E.2d 586, and in North Coast Cookies, Inc. v. Sweet Temptations, Inc. (1984), 16 Ohio App.3d 342, 16 OBR 391, 476 N.E.2d 388. Restatement Section 33, Comment *e* follows virtually identical language contained in Section 2–305(1) of the Uniform Commercial Code, which was adopted in Ohio as R.C. 1302.18(A). Moreover the Court of Appeals for Cuyahoga County applied R.C. 1302.18 by analogy to a contract for services involving an open price term in Winning Sheet Metal Mfg. Co. v. Heat Sealing Equip. Mfg. Co. (Sept. 30, 1982), Cuyahoga App. No. 44365, unreported, at 3–4, 1982 WL 5944.

The court therefore determined that a reasonable rate for Armco to pay to Oglebay for transporting Armco's iron ore during the 1986 shipping season was $6.00 per gross ton with an additional rate of twenty-five cents per gross ton when self-unloading vessels were used. The court based this determination upon the parties' extensive course of dealing, " * * * the detriment to the parties respectively, and valid comparisons of market price which reflect [the] economic reality of current depressed conditions in the American steel industry."

The court of appeals concluded that the trial court was justified in setting $6.25 per gross ton as a "reasonable rate" for Armco to pay Oglebay for the 1986 season, given the evidence presented to the trial court concerning various rates charged in the industry and given the intent of the parties to be bound by the agreement.

The court of appeals also held that an open price term could be filled by a trial court, which has the authority to review evidence and establish a "reasonable price," when the parties clearly intended to be bound by the contract. To support this holding, the court cited Restatement of the Law 2d, Contracts, supra, at 92, Section 33, and its comments, and 179, Section 362, and its comments.

Section 33, Comment *a* provides in part:

" * * * [T]he actions of the parties may show conclusively that they have intended to conclude a binding agreement, even though one or more terms are missing or are left to be agreed upon. In such cases courts endeavor, if possible, to attach a sufficiently definite meaning to the bargain.

"An offer which appears to be indefinite may be given precision by usage of trade or by course of dealing between the parties. Terms may be supplied by factual implication, and in recurring situations the law often supplies a term in the absence of agreement to the contrary. * * * " Id. at 92.

As the court of appeals noted, we have held that "agreements to agree," such as the pricing mechanisms in the 1957 contract, are enforceable when the parties have manifested an intention to be bound by their terms and when these intentions are sufficiently definite to be specifically enforced. Normandy Place Assoc., supra, 2 Ohio St.3d at 105–106, 2 OBR at

656,443N.E.2d at 164. We have also held that "[i]f it is found that the parties intended to be bound, the court should not frustrate this intention, if it is reasonably possible to fill in some gaps that the parties have left, and reach a fair and just result." Litsinger Sign Co. v. American Sign Co. (1967), 11 Ohio St.2d 1, 14, 40 O.O.2d 30, 37, 227 N.E.2d 609, 619.

The court of appeals conducted an extensive review of the evidence presented to the trial court and concluded that the $6.25 per gross ton figure was a "reasonable rate" in this situation. The court of appeals noted that Oglebay presented evidence from Jesse J. Friedman, an economic and financial expert, who testified that $7.44 per gross ton was a reasonable rate for such services. Further evidence showed that Armco paid $5.00 per gross ton to Oglebay for the 1985 season, even though the published rate for that season was $7.41 per gross ton.

There was also testimony that Oglebay quoted Armco $5.66 per gross ton as the rate for the 1987 season. The evidence also showed that LTV Steel, prior to its bankruptcy renegotiations with Oglebay, had paid Oglebay the published rate of $7.41 per gross ton. Evidence also indicated that American Steamship Co. had quoted Armco a $5.90 per gross ton rate for the 1986 season.

The court of appeals concluded that the $6.25 per gross ton figure fell acceptably between the rate range extremes proven at trial. The court found this to be a reasonable figure. We find there was competent, credible evidence in the record to support this holding and affirm the court of appeals on this question.

III

Armco also argues that the trial court lacks equitable jurisdiction to order the parties to negotiate or in the failure of negotiations, to mediate, during each annual shipping season through the year 2010. The court of appeals ruled that the trial court did not exceed its jurisdiction in issuing such an order.

3 Restatement of the Law 2d, Contracts (1981) 179, Section 362, entitled "Effect of Uncertainty of Terms," is similar in effect to Section 33 and states:

"Specific performance or an injunction will not be granted unless the terms of the contract are sufficiently certain to provide a basis for an appropriate order."

Comment *b* to Section 362 explains:

" * * * Before concluding that the required certainty is lacking, however, a court will avail itself of all of the usual aids in determining the scope of the agreement. * * * Expressions that at first appear incomplete may not appear so after resort to usage * * * or the addition of a term supplied by law * * *." Id. at 179.

Ordering specific performance of this contract was necessary, since, as the court of appeals pointed out, " * * * the undisputed dramatic changes in the market prices of great lakes shipping rates and the length of the contract would make it impossible for a court to award Oglebay accurate damages due to Armco's breach of the contract.'' We agree with the court of appeals that the appointment of a mediator upon the breakdown of court-ordered contract negotiations neither added to nor detracted from the parties' significant obligations under the contract.

It is well-settled that a trial court may exercise its equitable jurisdiction and order specific performance if the parties intend to be bound by a contract, where determination of long-term damages would be too speculative. See 3 Restatement of the Law 2d, Contracts, supra, at 171–172, Section 360(a), Comment *b*; Columbus Packing Co. v. State, ex rel. Schlesinger (1919), 100 Ohio St. 285, 294, 126 N.E. 291, 293–294. Indeed, the court of appeals pointed out that under the 1962 amendment, Armco itself had the contractual right to seek a court order compelling Oglebay to specifically perform its contractual duties.

The court of appeals was correct in concluding that ordering the parties to negotiate and mediate during each shipping season for the duration of the contract was proper, given the unique and long-lasting business relationship between the parties, and given their intent to be bound and the difficulty of properly ascertaining damages in this case. The court of appeals was also correct in concluding that ordering the parties to negotiate and mediate with each shipping season would neither add to nor detract from the parties' significant contractual obligations. This is because the order would merely facilitate in the most practical manner the parties' own ability to interact under the contract. Thus we affirm the court of appeals on this question.

The court of appeals had before it competent, credible evidence from which to conclude that the parties intended to be bound by the terms of the contract, to conclude that the $6.25 per gross ton figure was a "reasonable rate" under the circumstances, and to conclude that the trial court's exercise of continuing equitable jurisdiction was proper in this situation. Accordingly, we affirm the decision of the court of appeals.

Judgment affirmed.

NOTES

(1) The *Oglebay Norton* facts reveal a contract with relational characteristics. For example, the relationship was to last for 50 years, the price term, which was intended to track the market over time (rather than to allocate risk), depended ultimately upon cooperative behavior by the parties (agreeing to fix the price), the carrier was asked to and made "transaction specific investments" in modifying the vessels for Armco's needs, and close relationships between the parties (almost but not quite a joint venture) developed. As such, a court might be reluctant to terminate the contract unless both parties clearly wanted to and might try to preserve the relationship. How did the court respond to Armco's failure to agree on the price and its apparent desire to exit from the contract (presumably because of a very bad market for steel)? Did the

court consider Armco to be in breach of contract? If so, what was the breach? If not, how could the court appoint a mediator and order specific performance? See Richard E. Speidel, *The Characteristics and Challenges of Relational Contracts*, 94 Nw. U. L. Rev. 823, 833–37 (2000) (analyzing the opinion).

(2) *Indefiniteness and Open Terms under the UCC.* Although the contract in *Oglebay Norton* was not for the sale of goods, the court applies UCC provisions, seemingly by analogy. These provisions break decisively with the traditional approach to open and indefinite terms. UCC 2–204(3), which states the basic principle as to open terms agreements underlying other sections, reads as follows: "Even though one or more terms are left open a contract for sale does not fail for indefiniteness if the parties have intended to make a contract and there is a reasonably certain basis for giving an appropriate remedy."

Subsection (3) establishes two standards; viz. (1) the parties must have intended to make a contract; (2) there must be a reasonably certain basis for giving an appropriate remedy. Compliance with the first standard is judged primarily with reference to other Code provisions dealing with intent to contract; viz., UCC 2–204(1), UCC 2–206 and UCC 2–207. Enforcement hinges upon whether the parties completed their preliminary negotiations or intended that agreement on the open terms was to be a condition of contractual obligation. The second test, as elaborated in the Code comments, is not one of certainty as to what the parties were to do nor as to the exact amount of damages due the plaintiff. The fact that one or more terms are left to be agreed is not enough of itself to defeat an otherwise adequate agreement. Commercial standards on the point of indefiniteness are to be applied.

Obviously, liability and remedy issues are often intertwined in disputes over indefiniteness. The agreement may be too indefinite to warrant specific performance but not money damages, or, as in *Oglebay,* the court may, in the exercise of its equitable jurisdiction, appoint a mediator and order the parties to negotiate. Similarly, damages measured by lost expectations may be unwarranted, but not damages measured by costs reasonably incurred in reliance upon the other's promise. Finally, the plaintiff should have a restitutionary remedy for the value of benefits conferred on the defendant through part performance.

(3) *The Effect of an "Agreement To Agree" under the UCC and Restatement (Second).* Suppose, in an agreement for the sale of goods, the parties apparently concluded their negotiations but explicitly left the quantity and the price of the described goods "to be agreed." Later, the seller refused to negotiate over the terms and the deal fell through. Did the seller breach a "contract" for the sale of goods? With regard to the *quantity* term, the general standard of UCC 2–204(3) applies: "Even though one or more terms are left open a contract for sale does not fail for indefiniteness if the parties have intended to make a contract and there is a reasonably certain basis for giving an appropriate remedy." It is possible that the parties may have intended to contract on these facts, but such sturdy stuff as trade usage, or a prior course of dealing or performance by both parties under the contract would be required to support the inference of intent. Even so, if the parties have not agreed, from what source shall the court derive a quantity term to supply in the agreement? As interpreted, the Statute of Frauds, Section 2–201(1) limits enforcement to the quantity of goods shown in the writing (what is "shown" by an agreement

to agree?) and the problems of determining a reasonable quantity term in the absence of some agreement are virtually insuperable. Thus, even with an intent to contract, lack of agreement on the quantity term should support a conclusion that the contract failed "for indefiniteness." In short, there was no "reasonably certain basis for giving an appropriate remedy."

With regard to the *price* term, the particular standard is supplied by Section 2–305. If the parties intend "not to be bound unless the price be fixed or agreed and it is not fixed or agreed there is no contract." UCC 2–305(4). If the requisite intent is present and the "price is left to be agreed by the parties and they fail to agree," the "price is a reasonable price at the time for delivery." UCC 2–305(1)(b). At this point, Section 2–305 is not concerned with why the parties failed to agree or with whether either or both of them negotiated in good faith. The fact of a failure to agree coupled with the requisite intent to contract justifies the court's intervention to fill the "gap" with a "reasonable price." Although it is easier for a court to ascertain reasonable price than reasonable quantity, success is not guaranteed. Thus, in North Central Airlines, Inc. v. Continental Oil Co., 574 F.2d 582 (D.C.Cir. 1978), a contract for the sale of oil failed for indefiniteness when the agreed pricing standard became inoperable and there was no reasonable basis for determining a substitute price. But see D.R. Curtis Co. v. Mathews, 103 Idaho 776, 653 P.2d 1188 (App.1982), where the court upheld the trial court's substitute price, determined after the parties failed to agree, as not unreasonable.

Restatement (Second) contains rules and standards intended to cover all exchange transactions, not just contracts for the sale of goods. Further, Restatement (Second) does not explicitly provide different rules for different transactions. Thus, unlike the opinion of Judge Fuchsberg in the *Schumacher* case, supra, there is no attempt to suggest that the need for security in real estate transactions dictates a different approach to the "agreement to agree" issue than in the more "fluid" sale of goods situation. How, then, might a case like *Schumacher* be decided under Restatement (Second)? Again, the first question would be whether leaving the rent on renewal "to be agreed" precluded contract formation. Section 33(3) states that leaving such a term "open or uncertain may show that a manifestation of intention is not intended to be understood as an offer or as an acceptance." Although the agreement to agree may "strongly indicate that the parties do not intend to be bound," see Illustration 8 to Section 33, the course of performance of the parties and the lessee's not unreasonable reliance under the first lease clearly answer that question in the affirmative. If, then, the parties intended to be bound and failed to agree, Restatement (Second), like the UCC, directs the court to enforce the renewal lease if the terms are "reasonably certain." See Sections 33(1) & (2) and 34. The terms of a contract are "reasonably certain if they provide a basis for determining the existence of a breach and for giving an appropriate remedy." Section 33(2). Part performance under an agreement "may remove uncertainty," Section 34(2), or, because it is reliance on the contract, part performance or other action "may make a contractual remedy appropriate even though uncertainty is not removed." Section 34(2). Finally, Section 204 provides:

When the parties to a bargain sufficiently defined to be a contract have not agreed with respect to a term which is essential to a determination of their rights and duties, a term which is reasonable in the circumstances is supplied by the court.

It is clear, is it not, that Restatement (Second) would dictate a different result than that reached by the court in *Schumacher*? The parties intended to contract. Although the performance of the parties did not provide a basis for agreement on the renewal price, the lessee's reliance on the option to renew was reasonable. A fair market value for the leasehold interest could be determined with reasonable certainty. Finally, the lessor, by insisting upon a rental some $300 over the fair rental value, may be negotiating in bad faith. Cumulatively, don't these factors support the intervention of the court to supply a reasonable term over the "freedom from contract" argument advanced by Judge Fuchsberg?

(4) *Incorporation of Commercial Context.* At the time when the UCC was being enacted, the tension was between asserted "rules" that require full and complete agreement on all material terms before the agreement is enforceable and the standards, announced by the UCC and Restatement (Second), that turn the question of enforceability upon both the intention of the parties and the ability of the court to supply a "reasonable" term to fill the gap. Professor Speidel, in discussing the UCC approach, has stated:

> A more complete triumph of standards over rules is hard to imagine. Furthermore, such standards as "intention to conclude a contract," 'reasonable price,' and 'reasonably certain basis' for enforcement require particularization within the commercial circumstances made relevant by the definition of agreement. * * * [T]his method reflects Llewellyn's view that the law of the transaction is imbedded in the total situation and that the task of the 'law authority' is to discover it. Law is 'immanent' in existing patterns of conduct or relationships and, when discovered, provides a more reliable source of certainty than does the rigid, external system of classical contract law. The problem with standards is that they may lead the court to water without explaining how to drink. * * * [T]he drafters of the Code left off at critical points, leaving the judge to fill in from what the parties could extract from the commercial context. * * * [T]he method pointed to the commercial context without clarifying how the diverse data were to be assembled and used.

Richard E. Speidel, *Restatement Second: Omitted Terms and Contract Method,* 67 Cornell L.Rev. 785, 791–92 (1982).

Comment: Open Terms Other Than Price

Article 2 of the UCC is predominantly a collection of default rules. The phrase "unless otherwise agreed" appears dozens of times in the text. And § 1–302 makes clear that by default UCC provisions should be interpreted as defaults:

> Except as otherwise provided ... the effect of provisions of [the Uniform Commercial Code] may be varied by agreement.... The presence in certain provisions ... of the phrase "unless otherwise

agreed'', or words of similar import, does not imply that the effect of other provisions may not be varied by agreement under this section.

Moreover, § 2–204(3) clearly suggests that the code has an inclination toward filling gaps rather than striking down open ended contracts for indefiniteness:

> Even though one or more terms are left open a contract for sale does not fail for indefiniteness if the parties have intended to make a contract and there is a reasonably certain basis for giving an appropriate remedy.

Not all provisions, however, are contractable. Most importantly, the obligation of "good faith" may not be disclaimed even by express agreement. [Rev. § 1–302(b)]. But even here the code allows some contractual flexibility:

> The parties, by agreement, may determine the standards by which [good faith] is to be measured if those standards are not manifestly unreasonable. Id.

There are a number of Code sections, other than the one dealing with open price contracts, which help make contracts more complete if the contract is silent. For example, unless otherwise agreed, the Code ordains:

1. All of the goods are to be delivered at one time, not in several lots. UCC 2–307.

2. The buyer has the option of selecting the assortment of the goods; the seller has the option of determining the specifications or arrangements relating to shipment. UCC 2–311(2).*

3. The time for shipment or delivery or any other action under a contract ... shall be a reasonable time. UCC 2–309(1).

4. The place for delivery of goods is the seller's place of business or residence. UCC 2–308.

5. If the agreement authorizes the seller to send the goods to the buyer (and the location of buyer and seller in distant cities could amount to this authorization), the seller may use documents of title and ship under reservation. UCC 2–310(b).

6. Payment of the price is due on receipt of the goods, UCC 2–301, 2–310(a), 2–507.

7. The seller warrants that the title conveyed shall be good. UCC 2–312.

8. A merchant seller warrants that the goods are "merchantable." UCC 2–314.

9. With certain qualifications, duties may be delegated and rights may be assigned to third parties UCC 2–210.]

---

* But the Code establishes a mandatory rule that the specifications by that party "must be made in good faith and within limits set by commercial reasonableness." UCC § 2–311(1).

The result of these rules can be summarized thus:

The parties are free to work out the terms of their own contract. As long as those terms fall within the boundaries of conscionability and fair dealing, the courts will enforce those terms. However, failure to agree on each and every term will not result in an unenforceable agreement. The Code fleshes out the skeletal contract by providing terms which the drafters thought would most probably be in the minds of the parties.**

Comment: How Should the Law Set "Default" Rules?

If the parties have intended to contract but the agreement is incomplete, what "default" rules should be inserted to fill the gaps? The traditional answer is give the parties what they would have contracted for if they had expressly contracted. This approach is sometimes called the "hypothetical contracting" approach to default setting. But it is often devilishly difficult for courts to infer what particular contracting parties would have contracted for. Often the best a court might do is infer what a majority of contractors in a particular setting would have done. This is sometimes called the "majoritarian" approach to default setting. The default price provision seems quite consistent with this hypothetical/majoritarian approach. The parties would have probably contracted for a reasonable price—which is normally going to be cashed out as closely related to the market price. Indeed, anytime you see the word "reasonable" included in the description of a defaults, there is a good chance that hypothetical gap filler is at work.*

But as a descriptive matter the law sometimes chooses to fill gaps with terms that do not accord with the hypothetical contracting approach. While the law fills price gaps with the reasonable price, it does not tend to fill quantity gaps by trying to divine what would have been a reasonable quantity. Instead, the impact of the statute of frauds is often to create de facto a quantity default of zero.** Or the *contra proferentem* rule (which tends to resolve contractual ambiguity by interpreting the contract against the drafting party) seems to have the goal of penalizing sloppy drafting

---

** Nordstrom, Handbook of the Law of Sales 105–110 (1970). This comment grows out of Nordstrom's discussion.

* However, § 204 of the Restatement (Second) of Contract provides that terms that are "reasonable in the circumstances" should be used to fill "omitted essential terms," but expressly disclaims reliance on the hypothetical approach in the accompanying comment:

> Sometimes it is said that the search is for the term the parties would have agreed to if the question had been brought to their attention. Both the meaning of the words used and the probability that a particular term would have

been used if the question had been raised may be factors in determining what term is reasonable in the circumstances. But where there is in fact no agreement, the court should supply a term which comports with community standards of fairness and policy rather than analyze a hypothetical model of the bargaining process.

** UCC § 2–201 ("A writing is not insufficient because it omits or incorrectly states a term agreed upon; [but] the contract is not enforceable . . . beyond the quantity of goods show in such writing").

rather than trying to divine what the parties would have expressly contracted for if they had been asked to resolve the ambiguity themselves. Indeed, any of the interpretive "rules of construction" (which strive to resolve ambiguity on some basis other than an attempt to uncover the parties' intent)*** can be seen as departing from the hypothetical contracting standard.

Ian Ayres and Rob Gertner have suggested that these departures might at times make good sense. "Penalty" or "information-forcing" defaults which intentionally penalize a contractor failing to fill a gap can further both equity and efficiency by giving a contractor the incentive to expressly contract. Ayres & Gertner, *Filling Gaps in Incomplete Contracts: An Economic Theory of Default Rules,* 99 Yale L.J. 87 (1989). In essence, a "penalty" default rule is a rule that the contractors would not have wanted. Its presence in the right case will provide contractors "an incentive to contract around the default rule and therefore to choose affirmatively the contract provision they prefer. In contrast to the received wisdom, penalty defaults are purposely set at what the parties would not want—in order to encourage the parties to reveal information to each other or to third parties (especially the courts)." Id. at 91. "When strategic considerations cause a more knowledgeable party not to raise issues that could improve contractual efficiency, a default that penalizes the more informed party may encourage the revelation of information." Id. at 128.

More generally there are a host of reasons besides "information forcing" that might justify a "minoritarian" default—that is, a default that only a minority of contracting parties would actually prefer. Minoritarian rules might, for example, be justified by:

(1) differences in the private costs of contracting,

(2) differences in the private costs of failing to contract,

(3) differences in the public costs of filling gaps, and

(4) differences in private information about the law.

"The choice of an efficient default does not boil down merely to a choice between the majoritarian rule (for which most contractors would have contracted) and a penalty default designed to induce a contractor to reveal information about her type. Instead, efficiency-minded lawmakers will often need to consider [other] factors to decide whether it is more efficient to choose a default that only a minority values." Ian Ayres & Rob Gertner, Majoritarian v. Minoritarian Defaults, 51 Stan. L. Rev. 1591 (1999).

The "default" revolution has taken the academy by storm. See, e.g., James J. White, Default Rules in Sales and the Myth of Contracting Out, 48 Loy. L. Rev. 53 (2002); Cass R. Sunstein, Switching the Default Rule, 77 N.Y.U. L. Rev. 106 (2002); Edward J. Jange & Paul M. Schwartz, The Gramm–Leach–Bliley Act, Information Privacy, and the Limits of Default

---

*** See, e.g., Restatement (Second) of Contract § 207 ("In choosing among the reasonable meanings of a promise . . . a meaning that serves the public interest is generally preferred").

Rules, 86 Minn. L. Rev. 1219 (2002); Robert S. Scott, *A Relational Theory of Default Rules for Commercial Contracts*, 19 J.Legal Stud. 597 (1990); Richard Craswell, *Contract Law, Default Rules, and the Philosophy of Promising*, 88 Mich.L.Rev. 489 (1989).

Empro Manufacturing Co., Inc. v. Ball–Co Manufacturing, Inc.

United States Court of Appeals, Seventh Circuit, 1989.
870 F.2d 423.

■ EASTERBROOK, CIRCUIT JUDGE.

We have a pattern common in commercial life. Two firms reach concord on the general terms of their transaction. They sign a document, captioned "agreement in principle" or "letter of intent", memorializing these terms but anticipating further negotiations and decisions—an appraisal of the assets, the clearing of a title, the list is endless. One of these terms proves divisive, and the deal collapses. The party that perceives itself the loser then claims that the preliminary document has legal force independent of the definitive contract. Ours is such a dispute.

Ball–Co Manufacturing, a maker of specialty valve components, floated its assets on the market. Empro Manufacturing showed interest. After some preliminary negotiations, Empro sent Ball–Co a three-page "letter of intent" to purchase the assets of Ball–Co and S.B. Leasing, a partnership holding title to the land under Ball–Co's plant. Empro proposed a price of $2.4 million, with $650,000 to be paid on closing and a 10–year promissory note for the remainder, the note to be secured by the "inventory and equipment of Ball–Co." The letter stated "[t]he general terms and conditions of such proposal (which will be subject to and incorporated in a formal, definitive Asset Purchase Agreement signed by both parties)". Just in case Ball–Co might suppose that Empro had committed itself to buy the assets, paragraph four of the letter stated that "Empro's purchase shall be subject to the satisfaction of certain conditions precedent to closing including, but not limited to" the definitive Asset Purchase Agreement and, among five other conditions, "[t]he approval of the shareholders and board of directors of Empro".

Although Empro left itself escape hatches, as things turned out Ball–Co was the one who balked. The parties signed the letter of intent in November 1987 and negotiated through March 1988 about many terms. Security for the note proved to be the sticking point. Ball–Co wanted a security interest in the land under the plant; Empro refused to yield.

When Empro learned that Ball–Co was negotiating with someone else, it filed this diversity suit. Contending that the letter of intent obliges Ball–Co to sell only to it, Empro asked for a temporary restraining order. The district judge set the case for a prompt hearing and, after getting a look at the letter of intent, dismissed the complaint under Fed.R.Civ.P. 12(b)(6) for failure to state a claim on which relief may be granted. Relying on

Interway, Inc. v. Alagna, 85 Ill.App.3d 1094, 41 Ill.Dec. 117 (1st Dist.1980), the district judge concluded that the statement, appearing twice in the letter, that the agreement is "subject to" the execution of a definitive contract meant that the letter has no independent force.

Empro insists on appeal that the binding effect of a document depends on the parties' intent, which means that the case may not be dismissed— for Empro says that the parties intended to be bound, a factual issue. Empro treats "intent to be bound" as a matter of the parties' states of mind, but if intent were wholly subjective there would be no parol evidence rule, no contract case could be decided without a jury trial, and no one could know the effect of a commercial transaction until years after the documents were inked. That would be a devastating blow to business. Contract law gives effect to the parties' wishes, but they must express these openly. Put differently, "intent" in contract law is objective rather than subjective—a point *Interway* makes by holding that as a matter of law parties who make their pact "subject to" a later definitive agreement have manifested an (objective) intent not to be bound, which under the parol evidence rule becomes the definitive intent even if one party later says that the true intent was different. As the Supreme Court of Illinois said in Schek v. Chicago Transit Authority, 42 Ill.2d 362, 364, 247 N.E.2d 886, 888 (1969), "intent must be determined solely from the language used when no ambiguity in its terms exists".... Parties may decide for themselves whether the results of preliminary negotiations bind them, ... but they do this through their words.

Because letters of intent are written without the care that will be lavished on the definitive agreement, it may be a bit much to put dispositive weight on "subject to" in every case, and we do not read *Interway* as giving these the status of magic words. They might have been used carelessly, and if the full agreement showed that the formal contract was to be nothing but a memorial of an agreement already reached, the letter of intent would be enforceable. Borg–Warner Corp. v. Anchor Coupling Co., 16 Ill.2d 234, 156 N.E.2d 513 (1958). Conversely, Empro cannot claim comfort from the fact that the letter of intent does not contain a flat disclaimer, such as the one in *Feldman* pronouncing that the letter creates no obligations at all. The text and structure of the letter—the objective manifestations of intent—might show that the parties agreed to bind themselves to some extent immediately. *Borg–Warner* is such a case. One party issued an option, which called itself "firm and binding"; the other party accepted; the court found this a binding contract even though some terms remained open. After all, an option to purchase is nothing if not binding in advance of the definitive contract. The parties to *Borg–Warner* conceded that the option and acceptance usually would bind; the only argument in the case concerned whether the open terms were so important that a contract could not arise even if the parties wished to be bound, a subject that divided the court. See 156 N.E.2d at 930–36 (Schaefer, J., dissenting).

A canvass of the terms of the letter Empro sent does not assist it, however. "Subject to" a definitive agreement appears twice. The letter also recites, twice, that it contains the "general terms and conditions", implying that each side retained the right to make (and stand on) additional demands. Empro insulated itself from binding effect by listing, among the conditions to which the deal was "subject", the "approval of the shareholders and board of directors of Empro". The board could veto a deal negotiated by the firm's agents for a reason such as the belief that Ball–Co had been offered too much (otherwise the officers, not the board, would be the firm's final decisionmakers, yet state law vests major decisions in the board). The shareholders could decline to give their assent for any reason (such as distrust of new business ventures) and could not even be required to look at the documents, let alone consider the merits of the deal. See Earl Sneed, *The Shareholder May Vote As He Pleases: Theory and Fact,* 22 U.Pittsburgh L.Rev. 23, 31–36, 40–42 (1960) (collecting cases). Empro even took care to require the return of its $5,000 in earnest money "without set off, in the event this transaction is not closed", although the seller usually gets to keep the earnest money if the buyer changes its mind. So Empro made clear that it was free to walk.

Neither the text nor the structure of the letter suggests that it was to be a one-sided commitment, an option in Empro's favor binding only Ball–Co. From the beginning Ball–Co assumed that it could negotiate terms in addition to, or different from, those in the letter of intent. The cover letter from Ball–Co's lawyer returning the signed letter of intent to Empro stated that the "terms and conditions are generally acceptable" but that "some clarifications are needed in Paragraph 3(c) (last sentence)", the provision concerning Ball–Co's security interest. "Some clarifications are needed" is an ominous noise in a negotiation, foreboding many a stalemate. Although we do not know what "clarifications" counsel had in mind, the specifics are not important. It is enough that even on signing the letter of intent Ball–Co proposed to change the bargain, conduct consistent with the purport of the letter's text and structure.

The shoals that wrecked this deal are common hazards in business negotiations. Letters of intent and agreements in principle often, and here, do no more than set the stage for negotiations on details. Sometimes the details can be ironed out; sometimes they can't. Illinois, ... allows parties to approach agreement in stages, without fear that by reaching a preliminary understanding they have bargained away their privilege to disagree on the specifics. Approaching agreement by stages is a valuable method of doing business. So long as Illinois preserves the availability of this device, a federal court in a diversity case must send the disappointed party home empty-handed. Empro claims that it is entitled at least to recover its "reliance expenditures", but the only expenditures it has identified are those normally associated with pre-contractual efforts: its complaint mentions the expenses "in negotiating with defendants, in investigating and reviewing defendants' business, and in preparing to acquire defendants' business." Outlays of this sort cannot bind the other side any more than paying an expert to tell you whether the painting at the auction is a genuine Rembrandt compels the auctioneer to accept your bid.

AFFIRMED.

NOTES

(1) *Contract to Bargain.* In an excellent article, Professor Charles Knapp has analyzed transactions where final agreement has been delayed either to await the occurrence of future events which control future agreement (agreement to agree) or to permit negotiations which will settle the details of a transaction already fully agreed upon in its essential terms (formal contract is contemplated). *Borg–Warner,* a case distinguished by the court in *Empro,* is thought to be a case in the first category. He argues that in cases like these where the parties have reached agreement to such a degree that they regard themselves as bound to each other, neither can withdraw for an "unjustified" reason yet neither can be compelled to perform if, after good faith bargaining, actual agreement cannot be reached. Thus is created a "contract to bargain" which stresses that unjustified withdrawals will give rise to appropriate contract remedies but that essential obligations are met by bargaining in good faith for as long as may reasonably be required under the circumstances. He has this to say about the *Borg–Warner* case:

> A better case could hardly be imagined to demonstrate the dilemma created by the common law for the judge concerned both with justice to the parties and with well-structured legal reasoning. While a majority of the court was persuaded by the parties' intention to make a binding agreement at the time they exchanged the letters, they were forced to take the position either that the contract was complete and binding in the absence of provisions for continued employment of personnel, *including the second-largest stock-holder,* or that the whole agreement was binding and enforceable—even specifically enforceable—despite the failure of buyer and seller to reach final agreement on the terms of continued employment. As Justice Schaefer points out, the selling company must have been concerned with the welfare of those personnel, and indeed Conroy himself must have been vitally concerned over the prospects for his continued employment. Justice Schaefer, arguing against the imposition of liability, was forced to take the position that the plaintiff should not even get to the jury, despite the allegation that the parties believed they were concluding a binding contract, acted as though they believed it, and—with only one apparent exception—still believed it.

> By contrast, applying the contract to bargain framework to such a situation would permit the court to take notice of, and give effect to, the parties' intention to create a relation which was, at least to some extent, legally binding. Second, it would save the court from inserting "reasonable" terms in the agreement where the terms are of such importance that they should only be decided by the parties. Third, it would direct the attention of the court to another important fact in the case: *Why has the defendant refused to go through with the sale?* If he has simply changed his mind, or now thinks a better price can be found elsewhere, then he should be liable to the plaintiff for breach of contract. If, however, he has

withdrawn because negotiations have broken down on the terms of his employment contract, and he has bargained in good faith, then he should be subject to no liability.

Of course, the court may have properly characterized the agreement as a complete and fully binding contract. The common law, however, forces the court to choose one extreme or the other, and, by directing the court's attention to the completeness of the agreement, the law diverts attention from the good faith of the non-performing party, which should be the most important question of all.

Charles L. Knapp, *Enforcing the Contract to Bargain*, 44 N.Y.U.L.Rev. 673, 715–16 (1969). [Reprinted by permission of the New York University Law Review.]

(2) How did Empro make clear it was "free to walk"? How else might this objective have been achieved? Does it appear that Ball–Co withdrew from the negotiations "in bad faith"? Should it make any difference if they did? For a comprehensive discussion of problems in this area, see E. Allan Farnsworth, *Precontractual Liability and Preliminary Agreements: Fair Dealing and Failed Negotiations*, 87 COLUM.L.REV. 217 (1987).

PROBLEM: THE CASE OF THE DON KING/"BUSTER" DOUGLAS LEGAL BOUT

James "Buster" Douglas and his manager John Johnson, entered into a boxing promotion agreement on December 31, 1988 (the "Promotional Agreement" or "Agreement"), with Don King Productions, Inc. (DKP). The Promotional Agreement provided for payment of $25,000 to Douglas in return for his granting DKP the exclusive right to promote his professional boxing bouts for three years. The Agreement also stated that this term would be automatically extended in the event Douglas was recognized as world champion, "to cover the entire period you are world champion and a period of two years following" loss of the title. Compensation for the individual bouts contemplated by the Promotional Agreement was to be made subject to further negotiation and agreement, with the agreed-to terms to be set forth in the individually-negotiated bout agreements. The Promotional Agreement specified a floor level of compensation of $50,000, plus $10,000 in training expenses, for Douglas' fights, except that in the case of a title bout or defense, no floor was provided, but such a purse was to be "negotiated and mutually agreed upon."

During the first year of the agreement, Douglas participated in three bouts arranged by DKP, the last of which was the heavyweight championship bout held in Tokyo on February 10, 1990, in which Douglas "shocked the world" by defeating then-heavyweight champion, Mike Tyson. In accordance with the Promotional Agreement, which called for monetary terms of each bout to be negotiated and set forth in a separate bout agreement, Douglas and Johnson had entered into a bout agreement on August 14, 1989 (the "Bout Agreement") pursuant to which Douglas was to be paid $1.3 million. This Bout Agreement granted DKP an "exclusive option: to promote [Douglas'] next three bouts following the Tokyo bout, such option to be exercised by giving notice to Douglas no later than 30 days after the Tokyo bout." The Bout Agreement provided that Douglas would receive $1 million for each of these bouts, except that in the event Douglas was the winner of the Tokyo bout, subsequent bouts would be subject to negotiation of a higher purse.

DKP sought to exercise its option and hold a rematch between Douglas and Tyson in June, 1990 at Trump Plaza in Atlantic City. However, on February 21, 1990, Douglas and Johnson executed a contract with Golden Nugget, Inc. and The Mirage Casino–Hotel (collectively, "Mirage") to stage Douglas' next two fights at the Mirage in Las Vegas, with a guaranteed minimum purse of $25 million dollars for the first bout and $25 million for a second heavyweight championship bout. This contract was made contingent upon Douglas obtaining a release from any obligation to DKP or a judicial declaration that DKP's exclusive Promotional and Bout Agreements were void and unenforceable.

In seeking such a declaration, Douglas and Johnson contend that they are not bound by the foregoing "Promotional and Bout Agreements" with DKP because these "are indefinite as to the essential term of consideration." Assuming New York law controls, how would you expect a court to rule? See Don King Productions, Inc. v. Douglas (James "Buster"), 742 F.Supp. 741 (S.D.N.Y.1990).

Comment: Texaco, Pennzoil and Outposts of Contract Law

The celebrated litigation between Pennzoil and Texaco, which generated the largest civil judgment in history ($10.53 billion), represents an outpost in contract law on several fronts. Texaco, Inc. v. Pennzoil, Co., 729 S.W.2d 768 (Tex.App.1987), cert. denied 485 U.S. 994, 108 S.Ct. 1305, 99 L.Ed.2d 686 (1988). First, it underscores the viability of the tort claim of interference with contractual relations and thereby illustrates a potent intersection between contract and tort law. Second, the case effectively evokes the specter of pre-contractual liability, which, combined with the tort claim, raises difficult (and frightening) possibilities for the corporate lawyer. Third, the question of what remedy to apply (i.e., whether tort or contract) and on what basis received a debatable answer. Finally, a fourth concern not addressed by the court, but subsequently of great concern to lawyers, is how to avoid the dangers of this "pre-contract" liability while maintaining the board of director's fiduciary responsibility to the shareholders.

The following is Professor Epstein's succinct description of the facts:

[Pennzoil] saw in the demoralization at Getty Oil an opportunity to become a major player in the oil industry by gaining control of Getty Oil's extensive reserves.

The two companies reached a deal, the gist of which was that Pennzoil and the Getty Trust [owner of 40.2% of Getty Oil stock] were to establish a new corporate vehicle to purchase the Getty shares from the [Getty] museum [owner of 10.8% of Getty Oil stock] and the public at large for a price set at $110 per share, plus $5 in deferred compensation. Pennzoil would wind up with about a 43 percent stake, and the Trust with a 57 percent stake. In essence Pennzoil and the Getty Trust engineered a squeeze play meant to displace present management while providing a handsome profit for the museum and the public shareholders.

Champagne glasses tinkled in celebration, press releases were duly issued, and on January 4, 1984, the deal was reported in the newspapers. Much detailed drafting of complex corporate documents remained to be done, but that was never to come to pass. Within hours of the original announcement Texaco stepped in with an offer to purchase all shares of Getty at $125 per share (later raised to $128), for a total price of just over $10 billion. That offer was accepted with great alacrity by * * * the museum on January 5, but only after Texaco agreed to indemnify the Getty interests for any liability they might have had to Pennzoil. * * * Pennzoil then * * * su[ed] Texaco for the common law tort of inducement of breach of contract. The rest is history.

Epstein, *The Pirates of Pennzoil, A Comic Opera Made Possible by a Grant from the Texaco Corporation,* 9 Regulation (November-December, 1985) p. 18. The case inspired another famous line attributed to Mr. Berra. "When Texaco's Chairman, John K. McKinley, asked Getty Oil's Chairman Sidney Peterson whether Getty might still be available even though an 'agreement in principle' had been entered into with Pennzoil, Peterson responded that 'the fat lady had not yet sung.' "Temkin, *When Does the Fat Lady Sing?: An Analysis of 'Agreements in Principle' "* in *Corporate Acquisitions,* 55 Ford.L.Rev. 125, n. 1 (1986).

Pennzoil brought suit in Delaware against Getty for specific enforcement of the merger contract. The Delaware Chancery Court denied specific performance, stating that as it was a remedy of last resort Pennzoil should pursue its damage remedy under contract law.[1]

Unfortunately for Texaco, with the failure of the Delaware action, Pennzoil was left to try its tort claim (for interference with contractual relations) in Texas. Now tort damages, both expectation and punitive, could be sought.

There has been considerable criticism of the award of damages in the case, which took into account Pennzoil's expectations of acquiring the oil reserves rather than, as some have suggested, the value of the company it was acquiring in terms of the price of its stock. The different measures produce vastly different results.[2]

---

1. Several commentators have seized on this issue to call for a more liberal use of specific performance in the corporate acquisitions area. Dean Yudof and John Jeffers wrote: "[T]he Chancellor's decision indicates how foolish the ancient rules are about specific performance in the modern context. Specific performance should have been the remedy of choice, not the remedy of last resort, applicable only if damages were inadequate. The dissolution of the Getty/Texaco deal and adherence to the original Getty/Pennzoil contract would have obviated the necessity of valuing the huge assets in dispute. And that valuation process is more complex for the courts than specific performance would have been." Yudof & Jeffer, *Pennzoil v. Texaco,* 27 Alberta L.Rev. 77, 79 (1988).

2. "With respect to damages, Pennzoil presented an attractive formula premised on a substitution of assets (an equivalent of 1 billion barrels of oil) for stock (3/7 of Getty

It appears most corporate lawyers have looked at Pennzoil as an aberration. However, though the lesson may not be that one is liable under a "letter of intent" (or some such instrument) for contract damages for breach, it still may have something of value to teach. Practitioners may be somewhat lulled into a false sense of security by "practices of the trade" where the "gentleman's agreement" is that there is no contract until the formal writing. Lawyers must take into account that at some point a jury not privy to the "gentleman's agreement" might look over their shoulders. Aware of this, they should be careful to draft any letters, notes or memorandums of agreement so as to make clear at what point the client manifests assent and that prior to that time there is (emphatically) no contract.

Another complication is encountered when the company has agreed to be bought through a merger or some other type of transfer of control. Under Delaware law (most Fortune 500 companies are chartered in Delaware and are subject to Delaware law concerning duties to shareholders), when a corporation places itself for sale, the board owes a duty to its shareholders to maximize shareholder value. See Revlon, Inc. v. MacAndrews & Forbes Holdings Corp., Inc., 506 A.2d 173 (Del.1985). Essentially, the board must auction off the corporation to the highest bidder. If the board of directors were to enter into a contractual arrangement with another company to acquire their company without seeking competing bids, the board of directors might be held in breach of their fiduciary duty to the shareholders. This duty may override their ability to bind the corporation to a contract under agency law, in that the directors might not have the authority to bind the corporation in such a situation. In which case, the corporation might not be bound to the contract, and the directors might be held liable for breach for the company's failure to perform. Under agency law, the directors' breach is described as a breach of their warranty of authority. Though this complex area of the law is covered in several other law school courses, a brief exposure to the types of problems presented serves to illustrate the grey, outer fringe of contract law. See also Ansaldi, *Texaco, Pennzoil and the Revolt of the Masses: A Contracts Postmortem*, 27 Hous.L.Rev. 733 (1990).

(D) REMEDIES WHERE AGREEMENT INCOMPLETE OR INDEFINITE

In disputes over indefiniteness, liability and remedy issues are intertwined. For example, even though the agreement is presumptively *enforceable* because the parties "intended" to contract, the contract will fail for indefiniteness if the court is unable to determine whether there has been a

stock) with the difference between the purchase price and Pennzoil's historical development cost being $7.53 billion. The logic of Pennzoil's theory flows nicely; however, it lacks authoritative support for the substitution of assets for stock. Furthermore, it contradicts the recognized rules which set the measure of damages in such cases at the difference between the market value of the property (stock price) at the time of the breach and the contract price." Baron and Baron, *The Pennzoil–Texaco Dispute: An Independent Analysis*, 38 Baylor L.Rev. 253 (1986).

breach or find a "reasonably certain basis for giving an app remedy." UCC 2–204(3); Restatement (Second) § 33(1). Dependi the nature and the extent of the indefiniteness, however, there sliding scale of remedial protection. Thus, indefiniteness in some the agreement may preclude specific performance but not interf the plaintiff's ability to prove damages measured by lost expe Similarly, an open term may foreclose proof of lost profits with re certainty but not interfere with proof of costs reasonably inc...... ... reliance upon the defendant's promise or the value of benefits conferred on the defendant through part performance. The point is this. If the incomplete or indefinite agreement is enforceable by whatever test, the plaintiff may seek to protect the expectation interest through specific performance or damages. If these remedies are not available because of indefiniteness in the agreement, alternative remedies protect the reliance and, if all else fails, the restitution interests. We will return to this sliding scale of remedial protection for breach of an enforceable agreement in Chapter Six.

What is the remedial situation where the agreement is found to be unenforceable due to indefinite or incomplete terms? In a theory of contract rooted in such concepts as "consideration" and protecting "reasonable expectations," the plaintiff is not entitled to either specific performance or damages measured by lost profits. Protection of the expectation interest depends upon an enforceable bargain. Similarly, one could argue that a plaintiff assumes the risk of any reliance in preparation for or performance of an unenforceable bargain, whether or not the defendant is benefited. Notable exceptions to this argument exist when the plaintiff's part performance is under a severable rather than an entire contract or where the plaintiff has made a down payment which the defendant, in all fairness, ought not retain. Here, more general principles of restitution to avoid unjust enrichment begin to operate and are softened even more when the part performance is under an agreement that both parties intended and thought to be enforceable. See Arrowsmith, *Ineffective Transactions and Unjust Enrichment: A Framework for Analysis,* 9 Legal Stud. 121 (1989).

With this general background in mind, consider the following famous case and the notes.

Hoffman v. Red Owl Stores, Inc.

Supreme Court of Wisconsin, 1965.
26 Wis.2d 683, 133 N.W.2d 267.

The complaint alleged that Lukowitz, as agent for Red Owl, represented to and agreed with plaintiffs that Red Owl would build a store building in Chilton and stock it with merchandise for Hoffman to operate in return for which plaintiffs were to put up and invest a total sum of $18,000; that in reliance upon the above mentioned agreement and representations plaintiffs sold their bakery building and business and their grocery store and business; also in reliance on the agreement and representations Hoffman purchased the building site in Chilton and rented a residence for himself and his family in Chilton; plaintiffs' action in reliance on the representations and agreement disrupted their personal and business life; plaintiffs lost substantial amounts of income and expended large sums of money as expenses. Plaintiffs demanded recovery of damages for the breach of defendants' representations and agreements.

The action was tried to a court and jury. The facts hereafter stated are taken from the evidence adduced at the trial. Where there was a conflict in the evidence the version favorable to plaintiffs has been accepted since the verdict rendered was in favor of plaintiffs.

Hoffman assisted by his wife operated a bakery at Wautoma from 1956 until sale of the building late in 1961. The building was owned in joint tenancy by him and his wife. Red Owl is a Minnesota corporation having its home office at Hopkins, Minnesota. It owns and operates a number of grocery supermarket stores and also extends franchises to agency stores which are owned by individuals, partnerships and corporations. Lukowitz resides at Green Bay and since September, 1960, has been divisional manager for Red Owl in a territory comprising Upper Michigan and most of Wisconsin in charge of 84 stores. Prior to September, 1960, he was district manager having charge of approximately 20 stores.

In November, 1959, Hoffman was desirous of expanding his operations by establishing a grocery store and contacted a Red Owl representative by the name of Jansen, now deceased. Numerous conversations were had in 1960 with the idea of establishing a Red Owl franchise store in Wautoma. In September, 1960, Lukowitz succeeded Jansen as Red Owl's representative in the negotiations. Hoffman mentioned that $18,000 was all the capital he had available to invest and he was repeatedly assured that this would be sufficient to set him up in business as a Red Owl store. About Christmas time, 1960, Hoffman thought it would be a good idea if he bought a small grocery store in Wautoma and operated it in order that he gain experience in the grocery business prior to operating a Red Owl store in some larger community. On February 6, 1961, on the advice of Lukowitz and Sykes, who had succeeded Lukowitz as Red Owl's district manager, Hoffman bought the inventory and fixtures of a small grocery store in Wautoma and leased the building in which it was operated.

After three months of operating this Wautoma store, the Red Owl representatives came in and took inventory and checked the operations and found the store was operating at a profit. Lukowitz advised Hoffman to sell the store to his manager, and assured him that Red Owl would find a larger store for him elsewhere. Acting on this advice and assurance, Hoffman sold the fixtures and inventory to his manager on June 6, 1961. Hoffman was reluctant to sell at that time because it meant losing the summer tourist business, but he sold on the assurance that he would be operating in a new location by fall and that he must sell this store if he wanted a bigger one. Before selling, Hoffman told the Red Owl representatives that he had $18,000 for "getting set up in business" and they assured him that there would be no problems in establishing him in a bigger operation. The makeup of the $18,000 was not discussed; it was understood plaintiff's father-in-law would furnish part of it. By June, 1961, the towns for the new grocery store had been narrowed down to two, Kewaunee and Chilton. In Kewaunee, Red Owl had an option on a building site. In Chilton, Red Owl had nothing under option, but it did select a site to which plaintiff obtained an option at Red Owl's suggestion. The option stipulated a purchase price of $6,000 with $1,000 to be paid on election to purchase and the balance to be paid within 30 days. On Lukowitz's assurance that everything was all set plaintiff paid $1,000 down on the lot on September 15th.

On September 27, 1961, plaintiff met at Chilton with Lukowitz and Mr. Reymund and Mr. Carlson from the home office who prepared a projected financial statement. Part of the funds plaintiffs were to supply as their investment in the venture were to be obtained by sale of their Wautoma bakery building.

On the basis of this meeting Lukowitz assured Hoffman: " * * * [E]verything is ready to go. Get your money together and we are set." Shortly after this meeting Lukowitz told plaintiffs that they would have to sell their bakery business and bakery building, and that their retaining this property was the only "hitch" in the entire plan. On November 6, 1961, plaintiffs sold their bakery building for $10,000. Hoffman was to retain the bakery equipment as he contemplated using it to operate a bakery in connection with his Red Owl store. After sale of the bakery Hoffman obtained employment on the night shift at an Appleton bakery.

The record contains different exhibits which were prepared in September and October, some of which were projections of the fiscal operation of the business and others were proposed building and floor plans. Red Owl was to procure some third party to buy the Chilton lot from Hoffman, construct the building, and then lease it to Hoffman. No final plans were ever made, nor were bids let or a construction contract entered. Some time prior to November 20, 1961, certain of the terms of the lease under which the building was to be rented by Hoffman were understood between him and Lukowitz. The lease was to be for 10 years with a rental approximating $550 a month calculated on the basis of 1 percent per month on the building cost, plus 6 percent of the land cost divided on a monthly basis. At the end of the 10–year term he was to have an option to renew the lease for an additional 10–year period or to buy the property at cost on an instalment basis. There was no discussion as to what the instalments would be or with respect to repairs and maintenance.

On November 22nd or 23rd, Lukowitz and plaintiffs met in Minneapolis with Red Owl's credit manager to confer on Hoffman's financial standing and on financing the agency. Another projected financial statement was there drawn up entitled, "Proposed Financing For An Agency Store." This showed Hoffman contributing $24,100 of cash capital of which only $4,600 was to be cash possessed by plaintiffs. Eight thousand was to be procured as a loan from a Chilton bank secured by a mortgage on the bakery fixtures, $7,500 was to be obtained on a 5 percent loan from the father-in-law, and $4,000 was to be obtained by sale of the lot to the lessor at a profit.

A week or two after the Minneapolis meeting Lukowitz showed Hoffman a telegram from the home office to the effect that if plaintiff could get another $2,000 for promotional purposes the deal could go through for $26,000. Hoffman stated he would have to find out if he could get another $2,000. He met with his father-in-law, who agreed to put $13,000 into the business provided he could come into the business as a partner. Lukowitz told Hoffman the partnership arrangement "sounds fine" and that Hoffman should not go into the partnership arrangement with the "front office." On January 16, 1962, the Red Owl credit manager teletyped Lukowitz that the father-in-law would have to sign an agreement that the $13,000 was either a gift or a loan subordinate to all general creditors and that he would prepare the agreement. On January 31, 1962, Lukowitz teletyped the home office that the father-in-law would sign one or other of the agreements. However, Hoffman testified that it was not until the final meeting some time between January 26th and February 2nd, 1962, that he was told that his father-in-law was expected to sign an agreement that the $13,000 he was advancing was to be an outright gift. No mention was then made by the Red Owl representatives of the alternative of the father-in-law signing a subordination agreement. At this meeting the Red Owl agents presented Hoffman with the following projected financial statement:

"Capital required in operation:

"Cash	$ 5,000.00	
"Merchandise	20,000.00	
"Bakery	18,000.00	
"Fixtures	17,500.00	
"Promotional Funds	1,500.00	
"TOTAL:		$62,000.00

"Source of funds:

"Red Owl 7–day terms	$ 5,000.00	
"Red Owl Fixture contract (Term 5 years)	14,000.00	
"Bank loans (Term 9 years Union State Bank of Chilton	8,000.00	
"(Secured by Bakery Equipment)		
"Other loans (Term No-pay) No interest Father-in-law	13,000.00	
"(Secured by None)		
"(Secured by Mortgage on	2,000.00	
"Wautoma Bakery Bldg.)		
"Resale of land	6,000.00	
"Equity Capital: $ 5,000.00-Cash		
"Amount owner has 17,500.00-Bakery		
Equip. to invest:	22,500.00	
"TOTAL:		$70,500.00"

Hoffman interpreted the above statement to require of plaintiffs a total of $34,000 cash made up of $13,000 gift from his father-in-law, $2,000 on mortgage, $8,000 on Chilton bank loan, $5,000 in cash from plaintiff, and $6,000 on the resale of the Chilton lot. Red Owl claims $18,000 is the total of the unborrowed or unencumbered cash, that is, $13,000 from the father-in-law and $5,000 cash from Hoffman himself. Hoffman informed Red Owl he could not go along with this proposal, and particularly objected to the requirement that his father-in-law sign an agreement that his $13,000 advancement was an absolute gift. This terminated the negotiations between the parties.

[At the conclusion of the trial, the trial court determined that P and D engaged in negotiations looking toward the establishment of a franchise and that they had not reached final agreement on all details at the time P withdrew from negotiations. The jury, in response to specific questions, found that D represented that if P met certain conditions he would get a franchise, that P reasonably relied upon these representations and that P had fulfilled all conditions required at the time negotiations terminated. The jury also determined that $3,265 would reasonably compensate P for the sale of the bakery building, taking up the Chilton option and various moving and rental expenses and that $16,735 should be awarded for the sale of the Wautoma store fixtures and inventory. After appropriate motions, the trial court vacated the finding concerning the Wautoma store, affirmed the other findings and ordered a new trial on the Wautoma damage issue. D appealed the awarding of any compensation and P appealed the order for a new trial. After stating the issues to be, 1) whether the facts support a cause of action for promissory estoppel, and 2) whether the jury's findings with respect to damages were sustained by the evidence, the court, speaking through Chief Justice Currie, endorsed and adopted for Wisconsin "the doctrine of promissory estoppel ... which supplies a needed tool which courts may employ in a proper case to prevent injustice."]

* * *

Applicability of Doctrine to Facts of this Case

The record here discloses a number of promises and assurances given to Hoffman by Lukowitz in behalf of Red Owl upon which plaintiffs relied and acted upon to their detriment.

Foremost were the promises that for the sum of $18,000 Red Owl would establish Hoffman in a store. After Hoffman had sold his grocery store and paid the $1,000 on the Chilton lot, the $18,000 figure was changed to $24,100. Then in November, 1961, Hoffman was assured that if the $24,100 figure were increased by $2,000 the deal would go through. Hoffman was induced to sell his grocery store fixtures and inventory in June, 1961, on the promise that he would be in his new store by fall. In November, plaintiffs sold their bakery building on the urging of defendants and on the assurance that this was the last step necessary to have the deal with Red Owl go through.

We determine that there was ample evidence to sustain the answers of the jury to the questions of the verdict with respect to the promissory representations made by Red Owl, Hoffman's reliance thereon in the exercise of ordinary care, and his fulfillment of the conditions required of him by the terms of the negotiations had with Red Owl.

There remains for consideration the question of law raised by defendants that agreement was never reached on essential factors necessary to establish a contract between Hoffman and Red Owl. Among these were the size, cost, design, and layout of the store building; and the terms of the lease with respect to rent, maintenance, renewal, and purchase options. This poses the question of whether the promise necessary to sustain a cause of action for promissory estoppel must embrace all essential details of a proposed transaction between promisor and promisee so as to be the equivalent of an offer that would result in a binding contract between the parties if the promisee were to accept the same.

Originally the doctrine of promissory estoppel was invoked as a substitute for consideration rendering a gratuitous promise enforceable as a contract. See Williston, Contracts (1st ed.), p. 307, sec. 139. In other words, the acts of reliance by the promisee to his detriment provided a substitute for consideration. If promissory estoppel were to be limited to only those situations where the promise giving rise to the cause of action must be so definite with respect to all details that a contract would result were the promise supported by consideration, then the defendants' instant promises to Hoffman would not meet this test. However, sec. 90 of Restatement, 1 Contracts, does not impose the requirement that the promise giving rise to the cause of action must be so comprehensive in scope as to meet the requirements of an offer that would ripen into a contract if accepted by the promisee. Rather the conditions imposed are:

(1) Was the promise one which the promisor should reasonably expect to induce action or forbearance of a definite and substantial character on the part of the promisee?

(2) Did the promise induce such action or forbearance?

(3) Can injustice be avoided only by enforcement of the promise?

We deem it would be a mistake to regard an action grounded on promissory estoppel as the equivalent of a breach of contract action. As Dean Boyer points out, it is desirable that fluidity in the application of the concept be maintained. 98 University of Pennsylvania Law Review (1950), 459, at page 497. While the first two of the above listed three requirements of promissory estoppel present issues of fact which ordinarily will be resolved by a jury, the third requirement, that the remedy can only be invoked where necessary to avoid injustice, is one that involves a policy decision by the court. Such a policy decision necessarily embraces an element of discretion.

We conclude that injustice would result here if plaintiffs were not granted some relief because of the failure of defendants to keep their promises which induced plaintiffs to act to their detriment.

Damages

Defendants attack all the items of damages awarded by the jury. [The court affirmed the trial court's decision to uphold the jury's award of reliance damages in the amount of $3,265.]

* * *

We turn now to the damage item with respect to which the trial court granted a new trial, i.e., that arising from the sale of the Wautoma grocery store fixtures and inventory for which the jury awarded $16,735. The trial court ruled that Hoffman could not recover for any loss of future profits for the summer months following the sale on June 6, 1961, but that damages would be limited to the difference between the sales price received and the fair market value of the assets sold, giving consideration to any goodwill attaching thereto by reason of the transfer of a going business. There was no direct evidence presented as to what this fair market value was on June 6, 1961. The evidence did disclose that Hoffman paid $9,000 for the inventory, added $1,500 to it and sold it for $10,000 or a loss of $500. His 1961 federal income tax return showed that the grocery equipment had been purchased for $7,000 and sold for $7,955.96. Plaintiffs introduced evidence of the buyer that during the first eleven weeks of operation of the grocery store his gross sales were $44,000 and his profit was $6,000 or roughly 15 percent. On cross-examination he admitted that this was gross and not net profit. Plaintiffs contend that in a breach of contract action damages may include loss of profits. However, this is not a breach of contract action.

The only relevancy of evidence relating to profits would be with respect to proving the element of goodwill in establishing the fair market value of the grocery inventory and fixtures sold. Therefore, evidence of profits would be admissible to afford a foundation for expert opinion as to fair market value.

Where damages are awarded in promissory estoppel instead of specifically enforcing the promisor's promise, they should be only such as in the opinion of the court are necessary to prevent injustice. Mechanical or rule of thumb approaches to the damage problem should be avoided. In discussing remedies to be applied by courts in promissory estoppel we quote the following views of writers on the subject:

"Enforcement of a promise does not necessarily mean Specific Performance. It does not necessarily mean Damages for breach. Moreover the amount allowed as Damages may be determined by the plaintiff's expenditures or change of position in reliance as well as by the value to him of the promised performance. Restitution is also an 'enforcing' remedy, although it is often said to be based upon some kind of a rescission. In determining what justice requires, the court must remember all of its powers, derived from equity, law merchant, and other sources, as well as the common law. Its decree should be molded accordingly." 1A Corbin, Contracts, p. 221, sec. 200.

"The wrong is not primarily in depriving the plaintiff of the promised reward but in causing the plaintiff to change position to his detriment. It would follow that the damages should not exceed the loss caused by the change of position, which would never be more in amount, but might be less, than the promised reward." Seavey, Reliance on Gratuitous Promises or Other Conduct, 64 Harvard Law Review (1951), 913, 926.

"There likewise seems to be no positive legal requirement, and certainly no legal policy, which dictates the allowance of contract damages in every case where the defendant's duty is consensual." Shattuck, Gratuitous Promises—A New Writ?, 35 Michigan Law Review (1936), 908, 912.

At the time Hoffman bought the equipment and inventory of the small grocery store at Wautoma he did so in order to gain experience in the grocery store business. At that time discussion had already been had with Red Owl representatives that Wautoma might be too small for a Red Owl operation and that a larger city might be more desirable. Thus Hoffman made this purchase more or less as a temporary experiment. Justice does not require that the damages awarded him, because of selling these assets at the behest of defendants, should exceed any actual loss sustained measured by the difference between the sales price and the fair market value.

Since the evidence does not sustain the large award of damages arising from the sale of the Wautoma grocery business, the trial court properly ordered a new trial on this issue.

Order affirmed. Because of the cross-appeal, plaintiffs shall be limited to taxing but two-thirds of their costs.

NOTES

(1) In Earhart v. William Low Co., 25 Cal.3d 503, 158 Cal.Rptr. 887, 600 P.2d 1344 (1979), there was a completed agreement for construction subject to an express condition precedent; viz., the obtaining of adequate financing. Before the condition was satisfied, Defendant requested Plaintiff to commence performance of the conditional bargain but did not expressly promise to pay. The plaintiff's performance did not confer a direct benefit on the defendant and the express condition was never satisfied. Nevertheless, the court concluded that "compensation for a party's performance should be paid by the person whose request induced the performance." According to the court, it was a "pure fiction" to base recovery on a restitution theory. Rather, either the party requesting performance had a moral obligation to "restore to his original position a party who has acted to his detriment in reliance on a representation" or that recovery should be based upon "promissory estoppel" under Section 90. Under either approach, where there is an "urgent" request by the defendant and reasonable reliance by the plaintiff, the defendant is liable for the reasonable value of the plaintiff's part performance. Accord: Cyberchron Corp. v. Calldata Systems Development, Inc., 47 F.3d 39, 46–47 (2d Cir.1995)(plaintiff recovered actual expenditures in preparing to perform and performing work requested under a failed agreement to produce computer equipment, including overhead).

(2) The *Red Owl* case, which might be called the "high water mark" in the development of promissory estoppel, has received considerable attention in the literature. See, e.g., Henderson, *Promissory Estoppel and Traditional Contract Law*, 78 Yale L.J. 343, 376–87 (1969); Summers, *"Good Faith" in General Contract Law and the Sales Provisions of the Uniform Commercial Code*, 54 Va.L.Rev. 195, 216–27, 256–58 (1968). See also, Barnett & Becker, Promissory

Estoppe, Contract Formalities, and Misrepresentation, 15 Hofstra L.Rev. 443, 485–495 (1987); Feinman, *Critical Approaches to Contract Law,* 30 U.C.L.A.L.Rev. 829, 852–57 (1983). The case represents the farthest advance of contract, i.e., promise-based theory, into policing conduct in pre-contract negotiations. Neither UCC 1–205 nor Restatement (Second) § 205 impose a duty of good faith in the negotiation of a contract, although protection may be achieved through such doctrines as unconscionability and through remedies in restitution or tort. See Restatement (Second) § 205, Comment c. The contract remedy under *Red Owl* and similar cases has usually been limited to protection of the reliance interest. Profits that would have been earned if the contract had been formed have not been allowed. See, e.g., Wheeler v. White, 398 S.W.2d 93 (Tex.1965); Restatement (Second) § 90, Comment d. But for a case awarding lost profits where liability was based upon promissory estoppel, see Walters v. Marathon Oil Co., 642 F.2d 1098 (7th Cir.1981).

Copeland v. Baskin Robbins U.S.A.

California Court of Appeal, Second District, 2002.
96 Cal.App.4th 1251, 117 Cal.Rptr.2d 875.

■ JOHNSON, ACTING P.J.

We address an unsettled question in California: may a party sue for breach of a contract to negotiate an agreement or is such a "contract" merely an unenforceable "agreement to agree?" We hold a contract to negotiate an agreement is distinguishable from a so-called "agreement to agree" and can be formed and breached just like any other contract. We further hold, however, even if the plaintiff in this case could establish the defendant's liability for breach of contract he is limited to reliance damages—a form of recovery he has disavowed and defendant has shown he cannot prove. For this reason we affirm the trial court's judgment for defendant.

FACTS AND PROCEEDINGS BELOW

The following facts are undisputed.

Baskin Robbins operated an ice cream manufacturing plant in the city of Vernon. When the company announced its intention to close the plant, Copeland expressed an interest in acquiring it. The parties commenced negotiations. Copeland made clear from the outset his agreement to purchase the plant was contingent on Baskin Robbins agreeing to purchase the ice cream he manufactured there. Copeland testified at his deposition the ice cream purchase arrangement, known as "co-packing," was "critical" and "a key to the deal." Without co-packing, Copeland testified, "this deal doesn't work." Baskin Robbins does not deny the co-packing arrangement was an indispensable part of the contract to purchase the plant.

After several months of negotiations an agreement took shape under which Copeland would purchase the plant's manufacturing assets and sublease the plant property. Baskin Robbins would purchase seven million gallons of ice cream from Copeland over a three year period.

In May 1999 Baskin Robbins sent Copeland a letter which stated in relevant part "This letter details the terms which our Supply Chain executives have approved for subletting and sale of our Vernon manufacturing facility/equipment and a product supply agreement.... (1) Baskin Robbins will sell [Copeland] Vernon's ice cream manufacturing equipment ... for $1,300,000 cash.... (2) Baskin Robbins would agree, subject to a separate co-packing agreement and negotiated pricing, to provide [Copeland] a three year co-packing agreement for 3,000,000 gallons in year 1, 2,000,000 gallons in year 2 and 2,000,000 in year 3.... If the above is acceptable please acknowledge by returning a copy of this letter with a non-refundable check for three thousand dollars.... We should be able to coordinate a closing [within] thirty days thereafter." Copeland signed a statement at the bottom of the letter agreeing "[t]he above terms are acceptable" and returned the letter to Baskin Robbins along with the $3000 deposit.

After Copeland accepted the terms in the May 1999 letter the parties continued negotiating over the terms of the co-packing agreement. Among the issues to be settled were the price Baskin Robbins would pay for the ice cream, the flavors Copeland would produce, quality standards and controls, who would bear the loss from spoilage, and trademark protection. Copeland testified he believed in June 1999 he reached an oral agreement with Baskin Robbins on a price for the ice cream of his cost plus 85 cents per tub. He conceded, however, the parties had not agreed on how the cost component was to be determined and so far as he knew there was no written memorandum of this pricing agreement. None of the other issues were settled before Baskin Robbins allegedly breached the contract.

In July 1999, Baskin Robbins wrote to Copeland breaking off negotiations over the co-packing arrangement and returning his $3000 deposit. The letter explained Baskin Robbins' parent company had "recently ... made strategic decisions around the Baskin Robbins business" and "the proposed co-packing arrangement [is] out of alignment with our strategy." Therefore, Baskin Robbins informed Copeland, "we will not be engaging in any further negotiations of a co-packing arrangement[.]" Although Baskin Robbins offered to proceed with the agreement for the sale and lease of the Vernon plant assets it did not insist on doing so, apparently accepting Copeland's view the lack of a co-packing agreement was a "deal-breaker."

In his suit for breach of contract, Copeland alleged he and Baskin Robbins entered into a contract which provided Baskin Robbins would enter into a co-packing agreement with Copeland under the terms set out in the May 1999 letter and additional terms to be negotiated. Baskin–Robbins breached this contract by "unreasonably and wrongfully refusing to enter into any co-packing agreement with [Copeland]." As a result of this breach of contract Copeland suffered expectation damages "in the form of lost profits ... as well as lost employment opportunities and injury to his reputation." In response to a discovery request, Copeland stated his damages consisted of "lost profits from [the] three year co-packing agreement with defendants" as well as lost profits from other sales he could have made had he acquired the plant and the profit he could have earned from selling the plant equipment. Copeland's discovery responses did not provide or allege he could provide evidence of damages he suffered as a result of his relying on Baskin Robbins' promise to negotiate a co-packing agreement.

The trial court granted Baskin Robbins' motion for summary judgment based on the undisputed facts described above. The court concluded the May 1999 letter was susceptible to several interpretations but no matter how it was interpreted it failed as a contract because the essential terms of the co-packing deal were never agreed to and there was no reasonable basis upon which to determine them. Copeland filed a timely appeal from the subsequent judgment.

For the reasons discussed below we affirm the judgment albeit on a ground different from those relied upon by the trial court.

DISCUSSION

I. *A CAUSE OF ACTION WILL LIE FOR THE BREACH OF A CONTRACT TO NEGOTIATE AN AGREEMENT.*

When Baskin Robbins refused to continue negotiating the terms of the co-packing agreement Copeland faced a dilemma. "Many millions of dollars" in anticipated profits had melted away like so much banana ripple ice cream on a hot summer day. True enough, he could proceed with the contract for the purchase and lease of the Vernon plant's assets and use those assets to produce ice cream for other retailers. But, as he explained in his deposition, without the Baskin Robbins co-packing agreement he could not afford to purchase the assets and pay the on-going costs of operating the plant while he searched for other business. Alternatively he could attempt to sue Baskin Robbins for breach of the co-packing agreement on the theory the terms of the agreement set out in the May 1999 letter plus additional terms supplied by the court constituted an enforceable contract. Such a suit, however, had a slim prospect of success. While courts have been increasingly liberal in supplying missing terms in order to find an enforceable contract they do so only where the "reasonable intentions of the parties" can be ascertained. It is still the general rule that where any of the essential elements of a promise are reserved for the future agreement of both parties, no legal obligation arises until such "future agreement is made." City of Los Angeles v. Superior Court (1959) 51 Cal.2d 423, 433. Here, the parties agreed in the May 1999 letter as to the amount of ice cream Baskin Robbins would purchase over a three year period but, as Copeland candidly admitted, "a variety of complex terms" remained for agreement before the co-packing contract could be completed. These included price, the flavors to be manufactured, quality control standards, and responsibility for waste.

Copeland chose a third course. Rather than insist the parties had formed a co-packing contract and Baskin Robbins had breached it, he claimed the May 1999 letter constituted a contract to negotiate the remaining terms of the co-packing agreement and Baskin Robbins breached this contract by refusing without excuse to continue negotiations or, alternatively, by failing to negotiate in good faith. This path too has its difficulties. No reported California case has held breach of a contract to negotiate an agreement gives rise to a cause of action for damages.* On the other hand numerous California cases have expressed the view the law provides no remedy for breach of an "agreement to agree" in the future. We believe, however, these difficulties could be overcome in an appropriate case.

Initially, we see no reason why in principle the parties could not enter into a valid, enforceable contract to negotiate the terms of a co-packing agreement. A contract, after all, is "an agreement to do or not to do a certain thing." Civ.Code, § 1549 Persons are free to contract to do just about anything that is not illegal or immoral. Conducting negotiations to buy and sell ice cream is neither. * * *

A contract to negotiate the terms of an agreement is not, in form or substance, an "agreement to agree." If, despite their good faith efforts, the parties fail to reach ultimate agreement on the terms in issue the contract to negotiate is deemed performed and the parties are discharged from their obligations. Failure to agree is not, itself, a breach of the contract to negotiate. A party will be liable only if a failure to reach ultimate agreement resulted from a breach of that party's obligation to negotiate or to negotiate in good faith. For these reasons, criticisms of an "agreement to agree" as "absurd" and a "contradiction in terms" do not apply to a contract to negotiate an agreement.

In addition, it is important to note courts which have found purported contracts to be unenforceable "agreements to agree" have focused on the enforceability of the underlying substantive contract, not on whether the agreement to negotiate the terms of that contract is enforceable in its own right. In *Autry v. Republic Productions,* for example, after stating the law "provides no remedy for breach of an agreement to agree" the court explained this was so because "[t]he court may not imply what the parties will agree upon." *Autry v. Republic Productions, Inc.,* 30 Cal.2d at pp. 151–152. * * *

Most jurisdictions which have considered the question have concluded a cause of action will lie for breach of a contract to negotiate the terms of an agreement. * * *

---

* In *Racine & Laramie, Ltd. v. Department of Parks & Recreation* (1992) 11 Cal. App.4th 1026, 1035, the court posited, in dictum, such a cause of action could arise where, for example, the parties entered into an agreement they would "bargain in good faith for the purpose of reaching an agreement." In *Auerbach v. Great Western Bank* (1999) 74 Cal.App.4th 1172, 1177, 1190, the defendant stipulated its agreement to negotiate with the plaintiffs "concerning the possible modification" of the terms of their loan obligated it "to negotiate in good faith." Therefore, the court concluded, "we have no occasion to consider whether [Great Western]'s promise to engage in negotiations to modify the note is a valid contract as opposed to an unenforceable 'agreement to agree.' " [Citing the dictum in *Racine & Laramie, supra.*] In *Vestar Development II v. General Dynamics Corp.* (9th Cir.2001) 249 F.3d 958, 960–961, applying California law, the court concluded the question whether an agreement to negotiate a contract is enforceable is "unsettled" but held that in any event plaintiff had failed to allege compensable damages. (See discussion of damages issue below.)

Baskin Robbins maintains there are sound public policy reasons for not enforcing a contract to negotiate an agreement. In doing so, we would be injecting a covenant of good faith and fair dealing into the negotiation process whether or not the parties specifically agreed to such a term.* Citing Professor Farnsworth,** Baskin Robbins argues that instead of having a salutary effect on contract negotiations, imposing a regime of good faith and fair dealing would actually discourage parties from entering into negotiations, especially where the chances of success were slight. Alternatively, such an obligation might increase the pressure on the parties to bring the negotiations to a hasty, even if unsatisfactory conclusion, rather than risk being charged with the ill-defined wrong of bad faith negotiation. Most parties, Baskin Robbins suggests, would prefer to risk losing their out-of-pocket costs if the negotiation fails rather than risk losing perhaps millions of dollars in expectation damages if their disappointed negotiating partner can prove bad faith. Finally, Baskin Robbins argues, any precontractual wrong-doing can be adequately remedied by existing causes of action for unjust enrichment, promissory fraud and promissory estoppel.

We find Baskin Robbins' policy arguments unpersuasive.

Allowing a party to sue for breach of a contract to negotiate an agreement would not inject a covenant of good faith and fair dealing into the negotiation process in violation of the parties' intent. When two parties, under no compulsion to do so, engage in negotiations to form or modify a contract neither party has any obligation to continue negotiating nor to negotiate in good faith. Only when the parties are under a contractual compulsion to negotiate does the covenant of good faith and fair dealing attach, as it does in every contract. In the latter situation the implied covenant of good faith and fair dealing has the salutary effect of creating a disincentive for acting in bad faith in contract negotiations.

Professor Farnsworth's criticisms were not directed toward a cause of action for breach of a contract to negotiate the terms of an agreement. On the contrary, Farnsworth supports such a cause of action. Rather, his criticisms were directed at the theory propounded by some European courts and legal scholars that, even absent a contractual agreement to negotiate, a general obligation of fair dealing arises out of the negotiations themselves. We rejected this theory of liability in *Los Angeles Equestrian Center, Inc. v. City of Los Angeles* as did the court in *Racine & Laramie.*, 11 Cal.App.4th at pp. 1032–1033.

Arguing bad faith is an uncertain concept which could cost the defendant millions of dollars in expectation damages is also without merit. For the reasons we explain below, the appropriate remedy for breach of a contract to negotiate is not damages for the injured party's lost expectations under the prospective contract but damages caused by the injured

---

* In California, a covenant of good faith and fair dealing is implied in every contract. (*Foley v. Interactive Data Corp.* (1988) 47 Cal.3d 654, 684, 254 Cal.Rptr. 211, 765 P.2d 373.)

** Farnsworth, *Precontractual Liability and Preliminary Agreements: Fair Dealing and Failed Negotiations,* 87 Colum.L.Rev. 217 (1987).

reliance on the agreement to negotiate. Furthermore, we disagree ose who say the courts, unlike the National Labor Relations Board r arbitrators, are ill equipped to determine whether people are ing with each other in good faith.* While few of us will ever e a multi-million dollar contract, each of us participates in some negotiation nearly every day. In most cases the question whether the defendant negotiated in good faith will be a question of fact for the jury. In our view ordinary citizens applying their experience and common sense are very well equipped to determine whether the parties negotiated with each other in good faith. * * *

A cause of action for promissory fraud is based on "[a] promise made without any intention of performing it[.]"** In many cases the defendant may have intended to negotiate in good faith when it contracted to do so but changed its mind later when, for example, a more attractive contracting partner came along. * * * Thus, we conclude ... promissory fraud [does not] provide a party an adequate vehicle for relief when its negotiating partner breaks off negotiations or negotiates in bad faith.

The doctrine of promissory estoppel is generally used to enforce the defendant's clear and unambiguous promise when the plaintiff has reasonably and foreseeably relied on it. We agree a cause of action for promissory estoppel might lie if the defendant made a clear, unambiguous promise to negotiate in good faith and the plaintiff reasonably and foreseeably relied on that promise in incurring expenditures connected with the negotiation. We may also assume for the sake of argument such a cause of action could be based on an implied promise to negotiate in good faith. If these propositions are correct, then promissory estoppel is just a different rubric for determining the enforceability of a contract to negotiate an agreement.

Finally, we believe there are sound public policy reasons for protecting parties to a business negotiation from bad faith practices by their negotiating partners. Gone are the days when our ancestors sat around a fire and bargained for the exchange of stone axes for bear hides. Today the stakes are much higher and negotiations are much more complex. Deals are rarely made in a single negotiating session. Rather, they are the product of a gradual process in which agreements are reached piecemeal on a variety of issues in a series of face-to-face meetings, telephone calls, e-mails and letters involving corporate officers, lawyers, bankers, accountants, architects, engineers and others. As Professor Farnsworth observes, contracts today are not formed by discrete offers, counter-offers and acceptances. Instead they result from a gradual flow of information between the parties followed by a series of compromises and tentative agreements on major points which are finally refined into contract terms. These slow contracts are not only time-consuming but costly. For these reasons, the parties should have some assurance "their investments in time and money and

* See e.g., *Venture Associates v. Zenith Data Systems* (7th Cir.1996) 96 F.3d 275, 277. (*Venture Associates II.*)

** Civ.Code, § 1572(4); *Muraoka v. Budget Rent–A–Car Inc.* (1984) 160 Cal.App.3d 107, 119, 206 Cal.Rptr. 476.

effort will not be wiped out by the other party's footdragging or change of heart or taking advantage of a vulnerable position created by the negotiation." This concept is not new to California law. In *Drennan v. Star Paving Co.* the court applied the doctrine of promissory estoppel to hold that where a general contractor used the bid of a subcontractor in formulating its own successful bid for a job the court would imply a promise by the subcontractor not to revoke its bid in order "to preclude the injustice that would result if the offer could be revoked after the offeree had acted in detrimental reliance thereon." 51 Cal.2d at p. 414.

For obvious reasons, damages for breach of a contract to negotiate an agreement are measured by the injury the plaintiff suffered in relying on the defendant to negotiate in good faith. This measure encompasses the plaintiff's out-of-pocket costs in conducting the negotiations and may or may not include lost opportunity costs. The plaintiff cannot recover for lost expectations (profits) because there is no way of knowing what the ultimate terms of the agreement would have been or even if there would have been an ultimate agreement.

II. *BASKIN ROBBINS IS ENTITLED TO SUMMARY JUDGMENT BECAUSE IT HAS SHOWN COPELAND CANNOT ESTABLISH RELIANCE DAMAGES.*

[The Court's discussion of reliance damages is omitted.]

The judgment is affirmed.

CHAPTER FIVE

AVOIDANCE OF CONTRACTS

This chapter explores a variety of ways that parties can avoid legal obligation for promises that seem to satisfy the requirements for contract (e.g., bargained for consideration) that we have explored in Chapters Two and Four. Courts at times will refuse to enforce contracts because of (a) impermissible parties to the agreement, (b) impermissible defects in the bargaining process, or (c) impermissible terms in the agreement.

While it is possible to contract around many of the rules of agreement (e.g., the mail box rule), performance (e.g., payment of a reasonable price), and liability (e.g., expectation damages), the rules in this chapter are for the most part "mandatory" or "immutable"—in that the contracting parties do not have the freedom to waive these defenses.*

Our focus here is on defenses to contract that arise at the time the contract is formed. In the next chapter on performance, we will turn our attention to events occurring after formation—such as events which render performance impracticable—that may also be raised to avoid contractual obligation.

SECTION 1. CAPACITY TO CONTRACT: INFANCY; MENTAL INCOMPETENCE

A person must have legal capacity to contract. In the words of Restatement (Second) § 12(1), "No one can be bound by contract who has not legal capacity to incur at least voidable contractual duties. * * *" Several questions must be considered:

(1) Under what circumstances is a person so incapacitated that either no contract can arise from the bargain (contract "void") or a contract which does arise can be rescinded or avoided (contract "voidable")?

(2) What must be done to effectively rescind a "voidable" contract?

(3) What are the appropriate remedies available to both parties involved in the transaction?

---

* Immutable rules are sprinkled throughout the book. For example, "consideration" has to varying degrees been an immutable prerequisite for forming a legal obligation. And the next chapter will show that the duty of "good faith" immutably governs how parties must perform their contractual obligations.

A broader consideration is the extent that the "capacity" cases relate both to the objective of achieving fairness in the exchange and to the processes of change in the society, such as the legislative trend lowering the age of majority from twenty-one to eighteen and changes in the understanding and treatment of mental illness and drug addiction.[3] Collateral reading: Farnsworth §§ 4.2–4.8; Calamari and Perillo §§ 8–1—8–15; Murray §§ 21–27; Dobbs § 13.4.

(A) INFANCY

"Unless a statute provides otherwise, a natural person has the capacity to incur only voidable contractual duties until the beginning of the day before the person's eighteenth birthday." Restatement (Second) of Contracts, Sec. 14.

> We recognize what seems to be an injustice to the defendant to permit the minor-plaintiff to possess and enjoy the use of the automobile for almost a year, drive it into a telephone pole and wreck it, then haul it into a yard and elect to rescind the whole transaction. However, this is not an equitable proceeding and is controlled entirely by legal principles under which a minor has the right as to contracts made during minority to affirm or disaffirm his contracts other than those for necessaries. Those who deal with a minor must do so charged with the knowledge of the controlling principle of law which, as here, may work some injustice in individual cases but affords, in general, the protection of minors against their own improvidence at a time when they are presumed to be incapable of protecting themselves.

Thus did the Court of Appeals of Ohio, Madison County, reaffirm orthodox common law doctrine in Davis v. Clelland, 92 N.E.2d 827, 829 (Ohio App.1950). The minor (or infant, the term frequently used in the legal literature) has long been accorded special contractual immunity. The extent of protection has diminished somewhat in recent years, either by decision or statute, but nowhere today is the minor recognized as possessing full legal capacity to contract. In general, a minor's contracts are voidable; obligation may be avoided by timely and appropriate disaffirmance. The other party, if an adult, is bound, reflecting the risk of contracting with one who is under age. On the other hand, once the age of majority is reached, the minor, now an adult, can ratify or affirm the contract.

Bowling v. Sperry

Appellate Court of Indiana, Division No. 1, 1962.
133 Ind.App. 692, 184 N.E.2d 901.

■ MYERS, JUDGE.

This is an appeal from a judgment of the Noble Circuit Court in a civil action brought by appellant, Larry Bowling, by Norma Lemley as next

---

3. Article 19 of the Louisiana Civil Code provides: "All persons have capacity to contract, except unemancipated minors, interdicts, and persons deprived of reason at the time of contracting." For an analysis of this provision in the light of civil law antecedents, see Dugas, *The Contractual Capacity of Minors: A Survey of the Prior Law and the New Articles,* 62 Tul.L.Rev. 745 (1988).

friend, hereinafter referred to as Larry, against appellee, Max E. Sperry, d/b/a Sperry Ford Sales, to disaffirm and set aside a contract for the purchase of an automobile on the grounds of infancy.

Larry was a minor, sixteen years of age. On June 29, 1957, he purchased from appellee a 1947 Plymouth automobile for the sum of $140 cash. He paid $50 down on that day and returned on July 1, 1957, to pay the balance of $90 and take possession of the car. Appellee delivered to him a certificate of title and a written receipt. This receipt stated that as of June 29, 1957, Max Sperry Ford Sales sold to Larry Bowling a 1947 Plymouth for the amount of $140, cash, paid in full.

Larry drove the car several times during the following week and discovered that the main bearing was burned out. He had the car brought back to appellee's place of business where he was informed that it would cost him from $45 to $95 to make repairs. He declined to pay this amount and left the car on appellee's lot. Subsequently, he mailed a letter to appellee to the effect that he disaffirmed the contract of purchase and demanded the return of his money. Upon appellee's refusal to pay back the $140, this lawsuit followed.

Larry's complaint is based upon the fact that appellee sold him a car knowing that he was a minor; that he tendered back the car, rescinded the contract, and demanded the sum of $140. Appellee's answer was in two paragraphs, the first being in the nature of a general denial, pursuant to the provisions of Supreme Court Rule 1–3, and the second being an allegation that Larry was accompanied by his grandmother and aunt at the time of the purchase, and that the aunt paid appellee the sum of $90 of the purchase price. Upon trial of the case by the court, judgment was rendered in favor of appellee and against Larry.

It has been the rule in Indiana for many years that the contracts of minors are voidable and may be disaffirmed. It is not necessary that the other party be placed in *statu quo,* nor is it necessary that the minor tender back the money or property he has received before suing for the value or possession of the money or property given by him to the adult. All such voidable contracts by a minor in regard to personal property may be avoided at any time during his minority or upon his arrival at full age. . . .

The evidence showed that Larry's grandmother and aunt accompanied him to appellee's used car lot on June 29, 1957, when he selected the automobile, and that his aunt drove the car around the lot at that time. Furthermore, it was revealed that his aunt had loaned him $90 in order to make final payment on the car and that he had commenced to pay this back at $10 a week thereafter.

These facts, however, do not change the general rule. In so far as the agreement and sale is concerned, there was sufficient evidence to show that it was made between appellee and Larry, and no one else. It is of no consequence that his aunt and grandmother accompanied him at the time of purchase; and the fact that his aunt made payment of the $90 balance due could have no effect upon Larry's right to take advantage of his minority in an action to recover such payment.... Appellee was fully aware of Larry's age when the sale was negotiated. The written receipt was in Larry's name alone. This contract was squarely between an adult and a minor and falls within the rule pronounced above. Larry had every right to disaffirm it and set it aside.

Appellee claims there is doubt as to whether Larry received a certificate of title from appellee with his name on it. It is contended that the certificate was delivered in blank. As was said in the case of Wooldridge, by Next Friend, v. Hill, supra (at page 14 of 124 Ind.App., at page 648 of 114 N.E.2d): "It is of little consequence whether title to the property involved had passed to the infant or not." The certificate of title is only evidence of ownership, and in this case it would make no difference whether Larry had received a certificate in blank or with his name on it....

Appellee argues that an inference may be drawn from the evidence to show that the burned-out bearing was caused by Larry's operation of the car and his failure to put oil in the crankcase. Even if this were true, it is no defense to this action. There is no requirement in Indiana that before a disaffirmance is effected the parties must be placed in *statu quo*....

The question of whether or not the automobile was a necessary was injected into the trial of the case although appellee did not plead it as a defense. Some argument on this subject was made by the parties in the briefs. Section 58–102, Burns' Ind.Stat., 1961 Replacement, reads as follows:

"Capacity to buy and sell is regulated by the general law concerning capacity to contract, and to transfer and acquire property.

"Where necessaries are sold and delivered to an infant, or to a person who by reason of mental incapacity or drunkenness is incompetent to contract, he must pay a reasonable price therefor.

"Necessaries in this section means goods suitable to the condition in life of such infant or other person, and to his actual requirements at the time of delivery."

In the case of Price et al. v. Sanders et al. (1878), 60 Ind. 310, 314, the following is stated:

" 'Necessaries,' in the technical sense, mean such things as are necessary to the support, use or comfort of the person of the minor, as food, raiment, lodging, medical attendance, and such personal comforts as comport with his condition and circumstances in life, including a common school education; but it has been pithily and happily said, that necessaries do not include 'horses, saddles, bridles, liquors, pistols, powder, whips and fiddles.' "

Whether the goods are necessaries is a question of law, and if they are deemed as such, their quantity, quality and reasonable value are matters of fact....

It has been stated in 27 Am.Jur., Infants, § 17, pp. 760, 761, as follows:

"Aside from such things as are obviously for maintenance of existence, what are or what are not necessaries for an infant depends on what is reasonably necessary for the proper and suitable maintenance of the infant in view of his social position and situation in life, the customs of the social circle in which he moves or is likely to move, and the fortune possessed by him and by his parents. It has been said that articles of mere luxury or adornment cannot be included, but that useful articles, although of an expensive and luxurious character, may be included if they are reasonable in view of the infant's circumstances. The necessities to be procured by the contract must be personal necessities, that is, for the living or personal well-being of the infant. * * *

"What is furnished to the infant must be suitable, not only to his condition in life, but also to his actual requirements at the time—in other words, the infant must not have at the time of delivery an adequate supply from other sources. To be liable for articles as necessaries, an infant must be in actual need of them, and obliged to procure them for himself."

The evidence revealed that at the time of this transaction, Larry was living with his grandmother in Cromwell, Indiana, where he had lived for the past fifteen years; that his mother was dead and his father resided in Fort Wayne; that he was a student at Cromwell High School, but was on vacation; that he had a summer job working at a restaurant in the town of Syracuse, Indiana, which was eight or nine miles away from his home; that his usual means of transportation back and forth was with the cook; that on occasion he could "bum" rides with other people.

The acting manager for appellee, who had dealt with Larry, testified that when Larry's aunt and grandmother came to the sales lot on June 29, 1957, "they" said Larry needed something for him to get back and forth to work. He said it was his "understanding" that the car was needed for that purpose. Larry stated that during the short period of time he had possession of it, he only used it for pleasure, and did not drive it to work.

We are well aware of the overwhelming increase in the use and number of automobiles in this country since World War II. What once was a great luxury for only the wealthy has become a matter of common necessity for the ordinary workingman, farmer and businessman. The automobile is as important to the modern household as food, clothing and shelter. The problem here is whether the car in question was so needed by Larry, in view of his situation in life, his social status and his financial position, that he could not be maintained properly or suitably without it. The burden of showing this was upon appellee.... From the evidence presented, we do not think appellee met this burden. While every high school boy today wants a car of his own, and many of them own automobiles which under given circumstances may be considered as necessaries, we do not consider the car in this case so vital to Larry's existence that it could be classified as a necessary.

Judgment reversed, and cause remanded with instructions that the trial court sustain appellant's motion for a new trial on the ground that the judgment is contrary to law.

NOTES

(1) After this brief excursion into the world of minors' contracts, what are your reactions? Are just results being achieved? What reform(s), if any, are in order?

(2) What do you advise an adult client who proposes to contract with a minor? In *Bowling*, for example, would Sperry have been protected if Larry's grandmother had agreed to become jointly liable with him?

(3) In what respect might contractual immunity be legally disadvantageous for the minor?

(4) *Legal Responsibility of Emancipated Minor.*

The underpinnings of the general rule allowing the minor to disaffirm his contracts were undoubtedly the protection of the minor. It was thought that the minor was immature in both mind and experience and that, therefore, he should be protected from his own bad judgments as well as from adults who would take advantage of him. The doctrine of the voidability of "minors" contracts often seems commendable and just. If the beans that the young naive Jack purchased from the crafty old man in the fairy tale "Jack and the Bean Stalk" had been worthless rather than magical, it would have been only fair to allow Jack to disaffirm the bargain and reclaim his cow. However, in today's modern and sophisticated society the "infancy doctrine" seems to lose some of its gloss.

Paradoxically, we declare the infant mature enough to shoulder arms in the military, but not mature enough to vote; mature enough to marry and be responsible for his torts and crimes, but not mature enough to assume the burden of his own contractual indiscretions. In Wisconsin, the infant is deemed mature enough to use a dangerous instrumentality—a motor vehicle—at sixteen, but not mature enough to purchase it without protection until he is twenty-one.

No one really questions that a line as to age must be drawn somewhere below which a legally defined minor must be able to disaffirm his contracts for nonnecessities. The law over the centuries has considered this age to be twenty-one. Legislatures in other states have lowered the age. We suggest that the appellant might better seek the change it proposes in the legislative halls rather than this court. A recent law review article in the Indiana Law Journal explores the problem of contractual disabilities of minors and points to three different legislative solutions leading to greater freedom to contract. The first approach is one gleaned from the statutes of California and New York, which would allow parties to submit a proposed contract to a court which would remove the infant's right of disaffirmance upon a finding that the particular contract is fair. This suggested approach appears to be extremely impractical in light of the expense and delay that would necessarily accompany the procedure. A second approach would be to establish a rebuttable presumption of incapacity to replace the strict rule. This alternative would be an open invitation to litigation. The third suggestion is a statutory procedure that would allow a minor to petition a court for the removal of disabilities. Under this procedure a minor would only have to go to court once, rather than once for each contract as in the first suggestion.

Undoubtedly, the infancy doctrine is an obstacle when a major purchase is involved. However, we believe that the reasons for allowing that obstacle to remain viable at this point outweigh those for casting it aside. Minors require some protection from the pitfalls of the market place. Reasonable minds will always differ on the extent of the protection that should be afforded. For this court to adopt a rule that the appellant suggests and remove the contractual disabilities from a minor simply because he becomes emancipated, which in most cases would be the result of marriage, would be to suggest that the married minor is somehow vested with more wisdom and maturity than his single counterpart. However, logic would not seem to dictate this result especially when today a youthful marriage is oftentimes indicative of a lack of wisdom and maturity.

Kiefer v. Fred Howe Motors, Inc., 39 Wis.2d 20, 158 N.W.2d 288, 290–291 (1968).

(5) *Restoration or Restitution? Bowling* adheres to the prevailing view as to the degree of restitution required of a minor upon disaffirmance. The minor is obliged to return what he or she still has; i.e., in specie. There is no obligation to account for use or depreciation or to return an equivalent of what was received. Thus, the requirement is one of restoration, not restitution. See, e.g., Star Chevrolet Co. v. Green, 473 So.2d 157 (Miss.1985) (minor who wrecked vehicle not obliged to account for proceeds received from insurance company); But see Valencia v. White, 134 Ariz. 139, 654 P.2d 287 (App.1982) (discussion of various departures from the majority rule in cases from New Hampshire, Minnesota, Pennsylvania, New York and New Jersey).

(6) *Disaffirmance and Ratification.* "An infant cannot affirmatively ratify until he comes of age. After that date any manifestation by him of an intent to regard the bargain as binding will deprive him of the power to avoid the contract.... Mere silence or inaction by a former infant after attaining majority does not amount to ratification.... However, an infant should be required to disaffirm within a reasonable time after coming of age.... Disavowal of a contract by an infant need not be by any prescribed form or ceremony; the filing of an answer by him or in his behalf disaffirming the contract is sufficient in itself to accomplish the result." Mechanics Finance Co. v. Paolino, 29 N.J.Super. 449, 455–56, 102 A.2d 784 (1954).

In Bobby Floars Toyota, Inc. v. Smith, 48 N.C.App. 580, 269 S.E.2d 320 (1980), a minor made eleven monthly payments on the purchase of an automobile, ten of them after his eighteenth birthday. After noting that a reasonable time for disaffirmance depends upon the circumstances of each case, no hard-and-fast rule regarding time limits being capable of definition, the court concluded that ten months was enough time within which to elect between disaffirmance and ratification with respect to an item of personal property which is constantly depreciating in value. Cf. Keser v. Chagnon, 159 Colo. 209, 410 P.2d 637 (1966) (court upheld lower court's conclusion that the minor did not ratify by using the car (an Edsel) for sixty days after reaching his majority before disaffirming and returning the car ten days after that).

(7) *Recovery for Necessaries Furnished.* The law is replete with instances where the effect of a strict rule is mitigated by successful assertion of a claim of unjust enrichment. For example, a contract may be within the Statute of Frauds, and for that reason unenforceable, but the plaintiff may be able to proceed on a theory of quasi-contract. Granting relief on this basis does not, in the ordinary situation, thwart statutory purposes. In much the same way, a recovery for necessaries furnished to a minor is not viewed as inconsistent with the policy of contractual immunity. The suit is not on the contract. Rather, as one court put it, the minor "is held on a promise implied by law, and not, strictly speaking, on his actual promise.... [H]e is liable to pay only what the necessaries were reasonably worth, and not what he may improvidently have agreed to pay for them." Trainer v. Trumbull, 141 Mass. 527, 530, 6 N.E. 761, 762 (1886). Even if necessaries are involved, recovery is limited to unjust enrichment. But courts have been unwilling to expand the category of necessaries to include, for example, the necessitous character of an automobile. Accord: Warwick Municipal Employees Credit Union v. McAllister, 110 R.I. 399, 293 A.2d 516 (1972). Finally, if the goal is to preclude an unjust enrichment, then why limit recovery to necessary items? See Wolfe, *A Reevaluation of the Contractual Rights of Minors,* 57 UMKC L.Rev. 145 (1988).

(8) *Effect of Misrepresentation of Age: Tort; Estoppel.* If the minor is silent as to her age, the risk of her incapacity because of age strictly falls on the other side to the contract. In essence, a contractor has a duty to ascertain that the other side is not an infant—possibly by securing a representation from the other side about her age.

There are a number of approaches to the effect of a misrepresentation of age. At one extreme is the Massachusetts rule which states that minors are "not liable in tort for deceit arising from false representations as to ... age or for damages to the machines while in their possession and used by them." Raymond v. General Motorcycle Co., 230 Mass. 54, 119 N.E. 359 (1918). In the middle are the cases which hold that misrepresentation will not estop the minor from disaffirming but will justify damages in tort. See Mestetzko v. Elf Motor Co., 119 Ohio St. 575, 165 N.E. 93 (1929); Creer v. Active Automobile Exchange, 99 Conn. 266, 121 A. 888 (1923); Annot., *Liability for an Infant in Tort for Inducing Contract by Misrepresenting His Age,* 67 A.L.R. 1264 (1930). At the other extreme is estoppel: "When a minor has reached that stage of maturity which indicates that he is of full age, and enters into a contract falsely representing himself to be of age, accepting the benefits of the contract, he will be estopped to deny that he is not of age when the obligation of the contract is sought to be enforced against him." Johnson v. McAdory, 228 Miss. 453, 88 So.2d 106 (1956).

The estoppel approach has been codified by statute in Indiana: "When, in case of any loan or sale made by seller, creditor or secured party, the borrower, or any other person furnishing security on behalf of the borrower, shall, as an inducement to the seller, creditor or secured party to make the loan or sale, represent to it, in writing, that he or she is eighteen (18) years of age or older, whereas in fact such person or persons are under the age of eighteen (18) years, or shall otherwise make any false statement or representation to the seller, creditor or secured party and the seller, creditor or secured party is thereby deceived, and the loan or sale is made in reliance upon such representation, neither the person so representing, nor any one in his or her behalf, nor any person otherwise legally liable to pay such loan or sale, shall afterwards be allowed, as against such seller, creditor or secured party, to take advantage of the fact that the person making the representation was under eighteen (18) years of age, but each such person shall be estopped by such representation." Ind.Code 28–1–26.5–1.

PROBLEM: THE CASE OF THE BOLD GRADUATES

After receiving their high school diplomas, Matt and Pat, age seventeen, determined to strike out on their own. They decided to rent an apartment together, find jobs, and see if they could make it in the "real world." Their parents were pleased, but somewhat dubious. They assured the boys that "they would always be welcome at home."

On June 15, the boys signed a year lease with Landlord, Inc., calling for a $250 monthly rental, payable in advance, plus a security deposit of $250. They paid the first month's rent and the security deposit. However, they vacated the premises on July 15 and demanded a return of all monies paid. Were they entitled to repayment?

Tiring of life in the real world, the boys took off in the fall for State U. They again executed a one-year lease (monthly rental of $400 plus $400 security deposit). But, alas, their educational careers were short-lived, and they again decided to strike out for other parts. They confronted the landlord with a demand for the return of all payments. The landlord refused. He conceded that they were paid up for the period of their stay, but he insisted they were breaching the lease and were accountable for damages that would be sustained. How should the matter be resolved?

(B) MENTAL INCOMPETENCE

Restatement (Second) § 15 provides:

Mental Illness or Defect

(1) A person incurs only voidable contractual duties by entering into a transaction if by reason of mental illness or defect (a) he is unable to understand in a reasonable manner the nature and consequences of the transaction, or (b) he is unable to act in a reasonable manner in relation to the transaction and the other party has reason to know of his condition.

(2) Where the contract is made on fair terms and the other party is without knowledge of the mental illness or defect, the power of avoidance under Subsection (1) terminates to the extent that the contract has been so performed in whole or in part or the circumstances have so changed that avoidance would be unjust. In such a case a court may grant relief as justice requires.

The rationale of this section is explained as an effort to reconcile "two conflicting policies: the protection of justifiable expectations and of the security of transactions, and the protection of persons unable to protect themselves against imposition." Comment a. If a guardian is appointed, the problem is resolved: "A person has no capacity to incur contractual duties if his property is under guardianship * * *." Restatement (Second) § 13.

But without a guardian, the search for a mediating principle is complicated by the "wide variety of types and degrees of mental incompetency." This means that a "person may be able to understand almost nothing, or only simple or routine transactions, or he may be incompetent only with respect to a particular type of transaction." Also, even if his "understanding is complete, he may lack capacity to control his acts in the way that the normal individual can and does control them; in such cases the incapacity makes the contract voidable only if the other person has reason to know of his condition." Comment b.

In Ortelere v. Teachers' Retirement Bd., 25 N.Y.2d 196, 202, 303 N.Y.S.2d 362, 250 N.E.2d 460 (N.Y.1969), the Court of Appeals rejected the traditional standard of measurement, a "cognitive test," in which the focus was on whether an individual could comprehend and understand the nature of the transaction. The court instead fashioned an additional test, based upon Restatement (Second) of Contracts § 15 (1) (b), permitting a contract to be voided where a person, "by reason of mental illness or defect" is "unable to act in a reasonable manner in relation to the transaction." Thus, in New York, the test for contractual incapacity includes not only those who do not understand the nature and consequences of their actions, but those " 'whose contracts are merely uncontrolled reactions to their mental illness.' "

A few courts take the position that a contract with an incompetent will be enforced if the exchange is fair, unless the other party "recognizes the other's incapacity." If so, the other party is "guilty of a fraud." The more common rule is that the incompetent should be able to avoid the contract providing that he can restore the other party to his pre-contract position. This rule depends upon whether the other party acted in "good faith" and was unaware of the incapacity and stands "in stark contrast to the rule usually applied in cases of avoidance by minors, who are permitted to rescind a contract upon returning whatever depreciated value remains in their hands." Dobbs § 13.4. For a comprehensive analysis, see Meiklejohn, *Contractual and Donative Capacity*, 39 Case Wes.Res.L.Rev. 307 (1988–89).

Heights Realty, Ltd. v. Phillips

Supreme Court of New Mexico, 1988.
106 N.M. 692, 749 P.2d 77.

■ STOWERS, JUSTICE.

This case involves an exclusive listing contract between plaintiff-appellant, Heights Realty, Ltd. (Heights Realty), and Johnye Mary Gholson (Mrs. Gholson), the original named defendant. Heights Realty filed an amended complaint seeking its commission for having performed under the terms of the contract by having provided a buyer to purchase Mrs. Gholson's property. During the pendency of this action, Mrs. Gholson was adjudicated incompetent and E.A. Phillips (Phillips), the present defendant-appellee, was appointed conservator of her estate. Following a bench trial, the district court found Mrs. Gholson lacked the mental capacity to have validly executed the listing contract and entered judgment in favor of Phillips. On appeal, Heights Realty argues that the presumption of competency was not overcome by clear and convincing evidence. We disagree and affirm the judgment of the district court.

In 1984, Mrs. Gholson was interested in selling her North Valley property. She telephoned Heights Realty and spoke with Pat Eichenberg, a real estate broker and owner of Heights Realty and also an acquaintance of hers, who brought Mrs. Gholson an exclusive listing agreement. Mrs. Gholson was approximately eighty-four years old when she signed the contract on September 26, 1984, listing the property for one year in the amount of $250,000 with a cash down payment of $75,000. No other terms were included in the agreement. Subsequently, Mrs. Gholson changed her mind about the amount of the down payment and on October 10, 1984, signed an addendum increasing it to $100,000. In November 1984 an offer was made to purchase the property for $255,000. Mrs. Gholson did not accept that offer.

The question to be determined is whether substantial evidence was presented from which the trial court could properly conclude that the presumption of competency was overcome by clear and convincing evidence.

On appeal, this court reviews the record to determine whether there is substantial evidence to support the trial court's findings of fact. . . .

The test of mental capacity is whether a person is capable of understanding in a reasonable manner the nature and effect of the act in which the person is engaged. . . . The law presumes that every person is competent. To show the contrary, the burden of proof rests on the person asserting lack of capacity to establish the same by clear and convincing proof. . . . The burden remains on those alleging incompetency unless the case is brought within the exception in which previous incompetency is admitted or sufficiently shown and thus changes that burden. If incompetency of a general permanent nature has been shown to once exist for a period of time prior to the execution of the instrument under attack, it is presumed to continue until there is a showing by the person relying on the validity of that instrument that proves the existence of a lucid interval at the time of its execution. . . .

Although the test of mental capacity is applied as of the date that the attacked instrument is executed, evidence of a person's prior or subsequent condition is admissible to show the condition at the time in issue. . . . The combined weight of all the evidence in each case determines the result. The court is entitled to take into consideration the individual's physical condition; the adequacy of consideration; whether or not the transaction was improvident; the relation of trust and confidence between the parties to the transaction and the weakness of the mind of the alleged incompetent person as judged by all other acts within a reasonable time prior and subsequent to the act in question. . . .

Only Mrs. Eichenberg and Mrs. Gholson were present at the time of the signing of the exclusive listing agreement on September 26, 1984, and its addendum on October 10, 1984. Mrs. Eichenberg testified that Mrs. Gholson was "just as sharp as a tack" when the agreement was executed. She further testified that on the date the addendum was signed, Mrs. Eichenberg read the contents of it to Mrs. Gholson who had been lying down on the couch because she had injured her foot and that Mrs. Gholson appeared to have no problems understanding the addendum since she even corrected a misspelling in her name.

Testimony was presented that Mrs. Gholson owned approximately twelve acres with a residence in Albuquerque's North Valley at the time she decided to sell the property for financial reasons. Mrs. Gholson stated that she set the asking price of $250,000 by guessing at the value of the property and left open all other terms vital to the contract. Mrs. Gholson also testified that she had no recollection of signing the addendum because she "couldn't think of anything in sequence at that time." Evidence showed that no family or lawyer assisted her in executing the agreements. It appears from the record that the trial court discounted Mrs. Eichenberg's testimony.

Additional testimony as to Mrs. Gholson's mental capacity was elicited from her son-in-law, Phillips, and granddaughter, Louise Loomis, both of whom had for many years observed Mrs. Gholson's speech and conduct. Phillips testified that he first noticed behavior evidencing her gradual mental decline in 1959, after the death of her husband. He recounted a number of incidents: for example, beginning in May 1983, Mrs. Gholson began to mismanage the payment of her bills, confusing credit with debit balances; she set off her burglar alarm and left it running; she locked herself out of her automobile while the engine was still on; and she failed to recall the death of her younger brother, with whom she had been extremely close, on September 19, 1984. Phillips characterized her as being constantly confused.

Louise Loomis testified that she always maintained a close and intimate relationship with her grandmother. She described the degeneration of Mrs. Gholson's mind over a period of years. In particular, she stated that around 1979 or 1980, her grandmother began to have problems comprehending matters. Mrs. Loomis testified that by the summer of 1984 on a trip to Utah, her grandmother was unable to communicate with people or dial a telephone number for room service and that shortly thereafter, Mrs. Gholson could not carry on her personal affairs nor make appointments with the hairdresser. She also developed erratic eating habits and was incapable of dealing with restaurant bills. Continuing, Mrs. Loomis testified that her grandmother became much more confused after she broke her foot in September of 1984. She opined that her grandmother did not have the mental capacity to understand a listing agreement.

Two psychiatrists testified, Dr. Farber for Heights Realty, and Dr. Muldawer on behalf of Mrs. Gholson. Dr. Farber neither met with nor examined Mrs. Gholson and only reviewed documents about her. Dr. Farber indicated that primarily he relied on Dr. Muldawer's handwritten notes and his deposition. Dr. Farber averred that he neither had sufficient evidence nor had he made a timely examination of her to enable him to say that she was incompetent, and therefore the presumption of competency had to prevail.

Dr. Muldawer testified that he examined Mrs. Gholson on January 11, 1985, reviewed relevant documents, and thereafter conferred with her relatives. He found that Mrs. Gholson showed a general decline in her cognitive skills about 1979 or 1980 involving her judgment, reasoning and memory. He further stated that this decline was slow and subtle and was evidenced by increasing forgetfulness and the general inability to take care of her own needs. He concluded that when she signed the listing agreement "she certainly didn't fully understand the terms" even though "in a broader sense she knew she was disposing of property." He then stated he could not use the word "conclusively" to describe Mrs. Gholson's lack of contractual capacity on September 26, 1984, but he could state that she was incompetent on that date within "reasonable medical probability."

A review of the trial record indicates, as properly found by the court below, that "on September 26, 1984 and thereafter Mrs. Gholson was suffering from a progressive, deteriorating mental disease which prevented her from understanding the nature and consequences of the * * * agreement and the Addendum thereto"; and that "on September 26, 1984 and thereafter, Mrs. Gholson was without lucid intervals."

There was a conflict in the general medical testimony adduced from Dr. Muldawer, who observed Mrs. Gholson, and Dr. Farber, who never observed her but relied on observations of another party. This type of medical testimony therefore, in and of itself, is not sufficient to overcome the presumption of competency.... The opinions expressed by Phillips and Mrs. Loomis were predicated on their many experiences with Mrs. Gholson tending to afford them opportunities to observe her mental capacity. Thus, there was substantial evidence presented from those who were in a position to observe Mrs. Gholson's conduct before and after the day the instrument in question was executed.

Even though some of the evidence adduced was conflicting, this goes to the question of credibility, a question solely for resolution by the trier of fact, who after hearing the testimony resolved the question in favor of Mrs. Gholson. This court will not resolve conflicts or substitute its judgment where the record as a whole substantially supports the trial court's findings of fact....

Although the trial court did not specifically state in its findings that the presumption of competency was overcome by clear and convincing evidence, it is implicit in those findings when the evidence is viewed in its entirety that this burden of proof had been sustained. We hold that substantial evidence was presented from which the trial court could properly conclude that the presumption of competency was overcome by clear and convincing evidence; consequently, Mrs. Gholson lacked mental capacity to enter into the exclusive listing agreement and its addendum. The judgment of the district court is affirmed.

NOTES

(1) Is adequacy of consideration relevant to the issue of mental capacity? See Restatement (Second), § 15, comment b: "Where a person has some understanding of a particular transaction which is affected by mental illness or defect, the controlling consideration is whether the transaction in its result is one which a reasonably competent person might have made." See also Green, *Proof of Mental Incompetence and the Unexpressed Major Premise,* 53 Yale L.J. 271, 304–5 (1944); Alexander and Szasz, *From Contract to Status via Psychiatry,* 13 Santa Clara Law. 537, 557–8 (1973). What evidence was there here that the listing agreement was improvident or unfair?

(2) *Inadequacy of Consideration Plus Something Else.* "[I]nadequacy of price *within itself,* and disconnected from all other facts, cannot be a ground for setting aside a contract, or affording relief against it. There must be something else besides the mere inadequacy of consideration or inequality in the bargain, to justify a court in granting relief by setting aside the contract. *What this something else besides the inadequacy* should be, perhaps no court ought to say, lest the wary and cunning, by employing other means than those named, should escape with their fraudulent gains. I, however, will venture to say, that it ought, in connection with the inadequacy of consideration, to superinduce the belief that there had been either a suppression of the truth, the suggestion of falsehood, abuse of confidence, a violation of duty arising out of some fiduciary relation between the parties, the exercise of undue influence, or the taking of an unjust and inequitable advantage of one whose peculiar situation at the time would be calculated to render him an easy prey to the cunning and the artful. But if no one of these appears, or if no fact is proved that will lead the mind to the conclusion, that the party against whom relief is sought has suppressed some fact that he ought to have disclosed, or that he has suggested some falsehood, or abused in some manner the confidence reposed in him, or that some fiduciary relation existed between the parties, or that the party complaining was under his influence, or at the time of the trade was in a condition, *from any cause,* that would render him an easy victim to the unconscientious, then relief cannot be afforded; for inadequacy of consideration, *standing alone and unsupported by any thing else, can authorize no court, governed by the rules of the English law, to set aside a contract....*" Judge v. Wilkins, 19 Ala. 765, 772 (1851), quoted in Williamson v. Matthews, 379 So.2d 1245, 1247 (Ala.1980) (emphasis in original).

(3) What result if the conservator, pleased with the offer procured by Heights Realty, had proceeded to sell to the offeror? Would this rule out the incompetency defense? Would there be a basis for recovery by the realty company?

(4) *The Case of the Adjudged Incompetent.* Manzelle Johnson was declared incompetent, and her nephew, Obbie Neal, was appointed her guardian. Obbie persuaded Mrs. Johnson to deed real property to him in his individual capacity,

and he, in turn, conveyed the property to Charles Weatherly, a bona fide purchaser. Obbie was later removed as guardian, and the new guardian sued to cancel the deeds and to collect profits from the land which accrued to Weatherly. Weatherly counterclaimed for the amount of consideration paid for the land and the value of improvements which he had made. What result? See Beavers v. Weatherly, 250 Ga. 546, 299 S.E.2d 730 (1983).

CitiFinancial, Inc. v. Brown

United States District Court, N.D. Mississippi, 2001.
2001 WL 1530352, reversed, 304 F.3d 469 (5th Cir.2002).

◼ DAVIDSON, CHIEF J.

Presently before the court are the following: (1) the Plaintiffs' Verified Petition seeking an order compelling arbitration pursuant to 9 U.S.C. § 4, and to stay the state court proceeding brought in Noxubee County, Mississippi, by the Defendant, John Brown, against the Plaintiffs; * * * Upon due consideration, the court finds that the Plaintiffs' Verified Petition seeking an order compelling arbitration and their motion for summary judgment shall be denied. All other motions are thereafter moot and shall be denied as such.

A.   Factual Background

In December, 1998, the Defendants, Catherine and John Brown, mother and son, obtained a loan from the Plaintiff, CitiFinancial, Inc. This loan consolidated the Browns' debts and lowered their monthly payments. The Browns' loan agreement contained an Arbitration Provision, requiring the Browns to arbitrate any claims they might have against CitiFinancial, its affiliate corporations, or their employees or agents. Despite this agreement, John Brown commenced a civil action in the Circuit Court of Noxubee County, Mississippi, against CitiFinancial, claiming fraud and breach of contract. His mother, Catherine Brown, is not a party to the Circuit Court action. Thereafter, CitiFinancial filed a petition to compel arbitration in this court pursuant to 9 U.S.C. § 4. The Browns' primary defense to this petition to compel arbitration is that John Brown is incompetent and therefore his arbitration agreement is void.

John Brown is a 42 year old man who has been profoundly retarded since birth. He weighs only 90 pounds, is functionally deaf, has poor eye sight and is language impaired. His intellectual performance is equivalent to that of a three year old and he can neither read nor write. He lives with his mother, Catherine Brown, who is his primary care giver. Even so, CitiFinancial required him to sign the loan agreement containing the arbitration clause by printing his name on a piece of paper and having him copy it on the appropriate line.

B.   Relevant Standards

[The court discussed the standard of enforceability for a written agreement to arbitrate under Section 2 of the Federal Arbitration Act, 9 U.S.C. sec. 1–16, which provides that a written provision in a contract that evidences a transaction involving commerce, to settle by arbitration a controversy arising out of that contract, is valid, irrevocable, and enforceable. In the Fifth Circuit, there is a two step inquiry: First, the court must determine whether the parties agreed to arbitrate the dispute and, if so, second, it must then consider whether any federal statute or policy renders the claims nonarbitrable. In the words of the court, a "party seeking to avoid arbitration must allege and prove that the arbitration clause itself was a product of fraud or coercion; alternatively, that party can allege and prove that another ground exists at law or in equity that would allow the contract to be revoked."]

C. Discussion

The parties do not dispute that their agreement contains the following mandatory arbitration clause: * * * [The court quoted the arbitration clause.]

As for the first step in the court's analysis, the court finds that the parties never agreed to arbitrate and John Brown did not waive his right to seek adjudication of his claims in court, as he was incompetent to do so. "The fundamental idea of a contract is that it requires the assent of two minds. But a lunatic, or a person *non compo menti,* has nothing which the law recognizes as a mind, and it would seem, therefore, upon principle, that he cannot ma [*sic]* contract which may have any efficacy as such." *Dexter v. Hall,* 82 U.S. 9 (1872).

According to Mississippi law, one basis for refusing to enforce a contract is the lack of capacity of a party. "The contracts of persons *non compos mentis* are absolutely void, whether executed or executory—mere nullities." *Ricketts v. Jollitt,* 62 Miss. 440 (1884). This is so because "without consent of both parties there [can] be no contract, and without capacity to comprehend the ... nature, and terms of the proposed contract, there [can] be no consent." *Hill v. McLaurin,* 1854 WL 231 (Miss.Err. & App.1858) *See also Gross v. Jones,* 52 So. 802 (Miss.1907) (party who was of unbalanced mind and whose "whole business life and dealing was characterized by childlike faith and implicit trust" was incapable of contracting). * * *

[The court considered and rejected several "brazen" arguments by CitiFinancial that, nevertheless, John Brown was obligated to arbitrate, including that Brown was competent because he brought suit under his own name, that Brown's mother, who was never appointed as guardian, signed the arbitration agreement as his guardian, and that Brown's mother's status as payee of his social security checks bound him to arbitrate.]

The Plaintiffs next argue that under *Prima Paint Corp. v. Flood & Conklin Manufacturing, Co.,* 388 U.S. 395 (1967), the issue as to whether John Brown was competent to enter into the arbitration agreement is a matter left to the arbitrator, and not the District Court. The court does not agree.

In *Prima Paint,* the United States Supreme Court held that a court asked to enforce an arbitration agreement must examine only those defenses that relate specifically and uniquely to the arbitration agreement itself. The court concluded that allegations of fraud in the inducement with regard to the formation of the overall contract in which the arbitration provision is contained are to be resolved by the arbitrator, not the court. . . .

Lower courts also held that *Prima Paint's* reasoning applies equally to contract defenses such as mistake, unconscionability and duress. . . . Federal courts have also held that the *Prima Paint* doctrine extends to the argument that a contracting party lacked the capacity to enter into an agreement because, for example, he was an infant. . . .

The Plaintiffs point to several cases in which the Mississippi Supreme Court states that contracts of infants are voidable, not void. . . . This court agrees. However, the case at hand involves incompetence based on mental capacity, not age. John Brown will not outgrow his mental retardation and will presumably never be able to reaffirm this contract. The Mississippi Supreme Court only addresses incompetence in the cited cases by stating that the same principles apply to each. However, when the Mississippi Supreme Court was asked directly concerning an incompetent's contracts they stated "[t]he contracts of persons *non compos mentis* are absolutely void, whether executed or executory—mere nullities." *Ricketts v. Jollitt,* 62 Miss. 440 (1884). The court finds that John Brown lacked capacity to enter into an arbitration agreement, based on his mental condition and therefore, it is void.

Further, the court finds that the issue of John Brown's mental incompetence goes directly to the making of the arbitration agreement. If he could not read or understand the arbitration agreement, he certainly could not consent to it. Under *Prima Paint,* if an issue "goes to the 'making' of the agreement to arbitrate the federal court may proceed to adjudicate it." *Prima Paint,* 388 U.S. at 404. * * *

The Plaintiffs last argue that Catherine and John Brown have accepted the benefits under the loan agreement and therefore are estopped from avoiding the arbitration clause contained in the loan agreement. * * *

The court recognizes that returning the consideration he received under the contract is an issue to be resolved, however, it is not a condition precedent to the contract being voided. "[W]here an insane person disaffirms a contract entered into, he must restore the consideration received, if he still has it. But it is not a condition precedent to disaffirming it. And, if he has squandered the consideration entirely, he can disaffirm without restoring the consideration so dissipated." *Woolbert v. Lee Lumber, Co.,* 117 So. 354, 359 (Miss.1928). Accordingly, the court finds that the issues of whether John Brown received any consideration or any should be returned to the Plaintiffs is best decided in the state court and is not a condition precedent to the voiding of this arbitration agreement. * * *

[The court denied the petition to seek an order compelling arbitration. This decision was reversed on appeal on the ground that the merits of Brown's capacity defense were for the arbitrators rather than the district court to decide. Primerica Life Ins. Co. v. Brown, 304 F.3d 469 (5th Cir.2002).]

Ervin v. Hosanna Ministry, Inc.

Superior Court of Connecticut, 1995.
1995 WL 681532 (Unpublished).

■ SKOLNICK, JUDGE.

The plaintiffs, Jacqueline Ervin and Curtis Ervin, commenced this action against the defendant Hosanna Ministry, Inc., a/k/a/ Hosanna Ministries, Inc., ("Hosanna Ministry"), and Obie Ponton, on October 3, 1994. The plaintiffs allege that on or about December, 1992, Jacqueline Ervin was admitted into the care and custody of the defendant Hosanna Ministry for treatment and rehabilitation with respect to her alcohol/drug addictions. The plaintiffs further allege that funds were paid for Jacqueline Ervin's acceptance and admittance into the program.... * * *

[The plaintiffs alleged *inter alia* "negligence on the part of Hosanna for its failure to maintain its premises in reasonably safe condition resulting in injury to the plaintiff."]

On July 11, 1995, the defendants filed a motion for summary judgment on the basis that Jacqueline Ervin waived her right to bring any claim based upon the defendants' intentional, reckless, or negligent conduct by "freely" and "with full comprehension" signing a general release on January 17, 1993....

On July 26, 1995, the plaintiffs filed an objection to the defendants' motion for summary judgment along with the affidavit of Jacqueline Ervin. The objection to summary judgment essentially asserts that the plaintiff has no recollection of signing the release, was in a diminished capacity if she did sign the release, and that there were fraudulent misrepresentations made to the plaintiff at the time of admittance into Hosanna Ministry's drug/alcohol rehabilitation program, and these misrepresentations induced her to enroll in the program....

The court feels that there are several issues of material fact for a trier to determine such as whether the plaintiff actually signed the general release,* or, in the alternative, whether she signed the release "freely" or

---

* The relevant portion of the general release is as follows:

"I, the undersigned, being an adult, being *completely free of the influence of alcohol and drugs* of any kind whatsoever, and having had explained to me the importance of this paper as evidence of my present and future intent to forgive and release Hosanna Ministry, Inc., and all its officers, director employees and agents of and from all claims which I, at any time, may have against it, them or any of them;

AND IN CONSIDERATION of and for my being freely admitted into the Hosanna ministry; the free lodging, board, vocational biblical, educational and general training and education which I shall receive; the *free rehabilitation from drug and alcohol dependence* and from other forms of socially deviant behavior which I shall receive; the free rehabilitation "with full comprehension.''*

"Whether or not a provision forms part of a contract is ordinarily a factual question for the trier." *Carter v. Reichlin Furriers,* 34 Conn. Sup. 661, 665,(Appellate Sess. 1977).... The court believes that plaintiff's affidavit raises a genuine issue of material fact as to her assent to the general release. As plaintiff's affidavit indicates that she has no "recollection" of signing a waiver or release, an issue of fact exists as to whether she actually signed the release and assented to its terms.

Even if the court were to conclude, for the purposes of summary judgment consideration, that Jacqueline Ervin actually signed the general release, an issue of material fact would remain as to whether Jacqueline Ervin's signature was made "freely" and with "full comprehension." If, as claimed in her affidavit, she was under the influence of drugs, she may have lacked the mental capacity to execute such a general release of all claims. If the plaintiff was intoxicated or lacked mental capacity due to her addictions, then an issue exists as to whether she assented to the agreement.

"[I]n Connecticut a party may avoid certain contractual obligations on the ground that at the time they were entered into he or she was mentally incapacitated." *Cotrell v. Connecticut Bank & Trust Co.,* 175 Conn. 257 (1978). According to the Restatement (Second), Contracts, a party cannot be bound to a contract if they were intoxicated when they entered into the contract. The rationale for this is that "compulsive alcoholism may be a form of mental illness.... If drunkenness is *so extreme* as to prevent any manifestation of assent, there is no capacity to contract." (Emphasis added.) Restatement (Second), Contracts § 16, comment (a)(1981). "Otherwise the other party is affected only by intoxication of which he has reason to know." Restatement (Second), Contracts § 16, comment (b)(1981).

Due to her alcohol/drug addictions the plaintiff attests that she has no recollection of signing a waiver or release of claims dated January 17, 1993. Therefore, an issue of material fact exists as to whether Jacqueline Ervin had the mental capacity to execute such a release.

from drug and alcohol dependence and from other forms of socially deviant behavior which I shall receive; the free social and spiritual guidance and counseling which I shall receive and fully intending to be legally bound;

AND ON BEHALF of myself and my heirs, executors, administrators and assigns I do hereby *fully forgive, release and discharge* Hosanna Ministry, Inc. and its officers, directors, employees and agents...." (Emphasis added.)

* The relevant portions of the plaintiff's affidavit are as follows:

"For some time prior to December 1992/January 1993, I suffered from addictions to drugs (crack-cocaine) and alcohol....

Due to the fact that I was suffering from the aforementioned drug/alcohol addictions, I have no recollection of signing a waiver or release....

Due to the aforementioned fraudulent representations made to me as well as my drug/alcohol addiction, I do not recall and do not consider valid the release of claims purportedly signed by me and dated January 17, 1993...."

"The test of mental capacity to make a contract or deed is whether at the time of execution of the instrument the maker possessed understanding sufficient to comprehend the nature, extent and consequences of the transaction." *Nichols v. Nichols,* 79 Conn. 644, 657 (1907). Evidence may be considered as to the mind of the alleged incompetent "before, at, and after his contract, in order to ascertain his real condition at the moment of entering into an agreement." *Cooper v. Burby,* supra, 7 CSCR 592.

Because of the existence of several issues of material fact, the defendants' motion for summary judgment is hereby denied.

NOTES

(1) *Incapacity Due to Intoxication.* "Our rule regarding intoxication is much the same. The drunkenness of a party at the time of making a contract may render the contract voidable, but it does not render it void; and to render the contract voidable, it must be made to appear that the party was intoxicated to such a degree that he was, at the time of the contracting, incapable of exercising judgment, understanding the proposed engagement, and of knowing what he was about when he entered into the contract sought to be avoided.... Proof merely that the party was drunk on the day the sale was executed does not per se, show that he was without contractual capacity; there must be some evidence of a resultant condition indicative of that extreme impairment of the faculties which amounts to contract incapacity." Williamson v. Matthews, 379 So.2d 1245, 1247–48 (Ala.1980). See Restatement (Second) § 16.

PROBLEM: THE CASE OF THE DRUG INFLUENCED SELLER

Alvin, a graduate student, age 25, owned a gold and silver belt which was given to his grandfather when he was welterweight champion of the world. The belt was worth about $500, but had great sentimental value to Alvin. On the evening of October 20, Alvin, alone in his apartment, took an LSD tablet. Shortly thereafter, he began to hallucinate and, soon, a "voice" told him that he must sell the belt and donate the proceeds to charity. Alvin went promptly to Bart's Pawnship and sold the belt for $475. When the effects of the drug had gone, Alvin realized what had happened. Bart, however, refused to return the belt, claiming that he "bought it fair and square."

Alvin brought suit to rescind the contract for sale and to recover the belt. At the trial, Plaintiff's expert testified that LSD, like other hallucinogens, can produce a range of mental states, including hallucinations, delusions, and partial amnesia. He also stated that the effects of the drug may range from a loss of time and space perception to panic, paranoid delusions and reactions very similar to schizophrenia. He then concluded that at the time of the sale, Plaintiff was under the influence of the drug and "was not aware of the quality and nature of his act." On cross-examination, it was brought out that Plaintiff had no mental disease or defect and that he had used LSD on previous occasions. Defendant's testimony, corroborated by another witness, was that Plaintiff entered his store, offered to sell the belt for $600 and after about ten minutes of bargaining, agreed to take $475. Defendant testified that Plaintiff acted a "little strange" but that he was lucid and bargained very well. At the close of the evidence, Defendant made a motion for a directed verdict which the trial court granted. In an oral opinion from the bench, the judge stated that he was relying on Restatement (Second) § 16 on "intoxicated persons" and that although he believed that Plaintiff was, at the time of the sale, unable to understand in a reasonable manner the nature and consequences of the transaction, he found that Defendant had no reason to know about the lessened capacity. Also, he opined that Plaintiff must bear some of the responsibility, since he elected to take LSD. Accordingly, the motion was granted and a judgment was entered for Defendant.

On appeal, what result?

SECTION 2.   DEFECTS IN BARGAINING PROCESS

In Chapters Two and Four, you studied the ordinary requisites of promissory liability. By and large, an assumption has been indulged that the negotiating parties have roughly equal intelligence, information and economic resources and that one party has not abused any superiority in bargaining power or ability. When these traditional conditions have been met and the indulged assumptions not shaken, courts have been perfectly willing to enforce what the parties have agreed is a "fair exchange," refusing, as they say, to inquire into "adequacy." Put another way, in the absence of mistake or misunderstanding, a breach of contract after the parties have complied with the paradigm of "offer-acceptance" and "consideration" is likely to trigger remedies designed to protect the value of the bargain.

In this section, the focus is upon acts or omissions by one party which seriously disrupt the bargaining process. This conduct varies in type and is placed under such labels as mistake, fraud, constructive fraud, misrepresentation, undue influence, duress, bad faith and unconscionability. When these are present, a court may be persuaded to give relief from the bargain even though the traditional conditions of promissory liability have been met.

Granting relief when there are defects in the bargaining process can be grounded on efficiency as well as equity. When both sides consent to the quid pro quo of a contract, there is a strong "revealed preference" argument for presuming that the contract is expected to enhance social welfare. Since each party indicates by consenting that the exchange of promises makes her better off, third-parties (such as courts) can infer—absent negative externalities—that the contract represents a Pareto enhancement in social welfare. [The Pareto criterion is satisfied because the contractors each signal that they expect to be made better off by the contract and no one else in society is made worse off.] But if there are defects in the bargaining process, then the revealed-preference presumption fails. We can no longer infer that each contractor is made better off by her exchange of promises. And accordingly third-parties can no longer be confident that the exchanged promises are welfare enhancing.

The materials in this section explore the grounds for relief based on procedural defects, and the available remedies. There is considerable overlap here with other law school courses; notably, torts, specialized consumer and commercial law courses, and trade regulation.

(A) UNILATERAL AND MUTUAL MISTAKE

Failure of the parties to possess sufficient or accurate information about a "basic assumption on which the contract was made" undermines our confidence that the bargaining process will produce an equitable or efficient outcome. The discovery of a mistake, that is, "a belief that is not in accord with the facts," Restatement (Second) § 151, by one (unilateral) or both (mutual) parties can provide a basis for rescinding a contract.

The Restatement (Second) of Contract §§ 152 and 153 summarize the condition under which "mistake" will lead courts to void contractual obligations:

§ 152   When Mistake of Both Parties Makes a Contract Voidable

(1) Where a mistake of both parties at the time a contract was made as to a basic assumption on which the contract was made has a material effect on the agreed exchange of performances, the contract is voidable by the adversely affected party unless he bears the risk of the mistake. . . .

§ 153   When Mistake of One Party Makes a Contract Voidable

Where a mistake of one party at the time a contract was made as to a basic assumption on which he made the contract has a material effect on the agreed exchange of performances that is adverse to him, the contract is voidable by him if he does not bear the risk of the mistake ... , and

(a) the effect of the mistake is such that enforcement of the contract would be unconscionable, or (b) the other party had reason to know of the mistake or his fault caused the mistake.

Is it clear whether unilateral or mutual mistake will be easier to prove in practice?

While the Restatement might seem to crisply describe the preconditions for voiding the contract, as an empirical matter courts only rarely (and somewhat erratically) void contracts because of mistake. This may be because (unlike the intentional abuses of fraud, duress and unconscionability) the mistaken beliefs at issue in "mistake" cases may not be the defendant's fault.

Even though excuse for mistake concerns mistaken assumptions about reality at the time of contracting, the mere fortuity that the mistake concerned events occurring after the contract was formed will transform the issue into one of "impossibility of performance" or frustration of purpose, see infra, Chapter Five. Collateral reading: Lon L. Fuller, *Mistake and Error in the Law of Contracts*, 33 Emory L.Rev. 41 (1984); Farnsworth §§ 9.1–9.4; Calamari and Perillo §§ 9–25 to 9–36; Murray § 91.

Boise Junior College District v. Mattefs Construction Co.

Supreme Court of Idaho, 1969.
92 Idaho 757, 450 P.2d 604.

■ Spear, Justice. The issue presented is whether, under the circumstances of this case, a contractor is entitled to the equitable relief of rescission when it has submitted a bid which contains a material clerical mistake. We conclude that such relief is available.

Mattefs Construction Company (hereinafter termed respondent) was one of ten bidders on a construction contract to be let by Boise Junior College District (hereinafter referred to as appellant). Along with its bid respondent submitted the customary bid bond containing a promise to pay the difference between its bid and the next higher bid actually accepted if respondent refused to enter into a contract with appellant. Contract specifications also provided that the bid could be not withdrawn for 45 days after it was opened.

The architect's estimate of costs on the building project was $150,000, but when the bids were opened seven of them ran in excess of $155,000 while three of them were less than $150,000. Fulton Construction Company bid $134,896. The respondent bid $141,048. The third bid by Cain and Hardy, Inc., was $148,915. When Fulton refused to sign a contract it was tendered to respondent who likewise refused to sign it. Ultimately the contract was awarded to Cain and Hardy, Inc., the third lowest bidder and appellant proceeded to attempt collection on respondent's bid bond.

One who errs in preparing a bid for a public works contract is entitled to the equitable relief of rescission if he can establish the following conditions: (1) the mistake is material; (2) enforcement of a contract pursuant to the terms of the erroneous bid would be unconscionable; (3) the mistake did not result from violation of a positive legal duty or from culpable negligence; (4) the party to whom the bid is submitted will not be prejudiced except by the loss of his bargain; and (5) prompt notice of the error is given. These principles are established by substantial authority, i.e., Annot., 52 A.L.R.2d 792, § III; . . . That appellant recognizes these principles is evident, because it has raised questions as to the existence of each one of these elements by its assignments of error. Therefore, we shall consider each of these conditions necessary for equitable relief, in the context of the objections raised.

I

Appellant contends that the trial court erred in determining that omission of the glass bid was a material mistake. The trial court found:

"This was the second largest sub bid item in the whole contract, only the mechanical sub bid being larger. It amounted to about 14% of the contract and was thus a material item."

Thus, the issue is whether, as a matter of law, a 14% error in bid is a material error. We have no difficulty in reaching the conclusion that omission of an item representing 14% of the total bid submitted is substantial and material. Appellant cites a number of cases wherein courts have directly or indirectly determined that material error was not involved, in spite of mistakes which ranged up to 50%, i.e., Modany Bros. v. State Public School Building Authority, 417 Pa. 39, 208 A.2d 276 (1965); ... However, we are persuaded we should adopt a rule which is not so harsh and turn instead to authority such as Elsinore Union Elementary School Dist. v. Kastorff, 54 Cal.2d 380 (1960), in which the court stated:

"Plaintiff suggests that in any event the amount of the plumbing bid omitted from the total was immaterial. The bid as submitted was in the sum of $89,994, and whether the sum for the omitted plumbing was $6,500 or $9,285 (the two sub bids), the omission of such a sum is plainly material to the total. In Lemoge Electric v. County of San Mateo, 46 Cal.2d 659, 661–662 (1956) the error which it was declared would have entitled plaintiff to rescind was the listing of the cost of certain materials as $104.52, rather than $10,452, in a total bid of $172,421. Thus the percentage of error here was larger than in Lemoge, and was plainly material."

II

An error in the computation of a bid may be material, representing a large percentage of the total bid submitted, and yet requiring compliance with the bid may not be unconscionable. Thus, omission of a $25,000 item in a $100,000 bid would be material, but if the $100,000 bid included $50,000 in profit, no hardship would be created by requiring the contractor to comply with the terms of his bid.

This does not represent the case at bar. Here the record reveals that if respondent were forced to comply with the terms of its bid it would lose at least $10,000. Respondent's costs, including the omitted item, would be roughly $151,000 while the total amount of its bid was only $141,000. Enforcement of the bid is deemed unconscionable as working a substantial hardship on the bidder where it appears he would incur a substantial pecuniary loss. Donaldson v. Abraham, 68 Wash. 208 (1912). This is particularly so where, as here, no injury is caused by withdrawal of the bid. (See sec. IV, infra.)

III

One who seeks equitable relief from error must establish that such error does not result from violation of a positive legal duty or from culpable negligence.

" * * * [This] generally means carelessness or lack of good faith in calculation which violates a positive duty in making up a bid, so as to amount to gross negligence, or wilful negligence, when it takes on a sinister meaning and will furnish cause, if established, for holding a mistake of the offending bidder to be one not remediable in equity. *It is thus distinguished from a clerical or inadvertent error in handling items of a bid either through setting them down or transcription.*" (emphasis added) Annot., 52 A.L.R.2d 792, 794.

In several of its assignments appellant contends that the trial court erred in not finding that respondent was negligent to the point of being grossly negligent. ...

* * *

On the basis of these facts the trial court concluded:

"There was no willful or even negligent act by plaintiff's agents which prevented knowledge of the error from reaching Mr. Mattefs prior to the opening. In preparing the bid Mattefs Construction Company proceeded in the usual way and under the same last minute pressures that are experienced by all general contractors bidding on bids of this kind. Under the evidence I conclude that it was using ordinary care in its methods of bid preparation; that is, the same care that other contractors in the area use in making bids of the kind here involved. There was no evidence of any gross negligence or fraudulent or willful intent to omit this item for the purpose of obtaining any advantage in the bidding."

It is appellant's contention that the trial court erred in making these findings. It has long been the rule of this court that:

"Where the findings of the trial court are supported by substantial and competent, though conflicting, evidence, such findings will not be disturbed on appeal." ...

Additionally, the trial judge is the arbiter of conflicting evidence; his determination of the weight, credibility, inference and implications thereof is not to be supplanted by this court's impressions or conclusions from the written record. *Meridian Bowling Lanes, Inc. v. Brown*, supra. Also findings of fact shall not be set aside unless clearly erroneous. I.R.C.P. 52(a).

Thus, the finding of the trial court that the mistake of respondent was not due to the required type of negligence must be affirmed. As was held in the *Kemper* case:

"The type of error here involved is one which will sometimes occur in the conduct of reasonable and cautious businessmen, and, under all the circumstances, we cannot say as a matter of law that it constituted a neglect of legal duty such as would bar the right to equitable relief." 235 P.2d at p. 11.

IV

It is well settled by the authorities that a bid may not be withdrawn if such withdrawal would work a substantial hardship on the offeree. Many situations can be hypothesized where such a hardship would result. However, none appears here, nor has appellant attempted to prove any hardship. Appellant expected to pay $150,000 for the work it solicited. Its actual cost will be $149,000. It complains because it cannot have the work done for $141,000. Thus, appellant's injury consists of a failure to save $9,000 on its construction rather than saving $1,000.

" * * * [T]he city will not be heard to complain that it cannot be placed in statu quo because it will not have the benefit of an inequitable bargain.

[citations]" * * * *Kemper Const. Co.*, supra, at page 11. See also Kutsche v. Ford, 222 Mich. 442 (1923).

The most appellant can argue is that its damage is presumed by the requirement of a bid bond and that release of a bid bond and that release of a bidder whenever he makes a mistake will impair the purposes for which a bid bond is required....

* * *

The proper purpose of a provision against withdrawal of a bid was fully explained by the Maryland Court of Appeals, quoting from Geremia v. Boyarsky, 107 Conn. 387 (1928):

" 'It is objected that the rule should be different where, as here, there is a proviso forbidding the withdrawal of bids. To be sure, this puts a bidder on notice that there is a certain finality about bidding for a government contract. But this by no means should enable a governmental agency to take an unconscionable advantage of its special status as a government body. * * * The proper effect of the requirement that bids remain unrevoked is to assure the State that a bidder will be relieved of his obligation only when it is legally justifiable. That means that the State is in the same position as any acceptor when there is a question of rectifying an error. * * * Of course, it is obvious, as the State contends, that the system of public bidding, developed by experience and usual in public contracts, should not be broken down by lightly permitting bidders to withdraw because of change of mind. Such a course would be unfair to other straightforward bidders, as well as disruptive of public business. But it can hardly be a substantial impairment of such system to grant the relief— which would clearly be given as between private citizens—in a case where a bona fide mistake is proven and was known to the State before acceptance or any loss to it.' " City of Baltimore v. De Luca–Davis Construction Co., 124 A.2d at p. 565.

V

The final element of the right to equitable relief raised by appellant is actually an adjunct of the previous question of whether the offeree will be damaged by withdrawal of the bid. The requirement of prompt notice is separately stated here because appellant earnestly argues that it was not given such prompt notice. This contention is not supported by the evidence.

* * *

Relief from mistaken bids is consistently allowed where the acceptor has actual notice of the error prior to its attempted acceptance and the other elements necessary for equitable relief are present. M.F. Kemper Const. Co., 235 P.2d at page 10. We see no reason to deviate from this rule where, as here, the party opposing the grant of equitable relief can show no damage other than loss of benefit of an inequitable bargain. We conclude that appellant's position is no better here than it was when similar arguments were presented to the U.S. Supreme Court nearly 70 years ago. In quoting from the circuit court opinion, the court held:

" ' * * * If the defendants [appellants] are correct in their contention there is absolutely no redress for a bidder for public work, no matter how aggravated or palpable his blunder. The moment his proposal is opened by the executive board he is held as in a grasp of steel. There is no remedy, no escape. If, through an error of his clerk, he has agreed to do work worth $1,000,000 for $10, he must be held to the strict letter of his contract, while equity stands by with folded hands and sees him driven into bankruptcy. The defendants' [appellants'] position admits of no compromise, no exception, no middle ground.' " Moffett, Hodgkins & Clarke Co. v. City of Rochester, 178 U.S. 373 (1900).

This reasoning is equally applicable to the cause at bar.

Judgment affirmed. Costs to respondent.

NOTES

(1) *Effect Where There Is Knowledge of Mistake.* Since the offeree appeared to have actual notice of the error prior to acceptance, why was not this knowledge sufficient to terminate the power of acceptance?

Under the court's analysis in *Boise,* would the result have been the same if the offer had been accepted before the offeree knew of the error? Restatement (Second) § 153 takes the position that a material mistake by one party as to a "basic assumption on which he made the contract" makes the contract "voidable by him if * * * the effect of the mistake is such that enforcement of the contract would be unconscionable, or * * * the other party had reason to know of the mistake or his fault caused the mistake."

The offeree's actual or constructive knowledge of a mistake is often an important factor in judicial opinions granting relief to the mistaken party. Relief typically takes the form of rescission, an equitable remedy invalidating the contract. Thus, it is evidently conceded that a contract of some sort has been formed. Yet if the offeree knew or should have known about the mistake it is arguable that he or she had no power to accept the offer at all. In Rushlight Automatic Sprinkler Co. v. City of Portland, 189 Or. 194, 219 P.2d 732 (1950), the plaintiff's bid was substantially below the others because the cost of steel was mistakenly omitted. In allowing rescission, the court observed: "We believe that in this State an offer and acceptance are deemed to effect a meeting of the minds, even though the offeror made a material mistake in compiling his offer, provided the acceptor was not aware of the mistake and had no reason to suspect it. But if the offeree knew of the mistake, and it was basic, or if the circumstances were such that he, a reasonable man, should have inferred that a basic mistake was made, a meeting of the minds does not occur. The circumstances which should arouse the suspicions of the fair-minded offeree are many, as stated in § 94 of Williston on Contracts, Rev.Ed.: " ' ... And the same principle is applicable in any case where the offeree should know that the terms of the offer are unintended or misunderstood by the offeror. The offeree will not be permitted to snap up an offer that is too good to be true; no contract based on such an offer can then be enforced by the acceptor.'" 219 P.2d at 752–53.

Where the remedy of rescission is sought, it may make little difference whether the court concludes that there was no mutual assent or that the contract was voidable. But are there cases where this would not be true? Is *Boise* such a case? See *Problem: The Case of the Four Million Labels,* infra. See also Wil–Fred's Inc. v. Metropolitan Sanitary District of Greater Chicago, 57 Ill.App.3d 16, 14 Ill.Dec. 667, 372 N.E.2d 946 (1978), where the court considered the distinction traditionally made between a clerical or mathematical error and an error in business judgment. The court observed: "Generally, relief is refused for errors in judgment and allowed for clerical or mathematical mistakes. . . . Nonetheless, we believe, in fairness to the individual bidder, that the facts surrounding the error, not the label, i.e. 'mistake of fact' or 'mistake of judgment,' should determine whether relief is granted." 14 Ill.Dec. at 674. The court pointed out that the plaintiff's error in judgment derived, at least in part, from misleading specifications furnished by the defendant. But the court went on to state: "Furthermore, it was established that Wil–Fred's quotation was $233,775 lower than the next lowest bid. It is apparent that such a sizable discrepancy should have placed the Sanitary District on notice that plaintiff's bid contained a material error. . . . Accordingly equity will not allow the District to take advantage of Wil–Fred's low offer." 14 Ill.Dec. at 674. There is a hint here that a "palpable" error, however derived, may be sufficient to warrant relief. For a thorough treatment of the mistaken bid problem, see Ernest Jones, *The Law of Mistaken Bids,* 48 U.Cin.L.Rev. 43 (1979).

(2) *Effect of Bidder Negligence.*

The very term "mistake" connotes some degree of negligent conduct. * * * In most circumstances it would be illogical, if not impossible, to require a bidder who made a mistake in calculating a bid to establish that the mistake was one most reasonable bidders would make under the same or substantially similar circumstances. Requiring proof of freedom from negligence focuses substantial attention on the cause of the mistake; the question of the availability of equitable relief from a mistaken bid should focus primarily on the consequences of the mistake. * * * Numerous courts and commentators have concluded that in public construction contract cases in which a bidder seeks equitable relief from bond forfeiture provisions because of a mistaken bid, the fundamental issue is whether the bidder made an honest or good faith mistake and any question of gross or extreme negligence of the bidder should be considered only as evidence of the bidder's lack of good faith. * * * This approach recognizes that a bidder should not be allowed to rescind a mistaken bid if the bid were made in bad faith and emphasizes the desirability of ensuring that public projects proceed on the basis of accurate cost estimates. A contrary rule would encourage manipulative bidding practices and undermine the stability of the bidding process. Furthermore, evenhanded application of a good faith standard ensures fair treatment of all parties involved in dealings with municipal authorities, thereby enhancing the integrity of the bidding process.

Powder Horn Constructors, Inc. v. City of Florence, 754 P.2d 356, 362 (Colo. 1988).

(3) *Mistakes in Bids and Federal Government Contracting.* Applicable regulations oblige a contracting officer to examine all bids for mistakes. Federal Acquisition Regulation 14.406–1. In cases of apparent mistakes and in cases where the contracting officer has reason to believe that a mistake may have been made, the contracting officer shall request from the bidder a verification of the bid, calling attention to the suspected mistake. Id. Any clerical mistake, apparent on the face of the bid, may be corrected by the contracting officer before the award. FAR 14.406–2. If a bidder requests permission to correct a mistake and clear and convincing evidence establishes both the existence of the mistake and the bid actually intended, the agency head may make a determination permitting the bidder to correct the mistake; provided, that if this correction would result in displacing one or more lower bids, such a determination shall not be made unless the existence of the mistake and the bid actually intended are ascertainable substantially from the invitation and the bid itself. FAR 14.406–3.

Relief from the mistake is, of course, more difficult to obtain after the award of the contract. Here one is, in general, obliged to show by clear and convincing evidence either mutual mistake or a unilateral mistake of which the contracting officer had actual or constructive knowledge; i.e., knew or should have known of the error. FAR 14.406–4. For such mistakes, agencies are authorized to (1) rescind the contract or (2) reform the contract so as to delete the items involved in the mistake, or to increase the price if the contract price, as corrected, does not exceed that of the next lowest acceptable bid under the original invitation for bids. Id. The United States Claims Court recently denied relief from an accepted bid on a latrine repair project, where the 13% price disparity was quite close to the government's own estimate and where the government's representative neither knew nor had reason to know of the mistake. Fadeley v. United States, 15 Cl.Ct. 706 (1988). The court observed: "The granting of equitable relief is based upon a concern with the overreaching of a contractor by a contracting officer who suspects a mistake in the bid and is willing to accept it nevertheless. This is not the situation here. Therefore, Federal Acquisition Regulation 14.406–4 (1986), which allows for the reformation of a contract to reflect the correction of a prior, unilateral bid mistake when the contracting officer is charged with knowledge of that mistake is not applicable in the instant case." 15 Cl.Ct. at 712. The formation of government contracts by competitive bidding is treated in John W. Whelan & James F. Nagle, Federal Government Contracts: Cases and Materials 182–205 (2d ed. 2002).

(4) *Mistaken Admissions.*

"Two of the 9,691 envelopes that were mailed last month to applicants to next year's freshman class contained the wrong letter, and two high school seniors who were supposed to be sent rejection notices received acceptances. 'Somebody must have pulled the form letter off the wrong pile,' explained Spencer J. Reynolds '61, associate director of admission. To his knowledge, he said, this was the first such error in his nine years at Princeton, during which time some 76,000 applications have been processed.

"In one of the cases, the mistake was discovered when the recipient visited the campus and noticed that his name was not included in the list of admitted students posted in the admissions office. The other case came to light when the student called because his envelope had not contained a reply card. Since legally a letter of admission may be considered a binding contract, the university decided to honor the acceptances. One of the students is viewed as academically unqualified and has been advised that he probably could not handle the workload, while the other has been informed that he is thought capable of doing the work. As of Memorial Day, neither had yet notified the university of his decision." *Princeton Alumni Weekly,* May 27, 1975, p. 8.

PROBLEM: THE CASE OF THE FOUR MILLION LABELS

Reed, operator of a small photography store, had need of adhesive pricing labels. He began to prepare a purchase order for five different types of labels. In handwriting he filled in the blank spaces for four different types and in the quantity column noted opposite each "2M." At that point he was interrupted by a customer, and it was not until later that he finished writing the order. He described the fifth label as "Label as Attached," attached a copy of the desired label, and in the quantity column wrote "4MM." He then mailed the completed order to Monarch, a nationwide manufacturer and supplier of pricing and product identification labels.

The designation "M" is understood in the label industry to mean one thousand. "MM" stands for one million. Reed intended to order 4,000 of the fifth type; his use of "MM" was a mistake.

In previous transactions the largest order Monarch had received from Reed for any one item was 4,000. Indeed, the largest order Monarch ever received previously from any source was for one million labels. Without checking further, Monarch proceeded to fill the order. The first four items were in stock and were mailed to Reed. The fifth required a special printing. Reed did not become aware of any problem until a truck drove up to his store with seven cartons of labels weighing 622 pounds!

Reed refused to receive the merchandise; Monarch sued for the $2,680 purchase price. What result? Consider the matter pro and con before consulting Reed's Photo Mart v. Monarch Marking System Co., 475 S.W.2d 356 (Tex.Civ. App.1971), reversed 485 S.W.2d 905 (Tex.1972).

Beachcomber Coins, Inc. v. Boskett

Superior Court of New Jersey, Appellate Division, 1979.
166 N.J.Super. 442, 400 A.2d 78.

■ CONFORD, P.J.A.D. (retired and temporarily assigned).

Plaintiff, a retail dealer in coins, brought an action for rescission of a purchase by it from defendant for $500 of a dime purportedly minted in 1916 at Denver. Defendant is a part-time coin dealer. Plaintiff asserts a mutual mistake of fact as to the genuineness of the coin as Denver-minted, such a coin being a rarity and therefore having a market value greatly in excess of its normal monetary worth. Plaintiff's evidence at trial that the "D" on the coin signifying Denver mintage was counterfeited is not disputed by defendant. Although at trial defendant disputed that the coin tendered back to him by plaintiff was the one he sold, the implicit trial finding is to the contrary, and that issue is not raised on appeal.

The trial judge, sitting without a jury, held for defendant on the ground that the customary "coin dealing procedures" were for a dealer purchasing a coin to make his own investigation of the genuineness of the coin and to "assume the risk" of his purchase if his investigation is faulty. The judge conceded that the evidence demonstrated satisfaction of the ordinary requisites of the rule of rescission for mutual mistake of fact that both parties act under a mistake of fact and that the fact be "central" [material] to the making of the contract. The proofs were that the seller had himself acquired this coin and two others of minor value for a total of $450 and that his representative had told the purchaser that he would not sell the dime for less than $500. The principal of plaintiff firm spent from 15 to 45 minutes in close examination of the coin before purchasing it. Soon thereafter he received an offer of $700 for the coin subject to certification of its genuineness by the American Numismatic Society. That organization labelled it a counterfeit, and as a result plaintiff instituted the present action.

The evidence and trial judge's findings establish this as a classic case of rescission for mutual mistake of fact. As a general rule,

> * * * where parties on entering into a transaction that affects their contractual relations are both under a mistake regarding a fact assumed by them as the basis on which they entered into the transaction, it is voidable by either party if enforcement of it would be materially more onerous to him than it would have been had the fact been as the parties believed it to be. [Restatement, Contracts, § 502 at 961 (1932);* 13 Williston on Contracts (3 ed. 1970), § 1543, 74–75]

By way of example, the *Restatement* posits the following:

> A contracts to sell to B a specific bar of silver before them. The parties supposed that the bar is sterling. It has, however, a much larger admixture of base metal. The contract is voidable by B. [Op. cit. at 964].

Moreover, "negligent failure of a party to know or to discover the facts as to which both parties are under a mistake does not preclude rescission or reformation on account thereof." Restatement, op. cit., § 502 at 977. The law of New Jersey is in accord. See Riviere v. Berla, 89 N.J.Eq. 596, 597(E. & A. 1918); Dencer v. Erb, 142 N.J.Eq. 422, 429 (Ch.1948). In the *Riviere* case relief was denied only because the parties could not be restored to the

---

* No substantial change in the rule was effected by Restatement, Contracts 2d, § 294(1), Tent.Dr. No. 10 (1975) at 10. This provides:

    (1) Where a mistake of both parties at the time a contract was made as to a basic assumption on which the contract was made has a material effect on the agreed exchange of performances, the contract is voidable by the adversely affected party unless he bears the risk of the mistake under the rule stated in § 296.

The exceptions in § 296 are not here applicable [§ 294(1) is § 152(1) in the final draft. Ed.]

status quo ante. In the present case they can be. It is undisputed that both parties believed that the coin was a genuine Denver-minted one. The mistake was mutual in that both parties were laboring under the same misapprehension as to this particular, essential fact. The price asked and paid was directly based on that assumption. That plaintiff may have been negligent in his inspection of the coin (a point not expressly found but implied by the trial judge) does not, as noted above, bar its claim for rescission. Cf. Smith v. Zimbalist, 2 Cal.App.2d 324, 38 P.2d 170 (D.Ct.App. 1934).

Defendant's contention that plaintiff assumed the risk that the coin might be of greater or lesser value than that paid is not supported by the evidence. It is well established that a party to a contract can assume the risk of being mistaken as to the value of the thing sold. 13 Williston, Contracts, op. cit., § 1543A at 85. The *Restatement* states the rule this way:

> Where the parties know that there is doubt in regard to a certain matter and contract on that assumption, the contract is not rendered voidable because one is disappointed in the hope that the facts accord with his wishes. The risk of the existence of the doubtful fact is then assumed as one of the elements of the bargain. [Restatement, op. cit., § 502, Comment f at 964. See also Restatement, Contracts 2d, op. cit., § 296(b), Comment c at 4.]

However, for the stated rule to apply, the parties must be conscious that the pertinent fact may not be true and make their agreement at the risk of that possibility. . . . In this case both parties were certain that the coin was genuine. They so testified. Plaintiff's principal thought so after his inspection, and defendant would not have paid nearly $450 for it otherwise. A different case would be presented if the seller were uncertain either of the genuineness of the coin or of its value [if] genuine, and had accepted the expert buyer's judgment on these matters.

The trial judge's rationale of custom of the trade is not supported by the evidence. It depended upon the testimony of plaintiff's expert witness who on cross-examination as to the "procedure" on the purchase by a dealer of a rare coin, stated that the dealer would check it with magnification and then "normally send it to the American Numismatic Certification Service for certification." This testimony does not in our opinion establish that practice as a usage of trade "having such regularity of observance in a * * * trade as to justify an expectation that it will be observed with respect to the transaction in question," within the intent of the Uniform Commercial Code, N.J.S.A. 12A:1–205(2).*

The cited code provision contemplates that the trade usage is so prevalent as to warrant the conclusion that the parties contracted with reference to, and intended their agreement to be governed by it. . . . Our

---

* Note, also, that evidence of a trade usage is not admissible unless the offering party gives the other party advance notice to prevent unfair surprise. N.J.S.A. 12A:1– 105(6). Plaintiff received no notice that the judge intended to decide this case on the basis of the alleged trade usage.

reading of the testimony does not indicate any basis for findings either that this was a trade usage within the Code definition at all or that these parties in fact accepted it as such to the extent that they were agreeing that because of it the sale was an "as is" transaction. Indeed, the same witness testified there was a "normal policy" among coin dealers throughout the United States of a "return privilege" for altered coins. * * *

Reversed.

Sherwood v. Walker

Supreme Court of Michigan, 1887.
66 Mich. 568, 33 N.W. 919.

■ MORSE, J.

The main controversy depends upon the construction of a contract for the sale of the cow.... The Walkers are importers and breeders of polled Angus cattle. The plaintiff is a banker living at Plymouth, in Wayne county. He called upon the defendants at Walkerville for the purchase of some of their stock, but found none there that suited him. Meeting one of the defendants afterwards, he was informed that they had a few head upon their Greenfield farm. He was asked to go out and look at them, with the statement that they were probably barren, and would not breed. May 5, 1886, the plaintiff went out to Greenfield and saw the cattle. A few days thereafter, he called upon one of the defendants with the view of purchasing a cow, known as "Rose 2d of Aberlone." After considerable talk it was agreed that defendants would telephone Sherwood at his home in Plymouth in reference to the price. The second morning after this talk he was called up by telephone, and the terms of the sale were finally agreed upon. He was to pay five and one-half cents per pound, live weight, fifty pounds shrinkage ... He requested defendants to confirm the sale in writing, which they did ...

On the twenty-first of the same month the plaintiff went to defendants' farm at Greenfield, and presented the order and [confirmation letter to an employee of the Walkers,] who informed him that the defendants had instructed him not to deliver the cow. Soon after, the plaintiff rendered to Hiram Walker, one of the defendants, $80, and demanded the cow. Walker refused to take the money or deliver the cow. The plaintiff then instituted this suit. * * *

[At the trial, t]he defendants introduced evidence tending to show that at the time of the alleged sale it was believed by both the plaintiff and themselves that the cow was barren and would not breed; that she cost $850, and if not barren would be worth from $750 to $1,000; that after the date of the letter ... the defendants were informed by [an employee] that in his judgment the cow was with calf, and therefore they instructed him not to deliver her to plaintiff ... The cow had a calf in the month of October following ...]

It appears from the record that both parties supposed this cow was barren and would not breed, and she was sold by the pound for an insignificant sum as compared with her real value if a breeder. She was evidently sold and purchased on the relation of her value for beef, unless the plaintiff had learned of her true condition, and concealed such knowledge from the defendants ... The question arises whether the [defendants] had a right to [refuse to perform the contract] ... I am of the opinion that the [circuit] court erred in holding [that the contract should have been performed at the agreed upon price]. I know that this is a close question, and the dividing line between the adjudicated cases is not easily discerned. But it must be considered as well settled that a party who has given an apparent consent to a contract of sale may refuse to execute it, or he may avoid it after it has been completed, if the assent was founded, or the contract made, upon the mistake of a material fact,—such as the subject-matter of the sale, the price, or some collateral fact materially inducing the agreement; and this can be done when the mistake is mutual....

If there is a difference or misapprehension as to the substance of the thing bargained for; if the thing actually delivered or received is different in substance from the thing bargained for, and intended to be sold,—then there is no contract; but if it be only a difference in some quality or accident, even though the mistake may have been the actuating motive to the purchaser or seller, or both of them, yet the contract remains binding ... It has been held, in accordance with the principles above stated, that where a horse is bought under the belief that he is sound, and both vendor and vendee honestly believe him to be sound, the purchaser must stand by his bargain, and pay the full price, unless there was a warranty.

It seems to me, however, in the case made by this record, that the mistake or misapprehension of the parties went to the whole substance of the agreement. If the cow was a breeder, she was worth at least $750; if barren, she was worth not over $80. The parties would not have made the contract of sale except upon the understanding and belief that she was incapable of breeding, and of no use as a cow. It is true she is now the identical animal that they thought her to be when the contract was made; there is no mistake as to the identity of the creature. Yet the mistake was not of the mere quality of the animal, but went to the very nature of the thing. A barren cow is substantially a different creature than a breeding one. There is as much difference between them for all purposes of use as there is between an ox and a cow that is capable of breeding and giving milk. If the mutual mistake had simply related to the fact whether she was with calf or not for one season, then it might have been a good sale, but the mistake affected the character of the animal for all time, and for its present and ultimate use. She was not in fact the animal, or the kind of animal, the defendants intended to sell or the plaintiff to buy ... The court should have instructed the jury that if they found that the cow was sold, or contracted to be sold, upon the understanding of both parties that she was barren and useless for the purpose of breeding, and that in fact she was not barren, but capable of breeding, then the defendants had a right to rescind, and refuse to deliver, and the verdict should be in their favor.

The judgment of the court below must be reversed, and a new trial granted, with costs of this court to defendants.

■ SHERWOOD, J. (dissenting) ... There is no question but that the defendants sold the cow representing her of the breed and quality they believed the cow to be, and that the purchaser so understood it. And the buyer purchased her believing her to be of the breed represented by the sellers, and possessing all the qualities stated, and even more. He believed she would breed. There is no pretense that the plaintiff bought the cow for beef, and there is nothing in the record indicating that he would have bought her at all only that he thought she might be made to breed. Under the foregoing facts ... it is held that because it turned out that the plaintiff was more correct in his judgment as to one quality of the cow than the defendants, and a quality, too, which could not by any possibility be positively known at the time by either party to exist, the contract may be annulled by the defendants at their pleasure ... If the owner of a Hambletonian horse had speeded him, and was only able to make him go a mile in three minutes, and should sell him to another, believing that was his greatest speed, for $300, when the purchaser believed he could go much faster, and made the purchase for that sum, and a few days thereafter, under more favorable circumstances, the horse was driven a mile in 2 min. 16 sec., and was found to be worth $20,000, I hardly think it would be held, whether at law or in equity, by any one, that the seller in such case could rescind the contract ...

In this case neither party knew the actual quality and condition of this cow at the time of the sale ... The defendants thought [Rose could not be made to breed], but the plaintiff says that he thought she could be made to breed, but believed she was not with calf. The defendants sold the cow for what they believed her to be, and the plaintiff bought her as he believed she was, after the statements made by the defendants. No conditions whatever were attached to the terms of sale by either party ... It is not the duty of courts to destroy contracts when called upon to enforce them, after they have been legally made ... There was no difference between the parties, nor misapprehension, as to the substance of the thing bargained for, which was a cow supposed to be barren by one party, and believed not to be by the other. As to the quality of the animal, subsequently developed, both parties were equally ignorant, and as to this each party took his chances ... In this case the cow sold was the one delivered. What might or might not happen to her after the sale formed no element in the contract ...

Lenawee County Board of Health v. Messerly

Supreme Court of Michigan, 1982.
417 Mich. 17, 331 N.W.2d 203.

■ RYAN, JUSTICE.

In March of 1977, Carl and Nancy Pickles, appellees, purchased from appellants, William and Martha Messerly, a 600–square-foot tract of land upon which is located a three-unit apartment building. Shortly after the transaction was closed, the Lenawee County Board of Health condemned the property and obtained a permanent injunction which prohibits human habitation on the premises until the defective sewage system is brought into conformance with the Lenawee County sanitation code.

We are required to determine whether appellees should prevail in their attempt to avoid this land contract on the basis of mutual mistake and failure of consideration. We conclude that the parties did entertain a mutual misapprehension of fact, but that the circumstances of this case do not warrant rescission.

I

The facts of the case are not seriously in dispute. In 1971, the Messerlys acquired approximately one acre plus 600 square feet of land. A three-unit apartment building was situated upon the 600–square-foot portion. The trial court found that, prior to this transfer, the Messerlys' predecessor in title, Mr. Bloom, had installed a septic tank on the property without a permit and in violation of the applicable health code. The Messerlys used the building as an income investment property until 1973 when they sold it, upon land contract, to James Barnes who likewise used it primarily as an income-producing investment.

Mr. and Mrs. Barnes, with the permission of the Messerlys, sold approximately one acre of the property in 1976, and the remaining 600 square feet and building were offered for sale soon thereafter when Mr. and Mrs. Barnes defaulted on their land contract. Mr. and Mrs. Pickles evidenced an interest in the property, but were dissatisfied with the terms of the Barnes–Messerly land contract. Consequently, to accommodate the Pickleses' preference to enter into a land contract directly with the Messerlys, Mr. and Mrs. Barnes executed a quit-claim deed which conveyed their interest in the property back to the Messerlys. After inspecting the property, Mr. and Mrs. Pickles executed a new land contract with the Messerlys on March 21, 1977. It provided for a purchase price of $25,500. A clause was added to the end of the land contract form which provides:

> "17. Purchaser has examined this property and agrees to accept same in its present condition. There are no other or additional written or oral understandings."

Five or six days later, when the Pickleses went to introduce themselves to the tenants, they discovered raw sewage seeping out of the ground. Tests conducted by a sanitation expert indicated the inadequacy of the sewage system. The Lenawee County Board of Health subsequently condemned the property and initiated this lawsuit in the Lenawee Circuit Court against the Messerlys as land contract vendors, and the Pickleses, as vendees, to obtain a permanent injunction proscribing human habitation of the premises until the property was brought into conformance with the Lenawee County sanitation code. The injunction was granted, and the Lenawee County Board of Health was permitted to withdraw from the lawsuit by stipulation of the parties.

When no payments were made on the land contract, the Messerlys filed a cross-complaint against the Pickleses seeking foreclosure, sale of the property, and a deficiency judgment. Mr. and Mrs. Pickles then counter-claimed for rescission against the Messerlys, and filed a third-party complaint against the Barneses, which incorporated, by reference, the allegations of the counterclaim against the Messerlys. In count one, Mr. and Mrs. Pickles alleged failure of consideration. Count two charged Mr. and Mrs. Barnes with willful concealment and misrepresentation as a result of their failure to disclose the condition of the sanitation system. Additionally, Mr. and Mrs. Pickles sought to hold the Messerlys liable in equity for the Barneses' alleged misrepresentation. The Pickleses prayed that the land contract be rescinded.

After a bench trial, the court concluded that the Pickleses had no cause of action against either the Messerlys or the Barneses as there was no fraud or misrepresentation. This ruling was predicated on the trial judge's conclusion that none of the parties knew of Mr. Bloom's earlier transgression or of the resultant problem with the septic system until it was discovered by the Pickleses, and that the sanitation problem was not caused by any of the parties. The trial court held that the property was purchased "as is", after inspection and, accordingly, its "negative * * * value cannot be blamed upon an innocent seller". Foreclosure was ordered against the Pickleses, together with a judgment against them in the amount of $25,943.09.

Mr. and Mrs. Pickles appealed from the adverse judgment. The Court of Appeals unanimously affirmed the trial court's ruling with respect to Mr. and Mrs. Barnes but, in a two-to-one decision, reversed the finding of no cause of action on the Pickleses' claims against the Messerlys.... It concluded that the mutual mistake between the Messerlys and the Pickleses went to a basic, as opposed to a collateral, element of the contract, and that the parties intended to transfer income-producing rental property but, in actuality, the vendees paid $25,500 for an asset without value.[1]

We granted the Messerlys' application for leave to appeal. 411 Mich. 900 (1981).

II

We must decide initially whether there was a mistaken belief entertained by one or both parties to the contract in dispute and, if so, the resultant legal significance.

A contractual mistake "is a belief that is not in accord with the facts". 1 Restatement Contracts, 2d, § 151, p. 383. The erroneous belief of one or

---

1. The trial court found that the only way that the property could be put to residential use would be to pump and haul the sewage, a method which is economically unfeasible, as the cost of such a disposal system amounts to double the income generated by the property. There was speculation by the trial court that the adjoining land might be utilized to make the property suitable for residential use, but in the absence of testimony directed at that point, the court refused to draw any conclusions. The trial court and the Court of Appeals both found that the property was valueless, or had a negative value.

both of the parties must relate to a fact in existence at the time the contract is executed. Richardson Lumber Co. v. Hoey, 219 Mich. 643, 189 N.W. 923 (1922); Sherwood v. Walker, 66 Mich. 568, 580, 33 N.W. 919 (1887) (Sherwood, J., dissenting). That is to say, the belief which is found to be in error may not be, in substance, a prediction as to a future occurrence or non-occurrence. . . .

The Court of Appeals concluded, after a *de novo* review of the record, that the parties were mistaken as to the income-producing capacity of the property in question. . . . We agree. The vendors and the vendees each believed that the property transferred could be utilized as income-generating rental property. All of the parties subsequently learned that, in fact, the property was unsuitable for any residential use.

* * *

Having determined that when these parties entered into the land contract they were laboring under a mutual mistake of fact, we now direct our attention to a determination of the legal significance of that finding.

A contract may be rescinded because of a mutual misapprehension of the parties, but this remedy is granted only in the sound discretion of the court. . . . Appellants argue that the parties' mistake relates only to the quality or value of the real estate transferred, and that such mistakes are collateral to the agreement and do not justify rescission, citing A & M Land Development Co. v. Miller, 354 Mich. 681 (1959).

In that case, the plaintiff was the purchaser of 91 lots of real property. It sought partial rescission of the land contract when it was frustrated in its attempts to develop 42 of the lots because it could not obtain permits from the county health department to install septic tanks on these lots. This Court refused to allow rescission because the mistake, whether mutual or unilateral, related only to the value of the property.

"There was here no mistake as to the form or substance of the contract between the parties, or the description of the property constituting the subject matter. The situation involved is not at all analogous to that presented in Scott v. Grow, 301 Mich. 226 (1942). There the plaintiff sought relief by way of reformation of a deed on the ground that the instrument of conveyance had not been drawn in accordance with the intention and agreement of the parties. It was held that the bill of complaint stated a case for the granting of equitable relief by way of reformation. In the case at bar plaintiff received the property for which it contracted. The fact that it may be of less value than the purchaser expected at the time of the transaction is not a sufficient basis for the granting of equitable relief, neither fraud nor reliance on misrepresentation of material facts having been established." 354 Mich. 693–694.

Appellees contend, on the other hand, that in this case the parties were mistaken as to the very nature of the character of the consideration and claim that the pervasive and essential quality of this mistake renders rescission appropriate. They cite in support of that view Sherwood v.

Walker, 66 Mich. 568 (1887), the famous "barren cow" case. In that case, the parties agreed to the sale and purchase of a cow which was thought to be barren, but which was, in reality, with calf. When the seller discovered the fertile condition of his cow, he refused to deliver her. In permitting rescission, the Court stated: [The court quoted the last two paragraphs in the majority opinion, supra at 483.] * * *

As the parties suggest, the foregoing precedent arguably distinguishes mistakes affecting the essence of the consideration from those which go to its quality or value, affording relief on a per se basis for the former but not the latter. . . .

However, the distinctions which may be drawn from *Sherwood* and *A & M Land Development Co.* do not provide a satisfactory analysis of the nature of a mistake sufficient to invalidate a contract. Often, a mistake relates to an underlying factual assumption which, when discovered, directly affects value, but simultaneously and materially affects the essence of the contractual consideration. It is disingenuous to label such a mistake collateral. . . .

Appellant and appellee both mistakenly believed that the property which was the subject of their land contract would generate income as rental property. The fact that it could not be used for human habitation deprived the property of its income-earning potential and rendered it less valuable. However, this mistake, while directly and dramatically affecting the property's value, cannot accurately be characterized as collateral because it also affects the very essence of the consideration. "The thing sold and bought [income generating rental property] had in fact no existence". *Sherwood v. Walker*, 66 Mich. 578.

We find that the inexact and confusing distinction between contractual mistakes running to value and those touching the substance of the consideration serves only as an impediment to a clear and helpful analysis for the equitable resolution of cases in which mistake is alleged and proven. Accordingly, the holdings of *A & M Land Development Co.* and *Sherwood* with respect to the material or collateral nature of a mistake are limited to the facts of those cases.

Instead, we think the better-reasoned approach is a case-by-case analysis whereby rescission is indicated when the mistaken belief relates to a basic assumption of the parties upon which the contract is made, and which materially affects the agreed performances of the parties. . . . 1 Restatement Contracts, 2d, § 152, pp. 385–386.[2] Rescission is not available, howev-

---

2. The parties have invited our attention to the first edition of the Restatement of Contracts in their briefs, and the Court of Appeals cites to that edition in its opinion. However, the second edition was published subsequent to the issuance of the lower court opinion and the filing of the briefs with this Court. Thus, we take it upon ourselves to refer to the latest edition to aid us in our resolution of this case.

Section 152 delineates the legal significance of a mistake.

"§ 152. When Mistake of Both Parties Makes a Contract Voidable

"(1) Where a mistake of both parties at the time a contract was made as to a er, to relieve a party who has assumed the risk of loss in connection with the mistake....

All of the parties to this contract erroneously assumed that the property transferred by the vendors to the vendees was suitable for human habitation and could be utilized to generate rental income. The fundamental nature of these assumptions is indicated by the fact that their invalidity changed the character of the property transferred, thereby frustrating, indeed precluding, Mr. and Mrs. Pickles' intended use of the real estate. Although the Pickleses are disadvantaged by enforcement of the contract, performance is advantageous to the Messerlys, as the property at issue is less valuable absent its income-earning potential. Nothing short of rescission can remedy the mistake. Thus, the parties' mistake as to a basic assumption materially affects the agreed performances of the parties.

Despite the significance of the mistake made by the parties, we reverse the Court of Appeals because we conclude that equity does not justify the remedy sought by Mr. and Mrs. Pickles.

Rescission is an equitable remedy which is granted only in the sound discretion of the court.... A court need not grant rescission in every case in which the mutual mistake relates to a basic assumption and materially affects the agreed performance of the parties.

In cases of mistake by two equally innocent parties, we are required, in the exercise of our equitable powers, to determine which blameless party should assume the loss resulting from the misapprehension they shared.[4] Normally that can only be done by drawing upon our "own notions of what is reasonable and just under all the surrounding circumstances."[5]

Equity suggests that, in this case, the risk should be allocated to the purchasers. We are guided to that conclusion, in part, by the standards announced in § 154 of the Restatements of Contracts 2d, for determining when a party bears the risk of mistake. See fn. 12. Section 154(a) suggests that the court should look first to whether the parties have agreed to the allocation of the risk between themselves. While there is no express assumption in the contract by either party of the risk of the property becoming uninhabitable, there was indeed some agreed allocation of the

basic assumption on which the contract was made has a material effect on the agreed exchange of performances, the contract is voidable by the adversely affected party unless he bears the risk of the mistake under the rule stated in § 154.

"(2) In determining whether the mistake has a material effect on the agreed exchange of performances, account is taken of any relief by way of reformation, restitution, or otherwise."

4. This risk-of-loss analysis is absent in both *A & M Land Development Co.* and *Sherwood,* and this omission helps to explain, in

part, the disparate treatment in the two cases. Had such an inquiry been undertaken in *Sherwood,* we believe that the result might have been different. Moreover, a determination as to which party assumed the risk in *A & M Land Development Co.* would have alleviated the need to characterize the mistake as collateral so as to justify the result denying rescission. Despite the absence of any inquiry as to the assumption of risk in those two leading cases, we find that there exists sufficient precedent to warrant such an analysis in future cases of mistake.

5. Hathaway v. Hudson, 256 Mich. 702, quoting 9 C.J., p. 1161.

risk to the vendees by the incorporation of an "as is" clause into the contract which, we repeat, provided:

> "Purchaser has examined this property and agrees to accept same in its present condition. There are no other or additional written or oral understandings."

That is a persuasive indication that the parties considered that, as between them, such risk as related to the "present condition" of the property should lie with the purchaser. If the "as is" clause is to have any meaning at all, it must be interpreted to refer to those defects which were unknown at the time that the contract was executed. Thus, the parties themselves assigned the risk of loss to Mr. and Mrs. Pickles.

We conclude that Mr. and Mrs. Pickles are not entitled to the equitable remedy of rescission and, accordingly, reverse the decision of the Court of Appeals.

NOTES

(1) *Sherwood v. Walker* concerned the sale of a presumed barren cow named "Rose the Second of Aberlone." It is the classic mutual mistake case, renowned in prose and poetry. See Robert Birmingham, *A Rose by Any Other Word: Mutual Mistake in Sherwood v. Walker*, 21 U.C.D.L.Rev. 197 (1987).

The court noted that the mistake was not of the "mere quality of the animal, but went to the very nature of the thing." Moreover, "the thing sold and bought had in fact no existence." What was the point of making these distinctions? What are the competing policy considerations in cases of this type? What does *Lenawee*, the later Michigan case, add to *Sherwood v. Walker*?

What requirements are prescribed by Restatement (Second) for avoiding a contract on the grounds of mutual mistake? Can *Beachcomber* and *Lenawee* be reconciled on the basis of Restatement prescriptions?

(2) Professor Brainerd Currie's poem "Aberlone, Rose Of," is one of the delights of legal literature. See 10 The Student Lawyer 4 (1965). For your enjoyment and edification, the beginning and the ending are reprinted below.

Aberlone, Rose Of.

'Tis the middle of night on the Greenfield farm
And the creatures are huddled to keep them from harm.

Ah me!—Ah moo!

Respectively their quidsome balm
How mournfully they chew!
And one there is who stands apart
With hanging head and heavy heart,
Have pity on her sore distress,
This norm of bovine loveliness,
Her gentle limbs, her hornless brow
Proclaim no ordinary cow:
Fair as a pasture sweet with hay
Mown in the very month of May!

Nay, fairer yet! And yet more fair!
She stands alone, the short black hair
Heaving sometimes on her breast,
Shunned and despised by all the rest.
If one should ask her why she doth grieve
She would answer sadly, "I can't conceive."
Her shame is a weary weight like stone
For Rose the Second of Aberlone.
Her sire is of a noble line
Of most aristocratic kine:
Angus of Aberdeen, black and polled;
Their name is proud and their get pure gold.
Their procreation hath won renown,
But Rose the Second hath let them down.
Her forbears have labored for bitter meed,
For Rose is barren and will not breed.
Now the gate that is strait and the way that is narrow
Call for a cow to forgo being farrow.
In a cow one condones a trifle of loose
Morality if she will just reproduce,
The stars in their courses deliver us
From the cow that is non-frugiferous!
If a heifer aspires to a niche on high
She must certainly plan to fructify,
And when she reaches puberty
Must concentrate on uberty.
No honor is there for the boss of that ilk
That produceth no young and giveth no milk;
And this is the reason her kith make moan
For Rose the Second of Aberlone.

* * *

'Tis the middle of night before the exam,
And there's nothing to eat but a cold bit of ham,

Ah me!—Ah moo!

Mark how the eager students cram,
What coffee black they brew!
A dismal specter haunts this wake—
The law of mutual mistake;
And even the reluctant drone
Must cope with Rose of Aberlone.
She rules the cases, she stalks the page
Even in this atomic age.
In radioactive tracts of land,
In hardly collectible notes of hand,
In fiddles of dubious pedigree,
In releases of liability,
In zoning rules unknown to lessors,
In weird conceits of law professors,
In printers' bids and ailing kings,

In all mutations and sorts of things,
In many a hypothetical
With characters alphabetical,
In many a subtle and sly disguise
There lurks the ghost of her sad brown eyes.
That she will turn up in some set of facts is
Almost as certain as death and taxes:
For students of law must still atone
For the shame of Rose of Aberlone.

(3) *An Anomalous Situation.* In a case which the court said presents an "anomalous" situation, the *vendors* sought to rescind a contract for the sale of land based on a defect (leaking underground gasoline storage tanks) discovered after the agreement. The transaction involved the sale for $320,000 of a gas station and automobile parts store in East Lansing for use as a 7–Eleven store. The agreement contained an "as is" clause. The vendors sought to rescind because state environmental statutes make previous owners of sites liable for environmental contamination and responsible for cleanup. The court upheld the vendor's right to rescind based on mutual mistake. Garb–Ko, Inc. v. Lansing–Lewis Services, Inc., 167 Mich.App. 779, 423 N.W.2d 355 (1988). Asserting that the "as is" clause held no significance since the purchaser was not the adversely affected party, the court noted: "[Vendors] have a continuing obligation and responsibility for the contaminated property. One expert estimated that the cost of cleanup could be anywhere from $100,000 to $1,000,000. In order to contain further cleanup costs and third-party claims arising from use of the contaminated land, [Vendors] need control over the use of the property. Sale to plaintiff would not give them such control." 423 N.W.2d at 358.

(4) *The Treasure in the Dunghill: A Rabbinical Account.* Alexander of Macedon visited King Kazia beyond the dark mountains. He came forth, offering him golden bread on a golden tray. "Do I then need your gold?" he demanded. "Had you then nothing to eat in your own country that you have come here?" he retorted. "I came only because I wished to see how you dispense justice," was the reply. As he sat with him a man came with a complaint against his neighbour. "This man," he stated, "sold me a dunghill and I found a treasure in it." The buyer argued, "I bought a dunghill only," while the vendor maintained, "I sold the dunghill and all it contained." Said he [the king] to one: "Have you a son?" "Yes," replied he. "And have you a daughter?" he asked the other, "Yes," was the answer. "Then marry them and let the treasure belong to both." He noticed him [Alexander] sitting astonished, and asked him, "Have I then not judged well?" "Yes," he replied. "Had this happened among you, how would you have judged?" "I would have slain both and kept the treasure for myself." 1 Midrash Rabbah, ch. XXXIII (H. Freedman trans. 3d ed. 1983). Can you suggest other alternatives?

PROBLEMS: THE CASES OF THE UNKNOWN OIL DEPOSITS, MESTROVIC'S DRAWINGS, AND UNKNOWN INJURIES

(a) Vendor, a farmer, agreed in writing to sell forty acres of land to Purchaser, a neighbor, for $40,000 ($1,000 per acre). Before closing it was discovered that the land contained valuable oil deposits, which fact if known at the time of contracting, would have justified a price of $400,000 ($10,000 per acre). Does Vendor have a case for rescission? Cf. Tetenman v. Epstein, 66 Cal.App. 745, 226 P. 966 (1924).

(b) The 1st Source Bank, as executor of the estate of Olga Mestrovic, deceased widow of renowned Yugoslavian sculptor Ivan Mestrovic, entered into a contract to sell the family home to Terrence and Antoinette Wilkin. No mention was made of any works of art. After closing, the Wilkins complained that the premises were left in a cluttered condition and needed extensive cleaning. The Bank proposed that they would arrange to have the cleaning done by a rubbish removal service, or that the Wilkins could clean the house themselves and retain any items of personal property which remained. The Wilkins opted to do the work themselves, and in so doing found eight drawings and a sculpture apparently created by Ivan Mestrovic. Neither the Bank nor the Wilkins suspected that any works of art remained on the premises. In a contest of ownership between the Bank and the Wilkins, who wins? See Wilkin v. 1st Source Bank, 548 N.E.2d 170 (Ind.App.1990).

(c) O was injured in an accident at work. The employer's Insurance Company admitted liability and requested that O enter the hospital for tests on the extent of the injuries. At the conclusion of the hospital stay and after evaluating the doctor's report, Insurance Company offered O $40,000 in full settlement of any and all claims under the policy. O accepted the offer and signed a release which, among other things, stated that it was a "general release of all claims for personal injuries, known or unknown." Later, O became seriously ill due to an internal trauma that was not detected in the medical examination. O claims that the release should be set aside for mutual mistake. Do you agree? Compare Obaitan v. State Farm, 1997 WL 208959 (Del.Ch.1997) with Gortney v. Norfolk & Western Ry. Co., 216 Mich.App. 535, 549 N.W.2d 612 (1996).

Comment: Reformation for Mistake in Expression

Reformation, like rescission, is an equitable remedy. Unlike rescission, however, reformation is designed to restore the efficacy of a writing which does not reflect the earlier agreement of the parties, frequently oral, which they apparently intended to be reflected in the writing. It has been described as a "way station" to some other remedy, in that the ultimate objective of the plaintiff is to enforce the writing as reformed. In the classic case for reformation, the plaintiff must show by clear and convincing evidence that the parties had actually reached agreement over the term at issue, that both intended the term to be included in a subsequent writing, and because of "mutual mistake" in expression, the term was not included. See Schroeder v. Gebhart, 825 So.2d 442, 446 (Fla.App.2002); Simek v. Cashin, 292 A.D.2d 439, 738 N.Y.S.2d 393 (N.Y.A.D.2002); Wellman Savings Bank v. Adams, 454 N.W.2d 852 (Iowa 1990); Novak v. Smith, 197 Ill.App.3d 390, 143 Ill.Dec. 717, 554 N.E.2d 652 (1990); United Bank of Ariz. v. Ashland Dev. Corp., 164 Ariz. 312, 792 P.2d 775 (App.1990) (reformation granted); Frantl Industries, Inc. v. Maier Construction, Inc., 68 Wis.2d 590, 229 N.W.2d 610 (1975). Since the defendant will invariably deny that he intended the term to be included in the writing, the plaintiff must shoulder an uphill burden in establishing the mistake. The "fault" of the plaintiff in not carefully reading the writing before signing or of an agent selected to reduce the agreement to writing, however, will not bar reformation if the plaintiff can otherwise demonstrate that both parties believed that the writing expressed their true agreement. See Treadaway v. Camellia Convalescent Hospitals, Inc., 43 Cal.App.3d 189, 118 Cal.Rptr. 341 (1974). On the other hand, if the "mutual" mistake is in the formulation rather than the expression of the agreement, the proper remedy is rescission rather than reformation of the contract. See Restatement (Second) §§ 153–155; National Resort Communities v. Cain, 526 S.W.2d 510 (Tex. 1975) (mutual mistake in formulation). See also Calamari & Perillo sec. 9.31–9.36.

As time passes, a broader basis for reformation may be emerging in the cases. Under the traditional view, reformation is granted only where there is a mutual mistake in expression. See, e.g., Hoffman v. Chapman, 182 Md. 208, 34 A.2d 438 (1943) (rescission is proper remedy for unilateral mistake, fraud, duress or other inequitable conduct). A slightly broader basis is found in New York, where the "classic" case for reformation is said to include mutual mistake in expression or a "mistake on plaintiff's part and a fraud by defendant." Brandwein v. Provident Mutual Life Insurance Co., 3 N.Y.2d 491, 168 N.Y.S.2d 964, 146 N.E.2d 693 (1957). See Barash v. Pennsylvania Terminal Real Estate Corp., 26 N.Y.2d 77, 308 N.Y.S.2d 649, 256 N.E.2d 707 (1970). An even broader basis for reformation is stated in Kufer v. Carson, 230 N.W.2d 500, 504 (Iowa 1975), where the court stated:

> Ultimately equity will grant relief if an instrument as written fails to express the true agreement between the parties without regard to the cause of the failure to express the agreement as actually made, whether it is due to fraud, mistake in the use of language, or anything else which prevented the instrument from expressing the true intention of the parties.

But see Atlas Corp. v. United States, 895 F.2d 745 (Fed.Cir.1990), holding that reformation for mutual mistake is not available where the facts upon which the mistake was based were not knowable at the time of contracting: "It is true that even though the outcome of a fact is unknowable, the parties can make a mistake concerning that fact. But where the existence of a fact is unknowable, the parties cannot have a belief concerning that fact, and they cannot make a mistake about it." 895 F.2d at 751.

Finally, some courts have "reformed" contracts to purge them of defects in the formulation process, such as illegality and unconscionability. See Karpinski v. Ingrasci, 28 N.Y.2d 45, 320 N.Y.S.2d 1, 268 N.E.2d 751 (1971) (illegality) and Jones v. Star Credit Corp., supra at 68 (where the court adjusted the agreed price to the amount already paid under the contract). See also UCC 2–302(1); 2–719(2) & (3). At least one court has "reformed" a contract to relieve a party whose duty of performance was excused due to mutual mistake and commercial impracticability. See Aluminum Co. of America v. Essex Group, Inc., 499 F.Supp. 53 (W.D.Pa.1980). These developments purport to grant "reformation" to remedy problems other than mistake in the expression of the agreement and, as you can plainly see, have little to do with the intention of the parties.

Ayer v. Western Union Telegraph Co.

Supreme Judicial Court of Maine, 1887.
79 Me. 493, 10 A. 495.

■ EMERY, J. On report. The defendant telegraph company was engaged in the business of transmitting messages by telegraph between Bangor and Philadelphia, and other points. The plaintiff, a lumber dealer in Bangor, delivered to the defendant company in Bangor, to be transmitted to his correspondent in Philadelphia, the following message: "Will sell 800 M laths, delivered at your wharf, two ten net cash. July shipment. Answer quick." The regular tariff rate was prepaid by the plaintiff for such transmission. The message delivered by the defendant company to the Philadelphia correspondent was as follows: "Will sell 800 M laths, delivered at your wharf, two net cash. July shipment. Answer quick." It will be seen that the important word "ten" in the statement of price was omitted. The Philadelphia party immediately returned by telegraph the following answer: "Accept your telegraphic offer on laths. Cannot increase price spruce." Letters afterwards passed between the parties, which disclosed the error in the transmission of the plaintiff's message. About two weeks after the discovery of the error, the plaintiff shipped the laths, as per the message received by his correspondent, to-wit, at two dollars per M. He testified that his correspondent insisted he was entitled to the laths at that price, and they were shipped accordingly.

The defendant telegraph company offered no evidence whatever, and did not undertake to account for or explain the mistake in the transmission of the message. The presumption therefore is that the mistake resulted from the fault of the telegraph company. * * *

The fault and consequent liability of the defendant company being thus established, the only remaining question is the extent of that liability in this case. The plaintiff claims it extends to the difference between the market price of laths and the price at which they were shipped. The defendant claims its liability is limited to the amount paid for the transmission of the message. * * *

The defendant company ... claims that the plaintiff was not in fact damaged to a greater extent than the price paid by him for the transmission. It contends that the plaintiff was not bound by the erroneous message delivered by the company to the Philadelphia party, and hence need not have shipped the laths at the lesser price. This raises the question whether the message written by the sender, and intrusted to the telegraph company for transmission, or the message written out and delivered by the company to the receiver at the other end of the line, as and for the message intended to be sent, is the better evidence of the rights of the receiver against the sender. The question is important and not easy of solution. It would be hard that the negligence of the telegraph company, or an error in transmission resulting from uncontrollable causes, should impose upon the innocent sender of a message a liability he never authorized nor contemplated. It would be equally hard that the innocent receiver, acting in good faith upon the message as received by him, should through such error lose all claim upon the sender. If one, owning merchandise, write a message offering to sell at a certain price, it would seem unjust that the telegraph company could bind him to sell at a less price, by making that error in the transmission. On the other hand, the receiver of the offer may in good faith, upon the strength of the telegram as received by him, have sold all the merchandise to arrive, perhaps at the same rate. It would seem unjust that he should have no claim for the merchandise. If an agent receives instructions by telegraph from his principal, and in good faith acts upon them as expressed in the message delivered him by the company, it would seem he ought to be held justified, though there were an error in the transmission.

It is evident that in case of an error in the transmission of a telegram either the sender or receiver must often suffer loss. As between the two, upon whom should the loss finally fall? We think the safer and more equitable rule, and the rule the public can most easily adapt itself to, is that, as between the sender and receiver, the party who selects the telegraph as the means of communication shall bear the loss caused by the errors of the telegraph. The first proposer can select one of many modes of communication, both for the proposal and the answer. The receiver has no such choice, except as to his answer. If he cannot safely act upon the message he received through the agency selected by the proposer, business must be seriously hampered and delayed. The use of the telegraph has become so general, and so many transactions are based on the words of the telegram received, that any other rule would now be impracticable.

Of course, the rule above stated presupposes the innocence of the receiver, and that there is nothing to cause him to suspect an error. If there be anything in the message, or in the attendant circumstances, or in the prior dealings of the parties, or in anything else, indicating a probable error in the transmission, good faith on the part of the receiver may require him to investigate before acting. Neither does the rule include forged messages, for in such case the supposed sender did not make any use of the telegraph.
* * *

It follows that the plaintiff in this case is entitled to recover the difference between the two dollars and the market price, as to laths. The evidence shows that the difference was 10 cents per M. Judgment for plaintiff for $80, with interest from the date of the writ.

NOTES

(1) How is it that the existence of a contract between the sender and the recipient of the message is put in issue in this case versus the telegraph company?

(2) Was Ayer in any way responsible for the mistake? How, then, is there justification for holding him to a contract on the altered terms? Do reasons of business policy support the decision? Does the case accord with the objective theory of contractual assent? What about economic efficiency?

PROBLEM: MISTAKES IN TRANSMISSION; THE OUTER FRINGES OF THE OBJECTIVE TEST

Sam, a breeder of race horses, owned Flasher and Dasher, who, as two-year olds, had shown great promise. Brenda, a sportsperson, was interested in buying one or both. She visited Sam's farm and, after some discussion, offered to buy Dasher for $5,000 and Flasher for $6,000. Sam replied that "under no circumstances" would he sell Flasher, who was promised to his daughter on her next birthday, but that he would sell Dasher to Brenda for $7,000. Brenda replied that the price on Dasher was "too high" but that if Sam could lower it a bit, please contact her at home some 500 miles away.

(1) The next day, Sam decided to sell Dasher to Brenda for $6,000. Accordingly, he typed out an offer to sell and placed it in a properly addressed, stamped envelope. On his way to the mail box, Sam had a change of mind. Before he could return to his office, however, Sam was struck by a bicycle and knocked unconscious. A stranger, seeing the letter on the sidewalk, mailed it and upon receipt the next day, Brenda promptly telegraphed an acceptance and resold Dasher to Thad, a friend, for $8,000. Later, the fully conscious Sam telephoned to say that he did not intend to sell Dasher. Is there a contract to sell Dasher?

(2) Suppose that Sam had indicated an offer to sell Dasher for $6,000, but his secretary typed Flasher instead and Sam signed the letter without reading. Upon receipt, Brenda promptly telegraphed "accept your offer to sell Flasher" and resold Flasher to Thad for $8,000. Is there a contract to sell Flasher? How about Dasher? Compare Restatement, Second, sec. 20(2) with CISG Art. 8(1).

(3) Suppose that Sam went to a telegraph office and upon a standard form clearly wrote the following: "Will sell Dasher to you for $6,000." The form contained a limitation of liability approved by the Federal Communications Commission that the company would not be liable for mistakes or delays in transmission beyond the sum of $500, unless the message was sent at repeated message rates or was specially valued. The outer limit of liability for a repeated message was $5,000. Sam read the limitation and chose not to pay the extra charge for a repeated or specially valued message. Due to a mistake of the telegraph company, the telegram as sent offered to sell Dasher for $5,000. Brenda promptly telegraphed her acceptance and resold Dasher to Thad for $8,000. Is there a contract to sell Dasher for $5,000? Assuming that the telegraph company was negligent, what is its liability, if any, to Sam? To Brenda? To Thad?

(B) FRAUD AND THE DUTY TO DISCLOSE

Contract law concerns not only promises to do (or to refrain from doing) future acts, it also concerns representations of existing fact (and the implicit promise that all contractual representations are true). This section explores the legal consequences of intentionally misrepresenting facts (i.e., fraud) or failing to make a representation (i.e., failure to disclose).

Laidlaw v. Organ

Supreme Court of the United States, 1817.
15 U.S. 178, 2 Wheat. 178.

[Error to the district court for the Louisiana district. The plaintiff/buyer (defendant in error), Organ, filed suit against Laidlaw, the defendant/seller (plaintiff in error), seeking to recover possession of 111 hogsheads of tobacco that defendant took from plaintiff's possession. Defendant initially delivered the tobacco to plaintiff under a contract for $7,544.69, but later the defendant/seller "by force, and of their own wrong, took possession of the same." The defendant/seller alleged, however, that fraud in the inception nullified its duty to sell: "[O]n the night of the 18th of February, 1815, [messengers] brought from the British fleet news that a treaty of peace had been signed at Ghent by the American and British commissioners [ending the war of 1812 and consequently the British blockade of New Orleans]. This news was "made public in a handbill on Sunday morning, 8 o'clock, the 19th of February, 1815." Plaintiff called defendant "(with whom he had been bargaining for the tobacco mentioned in the petition, the evening previous,) ... soon after sunrise on the morning of Sunday, the 19th of February, 1815, before [defendant] had heard said news. [Defendant] asked if there was any news which was calculated to enhance the price or value of the article about to be purchased." The plaintiff apparently remained silent; "the purchase was then and there made ... and in consequence of said news the value of said article had risen from 30 to 50 per cent." The lower court found for the plaintiff.]

* * *

C. J. Ingersoll, for the plaintiffs in error. The first question is, whether the sale, under the circumstances of the case, was a valid sale; whether fraud, which vitiates every contract, must be proved by the communication of positive misinformation, or by withholding information when asked. Suppression of material circumstances within the knowledge of the vendee, and not accessible to the vendor, is equivalent to fraud, and vitiates the contract. Pothier, in discussing this subject, adopts the distinction of the forum of conscience, and the forum of law; but he admits that fides est servanda. The parties treated on an unequal footing, as the one party had received intelligence of the peace of Ghent, at the time of the contract, and the other had not. This news was unexpected, even at Washington, much more at New–Orleans, the recent scene of the most sanguinary operations of the war. In answer to the question, whether there was any news calculated to enhance the price of the article, the vendee was silent. This reserve, when such a question was asked, was equivalent to a false answer, and as much calculated to deceive as the communication of the most fabulous intelligence. Though the plaintiffs in error, after they heard the news of peace, still went on, in ignorance of their legal rights, to complete the contract, equity will protect them. . . .

Key, contra. . . . The only real question in the cause is, whether the sale was invalid because the vendee did not communicate information which he received precisely as the vendor might have got it had he been equally diligent or equally fortunate? And, surely, on this question there can be no doubt. Even if the vendor had been entitled to the disclosure, he waived it by not insisting on an answer to his question; and the silence of the vendee might as well have been interpreted into an affirmative as a negative answer. But, on principle, he was not bound to disclose. Even admitting that his conduct was unlawful, in foro conscientiae, does that prove that it was so in the civil forum? Human laws are imperfect in this respect, and the sphere of morality is more extensive than the limits of civil jurisdiction. The maxim of caveat emptor could never have crept into the law, if the province of ethics had been co-extensive with it. There was, in the present case, no circumvention or manaeuvre practised by the vendee, unless rising earlier in the morning, and obtaining by superior diligence and alertness that intelligence by which the price of commodities was regulated, be such. It is a romantic equality that is contended for on the other side. Parties never can be precisely equal in knowledge, either of facts or of the inferences from such facts, and both must concur in order to satisfy the rule contended for. The absence of all authority in England and the United States, both great commercial countries, speaks volumes against the reasonableness and practicability of such a rule.

C. J. Ingersoll, in reply. Though the record may not show that any thing tending to mislead by positive assertion was said by the vendee, in answer to the question proposed by Mr. Girault, yet it is a case of manaeuvre; of mental reservation; of circumvention. The information was monopolized by the messengers from the British fleet, and not imparted to the public at large until it was too late for the vendor to save himself. The rule of law and of ethics is the same. It is not a romantic, but a practical and legal rule of equality and good faith that is proposed to be applied.

Marshall, Ch. J. The question in this case is, whether the intelligence of extrinsic circumstances, which might influence the price of the commodity, and which was exclusively within the knowledge of the vendee, ought to have been communicated by him to the vendor? The court is of opinion that he was not bound to communicate it. It would be difficult to circumscribe the contrary doctrine within proper limits, where the means of intelligence are equally accessible to both parties. But at the same time, each party must take care not to say or do any thing tending to impose upon the other. The court thinks that the absolute instruction of the judge was erroneous, and that the question, whether any imposition was practised by the vendee upon the vendor ought to have been submitted to the jury. For these reasons the judgment must be reversed, and the cause remanded to the district court of Louisiana, with directions to award a venire facias de novo.

Venire de novo awarded.

NOTES

(1) Anthony Kronman in *Mistake, Disclosure, Information and the Law of Contracts*, 7 J. Legal Stud. 1 (1978) distinguishes between deliberately-acquired and casually-acquired information. Kronman argues that the law should not require contractual parties to disclose deliberately-acquired information so that private parties can profit from this type of private information and hence be encouraged to create it.

(2) Robert Cooter and Tom Ulen in Law and Economics 258–61 (1988), however have drawn a second useful distinction between "productive facts" ("information that can be used to increase wealth") and "redistributive facts" ("information creating a bargaining advantage that can be used to redistribute wealth in favor of the knowledgeable party but that does not lead to the creation of new wealth"). Which type of information is at stake in *Laidlaw*? See Steven Shavell, *Acquisition and Disclosure of Information Prior to Sale*, 25 Rand J. Econ. 20 (1994) (using this distinction to argue sellers should be required to disclose so that they do not have unduly high incentives to acquire information, but that buyers be allowed to conceal their information).

(3) *Laidlaw* teaches that by asking a question a promisee might create a duty of disclosure for a promissor. Alternatively, a promisee could demand an explicit representation from a promissor that she has no material non-public information concerning the contract. But a promisee might also indirectly create an duty of disclosure in the promissor (not by asking a question or demanding a representation but) merely by making a representation herself. See Restatement (Second) of Contracts § 161 (1981) (disclosure required if necessary to "correct a mistake of the other party as to a basic assumption on which that party is making the contract").

Vokes v. Arthur Murray, Inc.

District Court of Appeal of Florida, Second District, 1968.
212 So.2d 906.

■ PIERCE, JUDGE.

This is an appeal by Audrey E. Vokes, plaintiff below, from a final order dismissing with prejudice, for failure to state a cause of action, her fourth amended complaint, hereinafter referred to as plaintiff's complaint.

Defendant Arthur Murray, Inc., a corporation, authorizes the operation throughout the nation of dancing schools under the name of "Arthur Murray School of Dancing" through local franchised operators, one of whom was defendant J.P. Davenport whose dancing establishment was in Clearwater.

Plaintiff Mrs. Audrey E. Vokes, a widow of 51 years and without family, had a yen to be "an accomplished dancer" with the hopes of finding "new interest in life". So, on February 10, 1961, a dubious fate, with the assist of a motivated acquaintance, procured her to attend a "dance party" at Davenport's "School of Dancing" where she whiled away the pleasant hours, sometimes in a private room, absorbing his accomplished sales technique, during which her grace and poise were elaborated upon and her rosy future as "an excellent dancer" was painted for her in vivid and glowing colors. As an incident to this interlude, he sold her eight ½-hour dance lessons to be utilized within one calendar month therefrom, for the sum of $14.50 cash in hand paid, obviously a baited "come-on".

Thus she embarked upon an almost endless pursuit of the terpsichorean art during which, over a period of less than sixteen months, she was sold fourteen "dance courses" totalling in the aggregate 2302 hours of dancing lessons for a total cash outlay of $31,090.45, all at Davenport's dance emporium. All of these fourteen courses were evidenced by execution of a written "Enrollment Agreement—Arthur Murray's School of Dancing" with the addendum in heavy black print, "No one will be informed that you are taking dancing lessons. Your relations with us are held in strict confidence", setting forth the number of "dancing lessons" and the "lessons in rhythm sessions" currently sold to her from time to time, and always of course accompanied by payment of cash of the realm.

These dance lesson contracts and the monetary consideration therefor of over $31,000 were procured from her by means and methods of Davenport and his associates which went beyond the unsavory, yet legally permissible, perimeter of "sales puffing" and intruded well into the forbidden area of undue influence, the suggestion of falsehood, the suppression of truth, and the free exercise of rational judgment, if what plaintiff alleged in her complaint was true. From the time of her first contract with the dancing school in February, 1961, she was influenced unwittingly by a constant and continuous barrage of flattery, false praise, excessive compliments, and panegyric encomiums, to such extent that it would be not only inequitable, but unconscionable, for a Court exercising inherent chancery power to allow such contracts to stand.

She was incessantly subjected to overreaching blandishment and cajolery. She was assured she had "grace and poise"; that she was "rapidly improving and developing in her dancing skill"; that the additional lessons would "make her a beautiful dancer, capable of dancing with the most accomplished dancers"; that she was "rapidly progressing in the development of her dancing skill and gracefulness", etc., etc. She was given "dance aptitude tests" for the ostensible purpose of "determining" the number of remaining hours of instructions needed by her from time to time.

At one point she was sold 545 additional hours of dancing lessons to be entitled to award of the "Bronze Medal" signifying that she had reached "the Bronze Standard", a supposed designation of dance achievement by students of Arthur Murray, Inc.

Later she was sold an additional 926 hours in order to gain the "Silver Medal", indicating she had reached "the Silver Standard", at a cost of $12,501.35.

At one point, while she still had to her credit about 900 unused hours of instructions, she was induced to purchase an additional 24 hours of lessons to participate in a trip to Miami at her own expense, where she would be "given the opportunity to dance with members of the Miami Studio".

She was induced at another point to purchase an additional 126 hours of lessons in order to be not only eligible for the Miami trip but also to become "a life member of the Arthur Murray Studio", carrying with it certain dubious emoluments, at a further cost of $1,752.30.

At another point, while she still had over 1,000 unused hours of instruction she was induced to buy 151 additional hours at a cost of $2,049.00 to be eligible for a "Student Trip to Trinidad", at her own expense as she later learned.

Also, when she still had 1100 unused hours to her credit, she was prevailed upon to purchase an additional 347 hours at a cost of $4,235.74, to qualify her to receive a "Gold Medal" for achievement, indicating she had advanced to "the Gold Standard".

On another occasion, while she still had over 1200 unused hours, she was induced to buy an additional 175 hours of instruction at a cost of $2,472.75 to be eligible "to take a trip to Mexico".

Finally, sandwiched in between other lesser sales promotions, she was influenced to buy an additional 481 hours of instruction at a cost of $6,523.81 in order to "be classified as a Gold Bar Member, the ultimate achievement of the dancing studio".

All the foregoing sales promotions, illustrative of the entire fourteen separate contracts, were procured by defendant Davenport and Arthur Murray, Inc., by false representations to her that she was improving in her dancing ability, that she had excellent potential, that she was responding to instructions in dancing grace, and that they were developing her into a beautiful dancer, whereas in truth and in fact she did not develop in her dancing ability, she had no "dance aptitude", and in fact had difficulty in "hearing the musical beat". The complaint alleged that such representations to her "were in fact false and known by the defendant to be false and contrary to the plaintiff's true ability, the truth of plaintiff's ability being fully known to the defendants, but withheld from the plaintiff for the sole and specific intent to deceive and defraud the plaintiff and to induce her in the purchasing of additional hours of dance lessons". It was averred that the lessons were sold to her "in total disregard to the true physical, rhythm, and mental ability of the plaintiff". In other words, while she first exulted that she was entering the "spring of her life", she finally was awakened to the fact there was "spring" neither in her life nor in her feet.

The complaint prayed that the Court decree the dance contracts to be null and void and to be cancelled, that an accounting be had, and judgment entered against the defendants "for that portion of the $31,090.45 not charged against specific hours of instruction given to the plaintiff". The Court held the complaint not to state a cause of action and dismissed it with prejudice. We disagree and reverse.

The material allegations of the complaint must, of course, be accepted as true for the purpose of testing its legal sufficiency. Defendants contend that contracts can only be rescinded for fraud or misrepresentation when the alleged misrepresentation is as to a material fact, rather than an opinion, prediction or expectation, and that the statements and representations set forth at length in the complaint were in the category of "trade puffing", within its legal orbit.

It is true that "generally a misrepresentation, to be actionable, must be one of fact rather than of opinion". Tonkovich v. South Florida Citrus Industries, Inc., Fla.App.1966; Kutner v. Kalish, Fla.App.1965. But this rule has significant qualifications, applicable here. It does not apply where there is a fiduciary relationship between the parties, or where there has been some artifice or trick employed by the representor, or where the parties do not in general deal at "arm's length" as we understand the phrase, or where the representee does not have equal opportunity to become apprised of the truth or falsity of the fact represented. 14 Fla.Jur. Fraud and Deceit, § 28; Kitchen v. Long, 1914, 67 Fla. 72. As stated by Judge Allen of this Court in Ramel v. Chasebrook Construction Company, Fla.App.1961:

> " * * * A statement of a party having * * * superior knowledge may be regarded as a statement of fact although it would be considered as opinion if the parties were dealing on equal terms."

It could be reasonably supposed here that defendants had "superior knowledge" as to whether plaintiff had "dance potential" and as to whether she was noticeably improving in the art of terpsichore. And it would be a reasonable inference from the undenied averments of the complaint that the flowery eulogiums heaped upon her by defendants as a prelude to her contracting for 1944 additional hours of instruction in order to attain the rank of the Bronze Standard, thence to the bracket of the Silver Standard, thence to the class of the Gold Bar Standard, and finally to the crowning plateau of a Life Member of the Studio, proceeded as much or more from the urge to "ring the cash register" as from any honest or realistic appraisal of her dancing prowess or a factual representation of her progress.

Even in contractual situations where a party to a transaction owes no duty to disclose facts within his knowledge or to answer inquiries respecting such facts, the law is if he undertakes to do so he must disclose the *whole truth*.... From the face of the complaint, it should have been reasonably apparent to defendants that her vast outlay of cash for the many hundreds of additional hours of instruction was not justified by her slow and awkward progress, which she would have been made well aware of if they had spoken the "whole truth".

In Hirschman v. Hodges, etc., 1910, 59 Fla. 517, it was said that—

> " * * * what is plainly injurious to good faith ought to be considered as a fraud sufficient to impeach a contract",

and that an improvident agreement may be avoided—

" * * * because of surprise, or mistake, *want of freedom, undue influence, the suggestion of falsehood, or the suppression of truth*". (Emphasis supplied.)

We repeat that where parties are dealing on a contractual basis at arm's length with no inequities or inherently unfair practices employed, the Courts will in general "leave the parties where they find themselves". But in the case sub judice, from the allegations of the unanswered complaint, we cannot say that enough of the accompanying ingredients, as mentioned in the foregoing authorities, were not present which otherwise would have barred the equitable arm of the Court to her. In our view, from the showing made in her complaint, plaintiff is entitled to her day in Court.

It accordingly follows that the order dismissing plaintiff's last amended complaint with prejudice should be and is reversed.

Reversed.

NOTES

(1) *Fraud: Kaleidoscopic and Infinite.* "Fraud is kaleidoscopic, infinite. Fraud being infinite and taking on protean form at will, were courts to cramp themselves by defining it with a hard and fast definition, their jurisdiction would be cunningly circumvented at once by new schemes beyond the definition. Messieurs, the fraud-feasors, would like nothing half so well as for courts to say they would go thus far, and no further in its pursuit. * * * Accordingly definitions of fraud are of set purpose left general and flexible, and thereto courts match their astuteness against the versatile inventions of fraud-doers." Stonemets v. Head, 248 Mo. 243, 263, 154 S.W. 108, 114 (1913).

(2) *Statutory Protection.* Not only is fraud "kaleidoscopic," so also are the judicial attempts to reach the varieties of deceptive practices. The court in *Vokes* drew upon a tradition of case law under which the agreement might be rescinded. In a similar case, a Texas court awarded treble damages and attorney's fees, pursuant to a statute entitled "Deceptive Trade Practices— Consumer Protection Act." Bennett v. Bailey, 597 S.W.2d 532 (Tex.Civ.App. 1980). Statutes of this type figure prominently in contemporary litigation, granting additional rights not only to consumers but in some instances commercial parties as well. See infra at 514.

(3) Collateral Reading: Restatement (Second) §§ 159–173; Farnsworth §§ 4.10–4.15; Dobbs §§ 9.1–9.6; Calarmari & Perillo §§ 9–13—9–24; Murray § 95; Prosser (5th ed.) §§ 105–110.

Comment: Misrepresentation, Rescission and Restitution

A misrepresentation is "an assertion that is not in accord with the facts." Restatement (Second) § 159. The effect of such an assertion by one party inducing another to enter into a contract may be to provide the latter with a tort claim for damages, or alternatively, the aggrieved party may sue to rescind the contract because of the other's deceptive language or conduct. In general, the misrepresentation must be an assertion or affirmation of an existing fact (not an expression of opinion, a promise to do something in the future, or a prediction of future events) upon which the other party justifiably relies in entering the contract. The misrepresentation may be fraudulent or innocent. Moreover, the misrepresentation may be the assertion of a "half truth" or consist of the concealment of a fact (e.g., covering over the evidence of termite infestation to mislead prospective purchaser) or even the failure to disclose. Finally, the usual effect of wrongful misrepresentation is to render the contract "voidable," but courts have identified a kind of fraud in the "execution" (as distinguished from the ordinary fraud in the "inducement") which precludes the formation of any contract at all (or, as is sometimes said, a "void" contract). An example is where a party secures another's signature by misrepresenting the character of the document. See Restatement (Second) § 163.

A good statement of the law of "innocent misrepresentation" is found in Norton v. Poplos, 443 A.2d 1 (Del.1982)

> Essentially, the equitable remedy of rescission results in abrogation or "unmaking" of an agreement, and attempts to return the parties to the *status quo*. Common grounds for rescission of a contract for the sale of real property include fraud, misrepresentation and mistake. . . .
>
> But in addition to rescission for fraudulent misrepresentation, rescission also may be granted under certain circumstances for innocent misrepresentations made by a seller. Thus, as stated by Professor Williston:
>
> It is not necessary, in order that a contract may be rescinded for fraud or misrepresentation, that the party making the misrepresentation should have known that it was false. Innocent misrepresentation is sufficient for though the representation may have been made innocently, it would be unjust and inequitable to permit a person who has made false representations, even innocently, to retain the fruits of a bargain induced by such representations.
>
> Similarly, Restatement 2d of Contracts, § 164, states that,
>
>> If a party's manifestation of assent is induced by either a fraudulent *or material* misrepresentation by the other party upon which the recipient is justified in relying, the contract is voidable by the recipient." (Emphasis added.)
>
> See also Restatement, First § 476 (1932). Most American jurisdictions which have addressed this issue appear to recognize that an innocent material misrepresentation by a vendor which induces the sale of the property is ground for rescission of the contract. In addition to ordering rescission, a court will generally direct that a down payment by a buyer be returned on a theory of restitution. . . .
>
> A misrepresentation need not be in the form of written or spoken words. Stated simply, a misrepresentation is merely an "assertion not in accordance with the facts," Restatement 2d of Contracts, § 159, and such an assertion may be made by conduct as well as words. Id. Comment a. And although a statement or assertion may be facially true, it may constitute an actionable misrepresentation if it causes a

false impression as to the true state of affairs, and the actor fails to provide qualifying information to cure the mistaken belief.... Stated another way,

> [a] statement may be true with respect to the facts stated, but may fail to include qualifying matters necessary to prevent the implication of an assertion that is false with respect to other facts. For example a true statement that an event has recently occurred may carry the false implication that the situation has not changed since its occurrence. Such half-truth may be as misleading as an assertion that is wholly false."

Restatement 2d of Contracts, § 159, comment b."

One remedy for misrepresentation is to rescind the contract.

The purpose of rescission, whether through a legal or equitable action, is "restitutionary;" i.e., there is a dissolution or "undoing" of the contract and a restoration of the parties to their pre-contract position (*status quo ante*). Originally, rescission was exclusively an equitable remedy, but eventually law courts recognized the right to utilize rescission as a way of securing appropriate restitutionary relief. Whether equitable or legal rescission, an "adjustment of the equities" of the parties is a matter of major concern. For example, "when a party elects to rescind the contract, he is only entitled to a return to the status quo. This usually requires a plaintiff to restore *any benefit* he received under the contract, *including a return in specie of any property received and a reasonable rental value for the use of the property*, plus damages for waste if any. Likewise, *the defendant must restore any money paid by the plaintiff under the contract plus interest*, monetary reimbursement for reasonable repairs, expenditures and improvements made on the property by the plaintiff, and, where a business has been sold, a reasonable amount of compensation for the value of the plaintiff's labor and services rendered during the period of time which he operated and possessed the property...." Smeekens v. Bertrand, 262 Ind. 50, 58, 311 N.E.2d 431 (1974) (emphasis in original).

According to Professor Dan Dobbs: "The most common way in which fraud litigation reaches the courts is in the direct action for damages—the action that once would have been called the deceit action. However, fraud is also grounds for rescission of a transaction fraudulently induced. Where, as a result of one party's fraud, the other party is induced to sign an instrument that does not express their true agreement, the reformation remedy is the appropriate one.

The constructive trust is quite suited to fraud cases and often furnishes a useful remedy as does the equitable lien.

At other times, the fraud is not the basis of an action or claim at all, but is merely operable as a defense or as an estoppel.

In any kind of case the remedy available should carry out the substantive policy in question. In fraud cases perhaps more than others the relation between substance and remedy is an especially close one. If the plaintiff demands a relatively mild remedy—rescission—he may be given relief even if he does not show actual intent to deceive by the defendant. On the other hand, if he seeks a harsher damages measure, many courts will require him to show such an intent. It is for this reason quite impossible to separate completely the substantive and remedial rules in fraud cases. Dobbs § 9.1.

Hill v. Jones

Court of Appeals of Arizona, 1986.
151 Ariz. 81, 725 P.2d 1115.

■ MEYERSON, JUDGE.

Must the seller of a residence disclose to the buyer facts pertaining to past termite infestation? This is the primary question presented in this appeal. Plaintiffs Warren G. Hill and Gloria R. Hill (buyers) filed suit to rescind an agreement to purchase a residence. Buyers alleged that Ora G. Jones and Barbara R. Jones (sellers) had made misrepresentations concerning termite damage in the residence and had failed to disclose to them the existence of the damage and history of termite infestation in the residence. The trial court dismissed the claim for misrepresentation based upon a so-called integration clause in the parties' agreement.

Sellers then sought summary judgment on the "concealment" claim arguing that they had no duty to disclose information pertaining to termite infestation and that even if they did, the record failed to show all of the elements necessary for fraudulent concealment. The trial court granted summary judgment, finding that there was "no genuinely disputed issue of material fact and that the law favors the ... defendants." The trial court awarded sellers $1,000.00 in attorney's fees. Buyers have appealed from the judgment and sellers have cross-appealed from the trial court's ruling on attorney's fees.

I. FACTS

In 1982, buyers entered into an agreement to purchase sellers' residence for $72,000. The agreement was entered after buyers made several visits to the home. The purchase agreement provided that sellers were to pay for and place in escrow a termite inspection report stating that the property was free from evidence of termite infestation. Escrow was scheduled to close two months later.

One of the central features of the house is a parquet teak floor covering the sunken living room, the dining room, the entryway and portions of the halls. On a subsequent visit to the house, and when sellers were present, buyers noticed a small "ripple" in the wood floor on the step leading up to the dining room from the sunken living room. Mr. Hill asked if the ripple could be termite damage. Mrs. Jones answered that it was water damage. A few years previously, a broken water heater in the house had in fact caused water damage in the area of the dining room and steps which necessitated that some repairs be made to the floor. No further discussion on the subject, however, took place between the parties at that time or afterwards.

Mr. Hill, through his job as maintenance supervisor at a school district, had seen similar "ripples" in wood which had turned out to be termite damage. Mr. Hill was not totally satisfied with Mrs. Jones's explanation, but he felt that the termite inspection report would reveal whether the ripple was due to termites or some other cause.

The termite inspection report stated that there was no visible evidence of infestation. The report failed to note the existence of physical damage or evidence of previous treatment. The realtor notified the parties that the property had passed the termite inspection. Apparently, neither party actually saw the report prior to close of escrow.

After moving into the house, buyers found a pamphlet left in one of the drawers entitled "Termites, the Silent Saboteurs." They learned from a neighbor that the house had some termite infestation in the past. Shortly after the close of escrow, Mrs. Hill noticed that the wood on the steps leading down to the sunken living room was crumbling. She called an exterminator who confirmed the existence of termite damage to the floor and steps and to wood columns in the house. The estimated cost of repairing the wood floor alone was approximately $5,000.

Through discovery after their lawsuit was filed, buyers learned the following. When sellers purchased the residence in 1974, they received two termite guarantees that had been given to the previous owner by Truly Nolen, as well as a diagram showing termite treatment at the residence that had taken place in 1963. The guarantees provided for semi-annual inspections and annual termite booster treatments. The accompanying diagram stated that the existing damage had not been repaired. The second guarantee, dated 1965, reinstated the earlier contract for inspection and treatment. Mr. Jones admitted that he read the guarantees when he received them. Sellers renewed the guarantees when they purchased the residence in 1974. They also paid the annual fee each year until they sold the home.

On two occasions during sellers' ownership of the house but while they were at their other residence in Minnesota, a neighbor noticed "streamers" evidencing live termites in the wood tile floor near the entryway. On both occasions, Truly Nolen gave a booster treatment for termites. On the second incident, Truly Nolen drilled through one of the wood tiles to treat for termites. The neighbor showed Mr. Jones the area where the damage and treatment had occurred. Sellers had also seen termites on the back fence and had replaced and treated portions of the fence.

Sellers did not mention any of this information to buyers prior to close of escrow. They did not mention the past termite infestation and treatment to the realtor or to the termite inspector. There was evidence of holes on the patio that had been drilled years previously to treat for termites. The inspector returned to the residence to determine why he had not found evidence of prior treatment and termite damage. He indicated that he had

not seen the holes in the patio because of boxes stacked there. It is unclear
whether the boxes had been placed there by buyers or sellers. He had not
found the damage inside the house because a large plant, which buyers had
purchased from sellers, covered the area. After investigating the second
time, the inspector found the damage and evidence of past treatment. He
acknowledged that this information should have appeared in the report. He
complained, however, that he should have been told of any history of
termite infestation and treatment before he performed his inspection and
that it was customary for the inspector to be given such information.

Other evidence presented to the trial court was that during their
numerous visits to the residence before close of escrow, buyers had unrestricted access to view and inspect the entire house. Both Mr. and Mrs. Hill
had seen termite damage and were therefore familiar with what it might
look like. Mr. Hill had seen termite damage on the fence at this property.
Mrs. Hill had noticed the holes on the patio but claimed not to realize at
the time what they were for. Buyers asked no questions about termites
except when they asked if the "ripple" on the stairs was termite damage.
Mrs. Hill admitted she was not "trying" to find problems with the house
because she really wanted it.

II.   CONTRACT INTEGRATION CLAUSE

[The court held that an integration clause in the contract could not exclude
representations by the Owner, whether made before or after the contract
was signed, that were relevant to the defense of fraud.]

III.   DUTY TO DISCLOSE

The principal legal question presented in this appeal is whether a seller
has a duty to disclose to the buyer the existence of termite damage in a
residential dwelling known to the seller, but not to the buyer, which
materially affects the value of the property. For the reasons stated herein,
we hold that such a duty exists.

This is not the place to trace the history of the doctrine of caveat
emptor. Suffice it to say that its vitality has waned during the latter half of
the 20th century. . . . The modern view is that a vendor has an affirmative
duty to disclose material facts where:

1.   Disclosure is necessary to prevent a previous assertion from
being a misrepresentation or from being fraudulent or material;

2.   Disclosure would correct a mistake of the other party as to a
basic assumption on which that party is making the contract and if
nondisclosure amounts to a failure to act in good faith and in accordance with reasonable standards of fair dealing;

3.   Disclosure would correct a mistake of the other party as to the
contents or effect of a writing, evidencing or embodying an agreement
in whole or in part;

4.   The other person is entitled to know the fact because of a
relationship of trust and confidence between them.

Restatement (Second) of Contracts § 161 (1981) (Restatement); see Restatement (Second) of Torts § 551 (1977).

Arizona courts have long recognized that under certain circumstances there may be a "duty to speak." ... As the supreme court noted in the context of a confidential relationship, "[s]uppression of a material fact which a party is bound in good faith to disclose is equivalent to a false representation." Leigh v. Loyd, 74 Ariz. 84, 87 (1952); ...

Must you disclose materiality?

Are termites Material ?

Thus, the important question we must answer is whether under the facts of this case, buyers should have been permitted to present to the jury their claim that sellers were under a duty to disclose their (sellers') knowledge of termite infestation in the residence. This broader question involves two inquiries. First, must a seller of residential property advise the buyer of material facts within his knowledge pertaining to the value of the property? Second, may termite damage and the existence of past infestation constitute such material facts?

The doctrine imposing a duty to disclose is akin to the well-established contractual rules pertaining to relief from contracts based upon mistake. Although the law of contracts supports the finality of transactions, over the years courts have recognized that under certain limited circumstances it is unjust to strictly enforce the policy favoring finality. Thus, for example, even a unilateral mistake of one party to a transaction may justify rescission. Restatement § 153.

There is also a judicial policy promoting honesty and fair dealing in business relationships. This policy is expressed in the law of fraudulent and negligent misrepresentations. Where a misrepresentation is fraudulent or where a negligent misrepresentation is one of material fact, the policy of finality rightly gives way to the policy of promoting honest dealings between the parties. See Restatement § 164(1).

Under certain circumstances nondisclosure of a fact known to one party may be equivalent to the assertion that the fact does not exist. For example "[w]hen one conveys a false impression by the disclosure of some facts and the concealment of others, such concealment is in effect a false representation that what is disclosed is the whole truth." State v. Coddington, 135 Ariz. 480, 481 (App.1983). Thus, nondisclosure may be equated with and given the same legal effect as fraud and misrepresentation. One category of cases where this has been done involves the area of nondisclosure of material facts affecting the value of property, known to the seller but not reasonably capable of being known to the buyer.

Should they have noticed the damage?

Courts have formulated this "duty to disclose" in slightly different ways. For example, the Florida Supreme Court recently declared that "where the seller of a home knows of facts materially affecting the value of the property which are not readily observable and are not known to the buyer, the seller is under a duty to disclose them to the buyer." Johnson v. Davis, 480 So.2d 625, 629 (Fla.1985) (defective roof in three-year old home). In California, the rule has been stated this way:

[W]here the seller knows of facts materially affecting the value or desirability of the property which are known or accessible only to him and also knows that such facts are not known to, or within the reach of the diligent attention and observation of the buyer, the seller is under a duty to disclose them to the buyer.

Lingsch v. Savage, 213 Cal.App.2d 729, 735 (1963); contra Ray v. Montgomery, 399 So.2d 230 (Ala.1980); see generally W. Prosser & W. Keeton, The Law of Torts § 106 (5th ed. 1984).[2] We find that the Florida formulation of the disclosure rule properly balances the legitimate interests of the parties in a transaction for the sale of a private residence and accordingly adopt it for such cases.

As can be seen, the rule requiring disclosure is invoked in the case of material facts.[3] Thus, we are led to the second inquiry—whether the existence of termite damage in a residential dwelling is the type of material fact which gives rise to the duty to disclose. The existence of termite damage and past termite infestation has been considered by other courts to be sufficiently material to warrant disclosure. See generally Annot., 22 A.L.R.3d 972 (1968). * * *

Although sellers have attempted to draw a distinction between live termites[4] and past infestation, the concept of materiality is an elastic one which is not limited by the termites' health. "A matter is material if it is one to which a reasonable person would attach importance in determining his choice of action in the transaction in question." Lynn v. Taylor, 7 Kan.App.2d at 371. For example, termite damage substantially affecting the structural soundness of the residence may be material even if there is no evidence of present infestation. Unless reasonable minds could not differ, materiality is a factual matter which must be determined by the trier of fact. The termite damage in this case may or may not be material. Accordingly, we conclude that buyers should be allowed to present their case to a jury.

Sellers argue that even assuming the existence of a duty to disclose, summary judgment was proper because the record shows that their "silence ... did not induce or influence" the buyers. This is so, sellers contend, because Mr. Hill stated in his deposition that he intended to rely on the termite inspection report. But this argument begs the question. If sellers were fully aware of the extent of termite damage and if such information had been disclosed to buyers, a jury could accept Mr. Hill's

---

2. There are variations on this same theme. For example, Pennsylvania has limited the obligation of disclosure to cases of dangerous defects. Glanski v. Ervine, 269 Pa.Super. 182, 191 (1979).

3. Arizona has recognized that a duty to disclose may arise where the buyer makes an inquiry of the seller, regardless of whether or not the fact is material. Universal Inv. Co. v. Sahara Motor Inn, Inc., 127 Ariz. 213, 215

(1980). The inquiry by buyers whether the ripple was termite damage imposed a duty upon sellers to disclose what information they knew concerning the existence of termite infestation in the residence.

4. Sellers acknowledge that a duty of disclosure would exist if live termites were present. Obde v. Schlemeyer, 56 Wash.2d 449 (1960).

testimony that had he known of the termite damage he would not have purchased the house.

Sellers further contend that buyers were put on notice of the possible existence of termite infestation and were therefore "chargeable with the knowledge which [an] inquiry, if made, would have revealed." Godfrey v. Navratil, 3 Ariz.App. 47, 51 (1966). It is also true that "a party may ... reasonably expect the other to take normal steps to inform himself and to draw his own conclusions." Restatement § 161 comment d. Under the facts of this case, the question of buyers' knowledge of the termite problem (or their diligence in attempting to inform themselves about the termite problem) should be left to the jury.[5]

By virtue of our holding, sellers' cross-appeal is moot. Reversed and remanded.

NOTES

(1) *Duty of Disclosure in Contract Negotiations.* What is the scope of the duty to disclose material facts during contract negotiations? See Laidlaw v. Organ, *supra* at 498.

One statement of the guidelines was made in Simpson Timber Co. v. Palmberg Construction Co., 377 F.2d 380, 385 (9th Cir.1967): "It is well settled that in the absence of a duty to speak, silence as to a material fact does not of itself constitute fraud. ... On the other hand, once a duty to disclose has arisen, suppression of a material fact is tantamount to an affirmative misrepresentation. ... However, businessmen dealing at arm's length are rarely under a duty to speak." As another court observed with disquieting candor, in the absence of rather special circumstances the standards of conduct rise "no higher than the morals of the market place." Rader v. Boyd, 252 F.2d 585, 587 (10th Cir.1957).

The presence of a fiduciary or confidential relationship is a traditional reason for augmenting a party's duty to disclose. As stated by one court, the presence of a confidential relationship "imposes a duty on the party in whom the confidence is reposed to exercise the utmost good faith and to refrain from obtaining any advantage at the expense of the confiding party." Hyde v. Hyde, 78 S.D. 176, 99 N.W.2d 788 (1959). This status is open-ended and arises from special relationships of trust or confidence or an agreement, express or implied. Its existence is a question of fact, the proof of which may be aided by presumptions which the party in a position of superior knowledge must rebut. Its presence gives rise to a duty to speak and more. For example, in Vai v. Bank of America National Trust & Savings Association, 56 Cal.2d 329, 15 Cal.Rptr. 71, 364 P.2d 247 (1961), a community property settlement was invalidated where the husband failed to disclose property value information to his wife. Even more striking is Jackson v. Seymour, 193 Va. 735, 71 S.E.2d 181 (1952), where the court ordered a deed from sister to brother cancelled and the status

---

5. Sellers also contend that they had no knowledge of any existing termite damage in the house. An extended discussion of the facts on this point is unnecessary. Simply stated, the facts are in conflict on this issue.

quo restored when it appeared that the brother, after the deed was recorded, had cut and marketed timber worth at least ten times the agreed price for the land. The court stated:

> This is not the ordinary case in which the parties dealt at arm's length and the shrewd trader was entitled to the fruits of his bargain. The parties were brother and sister. He was a successful business man and she a widow in need of money and forced by circumstances * * * to sell a part of the lands which she had inherited. Because of their friendly and intimate relations she entrusted to him and he assumed the management and renting of a portion of this very land. He engaged tenants for such of the land as could be cultivated and collected the rents. She accepted his settlements without question.

> Moreover, it is undisputed that neither of the parties knew of the timber on the land and we have from the defendant's own lips the admission that as it turned out "afterwards" he had paid a grossly inadequate price for the property and that he would not have bought it from her for the small amount paid if he had then known of the true situation.

> To hold that under these circumstances the plaintiff is without remedy would be a reproach to the law. Nor do we think that a court of equity is so impotent." 71 S.E.2d at 184.

See also First National Bank in Lenox v. Brown, 181 N.W.2d 178 (Iowa 1970), where the bank made a loan knowing that the proceeds would be used to purchase an interest in personal property in which the bank held a perfected security interest. The court concluded that the bank and the plaintiff were in a relationship of "trust and confidence," that the "trusted party" had "superior knowledge of the facts" and therefore, "a duty to disclose all material facts of which he is aware, or at least those favorable to his own position and adverse to the other." 181 N.W.2d at 182. The mere recording of the security interest by the bank was an insufficient disclosure and, on these facts, "silence qualified as a misrepresentation."

Another traditional case involving a duty to "speak up" is where such disclosure is necessary to correct a previous statement or false impression. Beyond this, courts have been reluctant to recognize a disclosure obligation in an ordinary arm's length transaction. *Hill* is exceptional, but is a likely precursor of more to come. Consider, again, the potential impact of the following Restatement formulation which influenced the Arizona court: "A person's non-disclosure of a fact known to him is equivalent to an assertion that the fact does not exist in the following cases only: * * * (b) where he knows that disclosure of the fact would correct a mistake of the other party as to a basic assumption on which that party is making the contract and if non-disclosure of the fact amounts to a failure to act in good faith and in accordance with reasonable standards of fair dealing. * * *" Restatement (Second) § 161(b). For a discussion of developing doctrine requiring the vendor of a house to disclose its defects to prospective purchasers, see Curnes, *Protecting the Virginia Homebuyer: A Duty to Disclose Defects*, 73 Va.L.Rev. 459 (1987).

Finally, some have urged the imposition of a general obligation to exercise "good faith" in the *formation* of contracts, as is now prescribed by the Uniform Commercial Code for *performance* and *enforcement*. ("Every contract or duty within this Act imposes an obligation of good faith in its performance and enforcement." UCC 1–203.) What would be the relative advantages and disadvantages of such an approach? For a thoughtful treatment, set in the context of insurance litigation, see Holmes, *A Contextual Study of Commercial Good Faith: Good–Faith Disclosure in Contract Formation,* 39 U.Pitt.L.Rev. 381 (1978) ("Although the concept is not precise, detailed, or rigid as compared with others generally used in formulations of contract law, it is suggested that 'good faith' has a sufficiently common core of meaning, over a considerable range of applications, to make it functional in practical affairs. Properly perceived, 'good faith' is a single mode of analysis comprising a spectrum of related, factual considerations. The context of its use is critically important. In the context of disclosures required in contracting, for example, the following factual elements should be considered: the nature of the undisclosed fact, accessibility of knowledge, the nature of the contract, trade customs and prior course of dealing, conduct of the party in obtaining knowledge, and the status and relationship of the parties." (pp. 450–51). See also Kessler and Fine, *Culpa in Contrahendo, Bargaining in Good Faith, and Freedom of Contract: A Comparative Study,* 77 Harv.L.Rev. 401 (1964).

(2) *From Common Law "Fraud" to Statutory "Unfairness" and "Deception."* Every state has legislation, modeled generally upon Section 5 of the Federal Trade Commission Act, prohibiting "unfair" or "deceptive" trade practices or acts. See, generally, J. Sheldon, Unfair and Deceptive Acts and Practices (4th Ed. 2000), published by the National Consumer Law Center and containing extensive annotation and commentary. As originally enacted, these laws were designed to protect consumers, but in nearly half of the jurisdictions the protective mantle now extends to business entities as well. See Gilleran and Standfeld, *Little FTC Acts Emerge in Business Litigation,* 72 A.B.A.J. 58 (May, 1986). For a thorough study of this trend, see Shell, *Substituting Ethical Standards for Common Law Rules in Commercial Cases: An Emerging Statutory Trend,* 82 Nw.U.L.Rev. 1198 (1988). Professor Shell examines these laws in the context of a general movement away from specific rules and toward open-ended standards, resulting in the dramatic expansion of business liability under such concepts as promissory estoppel, unconscionability, and good faith.

Although these "unfair and deceptive acts or practices" laws (UDAP) vary from state to state, one can identify some common features; notably, (1) vague criteria; (2) private remedy.

First, the proscribed actions are described in general terms; e.g., "deceptive"; "unfair"; "unconscionable." Some statutes also enumerate specific prohibitions, violation of which is a *per se* violation of the statute. Some of these are specific in character; others are not. For example, in the Texas "laundry list" the following is a deceptive trade practice: "disconnecting, turning back, or resetting the odometer of any motor vehicle so as to reduce the number of miles indicated on the odometer gauge." But so is the following: "the failure to disclose information concerning goods or services which was known at the time of the transaction if such failure to disclose such information was intended to induce the consumer into a transaction into which the consumer would not have entered had the information been disclosed."

Second, a private remedy is provided. Unlike the FTC Act, these Little FTC acts provide a right of action to the aggrieved party. At a minimum, actual damages may be recovered, and this includes, in appropriate situations, consequential damages. In addition, provision is made in many of the statutes for a recovery of multiple damages, double or triple. Finally, most of the laws permit the recovery of attorney's fees and costs. In a case brought under the Massachusetts Unfair and Deceptive Trade Practice Act, a buyer of a computer system was awarded compensatory damages of $2.3 million, which the court doubled to $4.6 million, and attorney's fees of $270,000. Computer Systems Engineering, Inc. v. Qantel Corp., 571 F.Supp. 1365 (D.Mass.1983), affirmed 740 F.2d 59 (1st Cir.1984).

Similarly, in Linkage Corporation v. Trustees of Boston University, 425 Mass. 1, 679 N.E.2d 191 (1997), the court found that the University's actions under a contract, principally those of its president, John Silber, and provost, John Westling, constituted a willful and knowing violation of the Massachusetts Unfair and Deceptive Trade Act, G.F. c. 93A. The trial court was warranted in finding that "Boston University's actions in the months leading up to, and after, the termination [of a renewal agreement] were unethical and unscrupulous, and [the president's and the provost's] conduct, in particular, was unfair, oppressive, and deceptive." More particularly: [T]he University "repudiated binding agreements and usurped Linkage's business and work force in order to promote a purely self-serving agenda. The result was to end Linkage's vitality as a going concern, at least until it might be able to reconstitute itself with its main mission still intact." As a consequence, Linkage's damages of $2,411,852 were doubled under the punitive damage provision of G.L. c. 93A and Linkage was permitted to recover its attorney's fees and costs, some $899,382.

There is always tension between "rule" and "discretion." A specific rule provides certainty and predictability, whereas the exercise of discretion pursuant to general standards provides flexibility and adaptability. Is one a clearly superior method of governance in the commercial area? For a thoughtful weighing of competing arguments, see Richard Shell, supra. Professor Shell reaches the following conclusion:

> This article has concluded that state legislatures should reform state FTC Acts to balance this impulse toward doing justice with restrictions that will curb the potential for abuse inherent in this regulatory scheme. This conclusion does not rest on a finding that ethical standards are improper vehicles for regulation, but rather derives from a recognition that such open-ended standards, when combined with liberal awards of treble damages and attorneys' fees, create incentives for litigation that are inappropriate in the commercial setting. 82 Nw.U.L.Rev. at 1253–4.

(3) *RICO: Panacea or Nightmare?* On October 15, 1970, Congress enacted the Racketeer Influenced and Corrupt Organizations Act (RICO), which one writer has characterized as "perhaps the most powerful federal criminal enactment in American law." McIntosh, *Racketeer Influenced and Corrupt Organizations Act: Powerful New Tool of the Defrauded Securities Plaintiff*, 31 Kan.L.Rev. 7, 8 (1982). The statutory purpose is "to seek the eradication of organized crime in the United States by strengthening the legal tools in the evidence-gathering process, by establishing new penal prohibitions, and by providing enhanced sanctions and new remedies to deal with the unlawful activities of those engaged in organized crime." Pub.L. No. 91–452, 84 Stat. 922, 923 (Congressional Statement of Findings and Purpose).

Among the key provisions is that which allows a private litigant to recover treble damages, costs and attorney fees if it is established that the form of fraud constitutes a "pattern of racketeering activity" cognizable under the statute. There has been a growing realization that RICO remedies may be available in situations where no direct link to "organized crime" is proven. Hence, the potential of the statute in more ordinary commercial litigation is enormous and affords a defrauded party a civil remedy far more effective than that traditionally provided by, for example, federal securities law.

The widespread use of RICO by civil plaintiffs, particularly when using state and federal fraud statutes to satisfy the statute's predicate acts requirement, has generated heated controversy. Critics insist that the application of RICO to ordinary commercial disputes far exceeds Congressional intent. They maintain that RICO was intended to be used against the infiltration of legitimate business by organized crime, not ordinary commercial fraud. Further, it is argued that the statute's use in fraud suits has resulted in the unnecessary and unwise federalization of an area of law that should be left to the states. Finally, critics argue that the prospect of treble damages intimidates many defendants, causing them to settle frivolous claims out of court. In sum, the general thrust of the criticism is that RICO's broad language and draconian penalties help increase uncertainty in the marketplace and tend to discourage legitimate business activity.

Proponents, on the other hand, contend that Congress clearly intended the statute to be used against any criminal "enterprise," not just organized crime. Further, they maintain that RICO is expressly designed to supplement those federal and state fraud laws which were perceived to be inadequate. To the defenders of the statute, out of court settlements indicate the success of RICO by providing plaintiffs a statutory weapon which fills gaps left in existing legislation and the common law.

To date RICO has survived efforts to weaken or remove its fraud provisions. And while these provisions remain, RICO is certain to become more popular with civil plaintiffs. See Blakey and Perry, *An Analysis of the Myths that Bolster Efforts to Rewrite RICO and the Various Proposals for Reform: "Mother of God—Is This the End of RICO?"*, 43 Vand.L.Rev. 851 (1990).

PROBLEMS: UNCOMMUNICATIVE PARTIES AND THE DUTY TO DISCLOSE

(a) Mr. Mc, prospective purchaser, enters into negotiations to purchase a house belonging to Ms. M. Mc inquires of M's agent as to whether the house has ever had termites. Her agent answers that it has been inspected for termites and is due for another inspection shortly. The agent does not disclose that the prior inspection indicated termite infestation. Should the parties enter into a contract for the sale of the property, could the purchaser rescind? See Murphy v. McIntosh, 199 Va. 254, 99 S.E.2d 585 (1957).

(b) A Jewish congregation seeks to employ a rabbi to serve the congregation. Chaim W applies for the position. Neither in his resume nor during the employment negotiations does he disclose that he had previously been convicted of mail fraud and disbarred as an attorney. After he is hired and enters upon his duties, these facts of his past life come to light. Does the congregation have a right to rescind the contract? See Jewish Center of Sussex County v. Whale, 86 N.J. 619, 432 A.2d 521 (1981).

Yes, it's material

(c) Nurse N and Doctor K, employees of a local hospital, date each other frequently. The latter has genital herpes, but does not disclose this fact to Nurse N. They engage in sexual intercourse at a time when Dr. K knows the disease is active and would be transmitted. Nurse N contracts the disease. Does she have a cause of action for fraud? See B.N. v. K.K., 312 Md. 135, 538 A.2d 1175 (1988).

(d) D, an elderly person living alone, purchases a house from K. Neither K nor his agent tells D that a woman and her four children were murdered there ten years earlier. D learns of the gruesome episode from a neighbor after the sale. Can she rescind? See Reed v. King, 145 Cal.App.3d 261, 193 Cal.Rptr. 130 (1983).

No, immaterial
No Mistake

(e) Driller learns through an independent investigation that Owner's land contains valuable oil deposits. Knowing that Owner is not aware of this, Driller persuades him to enter into a contract to sell the land at a price much less than Owner would have insisted upon had he been aware of the oil potential. Should Owner be entitled to rescind? Would your answer be different if Driller obtained the information from trespassing upon Owner's land? Or if Driller had received "inside" information from a relative at a State agency? See Restatement (Second) § 161, Illus. 10.

(f) While looking through used books at a "flea market," Adam comes upon a Dickens first edition which carries a price tag of $5. Adam knows that the book will fetch several thousand dollars on the market and that Barbara, the proprietor, is unaware of this fact. Any duty to disclose?

(g) Employee interviews for a position in the accounting department of Employer. During the negotiations no mention is made to the prospective employee that plans are already in place for a sale of the company. Employee is hired on an "at will" basis, and shortly thereafter the sale is announced and new management takes over. Employee is among those let go. Did Employer have a duty to disclose information regarding the pending sale to Employee? Cf. Stowman v. Carlson Companies, Inc., 430 N.W.2d 490 (Minn.App.1988). Assume, instead, that Employee intends to work only until he can enter law school, but makes no mention of this to Employer. Should he be obliged to disclose this information?

1) Material

2) No, immaterial

(h) During an interview for summer employment, Jake, first-year law student, is questioned extensively about prior educational background and other personal matters. Jake knows that his chances for the job will be significantly reduced if he discloses that during his sophomore year in high school he was suspended from the basketball team for disciplinary reasons. Should he have a duty to volunteer this information? Should he be obliged to disclose that in college he was found guilty of plagiarism and placed on probation?

PROBLEM: RELEASE OF UNKNOWN INJURIES

On November 26, 1982, Vicente Morta suffered a collision that damaged his 1976 Mazda station wagon and caused him bodily injury. According to Morta, the car was "a total loss." Morta himself was knocked unconscious and taken by ambulance to the emergency room at Guam Memorial Hospital. After treating Morta, the attending physician assured him that he was fine and could go home. Afterwards, Morta continued to have pain in his muscles, chin and chest. He was treated three days later by a second physician at the Seventh Day Adventist Clinic, who also told him he was fine and the pain would eventually subside.

Morta sought compensation for his losses from appellant Korea Insurance Corporation (KIC), which insured the driver who had caused the accident. Morta was directed to Bernabe Santa Maria, a claims adjuster. Morta and Santa Maria happened to be from the same area of the Philippines and conversed in their native tongues, Tagalog and Ilocano. Morta testified that he had no problem understanding Santa Maria.

Santa Maria helped Morta complete the claim form, received from Morta his medical reports, examined the damaged Mazda and, acknowledging the liability of his insured, offered Morta $900. Morta testified that the settlement offer had several components: "Three Hundred Dollars for my car; $250 from loss of compensation of work, like that; and Two Hundred some for sufferings and injury that I suffered, you know. So, they told me, included also the medical bill from SDA and the towing expenses, that item."

Morta was not satisfied with that amount, claiming that the car alone had a blue-book value of $2300. Santa Maria told him that $900 was all he could pay. Morta did not jump at the offer; he thought it over and went to see a lawyer. He showed the lawyer the medical and police reports. The lawyer evaluated Morta's claim and advised him that he would be unlikely to recover much more than the $900 KIC had offered and that any attempt to do so would delay payment. Morta returned to Santa Maria's office and accepted the $900. Because the settlement check covered damages for the car as well as for personal injuries—in short, all of Morta's claims—Morta signed a standard release, which was less than a page long. The trial court described the release as follows:

> At the top, in characters a quarter-inch tall, was the word "RELEASE"; immediately beneath, in slightly smaller letters, were the words "OF ALL CLAIMS." A few concise sentences follow, clearly and unequivocally stating that Morta releases KIC from all claims "growing out of any and all known and unknown, foreseen and unforeseen bodily and personal injuries and property damage" arising out of the accident in question. Morta also acknowledges that "the injuries sustained are or may be permanent and progressive and that recovery therefrom is uncertain and indefinite...."
> In capital letters near the bottom is a certification that the signer has read and understands the terms of the release; immediately above the signature line, also in capitals, is a "caution" instructing the signer to read the release before signing it.

About a week after the settlement, Morta began to feel ill and dizzy. He was given medication by his doctor but soon thereafter he collapsed unconscious, awaking in a Honolulu hospital after undergoing emergency surgery for a blood clot in his brain. The medical bills amounted to approximately $11,000, all paid for by Morta's insurer, FHP, Inc.

Morta filed suit to recover damages resulting from this injury, disavowing the release on the ground, inter alia, that Santa Maria fraudulently misrepresented its contents. The jury returned a general verdict upholding the release and the superior court entered judgment to that effect.

Morta appealed and made the following arguments as to why the release was invalid:

(1) There was a mutual mistake of fact, in that both parties assumed that there were no unknown injuries. Either the release should be avoided or reformed to exclude the phrase "unknown injuries."

(2) There was a mistake by Morta, who did not know he was signing a release or, if he did, did not know the contents of the release and was surprised to learn that it purported to release unknown claims.

(3) There was fraud by the agent, who misrepresented the contents by failing to disclose and discuss the clause.

(4) Morta was unduly influenced by the agent [see Chapter 5, Section 2(C)].

(5) The release was signed under duress, [see Chapter 5, Section 2(C)] in that Morta needed the money and could not afford to refuse to sign and litigate the claim.

(6) The release was either against public policy [see Chapter 5, Section 3] or unconscionable [see Chapter 5, Section 2(D)].

How should these claims be resolved? See Morta v. Korea Insurance Corp., 840 F.2d 1452 (9th Cir.1988), from which these facts were taken.

Comment: Misrepresentation of Intent to Perform; Promissory Fraud

Basic principles. Under the doctrine of promissory fraud, many jurisdictions will impose punitive damages on promissors who at the time of promising don't intend to perform their promise. While promissory fraud is seldom taught in first year courses, it is frequently litigated and represents one of the few opportunities that plaintiffs have to claim punitive damages for breach of contract.

Promissory fraud at first seems to be a non sequitur. Promising to perform in the future seems not to concern a representation of an existing fact. So the mere act of promising seems to eliminate the possibility of misrepresenting an existing fact. But courts in most jurisdictions have found that by promising a promisor implicitly represents a *present intent* to perform the promise. In 1885, Lord Bowen famously opined in Edgington v. Fitzmaurice, 29 Ch. D. 459 (1885): "The state of a man's mind is as much a fact as the state of his digestion." And Restatement (Second) of Torts § 530, Comment c recites the now well accepted rule: "Since a promise necessarily carries with it the implied assertion of an intention to perform[,] it follows that a promise made without such an intention is fraudulent." Thus, if the promisor in fact does not intend to perform her promise, then her implicit representation of a present intent to perform is the basis for a fraud claim.

But the common law has been leery about giving promisee's an open ended opportunity to convert every breach of contract into a claim for punitive damages. The critical difficulty in any promissory fraud case is inferring the promissor's actual intent at the time of promising. Did George Bush really intend to veto any tax increase when he promised "Read My Lips"? Stephen D. Sencer, Note, *Read My Lips: Examining the Legal Implications of Knowingly False Campaign Promises*, 90 Mich. L. Rev. 428 (1991). Courts infer an initial lack of intent to perform chiefly because of:

(i) lack of changed circumstances between time of promising and time of breach;*

(ii) a pattern of repeated breaching over time (for example, Herald Hill's promise in *The Music Man* to train a boy's band, or the hundreds of breached cremation promises by a Georgia funeral home;**

(iii) impossibility of performance at time of promising;***

(iv) internal documents indicating no intent of performing.****

Judge Posner on the Scheme to Defraud Requirement. The concern that plaintiffs will use promissory fraud claims as a catch-all method of securing punitive damages has led Illinois to require plaintiffs to prove a "scheme to defraud". See Speakers of Sport, Inc. v. ProServ, Inc., 178 F.3d 862 (7th Cir. 1999) (Posner, J.) ("By requiring that the plaintiff show a pattern, by thus not letting him rest on proving a single promise, the law reduces the likelihood of a spurious suit; for a series of unfulfilled promises is better (though of course not conclusive) evidence of fraud than a single unfulfilled promise.")

Justice Holmes on Promissory Fraud. A "Holmsian" might argue that a promissor does not implicitly represent an intent to perform the promise but merely an intent to perform or pay damages. But Justice Holmes in Bailey v. Alabama, 219 U.S. 219, 31 S.Ct. 145, 55 L.Ed. 191 (1911), in dissent voted to affirm the conviction of an African American worker who had taken a $15 signing bonus to work for a year and then breached after a little more than month without paying back the bonus. The Alabama criminal statute in question provided that any person who, "with intent to injure or defraud his employer" enters into a written labor contract, and gets money in advance from the employer; and who then, "without refunding such money ... refuses or fails to perform such ... service," can be punished by a fine of double the damages suffered by the injured person. Half of the fine goes to the county, half to the "injured party." The act also established that (i) the refusal to perform or refund advanced money "shall

* See, e.g., Hammonds v. Turnipseed, 709 So.2d 39 (Ala.Civ.App.1997).

** See Trent Seibert, Legislator Considering Funeral Laws Reform Sought after Ga. Horror, Denver Post A8 (February 20, 2002)

*** See In re Mercer, 246 F.3d 391 (5th Cir.2001).

**** See The Wharf (Holdings) Lmt. v. United International Holdings, Inc., 532 U.S. 588, 121 S.Ct. 1776, 149 L.Ed.2d 845 (2001) (securities law § 10(b) violated by defendant Wharf's option sale when "[c]ontemporaneous internal Wharf documents suggested that Wharf had never intended to carry out its promise.")

be prima facie evidence of the intent to'' defraud the employer, and (ii) the worker was not allowed to testify ''as to his uncommunicated motives, purpose or intention.'' Holmes in dissent reasoned that the statute was not constitutionally infirm:

"I think it a mistake to say that this statute attaches its punishment to the mere breach of a contract to labor. It does nor purport to do so; what it purports to punish is fraudulently obtaining money by a false pretense of an intent to keep the written contract in consideration of which the money is advanced. (It is not necessary to cite cases to show that such an intent may be the subject of a material false representation.) But the import of the statute is supposed to be changed by the provision that a refusal to perform, coupled with a failure to return the money advanced, shall be prima facie evidence of fraudulent intent. I agree that if the statute created a conclusive presumption it might be held to make a disguised change in the substantive law. But it only makes the conduct prima facie evidence, a very different matter. Is it not evidence that a man had a fraudulent intent if he receives an advance upon a contract over night and leaves in the morning? I should have thought that it very plainly was.... For prima facie evidence is only evidence, and as such may be held by the jury insufficient to make out guilt...."

"I do not see how the result that I have reached thus far is affected by the rule ... that the prisoner cannot testify to his uncommunicated intentions, and therefore, it is assumed, would not be permitted to offer a naked denial of an intent to defraud. If there is an excuse for breaking the contract it will be found in external circumstances, and can be proved...."

"To sum up, I think that obtaining money by fraud may be made a crime as well as murder or theft; that a false representation, expressed or implied, at the time of making a contract of labor that one intends to perform it and thereby obtaining an advance, may be declared a case of fraudulently obtaining money as well as any other; that if made a crime it may be punished like any other crime, and that an unjustified departure from the promised service without repayment may be declared a sufficient case to go to the jury for their judgment; all without in any way infringing the Thirteenth Amendment or the statutes of the United States."

Justice O'Connor on Promissory Fraud. In Pinnacle Peak Developers v. TRW Inv. Corp., 129 Ariz. 385, 631 P.2d 540 (App.1980), then Judge Sandra Day O'Connor addressed the relationship between promissory fraud and promises that were not otherwise enforceable because of the statute of frauds or parol evidence rule:

A summary of the problem raised in a case such as this one is succinctly stated in James and Gray, Misrepresentation (pt. II), 37 Md. Law Rev. 488, at 507–08 (1978):

Although the notion of promissory fraud is well recognized, it may seriously collide with the policies underlying certain prophylactic legal rules like the Statute of Frauds and the parol evidence rule. Both these rules are designed to prevent fraudulent claims (or defenses) through excluding a type of evidence (viz., evidence of oral agreement) which is too easy to fabricate and too hard to meet. It could go without saying that these rules are not meant to shield fraud, but they may well have just that effect if they prevent a party from showing that he has been deceived by an oral promise, made to induce reliance and action but without the slightest intention of keeping it. Many courts allow oral proof of fraud in such a case and this seems sound because the affirmative burden of proving fraud (i.e., present intent not to keep the promise when it was made, or even the absence of an intent to keep it) would seem to be a substantial safeguard against trumped-up contracts. Moreover, the safeguard is enhanced by the prevailing procedural rules requiring clear and convincing evidence of fraud and holding that the mere nonperformance of a contract does not warrant an inference of the requisite fraudulent intent.

"The cases from other states are split widely on whether to permit parol evidence which contradicts a writing when fraud in the inducement is alleged. A number of courts appear to follow the Restatement of Contracts s 238 (1932), and allow evidence of promissory fraud, notwithstanding the parol evidence rule.... Other courts exclude evidence of promissory fraud which contradicts the terms of the written agreement on the basis of the parol evidence rule.

The debate involves the question: is the public better served by giving effect to the parties' entire agreement written and oral, even at the risk of injustice caused by the possibility of perjury ... , or does the security of transactions require that, despite occasional injustices, persons adopting a formal writing be required, on the penalty of voidness of their oral and written side agreements, to put their entire agreement in the formal writing? ...

A case by case study of a large number of cases nationwide dealing with the application of the parol evidence rule ... indicate[s] that, in practice, courts generally apply the parol evidence rule to exclude allegations of prior or contemporaneous oral promises which contradict the written agreement in cases involving "formal contracts" which were the result of negotiation between parties with some expertise and business sophistication.... There is a much greater tendency in the reported cases to allow such evidence in "informal contracts" between people who lack sophistication in business.... In cases involving abuse of the bargaining process, such as unconscionable contracts or contracts involving duress, the courts almost always disregard the parol evidence rule and allow evidence of the oral promises or representations.

The pleadings and affidavits in this case reflect that the parties each had experience in business transactions and that the written option agreement was prepared as the result of negotiations between the parties, who were represented by counsel. It involved a relatively substantial and sophisticated real estate transaction. The written option agreement was a 'formal contract.' The contradiction of the written agreement and the oral representation is clear.... The facts are such that courts in most jurisdictions would exclude the evidence of the prior oral statement on the basis of a strict application of the parol evidence rule. It is our opinion on rehearing that the trial court correctly granted summary judgment to appellee on Count II quieting title to the property covered by the option agreement in appellee.

The application of the parol evidence rule moves along a continuum based on the extent of the contradiction and the relative strength and sophistication of the parties and their negotiations.... There are circumstances under which evidence of a prior or contemporaneous contradictory oral representation or promise would be admissible not-withstanding the subsequent integrated written agreement of the parties...."

Promissory Fraud in Other Contexts. Colorable issues of promissory fraud arise in many other cases contained in this casebook. See Peevyhouse v. Garland Coal & Min Co., infra at 936 (promised land restoration was known to be infeasible); Hoffman v. Red Owl Stores, supra at 435 (repeated assurances that franchise would be offered); Alaska Packers' Ass'n v. Domenico, supra at 84 (employer promised modification that she did not intend to perform).

(C) DURESS AND UNDUE INFLUENCE

In the fraud materials just considered, the aggrieved party assented to the bargain without complete or accurate information. He or she justifiably relied upon false representations of material facts by the defendant. In the materials to follow, the aggrieved party, who is accurately informed and primed to resist a proposed deal, is told by the defendant "unless you agree to this bargain, I will see that X happens." Because X is presumably less pleasant than contracting, the aggrieved party, in the typical case, agrees to the bargain (which, by the way, may be perfectly fair) and later claims that the "apparent" assent was coerced. Put another way, it is claimed that one's "free will" was overcome by the threat and, therefore, the bargain is not enforceable. Although the factors in the analysis tend to be both complicated and infused with a bias against the duress defense, we will try in this short subsection to determine when the defense that choice was impaired by threat is likely to succeed.

Rubenstein v. Rubenstein

Supreme Court of New Jersey, 1956.
20 N.J. 359, 120 A.2d 11.

■ HEHER, JUSTICE. The judgment of the Appellate Division of the Superior Court affirming the Chancery Division's judgment dismissing the complaint was certified here for appeal at the instance of plaintiff.

The gravamen of the complaint is that plaintiff, while "in fear of his safety and under duress" practiced by his defendant wife, by a deed of conveyance in which she joined, conveyed to her wholly-owned corporation, Natalie's Realty Co., Inc., all his right, title and interest in a farm of 126

1/2 acres containing a 14–room dwelling house and several farm buildings, situate on the Freehold–Matawan Road in Marlboro Township, Monmouth County, known as the "Marlboro Manor Farm," of the value of $90,000, and a plot of ground and a factory building on Dowd Avenue in Farmingdale, Monmouth County, of the value of $12,000, both tracts then being held by plaintiff and his wife in a tenancy by the entirety. The intervener-respondent was made a party defendant as the purchaser of 110 acres of the farm property for $23,000 by contract made with Natalie and her corporate codefendant, a price said to be "far below its present market value."

The complaint charges that by the conveyances thus made plaintiff "has divested himself of all his real property and all his assets"; that "when he made the said conveyances and thereafter" Natalie "promised and agreed that she would support" their two infant children, Leon, 5 1/2 years of age, and Norman Thomas, 2 1/2 years old, "out of the incomes" of these properties; that the farm land which Natalie "proposes to sell has been under lease," yielding $2500 annually; and that the farm property, "if properly managed, would produce sufficient revenues to provide for the support, maintenance and education of the infant children," but if 110 acres be sold at the stated price "the property will be so depreciated in value that the interest of the infants will be seriously jeopardized." . . .

If these conveyances were procured by means of duress, they are inoperative and voidable. Actual violence is not an essential element of duress of the person, even at common law, because consent is the very essence of a contract and, if there be compulsion, there is no actual consent. And moral compulsion, such as that produced by threats to take life or to inflict great bodily harm, as well as that produced by imprisonment, came to be regarded everywhere as sufficient in law to destroy free agency, indispensable to the consent without which there can be no contract. Duress in its more extended sense means that degree of constraint or danger, either actually inflicted or threatened and impending, sufficient in severity or in apprehension to overcome the mind or will of a person of ordinary firmness, according to the earlier rule, but now, by the weight of modern authority, such as in fact works control of the will. There are two categories under the common law: duress per minas and duress of imprisonment. Duress per minas at common law "is where the party enters into a contract (1) For fear of loss of life; (2) For fear of loss of limb; (3) For fear of mayhem; (4) For fear of imprisonment"; and some of the later English cases confine the rule within these limits, while the American rule is more liberal and contracts procured by threats of battery to the person, or the destruction of property, were early held to be voidable on the ground of duress, "because in such a case there is nothing but the form of a contract, without the substance." Brown v. Pierce, 7 Wall. 205, 19 L.Ed. 134 (1869). In many cases it was found to be enough that there was moral compulsion "sufficient to overcome the mind and will of a person entirely competent, in all other respects, to contract," for "it is clear that a contract made under such circumstances is as utterly without the voluntary consent of the party menaced as if he were induced to sign it by actual violence; * * *.'' United States v. Huckabee, 16 Wall. 414 (1873).

It would seem to be basic to the legal concept of duress, proceeding as it does from the unreality of the apparent consent, that the controlling factor be the condition at the time of the mind of the person subjected to the coercive measures, rather than the means by which the given state of mind was induced, and thus the test is essentially subjective.

"The test of duress is not so much the means by which the party was compelled to execute the contract as it is the state of mind induced by the means employed—the fear which made it impossible for him to exercise his own free will * * *. The threat must be of such a nature and made under such circumstances as to constitute a reasonable and adequate cause to control the will of the threatened person, and must have that effect; and the act sought to be avoided must be performed by such person while in such condition." Fountain v. Bigham, 235 Pa. 35,(Sup.Ct.1912).

In the modern view, moral compulsion or psychological pressure may constitute duress if, thereby, the subject of the pressure is overborne and he is deprived of the exercise of his free will. The question is whether consent was coerced; that is, was the person complaining "induced by the duress or undue influence to give his consent, and would not have done so otherwise." Williston on Contracts (rev. ed.), section 1604. See Restatement, Contracts, section 492. It was said in the early books that there could not be duress by threats unless the threats were such as "to put a brave man in fear"; then came the qualified standard of something sufficient to overcome the will of a person of "ordinary firmness"; but the tendency of the more recent cases, and the rule comporting with reason and principle, is that any "unlawful threats" which do "in fact overcome the will of the person threatened, and induce him to do an act which he would not otherwise have done, and which he was not bound to do, constitute duress. The age, sex, capacity, relation of the parties and all the attendant circumstances must be considered. This follows the analogy of the modern doctrine of fraud which tends to disregard the question whether misrepresentations were such as would have deceived a reasonable person, and confines the question to whether the misrepresentations were intended to deceive and did so." Williston on Contracts, section 1605. Such is the trend of the cases in New Jersey.

But the pressure must be wrongful, and not all pressure is wrongful. And means in themselves lawful must not be so oppressively used as to constitute, e.g., an abuse of legal remedies. Williston on Contracts, sections 1606, 1607. The act or conduct complained of need not be "unlawful" in the technical sense of the term; it suffices if it is "wrongful in the sense that it is so oppressive under given circumstances as to constrain one to do what his free will would refuse." First State Bank v. Federal Reserve Bank, 174 Minn. 535,(Sup.Ct.1928).

Here, the trial judge said: "I will not allow [plaintiff] to testify to a state of mind." Again: "I think that we would be opening a door wide and entering into a very dangerous area if we were to allow a witness to say what his private thought was in response to an external force or statement."

We come now to the case made by plaintiff which fell before the motion to dismiss. All was serene, apparently, in the domestic relation until the older boy developed a mental condition diagnosed in the Fall of 1952 as "childhood schizophrenia." [The disclosure of the illness] led to sharp differences of opinion, e.g., as to the mode of treatment of the child, and eventually to an estrangement attended by the wife's insistent demands for the transfer of the husband's entire interest in the properties at issue, practically the whole of his possessions.

There is no occasion now to set down the plaintiff's evidence in detail. It suffices to say that he gave a circumstantial account of threats of gangster violence, arsenic poisoning, and a course of action designed to overcome his will, he affirms, culminating in his arrest for desertion and nonsupport. The arsenic threat, he said, had a background that filled him with an overpowering sense of foreboding and dread. His wife's father was then serving a life sentence in a Pennsylvania prison for murder committed while he was identified with an "arsenic ring" engaged in killings to defraud life insurers. The threats were first made in December 1952. The demand for the conveyances came in April 1953, and was refused. It was repeated at intervals until the following July, when the arsenic threat was made. He was seized with a great fear for his life and, so conditioned, he agreed the following day to make the conveyance. . . .

The trial judge said of the plaintiff: "I saw a witness who in many ways, in the way he testified, by voice, by his answers to direct questions and so on, who to me is possessed of an insecurity from within," one who "in life hasn't faced up reality frontally and boldly"; "as on the witness stand, he has in life tended to avoid important problems, and marriage was one"; the misfortune to the child had its effect, and the plaintiff "was running from it," although he "had every desire to do what he could" for the boy. And the suggestion was made that the defendant wife's "assumption of all liabilities against the (conveyed) property was not an unmixed blessing to him"; "A big load was shifted together with the assets."

These findings suggest psychological factors bearing on the subjective standard of free will. . . . There was a Prima facie showing here of a compulsive yielding to the demand for the conveyances, rather than the volitional act of a free mind, which called for a full disclosure by the defendant wife; and so it was error to entertain the motion to dismiss at the close of the plaintiff's case. The testimony of plaintiff stood unchallenged. Stress is laid upon the advantage of personal observation of the plaintiff witness in the assessment of his testimony; but this is peculiarly a case for explanation by the defendant under the same scrutiny, in particular as to dominance of will. Duress is a species of fraud, although unlike fraud, duress does not necessarily depend on the intent of the person exercising it. See Restatement, Contracts, section 492, Comment A.

The judgment is reversed; and the cause is remanded for further proceedings in conformity with this opinion.

Austin Instrument, Inc. v. Loral Corp.

Court of Appeals of New York, 1971.
29 N.Y.2d 124, 324 N.Y.S.2d 22, 272 N.E.2d 533.

■ FULD, CHIEF JUDGE. The defendant, Loral Corporation, seeks to recover payment for goods delivered under a contract which it had with the plaintiff Austin Instrument, Inc., on the ground that the evidence establishes, as a matter of law, that it was forced to agree to an increase in price on the items in question under circumstances amounting to economic duress.

In July of 1965, Loral was awarded a $6,000,000 contract by the Navy for the production of radar sets. The contract contained a schedule of deliveries, a liquidated damages clause applying to late deliveries and a cancellation clause in case of default by Loral. The latter thereupon solicited bids for some 40 precision gear components needed to produce the radar sets, and awarded Austin a subcontract to supply 23 such parts. That party commenced delivery in early 1966.

In May, 1966, Loral was awarded a second Navy contract for the production of more radar sets and again went about soliciting bids. Austin bid on all 40 gear components but, on July 15, a representative from Loral informed Austin's president, Mr. Krauss, that his company would be awarded the subcontract only for those items on which it was low bidder. The Austin officer refused to accept an order for less than all 40 of the gear parts and on the next day he told Loral that Austin would cease deliveries of the parts due under the existing subcontract unless Loral consented to substantial increases in the prices provided for by that agreement—both retroactively for parts already delivered and prospectively on those not yet shipped—and placed with Austin the order for all 40 parts needed under Loral's second Navy contract. Shortly thereafter, Austin did, indeed, stop delivery. After contacting 10 manufacturers of precision gears and finding none who could produce the parts in time to meet its commitments to the Navy,* Loral acceded to Austin's demands; in a letter dated July 22, Loral wrote to Austin that "We have feverishly surveyed other sources of supply and find that because of the prevailing military exigencies, were they to start from scratch as would have to be the case, they could not even remotely begin to deliver on time to meet the delivery requirements established by the Government. * * * Accordingly, we are left with no choice or alternative but to meet your conditions."

Loral thereupon consented to the price increases insisted upon by Austin under the first subcontract and the latter was awarded a second

---

* The best reply Loral received was from a vendor who stated he could commence deliveries sometime in October.

subcontract making it the supplier of all 40 gear parts for Loral's second contract with the Navy. Although Austin was granted until September to resume deliveries, Loral did, in fact, receive parts in August and was able to produce the radar sets in time to meet its commitments to the Navy on both contracts. After Austin's last delivery under the second subcontract in July, 1967, Loral notified it of its intention to seek recovery of the price increases.

On September 15, 1967, Austin instituted this action against Loral to recover an amount in excess of $17,750 which was still due on the second subcontract. On the same day, Loral commenced an action against Austin claiming damages of some $22,250—the aggregate of the price increases under the first subcontract—on the ground of economic duress. The two actions were consolidated and, following a trial, Austin was awarded the sum it requested and Loral's complaint against Austin was dismissed on the ground that it was not shown that "it could not have obtained the items in question from other sources in time to meet its commitment to the Navy under the first contract." A closely divided Appellate Division affirmed (316 N.Y.S.2d 528, 532). There was no material disagreement concerning the facts; as Justice Steuer stated in the course of his dissent below, "[t]he facts are virtually undisputed, nor is there any serious question of law. The difficulty lies in the application of the law to these facts." (316 N.Y.S.2d 534.)

The applicable law is clear and, indeed, is not disputed by the parties. A contract is voidable on the ground of duress when it is established that the party making the claim was forced to agree to it by means of a wrongful threat precluding the exercise of his free will. . . . The existence of economic duress or business compulsion is demonstrated by proof that "immediate possession of needful goods is threatened" . . . more particularly, in cases such as the one before us, by proof that one party to a contract has threatened to breach the agreement by withholding goods unless the other party agrees to some further demand. . . . However, a mere threat by one party to breach the contract by not delivering the required items, though wrongful, does not in itself constitute economic duress. It must also appear that the threatened party could not obtain the goods from another source of supply and that the ordinary remedy of an action for breach of contract would not be adequate.

We find without any support in the record the conclusion reached by the courts below that Loral failed to establish that it was the victim of economic duress. On the contrary, the evidence makes out a classic case, as a matter of law, of such duress.

It is manifest that Austin's threat—to stop deliveries unless the prices were increased—deprived Loral of its free will. As bearing on this, Loral's relationship with the Government is most significant. As mentioned above, its contract called for staggered monthly deliveries of the radar sets, with clauses calling for liquidated damages and possible cancellation on default. Because of its production schedule, Loral was, in July, 1966, concerned with meeting its delivery requirements in September, October and November, and it was for the sets to be delivered in those months that the withheld gears were needed. Loral had to plan ahead, and the substantial liquidated damages for which it would be liable, plus the threat of default, were genuine possibilities. Moreover, Loral did a substantial portion of its business with the Government, and it feared that a failure to deliver as agreed upon would jeopardize its chances for future contracts. These genuine concerns do not merit the label "self-imposed, undisclosed and subjective" which the Appellate Division majority placed upon them. It was perfectly reasonable for Loral, or any other party similarly placed, to consider itself in an emergency, duress situation.

Austin, however, claims that the fact that Loral extended its time to resume deliveries until September negates its alleged dire need for the parts. A Loral official testified on this point that Austin's president told him he could deliver some parts in August and that the extension of deliveries was a formality. In any event, the parts necessary for production of the radar sets to be delivered in September were delivered to Loral on September 1, and the parts needed for the October schedule were delivered in late August and early September. Even so, Loral had to "work * * * around the clock" to meet its commitments. Considering that the best offer Loral received from the other vendors it contacted was commencement of delivery sometime in October, which, as the record shows, would have made it late in its deliveries to the Navy in both September and October, Loral's claim that it had no choice but to accede to Austin's demands is conclusively demonstrated.

We find unconvincing Austin's contention that Loral, in order to meet its burden, should have contacted the Government and asked for an extension of its delivery dates so as to enable it to purchase the parts from another vendor. Aside from the consideration that Loral was anxious to perform well in the Government's eyes, it could not be sure when it would obtain enough parts from a substitute vendor to meet its commitments. The only promise which it received from the companies it contacted was for *commencement* of deliveries, not full supply, and, with vendor delay common in this field, it would have been nearly impossible to know the length of the extension it should request. It must be remembered that Loral was producing a needed item of military hardware. Moreover, there is authority for Loral's position that nonperformance by a subcontractor is not an excuse for default in the main contract. (See, e.g., McBride & Wachtel, Government Contracts, § 35.10, [11].) In light of all this, Loral's claim should not be held insufficiently supported because it did not request an extension from the Government.

Loral, as indicated above, also had the burden of demonstrating that it could not obtain the parts elsewhere within a reasonable time, and there can be no doubt that it met this burden. The 10 manufacturers whom Loral contacted comprised its entire list of "approved vendors" for precision gears, and none was able to commence delivery soon enough. As Loral was producing a highly sophisticated item of military machinery requiring parts made to the strictest engineering standards, it would be unreasonable to hold that Loral should have gone to other vendors, with whom it was either unfamiliar or dissatisfied, to procure the needed parts. As Justice Steuer noted in his dissent, Loral "contacted all the manufacturers whom it believed capable of making these parts" (316 N.Y.S.2d at p. 534), and this was all the law requires.

It is hardly necessary to add that Loral's normal legal remedy of accepting Austin's breach of the contract and then suing for damages would have been inadequate under the circumstances, as Loral would still have had to obtain the gears elsewhere with all the concomitant consequences mentioned above. In other words, Loral actually had no choice, when the prices were raised by Austin, except to take the gears at the "coerced" prices and then sue to get the excess back.

* * *

In sum, the record before us demonstrates that Loral agreed to the price increases in consequence of the economic duress employed by Austin. Accordingly, the matter should be remanded to the trial court for a computation of its damages.

The order appealed from should be modified, with costs, by reversing so much thereof as affirms the dismissal of defendant Loral Corporation's claim and, except as so modified, affirmed.

■ Bergan, Judge (dissenting).

Whether acts charged as constituting economic duress produce or do not produce the damaging effect attributed to them is normally a routine type of factual issue.

Here the fact question was resolved against Loral both by the Special Term and by the affirmance at the Appellate Division. It should not be open for different resolution here.

* * *

Machinery Hauling, Inc. v. Steel of West Virginia

Supreme Court of Appeals of West Virginia, 1989.
181 W.Va. 694, 384 S.E.2d 139.

■ Miller, Justice:

[Plaintiff buyer contracted with defendant seller to purchase steel and have it delivered to a third party. Defendant informed Plaintiff that the steel was unmerchantable and that the third party had rejected it and orally directed Plaintiff to return the last three undelivered loads to Defendant. Defendant's agent then (allegedly) told Plaintiff that if it did not pay $31,000, the price of the undelivered loads, it would cease doing business with Plaintiff, with a potential loss over over $1,000,000 per year.

In its complaint, the plaintiff alleged that Defendant and its agent "negligently attempted to extort money" from Plaintiff by their joint threat to sever business relations unless payment for the defective product was made and sought monetary damages for their "extortionate demands." The circuit court denied recovery. On appeal, the Supreme Court first held that there was no cause of action under the West Virginia criminal extortion statute because the threat was not an unlawful act: * * * "Steel was free to place its haulage business wherever it chose. Its statement to the plaintiff did not constitute an unlawful act."]

* * *

The more common analysis proceeds under a theory of business or economic loss. In the early common law, duress per minas, i.e., by threats, was available to void a contract where the threat involved imprisonment, mayhem, or loss of life or limb. Restatement (Second) of Torts § 871, comment f (1979); 25 Am.Jur.2d Duress & Undue Influence § 11 (1966). Through the years, there has been a steady expansion of duress principle such that direct dire harm is no longer essential, the focus instead being on whether the threat overbears the exercise of free will. Professor Williston, in discussing the status of business compulsion, has identified two basic elements: (1) the party who asserts business compulsion "must show that he has been the victim of a wrongful or unlawful act or threat," and (2) "[s]uch act or threat must be one which deprives the victim of his unfettered will." 13 Williston on Contracts § 1617 at 704 (1970).

Recently, courts have tended to avoid the term "free will" as applied to the victim, but instead have utilized the concept that the victim had "no reasonable alternative." This is found in Section 175(1) of the Restatement (Second) of Contracts (1981): "If a party's manifestation of assent is induced by an improper threat by the other party that leaves the victim no reasonable alternative, the contract is voidable by the victim." A more difficult issue is determining what type of threat is sufficient to invoke the rule. Courts tend to use as a shorthand summary, words such as "wrongful," "oppressive," or "unconscionable" to describe conduct, but the complexity of the term "threat" is demonstrated in Section 176 of the Restatement. The concept of "economic or business duress" may be generally stated as follows: Where the plaintiff is forced into a transaction as a result of unlawful threats or wrongful, oppressive, or unconscionable conduct on the part of the defendant which leaves the plaintiff no reasonable alternative but to acquiesce, the plaintiff may void the transaction and recover any economic loss....

Furthermore, while economic duress principles are more prevalent in contract cases, they are not limited solely to this area. Some courts have proceeded to analyze economic duress cases in terms of a tort theory. Under this theory, the duty is deemed to be the reasonable use of the superior economic power of the defendant. The breach is using such power unlawfully or unreasonably. The proximate cause is shown by the fact that the victim had no reasonable recourse but to acquiesce in the unlawful conduct of the defendant and is damaged thereby.... It is apparent that this tort theory is not substantially different from the economic duress theory under a contract analysis.

In several cases, we have utilized what amounts to a "business compulsion" analysis, although we characterized it only as "duress." [The court reviewed the West Virginia cases.] * * *

While we recognize the concept of business or economic duress, we do not find it exists in this case. There was no continuing contract between the plaintiff and the defendants. Thus, the demand by the defendants that the plaintiff pay $31,000 for the defective steel was not coupled with a threat to terminate an existing contract. Furthermore, the plaintiff did not accede to the defendants' demand and pay over the money.

The plaintiff's claim, stripped to its essentials, is that it has been deprived of its future prospects of doing business with the defendants. However, this future expectancy is not a legal right on which the plaintiff can anchor a claim of economic duress. * * *

Finally, there appears to be general acknowledgement that duress is not shown because one party to the contract has driven a hard bargain or that market or other conditions now make the contract more difficult to perform by one of the parties or that financial circumstances may have caused one party to make concessions. . . .

The questions certified to us by the Cabell County Circuit Court are, therefore, answered, and this case is dismissed from the docket.

Certified questions answered and dismissed.

NOTES

(1) *Duress: Wrongful Coercion.* Duress as such is seldom recognized as an independent tort. The victim does not usually maintain an action for damages. *Machinery Hauling* is exceptional in this respect. In the usual case, duress is pleaded as a defense or as a basis for avoiding a transaction and securing restitutionary relief. Moreover, the issue seldom arises in connection with initial contract formation; most often there is an attempt to bar enforcement of a contract modification or a settlement agreement. More on this later. See infra, Chapter Five, Section 4(C).

Normally, duress by physical compulsion prevents formation of a contract, Restatement (Second) § 174, whereas duress by threats makes a contract voidable. Restatement (Second) § 175 provides: "If a party's manifestation of assent is induced by an improper threat by the other party that leaves the victim no reasonable alternative, the contract is voidable by the victim." Collateral reading: Restatement (Second) §§ 174–176; Farnsworth §§ 4.16–4.19; Dobbs § 10.2; Calamari & Perillo §§ 9–2—9–8; Murray § 93.

(2) In *Austin Instruments,* Loral insisted that it was "left with no choice or alternative but to meet your [Austin's] conditions." What, precisely, were its alternatives? Was there a "reasonable" alternative?

(3) *When is a threat wrongful?* Can it ever be unlawful to threaten to do what one has a legal right to do? Quoting from an Oregon case, the court in *Machinery Hauling* states: "It is well established, however, that threats to do what the threatening person had a legal right to do does not constitute duress."

This is misleading. The Oklahoma Supreme Court recently offered this clarification: "Ordinarily a party may threaten to do what is lawful; however, a coercer's threats may be wrongful even though the threatened action would have been legal. The key factor, therefore, must be the fact that the threatened action is an unreasonable alternative to an injurious contractual demand in a bargaining situation. The wrongfulness of the coercer's conduct must be related to the unreasonableness of the alternatives which he presents to the weaker party, and the inherent wrongfulness of either alternative is relevant only insofar as it shows the unreasonableness of the alternatives. 'Unlawful' when applied to promises, agreements, contracts and considerations, means that the agreements are legally ineffective because they were obtained by bad faith coercion or compulsion, even though the acts may not be illegal per se." Centric Corporation v. Morrison–Knudsen Company, 731 P.2d 411, 419 (Okl.1986). A common example, and one referred to in *Machinery Hauling,* is the threat of criminal prosecution as an "improper means of inducing the recipient to make a contract ... a misuse, for personal gain, of power given for other legitimate ends." Restatement (Second) § 176, Comment c. Even a threat of civil process may, under exceptional circumstances, be abusive "if the threat is shown to have been made in bad faith." Id. Comment d. For other examples of wrongful threats to do what one has a legal right to do, see Berger v. Berger, 466 So.2d 1149 (Fla.App.1985) (husband threatens to inform Internal Revenue Service of wife's tax evasion if she does not sign settlement agreement); Wolf v. Marlton Corporation, 57 N.J.Super. 278, 154 A.2d 625 (1959) (purchaser under land contract threatens to sell to an "undesirable" in order to force vendor-developer to return deposit). Does *Machinery Hauling* fit here?

(4) *Undue Influence.* "While law courts developed the idea of duress, equity courts developed the parallel, but distinct, idea of undue influence." Dobbs § 10.3. Undue influence is characterized by "unfair" persuasion that may fall short of constituting actual duress. "The hallmark of such persuasion is high pressure, a pressure which works on mental, moral, or emotional weakness to such an extent that it approaches the boundaries of coercion." Odorizzi v. Bloomfield School District, 246 Cal.App.2d 123, 130, 54 Cal.Rptr. 533 (1966). Moreover, it is ordinarily limited to situations where there is a relationship of trust and confidence (e.g., parent and child; husband and wife; attorney and client), and one party is particularly susceptible to pressure by the other. However, undue influence has been found where a confidential relationship in the usual sense does not exist. The *Odorizzi* case, supra, is illustrative. In that case a school teacher was arrested on criminal charges of homosexual activity and after conferring with school officials submitted a letter of resignation the following day. A month later the charges were dismissed, and the teacher sued for rescission of the resignation and other appropriate relief. In upholding the teacher's position, the court observed that the pattern of "over-persuasion" usually involves several of the following elements: "(1) discussion of the transaction at an unusual or inappropriate time, (2) consummation of the transaction in an unusual place, (3) insistent demand that the business be finished at once, (4) extreme emphasis on untoward consequences of delay, (5) the use of multiple persuaders by the dominant side against a single servient party, (6) absence of third-party advisers to the servient party, (7) statements that there is no time to consult financial advisers or attorneys." 246 Cal.2d at 133, 54 Cal.Rptr. at 541. See: Farnsworth § 4.20; Calamari & Perillo §§ 9–9—

9–12; Murray § 94; Note, *Duress and Undue Influence—A Comparative Analysis,* 22 Baylor L.Rev. 572 (1970)

(D) UNCONSCIONABILITY

Section 2–302 of the Uniform Commercial Code provides:

(1) If the court as a matter of law finds the contract or any clause of the contract to have been unconscionable at the time it was made the court may refuse to enforce the contract, or it may enforce the remainder of the contract without the unconscionable clause, or it may so limit the application of any unconscionable clause as to avoid any unconscionable result.

(2) When it is claimed or appears to the court that the contract or any clause thereof may be unconscionable the parties shall be afforded a reasonable opportunity to present evidence as to its commercial setting, purpose and effect to aid the court in making the determination.

Comment 1, in an effort to explain, contains the following language:

This section is intended to make it possible for the courts to police explicitly against the contracts or clauses which they find to be unconscionable. In the past such policing has been accomplished by adverse construction of language, by manipulation of the rules of offer and acceptance or by determinations that the clause is contrary to public policy or to the dominant purpose of the contract. This section is intended to allow the court to pass directly on the unconscionability of the contract or particular clause therein and to make a conclusion of law as to its unconscionability. The basic test is whether, in the light of the general commercial background and the commercial needs of the particular trade or case, the clauses involved are so one-sided as to be unconscionable under the circumstances existing at the time of the making of the contract. Subsection (2) makes it clear that it is proper for the court to hear evidence upon these questions. The principle is one of the prevention of oppression and unfair surprise * * * and not of disturbance of allocation of risks because of superior bargaining power.

The mandate "to police explicitly against the contracts or clauses which they [the courts] find to be unconscionable" has generated intense interest and controversy across the land. For early statements of opposing views, see Arthur Leff, *Unconscionability and the Code—The Emperor's New Clause,* 115 U.Pa.L.Rev. 485 (1967) and Ellinghaus, *In Defense of Unconscionability,* 78 Yale L.J. 757 (1969).

There are some historical antecedents to UCC 2–302 reflected, for example, in the equitable maxim that "Equity will not enforce unconscionable bargains." See, e.g., Cutler Corp. v. Latshaw, 374 Pa. 1, 97 A.2d 234 (1953), where the court refused to enforce a confession of judgment clause buried in fine print on the back of a home repair contract. Moreover, there has evidently been a significant strain of American case law wherein courts have "limited and sometimes denied contractual obligation by reference to the fairness of the underlying exchange." Morton Horwitz, *The Historical Foundations of Modern Contract Law,* 87 Harv.L.Rev. 917, 123 (1974). But it is only with the advent of UCC 2–302, limited to transactions in goods, and Section 208 of the Restatement, Second of Contracts, that courts began in earnest to grapple with the ramifications of unconscionability doctrine and to spell out specific content.

A key question in the controversy concerns the extent that the prevention of "oppression and unfair surprise" adds to the evolving doctrines of fraud and duress and the expanding category of agreements or terms violative of public policy (infra at Chapter Six, Section Three).

The principal task is to identify the transaction types and the critical factors that increase the chances that a court will, at the very least, insist that there be a hearing on the unconscionability issue. This may turn on the attitude of the judge or court as well. For example, a judge who agrees with Professor Richard Epstein that it is improper for courts to "act as roving commissions to set aside those agreements whose substantive terms they find objectionable" and that the proper function of unconscionability is only to "police the process whereby private agreements are formed, and in that connection, only to facilitate the setting aside of agreements that are as a matter of probabilities likely to be vitiated by the classical defenses of duress, fraud or incompetence" is likely to have little receptivity to the unconscionability defense. See Richard Epstein, *Unconscionability: A Critical Reappraisal,* 18 J.Law & Econ. 293, 294–95 (1975).

Also, remember that the unconscionability doctrine is likely to be a transitional device in the movement, in a particular problem area, from lesser to greater legal control. Use by a court of the doctrine signals the breakdown of more traditional contract doctrine, such as the "duty to read" and, in many cases, heralds the coming of more comprehensive legislative and administrative regulation, some of which was discussed in the preceding section. For example, concerns about the presence and content of so-called "mandatory" arbitration clauses in consumer and other contracts have increased the claims that they are unconscionable, see infra at 557, and may result in legislative changes.

Like promissory estoppel, unconscionability operates in the interstices to achieve particularized fairness. But unlike promissory estoppel, fairness is achieved by restricting rather than expanding the scope of contractual liability. In short, its development and use are symptomatic of important changes in the society and, therefore, is worth some serious consideration.

(1) CONSUMER TRANSACTIONS

The notion that an unconscionable bargain should not be enforced is not foreign to the common law. See, e.g., the oft-quoted definition of an unconscionable bargain as one "such as no man in his senses and not under delusion would make on the one hand, and as no honest and fair man would accept on the other," Earl of Chesterfield v. Janssen, 2 Ves.Sr. 125, 28 Eng.Rpt. 82 (1750), quoted in Hume v. United States, 132 U.S. 406,

411, 10 S.Ct. 134, 33 L.Ed. 393 (1889). But this occasional language belies the normal assumption that "people should be entitled to contract on their own terms without the indulgence of paternalism by courts in the alleviation of one side or another from the effects of a bad bargain * * * [and] should be permitted to enter into contracts that actually may be unreasonable or which may lead to hardship on one side." Carlson v. Hamilton, 8 Utah 2d 272, 332 P.2d 989, 990–1 (1958).

At the risk of oversimplification, it is suggested that two developments have changed the perception of, if not the underlying assumptions about, unconscionability. The first was a tremendous expansion after World War II of the demand for and availability of consumer credit. One result was that more transactions between individuals who purchased or borrowed for personal, family or household purposes and professional sellers or lenders took place. The second was the perfection of the so-called "contract of adhesion," that is, a standard form contract drafted by one party and offered on a "take-it-or-leave-it" basis. As you study the following materials, keep the words of Karl N. Llewellyn in mind:

> The answer [to the question, how does a court decide when a party is unfairly surprised by a contract term], I suggest, is this: Instead of thinking about "assent" to boiler-plate clauses, we can recognize so far as concerns the specific, there is no assent at all. What has in fact been assented to, specifically, are the few dickered terms, and the broad type of the transaction, and but one thing more. That one thing more is a blanket assent (not a specific assent) to any not unreasonable or indecent terms the seller may have on his form, which do not alter or eviscerate the reasonable meaning of the dickered terms. The fine print which has not been read has no business to cut under the reasonable meaning of those dickered terms which constitute the dominant and only real expression of agreement, but much of it commonly belongs in. * * * [A]ny contract with boiler-plate results in two several contracts: the *dickered* deal, and the collateral one of *supplementary* boiler plate. Rooted in sense, history, and simplicity, it is an answer which could occur to anyone.

Karl N. Llewellyn, The Common Law Tradition: Deciding Appeals 370–71 (1960).

Williams v. Walker–Thomas Furniture Co.

District of Columbia Court of Appeals, 1964.
198 A.2d 914.

■ QUINN, ASSOCIATE JUDGE. Appellant, a person of limited education separated from her husband, is maintaining herself and her seven children by means of public assistance. During the period 1957–1962 she had a continuous course of dealings with appellee from which she purchased many household articles on the installment plan. These included sheets, curtains, rugs, chairs, a chest of drawers, beds, mattresses, a washing machine, and a stereo set. In 1963 appellee filed a complaint in replevin for possession of all the items purchased by appellant, alleging that her payments were in default and that it retained title to the goods according to the sales contracts. By the writ of replevin appellee obtained a bed, chest of drawers, washing machine, and the stereo set. After hearing testimony and examining the contracts, the trial court entered judgment for appellee.

Appellant's principal contentions on appeal are (1) there was a lack of meeting of the minds, and (2) the contracts were against public policy.

Appellant signed fourteen contracts in all. They were approximately six inches in length and each contained a long paragraph in extremely fine print. One of the sentences in this paragraph provided that payments, after the first purchase, were to be prorated on all purchases then outstanding. Mathematically, this had the effect of keeping a balance due on all items until the time balance was completely eliminated. It meant that title to the first purchase, remained in appellee until the fourteenth purchase, made some five years later, was fully paid.

[handwritten margin note: Title to Store until Last was paid in full]

At trial appellant testified that she understood the agreements to mean that when payments on the running account were sufficient to balance the amount due on an individual item, the item became hers. She testified that most of the purchases were made at her home; that the contracts were signed in blank; that she did not read the instruments; and that she was not provided with a copy. She admitted, however, that she did not ask anyone to read or explain the contracts to her.

We have stated that "one who refrains from reading a contract and in conscious ignorance of its terms voluntarily assents thereto will not be relieved from his bad bargain." Bob Wilson, Inc. v. Swann, D.C.Mun.App., 168 A.2d 198, 199 (1961). "One who signs a contract has a duty to read it and is obligated according to its terms." Hollywood Credit Clothing Co. v. Gibson, D.C.App., 188 A.2d 348, 349 (1963). "It is as much the duty of a person who cannot read the language in which a contract is written to have someone read it to him before he signs it, as it is the duty of one who can read to peruse it himself before signing it." Stern v. Moneyweight Scale Co., 42 App.D.C. 162, 165 (1914).

A careful review of the record shows that appellant's assent was not obtained "by fraud or even misrepresentation falling short of fraud." Hollywood Credit Clothing Co. v. Gibson, supra. This is not a case of mutual misunderstanding but a unilateral mistake. Under these circumstances, appellant's first contention is without merit.

[handwritten margin note: No meeting of the Minds]

Appellant's second argument presents a more serious question. The record reveals that prior to the last purchase appellant had reduced the balance in her account to $164. The last purchase, a stereo set, raised the balance due to $678. Significantly, at the time of this and the preceding purchases, appellee was aware of appellant's financial position. The reverse side of the stereo contract listed the name of appellant's social worker and her $218 monthly stipend from the government. Nevertheless, with full knowledge that appellant had to feed, clothe and support both herself and seven children on this amount, appellee sold her a $514 stereo set.

We cannot condemn too strongly appellee's conduct. It raises serious questions of sharp practice and irresponsible business dealings. A review of the legislation in the District of Columbia affecting retail sales and the pertinent decisions of the highest court in this jurisdiction disclose, however, no ground upon which this court can declare the contracts in question contrary to public policy. We note that were the Maryland Retail Installment Sales Act, Art. 83 §§ 128–153, or its equivalent, in force in the District of Columbia, we could grant appellant appropriate relief. We think Congress should consider corrective legislation to protect the public from such exploitive contracts as were utilized in the case at bar.

Affirmed.

Williams v. Walker–Thomas Furniture Co.

United States Court of Appeals, District of Columbia Circuit, 1965.
121 U.S.App.D.C. 315, 350 F.2d 445.

■ J. SKELLY WRIGHT, CIRCUIT JUDGE. Appellee, Walker–Thomas Furniture Company, operates a retail furniture store in the District of Columbia. During the period from 1957 to 1962 each appellant in these cases purchased a number of household items from Walker–Thomas, for which payment was to be made in installments. The terms of each purchase were contained in a printed form contract which set forth the value of the purchased item and purported to lease the item to appellant for a stipulated monthly rent payment. The contract then provided, in substance, that title would remain in Walker–Thomas until the total of all the monthly payments made equaled the stated value of the item, at which time appellants could take title. In the event of a default in the payment of any monthly installment, Walker–Thomas could repossess the item.

The contract further provided that "the amount of each periodical installment payment to be made by [purchaser] to the Company under this present lease shall be inclusive of and not in addition to the amount of each installment payment to be made by [purchaser] under such prior leases, bills or accounts; *and all payments now and hereafter made by [purchaser] shall be credited pro rata on all outstanding leases, bills and accounts* due the Company by [purchaser] at the time each such payment is made." (Emphasis added.) The effect of this rather obscure provision was to keep a balance due on every item purchased until the balance due on all items, whenever purchased, was liquidated. As a result, the debt incurred at the time of purchase of each item was secured by the right to repossess all the items previously purchased by the same purchaser, and each new item purchased automatically became subject to a security interest arising out of the previous dealings.

On May 12, 1962, appellant Thorne purchased an item described as a Daveno, three tables, and two lamps, having total stated value of $391.10. Shortly thereafter, he defaulted on his monthly payments and appellee sought to replevy all the items purchased since the first transaction in 1958. Similarly, on April 17, 1962, appellant Williams bought a stereo set of stated value of $514.95.* She too defaulted shortly thereafter, and appellee sought to replevy all the items purchased since December, 1957. The Court of General Sessions granted judgment for appellee. The District of Columbia Court of Appeals affirmed, and we granted appellants' motion for leave to appeal to this court.

Appellants' principal contention, rejected by both the trial and the appellate courts below, is that these contracts, or at least some of them, are unconscionable and, hence, not enforceable. In its opinion in Williams v. Walker–Thomas Furniture Company, 198 A.2d 914, 916 (1964), the District of Columbia Court of Appeals explained its rejection of this contention as follows:

[The court quoted the last two paragraphs of Judge Quinn's opinion, reported supra.]

We do not agree that the court lacked the power to refuse enforcement to contracts found to be unconscionable. In other jurisdictions, it has been held as a matter of common law that unconscionable contracts are not enforceable. While no decision of this court so holding has been found, the notion that an unconscionable bargain should not be given full enforcement is by no means novel. In Scott v. United States, 79 U.S. (12 Wall.) 443, 445 (1870), the Supreme Court stated:

"* * * * If a contract be unreasonable and unconscionable, but not void for fraud, a court of law will give to the party who sues for its breach damages, not according to its letter, but only such as he is equitably entitled to. * * * *"

Since we have never adopted or rejected such a rule, the question here presented is actually one of first impression.

Congress has recently enacted the Uniform Commercial Code, which specifically provides that the court may refuse to enforce a contract which it finds to be unconscionable at the time it was made. 28 D.C.Code § 2–302 (Supp. IV 1965). The enactment of this section, which occurred subsequent to the contracts here in suit, does not mean that the common law of the District of Columbia was otherwise at the time of enactment, nor does it preclude the court from adopting a similar rule in the exercise of its powers to develop the common law for the District of Columbia. In fact, in view of the absence of prior authority on the point, we consider the congressional adoption of § 2–302 persuasive authority for following the rationale of the cases from which the section is explicitly derived. Accordingly, we hold that where the element of unconscionability is present at the time a contract is made, the contract should not be enforced.

Unconscionability has generally been recognized to include an absence of meaningful choice on the part of one of the parties together with contract terms which are unreasonably favorable to the other party.

---

* At the time of this purchase her account showed a balance of $164 still owing from her prior purchases. The total of all the purchases made over the years in question came to $1,800. The total payments amounted to $1,400. [Footnote of the court.]

[handwritten margin notes: "DC hasn't adopted this yet"; "UCC enacted"; "UCC persuasive"; "Uncon. def."]

Whether a meaningful choice is present in a particular case can only be determined by consideration of all the circumstances surrounding the transaction. In many cases the meaningfulness of the choice is negated by a gross inequality of bargaining power. The manner in which the contract was entered is also relevant to this consideration. Did each party to the contract, considering his obvious education or lack of it, have a reasonable opportunity to understand the terms of the contract, or were the important terms hidden in a maze of fine print and minimized by deceptive sales practices? Ordinarily, one who signs an agreement without full knowledge of its terms might be held to assume the risk that he has entered a one-sided bargain. But when a party of little bargaining power, and hence little real choice, signs a commercially unreasonable contract with little or no knowledge of its terms, it is hardly likely that his consent, or even an objective manifestation of his consent, was ever given to all the terms. In such a case the usual rule that the terms of the agreement are not to be questioned should be abandoned and the court should consider whether the terms of the contract are so unfair that enforcement should be withheld.

In determining reasonableness or fairness, the primary concern must be with the terms of the contract considered in light of the circumstances existing when the contract was made. The test is not simple, nor can it be mechanically applied. The terms are to be considered "in the light of the general commercial background and the commercial needs of the particular trade or case." Corbin suggests the test as being whether the terms are "so extreme as to appear unconscionable according to the mores and business practices of the time and place...." We think this formulation correctly states the test to be applied in those cases where no meaningful choice was exercised upon entering the contract.

Because the trial court and the appellate court did not feel that enforcement could be refused, no findings were made on the possible unconscionability of the contracts in these cases. Since the record is not sufficient for our deciding the issue as a matter of law, the cases must be remanded to the trial court for further proceedings.

So ordered.

■ DANAHER, CIRCUIT JUDGE (dissenting). The District of Columbia Court of Appeals obviously was as unhappy about the situation here presented as any of us can possibly be. Its opinion in the *Williams* case, quoted in the majority text, concludes: "We think Congress should consider corrective legislation to protect the public from such exploitive contracts as were utilized in the case at bar."

My view is thus summed up by an able court which made no finding that there had actually been sharp practice. Rather the appellant seems to have known precisely where she stood.

There are many aspects of public policy here involved. What is a luxury to some may seem an outright necessity to others. Is public oversight to be required of the expenditures of relief funds? A washing machine, e.g., in the hands of a relief client might become a fruitful source of income. Many relief clients may well need credit, and certain business establishments will take long chances on the sale of items, expecting their pricing policies will afford a degree of protection commensurate with the risk. Perhaps a remedy when necessary will be found within the provisions of the "Loan Shark" law, D.C.Code §§ 26–601 et seq. (1961).

I mention such matters only to emphasize the desirability of a cautious approach to any such problem, particularly since the law for so long has allowed parties such great latitude in making their own contracts. I dare say there must annually be thousands upon thousands of installment credit transactions in this jurisdiction, and one can only speculate as to the effect that these cases will have.

* * *

NOTES

(1) Did Judge Wright hold that the contracts were unconscionable at the time of contracting? See UCC 2–302.

(2) Try to describe the views of Judge Quinn in the lower court and Judges Wright and Danaher in the Court of Appeals on whether a court should declare a contract unconscionable. What are the similarities and differences?

(3) State as clearly as you can Judge Wright's test for determining whether a contract is unconscionable. Would you expect the outcome of its application to vary with whether the contract was between a professional business person and an individual consumer or two business people?

(4) *Procedural vs. Substantive Unconscionability.* "Properly understood, [the principle of freedom of contract] does not require a court to enforce every contract brought before it. It does, however, demand that the reasons invoked for not enforcing the contract be of one of two sorts. Either there must be proof of some defect in the *process* of contract formation (be it duress, fraud or undue influence); or there must be, but only within narrow limits, some incompetence of the party against whom the agreement is to be enforced. The doctrine of unconscionability is important in both these respects because it can, if wisely applied, allow the courts to police these two types of problems, and thereby improve the general administration of the contract law. Yet when the doctrine of unconscionability is used in its *substantive* dimension, be it in a commercial or consumer context, it serves only to undercut a private right of contract in a manner that is apt to do more social harm than good. The result of the analysis is the same even if we view the question of unconscionability from the lofty perspective of public policy. '(I)f there is one thing which more than another public policy requires, it is that men of full age and competent understanding shall have the utmost liberty of contracting, and that their contracts when entered into freely and voluntarily shall be held sacred and shall be enforced by Courts of justice.' (Printing and Numerical Registering Co. v. Sampson, L.R. 19 Eq. 462, 465 (1875)." Richard Epstein, *Unconscionability: A Critical Reappraisal,* 18 J.Law & Econ. 293, 315 (1975).

(5) Another court took a shot at a definition.

Unconscionability has been defined as 'an absence of meaningful choice on the part of one of the parties, together with contract terms which are unreasonably favorable to the other party' ... To show that a provision is conscionable, the party seeking to uphold the provision must show that the provision bears some reasonable relationship to the risks and needs of the business. ... The indicators of procedural unconscionability generally fall into two areas: (1) lack of knowledge, and (2) lack of voluntariness. A lack of knowledge is demonstrated by a lack of understanding of the contract terms arising from inconspicuous print or the use of complex, legalistic language, ... disparity in sophistication of parties, ... and lack of opportunity to study the contract and inquire about contract terms.... A lack of voluntariness is demonstrated in contracts of adhesion when there is a great imbalance in the parties' relative bargaining power, the stronger party's terms are unnegotiable, and the weaker party is prevented by market factors, timing or other pressures from being able to contract with another party on more favorable terms or to refrain from contracting at all.

...

Substantive unconscionability is found when the terms of the contract are of such an oppressive character as to be unconscionable. It is present when there is a one-sided agreement whereby one party is deprived of all the benefits of the agreement or left without a remedy for another party's nonperformance or breach, ... a large disparity between the cost and price or a price far in excess of that prevailing in the market [place], ... or terms which bear no reasonable relationship to business risks assumed by the parties...."

Bank of Indiana, National Association v. Holyfield, 476 F.Supp. 104, 109–10 (S.D.Miss.1979).

(6) *Pop Bible Quiz*: Name unconscionable deals that Jacob cut with family members that were the bi-product of (1) lack of knowledge,* and (2) lack of voluntariness?** Extra credit: name other unconscionable deals with which Jacob was involved?***

(7) *Judge Posner on "Meaningful Choice."* "There can be no objection to using the one-sidedness of a transaction as evidence of deception, lack of agreement, or compulsion, none of which is shown here. The problem with unconscionability as a legal doctrine comes in making sense out of lack of 'meaningful choice' in a situation where the promisor was not deceived or compelled and really did agree to the provision that he contends was unconscio-

---

* "And Jacob said unto his father, I am Esau thy firstborn; I have done according as thou badest me: arise, I pray thee, sit and eat of my venison, that thy soul may bless me." Genesis 27:19.

** "And Esau said to Jacob, Feed me, I pray thee, with that same red [pottage]; for I [am] faint: therefore was his name called Edom. And Jacob said, Sell me this day thy birthright. And Esau said, Behold, I [am] at the point to die: and what profit shall this birthright do to me?" Genesis 25:30–31

*** See Genesis 29:16. See also Genesis 34:13–25 ("And the sons of Jacob answered Shechem and Hamor his father deceitfully, and said, because he had defiled Dinah their sister: And they said unto them, We cannot do this thing, to give our sister to one that is uncircumcised; for that were a reproach unto us ... And it came to pass on the third day, when they were sore, that two of the sons of Jacob, Simeon and Levi, Dinah's brethren, took each man his sword, and came upon the city boldly, and slew all the males.")

nable. Suppose that for reasons unrelated to any conduct of the promisee the promisor has very restricted opportunities. Maybe he is so poor that he can be induced to sell the clothes off his back for a pittance, or is such a poor credit risk that he can be made (in the absence of usury laws) to pay an extraordinarily high interest rate to borrow money that he wants desperately. Does he have a 'meaningful choice' in such circumstances? If not he may actually be made worse off by a rule of nonenforcement of hard bargains; for, knowing that a contract with him will not be enforced, merchants may be unwilling to buy his clothes or lend him money. Since the law of contracts cannot compel the making of contracts on terms favorable to one party, but can only refuse to enforce contracts with unfavorable terms, it is not an institution well designed to rectify inequalities in wealth." Posner, J. in Amoco Oil Company v. Ashcraft, 791 F.2d 519, 522 (7th Cir.1986).

(8) *Substantive Unconscionability As Evidence of Procedural Unconscionability.* Lop-sided agreements can actually be evidence of some procedural defect. If the court encounters a bargain that is so outrageous "such as no man in his senses and not under delusion would make," it may infer that the presence of a some defect in the bargaining process.

(9) *Remediability?* Which is easier for the law to cure—lack of information or lack of voluntariness? See UCC § 2–316(2) (modification of implied warranty of merchantability must be "conspicuous").

Comment: Renting–To–Own as a Modern Method to "Profit on Poverty"

[Retailers can often avoid consumer credit regulation by restructuring the transaction as "renting-to-own" where the consumer has the option to stop renting before attaining ownership of the chattel. Unlike traditional credit contracts, rent-to-own customers do not unconditionally promise to pay off a loan and therefore the transaction falls outside the definition of most consumer credit statutes. The following article describes the business practices of Rent–A–Center, a chain of stores (owned by Thorn Americans, Inc.) that controls 25% of the 2.8 billion U.S. Market.]

For low-income customers, Rent–A–Center has tremendous appeal. The chain gives them immediate use of brand-name merchandise, and the weekly payments are usually less than $20. But while in theory customers can eventually own the goods outright, the company says three out of every four are unable to meet all their payments.

Their failure is partially responsible for Thorn's success. The company earns considerably more by renting, repossessing and then re-renting the same goods than it does if the first customer makes all the payments. Derrick–Myers, who was fired as manager of the Rent–A–Center store in Victorville, California, recalls one particular Philco VCR, for example, that he says retailed for about $119—but that brought in more than $5,000 in a five-year period.

That means the most profitable customers are people like Minneapolis welfare mother Angela Adams, who says Rent–A–Center salespeople cajoled her into renting more than a dozen items at a monthly cost that reached about \$325. Though the salespeople knew how little she earned, "they pushed it on me," she says. When she fell behind in her payments in late 1991, Rent–A–Center sued her and repossessed the goods, ranging from a bedroom set to two VCRs. Ms. Adams is now a named plaintiff in one of the two class-action suits, this one pending in federal court in Minneapolis. Rent–A–Center declines comment.

"Even if a customer can't afford it and you know it and they know it, we'll rent to them anyway," says Rod Comeaux, a former store manager from Onley, VA., who was fired a year ago for unrelated reasons. "We can always get it back" and re-rent it to others, he says.

Rent–A–Center's Mr. Gates denies that salespeople put excessive pressure on customers or intentionally overload them with goods. On average, customers rent 2.85 items a month, at a total monthly cost of \$99.07, and they are able to cancel rentals at any time without a penalty, he points out. Store managers—who are required to obtain income and other financial information from customers—ideally should act as "financial planners" for customers, he says, adding that the "worst thing" employees can do is to rent to customers whose "eyes are bigger than their stomachs."

Rent–A–Center says its customer base is 25% to 30% black and 10% to 15% Hispanic, and just 15% are on welfare or government subsidies. But former store managers consistently maintain that the total on government assistance is more than 25%, with some claiming up to 70%. Indeed, they unanimously report that sales always spiked on "Mother's Day," as they call the day when welfare mother's get their checks. * * *

According to a thick training manual, salespeople are supposed to quote the weekly and monthly rental rates. The manual doesn't instruct employees to quote the total cost, and former store managers say they made sure they never did. In fact, in 40 states, the total isn't even on the price tag. (Ten states require that it be listed on price tags, a rule Rent–A–Center says it will honor in all 50 states by next month.) Instead, the manual instructs employees to focus on "features and benefits," such as Rent–A–Center's free delivery and repair, and most of all, the low weekly price.

But the advertised weekly price is designed to yield each store about 3½ times its cost of purchasing the merchandise from Rent–A–Center headquarters. The total is jacked up further by a one-time processing fee (typically \$7.50) and late fees (typically \$5). The total price is usually revealed only in the rental agreement that customers sign at the end of the sales process, former store managers say.

To boost Rent–A–Center's profits, employees also push a "customer protection" plan that offers minimal benefits but that 95% of customers end up subscribing to. "It's better than insurance," saleswoman Laura Daupino of the Bloomfield, N.J. store was overheard telling an unemployed welfare mother recently. Yet, unlike insurance, it doesn't replace stolen or destroyed items, or reimburse customers for their loss. It offers customers basically one benefit: It prevents Rent–A–Center from suing customers if goods are stolen or destroyed.

For Rent–A–Center, however, the benefit is considerably larger: The protection plan is a $29 million annual revenue booster, much of which drops to the bottom line, as does most of the $27 million racked up from the other fees, according to internal company financial documents.

Rent–A–Center has long justified his high prices by citing customer defaults and the costs associated with its free repairs. But part of Rent–A–Center's secret of success is that those costs are minimal. Internal documents show its service expenses ran 3.3% of rental revenue in fiscal 1993, though Rent–A–Center says the actual figure is closer to 10%. And its total inventory losses—from junked merchandise and "skips and stolens" (as in customers who skip town)—run a bit over 2% of revenue. * * *

Thorn executives say there is nothing insidious about Rent–A–Center's strategy of courting customers who are of limited means, and of treating them well. Customers receive "fantastic" service, say Sir Colin, who professes to be "always puzzled" why the rent-to-own industry is "badly regarded." Rent–A–Center, he adds, "treats them like kings and queens."

Customers like Carol Baker, a waitress at a resort hotel in Bolton Landing, N.Y., are appreciative. "The prices could be cheaper," says Ms. Baker, whose home is almost completely furnished by Rent–A–Center, "but they treat me like I'm a somebody."

Former employees and other customers see things differently. "The Rent–A–Center philosophy," says Mr. Comeaux, the former store manager in Virginia, "is that if you treat the customer like they're royalty, you can bleed them through the nose." * * *

Inevitably, some customers take on more than they can handle. So it is that behind every Rent–A–Center salesman lurks his doppelganger: Repo man.

Repossessions are never pretty, and the pre-Thorn era was no exception. But because of the ambitious targets, people who have worked under both regimes say, employees now push harder than ever. Customers typically make their payments every Saturday and, throughout the morning, store employees work the phones exacting promises from the tardy. In these conversations, former customers say, they have been harassed, intimidated and even threatened with violence. Robert Keeling, a former manager in Gasden, Ala., who was fired in March in part for carrying a gun, says that a "favorite ploy is falsely informing customers or their relatives that a warrant for arrest has been issued for the theft of rental property. * * *

On Halloween night in 1991, three Rent–A–Center employees in Utica, N.Y., dressed up, respectively, as the Cookie Monster, a gorilla and an alien life form and knocked on a customer's door. Once inside, they successfully repossessed a home-entertainment system on which payments hadn't been made in almost three months. Gary Gerhardt, the store manager who blessed this plan, calls the ruse "a last-ditch effort," adding, "it was the only way we could think to get someone in the door."

At the crack of dawn one Sunday, Mr. Myers, the store manager in Victorville, Calif., until March 1992, pulled off a particularly tough repossession by enlisting three burly Hell's Angles. He adds that in other instances he vented his spleen on delinquent customers who wouldn't come to the door by slathering superglue all over their deadbolts and doorknobs. (Messrs. Gerhardt and Myers both were fired, but over unrelated matters.)

The grueling routine grates on some Rent–A–Center employees. Mr. Baker, the former Maryland store manager, quite in disgust in 1991 after one of his employees repossessed a refrigerator from a welfare mother with an infant, plunking her meat and milk on the kitchen table. * * *

Yet another tactic in Rent–A–Center's repo repertoire is the "couch payment"—sexual favors exacted by employees in lieu of cash. Of 28 former store managers interviewed, six said the practice had occurred in their areas. [S]ome store employees have boasted that they "have gone out to the customers' homes, had sex with them, and then repo-ed the merchandise anyway." * * *

In its new ventures, Rent–A–Center will surely be able to count on its current customers, a loyal lot: Most feel they can't get quality goods any other way.

Nancy Thornley, an Ogden, Utah, housewife, for example, was diligently handing over about $261 a month in rental payments to Rent–A–Center in 1991 when she lost a leg to diabetes. Faced with a $1,000 bill for a prosthetic limb, she arranged to defer part of her rental tab, she says. But shortly after she returned home from the hospital, she was shocked with two store employees showed up without notice on a Saturday afternoon, accused her of being three months behind in payments and carted away all the goods, primarily basics such as a refrigerator and a couch.

"It was total humiliation," she says. "All my neighbors were watching."

A year later, though, Ms. Thornley was back, having been inundated by Rent–A–Center letters and "We Want You Back" coupons. She was reluctant to return, she says. But "I needed the item," a microwave oven, and couldn't afford to buy it. Says Ms. Thornley: "I felt like there was nowhere else to go."

Alix M. Freedman, *A Marketing Giant Uses Its Sales Prowess To Profit on Poverty*, Wall Street Journal, Sept. 22, 1993, p. A12. [Reprinted by permission of Wall Street Journal, © 1993 Dow Jones & Company, Inc. All Rights Reserved Worldwide.]

Comment: Contracts of Adhesion

Standard form contracts presented on a take-it-or-leave-it basis are often referred to as "contracts of adhesion." At common law, contracts of adhesion have been "presumptively enforceable." Todd D. Rakoff, *Contracts of Adhesion: an Essay in Reconstruction*, 96 Harv. L. Rev. 1173, 1185 (1983). ("[I]n the absence of extraordinary circumstances, the adherent can establish an excuse only by showing affirmative participation by the drafting party in causing misunderstanding."). But see Restatement (Second) of Contract § 211(3) regarding "Standardized Agreements": "Where the other party has reason to believe that the party manifesting ... assent would not do so if he knew that the writing contained a particular term, the term is not part of the agreement." [Could a general consumer survey establish such knowledge?]

Some jurisdictions narrowly define the category. For example in Washington: "An adhesion contract is usually (1) a standard form, (2) prepared by one party and submitted to another party on a 'take it or leave it' basis, (3) when the bargaining power between the parties was not truly equal." *Eelbode v. Chec Med. Ctrs., Inc.*, 97 Wash.App. 462, 472 n. 6, 984 P.2d 436 (1999)). Other jurisdictions define the category of adhesive contracts broadly as being conclusive proof of procedural unconscionability but then ask whether the bargain in sufficiently unconscionable in a substantive sense to warrant non-enforcement. For example, in California:

> A finding of a contract of adhesion is essentially a finding of procedural unconscionability. This conclusion does not end our inquiry, however, because "[t]he determination that a contract is adhesive ... does not necessarily mean that an arbitration provision contained therein is unenforceable." An arbitration provision in an adhesion contract is legally enforceable unless the provision (1) does not fall within the reasonable expectations of the weaker party, or (2) is unduly oppressive or unconscionable.... [T]he courts 'scrutinize such contracts with care' and refuse to honor the selection 'if to do so would result in substantial injustice to the adherent.'

Ehlers Elevators, Inc. v. Beta Seed Co., 2002 WL 31492719 (Cal.App.2002).

Jurisdictions that broadly define the category also tend to find that there are varying degrees of procedural unconscionability produced by an adhesive contract. For example, in Olson v. ARV Assisted Living, Inc., 2002 WL 31174254 (Cal.App.2002), the court in reviewing an arbitration agreement found:

> While the agreement was adhesive, there was no greater oppression in its presentation to Olson than is inherent in any arbitration agreement presented to any employee by any employer.... The agreement, however, is less than a model of clarity and could have more completely explained its implications, e.g., that Olson was giving up her right to a court trial or jury trial. On the other hand the agreement was not made opaque by technical or obscure language and its meaning was discoverable from its terms.... The agreement was, therefore, procedurally unconscionable but the degree of that unconscionability was relatively low.

Id. at 3. See the *Ferguson* case, *infra* at 557. Thus, while the phrase "contract of adhesion" is generally used in a pejorative sense, it is important to keep in mind that most adhesive contracts will be judicially enforced. Merely arguing that your client signed a standardized contract that was presented on a take-it-or-leave-it basis will not normally be sufficient to avoid the finding of an enforceable agreement.

Jones v. Star Credit Corp.

Supreme Court of New York, 1969.
59 Misc.2d 189, 298 N.Y.S.2d 264.

[The opinion is reprinted, supra at 68].

NOTES

(1) The Federal Trade Commission, by regulation, requires a "cooling off period" for door-to-door sales. In essence, the seller must inform the consumer in writing and in CONSPICUOUS type in the "same language, e.g., Spanish, as that principally used in the oral sales presentation" the following: "YOU, THE BUYER, MAY CANCEL THIS TRANSACTION AT ANY TIME PRIOR TO MIDNIGHT OF THE THIRD BUSINESS DAY AFTER THE DATE OF THIS TRANSACTION. SEE THE ATTACHED NOTICE OF CANCELLATION FORM FOR AN EXPLANATION OF THIS RIGHT." 16 C.F.R. sec. 429.1 (March 1, 1996).

In addition, Section 4(c) of the Uniform Consumer Sales Practices Act provides that "in determining whether an act or practice is unconscionable, the court shall consider circumstances such as the following of which the supplier knew or had reason to know: (1) that he took advantage of the inability of the consumer reasonably to protect his interests because of his physical infirmity, ignorance, illiteracy, inability to understand the language of an agreement or similar factors; (2) that when the consumer transaction was entered into the price grossly exceeded the price at which similar property or services were readily obtainable in similar transactions by like consumers; ... (4) that when the consumer transaction was entered into there was no reasonable probability of payment of the obligation in full by the consumer."

(2) In California Grocers v. Bank of America, 22 Cal.App.4th 205, 27 Cal.Rptr.2d 396 (1994), defendant bank charged customers a $3 fee for certain returned deposit items (DIRs). The California Grocers Association, a trade group of retail and wholesale grocers, attacked the fee. In holding that the fee was not unconscionable ("not so high as to shock the conscience"), the court relied upon two determinations: First, there was "free" competition among banks in California and the $3 fee was at the low end of similar fees charged by other banks; and Second, the "$3 fee is not so exorbitant as to shock the conscience." Even though the cost of processing a DIR was only $1.50, the markup was "only 100 percent." "This may be a generous profit, but it is wholly within the range of commonly accepted notions of fair profitability." The court noted that price unconscionability cases "generally involve much greater price-value disparities" and cited *Jones v. Star Credit* for the proposition that a "sale of a freezer at triple its retail value" was unconscionable." Id. At 402–403.

(3) The Supreme Court of Arizona has read UCC 2–302 in conjunction with UCC 2–719(3) to conclude that "a claim of unconscionability can be

established with a showing of substantive unconscionability alone, especially in cases involving either price-cost disparity or limitation of remedies." Further: "If only procedural irregularities are present, it may be more appropriate to analyze the claims under the doctrines of fraud, misrepresentation, duress, and mistake, although such irregularities can make a case of procedural unconscionability." Maxwell v. Fidelity Financial Services, 184 Ariz. 82, 907 P.2d 51 (1995). Do you agree with this reading of the Code?

Fleet v. United States Consumer Council, Inc.

United States District Court, E.D. Pennsylvania, 1989.
95 B. R. 319.

* * *

IV.   THE FEE CHARGED BY USCC CONSTITUTED AN UNCONSCIONABLE PRICE AND A FRAUD IN VIOLATION OF NJ UDAP

The NJ UDAP [Unfair & Deceptive Practices Act, N.J.S.A. 56:8–1 et seq.] prohibits any "unconscionable commercial practice," . . . as well as deceptive and fraudulent conduct used in the sale or advertisement of merchandise * * * . . .

While the term "unconscionability" is not specifically defined in either the NJ UDAP or the UCC, it has been characterized as "an amorphous concept obviously designed to establish a broad business ethic." [Kugler v. Romain, 279 A.2d 640 (N.J.1971)] Thus, the New Jersey Supreme Court, in *Romain*, concluded that the legislature expected the courts to interpret the concept of unconscionability "liberally so as to effectuate the public purpose, and to pour content into it on a case-by-case basis." . . . As one commentator noted:

> The Courts have always avoided hampering themselves by defining or laying down as a general proposition what shall be held to constitute fraud. Fraud is infinite in variety. The fertility of man's invention in devising new schemes of fraud is so great, that the courts have always declined to define it, or to define undue influence, which is one of its many varieties, reserving to themselves the liberty to deal with it under whatever form it may present itself.

KERR, FRAUD AND MISTAKE (7th ed. 1952) . . .

Despite the amorphous nature of the concept of unconscionability, it has been defined as establishing a standard of conduct contemplating "good faith, honesty in fact, and observance of fair dealings." . . . As the Court in *Romain* noted, "[t]he need for application of the standard is most acute when the professional seller is seeking the trade of those most subject to exploitation—the uneducated, the inexperienced and the people of low incomes."* The Uniform Consumer Sales Practice Act (hereinafter "UCSPA") provides that, in determining whether an act or practice is unconscio-

---

* The court in *Romain* recognized that [t]he deception, misrepresentation, and unconscionable practices engaged in by profes- sional sellers seeking mass distribution of many types of consumer goods frequently produce an adverse effect on large segments nable, the court should consider, among other factors, whether "the price grossly exceeded the price at which similar property or services were readily obtainable in similar transactions by like consumers." UCSPA, § 4(c)(2).

The Plaintiffs maintain that the fee charged by USCC was an unconscionable price for the services provided. The seminal New Jersey case on price unconscionability is *Romain.* That case involved the door-to-door sales of so-called educational books for children ... Sales efforts were directed at minority group consumers and consumers of limited education and economic means.... The seller was charging between \$250.00 and \$280.00 for books with a value of about \$110.00.... Evidence was presented that the books sold were of little or no educational value to children in the age-group and socio-economic position targeted by the seller....

The *Romain* court found the seller's price to be unconscionable, and further held that such price unconscionability constituted a consumer fraud prohibited by NJ UDAP.... In so holding, the court reasoned that:

> [i]n deciding whether defendant, contrary to the statute, used any deception, fraud, false pretense, or misrepresentation, or whether he concealed, suppressed or omitted any material fact in connection with the sales to book purchaser, the price charged the consumer is only one element to be consider. If the price is grossly excessive in relation to the seller's costs, and if in addition the good sold have little or no value to the consumer for the purpose for which he was persuaded to buy them and which the seller pretended they would serve, the price paid by the consumer takes on even more serious characteristics of imposition....

We find the facts in the present case to be even more indicative of imposition. The consumers who turned to USCC for help were financially troubled and distraught. Some were unemployed or disabled. Many were facing the loss of their homes through foreclosure. USCC, through its marketing scheme, represented that it could provide help to these consumers, help which USCC could not and did not provide. USCC then charged consumers \$195.00 to \$260.00 simply for referring them to an attorney. Such a referral could be obtained for free through a bar association lawyer referral service....

In light of the circumstances of the present case, we have no difficulty concluding that the fee charged by USCC constitutes an unconscionable price for its services and a fraud in violation of NJ UDAP. * * *

NOTES

(1) Litigants claiming price unconscionability have fared better under regulatory statutes than under UCC 2–302 standing alone; e.g. McRaild v.

of disadvantaged and poorly educated people, who are wholly devoid of expertise and least able to understand or to cope with the "sale-oriented," "extroverted" and unethical solici-tors bent on capitalizing upon their weakness, who therefore most need protection against predatory practices. 279 A.2d at 652.

Shepard Lincoln Mercury, 141 Mich.App. 406, 367 N.W.2d 404 (1985) (Michigan Consumer Protection Act; trade of an automobile valued at $17,000 and $11,000 in cash for a house determined to have a minimum value of $43,000); Town East Ford Sales, Inc. v. Gray, 730 S.W.2d 796 (Tex.App.1987) (gross disparity between market value and price paid); People by Abrams v. Two Wheel Corp., 71 N.Y.2d 693, 530 N.Y.S.2d 46, 525 N.E.2d 692 (1988) (New York "price gouging" statute which prohibits merchants from charging unconscionably excessive prices for essential consumer goods during disruptions in the market caused by such forces as strikes, power failures, weather conditions and other emergencies; sale of 100 generators at inflated prices ranging from 4% to 67% over the base prices); Ramirez–Eames v. Hover, 108 N.M. 520, 775 P.2d 722 (1989) (Uniform Owner–Resident Relations Act; agreement to pay $850 monthly rental for apartment, where market value was $725).

(2) *Procedural Aspects*. UCC 2–302 provides that if "the court as a matter of law" finds the contract to have been unconscionable "at the time it was made," it may refuse to enforce it. Thus, unconscionability is an issue of law to be decided by the court. Moreover, the focus is upon the situation as it existed at the time of the contract.

Ordinarily, a party will plead unconscionability as an affirmative defense. Although in some cases the pleadings may be sufficient to permit a court to resolve the issue on a motion for summary judgment, in the usual case there will be a hearing at which the parties present evidence for the trial judge's consideration. What kind of evidence? The Uniform Commercial Code does not say, other than that it should pertain to the contract's "commercial setting, purpose and effect," so as "to aid the court in making the determination." This is sufficient to indicate, however, that the scope of inquiry is broad. An Arizona court has commented as follows:

> It was the obvious intention of the drafters and our Legislature that the court have the widest latitude in hearing evidence on the issue of commercial setting in cases where unconscionability was claimed, either in whole or in part. * * * In this context, while serious questions can be raised, and have indeed been raised here, concerning the admissibility of some of the evidence under general contract law terms (the parole evidence rule), the trial court was obviously correct in allowing the widest latitude in receiving evidence on the issue of commercial setting and unconscionability.

Raybond Electronics, Inc. v. Glen–Mar Door Manufacturing Co., 22 Ariz.App. 409, 528 P.2d 160 (1974).

Subsection (2) of UCC 2–302 guarantees the right of the parties to present evidence of the contract's commercial setting, purpose, and effect. This may be of particular importance to one who seeks to defend against unconscionability, for evidence of commercial context may demonstrate that a contract or clause which superficially seems to be one-sided in character is actually quite reasonable when viewed in the totality of the circumstances. See, e.g., In re Elkins–Dell Manufacturing Co., 253 F.Supp. 864 (E.D.Pa.1966).

The burden of proof is said to be upon the one who claims the unconscionability. See, e.g., *Zapatha v. Dairy Mart, Inc.*, infra at 564. This means, in practice, that one claiming an unconscionability defense must come forward with the evidence showing a prima facie case. The burden would then seem to shift to the other party to persuade the court that the contract or clause was conscionable. See note 4, infra.

Finally, if there is a judicial finding of unconscionability, what are the remedial consequences? The Code states that the court "may refuse to enforce the contract, or it may enforce the remainder of the contract without the unconscionable clause, or it may so limit the application of any unconscionable clause as to avoid any unconscionable result." Essentially, the aggrieved party is limited to defensive weapons. As illustrated in *Jones*, however, the court may do more than simply refuse to enforce the contract or clause. There the court, in effect, reformed the contract by holding that the amount due was to be equal to the amount already paid. See also Vockner v. Erickson, 712 P.2d 379 (Alaska 1986) (land purchase agreement deemed unconscionable under section 208 of the revised Restatement; amount of installment payment changed).

There is, evidently, no right to recover damages under UCC 2–302. See, e.g., Cowin Equipment Co. v. General Motors Corporation, 734 F.2d 1581 (11th Cir.1984); Best v. United States National Bank, 78 Or.App. 1, 714 P.2d 1049 (1986) (court acknowledged that relief might possibly be predicated upon breach of an implied covenant of good faith and fair dealing). Although UCC 2–302 does not specifically authorize money damages, it does authorize a court to "enforce the contract without the unconscionable clause." Thus, after striking an unconscionable clause, a court may then award damages for breach of the contract without that clause. Langemeier v. National Oats, Inc., 775 F.2d 975 (8th Cir.1985). Finally, damages may be recovered under a state's deceptive trade practice statute, twelve of which specifically prohibit unconscionable practices. See J. Sheldon, Unfair and Deceptive Acts and Practices 112 (4th ed. 2000) (Alabama; District of Columbia; Kansas; Kentucky; Michigan; Nebraska; New Jersey; New Mexico; New York; Ohio; Texas; Utah).

PROBLEM: THE CASE OF THE LIFE–CARE CONTRACT

Kathleen MacKay, age 79, visited a number of retirement facilities in the Santa Fe and Albuquerque area. She liked La Vida Llena the best. She took several weeks to study the Residence Agreement which this facility used. She discussed the proposed agreement with her friends, but not with an attorney. On March 2, 1983 she signed the agreement and made a deposit toward the entry fee; on June 16, upon payment of the remainder of the $36,950 entry fee, she moved in. She became sick on December 29th of that year, and two days later she died.

Under the Residence Agreement, the entry fee entitled Mrs. MacKay to occupy a one-bedroom unit for the rest of her life, and guaranteed her admission to the La Vida Llena Nursing Care Center whenever required. She was also obliged to pay a monthly service fee of $537.00 to cover meals, laundry, etc. She had the right to terminate the agreement upon 30–days notice if she were unable to live alone and if monthly payments were current. La Vida Llena would then refund the entrance fee less "10% plus 1% for each month of residency." There was no refund of entry fee upon a resident's death.

Mrs. MacKay's personal representative sought a refund of the entrance fee on the ground that the agreement was an unconscionable adhesion contract.

What result? See Guthmann v. La Vida Llena, 103 N.M. 506, 709 P.2d 675 (1985).

Ferguson v. Countrywide Credit Industries, Inc.

United States Court of Appeals, Ninth Circuit, 2002.
298 F.3d 778.

■ PREGERSON, CIRCUIT JUDGE.

Misty Ferguson ("Ferguson") filed a complaint against Countrywide Credit Industries, Inc. ("Countrywide") and her supervisor, Leo DeLeon ("DeLeon"), alleging causes of action under federal and state law for sexual harassment, retaliation, and hostile work environment. Countrywide filed a petition for an order compelling arbitration of Ferguson's claims. The district court denied Countrywide's petition on the grounds that Countrywide's arbitration agreement is unenforceable based on the doctrine of unconscionability and that Ferguson cannot be compelled to arbitrate her Title VII employment discrimination claims. Countrywide appeals this decision. We have jurisdiction under 9 U.S.C. § 16(a)(1)(B). We review de novo a district court's denial of a motion to compel arbitration, . . . and affirm on the ground that the arbitration agreement is unconscionable.

I. FACTUAL and PROCEDURAL HISTORY

Ferguson filed a complaint against Countrywide and DeLeon, alleging causes of action for sexual harassment, retaliation, and hostile work environment under Title VII of the Civil Rights Act of 1964 and 1991, 42 U.S.C. §§ 2000e–2(a), 2000e 3 & 1981a(c), and the California Fair Employment and Housing Act, Cal. Gov't Code §§ 12900 *et seq.* ("FEHA").

Countrywide filed a petition to compel arbitration of Ferguson's claims. When Ferguson was hired she was required to sign Countrywide's Conditions of Employment, which states in relevant part: "I understand that in order to work at Countrywide I must execute an arbitration agreement." Countrywide's arbitration agreement ("the arbitration agreement") contains the following relevant clauses:

Paragraph 1. *Agreement to Arbitrate; Designated Claims:*

"Except as otherwise provided in this Agreement, the Company and Employee hereby consent to the resolution by arbitration of all claims or controversies for which a federal or state court . . . would be authorized to grant relief. . . ."

The arbitration agreement then outlines which claims are covered by the agreement* and which claims are not covered.** [In the agreement, the

---

Agreement to Arbitrate; Designated Claims: "The Claims covered by this Agreement include, but are not limited to, claims for wages or other compensation due; claims for breach of any contract or covenant, express or implied; tort claims; claims for discrimination or harassment on bases which include but are not limited to race, sex, sexual orientation, religion, national origin, age, marital status, disability or medical condiparties agreed, inter alia, to (i) waive all rights to a "trial before a jury;" (ii) have arbitration as "the parties' exclusive remedy;" and (iii) limit discovery "to three depositions and an aggregate of 30 discovery requests of any kind."]

She says she didn't sign

In her answer to Countrywide's petition to compel arbitration, Ferguson denied that she signed the arbitration agreement and requested a jury trial on that issue, pursuant to section 4 of the Federal Arbitration Act ("FAA"). Countrywide filed reply documents in support of the petition, and submitted evidence that Ferguson entered the agreement.

* * *

[The district court denied Countrywide's petition to compel arbitration. Although the court found that Ferguson raised a genuine dispute regarding the making of the arbitration agreement, it ruled that, assuming the agreement does exist: (1) the arbitration agreement is unenforceable because it is unconscionable under *Armendariz v. Foundation Health Psychcare Services, Inc.,* 24 Cal.4th 83 (Cal.2000); and (2) under the Ninth Circuit's holding in *Duffield v. Robertson Stephens & Co.,* 144 F.3d 1182, 1190 (9th Cir.1998), Ferguson cannot be compelled to arbitrate her Title VII claims. On appeal from the decision to compel arbitration, the court of appeals affirmed on the unconscionability ruling and found it unnecessary to rule on the arbitrability of the Title VII claims.]

Appeal = Aff.

Uncons.

II.   UNCONSCIONABILITY

A. The district court correctly concluded that Countrywide's arbitration agreement was unenforceable because it is unconscionable under California law.

The FAA compels judicial enforcement of a wide range of written arbitration agreements. Section 2 of the FAA provides, in relevant part, that arbitration agreements "shall be valid, irrevocable, and enforceable, save upon such grounds that exist at law or in equity for the revocation of any contract." 9 U.S.C. § 2. In determining the validity of an agreement to arbitrate, federal courts "should apply ordinary state-law principles that govern the formation of contracts." *First Options of Chicago, Inc. v. Kaplan,* 514 U.S. 938, 944, (1995). "Thus, generally applicable defenses, such as ... unconscionability, may be applied to invalidate arbitration

tion; claims for benefits ... and claims for violation of any federal, state or other governmental constitution, statute, ordinance, regulation, or public policy."

** *Claims Not Covered by This Agreement:* "This Agreement does not apply to or cover claims for workers' compensation or unemployment compensation benefits; claims resulting from the default of any obligation of the Company or the Employee under a mortgage loan which was granted and/or serviced by the Company; claims for injunctive and/or other equitable relief for intellectual property violations, unfair competition and/or the use and/or unauthorized disclosure of trade secrets or confidential information; or claims based upon an employee pension or benefit plan that either (1) contains an arbitration or other non-judicial resolution procedure, in which case the provisions of such plan shall apply, or (2) is underwritten by a commercial insurer which decides claims."

agreements without contravening § 2 [of the FAA]." *Doctor's Assocs., Inc. v. Casarotto,* 517 U.S. 681, 687 (1996).

California courts may invalidate an arbitration clause under the doctrine of unconscionability. This doctrine, codified by the California Legislature in California Civil Code § 1670.5(a), provides:

> if the court as a matter of law finds the contract or any clause of the contract to have been unconscionable at the time it was made, the court may refuse to enforce the contract, or may enforce the remainder of the contract without the unconscionable clause, or it may so limit the application of any unconscionable clause as to avoid any unconscionable result.

This statute, however, does not define unconscionability. Instead, we look to the California Supreme Court's decision in *Armendariz,* 24 Cal.4th 83, which provides the definitive pronouncement of California law on unconscionability to be applied to mandatory arbitration agreements, such as the one at issue in this case. In order to render a contract unenforceable under the doctrine of unconscionability, there must be both a procedural and substantive element of unconscionability.... These two elements, however, need not both be present in the same degree.... Thus, for example, "the more substantively oppressive the contract term, the less evidence of procedural unconscionability is required to come to the conclusion that the term is unenforceable." *Armendariz,* 99 Cal.Rptr.2d 745.

1. Procedural Unconscionability

Procedural unconscionability "concerns the manner in which the contract was negotiated and the circumstances of the parties at that time." *Kinney v. United Healthcare Servs., Inc.,* 83 Cal.Rptr.2d 348, 352–53 (Ct.App.1999). A determination of whether a contract is procedurally unconscionable focuses on two factors: oppression and surprise. " 'Oppression' arises from an inequality of bargaining power which results in no real negotiation and an absence of meaningful choice. 'Surprise' involves the extent to which the supposedly agreed-upon terms of the bargain are hidden in the prolix printed form drafted by the party seeking to enforce the disputed terms." *Stirlen v. Supercuts, Inc.,* 60 Cal.Rptr.2d 138, 145 (Ct.App.1997).

In *Circuit City Stores, Inc. v. Adams,* 279 F.3d 889, 892 (9th Cir.), *cert. denied,* 122 S.Ct. 2329 (2002), we held that the arbitration agreement at issue satisfied the elements of procedural unconscionability under California law. We found the agreement to be procedurally unconscionable because:

> Circuit City, which possesses considerably more bargaining power than nearly all of its employees or applicants, drafted the contract and uses it as its standard arbitration agreement for all of its new employees. The agreement is a prerequisite to employment, and job applicants are not permitted to modify the agreement's terms—they must take the contract or leave it....

In the present case, as in *Circuit City,* the arbitration agreement was imposed as a condition of employment and was non-negotiable.

Countrywide contends that there was no element of "surprise" or "oppression" in its arbitration agreement because Ferguson had "ample time to consider alternatives to Countrywide's terms of employment" and the contract was "written in plain language." A California appellate court recently rejected these arguments, holding that whether the plaintiff had an opportunity to decline the defendant's contract and instead to enter into a contract with another party that does not include the offending terms is not the relevant test for procedural unconscionability.... Instead, California courts have consistently held that where a party in a position of unequal bargaining power is presented with an offending clause without the opportunity for meaningful negotiation, oppression and, therefore, procedural unconscionability, are present. * * * Because Ferguson was in a position of unequal bargaining power and was presented with offending contract terms without an opportunity to negotiate, the district court in the instant case correctly found Countrywide's arbitration agreement procedurally unconscionable.

She couldn't bargain

2. Substantive Unconscionability

Substantive unconscionability "focuses on the terms of the agreement and whether those terms are so one-sided as to *shock the conscience....*"

a. One-sided coverage of arbitration agreement

Countrywide's arbitration agreement specifically covers claims for breach of express or implied contracts or covenants, tort claims, claims of discrimination or harassment based on race, sex, age, or disability, and claims for violation of any federal, state, or other governmental constitution, statute, ordinance, regulation, or public policy. On the other hand, the arbitration agreement specifically excludes claims for workers' compensation or unemployment compensation benefits, injunctive and/or other equitable relief for intellectual property violations, unfair competition and/or the use and/or unauthorized disclosure of trade secrets or confidential information....

Countrywide's arbitration agreement was unfairly one-sided and, therefore, substantively unconscionable because the agreement compels arbitration of the claims employees are most likely to bring against Countrywide ... [but] exempts from arbitration the claims Countrywide is most likely to bring against its employees. Further, we ... conclude that Countrywide's justifications for its one-sided arbitration agreement are not persuasive.

b. Arbitration Fees

In *Armendariz,* the California Supreme Court held that:

when an employer imposes mandatory arbitration as a condition of employment, the arbitration agreement or arbitration process cannot generally require the employee to bear any *type* of expense that the employee would not be required to bear if he or she were free to bring the action in court. This rule will ensure that employees bringing [discrimination] claims will not be deterred by costs greater than the usual costs incurred during litigation, costs that are essentially imposed on an employee by the employer.

Armendariz, 99 Cal.Rptr.2d 745.

Countrywide's arbitration agreement has a provision that requires the employee to "pay to NAF [National Arbitration Forum] its filing fee up to a maximum of $125.00 when the Claim is filed. The Company shall pay for the first hearing day. All other arbitration costs shall be shared equally by the Company and the Employee." Countrywide argues that this provision is not so one-sided as to "shock the conscience" and, therefore, is enforceable. However, *Armendariz* holds that a fee provision is unenforceable when the employee bears *any* expense beyond the usual costs associated with bringing an action in court. *Id.* As indicated in Ferguson's opposition to the petition to compel arbitration and in her brief, NAF imposes multiple fees which would bring the cost of arbitration for Ferguson into the thousands of dollars.* Moreover, on remand in *Circuit City,* we held that a fee allocation scheme which requires the employee to split the arbitrator's fees with the employer would alone render an arbitration agreement substantively unconscionable ... * * *

Making them pay for arb. costs is uncons.

c. One-sided discovery provision

Ferguson also argues that the discovery provision in the arbitration agreement is one-sided and, therefore, unconscionable. The discovery provision states that "[a] deposition of a corporate representative shall be limited to no more than four designated subjects," but does not impose a similar limitation on depositions of employees. Ferguson also notes that the arbitration agreement sets mutual limitations (e.g., no more than three depositions) and mutual advantages (e.g., unlimited expert witnesses) which favor Countrywide because it is in a superior position to gather information regarding its business practices and employees' conduct, and has greater access to funds to pay for expensive expert witnesses.

Ferguson urges this court to affirm the district court's ruling that the discovery provision is unconscionable on the ground that the limitations and mutual advantages on discovery are unfairly one-sided and have no commercial justification other than "maximizing employer advantage," which is an improper basis for such differences under *Armendariz,* 99 Cal.Rptr.2d 745. Countrywide argues to the contrary that the arbitration agreement provides for ample discovery by employees.

In *Armendariz,* the California Supreme Court held that employees are "at least entitled to discovery sufficient to adequately arbitrate their statutory claims, including access to essential documents and witnesses." *Armendariz,* 99 Cal.Rptr.2d 745, 6 P.3d at 684. Adequate discovery, however, does not mean unfettered discovery. As *Armendariz* recognized, an

---

* Parties to arbitration are often charged two or three thousand dollars per day in arbitration "forum fees," since arbitrators typically charge $300–400 per hour....

arbitration agreement might specify "something less than the full panoply of discovery provided in [California] Code of Civil Procedure." *Id.* * * *

[The court found that Countrywide's discovery provisions may afford Ferguson adequate discovery to vindicate her claims.]

Entire agreement is one-sided

Nevertheless, we recognize an insidious pattern in Countrywide's arbitration agreement. Not only do these discovery provisions appear to favor Countrywide at the expense of its employees, but the entire agreement seems drawn to provide Countrywide with undue advantages should an employment-related dispute arise. Aside from merely availing itself of the cost-saving benefits of arbitration, Countrywide has sought to advantage itself substantively by tilting the playing field. * * * [I]n the context of an arbitration agreement which unduly favors Countrywide at every turn, we find that their inclusion reaffirms our belief that the arbitration agreement as a whole is substantively unconscionable.

B.   The offending provisions of Countrywide's arbitration agreement cannot be severed or limited.

Countrywide argues that, if we conclude that certain provisions of its arbitration agreement are unconscionable, we should sever those offending provisions and enforce the remainder of the contract. Under California Civil Code § 1670.5(a):

> If the court as a matter of law finds the contract or any clause of the contract to have been unconscionable at the time it was made the court may refuse to enforce the contract, or it may enforce the remainder of the contract without the unconscionable clause, or it may so limit the application of any unconscionable clause as to avoid any unconscionable result.

Under this section, however, a court may, in its discretion, "refuse to enforce the contract as a whole if it is permeated by the unconscionability." Legislative Committee Comment on § 1670.5.

In *Armendariz,* the California Supreme Court declined to sever the unconscionable provisions of an arbitration agreement for two reasons, both of which are applicable to Countrywide's arbitration agreement. First, the court found that there was more than one unlawful provision and that "such multiple defects indicate a systematic effort to impose arbitration on an employee not simply as an alternative to litigation, but as an inferior forum that works to the employer's advantage." *Armendariz,* 6 P.3d at 696–97. Second, the agreement's lack of mutuality so permeated the contract that "the court would have to, in effect, reform the contract, not through severance or restriction, but by augmenting it with additional terms." *Id.* at 697.

The whole thing is uncon. Can't just enforce parts not affected.

In the instant case, the lack of mutuality regarding the type of claims that must be arbitrated, the fee provision, and the discovery provision, so permeate Countrywide's arbitration agreement that we are unable to sever its offending provisions. * * * For these * * * reasons, we find that Countrywide's arbitration agreement is so permeated with unconscionable clauses that we cannot remove the unconscionable taint from the agreement. * * *

The district court's denial of Countrywide's petition to compel arbitration on the ground that Countrywide's arbitration agreement is unenforceable under the doctrine of unconscionability is AFFIRMED.

NOTES

(1) In Circuit City Stores, Inc. v. Adams, 532 U.S. 105, 121 S.Ct. 1302, 149 L.Ed.2d 234 (2001), the Supreme Court held that the Federal Arbitration Act applied to all contracts of employment except those of transportation workers and those subject to collective bargaining agreements. In the context of the evolving FAA jurisprudence, this meant that an agreement to arbitrate all claims arising out of or relating to the employment relationship, including Title VII and other statutory discrimination claims, was arbitrable unless the arbitration clause was unenforceable under state contract law which, in California at least, is found in Armendariz v. Foundation Health Psychcare Services, Inc., 24 Cal.4th 83, 99 Cal.Rptr.2d 745, 6 P.3d 669 (2000)

On remand, the Ninth Circuit held that the arbitration clause was unconscionable because it was an adhesion contract (procedural) and because the clause (1) required arbitration of the employee's claims and not the employer's, (2) limited the employee's remedies available under state law, (3) required the employee to pay one-half of the arbitration costs, and (4) imposed a strict 1 year statute of limitations. Circuit City Stores, Inc. v. Adams, 279 F.3d 889 (9th Cir.2002), cert. denied, ___ U.S. ___, 122 S.Ct. 2329, 153 L.Ed.2d 160 (2002).

(2) Standard form arbitration clauses are present in more and more contracts between individuals and organizations. In addition to employment contracts, they appear in contracts between investors and broker-dealers, customers and banks, holders and credit card issuers, and patients and HMOs, to name a few.

On the face of it, it is difficult to see why these clauses are substantively unconscionable. Even though they are presented on a take it or leave it basis, the clauses are based upon agreement (to this extent they are not mandatory) and remove disputes from crowded court dockets to arbitrators, who allegedly can decide them more quickly with less expense. In fact, there is a strong policy favoring arbitration under the FAA. In short, arbitration clauses are a far cry from the "cross-collateral" and "add-on" clauses found in the contracts of Mrs. Williams.

One problem with this is, of course, that the individual, even if well informed, cannot bargain over the clause and cannot obtain the job, or the investment opportunity, or the bank account, or the credit card, without assenting to the clause. Another problem is that to the extent the agreement to arbitrate frequently includes regulatory provisions designed to protect the individual, such Title VII claims, the courts have sent them to arbitration, where decisions of the arbitrators on the merits are usually not subject to judicial review. The final problem is one identified by the court in this case, the clauses sometimes impose unreasonable cost burdens, see Brower v. Gateway 2000, Inc., 246 A.D.2d 246, 676 N.Y.S.2d 569 (N.Y.A.D.1998) (arbitration fees excessive), and are frequently drafted to favor the organization. They don't prevent the individual's rights from being vindicated before the arbitrators, but they impose limitations and burdens that impede vindication.

Thus, the adhesion aspect of the consent and the (potentially) one-sided nature of the clause itself when coupled with a core characteristic of arbitration, limited judicial review of the award, undercut the initial assumption that "arbitration is good." See generally Christine M. Reilly, *Achieving Knowing and Voluntary Consent in Pre–Dispute Mandatory Arbitration at the Contracting stage of Employment*, 90 Cal. L. Rev. 1203 (2002).

PROBLEM: REVISING UCC 2–302?

Section 2–302 of Revised Article 2 has not been changed: the text (with one cosmetic change) and, apparently the comments, will remain the same.

Assume you have been appointed a consultant to the revision process and asked to prepare a draft revision of UCC 2–302 that would state more clearly what contracts and terms are unconscionable and what are not. How would your draft read? Why?

(2) UNCONSCIONABILITY IN COMMERCIAL TRANSACTIONS

Should the defense of unconscionability be limited to consumer cases, that is, cases where individuals buy goods or services for personal, family, or household purposes? Or might it be used as well in commercial transactions? If so, should it make any difference whether the person in commerce is an individual or a small business or a large corporation?

To date the "merchant" has not been notably successful in invoking the defense. See, e.g., W.L. May Co., Inc. v. Philco–Ford Corp., 273 Or. 701, 543 P.2d 283 (1975) ("It may also be noted that both parties to the contract were sophisticated business people. This is clearly not the case of an innocent consumer who has unsuspectingly signed an adhesion contract." 543 P.2d at 287); Gillman v. Chase Manhattan Bank, 73 N.Y.2d 1, 537 N.Y.S.2d 787, 534 N.E.2d 824 (1988) (security agreement provision for issuance of letter of credit not unconscionable; a type of routine commercial transaction with which parties were necessarily familiar); County Asphalt, Inc. v. Lewis Welding & Engineering Corp., 323 F.Supp. 1300 (S.D.N.Y. 1970) ("[I]t is the exceptional commercial setting where a claim of unconscionability will be allowed * * *." 323 F.Supp. at 1308); Stanley A. Klopp, Inc. v. John Deere Co., 510 F.Supp. 807 (E.D.Pa.1981) ("Although commercial contracts can be unenforceable in whole or in part for unconscionability, it would be improper to borrow, without differentiation, concepts developed to protect consumers and employ them in favor of one commercial party over another." 510 F.Supp. at 810).

Nevertheless, neither the Code nor case law specifically limits UCC 2–302 and the principles underlying it to consumer transactions, and, as illustrated in the materials to follow, commercial entities can sometimes derive protection from unconscionability theory. Arguments based upon unconscionability appear regularly in commercial litigation, and courts are being called upon to examine the issue in a wide variety of contexts. See, generally, Mallor, *Unconscionability in Contracts Between Merchants,* 40 Sw.L.J. 1065 (1986).

Weaver v. American Oil Co.

Supreme Court of Indiana, 1971.
257 Ind. 458, 276 N.E.2d 144.

■ ARTERBURN, CHIEF JUSTICE.

In this case the appellee oil company presented to the appellant-defendant leasee, a filling station operator, a printed form contract as a lease to be signed, by the defendant, which contained, in addition to the normal leasing provisions, a "hold harmless" clause which provided in substance that the leasee operator would hold harmless and also indemnify the oil company for any negligence of the oil company occurring on the leased premises. The litigation arises as a result of the oil company's own employee spraying gasoline over Weaver and his assistant and causing them to be burned and injured on the leased premises. This action was initiated by American Oil and Hoffer (Appellees) for a declaratory judgment to determine the liability of appellant Weaver, under the clause in the lease. The trial court entered judgment holding Weaver liable under the lease.

Clause three [3] of the lease reads as follows:

"Lessor, its agents and employees shall not be liable for any loss, damage, injuries, or other casualty of whatsoever kind or by whomsoever caused to the person or property of anyone (including Lessee) on or off the premises, arising out of or resulting from Lessee's use, possession or operation thereof, or from defects in the premises whether apparent or hidden, or from the installation existence, use, maintenance, condition, repair, alteration, removal or replacement of any equipment thereon, whether due in whole or in part to negligent acts or omissions of Lessor, its agents or employees; and Lessee for himself, his heirs, executors, administrators, successors and assigns, hereby agrees to indemnify and hold Lessor, its agents and employees, harmless from and against all claims, demands, liabilities, suits or actions (including all reasonable expenses and attorneys' fees incurred by or imposed on the Lessor in connection therewith) for such loss, damage, injury or other casualty. Lessee also agrees to pay all reasonable expenses and attorneys' fees incurred by Lessor in the event that Lessee shall default under the provisions of this paragraph."

It will be noted that this lease clause not only exculpated the leasor oil company from its liability for its negligence, but also compelled Weaver to indemnify them for any damages or loss incurred as a result of its negligence. The appellate court held the exculpatory clause invalid, 261 N.E.2d 99, but the indemnifying clause valid, 262 N.E.2d 663. In our opinion, both these provisions must be read together since one may be used to effectuate the result obtained through the other. We find no ground for any distinction and we therefore grant the petition to transfer the appeal to this court.

This is a contract, which was submitted (already in printed form) to a party with lesser bargaining power. As in this case, it may contain unconscionable or unknown provisions which are in fine print. Such is the case now before this court.

The facts reveal that Weaver had left high school after one and a half years and spent his time, prior to leasing the service station, working at various skilled and unskilled labor oriented jobs. He was not one who should be expected to know the law or understand the meaning of technical terms. The ceremonious activity of signing the lease consisted of nothing more than the agent of American Oil placing the lease in front of Mr. Weaver and saying "sign", which Mr. Weaver did. There is nothing in the record to indicate that Weaver read the lease; that the agent asked Weaver to read it; or that the agent, in any manner, attempted to call Weaver's attention to the "hold harmless" clause in the lease. Each year following, the procedure was the same. A salesman, from American Oil, would bring the lease to Weaver, at the station, and Weaver would sign it. The evidence showed that Weaver had never read the lease prior to signing and that the clauses in the lease were never explained to him in a manner from which he could grasp their legal significance. The leases were prepared by the attorneys of American Oil Company, for the American Oil Company, and the agents of the American Oil Company never attempted to explain the conditions of the lease nor did they advise Weaver that he should consult legal counsel, before signing the lease. The superior bargaining power of American Oil is patently obvious and the significance of Weaver's signature upon the legal document amounted to nothing more than a mere formality to Weaver for the substantial protection of American Oil.

Had this case involved the sale of goods it would have been termed an "unconscionable contract" under sec. 2–302 of the Uniform Commercial Code as found in Burns' Ind.Stat. sec. 19–2–302, IC 1971, 26–1–2–302. * * *

According to the Comment to Official Text, the basic test of unconscionability is whether, in light of the general commercial background and the commercial needs of the particular trade or case, the clauses involved are so one-sided as to be unconscionable under the circumstances existing at the time of the making of the contract. Subsection two makes it clear that it is proper for the court to hear evidence upon these questions. * * *

The facts of this case reveal that in exchange for a contract which, if the clause in question is enforceable, may cost Mr. Weaver potentially thousands of dollars in damages for negligence of which he was not the cause, Weaver must operate the service station seven days a week for long hours, at a total yearly income of $5,000–$6,000. The evidence also reveals that *the clause was in fine print* and *contained no title heading* which would have identified it as an indemnity clause. It seems a deplorable abuse of justice to hold a man of poor education, to a contract prepared by the attorneys of American Oil, for the benefit of American Oil which was presented to Weaver on a "take it or leave it basis". * * *

The traditional contract is the result of free bargaining of parties who are brought together by the play of the market, and who meet each other on a footing of approximate economic equality. In such a society there is no danger that freedom of contract will be a threat to the social order as a whole. But in present-day commercial life the standardized mass contract has appeared. It is used primarily by enterprises with strong bargaining power and position. The weaker party, in need of the good or services, is frequently not in a position to shop around for better terms, either because the author of the standard contract has a monopoly (natural or artificial) or because all competitors use the same clauses.

* * *

When a party can show that the contract, which is sought to be enforced, was in fact an unconscionable one, due to a prodigious amount of bargaining power on behalf of the stronger party, which is used to the stronger party's advantage and is unknown to the lesser party, causing a great hardship and risk on the lesser party, the contract provision, or the contract as a whole, if the provision is not separable, should not be enforceable on the grounds that the provision is contrary to public policy. The party seeking to enforce such a contract has the burden of showing that the provisions were explained to the other party and *came to his knowledge* and there was in fact *a real and voluntary meeting of the minds and not merely an objective meeting.*

Unjust contract provisions have been found unenforceable, in the past, on the grounds of being contrary to public policy, where a party has a greater bargaining position. * * *

We do not mean to say or infer that parties may not make contracts exculpating one of his negligence and providing for indemnification, but it must be done *knowingly* and *willingly* as in insurance contracts made for that very purpose.

It is the duty of the courts to administer justice and that role is not performed, in this case, by enforcing a written instrument, not really an agreement of the parties as shown by the evidence here, although signed by the parties. The parole evidence rule must yield to the equities of the case. The appeal is transferred to this court and the judgment of the trial court is reversed with direction to enter judgment for the appellant.

[Dissenting opinion of Judge Prentice is omitted.]

NOTES

(1) Would the exculpatory/indemnification clause have escaped condemnation if Weaver had read the lease? To what extent was his "poor education" a factor in the case? What if commercial loss alone and not personal injury had been involved? *Cf.* UCC 2–719(3). Note that although this is a commercial contract the lessee is an individual—a sole proprietor. Is it the nature of the

contract (consumer or business) or the capacity of the party claiming excuse that controls?

(2) As counsel for the American Oil Company, what evidence of "commercial context" would you have liked the court to consider? What would you advise the client as to future lease negotiations? For a thorough treatment of *Weaver* and related cases, see Ellen Jordan, *Unconscionability at the Gas Station,* 62 Minn.L.Rev. 813 (1978).

Zapatha v. Dairy Mart, Inc.

Supreme Judicial Court of Massachusetts, 1980.
381 Mass. 284, 408 N.E.2d 1370.

■ WILKINS, JUSTICE.

Z = Employee

D = Employer

Δ WINS

RULE:
NOT UNCONS.

We are concerned here with the question whether Dairy Mart, Inc. (Dairy Mart), lawfully undertook to terminate a franchise agreement under which the Zapathas operated a Dairy Mart store on Wilbraham Road in Springfield. The Zapathas brought this action seeking to enjoin the termination of the agreement, alleging that the contract provision purporting to authorize the termination of the franchise agreement without cause was unconscionable and that Dairy Mart's conduct was an unfair and deceptive act or practice in violation of G.L. c. 93A. The judge ruled that Dairy Mart did not act in good faith, that the termination provision was unconscionable, and that Dairy Mart's termination of the agreement without cause was an unfair and deceptive act. We granted Dairy Mart's application for direct appellate review of a judgment that stated that Dairy Mart could terminate the agreement only for good cause and that the attempted termination was null and void. We reverse the judgments.

Mr. Zapatha is a high school graduate who had attended college for one year and had also taken college evening courses in business administration and business law. From 1952 to May, 1973, he was employed by a company engaged in the business of electroplating. He rose through the ranks to foreman and then to the position of operations manager, at one time being in charge of all metal finishing in the plant with 150 people working under him. In May, 1973, he was discharged and began looking for other opportunities, in particular a business of his own. Several months later he met with a representative of Dairy Mart. Dairy Mart operates a chain of franchised "convenience" stores. The Dairy Mart representative told Mr. Zapatha that working for Dairy Mart was being in business for one's self and that such a business was very stable and secure. Mr. Zapatha signed an application to be considered for a franchise. In addition, he was presented with a brochure entitled "Here's a Chance," which made certain representations concerning the status of a franchise holder.[1]

---

1. It included the following statements: " . . . you'll have the opportunity to own and run your own business . . . "; "We want to be sure we're hooking up with the right person.

A person who sees the opportunity in owning his own business . . . who requires the security that a multi-million dollar parent company can offer him . . . who has the good judgment

Dairy Mart approved Mr. Zapatha's application and offered him a store in Agawam. On November 8, 1973, a representative of Dairy Mart showed him a form of franchise agreement, entitled Limited Franchise and License Agreement, asked him to read it, and explained that his wife would have to sign the agreement as well.

Asked Him To Read It

Under the terms of the agreement, Dairy Mart would license the Zapathas to operate a Dairy Mart store, using the Dairy Mart trademark and associated insignia, and utilizing Dairy Mart's "confidential" merchandising methods. Dairy Mart would furnish the store and the equipment and would pay rent and gas and electric bills as well as certain other costs of doing business. In return Dairy Mart would receive a franchise fee, computed as a percentage of the store's gross sales. The Zapathas would have to pay for the starting inventory, and maintain a minimum stock of saleable merchandise thereafter. They were also responsible for wages of employees, related taxes, and any sales taxes. The termination provision, which is set forth in full in the margin,[2] allowed either party, after twelve months, to terminate the agreement without cause on ninety days' written notice. In the event of termination initiated by it without cause, Dairy Mart agreed to repurchase the saleable merchandise inventory at retail prices, less 20%.

Either party Could get out after 12 months

The Dairy Mart representative read and explained the termination provision to Mr. Zapatha. Mr. Zapatha later testified that, while he understood every word in the provision, he had interpreted it to mean that Dairy Mart could terminate the agreement only for cause. The Dairy Mart representative advised Mr. Zapatha to take the agreement to an attorney and said "I would prefer that you did." However, he also told Mr. Zapatha that the terms of the contract were not negotiable. The Zapathas signed the agreement without consulting an attorney. When the Zapathas took charge of the Agawam store, a representative of Dairy Mart worked with them to train them in Dairy Mart's methods of operation.

DM told them to see a lawyer

In 1974, another store became available on Wilbraham Road in Springfield, and the Zapathas elected to surrender the Agawam store. They executed a new franchise agreement, on an identical printed form, relating to the new location.

New location

and business sense to take advantage of the unique independence that Dairy Mart offers its franchisees ... We're looking for a partner ... who can take the tools we offer and build a life of security and comfort ... "

2. "(9) The term of this Limited Franchise and License Agreement shall be for a period of Twelve (12) months from date hereof, and shall continue uninterrupted thereafter. If DEALER desires to terminate after 12 months from date hereof, he shall do so by giving COMPANY a ninety (90) day written notice by Registered Mail of his intention to terminate. If COMPANY desires to terminate, it likewise shall give a ninety (90) day

notice, except for the following reasons which shall not require any written notice and shall terminate the Franchise immediately:

"(a) Failure to pay bills to suppliers for inventory or other products when due.

"(b) Failure to pay Franchise Fees to COMPANY.

"(c) Failure to pay city, state or federal taxes as said taxes shall become due and payable.

"(d) Breach of any condition of this Agreement."

In November, 1977, Dairy Mart presented a new and more detailed form of "Independent Operator's Agreement" to the Zapathas for execution. Some of the terms were less favorable to the store operator than those of the earlier form of agreement.[3] Mr. Zapatha told representatives of Dairy Mart that he was content with the existing contract and had decided not to sign the new agreement. On January 20, 1978, Dairy Mart gave written notice to the Zapathas that their contract was being terminated effective in ninety days. The termination notice stated that Dairy Mart "remains available to enter into discussions with you with respect to entering into a new Independent Operator's Agreement; however, there is no assurance that Dairy Mart will enter into a new Agreement with you, or even if entered into, what terms such Agreement will contain." The notice also indicated that Dairy Mart was prepared to purchase the Zapathas' saleable inventory.

The judge found that Dairy Mart terminated the agreement solely because the Zapathas refused to sign the new agreement. He further found that, but for this one act, Dairy Mart did not behave in an unconscionable manner, in bad faith, or in disregard of its representations. * * *

[Because the franchise agreement involves mostly transactions in services, the court is disinclined to find that the transaction is a "sale of goods" exclusively covered by the U.C.C. However, the court applies the U.C.C.'s statement of policy concerning good faith and unconscionability together with their common law counterparts.]

2. We consider first the plaintiffs' argument that the termination clause of the franchise agreement, authorizing Dairy Mart to terminate the agreement without cause, on ninety days' notice, was unconscionable by the standards expressed in G.L. c. 106, § 2–302. The same standards are set forth in Restatement (Second) of Contracts § 234 (Tent. Drafts Nos. 1–7, 1973). The issue is one of law for the court, and the test is to be made as of the time the contract was made. * * * In measuring the unconscionability of the termination provision, the fact that the law imposes an obligation of good faith on Dairy Mart in its performance under the agreement should be weighed. * * *

The official comment to § 2–302 states that "[t]he basic test is whether, in the light of the general commercial background and the commercial needs of the particular trade or case, the clauses involved are so one-sided as to be unconscionable under the circumstances existing at the time of the making of the contract. . . . The principle is one of prevention of oppression and unfair surprise . . . and not of disturbance of allocation of risks because

---

3. In his testimony, Mr. Zapatha said that he objected to a new provision under which Dairy Mart reserved the option to relocate an operator to a new location and to a requirement that the store be open from 7 A.M. to 11 P.M. every day. Previously the Zapathas' store had been open from 8 A.M. to 10 P.M.

There were other provisions, such as an obligation to pay future increases in the cost of heat and electricity, that were more burdensome to a franchisee. A few changes may have been to the advantage of the franchisee.

of superior bargaining power." Official Comment 1 to U.C.C. § 2–302.[4] Unconscionability is not defined in the Code, nor do the views expressed in the official comment provide a precise definition. The annotation prepared by the Massachusetts Advisory Committee on the Code states that "[t]he section appears to be intended to carry equity practice into the sales field." This court has not had occasion to consider in any detail the meaning of the word "unconscionable" in § 2–302. Because there is no clear, all-purpose definition of "unconscionable," nor could there be, unconscionability must be determined on a case by case basis (* * *), giving particular attention to whether, at the time of the execution of the agreement, the contract provision could result in unfair surprise and was oppressive to the allegedly disadvantaged party.

We start with a recognition that the Uniform Commercial Code itself implies that a contract provision allowing termination without cause is not per se unconscionable.... Section 2–309(3) provides that "[t]ermination of a contract by one party except on the happening of an agreed event requires that reasonable notification be received by the other party and an agreement dispensing with notification is invalid if its operation would be unconscionable." G.L. c. 106, § 2–309, as appearing in St.1957, c. 765, § 1. This language implies that termination of a sales contract without agreed "cause" is authorized by the Code, provided reasonable notice is given. * * * There is no suggestion that the ninety days' notice provided in the Dairy Mart franchise agreement was unreasonable.

We find no potential for unfair surprise to the Zapathas in the provision allowing termination without cause. We view the question of unfair surprise as focused on the circumstances under which the agreement was entered into.[5] The termination provision was neither obscurely worded, nor buried in fine print in the contract. Contrast Williams v. Walker–Thomas Furniture Co., 350 F.2d 445, 449 (D.C.Cir.1965). The provision was specifically pointed out to Mr. Zapatha before it was signed; Mr. Zapatha testified that he thought the provision was "straightforward," and he declined the opportunity to take the agreement to a lawyer for advice. The Zapathas had ample opportunity to consider the agreement before they

---

4. The comment has been criticized as useless and at best ambiguous (J. White & R. Summers, The Uniform Commercial Code, 116 [1972]), and § 2–302 has been characterized as devoid of any specific content. Leff, Unconscionability and the Code—(The Emperor's New Clause, 115 U.Pa.L.Rev. 485, 487–489 [1967]). On the other hand, it has been said that the strength of the unconscionability concept is its abstraction, permitting judicial creativity. See Ellinghaus, In Defense of Unconscionability, 78 Yale L.J. 757 (1969).

5. As we shall note subsequently, the concept of oppression deals with the substan-

tive unfairness of the contract term. This two-part test for unconscionability involves determining whether there was "an absence of meaningful choice on the part of one of the parties, together with contract terms which are unreasonably favorable to the other party." Williams v. Walker–Thomas Furniture Co., 350 F.2d 445, 449 (D.C.Cir.1965). See Corenswet, Inc. v. Amana Refrigeration, Inc., 594 F.2d 129, 139 (5th Cir.1979). The inquiry involves a search for components of "procedural" and "substantive" unconscionability. See generally Leff, Unconscionability and the Code—The Emperor's New Clause, 115 Pa. L.Rev. 485 (1967). * * *

signed it. Significantly, the subject of loss of employment was paramount in Mr. Zapatha's mind. He testified that he had held responsible jobs in one company from 1952 to 1973, that he had lost his employment, and that he "was looking for something that had a certain amount of security; something that was stable and something I could call my own." We conclude that a person of Mr. Zapatha's business experience and education should not have been surprised by the termination provision and, if in fact he was, there was no element of unfairness in the inclusion of that provision in the agreement. * * *

We further conclude that there was no oppression in the inclusion of a termination clause in the franchise agreement. We view the question of oppression as directed to the substantive fairness to the parties of permitting the termination provisions to operate as written. The Zapathas took over a going business on premises provided by Dairy Mart, using equipment furnished by Dairy Mart. As an investment, the Zapathas had only to purchase the inventory of goods to be sold but, as Dairy Mart concedes, on termination by it without cause Dairy Mart was obliged to repurchase all the Zapathas' saleable merchandise inventory, including items not purchased from Dairy Mart, at 80% of its retail value. There was no potential for forfeiture or loss of investment. * * *

[The court also held that Dairy Mart terminated the contract in good faith and that the termination clause or process did not constitute a deceptive practice or an unfair trade practice.]

Judgments reversed.

NOTES

(1) Section 208 of Restatement (Second) provides:

If a contract or term thereof is unconscionable at the time the contract is made a court may refuse to enforce the contract, or may enforce the remainder of the contract without the unconscionable term, or may so limit the application of any unconscionable terms as to avoid any unconscionable result.

For a general discussion, see Robert Hillman, *Debunking Some Myths About Unconscionability: A New Framework for U.C.C. Section 2–302,* 67 Cornell L.Rev. 1 (1981).

(2) Note that Justice Wilkins concludes that "oppression" relates to substantive rather than procedural unconscionability. This differs from the Ninth Circuit's interpretation of California law, where oppression is put in the procedural camp. What difference does this make? Which approach makes it easier to establishing unconscionability under UCC 2–302.

(3) *Beyond Commercial Transactions: Separation Agreements.* After fifteen years of marriage and the birth of three children, Charles and Kathleen Williams experienced marital difficulties and decided to separate. Kathleen's lawyer prepared a separation agreement which Charles signed without the advice of counsel, evidently with the hope that his signing might help lead to a resolution of their problems and bring about a reconciliation. Under the

agreement, Charles was required to transfer his interest in their home to Kathleen, together with the contents of the house and their automobile. In addition, Charles agreed to pay the mortgage on the house, the car loan, and all other marital obligations. In sum, under the agreement the wife was to receive property valued at approximately $131,000, while the husband was to retain property valued at about $1,100. Indeed, his total weekly financial obligations under the agreement exceeded his weekly net salary.

In a later divorce action, Charles sought to have the separation agreement set aside; Kathleen asked that it be incorporated into the divorce decree. The trial court found the agreement to be unconscionable, and this was upheld on appeal, the court citing Restatement (Second) § 208: "If a contract or term thereof is unconscionable at the time the contract is made a court may refuse to enforce the contract, or may enforce the remainder of the contract without the unconscionable term, or may so limit the application of any unconscionable term as to avoid any unconscionable result." Williams v. Williams, 306 Md. 332, 508 A.2d 985 (1986).

"In separation agreements particularly," a Virginia court has observed, "unconscionability may be of heightened importance." Derby v. Derby, 8 Va.App. 19, 378 S.E.2d 74, 79 (1989). The court elaborated:

> While no fiduciary duty exists between the parties, marriage and divorce create a relationship which is particularly susceptible to over-reaching and oppression. * * * Professor Homer Clark suggests three reasons for this special emphasis. First, the relationship between husband and wife is not the usual relationship that exists between parties to ordinary commercial contracts. Particularly when the negotiation is between the parties rather than between their lawyers, the relationship creates a situation ripe for subtle overreaching and misrepresentation. Behavior that might not constitute fraud or duress in an arm's length context may suffice to invalidate a grossly inequitable agreement where the relationship is utilized to overreach or take advantage of a situation in order to achieve an oppressive result. Second, Clark notes that unlike commercial contracts, the state itself has an interest in the terms and enforceability of separation agreements. If either spouse is left in necessitous circumstances by a separation agreement, that spouse and any children might become public charges. Finally, Clark notes that courts have recognized that the law should encourage the resolution of property issues through the process of negotiation rather than through litigation. "These processes are more likely to succeed if the parties and their lawyers know in advance that ... fairness will be insisted upon by the courts when they are called upon to approve the agreement." Clark, supra [The Law of Domestic Relations in the United States, 1987] § 19.2.

Coursey v. Caterpillar, Inc.

United States Court of Appeals, Sixth Circuit, 1995.
64 F.3d 662 (Unpublished).

[One of the questions before the court was whether a term in a commercial contract that excluded the seller's liability for consequential damages was unconscionable. UCC 2–719(3). The court first held that implied warranties had been properly disclaimed by the seller under UCC 2–316(2) and that the seller had made an express warranty that the goods were free from defects in material and workmanship, but the contract provided that repair and replacement for breach of that warranty was the exclusive remedy.]

* * *

Except in cases in which consumer goods cause personal injuries, the buyer carries the burden of proving the unconscionability of a limitation-of-remedy clause.... Unconscionability is rarely found to exist in a commercial setting....

The various factors considered by courts in deciding questions of unconscionability have been divided by the commentators into "procedural" and "substantive" categories ... Under the "procedural" rubric are facts which involve the "meeting of the minds" of the contracting parties: age, education, intelligence, business acumen and experience, relative bargaining power, who drafted the contract, whether the terms were explained to the weaker party, whether alterations in the printed terms were possible, and whether there were alternate sources of supply for the goods in question. The "substantive" heading embraces the contractual terms themselves, and requires a determination whether they were commercially reasonable. Most courts have taken a "balancing approach" to the unconscionability question and seem to require a certain quantum of procedural plus a certain quantum of substantive unconscionability to tip the scales in favor of unconscionability.

The plaintiffs failed to come forward with any evidence that the disclaimer of consequential damages was either procedurally or substantively unconscionable. The warranty provided for replacement of parts and labor in the event of mechanical failure and plaintiffs availed themselves of that warranty several times. If they did not like the terms of the warranty, they were free to purchase a tractor elsewhere. Nor have the plaintiffs demonstrated that the limitation of damages to replacement parts and labor is commercially unreasonable. The limitations clause was a conspicuous and unambiguous part of the sales transaction between two commercial entities. It was a limitation not unusual or unexpected in a commercial setting. Accordingly, the disclaimer of the remedy of consequential damages was valid and effective, [and defendants] were entitled to summary judgment with respect to plaintiff's claim for consequential damages.

NOTES

(1) What happens to the clause excluding liability for consequential damages if the seller is unable or unwilling to perform or satisfy the limited express warranty. Suppose, for example, after several tries the seller is unable to supply a needed replacement part and the machinery will not operate. Read UCC 2–719(2). If the limited remedy (repair and replacement) fails of its essential purpose, is the buyer entitled to consequential damages regardless of UCC 2–719(3)?

PROBLEM: THE CASE OF BISKO'S COMPUTER

As a result of your firm's superb handling of *The Case of the Recalcitrant Manufacturer,* the president of Bisko, Inc., John Baker, has returned for more legal advice. It seems that with the addition of the two new ovens the business prospered and the company's old accounting system was suffering from the strain. The company management decided it was time to enter the mysterious world of modern data processing. Caraway Co. had installed a computer system, and while the Bisko people did not really know all the advantages of computerization, they were determined to keep up with the competition. Baker contacted several computer companies, who responded by flooding them with literature and sending representatives to call.

Bisko was a family business, and no one knew very much about computers. One of Bisko's customers, who operated a chain of supermarkets, had told Baker that their Computron computer system had done extremely well and that they "would hate to think of going back to the old ways." After discussing the matter among themselves, the Bisko management decided to "go with" the Computron Company, if they could work out a satisfactory deal.

Computron sales representatives, after making a study of Bisko's needs, recommended the Ajax 0–500 plus the "software" that would perform five basic functions: (1) accounts receivable; (2) payroll; (3) inventory control; (4) invoicing; and (5) state taxes. The salesman said the whole system would be "up and running" within a few weeks and would be the equivalent of a "turn key" operation. (A turn key system is one that is ready to operate as soon as it is turned on.) Computron, he said, would train the Bisko personnel, and thereafter the system would require only minimal maintenance. He assured them that they would be amazed at the difference the system would make in business efficiency and that they would, of course, have Computron "behind them all the way."

On April 5, the parties executed a written contract for the purchase of the "hardware" (the Ajax 0–500), the "software" (the programs) and related services, all for a total price of $35,000. Five thousand was paid down, and the balance plus interest was to be paid in monthly installments stretching over a three year period. On the first page of the form, prepared by Computron and styled "Computron Computer Package Contract," appeared the basic information regarding names of parties, description of goods and services, price and payment terms, etc. The following clause also appeared on this page:

EXCEPT AS SPECIFICALLY PROVIDED IN THIS AGREEMENT, THERE ARE NO OTHER WARRANTIES, EXPRESS OR IMPLIED, INCLUDING BUT NOT LIMITED TO ANY IMPLIED WARRANTIES OF MERCHANTABILITY OR FITNESS FOR A PARTICULAR PURPOSE.

IN NO EVENT SHALL COMPUTRON COMPANY BE LIABLE FOR LOSS OF PROFITS OR OTHER ECONOMIC LOSS, INDIRECT, SPECIAL, CONSEQUENTIAL, OR SIMILAR DAMAGES ARISING OUT OF ANY BREACH OF THE AGREEMENTS OR OBLIGATIONS UNDER THIS AGREEMENT.

COMPUTRON COMPANY SHALL NOT BE LIABLE FOR ANY DAMAGES CAUSED BY DELAY IN DELIVERY, INSTALLATION OR

FURNISHING OF EQUIPMENT OR SERVICES UNDER THIS AGREE-
MENT BEYOND WHAT IS PROVIDED HEREIN.

On the second and last page was a provision that Computron warranted its
product for "one (1) year after delivery against defects in material, workmanship and operational failure from ordinary use" and that "services would be
performed in a skillful and workmanlike manner." It further provided that the
"sole and exclusive remedy for breach of this express warranty is repair or
replacement of the defective parts." The concluding paragraph was as follows:
"This contract states the entire obligation of seller in connection with this
transaction."

Computron delivered the Ajax 0–500 to Bisko on May 17 of last year, and
the system was brought on line later that month. From the very beginning
Bisko encountered problems with the Computron system. The figures on the
first batch of invoices were all wrong. Computron personnel, murmuring
reassurances, threw out this first run and produced a second which, when sent
out to Bisko's customers, produced a wave of complaints about billing inaccura-
cies. Since then, Baker reports, things have gone from bad to worse. In one case
a hardware defect caused the computer to destroy data stored in the memory.
Bisko then had to hire an accounting firm at great expense to reconstruct the
data. Computron has responded to each call for help, but they are seemingly
unable to get the "bugs" out of the system. In desperation, Baker comes to you.
"I've had it!" he tells you. "You've got to help me. It's too bad, I suppose, I
didn't contact you before we got into this computer business."

Senior partner calls you in, relates the foregoing, and asks your evaluation
of three UCC-related aspects; viz., 2–302; effectiveness of exclusive or limited
remedy; availability of consequential damages. Oblige her.

SECTION 3.   ILLEGALITY: AGREEMENTS UNENFORCEABLE ON GROUNDS OF PUBLIC POLICY

Another control upon promissory liability is imposed by the world
around the bargain: the promise or term of the agreement may not be
enforceable on grounds of "public policy." In these cases, the bargain will
probably satisfy the conditions established by the general law of contracts.
There will be an offer and acceptance, consideration will be present, the
agreement will satisfy the Statute of Frauds, and there will be no issues of
fraud, duress or unconscionability. But one of the parties or the court may
assert that the bargain itself, its performance or the objectives to be
achieved are "illegal" or against "public policy" and ought not be enforced.
At the same time, the defendant will argue that if the promise is not
enforceable the plaintiff should be denied restitution of any benefits conferred on the defendant by performance or part performance. If these
arguments are successful, the defendant will have avoided contractual
liability and may be permitted to retain any benefits received on the ground
that the contract in which he or she was involved was against public policy.
When and why this result is justified will be the subject of this subsection.

No – Had a choice whether to Enter or not

Terms were clear + not harsh + Warranty as long as they tried to service it

Some of the analytical difficulties are illustrated by a simple and clear example. Suppose that Abner and Boscoe agree that Boscoe will murder Clyde for $5,000, with $2,500 down and the balance when the job is done.* Without more, this is a simple, enforceable bilateral contract. But the performance by Boscoe and the bargain itself are felonies, the former being murder and the latter being a conspiracy to commit murder. What is the effect of this on enforceability?

The first Restatement took a firm position with a predictable result: "A bargain is illegal * * * if either its formation or its performance is criminal, tortious, or otherwise opposed to public policy." Section 512. Similarly, where both parties are equally involved in the illegality, the effect is that neither can "recover damages for breach thereof nor, by rescinding the bargain, recover the performance that he has rendered thereunder or its value." Section 598. But note that it was the Restatement rather than the criminal law statutes that declared the contract unenforceable and denied restitution. The statute, regulation or other source of public policy may say nothing about contracts and their enforceability. Thus, the jump from the conclusion that the bargain or its performance is a crime or a tort or "otherwise opposed to public policy" to the conclusion that it should not be enforced and restitution should be denied is not without difficulty.

Suppose, for example, that the performance of the bargain is a crime but its making is not. Or *vice versa*. What if one party is ignorant of the illegality? Suppose the crime is a misdemeanor rather than a felony. Suppose that the court concludes that the public policy is strong enough to deny enforcement of the bargain but not to deny restitution. The problems are varied, complex, and difficult.

The drafters of Restatement (Second) propose an interest balancing approach. Section 178(1) provides, first, that a "promise or other term of an agreement is unenforceable on grounds of public policy if legislation provides that it is unenforceable. * * * " Thus, if a constitution, statute, administrative regulation or local ordinance preempts the enforceability question by clear language, the court's job is to implement that legislative decision. See Comment a. But if there is no clear legislative mandate, the promise or term is still unenforceable if the "interest in its enforcement is clearly outweighed in the circumstances by a public policy against the enforcement of such terms." Section 178(1).

What are the factors to be weighed in the balance? Section 178(2) provides that in "weighing the interest in the enforcement of a term, account is taken of (a) the parties' justified expectations, (b) any forfeiture

---

* The TV show "Law and Order", which aired in Chicago on November 13, 2002, provided a more modern transaction. Party A wants Party B assassinated. Party A puts the word out through reliable sources and provides a telephone number on a "throw away cell phone." Reliable sources reach Party C, the hitman, who calls A on the cell phone. Party A tells Party C who is to be hit and Party C tells A that the job will be done after Party A transfers $50,000 to a designated offshore bank account. Party A transfers the funds, destroys the cell phone and waits for the results.

that would result if enforcement were denied, and (c) any special public interest in the enforcement of the particular term." Section 178(3) provides that in "weighing a public policy against enforcement of a term, account is taken of (a) the strength of that policy as manifested by legislation or judicial decisions, (b) the likelihood that a refusal to enforce the term will further that policy, (c) the seriousness of any misconduct involved and the extent to which it was deliberate, and (d) the directness of the connection between that misconduct and the term." Obviously, the outcome in our Abner–Boscoe "contract" will be the same under both Restatements, even though the court may balance interests under either Restatement approach. The virtue of the Restatement (Second) test is that it would seem to provide more flexibility in cases that are not so clear cut. Similarly, there is more discretion for a court to grant restitution to the plaintiff even though the bargain itself is unenforceable. See Sections 197–199.

For a recent application of the Restatement (Second) "balancing" test in a case involving the machinations of the "erstwhile president of Old Court Savings & Loan Association," see Springlake Corporation v. Symmarron Limited Partnership, 81 Md.App. 694, 569 A.2d 715 (1990). Observing that the "bent" of the Restatement seems to favor enforcement in the doubtful cases, the court summed up the competing factors as follows:

> In weighing the interest favoring enforcement, account is to be taken of the parties' "justified expectations," any forfeiture that would result if enforcement were denied, and "any special public interest in the enforcement of the particular term." Weighing against enforcement are the strength of the public policy, the likelihood that a refusal to enforce the promise will further that policy, the seriousness of the misconduct involved and the extent to which it was deliberate, and the directness of the connection between the misconduct and the promise. 569 A.2d at 702–3.

All of this analysis and balancing is relevant to a fundamental policy question: what is the purpose to be served in denying enforcement and restitution when the contract is against public policy? Assuming here that punishment may come through the criminal law process,* a principal reason advanced for denying judicial relief is that it will discourage illegal bargaining.

Opportunistic behavior tends to drive out contracting and different doctrines of contract law (such as the duty of good faith) can be seen as an attempt to constrain contractual opportunism. The refusal to enforce illegal contracts or order restitution has the socially valuable effect of *encouraging opportunism* with regard to substantively illegal agreements. Allowing

---

* Contrast the infrequent award of punitive damages for breach of contract, where the objective is to punish the contract breacher and to deter future conduct of a similar sort by the breacher and those similarly situated. In these cases, the underlying contract is not against public policy and the breach, even though egregious, is probably a tort rather than a crime.

Boscoe to abscond with the downpayment dampens Abner's interest in contracting.*

But in some contexts non-enforcement will increase the amount of the unwanted activity. For example, imagine that employers of undocumented workers are allowed to get away without paying wages. If employers know about this rule but undocumented workers do not, it is possible that there will be more "illegal" work. We might have less undocumented work if we enforced the employers wage promise. Indeed, we might have even less if we required employers (the side that is more likely to know about the law) to pay three times the contract wage to any worker who was subsequently found to be undocumented.

An alternative explanation for non-enforcement is that courts withhold judicial access to unworthy claimants to preserve their institutional integrity—or phrased in the more florid prose of Corbin, "in pious fear that the 'judicial ermine' might otherwise be spoiled."

Collateral reading: Farnsworth §§ 5.1–5.9; Calamari and Perillo §§ 22–1— 22–9; Murray § 98.

Sinnar v. Le Roy

Supreme Court of Washington, Department 2, 1954.
44 Wash.2d 728, 270 P.2d 800.

■ WEAVER, J.—Plaintiff brings this action to recover four hundred fifty dollars which he delivered to defendant upon the latter's promise either to get a beer license for plaintiff or return the money. Defendant appeals from a judgment against him.

Respondent owns and operates a grocery store on Jackson street, in Seattle. Prior to the transaction involved, he made application to the Washington state liquor control board for a license to sell beer, and paid sixty dollars license fee; the license was denied and the license fee returned.

Appellant, a customer, neighbor, and friend of respondent, is a business machine operator at Boeing Airplane Company. When the license was denied, the parties discussed the matter. Appellant testified:

"Well, I talked to—I told John [respondent] that I knew a fellow that worked for the—well, at that time I didn't know that the license come from the state, I thought beer licenses like these come from the city, and I knew this Mr. Lewis worked for the city in this County–City Building here for a number of years, and so then I talked to Mr. Lewis and he said that— (interrupted) ... after I told him I thought I could get the license, I told him I'd see about it, and then I called about it, and I called him, after telephone conversations back and forth to me, and then I called John

---

* See Juliet Kostritsky, *Illegal Contracts*   *Contract Theory,* 74 Ia.L.Rev. 115 (1988).
and Efficient Deterrence: A Study in Modern

[respondent] ... and I told him that it would cost him $450.00, and that's all I said and then I went on to work."

Both parties knew that a third party was to be involved. Appellant testified that he gave respondent's four hundred fifty dollars cash to a Mr. Lewis, who is not identified except as reference was made to him in appellant's testimony, herein quoted. Respondent did not receive a beer license.

He testified:

"Well, I told him to be careful who he gives the money to. I found out that this was just a sucker game, and knowing him as well as I did, I thought he'd do me some good. Q. What, if any, conditions were attached to the delivery of the money? A. Well, he told me the license or the money back. He said it was good as in the bank. ... I didn't care how. He was to get my license or the money back. I didn't care what he done with it, whether he bought a retired license or what."

Respondent testified several times that he told appellant to be "careful who he gave the money to." There is no indication in the evidence that the money was paid for professional services.

Appellant's assignments of error are presented upon the theory that this was an illegal transaction. The defense of illegality not having been pleaded, respondent argues that appellant is foreclosed from raising the question. We cannot agree with this conclusion.

"Illegality, if of a serious nature, need not be pleaded. If it appears in evidence the court of its own motion will deny relief to the plaintiff. The defendant cannot waive the defense if he wishes to do so. Indeed, if the court suspects illegality, it may examine witnesses and develop facts not brought out by the parties, and thereby establish illegality that precludes recovery by the plaintiff. If, however, the illegality is not serious, and neither public policy nor statute clearly requires denial of relief, courts refuse to give effect to facts showing illegality unless those facts are essential to establish a prima facie right of recovery or are pleaded by defendant." Restatement, Contracts, § 600, Comment a.

The only place such a license might have been secured was from the Washington state liquor control board. Laws of 1937, chapter 217, § 1, § 23–U, p. 1066 (Rem.Rev.Stat. (Sup.), § 7306–23U [cf. RCW 66.24.010]), provides:

"The holder of one or more licenses may assign and transfer the same to any qualified person under such rules and regulations as the board may prescribe: *Provided, however,* That no such assignment and transfer shall be made which will result in both a change of licensee and change of location; the fee for such assignment and transfer shall be ten dollars ($10.00)."

The illegality, which is claimed and argued in the instant case, is of a serious nature. The situation involves a beer license, which can be secured only from an agency of the state; it purports to deal with a matter which is exclusively within the realm of public policy. A party to such a situation cannot waive his right to set up the defense of illegality, and, if the evidence produced in support of the cause of action also establishes the illegality of the transaction, it should be considered by the trier of the facts, even though illegality has not been pleaded as a defense. . . .

* * *

In principle, we cannot distinguish the instant case from Goodier v. Hamilton, 172 Wash. 60, 63 (1933), wherein we said:

"It is within the realm of contemplation that a contract of this nature would readily suggest to one desirous of securing a highly compensatory result, to employ means which the law, good morals and public policy do not sanction. To anticipate and prevent a subversion of a proper administration of justice, the law should make it impossible for any such temptation to be carried into fruition by condemning a contract that contains the germ of possible corruption."

The record not only discloses that this transaction "contains the germ of possible corruption," but the evidence, and all inferences which may be drawn, lead us to conclude that the parties contemplated the use of means other than legal to accomplish the end desired.

A court will not knowingly aid in the furtherance of an illegal transaction, but will leave the parties where it finds them.

The judgment is reversed, with instructions to dismiss the action. Since the parties are in *pari delicto,* it is consistent with our decision that each bear his own costs.

NOTES

(1) Exactly where was the "illegality" in *Sinnar*—in the making of the contract, its performance, the objective to be achieved or what? Would the court come out differently on the enforceability issue using the Restatement (Second) balancing test, supra at 625? Restatement (Second) clearly supports the power of a court to raise the public policy issue *sua sponte*:

Even if neither party's pleading or proof reveals the contravention, the court may ordinarily inquire into it and decide the case on the basis of it if it finds it just to do so, subject to any relevant rules of pleading or proof by which it is bound.

Restatement (Second), Chapter 8, Topic 1, Introductory Note.

(2) *Restitutionary Exceptions.* The result in *Sinnar v. Le Roy* is that the defendant (or some unknown third person) is permitted to keep the plaintiff's $450. Yet both were equally involved in the wrongdoing. What policy justifies this result? This result—no restitution—is supported by Section 197 of Restatement (Second) as a general rule with some exceptions; e.g., (1) The denial of restitution causes "disproportionate forfeiture," Section 197; (2) The plaintiff was excusably ignorant of facts or of legislation "of a minor character, in the absence of which the promise would be enforceable," Section 198(a); (3) The plaintiff was "not equally in the wrong with the promisor," Section 198(b); and

(4) The plaintiff did not "engage in serious misconduct and * * * he withdraws from the transaction before the improper purpose has been achieved." Section 199(a). See Section 199(b), stating that restitution will also be allowed where the plaintiff did "not engage in serious misconduct and * * * allowance of the claim would put an end to a continuing situation that is contrary to the public interest."

See White v. McBride, 937 S.W.2d 796 (Tenn.1996), where the court found a contingency fee contract between a lawyer and his client "clearly excessive" under the applicable Code of Professional Responsibility and denied enforcement. The court also denied the plaintiff's claim for the reasonable value of the services rendered, and distinguished this case from the "innocent snafu" that might render a fee contract unenforceable:

> A violation of [the applicable rule] is an ethical transgression of a most flagrant sort as it goes directly to the heart of the fiduciary relationship that exists between attorney and client. To permit an attorney to fall back on the theory of *quantum meruit* when he unsuccessfully fails to collect a clearly excessive fee does absolutely nothing to promote ethical behavior. On the contrary, this interpretation would encourage attorneys to enter exorbitant fee contracts, secure that the safety net of *quantum meruit* is there in case of a subsequent fall.

(3) *Lord Mansfield Justifies.* The following statement of Lord Mansfield in Holman v. Johnson, [1775] 1 Cowp. 341, is most frequently advanced to justify disallowance of recovery where both parties are *in pari delicto*:

> The objection that a contract is immoral or illegal as between plaintiff and defendant, sounds at all times very ill in the mouth of the defendant. It is not for his sake, however, that the objection is ever allowed; but it is founded in general principles of policy, which the defendant has the advantage of, contrary to the real justice as between him and the plaintiff, by accident, if I may so say. The principle of public policy is this: Ex dolo malo non oritur actio. No court will lend its aid to a man who founds his cause of action upon an immoral or an illegal act. If, from the plaintiff's own stating or otherwise, the cause of action appears to arise ex turpi causa, or the transgression of a positive law of this country, there the court says he has no right to be assisted. It is upon that ground the court goes; not for the sake of defendant, but because they will not lend their aid to such a plaintiff. So if the plaintiff and defendant were to change sides, and the defendant was to bring his action against the plaintiff, the latter would then have the advantage of it; for where both parties are equally in fault, potior est conditio defendentis.

What judicial alternatives are available? Can you suggest a more acceptable approach? Cf. Wade, *Restitution of Benefits Acquired Through Illegal Transactions,* 95 U.Pa.L.Rev. 261 (1947); Grodecki, *In Pari Delicto Potior Est Conditio Defendentis,* 71 L.Q.Rev. 254 (1955). Both authors point out that Mansfield recognized that the *in pari delicto* maxim should not be applied rigidly and mechanically. For example, in Clarke v. Shee, [1774] 1 Cowp. 197, 200, he wrote:

> ' There are two sorts of prohibitions enacted by positive law, in respect of contracts. 1st. To protect weak or necessitous men from being overreached,

defrauded or oppressed. There the rule in pari delicto, potior est conditio defendentis, does not hold; and an action will lie; because where the defendant imposes upon the plaintiff it is not par delictum. * * * The next sort of prohibition is founded upon general reasons of policy and public expedience. There both parties offending are equally guilty; par est delictum, et potior est conditio defendentis.

(4) *Dean Wigmore Dissents.* "The real theory of *pari delicto* seems to be that the plaintiff loses his right by partaking in wrong-doing. * * * But the whole notion is radically wrong in principle and produces extreme injustice. If A owes B $5,000 why should he not pay it whether B has violated a statute or not? Where the issue is as to the rights of two litigants, it is unscientific to impose a penalty incidentally by depriving one of the litigants of his admitted right. It is unjust, also, for two reasons: first, one guilty party suffers, while another of equal guilt is rewarded; secondly, the penalty is usually utterly disproportionate to the offense. If there is one part of criminal jurisprudence which needs even more careful attention than it now receives it is the apportionment of penalty to offense. Yet the doctrine now under consideration requires, with monstrous injustice and blind haphazard, that the plaintiff shall be mulcted in the amount of his right, whatever that may be. Take for example the case of Gambriozo v. Maffet (2 Wash.C.C. 98), in which plaintiff and defendant were joint owners of a vessel. To avoid paying the tax on alien owners, the vessel was registered in the name of the defendant. For this illegality the plaintiff is denied the help of the courts in making the defendant account for the vessel's profits. In this way, and in a hundred similar ways, a fine of thousands of dollars may be imposed for petty violations of law. One cannot imagine why we have so long allowed such an unworthy principle to remain.

"The expedient that naturally suggests itself is merely to order the sum due to be paid into court and to deduct from it such a portion as may be named by the proper tribunal as the penalty for the violation of the law." Wigmore, *A Summary of Quasi–Contracts,* 25 Am.L.Rev. 695, 712–13 (1891).

(5) *Public Policy: An Elusive Concept.* "From the dawn of the common law tradition in England, courts have refused to implement those private contractual undertakings which, when measured against the prevailing mores and moods of society, contravene judicial perceptions of so-called "public policy." See 1 E. Coke, *Institutes of the Laws of England: A Commentary upon Littleton* *19 (Thomas ed. 1827) (*"nihil quod est inconveniens est licitum"*); Winfield, *Public Policy in the English Common Law,* 42 Harv.L.Rev. 76, 79 et seq. (1928). This Court stated early on that considerations of public policy are deemed paramount to private rights and where conflict between the two exists, private interests must yield to the public good. Wildey v. Collier, 7 Md. 273, 278–79, 61 Am.Dec. 346 (1854).

As the highest court in Maryland put it:

Public policy is that principle of the law which holds that no subject can lawfully do that which has a tendency to be injurious to the public, or against the public good, which may be termed, as it sometimes has been, the policy of the law, or public policy in relation to the administration of the law.' Egerton v. Earl Brownlow, 4 H.L.Cas. 1, 196 (1853).

... But beyond this relatively indeterminate description of the doctrine, jurists to this day have been unable to fashion a truly workable definition of public policy. Not being restricted to the conventional sources of positive law (constitutions, statutes and judicial decisions), judges are frequently called upon to discern the dictates of sound social policy and human welfare based on nothing more than their own personal experience and intellectual capacity. See 6A A. Corbin, *Contracts* § 1375, at 10 and 18 (1962). Inevitably, conceptions of public policy tend to ebb and flow with the tides of public opinion, making it difficult for courts to apply the principle with any degree of certainty. 1 W. Story, *A Treatise on the Law of Contracts* § 675 (5th ed. 1874).

[P]ublic policy ... is but a shifting and variable notion appealed to only when no other argument is available, and which, if relied upon today, may be utterly repudiated tomorrow.' Kenneweg v. Allegany County, 102 Md. 119, 125, 62 A. 249 (1905).

Fearing the disruptive effect that invocation of the highly elusive public policy principle would likely exert on the stability of commercial and contractual relations, Maryland courts have been hesitant to strike down voluntary bargains on public policy grounds, doing so only in those cases where the challenged agreement is patently offensive to the public good, that is, where "the common sense of the entire community would ... pronounce it" invalid. Estate of Woods, Weeks & Co., 52 Md. 520, 536 (1879); Trupp v. Wolff, 24 Md.App. 588, 616, cert. denied, 275 Md. 757 (1975).... This reluctance on the part of the judiciary to nullify contractual arrangements on public policy grounds also serves to protect the public interest in having individuals exercise broad powers to structure their own affairs by making legally enforceable promises, a concept which lies at the heart of the freedom of contract principle. Restatement (Second) of Contracts, Introductory Note to Ch. 14, at 46 (Tent. Draft No. 12, 1977); ...

In the final analysis, it is the function of a court to balance the public and private interests in securing enforcement of the disputed promise against those policies which would be advanced were the contractual term held invalid. Enforcement will be denied only where the factors that argue against implementing the particular provision clearly and unequivocally outweigh "the law's traditional interest in protecting the expectations of the parties, its abhorrence of any unjust enrichment, and any public interest in the enforcement" of the contested term. Restatement (Second) of Contracts § 320, Comment b (Tent. Draft No. 12, 1977).

Maryland–National, etc. v. Washington National Arena, 282 Md. 588, 386 A.2d 1216, 1227–28 (1978).

PROBLEM: THE CASE OF THE GREEN DOOR TAVERN

Patricia Myers operated the Green Door tavern in Granby, Missouri. Mrs. Myers had a three-year lease with option to purchase the premises from the owner John Hurn, Jr. and a beer by-the-drink license issued by the Missouri Division of Liquor Control.

Todd Clouse was a patron of the tavern. During one of his visits, Patricia's husband Jerry asked Clouse if he would be interested in purchasing an interest in the business. Negotiations followed which resulted in the signing of an "Employment/Management Contract" under which the Myers, as "Employers," agreed to hire Clouse to manage the business for a four-year period and pay him sixty percent of the net profit of the business as salary. In addition, Clouse was to receive, at the termination of the agreement or upon the exercise of the lease option to purchase, whichever came first, a 60 percent interest in the Green Door, with the Myers agreeing to exercise the option to purchase the property from Hurn within the lease period. Upon purchase of the property from Hurn, the Myers and Clouse were each to pay 50 percent of the purchase price. Finally, Clouse agreed to pay the Myers $15,000, $7,500 at the time of signing.

After executing the contract, Clouse paid the $7,500 and began operating the tavern. Two weeks later, however, the parties were summoned to the office of Larry Fuhr of the Missouri Liquor Commission. Fuhr questioned the agreement because an agreement with a licensed person (Patricia Myers) to operate a tavern, is in violation of Missouri law. Fuhr also objected to Jerry Myers' name on the contract because the latter, evidently a convicted felon, could have nothing to do with the operation of the tavern. The upshot was that Patricia surrendered her license to Fuhr.

Clouse later applied for and received a liquor license to operate the tavern in his own name, and he negotiated a new lease with Hurn. Clouse then requested that the Myers return his $7,500. They refused. He sued. What result? See Clouse v. Myers, 753 S.W.2d 316 (Mo.App.1988).

Homami v. Iranzadi

California Court of Appeal, Sixth District, 1989.
211 Cal.App.3d 1104, 260 Cal.Rptr. 6.

■ BRAUER, ASSOCIATE JUSTICE.

Ahmad Homami sued Mansoor Iranzadi to collect the balance due on a promissory note. Iranzadi claimed he had paid down the principal balance by approximately $40,000. Homami acknowledged receiving that amount but claimed the payments represented interest only. The note expressly provided: "This note shall bear no interest." But Homami testified at trial that the parties nonetheless had an oral agreement for the payment of 12 percent interest per annum. According to Homami the no interest provision on the note was only so that he could avoid reporting the income for state and federal income tax purposes.

The trial court granted judgment in favor of Homami. We reverse on the basis that Homami's claim is dependent upon an agreement for the express purpose of violating the law and defrauding state and federal governments.

FACTS

Homami and Iranzadi were brothers-in-law. At the time of this transaction, they had been involved in various business dealings together both in Iran and in the United States.

On January 9, 1984, Homami wrote a check for $250,000 to California Land Title in order to fund a real estate transaction on behalf of Iranzadi. The close of escrow was delayed until March 22, 1984. In the interim Homami kept the money available to make the loan.

The $250,000 loan was evidenced by two identical promissory notes dated March 22, 1984, in the amount of $125,000 each. Each note provided that it was all due and payable in two years and each recited that it would bear no interest. One note was secured by property known as the "Pinehill" property, and the other by property known as the "Outlook" property.

Iranzadi, who was not fluent in English, had granted Homami a power of attorney. Pursuant to this power Homami routinely wrote checks for his brother-in-law.

On March 25, 1984, three days after the loan was funded, Homami signed a check to himself for $2,104.68 on Iranzadi's account. The check bore a notation in Persian that it was for interest to March. According to Homami, this amount represented interest lost to him by virtue of the fact that he had kept the $250,000 accessible for two and a half months. He testified that Iranzadi had agreed to pay him the difference between the interest he was earning in his regular bank account and the 12 percent he would be receiving from Iranzadi.

Thereafter, checks were drawn to Homami on Iranzadi's account more or less on a monthly basis for approximately a year. For the first few months Homami signed the checks. The last six checks were signed by Iranzadi's son. With the exception of two payments, all of the checks were for $2,500. That would be the exact amount of monthly interest on a debt for $250,000 bearing a rate of 12 percent per annum. The total amount paid to Homami from Iranzadi, including the initial payment of $2,104.68, was $39,324.68.

On March 18, 1985, Homami and Iranzadi signed a document entitled "Modification Agreement" for each of the promissory notes. The modification agreements were identical except for their reference to the respective notes and deeds of trust. Each provided for the following modification of terms:

"1. The note shall be all due and payable on or before September 22, 1985.

2. The note shall bear no interest until June 22, 1985.

3. On June 22, 1985, interest shall commence at the rate of eighteen percent per annum; said interest shall be payable monthly commencing on July 22, 1985 and continue monthly thereafter until the maturity date expressed herein."

Thereafter, two more payments of $2,500 were made, on May 22, 1985 and June 23, 1985. No further payments of any amount were made.

On August 14, 1985, Homami filed notices of default on the ground that Iranzadi had failed to pay the monthly installment of interest due July 22, 1985. Foreclosures were commenced on both properties. Iranzadi found a buyer for the Pinehill property and escrow closed at the end of January, 1986. Homami was paid through that escrow the full principal balance of $125,000 on the one note, plus interest at 18 percent from June 22, 1985, as per the modification agreement, and foreclosure fees; however, Iranzadi expressly reserved the right to claim a credit for approximately $40,000, plus fees and costs, against the second note.

The Outlook property sold in June 1986. Homami submitted a demand for the full $125,000 plus interest on that amount from June 22, 1985, and foreclosure fees. Iranzadi, maintaining he had paid $39,324.68 on the principal balance between March 1984 and June 1985, claimed a credit in that amount. Escrow closed but the sum of $43,500 was held out of the proceeds and delivered to Albert Ham, a stakeholder, pending resolution of the dispute.

Homami filed suit October 15, 1986, alleging breach of a written contract. Attached to the complaint were the two promissory notes and modification agreements. Iranzadi filed a cross-complaint for declaratory relief, alleging that he had paid $39,324.68 towards reducing the principal, and seeking a determination of rights as to the monies held in trust. He also pleaded a cause of action for conversion of the $39,324.68 and prayed for compensatory relief and punitive damages against Homami.

At trial Homami testified that he and Iranzadi had orally agreed on an interest rate of 12 percent, and had also agreed that Iranzadi would not report interest paid and Homami would not have to report receiving the income. He testified that this arrangement was discussed and reiterated at a family meeting March 15, 1985. And he specifically stated that the reason the loan documents did not reflect any interest was so that he could avoid reporting income to the IRS.

Iranzadi, on the other hand, claimed that he and Homami had never discussed interest on the loan. He testified that in family dealings interest was never charged and that he had often loaned money to Homami without interest. He stated that he had authorized Homami to take $2,000 to $3,000 from his account every month to reduce the principal balance.

The trial court found that the payments made by Iranzadi to Homami totalling $39,324.68 represented interest only, and no principal reduction. Therefore Iranzadi still owed Homami that amount on the loan. The court rendered judgment in favor of Homami for $39,324.68 plus interest at 18 percent from June 30, 1986, the close of escrow, plus attorneys fees and costs. The judgment ordered that Albert Ham, the stakeholder, be awarded $588.11 for his costs and that he distribute the balance in the trust account to Homami in partial payment of the judgment.

DISCUSSION

[Iranzadi argues] that a contract which has as its object an illegal purpose is contrary to public policy and void. Since we find the last point to be dispositive, we need not address the remaining issues.

The Civil Code provides a starting place. A contract must have a lawful object. (Civ.Code, § 1550.) Any contract which has as its object the violation of an express provision of law is unlawful. (Civ.Code, § 1667, subd. (1).) The object of a contract is the thing which it is agreed, on the part of the party receiving the consideration, to do or not to do. (Civ.Code, § 1595.) The object must be lawful when the contract is made. (Civ.Code, § 1596.) And that part of the contract which is unlawful is void. (Civ.Code, § 1599.)

Courts have interpreted these statutes liberally. " 'The general principle is well established that a contract founded on an illegal consideration, or which is made for the purpose of furthering any matter or thing prohibited by statute, or to aid or assist any party therein, is void. This rule applies to every contract which is founded on a transaction *malum in se,* or which is prohibited by a statute on the ground of public policy.' " (C.I.T. Corp. v. Breckenridge (1944) 63 Cal.App.2d 198, 200.)

It makes no difference whether the contract has been partially or wholly performed. Rather, the test is " 'whether the plaintiff requires the aid of the illegal transaction to establish his case. If the plaintiff cannot open his case without showing that he has broken the law, the court will not assist him, whatever his claim in justice may be upon the defendant.' "[Id.]

Nor does it matter that the illegality has not been pleaded. "[I]f the question of illegality develops during the course of a trial, a court must consider it whether pleaded or not. . . . 'Whenever the evidence discloses the relations of the parties to the transaction to be illegal and against public policy, it becomes the duty of the court to refuse to entertain the action.' " (Russell v. Soldinger (1976) 59 Cal.App.3d 633, 642.)

Cases which have applied these principles fall into several broad categories. A common situation involves the unlicensed contractor, or other unlicensed professional, who seeks to collect money for services rendered. Courts have routinely refused to grant relief in such cases on the ground that the failure to comply with licensing requirements violates a law designed to protect and benefit the public. Therefore a party who has violated the law and entered into an agreement to perform services while unlicensed cannot obtain the aid of courts to enforce the agreement. . . .

In another factual context, courts have refused to grant relief to parties seeking to collect monies arising from illegal gambling activities. . . .

A third group of cases closer to our facts involves plaintiffs who have attempted to circumvent federal law. Generally these cases arise where nonveterans seek to obtain government benefits and entitlements available to veterans only, either by setting up a strawman veteran or otherwise by falsifying documents.

For example, in May v. Herron (1954) 127 Cal.App.2d 707, the Newmans transferred property to a veteran for the sole purpose of obtaining a Veteran's Priority under Federal Priorities Regulation No. 33. That regulation provided that veterans who wished to build houses for their own occupancy would receive preferential treatment in obtaining construction materials. The Newmans had been advised to obtain the illegal veteran's priority by their building contractor, who then entered into a contract with the veteran to build a house which he knew the Newmans intended to occupy. When the builder sued to recover a balance due on the construction contract, the court refused to come to his aid, finding that he had "initiated, suggested and directed a conspiracy to violate and circumvent a federal regulation which had the force of law." (Id. at p. 711.) The court concluded in this vein: "To permit a recovery here on any theory would permit plaintiff to benefit from his wilful and deliberate flouting of a law designed to promote the general public welfare." (Id. at p. 712.) * * *

The message from these cases couldn't be clearer. As the Supreme Court has expressed it: " 'No principle of law is better settled than that a party to an illegal contract cannot come into a court of law and ask to have his illegal objects carried out; nor can he set up a case in which he must necessarily disclose an illegal purpose as the groundwork of his claim.' " (Lee On v. Long, supra, 37 Cal.2d 499, 502.)

We do not perceive any meaningful difference between the unlawful agreements described in the above example and the tax evasion scheme perpetrated by Homami and Iranzadi in our case. Here Homami entered into a written agreement which specifically provided that he would be paid no interest. The purpose of the provision was to enable him to avoid compliance with state and federal income tax regulations. He then secretly collected interest income which he had no intention of reporting. And when a dispute developed, he sought the aid of the court to enforce the secret agreement so that he could keep the money he had collected.

[E]ven though a written contract is legal on its face, evidence may be introduced to establish its illegal character. (May v. Herron, supra, 127 Cal.App.2d 707, 710–711.) And if the substance of the transaction is illegal, it matters not when or how the illegality is raised in the course of the lawsuit. Whether the evidence comes from one side or the other, the disclosure is fatal to the case. The fact is that Homami, in order to state his claim to the funds held out of the escrow proceeds, was obliged to testify and did testify that he collected interest secretly in order to circumvent income tax laws. As the cases have repeatedly pointed out, "the test . . . is whether the plaintiff can establish his case otherwise than through the medium of an illegal transaction to which he himself was a party." (Schur v. Johnson (1934) 2 Cal.App.2d 680, 683–684.) It is clear that Homami could not do so.

Because his agreement violated the law, Homami is not entitled to the $39,624.86 he collected as unreported interest. That amount is to be credited to Iranzadi from the escrow proceeds. Distribution of the balance of the funds held in the trust account is to be determined by the court on remand.

NOTES

(1) In *Homami*, what is the public policy said to be violated? To what extent, if any, would the denial of judicial remedy promote this policy?

(2) The court in *Homami* refers to "the importance of deterring illegal conduct." Appraise the deterrent effect of the opinion.

(3) Illegality may not prevent the enforcement of a contract if the court construes the illegality not to be "serious". For example, in Town Planning and Engineering Assoc. v. Amesbury Specialty Co., 369 Mass. 737, 342 N.E.2d 706 (1976), an uncredentialed engineer was hired but subsequently not paid for engineering work. Even though a Massachusetts provides that engineering is to be performed only by registered engineers, the court found that the illegal behavior contracted for was *de minimus*.

(4) *Public Policy and the Role of the Judiciary.* If a constitutionally valid statute provides explicitly that a particular contract is "illegal" or otherwise opposed to public policy, the task of the court is relatively easy. The court responds, in appropriate ways, to the declared will of the legislature. Most contract illegality cases are not of this type, however. More likely the statute does not address the precise issue; there is, at most, merely an indication of general legislative policy. This means that the question of what sound policy requires regarding the allegedly illegal bargain is plainly a "judicial" question. Corbin § 1375. The court may state that it will be "guided" by a legislative declaration of policy, but it cannot escape the responsibility of doing justice in the particular case. In short, it is the court which must perform the task of elaborating the public policy of the jurisdiction, and this, of course, is frequently a difficult undertaking. See, generally, Walter Gellhorn, *Contracts and Public Policy,* 35 Colum.L.Rev. 679 (1935).

(5) *Discrimination as Grounds for Illegality.* 42 U. S. C. § 1981 prohibits race discrimination in the "mak[ing] and enforce[ment]" of contracts. Prohibitions against disparate racial treatment are unusual mandatory contract rules because the legality of one contract turns on the terms of another contract. Only by comparing terms or offers between contracts can one establish disparate treatment. In Patterson v. McLean Credit Union, 491 U.S. 164, 109 S.Ct. 2363, 105 L.Ed.2d 132 (1989), however, the Supreme Court held that § 1981 does not regulate disparate treatment in performance of contract. The court expressly rejected the notion that racial harassment in the conditions of employment is actionable under § 1981 when "it amounts to a breach of contract under state law." Do employers implicitly covenant not to racially harass? Would contracting around this covenant violate public policy?

(6) *A Cautionary Note.* In an English case, St. John Shipping Corp. v. Joseph Rank, Ltd., [1956] 3 All E.R. 683, the plaintiff sued for the balance of freight charges due for transporting wheat from Mobile, Alabama to Liverpool. The defendant insisted that it was not obliged to pay because the freighter had been overloaded in violation of a statute making it a criminal offense to load a ship so that the load line was submerged. In holding for the plaintiff, the court said that the question was "whether the statute is meant to prohibit the contract being sued upon." It is significant, however, that the court was influenced by practical considerations. Speaking for the court, Lord Devlin said:

> If a contract has as its whole object the doing of the very act which the statute prohibits, it can be argued that you can hardly make sense of a statute which forbids an act and yet permits to be made a contract to do it; that is a clear implication. But unless you get a clear implication of that sort, I think that a court ought to be very slow to hold that a statute

intends to interfere with the rights and remedies given by the ordinary law of contract.

Caution in this respect is, I think, especially necessary in these times when so much of commercial life is governed by regulations of one sort or another which may easily be broken without wicked intent. Persons who deliberately set out to break the law cannot expect to be aided in a court of justice, but it is a different matter when the law is unwittingly broken. To nullify a bargain in such circumstances frequently means that in a case—perhaps of such triviality that no authority would have felt it worth while to prosecute—a seller, because he cannot enforce his civil rights, may forfeit a sum vastly in excess of any penalty that a criminal court would impose; and the sum forfeited will not go into the public purse but into the pockets of someone who is lucky enough to pick up the windfall or astute enough to have contrived to get it. It is questionable how far this contributes to public morality * * *. It may be questionable also whether public policy is well served by driving from the seat of judgment anyone who has been guilty of a minor transgression. Commercial men who have unwittingly offended against one of a multiplicity of regulations may nevertheless feel that they have not thereby forfeited all right to justice, and may go elsewhere for it if courts of law will not give it to them. In the last resort they will, if necessary, set up their own machinery for dealing with their own disputes in the way that those whom the law puts beyond the pale, such as gamblers, have done." 3 All E.R. at 690–691. See Note, *The Doctrine of Illegality and Petty Offenders: Can Quasi–Contract Bring Justice?*, 42 Notre Dame Law. 46 (1966).

PROBLEMS: IMPACT UPON CONTRACT ENFORCEMENT OF STATUTORY VIOLATIONS

(a) *The Case of the Unregistered Apartment*. Tenant signed a one-year lease with Landlord, but decided not to occupy the premises. Landlord sues for damages. Tenants argues that the lease is void because the apartment was not registered as a residential unit, nor did the Landlord secure an occupancy permit, as required by city code. What result? See Noble v. Alis, 474 N.E.2d 109 (Ind.App.1985).

(b) *The Case of the Unmetered Fuel Oil Deliveries*. Buyer owned two homes to which Seller delivered fuel oil on several occasions. Not all of the deliveries were metered as required by law, and for which Seller was subject to fine and/or imprisonment. Seller sues for $5,000 worth of oil delivered but not metered. What result? See Rupert's Oil Service v. Leslie, 40 Conn.Sup. 295, 493 A.2d 926 (1985).

(c) *The Case of the Excessive Interest Charge*. Plaintiff, an investment company licensed by the Small Business Administration, loaned defendant $64,000. The loan was secured by a mortgage on defendant's residence. When the defendant defaulted on the loan, plaintiff sought to foreclose on the mortgage. The defendant argued that the plaintiff had charged interest above that allowed by regulations of the Small Business Administration, and this made the contract unenforceable. The trial court agreed. What result on appeal? See Lloyd Capital Corp. v. Pat Henchar, Inc., 152 A.D.2d 725, 544 N.Y.S.2d 178 (1989).

(d) *The Case of the Uncertified Carrier.* On four occasions Carrier transported Owner's horses in interstate commerce, but without having obtained a "certificate of public convenience and necessity" as required by the Interstate Commerce Commission Act. Can Owner interpose this statutory violation as a legal justification for not paying the Carrier? See Hull and Smith Horse Vans, Inc. v. Carras, 144 Mich.App. 712, 376 N.W.2d 392 (1985). See also Northern Indiana Public Service Company v. Carbon County Coal Company, 799 F.2d 265 (7th Cir.1986) (good commentary on "balancing" by Judge Posner in case involving violation of "anachronistic" provision of Mineral Lands Leasing Act of 1920).

(e) *The Case of the "No Bid" Contract.* Seller contacted Buyer, a community hospital, concerning the sale of radiator covers needed by the hospital for accreditation purposes. The county commissioners negotiated the contract with Seller but without going through the formal bidding process mandated by law. Seller sues for the $56,600 price. The county treasurer refuses to pay. Who wins? See Majestic Radiator Enclosure Company, Inc. v. County Commissioners of Middlesex, 397 Mass. 1002, 490 N.E.2d 1186 (1986).

(f) *The Case of the Delayed Title Delivery.* Buyer bought a boat from Seller, but after having experienced several problems with the boat sought to avoid the sale. Buyer argued that Seller's failure to deliver a certificate of title within 20 days, as mandated by state law, made the contract unenforceable. Is Buyer correct? Saulny v. RDY, Inc., 760 S.W.2d 813 (Tex.App.1988).

(g) *The Case of the Missing Repair Estimate.* Owner brought his Jaguar in for service and orally agreed to pay $187 for certain repairs. When he returned to pick up the car he agreed to pay $200 for further work which the mechanic recommended. Later the car was delivered to his home, accompanied by a repair bill for $500. Owner refused to pay, insisting that the contract was void because the service station failed to provide a written estimate as required by statute. Does Owner make a convincing argument? See Bennett v. Hayes, 53 Cal.App.3d 700, 125 Cal.Rptr. 825 (1975).

(h) *The Case of the Unlicensed Employment Agency.* Employer contracted with Employment Agency to find a computer programmer. The Agency found a qualified applicant, whom the employer later hired. However, Employer refused to pay the agreed upon fee, based upon Employment Agency's lack of license required by statute. What, if anything, should the Agency be able to recover? See T.E.C. & Associates, Inc. v. Alberto–Culver Company, 131 Ill.App.3d 1085, 87 Ill.Dec. 220, 476 N.E.2d 1212 (1985). See also U.S. Nursing Corp. v. Saint Joseph Medical Center, 39 F.3d 790 (7th Cir.1994) (unlicensed nursing service); Design Development, Inc. v. Brignole, 20 Conn.App. 685, 570 A.2d 221 (1990) (architect); Hoffman v. Dunn, 496 N.E.2d 818 (Ind.App.1986) (realtor); Haberman v. Elledge, 42 Wash.App. 744, 713 P.2d 746 (1986) (well driller).

(i) *Gambling.* R, a Virginia resident, lost $3.8 million over the course of several years gambling at defendant's casino in New Jersey where gambling is legal. R claimed that arrangements made by the defendant to induce her to return for more and more gambling (called "comps" in the trade) were illegal in Virginia and that she should be able to avoid them and recover the amount she gambled in restitution. The court held that it was irrelevant which state's law applied. Under New Jersey law, even though gambling was legal by statute, the "comp" arrangements were not contracts because there was no mutuality of obligation. Under Virginia law, there were no contract remedies because a gambling contract is void in Virginia, leaving the parties "in the plight in which they have seen fit to place themselves without undertaking to balance benefits or burdens." In neither state, therefore, was restitution of the amount gambled recoverable. Rahmani v. Resorts International Hotel, Inc., 20 F.Supp.2d 932 (E.D.Va.1998).

(j) *Political and Media Promises.* In Cohen v. Cowles Media Co. supra at 153, the court concluded, as a factual matter, that the newspaper/promisor did not intend to create a legally enforceable agreement. But what if a newspaper promises to compensate any source that it injures with negligent misrepresentations and expressly announces that it intends this agreement to be legally enforceable. Should the contract be unenforceable as being in conflict with the holding of *New York Times v. Sullivan*, 376 U.S. 254, 84 S.Ct. 710, 11 L.Ed.2d 686 (1964), or do newspapers instead have a constitutional right to stand behind the truthfulness of their representations? Is *Sullivan* merely a constitutional default? Do politicians have the opportunity to make their campaign promises legally binding?: "If elected, I promise to X (and I intend for this promise to be legally enforceable)." See John Solomon, Prize Fight, The New Republic 23 (November 15, 1999) (describing promise of RNC Chairman Haley Barbour to pay $1 million if reader can prove that Republicans are "cutting" Medicare, discussed supra at 263).

Comment: Validity of a Contract Limiting Liability for Negligence

Should one be able to contract so as to gain immunity from suit for any future wrong committed? For example, suppose A and B agree that the latter may not sue for damages growing out of a future assault committed by A upon B. Obviously, such an agreement would be violative of public policy. However, would an agreement absolving A from damages for negligent injury to B also be illegal? In most cases, it would not. See Williston § 1749A; Corbin § 1472. For a discussion of recent precedent and statutory regulation, see Cava and Wiesner, *Rationalizing a Decade of Judicial Responses to Exculpatory Clauses,* 28 Santa Clara L. Rev. 611 (1988).*

There is widespread recognition of the ability of parties whose bargaining power is not substantially unequal to contract against liability for negligence. Such arrangements are usually regarded as realistic efforts to allocate perceived risks. Thus, the drafters of Restatement (Second) observe that "a party to a contract can ordinarily exempt himself from liability for harm caused by his failure to observe the standard of reasonable care imposed by the law of negligence." Restatement (Second) § 195, Comment a. But they stipulate major exceptions. Section 195 reads as follows:

---

* A related question concerns the validity of indemnification or "hold harmless" provisions, whereby one secures another's promise to indemnify one against one's own negligence. "An indemnity clause purports to shift responsibility for the payment of damages from one party to another. * * * As such, an indemnity clause allocates the risk of loss or injury resulting from a particular venture between the parties to the agreement. An exculpatory clause relieves one party from the consequences of its own negligence. * * * Such clause relieves one party from responsibility for injuries incurred by the other party from a particular transaction or occurrence." Whitson v. Goodbodys, Inc., 773 S.W.2d 381 (Tex.App.1989) (upheld exculpatory clause in plaintiff's agreement with health club).

[margin note: Intentional]

(1) A term exempting a party from tort liability for harm caused intentionally or recklessly is unenforceable on grounds of public policy.

[margin note: PP]

(2) A term exempting a party from tort liability for harm caused negligently is unenforceable on grounds of public policy if

[margin note: Workers Comp]

    (a) the term exempts an employer from liability to an employee for injury in the course of his employment;

[margin note: duty of Pub. Service]

    (b) the term exempts one charged with a duty of public service from liability to one to whom that duty is owed for compensation for breach of that duty, or

[margin note: Class]

    (c) the other party is similarly a member of a class protected against the class to which the first party belongs.

[margin note: OK if bargained for ...]

(3) A term exempting a seller of a product from his special tort liability for physical harm to a user or consumer is unenforceable on grounds of public policy unless the term is fairly bargained for and is consistent with the policy underlying that liability.*

The courts' delineation of a "public service" exception is imprecise. What, for example, of an exculpatory clause in a contract for advertising is the "yellow pages"? See, Annot., *Liability of Telephone Company for Mistakes in or Omissions from its Directory*, 47 A.L.R.4th 883 (1986). Compare Richard A. Berjian, D.O., Inc. v. Ohio Bell Telephone Company, 54 Ohio St.2d 147, 375 N.E.2d 410 (1978) ("In the overwhelming majority of jurisdictions confronting the issue of whether the classified advertising service is a service within the scope of the duties owed by the telephone company to the public, courts have found such service to be a matter of private concern only, and, therefore, have held that telephone companies through use of exculpatory clauses in their service contracts can limit their liability for negligently failing to place a customer's order for advertising in the yellow pages." 375 N.E.2d at 415) with Morgan v. South Central Bell Telephone Co., 466 So.2d 107 (Ala.1985) ("We are satisfied that the plaintiffs did not have a meaningful choice relative to the inclusion of an exculpatory clause * * * and that the defendant had the bargaining power in a gross and unbalanced manner in determining the terms and conditions in the directory advertisement." 466 So.2d at 118).*

* Several states have legislated against particular types of exculpatory clauses; e.g., Illinois (real property leases); New York (comprehensive statutory scheme affecting lessors of real property, caterers, construction contractors, building service or maintenance contractors, architects, engineers, surveyors, garages and parking places, pools, gymnasiums, and public amusement places). In addition, many states have enacted some form of anti-indemnification statute applicable to construction contracts. See Smith, *Combatting Adhesion Contracts: Where Does the Buck Stop?*, 9 Construction Lawyer § 3, p. 3 (1989).

* In making this determination, the Alabama court referred to criteria stated in an influential California decision, Tunkl v. Regents of the University of California, 60 Cal.2d 92, 32 Cal.Rptr. 33, 383 P.2d 441 (1963). In invalidating an exculpatory clause in a contract between a charitable research hospital and a patient, the court offered the following guidelines: "It concerns a business of the type generally thought suitable for public regulation. The party seeking exculpation is engaged in performing a service of

Moreover, it is clear that exculpatory agreements are not favorites of the law. "The law expresses this disfavor either by indulging in a presumption against the parties' intention to contract for immunity against the consequences of their own negligence by requiring that such a provision for immunity in a contract must be expressed in clear and unequivocal language to be valid and effective." Williston § 1749A. *Colgan* is an example of this heightened scrutiny. See also Scott & Fetzer Company v. Montgomery Ward & Company, 112 Ill.2d 378, 98 Ill.Dec. 1, 493 N.E.2d 1022 (1986) (Exculpatory clauses "are not favored * * * and are to be strictly construed against the party they benefit * * * especially when that party was also the draftsman * * *. Such clauses must spell out the intention of the parties with great particularity and will not be construed to defeat a claim which is not explicitly covered by their terms." 493 N.E.2d at 1029–30).

Where the agreement is of an adhesion type between parties with disproportionate bargaining power, there may be a conceptual overlap of "illegality" and "unconscionability." See *Weaver v. American Oil Company*, supra at 561, involving a gas station lease with a fine print clause requiring lessee (Weaver) to indemnify lessor (American Oil Company) if anyone was injured by the lessor's negligence and holding the latter harmless for injuries to lessee. An American Oil Company employee spilled gasoline on Weaver and one of his employees. Both were injured when the gasoline ignited. The court reasoned, by analogy to UCC 2–302, that this disparity in bargaining power, the lack of awareness of the fine print clause by the lessee, and the hardship it imposed upon him, rendered the clause unconscionable. The court noted: "We do not mean to say or infer that parties may not make contracts exculpating one of his negligence and providing for indemnification, but it must be done *knowingly* and *willingly* as in insurance contracts made for that very purpose." 276 N.E.2d at 148. *Cf.* LaFrenz v. Lake County Fair Board, 172 Ind.App. 389, 360 N.E.2d 605 (1977) (written release, whereby fair board relieved of any liability resulting from wife being with her husband in pit area during a demolition derby, upheld; *Weaver* distinguished).

Under Section 402A of Restatement (Second) of Torts, a manufacturer's or seller's attempt to disclaim or limit liability for damages to person or property caused by a dangerously defective product is against public policy.

great importance to the public, which is often a matter of practical necessity for some members of the public. The party holds himself out as willing to perform this service for any member of the public who seeks it, or at least for any member coming within certain established standards. As a result of the essential nature of the service, in the economic setting of the transaction, the party invoking exculpation possesses a decisive advantage of bargaining strength against any member of the public who seeks his services. In exercising a superior bargaining power the party confronts the public with a standardized adhe-sion contract of exculpation and makes no provision whereby a purchaser may pay additional reasonable fees and obtain protection against negligence. Finally, as a result of the transaction, the person or property of the purchaser is placed under the control of the seller, subject to risk of carelessness by the seller or his agents." 60 Cal.2d at 98–101. For a recent application of the *Tunkl* criteria, see Wagenblast v. Odessa School District, 110 Wash.2d 845, 758 P.2d 968 (1988). For a critique of *Wagenblast*, see Recent Cases, 102 Harv.L.Rev. 729 (1989).

See Comment m. This policy is endorsed in Section 195(3) of Restatement (Second) for a "term exempting seller of a product from his special tort liability for physical harm to a user or consumer * * * unless the term is fairly bargained for and is consistent with the policy underlying that liability." Comment c states that the exception is for the "rare situation in which the term is consistent with the policy underlying the liability." Where a seller's breach of warranty causes economic loss rather than damage to person or property, "disclaimers" of warranty and limitations upon remedy are enforceable if not unconscionable. See UCC 2–302, 2–316(2) and 2–719(3). Put another way, there is no public policy against these risk allocation devices but, at the very least, they must be fairly bargained for. For a decision holding that these clauses were unconscionable in a commercial setting, see A & M Produce Co. v. FMC Corp., 135 Cal.App.3d 473, 186 Cal.Rptr. 114 (1982).

Data Management, Inc. v. Greene

Supreme Court of Alaska, 1988.
757 P.2d 62.

■ MATTHEWS, CHIEF JUSTICE.

FACTS

Data Management, Inc. employed James H. Greene and Richard Van Camp. The parties signed a contract containing a covenant not to compete. The covenant provides that the employees will not compete with Data Management in Alaska for five years after termination.[1]

Shortly after the employees' termination from Data Management, the company filed suit against them for breach of the covenant not to compete. Data Management sought a preliminary injunction enjoining Greene and Van Camp from rendering computing services to twenty-one named indi-

1. The covenant not to compete stated:

Inasmuch as the Employee will acquire or have access to information which is of a highly confidential and secret nature, it is agreed that for the terms of this agreement and for a period of 5 years after the termination of this agreement, Employee [sic] will not, within the State of Alaska, directly or indirectly, perform any similar services for any other person or firm located within the State of Alaska, without first obtaining the written consent and approval of the Employer, and that Employee will not own, manage, operate or control, be employed by, participate in, or be connected in any manner with the ownership, management, operation or control of any business similar to the type of business conducted by the Employer at the time of the termination of this contract or in competition with, directly or indirectly, the business of the Employer. In the event of an actual or threatened breach by the Employee of the provisions of this paragraph, the Employer shall be entitled to an injunction restraining the Employee from owning, managing, operating, controlling, [sic] being employed by, participating in, or being in any way so connected with any business similar to the type of business engaged in by the Employer. Nothing herein stated shall be construed as prohibiting the Employer from pursuing any other remedies available for such breach of threatened breach, including the recovery of damages from the Employee.

viduals.[2] The preliminary injunction was granted.

Subsequently, the court granted summary judgment to Greene and Van Camp. The court found that the anti-competition covenant was not severable and was wholly unenforceable. Data Management appeals.

DISCUSSION

We have not yet decided whether an overly broad covenant not to compete can be altered to render it legal. A survey of other jurisdictions reveals three different approaches.

The first approach is to hold that a covenant which is overbroad, and hence unconscionable, will not be enforced. This strict view was adopted by Arkansas in Rector–Phillips–Morse, Inc. v. Vroman, 253 Ark. 750 (1973). In that case, the court held that a three year covenant not to compete was too long. The court rejected the employer's request to alter the covenant from three years to six months. The court held, "our rule is that when a restriction such as this one is too far-reaching to be valid, the court will not make a new contract for the parties by reducing the restriction to a shorter time or to a smaller area." Id. 489 S.W.2d 1 at 4. Georgia has also adopted this position. See, Rollins Protective Serv. Co. v. Palermo, 287 S.E.2d 546, 549 (1982).

We do not favor this approach. The parties' contract is a bargain. One of the elements of that bargain is the covenant not to compete. As a general rule, courts should respect the rights of parties to enter into contracts, and should not interfere with their contractual relationships. There is a need to strike a balance between protecting the rights of parties to enter into contracts, and the need to protect parties from illegal contracts. Obliterating all overbroad covenants not to compete, regardless of their factual settings, is too mechanistic and may produce unduly harsh results. In response to objections like these, a second approach was developed.

The second approach is to hold that if words in an overbroad covenant not to compete can be deleted in such a way as to render it enforceable then the court may do so. This is the so-called "blue pencil" rule. See Restatement of Contracts § 518 (1932). This position was adopted by Indiana in Licocci v. Cardinal Associates, Inc., 432 N.E.2d 446, 452 (Ind. App.1982), vacated on other grounds, 445 N.E.2d 556 (Ind.1983) where the court stated, "if the covenant is clearly separated into parts and some parts are reasonable and others are not, the contract may be held divisible. The reasonable restrictions may then be enforced...."

This rule has been criticized as being too mechanical, in that it values the wording of the contract over its substance. For example, if a seller promised not to compete "anywhere in England," the whole provision would be void because the quoted clause cannot be narrowed by deleting any words. On the other hand, if the seller promised not to compete "in London or elsewhere in England," the covenant would be enforceable as to

---

2. Data Management argues that this is a reasonable modification of the covenant not to compete, and that the trial court erred in not so modifying the covenant.

London because "elsewhere in England" could be "blue penciled." The difference is merely semantic and we reject it.

The third approach, and the one we adopt, is to hold that if an overbroad covenant not to compete can be reasonably altered to render it enforceable, then the court shall do so unless it determines the covenant was not drafted in good faith. The burden of proving that the covenant was drafted in good faith is on the employer. This is the position taken in most United States jurisdictions[3] and by the Restatement (Second) of Contracts § 184(2) (1981).[4]

Ohio explained this approach in Raimonde v. Van Vlerah, 42 Ohio St.2d 21 (1975).

[M]any courts have abandoned the "blue pencil" test in favor of a rule of "reasonableness" which permits courts to determine, on the basis of all available evidence, what restrictions would be reasonable between the parties. Essentially, this test differs from the "blue pencil" test only in the manner of modification allowed. It permits courts to fashion a contract reasonable between the parties, in accord with their intention at the time of contracting, and enables them to evaluate all the factors comprising "reasonableness" in the context of employee covenants.

Among the factors properly to be considered are: "[t]he absence or presence of limitations as to time and space, * * * whether the employee represents the sole contact with the customer; whether the employee is possessed with confidential information or trade secrets; whether the covenant seeks to eliminate competition which would be unfair to the employer or merely seeks to eliminate ordinary competition; whether the covenant seeks to stifle the inherent skill and experience of the employee; whether the benefit to the employer is disproportional to the detriment to the employee; whether the covenant operates as a bar to the employee's sole means of support; whether the employee's talent which the employer seeks to suppress was actually developed during the period of employment; and whether the forbidden employment is merely incidental to the main employment."

Id. at 546–47.

This approach is consistent with U.C.C. § 2–302, as codified in Alaska under AS 45.02.302, which states:

(a) If the court as a matter of law finds the contract or a clause of the contract unconscionable at the time it was made, the court may

---

3. See Bess v. Bothman, 257 N.W.2d 791 (Minn.1977).

4. Restatement (Second) of Contracts § 184(2) (1981) states:

A court may treat only part of a term as unenforceable ... if the party who seeks to enforce the term obtained it in good faith and in accordance with reasonable standards of fair dealing.

The Restatement (Second) goes on to say, "this Section rejects the so-called 'blue pencil rule' of former § 518.... This rule is rejected because it is now contrary to the weight of authority and has been strongly criticized by scholarly writers." Id. at reporter's note.

refuse to enforce the contract, enforce the remainder of the contract without the unconscionable clause, or so limit the application of an unconscionable clause as to avoid an unconscionable result.

(b) If it is claimed or appears to the court that the contract or any clause of the contract may be unconscionable, the parties shall be given a reasonable opportunity to present evidence as to its commercial setting, purpose, and effect to aid the court in making the determination.

One criticism of this position is that employers are encouraged to overreach; if the covenant they draft is overbroad then the court redrafts it for them. While we recognize that the problem of overreaching exists, we think it can be overcome by stressing the good faith element of the test. The trial court must determine whether an employer has overreached willfully and, if so, the court should refuse to alter the covenant.

Accordingly, we REMAND this case to the trial court so it can determine whether Data Management acted in good faith, and if so, whether the covenant not to compete can be reasonably altered.[5]

NOTES

(1) *Covenant Not To Compete and the Concept of Partial Illegality.* A prolific source of "illegality" litigation has been the covenant not to compete, involving either the promise of a vendor of a business not to compete with the purchaser or the promise of an employee not to compete with his or her employer after termination of the employment. There are numerous decisions and a wealth of critical commentary treating various aspects of the matter. See, generally, Farnsworth § 5.3; Calamari and Perillo §§ 16–19—16–22; Murray § 98.

In an opinion which must surely rank among the most exhaustive (and exhausting!) on record, the court began as follows:

> When the defendant, Clifford Witter, a dance instructor, waltzed out of the employment of the plaintiff, the Arthur Murray Dance Studios of Cleveland, Inc., into the employment of the Fred Astaire Dancing Studios, the plaintiff waltzed Witter into court. For brevity, the two studios are called "Arthur Murray" and "Fred Astaire." At the time Witter took his contentious step, Arthur Murray had a string attached to him—a certain contract prohibiting Witter, after working for Arthur Murray no more, from working for a competitor. That Arthur Murray and Fred Astaire are rivals in dispensing Terpsichorean erudition is not disputed. Now Arthur Murray wants the court to pull that string and yank Witter out of Fred Astair's pedagogical pavilion.
>
> No layman could realize the legal complication involved in Witter's uncomplicated act. That is not one of those questions on which the legal

---

5. Because it found the overbroad covenant not to compete was unenforceable, the trial court denied Data Management's request for the liquidated damages provided for in the contract. If, on remand, the trial court finds it appropriate to alter the covenant not to compete to render it enforceable, it should also address the issue of liquidated damages.

researcher cannot find enough to quench his thirst. To the contrary there is so much authority it drowns him. It is a sea—vast and vacillating, overlapping and bewildering. One can fish out of it any kind of strange support for anything, if he lives so long. This deep and unsettled sea pertaining to an employee's covenant not to compete with his employer after termination of employment is really Seven Seas; and now that the court has sailed them, perhaps it should record those seas so that the next weary traveler may be saved the terrifying time it takes just to find them.

Arthur Murray Dance Studios of Cleveland v. Witter, 105 N.E.2d 685 (Ohio Com.Pl.1952).

In general, the courts focus upon two aspects of the covenant: (1) whether it protects some legitimate interest of the promisee; (2) whether it is reasonable in scope. Moreover, courts tend to be more favorably disposed to those covenants which are ancillary to the sale of a business than to those which restrict an employee's competitive activities. See Blake, *Employee Agreements Not to Compete,* 73 Harv. L.Rev. 625 (1960). For a criticism of this judicial inclination, see Callahan, *Post–Employment Restraint Agreements: A Reassessment,* 52 U.Chi.L.Rev. 703 (1985) (argument that treating employee covenants in an exceptional way, vis., presuming invalidity, may actually have an anti-competitive impact and work to employee's disadvantage).

A covenant ancillary to the sale of a business is usually seen as protective of the good will being sold. With respect to the employee covenant, where the party does not have a special or unique skill, the usual attempt is to protect by precluding the use of trade secrets, confidential information, customer lists and the like. For "[a]s a general rule, an employer is not entitled to protection from an employee's use of his knowledge, skill, or general information acquired or increased through experience or instruction while in the employment." Century Personnel, Inc. v. Brummett, 499 N.E.2d 1160, 1161 (Ind.App.1986). Compare Field v. Alexander & Alexander of Indiana, Inc., 503 N.E.2d 627 (Ind.App.1987) (upholding covenant not to compete by insurance salesman whereby latter obliged for a period of two years following termination to not solicit customers with whom employee had personal contact during previous two-year period) *with* American Shippers Supply Co. v. Campbell, 456 N.E.2d 1040 (Ind.App. 1983) (employer did not have a protectible interest in customer lists which could have been easily obtained from a telephone book or trade publication).

The reasonableness criterion deals primarily with the area covered and the duration. And it is here that efforts are frequently made, as in the instant case, to convince a court that the excessive parts should excised, leaving intact that which is reasonable both as to space and time. Efforts are thus made to sever or divide the legal portion from that which is illegal. The court here discusses three judicial responses. Which do you prefer? Why?

(2) *Mitigation of Strict Rule by Allowance of Restitution.* Courts recognize that rigorous application of the *in pari delicto* maxim may at times lead to results which are hardly consonant with sound public policy. Hence, the appearance of ameliorative doctrines, such as "partial illegality" discussed above, which permits enforcement of the legal portion. To quote Judge Cardozo, speaking of an unrelated matter but in a way which is apropos, courts are hesitant "to visit venial fault with oppressive retribution." *Jacob & Youngs v. Kent,* infra at 780. An effective method of avoiding application of the strict rule

is to establish that the parties are not equally at fault; i.e., they are not in *pari delicto*. An illustration is Webb v. Fulchire, 25 N.C. (3 Ired.) 485 (1843), where the victim of a "shell game" successfully sued to recover his losses, the court observing: "Surely, the artless fool, who seems to have been alike bereft of his senses and his money, is not to be deemed a partaker in the same crime, in *pari delicto,* with the juggling knave, who gulled and fleeced him." One may be able to establish a lack of parity of blame by showing one's ignorance of the illegality, the other party's fraud or deception, or membership in a class the public policy is designed to protect. Finally, one may avoid strict application by withdrawing from the contract before its illegal purpose has been attained. This is known as the doctrine of *locus poenitentiae*. See, generally, Dobbs § 13.5. For the Restatement's treatment of these various mitigating techniques, see supra at 629.

(3) *The Illegality Spectrum.* A thorough study of illegality in contracting could involve no less than a complete study of law and the sources from which it derives. As noted, a bargain is "illegal" if it contravenes "public policy." The term "public policy" is, of course, broad and comprehensive. In its ordinary signification, it encompasses, first of all, the declared law—constitutions, statutes, ordinances, regulations, judicial decisions, etc. But beyond this it includes conceptions and attitudes which order society itself and thereby shape its laws. Hence, in the present context public policy may be viewed as a framework or structure within which freedom of contract may be exercised. The following materials in this subsection, which pertain to still other aspects of the pervasive problem of "freedom and policy," oblige one to identify and evaluate certain basic policies which are largely presuppositional in character. These policies are among the basic premises, the fundamentals, of the legal and social systems.

Watts v. Watts

Supreme Court of Wisconsin, 1987.
137 Wis.2d 506, 405 N.W.2d 303.

■ SHIRLEY S. ABRAHAMSON, JUSTICE.

This is an appeal from a judgment of the circuit court for Dane County, William D. Byrne, Judge, dismissing Sue Ann Watts' amended complaint, pursuant to sec. 802.06(2)(f), Stats.1985–86, for failure to state a claim upon which relief may be granted. This court took jurisdiction of the appeal upon certification by the court of appeals under sec. (Rule) 809.61, Stats. 1985–86. * * *

The case involves a dispute between Sue Ann Evans Watts, the plaintiff, and James Watts, the defendant, over their respective interests in property accumulated during their nonmarital cohabitation relationship which spanned 12 years and produced two children. The case presents an issue of first impression and comes to this court at the pleading stage of the case, before trial and before the facts have been determined.

The plaintiff asked the circuit court to order an accounting of the defendant's personal and business assets accumulated between June 1969 through December 1981 (the duration of the parties' cohabitation) and to determine plaintiff's share of this property.

* * *

The circuit court dismissed the amended complaint, concluding that sec. 767.255, Stats.1985–86, authorizing a court to divide property, does not apply to the division of property between unmarried persons. * * *

We agree with the circuit court that the legislature did not intend sec. 767.255 to apply to an unmarried couple. We disagree with the circuit court's implicit conclusion that courts cannot or should not, without express authorization from the legislature, divide property between persons who have engaged in nonmarital cohabitation. Courts traditionally have settled contract and property disputes between unmarried persons, some of whom have cohabited. Nonmarital cohabitation does not render every agreement between the cohabiting parties illegal and does not automatically preclude one of the parties from seeking judicial relief, such as statutory or common law partition, damages for breach of express or implied contract, constructive trust and quantum meruit where the party alleges, and later proves, facts supporting the legal theory. The issue for the court in each case is whether the complaining party has set forth any legally cognizable claim.

* * *

We test the sufficiency of the plaintiff's amended complaint by first setting forth the facts asserted in the complaint and then analyzing each of the five legal theories upon which the plaintiff rests her claim for relief.

I.

The plaintiff commenced this action in 1982. The plaintiff's amended complaint alleges the following facts, which for purposes of this appeal must be accepted as true. The plaintiff and the defendant met in 1967, when she was 19 years old, was living with her parents and was working full time as a nurse's aide in preparation for a nursing career. Shortly after the parties met, the defendant persuaded the plaintiff to move into an apartment paid for by him and to quit her job. According to the amended complaint, the defendant "indicated" to the plaintiff that he would provide for her.

Early in 1969, the parties began living together in a "marriage-like" relationship, holding themselves out to the public as husband and wife. The plaintiff assumed the defendant's surname as her own. Subsequently, she gave birth to two children who were also given the defendant's surname. The parties filed joint income tax returns and maintained joint bank accounts asserting that they were husband and wife. The defendant insured the plaintiff as his wife on his medical insurance policy. He also took out a life insurance policy on her as his wife, naming himself as the beneficiary. The parties purchased real and personal property as husband and wife. The plaintiff executed documents and obligated herself on promissory notes to lending institutions as the defendant's wife.

During their relationship, the plaintiff contributed childcare and home-making services, including cleaning, cooking, laundering, shopping, running errands, and maintaining the grounds surrounding the parties' home. Additionally, the plaintiff contributed personal property to the relationship which she owned at the beginning of the relationship or acquired through gifts or purchases during the relationship. She served as hostess for the defendant for social and business-related events. The amended complaint further asserts that periodically, between 1969 and 1975, the plaintiff cooked and cleaned for the defendant and his employees while his business, a landscaping service, was building and landscaping a golf course.

From 1973 to 1976, the plaintiff worked 20–25 hours per week at the defendant's office, performing duties as a receptionist, typist, and assistant bookkeeper. From 1976 to 1981, the plaintiff worked 40–60 hours per week at a business she started with the defendant's sister-in-law, then continued and managed the business herself after the dissolution of that partnership. The plaintiff further alleges that in 1981 defendant made their relationship so intolerable that she was forced to move from their home and their relationship was irretrievably broken. Subsequently, the defendant barred the plaintiff from returning to her business.

The plaintiff alleges that during the parties' relationship, and because of her domestic and business contributions, the business and personal wealth of the couple increased. Furthermore, the plaintiff alleges that she never received any compensation for these contributions to the relationship and that the defendant indicated to the plaintiff both orally and through his conduct that he considered her to be his wife and that she would share equally in the increased wealth.

The plaintiff asserts that since the breakdown of the relationship the defendant has refused to share equally with her the wealth accumulated through their joint efforts or to compensate her in any way for her contributions to the relationship.

[The court rejects plaintiff's contentions that (1) she is entitled to an equitable division of property under Wisconsin's Family Code and (2) defendant should be estopped from asserting lack of legal marriage.]

IV.

The plaintiff's third legal theory on which her claim rests is that she and the defendant had a contract to share equally the property accumulated during their relationship. The essence of the complaint is that the parties had a contract, either an express or implied in fact contract, which the defendant breached.

Wisconsin courts have long recognized the importance of freedom of contract and have endeavored to protect the right to contract. A contract will not be enforced, however, if it violates public policy. A declaration that the contract is against public policy should be made only after a careful balancing, in the light of all the circumstances, of the interest in enforcing a particular promise against the policy against enforcement. Courts should be reluctant to frustrate a party's reasonable expectations without a corresponding benefit to be gained in deterring "misconduct" or avoiding inappropriate use of the judicial system. . . .

The defendant appears to attack the plaintiff's contract theory on three grounds. First, the defendant apparently asserts that the court's recognition of plaintiff's contract claim for a share of the parties' property contravenes the Wisconsin Family Code. Second, the defendant asserts that the legislature, not the courts, should determine the property and contract rights of unmarried cohabiting parties. Third, the defendant intimates that the parties' relationship was immoral and illegal and that any recognition of a contract between the parties or plaintiff's claim for a share of the property accumulated during the cohabitation contravenes public policy.

The defendant rests his argument that judicial recognition of a contract between unmarried cohabitants for property division violates the Wisconsin Family Code on Hewitt v. Hewitt, 77 Ill.2d 49 (1979). In Hewitt the Illinois Supreme Court concluded that judicial recognition of mutual property rights between unmarried cohabitants would violate the policy of the Illinois Marriage and Dissolution Act because enhancing the attractiveness of a private arrangement contravenes the Act's policy of strengthening and preserving the integrity of marriage. The Illinois court concluded that allowing such a contract claim would weaken the sanctity of marriage, put in doubt the rights of inheritance, and open the door to false pretenses of marriage. Hewitt, 77 Ill.2d at 65.

We agree with Professor Prince and other commentators that the *Hewitt* court made an unsupportable inferential leap when it found that cohabitation agreements run contrary to statutory policy and that the Hewitt court's approach is patently inconsistent with the principle that public policy limits are to be narrowly and exactly applied.[14]

Furthermore, the Illinois statutes upon which the Illinois supreme court rested its decision are distinguishable from the Wisconsin statutes. The Illinois supreme court relied on the fact that Illinois still retained "fault" divorce and that cohabitation was unlawful. By contrast, Wisconsin abolished "fault" in divorce in 1977 and abolished criminal sanctions for nonmarital cohabitation in 1983.[15]

---

14. Prince, *Public Policy Limitations in Cohabitation Agreements: Unruly Horse or Circus Pony,* 70 Minn.L.Rev. 163, 189–205 (1985).

15. Both Illinois and Wisconsin have abolished common law marriages. In our view this abolition does not invalidate a private cohabitation contract. Cohabitation agreements differ in effect from common law marriage. There is a significant difference between the consequences of achieving common law marriage status and of having an enforceable cohabitation agreement.

In Latham v. Latham, 274 Or. 421, 426–27 (1976), the Oregon supreme court found that the Legislature's decriminalization of cohabitation represented strong evidence that enforcing agreements made by parties during cohabitation relationships would not be contrary to Oregon public policy.

The defendant has failed to persuade this court that enforcing an express or implied in fact contract between these parties would in fact violate the Wisconsin Family Code. The Family Code, chs. 765–768 Stats. 1985–86, is intended to promote the institution of marriage and the family. We find no indication, however, that the Wisconsin legislature intended the Family Code to restrict in any way a court's resolution of property or contract disputes between unmarried cohabitants.

The defendant also urges that if the court is not willing to say that the Family Code proscribes contracts between unmarried cohabiting parties, then the court should refuse to resolve the contract and property rights of unmarried cohabitants without legislative guidance. The defendant asserts that this court should conclude, as the *Hewitt* court did, that the task of determining the rights of cohabiting parties is too complex and difficult for the court and should be left to the legislature. We are not persuaded by the defendant's argument. Courts have traditionally developed principles of contract and property law through the case-by-case method of the common law. While ultimately the legislature may resolve the problems raised by unmarried cohabiting parties, we are not persuaded that the court should refrain from resolving such disputes until the legislature gives us direction.[16] Our survey of the cases in other jurisdictions reveals that *Hewitt* is not widely followed.

We turn to the defendant's third point, namely, that any contract between the parties regarding property division contravenes public policy because the contract is based on immoral or illegal sexual activity. * * *

Courts have generally refused to enforce contracts for which the sole consideration is sexual relations, sometimes referred to as "meretricious" relationships. See In Matter of Estate of Steffes, 95 Wis.2d 490, 514 (1980), citing Restatement of Contracts Section 589 (1932). Courts distinguish, however, between contracts that are explicitly and inseparably founded on sexual services and those that are not. This court, and numerous other courts, have concluded that "a bargain between two people is not illegal merely because there is an illicit relationship between the two so long as the bargain is independent of the illicit relationship and the illicit relationship does not constitute any part of the consideration bargained for and is not a condition of the bargain." Steffes, supra, 95 Wis.2d at 514.

While not condoning the illicit sexual relationship of the parties, many courts have recognized that the result of a court's refusal to enforce contract and property rights between unmarried cohabitants is that one party keeps all or most of the assets accumulated during the relationship, while the other party, no more or less "guilty," is deprived of property which he or she has helped to accumulate.... * * *

---

16. We have previously acted in the absence of express legislative direction. See Estate of Fox, 178 Wis. 369 (1922), in which the court allowed relief under the doctrine of unjust enrichment to a woman who in good faith believed that she was married when she actually was not, discussed infra....

Having reviewed the complaint and surveyed the law in this and other jurisdictions, we hold that the Family Code does not preclude an unmarried cohabitant from asserting contract and property claims against the other party to the cohabitation. We further conclude that public policy does not necessarily preclude an unmarried cohabitant from asserting a contract claim against the other party to the cohabitation so long as the claim exists independently of the sexual relationship and is supported by separate consideration. Accordingly, we conclude that the plaintiff in this case has pleaded the facts necessary to state a claim for damages resulting from the defendant's breach of an express or an implied in fact contract to share with the plaintiff the property accumulated through the efforts of both parties during their relationship. Once again, we do not judge the merits of the plaintiff's claim; we merely hold that she be given her day in court to prove her claim.

V.

The plaintiff's fourth theory of recovery involves unjust enrichment. Essentially, she alleges that the defendant accepted and retained the benefit of services she provided knowing that she expected to share equally in the wealth accumulated during their relationship. She argues that it is unfair for the defendant to retain all the assets they accumulated under these circumstances and that a constructive trust should be imposed on the property as a result of the defendant's unjust enrichment. In his brief, the defendant does not attack specifically either the legal theory or the factual allegations made by the plaintiff.

Unlike claims for breach of an express or implied in fact contract, a claim of unjust enrichment does not arise out of an agreement entered into by the parties. Rather, an action for recovery based upon unjust enrichment is grounded on the moral principle that one who has received a benefit has a duty to make restitution where retaining such a benefit would be unjust . . . . .

Because no express or implied in fact agreement exists between the parties, recovery based upon unjust enrichment is sometimes referred to as "quasi contract," or contract "implied in law" rather than "implied in fact." Quasi contracts are obligations created by law to prevent injustice. . . .

In Wisconsin, an action for unjust enrichment, or quasi contract, is based upon proof of three elements: (1) a benefit conferred on the defendant by the plaintiff, (2) appreciation or knowledge by the defendant of the benefit, and (3) acceptance or retention of the benefit by the defendant under circumstances making it inequitable for the defendant to retain the benefit. . . .

The plaintiff has cited no cases directly supporting actions in unjust enrichment by unmarried cohabitants, and the defendant provides no authority against it. * * *

As we have discussed previously, allowing no relief at all to one party in a so-called "illicit" relationship effectively provides total relief to the other, by leaving that party owner of all the assets acquired through the efforts of both. Yet it cannot seriously be argued that the party retaining all the assets is less "guilty" than the other. Such a result is contrary to the principles of equity. Many courts have held, and we now so hold, that unmarried cohabitants may raise claims based upon unjust enrichment following the termination of their relationships where one of the parties attempts to retain an unreasonable amount of the property acquired through the efforts of both.

In this case, the plaintiff alleges that she contributed both property and services to the parties' relationship. She claims that because of these contributions the parties' assets increased, but that she was never compensated for her contributions. She further alleges that the defendant, knowing that the plaintiff expected to share in the property accumulated, "accepted the services rendered to him by the plaintiff" and that it would be unfair under the circumstances to allow him to retain everything while she receives nothing. We conclude that the facts alleged are sufficient to state a claim for recovery based upon unjust enrichment.

As part of the plaintiff's unjust enrichment claim, she has asked that a constructive trust be imposed on the assets that the defendant acquired during their relationship. A constructive trust is an equitable device created by law to prevent unjust enrichment. Wilharms v. Wilharms, 93 Wis.2d 671, 678 (1980). To state a claim on the theory of constructive trust the complaint must state facts sufficient to show (1) unjust enrichment and (2) abuse of a confidential relationship or some other form of unconscionable conduct. The latter element can be inferred from allegations in the complaint which show, for example, a family relationship, a close personal relationship, or the parties' mutual trust. These facts are alleged in this complaint or may be inferred. Gorski v. Gorski, 82 Wis.2d 248, 254–55 (1978). Therefore, we hold that if the plaintiff can prove the elements of unjust enrichment to the satisfaction of the circuit court, she will be entitled to demonstrate further that a constructive trust should be imposed as a remedy.

NOTES

(1) *Hewitt v. Hewitt: The Other Side.* The Wisconsin court is highly critical of *Hewitt v. Hewitt,* an opinion of the Illinois Supreme Court which espouses the traditional view respecting the enforcement of cohabitation agreements: The following is from that opinion:

> The issue of whether property rights accrue to unmarried cohabitants can not, however, be regarded realistically as merely a problem in the law of express contracts.

> * * * There are major public policy questions involved in determining whether, under what circumstances, and to what extent it is desirable to accord some type of legal status to claims arising from such relationships.

Of substantially greater importance than the rights of the immediate parties is the impact of such recognition upon our society and the institution of marriage. Will the fact that legal rights closely resembling those arising from conventional marriages can be acquired by those who deliberately choose to enter into what have heretofore been commonly referred to as "illicit" or "meretricious" relationships encourage formation of such relationships and weaken marriage as the foundation of our family-based society? In the event of death shall the survivor have the status of a surviving spouse for purposes of inheritance, wrongful death actions, workmen's compensation, etc.? And still more importantly: what of the children born of such relationships? What are their support and inheritance rights and by what standards are custody questions resolved? What of the sociological and psychological effects upon them of that type of environment? Does not the recognition of legally enforceable property and custody rights emanating from nonmarital cohabitation in practical effect equate with the legalization of common law marriage—at least in the circumstances of this case? And, in summary, have the increasing numbers of unmarried cohabitants and changing mores of our society.... reached the point at which the general welfare of the citizens of this State is best served by a return to something resembling the judicially created common law marriage our legislature outlawed in 1905?

* * * The real thrust of plaintiff's argument here is that we should abandon the rule of illegality because of certain changes in societal norms and attitudes. It is urged that social mores have changed radically in recent years, rendering this principle of law archaic. It is said that because there are so many unmarried cohabitants today the courts must confer a legal status on such relationships. This, of course, is the rationale underlying some of the decisions and commentaries. (See, e.g., Marvin v. [actor Lee] Marvin (1976), 18 Cal.3d 660, 683) If this is to be the result, however, it would seem more candid to acknowledge the return of varying forms of common law marriage than to continue displaying the naivete we believe involved in the assertion that there are involved in these relationships contracts separate and independent from the sexual activity, and the assumption that those contracts would have been entered into or would continue without that activity.

Even if we were to assume some modification of the rule of illegality is appropriate, we return to the fundamental question earlier alluded to: If resolution of this issue rests ultimately on grounds of public policy, by what body should that policy be determined? *Marvin*, viewing the issue as governed solely by contract law, found judicial policy-making appropriate. Its decision was facilitated by California precedent and that State's no-fault divorce law. In our view, however, the situation alleged here was not the kind of arm's length bargain envisioned by traditional contract principles, but an intimate arrangement of a fundamentally different kind. The issue, realistically, is whether it is appropriate for this court to grant a legal status to a private arrangement substituting for the institution of marriage sanctioned by the State. The question whether change is needed in the law governing the rights of parties in this delicate area of marriage-like relationships involves evaluations of sociological data and alternatives we believe best suited to the superior investigative and fact-finding facilities of the legislative branch in the exercise of its traditional authority to declare public policy in the domestic relations field.

Hewitt v. Hewitt, 77 Ill.2d 49, 31 Ill.Dec. 827, 394 N.E.2d 1204, 1207–10 (1979).

(2) In Wilcox v. Trautz, 427 Mass. 326, 693 N.E.2d 141, 146 (1998), the court adopted the view that:

> [U]nmarried cohabitants may lawfully contract containing property, financing, and other matters relevant to their relationship. Such a contract is subject to the rules of contract law and valid even if expressly made in contemplation of a common living arrangement, except to the extent that sexual services constitute the only, or dominant, consideration for the agreement, or that enforcement should be denied on some other public policy ground.

The court stated, however:

> Nothing we say here today is intended to derogate from the clear distinction we have made ... between the legal rights of married and unmarried cohabitants ... Nor should anything we have said be taken as a suggestion or intimation that we are retreating from our prior expressions regarding the importance of the institution of marriage and the strong public interest in ensuring that its integrity is not threatened.... We have never recognized common law marriage in this Commonwealth ... nor have we permitted the incidents of the marital relationship to attach to an arrangement of cohabitation without marriage.

Finally, the court noted that "if the parties eventually were to marry, the [cohabitation] agreement is no longer valid, and the rules concerning antenuptial, postnuptial, or separation agreements will then govern any agreement thereafter entered into by them."

See generally, Symposium, *Unmarried Partners and the Legacy of Marvin v. Marvin*, 79 N. Dame L. Rev. 1409 (2001).

Comment: Baby M—Are There Some Things Money Can't Buy?

In March of 1984, Mary Beth Whitehead responded to an advertisement in the Asbury Park Press asking for women willing to help infertile couples bear children. She was sent an "application," which she completed and returned. Being told that she had been "accepted," she was directed to the Manhattan law office of Noel Keane, a specialist in surrogate parenting law. He explained to Mrs. Whitehead that for each deal arranged he received $10,000, and the mother received $10,000, but only if she gave birth to, and surrendered, a healthy baby. If the baby was deformed, retarded, or damaged in any way, the couple could call the deal off, keep most of the $10,000, and return the baby to her.[1]

---

1. According to Mrs. Whitehead, Noel Keane claimed he had arranged three hundred births in the year Mrs. Whitehead was pregnant with Baby M. The facts in this paragraph are taken from Mary Beth White-head's account. See M. Whitehead, A Mother's Story (1989). The remaining facts are taken from the opinion of the Supreme Court of New Jersey, 109 N.J. 396, 537 A.2d 1227 (1988).

On February 6, 1985, Mrs. Whitehead entered into a written surrogacy contract with William Stern. The contract provided that through artificial insemination using Mr. Stern's sperm, Mrs. Whitehead would become pregnant, carry the child to term, bear it, deliver it to Mr. Stern and his wife, and thereafter do whatever was necessary to terminate her maternal rights so that Mrs. Stern could adopt the child. Mrs. Whitehead's husband, Richard, was also a party to the contract; Mrs. Stern was not. Mr. Stern agreed to pay Mrs. Whitehead $10,000 for her services, and in a separate contract, agreed to pay the Infertility Center of New York the sum of $7,000. Mrs. Whitehead agreed that she would "not abort the child once conceived except, if in the professional medical opinion of the inseminating physician, such action is necessary for the physical health of Mary Beth Whitehead or the child has been determined by said physician to be physically abnormal," and Mrs. Whitehead further agreed that "upon the request of said physician to undergo amniocentesis ... or similar tests to detect genetic and congenital defects." If such defects were detected, Mrs. Whitehead agreed to abort the fetus upon demand of Mr. Stern. 109 N.J. 396, 473, 537 A.2d 1227, 1268.

After several artificial inseminations over a period of months, Mrs. Whitehead finally became pregnant. On March 27, 1986, she gave birth to a baby girl whom she named Sara Elizabeth. Mrs. Whitehead realized almost at once that she could not part with the child. But she did surrender the baby to the Sterns on March 30 at the Whitehead home. The Sterns, who were childless and who feared that pregnancy was a health risk for Mrs. Stern, were overjoyed. They took the baby, whom they renamed Melissa, to their home.

There then followed a series of bitter conflicts and confrontations, culminating in a trial before Judge Sorkow of the Superior Court of New Jersey. See Matter of Baby M, 217 N.J.Super. 313, 525 A.2d 1128 (1987). After a thirty-two day trial over a period of two months, the court upheld the surrogate contract, ordering that Mrs. Whitehead's parental rights be terminated and that sole custody of the child be granted to Mr. Stern, and, after hearing brief testimony from Mrs. Stern, immediately entered an order allowing the adoption of Melissa by Mrs. Stern, all in accordance with the surrogacy contract. On appeal, the Supreme Court of New Jersey affirmed in part and reversed in part, remanding for further proceedings. It invalidated the contract and refused to terminate Mrs. Whitehead's parental rights. But it agreed that custody should be awarded to Mr. Stern, with visitation rights to Mrs. Whitehead. Matter of Baby M, 109 N.J. 396, 537 A.2d 1227 (1988).

In voiding the contract, Chief Justice Willentz, speaking for the court, stated emphatically: "This is the sale of a child, or at the very least, the sale of a mother's right to her child, the only mitigating factor being that one of the purchasers is the father. Almost every evil that prompted the prohibition on the payment of money in connection with adoptions exist here." 109 N.J. at 438.

Responding to the argument that Mrs. Whitehead had agreed to the surrogacy arrangement, supposedly fully understanding the consequences, the court noted:

> Putting aside the issue of how compelling her need for money may have been, and how significant her understanding of the consequences, we suggest that her consent is irrelevant. There are, in a civilized society, some things that money cannot buy. In America, we decided long ago that merely because conduct purchased by money was "voluntary" did not mean it was good or beyond regulation or prohibition. * * * There are in short, values that society deems more important than granting to wealth whatever it can buy, be it labor, love, or life. 109 N.J. at 440, 537 A.2d at 1249.

The court then alluded to potential long-term effects of surrogacy:

> The long-term effect of surrogacy contracts are not known, but feared—the impact on the child who learns her life was bought, that she is the offspring of someone who gave birth to her only to obtain money; the impact on the natural mother as the full weight of her isolation is felt along with the full reality of the sale of her body and her child; the impact on the natural father and the adoptive mother once they realize the consequences of their conduct. 109 N.J. at 441, 537 A.2d at 1250.

The court concluded this analysis as follows:

> The surrogate contract is based on principles that are directly contrary to the objective of our laws. It guarantees the separation of a child from its mother; it looks to adoption regardless of suitability; it totally ignores the child; it takes the child from the mother regardless of her wishes and maternal fitness; and it does all of this, it accomplishes all of its goals, through the use of money.

> Beyond that is the potential degradation of some women that may result from this arrangement. In many cases, of course, surrogacy may bring satisfaction, not only to the infertile couple, but to the surrogate mother herself. The fact, however, that many women may not perceive surrogacy negatively but rather see it as an opportunity does not diminish its potential for devastation to other women.

> In sum, the harmful consequences of the surrogacy arrangement appear to us all too palpable. In New Jersey the surrogate mother's agreement to sell her child is void. Its irrevocability infects the entire contract, as does the money that purports to buy it. 109 N.S. at 441–444, 537 A.2d at 1250.

The Baby M case has generated an enormous amount of commentary. For a sampling of competing views, see e.g. Carol Sanger, *(Baby) M's for the Many Things: Why I Start with Baby M*, 44 St. Louis L. J. 1443 (2000). *Colloquy: In Re Baby M*, 76 Geo.L.J. 1717–1844 (1988). See also *Annot., Validity and Construction of Surrogate Parenting Agreement*, 77 A.L.R. 4th 70 (1990). Relying heavily on contract theory, the Supreme Court of

California enforced a surrogacy contract in Johnson v. Calvert, 5 Cal.4th 84, 19 Cal.Rptr.2d 494, 851 P.2d 776 (1993).

Some Cutting Edge Problems:

If Mary Beth Whitehead had been selected in part because of her race, would the contract be voidable on the grounds of public policy for violating § 1981? Do constitutional privacy and associational rights trump the statutory prohibitions against race discrimination in contracting?

In today's brave new world, pro-creation requires sperm, an egg and a womb. Which of items should be alienable? At what point of time should buyer or seller have a right to void the contract? See A.Z. v. B.Z., 431 Mass. 150, 725 N.E.2d 1051, 1059 (2000)(refusing to enforce agreement providing that, on the parties' divorce, frozen embryos were to be given to the wife for implantation). Is specific performance ever appropriate? See E. A. Waldman, *Disputes Over Embryos: Of Contracts and Consents*, 32 Ariz. St. L. J. 897 (2000).

Should contracts to use or not to use contraceptives ever be enforceable (at least for money damages)? Should contract to abort or not to abort ever be enforceable (at least for money damages)? Could a woman or a man validly promise to indemnify a sexual partner for state imposed paternity obligations if a child is born? See *Erwin L.D. v. Myla Jean L.*, 41 Ark.App. 16, 847 S.W.2d 45 (1993); Melanie G. McCulley, *The Male Abortion: the Putative Father's Right to Terminate His Interests in and Obligations to the Unborn Child*, 7 J.L. & Pol'y 1, 55 (1998).

If a plaintiff established a defendant/promissor never intended to perform a pro-creative promise (say, to use contraceptives or not to abort if pregnant), should the defendant be liable for promissory fraud damages? See *Henson v. Sorrell*, 1999 WL 5630(Tenn.Ct.App.1999)(rejecting promissory fraud claim).

Wallis v. Smith

Court of Appeals of New Mexico, 2001.
130 N.M. 214, 22 P.3d 682.

■ Bosson, Judge.

Peter Wallis and Kellie Rae Smith were partners in a consensual sexual relationship. Allegedly, Smith misrepresented that she was practicing birth control when she was not, and Wallis unknowingly fathered her child. Wallis sued Smith for money damages, asserting four causes of action—fraud, breach of contract, conversion, and prima facie tort—that the district court dismissed for failure to state a claim upon which relief may be granted. Wallis appeals that dismissal. . . . We affirm the dismissal, holding that under these facts, the causes of action are not cognizable in New Mexico because they contravene the public policy of this state.

BACKGROUND

The following facts are taken from Wallis's complaint, which we must assume to be true for the purpose of determining whether a complaint states a viable claim for relief. Wallis and Smith began an intimate, sexual relationship some time before April 1997. They discussed contraceptive techniques and agreed that Smith would use birth control pills. Wallis and Smith further agreed that their sexual intimacy would last only as long as Smith continued to take birth control pills because Wallis made it clear that he did not want to father a child. Wallis participated in contraception only passively; he relied on Smith to use birth control and took no precautions himself.

As time went by, Smith changed her mind. She chose to stop taking birth control pills, but never informed Wallis of her decision. Wallis continued their intimate relationship, and Smith became pregnant. Smith carried the fetus to term and gave birth to a normal, healthy girl on November 27, 1998.

Wallis alleges that he has suffered, and will continue to suffer, substantial economic injury as a proximate result of his unintended fatherhood because New Mexico law requires him to pay child support for the next eighteen years. *See* NMSA 1978, § 40–11–15 (1997). Due to his statutory obligations, Wallis asserts that he has been injured by Smith's conduct, and requests compensatory and punitive damages from her. The district court determined that public policy prohibited the relief sought by Wallis, and dismissed the case with prejudice.

CONTRACEPTIVE FRAUD

* * * At the onset of our discussion it is important to distinguish the factual allegations of this case from other kinds of related lawsuits, and thus underscore the limited reach of this opinion. Wallis's complaint is not about sexually-transmitted disease, ... nor does it concern the damages arising from an unwanted pregnancy that led to an abortion, ... or an undesired pregnancy resulting in medical complications, ... This case is not even brought to recover the expense of giving birth.... Wallis's complaint is limited to compensatory damages for the "economic injury" of supporting a normal, healthy child.

Although Wallis insists that he is not attempting to circumvent his child support obligations, we cannot agree. It is self-evident that he seeks to recover for the very financial loss caused him by the statutory obligation to pay child support. At oral argument when pressed by the Court to clarify what damages Wallis was seeking, his counsel stated that Wallis was seeking not punitive, but compensatory damages measured by his "out of pocket loss." Therefore, this case boils down to whether sound public policy would permit our courts to require Smith to indemnify Wallis for child support under the circumstances of this case. * * *

Making each parent financially responsible for the conception and birth of children also illuminates a strong public policy that makes paramount the interests of the child. Our jurisprudence has abandoned the notion that the father of an "illegitimate" child could decline to accept the financial responsibility of raising that child.... Currently, the state exercises its *parens patriae* authority to protect the best interests of all children by ensuring that the parents provide "an adequate standard of support." NMSA 1978, § 40–4–11.1(B)(1) (1995). Placing a duty of support on each parent has the added benefit of insulating the state from the possibility of bearing the financial burden for a child. *See* § 40–11–15(D). In our view, it is difficult to harmonize the legislative concern for the child, reflected in the immutable duty of parental support, with Wallis's effort in this lawsuit to shift financial responsibility for his child solely to the mother.

* * * Some courts have dismissed contraceptive fraud cases on the ground that the claims tread too far into the realm of an individual's privacy interests.... We agree that individuals are entitled a sphere of privacy into which courts should not tread. A person's choice whether or not to use contraceptives understandably fits into this sphere. We also believe that the "privacy interests involved ... require a cautious approach," and therefore we elect to rely primarily on the prevailing public policy of child support, while at the same time recognizing the serious privacy concerns implicated and threatened by the underlying lawsuit....

Wallis's attempt to apply traditional contract and tort principles to his contraceptive agreement is unconvincing and, in the end, futile. The contract analogy fails because children, the persons for whose benefit child support guidelines are enacted, have the same needs regardless of whether their conception violated a promise between the parents.... * * *

Wallis tries to make the basis for liability not so much the birth of the child, but the fact that Smith lied, and perpetrated a fraud on him. *See* Paula C. Murray & Brenda J. Winslett, *The Constitutional Right to Privacy and Emerging Tort Liability for Deceit in Interpersonal Relationships*, 1986 U. Ill. L.Rev. 779, 832 (advocating recognition of contraceptive fraud suits). But not all misrepresentations are actionable.... * * *

Finally, Wallis argues that our courts have recognized tort claims which measure damages by the economic injury of supporting an unwanted child. *See Lovelace Med. Ctr. v. Mendez*, 111 N.M. 336, 345 (1991). However, *Lovelace* does not stand for the proposition that one parent can sue the other for the costs of raising a child. *Lovelace* held that a doctor has a duty to inform a couple that a surgical procedure to render one partner sterile was not successful, and the court determined the extent to which damages flow from the breach of that duty resulting in the birth of a healthy child. *See id.* at 342. * * *

Accordingly, we hold that the actions asserted here cannot be used to recoup the financial obligations of raising a child. We emphasize that this holding is gender neutral insofar as it precludes a monetary reimbursement for child support....

■ ALARID, JUDGE (specially concurring).

* * * If we recognize a claim based on intentional misrepresentation, we have started down the road towards establishing standards of conduct in reproductive relationships—one of the most important and private forms of interpersonal relations. In the absence of a clear balance favoring the imposition of legal duties of disclosure in reproductive relations between competent adult sex partners, candor in reproductive matters should be left to the ethics of the participants.

> [T]here are still many immoral acts which do not amount to torts, and the law has not yet enacted the golden rule. It is impossible to afford a lawsuit for every deed of unkindness or betrayal, and there is much evil in the world which must necessarily be left to other agencies of social control.

W. Page Keeton, Dan B. Dobbs, Robert E. Keeton, David G. Owen, *Prosser and Keeton on Torts* § 4 at 22 (5th ed.1984). In my view, Wallis has failed to demonstrate a clear balance in favor of recognition of a cause of action for contraceptive fraud/breach of promise to practice birth control.

* * * Today, the Court establishes the principle that contraception is a non-delegable duty in New Mexico. I see nothing unfair in applying this rule to Wallis. Had Wallis bothered to investigate the state of the law prior to beginning a sexual relationship with Smith in April 1997, he would have learned that the overwhelming majority of jurisdictions considering the issue have refused to recognize a cause of action for economic damages stemming from contraceptive fraud/breach of promise to practice birth control.

* * * Lastly, Wallis concedes that his complaint alleges damages for purely economic loss. I express no opinion at this time as to whether privacy interests would outweigh other considerations so as to foreclose causes of action based upon tortiously-inflicted physical harm to a sex partner. *See, e.g., Kathleen K. v. Robert B.,* 150 Cal.App.3d 992 (1984) (holding that right of privacy should not bar cause of action based upon sex partner's failure to advise other partner that he was infected with herpes).

PROBLEM: THE CASE OF DONNIS AND BENJAMIN'S COHABITATION AGREEMENT

Donnis G. Whorton and Benjamin F. Dillingham, III began dating and entered into a same-sex relationship, when Donnis was a college student pursuing a Bachelor of Arts degree. When they began living together, they orally agreed that Whorton's full-time occupation was to be Dillingham's chauffeur, bodyguard, social and business secretary, and partner and counselor in real estate investments. Additionally, Whorton was to be Dillingham's constant companion, confidant, traveling and social companion, and lover. In return, Dillingham agreed to be Whorton's lover and to financially support Whorton for life, and to open bank accounts, grant Whorton invasionary powers to savings accounts held in Dillingham's name, and permit Whorton to charge on Dillingham's personal accounts. (They specifically agreed that if any portion of the agreement was found to be legally unenforceable, it was severable and the balance of the provisions were to remain in full force and effect.).

Whorton allegedly complied with all of the terms of the agreement for seven years, at which point Dillingham barred him from his premises. Dillingham refuses to perform his part of the contract, and Whorton sues. What result? See Whorton v. Dillingham, 202 Cal.App.3d 447, 248 Cal.Rptr. 405 (1988).

The Whorton case and others in the United States and Canada are discussed and criticized in Sharmila Roy Grossman, *The Illusory Rights of Marvin v. Marvin for the Same Sex Couples versus the Preferable Canadian Approach,* 38 Cal. West. L. Rev. 547 (2002). On the issue of same-sex marriage, see David B. Cruz, *Disestablishing Sex and Gender*, 90 Cal. L. Rev. 997, 1078–1084 (2002). See also Craig W. Christensen, *Legal Ordering of Family Values: The Case of Gay and Lesbian Families*, 18 Cardozo L. Rev. 1299 (1997).

Comment: Aleatory, Gambling and Insurance Contracts

An aleatory promise is promise "under which his duty to perform is conditional on the occurrence of a fortuitous event," Restatement (Second) of Contracts S 76, cmt. c (1981). The term derives from the Latin "alea" for die (as in Caesar's comment on crossing the Rubicon: "Alia iacta est!" "The die is cast."). The common law generally enforces such promises. For example, A can promise to sell and B to buy goods if a war ends by a certain date.

But a subset of aleatory promises are not enforceable. American common law has generally regarded gambling agreements to be voidable as against public policy. See, e.g., Restatement (Second) of Contracts S 178, illustration 1 (1981). Ordinarily, a party to a wagering contract can withdraw while the agreement is still executory, and recover the money that he bet. Since wagers are against public policy, the winner of a wager cannot recover by court action money won and not paid. And money loaned or furnished for the purpose of being used in gambling cannot be recovered. Moreover, the loser in a wagering agreement cannot recover the money he lost in a court action. Some states may refuse to enforce credit card debts incurred for Internet gambling because enforcing the debt would be against the state's public policy. See Providian National Bank v. Haines, No. CV 980858 (Cal. Super. Ct. filed July 23, 1998) (unpublished)).

It is, however, not always easy to distinguish illegal wagering contracts from other "aleatory" contracts that have a legitimate commercial or other purpose and are not considered contrary to public policy. Likewise insurance contracts can often be recharacterized as wagers (and vice-versa): "I bet you, I don't die next year." or "I'm willing to offer you insurance that the Jets win the superbowl."

But courts often try to distinguish between unenforceable gambling contracts and enforceable aleatory or insurance contracts by focusing on whether the risk that is assumed by the promisor is created by the bargain itself. Insureds tend to buy insurance to compensate them for the possible occurrence of an existing risk. Gamblers by their contracts create the risk at issue. (As Corbin once said: "It can hardly be conceived that prior to their betting bargain it makes any difference to either party engaged in throwing dice which faces are up when the dice stops rolling" Corbin on Contracts, at sec. 1481). Also insureds tend to bargain for payments conditional upon something untoward happening; while gamblers tend to bargain for payments conditional upon something fortuitous happening (i.e., their favored team winning).

PROBLEM: THE CASE OF THE PROMISE TO REMAIN SILENT

During a dinner party before the beginning of the fall semester, Professor A mentions that he intends to offer his used car for sale to the hordes of incoming students. Professor B who has just arrived in town as a visiting lecturer responds that she herself is interested in buying the car and asks if she can borrow the car to have her mechanic "check it out." Professor A agrees, but only on condition that Professor B disclose nothing about what the mechanic finds. Professor A explains that the incoming students will not have an opportunity to have the car evaluated and Professor A doesn't want to have to disclose negative information about the car's quality.

Professor B agrees to remain silent and takes possession of the car. The next day, Professor B calls and tells A that she does not want to buy the car. Moreover, B volunteers that the mechanic found a problem with the car. A responds, "Don't tell me." B responds: "But it's a safety problem." A responds again, "Don't tell me."

A goes on to sell the car to an incoming graduate student (with limited English abilities). A does not disclose his prior agreement with B, nor does A disclose that B's mechanic found some type of a "safety problem"—but professor A does disclose all previously acquired material information about the car.

The graduate student is subsequently injured in accident caused by a safety problem uncovered in the initial mechanic's examination. Does Professor A face any potential legal liability for his conduct? Should the initial agreement to remain silent be unenforceable? If such agreements are unenforceable, how are future Professor A's likely to react?

SIX

ЯMANCE

DETERMINING SCOPE AND CONTENT OF

Ꭲ

There no general requirement that an agreement or promise be in writing to be enforceable as a contract. As we have seen, the Statute of Frauds imposes that requirement in particular cases, and the parties may, if they desire, condition liability upon the reducing of their agreement to a complete writing. Similarly, statutes occasionally give legal effect to written promises which comply with a stated form. See UCC 2–205. On the whole, however, the modern trend is toward informality in the formation of contracts. Indeed, UCC 1–201(3) defines agreement as the "bargain of the parties in fact as found in their language or by implication from other circumstances including course of dealing or usage of trade or course of performance * * *."

Nevertheless, many contracts are written in whole or in part. These written agreements may be the product of intensive and thorough bargaining between equal parties assisted by counsel or a standard form drafted exclusively by one party and offered to the other on a take-it-or-leave-it basis. They may contain all of the agreed terms or just part. They may be clear or ambiguous. Or, they may be the product of amateurs operating with little experience and without the advice of counsel. In short, the only sure thing is that the problems will be varied and the disputes plentiful.

In this section we are not primarily concerned with whether a contract has been formed, whether there has been a misunderstanding *à la Peerless*, or whether the parties have made a mistake in reducing their oral agreement to writing. Assuming that there is some written expression of the agreement, the basic questions are whether one party may prove prior or contemporaneously agreed terms or conditions which alter or add to the writing and how does a court determine the meaning of language in dispute which is admittedly part of the bargain. The first issue involves the "parol evidence rule" which determines the provability of a prior or contemporaneous oral agreement when the parties have assented to a written agreement. The second issue involves "interpretation," the ascertainment of the meaning to be given contract language. ("Interpretation of a promise or agreement or a term thereof is the ascertainment of its meaning." Restatement (Second) § 200.) As the selected materials will indicate, there is often a confusing overlap of these issues. Collateral reading: Farnsworth §§ 7.2–7.6 (parol evidence rule), 7.7–7.14 (interpretation); Murray §§ 82–85 (parol

[handwritten margin notes: "Informality UCC 1–203"; "Parol Evidence – proof of oral agreement prior to writing"]

evidence rule), 87–90 (interpretation); Calamari and Perillo §§ 3–2 through 3–8 (parol evidence rule), 3–9 through 3–18 (interpretation).

(A) INTEGRATED WRITINGS AND THE PAROL EVIDENCE RULE

The parol evidence rule depends upon the intention of the parties: did they intend a writing assented to by both to be integrated (final) as to some of the terms of the agreement (partial integration) or as to all of the terms of the agreement (total integration). If not, then evidence extrinsic to the writing of other agreed terms will be admitted under the usual rules of evidence. If so, then some agreed terms extrinsic to the writing will be excluded by the so-called parol evidence rule.

So far so good. But there are a series of troublesome questions: (1) How does a court determine whether the writing was integrated; (2) If integrated, how does a court determine which terms in the writing are final; (3) Does the parol evidence rule exclude evidence relevant to the interpretation of terms in the writing; and (4) What are the exceptions to the parol evidence rule, i.e. can evidence be admitted to show that the written contract was induced by fraud or mistake?

We will consider these questions in this Subsection.

Mitchill v. Lath

Court of Appeals of New York, 1928.
247 N.Y. 377, 160 N.E. 646.

■ ANDREWS, J. In the fall of 1923 the Laths owned a farm. This they wished to sell. Across the road, on land belonging to Lieutenant–Governor Lunn, they had an ice house which they might remove. Mrs. Mitchill looked over the land with a view to its purchase. She found the ice house objectionable. Thereupon "the defendants orally promised and agreed, for and in consideration of the purchase of their farm by the plaintiff, to remove the said ice house in the spring of 1924." Relying upon this promise, she made a written contract to buy the property for $8,400, for cash and a mortgage and containing various provisions usual in such papers. Later receiving a deed, she entered into possession and has spent considerable sums in improving the property for use as a summer residence. The defendants have not fulfilled their promise as to the ice house and do not intend to do so. We are not dealing, however, with their moral delinquencies. The question before us is whether their oral agreement may be enforced in a court of equity.

This requires a discussion of the parol evidence rule—a rule of law which defines the limits of the contract to be construed. (Glackin v. Bennett, 226 Mass. 316.) It is more than a rule of evidence, and oral testimony, even if admitted, will not control the written contract (O'Malley v. Grady, 222 Mass. 202), unless admitted without objection. (Brady v. Nally, 151 N.Y. 258.) It applies, however, to attempts to modify such a contract by parol. It does not affect a parol collateral contract distinct from and independent of the written agreement. It is, at times, troublesome to draw the line. Williston, in his work on Contracts (sec. 637) points out the difficulty. "Two entirely distinct contracts," he says, "each for a separate consideration may be made at the same time and will be distinct legally. Where, however, one agreement is entered into wholly or partly in consideration of the simultaneous agreement to enter into another, the transactions are necessarily bound together. * * * Then if one of the agreements is oral and the other is written, the problem arises whether the bond is sufficiently close to prevent proof of the oral agreement." That is the situation here. It is claimed that the defendants are called upon to do more than is required by their written contract in connection with the sale as to which it deals.

The principle may be clear, but it can be given effect by no mechanical rule. As so often happens, it is a matter of degree, for, as Professor Williston also says, where a contract contains several promises on each side it is not difficult to put any one of them in the form of a collateral agreement. If this were enough, written contracts might always be modified by parol. Not form, but substance, is the test.

In applying this test the policy of our courts is to be considered. We have believed that the purpose behind the rule was a wise one not easily to be abandoned. Notwithstanding injustice here and there, on the whole it works for good. Old precedents and principles are not to be lightly cast aside unless it is certain that they are an obstruction under present conditions. New York has been less open to arguments that would modify this particular rule, than some jurisdictions elsewhere. Thus in Eighmie v. Taylor (98 N.Y. 288) it was held that a parol warranty might not be shown although no warranties were contained in the writing.

Under our decisions before such an oral agreement as the present is received to vary the written contract at least three conditions must exist, (1) the agreement must in form be a collateral one; (2) it must not contradict express or implied provisions of the written contract; (3) it must be one that parties would not ordinarily be expected to embody in the writing; or put in another way, an inspection of the written contract, read in the light of surrounding circumstances must not indicate that the writing appears "to contain the engagements of the parties, and to define the object and measure the extent of such engagement." Or again, it must not be so clearly connected with the principal transaction as to be part and parcel of it.

The respondent does not satisfy the third of these requirements. It may be, not the second. We have a written contract for the purchase and sale of land. The buyer is to pay $8,400 in the way described. She is also to pay her portion of any rents, interest on mortgages, insurance premiums and water meter charges. She may have a survey made of the premises. On their part the sellers are to give a full covenant deed of the premises as described, or as they may be described by the surveyor if the survey is had, executed and acknowledged at their own expense; they sell the personal property on the farm and represent they own it; they agree that all amounts paid them on the contract and the expense of examining the title shall be a lien on the property; they assume the risk of loss or damage by fire until the deed is delivered; and they agree to pay the broker his commissions. Are they to do more? Or is such a claim inconsistent with these precise provisions? It could not be shown that the plaintiff was to pay $500 additional. Is it also implied that the defendants are not to do anything unexpressed in the writing?

That we need not decide. At least, however, an inspection of this contract shows a full and complete agreement, setting forth in detail the obligations of each party. On reading it, one would conclude that the reciprocal obligations of the parties were fully detailed. Nor would his opinion alter if he knew the surrounding circumstances. The presence of the ice house, even the knowledge that Mrs. Mitchill thought it objectionable, would not lead to the belief that a separate agreement existed with regard to it. Were such an agreement made it would seem most natural that the inquirer should find it in the contract. Collateral in form it is found to be, but it is closely related to the subject dealt with in the written agreement—so closely that we hold it may not be proved.

Where the line between the competent and the incompetent is narrow the citation of authorities is of slight use. Each represents the judgment of the court on the precise facts before it. How closely bound to the contract is the supposed collateral agreement is the decisive factor in each case. * * *

We do not ignore the fact that authorities may be found that would seem to support the contention of the appellant. . . . * * * But the fixed form of a deed makes it inappropriate to insert collateral agreements, however closely connected with the sale. This may be cause for an exception. Here we deal with the contract on the basis of which the deed to Mrs. Mitchill was given subsequently, and we confine ourselves to the question whether its terms may be modified.

* * *

Our conclusion is that the judgment of the Appellate Division and that of the Special Term should be reversed and the complaint dismissed, with costs in all courts.

■ LEHMAN, J. (dissenting). I accept the general rule as formulated by Judge ANDREWS. I differ with him only as to its application to the facts shown in the record. * * *

Judge Andrews has formulated a standard to measure the closeness of the bond. Three conditions, at least, must exist before an oral agreement may be proven to increase the obligation imposed by the written agreement. I think we agree that the first condition that the agreement "must in form be a collateral one" is met by the evidence. I concede that this condition is met in most cases where the courts have nevertheless excluded evidence of the collateral oral agreement. The difficulty here, as in most cases, arises in connection with the two other conditions.

The second condition is that the "parol agreement must not contradict express or implied provisions of the written contract." Judge Andrews voices doubt whether this condition is satisfied. The written contract has been carried out. The purchase price has been paid; conveyance has been made; title has passed in accordance with the terms of the written contract. The mutual obligations expressed in the written contract are left unchanged by the alleged oral contract. When performance was required of the written contract, the obligations of the parties were measured solely by its terms. By the oral agreement the plaintiff seeks to hold the defendants to other obligations to be performed by them thereafter upon land which was not conveyed to the plaintiff. The assertion of such further obligation is not inconsistent with the written contract unless the written contract contains a provision, express or implied, that the defendants are not to do anything not expressed in the writing. Concededly there is no such express provision in the contract, and such a provision may be implied, if at all, only if the asserted additional obligation is "so clearly connected with the principal transaction as to be part and parcel of it," and is not "one that the parties would not ordinarily be expected to embody in the writing." The hypothesis so formulated for a conclusion that the asserted additional obligation is inconsistent with an implied term of the contract is that the alleged oral agreement does not comply with the third condition as formulated by Judge Andrews. In this case, therefore, the problem reduces itself to the one question whether or not the oral agreement meets the third condition.

I have conceded that upon inspection the contract is complete. "It appears to contain the engagements of the parties, and to define the object and measure the extent of such engagement;" it constitutes the contract between them and is presumed to contain the whole of that contract. (Eighmie v. Taylor, 98 N.Y. 288.) That engagement was on the one side to convey land; on the other to pay the price. The plaintiff asserts further agreement based on the same consideration to be performed by the defendants after the conveyance was complete, and directly affecting only other land. It is true, as Judge Andrews points out, that "the presence of the ice house, even the knowledge that Mrs. Mitchill thought it objectionable, would not lead to the belief that a separate agreement existed with regard to it;" but the question we must decide is whether or not, *assuming* an agreement was made for the removal of an unsightly ice house from one parcel of land as an inducement for the purchase of another parcel, the parties would ordinarily or naturally be expected to embody the agreement for the removal of the ice house from one parcel in the written agreement to convey the other parcel. Exclusion of proof of the oral agreement on the ground that it varies the contract embodied in the writing may be based only upon a finding or presumption that the written contract was intended to cover the oral negotiations for the removal of the ice house which lead up to the contract of purchase and sale. To determine what the writing was intended to cover "the document alone will not suffice. What it was intended to cover cannot be known till we know what there was to cover. The question being whether certain subjects of negotiation were intended to be covered, we must compare the writing and the negotiations before we can determine whether they were in fact covered." (Wigmore on Evidence [2d ed.], section 2430.)

The subject-matter of the written contract was the conveyance of land. The contract was so complete on its face that the conclusion is inevitable that the parties intended to embody in the writing all the negotiations covering at least the conveyance. The promise by the defendants to remove the ice house from other land was not connected with their obligation to convey, except that one agreement would not have been made unless the other was also made. The plaintiff's assertion of a parol agreement by the defendants to remove the ice house was completely established by the great weight of evidence. It must prevail unless that agreement was part of the agreement to convey and the entire agreement was embodied in the writing.

* * *

The rule of integration undoubtedly frequently prevents the assertion of fraudulent claims. Parties who take the precaution of embodying their oral agreements in a writing should be protected against the assertion that other terms of the same agreement were not integrated in the writing. The limits of the integration are determined by the writing, read in the light of the surrounding circumstances. A written contract, however complete, yet covers only a limited field. I do not think that in the written contract for the conveyance of land here under consideration we can find an intention to cover a field so broad as to include prior agreements, if any such were made, to do other acts on other property after the stipulated conveyance was made.

In each case where such a problem is presented, varying factors enter into its solution. Citation of authority in this or other jurisdictions is useless, at least without minute analysis of the facts. The analysis I have made of the decisions in this State leads me to the view that the decision of the courts below is in accordance with our own authorities and should be affirmed.

■ CARDOZO, CH. J., POUND, KELLOGG and O'BRIEN, JJ., concur with ANDREWS, J.; LEHMAN, J., dissents in opinion in which CRANE, J., concurs.

Judgment accordingly.

Masterson v. Sine

Supreme Court of California, 1968.
68 Cal.2d 222, 65 Cal.Rptr. 545, 436 P.2d 561.

■ TRAYNOR, CHIEF JUSTICE. Dallas Masterson and his wife Rebecca owned a ranch as tenants in common. On February 25, 1958, they conveyed it to Medora and Lu Sine by a grant deed "Reserving unto the Grantors herein an option to purchase the above described property on or before February 25, 1968" for the "same consideration as being paid heretofore plus their depreciation value of any improvements Grantees may add to the property from and after two and a half years from this date." Medora is Dallas' sister and Lu's wife. Since the conveyance Dallas has been adjudged bankrupt. His trustee in bankruptcy and Rebecca brought this declaratory relief action to establish their right to enforce the option.

The case was tried without a jury. Over defendants' objection the trial court admitted extrinsic evidence that by "the same consideration as being paid heretofore" both the grantors and the grantees meant the sum of $50,000 and by "depreciation value of any improvements" they meant the depreciation value of improvements to be computed by deducting from the total amount of any capital expenditures made by defendants grantees the amount of depreciation allowable to them under United States income tax regulations as of the time of the exercise of the option.

The court also determined that the parol evidence rule precluded admission of extrinsic evidence offered by defendants to show that the parties wanted the property kept in the Masterson family and that the option was therefore personal to the grantors and could not be exercised by the trustee in bankruptcy.

The court entered judgment for plaintiffs, declaring their right to exercise the option, specifying in some detail how it could be exercised, and reserving jurisdiction to supervise the manner of its exercise and to determine the amount that plaintiffs will be required to pay defendants for their capital expenditures if plaintiffs decide to exercise the option.

Defendants appeal. They contend that the option provision is too uncertain to be enforced and that extrinsic evidence as to its meaning should not have been admitted. The trial court properly refused to frustrate the obviously declared intention of the grantors to reserve an option to repurchase by an overly meticulous insistence on completeness and clarity of written expression. ... It properly admitted extrinsic evidence to explain the language of the deed ... to the end that the consideration for the option would appear with sufficient certainty to permit specific enforcement. ... The trial court erred, however, in excluding the extrinsic evidence that the option was personal to the grantors and therefore nonassignable.

When the parties to a written contract have agreed to it as an "integration"—a complete and final embodiment of the terms of an agreement—parol evidence cannot be used to add to or vary its terms. ... When only part of the agreement is integrated, the same rule applies to that part, but parol evidence may be used to prove elements of the agreement not reduced to writing. ...

The crucial issue in determining whether there has been an integration is whether the parties intended their writing to serve as the exclusive embodiment of their agreement. The instrument itself may help to resolve that issue. It may state, for example, that "there are no previous understandings or agreements not contained in the writing," and thus express the parties' "intention to nullify antecedent understandings or agreements." (See 3 Corbin, Contracts (1960) § 578, p. 411.) Any such collateral agreement itself must be examined, however, to determine whether the parties intended the subjects of negotiation it deals with to be included in, excluded from, or otherwise affected by the writing. Circumstances at the time of the writing may also aid in the determination of such integration. . . .

California cases have stated that whether there was an integration is to be determined solely from the face of the instrument . . . and that the question for the court is whether it "appears to be a complete * * * agreement * * *." (See Ferguson v. Koch (1928) 204 Cal. 342, 346, . . .) Neither of these strict formulations of the rule, however, has been consistently applied. The requirement that the writing must appear incomplete on its face has been repudiated in many cases where parol evidence was admitted "to prove the existence of a separate oral agreement as to any matter on which the document is silent and which is not inconsistent with its terms"—even though the instrument appeared to state a complete agreement. . . . Even under the rule that the writing alone is to be consulted, it was found necessary to examine the alleged collateral agreement before concluding that proof of it was precluded by the writing alone. (See 3 Corbin, Contracts (1960) § 582, pp. 444–446.) It is therefore evident that "The conception of a writing as wholly and intrinsically self-determinative of the parties' intent to make it a sole memorial of one or seven or twenty-seven subjects of negotiation is an impossible one." (9 Wigmore, Evidence (3d ed. 1940) § 2431, p. 103.) For example, a promissory note given by a debtor to his creditor may integrate all their present contractual rights and obligations, or it may be only a minor part of an underlying executory contract that would never be discovered by examining the face of the note.

In formulating the rule governing parol evidence, several policies must be accommodated. One policy is based on the assumption that written evidence is more accurate than human memory. . . . This policy, however, can be adequately served by excluding parol evidence of agreements that directly contradict the writing. Another policy is based on the fear that fraud or unintentional invention by witnesses interested in the outcome of the litigation will mislead the finder of facts. . . . McCormick has suggested that the party urging the spoken as against the written word is most often the economic underdog, threatened by severe hardship if the writing is enforced. In his view the parol evidence rule arose to allow the court to control the tendency of the jury to find through sympathy and without a dispassionate assessment of the probability of fraud or faulty memory that the parties made an oral agreement collateral to the written contract, or that preliminary tentative agreements were not abandoned when omitted from the writing. (See McCormick, Evidence (1954) § 210.) He recognizes, however, that if this theory were adopted in disregard of all other considerations, it would lead to the exclusion of testimony concerning oral agreements whenever there is a writing and thereby often defeat the true intent of the parties. See McCormick, op. cit. supra, § 216, p. 441.

If Evidence

is Credible...

admit it

§240

ucc

2.202

Evidence of oral collateral agreements should be excluded only when the fact finder is likely to be misled. The rule must therefore be based on the credibility of the evidence. One such standard, adopted by section 240(1)(b) of the Restatement of Contracts, permits proof of a collateral agreement if it "is such an agreement as might *naturally* be made as a separate agreement by parties situated as were the parties to the written contract." (Italics added; ... The draftsmen of the Uniform Commercial Code would exclude the evidence in still fewer instances: "If the additional terms are such that, if agreed upon, they would *certainly* have been included in the document in the view of the court, then evidence of their alleged making must be kept from the trier of fact." (Com. 3, § 2–202, italics added.)[1]

The option clause in the deed in the present case does not explicitly provide that it contains the complete agreement, and the deed is silent on the question of assignability. Moreover, the difficulty of accommodating the formalized structure of a deed to the insertion of collateral agreements makes it less likely that all the terms of such an agreement were included. ... The statement of the reservation of the option might well have been placed in the recorded deed solely to preserve the grantors' rights against any possible future purchasers and this function could well be served without any mention of the parties' agreement that the option was personal. There is nothing in the record to indicate that the parties to this family transaction, through experience in land transactions or otherwise, had any warning of the disadvantages of failing to put the whole agreement in the deed. This case is one, therefore, in which it can be said that a collateral agreement such as that alleged "might naturally be made as a separate agreement." *A fortiori*, the case is not one in which the parties "would certainly" have included the collateral agreement in the deed.

It is contended, however, that an option agreement is ordinarily presumed to be assignable if it contains no provisions forbidding its transfer or indicating that its performance involves elements personal to the parties. ... The fact that there is a written memorandum, however, does not necessarily preclude parol evidence rebutting a term that the law would otherwise presume. * * *

§ 240

applies

In the present case defendants offered evidence that the parties agreed that the option was not assignable in order to keep the property in the Masterson family. The trial court erred in excluding that evidence.

The judgment is reversed.

■ PETERS, TOBRINER, MOSK, and SULLIVAN, JJ., concur.

---

1. Corbin suggests that, even in situations where the court concludes that it would not have been natural for the parties to make the alleged collateral oral agreement, parol evidence of such an agreement should nevertheless be permitted if the court is convinced that the unnatural actually happened in the case being adjudicated. (3 Corbin, Contracts, § 485, pp. 478, 480; cf. Murray, The Parol Evidence Rule: A Clarification (1966) 4 Duquesne L.Rev. 337, 341–342.) This suggestion may be based on a belief that judges are not likely to be misled by their sympathies. If the court believes that the parties intended a collateral agreement to be effective, there is no reason to keep the evidence from the jury.

[In a dissenting opinion, Justice Burke, with whom Justice McComb concurred, insisted that the majority opinion, 1) undermined the parol evidence rule as it has been known in California since 1872, 2) rendered suspect instruments of conveyance absolute on their face, 3) materially lessened the reliance which might be placed upon written instruments affecting title to real estate, and 4) opened the door, albeit unintentionally, to a new technique for the defrauding of creditors.]

NOTES

(1) What were factual differences in *Mitchill v. Lath* and *Masterson v. Sine*? Do those differences explain the different outcomes in the cases? If not, what might be a persuasive explanation.

(2) Sections 209–218 of the Restatement, Second, of Contracts deal with the parol evidence rule. Study those sections, please. Do they support a different result in *Mitchill v. Lath*? In *Masterson v. Sine*?

(3) Critics of the parol evidence rule have insisted that it ought not be regarded as a "rule of form." E.g., Justin Sweet, *Contract Making and Parol Evidence: Diagnosis and Treatment of a Sick Rule,* 53 Cornell L.Rev. 1036, 1060 (1968). An emphasis upon the "formal aspects" of the rule tends to restrict the use of parol evidence and to protect the exclusivity of the written terms. The avowed goal is the maintenance of the security of transactions as the "four corners" of the writing is looked to as defining the scope of obligation. Interested parties may thereby gain some assurance that evidence of informal expression may not be introduced to alter the apparent obligation. Note how the dissenting judge in *Masterson* is fearful of the majority opinion's effect in lessening the reliance which may be placed upon written instruments. But the cost of this protection may be too high. Does it not bespeak disinterest in determining the real agreement of the parties? If, as in *Mitchill*, the defendants for the same consideration promised to remove the ice house, why should they not be legally obliged to do so? It must be borne in mind that the admission of the proffered evidence would not have conclusively established the fact. The vendors could, of course, have offered evidence disputing the existence of such an oral promise, and the resultant credibility issue would have been decided in the usual way.

(4) *Does the Parol Evidence Rule Give Preference to Written Evidence of Contract Terms?*

"The law should give effect to the contract. In an important kind of trouble case, the parties dispute over contract terms. The contract might be entirely oral, or it might be partly oral and partly in writing. If the contract is not unenforceable under the statute of frauds, a court will have to ascertain its terms. Partly to guard against the uncertainties of litigation over oral contract terms, parties frequently undertake to put their contracts in writing. But there can be no magic in this. One party may later contend that the writing does not embody the terms agreed on; a writing cannot prevent disputes over terms. Moreover, a writing cannot by itself tell us what any of the terms really were. A writing is only potential evidence to be introduced in court, should the parties go to court to resolve a dispute over terms.

"Courts are frequently called on to resolve disputes over terms. The novice might expect that the process of adjudication here would be the same as in any other type of case in which facts are disputed: the parties would introduce all relevant evidence as to terms, including any writing, and the trier of fact would then determine what terms the parties actually contracted for. Also there would be the usual division of labor between judge and jury. Judges would, for example, rule on relevancy and admissibility, and they would be empowered to grant a motion for a non-suit, for a directed verdict, or for a judgment *n.o.v.* Thus, the usual protections against unreasonable jury determinations would be available to help assure that in the end, the court gives effect to the contract of the parties as actually agreed.

"But Anglo–American law does not handle all disputes over contract terms in this way. Our courts apply a so-called 'parol evidence rule' when some of the evidence of terms is embodied in a writing. The usual effect of this is to give preference to the written version of terms. Writings are more reliable than memories to show contract terms, and forgery is supposedly easier to detect than is lying on the witness stand. These are the principal premises of a parol evidence rule. Early critics of the rule challenged these premises and emphasized that the rule is inconsistent with our usual processes of proof. If juries are to be 'trusted' in disputes over contract terms not involving writings, then why should they not hear all the evidence, even where writings are involved, and decide accordingly? The debate still rages.

White and Summers, Uniform Commercial Code 94–95 (3d ed. 1988).

This text is slightly revised in White and Summers, Uniform Commercial Code 88–89 (5th ed. 2000), where the authors have replaced the phrase "The debate still rages" with the following: "One reason is the same social Darwinist reasons given [for the statute of frauds]; to train contracting parties to memorialize their agreements and so to minimize disputes between them and in the courts."

Alaska Northern Development, Inc. v. Alyeska Pipeline Service Co.

Supreme Court of Alaska, 1983.
666 P.2d 33, cert. denied 464 U.S. 1041, 104 S.Ct. 706, 79 L.Ed.2d 170 (1984).

Opinion

■ COMPTON, JUSTICE.

Alaska Northern Development, Inc. ("AND") appeals a judgment in favor of Alyeska Pipeline Service Co. ("Alyeska") in a dispute involving contract formation and interpretation. For the reasons stated below, we affirm.

I.   FACTUAL AND PROCEDURAL BACKGROUND

In late October or early November 1976, David Reed, a shareholder and corporate president of AND, initiated discussion with Alyeska personnel in Fairbanks regarding the purchase of surplus parts. The Alyeska employees with whom Reed dealt were Juel Tyson, Clarence Terwilleger and Donald Bruce.

After a series of discussions, Terwilleger indicated that Reed's proposal should be put in writing so it could be submitted to management. With the assistance of AND's legal counsel, Reed prepared a letter of intent dated December 10, 1976. In this letter, AND proposed to purchase "the entire Alyeska inventory of Caterpillar parts." The place for the purchase price was left blank.

Alyeska responded with its own letter of intent dated December 11, 1976. The letter was drafted by Bruce and Tyson in consultation with William Rickett, Alyeska's manager of Contracts and Material Management. Again, the price term was absent. The letter contained the following language, which is the focus of this lawsuit: "Please consider this as said letter of intent, *subject to the final approval of the owner committee.*" (Emphasis added.)

Reed was given an unsigned draft of the December 11 letter, which was reviewed by AND's legal counsel. Reed then met with Rickett, and they agreed on sixty-five percent of Alyeska's price as the price term to be filled in the blank on the December 11 letter. Rickett filled in the blank as agreed and signed the letter. In March 1977, the owner committee rejected the proposal embodied in the December 11 letter of intent.

AND contends that the parties understood the subject to approval language to mean that the Alyeska owner committee would review the proposed agreement only to determine whether the price was fair and reasonable. Alyeska contends that Reed was never advised of any such limitation on the authority of the owner committee. In April 1977, AND filed a complaint alleging that there was a contract between AND and Alyeska, which Alyeska breached. The complaint was later amended to include counts for reformation and punitive damages.

Alyeska moved for summary judgment on the punitive damages and breach of contract counts. The superior court granted summary judgment in favor of Alyeska on the punitive damages count. The court initially denied Alyeska's motion for summary judgment on the breach of contract claim; however, based on a review of the case after discovery had closed, the court announced at a hearing on September 26, 1980, that it would reverse its earlier ruling and grant Alyeska's motion. The court confirmed this ruling at a hearing on November 5, 1980, after consideration of AND's Motion for Clarification.

* * *

II. APPLICATION OF THE PAROL EVIDENCE RULE

The superior court held that the parol evidence rule of the Uniform Commercial Code, section 2–202, codified as AS 45.02–202,[3] applied to the

---

3. As 45.02.202 provides:

Final written expression; parol or ex trinsic evidence. Terms with respect to

which the confirmatory memoranda of the parties agree, or which are otherwise set out in a writing intended by the

December 11 letter and therefore no extrinsic evidence could be presented to a jury which limited the owner committee's right of approval. AND contends that the court erred in applying the parol evidence rule. We disagree.

In order to exclude parol evidence concerning the inclusion of additional terms to a writing, a court must make the following determinations. First, the court must determine whether the writing under scrutiny was integrated, i.e., intended by the parties as a final expression of their agreement with respect to some or all of the terms included in the writing. Second, the court must determine whether evidence of a prior or contemporaneous agreement contradicts or is inconsistent with the integrated portion. If the evidence is contradictory or inconsistent, it is inadmissible. If it is consistent, it may nevertheless be excluded if the court concludes that the consistent term would necessarily have been included in the writing by the parties if they had intended it to be part of their agreement. AS 45.02.202; Braund, Inc. v. White, 486 P.2d 50, 56 (Alaska 1971); U.C.C. § 2-202 comment 3 (1977).

A. Was the December 11 Letter a Partial Integration?

An integrated writing exists where the parties intend that the writing be a final expression of one or more terms of their agreement. Kupka v. Morey, 541 P.2d 740, 747 n. 8 (Alaska 1975); Restatement (Second) of Contracts § 209(a) (1979). Whether a writing is integrated is a question of fact to be determined by the court in accordance with all relevant evidence. Restatement (Second) of Contracts § 209 comment c (1979).

In granting summary judgment on the breach of contract claim, the superior court stated that it had carefully considered all relevant evidence, including oral and written records of all facets of the business deal in question, to arrive at its finding that the agreement was partially integrated.[4] After the six-week trial on the reformation issue, the superior court reaffirmed this finding:

parties as a final expression of their agreement with respect to the terms included in the writing, may not be contradicted by evidence of a prior agreement or of a contemporaneous oral agreement, but may be explained or supplemented

(1) by course of dealing or usage of trade (AS 45.01.205) or by course of performance (AS 45.02.208); and

(2) by evidence of consistent additional terms unless the court finds the writing was intended also as a complete and exclusive statement of the terms of the agreement.

4. At the hearing on AND's Motion for Clarification, the superior court stated:

[I]t seems to me absolutely conclusive on this evidence, and I'm making this as a finding of fact, that this agreement is partially integrated, and I'm not making it by reference only to the four corners of the—of the writings but reference to all the extrinsic evidence that has been proffered to me, read everybody's deposition, considered in detail all the processes of negotiations, everything that was said and done by everybody as related by them up till the time that Rickett included the language in the letter and turned it over to Reed. So we're not here talking about the for [sic] corners or ambiguity or anything like that. We're talking about all the extrinsic evidence,

35. The plaintiff initially contends that the letter of December 11, 1976 (the letter) was not integrated or partially integrated and therefore the court was in error in granting summary judgment in favor of defendant on the contract counts of the plaintiff's complaint on September 26, 1980.

36. After considering the evidence submitted at trial, the court reaffirms its prior conclusion that the letter was integrated as to the Owners Committee's approval clause.

37. The parties intended to write down their discussions in a comprehensive form which allowed Reed to seek financing and allow the primary actors (Tyson, Bruce, Terwilleger, Rickett) to submit the concept embodied by the letter to higher management....

38. There are three subjects upon which plaintiff seeks reformation.... As to the first, [limiting the Owner Committee to a consideration of price] which has been plaintiff's primary focus, the court finds that such reference was integrated such that the parole [sic] evidence rule would bar any inconsistent testimony. Testimony that the owners were limited to "price" in their review is inconsistent....

41. With respect to the Owners Committee's approval clause, according to the plaintiff's contention the owners were entitled to review the transaction, on whatever basis, only one time. This was testified to by both Mr. Reed and argued by plaintiff in closing.... It was also conceded in closing that the review by the owners, on whatever standard, would occur prior to any formal contract being negotiated and executed.... This is also consistent with the testimony of each of the participants.

42. In addition, Mr. Reed, in consultation with Ed Merdes and Henry Camarot, his attorneys, tendered the letter of March 4, 1977, as a document which could serve as "the contract...." The March 4 letter contains no further reference to the Owners Committee's approval function.... Therefore, I find that as to the Owners Committee's approval ... the letter of December 11 constitutes an integration or partial integration.... This having been established, the analysis outlined by the court on September 26, 1980, when granting defendant's motion for summary judgment on the contract claims is applicable.

After reviewing the record, we cannot say that this finding of a partial integration was clearly erroneous.

* * *

meaning on balance to a conclusion more probable than not that this is a partially integrated agreement.

B. *Does the Excluded Evidence Contradict the Integrated Terms?*

Having found a partial integration, the next determination is whether the excluded evidence contradicts the integrated portion of the writing. Comment b to section 215 of the Restatement (Second) of Contracts is helpful in resolving this issue.[5] Comment b states:

> An earlier agreement may help the interpretation of a later one, but it may not contradict a binding later integrated agreement. Whether there is a contradiction depends . . . on whether the two are consistent or inconsistent. This is a question which often cannot be determined from the face of the writing; the writing must first be applied to its subject matter and placed in context. The question is then decided by the court as part of a question of interpretation. Where reasonable people could differ as to the credibility of the evidence offered and the evidence if believed could lead a reasonable person to interpret the writing as claimed by the proponent of the evidence, the question of credibility and the choice among reasonable inferences should be treated as questions of fact. But the asserted meaning must be one to which the language of the writing, read in context, is reasonably susceptible. If no other meaning is reasonable, the court should rule as a matter of law that the meaning is established.

According to comment b, therefore, a question of interpretation may arise before the contradiction issue can be resolved. If the evidence conflicts, the choice between competing inferences is for the trier of fact to resolve. . . . The meaning is determined as a matter of law, however, if "the asserted meaning [is not] one to which the language of the writing, read in context, is reasonably susceptible." Restatement (Second) of Contracts § 215 comment b (1979). . . .

AND contends that the superior court erred in granting summary judgment because the evidence conflicted as to the meaning of the owner committee approval clause. It concludes that under *Alyeska* it was entitled to a jury trial on the interpretation issue. Alyeska contends, and the superior court ruled, that a jury trial was inappropriate because, as a matter of law, AND's asserted meaning of the clause at issue was not reasonably susceptible to the language of the writing. The superior court stated:

> The Court is making the . . . ruling that the offer of evidence to show that Rickett's letter really meant to limit owner committee approval to the price term alone . . . is not reasonably susceptible—or the writing is not reasonably susceptible to that purpose. And therefore, that extrinsic evidence operates to contradict the writing, not specific words in the writing, but the words in the context of the totality of the writing and the totality of the extrinsic evidence.

---

5. Restatement (Second) of Contracts § 215, which parallels the rule stated in U.C.C. § 2–202, reads: "Except as stated in the preceding Section, where there is a binding agreement, either completely or partially integrated, evidence of prior or contemporaneous agreements or negotiations is not admissible in evidence to contradict a term of the writing."

We agree that the words used in the December 11 letter are not reasonably susceptible to the interpretation advanced by AND. Therefore, we find no merit to AND's contention that it was entitled to a jury trial on the interpretation issue.

After rejecting the extrinsic evidence for purposes of interpretation, the superior court found AND's offered testimony, that the owner committee's approval power was limited to approval of the price, to be inconsistent with and contradictory to the language used by the negotiators in the December 11 letter. AND contends that the offered testimony did not contradict, but rather explained or supplemented the writing with consistent additional terms. For this contention, AND relies on the standard articulated in Hunt Foods & Industries, Inc. v. Doliner, 270 N.Y.S.2d 937 (N.Y.App.1966). In Hunt Foods, the defendant signed an option agreement under which he agreed to sell stock to Hunt Foods at a given price per share. When Hunt Foods attempted to exercise the option, the defendant contended that the option could only be exercised if the defendant had received offers from a third party. The court held that section 2–202 did not bar this evidence from being admitted because it held that the proposed oral condition to the option agreement was not "inconsistent" within the meaning of section 2–202; to be inconsistent, "the term must contradict or negate a term of the writing. A term or condition which has a lesser effect is provable." Id. 270 N.Y.S.2d at 940.

The narrow view of consistency expressed in Hunt Foods has been criticized. In Snyder v. Herbert Greenbaum & Associates, Inc., 38 Md.App. 144 (Md.App.1977), the court held that the parol evidence of a contractual right to unilateral rescission was inconsistent with a written agreement for the sale and installation of carpeting. The court defined "inconsistency" as used in section 2–202(b) as "the absence of reasonable harmony in terms of the language and respective obligations of the parties." Id. 380 A.2d at 623 (emphasis in original) (citing U.C.C. § 1–205(4)) . . .

We agree with this view of inconsistency and reject the view expressed in *Hunt Foods*.[6] Under this definition of inconsistency, it is clear that the proffered parol evidence limiting the owner committee's right of final approval to price is inconsistent with the integrated term that unconditionally gives the committee the right to approval. Therefore, the superior court was correct in refusing to admit parol evidence on this issue.[7] * * *

---

6. Hunt Foods was implicitly rejected in Johnson v. Curran, 633 P.2d 994, 996–97 (Alaska 1981) (parol evidence concerning an early termination right based on nightclub owner's dissatisfaction with the band's performance was inconsistent with parties' written contract specifying definite time without mention of any right of early termination and thus inadmissible).

7. Our affirmance of the superior court's holding that the proposed version is inconsistent with the integrated clause obviates discussion of whether the addition, if consistent, would have been included in the December 11 letter. Furthermore, we decline to reach AND's contentions regarding the applicability of U.C.C. § 2–207 because AND never raised the § 2–207 argument at the superior court level. See, e.g., Jeffries v. Glacier State Telephone Co., 604 P.2d 4, 11 (Alaska 1979).

Affirmed.

NOTES

(1) Read UCC 2–202 and the comments. What test did the court use to determine whether the writing was partially integrated? If the writing was not detailed and complete on its face, why did the court decide it was integrated with regard to some of the terms? Assuming that it was partially integrated, what test did the court use to decide whether the oral condition was a "consistent additional term?" Is a term in "reasonable harmony" with the writing if it would have naturally and normally be made a separate agreement? Or is the test whether the oral condition "would certainly" have been included in the writing?

See Restatement (Second) § 216(2) which provides: "An agreement is not completely integrated if the writing omits a consistent additional agreed term which is * * * (b) such a term as in the circumstances might naturally be omitted from the writing."

In A. Kemp Fisheries, Inc. v. Castle & Cooke, Inc., 852 F.2d 493 (9th Cir.1988), reprinted infra at 640, the court, applying California law, held that a Charter Agreement between the parties was an integrated writing, even though it did not contain a "merger" clause. In making this determination, the court considered:

> [T]he language and completeness of the written agreement and whether it contains an integration clause, the terms of the alleged ... agreement and whether they contradict those in the writing, whether the ... agreement might naturally be made as a separate agreement, and whether the jury might be misled by the introduction of the parol testimony. A court also considers the circumstances surrounding the transaction and its subject matter, nature and object. 852 F.2d at 495.

(2) The plaintiff in *Alaska Northern* attempted an endrun around the parol evidence rule by introducing evidence of the oral agreement for the purpose of interpreting a term already in the contract. Normally, evidence for this purpose is admitted. See Restatement, Second, Contracts 212. How did the court stop this end run? Do you agree?

Revised 2–202(2) provides that "terms in a record may be explained by evidence of course of performance, course of dealing, or usage of trade without a preliminary determination by the court that the language used is ambiguous." Would this revision have helped the court in the *Alaska Northern* case?

PROBLEM: PAROL EVIDENCE UNDER CISG

An Italian seller of ceramic tiles and an American buyer, acting through agents, negotiated an oral agreement of sale that contained agreement on price, quality, quantity, delivery, and payment. The parties then reduced the negotiated terms to writing on a form prepared by the seller. On the front over the signature line there was language incorporating terms on the back of the writing into the contract. One of the terms on the back provided:

Default in delay in payment within the time agreed upon gives [Seller] the right to ... suspend or cancel the contract itself and to cancel possible other pending contracts and the buyer does not have the right to indemnification or damages.

The agents signed the writing, but there was evidence, confirmed by affidavits, that at the time of signing neither agent intended that terms on the back of the writing were part of the contract. Later, there was a dispute over late payment and the seller invoked the delay in payment term. As a defense, the buyer introduced evidence that neither party intended the back to be part of the contract, although language on the front was not modified to make this intention clear.

(1) Is this evidence admissible under CISG to exclude the default in payment clause? See CISG Art. 8. To check your reasoning, see MCC–Marble Ceramic Center, Inc. v. Ceramica Nuova d'Agostino, S.p.A., 144 F.3d 1384 (11th Cir.1998) (no parol evidence rule under CISG).

(2) If the contract was between an American seller and buyer, would the evidence be admissible under UCC 2–202? If both parties have the same intention, should that control when it is inconsistent with a term in the writing? See Restatement, Second, Contracts 20(2).

Luther Williams, Jr., Inc. v. Johnson

District of Columbia Court of Appeals, 1967.
229 A.2d 163.

■ QUINN, JUDGE. Appellant (plaintiff below) sought to recover $670 as liquidated damages under a contract for improvements on appellees' home. Appellees' defense was that the contract never came into existence because of an unfulfilled condition precedent. This appeal raises the sole question of whether the parol evidence rule required exclusion of all testimony regarding the alleged condition.

At the trial, Luther Williams, Jr., president of appellant corporation, testified that prior to the signing of the contract, he offered to arrange any necessary financing for appellees, but was advised that they had their own. He was further informed that the down payment would be made in a few days when they received their funds. After drawing plans and contacting appellees several times, he was told that their financing had not been obtained and that they had procured another contractor to make certain improvements on the property.

Appellees testified that they signed the contract thinking it was merely an estimate; that they told Mr. Williams the improvements would depend upon approval of their financing by their bank; and that it was their understanding with him that they would not become obligated until they had procured the funds. Appellant objected to the introduction of all testimony concerning a parol agreement regarding financing, and later objected to jury instructions on that subject. The objections were overruled, and the jury returned a verdict for appellees.

As previously stated, the issue here is a narrow one, namely, whether the admission of testimony concerning the oral condition precedent violated the parol evidence rule. Briefly stated, that rule provides that when the parties to a contract reduce their agreement to writing, that writing is presumed to be the final repository of all prior negotiations, and testimony concerning prior or contemporaneous oral agreements which tends to vary, modify or contradict the terms of the writing is inadmissible. See 3 Corbin, Contracts § 573 (1960); 4 Williston, Contracts, § 631 (3d ed. 1961).

In this jurisdiction, however, it is well settled that a written contract may be conditioned on an oral agreement that the contract shall not become binding until some condition precedent resting in parol shall have been performed. ... Furthermore, parol testimony to prove such a condition is admissible when the contract is silent on the matter, the testimony does not contradict nor is it inconsistent with the writing, and if under the circumstances it may properly be inferred that the parties did not intend the writing to be a complete statement of their transaction. ...

The contract in question contained the following clause:

"This contract embodies the entire understanding between the parties, and there are no verbal agreements or representations in connection therewith."

Two problems thus arise when applying the above rules to the instant case. First, in the light of an "integration clause," can evidence be admitted to show that the parties did not intend the writing to be a complete statement of their transaction? Second, can it be said that the testimony regarding the condition precedent does not contradict the writing when the contract states there are no agreements other than those contained in the writing?

As to the first question, it has always been presumed that a written contract is the final repository of the agreement of the parties. 4 Williston, op. cit. supra § 631 at 953–954. In this regard, an integration clause merely strengthens this presumption. However, intent is a question of fact, and to determine the intent of the parties, it is necessary to look not only to the written instrument, but to the circumstances surrounding its execution.

In Mitchell v. David, supra, we quoted with approval from 9 Wigmore, Evidence § 2430 (3d ed. 1940) as follows:

"Whether a particular subject of negotiation is embodied by the writing *depends wholly upon the intent of the parties* thereto. In this respect the contrast is between voluntary integration and integration by law. Here the parties are not obliged to embody their transaction in a single document; yet they may, if they choose. Hence it becomes merely a question whether they have intended to do so."

"This intent must be sought where always intent must be sought, namely, in the *conduct* and *language* of the parties and the *surrounding circumstances*. The document alone will not suffice. What it was intended to cover cannot be known till we know what there was to cover. The question being whether certain subjects of negotiation were intended to be covered, we must compare the writing and the negotiations before we can determine whether they were in fact covered. Thus the apparent paradox is committed of receiving proof of certain negotiations in order to determine whether to exclude them; and this doubtless has sometimes seemed to lower the rule to a quibble. But the paradox is apparent only. The explanation is that these alleged negotiations are received only provisionally. Although in form the witnesses may be allowed to recite the facts, yet in truth the facts will be afterwards treated as immaterial and legally void, if the rule is held applicable. There is a preliminary question for the judge to decide as to the intent of the parties, and upon this he hears evidence on both sides; his decision here, *pro* or *con,* concerns merely this question preliminary to the ruling of law. If he decides that the transaction was covered by the writing, he does not decide that the excluded negotiations did not take place, but merely that *if* they did take place they are nevertheless legally immaterial. If he decides that the transaction was not intended to be covered by the writing, he does not decide that the negotiations did take place, but merely that *if* they did, they are legally effective, and he then leaves to the jury the determination of fact whether they did take place." 51 A.2d at 378. . . . We are still of the opinion that this expresses the better practice.

As to the second question, we are aware that some courts have answered it in the negative. . . . We believe, however, that this is an erroneous interpretation of Restatement, Contracts § 241 (1932) which provides as follows:

"Where parties to a writing which purports to be an integration of a contract between them orally agree, before or contemporaneously with the making of the writing, that it shall not become binding until a future day or until the happening of a future event, the oral agreement is operative *if there is nothing in the writing inconsistent therewith.*" (Emphasis added.)

To explain this section, the following illustration is given:

"A and B make and sign a writing in which A promises to sell and B promises to buy goods of a certain description at a stated price. The parties at the same time orally agree that the writing shall not take effect unless within ten days their local railroad has cars available for shipping the goods. The oral agreement is operative according to its terms. If, however, the writing provides 'delivery shall be made within thirty days' from the date of the writing, the oral agreement is inoperative."

In our opinion, it is clear from the example that what is intended is not the exclusion of evidence because of the existence of an "integration clause," 3 Corbin, op. cit. supra § 578 at 405–407, but an exclusion only if the alleged parol condition contradicts some other specific term of the written agreement. . . . In the instant case, no provision was made regarding financing. Therefore, the parol condition would not contradict the terms of the writing.

For the above-stated reasons, we hold that it was not error to admit testimony tending to show that the writing was not intended to be a complete statement of the agreement of the parties and to instruct the jury to find for appellees if they determined that the negotiations regarding the condition precedent had taken place and that the contract was not to become binding unless the financing was first obtained.

Affirmed.

NOTES

(1) *Conclusiveness of merger clause.* The writing in *Luther Williams* contains an added element not present in preceding cases of this section; *viz.,* a provision usually referred to as a "merger" or "integration" clause. What is its significance relative to ascertaining whether the writing is a complete or only a partial integration? Is it conclusive evidence of intention or only presumptive evidence?

In a commercial transaction, is the presence of a "merger" clause conclusive on the intention of the parties to have a total integration of the writing? In ARB, Inc. v. E–Systems, Inc., 663 F.2d 189, 198–199 (D.C.Cir.1980), the answer, under Maryland law at least, was no. Integration clauses are not "absolutely conclusive." Rather, they are:

[I]ndicative of the intention of the parties to finalize their complete understanding in the written contract ... that there was no other prior or contemporaneous agreement not included in the written contract. Thus, the court should consider the circumstances surrounding the making of the contract ... to discover whether the integration clause in question does, in fact, express the genuine intention of the parties to make the written contract the complete and exclusive statement of their agreement. These circumstances include the length and detail of the contract, the length and nature of the negotiations preceding execution and the absence of "persuasive evidence supporting a determination that the parties intended, at the time of contracting, that non-written terms be part of the overall agreement.

Accord: Betaco, Inc. v. Cessna Aircraft Co., 103 F.3d 1281 (7th Cir.1996) (merger clause not conclusive, but presumption not rebutted by evidence).

(2) *Effect of Merger Clause in Consumer Sales.* According to Professor Justin Sweet, the exclusive purpose of the parol evidence rule is to protect "truly integrated writings." Justin Sweet, *Contract Making and Parol Evidence: Diagnosis and Treatment of a Sick Rule,* 53 Cornell L.Rev. 1036, 1060 (1967). In most cases a merger clause contained in a writing which has objectively been assented to by both parties is the best evidence of an intention to integrate. In a wide range of retail sales to consumers, however, the merger clause buried in the boiler plate of a written contract can be a potent weapon in the hands of the seller.

For example, in the pre-sale "dickering" the seller may make an oral, express warranty which becomes part of the basis of the buyer's bargain. UCC 2–313(1). Later, the buyer signs a written contract for sale containing the merger clause which, of course, was not read, not called to his or her attention and, even if read, would not clearly indicate that a material, inducing term of the sale was being excluded. If the merger clause is viewed as an attempt to "disclaim" the express warranty, the warranty prevails under UCC 2–316(1). If the merger clause is viewed as an attempt totally to integrate the writing, UCC 2–202 applies and would appear to protect the seller. Is the use by a professional seller of a merger clause in consumer transactions without full disclosure of its presence and meaning unconscionable?

Restatement (Second) § 211(3) provides:

Where the other party has reason to believe that the party manifesting such assent would not do so if he knew that the writing contained a particular term, the term is not part of the agreement." The drafters appended the following comment: "[A] party who adheres to the other party's standard terms does not assent to a term if the other party has reason to believe that the adhering party would not have accepted the agreement if he had known that the agreement contained the particular term. Such a belief or assumption may be shown by the prior negotiations or inferred from the circumstances. Reason to believe may be inferred from the fact that the term is bizarre or oppressive, from the fact that it eviscerates the non-standard terms explicitly agreed to, or from the fact that it eliminates the dominant purpose of the transaction. The inference is reinforced if the adhering party never had an opportunity to read the term, or if it is illegible or otherwise hidden from view. This rule is closely related to the policy against unconscionable terms and the rule of interpretation against the draftsman. See §§ 206 and 208. Restatement (Second) § 211, Comment f.

See also Birnbaum, Stahl & West, *Standardized Agreements and the Parol Evidence Rule: Defining and Applying the Expectations Principle*, 26 Ariz. L.Rev. 793 (1984).

(3) *Evidence of Nonexistence or Invalidity of Agreement.* The parol evidence rule contemplates the protection of a writing embodying the terms of a contract. If there is no contract the Rule's protective shield is obviously unavailable. Thus, evidence establishing invalidity of the purported agreement, such as lack of consideration, fraud, mistake, duress or illegality, is readily admitted. A difficulty is encountered, however, where there is a valid contract in the ordinary sense, but a party asserts an oral "condition" to the assumed duty. Evidence of this condition does not establish the non-existence of the underlying contract; rather, it establishes a condition or qualification of the duty to perform. (See infra, Section B). If the evidence of an oral condition is to be admitted, and the authorities are conflicting, it should be upon a ground other than that of showing the non-existence of a contract. How is this type of problem resolved under UCC 2–202? See also Restatement (Second) § 217: "Where the parties to a written agreement agree orally that performance of the agreement is subject to the occurrence of a stated condition, the agreement is not integrated with respect to the oral condition."

Comment: Warranties, Disclaimers and the Parol Evidence Rule

In contracts for the sale of goods, the seller may make four warranties of quality: express warranties, UCC 2–313; an implied warranty of merchantability, UCC 2–314; an implied warranty of fitness for particular purpose, UCC 2–315; and a warranty of good title, UCC 2–312(1). These warranties, when made, are clearly terms of the agreement. The Code also regulates efforts by the seller to exclude or modify warranties made. For example, "to exclude or modify the implied warranty of merchantability or any part of it the language must mention merchantability and in case of a writing must be conspicuous * * *." UCC 2–316(2). Similarly, a warranty that "title shall be good and its transfer rightful" can be excluded or modified "only by specific language" or by special circumstances defined in UCC 2–312(2). In short, a warranty made may be very difficult to take away by a disclaimer. See Rev. 2–316(2), where tougher rules for disclaimers in consumer contracts are stated.

In the case of express warranties, it is impossible: if words or conduct creating an express warranty and words or conduct "tending to negate or limit warranty" cannot be construed as consistent with each other, "negation or limitation is inoperative to the extent that such construction is unreasonable." UCC 2–316(1).

How does the parol evidence rule, UCC 2–202, mesh with the giving and taking of warranties? *First,* if a disclaimer is effective, the parol evidence rule is irrelevant. The warranty has been excluded from the agreement by other means. *Second,* suppose the seller has made an implied warranty of merchantability and it has not been disclaimed. Since the warranty is a term of the agreement, one could argue that it is subject to exclusion under UCC 2–202 if the parties intended the writing to be a "complete and exclusive statement of the terms of the agreement." UCC 2–202(b). The problem is that this implied warranty emerges from the very roots of the bargain and UCC 2–316(2) sets a high standard for its exclusion. A good court, therefore, might be hesitant to exclude an implied warranty of merchantability by virtue of a general "merger" clause, even though that clause was conspicuous. In short, to protect this particular warranty, the court should insist upon the same level of detail and conspicuousness in the manifestation of intention to integrate the writing as UCC 2–316(2) requires for a disclaimer. Third, UCC 2–316(1), which makes it impossible to disclaim an express warranty, states that the matter is "subject to the provisions of this Article on parol or extrinsic evidence (Section 2–202)."

Suppose, then, this situation. The used car salesman has made "affirmations of fact" about the condition of a particular used car and they become "part of the basis" of the buyer's bargain. UCC 2–313(1). Later, the buyer signs a writing that attempts to disclaim all express warranties except a promise to share 50–50 in all repairs needed during the first 30 days and contains a general merger clause that provides: THIS WRITING IS THE FINAL AND EXCLUSIVE STATEMENT AND EXPRESSION OF ALL OF THE TERMS OF THE AGREEMENT. Buyer signs the agreement but, 60 days later, discovers a major defect that is inconsistent with the salesman's oral representation. Is the seller protected? The answer is no if the court concludes that the writing was not intended as a total integration and the oral representations can be admitted as "consistent additional terms." Similarly, the parol evidence rule does not apply at all if the representations were fraudulent. Further, there is a hint in some cases that even if a total integration was intended, the oral representation may not be excluded if the buyer was surprised by an "unexpected and unbargained for" exclusion. See Jordan v. Doonan Truck & Equipment, Inc., 220 Kan. 431, 552 P.2d 881 (1976). At least one court has concluded that an inconspicuous and broadly worded merger clause is unconscionable to the extent it is asserted to exclude oral express warranties. See Seibel v. Layne & Bowler, Inc., 56 Or.App. 387, 641 P.2d 668 (1982) review denied 293 Or. 190, 648 P.2d 852 (1982). The court endorsed the merger clause proposed by White and Summers, Uniform Commercial Code 111–112 (3d ed. 1988) [compare the "merger clause" in the fifth edition at 104, which deletes the last sentence.]:

> THIS AGREEMENT SIGNED BY BOTH PARTIES AND SO INITIALED BY BOTH PARTIES IN THE MARGIN OPPOSITE THIS PARAGRAPH CONSTITUTES A FINAL WRITTEN EXPRESSION OF ALL THE TERMS OF THIS AGREEMENT AND IS A COMPLETE AND EXCLUSIVE STATEMENT OF THOSE TERMS. ANY AND ALL REPRESENTATIONS, PROMISES, WARRANTIES OR STATEMENTS BY SELLER'S AGENT THAT DIFFER IN ANY WAY FROM THE TERMS OF THIS WRITTEN AGREEMENT SHALL BE GIVEN NO FORCE OR EFFECT.

Would this "merger" clause exclude implied warranties?

PROBLEM: THE CASE OF THE UNEXPECTED SPOUSE

After ten years of marriage, Ira Soper deserted his wife in Ohio under circumstances contrived to persuade that he had committed suicide. After that, he surfaced in Minneapolis under the name of John Young and became established in business and in a social way. Two years later he married a widow, but she died three years later. Two years later he married another widow and they lived together as husband and wife for five years until Soper died, this time for real, by his own hand. Prior to his death, however, he had entered into a stock insurance plan with his business partner. Under this plan, upon the death of either partner the survivor could acquire the other's business interest from the estate and the surviving "wife" was to be compensated by life insurance to be taken out by each partner on his life, premiums to be paid by the company. The resulting written insurance "trust" provided that upon the death of the Depositor the "trust company shall deliver the stock certificates of the deceased Depositor to the surviving Depositor and it shall deliver the proceeds of the insurance on the life of the deceased Depositor to the wife of the deceased Depositor if living ... " The insurance proceeds were duly paid by the trust officer to Gertrude Young, the woman with whom the deceased had been living as her husband. Shortly thereafter, Adeline, the first Mrs. Soper appeared and established that she was the legal spouse of the deceased. Mrs. Soper had an administrator appointed for the estate of the deceased and brought suit against Mrs. Young to recover the insurance proceeds.

Based upon the preceding materials and the materials to come in Chapter 6:

(1) What are the strongest arguments in favor of Adeline Soper?

(2) What are the strongest arguments in favor of Gertrude Young?

(3) How should the Court rule? See In re Soper's Estate, 196 Minn. 60, 264 N.W. 427 (1935).

(B) INTERPRETATION

Pacific Gas & Electric Co. v. G. W. Thomas Drayage & Rigging Co.   (π)   (Δ)

Supreme Court of California, 1968.
69 Cal.2d 33, 69 Cal.Rptr. 561, 442 P.2d 641.

■ TRAYNOR, CHIEF JUSTICE. Defendant appeals from a judgment for plaintiff in an action for damages for injury to property under an indemnity clause of a contract.

In 1960 defendant entered into a contract with plaintiff to furnish the labor and equipment necessary to remove and replace the upper metal cover of plaintiff's steam turbine. Defendant agreed to perform the work "at [its] own risk and expense" and to "indemnify" plaintiff "against all loss, damage, expense and liability resulting from * * * injury to property, arising out of or in any way connected with the performance of this contract." Defendant also agreed to procure not less than $50,000 insurance to cover liability for injury to property. Plaintiff was to be an additional named insured, but the policy was to contain a cross-liability clause extending the coverage to plaintiff's property.

During the work the cover fell and injured the exposed rotor of the turbine. Plaintiff brought this action to recover $25,144.51, the amount it subsequently spent on repairs. During the trial it dismissed a count based on negligence and thereafter secured judgment on the theory that the indemnity provision covered injury to all property regardless of ownership.

Defendant offered to prove by admissions of plaintiff's agents, by defendant's conduct under similar contracts entered into with plaintiff, and by other proof that in the indemnity clause the parties meant to cover injury to property of third parties only and not to plaintiff's property. Although the trial court observed that the language used was "the classic language for a third party indemnity provision" and that "one could very easily conclude that * * * its whole intendment is to indemnify third parties," it nevertheless held that the "plain language" of the agreement also required defendant to indemnify plaintiff for injuries to plaintiff's property. Having determined that the contract had a plain meaning, the court refused to admit any extrinsic evidence that would contradict its interpretation.

When a court interprets a contract on this basis, it determines the meaning of the instrument in accordance with the " * * * * extrinsic evidence of the judge's own linguistic education and experience." (3 Corbin on Contracts (1960 ed.) [1964 Supp. § 579, p. 225, fn. 56].) The exclusion of testimony that might contradict the linguistic background of the judge reflects a judicial belief in the possibility of perfect verbal expression. (9

Wigmore on Evidence (3d ed. 1940) § 2461, p. 187.) This belief is a remnant of a primitive faith in the inherent potency and inherent meaning of words.

The test of admissibility of extrinsic evidence to explain the meaning of a written instrument is not whether it appears to the court to be plain and unambiguous on its face, but whether the offered evidence is relevant to prove a meaning to which the language of the instrument is reasonably susceptible. . . .

A rule that would limit the determination of the meaning of a written instrument to its four-corners merely because it seems to the court to be clear and unambiguous, would either deny the relevance of the intention of the parties or presuppose a degree of verbal precision and stability our language has not attained.

Some courts have expressed the opinion that contractual obligations are created by the mere use of certain words, whether or not there was any intention to incur such obligations. Under this view, contractual obligations flow, not from the intention of the parties but from the fact that they used certain magic words. Evidence of the parties' intention therefore becomes irrelevant.

In this state, however, the intention of the parties as expressed in the contract is the source of contractual rights and duties. A court must ascertain and give effect to this intention by determining what the parties meant by the words they used. Accordingly, the exclusion of relevant, extrinsic evidence to explain the meaning of a written instrument could be justified only if it were feasible to determine the meaning the parties gave to the words from the instrument alone.

If words had absolute and constant referents, it might be possible to discover contractual intention in the words themselves and in the manner in which they were arranged. Words, however, do not have absolute and constant referents. "A word is a symbol of thought but has no arbitrary and fixed meaning like a symbol of algebra or chemistry, * * *." (Pearson v. State Social Welfare Board (1960) 54 Cal.2d 184, 195.) The meaning of particular words or groups of words varies with the " * * * verbal context and surrounding circumstances and purposes in view of the linguistic education and experience of their users and their hearers or readers (not excluding judges). * * * A word has no meaning apart from these factors; much less does it have an objective meaning, one true meaning." (Corbin, The Interpretation of Words and the Parol Evidence Rule (1965) 50 Cornell L.Q. 161, 187.) Accordingly, the meaning of a writing " * * * can only be found by interpretation in the light of all the circumstances that reveal the sense in which the writer used the words. The exclusion of parol evidence regarding such circumstances merely because the words do not appear ambiguous to the reader can easily lead to the attribution to a written instrument of a meaning that was never intended." . . .

Although extrinsic evidence is not admissible to add to, detract from, or vary the terms of a written contract, these terms must first be determined before it can be decided whether or not extrinsic evidence is being offered for a prohibited purpose. The fact that the terms of an instrument appear clear to a judge does not preclude the possibility that the parties chose the language of the instrument to express different terms. That possibility is not limited to contracts whose terms have acquired a particular meaning by trade usage, but exists whenever the parties' understanding of the words used may have differed from the judge's understanding.

Accordingly, rational interpretation requires at least a preliminary consideration of all credible evidence offered to prove the intention of the parties. (Civ.Code, § 1647; Code Civ.Proc. § 1860; see also 9 Wigmore on Evidence, op. cit. supra, § 2470, fn. 11, p. 227.) Such evidence includes testimony as to the "circumstances surrounding the making of the agreement * * * including the object, nature and subject matter of the writing * * *" so that the court can "place itself in the same situation in which the parties found themselves at the time of contracting." (Universal Sales Corp. v. Cal. Press Mfg. Co., supra, 20 Cal.2d 751, 761, 128 P.2d 665, 671; . . .) If the court decides, after considering this evidence, that the language of a contract, in the light of all the circumstances, is "fairly susceptible of either one of the two interpretations contended for * * *." (Balfour v. Fresno C. & I. Co. (1895) 109 Cal. 221, 225 . . .) extrinsic evidence relevant to prove either of such meanings is admissible.

In the present case the court erroneously refused to consider extrinsic evidence offered to show that the indemnity clause in the contract was not intended to cover injuries to plaintiff's property. Although that evidence was not necessary to show that the indemnity clause was reasonably susceptible of the meaning contended for by defendant, it was nevertheless relevant and admissible on that issue. Moreover, since that clause was reasonably susceptible of that meaning, the offered evidence was also admissible to prove that the clause had that meaning and did not cover injuries to plaintiff's property. Accordingly, the judgment must be reversed.

* * *

A. Kemp Fisheries, Inc. v. Castle & Cooke, Inc.

United States Court of Appeals, Ninth Circuit, 1988.
852 F.2d 493.

■ EUGENE A. WRIGHT, CIRCUIT JUDGE:

In this case we consider whether the court properly admitted parol evidence to determine the terms of the Charter Agreement between A. Kemp Fisheries, Inc. and Bumble Bee Samoa, Inc., a subsidiary of Castle & Cooke, Inc. We conclude that the court applied the parol evidence rule incorrectly and reverse its judgment.

BACKGROUND

A. Kemp Fisheries Inc. and Bumble Bee Samoa, Inc., a fully owned subsidiary of Castle & Cooke, Inc., agreed that Kemp would charter, with an option to purchase, the M/V CITY OF SAN DIEGO. Kemp needed the vessel to fish for herring and salmon in Alaska from April to August 1983. In February of that year they signed a letter of intent that incorporated certain telexes exchanged in their negotiations. This letter served as their agreement "[p]ending preparation and execution of final documentation required for the bareboat charter and option to purchase." To compensate Bumble Bee for removing the vessel from the market Kemp paid a nonrefundable deposit of $50,000.

After reviewing drafts of the agreement with Kemp's attorney, Bumble Bee sent the final bare boat Charter Agreement late in March. Louis Kemp, the charterer's president, found that the agreement differed from his understanding of the arrangement. Specifically, he understood that Bumble Bee had agreed that the engines would be in good working order and had represented orally that the freezing system would meet Kemp's specific needs. The agreement contained no such provisions and in fact, disclaimed all warranties, express or implied. Despite his reservations, Kemp signed it without voicing his concerns to Bumble Bee. He took the vessel in early April and sailed to Alaska for the May herring season.

In the midst of herring season, two of the three auxiliary engines that powered the SAN DIEGO's freezing system broke down. After repairing one engine, Kemp switched from freezing to curing the herring because it lacked confidence that the engine would last. Kemp sold the cured herring for a price below that for frozen herring.

In preparation for salmon season at the end of June, Kemp repaired the auxilliary engines and rented an additional engine. Although the engines were operating at full power and suffered no breakdowns, the salmon froze in a block and the flesh was "honey combed." Kemp's buyer rejected most of it. Kemp took it to a shore-based freezing plant in Bellingham where it was thawed and refrozen. It sold the salmon for 75 cents a pound, 50 cents less than the price it would have received for properly frozen salmon.

Kemp sued Bumble Bee and Castle & Cooke in admiralty for breach of the Charter Agreement, intentional and negligent misrepresentation, estoppel, and rescission. It claimed that Bumble Bee agreed to provide engines in good working order and represented that the freezing system would meet its specific needs.

The trial judge found that the Charter Agreement signed in March was ambiguous and admitted parol evidence to clarify the parties' intent. She concluded that the letter of intent and referenced telexes reflected the parties' final intent and indicated that no other negotiations would occur. From evidence of their negotiations, she found that Bumble Bee warranted the vessel to be seaworthy and the engines to be in good working condition, and represented orally that the vessel's freezing system could meet Kemp's specific requirements. She held Bumble Bee liable for all of Kemp's damages because the "inability of the M/V CITY OF SAN DIEGO to freeze herring and salmon within the parameters specified by Bumble Bee is solely the result of Bumble Bee's breach of warranties.'' Bumble Bee appeals.

ANALYSIS

A. *Integration*

The Charter Agreement is an integrated contract. The agreement itself is complete and comprehensive. It covers in great detail the various rights and responsibilities of the parties. Although the Charter does not contain an integration clause, the letter of intent shows clearly that the parties intended that the Charter would be the "final documentation" of their agreement.

The alleged agreements regarding the warranties of the vessel's seaworthiness, engines, and freezing system are not collateral agreements that would normally be made in a separate contract. These alleged understandings directly contradict the Charter's waiver of all warranties. In addition, the agreement specifies Bumble Bee's responsibility for testing and repairing the freezing system and preparing the vessel for Kemp. If Bumble Bee warranted the freezing system and the engines, the Charter Agreement would typically provide that.

The circumstances surrounding this transaction also support our conclusion that the contract is integrated. Kemp and Bumble Bee are corporations familiar with business transactions. Kemp's attorney reviewed the Charter with Bumble Bee in the month before it signed. Bumble Bee incorporated some of Kemp's changes into the final Charter presented in March. Kemp had ample opportunity to express its understanding of the deal. Nothing suggests that this agreement was not recognized by both parties as final and complete.

B. *Ambiguity*

The judge admitted parol evidence to resolve ambiguities and contradictions within sub-paragraphs 3B, E and F. Sub-paragraph 3B provides:

B. Prior to delivery of the Vessel, Owner shall maintain the Vessel in good condition and shall cause the Vessel to be surveyed, on its own account, by a competent surveyor chosen by Owner, which survey shall show that the Vessel meets TA 2003 insurance requirements and is in all respects tight, staunch, strong and seaworthy.

Sub-paragraphs 3E and F provide:

E. Delivery to Charterer shall constitute full performance by Owner of all of Owner's obligations hereunder, and thereafter Charterer shall not be entitled to make or assert any claim against Owner on account of any representations or warranties, express or implied, with respect to the Vessel.

F. Charterer's acceptance of delivery of the Vessel, its equipment, gear and nonconsumable stores shall constitute conclusive evidence that the same have been inspected by Charterer and are accepted by Charterer as suitable for the intended use hereunder and, as between

(margin notes) Charter is Complete

PE Contradicts the Writing

integrated + Final →
Kemp made no attempt to alter it

PE

the parties, the seaworthiness and suitability of the Vessel, its equipment, gear and nonconsumable stores are deemed admitted.

The judge construed sub-paragraph 3B as an express warranty of seaworthiness and sub-paragraphs 3E and F as a waiver of that warranty. To resolve this conflict, she turned to parol evidence.

The court erred. The parol evidence rule requires that courts consider extrinsic evidence to determine whether the contract is ambiguous. . . . But if the extrinsic evidence advances an interpretation to which the language of the contract is not reasonably susceptible, the evidence is not admissible. Drayage, 69 Cal.Rptr. at 564: "The test of admissibility of extrinsic evidence to explain the meaning of a written instrument is . . . whether the offered evidence is relevant to prove a meaning to which the language of the instrument is reasonably susceptible." Cf. *Trident*, at 570 n. 6.[2] The Charter Agreement is not "reasonably susceptible" to the court's interpretation that it warrants the seaworthiness of the vessel, the condition of the engines, and the capacity of the freezing system.

Sub-paragraph 3B concerns the condition of the vessel prior to delivery. It imposes on Bumble Bee an obligation to maintain the vessel in "good," not seaworthy condition, and to see that a "competent surveyor" surveys it to show that it is "tight, staunch, strong and seaworthy" for insurance purposes. It guarantees neither the accuracy of the survey nor the seaworthiness of the vessel.

Sub-paragraphs 3E and F address Bumble Bee's obligations after delivery. They provide that once Kemp accepts delivery, Bumble Bee's responsibility for the condition of the vessel ceases. They make clear that Kemp's acceptance of delivery releases Bumble Bee from responsibility for the vessel's condition and cannot be interpreted reasonably to warrant seaworthiness.

Nor should the court similarly have admitted evidence that Bumble Bee warranted the condition of the engines and the capacity of the freezing system. Paragraphs 3B, E and F do not even mention the engines or the freezing system and are not "reasonably susceptible" to that interpretation.

The court erred in admitting parol evidence and in enforcing warranties of seaworthiness, the engines, and freezing capacity. The Charter Agreement contains none of these warranties. * * *

---

2. The broad language in *Trident* suggests that under California law courts must always admit extrinsic evidence to determine the meaning of disputed contract language. *Trident* held only that courts may not dismiss on the pleadings when one party claims that extrinsic evidence renders the contract ambiguous. The case must proceed beyond the pleadings so that the court may consider the evidence. If, after considering the evidence, the court determines that the contract is not reasonably susceptible to the interpretation advanced, the parol evidence rule operates to exclude the evidence. The court may then decide the case on a motion for summary judgment. See *Trident* at 570 n. 6. The court decided this case on a fully developed record.

CONCLUSION

The judgment is REVERSED and is rendered for the defendant. The Charter Agreement is an integrated contract and contained all the parties' agreements. It is not ambiguous and the court erred in admitting parol evidence on the warranty of seaworthiness, the capacity of the freezing system, and the engines. Bumble Bee effectively waived the implied warranty of seaworthiness and all other warranties. Bumble Bee is not liable for Kemp's losses.

NOTES

(1) *Context evidence or "plain meaning" rule?* Section 212 of the Restatement (Second), in Comment b, takes a position that is consistent with that expressed by Judge Traynor:

> It is sometimes said that extrinsic evidence cannot change the plain meaning of a writing, but meaning can almost never be plain except in a context. Accordingly, the rule stated in Subsection (1) [pertaining to interpretation of integrated agreements] is not limited to cases where it is determined that the language used is ambiguous. Any determination of meaning or ambiguity should only be made in the light of the relevant evidence of the situation and relations of the parties, the subject matter of the transaction, preliminary negotiations and statements made therein, usages of trade, and the course of dealing between the parties.

Thus, Judge Traynor in *Pacific Gas* would have the trial judge hold a preliminary hearing to examine the proffered evidence, whether it be course of performance, a prior course of dealing, trade usage, or other circumstances, to determine whether the language of the contract is reasonably susceptible to the meaning claimed to be supported by the evidence. It is here that evidence is either admitted or excluded. Put differently, the only way to know whether there is an ambiguity is to first look at the extrinsic evidence. If the parties have drafted a clear and complete agreement, the odds favor exclusion of all but the most compelling evidence, such as a course of performance indicating how both parties interpreted the term or a trade usage to which both parties are bound.

Nevertheless, many courts still purport to apply what might be called the "plain meaning rule." A good example, W.W.W. Associates, Inc. v. Giancontieri, 77 N.Y.2d 157, 565 N.Y.S.2d 440, 566 N.E.2d 639 (1990), where the court said:

> We conclude ... that the extrinsic evidence tendered by plaintiff is not material. In its reliance on extrinsic evidence to bring itself within the 'party benefited' cases, plaintiff ignores a vital first step in the analysis: before looking to evidence of what was in the parties' minds, a court must give due weight to what was in the contract.

> A familiar and eminently sensible proposition of law is that, when parties set down their agreement in a clear, complete document, their writing should as a rule be enforced according to its terms. Evidence outside the four corners of the document as to what was really intended but unstated or misstated is generally inadmissible to add to or vary the writing....
> That rule imparts 'stability to commercial transactions by safeguarding

against fraudulent claims, perjury, death of witnesses ... infirmity of memory ... [and] the fear that the jury will improperly evaluate the extrinsic evidence.' [internal citation omitted]. Such considerations are all the more compelling in the context of real property transactions, where commercial certainty is a paramount concern.

Whether or not a writing is ambiguous is a question of law to be resolved by the courts.... In the present case, the contract, read as a whole to determine its purpose and intent ... plainly manifests the intention that defendants, as well as plaintiff, should have the right to cancel after June 1, 1987 if the litigation had not concluded by that date; and it further plainly manifests the intention that all prior understandings be merged into the contract, which expresses the parties' full agreement.... * * * Thus, we conclude there is no ambiguity as to the cancellation clause in issue, read in the context of the entire agreement, and that it confers a reciprocal right on both parties to the contract.

The question next raised is whether extrinsic evidence should be considered in order to create an ambiguity in the agreement. That question must be answered in the negative. It is well settled that 'extrinsic and parol evidence is not admissible to create an ambiguity in a written agreement which is 'complete and clear and unambiguous upon its face.'....

Which position do you prefer?

(2) *Holmes on the Interpretation Process.* "A word is not a crystal, transparent and unchanged; it is the skin of a living thought and may vary greatly in color and content according to the circumstances and the times in which it is used." Holmes, J. in Towne v. Eisner, 245 U.S. 418, 425, 38 S.Ct. 158, 62 L.Ed. 372 (1918). For this reason, no sooner do courts advance a general rule of strict construction than are exceptions made:

Words are the conduits by which thoughts are communicated, yet scarcely any of them have such a fixed and single meaning that they are incapable of denoting more than one thought.... One meaning crowds a word full of significance, while another almost empties the utterance of any import.... Thus one is justified in saying that the language of the dictionaries is not the only language spoken in America. For instance, the word 'thousand' as commonly used has a very specific meaning; it denotes ten hundreds or fifty scores, but the language of the various trades and localities has assigned to it meanings quite different from that just mentioned. Thus in the bricklaying trade a contract which fixes the bricklayer's compensation at '$5.25 a thousand' does not contemplate that he need lay actually 1,000 bricks in order to earn $5.25, but that he should build a wall of a certain size.... And, where the custom of a locality considers 100 dozen as constituting a thousand, one who has 19,200 rabbits upon a warren under an agreement for their sale at the price of 60 pounds for each thousand rabbits will be paid for only 16,000 rabbits....

Hurst v. W.J. Lake & Co., 141 Or. 306, 16 P.2d 627, 629 (1932).

(3) *Interpretation Under the UCC.* Under the UCC, one must distinguish rules for construing the statute itself from rules for interpreting agreements of the parties otherwise within the scope of the statute.

With regard to the former, UCC 1–102(1) [Rev.1–103(a)] provides that this "Act shall be liberally construed and applied to promote" the underlying purposes and policies set forth in UCC 1–102(2), e.g., "to permit the continued expansion of commercial practices through custom, usage and agreement of the parties." UCC 1–102(2)(b). In addition, Comment 1 to UCC 1–102 states that the text of each section should be read in the light of the purpose and policy of the rule or principle in question, as also of the Act as a whole, and the application of the language should be construed narrowly or broadly, as the case may be, in conformity with the purposes and policies involved.

Like contract interpretation, there is also a hierarchy of statutory interpretation—statutory language and definitions first, the Official Comments second, judicial interpretation third, views of commentators and experts fourth, and legislative history fifth. See John M. Breen, *Statutory Interpretation and the Lessons of Llewellyn,* 33 Loyola L.A. L. Rev. 263 (2000).

With regard to contract interpretation, the UCC provides no comprehensive approach to the interpretation of agreements. However, Subsection (a) of UCC 2–202 provides that terms in an integrated writing may be *explained* or *supplemented* "by course of dealing or usage of trade (Section 1–205) or by course of performance (Section 2–208)." Moreover, Revised 2–202(2) now provides:

> Terms in a record may be explained by evidence of course of performance, course of dealing, or usage of trade without a preliminary determination by the court that the language used is ambiguous.

The Code thereby explicitly encourages the use of these important extrinsic aids in the interpretation process and UCC 1–205 [Rev. 1–303] establishes an interpretation hierarchy. This approach is applauded by Amy Kastelly, *Stock Equipment for the Bargain in Fact: Trade Usage, "Express Terms," and Consistency Under Section 1–205 of the UCC,* 64 N.C.L.Rev. 777 (1986) but criticized by Lisa Bernstein, *The Questionable Empirical Basis of Article 2's Incorporation Strategy: A Preliminary Study,* 66 U. Chi. L. Rev. 781 (1999).

The "course of performance" provision, UCC 2–208(1), has been moved from Revised Article 2 to Revised 1–303(a). Rev. 1–303 (rather than former 1–205) also deals with "course of dealing" and "usage of trade." Read Rev. 1–303 carefully in preparation for the Frigaliment case, infra at 648.

(4) Assuming that the parol evidence rule and judicial utterances about the "plain meaning" of language will not be unduly restrictive upon the production of relevant evidence, the next problem is to understand how the court goes about the interpretation process. The following comment and case deals with this process. As you analyze the opinion, consider the following factors: 1. the nature of the negotiation process leading up to the agreement—were lawyers involved, did both parties participate, was it careful and thorough, etc.; 2. the type of evidence which the court admits as relevant—trade usage, conduct of the parties, statements in the course of negotiations, prior course of dealing, etc.; 3. the various "maxims," if any, employed by the court to assist in ascertaining meaning; 4. the "test," if any, employed by the court to determine whether the plaintiff's or the defendant's understanding of what the language meant is to be preferred and the role of the jury in this process.

Comment: The Hierarchy of Interpretation Rules

One way to conceive of the interpretative process is as the sequential application of a hierarchical series of rules to resolve contractual ambiguity. Courts begin with the express wording of the oral or written agreement:

> If the language of the contract is plain and unambiguous, there is no room for interpretation or construction. The court merely gives effect to the intentions of the parties as clearly expressed in the contract.... Where no explicit, unambiguous answer as to the meaning of the contract is available from within the four corners of the instrument (or, in the absence of a writing, from the express oral agreement), the surrounding circumstances become relevant and extrinsic evidence is admissible. However, there is a hierarchy among the available "external" sources as well.... The next three layers of the pyramid are, accordingly, course of performance, course of dealing, and usages of trade.... A course of performance overrides an inconsistent course of dealing, which in turn overrides an inconsistent usage of trade....

If a question regarding the meaning of the contract is not answered by any of the above four sources, one has to resort to legal supplementary rules, either statutory or judge-made, to fill the gap. Specific rules (e.g., rules respecting commercial sales) take priority over general ones (e.g., those applicable to any contract). Traditionally, supplementary rules were conceived of as based on the parties' presumed or hypothetical intentions and were thus labeled "implied terms." Current discourse on such "default rules" and "gap fillers" also falls in line with the conventional conception of the hierarchy. Such rules—in sharp contradistinction to mandatory rules—are relevant only when no answer may be found in any of the former sources.

At times, the meaning of the contract is ascertainable neither by reference to any of the elements constituting the "bargain in fact" (the contract's language, course of performance, course of dealing, and usage of trade), nor by application of default rules. In such extreme cases the gap in the agreement and in the applicable legal rules is filled by reference to general standards of reasonableness and good faith. In such a case "a term which is reasonable in the circumstances is supplied by the court." The official comments to the Restatement stress the normative character of this task: "where there is in fact no agreement [respecting an essential issue], the court should supply a term which comports with community standards of fairness and policy rather than analyze a hypothetical model of the bargaining process."
. . .

As one proceeds down the hierarchy, the level of generality and abstraction of the sources increases: first comes the specific transaction, followed by the totality of transactions made between the same parties, trade usage, legal rules applicable to similar contracts, general rules of contract law, and finally, the general standard of reasonableness. As one descends the hierarchy, there is a move away from the parties' individual will towards social values. The "community standards of fairness and policy," according to which the court should supply an omitted term, connote moral and social values of fairness, equity, decency, trust, taking the other party's interests into consideration, mutual cooperation, and good faith.

Eyal Zamir, *The Inverted Hierarchy of Contract Interpretation and Supplementation*, 97 Colum. L. Rev. 1710, 1718–19 (1997).

After courts exhaust the attempt to discover indicia of the contractors' intent (through plain meaning and extrinsic evidence), they turn then to various "rules of construction"—maxims such as the *contra proferentem* injunction to interpret ambiguities against the drafter (Restatement § 206) or the maxim to interpret contracts so that they "comport with community standards of fairness and policy" (Restatement § 204, Comment d).

A question arises, however, as to *who*—judge or jury—applies particular rules in the hierarchy. While judges are generally given the power to interpret the express words of the contract, juries are often given the task to interpret extrinsic evidence. See Restatement (Second) of Contracts § 212(2) (interpretation of an integrated agreement is to be determined as a question of law unless "it depends on the credibility of extrinsic evidence or on a choice among reasonable inferences to be drawn from extrinsic evidence").

But what happens if the extrinsic evidence sent to a jury is not sufficient to resolve the ambiguity? The judge should normally move on to applying the "rule of construction" tie breakers. But to do this would require a bifurcated trial (something we do not see). Mark P. Gergen, *The Jury's Role in Deciding Normative Issues in the American Common Law*, 68 Fordham L. Rev. 407 (1999).

Frigaliment Importing Co. v. B.N.S. International Sales Corp.

United States District Court, S.D. New York, 1960.
190 F.Supp. 116.

■ FRIENDLY, CIRCUIT JUDGE. The issue is, what is chicken? Plaintiff says "chicken" means a young chicken, suitable for broiling and frying. Defendant says "chicken" means any bird of that genus that meets contract specifications on weight and quality, including what it calls "stewing chicken" and plaintiff pejoratively terms "fowl". Dictionaries give both meanings, as well as some others not relevant here. To support its interpretation, plaintiff sends a number of volleys over the net; defendant essays to return them and adds a few serves of its own. Assuming that both parties were acting in good faith, the case nicely illustrates Holmes' remark "that the making of a contract depends not on the agreement of two minds in one intention, but on the agreement of two sets of external signs—not on the parties' having *meant* the same thing but on their having *said* the same thing." The Path of the Law, in Collected Legal Papers, p. 178. I have concluded that plaintiff has not sustained its burden of persuasion that the contract used "chicken" in the narrower sense.

The action is for breach of the warranty that goods sold shall correspond to the description, New York Personal Property Law, McKinney's Consol.Laws, c. 41 § 95. Two contracts are in suit. In the first, dated May 2, 1957, defendant, a New York sales corporation, confirmed the sale to plaintiff, a Swiss corporation, of

> "US Fresh Frozen Chicken, Grade A, Government Inspected, Eviscerated
>
> 2½–3 lbs. and 1½–2 lbs. each
>
> all chicken individually wrapped in cryovac, packed in secured fiber cartons or wooden boxes, suitable for export
>
> 75,000 lbs. 2½-3 lbs. . . . . @ $33.00
> 25,000 lbs. 1½-2 lbs. . . . . @ $36.50
>
> per 100 lbs. FAS New York
>
> scheduled May 10, 1957 pursuant to instructions from Penson & Co., New York."

The second contract, also dated May 2, 1957, was identical save that only 50,000 lbs. of the heavier "chicken" were called for, the price of the smaller birds was $37 per 100 lbs., and shipment was scheduled for May 30. The initial shipment under the first contract was short but the balance was shipped on May 17. When the initial shipment arrived in Switzerland, plaintiff found, on May 28, that the 2½-3 lbs. birds were not young chicken suitable for broiling and frying but stewing chicken or "fowl"; indeed, many of the cartons and bags plainly so indicated. Protests ensued. Nevertheless, shipment under the second contract was made on May 29, the 2½-3 lbs. birds again being stewing chicken. Defendant stopped the transportation of these at Rotterdam.

This action followed. Plaintiff says that, notwithstanding that its acceptance was in Switzerland, New York law controls under the principle of Rubin v. Irving Trust Co., 1953, 305 N.Y. 288, 305, 113 N.E.2d 424, 431; defendant does not dispute this, and relies on New York decisions. I shall follow the apparent agreement of the parties as to the applicable law.

Since the word "chicken" standing alone is ambiguous, I turn first to see whether the contract itself offers any aid to its interpretation. Plaintiff says the 1½-2 lbs. birds necessarily had to be young chicken since the older birds do not come in that size, hence the 2½-3 lbs. birds must likewise be young. This is unpersuasive—a contract for "apples" of two different sizes could be filled with different kinds of apples even though only one species came in both sizes. Defendant notes that the contract called not simply for chicken but for "US Fresh Frozen Chicken, Grade A, Government Inspected." It says the contract thereby incorporated by reference the Department of Agriculture's regulations, which favor its interpretation; I shall return to this after reviewing plaintiff's other contentions.

[handwritten margin note: Π claims chicken should be "young" But ... Apples come in diff. types]

The first hinges on an exchange of cablegrams which preceded execution of the formal contracts. The negotiations leading up to the contracts were conducted in New York between defendant's secretary, Ernest R. Bauer, and a Mr. Stovicek, who was in New York for the Czechoslovak government at the World Trade Fair. A few days after meeting Bauer at the fair, Stovicek telephoned and inquired whether defendant would be interested in exporting poultry to Switzerland. Bauer then met with Stovicek, who showed him a cable from plaintiff dated April 26, 1957, announcing that they "are buyer" of 25,000 lbs. of chicken 2½–3 lbs. weight, Cryovac packed, grade A Government inspected, at a price up to 33per pound, for shipment on May 10, to be confirmed by the following morning, and were interested in further offerings. After testing the market for price Bauer accepted, and Stovicek sent a confirmation that evening. Plaintiff stresses that, although these and subsequent cables between plaintiff and defendant, which laid the basis for the additional quantities under the first and for all of the second contract, were predominantly in German, they used the English word "chicken"; it claims this was done because it understood "chicken" meant young chicken whereas the German word, "Huhn," included both "Brathuhn" (broilers) and "Suppen-huhn" (stewing chicken), and that defendant, whose officers were thoroughly conversant with German, should have realized this. Whatever force this argument might otherwise have is largely drained away by Bauer's testimony that he asked Stovicek what kind of chickens were wanted, received the answer "any kind of chickens," and then, in German, asked whether the cable meant "Huhn" and received an affirmative response. Plaintiff attacks this as contrary to what Bauer testified on his deposition in March, 1959, and also on the ground that Stovicek had no authority to interpret the meaning of the cable. The first contention would be persuasive if sustained by the record, since Bauer was free at the trial from the threat of contradiction by Stovicek as he was not at the time of the deposition; however, review of the deposition does not convince me of the claimed inconsistency. As to the second contention, it may well be that Stovicek lacked authority to commit plaintiff for prices or delivery dates other than those specified in the cable; but plaintiff cannot at the same time rely on its cable to Stovicek as its dictionary to the meaning of the contract and repudiate the interpretation given the dictionary by the man in whose hands it was put ..... Plaintiff's reliance on the fact that the contract forms contain the words "through the intermediary of: _____", with the blank not filled, as negating agency, is wholly unpersuasive; the purpose of this clause was to permit filling in the name of an intermediary to whom a commission would be payable, not to blot out what had been the fact.

Plaintiff's next contention is that there was a definite trade usage that "chicken" meant "young chicken." Defendant showed that it was only beginning in the poultry trade in 1957, thereby bringing itself within the principle that "when one of the parties is not a member of the trade or other circle, his acceptance of the standard must be made to appear" by proving either that he had actual knowledge of the usage or that the usage

is "so generally known in the community that his actual individual knowledge of it may be inferred." 9 Wigmore, Evidence (3d ed. 1940) § 2464.
Here there was no proof of actual knowledge of the alleged usage; indeed, it
is quite plain that defendant's belief was to the contrary. In order to meet
the alternative requirement, the law of New York demands a showing that
"the usage is of so long continuance, so well established, so notorious, so
universal and so reasonable in itself, as that the presumption is violent that
the parties contracted with reference to it, and made it a part of their
agreement." Walls v. Bailey, 1872, 49 N.Y. 464, 472–473.

Plaintiff endeavored to establish such a usage by the testimony of
three witnesses and certain other evidence. Strasser, resident buyer in New
York for a large chain of Swiss cooperatives, testified that "on chicken I
would definitely understand a broiler." However, the force of this testimony was considerably weakened by the fact that in his own transactions the
witness, a careful businessman, protected himself by using "broiler" when
that was what he wanted and "fowl" when he wished older birds. Indeed,
there are some indications, dating back to a remark of Lord Mansfield, Edie
v. East India Co., 2 Burr. 1216, 1222 (1761), that no credit should be given
"witnesses to usage, who could not adduce instances in verification." 7
Wigmore, Evidence (3d ed.1940), § 1954; ... While Wigmore thinks this
goes too far, a witness' consistent failure to rely on the alleged usage
deprives his opinion testimony of much of its effect. Niesielowski, an officer
of one of the companies that had furnished the stewing chicken to defendant, testified that "chicken" meant "the male species of the poultry
industry. That could be a broiler, a fryer or a roaster", but not a stewing
chicken; however, he also testified that upon receiving defendant's inquiry
for "chickens", he asked whether the desire was for "fowl or frying
chickens" and, in fact, supplied fowl, although taking the precaution of
asking defendant, a day or two after plaintiff's acceptance of the contracts
in suit, to change its confirmation of its order from "chickens," as defendant had originally prepared it, to "stewing chickens." Dates, an employee
of Urner–Barry Company, which publishes a daily market report on the
poultry trade, gave it as his view that the trade meaning of "chicken" was
"broilers and fryers." In addition to this opinion testimony, plaintiff relied
on the fact that the Urner–Barry service, the Journal of Commerce, and
Weinberg Bros. & Co. of Chicago, a large supplier of poultry, published
quotations in a manner which, in one way or another, distinguish between
"chicken," comprising broilers, fryers and certain other categories, and
"fowl," which, Bauer acknowledged, included stewing chickens. This material would be impressive if there were nothing to the contrary. However,
there was, as will now be seen.

Defendant's witness Weininger, who operates a chicken eviscerating
plant in New Jersey, testified "Chicken is everything except a goose, a
duck, and a turkey. Everything is a chicken, but then you have to say, you
have to specify which category you want or that you are talking about." Its
witness Fox said that in the trade "chicken" would encompass all the
various classifications. Sadina, who conducts a food inspection service,
testified that he would consider any bird coming within the classes of

"chicken" in the Department of Agriculture's regulations to be a chicken. The specifications approved by the General Services Administration include fowl as well as broilers and fryers under the classification "chickens." Statistics of the Institute of American Poultry Industries use the phrases "Young chickens" and "Mature chickens," under the general heading "Total chickens." and the Department of Agriculture's daily and weekly price reports avoid use of the word "chicken" without specification.

Defendant advances several other points which it claims affirmatively support its construction. Primary among these is the regulation of the Department of Agriculture, 7 C.F.R. §§ 70.300–70.370, entitled, "Grading and Inspection of Poultry and Edible Products Thereof." and in particular § 70.301 which recited:

"*Chickens*. The following are the various classes of chickens:

(a) Broiler or fryer . . .

(b) Roaster . . .

(c) Capon . . .

(d) Stag . . .

(e) Hen or stewing chicken or fowl . . .

(f) Cock or old rooster . . .

Defendant argues, as previously noted, that the contract incorporated these regulations by reference. Plaintiff answers that the contract provision related simply to grade and Government inspection and did not incorporate the Government definition of "chicken," and also that the definition in the Regulations is ignored in the trade. However, the latter contention was contradicted by Weininger and Sadina; and there is force in defendant's argument that the contract made the regulations a dictionary, particularly since the reference to Government grading was already in plaintiff's initial cable to Stovicek.

Defendant makes a further argument based on the impossibility of its obtaining broilers and fryers at the 33 cents price offered by plaintiff for the 2 1/2–3 lbs. birds. There is no substantial dispute that, in late April, 1957, the price for 2 1/2–3 lbs. broilers was between 35 and 37 cents per pound, and that when defendant entered into the contracts, it was well aware of this and intended to fill them by supplying fowl in these weights. It claims that plaintiff must likewise have known the market since plaintiff had reserved shipping space on April 23, three days before plaintiff's cable to Stovicek, or, at least, that Stovicek was chargeable with such knowledge. It is scarcely an answer to say, as plaintiff does in its brief, that the 33 cents price offered by the 2 1/2–3 lbs. "chickens" was closer to the prevailing 35 cents price for broilers than to the 30 cents at which defendant procured fowl. Plaintiff must have expected defendant to make some profit—certainly it could not have expected defendant deliberately to incur a loss.

Finally, defendant relies on conduct by the plaintiff after the first shipment had been received. On May 28 plaintiff sent two cables complaining that the larger birds in the first shipment constituted "fowl." Defendant answered with a cable refusing to recognize plaintiff's objection and announcing "We have today ready for shipment 50,000 lbs. chicken 2 1/2–3 lbs. 25,000 lbs. broilers 1 1/2–2 lbs.," these being the goods procured for shipment under the second contract, and asked immediate answer "whether we are to ship this merchandise to you and whether you will accept the merchandise." After several other cable exchanges, plaintiff replied on May 29, "Confirm again that merchandise is to be shipped since resold by us if not enough pursuant to contract chickens are shipped the missing quantity is to be shipped within ten days stop we resold to our customers pursuant to your contract chickens grade A you have to deliver us said merchandise we again state that we shall make you fully responsible for all resulting costs."* Defendant argues that if plaintiff was sincere in thinking it was entitled to young chickens, plaintiff would not have allowed the shipment under the second contract to go forward, since the distinction between broilers and chickens drawn in defendant's cablegram must have made it clear that the larger birds would not be broilers. However, plaintiff answers that the cables show plaintiff was insisting on delivery of young chickens and that defendant shipped old ones at its peril. Defendant's point would be highly relevant on another disputed issue—whether if liability were established, the measure of damages should be the difference in market value of broilers and stewing chicken in New York or the larger difference in Europe, but I cannot give it weight on the issue of interpretation. Defendant points out also that plaintiff proceeded to deliver some of the larger birds in Europe, describing them as "poulets"; defendant argues that it was only when plaintiff's customers complained about this that plaintiff developed the idea that "chicken" meant "young chicken." There is little force in this in view of plaintiff's immediate and consistent protests.

When all the evidence is reviewed, it is clear that defendant believed it could comply with the contracts by delivering stewing chicken in the 2½–3 lbs. size. Defendant's subjective intent would not be significant if this did not coincide with an objective meaning of "chicken." Here it did coincide with one of the dictionary meanings, with the definition in the Department of Agriculture Regulations to which the contract made at least oblique reference, with at least some usage in the trade, with the realities of the market, and with what plaintiff's spokesman had said. Plaintiff asserts it to be equally plain that plaintiff's own subjective intent was to obtain broilers and fryers; the only evidence against this is the material as to market prices and this may not have been sufficiently brought home. In any event it is unnecessary to determine that issue. For plaintiff has the burden of showing that "chicken" was used in the narrower rather than in the broader sense, and this it has not sustained.

This opinion constitutes the Court's findings of fact and conclusions of law. Judgment shall be entered dismissing the complaint with costs.

---

* These cables were in German; "chicken", "broilers" and, on some occasions, "fowl," were in English.

NOTES

(1) Judge Friendly concluded in *Frigaliment* that the seller should win because its understanding coincided with an "objective" meaning of "chicken," and the buyer failed to show that the word was "used in the narrower rather than in the broader sense." Professor Corbin applauded this result, adding that the buyer also failed to prove that the seller "knew or had reason to know that plaintiff intended to buy broilers only." Arthur Corbin, *The Interpretation of Words and the Parol Evidence Rule,* 50 Cornell L.Q. 161, 169–70 (1964). Thus, extrinsic evidence both demonstrated that the word "chicken" was ambiguous and that the seller's understanding of "chicken" was, apparently, reasonable and the buyer's was not. Judge Friendly, however, had second thoughts about *Frigaliment.* Dissenting in Dadourian Export Corp. v. United States, 291 F.2d 178, 187 n. 4 (2d Cir.1961), he suggested that the "chicken" case should have been resolved under the *Peerless* doctrine (no contract unless both parties have same meaning in mind) "with the loss still left on the plaintiff because of the defendant's not unjustifiable reliance." Does this make sense? Professor William Young has argued that *Peerless* should be limited to cases of "true equivocation," i.e., where a full exposure to objective evidence in context fails to establish that one party's understanding is more reasonable than the other's. William Young, *Equivocation in the Making of Agreements,* 64 Colum.L.Rev. 619 (1964). Is the "chicken" case within this category?

In Shrum v. Zeltwanger, 559 P.2d 1384 (Wyo.1977), the court addressed the equally momentous question: "What is a cow?" The parties disagreed as to whether the term included a "heifer" which had never had a calf. The court overturned a summary judgment award for the buyer. Concluding that the word "cow" had "within the corral of this case, no plain and ordinary meaning," the matter should go to trial, presumably in order to determine which party offered the better interpretation. See also A.J. Cunningham Packing Corp. v. Florence Beef Co., 785 F.2d 348 (1st Cir.1986) (seller's interpretation of "75% chemically lean beef" preferred).

(2) *Chickens, Contract Interpretation and Restatement (Second).* In the interpretation of a promise or agreement, the key test under Restatement (Second) of whose meaning prevails is found in Section 201(2):

> Where the parties have attached different meanings to a promise or agreement or a term thereof, it is interpreted in accordance with the meaning attached by one of them if at the time the agreement was made
>
> > (a) that party did not know of any different meaning attached by the other, and the other knew the meaning attached by the first party; or
> >
> > (b) that party had no reason to know of any different meaning attached by the other, and the other had reason to know the meaning attached by the first party.

Subsection 3 provides that except as provided "in this section, neither party is bound by the meaning attached by the other, even though the result may be a failure of mutual assent." Comment d states that Subsection (2) follows the terminology of § 20, referring to the understanding of each party as the meaning "attached" by him to a term of a promise of agreement, and provides the following illustration:

4.   A agrees to sell and B to buy a quantity of eviscerated "chicken." A tenders "stewing chicken" or "fowl;" B rejects on the ground that the contract calls for "broilers" or "fryers." Each party makes a claim for damages against the other. It is found that each acted in good faith and that neither had reason to know of the difference in meaning. Both claims fail.

Does this illustration correctly summarize the conclusion of Judge Friendly in the *Frigaliment* case?

Sections 202 and 203 of Restatement (Second) provide some general rules and standards of preference to be followed in the process of interpretation. Section 202 provides:

§ 202.   Rules in Aid of Interpretation

(1) Words and other conduct are interpreted in the light of all the circumstances, and if the principal purpose of the parties is ascertainable it is given great weight.

(2) A writing is interpreted as a whole, and all writings that are part of the same transaction are interpreted together.

(3) Unless a different intention is manifested,

   (a) where language has a generally prevailing meaning, it is interpreted in accordance with that meaning;

   (b) technical terms and words of art are given their technical meaning when used in a transaction within their technical field.

(4) Where an agreement involves repeated occasions for performance by either party with knowledge of the nature of the performance and opportunity for objection to it by the other, any course of performance accepted or acquiesced in without objection is given great weight in the interpretation of the agreement.

(5) Wherever reasonable, the manifestations of intention of the parties to a promise or agreement are interpreted as consistent with each other.

Finally, in Section 206, entitled "Interpretation Against the Draftsman," we have the Restatement (Second) version of the much used *contra proferentem* rule: "In choosing among the reasonable meanings of a promise or agreement or a term thereof, that meaning is generally preferred which operates against the party who supplies the words or from whom a writing otherwise proceeds."

With the option of the *Peerless* result on the one extreme and the rule of construction against the drafter on the other, does Restatement (Second) provide much help in the middle for a judge with a "chicken" case? Using the Restatement (Second) approach to contract interpretation, can you improve upon the reasoning and result in *Frigaliment?* See, generally, Robert Braucher, *Interpretation and Legal Effect in the Second Restatement of Contracts,* 81 Colum.L.Rev. 13 (1981).

(3) *A Contra Proferentem Sampler.* Mastrobuono v. Shearson Lehman Hutton, Inc., 514 U.S. 52, 115 S.Ct. 1212, 131 L.Ed.2d 76 (1995)(broker who drafted an ambiguous document on choice of law governing arbitration "cannot now claim the benefit of the doubt" because the party who did not choose the

language must be protected "from an unintended or unfair result"); E.I. du Pont de Nemours and Co. v. Shell Oil Co., 498 A.2d 1108 (Del.1985) ("Where all parties to a contract are knowledgeable, there is no reason for imposing sanctions against the party who drafted the final provision." 498 A.2d at 1114); Matter of Estate of Orris, 622 P.2d 337 (Utah 1980) ("Where the draftsman is an attorney, as well as a party, strict construction is particularly apt." 622 P.2d at 339–40); Neal v. State Farm Insurance Co., 188 Cal.App.2d 690, 10 Cal.Rptr. 781(1961) ("The rule that any ambiguities caused by the draftsman of the contract must be resolved against the party * * * applies with peculiar force in the case of a contract of adhesion." 188 Cal.App.2d at 695); Franklin Life Insurance Co. v. Commonwealth Edison Co., 451 F.Supp. 602 (S.D.Ill.1978) ("[T]he idea of construing a contract against the drafter is not a result oriented rule but rather a rule which provides an answer when all other methods of construction and interpretation still leave the contract ambiguous." 451 F.Supp. at 616); Wilner's, Inc. v. Fine, 153 Ga.App. 591, 266 S.E.2d 278 (1980) ("It is also a well established rule that ambiguities in writings are to be construed most strongly against the author or the party for whose benefit the writing was prepared, which, in this case, is the landlord." 266 S.E.2d at 280); Gaunt v. John Hancock Mutual Life Insurance Co., 160 F.2d 599 (2d Cir.1947) ("[T]he canon contra proferentem is more rigorously applied in insurance than in other contracts, in recognition of the difference between the parties in their acquaintance with the subject matter." 160 F.2d at 602).

(4) *The "reasonable expectations" test.* In insurance contracts, where adhesion terms dominate, the courts will sometimes interpret a term in light of the reasonable expectations of the individual who signed the policy. A good but somewhat dated example of this is Gray v. Zurich Insurance, 65 Cal.2d 263, 54 Cal.Rptr. 104, 419 P.2d 168 (1966), where the question was whether the insurance company had a duty to defend its insured where the claim, if proven (intentional wrongdoing), would be excluded from coverage. The court said:

> In interpreting an insurance policy we apply the general principle that doubts as to meaning must be resolved against the insurer and that any exception to the performance of the basic underlying obligation must be so stated as clearly to apprise the insured of its effect.

> These principles of interpretation of insurance contracts have found new and vivid restatement in the doctrine of the adhesion contract. As this court has held, a contract entered into between two parties of unequal bargaining strength, expressed in the language of a standardized contract, written by the more powerful bargainer to meet its own needs, and offered to the weaker party on a "take it or leave it basis" carries some consequences that extend beyond orthodox implications. Obligations arising from such a contract inure not alone from the consensual transaction but from the relationship of the parties.

> Although courts have long followed the basic precept that they would look to the words of the contract to find the meaning which the parties expected from them, they have also applied the doctrine of the adhesion contract to insurance policies, holding that in view of the disparate bargaining status of the parties we must ascertain that meaning of the contract which the insured would reasonably expect. Thus as Kessler stated in his classic article on adhesion contracts: "In dealing with standardized contracts

courts have to determine what the weaker contracting party could legitimately expect by way of services according to the enterpriser's 'calling', and to what extent the stronger party disappointed reasonable expectations based on the typical life situation." (Kessler, Contracts of Adhesion (1943) 43 Colum.L.Rev. 629, 637.) * * *

When we test the instant policy by these principles we find that its provisions as to the obligation to defend are uncertain and undefined; in the light of the reasonable expectation of the insured, they require the performance of that duty. At the threshold we note that the nature of the obligation to defend is itself necessarily uncertain. Although insurers have often insisted that the duty arises only if the insurer is bound to indemnify the insured, this very contention creates a dilemma. No one can determine whether the third party suit does or does not fall within the indemnification coverage of the policy until that suit is resolved; in the instant case, the determination of whether the insured engaged in intentional, negligent or even wrongful conduct depended upon the judgment in the Jones suit, and, indeed, even after that judgment, no one could be positive whether it rested upon a finding of plaintiff's negligent or his intentional conduct. The carrier's obligation to indemnify inevitably will not be defined until the adjudication of the very action which it should have defended. Hence the policy contains its own seeds of uncertainty; the insurer has held out a promise that by its very nature is ambiguous. * * *

In summary, the individual consumer in the highly organized and integrated society of today must necessarily rely upon institutions devoted to the public service to perform the basic functions which they undertake. At the same time the consumer does not occupy a sufficiently strong economic position to bargain with such institutions as to specific clauses of their contracts of performance, and, in any event, piecemeal negotiation would sacrifice the advantage of uniformity. Hence the courts in the field of insurance contracts have tended to require that the insurer render the basic insurance protection which it has held out to the insured. This obligation becomes especially manifest in the case in which the insurer has attempted to limit the principal coverage by an unclear exclusionary clause. We test the alleged limitation in the light of the insured's reasonable expectation of coverage; that test compels the indicated outcome of the present litigation. * * *

The Supreme Court of New Jersey formulated the doctrine of reasonable expectations in insurance contracts as follows: "When members of the public purchase policies of insurance they are entitled to the broad measure of protection necessary to fulfill their reasonable expectations." Kievit v. Loyal Protective Life Insurance Co., 34 N.J. 475, 170 A.2d 22, 26 (1961). In Oklahoma, however, the Supreme Court has taken the position that the reasonable expectations doctrine may apply only to the construction of ambiguous insurance contracts or to contracts containing exclusions masked by technical or obscure language or hidden policy provisions. Max True Plastering Co. v. United States Fidelity & Guaranty Co., 912 P.2d 861 (Okl.1996). For helpful discussion, see Kenneth Abraham, *Judge–Made Law and Judge–Made Insurance: Honoring the Reasonable Expectations of the Insured,* 67 Va.L.Rev. 1151 (1981).

More recently, the "reasonable expectations" test as a general interpretive tool has been strongly criticized. See James J. White, *Form Contracts Under Revised Article* 2, 75 Wash. U. L. Q. 315 (1997), who doubted the wisdom of Section 2–206(b) in the November, 1996 Draft of Revised Article 2. That provision, which has since disappeared from the draft, provided:

> If a consumer manifests assent to a standard form, a term contained in the form which the consumer could not reasonably have expected is not part of the contract unless the consumer expressly agrees to it.

Compare Restatement, Second, § 211(3).

SECTION 2.   THE DUTY OF GOOD FAITH

(A) SCOPE AND CONTENT OF GOOD FAITH DUTY

Courts are also called upon to interpret the content of the implicit and mandatory duty of promisors to perform their contractual obligations in "good faith." In this Section we will first examine the scope and content of the duty of good faith in general and then test its application in four settings where claims of bad faith are frequently made: (1) Prevention, hindrance, or failure to cooperate; (2) Exercise of discretion granted by the contract; (3) Contract modifications; and (4) Termination of the contract for reasons other than breach.

It is now well established that "every contract imposes upon each party a duty of good faith and fair dealing in its performance and its enforcement." Restatement (Second) § 205; UCC 1–203 (obligation of good faith in its performance and enforcement) [Rev. 1–304]. This duty, which is imposed by law, cannot be "disclaimed by agreement," but the parties can determine the standards of good faith if those standards are not manifestly unreasonable. UCC 1–102(3) [Rev. 1–302(b)]. What is not always clear is (1) to what aspects of the transaction does the duty of good faith apply, (2) what is bad faith performance, and (3) what remedies are available when one party performs in bad faith? To put the matter more practically, what is bad faith and what can the other party do about it?

The consensus is that good faith, at a minimum, means "honesty in fact in the conduct or transaction involved," UCC 1–201(19), and, since the duty of good faith must be met "in a variety of contexts," its meaning should vary "somewhat with the context." Section 205, Restatement, Second, Comment a. Moreover, in Revised UCC 2–103(1)(b) good faith means both "honesty in fact and the observance of reasonable commercial standards of fair dealing in the trade." Thus, [according to the Restatement, Second] the duty of "fair dealing" means more than just honesty in fact. According to Comment a:

> Good faith performance or enforcement of a contract emphasizes faithfulness to an agreed common purpose and consistency with the justified expectations of the other party; it excludes a variety of types of conduct characterized as involving "bad faith" because they violate

community standards of decency, fairness or reasonableness. The appropriate remedy for a breach of the duty of good faith also varies with the circumstances.

And, according to Comment d:

Subterfuges and evasions violate the obligation of good faith in performance even though the actor believes his conduct to be justified. But the obligation goes further: bad faith may be overt or may consist of inaction, and fair dealing may require more than honesty. A complete catalogue of types of bad faith is impossible, but the following types are among those which have been recognized in judicial decisions: evasion of the spirit of the bargain, lack of diligence and slacking off, willful rendering of imperfect performance, abuse of power to specify terms, and interference with or failure to cooperate in the other party's performance.

Professor Robert S. Summers, in a careful article, has applauded the Restatement (Second) approach to the duty of good faith, primarily because it permits examples of bad faith to emerge over time from context to context. Put another way, the meaning of good faith is best determined by the conduct *excluded* rather than through an *a priori,* structured definition. Summers, *The General Duty of Good Faith—Its Recognition and Conceptualization,* 67 Cornell L.Rev. 810 (1982). He then criticizes as "misguided" three attempts to define good faith:

(1) Good faith is an absence of intention to harm a legally protected pecuniary interest;

(2) Good faith performance occurs when a party's discretion is exercised for any purpose within the reasonable contemplation of the parties at the time of formation to capture opportunities that were preserved upon entering the contract, interpreted objectively;*

---

* For development of the "foregone opportunities" thesis, see Burton, *Breach of Contract and the Common Law Duty to Perform in Good Faith,* 94 Harv.L.Rev. 369 (1980); *Good Faith Performance of a Contract Within Article 2 of the Uniform Commercial Code,* 67 Ia.L.Rev. 1 (1981). Burton asserts:

"Contract formation principles require that each party undertake to forgo in some way its future freedom to pursue opportunities alternative to the contract. A party who acts after formation to recapture a forgone opportunity often is in breach of the contract by failing to perform in good faith. ...(F)orgone opportunities (are) those alternative opportunities that would be regarded as forgone at formation by reasonable business persons operating in a commercial setting—an objective standard. Whether a party

acted after formation to recapture forgone opportunities is a question of subjective intention."

67 Ia.L.Rev. at 24. Another way of shooting at the same target is through the concept of "opportunism," defined by Professor Oliver Williamson to be a "variety of self-interest seeking" that "extends simple self-interest seeking to include self-interest seeking with guile." Williamson, *Transaction Cost Economics: The Governance of Contractual Relations,* 22 J.L. & Econ. 233, 234, n. 3 (1979). See Muris, *Opportunistic Behavior and the Law of Contracts,* 65 Minn.L.Rev. 521 (1981), where opportunism is defined as behavior by party A which is contrary to party B's understanding but not necessarily contrary to the explicit terms of the agreement and which results in a transfer of resources.

(3) Good faith and fair conduct consists of action according to reasonable standards set by customary practices and by known individual expectations. 67 Cornell L.Rev. at 829.

Professor Summers concedes that the "general duty of good faith and fair dealing is no more than a minimal requirement (rather than a high ideal)," but applauds it as an explicit recognition of the need for "contractual morality," the increased recognition of which "is one of the hallmarks of the law of our time." 67 Cornell L.Rev. at 811.

A recent proposed revision in UCC Article 1 defines good faith for all transactions and all parties (except those within Article 5) to mean "honesty in fact and the observance of reasonable commercial standards of fair dealing." Rev. UCC 1–201(20). Is this an improvement?

Centronics Corporation v. Genicom Corporation

Supreme Court of New Hampshire, 1989.
132 N.H. 133, 562 A.2d 187.

■ SOUTER, JUSTICE.

A contract between the buyer and seller of business assets provided for arbitration of any dispute about the value of the property transferred, to which the purchase price was pegged, and required an escrow deposit of a portion of the price claimed by the seller pending final valuation. The seller has charged the buyer with breach of an implied covenant of good faith in refusing, during arbitration, to release a portion of the escrow fund claimed to be free from "dispute." The Superior Court (Hollman, J.) granted summary judgment to the buyer, which we affirm.

* * *

Distribution from the escrow fund was to be governed by two sets of provisions. Insofar as the escrow agreement relates to the issue before us, it simply provided that "[i]n accordance with Section 2.07 of the Purchase Agreement, the Escrow Agent shall hold the Escrow Fund in its possession until instructed in writing" by respective New York counsel for Centronics and Genicom "to distribute the same or some portion thereof to Centronics or [Genicom] as the case may be," whereupon the escrow agent was to make the distribution as ordered. Section 2.07 of the Purchase Agreement, entitled "Final Payment of Purchase Price," began with a provision that "[f]inal settlement and payment of the Purchase Price shall be made not later than ten days after determination of [CCNBV, consolidated closing net book value] and computation of the Purchase Price," whether by agreement of the parties or decision of the arbitrator. There followed detailed instructions for payment out of escrow and final settlement between the parties, which are of no significance in the matter before us, being intended to provide for the payment to Centronics of whatever balance it might be owed on the purchase price, and the distribution to Genicom of any amount it might be found to have overpaid.

* * *

Genicom moved for summary judgment on the theory that, given the dispute over CCNBV, the terms of the parties' agreements required payments out of escrow only upon completion of arbitration, thus barring the implication of any duty to authorize a distribution before that event. Centronics objected and sought its own summary judgment, grounded on affidavits said to indicate that Genicom's refusal was meant to pressure Centronics into conceding a disputed item worth a substantial amount.

The trial court ruled for Genicom, after construing the contract to provide that the "only way funds can be released is upon final determination of the purchase price, which, as the parties agree, is in the hands of the arbitrator.

The instant suit is no more than [an] attempt on the part of [Centronics] to rewrite the contract. Essentially, [Centronics] asks this Court to read between the lines of § 2.07 and insert therein a provision regarding partial disbursal of funds from escrow in light of the protracted arbitration. While it is true that the parties contemplated a short time period for resolution of disputes through binding arbitration, the Court cannot insert a provision in the contract for partial payments where such provision does not exist.

[Centronics] should have demanded a mechanism for partial payments from the Escrow Fund if the arbitration process lagged, or if the factual situation regarding adjustments to the final purchase price occurred as it did. The Court will not renegotiate the contract between the parties to obtain this result. To the extent [Centronics] made a less advantageous contract, it must now abide by the terms of that contract as originally agreed."

Centronics reads the foregoing order as denying that any obligation of good faith is implied in the parties' contract. We read it differently, as concluding that the express terms of the contract are inconsistent with the claim that an obligation of good faith and fair dealing, or any other sort of implied obligation, either requires Genicom to agree to an interim distribution or bars Genicom from refusing to agree except in return for Centronics's concession on a disputed item. We consequently view this appeal as raising the related questions of whether the trial judge misunderstood the implied obligation of good faith or misconstrued the contract. We conclude that he did neither.

Although an obligation of good faith is imposed by statute in the performance and enforcement of every contract or duty subject to the Uniform Commercial Code, see RSA 382–A:1–203; 382–A:1–201(19), the parties before us have addressed the implied contractual obligation of good faith at common law, and our first concern in this case is to identify the jurisdiction whose common law is to be applied. Although the parties agreed that their contractual relations were to be governed by New York law, and although Centronics's brief cites two cases from the Second Circuit applying the law of that State, Centronics's principal reliance is on New Hampshire cases. Since the New York decisions are not at odds with our own, as we will indicate below, and since neither party has suggested that the relevant substantive law differs between the two jurisdictions, we will assume that to whatever extent the governing foreign law has not been proven it is identical to our own. . . .

Our own common law of good faith contractual obligation is not, however, as easily stated as we might wish, there being not merely one rule of implied good faith duty in New Hampshire's law of contract, but a series of doctrines, each of them speaking in terms of an obligation of good faith but serving markedly different functions. Since the time of our first contract decision couched in terms of good faith, Griswold v. Heat Corporation, 108 N.H. 119 (1967), we have relied on such an implied duty in three distinct categories of contract cases: those dealing with standards of conduct in contract formation, with termination of at-will employment contracts, and with limits on discretion in contractual performance, which is at issue in the instant case. Although decisions in the first and second categories are not directly relevant here, a short detour through their cases will serve clarity by indicating the categorical distinctions.

In our decisions setting standards of conduct in contract formation, the implied good faith obligations of a contracting party are tantamount to the traditional duties of care to refrain from misrepresentation and to correct subsequently discovered error, insofar as any representation is intended to induce, and is material to, another party's decision to enter into a contract in justifiable reliance upon it.

By way of contrast, the good faith enforced in the second category of our cases is an obligation implied in the contract itself, where it fulfills the distinctly different function of limiting the power of an employer to terminate a wage contract by discharging an at-will employee. Under the rule evolved from Monge v. Beebe Rubber Co., 114 N.H. 130 (1974) . . . , an employer violates an implied term of a contract for employment at-will by firing an employee out of malice or bad faith in retaliation for action taken or refused by the employee in consonance with public policy. . . . Although good faith in this context has not been rigorously defined, bad faith has been spoken of as equivalent to malice, . . . and treated virtually as a subject of equitable estoppel in labor relations, . . . Indeed, the concepts of good and bad faith applied in these cases are best understood not as elements of general contract law as such, but as expressions of labor policy. . . .

The differences between the obligations of good faith exemplified even in these first two groups of cases are enough to explain why the commentators despair of articulating any single concept of contractual good faith, even after the more than fifty years of litigation following in the wake of the American common law's first explicit recognition of an implied good faith contractual obligation in Kirke La Shelle Co. v. Paul Armstrong Co., 263 N.Y. 79, 87 (1933). See Summers, *"Good Faith" in General Contract*

Law and the Sales Provisions of the Uniform Commercial Code, 54 Va. L.Rev. 195, 196 (1968); Summers, *The General Duty of Good Faith—Its Recognition and Conceptualization,* 67 Cornell L.Rev. 810, 819 (1982); Burton, *More on Good Faith Performance of a Contract: A Reply to Professor Summers,* 69 Iowa L.Rev. 497, 511 (1984); Restatement, supra at § 205, comments a, d, e.

Even within the narrower confines of the third category of cases, those governing discretion in contractual performance, the one notable attempt to conceptualize implied good faith in a single, general definition, Burton, *Breach of Contract and the Common Law Duty to Perform in Good Faith,* 94 Harv.L.Rev. 369 (1980), discussed infra, is opposed by the view that the obligation of good faith performance is better understood simply as excluding behavior inconsistent with common standards of decency, fairness, and reasonableness, and with the parties' agreed-upon common purposes and justified expectations, see Summers, 67 Cornell L.Rev. at 820, 826; Restatement, supra at § 205, comment a. This view is consonant with our own cases in the third category, a canvass of which should inform our consideration of what good faith may or may not demand of Genicom in the circumstances before us.

[The court reviewed the New Hampshire cases.]

* * *

Despite the variety of their fact patterns, these cases illustrate a common rule: under an agreement that appears by word or silence to invest one party with a degree of discretion in performance sufficient to deprive another party of a substantial proportion of the agreement's value, the parties' intent to be bound by an enforceable contract raises an implied obligation of good faith to observe reasonable limits in exercising that discretion, consistent with the parties' purpose or purposes in contracting. A claim for relief from a violation of the implied covenant of good faith contractual performance therefore potentially raises four questions:

1.   Does the agreement ostensibly allow to or confer upon the defendant a degree of discretion in performance tantamount to a power to deprive the plaintiff of a substantial proportion of the agreement's value? Contracts may be broken in a multitude of ways and theories of relief are correspondingly numerous, but the concept of good faith in performance addresses the particular problem raised by a promise subject to such a degree of discretion that its practical benefit could seemingly be withheld.

2.   If the ostensible discretion is of that requisite scope, does competent evidence indicate that the parties intended by their agreement to make a legally enforceable contract? * * *

3.   Assuming an intent to be bound, has the defendant's exercise of discretion exceeded the limits of reasonableness? The answer to this question depends on identifying the common purpose or purposes of the contract, against which the reasonableness of the complaining party's expectations may be measured, and in furtherance of which

community standards of honesty, decency and reasonableness can be applied.

4. Is the cause of the damage complained of the defendant's abuse of discretion, or does it result from events beyond the control of either party, against which the defendant has no obligation to protect the plaintiff? Although this question is cast in the language of causation, it may be seen simply as the other face of question three. Suffice it to say here that its point is to emphasize that the good faith requirement is not a fail-safe device barring a defendant from the fruits of every plaintiff's bad bargain, or empowering courts to rewrite an agreement even when a defendant's discretion is consistent with the agreement's legally contractual character.

Applying this analytical sequence to the instant case takes us no further than the first of the four questions, whether the agreement effectively confers such discretion on Genicom over the timing of distributions from the escrow fund that, in the absence of some good faith limitation, Genicom could deny Centronics a substantial proportion of the contract's benefit. Was Genicom, that is, given authority to deprive Centronics indefinitely of a portion of the agreed consideration for the business assets previously transferred? The answer is obviously no * * * [This contract] contains express and unequivocal provisions governing the timing of payment, which must occur no later than ten days after final resolution of the purchase price, presumably on conclusion of the mandatory arbitration.... Genicom has no discretion to withhold approval for pay-out beyond that time, or to affect the timing of the arbitration itself. If, indeed, either party were dragging its heels in the conduct of the arbitration, it should go without saying that the dilatory conduct would be seen as a breach of contract, whether expressed in the language of bad faith or in traditional terms of the obligation to act within a reasonable time. See Restatement, supra at § 205, comment d. In short, because contractual provisions mandating payment on conclusion of the valuation process determine the date on which Centronics will get its due, it is clear that what Centronics claims to be Genicom's discretion over the timing of distribution is in reality a power that each party may exercise, but only jointly with the other, to agree to remove some or all of the escrowed funds from the ambit of the otherwise mandatory pay-out provisions.

Although this discussion reflects the analytical structure of the prior good faith performance cases cited by Centronics and followed here, we should also note that the same result would obtain from applying an alternative analysis proposed by Professor Burton, referred to above, which Centronics has also urged us to employ. Burton's functional analysis of the obligation to observe good faith in discretionary contract performance applies objective criteria, see Burton, 94 Harv.L.Rev. at 390–91, to identify the unstated economic opportunities intended to be bargained away by a promisor as a cost of performance, and it identifies bad faith as a promisor's discretionary action subjectively intended, id. at 386, 389, to recapture such an opportunity, thereby refusing to pay an expected performance cost, id. at 373. Centronics argues that its uncontradicted summary judgment affidavits establish that Genicom showed bad faith in Burton's sense, because its refusal to authorize distribution of the so-called undisputed amounts was an "attempt to recapture [the] degree of control concerning the amount of the final purchase price [which] it had agreed to place ... in the arbitrator's hands ... and thereby unjustifiably attain funds to which it was not entitled."

Genicom, of course, denies the uncontradicted evidentiary force that Centronics claims for its affidavits. But even assuming, *arguendo,* that the affidavits are uncontradicted and tend to prove what Centronics asserts, there are two respects in which the facts would fail the Burton test of bad faith as an exercise of discretion meant to recapture an opportunity foregone at the creation of the contract.

It is significant, first, that Genicom's refusal to consent to the distribution from escrow neither recaptures nor gains Genicom anything. In and of itself, the refusal removes no issue from the contingencies of arbitration and gives Genicom no present or future right to the money it wishes to obtain. Genicom's behavior thus contrasts sharply with examples of bad faith given by Burton, in which the discretionary delay preserved the actual use of funds or other valuable resources to the party exercising the discretion. See Burton, 94 Harv.L.Rev. at 394–402. The point is that only when the discretionary act recaptures an economic opportunity does the exercise of discretion pass from the realm of applying leverage for the sake of inducing further agreement into the sphere of bad faith, in which no agreement is necessary to realize the offending party's advantage.

* * *

A second and more fundamental flaw infects Centronics's reliance on the Burton analysis, however. It will be recalled that Burton's conception of bad faith in performance is the exercise of discretion for the purpose of recapturing opportunities foregone or bargained away at the time of contracting, with the identification of such foregone opportunities depending on objective analysis of the parties' "[e]xpectations [as they] may be inferred from the express contract terms in light of the ordinary course of business and customary practice...." Burton, 94 Harv.L.Rev. at 389. Hence, if an objective basis exists to infer that the parties never bargained away the right of either of them to condition any distribution on completing the arbitration of any disputes, then Genicom can not be guilty of bad faith by so insisting, whatever its subjective motive may be. We infer that the opportunity for such insistence never was bargained away.

Although the contract documents do not concisely state there will be no interim distribution, the texts come very close to such a provision. We have previously quoted the language of the escrow agreement that "[i]n accordance with Section 2.07 of the Purchase Agreement," the escrow agent shall hold the fund until instructed by the buyer's and seller's counsel to make a distribution. Section 2.07 was also quoted above. Its topic heading is "Final Payment of Purchase Price," and it provides that final payment and settlement shall be made within ten days of the final determination of net book value and purchase price, which will presumably be at the close of arbitration. "Final Payment . . . " is apparently so called to distinguish it from the "Payment to Sellers on Closing Date," required by § 2.03 of the agreement, since there is no other provision calling for any payment or distribution. The text thus supports the claim that the parties intended the escrow agent to leave the fund intact until the point of the final payment, if any, that would be due to Centronics ten days after the final price determination.

This reading is confirmed by an understanding of the evident business purposes to be served by such a restriction on payout. We explained above that the original escrow of $5,000,000 was to be increased by Genicom's deposit of an Adjustment Amount, which in effect was equal to the amount of Centronics's proposed revision of the final purchase price in excess of the preliminary purchase price. Although Centronics was obligated to follow accepted accounting procedures when it revised the balance sheet to calculate any adjustment, the revision was to be unaudited and Genicom had no control over the setting of this amount.

Genicom, however, was not left entirely subject to Centronics's natural temptation to state a higher, rather than a lower, Adjustment Amount. It is reasonable to suppose each party appreciated that the extent of disagreement and the resulting duration of arbitration would be roughly proportional to the size of the Adjustment Amount. If Centronics had to wait upon the outcome of arbitration before it received any escrowed funds, then Genicom would be able to rely on Centronics's own self-interest to limit the probable length of arbitration by limiting the amount of the adjustment potentially subject to arbitration.

It is also reasonable to assume that neither party expected the other to emerge from arbitration with the whole escrow fund. Each therefore had reason to seek some mechanism for inducing the other side to promote speedy arbitration and the prompt distribution of escrowed money. Such a mechanism would be provided by a scheme conditioning any distribution on completing arbitration, since each would thus be induced to hasten the process for their common benefit.

The probability is, therefore, that each party expected the escrow to remain intact throughout arbitration, as the reason for Genicom's agreement that Centronics would have discretion to state the amount of the adjustment, and as the inducement to a prompt effectuation of their common object of obtaining whatever would be due to each from the fund so escrowed. Whether, therefore, we rely on the analysis underlying our own prior cases, or on the rule as espoused by Burton, we affirm the trial judge's conclusion that Centronics is seeking a revision of the contract, not the enforcement of good faith in its performance.

Affirmed.

All concurred.

NOTES

(1) In *Centronics Corporation,* Judge Souter (now Mr. Justice) discussed the "good faith" scholarship of Robert Summers and Steven Burton. Exactly how do Summers and Burton differ in determining bad faith? Which view prevailed in *Centronics?* See Steve Burton & Eric Andersen, Contractual Good Faith 38–40 (1995), wherein Professor Burton claims victory.

(2) Suppose Genicom had been in bad faith in refusing to release the escrow funds. What remedy would be available to Centronics? Is bad faith simply another way to describe a breach by failing to perform an agreed part of the bargain?

(3) *Good Faith Duty in Formation.* Judge Souter suggested that implied duty of good faith in formation is "tantamount to the traditional duties of care to refrain from misrepresentation and to correct subsequently discovered error." Have you seen any evidence to support this conclusion in the materials studied to here? See El Paso Natural Gas Co. v. Minco Oil & Gas, Inc., 8 S.W.3d 309 (Tex.1999) (holding that under UCC parties are not subject to the statutory duty of good faith in procuring or forming a contract).

(4) *The UCC Position.* In Commentary No. 10 of the Permanent Editorial Board of the Uniform Commercial Code, dated February 10, 1994, the PEB concluded that UCC 1–203 did not create an independent cause of action for bad faith by parties to a contract for sale. Rather, the duty of good faith relates to performance or enforcement of the agreement of the parties and resort to principles of law and equity outside of the UCC is not proper. As a result, the PEB adopted the following new (1994) comment to UCC 1–203:

> This section does not support an independent cause of action for failure to perform or enforce in good faith. Rather, this section means that a failure to perform or enforce, in good faith, a specific duty or obligation under the contract, constitutes a breach of that contract or makes unavailable, under the particular circumstances, a remedial right or power. This distinction makes it clear that the doctrine of good faith merely directs a court towards interpreting contracts within the commercial context in which they are created, performed, and enforced, and does not create a separate duty of fairness and reasonableness which can be independently breached.

This Comment is preserved in Comment 1 to Rev. 1–304.

Comment: Contrasting Models of Good Faith Performance: The Unidroit Principles.

The American Model. American contract law imposes a non-variable duty of "good faith [and fair dealing] on the performance and enforcement of a contract." Unfortunately, the scope of this duty is limited. It does not apply to pre-contract negotiations.

Moreover, it is not a free-floating duty. Rather, it applies to the performance of agreed terms in the contract. For example, if the contract contains a clear and complete termination clause and one party follows that clause in terminating the contract, a court is likely to say that the termination was in good faith. If, however, the contract reserves discretion in performance to one or both parties, the exercise of that discretion must be in good faith. On the other hand, in the absence of a term in the contract, the parties have no common-law duty to negotiate in good faith after a disruptive event such as the failure of an agreed pricing mechanism, much less a duty to agree on an adjustment.

Combined with limitations on the duty of good faith is spirited disagreement among the commentators over what constitutes bad faith and a tendency in the courts to resist a finding of bad faith even where the duty is imposed. The result is that the potential of the duty of good faith for contracts, not to mention relational contracts, has arguably not been realized in the United States.

The Unidroit Model. A more expansive model of good faith, one which is consistent with relational contract theory, is found in the Unidroit Principles of International Commercial Contracts. The good faith model is expressed as follows:

> Article 1.7(1) provides that "each party must act in accordance with good faith and fair dealing in international trade," and Comment 1 makes it clear that the "parties' behaviour throughout the life of the contract, including the negotiation process, must conform to good faith and fair dealing."

> Article 2.15(1), however, suggests that a party is free not to negotiate (freedom from negotiation) and, if negotiations are undertaken, "is not liable for failure to reach an agreement." However, 2.15(2) states that a party who "negotiates or breaks off negotiations in bad faith is liable for the losses caused to the other party," and 2.15(3) states that it is "bad faith, in particular, for a party to enter into or continue negotiations when intending not to reach an agreement with the other party." These principles apply across the board to the formation process and the performance, adjustment, or termination of the contract.

> The duty to negotiate in good faith, therefore, applies if the parties voluntarily commence to negotiate or if the contract requires them to negotiate or bargain. Suppose neither of those conditions is satisfied. When is a duty to negotiate in good faith imposed?

> One answer is found in Article 5.2, which suggests that the obligation to negotiate may be implied from the nature and purpose of the contract, from practices established between the parties, from good faith and fair dealing, or from reasonableness. This is consistent with the notion in relational contracts that norms of behavior, including a duty to negotiate in good faith, may be generated from the relationship itself.

> A second answer is found in the sections of the Unidroit Principles dealing with the concept of hardship where "the performance of a contract becomes more onerous for one of the parties." Assuming that the definition of hardship in Article 6.2.2 is satisfied, the "disadvantaged party is entitled to request renegotiations ... without undue delay." Article 6.2.3 states what a court may do "upon failure to reach agreement within a reasonable time," but does not explicitly say

whether the nondisadvantaged party must negotiate if requested. Comment 5, however, provides:

> Although nothing is said in this article to that effect, both the request for renegotiations by the disadvantaged party and the conduct of both parties during the renegotiation process are subject to the general principle of good faith (Art. 1.7) and to the duty of cooperation (Art. 5.3).

Thus, the disadvantaged party must honestly believe that a case of hardship actually exists and not request renegotiations as a purely tactical maneuver. Similarly, once the request has been made, both parties must conduct the renegotiations in a constructive manner, in particular by refraining from any form of obstruction and by providing all the necessary information. Under a fair reading of the Unidroit Principles, therefore, one party has a duty to negotiate with the other in good faith, regardless of what the contract provides, in three situations: (1) where one party voluntarily commences to negotiate with the other party; (2) where the duty is implied from the relationship; and (3) where, after hardship has occurred, the other (disadvantaged) party makes a timely request to renegotiate the contract or its terms. The parties, however, may fail without penalty to agree in good faith. There is no duty to agree. Nevertheless, this duty to negotiate is not likely to arise unless the parties are performing a contract with relational characteristics.*

Richard E. Speidel, *The Characteristics and Challenges of Relational Contracts*, 94 Nw U. L. Rev. 823, 840–843 (2000).

For a trenchant critique of the American Model of good faith, see Michael P. Van Alstine, Of Textualism, Party Autonomy, and Good Faith, 40 Wm. & Mary L. Rev. 1223 (1999).

(B) PREVENTION, HINDRANCE, AND THE DUTY OF COOPERATION

A useful way to think about the problem posed in this section—prevention, hindrance and the duty of cooperation—is in terms of duties imposed by the courts upon parties to exchange relationships in the

---

* Although difficult to define, relational contracts are thought to have certain characteristics: (1) Extended duration, (2) Open terms with performance discretion conferred on one or both parties, (3) Future cooperative behavior is expected and, perhaps, facilitated by agreed governance or dispute resolution mechanisms, (4) Benefits and burdens of the contract are frequently shared rather than allocated to one party, (5) Transaction specific investments, i.e., investments unique to the particular relationship, may be made, and (6) Close, whole, personal relationships may form an integral aspect of the relationship.

See Speidel, 94 Nw. U. L. Rev. at 828–831, drawing on the work of Professor Ian R. Macneil. See also Paul J. Gudel, *Relational Contracts Theory and the Concept of Exchange*, 46 Buff. L. Rev. 763 (1998).

Using this descriptive model, an example of a relational contract is that found in Oglebay Norton Co. v. Armco, Inc., 52 Ohio St.3d 232, 556 N.E.2d 515 (1990), reprinted supra at 413. It is thought that the UNIDROIT model of good faith is preferable to the American model in dealing with performance under relational contracts.

absence of and, maybe, in spite of an expression of contrary agreement. Whether you say that these duties are implied or imposed is not as important as understanding when and why these relational duties will be found and enforced by the courts. Thus, the doctrines of "prospective inability" to perform and "anticipatory" repudiation both emerge from the perception that the defendant has done something to impair the plaintiff's expectation of receiving due performance, and that the plaintiff's interests, whether you call them expectation, reliance or restitution, should have some protection, be it defensive, affirmative or both. Despite the "implied promise" terminology, Lord Campbell put it very well when he said "where there is a contract to do an act on a future day, there is a relation constituted between the parties in the meantime by the contract and that they impliedly promise that * * * neither will do anything to the prejudice of the other inconsistent with that relation." *Hochster v. De La Tour*, infra at 863. This basic notion has been particularized in a contemporary decision which does not improve too much on the original:

> It is a fundamental principle of law that in every contract there exists an implied covenant of good faith and fair dealing.... Furthermore, each contract contains an implicit understanding that neither party will intentionally do anything to prevent the other party from carrying out his part of the agreement. * * * "It is likewise implied in every contract that there is a duty of cooperation on the part of both parties. *Thus, whenever the cooperation of the promisee is necessary for the performance of the promise, there is a condition implied that the cooperation will be given.*"

Lowell v. Twin Disc., Inc., 527 F.2d 767, 770 (2d Cir.1975) (emphasis in original).

As with a repudiation or breach by a material nonperformance, breach by prevention or hindrance or a failure to cooperate both excuses the aggrieved party from any duty to continue performance and gives a cause of action for damages.

Patterson v. Meyerhofer

Court of Appeals of New York, 1912.
204 N.Y. 96, 97 N.E. 472.

■ WILLARD, BARTLETT, J. The parties to this action entered into a written contract whereby the plaintiff agreed to sell and the defendant agreed to buy four several parcels of land with the houses thereon for the sum of $23,000, to be paid partly in cash and partly by taking title subject to certain mortgages upon the property. When she executed this contract, the defendant knew that the plaintiff was not then the owner of the premises which he agreed to sell to her but that he expected and intended to acquire title thereto by purchasing the same at a foreclosure sale. Before this foreclosure sale took place the defendant stated to the plaintiff that she would not perform the contract on her part but intended to buy the premises for her own account without in any way recognizing the said contract as binding upon her, and this she did, buying the four parcels for $5,595 each. The plaintiff attended the foreclosure sale, able, ready and willing to purchase the premises, and he bid for the same, but in every instance of a bid made by him the defendant bid a higher sum. The result was that she acquired each lot for $155 less than she had obligated herself to pay the plaintiff therefor under the contract or $620 less in all.

In the foreclosure sale was included a fifth house, which the defendant also purchased. This was not mentioned in the written contract between the parties, but according to the complaint there was a prior parol agreement which provided that the plaintiff should buy all five houses at the foreclosure sale and should convey only four of them to the defendant, retaining the fifth house for himself.

Upon these facts the plaintiff brought the present action demanding judgment that the defendant convey to him the fifth house and declaring that he had a lien upon the premises purchased by her at the foreclosure sale and that she holds the same in trust for the plaintiff subject to the contract. The complaint also prays that the plaintiff be awarded the sum of $620 damages, being the difference between the price which the defendant paid at the foreclosure sale for the four houses mentioned in the contract and the price which she would have had to pay the plaintiff thereunder.

The learned judge who tried the case at Special Term rendered judgment in favor of the defendant, holding that under the contract of sale there was no relation of confidence between the vendor and vendee. "In the present case," he said, "each party was free to act for his own interest, restricted only by the stipulations of the contract." He was, therefore, of the opinion that "the defendant had a right to buy in at the auction and that she is entitled to hold exactly as though she had been a stranger and that the plaintiff is not entitled to recover the difference between the price paid at the auction and the contract price."

I am inclined to agree with the trial court that no relation of trust can be spelled out of the transactions between the parties. There is no finding of any parol agreement in respect to the fifth house which has been mentioned, and even if there had been such an agreement resting merely in parol, I do not see that it would have been enforceable. As to the four parcels which constituted the subject-matter of the written contract, the defendant avowed her intention to ignore that contract before bidding for them, and cannot be regarded as having gone into possession *under* the plaintiff as vendor, but did so rather in defiance of any right of his; hence, there is no likeness to the cases of Galloway v. Finley (12 Peters, [U.S.], 264) and Bush v. Marshall (6 How. [U.S.], 284) relied upon by the appellant. In those cases, it is true, vendees who had bought up better titles than those of their vendors were treated as trustees for the latter; but the contracts of sale had been carried out and the vendees were in full possession of the lands before they acquired the superior outstanding title; and both decisions were expressly placed on the ground that under such circumstances the vendor and vendee stand in the relation of landlord and tenant and the vendee cannot disavow the vendor's title.

There is no need of judicially declaring any trust in the defendant, however, to secure to the plaintiff the profit which he would have made if the defendant had not intervened as purchaser at the foreclosure sale and had fulfilled the written contract on her part. This is represented by his claim for $620 damages. That amount, under the facts as found, I think the plaintiff was entitled to recover. He has demanded it in his complaint and he should not be thrown out of court because he has also prayed for too much equitable relief.

In the case of every contract there is an implied undertaking on the part of each party that he will not intentionally and purposely do anything to prevent the other party from carrying out the agreement on his part.

This proposition necessarily follows from the general rule that a party who causes or sanctions the breach of an agreement is thereby precluded from recovering damages for its non-performance or from interposing it as a defense to an action upon the contract....

"Where a party stipulates that another shall do a certain thing, he thereby impliedly promises that he will himself do nothing which may hinder or obstruct that other in doing that thing." (Gay v. Blanchard, 32 La.Ann. 497.)

By entering into the contract to purchase from the plaintiff property which she knew he would have to buy at the foreclosure sale in order to convey it to her, the defendant impliedly agreed that she would do nothing to prevent him from acquiring the property at such sale. The defendant violated the agreement thus implied on her part by bidding for and buying the premises herself. Although the plaintiff bid therefor she uniformly outbid him. Presumably if she had not interfered he could have bought the property for the same price which she paid for it. He would then have been able to sell it to her for the price specified in the contract (assuming that she fulfilled the contract), which was $620 more. This sum, therefore, represents the loss which he has suffered. It is the measure of the plaintiff's damages for the defendant's breach of contract.

I see no escape from this conclusion. It is true that the contract contemplated that the four houses should go to the defendant and they have gone to her; but that is not all. The contract contemplated that they should go to the plaintiff first. In that event the plaintiff would have received $620 which he has not got. This would have had to be paid by the defendant if she had fulfilled her contract; and she should be required to pay it now unless she can present some better defense than is presented in this record. This will place both parties in the position contemplated by the contract. The defendant will have paid no more than the contract obligated her to pay; the plaintiff will have received all to which the contract entitled him. I leave the fifth house out of consideration because as to that it seems to me there was no enforceable agreement.

For these reasons the judgments of the Appellate Division and the Special Term should be reversed and a new trial granted, with costs to abide the event.

Iron Trade Products Co. v. Wilkoff Co.

Supreme Court of Pennsylvania, 1922.
272 Pa. 172, 116 A. 150.

■ OPINION BY MR. JUSTICE WALLING. In July, 1919, plaintiff entered into a written contract with defendant for the purchase of twenty-six hundred tons of section relaying rails, to be delivered in New York harbor at times therein specified, for $41 a ton. Defendant failed to deliver any of the rails and plaintiff brought this suit, averring, by reason of such default, it had been compelled to purchase the rails elsewhere (two thousand tons thereof at $49.20 per ton and six hundred tons at $49 per ton), also that the market or current price of the rails at the time and place of delivery was approximately $50 per ton, and claiming as damages the difference between what it had been compelled to pay and the contract price. Defendant filed an affidavit of defense and a supplement thereto, both of which the court below held insufficient and entered judgment for plaintiff; from which defendant brought this appeal.

In effect, the affidavit of defense avers the supply of such rails was very limited, there being only two places in the United States (one in Georgia and one in West Virginia) where they could be obtained in quantities to fill the contract, and that, pending the time for delivery, defendant was negotiating for the required rails when plaintiff announced to the trade its urgent desire to purchase a similar quantity of like rails, and, in fact, bought eight hundred and eighty-seven tons and agreed to purchase a much larger quantity from the parties with whom defendant had been negotiating; further averring this conduct on behalf of plaintiff reduced the available supply of relaying rails and enhanced the price to an exorbitant sum, rendering performance by defendant impossible. The affidavit, however, fails to aver knowledge on part of plaintiff that the supply of rails was limited or any intent on its part to prevent, interfere with or embarrass defendant in the performance of the contract; and there is no suggestion of any understanding, express or implied, that defendant was to secure the rails from any particular source, or that plaintiff was to refrain from purchasing other rails; hence, it was not required to do so. The true rule is stated in Williston on Contracts, p. 1308, as quoted by the trial court, viz: "If a party seeking to secure all the merchandise of a certain character which he could, entered into a contract for a quantity of the required goods, and subsequently made performance of the contract by the seller more difficult by making other purchases which increased the scarcity of the available supply, his conduct would furnish no excuse for refusal to perform the prior contract." Mere difficulty of performance will not excuse a breach of contract: ... Defendant relies upon the rule stated in United States v. Peck, 102 U.S. 64, that, "The conduct of one party to a contract which prevents the other from performing his part is an excuse for nonperformance." The cases are not parallel; here, plaintiff's conduct did not prevent performance by defendant, although it may have added to the difficulty and expense thereof. There is no averment that plaintiff's purchases exhausted the supply of rails, and the advance in price caused thereby is no excuse.

The Peck case stands on different ground, there Peck contracted to sell the government a certain quantity of hay for the Tongue River station, and the trial court found it was mutually understood the hay was to be cut on government lands called "the Big Meadows," in the Yellowstone Valley, which was the only available source of supply; also that thereafter the government caused all of that hay to be cut for it by other parties. In view of this Peck was relieved from his contract.

[The court held that the plaintiff was entitled to damages measured by the difference between the contract price and the price paid to obtain substitute goods on the market.]

The assignments of error are overruled and the judgment is affirmed.

NOTES

(1) *Implied Covenant of Good Faith.* Whether the inquiry concerns discharge of duty, excuse for failure of condition, or action for breach, cases of this type are said to apply, in the last analysis, the principle that "in every contract there is an implied covenant that neither party shall do anything which will have the effect of destroying or injuring the right of the other party to receive the fruits of the contract, which means that in every contract there exists an implied covenant of good faith and fair dealing." Kirke La Shelle Co. v. Paul Armstrong Co., 263 N.Y. 79, 87, 188 N.E. 163 (1934). See Edwin W. Patterson, *Constructive Conditions in Contracts,* 42 Colum.L.Rev. 903, 928–42 (1942) (tracing history).

(2) In both *Patterson v. Meyerhofer* and *Iron Trade Products Co. v. Wilkoff Co.* and in *United States v. Peck,* discussed in *Wilkoff,* one party to the contract actively competed with the other to obtain what was promised under the contract. In each instance, the competition, which was in the defendant's best interest, was successful, either preventing or hindering the other party in performance. But liability was imposed only in *Patterson.* Can the cases be reconciled? Is the difference to be found in the motive behind the conduct or, perhaps, the knowledge possessed by the defendant at the time? Or, does the answer lie in a theory of risk assumption, based upon the language of the contract, the capacity of the parties, the nature of the performance, market conditions and what both parties knew or had reason to know about the exchange?

(3) *The Case of the Opportunistic Tenant.* Landlord leased premises to Tenant for use as a gasoline station at a rental of five cents for each gallon of gasoline sold. Midway during the five-year term, Tenant purchased adjoining property upon which he built and operated a new station. Prior to operation of the new station gallonage totaled approximately 40,000 per month; since that time the average has declined to around 4,000. There was no covenant in the lease prohibiting operation of a new station. Landlord consults you relative to his right, if any, to cancel the lease. What do you advise? Cf. Seggebruch v. Stosor, 309 Ill.App. 385, 33 N.E.2d 159 (1941).

(4) *The Case of the Interfering Homeowner.* Builder and Mr. and Mrs. Homeowner contracted for the construction of a new house, to be built according to certain plans and specifications at a cost of $100,000. Work began

one week later. Almost at once Mrs. Homeowner began making daily visits to the site, each time contacting the foreman in charge relative to what, how, why, etc. was going on. After enduring this for a week, the foreman reported to Builder that he simply "couldn't stand having her around all the time, yakking and getting in the way." Builder asked if she had interfered with the work, to which he replied: "Well, yes, in a way—but the main thing is she's just a damned nuisance." Builder consults you, asking: "What can I do about this?" Advise him. Cf. Li Volsi Construction Co. v. Shepard, 133 Conn. 133, 48 A.2d 263 (1946); Gamble v. Woodlea Construction Co., 246 Md. 260, 228 A.2d 243 (1967).

(5) A *Prevention–Hindrance Sampler: Its Bad Faith Stupid.*

Sons of Thunder, Inc. v. Borden, Inc., 148 N.J. 396, 690 A.2d 575 (1997) (bad faith performance evidenced by extortion, deception, and price cutting).

Ashland Management Inc. v. Janien, 82 N.Y.2d 395, 604 N.Y.S.2d 912, 624 N.E.2d 1007 (1993)(firm's refusal to negotiate confidentiality agreement in contract with employee is bad faith).

R.J. Kuhl Corp. v. Sullivan, 13 Cal.App.4th 1589, 17 Cal.Rptr.2d 425 (1993)(collusive acts to avoid broker's fee).

Beck v. Mason, 580 N.E.2d 290 (Ind.App.1991)(vendees failed to fulfill good faith duty to obtain financing).

Cenac v. Murry, 609 So.2d 1257 (Miss.1992)(bizarre behavior by vendor who, under installment contract containing a forfeiture clause to sell country store, interferes with operation of store; bad faith is breach for which damages are recoverable).

Anthony's Pier Four, Inc. v. HBC Associates, 411 Mass. 451, 583 N.E.2d 806 (1991)(unreasonable refusal by owner under a development contract to approve developer's master plan).

United States National Bank of Oregon v. Boge, 311 Or. 550, 814 P.2d 1082 (1991)(question of fact whether bank's refusal to give payoff information to borrower in order to prevent him from paying notes was in bad faith).

Larson v. Larson, 37 Mass.App.Ct. 106, 636 N.E.2d 1365 (1994)(where separation agreement calculates support obligation on husband's earned income, bad faith for husband to retire prematurely without making some other provision for support).

KW Plastics v. United States Can Co.

Middle District, Alabama, 2001.
131 F.Supp.2d 1289.

* * *

Alabama law recognizes the tort of intentional interference with prospective business relationships. The elements of a claim include: (1) the existence of a contract or business relation; (2) the defendant's knowledge of the contract or business relation; (3) intentional interference by the defendant with the contract or business relation; and (4) proximate damages ... "It is the right to do business in a fair setting that is protected." *Utah Foam Prods., Inc. v. Polytec, Inc.,* 584 So.2d 1345, 1352–53 (Ala.1991).

In defining the scope of this cause of action, Alabama courts have relied on the Restatement (Second) of Torts.... The Restatement divides recoverable damages for tortious interference into three categories: (1) the pecuniary loss of the benefits of the contract or the prospective relation; (2) consequential losses for which the interference is a legal cause; and (3) emotional distress or actual harm to reputation if either is reasonably to be expected to result from the interference. *See* Restatement (Second) Of Torts § 774A (1979).

Under Alabama law, a plaintiff seeking damages must provide sufficient evidence for the jury to estimate lost profits with reasonable certainty.... A thorough discussion of this state's decision to adopt this standard and reject the "new business" rule would be tedious and unnecessary, although the court refers the parties to *Super Valu Stores, Inc. v. Peterson,* 506 So.2d 317, 326–33 (Ala.1987), which reads like a treatise on this point. Under the "reasonable certainty" requirement, "the loss of profits ... must be capable of ascertainment with reasonable, or sufficient, certainty, or there must be some basis on which a reasonable estimate of the amount of the profit can be made...." * * *

NOTES

(1) *Tort of inducing breach of contract.* Assuming that Alabama law, stated supra, is a conventional statement of the law of tortious interference, suppose, in *Patterson v. Meyerhofer,* that Defendant was late to the auction and Plaintiff was able to purchase the parcels at the expected price. Suppose, further, that Defendant was able to induce Auctioneer to deed over the parcels to her for a total payment $620 more than Plaintiff had bid. Plaintiff would, at a minimum, have two contract claims in these circumstances: 1) against Auctioneer for repudiation of the contract to sell the parcels; and 2) against Defendant for breach by prevention of her contract to purchase from Plaintiff. (Surely the acceptability of the defendant's conduct does not improve simply because she missed the auction.) In addition, Plaintiff, in all probability, has a claim in tort against Defendant for inducing Auctioneer to breach the contract with Plaintiff.

In pursuing the tort claim, the plaintiff on the *Patterson* facts, should allege: (1) There was an existing contract or a protected expectancy of a future economic benefit between Plaintiff and the Auctioneer of which Defendant had knowledge; (2) Defendant's inducement actually caused Auctioneer to breach the contract, and Plaintiff was damaged by the breach; and (3) Defendant's conduct was intentional rather than inadvertent or careless and it was intentional because the defendant had reason to know or to anticipate that its conduct would induce Auctioneer to breach the contract [see *Texaco, Inc. v. Pennzoil, Co.,* 729 S.W.2d 768, 796–809 (Tex.App.1987), cert. denied 485 U.S. 994, 108 S.Ct. 1305, 99 L.Ed.2d 686 (1988) (Defendant had knowledge of agreement and actively induced breach), discussed supra at 432.

In addition, the plaintiff should be prepared to deal with a defense that the defendant's conduct was "privileged," that is, taken in good faith to protect a legally protected interest of its own which it believes may otherwise be impaired or destroyed by the performance of the contract. See Restatement (Second) of Torts § 773 (1979). If the defendant was engaged in a good faith effort to protect its self-interest, the action might not be tortious because it protects a valid interest.

Finally, if the elements are established and the conduct is not privileged, a wide range of remedies, including injunction, damages for loss of bargain, consequential damages, including mental anguish and damage to reputation, and even punitive damages, are available.

For additional reading, see Restatement (Second) of Torts §§ 766–774 (1979); Deepa Varadarakan. Tortious Interference and the Law of Contract: The Case for Specific Performance Revisited, 111 Yale L. J. 735 (2001).

Stockton v. Sowerwine

Supreme Court of Wyoming, 1984.
690 P.2d 1202.

■ BROWN, JUSTICE.

This appeal involves the question of an implied covenant of good faith in an option contract to repurchase certain real estate. The trial court found that appellant Mark L. Stockton (Stockton hereinafter) had exhibited bad faith in hindering appellee E.O. Sowerwine, III (Sowerwine hereinafter) in the exercise of his option to repurchase the land, and ordered specific performance of the contract. * * * We will affirm.

Before June, 1981, appellee's father, E.O. Sowerwine, Jr., owned the property subject to this lawsuit. He had numerous financial problems and in order to save his ranch, was provided $300,000 from Stockton to discharge pressing obligations. Upon receiving the $300,000 from Stockton, appellee's father deeded to Stockton 1,510 acres of the ranch with a one-year option to repurchase 1,505 acres as set forth in an Agreement and Option to Repurchase, dated June 15, 1981. The parties agreed that upon exercise of the option Stockton could keep five acres of his choice from the 1,510 acres. The action arose after Sowerwine alleged that Stockton wrongfully hindered him in the exercise of the option. The trial court found generally for Sowerwine, specifically finding that:

" * * * Defendant's [appellant's] actions display a conscious, methodical obstructive course of action towards the Plaintiff [appellee] and his attempts to exercise the option and such actions resulted in the actual hindrance of the Plaintiff."

The option to repurchase ran for one year until June 22, 1982, and required that appellee's father tender to Stockton the amount of $303,000, the original purchase price plus the "points" which were paid by Stockton to obtain his loan from the bank, together with interest at the rate of 19%, in addition to all expenses incurred by Stockton relating to his ownership of the property, plus $20,000. There was evidence indicating that the property's value was in excess of $1,000,000. Also, Stockton had the right to retain five acres of the property. On April 1, 1982, appellee's father had not yet obtained refinancing, and at that time the option was assigned to appellee.

In the following months, Sowerwine applied to the Federal Land Bank of Omaha for a loan to obtain refinancing. The Federal Land Bank issued a notice of loan approval on June 9, 1982. The following day, June 10, 1982, Sowerwine wrote Stockton of his intent to exercise the option. This letter was received by Stockton on June 12, 1982. On June 11, 1982, Sowerwine requested a list of the expenses incurred by Stockton, as well as a legal description of the five acres that Stockton desired to retain, in order to close the loan with the Federal Land Bank of Omaha. Stockton refused to provide Sowerwine with the list of expenses and the legal description of the five acres which Stockton desired to retain. On June 12, 1982, Stockton told Sowerwine that he could not provide a legal description because he did not know which five acres he wanted to retain. However, Paul Campbell, a surveyor in Cody, Wyoming, testified that he had been contacted by Stockton in the summer of 1981 and again in June of 1982; Stockton had told him which five acres of the property he wished to retain, and discussed the possibility of having those five acres surveyed. Also, on June 12, 1982, Stockton and his counsel told Sowerwine, who did not have an attorney with him, that the option was not assignable and that he, Sowerwine, could not exercise such option. At trial, however, both Stockton and his counsel admitted that both assertions were incorrect.

Since Stockton refused to give a legal description of the five acres which he wished to retain, and since the closing date of June 22, 1982, was approaching, Sowerwine sought interim financing at the Stockgrowers State Bank in Worland, Wyoming, among others. Sowerwine's application for the loan was considered by the bank's discount committee on June 15, 1982. One day earlier Stockton, also a bank president, wrote a letter to the president of the Stockgrowers State Bank, wherein he informed the bank of the existence of certain restrictive covenants upon the land, averred that he did not see how the Federal Land Bank could make a loan on land which was restricted, and suggested that the president call the Land Bank to discuss this issue. This letter was not mailed, but was hand delivered after Stockton drove 90 miles to do so. The discount committee of the Stockgrowers State Bank considered Sowerwine's loan application on June 15, 1982, and rejected it. The rejection was based, in large part, upon Stockton's letter to the bank regarding the existence of the covenants. The minutes of the discount committee reflect:

" * * * Because of a covenance [sic], there is to be no livestock on the land and if this is the case, then the Federal Land Bank won't loan the money. Stockton will give back the sprinkler system if Sauerwine [sic] will release the covenance [sic]. Son wants land to add to his 465 acres. No we are not interested."

At trial the president of Stockgrowers State Bank and the loan officer in charge of Sowerwine's application testified that the existence of the restrictive covenants was a major factor in their refusal to grant the loan to Sowerwine.

The facts show that on the last day the option could be exercised, June 22, 1982, the Federal Land Bank was ready to close its loan and grant the money to Sowerwine just as soon as it received a complete legal description of the property. This could not be done since Stockton refused to furnish Sowerwine a legal description of the five acres which he wished to retain. Sowerwine had deposited sufficient money in the Stockgrowers State Bank to cover any excess of the repurchase price over the loan amount and to cover any expenses incurred by Stockton incidental to his ownership of the property, including the expense of surveying the five acres. However, Stockton still refused to provide Sowerwine with an itemized list of expenses, even though such list had been prepared since June 16, 1982. The list was not given to Sowerwine until the option period had expired.

The trial court found that Stockton had intentionally violated the implied covenant of good faith in his hindrance of Sowerwine's attempt to validly exercise his option under the contract,....

* * *

In his treatise on contracts, Professor Williston states:

"It is a principle of fundamental justice that if a promisor is himself the cause of the failure of performance, either of an obligation due him or of a condition upon which his own liability depends, he cannot take advantage of the failure.

"In reflecting upon this jural proposition, a federal court has observed that 'Where liability under a contract depends upon a condition precedent one cannot avoid his liability by making the performance of the condition precedent impossible, or by preventing it.' The illustrations of this principle are legion." 5 Williston on Contracts, § 677, pp. 224–225 (3rd ed. 1961).

The above language was quoted with approval by this court in *Gibson v. J.T. Allen Agency,* Wyo., 407 P.2d 708, 710 (1965):

" * * * 'One who prevents or makes impossible the performance or happening of a condition precedent upon which his liability by the terms of a contract is made to depend cannot avail himself of its nonperformance.' "
. . .

Referring again to Williston on Contracts, § 677A, it is stated:

"It is as effective an excuse of performance of a condition that the promisor has hindered performance as that he has actually prevented it. * * * Where a party stipulates that another shall do a certain thing, he thereby impliedly promises that he will himself do nothing which will hinder or obstruct that other in doing that thing.

"And if the situation is such that the cooperation of one party is an essential prerequisite to performance by the other, there is not only a condition implied in fact qualifying the promise of the latter, but also an implied promise by the former to give the necessary cooperation."

* * *

This court has previously dealt with the issue of good faith in its relation to real estate contracts in *Wendling v. Cundall,* Wyo., 568 P.2d 888, 890 (1977):

" * * * The Uniform Commercial Code as adopted in Wyoming, ... would not encompass this transaction relating to real estate. The legislature did, however, define 'good faith' as those terms would apply to most other commercial transactions conducted by persons owing no fiduciary or other special obligation to one another. Pursuant to § 34–1–201(19), W.S., 'Good faith' means honesty in fact in the conduct or transaction concerned. * * * Absent some compelling reason, which is not present here, it is appropriate to have a similar definition of good faith applicable to transactions like this as pertains to those governed by the Uniform Commercial Code and the law merchant. We subscribe to the proposition that this test requires honesty of intent rather than diligence or nonnegligence. * * * "

* * * Applying those principles to the present case, we find that the record is replete with examples of Stockton's attempts to hinder Sowerwine's exercise of the option. Indeed, Stockton's attorney admitted that Stockton did not want the option to be exercised. Such intent is manifest through his attempt to block the interim financing which Sowerwine had applied for through the Stockgrowers State Bank, as well as his refusal to give Sowerwine a description of the five acres which he intended to retain, even though he had previously contacted a surveyor and told him the acres he wanted surveyed which he wished to retain. Furthermore, Stockton's intent is evidenced by his refusal to give Sowerwine an itemized list of expenses which Stockton had incurred incident to his ownership of the property which was needed to determine the repurchase price, even though such list had already been prepared.

In this case we find that the trial court was justified in concluding that Stockton had purposely hindered Sowerwine in his attempts to rightfully exercise his option under the contract.

Affirmed.

PROBLEM: THE CASE OF THE UNCOOPERATIVE VENDOR

In the process of negotiating a contract for the sale of land, Vendee indicated that he hoped to secure a loan on the property to be guaranteed by the Veterans Administration. Vendor, on the other hand, was opposed to dealing with the VA and preferred other financing arrangements. The issue was resolved by the insertion of the following clauses in the contract:

"(18) It is understood and agreed that this home is to be bought and financed under the G.I. Bill of Rights and is subject to approval by Veterans Administration of purchase price not to exceed Twenty One Thousand Nine Hundred Fifty ($21,950.00); said Eighteen Thousand Dollar First Deed of Trust herein mentioned has already been committed by the First Federal Savings &

Loan Assoc. of Washington, D.C., and said loan must be placed with this company, otherwise secondary financing will be arranged.

"(21) The purchaser agrees to accept the following financing in the event the house is not financed under the aforementioned G.I. financing * * *."

Shortly before the agreed closing date, the VA issued a certificate of "reasonable value" which appraised the property at some $4,450 less than the contract price. Since the purchase price exceeded valuation, it appeared that the VA guarantee would not be available. Vendor then informed Vendee that since the VA had disapproved the loan they should proceed in making settlement under the agreed alternative financing. Vendee then requested that Vendor furnish a schedule of his actual construction costs as a basis of appealing to the VA for a higher appraisal. Vendor refused and Vendee subsequently canceled the contract. After the settlement date passed without a closing, Vendor declared the 10% deposit forfeited and retained it as liquidated damages. Vendee sues to recover the deposit. What result?

Market Street Associates Limited Partnership v. Frey

United States Court of Appeals,Seventh Circuit, 1991.
941 F.2d 588.

■ POSNER, CIRCUIT JUDGE.

Market Street Associates Limited Partnership and its general partner appeal from a judgment for the defendants, General Electric Pension Trust and its trustees, entered upon cross-motions for summary judgment in a diversity suit that pivots on the doctrine of "good faith" performance of a contract. Cf. Robert Summers, " 'Good Faith' in General Contract Law and the Sales Provisions of the Uniform Commercial Code," 54 *Va.L.Rev.* 195, 232–43 (1968). Wisconsin law applies—common law rather than Uniform Commercial Code, because the contract is for land rather than for goods, UCC § 2–102; Wis.Stat. § 402.102, and because it is a lease rather than a sale and Wisconsin has not adopted UCC art. 2A, which governs leases. * * *

We come at last to the contract dispute out of which the case arises. In 1968, J.C. Penney Company, the retail chain, entered into a sale and leaseback arrangement with General Electric Pension Trust in order to finance Penney's growth. Under the arrangement Penney sold properties to the pension trust which the trust then leased back to Penney for a term of 25 years. Paragraph 34 of the lease entitles the lessee to "request Lessor [the pension trust] to finance the costs and expenses of construction of additional Improvements upon the Premises," provided the amount of the costs and expenses is at least $250,000. Upon receiving the request, the pension trust "agrees to give reasonable consideration to providing the financing of such additional Improvements and Lessor and Lessee shall negotiate in good faith concerning the construction of such Improvements and the financing by Lessor of such costs and expenses." Paragraph 34 goes on to provide that, should the negotiations fail, the lessee shall be entitled to repurchase the property at a price roughly equal to the price at which

Penney sold it to the pension trust in the first place, plus 6 percent a year for each year since the original purchase. So if the average annual appreciation in the property exceeded 6 percent, a breakdown in negotiations over the financing of improvements would entitle Penney to buy back the property for less than its market value (assuming it had sold the property to the pension trust in the first place at its then market value).

One of these leases was for a shopping center in Milwaukee. In 1987 Penney assigned this lease to Market Street Associates, which the following year received an inquiry from a drugstore chain that wanted to open a store in the shopping center, provided (as is customary) that Market Street Associates built the store for it. Whether Market Street Associates was pessimistic about obtaining financing from the pension trust, still the lessor of the shopping center, or for other reasons, it initially sought financing for the project from other sources. But they were unwilling to lend the necessary funds without a mortgage on the shopping center, which Market Street Associates could not give because it was not the owner but only the lessee. It decided therefore to try to buy the property back from the pension trust. Market Street Associates' general partner, Orenstein, tried to call David Erb of the pension trust, who was responsible for the property in question. Erb did not return his calls, so Orenstein wrote him, expressing an interest in buying the property and asking him to "review your file on this matter and call me so that we can discuss it further." At first, Erb did not reply. Eventually Orenstein did reach Erb, who promised to review the file and get back to him. A few days later an associate of Erb called Orenstein and indicated an interest in selling the property for $3 million, which Orenstein considered much too high.

That was in June of 1988. On July 28, Market Street Associates wrote a letter to the pension trust formally requesting funding for $2 million in improvements to the shopping center. The letter made no reference to paragraph 34 of the lease; indeed, it did not mention the lease. The letter asked Erb to call Orenstein to discuss the matter. Erb, in what was becoming a habit of unresponsiveness, did not call. On August 16, Orenstein sent a second letter—certified mail, return receipt requested—again requesting financing and this time referring to the lease, though not expressly to paragraph 34. The heart of the letter is the following two sentences: "The purpose of this letter is to ask again that you advise us immediately if you are willing to provide the financing pursuant to the lease. If you are willing, we propose to enter into negotiation to amend the ground lease appropriately." The very next day, Market Street Associates received from Erb a letter, dated August 10, turning down the original request for financing on the ground that it did not "meet our current investment criteria": the pension trust was not interested in making loans for less than $7 million. On August 22, Orenstein replied to Erb by letter, noting that his letter of August 10 and Erb's letter of August 16 had evidently crossed in the mails, expressing disappointment at the turn-down, and stating that Market Street Associates would seek financing elsewhere. That was the last contact between the parties until September 27, when Orenstein sent Erb a letter stating that Market Street Associates was exercising the option granted it by paragraph 34 to purchase the property upon the terms specified in that paragraph in the event that negotiations over financing broke down.

The pension trust refused to sell, and this suit to compel specific performance followed. Apparently the price computed by the formula in paragraph 34 is only $1 million. The market value must be higher, or Market Street Associates wouldn't be trying to coerce conveyance at the paragraph 34 price; whether it is as high as $3 million, however, the record does not reveal.

The district judge granted summary judgment for the pension trust on two grounds that he believed to be separate although closely related. The first was that, by failing in its correspondence with the pension trust to mention paragraph 34 of the lease, Market Street Associates had prevented the negotiations over financing that are a condition precedent to the lessee's exercise of the purchase option from taking place. Second, this same failure violated the duty of good faith, which the common law of Wisconsin, as of other states, reads into every contract.... In support of both grounds the judge emphasized a statement by Orenstein in his deposition that it had occurred to him that Erb mightn't know about paragraph 34, though this was unlikely (Orenstein testified) because Erb or someone else at the pension trust would probably check the file and discover the paragraph and realize that if the trust refused to negotiate over the request for financing, Market Street Associates, as Penney's assignee, would be entitled to walk off with the property for (perhaps) a song. The judge inferred that Market Street Associates didn't want financing from the pension trust—that it just wanted an opportunity to buy the property at a bargain price and hoped that the pension trust wouldn't realize the implications of turning down the request for financing. Market Street Associates should, the judge opined, have advised the pension trust that it was requesting financing pursuant to paragraph 34, so that the trust would understand the penalty for refusing to negotiate.

We begin our analysis by setting to one side two extreme contentions by the parties. The pension trust argues that the option to purchase created by paragraph 34 cannot be exercised until negotiations over financing break down; there were no negotiations; therefore they did not break down; therefore Market Street Associates had no right to exercise the option. This argument misreads the contract. Although the option to purchase is indeed contingent, paragraph 34 requires the pension trust, upon demand by the lessee for the financing of improvements worth at least $250,000, "to give reasonable consideration to providing the financing." The lessor who fails to give reasonable consideration and thereby prevents the negotiations from taking place is breaking the contract; and a contracting party cannot be allowed to use his own breach to gain an advantage by impairing the rights that the contract confers on the other party.... Often, it is true, if one party breaks the contract, the other can walk away from it without liability, can in other words exercise self-help.

But he is not required to follow that course. He can stand on his contract rights.

But what exactly are those rights in this case? The contract entitles the lessee to reasonable consideration of its request for financing, and only if negotiations over the request fail is the lessee entitled to purchase the property at the price computed in accordance with paragraph 34. It might seem therefore that the proper legal remedy for a lessor's breach that consists of failure to give the lessee's request for financing reasonable consideration would not be an order that the lessor sell the property to the lessee at the paragraph 34 price, but an order that the lessor bargain with the lessee in good faith. But we do not understand the pension trust to be arguing that Market Street Associates is seeking the wrong remedy. We understand it to be arguing that Market Street Associates has no possible remedy. That is an untenable position.

Market Street Associates argues, with equal unreason as it seems to us, that it could not have broken the contract because paragraph 34 contains no express requirement that in requesting financing the lessee mention the lease or paragraph 34 or otherwise alert the lessor to the consequences of his failing to give reasonable consideration to granting the request. There is indeed no such requirement (all that the contract requires is a demand). But no one says there is. The pension trust's argument, which the district judge bought, is that either as a matter of simple contract interpretation or under the compulsion of the doctrine of good faith, a provision requiring Market Street Associates to remind the pension trust of paragraph 34 should be read into the lease.

It seems to us that these are one ground rather than two. A court has to have a reason to interpolate a clause into a contract. The only reason that has been suggested here is that it is necessary to prevent Market Street Associates from reaping a reward for what the pension trust believes to have been Market Street's bad faith. So we must consider the meaning of the contract duty of "good faith." The Wisconsin cases are cryptic as to its meaning though emphatic about its existence, so we must cast our net wider. We do so mindful of Learned Hand's warning, that "such words as 'fraud,' 'good faith,' 'whim,' 'caprice,' 'arbitrary action,' and 'legal fraud' ... obscure the issue." *Thompson–Starrett Co. v. La Belle Iron Works,* 17 F.2d 536, 541 (2d Cir.1927). Indeed they do ...

The particular confusion to which the vaguely moralistic overtones of "good faith" give rise is the belief that every contract establishes a fiduciary relationship. A fiduciary is required to treat his principal as if the principal were he, and therefore he may not take advantage of the principal's incapacity, ignorance, inexperience, or even naivete.... If Market Street Associates were the fiduciary of General Electric Pension Trust, then (we may assume) it could not take advantage of Mr. Erb's apparent ignorance of paragraph 34, however exasperating Erb's failure to return Orenstein's phone calls was and however negligent Erb or his associates were in failing to read the lease before turning down Orenstein's request for financing.

But it is unlikely that Wisconsin wishes, in the name of good faith, to make every contract signatory his brother's keeper, especially when the brother is the immense and sophisticated General Electric Pension Trust, whose lofty indifference to small (= < $7 million) transactions is the signifier of its grandeur. In fact the law contemplates that people frequently will take advantage of the ignorance of those with whom they contract, without thereby incurring liability. *Restatement, supra,* § 161, comment d. The duty of honesty, of good faith even expansively conceived, is not a duty of candor. You can make a binding contract to purchase something you know your seller undervalues.... That of course is a question about formation, not performance, and the particular duty of good faith under examination here relates to the latter rather than to the former. But even after you have signed a contract, you are not obliged to become an altruist toward the other party and relax the terms if he gets into trouble in performing his side of the bargain.... Otherwise mere difficulty of performance would excuse a contracting party—which it does not....

But it is one thing to say that you can exploit your superior knowledge of the market—for if you cannot, you will not be able to recoup the investment you made in obtaining that knowledge—or that you are not required to spend money bailing out a contract partner who has gotten into trouble. It is another thing to say that you can take deliberate advantage of an oversight by your contract partner concerning his rights under the contract. Such taking advantage is not the exploitation of superior knowledge or the avoidance of unbargained-for expense; it is sharp dealing. Like theft, it has no social product, and also like theft it induces costly defensive expenditures, in the form of overelaborate disclaimers or investigations into the trustworthiness of a prospective contract partner, just as the prospect of theft induces expenditures on locks. See generally Steven J. Burton, "Breach of Contract and the Common Law Duty to Perform in Good Faith," 94 *Harv.L.Rev.* 369, 393 (1980).

The form of sharp dealing that we are discussing might or might not be actionable as fraud or deceit. That is a question of tort law and there the rule is that if the information is readily available to both parties the failure of one to disclose it to the other, even if done in the knowledge that the other party is acting on mistaken premises, is not actionable ..... All of these cases, however, * * * involve failure to disclose something in the negotiations leading up to the signing of the contract, rather than failure to disclose after the contract has been signed. * * * The distinction is important, as we explained in *Maksym v. Loesch,* 937 F.2d 1237, 1242 (7th Cir.1991). Before the contract is signed, the parties confront each other with a natural wariness. Neither expects the other to be particularly forthcoming, and therefore there is no deception when one is not. Afterwards the situation is different. The parties are now in a cooperative relationship the costs of which will be considerably reduced by a measure of trust. So each lowers his guard a bit, and now silence is more apt to be deceptive....

Moreover, this is a contract case rather than a tort case, and conduct that might not rise to the level of fraud may nonetheless violate the duty of good faith in dealing with one's contractual partners and thereby give rise to a remedy under contract law. Burton, *supra*, at 372 n. 17. This duty is, as it were, halfway between a fiduciary duty (the duty of *utmost* good faith) and the duty merely to refrain from active fraud. Despite its moralistic overtones it is no more the injection of moral principles into contract law than the fiduciary concept itself is.... It would be quixotic as well as presumptuous for judges to undertake through contract law to raise the ethical standards of the nation's business people. The concept of the duty of good faith like the concept of fiduciary duty is a stab at approximating the terms the parties would have negotiated had they foreseen the circumstances that have given rise to their dispute. The parties want to minimize the costs of performance. To the extent that a doctrine of good faith designed to do this by reducing defensive expenditures is a reasonable measure to this end, interpolating it into the contract advances the parties' joint goal.

It is true that an essential function of contracts is to allocate risk, and would be defeated if courts treated the materializing of a bargained-over, allocated risk as a misfortune the burden of which is required to be shared between the parties (as it might be within a family, for example) rather than borne entirely by the party to whom the risk had been allocated by mutual agreement. But contracts do not just allocate risk. They also (or some of them) set in motion a cooperative enterprise, which may to some extent place one party at the other's mercy. * * * The office of the doctrine of good faith is to forbid the kinds of opportunistic behavior that a mutually dependent, cooperative relationship might enable in the absence of rule. " 'Good faith' is a compact reference to an implied undertaking not to take opportunistic advantage in a way that could not have been contemplated at the time of drafting, and which therefore was not resolved explicitly by the parties." *Kham & Nate's Shoes No. 2, Inc. v. First Bank, supra,* 908 F.2d at 1357.

The contractual duty of good faith is thus not some newfangled bit of welfare-state paternalism or (*pace* Duncan Kennedy, "Form and Substance in Private Law Adjudication," 89 *Harv.L.Rev.* 1685, 1721 (1976)) the sediment of an altruistic strain in contract law, and we are therefore not surprised to find the essentials of the modern doctrine well established in nineteenth-century cases, ... * * *

The emphasis we are placing on postcontractual versus precontractual conduct helps explain the pattern that is observed when the duty of contractual good faith is considered in all its variety, encompassing not only good faith in the *performance* of a contract but also good faith in its *formation,* Summers, *supra,* at 220–32, and in its *enforcement.*... The formation or negotiation stage is precontractual, and here the duty is minimized. It is greater not only at the performance but also at the enforcement stage, which is also postcontractual.... * * * At the formation of the contract the parties are dealing in present realities; performance still lies in the future. As performance unfolds, circumstances change, often unforeseeably; the explicit terms of the contract become progressively less apt to the governance of the parties' relationship; and the role of implied conditions—and with it the scope and bite of the good-faith doctrine—grows.

We could of course do without the term "good faith," and maybe even without the doctrine. We could, as just suggested, speak instead of implied conditions necessitated by the unpredictability of the future at the time the contract was made. Farnsworth, "Good Faith Performance and Commercial Reasonableness under the Uniform Commercial Code," 30 *U.Chi.L.Rev.* 666, 670 (1963). Suppose a party has promised work to the promisee's "satisfaction." As Learned Hand explained, "he may refuse to look at the work, or to exercise any real judgment on it, in which case he has prevented performance and excused the condition." *Thompson–Starrett Co. v. La Belle Iron Works, supra,* 17 F.2d at 541 ..... That is, it was an implicit condition that the promisee examine the work to the extent necessary to determine whether it was satisfactory; otherwise the performing party would have been placing himself at the complete mercy of the promisee. The parties didn't write this condition into the contract either because they thought such behavior unlikely or failed to foresee it altogether. In just the same way—to switch to another familiar example of the operation of the duty of good faith—parties to a requirements contract surely do not intend that if the price of the product covered by the contract rises, the buyer shall be free to increase his "requirements" so that he can take advantage of the rise in the market price over the contract price to resell the product on the open market at a guaranteed profit.... If they fail to insert an express condition to this effect, the court will read it in, confident that the parties would have inserted the condition if they had known what the future held. Of similar character is the implied condition that an exclusive dealer will use his best efforts to promote the supplier's goods, since otherwise the exclusive feature of the dealership contract would place the supplier at the dealer's mercy. *Wood v. Duff–Gordon,* 222 N.Y. 88 (1917) (Cardozo, J.).

But whether we say that a contract shall be deemed to contain such implied conditions as are necessary to make sense of the contract, or that a contract obligates the parties to cooperate in its performance in "good faith" to the extent necessary to carry out the purposes of the contract, comes to much the same thing. They are different ways of formulating the overriding purpose of contract law, which is to give the parties what they would have stipulated for expressly if at the time of making the contract they had had complete knowledge of the future and the costs of negotiating and adding provisions to the contract had been zero.

The two formulations would have different meanings only if "good faith" were thought limited to "honesty in fact," an interpretation perhaps permitted but certainly not compelled by the Uniform Commercial Code, see Summers, *supra,* at 207–20—and anyway this is not a case governed by the UCC. We need not pursue this issue. The dispositive question in the present case is simply whether Market Street Associates tried to trick the pension trust and succeeded in doing so. If it did, this would be the type of opportunistic behavior in an ongoing contractual relationship that would violate the duty of good faith performance however the duty is formulated. There is much common sense in Judge Reynolds' conclusion that Market Street Associates did just that. The situation as he saw it was as follows. Market Street Associates didn't want financing from the pension trust (initially it had looked elsewhere, remember), and when it learned it couldn't get the financing without owning the property, it decided to try to buy the property. But the pension trust set a stiff price, so Orenstein decided to trick the pension trust into selling at the bargain price fixed in paragraph 34 by requesting financing and hoping that the pension trust would turn the request down without noticing the paragraph. His preliminary dealings with the pension trust made this hope a realistic one by revealing a sluggish and hidebound bureaucracy unlikely to have retained in its brontosaurus's memory, or to be able at short notice to retrieve, the details of a small lease made twenty years earlier. So by requesting financing without mentioning the lease Market Street Associates might well precipitate a refusal before the pension trust woke up to paragraph 34. It is true that Orenstein's second letter requested financing "pursuant to the lease." But when the next day he received a reply to his first letter indicating that the pension trust was indeed oblivious to paragraph 34, his response was to send a lulling letter designed to convince the pension trust that the matter was closed and could be forgotten. The stage was set for his thunderbolt: the notification the next month that Market Street Associates was taking up the option in paragraph 34. Only then did the pension trust look up the lease and discover that it had been had.

The only problem with this recital is that it construes the facts as favorably to the pension trust as the record will permit, and that of course is not the right standard for summary judgment. The facts must be construed as favorably to the nonmoving party, to Market Street Associates, as the record permits (that Market Street Associates filed its own motion for summary judgment is irrelevant, as we have seen). When that is done, a different picture emerges. On Market Street Associates' construal of the record, $3 million was a grossly excessive price for the property, and while $1 million might be a bargain it would not confer so great a windfall as to warrant an inference that if the pension trust had known about paragraph 34 it never would have turned down Market Street Associates' request for financing cold. And in fact the pension trust may have known about paragraph 34, and either it didn't care or it believed that unless the request mentioned that paragraph the pension trust would incur no liability by turning it down. Market Street Associates may have assumed and have been entitled to assume that in reviewing a request for financing from one of its lessees the pension trust would take the time to read the lease to see whether it bore on the request. Market Street Associates did not desire financing from the pension trust initially—that is undeniable—yet when it discovered that it could not get financing elsewhere unless it had the title to the property it may have realized that it would have to negotiate with the pension trust over financing before it could hope to buy the property at the price specified in the lease.

On this interpretation of the facts there was no bad faith on the part of Market Street Associates. It acted honestly, reasonably, without ulterior motive, in the face of circumstances as they actually and reasonably appeared to it. The fault was the pension trust's incredible inattention, which misled Market Street Associates into believing that the pension trust had no interest in financing the improvements regardless of the purchase option. We do not usually excuse contracting parties from failing to read and understand the contents of their contract; and in the end what this case comes down to—or so at least it can be strongly argued—is that an immensely sophisticated enterprise simply failed to read the contract. On the other hand, such enterprises make mistakes just like the rest of us, and deliberately to take advantage of your contracting partner's mistake during the performance stage (for we are not talking about taking advantage of superior knowledge at the formation stage) is a breach of good faith. To be able to correct your contract partner's mistake at zero cost to yourself, and decide not to do so, is a species of opportunistic behavior that the parties would have expressly forbidden in the contract had they foreseen it. The immensely long term of the lease amplified the possibility of errors but did not license either party to take advantage of them.

The district judge jumped the gun in choosing between these alternative characterizations. The essential issue bearing on Market Street Associates' good faith was Orenstein's state of mind, a type of inquiry that ordinarily cannot be concluded on summary judgment, and could not be here. If Orenstein believed that Erb knew or would surely find out about paragraph 34, it was not dishonest or opportunistic to fail to flag that paragraph, or even to fail to mention the lease, in his correspondence and (rare) conversations with Erb, especially given the uninterest in dealing with Market Street Associates that Erb fairly radiated. To decide what Orenstein believed, a trial is necessary. As for the pension trust's intimation that a bench trial (for remember that this is an equity case, since the only relief sought by the plaintiff is specific performance) will add no illumination beyond what the summary judgment proceeding has done, this overlooks the fact that at trial the judge will for the first time have a chance to see the witnesses whose depositions he has read, to hear their testimony elaborated, and to assess their believability.

The judgment is reversed and the case is remanded for further proceedings consistent with this opinion.

REVERSED AND REMANDED.

(C) EXERCISE OF RESERVED DISCRETION

Omni Group, Inc. v. Seattle–First National Bank
Court of Appeals of Washington, 1982.
Reprinted supra at 1037.

Billman v. Hensel
Court of Appeals of Indiana, Third District, 1979.
181 Ind.App. 272, 391 N.E.2d 671.

■ GARRARD, PRESIDING JUDGE.

The Hensels, as sellers, entered into a contract to sell their home to the Billmans (the buyers) for $54,000 cash. A condition of the contract was the ability of the buyers to secure a conventional mortgage on the property for not less than $35,000 within thirty (30) days. When the buyers did not complete the purchase, the sellers commenced this suit to secure a thousand dollars ($1,000) earnest money/liquidated damage deposit required by the contract. The buyers defended upon the basis that they were relieved from performing. The case was tried by the court and judgment was entered in favor of the sellers. The sole question raised on appeal is whether the court properly determined that the buyers were not excused from performance. We affirm.

The parties do not dispute, nor do we, that the "subject to financing" clause constituted a condition precedent in the contract.... It is also undisputed that the buyers did not, in fact, secure a mortgage loan commitment within the contractual period.

The evidence at trial disclosed that on September 30, the day following execution of the contract, Mr. Billman met with an agent of the Lincoln National Bank and Trust Company of Fort Wayne. Billman was told that he could not obtain a mortgage loan of $35,000 unless he could show he had the difference between the purchase price and the amount of the mortgage. After totaling his available resources, including a 90 day short term note for $10,000 representing the proceeds from the sale of his present home, Billman was $6,500 short of the required $19,000 balance. On October 1st, the Hensels deposited the earnest money check into their account. Billman called Mr. Hensel to tell him that he was close on the financing and requested permission to show the home to his parents on October 3rd.

The Billmans and Mr. Billman's parents went through the house by themselves. The Hensels overheard Mr. Billman's father tell Mr. Billman that "I think I'd be careful with this . . . I'm afraid of it." The Billmans returned without the parents later that same day. Mr. Billman told the Hensels that the deal was off because his parents were unable to loan him the $5,000 needed to complete his financing. The next day, Mr. Hensel told Mr. Billman that he would reduce the price of the home by $5,000. Mr. Billman refused to consider such a reduction, stating that he still needed another $1,500. The Billmans did not deposit funds to cover the check given as earnest money, and Mrs. Billman stopped payment on the check on October 4th.

The Billmans contacted only one financial institution concerning a mortgage loan, and made no formal loan application whatever. They limited discussion to a loan of $35,000 although they subsequently claimed to have required more. When Billman told Hensels he was canceling the sale, he stated the reason was that his parents would not give him $5,000 for the purchase. However, prior to that time he had not mentioned relying upon any assistance and had instead assured Hensels they had all the money needed to complete the sale. Then when Hensels offered to reduce the price by the figure Billman had mentioned, he stated he needed yet an additional $1,500.

We believe the better view to be that such subject to financing clauses impose upon the buyers an implied obligation to make a reasonable and good faith effort to satisfy the condition. . . .

Such an interpretation not only comports with the reasonable expectations of the parties, but is a logical extension of the sound rule of contract law that a promisor cannot rely upon the existence of a condition precedent to excuse his performance where the promisor, himself, prevents performance of the condition. . . .

We recognize that the First District's decision in Blakley v. Currence (1977), Ind.App., 361 N.E.2d 921 refused to impose such an obligation where the condition was not expressed in terms of the *ability* of the buyers to secure financing. We need not reach that question on the facts before us, although we believe the rule in *Blakley* should be limited to the facts there present.

Here the condition imposed was that the buyers be *able* to secure a conventional mortgage of *not less than* $35,000. From the evidence recited above the court was justified in concluding that the sellers had carried their burden of proof by establishing that the buyers did not make a reasonable and good faith effort to secure the necessary financing,[1] and therefore could not rely upon the condition to relieve their duty to perform.

Affirmed.

Neumiller Farms, Inc. v. Cornett

Supreme Court of Alabama, 1979.
368 So.2d 272.

■ SHORES, JUSTICE.

Jonah D. Cornett and Ralph Moore, Sellers, were potato farmers in DeKalb County, Alabama. Neumiller Farms, Inc., Buyer, was a corporation engaged in brokering potatoes from the growers to the makers of potato chips. The controversy concerns Buyer's rejection of nine loads of potatoes out of a contract calling for twelve loads. A jury returned a verdict of $17,500 for Sellers based on a breach of contract. Buyer appealed. We affirm.

From the evidence, the jury could have found the following:

On March 3, 1976, the parties signed a written contract whereby Sellers agreed to deliver twelve loads of chipping potatoes to Buyer during July and August, 1976, and Buyer agreed to pay $4.25 per hundredweight. The contract required that the potatoes be United States Grade No. 1 and "chipt [sic] to buyer satisfaction." As the term was used in this contract, a load of potatoes contains 430 hundredweight and is valued at $1,827.50.

---

1. Note that ordinarily this burden will fall upon the buyer who must bring suit seeking return of his earnest money.

(Market Price Drop)

Buyer accepted only 9 loads

Seller bought from diff. Guy + Buyer still upset ↳ even though Seller had bought from ~~buyer~~ Hartline prior !

✱ Buyer → excuse b/c of price drop

Sellers' potato crop yielded twenty to twenty-four loads of potatoes and Buyer accepted three of these loads without objection. At that time, the market price of chipping potatoes was $4.25 per hundredweight. Shortly thereafter, the market price declined to $2.00 per hundredweight.

When Sellers tendered additional loads of potatoes, Buyer refused acceptance, saying the potatoes would not "chip" satisfactorily. Sellers responded by having samples of their crop tested by an expert from the Cooperative Extension Service of Jackson County, Alabama, who reported that the potatoes were suitable in all respects. After receiving a letter demanding performance of the contract, Buyer agreed to "try one more load." Sellers then tendered a load of potatoes which had been purchased from another grower, Roy Hartline. Although Buyer's agent had recently purchased potatoes from Hartline at $2.00 per hundredweight, he claimed dissatisfaction with potatoes from the same fields when tendered by Sellers at $4.25 per hundredweight. Apparently the jury believed this testimony outweighed statements by Buyer's agents that Sellers' potatoes were diseased and unfit for "chipping."

Subsequently, Sellers offered to purchase the remaining nine loads of potatoes from other growers in order to fulfill their contract. Buyer's agent refused this offer, saying " ... 'I'm not going to accept any more of your potatoes. If you load any more I'll see that they're turned down.' ... 'I can buy potatoes all day for $2.00.' " No further efforts were made by Sellers to perform the contract.

At the time of Buyer's final refusal, Sellers had between seventeen and twenty-one loads of potatoes unharvested in their fields. Approximately four loads were sold in Chattanooga, Tennessee; Atlanta, Georgia; and local markets in DeKalb County. Sellers' efforts to sell their potato crop to other buyers were hampered by poor market conditions. Considering all of the evidence, the jury could properly have found that Sellers' efforts to sell the potatoes, after Buyer's final refusal to accept delivery, were reasonable and made in good faith.

This case presents three questions: 1) Was Buyer's refusal to accept delivery of Sellers' potatoes a breach of contract? 2) If so, what was the proper measure of Sellers' damages? and 3) Was the $17,500 jury verdict within the amount recoverable by Sellers under the proper measure of damages?

§ 7–2–703, Code of Alabama 1975 (UCC), specifies an aggrieved seller may recover for a breach of contract "Where the buyer *wrongfully* rejects ... goods...." (Emphasis Added) We must determine whether there was evidence from which the jury could find that the Buyer acted wrongfully in rejecting delivery of Sellers' potatoes.

A buyer may reject delivery of goods if either the goods or the tender of delivery fails to conform to the contract. § 7–2–601, Code of Alabama 1975. In the instant case, Buyer did not claim the tender was inadequate. Rather, Buyer asserted the potatoes failed to conform to the requirements of the contract; i.e., the potatoes would not chip to buyer satisfaction.

The law requires such a claim of dissatisfaction to be made in good faith, rather than in an effort to escape a bad bargain. . . .

Buyer, in the instant case, is a broker who deals in farm products as part of its occupation and, therefore, is a "merchant" with respect to its dealings in such goods. § 7–2–104, Code of Alabama 1975. In testing the good faith of a merchant, § 7–2–103, Code of Alabama 1975, requires " . . . honesty in fact and the observance of reasonable commercial standards of fair dealing in the trade." A claim of dissatisfaction by a merchant-buyer of fungible goods must be evaluated using an objective standard to determine whether the claim is made in good faith. Because there was evidence that the potatoes would "chip" satisfactorily, the jury was not required to accept Buyer's subjective claim to the contrary. A rejection of goods based on a claim of dissatisfaction, which is not made in good faith, is ineffectual and constitutes a breach of contract for which damages are recoverable.

* * *

[The court concluded that the trial court had properly applied the measure of damages in UCC 2–708 and affirmed the jury verdict for the seller in the amount of $17,500.]

NOTES

(1) As *Omni Group* indicates, where the agreement reserves discretion in performance to one party, the first question may be whether there is a contract at all. If, because of the reserved discretion, the apparent promise is found to be illusory, there is no consideration. The combination, however, of a commitment to do something and the general duty of good faith in performance, is normally enough to provide consideration. See, e.g., Bleecher v. Conte, 29 Cal.3d 345, 213 Cal.Rptr. 852, 698 P.2d 1154 (1981), where, in a complicated land transaction, the court found consideration in the buyer's promise to "do everything in their power to expedite the recordation of the final map" and to "proceed with diligence." But see Artex, Inc. v. Omaha Edible Oils, Inc., 231 Neb. 281, 436 N.W.2d 146 (1989) (contract interpreted to give defendant absolute discretion to refuse work).

(2) *Condition of Personal Satisfaction: Subjective or Objective Standard?* When a promisor conditions a duty to perform upon being satisfied with the other party's performance or "with respect to something else," see Restatement (Second) § 228, the expression of dissatisfaction must be in good faith. A common example of bad faith is where the promisor is dissatisfied with the overall bargain rather than the other party's performance. If, for example, the market price for goods has dropped well below the contract price, the buyer may claim dissatisfaction with the seller's performance in order to wriggle out of a bad deal. A more complex problem is the standard of good faith to be insisted upon—should it be "subjective" or "objective?" What was the test applied in *Mattei v. Hopper*, discussed in *Omni Group*, and in *Neumiller Farms?* In either *Omni Group* or *Neumiller*, could an expression of honest dissatisfaction have avoided liability under the contract? Under Restatement (Second) § 228, if it is "practicable to determine whether a reasonable person in the position of the obligor would be satisfied, an interpretation is preferred

under which the condition occurs if such a reasonable person in the position of the obligor would be satisfied."

For cases applying the "objective" test for measuring conditions of satisfaction, see Kennedy Associates, Inc. v. Fischer, 667 P.2d 174 (Alaska 1983) (trial court erred in applying subjective good faith standard to lender's dissatisfaction with condition of commercial rental property under clause making property "subject to approval"); Empire South, Inc. v. Repp, 51 Wash.App. 868, 756 P.2d 745, 748–750 (1988) (reasonable person in buyer's position would have been satisfied with used goods); Hall v. W.L. Brady Investments, Inc., 684 S.W.2d 379, 387 (Mo.App.1984) (question whether reasonable person would be satisfied with value of collateral for security).

In *Kennedy Associates,* supra, the court stated:

> The question of whether a court should utilize an objective rather than a subjective standard of good faith in gauging the validity of reliance upon a satisfaction clause dependent upon commercial judgment is one of first impression in this jurisdiction. It is well-established that where the condition requires satisfaction as to commercial value or quality, operative fitness, or mechanical utility, an objective standard is to be used in determining whether the clause has been satisfied ... On the other hand, if a judgment dependent upon personal taste or fancy, such as design of a dress or execution of a portrait is involved, a subjective test is appropriate ... The difficulty of the case before us lies in the fact that it arises in a commercial context but involves a judgment dependent upon consideration of a multiplicity of factors.... We conclude that the superior court should have applied an objective standard in determining whether the paragraph 14(i) condition was satisfied. Our choice of standard is predicated on the principle that a forfeiture of contractual rights is to be avoided, whenever possible. Therefore, just as "conditions" are to be construed as covenants, unless the parties have clearly agreed otherwise, so must a preference be given to application of an objective test of reasonable satisfaction whenever practicable and not precluded by the express terms of the parties' agreement. 667 P.2d at 181–82.

(3) If, in *Neumiller,* the buyer's dissatisfaction had been in good faith, the seller would have failed to deliver conforming goods. The buyer, then, could reject the tender of delivery, UCC 2–601, cancel the contract and pursue remedies for breach. See UCC 2–711(1). Since the dissatisfaction was in bad faith, the rejection was "wrongful," enabling the seller to pursue remedies for breach under UCC 2–703. We will have more to say about the buyer's remedies of rejection and revocation of acceptance later on in Chapter Seven.

(4) See, generally, James Brook, *Conditions of Personal Satisfaction in the Law of Contracts,* 27 N.Y.L.Sch.L.Rev. 103 (1981).

Comment: Lender Liability And The Duty To Act In Good Faith

A specialized context from which good faith disputes arise is the relationship between a lender and its customers; the termination of a line of credit by the lender may be bad faith, subjecting the lender to liability for the customer's commercial losses but not exemplary damages. See Reid v. Key Bank of Southern Maine, Inc., 821 F.2d 9 (1st Cir.1987), finding bad faith under the "subjective" definition of good faith (honesty in fact), where a minority customers line of credit was abruptly terminated without notice in circumstances where there was a continuing relationship between the parties, the customer was not in default and his overall financial position has not changed. Two other leading cases in the development of bad faith "lender liability" are K.M.C. Co., Inc. v. Irving Trust Co., 757 F.2d 752 (6th Cir.1985) (bad faith refusal to make advance under "discretionary" clause) and 999 v. C.I.T. Corp., 776 F.2d 866 (9th Cir.1985) (bad faith refusal to honor commitment to finance).

Assuming that a contract exists between the parties and the contract does not clearly give the lender power to take action at any time for any reason, recurring questions include the standard of good faith to be applied and whether bad faith has been proved in the particular case. See, e.g., United States v. H & S Realty Co., 837 F.2d 1 (1st Cir.1987) (no proof that bank had dishonest motives or intent to harm customer); Garrett v. BankWest, Inc., 459 N.W.2d 833 (S.D.1990) (refusal to make payment not bad faith where agreement not breached and refusal neither violated the spirit of the contract nor the justified expectations of the parties); Gilbert Central Corp. v. Overland National Bank, 232 Neb. 778, 442 N.W.2d 372 (1989) (refusal of lender to perform commitment raises genuine issue of material fact on good faith); United States National Bank of Oregon v. Boge, 102 Or.App. 262, 794 P.2d 801 (1990) (delay in responding to customer's request for information not bad faith); Price v. Wells Fargo Bank, 213 Cal.App.3d 465, 261 Cal.Rptr. 735 (1989) (absent fiduciary duty, "hard line" in repayment negotiations with informed customer not bad faith). See, generally, Patterson, *Good Faith, Lender Liability and Discretionary Acceleration: Of Llewellyn, Wittgenstein, and the Uniform Commercial Code*, 68 Tex.L.Rev. 169 (1989); Lawrence, *Lender Control Liability: An Analytical Model Illustrated with Applications to the Relational Theory of Secured Financing*, 62 S.Cal.L.Rev. 1387 (1989). See also, Chaitman, *The Ten Commandments for Avoiding Lender Liability*, 22 U.C.C.L.J. 3 (1989).

At issue in these cases is the scope of the lender's duty to act in good faith. Should the duty be subjective or objective? If objective, should it incorporate community standards of fair dealing, including concerns about racial discrimination, see Burton, *Racial Discrimination in Contract Performance: Patterson and a State Law Alternative*, 25 Harv.Civ.Rights Civ. Lib.L.Rev. 431 (1990), or should the test be limited to an interpretation of the contract terms, allowing the market to resolve other aspects of the dispute? See Comment, *What's So Good About Good Faith? The Good Faith Performance Obligation in Commercial Lending*, 55 U.Chi.L.Rev. 1335 (1988). Or, is there a middle ground?

Consider the argument of Professor Dan Fischel, which follows

Courts faced with a lender liability case must decide whether the challenged conduct of the lender was consistent with the agreement between the parties. This inquiry is primarily a matter of contract interpretation. What remains unclear, however, is whether courts should look beyond the contract itself and the usual tools of contract interpretation to some other body of authority in order to define the rights and duties between the parties. This question is important because borrowers in recent lender liability cases have argued that lenders' conduct violated the duty of good faith and fiduciary duties to the borrower. However, precisely what these concepts mean and what their relationship is to contract law is not clearly understood....

The doctrine of good faith has a long history in contract law. Section 1–203 of the Uniform Commercial Code provides that "[e]very contract or duty within this Act imposes an obligation of good faith in its performance or enforcement." Similarly, Section 205 of the Restatement (Second) of Contracts states that a duty of good faith should be imposed in all contracts.

However, notwithstanding the extensive literature on the subject, no consensus exists on precisely what the duty of good faith means. At one extreme, some commentators have argued that the duty should be limited to a prohibition of intentional dishonesty. Under this view, the duty of good faith adds little to the prohibition against fraud other than a vague exhortation for moral behavior. At the other extreme, several commentators have concluded that good faith should be interpreted expansively to incorporate community standards of fairness and decency. The obvious difficulty with this position is the lack of any accepted understanding of the meaning of these terms. Moreover, this lack of content creates an added risk that the fairness and decency standard will be applied arbitrarily to the detriment of lenders and borrowers alike. For example, a borrower-plaintiff might be able to invalidate default provisions used by borrowers to obtain more favorable credit terms on the grounds that they are "unfair," but this act would ultimately hurt borrowers as a class by raising the cost of credit.

An intermediate position is to interpret the duty of good faith as equivalent to a prohibition of opportunistic behavior. Under this view, lenders are entitled to the benefit of their bargain but are precluded from using contractual terms as a pretense for extracting benefits for which they have not bargained. For example, a lender ... could terminate funding if the default risk increased, but, absent a risk increase, the duty of good faith would prevent the same lender from threatening to terminate funding in order to force the borrower to pay a higher interest rate.

Once again, the rationale for imposing a duty of good faith on lenders relates to the impossibility of drafting a contract covering every possible contingency. If contracts could be negotiated and enforced without any cost, the parties could negotiate an agreement which would preclude attempts by the lender to behave opportunistically. Because of the costs of negotiating and enforcing agreements, however, the parties cannot prevent all opportunistic behavior by contract. Thus the duty of good faith acts as an implied contractual term to achieve what the parties themselves cannot given the costs involved.

While this interpretation of the duty of good faith has a certain appeal, it is not without difficulty. The problem is that distinguishing opportunistic from non-opportunistic behavior can be very complicated if not impossible. A lender will never concede that its actions were designed to obtain a benefit not bargained for in the initial agreement. On the contrary, the lender will claim that its refusal to continue funding was based on its assessment of the debtor and the probability of default. Moreover, not only will distinguishing between these two explanations be difficult, but also the attempt to distinguish them will impair the contractual protection given to the lender in the first instance.

Recall that provisions giving the lender sole discretion whether to continue funding and to call any amounts outstanding are best understood as bonding mechanisms used by the borrower to obtain more favorable credit terms. The strength of the bond, however, is weakened if the borrower can argue to a court that the exercise of discretion granted to the lender by the agreement was not done in good faith. This recourse defeats one of the key features of the bond: that the lender, and not a court, decides whether to continue the relationship with a particular borrower. On the other hand, allowing the lender absolute discretion, as discussed above, creates an incentive for the lender to behave opportunistically.

Thus there is a trade-off. The more absolute the discretion of the lender, the stronger the bond of the borrower but the greater the incentive of the lender to behave opportunistically. Conversely, the more expansive the interpretation of the duty of good faith to control opportunistic behavior by the lender, the weaker is the bond of the borrower and the less able the borrower is to use the bond to obtain more favorable credit terms.

Daniel Fischel, *The Economics of Lender Liability*, 99 Yale L.J. 131, 140–42 (1989).

Feld v. Henry S. Levy & Sons, Inc.

Court of Appeals of New York, 1975.
37 N.Y.2d 466, 373 N.Y.S.2d 102, 335 N.E.2d 320.

■ COOKE, JUDGE.

Plaintiff operates a business known as the Crushed Toast Company and defendant is engaged in the wholesale bread baking business. They entered into a written contract, as of June 19, 1968, in which defendant agreed to sell and plaintiff to purchase "all bread crumbs produced by the Seller in its factory at 115 Thames Street, Brooklyn, New York, during the period commencing June 19, 1968, and terminating June 18, 1969", the agreement to "be deemed automatically renewed thereafter for successive renewal periods of one year" with the right to either party to cancel by giving not less than six months notice to the other by certified mail. No notice of cancellation was served. Additionally, pursuant to a contract stipulation, a faithful performance bond was delivered by plaintiff at the inception of the contractual relationship, and a bond continuation certificate was later submitted for the yearly term commencing June 19, 1969.

Bread Crumbs are a made item

Interestingly, the term "bread crumbs" does not refer to crumbs that may flake off bread; rather, they are a manufactured item, starting with stale or imperfectly appearing loaves and followed by removal of labels, processing through two grinders, the second of which effects a finer granulation, insertion into a drum in an oven for toasting and, finally, bagging of the finished product.

Crumb making became too uneconomical

change Price?

6 ¢ to 7 ¢ ?

Subsequent to the making of the agreement, a substantial quantity of bread crumbs, said to be over 250 tons, were sold by defendant to plaintiff but defendant stopped crumb production on about May 15, 1969. There was proof by defendant's comptroller that the oven was too large to accommodate the drum, that it was stated that the operation was "very uneconomical", but after said date of cessation no steps were taken to obtain more economical equipment. The toasting oven was intentionally broken down, then partially rebuilt, then completely dismantled in the summer of 1969 and, thereafter, defendant used the space for a computer room. It appears, without dispute, that defendant indicated to plaintiff at different times that the former would resume bread crumb production if the contract price of 6 cents per pound be changed to 7 cents, and also that, after the crumb making machinery was dismantled, defendant sold the raw materials used in making crumbs to animal food manufacturers.

Special Term denied plaintiff's motion for summary judgment on the issue of liability and turned down defendant's counter-request for a summary judgment of dismissal. From the Appellate Division's order of affirmance, by a divided court, both parties appeal.

Output K = Sell Goods or Services a party may produce or perform ...

2-306 (1)

Act in GF to perform

Defendant contends that the contract did not require defendant to manufacture bread crumbs, but merely to sell those it did, and, since none were produced after the demise of the oven, there was no duty to then deliver and, consequently from then on, no liability on its part. Agreements to sell all the goods or services a party may produce or perform to another party are commonly referred to as "output" contracts and they usually serve a useful commercial purpose in minimizing the burdens of product marketing (see 1 Williston, Contracts [3d ed.], § 104A). The Uniform Commercial Code rejects the ideas that an output contract is lacking in mutuality or that it is unenforceable because of indefiniteness in that a quantity for the term is not specified.... Uniform Commercial Code, [2–306(1), comment] states in part: "Under this Article, a contract for output * * * is not too indefinite since it is held to mean the actual good faith output * * * of the particular party. Nor does such a contract lack mutuality of obligation since, under this section, the party who will determine quantity is required to operate his plant or conduct his business in good faith and according to commercial standards of fair dealing in the trade so that his output * * * will proximate a reasonably foreseeable figure." ...

The real issue in this case is whether the agreement carries with it an implication that defendant was obligated to continue to manufacture bread crumbs for the full term. Section 2–306 of the Uniform Commercial Code, entitled "Output, Requirements and Exclusive Dealings" provides:

"(1) A term which measures the quantity by the output of the seller or the requirements of the buyer means such actual output or requirements as may occur in good faith except that no quantity unreasonably disproportionate to any stated estimate or in the absence of a stated estimate to any normal or otherwise comparable prior output or requirements may be tendered or demanded.

"(2) *A lawful agreement* by either the seller or the buyer *for exclusive dealing* in the kind of goods concerned *imposes* unless otherwise agreed an obligation *by the seller to use best efforts to supply the goods* and by the buyer to use best efforts to promote their sale." (Emphasis supplied.)

The Official Comment thereunder reads in part: "Subsection (2), on exclusive dealing, makes explicit the commercial rule embodied in this Act under which the parties to such contracts are held to have impliedly, even when not expressly, bound themselves to use reasonable diligence as well as good faith in their performance of the contract. * * * An exclusive dealing agreement brings into play all of the good faith aspects of the output and requirement problems of subsection (1). It also raises questions of insecurity and right to adequate assurance under this Article."

Section 2–306 is consistent with prior New York case law.... Under the Uniform Commercial Code, the commercial background and intent must be read into the language of any agreement and good faith is demanded in the performance of that agreement ... , and, under the decisions relating to output contracts, it is clearly the general rule that good faith cessation of production terminates any further obligations thereunder and excuses further performance by the party discontinuing....

This is not a situation where defendant ceased its main operation of bread baking.... Rather, defendant contends in a conclusory fashion that it was "uneconomical" or "economically not feasible" for it to continue to make bread crumbs. Although plaintiff observed in his motion papers that defendant claimed it was not economically feasible to make the crumbs, plaintiff did not admit that as a fact. In any event, "economic feasibility", an expression subject to many interpretations, would not be a precise or reliable test.

There are present here intertwined questions of fact, whether defendant performed in good faith and whether it stopped its manufacture of bread crumbs in good faith, neither of which can be resolved properly on this record. The seller's duty to remain in crumb production is a matter calling for a close scrutiny of its motives (1 Hawkland, A Transactional Guide to the Uniform Commercial Code, p. 52, see, also, p. 48), confined here by the papers to financial reasons. It is undisputed that defendant leveled its crumb making machinery only after plaintiff refused to agree to a price higher than that specified in the agreement and that it then sold the

no #'s
to tell if
it wasn't
feasible

raw materials to manufacturers of animal food. There are before us no componential figures indicating the actual cost of the finished bread crumbs to defendant, statements as to the profits derived or the losses sustained, or data specifying the net or gross return realized from the animal food transactions.

The parties by their contract gave the right of cancellation to either by providing for a six months' notice to the other. The apparent purpose of such a stipulation was to provide an opportunity to either the seller or buyer to conclude their dealings in the event that the transactions were not as profitable or advantageous as desired or expected, or for any other reason. Correspondingly, such a notice would also furnish the receiver of it a chance to secure another outlet or source of supply, as the case might be. Short of such a cancellation, defendant was expected to continue to perform in good faith and could cease production of the bread crumbs, a single facet of its operation, only in good faith. Obviously, a bankruptcy or genuine imperiling of the very existence of its entire business caused by the production of the crumbs would warrant cessation of production of that item; the yield of less profit from its sale than expected would not. Since bread crumbs were but a part of defendant's enterprise and since there was a contractual right of cancellation, good faith required continued production until cancellation, even if there be no profit. In circumstances such as these and without more, defendant would be justified, in good faith, in ceasing production of the single item prior to cancellation only if its losses from continuance would be more than trivial, which, overall, is a question of fact.

The order of the Appellate Division should be affirmed, without costs.

NOTES

(1) The *Feld* case was governed by Section 2–306(1) of the UCC. To what extent is the exercise of discretion by an "output" seller and a "requirements" buyer governed by circumstances existing at the time of contracting? What test(s) does the court use to define bad faith at the time of performance? In any case, is the approach consistent with the view that bad faith exists when either the seller or buyer exercises discretion to recapture opportunities foregone at the time of contracting?

(2) *The Case of Good Faith but Disproportionate Demand.* Seller and Buyer enter a five-year "requirements" contract. During the first three years, Buyer ordered and Seller supplied an average of 10,000 units. Thereafter, there was a sharp turndown in the market. During the fourth year, Buyer ordered 1,000 units and in the fifth year, no units were ordered. Seller, conceding that Buyer was in good faith, argues that the orders in both years were "substantially disproportionate" to orders during the first three years. Accordingly, under UCC 2–306(1), Buyer was in breach for the last two years. How should the court rule? See Posner, J. in Empire Gas Corp. v. American Bakeries Co., 840 F.2d 1333 (7th Cir.1988) (suggesting buyer has no liability because good faith is not limited by substantial disproportion language); Orange & Rockland Utilities v. Amerada Hess Corp., 59 A.D.2d 110, 397 N.Y.S.2d 814 (1977) (buyer's

decision under requirements contract to take advantage of its cheap supply of oil by dramatically increasing its requirements was not made in good faith). Comment, *And Then There Were None: Requirements Contracts and the Buyer Who Does Not Buy,* 64 Wash.L.Rev. 871 (1989).

(3) *Output contracts.* In Canusa Corporation v. A & R Lobosco, Inc., 986 F.Supp. 723 (E.D.N.Y.1997), the parties entered into a five year output contract in which there was an "estimate" that Seller would ship "at a minimum" 1,500 tons of old news print (ONP 8) per month. Seller never met this estimate and, after extended discussions and an attempt to modify, the relationship broke down and Buyer sued Seller for damages based upon the quantity in the estimate. There was evidence, however, that the amounts actually tendered were Seller's output in good faith. The court held that in an output contract under UCC 2–306(1), good faith rather than the estimate controlled Seller's obligations: otherwise "adherence to the estimate in the contract would essentially convert all output contracts with an estimate into fixed contracts." This interpretation was extracted from the reasoning of several cases dealing with UCC 2–306:

> First as the *Feld* court [*Feld v. Henry S. Levy & Sons, Inc.,* reprinted supra] noted, good faith is the general standard by which output contracts are measured.... Second, as the *Empire Gas* court [*Empire Gas Corp. v. American Bakeries Co.,* cited in note 2 above] found, the "unreasonably disproportionate" language in sec. 2–306 is a specific construction of good faith in the context of increased output or demand, and has no relationship to a good faith analysis of a decrease.... In a requirements contract, the seller takes the risk that the buyer may in good faith reduce its requirements to zero ... Given the premise that a seller will want to maximize its output, the good faith standard provides a sufficient test to measure a reducing seller's performance against.... So too, in an output contract, the buyer takes the risk that the seller may reduce its production to zero.... Applying good faith rather than an estimate does not give a seller an unbargained for advantage; rather, it merely preserves the essential character of contracts that lack a fixed term, albeit through the somewhat elusive concept of good faith.

On the issues posed by UCC 2–306 and more, see Victor P. Goldberg, *Discretion in Long–Term Open Quantity Contracts: Reigning in Good Faith,* 35 U.C. Davis L. Rev. 319 (2002) (suggesting tailor-made contract clauses to reduce uncertainty without precluding flexibility).

PROBLEM: THE CASE OF THE URANIUM OXIDE DEBACLE

In May, 1976, S, a manufacturer, and B, a utility, entered into a ten year contract for the supply of uranium oxide, a fuel source for nuclear reactors. B agreed to purchase 50% of the annual output of S's plant at the higher of two prices, either a fixed price of $35 per pound subject to escalation based upon production costs, or an adjusted market price, then $37 per pound. S's factory had a capacity of 600,000 pounds per year. During the first five years of the contract, S averaged 500,000 pounds per year in output. B took and paid for an average of 250,000 pounds per year. The balance of the output went to meet the "requirements" of C, a prime contractor with the United States. In the "requirements" contract with C, it was estimated that the government would need and C would order from S between 200,000 and 250,000 pounds per year. In May, 1981, the market price of uranium oxide, after a 12 month steady decline, bottomed out at $20 per pound. The escalated price in the contract between S and B, however, was at $39 per pound. At the same time, B's requirements for uranium oxide had dropped off due to a slow down in the construction of nuclear reactors. In effect, B was paying $39 per pound for goods worth $20 on the open market and could use only 100,000 of the 250,000 delivered. In June, 1981, the United States terminated its contract with C for convenience under a clause in the government contract. C informed S that, since it no longer had requirements, it was cancelling its contract. At the same time, B had requested S either to reduce the quantity of goods produced or to grant an adjustment in the price. S refused and, from June, 1981 until June, 1982, S continued to produce uranium oxide at previous levels, some 500,000 pounds per year. S shipped 50% of the output to B and stored the excess against a time when the market would improve. S claimed that it was more efficient to continue production at the previous output even though it had no current customers who would take the excess over B's contract. Consider the following questions.

(1) S is considering a suit against C for breach of contract. If suit were filed, what are the probabilities of success?

(2) B, upon learning that C had canceled, refused to take and pay for 50% of S's output, claiming that S's maintaining the pre-cancellation level of output was a breach of contract. Is B correct?

Comment: Effect of "Best Efforts" Agreement on Contracts for Indefinite Quantity

The fact that the parties have entered an "output" or a "requirements" contract does not necessarily mean that one party must use "best efforts" to have output or requirements. To impose that obligation, the parties must agree to use "best efforts" in addition to satisfying their obligation to perform the contract in good faith. That obligation may be found in the bargain, see Perma Research and Development v. Singer Co., 542 F.2d 111 (2d Cir.1976), cert. denied 429 U.S. 987, 97 S.Ct. 507, 50 L.Ed.2d 598 (1976) ("best efforts" obligation implied), or presumed from the fact that the parties have entered into an "exclusive dealing" contract. Thus, UCC 2–306(2) provides that a "lawful agreement by either the seller or the buyer for exclusive dealing in the kind of goods concerned imposes unless otherwise agreed an obligation by the seller to use best efforts to supply the goods and by the buyer to use best efforts to promote their sale."

The question whether a party has used "best efforts" in a particular dispute has bothered the courts and commentators. See Allan Farnsworth, *On Trying to Keep One's Promises: The Duty of Best Efforts in Contract Law*, 46 U.Pitt.L.Rev. 117 (1983). If the parties have not specified the level of "best efforts" in the contract, the courts have, in most cases, applied an objective standard and asked whether the defendant has made reasonable efforts in the circumstances. See, e.g., Bloor v. Falstaff Brewing Corp., 601 F.2d 609 (2d Cir.1979); Victor P. Goldberg, *In Search of Best Efforts:*

Reinterpreting Bloor v. Falstaff, 44 St. Louis U. L.J. 1465 (2000); Goetz & Scott, *Principles of Relational Contracts,* 67 Va.L.Rev. 1089, 1149–50 (1981) (arguing that "best efforts" should require that level of effort "necessary to maximize the joint net product flowing from the ... relationship.") This is an important inquiry for both questions of liability and remedy. Thus, if the defendant has no duty to use "best efforts" or has satisfied that duty and is otherwise in good faith, there is no breach of contract. If, however, the defendant is in good faith but has not used "best efforts," the plaintiff should recover damages. As Judge Posner put it in Agfa–Gevaert, A.G. v. A.B. Dick Co., 879 F.2d 1518, 1523–24 (7th Cir.1989):

> When a distributor obligates himself to use his best efforts to promote a product and then breaks his contract, the remedial question is indeed how much he would have sold had he used his best efforts, implying diligent and energetic promotion.... But when he agrees merely to take his requirements of a particular product from his seller, and breaks his contract by satisfying those requirements elsewhere, the question is how much he bought from his alternative supplier(s) ... What he required, he bought; what he did not buy, he must not have required.

(D) MODIFICATION

Angel v. Murray

Supreme Court of Rhode Island, 1974.
Supra at 87.

Roth Steel Products v. Sharon Steel Corp.

United States Court of Appeals, Sixth Circuit, 1983.
705 F.2d 134.

[In November, 1972, Roth contracted to purchase 200 tons of "hot rolled" steel per month from Sharon through December, 1973. The price was $148 per ton. Sharon also "indicated" that it could sell "hot rolled" steel on an "open schedule" basis for $140 and discussed the "probability" that Sharon could sell 500 tons of "cold rolled" steel at prices varying with the type ordered. At that time, the steel industry was operating at 70% of capacity, steel prices were "highly competitive" and Sharon's quoted prices to Roth were "substantially lower" than Sharon's book price for steel. In early 1973, market conditions changed dramatically due to the development of an attractive export market and an increased domestic demand for steel. During 1973 and 1974, the steel industry operated at full capacity, steel prices rose and nearly every producer experienced substantial delays in filling orders. In March, 1973, Sharon notified all purchasers, including Roth, that it was discontinuing price concessions given in 1972. After negotiations, the parties agreed that Roth would pay the agreed price until June 30, 1973 and a price somewhere between the agreed price and Sharon's published prices for the balance of 1973. Roth was initially reluctant to agree to this modification, but ultimately agreed "primarily because they were unable to purchase sufficient steel elsewhere to meet their production requirements." Sharon was supplying one-third of Roth's requirements and all other possible suppliers were "operating at full capacity and ... were fully booked." The parties proceeded under this modification during the balance of 1973, although Sharon experienced difficulties in filling orders on time. During 1974, the parties did business on an entirely different basis. Roth would order steel, Sharon would accept the order at the price "prevailing at the time of shipment." During 1974 and 1975, Sharon's deliveries were chronically late, thereby increasing the price to Roth in a rising market. Roth, however, acquiesced in this pattern because it believed Sharon's assurances that late deliveries resulted from shortages of raw materials and the need for equitable allocation among customers and because there was "no practical alternative source of supply." This acquiescence was jolted in May, 1974 when Roth learned that Sharon was allocating substantial quantities of rolled steel to a subsidiary for sale at premium prices. After several more months of desultory performance on both sides, Roth sued Sharon for breach of contract, with special emphasis upon the modified contract for 1973. Sharon raised several defenses, including impracticability and, in the alternative, the agreed modification. The district court, after a long trial, held, *inter alia,* that Sharon was not excused from the 1973 contract on the grounds of impracticability and that the modification was unenforceable. A judgment for $555,968.46 was entered for Roth.

On appeal, the court of appeals affirmed the district court's decision on the impracticability, modification and other issues, but remanded the case for factual findings on whether Roth gave Sharon timely notice of breach. On the impracticability defense under UCC 2–615(a), the court held that "Sharon's inability to perform was a result of its policy accepting far more orders than it was capable of fulfilling, rather than a result of the existing shortage of raw materials." In refusing to enforce the modification of the 1973 contract, the court had this to say.]

■ CELEBREZZE, SENIOR CIRCUIT JUDGE.

* * *

C. In March, 1973, Sharon notified its customers that it intended to charge the maximum permissible price for all of its products; accordingly, all price concessions, including those made to the plaintiffs, were to be rescinded effective April 1, 1973. On March 23, 1973, Guerin indicated to Metzger that the plaintiffs considered the proposed price increase to be a breach of the November, 1972 contract. In an effort to resolve the dispute, Guerin met with representatives of Sharon on March 28, 1973 and asked Sharon to postpone any price increases until June or July, 1973. Several days later, Richard Mecaskey, Guerin's replacement, sent a letter to Sharon which indicated that the plaintiffs believed that the November, 1972 agreement was enforceable and that the plaintiffs were willing to negotiate a price modification if Sharon's cost increases warranted such an action. As a result of this letter, another meeting was held between Sharon and the plaintiffs. At this meeting, Walter Gregg, Sharon's vice-president and chairman of the board, agreed to continue charging the November, 1972 prices until June 30, 1973 and offered, for the remainder of 1973, to charge prices that were lower than Sharon's published prices but higher than the 1972 prices. Although the plaintiffs initially rejected the terms offered by Sharon for the second half of 1973, Mecaskey reluctantly agreed to Sharon's terms on June 29, 1973.

Before the district court, Sharon asserted that it properly increased prices because the parties had modified the November, 1973 contract to reflect changed market conditions. The district court, however, made several findings which, it believed, indicated that Sharon did not seek a modification to avoid a loss on the contract. The district court also found that the plaintiffs' inventories of rolled steel were "alarmingly deficient" at the time modification was sought and that Sharon had threatened to cease selling steel to the plaintiffs in the second-half of 1973 unless the plaintiffs agreed to the modification. Because Sharon had used its position as the plaintiffs' chief supplier to extract the price modification, the district court concluded that Sharon had acted in bad faith by seeking to modify the contract. In the alternative, the court concluded that the modification agreement was voidable because it was extracted by means of economic duress; the tight steel market prevented the plaintiffs from obtaining steel elsewhere at an affordable price and, consequently, the plaintiffs were forced to agree to the modification in order to assure a continued supply of steel. See e.g. Oskey Gasoline & Oil Co. v. Continental Oil Co., 534 F.2d 1281 (8th Cir.1976). Sharon challenges these conclusions on appeal.

The ability of a party to modify a contract which is subject to Article Two of the Uniform Commercial Code is broader than common law, primarily because the modification needs no consideration to be binding. ORC § 1302.12 (UCC § 2–209(1)). A party's ability to modify an agreement is limited only by Article Two's general obligation of good faith. ...In determining whether a particular modification was obtained in good faith, a court must make two distinct inquiries: whether the party's conduct is consistent with "reasonable commercial standards of fair dealing in the trade," ... and whether the parties were in fact motivated to seek modification by an honest desire to compensate for commercial exigencies; ... ORC § 1302.01(2) (UCC § 2–103). The first inquiry is relatively straightforward; the party asserting the modification must demonstrate that his decision to seek modification was the result of a factor, such as increased costs, which would cause an ordinary merchant to seek a modification of the contract. See Official Comment 2, ORC § 1302.12 (UCC § 2–209) (reasonable commercial standards may require objective reason); J. White & R. Summers, Handbook of Law under the UCC at 41. The second inquiry, regarding the subjective honesty of the parties, is less clearly defined. Essentially, this inquiry requires the party asserting the modification to demonstrate that he was, in fact, motivated by a legitimate commercial reason and that such a reason is not offered merely as a pretext. ...Moreover, the trier of fact must determine whether the means used to obtain the modification are an impermissible attempt to obtain a modification by extortion or overreaching. . . .

Sharon argues that its decision to seek a modification was consistent with reasonable commercial standards of fair dealing because market exigencies made further performance entail a substantial loss. The district court, however, made three findings which caused it to conclude that economic circumstances were not the reason that Sharon sought a modification: it found that Sharon was partially insulated from raw material price increases, that Sharon bargained for a contract with a slim profit margin and thus implicitly assumed the risk that performance might come to involve a loss, and that Sharon's overall profit in 1973 and its profit on the contract in the first quarter of 1973 were inconsistent with Sharon's position that the modification was sought to avoid a loss. Although all of these findings are marginally related to the question whether Sharon's conduct was consistent with reasonable commercial standards of fair dealing, we do not believe that they are sufficient to support a finding that Sharon did not observe reasonable commercial standards by seeking a modification. In our view, these findings do not support a conclusion that a reasonable merchant, in light of the circumstances, would not have sought a modification in order to avoid a loss. For example, the district court's finding that Sharon's steel slab contract[26] insulated it from industry wide cost increases is correct, so far as it goes. Although Sharon was able to purchase steel slabs at pre–1973 prices, the district court's findings also indicate that it was not able to purchase, at those prices, a sufficient tonnage of steel slabs to meet its production requirements.[27] The district court also found that Sharon experienced substantial cost increases for other raw materials, ranging from 4% to nearly 20%. In light of these facts, the finding regarding the fixed-price contract for slab steel, without more, cannot support an inference that Sharon was unaffected by the market shifts that occurred in 1973. Similarly, the district court's finding that Sharon entered a contract in November, 1972 which would yield only a slim profit does not support a conclusion that Sharon was willing to risk a loss on the contract. Absent a finding that the market shifts and the raw material price increases were foreseeable at the time the contract was formed—a finding which was not made—Sharon's willingness to absorb a

---

26. Sharon was a party to a contract with United States Steel which allowed it to make monthly purchases of slab steel ranging from a minimum of 25,000 tons per month to a maximum of 45,000 tons per month. It was also a party to a contract with Wierton Steel which allowed it to purchase slab steel in amounts varying between 10,000 to 20,000 tons per month. Both of these contracts were entered prior to 1973, at a very attractive price. When the market strengthened in 1973, however, Sharon was unable to obtain the maximum monthly tonnages permitted under these contracts: U.S. Steel delivered only 30,000 tons per month and Wierton 10,000 tons per month.

27. The district court found that Sharon suffered a continuing shortage of slab steel. It found that in 1972 (when Sharon was operating at substantially less than full capacity) it received 602,277 tons of slab steel; that in 1973, it received 506,596 tons of slab steel; and that in 1974 it received 373,-898 tons. Thus, the record is clear that Sharon was in a difficult position. As demand for steel increased, and as Sharon's mills began to work at a higher capacity, its supply of slab steel steadily diminished.

loss cannot be inferred from the fact that it contracted for a smaller profit than usual. Finally, the findings regarding Sharon's profits are not sufficient, by themselves, to warrant a conclusion that Sharon was not justified in seeking a modification. Clearly, Sharon's initial profit on the contract[28] is an important consideration; the district court's findings indicate, however, that at the time modification was sought substantial future losses were foreseeable.[29] A party who has not actually suffered a loss on the contract may still seek a modification if a future loss on the agreement was reasonably foreseeable. Similarly, the overall profit earned by the party seeking modification is an important factor; this finding, however, does not support a conclusion that the decision to seek a modification was unwarranted. The more relevant inquiry is into the profit obtained through sales of the product line in question. This conclusion is reinforced by the fact that only a few product lines may be affected by market exigencies;[30] the opportunity to seek modification of a contract for the sale of goods of a product line should not be limited solely because some other product line produced a substantial profit.

In the final analysis, the single most important consideration in determining whether the decision to seek a modification is justified in this context is whether, because of changes in the market or other unforeseeable conditions, performance of the contract has come to involve a loss. In this case, the district court found that Sharon suffered substantial losses by performing the contract *as modified*. See note 29, supra. We are convinced that unforeseen economic exigencies existed which would prompt an ordinary merchant to seek a modification to avoid a loss on the contract; thus, we believe that the district court's findings to the contrary are clearly erroneous. . . .

The second part of the analysis, honesty in fact, is pivotal. The district court found that Sharon "threatened not to sell Roth and Toledo any steel if they refused to pay increased prices after July 1, 1973" and, consequently, that Sharon acted wrongfully. Sharon does not dispute the finding that it threatened to stop selling steel to the plaintiffs. Instead, it asserts that such a finding is merely evidence of bad faith and that it has rebutted any inference of bad faith based on that finding. We agree with this analysis; although coercive conduct is evidence that a modification of a contract is sought in bad faith, that prima facie showing may be effectively rebutted by the party seeking to enforce the modification. . . . Although we agree with Sharon's statement of principles, we do not agree that Sharon has rebutted the inference of bad faith that rises from its coercive conduct. Sharon

---

28. The district court noted that in the first three months of 1973, Sharon made $3,089.00 on sales to Roth and lost $263.00 on steel sold to Toledo. Although Sharon lost significant sums of money on its contract with the plaintiffs, Sharon enjoyed overall profits in 1973, with net earnings of $11,566,000 on net sales of $338,205,000.

29. The evidence indicates, and the district court found, that with the exception of

hot rolled sheets Sharon absorbed a loss on every rolled steel product which it sold to the defendants in 1973, even though the modified prices were in effect during the third and the fourth quarters.

30. Apparently, Sharon's record overall profit was the result of other operations. It obtained a pre-tax profit of less than one percent on its total sales of rolled steel.

asserts that its decision to unilaterally raise prices was based on language in the November 17, 1972 letter which allowed it to raise prices to the extent of any general industry-wide price increase. Because prices in the steel industry had increased, Sharon concludes that it was justified in raising its prices. Because it was justified in raising the contract price, the plaintiffs were bound by the terms of the contract to pay the increased prices. Consequently, any refusal by the plaintiffs to pay the price increase sought by Sharon must be viewed as a material breach of the November, 1972 contract which would excuse Sharon from any further performance. Thus, Sharon reasons that its refusal to perform absent a price increase was justified under the contract and consistent with good faith.

This argument fails in two respects. First, the contractual language on which Sharon relies only permits, at most, a price increase for cold rolled steel; thus, even if Sharon's position were supported by the evidence, Sharon would not have been justified in refusing to sell the plaintiffs hot rolled steel because of the plaintiffs' refusal to pay higher prices for the product. More importantly, however, the evidence does not indicate that Sharon ever offered this theory as a justification until this matter was tried. Sharon's representatives, in their testimony, did not attempt to justify Sharon's refusal to ship steel at 1972 prices in this fashion. Furthermore, none of the contemporaneous communications contain this justification for Sharon's action. In short, we can find no evidence in the record which indicates that Sharon offered this theory as a justification at the time the modification was sought. Consequently, we believe that the district court's conclusion that Sharon acted in bad faith by using coercive conduct to extract the price modification is not clearly erroneous. Therefore, we hold that Sharon's attempt to modify the November, 1972 contract, in order to compensate for increased costs which made performance come to involve a loss, is ineffective because Sharon did not act in a manner consistent with Article Two's requirement of honesty in fact when it refused to perform its remaining obligations under the contract at 1972 prices.[31]

* * *

NOTES

(1) In *Roth Steel Products,* the court held that Sharon was *not* entitled to any relief under UCC 2–615(a). If Sharon had been entitled to "some relief," would the modification have been enforceable under UCC 2–209(1)?

---

31. The district court also found, as an alternative ground, that the modification was voidable because the plaintiffs agreed to the modification due to economic duress. See, e.g., Oskey Gasoline & Oil Co. v. Continental Oil, 534 F.2d 1281 (8th Cir.1976). Because we conclude that the modification was ineffective as a result of Sharon's bad faith, we do not reach the issue whether the contract modification was also voidable because of economic duress. We note, however, that proof that coercive means were used is necessary to establish that a contract is voidable because of economic duress. Normally, it cannot be used to void a contract modification which has been sought in good faith; if a contract modification has been found to be in good faith, then presumably no wrongful coercive means have been used to extract the modification.

(2) Would the modification have been enforceable under Section 89 of Restatement (Second), discussed and applied in *Angel v. Murray*? How does one draw the line between "circumstances not anticipated by the parties when the contract was made," Section 89(a), and the "occurrence of an event the non-occurrence of which was basic assumption on which the contract was made," Section 261?

(3) Note that *Roth Steel Products* invalidated the modification because of Sharon's bad faith rather than because of economic duress. The court suggests that proof of coercive means will not invalidate a modification made in good faith. See Note 31. What, then, was the bad faith in *Roth Steel Products*? Is this concept consistent with the view that a modification is in bad faith when one party uses a refusal to perform as a lever to recapture an opportunity foregone at the time of contracting?

(4) Some courts have relied exclusively upon concepts of economic duress when evaluating modifications. See, e.g., Austin Instrument, Inc. v. Loral Corp., 29 N.Y.2d 124, 324 N.Y.S.2d 22, 272 N.E.2d 533 (1971), reprinted *supra* at 527, where the court said:

> [A] mere threat by one party to breach the contract by not delivering the required items, though wrongful, does not in itself constitute economic duress. It must also appear that the threatened party could not obtain the goods from another source of supply and that the ordinary remedy of an action for breach of contract would not be adequate.

324 N.Y.S.2d at 24.

The "economic duress" approach is strongly favored by some commentators. See, e.g., Robert Hillman, *Contract Modification Under the Restatement (Second) of Contracts,* 67 Cornell L.Rev. 680 (1982); Henry Mather, *Contract Modification under Duress,* 33 S.Car.L.Rev. 615 (1982). In *Roth Steel Products,* Roth was clearly unable to obtain the promised steel from another source and ordinary damage remedies would appear to have been inadequate. Was Sharon's refusal (which was not excused under UCC 2–615(a)) to deliver steel unless Roth agreed to a price modification "wrongful?"

(5) *Duty to negotiate or modify*? Under American law, a party advantaged by changed circumstances has no duty to negotiate with the disadvantaged party unless the contract so requires. Even then, the duty is to negotiate in good faith, not to agree to a modification. The UNIDROIT model of good faith, see supra at 668, may require a duty to negotiate in good faith upon request by the disadvantaged party but does not require a modification. Should there ever be a duty to modify the contract? If not, should a court, to restore balance, modify or revise the contract? We will return to these questions in Chapter Six, Section 4. For now, consider the following argument:

> [C]an a case be made for imposing a duty on the advantaged party to accept a "fair and equitable" adjustment proposal made by the disadvantaged party? If so, what remedies are appropriate? * * * [A] tentative case can be made that does not convert the law of contracts into a pervasive duty to be altruistic.
>
> First, the disadvantaged party must propose a modification that would be enforceable if accepted by the advantaged party. Under the Restatement (Second), this occurs if the disrupted contract is not "fully performed on

either side" and if the modification is "fair and equitable in view of circumstances not anticipated by the parties when the contract was made." The changed circumstances are similar to but less than those required to discharge a contract for impracticability. This first requirement both neutralizes any opportunism by the disadvantaged party, *e.g.,* duress, and affirms that agreed adjustments are preferred—that contract is available to resolve the dilemma and has been employed by the disadvantaged party.

Second, it must be clear that the disadvantaged party did not assume the risk of the unanticipated event by agreement, or under the test stated in the UCC in section 2–615(a), or otherwise. If the disadvantaged party did assume the risk, then the advantaged party has no duty to accept any proposed modification. The risk assumption question is complicated, and the answer will probably not be clear at the time that the adjustment is proposed. Why should the advantaged party be held to reject at his peril? Because it is in this precise situation—where there are substantial unbargained-for gains and losses caused by unanticipated events—that a case for the duty to rescue can be made. In this setting where the risk of changed circumstances has not been allocated to either party, a refusal to adjust by the advantaged party leaves all of the loss on the disadvantaged party and permits the advantaged party to salt away all of the gains. Short of discharging the contract and leaving the parties to restitution, a duty to adjust is necessary to avoid opportunism.

Thus, imposing the duty here is consistent with emerging notions of good faith performance and   ...   loss avoidance. More importantly, it is an imposition with little damage to the requirement of consent in contract law. Since there is a "gap" in the agreement on risk allocation, even that staunch defender of the "promise principle," Professor Charles Fried, argues that the parties have "some obligation to share unexpected benefits and losses in the case of an accident" in the course of a joint enterprise where they are not strangers to each other.[59] This "sharing principle" is derived from a more general principle of altruism and is similar to what has been called the duty of "easy rescue" in the law of torts.

Last, this conclusion is bolstered by what might be the imperatives of an emerging theory of relational contract law. In *ALCOA,* the parties, at the time of contracting, were unable adequately to deal with certain changed circumstances over the duration of a seventeen-year contract. Yet preserving the contract was important to the parties and to third parties dependent upon its performance but not represented in the litigation. Ian Macneil has argued that in situations such as this there are relational norms that the contract should be preserved and conflict harmonized by adjustment. These norms put a high premium upon developing mechanisms for adjustment over time and good faith efforts to adjust in the light of change.[61] Thus, if in an *ALCOA*-type case [soaring performance costs exceed agreed price adjustment clause, buyer gets a windfall by selling finished product in escalating market], the court concludes that the disad-

59. C. Fried, supra note 52, at 72–73. See Coons, *Compromise as Precise Justice,* 68 Calif.L.Rev. 250 (1980).

61. [See, generally, I. Macneil, The New Social Contract 36–70 (1980).]

vantaged party is entitled to "some relief" but not discharge, and the advantaged party has refused to accept a reasonable adjustment in light of risks that the disadvantaged party did not assume, relational theory also supports a court imposed adjustment to preserve the contract, to adjust the price and to avoid the twin devils of unbargained-for hardship and unjust enrichment.

Richard E. Speidel, *The New Spirit of Contract,* 2 J.Law & Commerce 193, 202, 205–08 (1982).

(E) TERMINATION OF CONTRACTUAL RELATIONS FOR OTHER THAN BREACH

(1) COMMERCIAL CONTRACTS

Zapatha v. Dairy Mart, Inc.

Supreme Judicial Court of Massachusetts, 1980.
Supra at 564.

* * *

[The facts are stated supra at 564. The franchise contract contained the following termination clause:

(9) The term of this Limited Franchise and License Agreement shall be for a period of Twelve (12) months from date hereof, and shall continue uninterrupted thereafter. If DEALER desires to terminate after 12 months from date hereof, he shall do so by giving COMPANY a ninety (90) day written notice by Registered Mail of his intention to terminate. If COMPANY desires to terminate, it likewise shall give a ninety (90) day notice, except for the following reasons which shall not require any written notice and shall terminate the Franchise immediately:

(a) Failure to pay bills to suppliers for inventory or other products when due.

(b) Failure to pay Franchise Fees to COMPANY.

(c) Failure to pay city, state or federal taxes as said taxes shall become due and payable.

(d) Breach of any condition of this Agreement.

The contract also provided that in the event of a termination without cause Dairy Mart agreed to repurchase the saleable merchandise inventory at retail prices, less 20%. After holding that the termination clause was not unconscionable at the time of contracting, the Court considered whether the termination was in bad faith.]

* * *

3.   We see no basis on the record for concluding that Dairy Mart did not act in good faith, as that term is defined in the sales article ("honesty in fact and the observance of reasonable commercial standards of fair dealing in the trade"). G.L. c. 106, § 2–103(1)(b). There was no evidence that Dairy Mart failed to observe reasonable commercial standards of fair

dealing in the trade in terminating the agreement. If there were such standards, there was no evidence of what they were.

The question then is whether there was evidence warranting a finding that Dairy Mart was not honest "in fact." The judge concluded that the absence of any commercial purpose for the termination other than the Zapathas' refusal to sign a new franchise agreement violated Dairy Mart's obligation of good faith. Dairy Mart's right to terminate was clear, and it exercised that right for a reason it openly disclosed. The sole test of "honesty in fact" is whether the person was honest. * * * We think that, whether or not termination according to the terms of the franchise agreement may have been arbitrary, it was not dishonest. * * *

4. Although what we have said disposes of arguments based on application by analogy of provisions of the sales article of the Uniform Commercial Code, there remains the question whether the judge's conclusions may be supported by some general principle of law. The provisions of the Uniform Commercial Code with which we have dealt by analogy in this opinion may not have sufficient breadth to provide protection from conduct that has produced an unfair and burdensome result, contrary to the spirit of the bargain, against which the law reasonably should provide protection. . . . [7]

The law of the Commonwealth recognizes that under some circumstances a party to a contract is not free to terminate it according to its terms. In Fortune v. National Cash Register Co., 373 Mass. 96, 104–105, 364 N.E.2d 1251 (1977), we held that where an employer terminated an at will employment contract in order to deprive its employee of a portion of a commission due to him, the employer acted in bad faith. There, the employer correctly argued that termination of the employee was expressly permitted by the contract, and that all amounts payable under the terms of the contract at the time of termination had been paid. We concluded, however, that the law imposed an obligation of good faith on the employer and that the employer violated that obligation in terminating the relationship in order to avoid the payment of amounts earned, but not yet payable. The Legislature has limited the right of certain franchisors to terminate franchise agreements without cause.[8] On the other hand, the Legislature

---

7. The unconscionability provision of G.L. c. 106, § 2–302, concerns circumstances determined at the time of the making of the agreement and relates only to the unconscionability of a term or terms of the contract. The "good faith" obligation of G.L. c. 106, § 1–203, deals with "honesty in fact," a question of the state of mind of the merchant or of his adherence to whatever reasonable commercial standards there may be in his trade. A merchant's conduct might not be dishonest and might adhere to reasonable standards, if any, in his trade and thus might be in good faith under § 1–203, and yet be unfair and unreasonably burdensome.

8. See G.L. c. 93B, § 4(3)(e), (4) concerning the cancellation or nonrenewal of a motor vehicle dealer's franchise and requiring good cause for manufacturer's or distributor's action; G.L. c. 93E, §§ 5, 5A, requiring cause for a supplier's termination or nonrenewal of a gasoline station dealer's agreement and imposing an obligation on the supplier to repurchase merchantable products sold to the dealer. * * *

The special status of service station operators has prompted some courts to adopt has not adopted limitations on the right to terminate all franchise agreements in general, and its failure to do so is understandable because of the varied nature of franchise arrangements, where such varying factors exist as the relative bargaining power of the parties, the extent of investment by franchisees, and the degree to which the franchisee's goodwill, as opposed to that of the franchisor, is involved in the business operation. * * *

We are most concerned, as was the judge below, with the introductory circular that Dairy Mart furnished Mr. Zapatha. The judge ruled that the introductory circular contained misleading information concerning the Zapathas' status as franchisees. However, we cannot find in that document any deception or unfairness that has a bearing on the right of Dairy Mart to terminate the agreement as it did. A representative read the termination clause to Mr. Zapatha before the Zapathas signed the agreement. Mr. Zapatha declined an invitation to take the agreement to a lawyer. He understood individually every word of the termination clause. Moreover, when Dairy Mart terminated the agreement, it offered to negotiate further, and the Zapathas did not take the opportunity to do so. * * *

Dairy Mart lawfully terminated the agreement because there was no showing that in terminating it Dairy Mart engaged in any unfair, deceptive, or bad faith conduct.

Judgments reversed.

NOTES

(1) In *Zapatha,* Dairy Mart reserved broad power to terminate the franchise without regard to cause and followed the clause to the letter in exercising that power. How did the court justify imposing a duty of good faith on the exercise of that power? The answer, presumably, is that Dairy Mart must exercise discretion in deciding to invoke the clause. The discretion must be exercised in good faith, and this requires an inquiry into the reasons for the exercise and suggests that there are good and bad reasons.

If terminating because the franchisee refuses to modify the franchise on terms more favorable to the franchisor is not a bad reason (i.e., bad faith), what is? Suppose that the franchisor discriminated against a minority franchisee? Suppose the termination was in retaliation because the franchisee had reported salmonella in the ice cream to state health authorities? Suppose the purpose of the termination was to capture a thriving franchise for the benefit of the president's brother-in-law?

Does it help in Zapatha that both parties could terminate under the clause, that a terminated party had 90 days after notice of termination to liquidate its affairs, and that Dairy Mart agreed to repurchase Zapatha's post-termination inventory?

common law rules requiring good cause for termination in spite of contract language that seemed to allow termination without cause.

(2) Some courts have declined to impose a duty of good faith in terminating franchise and distributorship contracts. See Corenswet, Inc. v. Amana Refrigeration, Inc., 594 F.2d 129 (5th Cir.1979), cert. denied 444 U.S. 938, 100 S.Ct. 288, 62 L.Ed.2d 198 (1979), where the court refused to impose a good faith limitation upon the power to terminate an exclusive distributorship where the contract permitted termination by either party "at any time for any reason" on the giving of ten days notice. The court thought that the good faith duty always required the evaluation of the terminating party's motives and that a termination "without cause will almost always be characterizable as 'bad faith' termination." 594 F.2d at 138. Are you persuaded? Does this interpretation leave the employee with any protection against malicious or retaliatory terminations. See Robert Hillman, *An Analysis of the Cessation of Contractual Relations*, 68 Cornell L.Rev. 617, 642–57 (1983); Note, *Franchise Termination: An Analysis of the Implied Covenant of Good Faith in Franchise Agreements*, Am.J.Trial Advoc. 325 (1988).

(2) Federal and state laws have increasingly regulated the power to terminate a franchise relationship. For example, the Automobile Dealer's Day in Court Act, 15 U.S.C.A. § 1221 et seq., provides that a dealer may sue for damages "by reason of the failure of said automobile manufacturer ... to act in good faith in performing or complying with any of the terms and provisions of the franchise or in terminating, canceling or not renewing the franchise with said dealer...." Id. at § 1222. Good faith, however, is narrowly defined as the "duty of each party ... to guarantee ... freedom from coercion, intimidation, or threat of coercion or intimidation from the other party ... " Id. at § 1221(e). See Hubbard Chevrolet Co. v. General Motors Corp., 873 F.2d 873, 876–77 (5th Cir.1989) (federal good faith duty does not override or contradict clear reservation of power in contract). For an analysis of federal law and the effect of state "franchise relationship laws," see Pitegoff, *Franchise Relationship Laws: A Minefield for Franchisors*, 45 Bus.Law. 289 (1989). See also, Sutherland, *The Risks and Exposures Associated with Franchise Noncompliance*, 42 Bus.Law. 369 (1987).

(4) *American Model of Good Faith Revisited*. In other business relationships, terminations that follow the letter of a termination clause in the contract have been sustained even though there was evidence of opportunistic (bad faith) behavior by the terminator.

In Sons of Thunder, Inc. v. Borden, Inc., 148 N.J. 396, 690 A.2d 575 (1997), the defendant terminated a fishing contract with the plaintiff under a termination clause "standard" in the industry. The court drew a line between bad faith performance and bad faith termination that permitted it to hold that (1) the defendant performed the contract in bad faith (by hindrance and failure to cooperate) and was liable for damages, but (2) a termination which followed the letter of the termination clause was in good faith regardless of the defendant's motives. The court stated that the "implied covenant of good faith and fair dealing cannot override an express termination clause." Id. At 586. The question was whether the defendant "performed its obligations [under the termination clause] in good faith." The answer was yes if the termination clause was followed.

A similar analysis and result was reached by the Alaska Supreme Court in United Airlines, Inc. v. Good Taste, Inc., 982 P.2d 1259 (Alaska 1999) (applying

Illinois law).* The court, in reversing a verdict for Good Taste, interpreted the termination clause to be clear and unambiguous. It then found that United Airlines had followed the letter of the termination clause and rejected the finding of the trial court that, under Illinois law, United had engaged in bad faith (opportunistic) conduct associated with the termination. Under Illinois law:

> [T]erminable-at-will contracts are generally held to permit termination for any reason, good cause or not, or for no cause at all. Mindful that every contract carries the duty of good faith and fair dealing, as a matter of law, absent express disavowal by the parties, the duty of good faith and fair dealing does not override the clear right to terminate at will, since no obligation can be implied which would be inconsistent with and destructive of the unfettered right to terminate at will. Id. at 1266, quoting from Jepperson v. Minnesota Mining & Manufacturing Co., 681 N.E.2d 67, 71 (Ill.App.1997), aff'd, 700 N.E.2d 1014 (Ill. 1998).**

According to Dennis Patterson, the vice of cases like this is that control of the so-called immutable duty of good faith is given to private parties, more particularly, those who draft termination clauses and require others to assent to them. Dennis Patterson, *A Fable From The Seventh Circuit: Frank Easterbrook on Good Faith,* 76 Iowa L. Rev. 503 (1991). Do you agree?

(2) EMPLOYMENT CONTRACTS

Hillesland v. Federal Land Bank Association Of Grand Forks

Supreme Court of North Dakota, 1987.
407 N.W.2d 206.

■ ERICKSTAD, CHIEF JUSTICE.

Elmer Hillesland appeals from a district court summary judgment dismissing his action against the Federal Land Bank Association of Grand Forks [the Association] and the Federal Land Bank of St. Paul [the Bank]. We affirm.

Hillesland began working at the Association in 1956. He received several promotions and in 1972 was named Chief Executive Officer. He held that position until his discharge on June 15, 1983.

Through his position with the Association Hillesland in early 1983 learned that Ray and Eva Westby, customers of the Association, were experiencing financial difficulties. He also learned that they had received an offer to purchase their farm from another Association customer. Hillesland contacted the Westbys to offer financial counseling. They responded by expressing their desire to sell the farm. Although the parties dispute

---

* One of your co-authors was associated with the attorneys for the losing party, Good Taste (aka Saucy Sisters), a caterer for United Airlines.

** A careful reading of these opinions reveals that the statement of the court of appeals was dictum and that the decision affirmed by the Supreme Court did not involve the termination clause.

whether Hillesland initiated the discussions of sale of the property, it is undisputed that these discussions eventually led to an offer to purchase the Westby farm by Hillesland's sons, David and Don.

In accordance with standard Association procedure, Hillesland submitted details of the proposed transaction on a "Prohibited Acts Report and Action" form to the Association board of directors for approval. After meeting in a closed session with the Westbys, the board approved the transaction. Hillesland then submitted the matter to the Bank's Review Committee in St. Paul. In its report, the Review Committee stated that it was "not in a position to disapprove" the transaction, but it did express concern over the appearance of a conflict of interest and prohibited any further direct involvement in the transaction by Hillesland. The sale of the land to Hillesland's sons was completed shortly thereafter.

The Bank subsequently launched an investigation into the matter. On June 15, 1983, two representatives of the Bank appeared at a meeting of the Association board of directors in Grand Forks and advised Hillesland that he was being discharged from his employment with the Association. The Bank's rationale for Hillesland's termination was that he had violated written standards of conduct, had damaged the image and reputation of the Association and the Bank, and had exercised poor business judgment.

Hillesland commenced this action against the Association and the Bank alleging violation of provisions of the Farm Credit Act, breach of contract, age discrimination, and tortious interference by the Bank with Hillesland's employment contract with the Association. The district court granted summary judgment dismissing Hillesland's action, and he appeals.

[The court held, inter alia, that there was (1) no implied private right of action under the Farm Credit Act, 12 U.S.C. sec. 2227(a)(3), (2) no age discrimination, and (3) no claim against the Bank for tortious interference with contract.]

* * *

BREACH OF CONTRACT

Hillesland contends that the trial court erred in dismissing his breach of contract claim because there are material fact issues remaining which preclude summary judgment. * * *

Section 34–03–01, N.D.C.C., is North Dakota's codification of the "at will" doctrine:

"Termination of employment at will—Notice required. An employment having no specified term may be terminated at the will of either party on notice to the other, except when otherwise provided by this title."

In order to support his claim for breach of an employment contract Hillesland must produce evidence that there existed a contract for employment for a specified term or that he would only be terminated for cause. Hillesland asserts that he was employed permanently, to be fired only if he did not satisfactorily perform.

The only evidence relied upon by Hillesland to support his contention that he had a contract for permanent, lifetime employment was conclusory statements in his deposition that he had received the "impression" from his job interview in 1956 that he had been hired for a "permanent type" and "career type position." Hillesland could not recall the substance of the interview but only his "impressions." Hillesland admitted that he had never been told by anyone that he would only be terminated for cause.

In *Wadeson v. American Family Mutual Insurance Co.,* 343 N.W.2d 367, 371 (N.D.1984), we held that similar statements did not create a contractual agreement to discharge only for good cause:

"The fact that American Family 'publications' represented employment with American Family as a 'lifetime opportunity' and 'permanent and stable business', as Wadeson asserts, does not bring Wadeson's employment within the scope of cases ... where the employer had specifically said that discharge would only be for good cause. We do not read such statements used in recruiting new agents to be promises either of permanent employment or that one will be discharged only for good cause."

Hillesland has failed to draw our attention to any evidence in the record which raises a material factual issue regarding an alleged contractual agreement taking Hillesland's employment outside the at-will rule of Section 34–03–01, N.D.C.C. We conclude that the trial court did not err in granting summary judgment on this issue.

IMPLIED COVENANT OF GOOD FAITH AND FAIR DEALING

Hillesland contends that there is an implied covenant of good faith and fair dealing in all employment contracts and that the Bank and the Association breached that covenant when they terminated his employment. Hillesland alleges that there are material factual issues to be resolved on this issue which preclude summary judgment.

A brief historical perspective of the employment-at-will doctrine is helpful at this point. Prior to the mid-nineteenth century the prevailing theory was the "English rule," which provided that an employment without a set term was presumed to be for one year.... Toward the end of the century the at-will rule was gaining popularity, and by the beginning of the twentieth century the at-will doctrine prevailed in the United States ... The classic statement of the at-will rule is that an employer may discharge an employee "for good cause, for no cause or even for cause morally wrong, without being thereby guilty of legal wrong." *Payne v. Western & Atlantic Railroad Co.,* 81 Tenn. 507, 519–520 (1884) ...

Congress and the legislatures of many states have enacted statutory provisions intended to afford some measure of protection to employees. *See, e.g.,* § 14–02.4–03, N.D.C.C. (employer may not discharge an employee because of race, color, religion, sex, national origin, age, physical or mental handicap, or status with respect to marriage or public assistance). Judicially created exceptions to or modifications of the at-will rule have also emerged to ameliorate the sometimes harsh consequences of strict adherence to the at-will rule. The two most common modifications are the public policy exception, which allows a discharged employee to recover if his termination violates a well established and important public policy, and the imposition of an implied covenant of good faith and fair dealing into the employment contract.

As previously noted, the at-will rule is statutory in this state. Section 34–03–01, N.D.C.C., provides in pertinent part: "An employment having no specified term may be terminated at the will of either party on notice to the other." Our statute is derived from the virtually identical California statute, Cal.Lab.Code § 2922. Hillesland urges this court to imply into North Dakota employment contracts a covenant of good faith and fair dealing, as the California courts have done pursuant to that state's employment-at-will statute. Although we would normally attach great significance to a sister state's construction of a statute which served as the model for our state's provision, we decline to do so in this case.

The seminal California case is *Cleary v. American Airlines, Inc.,* 111 Cal.App.3d 443 (1980). Cleary had been employed by American for eighteen years when he was dismissed in 1976. Although American claimed that Cleary was fired for theft, leaving his work area without authorization, and threatening a fellow employee, Cleary alleged that his termination resulted from his union activities. Cleary also asserted that American failed to follow its own regulations setting forth procedures for discipline and discharge of employees.

The Court of Appeal held that there was an implied covenant of good faith and fair dealing in every employment contract under California law and that Cleary had sufficiently pleaded facts of breach of that covenant to state a viable cause of action sounding in both tort and contract. The court relied heavily upon two factors—the length of Cleary's employment and the existence of express procedures regarding termination in the company regulations. Thus, the court held that "the longevity of the employee's service, together with the expressed policy of the employer, operate as a form of estoppel, precluding any discharge of such an employee by the employer without good cause." *Cleary v. American Airlines, Inc., supra,* 111 Cal.App.3d at 455–456.

In later cases, the California Court of Appeal has grappled with the appropriate application of *Cleary* in a variety of fact situations. For example, in *Khanna v. Microdata Corp.,* 170 Cal.App.3d 250, 262 (1985), the First District Court of Appeal held that the application of the implied covenant was not limited to those situations where the employment was long-term and the employer acted contrary to its own stated procedures for discharge:

> "We cannot agree with appellant that the factors relied on by the court in *Cleary* are the *sine qua non* to establishing a breach of the covenant of good faith and fair dealing implied in every employment contract. The cases subsequent to *Cleary* discussing the breach of the implied covenant in employment contracts have indicated that the theory of recovery articulated in *Cleary* is not dependent on the particular factors identified in that case.... To the contrary, a breach of the

implied covenant of good faith and fair dealing in employment contracts is established whenever the employer engages in 'bad faith
action extraneous to the contract, combined with the obligor's intent to
frustrate the [employee's] enjoyment of contract rights.' ... The facts
in *Cleary* establish only one manner among many by which an employer might violate this covenant."

A few months later, the Second District Court of Appeal expressly
disagreed with the holding in *Khanna,* concluding that to prove a violation
of the covenant the employee "must show longevity of service, and breach
of an express employer policy regarding the adjudication of employee
disputes." *Foley v. Interactive Data Corp.,* 219 Cal.Rptr. 866, 871 (1985),
review granted, 222 Cal.Rptr. 740 (1986). Noting that Foley's seven years at
the company "fell short of the necessary longevity" and that Foley did not
"adequately allege express formal procedures for terminating employees,"
the court held that dismissal of Foley's action was appropriate. *Foley,
supra,* 219 Cal.Rptr. at 871.

In those other jurisdictions which have found an implied-in-law covenant of good faith and fair dealing in employment contracts the application
of the rule has been far from uniform. The Arizona Supreme Court,
although holding that an implied covenant of good faith and fair dealing did
apply to employment contracts, disagreed with the California rule that the
covenant created a duty to terminate only in good faith:

> "We find neither the logic of the California cases nor their factual
> circumstances compelling for recognition of so broad a rule in the case
> before us. Were we to adopt such a rule, we fear that we would tread
> perilously close to abolishing completely the at-will doctrine and estab-
> lishing by judicial fiat the benefits which employees can and should get
> *only* through collective bargaining agreements or tenure provisions....
> While we do not reject the propriety of such a rule, we are not
> persuaded that it should be the result of judicial decision." *Wagenseller
> v. Scottsdale Memorial Hospital,* 147 Ariz. 370 (1985).

The court intimated that in Arizona the covenant would be breached
only by a termination which contravened public policy. *Wagenseller, supra,*
710 P.2d at 1041.

Similarly, in *Magnan v. Anaconda Industries, Inc.,* 193 Conn. 558, 479
A.2d 781 (1984), the Supreme Court of Connecticut recognized that the
covenant applied to employment contracts, but held that it should not be
applied to transform an at-will employment into one terminable only for
cause. To do so, the court stated, would be to "render the court a
bargaining agent for every employee not protected by statute or collective
bargaining agreement." *Magnan, supra,* 479 A.2d at 788. The court concluded that an at-will employee could challenge his dismissal only when the
reason for discharge involved a violation of an important public policy.
Magnan, supra, 479 A.2d at 789.

* * *

Given the somewhat erratic development of this doctrine in the courts, we decline to follow either the California formulation or any of the variant theories developed in other jurisdictions. We choose to align ourselves with the emerging majority of our sister states which have rejected the implication of a covenant of good faith and fair dealing in employment contracts. . . .

We agree entirely with the policies and reasoning enunciated by the Supreme Court of Washington, sitting en banc, in *Thompson v. St. Regis Paper Co., supra,* 685 P.2d at 1086–1087:

> "A number of courts have utilized a contract theory as a means of ameliorating the harshness of the rule. One contract theory utilized by a limited number of these courts is the adoption of a 'bad faith' exception. . . . Generally, these courts hold that in every employment contract there is an implied covenant of good faith and fair dealing which limited the employer's discretion to terminate an at will employee. Appellant urges us to adopt this approach.

> "We do not adopt this exception. An employer's interest in running his business as he sees fit must be balanced against the interest of the employee in maintaining his employment and this exception does not strike the proper balance. We believe that to imply into each employment contract a duty to terminate in good faith would . . . subject each discharge to judicial incursions into the amorphous concept of bad faith. . . . Moreover, while an employer may agree to restrict or limit his right to discharge an employee, to imply such a restriction on that right from the existence of a contractual right, which, by its terms has no restrictions, is internally inconsistent. . . . Such an intrusion into the employment relationship is merely a judicial substitute for collective bargaining which is more appropriately left to the legislative process." * * *

The Legislature has clearly spoken in Section 34–03–01, N.D.C.C. Adoption of the exception urged by Hillesland would effectively abrogate the at-will rule as applied in this state. We refuse to recognize a cause of action for breach of an implied covenant of good faith and fair dealing where, as in this case, the claimant relies upon an employment contract which contains no express term specifying the duration of employment. Accordingly, we conclude that the district court did not err in granting summary judgment against Hillesland on this issue.

* * *

The judgment of the district court is affirmed.

■ PEDERSON, SURROGATE JUSTICE, dissenting in part.

I agree with the opinion authored by Chief Justice Erickstad in all respects except for the dicta disposition of issue number 3,—Implied Covenant of Good Faith and Fair Dealing.

As I read the pleadings in this case, the termination was not "without cause" but for the exercise of poor judgment. I believe, nevertheless, that in all relationships between civilized persons, there is an obligation to not act in bad faith. Under circumstances that are appropriate, where there is an aggravated breach, unconscionable conduct, the court should provide a remedy.

NOTES

(1) The North Dakota statute codifies the common law "termination at will" doctrine. Suppose there had been no statute. Do you think the court would have reached the same result? Assuming that the employer did have a duty to exercise the discretion to terminate at will in good faith, was there bad faith on the facts of this case?

(2) The court discusses the opinion of the appellate court in Foley v. Interactive Data Corp., which was reversed in part by the California Supreme Court. Foley v. Interactive Data Corp., 47 Cal.3d 654, 254 Cal.Rptr. 211, 765 P.2d 373 (1988). In *Foley*, a decision that belies simple description, the employee sought punitive damages for an alleged wrongful discharge. The majority first rejected the contention that a public policy external to the contract barred the termination, 47 Cal.3d at 665–72. Next, the court concluded that the presumption favoring termination at will, found in Section 2922 of the California Labor Code, was overcome by the allegation of facts from which a jury might conclude that the employer had impliedly agreed to discharge only for cause. Id. at 674–82. Next, the court held that although the employer was subject to a covenant of good faith, a bad faith discharge did not constitute a tort. [Accord: Noye v. Hoffmann–La Roche, Inc., 238 N.J.Super. 430, 570 A.2d 12 (1990).] Rather, since the duty of good faith facilitated performance of contract duties, express or implied, bad faith (a discharge for other than cause) was a breach of contract for which contract remedies were available. Id. at 683–700. A careful reading of the majority, concurring and dissenting opinions reveals sharp disagreements on where the line between contract and tort should be drawn in disputes outside of the insurance area. Nevertheless, one commentator, an attorney for employers, applauds Foley for clarifying the role of courts and contract law in California, thus inviting legislative solutions to the more egregious terminations by employers. Donald E. Warner, Jr., *Foley Starts Setting Things Straight*, 3 LA Lawyer 59 (March, 2002).

(3) *Is "just cause" a better default?* Pauline Kim has shown that employees are generally misinformed about the current default—believing that when contract was silent, they could only be fired for just cause. Pauline T. Kim, Bargaining with Imperfect Information: A Study of Worker Perceptions of Legal Protection in an At–Will World, 83 Cornell L. Rev. 105 (1997). When a contract was silent, ninety percent of employees surveyed believed that it was "unlawful" to fire an employee based on personal dislike. And over eighty percent believed that it was illegal for an employer to fire an employee in order to hire another willing to do the same job for a lower wage. See also Richard Freeman & Joel Rogers, What Workers Want 118–22 (1999) (eighty-three percent of respondents believed it was unlawful to fire an employee "for no reason").

As a repeat player, the employer is much more likely to know the default—the meaning of contractual silence. Wouldn't it make more sense to use the *contra proferentem* or a "penalty default" principle and set the default against the more knowledgeable party?

(4) *Is "employment at will" really just a default in Missouri?* Defenses of employment at will usually stress that it is just a default—meaning that the parties are free to contract for more security if they so wish. But a few jurisdictions have erected barriers to contracting around the rule. For example, imagine that you worked in Missouri and your employer gave you a handbook that expressly stated you would only be fired "for cause." It turns out that you would still be considered an at will employee—who could be fired without cause. For two reasons! First, publishing an employee handbook does not constitute a contractual offer and no promise of job security can be derived from its provisions. Second, a court in the great state of Missouri has even rejected a written contract with an express "just-cause" clause as insufficient to overcome the at-will presumption. Main v. Skaggs Community Hosp., 812 S.W.2d 185, 189 (Mo.Ct.App.1991) "Given this judicial hostility to indefinite term, just-cause contracts, it appears that in Missouri, the at-will presumption can be overcome only by a clear agreement of employment for a fixed term." Kim, 83 Cornell L. Rev. at 114. Query: Can tenured professors at Wash. U. be fired without cause?

Comment: Erosion of "Employment at Will" Doctrine

For more than a century, American courts firmly adhered to the view that an employment contract of no fixed duration was terminable "at will." This meant that an employee who was not subject to a collective bargaining agreement could quit or be fired for a good reason, a bad reason, or no reason at all. See Richard Epstein, *In Defense of the Contract at Will,* 51 U.Chi.L.Rev. 947 (1984).

In recent years, the employer's power to discharge has been limited significantly by both statute and judicial opinion. For example, federal and some state statutes protect an employee against discriminatory discharges based upon race, sex and age. See Kauff and Silverstein, Recent Developments in the Law of Unjust Dismissal 7–26 (1988). Kauff and Silverstein summarize their findings as of 1988:

> Today approximately thirty states have held that the presumption of at-will employment can be contractually altered through statements made in employee handbooks or manuals. Other contract theories, such as promissory or equitable estoppel, independent consideration, and implied covenant of good faith and fair dealing, have also been found to rebut the at-will presumption and thus impair the employer's otherwise unfettered right to discharge. In tort, a majority of states now recognize that an at-will employee cannot be terminated where the reason to termination contravenes some express or implied public policy. Id. at 26.

For a more recent discussion of history and trends, see Stephen F. Befort, *Labor and Employment Law at the Millenium: A Historical Review and Critical Assessment,* 43 B.C. L. Rev. 351 (2002). See also, Glenn Weisenber-

ger, *Remedies for Employer's Wrongful Dischar*
Employment of an Indefinite Duration, 21 Ind.L.F

In light of these developments, one can s
leaving such an important issue of employment
tive bargaining agreements to the law of contrac
of the duty of good faith, employers are prote
nation at will" default rule or their power to ir
provision in the contract. Even with a duty c
posed for a court asked to administer that va;
labor market or to develop appropriate tort star
retaliatory discharge, to protect employee legit
ing, to say the least. You should not be surp
and federal legislation enacted to redress the l
of administrative agencies to which the employee can ιuιιι..
attention has shifted from the end of the relationship (by termination) to
the beginning, where employers are increasingly insisting that employees
agree to arbitrate all claims arising out of the relationship, including rights
created by statute. The vocal resistance to this move is evidenced by
increased attacks on arbitration clauses in the courts. See Christine M.
Reilly, *Achieving Knowing and Voluntary Consent in Pre–Dispute Mandatory Arbitration Agreements at the Contracting Stage,* 90 Cal. L. Rev. 1203
(2002).

SECTION 3. ALLOCATION OF RISK: WARRANTIES AND CONDITIONS

As we have seen, an agreed exchange of bargained for promises creates
a contract to exchange future performances. The parties will normally
agree on such things as the nature and quality of the performance, the time
for performance, the amount of payment, and how and when payment is to
be made. The failure without excuse by one party to perform its promise is
a breach of contract.

The parties may agree, however, to "hedge their bets" by expressly
conditioning a promise. Thus, a buyer may condition its duty to pay upon
being "satisfied" by the seller's performance or a seller may condition its
duty to pay upon receiving notice that the goods are completed. These
conditions provide defensive protection, in that unless the buyer is satisfied
or the seller receives notice, there is no duty to perform. Put differently,
the failure of an express condition discharges the promisor from its duty to
perform but normally does not give a cause of action for damages. We will
explore how these principles work in the next Subsection.

A warranty, however, operates differently. A warranty is a promise
that a representation is true.* A warranty (1) is made by one party to

---

* At times, the word "warranty" will be
used imprecisely as a synonym for "promise"
concerning future events—as in: "I warrant
that this battery will not fail."

about existing or past facts that are knowable but not necessarily ... and which (2) becomes a term in the contract. See UCC 2–313(1) ...rmation of fact about goods must become "part of the basis of the ...argain"). For example, a seller might represent to a buyer that "this cow is fertile and can conceive," an owner might represent to a contractor that "there are no subsurface rock conditions that will impede construction," or a subcontractor may represent to a prime contractor that "my men are licensed and fully insured." If the representation is false, there is a breach of the implied warranty that all representations of fact are true. As Judge Learned Hand once put it, a warranty "amounts to a promise to indemnify the promisee for any loss if the fact warranted proves untrue, for obviously the promisor cannot control what is already in the past." Metropolitan Coal Co. v. Howard, 155 F.2d 780, 784 (2d Cir.1946).

While the affirmative protection of warranty might seem to provide a stronger assurance than conditions, the failure of a condition by relieving the promisor of the duty to perform can work a great forfeiture to the promisee. In some contexts, the defensive protection of being able to withhold your own performance might provide stronger assurance that the other side will perform her promises, then the offensive right to be able to sue for damages.

For example, if a condition to a buyer's duty to pay is that the seller tender goods that perfectly comply with the terms of the agreement, then a slight deviation in performance could potentially relieve the buyer from any contractual obligation to pay for goods in its possession (although non-contractual or quasi-contractual bases such as restitution or quantum meruit may pertain). We will see that common law courts have developed a number of ways to avoid such forfeitures.

As you confront these materials on conditions and warranties, consider what mixture of protections are likely to maximize the gains from trade.

(A) REPRESENTATIONS AND WARRANTIES OF QUALITY

Modern corporate contracts (involving, inter alia, mergers and acquisitions or sales of assets) are carefully structured around the representations and warranties of each side. By warranting that an existing fact is true or promising that a future event will happen, a party can expose itself to breach of contract damages if the warranty fails—and thus can better assure the other side of its performance.

This section focuses on representations and warranties of quality in consumer transactions.

(1) EXPRESS WARRANTIES

To begin, students should remember that representations are not promises, but representations *of existing fact*. Misrepresentations of fact, however, can give rise to contractual liability (and sometimes tort liability) when affirmations of fact about the goods become part of the bargain. The buyer can count on the truth of those affirmations. Thus, UCC § 2–313 establishes:

(1) Express warranties by the seller are created as follows:

(a) Any affirmation of fact or promise made by the seller to the buyer which relates to the goods and becomes part of the basis of the bargain creates an express warranty that the goods shall conform to the affirmation or promise.

(b) Any description of the goods which is made part of the basis of the bargain creates an express warranty that the goods shall conform to the description.

(c) Any sample or model which is made part of the basis of the bargain creates an express warranty that the whole of the goods shall conform to the sample or model.

(2) It is not necessary to the creation of an express warranty that the seller use formal words such as "warrant" or "guarantee" or that he have a specific intention to make a warranty, but an affirmation merely of the value of the goods or a statement purporting to be merely the seller's opinion or commendation of the goods does not create a warranty.

Thus, representations ("affirmations of fact") or simply descriptions of the good create express warranties that the representation is true. There is an irreducible minimum representation involved in any contract—because as a practical matter there must be some minimal description of the good or service being sold.

On the other hand, the words and phrases identified in subsection (2) are excluded from the contract because they are, in effect, "puffing." Why does the section exclude "an affirmation merely of the value of the goods"? What is the meaning of "merely" in this context?

Revised Article 2 made two changes.

First, the scope of UCC 2–313 is expanded to include "remedial promises," defined as a "promise by the seller to repair or replace the goods or to refund all or part of the price upon the happening of a specified event." UCC 2–103(1)(n). Rev. 2–313(4) provides that: "Any remedial promise made by the seller to the immediate buyer creates an obligation that the promise will be performed upon the happening of the specified event." The seller, of course, decides whether to make a remedial promise at all or, if made, what the content shall be.

Second, two new sections, UCC 2–313A and UCC 2–313B, were added to clarify that a manufacturer who makes an express warranty to the public, either in a document passed through a dealer to a buyer or in advertising directly to potential buyers, may be liable in damages to the remote buyer if the goods do not conform to the express warranty. These new sections are complicated and hedged with limitations. Read them carefully.

(2) IMPLIED WARRANTIES

Besides express warranties, the common law has long enforced implied warranties of quality. For example, a seller implicitly represents that she owns the goods subject to the contract (and implicitly warrants that this implicit representation is true). Compare UCC § 2–312. The UCC has created two important additional implied warranties: the implied warranty of merchantability, which arises when a merchant sells described goods to a buyer, and the implied warranty of fitness for a particular purpose, which arises after a buyer has disclosed his or her particular needs or purposes for the goods and relies upon the seller's skill and judgment to supply them.

§ 2–314. Implied Warranty: Merchantability;

(1) Unless excluded or modified (Section 2–316), a warranty that the goods shall be merchantable is implied in a contract for their sale if the seller is a merchant with respect to goods of that kind. . . .

§ 2–315. Implied Warranty: Fitness for Particular Purpose

Where the seller at the time of contracting has reason to know any particular purpose for which the goods are required and that the buyer is relying on the seller's skill or judgment to select or furnish suitable goods, there is unless excluded or modified under the next section an implied warranty that the goods shall be fit for such purpose.*

Notice that a warranty of merchantability is only implied for merchants of "goods of that kind," while an implied warranty of fitness for a particular purpose could potentially apply to non-merchants as well.

The concept of "merchantability" is not self-defining, and while § 2–314(2) provides a 6–part disjunctive definition, the core representation is that the goods "are fit for the ordinary purposes for which such goods are used." § 2–314(2)(c).

Thus, we see that unless disclaimed, merchants implicitly warrant that goods are fit for "ordinary purposes" and other sellers fulfilling the requirements of § 2–315 implicitly warrant that goods are fit for a "particular purpose." The official comment explains the distinction:

A "particular purpose" differs from the ordinary purpose for which the goods are used in that it envisages a specific use by the buyer which is peculiar to the nature of his business whereas the ordinary purposes for which goods are used are those envisaged in the concept of merchantability and go to uses which are customarily made of the goods in question. For example, shoes are generally used for the purpose of walking upon ordinary ground, but a seller may know that a particular pair was selected to be used for climbing mountains. § 2–315, Comment 2.

---

* Does the warranty of fitness operate as an "information-forcing" or "penalty" default rule (which forces sellers to disclose private information when the good is not fit for a particular purpose? Compare CISG Art. 35, which treats these express and implied warranties in one section without mentioning the word warranty.

Why does the implied warranty of merchantability only apply to merchants? Why is the implied warranty of fitness for a particular purpose limited to occasions where the buyer is relying on the seller's skill or judgement?

PROBLEM: THE CASE OF THE DISAPPOINTED SKIER

Francine, an intermediate skier, went shopping for a pair of Ski Boots. She talked with friends and read some advertising literature and concluded that the Bordica Alpine was the ski boot for her. She then went to the Bordica outlet at the Mall and talked with Sales Person Bob. Bob fitted her with a Bordica Alpine 200 for women, telling her, inter alia, that "This is the best boot on the market—you can go anywhere with it—it is toasty on frigid days—the support on your ankles is superb." Persuaded, Francine bought a pair for $350. In January, Francine went to Vail on a ski trip. The temperature was around 0 degrees F. On the first day, she spent several hours in a back bowl over 10,000 feet high. After feeling pain and discomfort in her right foot, she started down the mountain. It was slow going. Just as she reached the top of the last easy glide to the bottom, the bindings on the left ski boot gave way, pitching her to the ground and breaking her ankle. After removing her boots, the medical attendant discovered severe frostbite on the right foot.

(1) Francine consults you for advice. What are her best arguments that Bob made warranties to her about the boots that were breached?

(2) If Bob breached warranties that resulted in personal injuries to Francine, are those losses recoverable under Article 2? See UCC 2–715(2)(b), 2–719(3).

(3) LIMITATIONS OF WARRANTIES AND REMEDIES

The *implicit* warranties of § 2–314 and § 2–315 are default rules (presumed in the absence of express agreement to the contrary) which the parties are free to contract around. But the UCC (and other statutes governing consumer contracts) govern the method that the parties must use to contracting out of implied warranties and at times the extent to which the warranties or the remedies for breach of the warranties can be disclaimed. § 2–316 says in part:

> (2) Subject to subsection (3), to exclude or modify the implied warranty of merchantability or any part of it the language must mention merchantability and in case of a writing must be conspicuous, and to exclude or modify any implied warranty of fitness the exclusion must be by a writing and conspicuous. Language to exclude all implied warranties of fitness is sufficient if it states, for example, that "There are no warranties which extend beyond the description on the face hereof."

> (3) Notwithstanding subsection (2)

> (a) unless the circumstances indicate otherwise, all implied warranties are excluded by expressions like "as is", "with all faults" or other language which in common understanding calls the buyer's

attention to the exclusion of warranties and makes plain that there is no implied warranty; and

(b) when the buyer before entering into the contract has examined the goods or the sample or model as fully as he desired or has refused to examine the goods there is no implied warranty with regard to defects which an examination ought in the circumstances to have revealed to him. . . .

Thus, to disclaim the implied warranty of merchantability, a seller must either conspicuously use the shibboleth, "merchantability" or use words which clearly disclaim all implicit warranties.

Revised UCC 2–316(2) has increased the conditions that must be met in consumer contracts before disclaimers of implied warranties are enforceable. Where an implied warranty of merchantability is involved, "the language must be in a record, be conspicuous, and state 'The seller undertakes no responsibility for the quality of the goods except as otherwise provided in this contract.'" Where an implied warranty of fitness is involved, the contract must state "The seller assumes no responsibility that the goods will be fit for any particular purpose for which you may be buying these goods except as otherwise provided in the contract." The test for disclaimers in other contracts remains the same, except that language satisfying the conditions for consumer contracts satisfies the requirements for any other contract.

Despite the improvements in disclosure in Rev. 2–316, the underlying premise that both buyer and seller are freely consenting to the warranty disclaimer may be belied by the pre-printed, non-negotiable nature of the seller's offer. Nowhere is concerns about "contracts of adhesion" greater than with provisions disclaiming warranties and/or limiting remedies. See Comment on Adhesion Contracts, *supra* at ___.

Henningsen v. Bloomfield Motors

Supreme Court of New Jersey, 1960.
32 N.J. 358, 161 A.2d 69.

[Helen Henningsen, the wife of the purchaser, Claus Henningsen, was held to be entitled to recover for personal injury against both the dealer, Bloomfield Motors, and the manufacturer, Chrysler Corporation. In a landmark decision, the court held that lack of privity would not bar Mrs. Henningsen's suit. The influence of the case would have been even greater had there not emerged a short time later a nonwarranty alternative for those injured by a defective product unreasonably dangerous to the user or consumer or to his or her property. See Restatement (Second) of Torts, 402A (strict liability in tort). The court also invalidated a disclaimer of warranty clause in the contract, a clause which purported to limit warranty protection to the purchaser and to the replacement of defective parts. In concluding that Chrysler's attempted disclaimer of an implied warranty of merchantability is so inimical to the public good as to compel an adjudication of its invalidity, the court spoke as follows:]

* * *

[W]hat effect should be given to the express warranty in question which seeks to limit the manufacturer's liability to replacement of defective parts, and which disclaims all other warranties, express or implied? In assessing its significance we must keep in mind the general principle that, in the absence of fraud, one who does not choose to read a contract before signing it, cannot later relieve himself of its burdens.... And in applying that principle, the basic tenet of freedom of competent parties to contract is a factor of importance. But in the framework of modern commercial life and business practices, such rules cannot be applied on a strict doctrinal basis. The conflicting interests of the buyer and seller must be evaluated realistically and justly, giving due weight to the social policy evinced by the Uniform Sales Act, the progressive decisions of the courts engaged in administering it, the mass production methods of manufacture and distribution to the public, and the bargaining position occupied by the ordinary consumer in such an economy. This history of the law shows that legal doctrines, as first expounded, often prove to be inadequate under the impact of later experience. In such case, the need for justice has stimulated the necessary qualifications or adjustments. ...

* * * As we have said, warranties originated in the law to safeguard the buyer and not to limit the liability of the seller or manufacturer. It seems obvious in this instance that the motive was to avoid the warranty obligations which are normally incidental to such sales. The language gave little and withdrew much. In return for the delusive remedy of replacement of defective parts at the factory, the buyer is said to have accepted the exclusion of the maker's liability for personal injuries arising from the breach of the warranty, and to have agreed to the elimination of any other express or implied warranty. An instinctively felt sense of justice cries out against such a sharp bargain. But does the doctrine that a person is bound by his signed agreement, in the absence of fraud, stand in the way of any relief?

In the modern consideration of problems such as this, Corbin suggests that practically all judges are "chancellors" and cannot fail to be influenced by any equitable doctrines that are available. And he opines that "there is sufficient flexibility in the concepts of fraud, duress, misrepresentation and undue influence, not to mention differences in economic bargaining power" to enable the courts to avoid enforcement of unconscionable provisions in long printed standardized contracts. 1 Corbin on Contracts (1950) § 128, p. 188. Freedom of contract is not such an immutable doctrine as to admit of no qualification in the area in which we are concerned. * * *

The traditional contract is the result of free bargaining of parties who are brought together by the play of the market, and who meet each other on a footing of approximate economic equality. In such a society there is no danger that freedom of contract will be a threat to the social order as a whole. But in present-day commercial life the standardized mass contract has appeared. It is used primarily by enterprises with strong bargaining power and position. * * * Such standardized contracts have been described as those in which one predominant party will dictate its law to an undetermined multiple rather than to an individual. They are said to resemble a law rather than a meeting of the minds.... * * *

The warranty before us is a standardized form designed for mass use. It is imposed upon the automobile consumer. He takes it or leaves it, and he must take it to buy an automobile. No bargaining is engaged in with respect to it. In fact, the dealer through whom it comes to the buyer is without authority to alter it; his function is ministerial—simply to deliver it. The form warranty is not only standard with Chrysler but, as mentioned above, it is the uniform warranty of the Automobile Manufacturers Association. * * *

The gross inequality of bargaining position occupied by the consumer in the automobile industry is thus apparent. There is no competition among the car makers in the area of the express warranty. Where can the buyer go to negotiate for better protection? Such control and limitation of his remedies are inimical to the public welfare and, at the very least, call for great care by the courts to avoid injustice through application of strict common-law principles of freedom of contract. Because there is no competition among the motor vehicle manufacturers with respect to the scope of protection guaranteed to the buyer, there is no incentive on their part to stimulate good will in that field of public relations. Thus, there is lacking a factor existing in more competitive fields, one which tends to guarantee the safe construction of the article sold. Since all competitors operate in the same way, the urge to be careful is not so pressing. ...

Although the courts, with few exceptions, have been most sensitive to problems presented by contracts resulting from gross disparity in buyer-seller bargaining positions, they have not articulated a general principle condemning, as opposed to public policy, the imposition on the buyer of a skeleton warranty as a means of limiting the responsibility of the manufacturer. They have endeavored thus far to avoid a drastic departure from age-old tenets of freedom of contract by adopting doctrines of strict construction, and notice and knowledgeable assent by the buyer to the attempted exculpation of the seller....

The rigid scrutiny which the courts give to attempted limitations of warranties and of the liability that would normally flow from a transaction is not limited to the field of sales of goods. Clauses on baggage checks restricting the liability of common carriers for loss or damage in transit are not enforceable unless the limitation is fairly and honestly negotiated and understandingly entered into. If not called specifically to the patron's attention, it is not binding. It is not enough merely to show the form of a contract; it must appear also that the agreement was understandingly made.... The same holds true in cases of such limitations on parcel check room tickets, ... and on storage warehouse receipts, ... on automobile parking lot or garage tickets or claim checks; ... as to exculpatory clauses in leases releasing a landlord of apartments in a multiple dwelling house from all liability for negligence where inequality of bargaining exists, see Annotation, 175 A.L.R. 8 (1948). * * *

It is true that the rule governing the limitation of liability cases last referred to is generally applied in situations said to involve services of a public or semi-public nature. Typical, of course, are the public carrier or storage or parking lot cases.... But in recent times the books have not been barren of instances of its application in private contract controversies, witness, e.g., ... In the last named matter [Cutler v. Latshaw], which has been noted earlier, the court relied upon the public interest cases as authority. It said:

> "Although these cases have to do with limitation on the liability of common carriers, their reasoning applies with equal force to the facts in the case at bar. When a party to a contract seeks to bind the other party with the unyielding thongs of a warrant of attorney-confession of judgment, a device not ordinarily expected by a homeowner in a simple agreement for alterations and repairs, the inclusion of such a self-abnegating provision must appear in the body of the contract and cannot be incorporated by casual reference with a designation not its own." 97 A.2d at page 238.

Basically, the reason a contracting party offering services of a public or *quasi*-public nature has been held to the requirements of fair dealing, and, when it attempts to limit its liability, of securing the understanding consent of the patron or consumer, is because members of the public generally have no other means of fulfilling the specific need represented by the contract. Having in mind the situation in the automobile industry as detailed above, and particularly the fact that the limited warranty extended by the manufacturers is a uniform one, there would appear to be no just reason why the principles of all of the cases set forth should not chart the course to be taken here.

The task of the judiciary is to administer the spirit as well as the letter of the law. On issues such as the present one, part of that burden is to protect the ordinary man against the loss of important rights through what, in effect, is the unilateral act of the manufacturer. The status of the automobile industry is unique. Manufacturers are few in number and strong in bargaining position. In the matter of warranties on the sale of their products, the Automotive Manufacturers Association has enabled them to present a united front. From the standpoint of the purchaser, there can be no arms length negotiating on the subject. Because his capacity for bargaining is so grossly unequal, the inexorable conclusion which follows is that he is not permitted to bargain at all. He must take or leave the automobile on the warranty terms dictated by the maker. He cannot turn to a competitor for better security.

Public policy is a term not easily defined. Its significance varies as the habits and needs of a people may vary. It is not static and the field of application is an ever increasing one. A contract, or a particular provision therein, valid in one era may be wholly opposed to the public policy of another. ... Courts keep in mind the principle that the best interests of society demand that persons should not be unnecessarily restricted in their freedom to contract. But they do not hesitate to declare void as against public policy contractual provisions which clearly tend to the injury of the public in some way.

NOTES

(1) Was the court correct in concluding that there "is no competition among the car makers in the area of the express warranty?" To what aspect of unconscionability would the lack of competition go?

(2) Did the consumer have an opportunity to avoid bearing the risk—possibly by contracting with a third party?

(3) Does the uniform usage of a clause among all car manufacturer's tend to establish unconscionability or is it a sign of a competitive market?

(4) "Sellers of 'hard goods'—appliances, machines—supply warranty clauses whose central features vary little across industries. These standard clauses (i) disclaim all implied warranties; (ii) expressly warrant the goods against defects in material and workmanship; (iii) limit the buyer's remedies, should the express warranty be breached, to the repair or replacement of defective parts, with the seller having the option of which remedy to use; (iv) limit the time within which claims under the express warranty can be made; (v) exclude liability for consequential damages." Richard E. Speidel & Linda J. Rusch, Commercial Transactions: Sales, Leases and Licenses 640–653 (2001). Are these "central features" efficient? equitable? See Chapter Seven, Section 5(B) for a case dealing with this standard "warranty package."

(5) *Personal injury resulting from breach of warranty*. Article 2 includes as consequential damages resulting from a seller's breach "injury to person and property proximately resulting from any breach of warranty." UCC 2–715(2)(b) Beyond that, two other sections deal with personal injury claims, UCC 2–719(3), providing that agreements excluding liability for personal injuries are "prima facie unconscionable," and UCC 2–318, providing three Alternative limitations on the defense of "no privity of contract" where foreseeable users (Mrs. Henningsen) or subpurchasers are involved. Thus, Mrs. Henningsen would have a personal injury claim in strict tort liability in most states and, to the extent that tort law is not preemptive, a warranty claim under Article 2. Whether the seller's effort to disclaim warranties, express or implied (as opposed to excluding liability for personal injury damages) would be tested under UCC 2–316(2) and the general section on Unconscionability. UCC 2–302.

In 1998, the American Law Institute published the Restatement (Third) of Products Liability. The revision of Article 2 should be completed by the Summer of 2003. How is the overlap between warranty and tort law accommodated where personal injuries and property damage result from a breach of warranty or a defective product? Neither document makes this clear. Thus if goods which are both unmerchantable under UCC 2–314 and defective under the Restatement cause personal injuries, the plaintiff, presumably, could sue in either warranty or tort or, perhaps, both. If a breach of warranty is established, however, the buyer must satisfy the usual conditions in Article 2 for the proof of that claim, i.e., notice within a reasonable time after the non-conformity is or should have been discovered, UCC 2–607(3)(a), privity of contract, UCC 2–318, satisfying the four year statute of limitations, UCC 2–715(1), and the absence of a valid disclaimer of warranty, UCC 2–316(2). These conditions do not exist in the law of torts. Agreements excluding liability for personal injuries, however, are still "prima facie" unconscionable.

Murray v. Holiday Rambler, Inc.

Supreme Court of Wisconsin, 1978.
83 Wis.2d 406, 265 N.W.2d 513.

■ CONNOR T. HANSEN, J. On January 23, 1974, the plaintiffs purchased a 22–foot 1973 Avenger motor home for a total sales price, including sales tax, license fees and trade-in allowance on another motor home owned by the plaintiffs, of $11,007.15. * * *

The document signed by Mr. Murray purported to exclude all warranties, express or implied.... The reverse side of this document stated:

MANUFACTURER'S UNDERTAKING—AVENGER CORPORATION

THERE ARE NO WARRANTIES EXPRESSED OR IMPLIED AND PARTICULARLY THERE ARE NO WARRANTIES OF MERCHANT-ABILITY OR FITNESS FOR A PARTICULAR PURPOSE MADE BY AVENGER CORPORATION FOR ITS PRODUCTS.

AVENGER CORPORATION, as the manufacturer, in lieu thereof undertakes and agrees that the product identified on the Pre–Delivery and Acceptance Declaration (reverse side) was free of defects in material and workmanship at the time of its delivery to the dealer and the initial user and owner; and * * *

If such Avenger product or its component parts (other than tires) shall fail within one year from the date of delivery to the original user because the product or component part was defective when installed; and

If the owner-user will return the trailer to a service facility authorized by Avenger Corporation within fifty-two (52) weeks after initial delivery, *Avenger Corporation will in the method it determines to be necessary replace, or repair, at its sole option any such defective product or component at its own cost and expense.*

THERE ARE NO OTHER WARRANTIES OF ANY KIND, EXPRESS OR IMPLIED, AND NO OTHER OBLIGATIONS, EITHER EXPRESS OR IMPLIED, INCLUDING SPECIFICALLY ANY OBLIGATION FOR INCIDENTAL EXPENSES OF ANY NATURE UNDERTAKEN BY AVENGER CORPORATION AS THE MANUFACTURER. (Emphasis added.)

* * * [W]here the limited remedy fails of its essential purpose, the limitation will be disregarded and ordinary UCC remedies will be available. Sec. 402.719(2), Stats. The purpose of an exclusive remedy of repair or replace-

ment, from the buyer's standpoint, is to give him goods which conform to the contract—in this case, a motor home substantially free of defects—within a reasonable time after a defect is discovered.

> [E]very buyer has the right to assume his new car, with the exception of minor adjustments, will be 'mechanically new and factory furnished, operate perfectly, and be free of substantial defects' ... After the purchase of an automobile, the same should be put in good running condition; that is the seller does not have an unlimited time for the performance of the obligation to replace and repair parts. The buyer of an automobile is not bound to permit the seller to tinker with the article indefinitely in the hope that it may ultimately be made to comply with the warranty.... At some point in time, if major problems continue to plague the automobile, it must become obvious to all people that a particular vehicle simply cannot be repaired or parts replaced so that the same is made free of defect...." Orange Motors of Coral Gables v. Dade Co. Dairies, 258 So.2d 319, 320, 321 (Fla.App.1972).

@ some point it's a Lemon

Although individual nonconformities may not be substantial in and of themselves, the obligation to repair or replace parts may fail of its essential purpose where the cumulative effect of all the nonconformities substantially impairs the value of the goods to the buyer....

Where the seller is given reasonable opportunity to correct the defect or defects, and the vehicle nevertheless fails to operate as should a new vehicle free of defects, the limited remedy fails of its essential purpose.... The buyer may then invoke any of the remedies available under the UCC, including the right to revoke acceptance of the goods, under sec. 2–608 of the UCC (sec. 402.608, Stats.). * * *

if seller tries to fix but it's impossible ... buyer can revoke 2-608

The testimony favorable to the verdict showed the following: Mr. Murray experienced problems with the lights and battery of the vehicle on the day he took possession and, although repairs were attempted, the lights continued to dim, the electrical system went dead on several occasions, and the generator did not charge the battery properly. The wiring of an outdoor light short-circuited where it passed through a sharp-edged metal wall. There were problems with the clock. There was an exposed, allegedly non-energized, 120–volt wire coming from the main electrical panel. Plaintiffs' expert witness testified that the wiring in the 12–volt electrical system was of an insufficient gauge for the type of fuses used by the manufacturer, that this wiring was not in conformity with the applicable electrical code, and that there was a danger of overheating in the electrical system.

Exposed Wire!

The original gas tank and an auxiliary gas tank, installed by KOA [the authorized Holiday Rambler dealer from whom Murray bought the motor home] at the Murrays' request prior to delivery, were both apparently improperly vented. As a result, it was extremely difficult to fill the tanks; gasoline would spew out of the tanks when the caps were removed; and gasoline fumes came up into the passenger compartment. Mr. Murray testified that on one occasion, service station attendants were able to put only twenty cents' worth of gasoline into both tanks. Apparently as a result

KOA - dealer bad Gas Tanks

of problems with the carburetor, the vehicle would stall. Dirt and soldering flux were found in the fuel filter, which was replaced, as was the fuel pump.

There were problems with the air suspension system. There was testimony that this resulted in uneven distribution of weight on the tandem set of wheels in the rear of the vehicle, putting insufficient weight on the front wheels and causing steering problems. Repairs were made to the suspension system, but the steering problems persisted. Mr. Murray complained that the front brakes were not operating properly, and despite adjustments, had difficulty with the front wheels.

Suspension + steering problems also

KOA apparently remedied various problems with the furnace and refrigerator, with an oil filter, and with a rattling engine cowling. KOA corrected the LP fuel tank gauge, which, as installed at the factory, indicated "full" when the tank was empty, and vice versa; KOA also supplied a missing handle for the tank and drained water which was inside the tank when it left the factory.

Unusual pressure caused a water line to come uncoupled. Mr. Murray advised KOA about this problem but repaired it himself.

There was also testimony regarding problems with folding seats, the furnace fan, the exhaust fan above the stove, a splash board which came unfastened, and the oven door, which fell off. Although there was conflicting testimony as to whether these parts were defective, the testimony of the Murrays with regard to these problems was not inherently incredible.
* * *

Interior Issues

Although the Murrays agreed that KOA had never refused to attempt a requested repair, this testimony does not affect their right to revoke acceptance. The limited remedy of repair or replacement of defective parts fails of its essential purpose whenever, despite reasonable opportunity for repair, the goods are not restored to a nondefective condition within a reasonable time, whether or not the failure to do so is willful. * * *

The jury awarded the plaintiffs $2,500 for loss of use of the motor home from the date of revocation of acceptance, August 15, 1974, to the date of the verdict. KOA argues that the plaintiffs were precluded by the terms of the limited warranty from recovering any incidental or consequential damages, including any damages for loss of use of the vehicle.

KOA - limited warranty → no incidentals

Where the exclusive limited remedy of the contract fails of its essential purpose, however, the buyer is entitled to invoke any of the remedies available under the UCC. Sec. 402.719(2), Stats. This includes the right to recover consequential damages under sec. 402.715.

UCC - Right to Consequentials

Consequential damages include any loss caused by general or particular needs of the buyer of which the seller had reason to know at the time of contracting and which could not reasonably be prevented by cover or otherwise. Sec. 402.715(1), Stats. Consequential damages have specifically been held to include damages for loss of use of an inoperable motor vehicle. Bob Anderson Pontiac, Inc. v. Davidson (Ind.App.1973), 293 N.E.2d 232.
* * *

Consequentials = seller knew + couldn't cover

Δ =
Russo Case
still had to
pay Car Value
But ... Not
Rental Car
fees ...

The defendant, KOA, relies upon Russo v. Hilltop Lincoln–Mercury, Inc. (Mo.App.1972), 479 S.W.2d 211. There, defective wiring had caused an automobile to be totally burned. The Missouri Court of Appeals held that, because the car could not be repaired, the limited warranty remedy of repair or replacement of defective parts was inapplicable. Accordingly, the buyer was allowed to recover, not merely the replacement cost of the defective wiring, but rather the full value of the car.

Implicit in this holding was a determination that the limited warranty remedy had failed of its essential purpose. Nevertheless, when the Missouri court turned to the buyer's claim for damages for the rental cost of a replacement car, the court held that such damages were excluded by the terms of the warranty and that this exclusion had not failed of its essential purpose.

Russo is
inconsistent
w/ UCC's
Intent

This result is inconsistent with the many decisions which have held that consequential damages may be recovered where a limited contractual remedy excluding such damages has failed. . . . Moreover, the result of the Russo Case, supra, which permitted the buyer to recover some UCC damages but not others, is inconsistent with the apparent intention of the drafters. Sec. 402.719(2), Stats., provides that once a limited remedy fails of its essential purpose "remedy may be had as provided in this code." In such a case the exclusive contractual remedy " . . . must give way to the general remedy provision of this Article [chapter 402, Stats.]." Official Comment 1, sec. 2–719 UCC.

Thus, although an express warranty excludes consequential damages, when the exclusive contractual remedy fails, the buyer may recover consequential damages under sec. 402.715, Stats., as though the limitation had never existed.

[The court found, however, that plaintiff failed to prove that the loss of use caused $2500 in damages and awarded plaintiffs $500.]

NOTES

(1) Was the seller unreasonable in not replacing the motor home? Should good faith attempts to repair be a defense? In commercial contracts, most courts interpret UCC 2–719(2) to preserve the term excluding liability for consequential damages even though the limited remedy has failed of its essential purpose. That exclusion will be enforced unless it is unconscionable. UCC 2–719(3). See Rheem Mfg. Co. v. Phelps Heating & Air Conditioning, Inc., 746 N.E.2d 941 (Ind.2001). See also Lewis Refrigeration Co. v. Sawyer Fruit, Vegetable and Cold Storage Co., infra at Chapter Seven, Section 5(B).

(2) *Research exercise.* A number of states have either amended the UCC or enacted separate legislation to prohibit warranty disclaimers in consumer sales. Even more states have passed immutable "lemon laws" that permit consumers to return new cars that dealers cannot repair. Check the relevant statutes of the state where you intend to practice and report your findings.

(4) The Magnuson–Moss Warranty Act, 15 U.S.C.A. sec. 2301 et seq, provides that "No supplier may disclaim . . . any implied warranty to a

consumer ... [if] such supplier makes any written warranty...." 15 U.S.C. § 2808(a) (1976). Section (b), however, provides that "implied warranties may be limited in duration to the duration of a written [express] warranty of reasonable duration, if such limitation is conscionable and is set for in clear and unmistakable language and prominently displayed on the face of the warranty." These limitations apply regardless of whether the written warranty is a full or limited warranty.

Magnuson Moss also requires sellers to disclose whether their warranties are "full" or "limited. A "full" warranty does not limit the duration of implied warranties; requires the warrantor to remedy defects within a reasonable time at no extra charge to the consumer; permits consumers to rescind or obtain a new product if the item sold cannot be conveniently repaired; and requires any exclusion of consequential damages to be stated in conspicuous language. All other warranties are "limited." 15 U.S.C. §§ 2303–2304 (1976):

> This disclosure requirement seeks to increase the warranty coverage available to consumers in two ways. First, Congress hoped that firms would be embarrassed to describe their warranties as "limited" and so would make full" warranties. Almost all firms, however, offer only "limited" warranties, apparently interpreting "full" to mean "too much." Second, if the concise labels "full" and "limited" would succinctly communicate to consumers the scope of warranty coverage, consumers could compare the coverage of different firms at greatly reduced cost.... But because almost all firms use limited warranties, ... no more information exists now than existed before passage of the Act. Alan Schwartz & Robert E. Scott, Commercial Transactions: Principles and Policies 226 (2d ed. 1991).

(5) In consumer contracts, Article 2 occupies an uneasy position between federal law, the Magnuson–Moss Warranty Act, and the state lemon laws. For example, suppose the manufacturer is unable after a reasonable number of tries to repair or replace defective parts in an expensive consumer good. Under Mag–Moss, the consumer is entitled to a new, replacement product only if the warrantor has made a "full" warranty. 15 U.S.C.A. § 2304(a). But the statute gives the warrantor a choice on this and almost no one chooses to make a full warranty. Under state lemon laws, replacement is available but the statutes apply to new cars only. Thus, in most cases, the consumer buyer is left with Article 2 which, at best, would permit the buyer to revoke acceptance, UCC 2–608, recover any of the price paid, and seek damages. UCC 2–711. The remedy of replacement from the seller is not available under Article 2, although the buyer could purchase new goods from another seller. UCC 2–712.

Section 2–811(b) of the 1999 draft of Revised Article 2 made a token effort to increase consumer protection in the gap:

> If, because of a breach of contract or other circumstances, an exclusive, agreed remedy fails substantially to achieve the intended purposes of the parties, the following rules apply: ... (2) In a consumer contract, an aggrieved party may reject the goods or revoke acceptance and, to the extent of the failure, may resort to all remedies under this Article."

This language does not appear in the 2002 draft of Revised Article 2.

(B) Express Conditions

(1) NATURE AND EFFECT

A rational person making commitments for the future is likely to take at least three things into account: first, what must one receive from the other party in exchange for one's promise or performance, and second, assuming that the return performance is satisfactory, what events could occur that would impair the incentive to complete the exchange and third, what can be done about them? Naturally, if the other party refuses to commit in a satisfactory way or, after making the promise, fails to perform, our rational person has protection. This protection is explained in terms of "no contract was ever formed" or "the defendant has breached the contract." But if a contract has been created and the defendant is not in breach, what protection is available when an event occurs which impairs the value of the bargain to the other?

A general answer is that if the agreement does not provide for this event, i.e., there is a "gap" in the agreement after legitimate processes of ascertaining and interpreting the agreement have been exhausted, the disappointed party faces an uphill battle. Here, as we shall see, the battle to escape from the contract is waged under such labels as "mutual mistake," "constructive conditions of exchange," and "impossibility or frustration of performance." The court is asked to fill this gap in the agreement and to protect the aggrieved party from severe disruptions, the risk of which he or she should not, under the circumstances, be made to assume.

But suppose the risk is foreseen by one party and expressly provided for in the agreement. For example, suppose that Uncle, a noted historian, has a nephew in law school and that Nephew has absolutely no interest in "cultural" courses, such as legal history or jurisprudence. After an appropriate bit of bargaining, Uncle induces Nephew to promise to take Professor Holmes' course in Common Law Miracles by promising to pay him $500, "provided that he take the course for a grade and earn a grade of B or better." Nephew takes the course and earns a grade of C+. What is the legal position of the parties at this point? Can Uncle, if he chooses, refuse to pay the $500 without liability for breach of contract?

The argument on both sides might run something like this. Uncle will argue that the "B or better" requirement was an express condition to his duty to pay $500. In Restatement (Second) parlance, it was "an event, not certain to occur, which must occur, unless its non-occurrence is excused, before performance under a contract becomes due." Section 224. See, generally, Arthur Corbin, *Conditions in the Law of Contracts*, 28 Yale L.J. 739 (1919). Moreover, the event was made a condition "by agreement of the parties." Section 226. Since the event did *not* occur (Nephew earned a C plus), two legal consequences follow: First, Uncle's unconditional duty to pay $500 never arose; and Second, the duty (and, thus, the contract) is discharged "when the condition can no longer occur." Section 225(1) & (2). Uncle's legal position is purely defensive—he avoids the duty to pay because the condition failed. As a consequence, Nephew bears the risk of the investment to earn "B or better" in a situation where Uncle has received no tangible benefit from that effort.

Nephew's counter-arguments, most of which will emerge more clearly in the materials to follow, might take these forms: (1) The event was not a condition at all. Rather, it was a matter of convenience that did not affect the rights and duties of the parties. (2) The event was promised by Nephew as a part of the agreed exchange. Although Uncle's duty to pay is "constructively" conditioned upon performance of the promise, the "constructive" condition is satisfied by substantial rather than literal compliance. In short, C+ is close enough. (3) The condition was excused, i.e., deleted from the agreement, either because Uncle "waived it" or because its excuse is necessary to avoid forfeiture.

With these arguments in mind, consider the following materials. After due consideration, who has the better of it, Uncle or Nephew?

Dove v. Rose Acre Farms, Inc.

Court of Appeals of Indiana, First District, 1982.
434 N.E.2d 931.

■ NEAL, JUDGE.

Plaintiff-appellant Mark Dove (Dove) appeals a negative judgment of the Decatur Circuit Court in favor of defendant-appellee Rose Acre Farms, Inc. in a trial before the court without the intervention of a jury.

We affirm.

STATEMENT OF THE FACTS

The evidence most favorable to support the judgment and the facts found specially by the trial court are as follows. Dove had been employed by Rose Acre Farms, operated by David Rust (Rust), its president and principal owner, in the summers and other times from 1972 to 1979. The business of Rose Acre was the production of eggs, and, stocked with 4,000,000 hens and staffed with 300 employees, it produced approximately 256,000 dozen eggs per day. Rust had instituted and maintained extensive bonus programs, some of which were for one day only, or one event or activity only. For example, one bonus was the white car bonus; if an employee would buy a new white car, keep it clean and undamaged, place a Rose Acre sign on it, commit no tardiness or absenteeism, and attend one management meeting per month, Rose Acre would pay $100 per month for 36 months as a bonus above and beyond the employee's regular salary, to apply on payments. Any slight violation, such as being a minute late for work, driving a dirty or damaged car, or missing work for any cause, would work a forfeiture of the bonus. Other bonuses consisted of egg production bonuses, deed conversion bonuses, house management bonuses, and a silver feather bonus. This last bonus program required the participant to wear a silver feather, and a system of rewards and penalties existed for employees who participated. While the conditions of the bonuses varied, one condition existed in all bonus programs: during the period of the bonus, the employee must not be tardy for even a minute, and must not miss work any day for any cause whatever, even illness. If the employee missed any days during the week, he was sometimes permitted to make them up on Saturday and/or Sunday. Any missed work not made up within the same week worked a forfeiture of the bonus. These rules were explained to the employees and were stated in a written policy. The bonus programs were voluntary, and all the employees did not choose to participate in them. When a bonus was offered a card was issued to the participant stating his name and the terms and amount of the bonus. Upon completion of the required tasks, the card was attached to the pay sheet, and the bonus was added to the paycheck. Rust was strict about tardiness and absenteeism, whether an employee was on a bonus program or not. If an employee was tardy, his pay would be docked to the minimum wage, or he would be sent home and lose an entire day. A minute's tardiness would also deprive the employee of a day for purposes of seniority. As was stated in the evidence, bonuses were given for the "extra mile" or actions "above and beyond the call of duty." The purpose of the bonus programs and penalties was to discourage absenteeism and tardiness, and to promote motivation and dependability.

In June 1979, Rust called in Dove and other construction crew leaders and offered a bonus of $6,000 each if certain detailed construction work was completed in 12 weeks. As Dove conceded in his own testimony, the bonus card indicated that in addition to completing the work, he would be required to work at least five full days a week for 12 weeks to qualify for the bonus. On the same day Dove's bonus agreement, by mutual consent, was amended to ten weeks with a bonus of $5,000 to enable him to return to law school by September 1. Dove testified that there was no ambiguity in the agreement, and he understood that to qualify for the bonus he would have to work ten weeks, five days a week, commencing at starting time and quitting only at quitting time. Dove testified that he was aware of the provisions concerning absenteeism and tardiness as they affected bonuses, and that if he missed any work, for any reason, including illness, he would forfeit the bonus. The evidence disclosed that no exception had ever been made except as may have occurred by clerical error or inadvertence.

In the tenth week Dove came down with strep throat. On Thursday of that week he reported to work with a temperature of 104°, and told Rust that he was unable to work. Rust told him, in effect, that if he went home, he would forfeit the bonus. Rust offered him the opportunity to stay there and lay on a couch, or make up his lost days on Saturday and/or Sunday. Rust told him he could sleep and still qualify for the bonus. Dove left to seek medical treatment and missed two days in the tenth week of the bonus program.

Rust refused Dove the bonus based solely upon his missing the two days of work. While there was some question of whether the construction job was finished, Rust does not seem to have made that issue the basis of his refusal. Bonuses to other crew leaders were paid. The trial court denied

---

Margin handwritten notes:

All Bonuses required being on-time + no missed days for ANY Excuse

Rust was Strict

6K 12 wks

Dove's:
10 wks
5K

- Dove Got sick in Wk 10
- Rust: You Can sleep here
- Dove left

Dove's recovery and, in the conclusions of law, stated that Dove had not shown that all of the conditions of the bonus contract had been met. Specifically, Dove failed to work five full days a week for ten weeks.

* * *

Dove argues that the bonus agreement was implemented to (1) insure his presence on the construction site, and (2) cut the cost of construction through maximum production by workers. He next contends that Rose Acre got what it bargained for, that is the completion of the project. He argues that he was present on the job, including the hours he worked late, at least 750 hours during the ten weeks, while regular working hours would amount to only 500 hours. Therefore, he concludes, there was substantial compliance with the agreement, and he should not be penalized because he failed to appear on the last two days because of illness.

* * *

We are constrained to observe, in the case before us, that the bonus rules at Rose Acre were well known to Dove when he agreed to the disputed bonus contract. He certainly knew Rust's strict policies and knew that any absence for any cause whatever worked a forfeiture of the bonus. With this knowledge he willingly entered into this bonus arrangement, as he had done in the past, * * *; he must be held to have agreed to all of the terms upon which the bonus was conditioned. If the conditions were unnecessarily harsh or eccentric, and the terms odious, he could have shown his disdain by simply declining to participate, for participation in the bonus program was not obligatory or job dependent.

Contrary to Dove's assertion that completion of a task was the central element of the bonus program, we are of the opinion that the rules regarding tardiness and absenteeism were a central theme. Rust stated that the purpose of the bonus program was to discourage tardiness and absenteeism and to promote motivation and dependability. Indeed, some of the bonus programs such as the white car bonus and the silver feather bonus were apparently an effort on the part of Rust to establish among the employees an identity with Rose Acre and to create an *esprit de corps*. The direct tangible benefits to Rose Acre would be unmeasurable, and the burden upon the employees would be equally unmeasurable. Yet, Rust was willing to pay substantial bonuses in the implementation of his program, and the employees, including Dove, were quite as willing to take the money.

No fraud or bad faith has been shown on the part of Rose Acre, and no public policy arguments have been advanced to demonstrate why the bonus contract should not be enforced as agreed between the parties. * * *

Dove argues that he should be relieved of strict performance because his illness rendered his performance impossible.

[The court discussed and distinguished two cases]

* * *

None of these cases involved a contract for personal services, though dicta contained general language applicable to such contracts. Generally, impossibility of performance is a defense to an action for damages.... Dove has not demonstrated how the doctrine is applicable here. Certainly a plaintiff cannot, upon failing to perform his part of the contract, sue his adversary for damages alleging that his own non-performance was because of impossibility. Suppose Dove, because of illness, could not work at all. Could he sue for wages? * * *

For the reasons given above, we hold that Dove failed to perform all of the conditions of the contract and is not entitled to recover any portion of the bonus. The judgment is affirmed.

NOTES

(1) What is the "condition" in *Dove?* What was the legal effect of its non-occurrence? Is it relevant that the "condition" was a performance by Dove that was necessary to create a bonus contract?

(2) "An obligor will often qualify his duty by providing that performance will not become due unless a stated event, which is not certain to occur, does occur. Such an event is called a condition. An obligor may make an event a condition of his duty in order to shift to the obligee the risk of its nonoccurrence. In this case the event may be within the control of the obligee (e.g., his furnishing security), or of the obligor (e.g., his satisfaction with the obligee's performance), or of neither (e.g., the accidental destruction of the subject matter)." Restatement (Second), Chapter 9, Topic 5, Introductory Note.

(3) *Condition Precedent and Condition Subsequent.* A standard classification is based on the distinction between conditions which are "precedent" and those which are "subsequent." The reference point is the accrual of the cause of action; i.e., the point in time when the obligor is under a duty to render an immediate performance. Conditions precedent must be satisfied before a contractual duty of this type comes into existence; the effect of the occurrence of a condition subsequent is to extinguish or discharge such a duty. For example, in Abolin v. Farmers' American Mutual Fire Insurance Co., 100 Pa.Super. 433 (1930), a fire insurance policy provided that "no suit or action on this policy for the recovery of any claim shall be sustainable in any court of law or equity * * * unless commenced within twelve months next after the fire * * * for which claim is made." After a fire occurred and proof of loss was made, both conditions precedent, the company was under a duty to make payment. But payment was not made, and the insured did not bring suit to collect within twelve months of the fire. Applying the foregoing provision, the court denied recovery. The company's duty was discharged by the failure to bring suit within the stipulated period. Such failure, in traditional usage, amounts to the occurrence of a condition subsequent in the contract.

Conditions subsequent are comparatively rare in contracts, and at times those which are treated in the cases as "subsequent" are clearly "precedent." See, e.g., Capitol Land Co. v. Zorn, 134 Ind.App. 431, 184 N.E.2d 152 (1962). Noting the relationship of the traditional condition subsequent to the discharge of obligation, the drafters of Restatement (Second) do not use the term and confine their use of "condition" to those of the precedent variety. See Restatement (Second) § 224, Comment e, § 230, Comment a.

Actually, the need for distinguishing between events which are "precedent" and "subsequent" in the above sense derives from procedural requirements. Under Rule 9(c) of the Federal Rules of Civil Procedure it is sufficient that the plaintiff allege generally in the complaint that all conditions precedent have been performed or have occurred. The defendant, on the other hand, is obliged to deny specifically and with particularity that they have not. A failure to plead accordingly will prevent using the failure of condition as a defense in the federal courts. See, e.g., Ginsburg v. Insurance Company of North America, 427 F.2d 1318, 1321–22 (6th Cir.1970). Federal courts take a similar approach on conditions subsequent. Thus, if a party fails in a required responsive pleading to raise an issue regarding the existence of a condition subsequent, that party may not later rely on the condition subsequent as a defense. Title Guaranty & Surety Co. v. Nichols, 224 U.S. 346, 32 S.Ct. 475, 56 L.Ed. 795 (1912). Since several states have promulgated pleading requirements based on the Federal Rules or have comparable provisions relative to the pleading of conditions, similar alertness is demanded in other jurisdictions. See, e.g., Travers v. Travelers Insurance Co., 385 Mass. 811, 434 N.E.2d 208 (1982).

Wal–Noon Corp. v. Hill

Court of Appeals of California, 1975.
45 Cal.App.3d 605, 119 Cal.Rptr. 646.

■ PUGLIA, PRESIDING JUSTICE.

* * *

In August of 1957, the parties entered into a lease agreement for the construction and occupancy of a building. The major portion of the building was to be occupied and used by plaintiffs for a market and the remainder was to be sublet by plaintiffs for various satellite enterprises. Construction was completed in 1959.

In 1967 or 1968 the roof started to leak over the market portion of the building. Shortly thereafter complaints were made to plaintiffs by other tenants of similar leaky conditions. On several occasions, repairs were made to the roof at plaintiffs' expense. After approximately 12 to 15 repairs, plaintiffs were advised by roofers whom they consulted that repair was no longer practicable and that a new roof should be installed. Plaintiffs sought and obtained competitive bids for replacing the roof and awarded the job to the lowest bidders. Replacement was accomplished in two stages, the satellite portion being done by one company in September 1968 at a cost of $4,800, and the market portion by another in August 1969 at a cost of $4,000.

The lease in part provided as follows: "MAINTENANCE AND RE-PAIRS. The Lessors agree, at their own cost and expense, to make all repairs to the roof and exterior walls (except glazing and painting replacements and/or repairs which Lessees agree to do) of the new building, provided, however, that the Lessors shall have no obligation to make any repairs to the new building made necessary by the negligence or improper use thereof by the Lessees, their sub-lessees, agents or employees. Except as herein qualified, Lessees shall keep the leased premises in good order and condition at their own expense and surrender the same in good order and condition upon the expiration or sooner termination of this lease, reasonable wear from proper use thereof and damage from the elements excepted. . . .

"WRITTEN COMMUNICATIONS. All notices, demands, consents and denials hereunder by either party to the other shall be in writing and shall be sufficiently given and served if either personally served, or if sent by United States registered mail, return receipt requested, postage prepaid, in a sealed envelope addressed as follows:

"If sent by mail to Lessors, the same shall be addressed to the Lessors at 4920 15th Avenue, Sacramento, California;

"If sent by mail to Lessees, the same shall be addressed to the Lessees at the leased premises.

"Either the Lessors or the Lessees may change such address by notice in writing to the other party of such new address as the Lessors or the Lessees may desire used for such purpose. All rent or other sums payable hereunder may be paid to Lessors at the above listed address for notices.

" . . .

"INTERPRETATION. The various headings and numbers herein and the groupings of the provisions of this lease into separate articles and paragraphs shall not be construed to limit or restrict either the meaning or application of any provision hereof, and are for the purpose of convenience only."

Prior to the repairs to and later replacement of the roof, plaintiffs did not review the lease to determine upon which party the obligation for such work was placed. However, in 1971, the plaintiffs finally became aware of the lease provision which allocated the responsibility for such repair and replacement to defendant lessors. Thereafter plaintiffs requested that defendants reimburse them for the sums expended to replace the roof. Defendants refused and this action was thereafter instituted.

The complaint filed by plaintiffs was phrased purely in terms of contract, as was defendants' answer. The action proceeded to trial on that theory, plaintiffs seeking to establish the provisions of the lease and the circumstances surrounding repair and replacement of the roof. Defendants sought to show that they were prejudiced by plaintiffs' failure to notify them of the defective condition of the roof at a time when they could exercise their contractual right to control repair or replacement.

The contractor who replaced the roof over the market testified that he was asked by plaintiffs to estimate cost of replacement but did not recall if he was asked to estimate cost of repair. He also stated that some of the roof damage possibly could have been caused in servicing the air conditioning equipment placed on the roof by plaintiffs and further, that some of the roof damage was attributable to water overflow from this equipment. The roof that he installed had a 15–year life expectancy. He testified that for an additional $1,200 to $1,300 a roof with a 20–year life expectancy could have been installed. He also testified that roofs can always be repaired, although in some cases it may not be economically feasible to do so.

The contractor who re-roofed the satellite area testified that plaintiffs did not ask him the cost of repair but only for an estimate of replacement cost. He also was of the opinion that some of the damage to the roof could have been caused in servicing the air conditioning equipment. The roof which he installed had a two-year warranty but this could have been extended to 20 years by the purchase at the time of installation of a bond for approximately $600.

Defendant Hill testified that he had no knowledge of leaks in the roof, the need for repairs, or that the roof had been replaced until he was so advised by plaintiffs in February 1971. He was of the opinion that the original roof on the building had a 20–year life expectancy, and that recourse might have been available against the installing contractor had he been timely notified. He testified that as a contractor himself, he might have been able to obtain more advantageous terms for required repairs or replacement. Hill further testified that an examination of the damage to the old roof might have disclosed the cause thereof and that if caused by plaintiffs' activities relating to the air conditioning system, he would not be liable under the lease for repairs or replacement.

The trial court prepared its own findings of fact and conclusions of law. It found that the lease required defendants to repair the roof except for repairs necessitated by plaintiffs' negligent or improper use; that repairs become necessary for which plaintiffs spent $8,941; and that defendants had neither notice from plaintiffs nor knowledge of the need for repairs prior to completion of the work.

From those facts the court concluded that plaintiffs breached the contract by failing to give notice; that they were, however, entitled to restitution because defendants had been unjustly enriched; that an offset equal to one-third of the replacement cost was equitable; and that plaintiffs were therefore entitled to judgment against defendants for $5,867 plus legal interest from the date demand was made for reimbursement under the lease. The court further concluded that plaintiffs were not entitled to attorney's fees "Inasmuch as this action was not predicated on the lease, and plaintiffs in any event had breached the lease, . . . "

Plaintiffs take the position on appeal that the judgment as rendered by the trial court "is outside the scope of the pleadings and the theory of the case as presented at the trial" and that the "case should stand or fall upon the contractual provisions of the lease." Plaintiffs then argue that the trial court erred in finding them in breach of the lease for failure to give notice and in denying them full recovery thereunder. The argument is made that the lease provision governing the form and manner of giving notice cannot be expanded into a condition precedent that notice to repair in fact be given.

The plaintiffs are, of course, correct that the lease does not contain an express provision that defendants be given notice to repair. However, it is impossible to conceive of how the intentions of the parties as expressed in the covenant to repair could be implemented if notice were not required. Defendants' duty to repair was not unconditional. It did not extend to repairs made necessary by the negligence or improper use of the premises by the lessees, their agents or employees. Such repairs were by necessary implication the responsibility of lessees who were by the lease obligated to keep the premises "in good order and condition at their own expense...." Clearly the parties did not intend that when repairs became necessary the lessees could unilaterally and conclusively determine the responsibility therefor and allocate the burden thereof as between lessor and lessee. If the interpretation of the lease urged by plaintiffs were accepted, however, it would permit plaintiffs to alter conditions without the lessors' knowledge and to their disadvantage, at the same time eliminating any real opportunity for the lessors to dispute their liability under the lease.

As an actual consequence of plaintiffs' unilateral action herein, defendants were irreparably handicapped in presenting a defense. Confronted with a *fait accompli,* defendants, in an effort to prove plaintiffs' responsibility for the roof damage or alternatively, to contest the necessity for repairs of the extent accomplished, were necessarily consigned to reliance upon evidence of a conjectural quality.

Moreover, it is necessarily implied in the covenant to repair at lessors' "own cost and expense" that the right to determine and control the nature, quality, course and manner, as well as the cost of repairs, is a concomitant of the burden so to do. The unilateral action of plaintiffs herein deprived defendants of this important right.

That which is necessarily implied in the language of a contract is as much a part of it as that which is expressed.... In the case at bench, notice as a condition precedent to the lessors' obligation to repair is not only clearly apparent from the terms of the written lease, it is indispensable to effectuate the intentions of the parties.... It has been held that unless explicitly excluded therein, performance under an express covenant to repair is conditional upon notice from the tenant.... Accordingly, we hold that notice is an indispensable condition precedent to defendants' duty to perform under the covenant to repair.

In the sense that the implied condition precedent of notice to repair does not in itself constitute a promise or covenant, plaintiffs are correct that the trial court erred in concluding that they breached the lease. (See 3A Corbin on Contracts (1960) § 634, p. 33.) However, the "error" is one of semantics, not substance. It is a minor departure from strict legal parlance and avails plaintiffs nothing, because their recovery upon the lease-contract is dependent upon alleging and proving performance of all conditions precedent to defendants' duty to repair.... It is conceded by plaintiffs, and the trial court so found, that no notice was given defendants prior to completion of the repairs. Accordingly, the trial court was correct in denying recovery to plaintiffs under the lease.

* * *

[The court rejected Plaintiffs' claim, in the alternative, that their expenditures for the new roof should be granted on the quasi-contractual theory of money paid by mistake. The court concluded that there "cannot be a valid, express contract and an implied contract, each embracing the same subject matter, existing at the same time." The reason was that "where the parties have freely, fairly and voluntarily bargained for certain benefits in exchange for undertaking certain obligations, it would be inequitable to imply a different liability and to withdraw from one party benefits for which he has bargained and to which he is entitled," i.e., the "right of control over repairs for which they are therein held responsible."]

NOTES

(1) How did the condition in *Wal-Noon* differ from that in *Dove?* Was the defendant in either case unjustly enriched by being allowed to keep benefits conferred by the plaintiff before the condition failed? See Suburban Transfer Serv., Inc. v. Beech Holdings, Inc., 716 F.2d 220, 222–227 (3d Cir.1983) (quasi-contract claim rejected where subject within scope of failed express condition). What about unreimbursed reliance?

(2) In *Wal–Noon,* the trial court held that the lessee "breached" the contract by failing to give notice. Was this holding correct? How does a court decide whether an event within the control of one party was promised as part of the agreed exchange? See the next case. See also, Willis, *Promissory and Non–Promissory Conditions,* 16 Ind.L.J. 349 (1941).

In re Carter's Claim

Supreme Court of Pennsylvania, 1957.
390 Pa. 365, 134 A.2d 908.

■ Opinion by MR. JUSTICE BENJAMIN R. JONES.

This is an appeal from a judgment entered upon an arbitrator's award in a proceeding under the Act of 1927.

In June 1954 the Edwin J. Schoettle Co., a Pennsylvania corporation, and its six subsidiaries were available for purchase. Lester L. Kardon, interested in purchasing the company and five of its subsidiaries, opened negotiations for that purpose. The negotiations extended from June 24, 1954 to September 17, 1954, on which latter date the parties entered into a written agreement under the terms of which Kardon (hereinafter called the buyer) purchased all the issued and outstanding capital stock of Schoettle Co. and all its subsidiaries (hereinafter called sellers). The total purchase price set forth in the agreement of sale (excluding certain real estate) was $2,100,000 of which amount $187,863.60 was set aside under paragraph 11 of the agreement to be held by the Provident Trust Company of Philadelphia as escrow agent to indemnify the buyer against "the liabilities of sellers by reason of any and all provisions of this agreement."

The present litigation arises from the fact that the buyer has presented a claim against the escrow fund for $69,998.42 as a "liability" of the seller under the agreement. Payment of this claim having been disputed by the sellers, both parties, under the provisions of the agreement, submitted to arbitration and Judge Gerald F. Flood was selected as arbitrator. On October 26, 1956 Judge Flood, as arbitrator, and after hearing, awarded to the buyer $3,182.88. Buyer's motion to correct the arbitrator's award was dismissed by the Court of Common Pleas No. 6 of Philadelphia County and judgment was entered in the amount of $3,182.88 in conformity with the arbitrator's award. From that judgment this appeal ensued.

The resolution of this controversy depends upon the interpretation of certain portions of the 25–page written agreement of September 17, 1954. The pertinent portions of this agreement are paragraphs 5(g), 9(a), 9(b), 9(c), 10(d) and 15, which read as follows: "5. *Representations and warranties.* Sellers *represent* and *warrant* as follows: [emphasis supplied] ... (g) *Absence of certain changes.* Since June 30, 1954, there have not been (i) any changes in Company's or its subsidiaries' financial condition, assets, liabilities, or businesses, other than changes in the ordinary course of business, none of which have been materially adverse, and changes required or permitted hereunder; (ii) any damage, destruction, or loss, whether or not covered by insurance, materially and adversely affecting the properties or businesses of Company and its subsidiaries as an entirety; (iii) any declaration, or setting aside, or payment of any dividend or other distribution in respect of Company's capital stock or that of any subsidiary (except that prior to the date hereof, Company has declared and paid a dividend of Sixteen and Two Thirds Cents ($.16⅔) per share on all issued and outstanding shares of its said capital stock), or any direct or indirect redemption, purchase, or other acquisition of any such stock; or (iv) any increase in the compensation payable or to become payable by Company or any subsidiary to any of their officers, employees, or agents, or any bonus payment or arrangement made to or with any of them.

* * *

"9. *Conditions precedent.* All obligations of Buyer under this agreement are subject to the fulfillment, prior to or at the closing of each of the following *conditions:* [emphasis supplied]. (a) *Financial condition at closing.* As of the time of closing the financial condition of the Company and its subsidiaries in the aggregate shall be no less favorable than the financial condition shown on the statements of said corporations dated June 30, 1954 and warranted to be true and complete in paragraph 5(e) hereof. (b) *Representations and warranties true at closing.* Sellers' representations and warranties contained in this agreement shall be true at the time of closing as though such representations and warranties were made at such time. (c) *Performance.* Sellers shall have performed and complied with all agreements and conditions required by this agreement to be performed or complied with by them prior to or at the closing.

* * *

"10. *Indemnification.* Sellers shall indemnify and hold harmless Buyer, subject to the limitations of paragraph 11 hereof, against and in respect of: * * * (d) any damage or deficiency resulting from any misrepresentation, breach of warranty, or nonfulfillment of any agreement on the part of Sellers, or any of them, under this agreement, or from any misrepresentation in or omission from any certificate or other instrument furnished or to be furnished to Buyer hereunder;

"15. *Survival of representations.* All representations, warranties and agreements made by Sellers and Buyer in this agreement or pursuant hereto shall survive closing, subject to the provisions of paragraph 11 hereof."

The buyer (appellant) contends that the financial condition on the date of purchase—September 17, 1954—was less favorable than that reflected in the company's financial statement of June 30, 1954 and, therefore, he is entitled to reimbursement out of the escrow fund for the amount of the deficiency. Sellers (appellees) deny any reduction in the financial condition and further argue that, even if there were any reduction, buyer has no right to reimbursement under the agreement unless such reduction resulted from occurrences outside the ordinary course of business or which caused a materially adverse change in the company's financial condition. Actually the buyer's position is that paragraph 9(a), supra, constituted a "warranty" on the sellers' part that the financial condition of the company and its subsidiaries was not less favorable than demonstrated by the financial statement of June 30, 1954 and, therefore, sellers having breached the warranty the buyer is entitled to claim the difference between the net worth on June 30, 1954 and September 17, 1954. On the other hand, sellers take the position that their engagement under paragraph 9(a) constituted a "condition" and not a warranty and the buyer had simply the right to refuse a consummation of the sale if the "condition" was not fulfilled; when the buyer elected to consummate the sale it waived the "condition."

* * *

This written agreement was carefully and meticulously prepared by able and competent counsel after long and thorough negotiations. Each general paragraph of the agreement is headed by a title descriptive of the contents of each paragraph. Paragraph 5, entitled "Representations and Warranties", expressly states that the sellers "represented and warranted" fifteen separate and carefully spelled out factual situations. Paragraph 9, entitled "Conditions precedent" expressly states that "All obligations of buyer under this agreement are subject to the fulfillment, prior to or at the closing, of each of the following *conditions.*" It is to be noted that included among the "*conditions*" was the financial condition of the company and its subsidiaries at the time of closing, that the fulfillment of the "conditions" was to take place not subsequent to but "prior to or at the closing" and that the buyer's obligations, not the sellers', were made subject to the fulfillment of the condition. This agreement, in distinct and indubitable language, distinguishes between such engagements on the sellers' part as constitute "Warranties" and such engagements as constitute "Conditions".

Assuming, arguendo, that the company and its subsidiaries' financial condition was less favorable on September 17, 1954 than the financial condition shown on the statement dated June 30, 1954, what under this agreement was the buyer's remedy? The buyer claims that such fact constituted a breach of warranty which gave to him the right to recover the amount of the reduced net worth, while the sellers claim that the buyer had the choice on September 17, 1954 either to accept the situation or to refuse to proceed under the agreement.

The buyer argues that it was impossible to ascertain at the date of closing whether or not the net worth of the company and its subsidiaries had been reduced, and that only by an examination after date of closing could this fact be ascertained and, therefore, both parties must have intended that the buyer have a reasonable time after the date of closing to ascertain this fact. Such an argument not only finds no support in the wording of the agreement but, on the contrary, is in direct conflict with the express terms of the agreement. Such a contention would require that we read into the agreement that which is in direct variance with the clear and unambiguous language employed to express the parties' intent.

* * *

The arbitrator concluded that to construe paragraph 9(a) as creative of a promise for the breach of which the buyer could recover damages—i.e., a warranty—would be inconsistent with paragraph 5(g). With this conclusion we are in full agreement. The sellers in paragraph 5(g) represented and warranted, inter alia, that there had not been any changes in the financial condition of the company or its subsidiaries other than changes in the ordinary course of business, none of which had been materially adverse and were changes required or permitted under the agreement. Paragraph 9(a) covers an entirely different situation in that it referred to such changes in the financial condition of the company and its subsidiaries in the ordinary course of business which were materially adverse and not permitted under the agreement; if this situation arose the agreement specifically provided that the buyer was under no obligation to complete the purchase. A comparison of paragraph 5(g) with paragraph 9(a) clearly leads to this conclusion; to place upon paragraph 9(a) any other construction than that placed upon it by the arbitrator would amount to a redundancy.

A resolution of the instant controversy depends entirely upon an interpretation of the language of this agreement. The language employed by the parties is manifestly indicative of that which was intended and the meaning of the agreement—free as it is of ambiguity and doubt—is to be determined by what the agreement states. The parties carefully and scrupulously delineated between the sellers' undertakings which were intended to be "warranties" and those which were intended to be "conditions." It is crystal clear that the undertaking under paragraph 9(a) was simply a "condition" and not a "warranty" and once the buyer elected to accept this agreement the provisions of paragraph 9(a) ceased to be operative and the buyer had no right to recover any damages.

The judgment of the Court below is affirmed. Costs to be paid by appellant.

NOTES

(1) Why was it important to differentiate warranties and conditions precedent in *In re Carter's Claim?* Note that the court appears to use the "plain meaning rule" of contract interpretation. Was that justified on these facts?

(2) It is sometimes said that failure of an express condition precedent gives the promisor a "shield" but not a "sword;" he or she can avoid the contract but has no claim for damages. Why was this defensive protection denied to the buyer in *In re Carter's Claim?*

(3) In some cases, the courts will construe the contract to impose a duty to give a notice that must occur before the other party has a duty to perform. Failure to give the notice is a breach of contract. For example, Internatio–Rotterdam v. River Brand Rice Mills, 259 F.2d 137 (2d Cir.1958), cert. denied 358 U.S. 946, 79 S.Ct. 352, 3 L.Ed.2d 352 (1959), a buyer who had contracted to buy rice failed by twelve hours to give seller two-weeks notice (where to ship). Because the price of rice was rising, the seller rescinded the contract. The court, examining conditions at the time the contract was made in July rather than the time of performance in December, held that the notice requirement was "the essence of the contract" and found that the defendant's refusal to sell was not a breach. In essence, the notice condition had failed and the defendant was discharged from the contract.

Professor Robert Childres concluded that the "question should have been whether the delivery period was material; or more precisely, whether it was sufficiently material to justify seller's canceling the deal." Further, "if this had been the question, it seems clear that the buyer would have won, that the seller could not have established any material prejudice from the buyer's less than twelve-hour delay." Robert Childres, *Conditions in the Law of Contracts,* 45 N.Y.U.L.Rev. 33, 57 (1970). Do you agree with this analysis?

In Continental Grain Co. v. Simpson Feed Co., 102 F.Supp. 354 (E.D.Ark. 1951), affirmed 199 F.2d 284 (8th Cir.1952), the issue was whether the buyer's 48–hour delay in furnishing shipping instructions "was sufficiently material" to justify the seller in attempting to cancel the contract. In holding that it was not, the court stated that whether undisputed facts amounted to a material breach was a question of law to be decided by the court. After reviewing the facts and identifying the factors listed in first Restatement § 275 which were relevant to materiality, the court concluded: (1) While installment deliveries were contemplated, time was not of the essence except to the extent that the defendant was obligated to complete its deliveries by the end of the agreed period; (2) Plaintiff's delay was not accompanied by any repudiation or manifested inability to perform; (3) Defendant suffered no substantial damage from the delay, nor did it run the risk of future damage—the market was rising and any loss from demurrage was outweighed by plaintiff's loss of bargain; (4) Plaintiff's delay was neither willful nor negligent; (5) "In truth, the defendant entered into a contract with the plaintiff which became disadvantageous when the soybean market rose, and from all of the facts and circumstances in the case we can not escape the conclusion that the defendant simply seized upon what was at most an inconsequential breach on the part of the plaintiff as an excuse for release from that contract."

(4) *Promise or Condition?* It is, of course, possible in a case like *River Brand Rice* for the parties explicitly to make a timely call or prompt sailing a condition precedent to the obligor's duty. If so and the condition fails, the promisor is discharged without regard to whether it was materially prejudiced. But if there is doubt about whether this has been done and the event is within the other party's control, Restatement (Second) § 227(2) prefers an interpretation that "a duty is imposed on an obligee that an event occur" rather than that the "event is made a condition of the obligor's duty." According to Comment d, the "preferred interpretation avoids the harsh results that might otherwise result from the nonoccurrence of a condition and still gives adequate protection to the obligor under the rules * * * relating to promises for an exchange of performances * * * [where] the obligee's failure to perform his duty has, if it is material, the effect of the nonoccurrence of a condition of the obligor's duty." See Howard v. Federal Crop Insurance Corp., 540 F.2d 695 (4th Cir.1976), where the court said:

> There is a general legal policy opposed to forfeitures.... Insurance policies are generally construed most strongly against the insurer.... When it is doubtful whether words create a promise or a condition, they will be construed as creating a promise.

This preference, however, does not apply to contracts "of a type under which only the obligor generally undertakes duties." Restatement (Second) § 227, comment d. Insurance is regarded as a contract of this type, where the usual interpretation is that the insured has no enforceable duty to pay premiums. Rather, if the risk insured against occurs, the insurance company's duty to pay under the policy is expressly conditioned upon the payment of premiums. Unless special arrangements with third parties have been made, however, the insured's failure to pay is a failure of condition rather than a breach of contract. See General Credit Corp. v. Imperial Casualty & Indemnity Co., 167 Neb. 833, 95 N.W.2d 145 (1959).

(5) *Time of payment as condition or convenience.* North American Graphite Corp. v. Allan, 184 F.2d 387 (D.C.Cir.1950), concerned an employment contract under which the bulk of the plaintiff's compensation was not payable until completion of a project. Following completion of most of the plaintiff's services, defendant fired him and abandoned the project. The court in *Allan* conceded that the parties could have made payment for services contingent upon successful operation of the mine, but did not clearly do so. Thus, the completion of the project language was intended as a convenient time for payment not as a condition precedent.

The case turns upon the court's interpretation of the contract—upon "the intention of the parties" as "gathered from the language used, the situation of the parties, and the subject matter of the contract, as presented by the evidence." It should not be surprising, therefore, that in situations of this type decisions may at times be difficult to reconcile, at least on the basis of the rather meager data ordinarily appearing in an appellate court opinion. For example, in Mascioni v. I.B. Miller, Inc., 261 N.Y. 1, 184 N.E. 473 (1933), a prime contractor's promise to a subcontractor of "[p]ayment to be made as received from the owner" was held to condition liability. However, the vast majority of decisions are in accord with Dancy v. William J. Howard, Inc., 297 F.2d 686 (7th Cir.1961), where the promise of a prime contractor to make final payment after he "has received final payment for construction" was said not to make such receipt of final payment a condition precedent, "but rather fixed it as a convenient time for payment." See also Main Electric, Ltd. v. Printz Services Corp., 980 P.2d 522 (Colo.1999) (construction against condition to avoid forfeiture). How clear must the language be to avoid the presumption against conditions?

PROBLEM: THE CASE OF THE INSOLVENT OWNER

S entered a subcontract with P for excavation work to be performed on land owned by O. P had the prime contract with O for the overall project, the development of a shopping center. The contract between S and P provided in part:

Article 5: Material and work invoices submitted before the 25th of the current month will be paid by the 28th of the following month, provided the material so delivered is acceptable, and if payment for invoiced material has been received by [P] under its general contract.

Article 18: ... [I]f the work has been satisfactorily performed and invoice as rendered is approved and if payment for such labor and material so invoiced has been received by [P] under its general contract, the subcontractor will be paid 85% of invoice as approved, less any payments previously made on account for previous periods. No payments made shall be considered as evidence of acceptance of the work either in whole or in part until the work is completed and accepted, whereupon final payment will be made within thirty (30) days of such acceptance upon receipt of all or any bonds, guarantees required.

O became insolvent and the project was terminated before S was paid in full for work done. S filed a mechanic's lien on O's property. The trustee in the insolvency proceeding found that S was owed $84,000 for work done, but ruled that the claim against O and its land was subordinated to other creditors of O. S then sued P under the subcontract. P alleged that it had not been paid in full by O before the insolvency and argued that under the subcontract payment by O was a condition precedent to its duty to pay S. What result? See A.A. Conte, Inc. v. Campbell–Lowrie–Lautermilch, 132 Ill.App.3d 325, 87 Ill.Dec. 429, 477 N.E.2d 30 (1985).

Omni Group, Inc. v. Seattle–First National Bank

Court of Appeals of Washington, 1982.
32 Wash.App. 22, 645 P.2d 727.

Reprinted supra at 103.

(2) EXCUSE OF EXPRESS CONDITIONS

On the one hand, the law of conditions fosters a policy favoring freedom *from* contract. If an express condition precedent has failed, the promisor has a defense and may be discharged from the contract without any obligation to compensate the promisee for part-performance. Whether the promisor was in fact prejudiced by the failure is immaterial. On the other hand, a strict application of the law of conditions can produce a perceived forfeiture, especially where the promisor is not actually prejudiced by the failure of a condition and the promisee has engaged in extensive preparation to perform or part-performance. Put differently, if the condition turns out to be immaterial to the promisor and the promisee has relied or conferred a benefit on the promisor, discharging the promisor may provide a severe test for the "freedom from" contract policy.

A good example of this "severe test" is Inman v. Clyde Hall Drilling Co., 369 P.2d 498 (Alaska 1962), where the court discharged an employer from a claim by a terminated employee because the employee failed to satisfy a 30–day condition of notice, even though the lawsuit was filed and service was made within the 30–day period and there was no evidence that the promisor was prejudiced by the delay. The court stated:

> Service of the complaint probably gave the Company actual knowledge of the claim. But that does not serve as an excuse for not giving the kind of written notice called for by the contract. Inman agreed that no suit would be instituted "prior to six (6) months *after the filing of the written notice of claim.*" (emphasis ours) If this means what it says (and we have no reason to believe it does not), it is clear that the commencement of an action and service of the complaint was not an effective substitute for the kind of notice called for by the agreement. To hold otherwise would be to simply ignore an explicit provision of the contract and say that it had no meaning. We are not justified in doing that.

As we have seen, one way to deal with the forfeiture problem is to argue that a condition precedent was not intended. But this will not work if the contract was clearly drafted. Another way to temper forfeiture is to excuse the condition on some other ground. Some possible grounds for excuse include: (1) An agreement by both parties modifying the contract to discharge the condition; (2) Conduct by the party for whose benefit the condition was made that "waives" the condition; (3) Changed circumstances that make compliance by the promisee with the condition impracticable; and (4) Discharge by the court. In this subsection, we will explore when these grounds for excuse of condition are available.

Clark v. West

Court of Appeals of New York, 1908.
193 N.Y. 349, 86 N.E. 1.

On February 12th, 1900, the plaintiff and defendant entered into a written contract under which the former was to write and prepare for publication for the latter a series of law books the compensation for which was provided in the contract. After the plaintiff had completed a three-volume work known as "Clark & Marshall on Corporations," the parties disagreed. The plaintiff claimed that the defendant had broken the contract by causing the book to be copyrighted in the name of a corporation, which was not a party to the contract, and he brought this action to recover what he claims to be due him, for an accounting and other relief. The defendant demurred to the complaint on the ground that it did not state facts sufficient to constitute a cause of action. The Special Term overruled the demurrer, but upon appeal to the Appellate Division, that decision was reversed and the demurrer sustained.

Those portions of the contract which are germane to the present stage of the controversy are as follows: "The plaintiff agreed to write a series of books relating to specified legal subjects; the manuscript furnished by him was to be satisfactory to the defendant; the plaintiff was not to write or edit anything that would interfere with the sale of books to be written by him under the contract and he was not to write any other books unless requested so to do by the defendant, in which latter event he was to be paid $3,000 a year." The contract contained a clause which provided that 'The first party (the plaintiff) agrees to totally abstain from the use of intoxicating liquors during the continuance of this contract, and that the payment to him in accordance with the terms of this contract of any money in excess of $2 per page is dependent on the faithful performance of this as well as the other conditions of this contract. * * *'

In a later paragraph it further recited that, "In consideration of the above promises of the first party (the plaintiff), the second party (the defendant) agrees to pay to the first party $2 per page, * * * on each book prepared by the first party under this contract and accepted by the second party, and if said first party abstains from the use of intoxicating liquor and otherwise fulfills his agreements as hereinbefore set forth, he shall be paid an additional $4 per page in manner hereinbefore stated." * * *

The plaintiff in his complaint alleges completion of the work on corporations and publication thereof by the defendant; the sale of many copies thereof from which the defendant received large net receipts; the number of pages it contained (3,469), for which he had been paid at the rate of $2 per page, amounting to $6,938, and that defendant has refused to pay him any sum over and above that amount, or any sum in excess of $2 per page. Full performance of the agreement on plaintiff's part is alleged, except that he "did not totally abstain from the use of intoxicating liquor during the continuation of said contract, but such use by the plaintiff was not excessive and did not prevent or interfere with the due and full performance by the plaintiff of all the other stipulations in said contract." The complaint further alleges a waiver on the part of the defendant of the plaintiff's stipulation to totally abstain from the use of intoxicating liquors * * *.

The defendant's breach of the contract is then alleged which is claimed to consist in his having taken out a copyright upon the plaintiff's work on corporations in the name of a publishing company which had no relation to the contract, and the relief asked for is that the defendant be compelled to account, and that the copyright be transferred to the plaintiff or that he recover its value.

The appeal is by permission of the Appellate Division and the following questions have been certified to us: 1. Does the complaint herein state facts sufficient to constitute a cause of action? 2. Under the terms of the contract alleged in the complaint, is the plaintiff's total abstinence from the use of intoxicating liquors a condition precedent which can be waived so as to render defendant liable upon the contract notwithstanding plaintiff's use of intoxicating liquors? 3. Does the complaint herein allege facts constituting a valid and effective waiver of plaintiff's non-performance of such condition precedent?

■ Werner, J. * * * Briefly stated, the defendant's position is that the stipulation as to plaintiff's total abstinence is the consideration for the payment of the difference between $2 and $6 per page and therefore could not be waived except by a new agreement to that effect based upon a good consideration; that the so-called waiver alleged by the plaintiff is not a waiver but a modification of the contract in respect to its consideration. The plaintiff on the other hand argues that the stipulation for his total abstinence was merely a condition precedent intended to work a forfeiture of the additional compensation in case of a breach and that it could be waived without any formal agreement to that effect based upon a new consideration.

The subject-matter of the contract was the writing of books by the plaintiff for the defendant. The duration of the contract was the time necessary to complete them all. The work was to be done to the satisfaction of the defendant, and the plaintiff was not to write any other books except those covered by the contract unless requested so to do by the defendant, in which latter event he was to be paid for that particular work by the year. The compensation for the work specified in the contract was to be $6 per page, unless the plaintiff failed to totally abstain from the use of intoxicating liquors during the continuance of the contract, in which event he was to receive only $2 per page. That is the obvious import of the contract construed in the light of the purpose for which it was made, and in accordance with the ordinary meaning of plain language. It is not a contract to write books in order that the plaintiff shall keep sober, but a contract containing a stipulation that he shall keep sober so that he may write satisfactory books. When we view the contract from this standpoint it will readily be perceived that the particular stipulation is not the consideration for the contract, but simply one of its conditions which fits in with those relating to time and method of delivery of manuscript, revision of proof, citation of cases, assignment of copyrights, keeping track of new cases and citations for new editions, and other details which might be waived by the defendant, if he saw fit to do so. This is made clear, it seems to us, by the provision that, "In consideration of the above promises," the defendant agrees to pay the plaintiff $2 per page on each book prepared by him, and if he "abstains from the use of intoxicating liquor and otherwise fulfills his agreements as hereinbefore set forth, he shall be paid an additional $4 per page in manner hereinbefore stated." The compensation of $2 per page, not to exceed $250 per month, was an advance or partial payment of the whole price of $6 per page, and the payment of the two-thirds, which was to be withheld pending the performance of the contract, was simply made contingent upon the plaintiff's total abstention from the use of intoxicants during the life of the contract. * * * It is obvious that the parties thought that the plaintiff's normal work was worth $6 per page. That was the sum to be paid for the work done by the plaintiff and not for total abstinence. If the plaintiff did not keep to the condition as to total abstinence, he was to lose part of that sum. * * * This, we think, is the fair interpretation of the contract, and it follows that the stipulation as to the plaintiff's total abstinence was nothing more nor less than a condition precedent. If that conclusion is well founded there can be no escape from the corollary that this condition could be waived; and if it was waived the defendant is clearly not in a position to insist upon the forfeiture which his waiver was intended to annihilate. The forfeiture must stand or fall with the condition. If the latter was waived, the former is no longer a part of the contract. Defendant still has the right to counterclaim for any damages which he may have sustained in consequence of the plaintiff's breach, but he cannot insist upon strict performance . . .

This whole discussion is predicated of course upon the theory of an express waiver. We assume that no waiver could be implied from the defendant's mere acceptance of the books and his payment of the sum of $2 per page without objection. It was the defendant's duty to pay that amount in any event after acceptance of the work. The plaintiff must stand upon his allegation of an express waiver and if he fails to establish that he cannot maintain his action.

The theory upon which the defendant's attitude seems to be based is that even if he has represented to the plaintiff that he would not insist upon the condition that the latter should observe total abstinence from intoxicants, he can still refuse to pay the full contract price for his work. The inequity of this position becomes apparent when we consider that this contract was to run for a period of years, during a large portion of which the plaintiff was to be entitled only to the advance payment of $2 per page, the balance being contingent, among other things, upon publication of the books and returns from sales. Upon this theory the defendant might have waived the condition while the first book was in process of production, and yet, when the whole work was completed, he would still be a position to insist upon the forfeiture because there had not been strict performance. Such a situation is possible in a case where the subject of the waiver is the very consideration of a contract, Organ v. Stewart, 60 N.Y. 413, 420, but not where the waiver relates to something that can be waived. In the case at bar, as we have seen, the waiver is not of the consideration or subject-matter, but of an incident to the method of performance. The consideration remains the same. The defendant has had the work he bargained for, and it is alleged that he has waived one of the conditions as to the manner in which it was to have been done. He might have insisted upon literal performance and then he could have stood upon the letter of his contract. If, however, he has waived that incidental condition, he has created a situation to which the doctrine of waiver very precisely applies.

The cases which present the most familiar phases of the doctrine of waiver are those which have arisen out of litigation over insurance policies where the defendants have claimed a forfeiture because of the breach of some condition in the contract, . . . but it is a doctrine of general application which is confined to no particular class of cases. A waiver has been defined to be the intentional relinquishment of a known right. It is voluntary and implies an election to dispense with something of value, or forego some advantage which the party waiving it might at its option have demanded or insisted upon. * * * While the principle may not be easily classified, it is well established that, if the words and acts of the insurer reasonably justify the conclusion that with full knowledge of all the facts it intended to abandon or not to insist upon the particular defense afterwards relied upon, a verdict or finding to that effect establishes a waiver, which, if it once exists, can never be revoked.' The doctrine of equitable estoppel, or estoppel *in pais*, is that a party may be precluded by his acts and conduct from asserting a right to the detriment of another party who, entitled to rely on such conduct, has acted upon it. * * * As already said, "the doctrine of waiver is to relieve against forfeiture; it requires no consideration for a waiver, nor any prejudice or injury to the other party." . . .

It remains to be determined whether the plaintiff has alleged facts which, if proven, will be sufficient to establish his claim of an express waiver by the defendant of the plaintiff's breach of the condition to observe total abstinence. In the 12th paragraph of the complaint, the plaintiff alleges facts and circumstances which we think, if established, would prove defendant's waiver of plaintiff's performance of that contract stipulation. These facts and circumstances are that long before the plaintiff had completed the manuscript of the first book undertaken under the contract, the defendant had full knowledge of the plaintiff's non-observance of that stipulation, and that with such knowledge he not only accepted the completed manuscript without objection, but "repeatedly avowed and represented to the plaintiff that he was entitled to and would receive said royalty payments (i.e., the additional $4 per page), and plaintiff believed and relied upon such representations, * * * and at all times during the writing of said treatise on corporations, and after as well as before publication thereof as aforesaid, it was mutually understood, agreed, and intended by the parties hereto that, notwithstanding plaintiff's said use of intoxicating liquors, he was nevertheless entitled to receive and would receive said royalty as the same accrued under said contract." * * *

The three questions certified should be answered in the affirmative, the order of the Appellate Division reversed, the interlocutory judgment of the Special Term affirmed, with costs in both courts, and the defendant be permitted to answer the complaint within twenty days upon payment of costs.

NOTES

(1) *Excuse of Conditions by "Waiver."* Since a condition is a term of the contract, it can be deleted or modified by a subsequent agreement between the parties. If, however, the condition, to use Restatement (Second) language, is a "material part of the agreed exchange," see Section 84(1)(a), the agreement must satisfy the usual requirements for an enforceable modification, including, upon occasion, consideration. See UCC 2–209(1); Restatement (Second) § 89.

It is frequently asserted, however, that a condition can be excused by conduct by one party to the contract which falls short of an agreed modification. An umbrella covering some of these situations is the word "waiver," which has been defined generally as the "voluntary relinquishment of a known right." Analysis reveals that where express conditions are involved, "waiver" is associated with three recurring fact patterns, aptly illustrated by insurance contracts:

(1) Plaintiff-insured has not satisfied an express condition that notice be given within 30 days after a covered accident, but Defendant-insurer, with full knowledge, elects to process the claim rather than to deny payment. Because of the "election" after the condition has failed, the insurer cannot thereafter insist upon the condition. See, e.g., Lee v. Casualty Co. of America, 90 Conn. 202, 96 A. 952 (1916); Restatement (Second) § 84(1) (conduct of insurer is a "promise to perform all * * * of a conditional duty under an antecedent contract in spite of the non-occurrence of the condition * * * "). According to Allan Farnsworth, the insurer is precluded from raising the condition by election. E. Allan Farnsworth, Changing Your Mind: The Law of Regretted Decisions 181–192 (1998).

(2) Immediately after the accident, Defendant-insurer tells Plaintiff-insured not to worry about the 30–day notice condition. Relying on this, Plaintiff submitted notice within 45 days of the accident and defendant refused to process the claim. The condition is waived because Plaintiff has materially changed his or her position in reliance upon Defendant's representation. See UCC 2–209(5); Restatement (Second) §§ 84(2) & 89(c). According to Professor Farnsworth, the insurer is precluded from raising the condition by equitable estoppel. E. Allan Farnsworth, supra at 163–173.

(3) After Plaintiff has substantially performed the contract, Defendant states that it will not insist upon a non-material condition. The condition is waived without "election" or "estoppel." Imperator Realty Co. v. Tull, 228 N.Y. 447, 127 N.E. 263 (1920). More broadly, when one party has promised or represented that he or she will not insist upon express conditions, "waiver" becomes a judicial device to avoid forfeiture in particular cases where an agreed modification cannot be found. See E. Allan Farnsworth, supra at 154–162. See also, Edward Rubin, *Toward a General Theory of Waiver,* 28 U.C.L.A.L.Rev. 478 (1981).

(2) *Effect of Term Requiring Written Modification.* A contract term that prohibits a non-written modification can be waived without a writing at common law. See First Nat. Bank of Pa. v. Lincoln Nat. Life Ins. Co., 824 F.2d 277, 280 (3d Cir.1987). UCC 2–209(2), however, provides that "A signed agreement which excludes modification or rescission except by a signed writing

cannot be otherwise modified or rescinded ... " Does this foreclose a non-written waiver?

In Wisconsin Knife Works v. National Metal Crafters, 781 F.2d 1280 (7th Cir.1986), the court, relying on UCC 2–209(4), held it did not. An "attempt at modification or rescission [which] does not satisfy the requirements of subsection (2) ... can operate as a waiver." The court, however, disagreed on the type of waiver required. The majority, speaking through Judge Posner, concluded that the waiver conduct must induce reliance by the other party. See UCC 2–209(5). Judge Easterbrook, in dissent, found that UCC 2–209 incorporated a broader concept of waiver. In short, proof of reliance was not required if the promisor, with knowledge of the failed condition, elected not to insist on it and proceeded with performance. Although a recent case sides with Judge Easterbrook's interpretation, BMC Industries, Inc. v. Barth Industries, Inc., 160 F.3d 1322 (11th Cir.1998), cert. denied, 526 U.S. 1132, 119 S.Ct. 1807, 143 L.Ed.2d 1010 (1999), the language in Revised UCC 2–209 remains unchanged.

(3) *Effect of Anti–Waiver Clause.* In M.J.G. Properties, Inc. v. Hurley, 27 Mass.App.Ct. 250, 537 N.E.2d 165 (1989), the lessee covenanted that it would use the property consistent with applicable zoning ordinances. The lease also provided that upon any breach of covenant, the lessor could repossess the premises "at any time" notwithstanding any waiver. After three breaches, the lessor sought to repossess the property. The lessee argued and the trial court agreed that the lessor, despite the "anti-waiver" clause, had waived its power to repossess. On appeal, the judgment was affirmed. The court stated:

> On the record before us, the trial judge was presented with the following evidence; two breaches occurring in 1985 had been ignored by the lessor, and no mention of them had been made to the lessee; nothing was said about a third breach for seven months, after which time the lessor attempted to terminate the lease; in the meantime two actions in small claims court were brought against the lessee on other grounds (one for increased rent); rent was accepted without reservation throughout the period prior to notice of termination; notice of termination came only after the lessee had exercised the option to extend. On this evidence, considering the antiwaiver clause as relevant but not dispositive, we cannot say, especially in view of the incomplete record before us ... that the judge erred in finding a waiver by the lessor. Id. at 167.

Ferguson v. Phoenix Assurance Company Of New York

Supreme Court of Kansas, 1962.
189 Kan. 459, 370 P.2d 379.

■ SCHROEDER

This is an action against an insurance company on a Storekeepers Burglary and Robbery Policy for loss of money by *safe burglary.* The question presented on appeal is whether the loss is covered by the provisions of the policy.

The facts have been stipulated and are not in controversy. The plaintiff, Forrest D. Ferguson (appellee), was insured under a "Storekeepers Burglary and Robbery Policy" issued by the Phoenix Assurance Company of New York (defendant-appellant). He operated the Rexall drug store in Council Grove, Kansas. During the night of March 8, 1960, the insured's place of business was broken into by forcing the front door open, as evidenced by tool marks. As a result of the burglary there was actual damage to the premises in the amount of $70; narcotics were taken from a storage drawer from within the premises of the value of $32.59; and money was taken from within the safe in the sum of $433.76.

Before the case was tried the insurance company confessed judgment in the amount of $152.59. This comprised the $70, the $32.59, and $50 for the loss of money from within the safe. The only amount in dispute is the remaining $383.76 taken from the safe.

The safe used in the drug store herein had two doors, the outer one was locked by means of a combination lock and the inner one by means of a key. Both doors to the safe were locked. In gaining access to the safe the outer door was opened by manipulating the combination thereof, and the inner door was opened by punching out the lock. There were no visible marks upon the exterior of the outer door of the safe to show the use of force or violence in gaining access through this door, but the inner door did disclose marks of force and violence upon its exterior, evidencing the use of tools in gaining access.

The policy of insurance entitled "Storekeepers Burglary and Robbery Policy" limited liability to $1,000 under each of the seven "Insuring Agreements." Among them is the following:

"IV. Burglary; Safe Burglary

"To pay for loss by safe burglary of money, securities and merchandise within the premises and for loss, not exceeding $50, by burglary of money and securities within the premises."

The policy in chronological sequence then listed the "Exclusions." The only one having any bearing upon this case reads:

"This policy does not apply:

"(a) to loss due to any fraudulent, dishonest or criminal act by any insured, a partner therein, or an officer, employee, director, trustee or authorized representative thereof, [while working or otherwise and] whether acting alone or in collusion with others; provided, this exclusion does not apply to [kidnapping,] safe burglary or robbery or attempt thereat by other than an insured or a partner therein;"

This exclusion was amended by an attached rider to include the words set forth in the brackets.

The policy then set forth the "Conditions" among which was: "1. Definitions . . . (j) Safe Burglary." The definition of the term "Safe Burglary," however, was amended by a rider attached to the policy. The amended definition, which is substantially identical to the original, reads:

" 'Safe Burglary' means (1) the felonious abstraction of insured property from within a vault or safe, the door of which is equipped with a combination lock, located within the premises by a person making felonious entry into such vault or such safe and any vault containing the safe, when all doors thereof are duly closed and locked by all combination locks thereon, provided such *entry shall be made by actual force and violence*, *of which force and violence there are visible marks made by tools, explosives, electricity or chemicals upon the exterior of (a) all of said doors of such vault or such safe and any vault containing the safe, if entry is made through such doors*, or (b) the top, bottom or walls of such vault or such safe and any vault containing the safe through which entry is made, if not made through such doors, or (2) the felonious abstraction of such safe from within the premises.'' (Emphasis added.)

The trial court said there was no question but that a burglary occurred, the money was taken, and the insurance was carried for that particular purpose. It held the provision relied upon by the insurer was "an escape clause" and allowed full recovery under the policy for the money taken from the safe. Judgment was entered for $536.35, as requested in the petition, plus $300 for attorney fees to be assessed as costs against the insurance company.

Appeal has been duly perfected by the insurance company presenting as the only dispute the construction of the insurance policy in question as it relates to safe burglary.

A study of the policy discloses that if the appellee is entitled to recover the loss must fall within provision No. IV of the "Insuring Agreements."

* * * The appellant contends the definition of safe burglary in the policy is clear and unambiguous. It says, since entry was made to the safe in question through the doors thereof, and there were no visible marks of force and violence made by tools, explosives, electricity or chemicals upon the exterior of the outer door through which entry was made, the loss was not insured under the plain meaning of the policy. * * *

The appellee contends the appellant's interpretation of safe burglary within the terms of the policy is not applicable and is illogical and contrary to the public policy of this state. It is argued the appellee is entitled to recover for the loss as a result of the burglary of his safe, when the facts are that the inner door of the safe was locked by a key and the safe entered by force and violence of which there were visible marks on the exterior of such inner door.

The appellee argues if the insurance company did not intend to pay for loss of money by safe burglary under the facts in this case, it should have had another item under its "Exclusions," stating in substance "that the company will not pay for any loss if a combination to a safe has been worked by manipulation." (See the policy provisions in ... *Assurance Corp. v. Heller*, [1953], 127 Colo. 64, 253 P. 2d 966.)

It is a generally accepted rule that insurance policies are to be construed in favor of the insured and against the company. This rule, however, is to be invoked only where there exists rational grounds for construction of the policy.... [But] courts are not at liberty to indulge in a construction that would give an unnatural meaning to the language in order to accomplish results that could not be shown to have been in the minds of the parties. * * *

In *Security State Bank v. Royal Indemnity Co.*, 127 Kan. 230, 273 Pac. 430, the policy of insurance required the insured to provide a guard for each custodian while conveying insured property outside the premises as a precaution to prevent loss. The insured failed to send a guard with a messenger who was robbed, and sought to recover. The court said:

" . . . We are of the opinion that the failure of the plaintiff to comply with the provision of the policy with respect to sending a guard with the messenger increased the risk of loss by robbery and may reasonably be said to have constituted a direct cause of the loss in question. . . ." (p. 231.)

This condition in the policy was recognized by the court as *substantive* and required fulfillment before liability attached.

It is not uncommon for insurance companies to include in theft or burglary insurance policies provisions restricting their liability to cases where the insured produces some form of specified evidence that the loss was due to theft or burglary. The reason for such restrictions, quite obviously, is to protect the companies from what are commonly known as "inside jobs," and from frauds that would inevitably result, but for such protection. (*United Sponging Co. v. Preferred Acc. Ins. Co.* [1916], 161 N. Y. S. 309.) * * *

Δ was protecting itself from "Inside Jobs"

The clause with which the court is concerned in the instant case specifies that there be "visible marks" upon the exterior of all doors of a safe, if entry is made through such doors.

The first question to be determined is whether this clause is designed to set forth a rule of evidence, or whether it is designed to set forth a rule of substantive law—a condition precedent limiting the liability of the insurance company. * * *

It is to be noted the indemnifying provision, "Insuring Agreement No. IV.," imposes no restriction or limitation. By this provision the company, under a policy entitled "Storekeepers Burglary and Robbery Policy," agrees "To pay for loss by safe burglary of money, securities and merchandise within the premises." Furthermore, no limitation or restriction is to be found among the "Exclusions," except the loss occasioned by "inside jobs"—safe burglary committed by the insured or a partner. Thereafter, as a *condition* in the policy, safe burglary is defined as the felonious abstraction of insured property from within a safe located within the insured premises by a person *making felonious entry into such safe by actual force and violence*. It requires that the door of such safe be equipped with a combination lock and that all doors thereof be duly closed and locked by all combination locks thereon.

There is no provision in the policy that force and violence are necessary to gain entry through each of the doors to the safe. The crucial clause here under consideration reads: "of which force and violence there are visible marks made by tools, explosives, electricity or chemicals upon the exterior of (*a*) all of said doors." The term "force and violence" used in this clause refers to the "actual force and violence" used in "making *felonious entry into*" *the safe*. The recital that there be *visible marks* upon the exterior of all of the doors to the safe has reference only to *evidence* of the force and violence used in making the felonious entry into the safe. In other words, the substantive condition of the proviso is that entry into the safe be made by actual force and violence. The further condition that there be visible marks upon the exterior of all doors to the safe, if entry is made through such doors, is merely evidentiary to show an entry into the safe by actual force and violence. * * *

As we interpret the "Storekeepers Burglary and Robbery Policy" of insurance presently before the court, the "visible marks" clause imposes a rule of evidence upon the assured to establish that entry was made into the safe by actual force and violence. Whether such force and violence need be only a contributing factor in making entry into the safe is not a point at issue. On the admitted facts here confronting the court actual force and violence were used in making entry into the appellee's safe and there were visible marks of such force and violence upon the exterior of the inner door, but there were no marks of force or violence upon the exterior of the outer door which was opened by manipulating the combination.

The question then resolves into whether an insurance company, in order to protect itself from "inside jobs" and frauds, may impose a rule of evidence which is binding upon the assured by a provision in the policy.

It is a well-established rule of insurance contracts that the insurance carrier can and must be able to select the risks it insures. But a provision intended to determine the character of evidence necessary to show liability is another matter. The cases generally hold, if the parties to an insurance contract adopt a provision which contravenes no principle of public policy and contains no element of ambiguity, the courts have no right to relieve one of them from disadvantageous terms, which he has actually made, by a process of interpretation. Upon this principle the insurance carrier has a perfect right, if it sees fit, to require proof even of so-called evidentiary facts as an indispensable basis for recovery. Where the provision is not in contravention of public policy and not ambiguous, the only inquiry can be whether the parties have assented to the incorporation in their agreement of a provision which clearly calls for such evidentiary proof. * * *

We hold that where a rule of evidence is imposed by a provision in an insurance policy, as here, the assertion of such rule by the insurance carrier, beyond the reasonable requirements necessary to prevent fraudulent claims against it in proof of the substantive conditions imposed by the policy, contravenes the public policy of this state. This becomes apparent when the statement of the rule in the policy itself, or its assertion by the insurance carrier, is designed to prevent recovery on an obviously justifiable claim.

On the facts in this case money was taken from the assured's safe by an admitted entry into the safe by actual force and violence, which was evidenced by visible marks upon the inner door of the safe. Under these circumstances the assertion by the insurance carrier of the evidentiary requirement, that there be visible marks of force and violence upon the exterior of the outer door, is obviously designed to defeat recovery on a just claim under the policy which insured the felonious abstraction of money from within the safe, by a person making felonious entry into such safe by actual force and violence, where both doors of the safe were duly closed and locked.

Had the insurance carrier desired to exclude loss by safe burglary where the combination of the outer door is worked by manipulation, such provision should have been incorporated under the "Exclusions" in the policy. The appellant asserts in its brief that the appellee is demanding payment "for a loss that clearly was *excluded* in the contract," (Emphasis added) thus recognizing the need for an *exclusion* in the policy to support its contention, but without actually having made such exclusion in the policy.

The judgment of the lower court is affirmed.

■ PRICE, J., dissenting:

Concededly, this policy of insurance contains a restrictive "safe burglary" clause—just as many other types of policies contain restrictions. In this day and age a person gets just about what he pays for—whether it be insurance protection or anything else—and that is what happened here. The clause in question is *plain, clear* and *unambiguous*, and, such being the case, should be enforced according to its terms in harmony with the universal rule pertaining to insurance contracts. In my opinion this court has no business making another contract for the parties—its function is to enforce the contract as made.

I would reverse the judgment.

NOTES

(1) *A Hidden Purpose?* In the 1989 movie, *Breaking In,* Burt Reynolds plays a veteran safecracker who reluctantly takes on a novice thief. The first lesson Reynolds's character imparts to his student is to "always check the catch." People get lazy when closing safes and intentionally choose not to spin the dial so that they can easily reopen the safe by only turning the dial once (instead of three times). "Checking the catch" means to check whether someone failed to spin the dial—so that the safecracker can just open the safe without cracking it. This suggests an alternative rationale for the insurance policy's "visible marks" limitations. The policy might have not only been trying to exclude inside jobs but also outside jobs that were facilitated by the insured's negligence—failing to spin the dial.

(2) *A Performance/Enforcement Dichotomy.* "Accordingly, an essential first step in the good faith enforcement analysis [of conditions] is to decide whether a particular contract provision invoked by a party is a performance term. Performance terms are included in an agreement for the purpose of defining the primary benefits the parties intended to flow to one of them as a result of the contract. The most obvious performance terms are promises, express or

implied-in-fact, that a certain action, such as the delivery of goods or the rendering of services, will be taken. Performance terms also can take the form of conditions, as when a fire insurance contract provides that payment to the insured is due only if (i.e., on the condition that) the covered premises are damaged by fire. Such a term is essential in defining the primary benefits and duties of the parties.

"Other express conditions will be enforcement terms. The purpose for their inclusion in the agreement is not to define the primary benefits due under a contract. Rather, they enhance the security of one of the parties by providing incentives for the proper completion of performance or alternatives in its absence. The most obvious examples include liquidated damages clauses or terms permitting cancellation upon breach. But other, less obvious enforcement terms also commonly exist. Such terms are not confined to responses to a breach of contract for which a party otherwise might be held to answer in damages. They include any term that helps to secure to at least one of the parties the likelihood that the performance stratum of the world of the contract will come to pass as expected.

* * * If the condition is an enforcement term, however, it should be given effect only if doing so would advance the purpose for which it was included in the agreement, without unnecessary cost to the party against whom enforcement is sought."

Steven J. Burton & Eric G. Andersen, The World of a Contract, 75 Iowa L. Rev. 861 (1990) Was the "visible marks" condition a performance or enforcement term?

PROBLEM: EXCUSE OF CONDITION TO AVOID DISPROPORTIONATE FORFEITURE.

Harry, a dentist, leased a suite in a building from Denise. When Denise refused to renew the lease at end of term, Harry removed his equipment in such a manner that the suite was damaged. Denise's insurance company, Federal, paid for the damage and then, on December 1, 1999, as subrogee sued Harry for the loss. On December 1, 2002, Harry, for the first time, notified its insurance company, Chubb, of Federal's claim and on March 1, 2003 filed a motion to implead Chubb. This motion was granted.

Thereafter, Chubb made a motion for summary judgment, raising two defenses under terms of the insurance policy. The first of these provisions states: "In the event of an occurrence, written notice ... shall be given by or for the insured to the company ... as soon as practicable." The other states: "If claim is made or suit is brought against the insured, the insured shall immediately forward to the company every demand, notice, summons, or other process received by him or his representative." Harry admitted that he had not complied with these terms, but argued that they should be excused because Chubb had not alleged that it was prejudiced by the failure. Chubb, on the other hand, argued that the notice condition was for its benefit, that the condition had not been waived, and that it was entitled to a presumption that failure of the condition was prejudicial. Even so, argued Chubb, the burden is on Harry to prove that there was no prejudice. See Aetna Casualty and Surety

Co. v. Murphy, 206 Conn. 409, 538 A.2d 219 (1988). The trial court agreed and granted the summary judgment.

You represent Harry, who wants you to appeal the decision. Your associate has called attention to Restatement, Second, Section 229, which provides: "To the extent that the non-occurrence of a condition would cause disproportionate forfeiture, a court may excuse the non-occurrence of that condition unless its occurrence was a material *part* of the agreed exchange." If you appeal, what are Harry's best arguments? Are they likely to prevail?

Comment: Limitations on the Waiver Doctrine.

Conditions precedent, express or implied, to a promisor's duty to perform are terms of the contract: they are part of the agreed exchange. Sometimes the other party promises that they will occur but most of the time she does not. In other words, in most cases the failure of a condition is not a breach of contract by the other party. Rather, failure gives the promisor a defense only.

If the promisor waives a condition inserted for its own benefit, a modification of the contract has occurred. But it is a unilateral modification: agreement by the promisee is not required. Are there any limitations on the scope of a modification by waiver?

Suppose that P, a consultant, was retained by D, a manufacturer, to give advice on how utility rates might be reduced by increased efficiency at D's plants. Compensation depended, in part upon the degree of increased efficiency resulting from the advice. P was to advise D about the plant at St. Joseph as well as others but St. Joseph, because of evaluations already under way, was excluded by the contract from the compensation base. P made recommendations about St. Joseph and increased efficiency resulted. Relying upon an exchange of letters after the contract was formed but before the evaluation was completed, P claimed that D, by stating that compensation would be paid for St. Joseph, had waived the limitation in the contract. There was no evidence of new consideration or that P had relied upon D's letter. The court affirmed a directed verdict for the defendant.

> The theory of "waiver" upon which appellant now bases its right to recover compensation has no application to this case. A party may waive performance of a condition inserted for his benefit and thereby make unconditional the other party's duty under an agreement, but he cannot by waiver of a condition precedent to his own liability create obligation in himself where none previously existed. To create such an obligation requires a new contract and new consideration.... "One cannot 'waive' himself into a duty to make a gift of money...."

National Utility Service, Inc. v. Whirlpool Corp., 325 F.2d 779, 781 (2d Cir.1963).

(C) CONSTRUCTIVE CONDITIONS OF EXCHANGE

This section continues the study of a series of performance issues where there is no clear agreement in the contract.

The first issue deals with the *order* in which the agreed exchange is to be performed. Which party is obligated to tender performance or to perform first? The question is important, for if Party A must perform first, Party B will have no duty under the contract until Party A has tendered or performed. Put differently, Party A's performance of the agreed exchange is a condition precedent to Party B's duty.

If Party A is obligated to go first, the second issue is quantitative: How much performance must Party A tender or render before Party B has a duty under the contract? Is literal performance required, or will "substantial" performance be sufficient? If the latter, by what standard will "substantial" performance be measured? Again, this is an important inquiry. If Party A's breach is substantial (material), Party B can cancel the contract and pursue remedies based upon Party A's total breach. If Party A's performance is not substantial, Party B cannot cancel and must perform, subject to an offset for any damages caused by Party A's minor breach.

A final problem involves restitution. If Party A has committed a material breach yet Party B's losses have been fully compensated, may Party A have restitution of any net benefits from Party A's part-performance retained by Party B? If so, how is restitution to be measured?

(1) HISTORICAL DEVELOPMENT

Suppose that an owner contracted to sell described land to a vendee for a stated price. The written agreement provided that the price was to be paid on June 1 but nothing was said about when the owner was to tender a deed. On June 1, the owner demanded payment but the vendee refused until a deed in proper form was tendered. The owner then sued for the price without tendering or alleging that the deed had been tendered. Can the vendor recover? Until the middle of the eighteenth century, the answer in England was yes, especially where the vendee ultimately had an action against the owner for failure to convey the land. See, e.g., Pordage v. Cole, 1 Wms. Saunders 319 (K.B.1669). In the absence of an agreement that the owner shall tender before the price was due, it was thought that the vendee "relied upon his remedy, and did not intend to make the performance a condition precedent." See Serjeant Williams' note to *Pordage v. Cole* in 1 Wms. Saunders 320. The legal result was that the exchange of promises, although mutual, was presumed to be independent rather than dependent. Professor Patterson explained this result by the interaction of three factors: (1) The literal-mindedness of the early law; (2) The failure of the common law courts to recognize the exchange function of many contracts; (3) The inhibiting effect of the forms of action available for contract litigation. Patterson, *Constructive Conditions in Contracts,* 42 Colum.L.Rev. 903, 907–910 (1943). According to Patterson, although the "courts were willing to seize upon any language which could be tortured into an express condition of exchange," in the absence of such language, they refused to "construct conditions of exchange." This was "serious because * * * procedure did not recognize the counterclaim; the defendant's remedy was to sue the plaintiff in a separate action for breach of contract." The practical effect of the rule was that the vendee was required to extend credit to the vendor and to rely upon his legal remedies if a tender of the deed was not forthcoming.

Kingston v. Preston*

King's Bench, 1773.
2 Doug. 689, 99 Eng.Rep. 437.

[This] was an action of debt for non-performance of covenants contained in certain articles of agreement between the plaintiff and the defendant. The declaration stated: That, by articles made the 24th of March, 1770, the plaintiff, for the considerations thereinafter mentioned, covenanted with the defendant to serve him for one year and a quarter next ensuing, as a covenant-servant, in his trade of a silkmercer, at 200 a year, and, in consideration of the premises, the defendant covenanted that, at the end of the year and a quarter, he would give up his business of a mercer to the plaintiff, and a nephew of the defendant, or some other person to be nominated by the defendant, and give up to them his stock in trade at a fair valuation; and that, between the young traders, deeds of partnership should be executed for fourteen years, and from and immediately after the execution of the said deeds the defendant would permit the said young traders to carry on the said business in the defendant's house. Then the declaration stated a covenant by the plaintiff, that he would accept the business and stock in trade, at a fair valuation, with the defendant's nephew, or such other person, & c., and execute such deeds of partnership, and, further, that the plaintiff should and would, at and before the sealing and delivery of the deeds, cause and procure good and sufficient security to be given to the defendant to be approved of by the defendant for the payment of 250 monthly to the defendant in lieu of a moiety of the monthly produce of the stock in trade, until the value of the stock should be reduced to 4000. Then the plaintiff averred that he had performed and been ready to perform his covenants, and assigned for breach on the part of the defendant, that he had refused to surrender and give up his business at the end of the said year and a quarter. The defendant pleaded: 1. That the plaintiff did not offer sufficient security; and 2. That he did not give sufficient security for the payment of the 250 & c. And the plaintiff demurred generally to both pleas. On the part of the plaintiff, the case was argued by Mr. Buller, who contended that the covenants were mutual and independent, and therefore a plea of the breach of one of the covenants to be performed by the plaintiff was no bar to an action for a breach by the defendant of one which he had bound himself to perform, but that the defendant might have his remedy for the breach by the plaintiff in a separate action. On the other side, Mr. Grose insisted that the covenants were dependent in their nature, and therefore performance must be al-

---

* [The Report of the case is taken from the argument of counsel for the plaintiff in Jones v. Barkley, 2 Doug. 689–92 (1781).]

leged. The security to be given for the money was manifestly the chief object of the transaction, and it would be highly unreasonable to construe the agreement so as to oblige the defendant to give up a beneficial business, and valuable stock-in-trade, and trust to the plaintiff's personal security (who might, and, indeed, was admitted to be worth nothing), for the performance of his part.

In delivering the judgment of the Court, Lord Mansfield expressed himself to the following effect: There are three kinds of covenants: 1. Such as are called mutual and independent, where either party may recover damages from the other for the injury he may have received by a breach of the covenants in his favor and where it is no excuse for the defendant to allege a breach of the covenants on the part of the plaintiff. 2. There are covenants which are conditions and dependent, in which the performance of one depends on the prior performance of another, and, therefore, till this prior condition is performed, the other party is not liable to an action on his covenant. 3. There is also a third sort of covenants, which are mutual conditions to be performed at the same time; and in these, if one party was ready and offered to perform his part, and the other neglected or refused to perform his, he who was ready and offered has fulfilled his engagement, and may maintain an action for the default of the other; though it is not certain that either is obliged to do the first act. His Lordship then proceeded to say, that the dependence or independence of covenants was to be collected from the evident sense and meaning of the parties, and that, however transposed they might be in the deed, their precedency must depend on the order of time in which the intent of the transaction requires their performance. That, in the case before the Court, it would be the greatest injustice if the plaintiff should prevail. The essence of the agreement was, that the defendant should not trust to the personal security of the plaintiff, but, before he delivered up his stock and business, should have good security for the payment of the money. The giving such security, therefore, must necessarily be a condition precedent. Judgment was accordingly given for the defendant, because the part to be performed by the plaintiff was clearly a condition precedent.

Goodison v. Nunn

King's Bench, 1792.
4 T.R. 762, 100 Eng.Rep. 1288.

■ LORD KENYON, CH.J.—This case is extremely clear, whether considered on principles of strict law or of common justice. The plaintiff engaged to sell an estate to the defendant, in consideration of which the defendant undertook to pay 210; and, if he did not carry the contract into execution, he was to pay 21; and now not having conveyed his estate, or offered to do so, or taken any one step towards it, the plaintiff has brought this action for the penalty. Suppose the purchase-money of an estate was 40,000 it would be absurd to say that the purchaser might enforce a conveyance without payment, and compel the seller to have recourse to him, who perhaps might be an insolvent person. The old cases, cited by the plaintiff's counsel, have been accurately stated; but the determinations in them outrage common sense. I admit the principle on which they profess to go: but I think that the Judges misapplied that principle. It is admitted in them all that where they are dependent covenants, no action will lie by one party unless he have performed, or offered to perform his covenant. Then the question is, whether these are, or are not, dependent covenants. I think they are; the one is to depend on the other; when the one party conveyed his estate he was to receive the purchase-money; and when the other parted with his money he was to have the estate. They were reciprocal acts, to be performed by each other at the same time. It seems, from the case in Strange, that the Judges were surprised at the old decisions; and in order to get rid of the difficulty, they said that a tender and refusal would amount to a performance: it is true they went farther, and said that "in consideration of the premises," meant only in consideration of the covenant to transfer, and not in consideration of the actual transferring of the stock: but to the latter part of that judgment I cannot accede. It is our duty, when we see that principles of law have been misapplied in any case, to overrule it. The principle is admitted in all the cases alluded to, that, if they be dependent covenants, performance, or the offer to perform, must be pleaded on the one part, in order to found the action against the other. The mistake has been in the misapplication of that principle in the cases cited; and I am glad to find that the old cases have been over-ruled; and that we are now warranted by precedent as well as by principle to say that this action cannot be maintained.

* * *

Judgment for the defendant.

NOTES

(1) In *Kingston*, the plaintiff failed to perform a material part of his promised performance; i.e., he committed a "material" breach. Yet he sought to enforce the contract against the defendant. On what theory? Upon what basis did the court protect the defendant? Did the result depend upon the intention of the parties? Or on something else? See Edwin W. Patterson, *Constructive Conditions in Contracts*, 42 Colum.L.Rev. 903 (1942).

(2) Professor William McGovern rejects the "general consensus" that promises were treated as independent until the time of Lord Mansfield. See, e.g., K & G Construction Co. v. Harris, 223 Md. 305, 312–13, 164 A.2d 451 (1960). He identified several types of contracts where promises were treated as dependent prior to *Kingston* and concluded that there was a fundamental similarity between medieval and modern law which was "obscured by the wide latitude given to medieval juries in deciding whether or not money was owed." McGovern, *Dependent Promises in the History of Leases and Other Contracts*, 52 Tulane L.Rev. 659, 703 (1978). McGovern also found that in "some early cases * * * promises were held to be independent, just as they are today" and concluded that, in the absence of agreement, this construction was sound so long as the remedies available to the aggrieved party, whether through setoff or

counterclaim, were adequate. To construct a condition of dependency where none was agreed "violates the principle that parties to a contract should be put in the position they would have enjoyed if the contract had been performed." Id. at 703–704. For a broader, more complex study seeking to explain, among other things, the development of independent covenants in seventeenth-century English contract law, see Clinton Francis, *The Structure of Judicial Administration and the Development of Contract Law in Seventeenth–Century England,* 83 Colum.L.Rev. 35 (1983).

Palmer v. Fox

Supreme Court of Michigan, 1936.
274 Mich. 252, 264 N.W. 361.

■ TOY, J. This is an action at law to recover the balance of the purchase price due on a land contract, made on September 28, 1925, between the Louis G. Palmer & Company, a corporation, as vendor, and the defendant, as vendee, for the sale of a certain lot in Palmer Grove Park Subdivision Number Two, in the city of Detroit. The contract provided for a purchase price of $1,650, of which $247.50 was to be paid at the execution thereof, and the balance to be paid in monthly installments of $16.50 each; the entire amount to be paid "on or before five years from the date hereof." The defendant made the initial payment and also made the monthly payments as called for in the contract up to and including that of February 11, 1931.

The vendor assigned its interest in the contract to Grace H. Palmer, on March 1, 1930, and she commenced this action on February 7, 1933, for the balance of the purchase price due in the amount of $709.02, plus interest. In July, 1933, a trusteeship was created making Louis G. Palmer trustee for Grace H. Palmer, and another, and during the trial of this cause he was substituted as party plaintiff.

The defendant claimed that the vendor and its assignees failed to perform the covenants in the contract to make stated improvements in the subdivision, and especially, in failing to cinderize or gravel all the streets therein. Defendant further claimed that plaintiff could not recover because of the failure to tender a deed to the premises before commencement of this action.

The court below tried the case without a jury, and found for the plaintiff in the amount of $709.02 principal and $146.89 interest, or a total of $855.91, whereupon judgment was entered for that amount.

Defendant appeals to this court.

The land contract contained a covenant as follows:

"The vendor agrees at its own expense to furnish cement sidewalks and to grade all streets; and either cinderize or gravel the streets, except Plymouth Avenue, at its election, and to furnish water mains and lateral sewers in the streets or alleys of said subdivision. If the water and sewer are put in by the city, the assessment against the property shall be paid by the vendor."

The contract also provided that upon receiving payment of principal and interest in full and upon surrender of the contract, the vendor would execute and deliver to the vendee a warranty deed of the premises, subject to certain covenants and restrictions. The contract further provided, "that time is of the essence of this contract."

The lot contracted for fronts on a street in said subdivision known as Westwood avenue (formerly Martin avenue). The testimony showed that said street had been graded but never cinderized or graveled. The proof further showed that the other improvements called for in the contract had been made, although there is some dispute as to whether certain other streets in the subdivision had been fully cinderized or graveled. However, it is conceded by both parties that Westwood avenue in said subdivision was never cinderized or graveled as covenanted in the contract. Defendant contends that the failure to cinderize this street of the subdivision, on which the lot in question abuts, is a material breach of the covenant requiring this improvement, and that such covenant being a dependent one, plaintiff cannot recover in this action.

Plaintiff contends that the covenant by defendant to pay is independent of plaintiff's covenant to furnish improvements, and that whether the covenant to put in improvements "is dependent or independent, is immaterial in view of the fact that the plaintiff's failure to cinderize the street before the defendant's lot, under said covenant, is not a material breach."

Was the covenant of vendor to make improvements, in the instant case, a dependent covenant?

In Folkerts v. Marysville Land Co., 236 Mich. 294, this court conceded that:

"It appears to be a more or less difficult task in some cases to say whether the covenants are independent or dependent."

In that case the court set forth the language contained in 6 R.C.L. p. 861, as being the general rule for determining this question, and we quote therefrom, in part, as follows:

"But the modern rule is that stipulations are to be construed to be dependent or independent according to the intention of the parties and the good sense of the case. Technical words should give way to such intention. Courts will not and ought not to construe covenants and agreements as independent, and still enforce performance by the other party, unless there is no other mode of construing the instrument, and unless it clearly appears to have been the deliberate intention of the parties at the time the instrument was executed. In brief, the courts will construe covenants to be dependent, unless a contrary intention clearly appears. A party should not be forced to pay out his money, unless he can get that for which he stipulated. * * * Where the acts or covenants of the parties are concurrent, and to be done or performed at the same time, the covenants are dependent, and neither party can maintain an action against the other, without averring and proving performance on his part.''

Were the covenants here concurrent? We think so.

It must be remembered that plaintiff brings this action to recover the balance due under the land contract. In the contract the defendant agreed to make payment "on or before five years from the date hereof." Plaintiff agreed to make certain improvements, and although no time was stated as to when such improvements were to be made, we think that the intention of the parties, in relation thereto, clearly appears from the language of the contract, as well as from extraneous facts contained in the record, that such improvements were to be made within the five-year period. Certainly they must be made within a reasonable time. Brow v. Gibraltar Land Co., 249 Mich. 662, 229 N.W. 604.

The contract contains a provision that *after* payment and "upon the surrender of this contract," the vendor will execute and deliver to the vendee a warranty deed to the premises. Logically, it would follow, then, that if the vendee must surrender the contract, every covenant of the contract, or at least every material covenant, must necessarily be effected before such surrender. Especially does such inference apply, where the contract itself does not provide for the performing of any of the agreements after the surrender of the contract. When the contract is surrendered by the vendee, it follows that any rights he has thereunder are likewise surrendered. So, if the vendee must surrender the contract before he may receive a deed, it must have been intended that all other covenants in the contract must necessarily be performed prior to such surrender. Therefore, the covenant to improve the property must have been intended by the terms of the contract to have run concurrently with the covenant to pay the full purchase price within five years.

It further appears from the record that plaintiff put in all the improvements called for by the contract during the period of five years, excepting the cinderizing or graveling of streets, or at least of one street, as hereinbefore stated. This partial performance by the vendor indicates its knowledge of the necessity of performing its covenants.

In the case of Folkerts v. Marysville Land Co., supra, this court, after quoting the statement from Ruling Case Law, hereinbefore in part set forth, said:

"Looking at the contracts which plaintiffs made, with these tests in mind, we are persuaded that the covenants to make improvements are dependent. The reasons which have moved us to this position are, in part, as follows: (a) The contract does not, upon its face, show that the covenants are independent. (b) The time stipulated for the performance by each party is concurrent. * * * (c) These plaintiffs purchased these lots for a home."

In the instant case, we have a contract that does not, upon its face, show that the covenants are independent; we also have the inferred intention of the parties that the covenants were to be performed concurrently. But here we do not have a vendee who purchased the lot for a home.

On the contrary, the defendant testified that he purchased the property for investment purposes.

While, under the reasoning of this court in the case of Folkerts v. Marysville Land Co., supra, the fact that the vendees had purchased the property for a home was a circumstance considered in determining the intention of the parties, it was not conclusive. Nor does it appear that such circumstance was in and of itself decisive. While it is true that the defendant in the instant case purchased the lot for investment purposes, yet can it be consistently urged that he therefore intended that he should get less than that for which he bargained?

We infer from the record that at the time of the execution of the land contract there were no improvements in the subdivision. It does not seem plausible that defendant would have purchased the lot if it was to remain in that same condition. He had a right to expect, and in all probability did expect, that by the time he had the lot paid for, all of the improvements would be in, and that instead of owning a lot in a subdivision marked by surveyors' stakes, he would have a lot on a street in a subdivision with water mains, lateral sewers, cement sidewalks and graded and surfaced streets, all materially present and not merely outlined on a plat or prospectus. The agreed consideration was to be paid, not for the lot as it was when the contract was made, but as it would be when the stipulated improvements were completed.

The making of the improvements was an essential part of the consideration supporting defendant's agreement to pay the purchase price. That the defendant intended to buy, and that the vendor agreed to sell a lot in a subdivision with improvements, is clear from the provisions of the contract. The defendant's covenant to pay the balance of the purchase price and to surrender the contract was dependent upon the vendor's covenant to make the specified improvements and to deliver a deed to the lot.

* * *

We therefore conclude that the covenant to improve and the covenant to pay the purchase price were dependent covenants.

But, contends plaintiff, it is immaterial whether or not the covenant to make improvements is dependent or independent "in view of the fact that the plaintiff's failure to cinderize the street before the defendant's lot, under said covenant, is not a material breach." On this point, in the trial court, plaintiff introduced testimony to the effect that the cost to cinderize the street in *front* of the lot in question would be only about $7. But the contract called for more than the cinderizing of the street in front of the lot purchased by defendant. It required the vendor to "either cinderize or gravel the streets." Merely to have cinderized or not to have cinderized that portion of the street in front of defendant's lot is beside the point.

The necessity of surfacing the streets in the subdivision, in order to improve the premises, is apparent, and insofar as defendant's rights are concerned, the surfacing of the entire street upon which his lot abutted was of paramount importance to him. The putting in of water mains, sidewalks, and sewers was of little avail, if the street remained unsurfaced so that he and others might not have a convenient way to and from his property. Merely to have surfaced the street in front of the one lot would be absurd. We think that the noncompliance by plaintiff in this respect amounts to a substantial and material breach of the covenant to improve.

The plaintiff and his assignors, therefore, being guilty of a substantial breach of a dependent covenant, cannot maintain this action.

It is not necessary to decide whether or not the tender of a deed to the property in question, made in the declaration of the plaintiff and again at the time of trial, is a sufficient tender, or whether any tender was necessary to be made before instituting this action, as decision has turned on the other questions presented.

The judgment is reversed, without new trial, with costs to defendant.

NOTES

(1) Review the agreement in *Palmer v. Fox*. When was the vendee to pay the price? When was the vendor to deliver a warranty deed? When was the vendor to complete the improvements? If the vendor did not agree to complete the improvements before the vendee's final payment, how does the court conclude that completion was a condition to payment?

(2) *Independent and Dependent Promises.* "Promises and counterpromises made by the respective parties to a contract have certain relations to one another, which determine many of the rights and liabilities of the parties. Broadly speaking, they are (1) independent of each other, or (2) mutually dependent, one upon the other. They are independent of each other if the parties intend that *performance* by each of them is in no way conditioned upon *performance* by the other. * * * In other words, the parties exchange promises for promises, not the *performance* of promises for the *performance* of promises. * * * A failure to perform an independent promise does not excuse non-performance on the part of the adversary party, but each is required to perform his promise, and, if one does not perform, he is liable to the adversary party for such nonperformance. * * * Promises are mutually dependent if the parties intend *performance* by one to be conditioned upon *performance* by the other, and, if they be mutually dependent, they may be (a) precedent, i.e., a promise that is to be performed before a corresponding promise on the part of the adversary party is to be performed, (b) subsequent, i.e., a corresponding promise that is not to be performed until the other party to the contract has performed a precedent covenant, or (c) concurrent, i.e., promises that are to be performed at the same time by each of the parties, who are respectively bound to perform each. * * * In the early days, it was settled law that covenants and mutual promises in a contract were *prima facie* independent, and that they were to be so construed in the absence of language in the contract clearly showing that they were intended to be dependent. * * * In the case of Kingston v. Preston, 2 Doug. 689, decided in 1774, Lord Mansfield, contrary to three centuries of opposing precedents, changed the rule, and decided that performance of one covenant might be dependent on prior performance of another, although the contract contained no express condition to that effect. * * * The

modern rule, which seems to be of almost universal application, is that there is a presumption that mutual promises in a contract are dependent and are to be so regarded, whenever possible." K & G Construction Company v. Harris, 223 Md. 305, 312–13, 164 A.2d 451 (1960) (emphasis in original).

(3) *Presumption of Dependency.* Why is there a "presumption that mutual promises in a contract are dependent and are to be so regarded, whenever possible?" As Holmes put it: "You can always imply a condition in a contract. But why do you imply it?" Holmes, *The Path of the Law,* 10 Harv.L.Rev. 457, 466 (1897). According to one court, the "doctrine of constructive dependency of promises should * * * be rested solely on their fairness, and not on any intention of the parties where they express none." Thus, the determination of mutual dependency should arise from the "inherent justice of the situation and not the unexpressed intention of the parties." Giumarra v. Harrington Heights, Inc., 33 N.J.Super. 178, 191, 109 A.2d 695 (1954). But, again, if the parties in *Palmer v. Fox* did not agree that the improvements should be completed before payment, what is the inherent injustice in requiring the vendee to pay before the improvements are completed? According to Restatement (Second), the answer turns on two general considerations: First, dependency "offers both parties maximum security against disappointment of their expectations of a subsequent exchange of performances by allowing each party to defer his own performance until he has been assured that the other will perform"; second, dependency "avoids placing on either party the burden of financing the other before the latter has performed." Section 234, Comment a. Do these considerations justify the result in *Kingston*? In *Goodison*? In *Palmer*? Compare Rowe v. Great Atlantic & Pacific Tea Co., Inc., 46 N.Y.2d 62, 412 N.Y.S.2d 827, 385 N.E.2d 566 (1978), where the court refused to "imply" a covenant limiting the lessee's power to assign the lease.

> [A] party who asserts the existence of an implied-in-fact covenant bears a heavy burden, for it is not the function of the courts to remake the contract agreed to by the parties, but rather to enforce it as it exists. Thus, a party making such a claim must prove not merely that it would have been better or more sensible to include such a covenant, but rather that the particular unexpressed promise sought to be enforced is in fact implicit in the agreement viewed as a whole. This is especially so where, as here, the implied covenant sought to be recognized and enforced is of a type not favored by the courts. * * * Such a covenant is to be recognized only if it is clear that a reasonable landlord would not have entered into the lease without such an understanding, for it is only in such a situation that it can be said with the requisite certainty that to refuse to recognize such a covenant would be to deprive the landlord of the fruits of his bargain.

412 N.Y.S.2d at 831.

(4) The modern view on the order of performance is stated in Restatement (Second) § 234:

> (1) Where all or part of the performances to be exchanged under an exchange of promises can be rendered simultaneously, they are to that extent due simultaneously, unless the language or the circumstances indicate the contrary.

(2) Except to the extent stated in Subsection (1), where the performance of only one party under such an exchange requires a period of time, his performance is due at an earlier time than that of the other party, unless the language or the circumstances indicate the contrary.

In Bell v. Elder, 782 P.2d 545 (Utah App.1989), the parties contracted to buy and sell real estate. The agreement did not provide a date for performance or state which party was to perform first. Before a reasonable time for performance had passed, the vendee, without first tendering payment, brought suit to cancel the contract and obtain restitution. The court dismissed the lawsuit.

Although the contract ... does not specify a precise deadline, performance was nevertheless due within a reasonable time ... If neither party performed its exchanged promise within that time, both promises are discharged.... Neither of these parties argues that the time for performance exceeds a reasonable time. Since performance of these obligations was due concurrently, neither party could claim a breach by the other until the party claiming the breach tendered performance of its concurrent obligation. The rule requiring such a tender has been explained in a case in which a real estate purchaser and seller each demanded and awaited performance by the other of their respective obligations to pay the price and deliver the property. The Supreme Court's words in that case apply here as well: "This is precisely the sort of deadlock meant to be resolved by the requirement of tender ... During the executory period of a contract whose time of performance is uncertain but which contemplates simultaneous performance by both parties, ... neither party can be said to be in default ... until the other party has tendered his performance. In other words, the party who desires to use legal process to exercise his legal remedies under such a contract must make a tender of his own agreed performance in order to put the other party in default." 782 P.2d at 548.

(5) *Leases.* Under what circumstances can a lessee terminate a lease upon a "material" breach of a covenant by the lessor? At common law, a lease was regarded as a conveyance of property rather than a contract. Rent was regarded as a payment "yielded" by the land, not as a contract for the payment of money. See Jersey Boulevard Corp. v. Lerner Stores Corp., 168 Md. 532, 178 A. 707 (1935). For this reason, covenants between lessor and lessee were regarded as independent unless otherwise expressly agreed. See, e.g., Rock County Savings & Trust Co. of Janesville v. Yost's, Inc., 36 Wis.2d 360, 153 N.W.2d 594 (1967); Uniform Residential Landlord and Tenant Act § 1.102, Comment. But see, McGovern, *Dependent Promises in the History of Leases and Other Contracts,* 52 Tul.L.Rev. 659, 703 (1978), who argues that the difference between modern and medieval law on dependency in leases has been "greatly exaggerated."

The modern view in both residential and commercial leases is that the promise to pay rent is dependent upon such lessor covenants as repair, habitability or assignability and that the lessee may withhold rent or terminate the lease if "deprived of a significant inducement to the making of the lease." Restatement (Second) Property § 7.1 (1977). As one court put it, the "actual subject matter of most leases, commercial or residential, is the building leased, not the land upon which it stands, and that therefore contract law rather than property law should be applied to disputes between landlords and tenants." Pawco Inc. v. Bergman Knitting Mills, 283 Pa.Super. 443, 424 A.2d 891 (1980). Thus, the duty of the lessee to pay rent or to remain in the lease is dependent upon "substantial performance" of the lessor's covenants, express or implied, with regard to the quality of the premises, thereby depriving the lessor of a traditional advantage when disputes over the lease arise. See, e.g., Teodori v. Werner, 490 Pa. 58, 415 A.2d 31 (1980); Shaw v. Mobil Oil Corp., 272 Or. 109, 535 P.2d 756 (1975), applying the "modern" view in commercial leases.

PROBLEM: THE CASE OF THE DEFAULTING PURCHASER

On March 1, Vendor contracted to sell land to Vendee for $8,000. Vendee paid $2,000 at the time of contracting and agreed to pay $1,000 by the first of each succeeding month until the total price was paid. Vendor agreed to convey the property on September 1, the day the final payment was due.

(a) Suppose Vendee failed to make the June 1 payment. Can Vendor recover the payment without tendering a deed?

(b) Assume that Vendee failed to make the July, August and September payments. Can Vendor recover these payments without tendering a deed? Can he recover the July and August payments alone? See Restatement (Second) § 234 and Illustrations 6, 7 and 12. See also Ideal Family and Youth Ranch v. Whetstine, 655 P.2d 429 (Colo.App.1982) (vendor agreed to put deed in escrow before vendee had duty to pay installments).

(2) THE AVOIDANCE OF FORFEITURE

Suppose a contractor agrees to construct a new garage for Owner for $25,000. Nothing is said about when payment should be made. Under the modern view of constructive conditions, "where the performance of only one party under an exchange requires a period of time, his performance is due at an earlier time than that of the other party, unless the language or the circumstances indicate the contrary." Restatement (Second) sec. 234(2). Contractor, then, must perform first. Suppose, however, that contractor demands part payment after 50% of the work has been completed and owner contends that contractor must either fully or substantially perform the work before any payment is due. Without more, owner is correct. Unless the contract is divisible or the parties have agreed upon installment payments or trade usage is to the contrary, contractor must first satisfy the constructive condition of exchange. As the court stated in Stewart v. Newbury, 220 N.Y. 379, 115 N.E. 984 (1917): "Where a contract is made to perform work and no agreement is made as to payment, the work must be substantially performed before payment can be demanded."

What is the "inherent fairness" in a rule that requires the construction contractor to extend credit to the owner? Is it enough to conclude that the operative rule is centuries old, the parties can, by agreement, mitigate its harshness and, in any event, "it is just as fair as the opposite rule would be?" See Section 234, Comment e. In this section, we will look at some of the ways that this harsh interpretation can be softened.

[handwritten margin notes: "→ diminution = 0", "R3482A"]

[handwritten left margin notes: "π wins →", "no proof of E. Waste", "π - Contractor", "D - buyer homeowner", "Facts:", "K= Reading pipe not fulfilled", "Fixed only @ excessive cost", "The pipes are the same", "TC = excluded", "the Evidence + found for D"]

Jacob & Youngs v. Kent

Court of Appeals of New York, 1921.
230 N.Y. 239, 129 N.E. 889.

■ CARDOZO, J. The plaintiff built a country residence for the defendant at a cost of upwards of $77,000, and now sues to recover a balance of $3,483.46, remaining unpaid. The work of construction ceased in June, 1914, and the defendant then began to occupy the dwelling. There was no complaint of defective performance until March, 1915. One of the specifications for the plumbing work provides that "all wrought iron pipe must be well galvanized, lap welded pipe of the grade known as 'standard pipe' of Reading manufacture." The defendant learned in March, 1915, that some of the pipe, instead of being made in Reading, was the product of other factories. The plaintiff was accordingly directed by the architect to do the work anew. The plumbing was then encased within the walls except in a few places where it had to be exposed. Obedience to the order meant more than the substitution of other pipe. It meant the demolition at great expense of substantial parts of the completed structure. The plaintiff left the work untouched, and asked for a certificate that the final payment was due. Refusal of the certificate was followed by this suit.

The evidence sustains a finding that the omission of the prescribed brand of pipe was neither fraudulent nor willful. It was the result of the oversight and inattention of the plaintiff's subcontractor. Reading pipe is distinguished from Cohoes pipe and other brands only by the name of the manufacturer stamped upon it at intervals of between six and seven feet. Even the defendant's architect, though he inspected the pipe upon arrival, failed to notice the discrepancy. The plaintiff tried to show that the brands installed, though made by other manufacturers, were the same in quality, in appearance, in market value and in cost as the brand stated in the contract—that they were, indeed, the same thing, though manufactured in another place. The evidence was excluded, and a verdict directed for the defendant. The Appellate Division reversed, and granted a new trial.

We think the evidence, if admitted, would have supplied some basis for the inference that the defect was insignificant in its relation to the project. The courts never say that one who makes a contract fills the measure of his duty by less than full performance. They do say, however, that an omission, both trivial and innocent, will sometimes be atoned for by allowance of the resulting damage, and will not always be the breach of a condition to be followed by a forfeiture.... The distinction is akin to that between dependent and independent promises, or between promises and conditions.... Some promises are so plainly independent that they can never by fair construction be conditions of one another.... Others are so plainly dependent that they must always be conditions. Others, though dependent and thus conditions when there is departure in point of substance, will be viewed as independent and collateral when the departure is insignificant.... Considerations partly of justice and partly of presumable intention are to tell us whether this or that promise shall be placed in one class or in another. The simple and the uniform will call for different remedies

from the multifarious and the intricate. The margin of departure within
the range of normal expectation upon a sale of common chattels will vary
from the margin to be expected upon a contract for the construction of a
mansion or a "skyscraper." There will be harshness sometimes and oppression in the implication of a condition when the thing upon which labor has
been expended is incapable of surrender because united to the land, and
equity and reason in the implication of a like condition when the subject-
matter, if defective, is in shape to be returned. From the conclusion that
promises may not be treated as dependent to the extent of their uttermost
minutiae without a sacrifice of justice, the progress is a short one to the
conclusion that they may not be so treated without a perversion of
intention. Intention not otherwise revealed may be presumed to hold in
contemplation the reasonable and probable. If something else is in view, it
must not be left to implication. There will be no assumption of a purpose to
visit venial faults with oppressive retribution.

Those who think more of symmetry and logic in the development of
legal rules than of practical adaptation to the attainment of a just result
will be troubled by a classification where the lines of division are so
wavering and blurred. Something, doubtless, may be said on the score of
consistency and certainty in favor of a stricter standard. The courts have
balanced such considerations against those of equity and fairness, and
found the latter to be the weightier. The decisions in this state commit us
to the liberal view, which is making its way, nowadays, in jurisdictions slow
to welcome it.... Where the line is to be drawn between the important and
the trivial cannot be settled by a formula. "In the nature of the case precise
boundaries are impossible" (2 Williston on Contracts, sec. 841). The same
omission may take on one aspect or another according to its setting.
Substitution of equivalents may not have the same significance in fields of
art on the one side and in those of mere utility on the other. Nowhere will
change be tolerated, however, if it is so dominant or pervasive as in any
real or substantial measure to frustrate the purpose of the contract....
There is no general license to install whatever, in the builder's judgment,
may be regarded as "just as good" (Easthampton L. & C. Co., Ltd., v.
Worthington, 186 N.Y. 407, 412). The question is one of degree, to be
answered, if there is doubt, by the triers of the facts.... and, if the
inferences are certain, by the judges of the law ... We must weigh the
purpose to be served, the desire to be gratified, the excuse for deviation
from the letter, the cruelty of enforced adherence. Then only can we tell
whether literal fulfillment is to be implied by law as a condition. This is not
to say that the parties are not free by apt and certain words to effectuate a
purpose that performance of every term shall be a condition of recovery.
That question is not here. This is merely to say that the law will be slow to
impute the purpose, in the silence of the parties, where the significance of
the default is grievously out of proportion to the oppression of the forfeiture. The willful transgressor must accept the penalty of his transgression.... For him there is no occasion to mitigate the rigor of implied
conditions. The transgressor whose default is unintentional and trivial may
hope for mercy if he will offer atonement for his wrong....

In the circumstances of this case, we think the measure of the allowance is not the cost of replacement, which would be great, but the difference in value, which would be either nominal or nothing. Some of the exposed sections might perhaps have been replaced at moderate expense. The defendant did not limit his demand to them, but treated the plumbing as a unit to be corrected from cellar to roof. In point of fact, the plaintiff never reached the stage at which evidence of the extent of the allowance became necessary. The trial court had excluded evidence that the defect was unsubstantial, and in view of that ruling there was no occasion for the plaintiff to go farther with an offer of proof. We think, however, that the offer, if it had been made, would not of necessity have been defective because directed to difference in value. It is true that in most cases the cost of replacement is the measure. . . . The owner is entitled to the money which will permit him to complete, unless the cost of completion is grossly and unfairly out of proportion to the good to be attained. When that is true, the measure is the difference in value. Specifications call, let us say, for a foundation built of granite quarried in Vermont. On the completion of the building, the owner learns that through the blunder of a subcontractor part of the foundation has been built of granite of the same quality quarried in New Hampshire. The measure of allowance is not the cost of reconstruction. "There may be omissions of that which could not afterwards be supplied exactly as called for by the contract without taking down the building to its foundations, and at the same time the omission may not affect the value of the building for use or otherwise, except so slightly as to be hardly appreciable" (Handy v. Bliss, 204 Mass. 513, 519. The rule that gives a remedy in cases of substantial performance with compensation for defects of trivial or inappreciable importance, has been developed by the courts as an instrument of justice. The measure of the allowance must be shaped to the same end.

The order should be affirmed, and judgment absolute directed in favor of the plaintiff upon the stipulation, with costs in all courts.

■ McLAUGHLIN, J. (dissenting). I dissent. The plaintiff did not perform its contract. Its failure to do so was either intentional or due to gross neglect which, under the uncontradicted facts, amounted to the same thing, nor did it make any proof of the cost of compliance, where compliance was possible.

Under its contract it obligated itself to use in the plumbing, only pipe (between 2,000 and 2,500 feet) made by the Reading Manufacturing Company. The first pipe delivered was about 1,000 feet and the plaintiff's superintendent then called the attention of the foreman of the subcontractor, who was doing the plumbing, to the fact that the specifications annexed to the contract required all pipe used in the plumbing to be of the Reading Manufacturing Company. They then examined it for the purpose of ascertaining whether this delivery was of that manufacture and found it was. Thereafter, as pipe was required in the progress of the work, the foreman of the subcontractor would leave word at its shop that he wanted a specified number of feet of pipe, without in any way indicating of what manufacture. Pipe would thereafter be delivered and installed in the building, without any examination whatever. Indeed, no examination, so far as appears, was made by the plaintiff, the subcontractor, defendant's architect, or any one else, of any of the pipe except the first delivery, until after the building had been completed. Plaintiff's architect then refused to give the certificate of completion, upon which the final payment depended, because all of the pipe used in the plumbing was not of the kind called for by the contract. After such refusal, the subcontractor removed the covering or insulation from about 900 feet of pipe which was exposed in the basement, cellar and attic, and all but 70 feet was found to have been manufactured, not by the Reading Company, but by other manufacturers, some by the Cohoes Rolling Mill Company, some by the National Steel Works, some by the South Chester Tubing Company, and some which bore no manufacturer's mark at all. The balance of the pipe had been so installed in the building that an inspection of it could not be had without demolishing, in part at least, the building itself.

I am of the opinion the trial court was right in directing a verdict for the defendant. The plaintiff agreed that all the pipe used should be of the Reading Manufacturing Company. Only about two-fifths of it, so far as appears, was of that kind. If more were used, then the burden of proving that fact was upon the plaintiff, which it could easily have done, since it knew where the pipe was obtained. The question of substantial performance of a contract of the character of the one under consideration depends in no small degree upon the good faith of the contractor. If the plaintiff had intended to, and had complied with the terms of the contract except as to minor omissions, due to inadvertence, then he might be allowed to recover the contract price, less the amount necessary to fully compensate the defendant for damages caused by such omissions. (Woodward v. Fuller, 80 N.Y. 312; Nolan v. Whitney, 88 N.Y. 648.) But that is not this case. It installed between 2,000 and 2,500 feet of pipe, of which only 1,000 feet at most complied with the contract. No explanation was given why pipe called for by the contract was not used, nor was any effort made to show what it would cost to remove the pipe of other manufacturers and install that of the Reading Manufacturing Company. The defendant had a right to contract for what he wanted. He had a right before making payment to get what the contract called for. It is no answer to this suggestion to say that the pipe put in was just as good as that made by the Reading Manufacturing Company, or that the difference in value between such pipe and the pipe made by the Reading Manufacturing Company would be either "nominal or nothing." Defendant contracted for pipe made by the Reading Manufacturing Company. What his reason was for requiring this kind of pipe is of no importance. He wanted that and was entitled to it. It may have been a mere whim on his part, but even so, he had a right to this kind of pipe, regardless of whether some other kind, according to the opinion of the contractor or experts, would have been "just as good, better, or done just as well." He agreed to pay only upon condition that the pipe installed were made by that company and he ought not to be compelled to pay unless that condition be performed. . . . The rule, therefore, of substantial performance, with damages for unsubstantial omissions, has no application. . . .

* * *

I am of the opinion the trial court did not err in ruling on the admission of evidence or in directing a verdict for the defendant.

For the foregoing reasons I think the judgment of the Appellate Division should be reversed and the judgment of the Trial Term affirmed.

Order affirmed, etc.

NOTES

(1) The dissenting judge insists that "[t]he plaintiff did not perform its contract." Does Judge Cardozo disagree? If not, where is the express condition in this case? Arguably, the plaintiff satisfied a "constructive" condition of substantial performance that was precedent to the defendant's duty to pay the last installment.

(2) Is the issue here one of liability, remedy, or both?

(3) Could the contract have been drafted so as to preclude any recovery if Reading pipe was not installed? How would you draft a clause that ensures the protection of Kent's idiosyncratic preference?

(4) Does the character of the breach have an effect upon availability of remedy? Should it? What were the remedial choices before the court?

(5) While buyer's duty to pay is normally conditioned on seller's substantial performance (unless otherwise agreed), the seller's duty to sell is normally conditioned on perfect tender of full payment. Should there be exceptions to this rule where the buyer is a day late or a dollar short? Cf. Lane Enterprises, Inc. v. L.B. Foster Co., 700 A.2d 465 (Pa.Super.1997) (finding that buyer breached duty to pay by withholding "$7,082.22 out of a $133,922.40 purchase order" but that this breach was not a material breach which justified the seller's cancellation of the contract).

O. W. Grun Roofing and Construction Co. v. Cope

Court of Civil Appeals of Texas, 1975.
529 S.W.2d 258.

■ CADENA, JUSTICE. Plaintiff, Mrs. Fred M. Cope, sued defendant, O.W. Grun Roofing & Construction Co., to set aside a mechanic's lien filed by defendant and for damages in the sum of $1,500.00 suffered by plaintiff as a result of the alleged failure of defendant to perform a contract calling for the installation of a new roof on plaintiff's home. Defendant, in addition to a general denial, filed a cross-claim for $648.00, the amount which plaintiff agreed to pay defendant for installing the roof, and for foreclosure of the mechanic's lien on plaintiff's home.

Following trial to a jury, the court below entered judgment awarding plaintiff $122.60 as damages for defendant's failure to perform the contract; setting aside the mechanic's lien; and denying defendant recovery on its cross-claim. It is from this judgment that defendant appeals.

The jury found (1) defendant failed to perform his contract in a good and workmanlike manner; (2) defendant did not substantially perform the contract; (3) plaintiff received no benefits from the labor performed and the materials furnished by defendant; the reasonable cost of performing the contract in a good and workmanlike manner would be $777.60. Although the verdict shows the cost of proper performance to be $777.60, the judgment describes this finding as being in the amount of $770.60, and the award of $122.60 to plaintiff is based on the difference between $770.60 and the contract price of $648.00.

Reasonable Cost 777.60

770.60 - 648 = 122.60 award

* * *

The written contract required defendant to install a new roof on plaintiff's home for $648.00. The contract describes the color of the shingles to be used as "russet glow," which defendant defined as a "brown varied color." Defendant acknowledges that it was his obligation to install a roof of uniform color.

After defendant had installed the new roof, plaintiff noticed that it had streaks which she described as yellow, due to a difference in color or shade of some of the shingles. Defendant agreed to remedy the situation and he removed the nonconforming shingles. However, the replacement shingles do not match the remainder, and photographs introduced in evidence clearly show that the roof is not of a uniform color. Plaintiff testified that her roof has the appearance of having been patched, rather than having been completely replaced. According to plaintiff's testimony, the yellow streaks appeared on the northern, eastern and southern sides of the roof, and defendant only replaced the non-matching shingles on the northern and eastern sides, leaving the southern side with the yellow streaks still apparent. The result is that only the western portion of the roof is of uniform color.

Roof was to be of Uniform Color

Δ tried to fix it but it looked "Patched"

When defendant originally installed the complete new roof, it used 24 "squares" of shingles. In an effort to achieve a roof of uniform color, five squares were ripped off and replaced. There is no testimony as to the number of squares which would have to be replaced on the southern, or rear, side of the house in order to eliminate the original yellow streaks. Although there is expert testimony to the effect that the disparity in color would not be noticeable after the shingles have been on the roof for about a year, there is testimony to the effect that, although some nine or ten months have elapsed since defendant attempted to achieve a uniform coloration, the roof is still "streaky" on three sides. One of defendant's experts testified that if the shingles are properly applied the result will be a "blended" roof rather than a streaked roof.

24 Squares 5 replaced

In view of the fact that the disparity in color has not disappeared in nine or ten months, and in view of the fact that there is testimony to the effect that it would be impossible to secure matching shingles to replace the nonconforming ones, it can reasonably be inferred that a roof of uniform coloration can be achieved only by installing a completely new roof.

The evidence is undisputed that the roof is a substantial roof and will give plaintiff protection against the elements.

The principle which allows recovery for part performance in cases involving dependent promises may be expressed by saying that a material breach or a breach which goes to the root of the matter or essence of the contract defeats the promisor's claim despite his part performance, or it may be expressed by saying that a promisor who has substantially performed is entitled to recover, although he has failed in some particular to comply with his agreement. The latter mode of expressing the rule is generally referred to as the doctrine of substantial performance and is especially common in cases involving building contracts, although its application is not restricted to such contracts.

It is difficult to formulate definitive rules for determining whether the contractor's performance, less than complete, amounts to "substantial performance," since the question is one of fact and of degree, and the answer depends on the particular facts of each case. But, although the decisions furnish no rule of thumb, they are helpful in suggesting guidelines. One of the most obvious factors to be considered is the extent of the nonperformance. The deficiency will not be tolerated if it is so pervasive as to frustrate the purpose of the contract in any real or substantial sense. The doctrine does not bestow on a contractor a license to install whatever is, in his judgment, "just as good." The answer is arrived at by weighing the purpose to be served, the desire to be gratified, the excuse for deviating from the letter of the contract and the cruelty of enforcing strict adherence or of compelling the promisee to receive something less than for which he bargained. Also influential in many cases is the ratio of money value of the tendered performance and of the promised performance. In most cases the contract itself at least is an indication of the value of the promised performance, and courts should have little difficulty in determining the cost of curing the deficiency. But the rule cannot be expressed in terms of a fraction, since complete reliance on a mathematical formula would result in ignoring other important factors, such as the purpose which the promised performance was intended to serve and the extent to which the nonperformance would defeat such purpose, or would defeat it if not corrected. See, generally, 3A Corbin, Contracts Secs. 700–07 (1960).

Although definitions of "substantial performance" are not always couched in the same terminology and, because of the facts involved in a particular case, sometimes vary in the recital of the factors to be considered, the following definition by the Commission of Appeals in Atkinson v. Jackson Bros., 270 S.W. 848, 851 (Tex.Comm.App.1925), is a typical recital of the constituent elements of the doctrine:

> To constitute substantial compliance the contractor must have in good faith intended to comply with the contract, and shall have substantially done so in the sense that the defects are not pervasive, do not constitute a deviation from the general plan contemplated for the

work, and are not so essential that the object of the parties in making the contract and its purpose cannot, without difficulty, be accomplished by remedying them. Such performance permits only such omissions or deviations from the contract as are inadvertent and unintentional, are not due to bad faith, do not impair the structure as a whole, and are remediable without doing material damage to other parts of the building in tearing down and reconstructing.

* * *

What was the general plan contemplated for the work in this case? What was the object and purpose of the parties? It is clear that, despite the frequency with which the courts speak of defects that are not "pervasive," which do not constitute a "deviation from the general plan," and which are "not so essential that the object of the parties in making the contract and its purpose cannot, without difficulty, be accomplished by remedying them," when an attempt is made to apply the general principles to a particular case difficulties are encountered at the outset. Was the general plan to install a substantial roof which would serve the purpose which roofs are designed to serve? Or, rather, was the general plan to install a substantial roof of uniform color? Was the object and purpose of the contract merely to furnish such a roof, or was it to furnish such a roof which would be of a uniform color? It should not come as a shock to anyone to adopt a rule to the effect that a person has, particularly with respect to his home, to choose for himself and to contract for something which exactly satisfies that choice, and not to be compelled to accept something else. In the matter of homes and their decoration, as much as, if not more than, in many other fields, mere taste or preference, almost approaching whimsy, may be controlling with the homeowner, so that variations which might, under other circumstances, be considered trifling, may be inconsistent with that "substantial performance" on which liability to pay must be predicated. Of mere incompleteness or deviations which may be easily supplied or remedied after the contractor has finished his work, and the cost of which to the owner is not excessive and readily ascertainable, present less cause for hesitation in concluding that the performance tendered constitutes substantial performance, since in such cases the owner can obtain complete satisfaction by merely spending some money and deducting the amount of such expenditure from the contract price.

In the case before us there is evidence to support the conclusion that plaintiff can secure a roof of uniform coloring only by installing a completely new roof. We cannot say, as a matter of law, that the evidence establishes that in this case that a roof which so lacks uniformity in color as to give the appearance of a patch job serves essentially the same purpose as a roof of uniform color which has the appearance of being a new roof. We are not prepared to hold that a contractor who tenders a performance so deficient that it can be remedied only by completely redoing the work for which the contract called has established, as a matter of law, that he has substantially performed his contractual obligation.

* * *

Finally, defendant argues that it was entitled to judgment at least on the theory of quantum meruit on its cross claim because the evidence establishes as a matter of law that defendant installed a good weatherproof roof which was guaranteed for 15 years, and that such roof was installed properly in accordance with factory specifications and was of use and benefit to plaintiff.

The evidence does not conclusively establish that the shingles were properly installed. There is evidence to the effect that if shingles of this type are properly installed the result will be a roof which "blends," rather than a roof with clearly discordant streaks. In any event, the evidence does not conclusively establish that plaintiff has received any benefit from defendant's defective performance. As already pointed out, there is evidence that plaintiff will have to install a completely new roof. Because of defendant's deficient performance, plaintiff is now in a position which requires that she pay for a new roof.

Nor does the evidence conclusively establish that plaintiff accepted the claimed benefit. She complained immediately and has expressed dissatisfaction at all times. We cannot infer an acceptance from the fact that plaintiff continued to live in the house. She was living in the house before defendant installed the new roof, and we know of no rule which would require that, in order to avoid a finding of implied acceptance, plaintiff was obligated to move out of her home.

The judgment of the trial court is affirmed.

NOTES

(1) *Jacob & Youngs v. Kent* and *O.W. Grun Roofing & Construction Co. v. Cope* squarely faced the following question: did the contractor satisfy the constructive condition that the work be substantially completed before the owner has a duty to pay? Consider the following questions:

(a) What was the agreement on payment in *Jacob & Youngs* and how does it differ from *O.W. Grun*?

(b) Why should the constructive condition ever be satisfied by less than a complete performance that conformed to the contract requirements? For example, if the contract required the construction of a "country house" with "standard pipe of Reading Manufacture," why should the owner be expected to pay for something different?

(c) If, at the time of contracting, the contractor did not know or have reason to know the owner's particular purpose in requiring "Reading" pipe and most "reasonable" owners would have been satisfied by either brand, how is the owner's particular purpose to be protected under the contract? By employment of a more attentive architect? By clearer and more complete contract drafting? Can you draft a clause that would protect Mr. Kent against the mitigating force of the doctrine of substantial performance? Compare Della Ratta, Inc. v. American Better Community Developers, Inc., 38 Md.App. 119, 380 A.2d 627 (1977), where the court held that in a wholly executory contract, the doctrine of substantial performance did not apply to the satisfaction of an express condition. The smaller the deviation and the greater the extent of forfeiture, however, the greater the odds that even an express condition will be excused. See Restatement (Second) § 229.

(3) *The Effect of Bad Faith.* Judge Cardozo, in *Jacob & Youngs v. Kent,* suggested that the quality of the breacher's conduct was relevant to the "substantial performance" question: The "willful transgressor must accept the penalty of his transgression" but the "transgressor whose default is unintentional and trivial may hope for mercy if he will offer atonement for his wrong." Section 241 of the Restatement (Second) is in accord: the "extent to which the behavior of the party failing to perform or to offer to perform comports with standards of good faith and fair dealing" is a circumstance relevant to the question. Which of the following cases would fall on the bad faith side of the line:

    (a) P substituted Pipe X for Pipe Y knowing that the contract called for Pipe Y and that D strongly desired Pipe Y with the intention of harming D.

    (b) P substituted Pipe X for Pipe Y concealing the switch from the architect. P assumed that D was indifferent to which brand was used and hoped to save money for himself under the fixed-price contract by using Pipe X, which could be procured more cheaply.

    (c) P substituted Pipe X for Pipe Y after honestly but carelessly concluding that the specifications called for "brand name or equal."

(4) *Trivial Breach.* In Foundation Dev. Corp. v. Loehmann's, Inc., 163 Ariz. 438, 788 P.2d 1189 (1990), Loehmans, the anchor tenant in a shopping center under a 20–year lease failed by two days to pay a disputed charge within the ten days specified in the lease. Because of this tardy payment, the lessor exercised it contractual right to terminate the lease. The court finds that lessor did not have the right to terminate for a "trivial breach" but does not explain what words would have been sufficient to make timely payment a condition of further rental. The court dismisses "stock phrases" such as "time is of the essence" as indicating an intent to create such a condition. What non-stock phrases would have been sufficient?

(5) The role of the architect as project manager and the function of arbitration in construction contracts is treated in Chapter 8, Section 2.

PROBLEM: READING PIPE AND THE WAIVER OF CONDITIONS

In *Jacob & Youngs v. Kent,* the court concluded that the installation of the particular brand of pipe, Reading pipe, was not a condition precedent to the duty of the owner to pay the balance due under the construction contract. But Judge Cardozo, speaking for the majority, did observe: "This is not to say that the parties are not free by apt and certain words to effectuate a purpose that performance of every term shall be a condition of recovery." What if, for some reason (e.g., it is intended as a showhouse for Reading pipe, or his wife once won a Miss Reading Pipe contest), the owner did indeed want the installation of this brand of pipe to be a condition? Could it be done? How?

Assume that installation of Reading pipe was thus made a condition precedent, but that the contractor cannot procure Reading pipe. He approaches the owner, advising him that Cohoes pipe, a brand of equal quality, is available. Owner is agreeable to the substitution, but after installation of the substitute, stands by the original contract provision making installation of Reading pipe a condition of recovery? Will owner prevail?

Assume instead that the owner does the totally unexpected; *viz.,* he says that not only is it all right to omit the installation of Reading pipe, there is no need to install any pipe at all or to even construct the building. The owner will pay anyway. Can contractor hold owner to this commitment?

As alternative to the above scenarios, suppose that contractor went ahead with the installation of Cohoes pipe without discussing the matter with the owner. Is the latter obligated to pay? Would it make a difference if the owner, after becoming aware of the substitution, indicated that he would still pay? Even if obliged to pay, could the owner still recover damages if the Cohoes pipe was inferior to the Reading pipe?

Finally, assume that the contractor did not install any pipe at all, but the owner (again, doing the unlikely thing) said that he would still pay. Would the owner be bound by this commitment?

PROBLEM: THE CASE OF THE DEFICIENT VALVE TESTER

B manufactured valves for use in automobile engines. The valves were required to meet high performance standards before they could be used by automobile manufacturers. In order to increase the efficiency of its operation, B entered negotiations with S for the design and manufacture of a valve testing machine. B explained its needs to S, elaborating on the automobile manufacturer's requirements, and stated that it needed a machine that would test the valves with no more than a 5% margin for error. In short, B expected a testing accuracy rate of at least 95%. S agreed to this requirement and it appeared in the written contract. Six months later, the machine was completed and B put it through a rigorous inspection and test. The result was that the machine consistently achieved a 93–94% accuracy rate, with occasional batches testing out at 95%. B then claimed that S had breached an express warranty that the machine would achieve a 95% accuracy rate, see UCC 2–313(1), and that B could "reject" the goods, UCC 2–601, cancel the contract for breach, see UCC 2–711(1), and sue for damages. S concedes that the warranty was breached, but claimed that there was substantial performance. Thus, B was required to accept and pay for the goods, UCC 2–709(1), with an adjustment for any damages caused by the breach. See UCC 2–717. B responded that the doctrine of substantial performance has been rejected by the UCC, and B was entitled to a "perfect" tender.

Consult the following Code sections from Article 2 and give us your opinion: UCC 2–601, 2–504, 2–508, 2–608, 2–612, 2–719 and the sections on good faith, UCC 1–203 [Rev. 1–304], 1–201(19) [Rev. 1–201(20), defining good faith to mean "honesty in fact and the observance of reasonable commercial standards of fair dealing"] and 2–103(1)(b).

Lowy v. United Pacific Insurance Co.

Supreme Court of California, 1967.
67 Cal.2d 87, 60 Cal.Rptr. 225, 429 P.2d 577.

■ McComb, Associate Justice. Plaintiffs appeal from a judgment in favor of defendant Arnold Wolpin (hereinafter referred to as "defendant") on a cross-complaint for damages for breach of an excavation and grading contract.

Facts: Plaintiffs, owners and subdividers, entered into a contract with defendant, a licensed contractor, for certain excavation and grading work on lots and streets, together with street improvement work consisting of paving the streets and installing curbs and gutters, in a subdivision containing 89 residential lots.

After defendant had performed 98 percent of the contracted excavation and grading work, a dispute arose between the parties regarding payment of $7,200 for additional work, consisting of importing dirt for fills, necessitated by changes made by plaintiffs in the plans.

Defendant ceased performance. Plaintiffs immediately employed others to do street improvement work called for by the contract and thereafter sued defendant and his bonding company for breach of contract. Defendant answered and cross-complained for damages for breach of contract and reasonable services rendered. The trial court determined that plaintiffs were entitled to nothing against defendant and his bonding company and allowed defendant recovery on his cross-complaint.

Questions: First. *Was the contract between the parties divisible and the doctrine of substantial performance applicable?*

Yes.

The contract provided, in part, as follows: "[Defendant] agrees to provide and pay for all materials, labor, tools, equipment, light, transportation and other facilities necessary for the execution, in a good and workmanlike manner, of all the following described work: Excavation, Grading and Street Improvements in Tracts No. 26589 and 19517 in accordance with plans and specifications * * * and Exhibit 'A' attached hereto. * * *

"The price which [plaintiffs] shall pay [defendant] for performing his obligations, as aforesaid or as hereunder set forth, is at the following prices indicated: * * *

"See Exhibits *'A' and 'B'* attached hereto." (Italics added.)

Exhibit "A" states in part: "[Defendant] agrees to furnish all equipment, labor and material necessary for street improvements, onsite and offsite grading, grade and excavation and erosion control on Tracts 26589 and 19517 * * * for the lump sum price of Seventy–Three Thousand, Five Hundred Dollars ($73,500.00) including, without limitation, *all grading, compaction, cleaning, grade and erosion control and dumping,* all of which are to be performed to satisfaction of [plaintiffs]. * * * " (Italics added.)

The construction of pavement, curbs and gutters is not included in the list of specific items for which the sum of $73,500 is to be paid.

Exhibit "B" lists 45 unit prices ranging from $.04 to $4.50 per unit for use in the computation of the amount to be charged for the performance of that part of the street improvement work consisting of paving the streets and installing curbs and gutters. The unit prices are entirely unrelated to excavation and grading.

The contract further provides: "In invoicing [plaintiffs], multiply all the final quantities by the unit prices set forth in Exhibit 'B.' All quantities will be determined by Delta Engineering & Surveying Co. and approved by [defendant] and [plaintiffs], *with the exception of grading, etc., mentioned in Exhibit 'A' of this Agreement, which is a lump sum price for a complete job without any limitations.*" (Italics added.)

The latter paragraph of the contract shows clearly that the lump sum of $73,500 was not intended to include payment for paving the streets and installing curbs and gutters.

The trial court found that under the contract there were two phases of work to be performed, (1) grading and (2) street improvements; that defendant performed all the terms and conditions thereof relating to grading, except work which could be completed for $1,470, being 2 percent of the total grading cost contracted for; that defendant performed additional grading work, reasonably worth $7,200, necessitated by changes in plans on the part of plaintiffs and not attributable to defendant, which additional work was also authorized by plaintiffs through their superintendent; that plaintiffs breached the contract by employing others to do street improvement work and by not making payments to defendant for grading work done by him when due, thereby excusing further performance by defendant; and that defendant was entitled to recover on his cross-complaint for damages, as follows:

Contract price for grading	$73,500.00
Additional work	7,200.00
	80,700.00
Less amount paid defendant	− 60,227.50
	20,472.50
Less credit for uncompleted work	− 1,470.00
	19,002.50
Less credit for items paid for defendant's account	− 1,166.00
Balance owing defendant	$17,836.50

The trial court also found that defendant was entitled to reasonable attorney's fees in the sum of $4,000, the contract providing for reasonable attorney's fees to be awarded to the prevailing party in any action brought to enforce the terms and conditions thereof.

The trial court further found that defendant had breached that portion of the contract relating to street improvement work and was not entitled to recover damages for loss of profits in connection therewith.

As indicated above, the contract required the performance of two kinds of work. First, certain excavation and grading work was to be done on lots and streets. Thereafter, street improvement work, consisting of paving the streets and installing curbs and gutters, was required.

Plaintiffs agreed to pay defendant for the excavation and grading work (including street grading work) the sum of $73,500, as set forth in Exhibit

"A" of the contract and they agreed to pay defendant for the paving of the streets and the installation of curbs and gutters (all commonly called "street improvement work") pursuant to the unit prices set forth in Exhibit "B" of the contract.

Accordingly, since the consideration was apportioned, the contract was a severable or divisible one. . . . *

Before defendant commenced the excavation and grading work, for which a lump sum price of $73,500 was set by the contract, he gave a surety bond for $73,500. When the excavation and grading work was nearing completion, and it was almost time for work under the second phase to begin, plaintiffs requested that defendant provide a surety bond for "street improvements" in the sum of $125,000, stating that "no work should be performed on any portion of the street improvement portion of the contract until such bond is furnished." Thus, it is clear that the parties treated the contract as a divisible one.

Under the circumstances, the fact that defendant did not perform the second phase of the contract does not prevent his recovering for work done under the first phase.

Defendant did not entirely perform under the first phase of the contract. However, the doctrine of substantial performance, ordinarily applied to building contracts, is here applicable, since the evidence shows that defendant completed 98 percent of the work under the first phase and was prevented from completing the balance through the fault of plaintiffs.

Where a person agrees to do a thing for another for a specified sum of money, to be paid on full performance, he is not entitled to any part of the sum until he has himself done the thing he agreed to do, unless full performance has been excused, prevented, or delayed by the act of the other party. (Thomas Haverty Co. v. Jones, 185 Cal. 285, 288–289.)

In Thomas Haverty Co. v. Jones, supra, at page 289, we held that in the case of a building contract where the owner has taken possession of the building and is enjoying the fruits of the contractor's work in the performance of the contract, if there has been a substantial performance thereof by the contractor in good faith, if the failure to make full performance can be compensated in damages to be deducted from the price or allowed as a counterclaim, and if the omissions and deviations were not wilful or fraudulent and do not substantially affect the usefulness of the building or the purpose for which it was intended, the contractor may, in an action upon the contract, recover the amount of the contract price remaining

---

* Williston defines a divisible contract, as follows: "A contract under which the whole performance is divided into two sets of partial performance, each part of each set being the agreed exchange for a corresponding part of the set of performances to be rendered by the other promisor, is called a divisible contract. Or, as expressed in the cases:

" 'A contract is divisible where by its terms, 1, performance of each party is divided into two or more parts, and 2, the number of parts due from each party is the same, and 3, the performance of each part by one party is the agreed exchange for a corresponding part by the other party.' " (6 Williston, Contracts (3d ed. 1962) § 860, pp. 252–254.)

unpaid, less the amount allowed as damages for the failure of strict performance.

Reference to the computation of items, both debit and credit, set forth in the findings in the present case, reveals an almost literal compliance with the formula approved in the *Haverty* case, supra; and there is substantial evidence to support the trial court's finding that plaintiffs themselves breached the contract and thus made impossible full performance on defendant's part.

* * *

The judgment is affirmed.

Plaintiffs are ordered to pay to defendant Wolpin additional attorney's fees on this appeal in an amount to be determined by the trial court.

NOTES

(1) Did the contractor in *Lowy* substantially perform the entire contract? If not, how did he recover the adjusted contract price for the excavation and grading work on the lots and streets?

(2) It is commonly stated that whether a contract is divisible depends upon the intention of the parties, and the intent to have a divisible contract may be inferred from such factors as the ease with which the agreed consideration can be apportioned to separate performances, the fungibility of those performances and the lack of evidence that the parties would have refused to deal for less than the whole. See Management Services Corp. v. Development Associates, 617 P.2d 406, 408 (Utah 1980) (contract to purchase eight lots divisible). Section 240 of Restatement (Second), however, states that the question is whether the "performances to be exchanged under an exchange of promises can be apportioned into corresponding pairs of part performances so that the parts of each pair are properly regarded as agreed equivalents. * * *" According to Comment d, the "process of apportionment is essentially one of calculation and the rule can only be applied where calculation is feasible." Even so, the contract is not divisible unless it is "proper to regard the parts of each pair as agreed equivalents" and, in many cases, the "parties * * * cannot even be said to have had any actual intention on the point." Comment e. Motivated by a desire to avoid forfeiture, the court's decision will "usually depend on considerations of fairness," such as the receipt by the aggrieved party of a part performance "worth to him roughly the same fraction of what full performance would have been worth. * * *" Put another way, the "injured party will not be required to pay for a part of the performance that he has received if he cannot make full use of that part without the remainder of the performance" and, in making this determination, a court "must * * * take account of the possibility that the remainder of the performance can be easily obtained from some other source."

(3) UCC 2–307 provides: "Unless otherwise agreed all goods called for by a contract for sale must be tendered in a single delivery and payment is due only on such tender but where the circumstances give either party the right to make or demand delivery in lots the price if it can be apportioned may be demanded for each lot." Thus, where the circumstances indicate that a party has a right

to delivery in lots, the price may be demanded for each lot if it is apportionable. 2–307, comment 4. In the next chapter attention is given to the related problem of whether the breach of an installment discharges the other party from contractual obligation.

PROBLEMS: DIVISIBLE OR ENTIRE CONTRACT?

1. *The Case of the Unpaid Contractor.* Contractor (C) and Owner (O) entered into a home remodeling contract, containing the following provision respecting price and payment: "All above material, and labor to erect and install same to be supplied for $30,000 to be paid as follows: $1,500 on signing of contract, $10,000 upon delivery of materials and starting of work, $15,000 on completion of rough carpentry and rough plumbing, $3,500 on completion. C, upon completion of the rough work, demanded payment of the third installment and O refused. C then sued O for $15,000 and, at trial, failed to offer proof as to actual damages. O moved to dismiss. Although conceding that its failure to pay was a breach, O argued that C was not entitled to the third payment, but to only such amount as it could establish by way of actual loss sustained from the breach. Which view should prevail? See New Era Homes Corp. v. Forster, 299 N.Y. 303, 86 N.E.2d 757 (1949), infra at 901.

2. *The Case of the Defaulting Thresher.* Plaintiffs (P), owners of a threshing outfit, agreed with the defendant (D), a farmer, to thresh his grain at the following rates: wheat, $1.00 per bushel; oats, $.60 per bushel; flax, $1.50 per bushel. After threshing about 50% of the crop, P moved its equipment to another location because they were losing money on the job with D. D was obliged to complete the threshing of its grain at a higher price through other parties. Is P entitled to recover for the work done at the agreed price per bushel on the ground that the contract was "divisible"? See Johnson v. Fehsefeldt, 106 Minn. 202, 118 N.W. 797 (1908). If not, is there another basis upon which they might seek relief? See the cases which follow.

3. *The Case of the Failed Resort Bid.* Young and Tate agreed to invest in a proposed resort project. The first stage involved putting together a bid to be made to the State. Among other things, the agreement provided that Young, because of her better credit, was to provide $50,000 for this first stage, $25,000 on January 2, 1985, and the next $25,000 "as needed." The agreement also provided that Tate "will assume liability for the first $25,000." The first payment was made, but when Tate's agent requested the second payment, Young, without justification, refused to pay. Tate then spent $32,000 in furtherance of the bid, which was ultimately rejected by the State. Young sued Tate to recover the $25,000 paid and Tate counterclaimed to recover $25,000 of the expenses incurred after Young refused to make the second payment. Assuming that Young's refusal was a breach of contract, what result? See Young v. Tate, 232 Neb. 915, 442 N.W.2d 865 (1989).

Britton v. Turner

Supreme Court of Judicature of New Hampshire, 1834.
6 N.H. 481.

Assumpsit for work and labour, performed by the plaintiff, in the service of the defendant, from March 9th, 1831, to December 27, 1831.

The declaration contained the common counts, and among them a count in *quantum meruit,* for the labor, averring it to be worth one hundred dollars.

At the trial in the C.C. Pleas, the plaintiff proved the performance of the labor as set forth in the declaration.

The defence was that it was performed under a special contract—that the plaintiff agreed to work one year, from some time in March, 1831, to March 1832, and that the defendant was to pay him for said year's labor the sum of one hundred and twenty dollars; and the defendant offered evidence tending to show that such was the contract under which the work was done.

Evidence was also offered to show that the plaintiff left the defendant's service without his consent, and it was contended by the defendant that the plaintiff had no good cause for not continuing in his employment.

There was no evidence offered of any damage arising from the plaintiff's departure, farther than was to be inferred from his non fulfillment of the entire contract.

The court instructed the jury, that if they were satisfied from the evidence that the labor was performed, under a contract to labor a year, for the sum of one hundred and twenty dollars, and if they were satisfied that the plaintiff labored only the time specified in the declaration, and then left the defendant's service, against his consent, and without any good cause, yet the plaintiff was entitled to recover, under his *quantum meruit* count, as much as the labor he performed was reasonably worth, and under this direction the jury gave a verdict for the plaintiff for the sum of $95.

The defendant excepted to the instructions thus given to the jury.

■ PARKER, J. delivered the opinion of the court. It may be assumed, that the labor performed by the plaintiff, and for which he seeks to recover a compensation in this action, was commenced under a special contract to labor for the defendant the term of one year, for the sum of one hundred and twenty dollars, and that the plaintiff has labored but a portion of that time, and has voluntarily failed to complete the entire contract.

It is clear, then, that he is not entitled to recover upon the contract itself, because the service, which was to entitle him to the sum agreed upon, has never been performed.

But the question arises, can the plaintiff, under these circumstances, recover a reasonable sum for the service he has actually performed, under the count in *quantum meruit.*

Upon this, and questions of a similar nature, the decisions to be found in the books are not easily reconciled.

It has been held, upon contracts of this kind for labor to be performed at a specified price, that the party who voluntarily fails to fulfil the contract by performing the whole labor contracted for, is not entitled to recover any thing for the labor actually performed, however much he may have done towards the performance, and this has been considered the settled rule of law upon this subject. . . .

That such rule in its operation may be very unequal, not to say unjust, is apparent.

A party who contracts to perform certain specified labor, and who breaks his contract in the first instance, without any attempt to perform it, can only be made liable to pay the damages which the other party has sustained by reason of such non performance, which in many instances may be trifling—whereas a party who in good faith has entered upon the performance of his contract, and nearly completed it, and then abandoned the further performance—although the other party has had the full benefit of all that has been done, and has perhaps sustained no actual damage—is in fact subjected to a loss of all which has been performed, in the nature of damages for the nonfulfillment of the remainder, upon the technical rule, that the contract must be fully performed in order to [justify] a recovery of any part of the compensation.

By the operation of this rule, then, the party who attempts performance may be placed in a much worse situation than he who wholly disregards his contract, and the other party may receive much more, by the breach of the contract, than the injury which he has sustained by such breach, and more than he could be entitled to were he seeking to recover damages by an action.

The case before us presents an illustration. Had the plaintiff in this case never entered upon the performance of his contract, the damage could not probably have been greater than some small expense and trouble incurred in procuring another to do the labor which he had contracted to perform. But having entered upon the performance, and labored nine and a half months, the value of which labor to the defendant as found by the jury is $95, if the defendant can succeed in this defence, he in fact receives nearly five sixths of the value of a whole year's labor, by reason of the breach of contract by the plaintiff, a sum not only utterly disproportionate to any probable, not to say possible damage which could have resulted from the neglect of the plaintiff to continue the remaining two and a half months, but altogether beyond any damage which could have been recovered by the defendant, had the plaintiff done nothing towards the fulfillment of his contract.

* * *

It is said, that where a party contracts to perform certain work, and to furnish materials, as for instance, to build a house, and the work is done, but with some variations from the mode prescribed by the contract, yet if the other party has the benefit of the labor and materials he should be bound to pay so much as they are reasonably worth. . . .

Those cases are not to be distinguished, in principle, from the present, unless it be in the circumstance, that where the party has contracted to furnish materials, and do certain labor, as to build a house in a specified manner, if it is not done according to the contract, the party for whom it is built may refuse to receive it—elect to take no benefit from what has been performed—and therefore if he does receive, he shall be bound to pay the value—whereas in a contract for labor, merely, from day to day, the party is continually receiving the benefit of the contract under an expectation that it will be fulfilled, and cannot, upon the breach of it, have an election to refuse to receive what has been done, and thus discharge himself from payment.

But we think this difference in the nature of the contracts does not justify the application of a different rule in relation to them.

The party who contracts for labor merely, for a certain period, does so with full knowledge that he must, from the nature of the case, be accepting part performance from day to day, if the other party commences the performance, and with knowledge also that the other may eventually fail of completing the entire term.

If under such circumstances he actually receives a benefit from the labor performed, over and above the damage occasioned by the failure to complete, there is as much reason why he should pay the reasonable worth of what has thus been done for his benefit, as there is when he enters and occupies the house which has been built for him, but not according to the stipulations of the contract, and which he perhaps enters, not because he is satisfied with what has been done, but because circumstances compel him to accept it such as it is, that he should pay for the value of the house.

* * *

In fact we think the technical reasoning, that the performance of the whole labor is a condition precedent, and the right to recover any thing dependent upon it—that the contract being entire there can be no apportionment—and that there being an express contract no other can be implied, even upon the subsequent performance of service—is not properly applicable to this species of contract, where a beneficial service has been actually performed; for we have abundant reason to believe, that the general understanding of the community is, that the hired laborer shall be entitled to compensation for the service actually performed, though he do not continue the entire term contracted for, and such contracts must be presumed to be made with reference to that understanding, unless an express stipulation shows the contrary.

* * *

It is easy, if parties so choose, to provide by an express agreement that nothing shall be earned, if the laborer leaves his employer without having performed the whole service contemplated, and then there can be no pretence for a recovery if he voluntarily deserts the service before the expiration of the time.

The amount, however, for which the employer ought to be charged, where the laborer abandons his contract, is only the reasonable worth, or the amount of advantage he receives upon the whole transaction, ... and, in estimating the value of the labor, the contract price for the service cannot be exceeded. . . .

* * *

The benefit and advantage which the party takes by the labor, therefore, is the amount of value which he receives, if any, after deducting the amount of damage * * *.

* * *

This rule, by binding the employer to pay the value of the service he actually receives, and the laborer to answer in damages where he does not complete the entire contract, will leave no temptation to the former to drive the laborer from his service, near the close of his term, by ill treatment, in order to escape from payment; nor to the latter to desert his service before the stipulated time, without a sufficient reason; and it will in most instances settle the whole controversy in one action, and prevent a multiplicity of suits and cross actions.

* * *

Applying the principles thus laid down, to this case, the plaintiff is entitled to judgment on the verdict.

The defendant sets up a mere breach of the contract in defence of the action, but this cannot avail him. He does not appear to have offered evidence to show that he was damnified by such breach, or to have asked that a deduction should be made upon that account. The direction to the jury was therefore correct, that the plaintiff was entitled to recover as much as the labor performed was reasonably worth, and the jury appear to have allowed a *pro rata* compensation, for the time which the plaintiff labored in the defendant's service.

* * *

Judgment on the verdict.

NOTES

The "constructive" condition dilemma facing Judge Parker in *Britton v. Turner* has been resolved by legislation in many states: the employer must pay the employee's wages at regular intervals regardless of "substantial" performance. See, e.g., Ill.Rev.Stat., ch. 48, §§ 39m–3 (all wage earners other than executives, administrators, professionals and commission agents must be paid on a semi-monthly basis.) The employer's failure to pay as required may be a crime. See Holmes v. Tradigrain, Inc., 411 So.2d 1132 (La.App.1982); Putnam v. Oregon Department of Justice, 58 Or.App. 111, 647 P.2d 949 (1982). For an illustration of the type of question that can arise under these statutes, see Suastez v. Plastic Dress–Up Co., 31 Cal.3d 774, 183 Cal.Rptr. 846, 647 P.2d 122 (1982), where the California Supreme Court held that a proportionate right to a paid vacation vested in the employee as labor was rendered and, once vested, was protected from forfeiture by the applicable legislation.

Comment: Recovery in Restitution by a Plaintiff in Default

Britton v. Turner permitted a plaintiff who had arguably committed a material breach to recover the reasonable value of work done up to the breach, "less whatever damages the other party has suffered." See also Kulseth v. Rotenberger, 320 N.W.2d 920 (N.D.1982); Kirkland v. Archbold, 113 N.E.2d 496 (Ohio App.1953); Pinches v. Swedish Evangelical Lutheran Church, 55 Conn. 183, 10 A. 264 (1887). Put another way, although a plaintiff cannot recover "on the contract," he or she can recover in restitution the net benefit retained by the defendant after full compensation for plaintiff's breach of contract. That benefit, however, is limited by the contract price. Section 357 of the first Restatement adopted the "net benefit" test, stating that the "measure of the defendant's benefit from the plaintiff's part performance is the amount by which he has been enriched as a result of such performance * * *." Section 357(3).

The first Restatement, however, provided that restitution was not available if the plaintiff's breach was "wilful and deliberate." Section 357(1). The apparent purpose of this limitation was to direct attention to the moral justification for the breach: an intentional breach is not regarded as wilful and deliberate if it was "due to hardship, insolvency, or circumstances that tend appreciably toward moral justification." Comment e. See G. Palmer, Law of Restitution § 5.1 (1978). Section 374(1) of Restatement (Second), however, does not make restitution turn upon the morality of the plaintiff's breach. If the defendant is justified in refusing to perform because of the plaintiff's material breach, the "party in breach is entitled to restitution for any benefit that he has conferred by way of part performance or reliance in excess of the loss that he has caused by his own breach." See Section 370, for the general requirement that a benefit be conferred for restitution. Section 371 provides the "measure" of the restitution interest. If money rather than specific restitution is sought, "it may as justice requires be measured by either (a) the reasonable value to the other party of what he received in terms of what it would have cost him to obtain it from a person in the claimant's position, or (b) the extent to which the other party's property has been increased in value or his other interests advanced." In no case, however, "will the party in breach be allowed to recover more than a ratable portion of the total contract price where such a portion can be determined." Section 374, Comment b. Does this approach rule out consideration of the moral justification for the breach? The answer is probably no when judicial discretion in measuring the restitution interest is taken into account. The measurement is made "as justice requires" and when the "party seeking restitution has himself committed a material breach * * * uncertainties as to the amount of the benefit may properly be resolved against him." Section 371, Comment a. See Illustration 1. This open-endedness is consistent with Professor Palmer's conclusion that although restitution should not always be denied when the breach is in bad faith, it "does mean that it should be allowed less readily." In short, "the retention of some enrichment may well be just when it is brought about by plaintiff's willful and deliberate breach." G. Palmer at § 5.15, p. 685.

This, apparently, is still the law in New York, at least in real estate contracts, where the vendor is permitted to keep the down payment in a contract to purchase where the vendee commits a willful breach. In Maxton Builders, Inc. v. Lo Galbo, 68 N.Y.2d 373, 509 N.Y.S.2d 507, 502 N.E.2d 184 (1986), the court recognized the "modern rule" that permitted restitution of the excess retained over damages but refused to overrule earlier authority to the contrary.

In the leading case, Lawrence v. Miller, 86 N.Y. 131 . . . decided by this court in 1881, we denied the assignee of the defaulting vendee recovery of a $2,000 down payment, reasoning that the vendor acquired the money rightfully, failed in no duty to the vendee, and the money would have been his but for the vendee's breach. We stated (at p. 140): "To allow a recovery of this money would be to sustain an action by a party on his own breach of his own contract, which the law does not allow * * * Nor can the specious view be taken, presented by the plaintiff, that the defendant is entitled to no more than he has actually been damaged."

Much of the criticism of *Lawrence v. Miller* (supra) is directed at the rule on which it is based, which broadly holds that a party who defaults on a contract cannot recover the amount or value of part performance. . . . This parent rule is applicable to contracts generally, and has been applied to a wide variety of circumstances including the sale of goods, employment contracts for a fixed term, construction contracts, and installment land sales. . . . In all of these cases the common law would deny any relief to the defaulting party even when there had been substantial, or nearly complete performance. It was these holdings especially which prompted the criticism calling for reform of the parent rule on the ground that it produced a forfeiture "and the amount of the forfeiture increases as performance proceeds, so that the penalty grows larger as the breach grows smaller." . . .

The "modern rule" advocated by the critics permits the party in default to recover for part performance in excess of actual damages, but places the burden on him to prove the net benefit conferred . . . The rule was designed primarily to protect the party who had made a number of payments or substantial performance before default, and provides little relief to the defaulting purchaser seeking to recover a down payment or first installment. * * *

The Restatement (Second) of Contracts adopts the "modern rule", but recognizes an exception for liquidated damages, and also for "money paid" under an understanding or "usage" that it be retained in the event of a breach (§ 374 comment c). The illustration involves the right of a seller on a real estate contract to retain the first installment equal to 10% of the contract price, upon the buyer's default. * * *

We have previously noted that a court should not depart from its prior holdings "unless impelled by '*the most cogent reasons*' " (Baker v. Lorillard, 4 N.Y. 257, 261). This standard is particularly apt in cases involving the legal effect of contractual relations. In fact, when contractual rights are at issue, 'where it can reasonably be assumed that settled rules are necessary and necessarily relied upon, stability and adherence to precedent are generally more important than a better or even a "correct" rule of law' (Matter of Eckart, 39 N.Y.2d 493, 500). The rule permitting a party in default to seek restitution for part performance has much to commend it in its general applications. But as applied to real estate down payments approximating 10% it does not appear to offer a better or more workable rule than the long-established "usage" in this State with respect to the seller's right to retain a down payment upon default. * * *

Finally, real estate contracts are probably the best examples of arm's length transactions. Except in cases where there is a real risk of overreaching, there should be no need for the courts to relieve the parties of the consequences of their contract. If the parties are dissatisfied with the rule of *Lawrence v. Miller* (supra), the time to say so is at the bargaining table. * * *

PROBLEMS: RESTITUTIONARY RELIEF AND THE WRONGDOER

(1) A contracted with B to construct a swimming pool on B's land for $15,000. The specifications required a designated system for the walls and floor that was guaranteed for 20 years. A, in order to shave costs on the fixed-price contract, deliberately installed a different and somewhat inferior system, which was guaranteed for 10 years. B refused to pay the contract price and A sued for either the price or restitution. The trial court determined that although B had a functional pool for at least 10 years, A had committed a material breach. The trial court also determined that the cost to replace the system would be $20,000 and that the difference in value of the land with a pool as promised by A and the pool actually constructed was $5,000. In order to avoid "economic waste," the trial court then awarded B $5,000 damages for breach of contract. In considering A's claim for restitution, the trial court determined that: (a) the reasonable value to B of the pool constructed in terms of what it would have cost to obtain it from another pool contractor was $12,000; and (b) the difference in value of B's land with the pool actually constructed and without a pool was $5,000. What, if anything, should A recover in restitution from B?

(2) B ordered complex medical diagnostic equipment from S for $500,000 and paid $300,000 down at the time of contracting. S completed manufacturing the machine, but B, because its needs had changed, refused to accept delivery. S sued for damages and, as a lost volume seller, proved that the profit plus reasonable overhead it would have made on the contract was $80,000. B sought to recover the down payment. Assuming that S's damages are $80,000, what if anything, can B recover? See UCC 2–718 (2–4).

SECTION 4.   CHANGED CIRCUMSTANCES; IMPRACTICABILITY AND FRUSTRATION OF PURPOSE

The law of impracticability and frustration can be thought of us another type of implied condition. One's duty to perform a contract is normally—that is, by default—conditioned not only upon the absence of a material breach by the other side, but also conditioned upon performance not becoming impracticable.

And as with our earlier discussion of express and implied conditions, conditioning the duty to perform on the non-occurrence of certain events (impractiability and frustration of purpose) is a powerful way that the parties can allocate risks concerning those events. The risk allocation problems treated in this section are suggested by a familiar hypothetical. Suppose that S has sold goods to B and agreed to have them transported to a port on the Gulf of Aden by a specified date. S then contracts with C, a shipping company, to pick up the goods in Galveston, Texas and transport them to the Gulf of Aden by the specified date for a fixed price of $50,000. After the ship was underway and just as it was entering the Mediterranean Sea, word was received that due to a flare up of hostilities in the Middle East, the Suez Canal had been closed indefinitely. C informed S of this event and offered to transport the goods to their destination via the Cape of Good Hope, a trip that would cost C $100,000 more than the agreed contract price and would delay delivery by two weeks. S refused the offer to modify the contract and insisted that C complete the contract of carriage via the Cape at the original contract price and pay any damages caused by the delay. C then broke off discussions and returned to Galveston with the goods. S sued for damages caused by C's alleged breach of contract and C countered with the defense that performance was excused by a changed circumstance, the closing of the Suez Canal. How should this case be resolved?

In approaching this question, analysis is aided if the following questions are asked and answered.

First, what was the nature of the risk event and what was its impact on the contractual relationship? Was the "event" a condition which existed at the time of contracting or a circumstance which arose thereafter? Was the impact of the event that performance as agreed was prevented or made more costly or that the incentive of one party to perform was impaired because its purpose in entering the contract was frustrated?

Second, was the party seeking relief at "fault" in that it caused the event or failed to take reasonable steps either to avoid it or to minimize the impact?

Third, if the party seeking relief was not at "fault," did the agreement allocate the risk of the event to one or the other or both parties? The form of agreement may include an express condition, an "excuse" or *force majeure* clause[1] or a more elaborate risk allocation system, including

---

1. Here is an example of such a clause:
EXCUSABLE DELAY:
Shipper shall not be responsible nor deemed to be in default on account of delays in performance of this Agreement due to causes beyond Shipper's control and not occasioned by its fault or negligence, including but not being limited to civil war, insurrections, strikes, riots, fires, floods, explosions, earthquakes, serious accidents, and any act of government, acts of God or the public enemy,

insurance. Or it may be concluded that because the risk was discussed or foreshadowed in the negotiations, it was "tacitly" agreed to by the promisor who made an unconditional promise to perform at a fixed price.[2]

Fourth, if there was no agreement, express or implied, allocating the risk, how is the court to fill the "gap" in risk allocation? One method is for the court to refuse to impose any risk allocation terms on the parties. In short, the maker of an unconditional promise bears the full risk of the event and its impact. A more flexible test, adopted by Section 261 of Restatement (Second), is as follows:

> Where, after a contract is made, a party's performance is made impracticable without his fault by the occurrence of an event the non-occurrence of which was a basic assumption on which the contract was made, his duty to render that performance is discharged, unless the language or the circumstances indicate the contrary.

Note that the test applies in the absence of "fault" by the party seeking relief or "language or circumstances" to the contrary. Note, also, that the test has two parts: (1) The non-occurrence of the event must have been a basic assumption on which the contract was made; and (2) the event must have made performance "impracticable." The Restatement (Second) test, derived from UCC 2–615(a), governs whether the event existed at the time of contracting, Section 266, occurred after contract formation, Section 261, or frustrated the purpose of the party seeking relief rather than made performance impracticable, Section 265.

Fifth, what is the nature and scope of relief when the conditions of Section 261 or UCC 2–615(a) are satisfied? Is relief limited to discharge of the contract with appropriate restitution or must the parties continue performance under terms adjusted by the court to reflect the risk? Is there a remedial middle ground?

Sixth, suppose, in our hypothetical, that S accepted C's offer to modify the contract by agreement. Would that modification be enforceable? Suppose that the advantaged party refused to negotiate over a proposed modification. Would that ever be bad faith?

Keep these questions in mind as you search for answers in the following materials. Remember that the problem is far more complex and controversial than the effort to excuse a condition for unjust forfeiture or to determine what is bad faith in the exercise of performance discretion. To some, too much excuse undermines the stability of contracts, reallocates

---

failure of transportation, epidemics, quarantine restrictions, failure of vendors or other shippers to perform their contracts or labor troubles causing cessation, slowdown, or interruption of work, provided such cause is beyond Shipper's control.

See Eastern Air Lines, Inc. v. McDonnell Douglas Corp., 532 F.2d 957, 988 (5th Cir. 1976).

2. See UCC 2–615, Comment 8; Barbarossa & Sons, Inc. v. Iten Chevrolet, Inc., 265 N.W.2d 655 (Minn.1978) (seller tacitly assumes a material risk foreseen at the time of contracting as a "real possibility" by failing explicitly to provide against it in the agreement); Harper & Associates v. Printers, Inc., 46 Wash.App. 417, 730 P.2d 733 (1986).

risks already insured against in an inefficient manner and invites courts to "make" contracts that the parties could and should have made for themselves. Thus, despite sound analysis and a flexible test for excuse, you should not be surprised to discover that there is considerable judicial talk about granting relief but precious little evidence that relief has been granted. This was the sad lesson learned by the carriers in the litigation that followed the two occasions when, due to hostilities, the Suez Canal was closed.[3]

(A) EXISTING IMPRACTICABILITY

Mineral Park Land Co. v. Howard

Supreme Court of California, 1916.
172 Cal. 289, 156 P. 458.

■ SLOSS, J. The defendants appeal from a judgment in favor of plaintiff for $3,650. The appeal is on the judgment roll alone.

The plaintiff was the owner of certain land in the ravine or wash known as the Arroyo Seco, in South Pasadena, Los Angeles county. The defendants had made a contract with the public authorities for the construction of a concrete bridge across the Arroyo Seco. In August, 1911, the parties to this action entered into a written agreement whereby the plaintiff granted to the defendants the right to haul gravel and earth from plaintiff's land, the defendants agreeing to take therefrom all of the gravel and earth necessary in the construction of the fill and cement work on the proposed bridge, the required amount being estimated at approximately 114,000 cubic yards. Defendants agreed to pay 5 cents per cubic yard for the first 80,000 yards, the next 10,000 yards were to be given free of charge, and the balance was to be paid for at the rate of 5 cents per cubic yard.

The complaint was in two counts. The first alleged that the defendants had taken 50,131 cubic yards of earth and gravel, thereby becoming indebted to plaintiff in the sum of $2,506.55, of which only $900 had been paid, leaving a balance of $1,606.55 due. The findings support plaintiff's

---

3. The litigation following two earlier Suez Canal closings produced results against the interest of the ship owner. In short, they were held to have assumed the risk of the event and the extra costs that ensued. See, e.g., American Trading & Production Corp. v. Shell International Marine Ltd., 453 F.2d 939 (2d Cir.1972); Transatlantic Financing Corp. v. United States, 124 U.S.App.D.C. 183, 363 F.2d 312 (1966). The general problem, English cases and the special problems of international trade are well discussed in Robert Birmingham, *A Second Look at the Suez Canal Cases: Excuse for Nonperformance of Contractual Obligations in the Light of Eco-* *nomic Theory*, 20 Hastings L.J. 1393 (1969); Oscar Schlegal, *Of Nuts, and Ships and Sealing Wax, Suez and Frustrating Things–The Doctrine of Impossibility of Performance*, 23 Rutgers L.Rev. 419 (1969); Harold Berman, *Excuse for Nonperformance in the Light of Contract Practices in International Trade*, 63 Colum.L.Rev. 1413 (1963). As Judge Mulligan put it: "Matters involving impossibility or impracticability of performance of contract are concededly vexing and difficult. One is even urged on the allocation of such risks to pray for the 'Wisdom of Solomon.' ... [and rely upon] the efficacy of prayer." 453 F.2d at 944.

claim in this regard, and there is no question of the propriety of so much of the judgment as responds to the first count. The second count sought to recover damages for the defendants' failure to take from plaintiff's land any more than the 50,131 yards.

It alleged that the total amount of earth and gravel used by defendants was 101,000 cubic yards, of which they procured 50,869 cubic yards from some place other than plaintiff's premises. The amount due the plaintiff for this amount of earth and gravel would, under the terms of the contract, have been $2,043.45. The count charged that plaintiff's land contained enough earth and gravel to enable the defendants to take therefrom the entire amount required, and that the 50,869 yards not taken had no value to the plaintiff. Accordingly the plaintiff sought, under this head, to recover damages in the sum of $2,043.45.

The answer denied that the plaintiff's land contained any amount of earth and gravel in excess of the 50,131 cubic yards actually taken, and alleged that the defendants took from the said land all of the earth and gravel available for the work mentioned in the contract.

The court found that the plaintiff's land contained earth and gravel far in excess of 101,000 cubic yards of earth and gravel, but that only 50,131 cubic yards, the amount actually taken by the defendants, was above the water level. No greater quantity could have been taken "by ordinary means," or except by the use, at great expense, of a steam dredger, and the earth and gravel so taken could not have been used without first having been dried at great expense and delay. On the issue raised by the plea of defendants that they took all the earth and gravel that was available the court qualified its findings in this way: It found that the defendants did take all of the available earth and gravel from plaintiff's premises, in this, that they took and removed "all that could have been taken advantageously to defendants, or all that was practical to take and remove from a financial standpoint"; that any greater amount could have been taken only at a prohibitive cost, that is, at an expense of 10 or 12 times as much as the usual cost per yard. It is also declared that the word "available" is used in the findings to mean capable of being taken and used advantageously. It was not "advantageous or practical" to have taken more material from plaintiff's land, but it was not impossible. There is a finding that the parties were not under any mutual misunderstanding regarding the amount of available gravel, but that the contract was entered into without any calculation on the part of either of the parties with reference to the amount of available earth and gravel on the premises.

The single question is whether the facts thus found justified the defendants in their failure to take from the plaintiff's land all of the earth and gravel required. This question was answered in the negative by the court below. The case was apparently thought to be governed by the principle—established by a multitude of authorities—that where a party has agreed, without qualification, to perform an act which is not in its nature impossible of performance, he is not excused by difficulty of performance, or by the fact that he becomes unable to perform.

It is, however, equally well settled that, where performance depends upon the existence of a given thing, and such existence was assumed as the basis of the agreement, performance is excused to the extent that the thing ceases to exist or turns out to be nonexistent. * * *

We think the findings of fact make a case falling within the rule of these decisions. The parties were contracting for the right to take earth and gravel to be used in the construction of the bridge. When they stipulated that all of the earth and gravel needed for this purpose should be taken from plaintiff's land, they contemplated and assumed that the land contained the requisite quantity, available for use. The defendants were not binding themselves to take what was not there. And, in determining whether the earth and gravel were "available," we must view the conditions in a practical and reasonable way. Although there was gravel on the land, it was so situated that the defendants could not take it by ordinary means, nor except at a prohibitive cost. To all fair intents then, it was impossible for defendants to take it.

"A thing is impossible in legal contemplation when it is not practicable; and a thing is impracticable when it can only be done at an excessive and unreasonable cost." 1 Beach on Contr. § 216. We do not mean to intimate that the defendants could excuse themselves by showing the existence of conditions which would make the performance of their obligation more expensive than they had anticipated, or which would entail a loss upon them. But, where the difference in cost is so great as here, and has the effect, as found, of making performance impracticable, the situation is not different from that of a total absence of earth and gravel.

On the facts found, there should have been no recovery on the second count.

The judgment is modified by deducting therefrom the sum of $2,043.45, and, as so modified, it stands affirmed.

We concur: SHAW, J.; LAWLOR, J.

NOTES

(1) Section 456 of the first Restatement, entitled "Existing Impossibility," provided that, unless a contrary intention was manifested, a "promise imposes no duty if performance of the promise is impossible because of facts existing when the promise is made of which the promisor neither knows nor has reason to know." The word "impossibility" was defined to include both "strict impossibility" and "impracticability because of extreme and unreasonable difficulty, expense, injury or loss involved." Section 460(1) provided that where the "existence of a specific thing * * * is, either by the terms of a bargain or in the contemplation of both parties necessary for the performance of a promise in the bargain, a duty to perform the promise (a) never arises if at the time the bargain is made the existence of the thing within the time for seasonable performance is impossible * * *." Which of these sections catches the essence of *Mineral Park v. Howard?* Is it correct to conclude in *Mineral Park* that it

was irrelevant which party assumed the risk of the subsurface conditions and that the real question was whether the performance was impracticable?

(2) For modern counterparts of *Mineral Park,* see Mat–Su/Blackard/Stephan & Sons v. State, 647 P.2d 1101 (Alaska 1982) (risk of inadequate gravel allocated by contract to contractor); Beck v. J.M. Smucker Co., 277 Or. 607, 561 P.2d 623 (1977) (subsurface sand).

United States v. Wegematic Corp.

United States Court of Appeals, Second Circuit, 1966.
360 F.2d 674.

■ Before LUMBARD, CHIEF JUDGE, and FRIENDLY and ANDERSON, CIRCUIT JUDGES.

■ FRIENDLY, CIRCUIT JUDGE. The facts developed at trial in the District Court for the Southern District of New York, fully set forth in a memorandum by Judge Graven, can be briefly summarized: In June 1956 the Federal Reserve Board invited five electronics manufacturers to submit proposals for an intermediate-type, general-purpose electronic digital computing system or systems; the invitation stressed the importance of early delivery as a consideration in determining the Board's choice. Defendant, a relative newcomer in the field, which had enjoyed considerable success with a smaller computer known as the ALWAC III–E, submitted a detailed proposal for the sale or lease of a new computer designated as the ALWAC 800. It characterized the machine as "a truly revolutionary system utilizing all of the latest technical advances," and featured that "maintenance problems are minimized by the use of highly reliable magnetic cores for not only the high speed memory but also logical elements and registers." Delivery was offered nine months from the date the contract or purchase order was received. In September the Board acted favorably on the defendant's proposal, ordering components of the ALWAC 800 with an aggregate cost of $231,800. Delivery was to be made on June 30, 1957, with liquidated damages of $100 per day for delay. The order also provided that in the event the defendant failed to comply "with any provision" of the agreement, "the Board may procure the services described in the contract from other sources and hold the Contractor responsible for any excess cost occasioned thereby." Defendant accepted the order with enthusiasm.

The first storm warning was a suggestion by the defendant in March 1957 that the delivery date be postponed. In April it informed the Board by letter that delivery would be made on or before October 30 rather than as agreed, the delay being due to the necessity of "a redesign which we feel has greatly improved this equipment"; waiver of the stipulated damages for delay was requested. The Board took the request under advisement. On August 30 defendant wrote that delivery would be delayed "possibly into 1959"; it suggested use of ALWAC III–E equipment in the interim and waiver of the $100 per day "penalty." The Board also took this request under advisement but made clear it was waiving no rights. In mid-October defendant announced that "due to engineering difficulties it has become impracticable to deliver the ALWAC 800 Computing System at this time";

it requested cancellation of the contract without damages. The Board set about procuring comparable equipment from another manufacturer; on October 6, 1958, International Business Machines Corporation delivered an IBM 650 computer, serving substantially the same purpose as the ALWAC 800, at a rental of $102,000 a year with an option to purchase for $410,450.

In July 1958 the Board advised defendant of its intention to press its claim for damages; this suit followed. The court awarded the United States $46,300 for delay under the liquidated damages clause, $179,450 for the excess cost of the IBM equipment, and $10,056 for preparatory expenses useless in operating the IBM system—a total of $235,806, with 6% interest from October 6, 1958.

The principal point of the defense, which is the sole ground of this appeal, is that delivery was made impossible by "basic engineering difficulties" whose correction would have taken between one and two years and would have cost a million to a million and a half dollars, with success likely but not certain. Although the record does not give an entirely clear notion what the difficulties were, two experts suggested that they may have stemmed from the magnetic cores, used instead of transistors to achieve a solid state machine, which did not have sufficient uniformity at this stage of their development. Defendant contends that under federal law, which both parties concede to govern, see Cargill, Inc. v. Commodity Credit Corp., 275 F.2d 745, 751–753 (2 Cir.1960), the "practical impossibility" of completing the contract excused its defaults in performance.

* * *

We find persuasive the defendant's suggestion of looking to the Uniform Commercial Code as a source for the "federal" law of sales....

Section 2–615 of the UCC, entitled "Excuse by failure of presupposed conditions," provides that:

> "Except so far as a seller may have assumed a greater obligation * * * delay in delivery or non-delivery * * * is not a breach of his duty under a contract for sale if performance as agreed has been made impracticable by the occurrence of a contingency the nonoccurrence of which was a basic assumption on which the contract was made * * *."

The latter part of the test seems a somewhat complicated way of putting Professor Corbin's question of how much risk the promisor assumed. Recent Developments in the Law of Contracts, 50 Harv.L.Rev. 449, 465–66 (1937); 2 Corbin, Contracts § 1333, at 371. We see no basis for thinking that when an electronics system is promoted by its manufacturer as a revolutionary breakthrough, the risk of the revolution's occurrence falls on the purchaser; the reasonable supposition is that it has already occurred or, at least, the manufacturer is assuring the purchaser that it will be found to have when the machine is assembled. As Judge Graven said: "The Board in its invitation for bids did not request invitations to conduct a development program for it. The Board requested invitations from manufacturers for the furnishing of a computer machine." Acceptance of defendant's argument would mean that though a purchaser makes his choice because of the attractiveness of a manufacturer's representation and will be bound by it, the manufacturer is free to express what are only aspirations and gamble on mere probabilities of fulfillment without any risk of liability. In fields of developing technology, the manufacturer would thus enjoy a wide degree of latitude with respect to performance while holding an option to compel the buyer to pay if the gamble should pan out. . . . We do not think this the common understanding—above all as to a contract where the manufacturer expressly agreed to liquidated damages for delay and authorized the purchaser to resort to other sources in the event of non-delivery. . . . If a manufacturer wishes to be relieved of the risk that what looks good on paper may not prove so good in hardware, the appropriate exculpatory language is well known and often used.

Beyond this the evidence of true impracticability was far from compelling. The large sums predicted by defendant's witnesses must be appraised in relation not to the single computer ordered by the Federal Reserve Board, evidently for a bargain price, but to the entire ALWAC 800 program as originally contemplated. Although the record gives no idea what this was, even twenty-five machines would gross $10,000,000 if priced at the level of the comparable IBM equipment. While the unanticipated need for expending $1,000,000 or $1,500,000 on redesign might have made such a venture unattractive, as defendant's management evidently decided, the sums are thus not so clearly prohibitive as it would have them appear. What seemingly did become impossible was on-time performance; the issue whether if defendant had offered prompt rectification of the design, the Government could have refused to give it a chance and still recover not merely damages for delay but also the higher cost of replacement equipment, is not before us.

Affirmed.

NOTES

(1) Excuse issues arise under government contracts when a contractor performing a fixed-price contract claims that it is "impossible" or impracticable to achieve the promised result under the specifications. Normally, the contractor will not be excused under the contract "default" clause or other standard risk allocation clauses. See, e.g., 32 C.F.R. 7:12, § 7.103(11) (fixed-price supply contract). See also Austin Co. v. United States, 161 Ct.Cl. 76, 314 F.2d 518 (1963), cert. denied 375 U.S. 830, 84 S.Ct. 75, 11 L.Ed.2d 62 (1963), holding that the contractor assumed the risk if the default clause did not provide an excuse and the contractor agreed to produce a particular result at a fixed-price.

As Judge Friendly indicated in *Wegematic*, however, appropriate sections of the Uniform Commercial Code may be used as a source of federal contract law. What "test" for excuse did Judge Friendly adopt in *Wegematic*? If the risk of not achieving the promised result was properly on the contractor, was the court correct in considering whether "performance as agreed" was made impracticable?

(2) If the government has furnished detailed specifications which the contractor must follow ("performance" specifications) or specifications which require a particular result ("design" specifications) and the contractor is unable to perform on time, the risk is placed upon the government if the specifications were "defective" or an implied warranty of "suitability" was made. Here, if the "technical impossibility" makes performance "impracticable, or unfeasible or commercially senseless," the contractor will be excused. J.A. Maurer, Inc. v. United States, 202 Ct.Cl. 813, 485 F.2d 588, 594–96 (1973). Similarly, if the contractor actually completes performance at a cost in excess of the contract price, it will be excused for any delay and compensated for additional costs under the Changes Clause in the contract. See Foster Wheeler Corp. v. United States, 206 Ct.Cl. 533, 513 F.2d 588 (1975). Finally, the government may be liable for extra costs incurred in achieving promised results when contracting officials have failed to disclose material information about performance at the time of contracting under circumstances where the government knew that the contractor was unaware of the information and not likely to find out. See, e.g., Broad Ave. Laundry & Tailoring Co. v. United States, 681 F.2d 746, 750–51 (Ct.Cl.1982). For a useful overview, see John M. Vogel, *Impossibility of Performance—A Closer Look,* 9 Pub.Contract L.J. 110 (1977).

(3) *Subsurface Conditions.* When a contractor encounters unexpected subsurface conditions upon the land of another which delay or increase the cost of performance, the usual rule is that the contractor assumes the risk unless the owner, whether a private party or the government, has agreed to assume the risk, misrepresented the conditions or failed to disclose known difficulties. See, e.g., Carnegie Steel Co. v. United States, 240 U.S. 156, 36 S.Ct. 342, 60 L.Ed. 576 (1916); Rolin v. United States, 142 Ct.Cl. 73, 160 F.Supp. 264 (1958); Stees v. Leonard, 20 Minn. 494 (1874). See also Restatement (Second) § 266, Illus. 8. Impracticability alone is not an excuse: both parties must assume that the conditions did not exist. Compare *Mineral Park v. Howard,* supra. In order to avoid "padded" prices by contractors and the delays incident to disputes over subsurface conditions, the government has developed a standard clause dealing with these risks:

DIFFERING SITE CONDITIONS

(a) The Contractor shall promptly, and before such conditions are disturbed, notify the Contracting Officer in writing of: (1) subsurface or latent physical conditions at the site differing materially from those indicated in this contract, or (2) unknown physical conditions at the site, of an unusual nature, differing materially from those ordinarily encountered and generally recognized as inhering in work of the character provided for in this contract. The Contracting Officer shall promptly investigate the conditions, and if he finds that such conditions do materially so differ and cause an increase or decrease in the Contractor's cost of, or the time required for, performance of any part of the work under this contract, whether or not changed as a result of such conditions, an equitable adjustment shall be made and the contract modified in writing accordingly.

(b) No claim of the Contractor under this clause shall be allowed unless the Contractor has given the notice required in (a) above; *provided,* however, the time prescribed therefor may be extended by the Government.

(c) No claim by the Contractor for an equitable adjustment hereunder shall be allowed if asserted after final payment under this contract.

32 C.F.R. § 7.602.4.

(4) *Existing Impracticability v. Mutual Mistake.* Section 266(1) of Restatement (Second) provides:

> Where, at the time a contract is made, a party's performance under it is impracticable without his fault because of a fact of which he has no reason to know and the non-existence of which is a basic assumption on which the contract is made, no duty to render that performance arises, unless the language or circumstances indicate the contrary.

Section 152(1), on the other hand, provides that a contract is "voidable" by an adversely affected party "where a mistake of both parties at the time the contract was made has a material effect on the agreed exchange of performances" unless he bears the risk under the agreement, or has proceeded with limited knowledge of the facts to which the mistake relates but "treats his limited knowledge as sufficient" or the risk is allocated to him "by the court on the ground that it is reasonable in the circumstances to do so." Section 154. See Roy v. Stephen Pontiac–Cadillac, Inc., 15 Conn.App. 101, 543 A.2d 775 (1988) (buyer "had reason to know" that seller could not deliver truck actually ordered).

Suppose that you represented the contractor in *Mineral Park v. Howard* and Restatement (Second) was available. Which theory of risk allocation would you pursue, "Existing Impracticability" or "Mutual Mistake?" A question to consider is whether either theory should be applied to circumstances which arise after the contract is formed. For example, is it correct to draw a distinction between facts that are knowable and not known and facts that are not knowable and not known?

PROBLEM: A BUILDER IN THE QUAGMIRE OF IMPRACTICABILITY

Part of this problem reviews excuse where disrupting facts were existing but not known. Other parts anticipate the next Section, where disrupting facts were neither knowable nor known.

Fenstermacher (F), a builder, contracted with Harry (H), a homeowner, to construct a residence on Harry's land. The contract price was $300,000, and the home was to be constructed according to detailed plans and specifications prepared by Harry's architect. The home was to be constructed on the only feasible spot on the lot. In the following situations, assess the probability that F will be discharged or obtain some relief in performing the contract.

(1) F started bulldozing and quickly discovered a massive and unforeseen (by F) rock formation some four feet under the surface. F had performed no tests before commencing performance. F estimates that it will cost an extra $100,000 to remove the rock.

(2) When F had laid the foundations and completed the home up to the first floor, it became clear that one corner was sinking. Unknown to F and H,

the soil under that corner turned to "jelly" after a hard rain. After spending $25,000 to remedy the situation, the house was still subsiding. Experts will testify that the problem, if detected in advance, could have been avoided with an expenditure of about $50,000 and that another $50,000 will be required to remedy the problem at this stage. F refuses to continue performance unless H agrees to adjust the contract price.

(3) After construction began, a new county zoning ordinance was adopted. The county attorney claimed that Harry's proposed residence was now on a lot that was too small and obtained an injunction against continued construction. F stopped work. Six months later, the injunction was dissolved after H, through his attorney, obtained a final ruling that the ordinance did not have retroactive effect. By this time, F had his building crew on other projects and refused to continue performance. Evidence will support the claim that F's overall construction costs have increased 10% in the six month period.

(4) After the home was 60% completed and without the fault or negligence of either party, a fire burned the structure to the ground. F had been paid $50,000 as progress payments. F was not insured, although it was customary for the builder to obtain insurance on the structure until closing. Is F excused or must he rebuild under the contract without a price adjustment? What about the progress payments?

(5) When the house was 60% completed, F died of a heart attack. F had been paid $50,000 up to that time. H contracted with C to complete the work for $300,000 and, when the work was done, sued F's executor for $50,000 damages for "breach" of contract. You may assume that F's executor had, upon H's request, refused to complete performance after F's death.

(B) SUPERVENING IMPRACTICABILITY

Taylor v. Caldwell

King's Bench, 1863.
3 B. & S. 826, 122 Eng.Rep. 309.

■ BLACKBURN, J. In this case the plaintiffs and defendants had, on the 27th May, 1861, entered into a contract by which the defendants agreed to let the plaintiffs have the use of The Surrey Gardens and Music Hall on four days then to come, viz., the 17th June, 15th July, 5th August and 19th August, for the purpose of giving a series of four grand concerts, and day and night fetes at the Gardens and Hall on those days respectively; and the plaintiffs agreed to take the Gardens and Hall on those days, and pay £100 for each day.

The parties inaccurately call this a "letting," and the money to be paid a "rent"; but the whole agreement is such as to shew that the defendants were to retain the possession of the Hall and Gardens so that there was to be no demise of them, and that the contract was merely to give the plaintiffs the use of them on those days. Nothing however, in our opinion, depends on this. The agreement then proceeds to set out various stipulations between the parties as to what each was to supply for these concerts and entertainments, and as to the manner in which they should be carried on. The effect of the whole is to shew that the existence of the Music Hall in the Surrey Gardens in a state fit for a concert was essential for the fulfillment of the contract, such entertainment as the parties contemplated in their agreement could not be given without it.

After the making of the agreement, and before the first day on which a concert was to be given, the Hall was destroyed by fire. This destruction, we must take it on the evidence, was without the fault of either party, and was so complete that in consequence the concerts could not be given as intended. And the question we have to decide is whether, under these circumstances, the loss which the plaintiffs have sustained is to fall upon the defendants. The parties when framing their agreement evidently had not present to their minds the possibility of such a disaster, and have made no express stipulation with reference to it, so that the answer to the question must depend upon the general rules of law applicable to such a contract.

There seems no doubt that where there is a positive contract to do a thing, not in itself unlawful, the contractor must perform it or pay damages for not doing it, although in consequence of unforeseen accidents, the performance of his contract has become unexpectedly burdensome or even impossible. . . . But this rule is only applicable when the contract is positive and absolute, and not subject to any condition either express or implied; and there are authorities which, as we think, establish the principle that where, from the nature of the contract, it appears that the parties must from the beginning have known that it could not be fulfilled unless when the time for the fulfillment of the contract arrived some particular specified thing continued to exist, so that, when entering into the contract, they must have contemplated such continuing existence as the foundation of what was to be done; there, in the absence of any express or implied warranty that the thing shall exist, the contract is not to be construed as a positive contract, but as subject to an implied condition that the parties shall be excused in case, before breach, performance becomes impossible from the perishing of the thing without default of the contractor.

There seems little doubt that this implication tends to further the great object of making the legal construction such as to fulfill the intention of those who entered into the contract. For in the course of affairs men in making such contracts in general would, if it were brought to their minds, say that there should be such a condition.

Accordingly, in the Civil law, such an exception is implied in every obligation of the class which they call obligatio de certo corpore. The rule is laid down in the Digest, lib. xlv., tit. 1, d verborum obligationibus, 1. 33. "Si Stichus certo die dari promissus, ante diem moriatur: non tenetur promissor." The principle is more fully developed in 1. 23. "Si ex legati causa, aut ex stipulatu hominem certum mihi debeas: non aliter post mortem ejus tenearis mihi, quam si per te steterit, quominum vivo eo eum mihi dares: quod ita fit, si aut interpellatus non didisti, aut occidisti eum." The examples are of contracts respecting a slave, which was the common illustration of a certain subject used by the Roman lawyers, just as we are apt to take a horse; and no doubt the propriety, one might almost say necessity, of the implied condition is more obvious when the contract relates to a living animal, whether man or brute, than when it relates to some inanimate thing (such as in the present case a theatre) the existence of which is not so obviously precarious as that of the live animal, but the principle is adopted in the Civil law as applicable to every obligation of which the subject is a certain thing. The general subject is treated of by Pothier, who in his Traite des Obligations, partie 3, chap. 6, art. 3, § 668 states the result to be that the debtor corporis certi is freed from his obligation when the thing has perished, neither by his act, nor his neglect, and before he is in default, unless by some stipulation he has taken on himself the risk of the particular misfortune which has occurred.

Although the Civil law is not of itself authority in an English Court, it affords great assistance in investigating the principles on which the law is grounded. And it seems to us that the common law authorities establish that in such a contract the same condition of the continued existence of the thing is implied by English law.

There is a class of contracts in which a person binds himself to do something which requires to be performed by him in person; and such promises, e.g. promises to marry, or promises to serve for a certain time, are never in practice qualified by an express exception of the death of the party; and therefore in such cases the contract is in terms broken if the promisor dies before fulfillment. Yet it was very early determined that, if the performance is personal, the executors are not liable; Hyde v. The Dean of Windsor (Cro.Eliz. 552, 553). See 2 Wms.Exors. 1560, 5th ed., where a very apt illustration is given. "Thus," says the learned author, "if an author undertakes to compose a work, and dies before completing it, his executors are discharged from this contract: for the undertaking is merely personal in its nature, and, by the intervention of the contractor's death, has become impossible to be performed." For this he cites a dictum of Lord Lyndhurst in Marshall v. Broadhurst (1 Tyr. 348, 349), and a case mentioned by Patteson J. in Wentworth v. Cock (10 A. & E. 42, 45–46). In Hall v. Wright (E.B. & E. 746, 749), Crompton J., in his judgment, puts another case. "Where a contract depends upon personal skill, and the act of God renders it impossible, as, for instance, in the case of a painter employed to paint a picture who is struck blind, it may be that the performance might be excused."

It seems that in those cases the only ground on which the parties or their executors, can be excused from the consequences of the breach of the contract is, that from the nature of the contract there is an implied condition of the continued existence of the life of the contractor, and, perhaps in the case of the painter of his eyesight. In the instances just given, the person, the continued existence of whose life is necessary to the fulfilment of the contract, is himself the contractor, but that does not seem in itself to be necessary to the application of the principle; as is illustrated by the following example. In the ordinary form of an apprentice deed the apprentice binds himself in unqualified terms to "serve until the full end and term of seven years to be fully complete and ended," during which term it is covenanted that the apprentice his master "faithfully shall serve," and the father of the apprentice in equally unqualified terms binds himself for the performance by the apprentice of all and every covenant on his part. (See the form, 2 Chitty on Pleading, 370, 7th ed. by Greening.) It is undeniable that if the apprentice dies within the seven years, the covenant of the father that he shall perform his covenant to serve for seven years is not fulfilled, yet surely it cannot be that an action lie against the father? Yet the only reason why it would not is that he is excused because of the apprentice's death.

These are instances where the implied condition is of the life of a human being, but there are others in which the same implication is made as to the continued existence of a thing. For example, where a contract of sale is made amounting to a bargain and sale, transferring presently the property in specific chattels, which are to be delivered by the vendor at a future day; there, if the chattels, without fault of the vendor, perish in the interval, the purchaser must pay the price and the vendor is excused from performing his contract to deliver, which has thus become impossible.

* * *

It may, we think, be safely asserted to be now English law, that in all contracts of loan of chattels or bailments if the performance of the promise of the borrower or bailee to return the things lent or bailed, becomes impossible because it has perished, this impossibility (if not arising upon the fault of the borrower or bailee from some risk which he has taken upon himself) excuses the borrower or bailee from the performance of his promise to redeliver the chattel.

The great case of Coggs v. Bernard (1 Smith's L.C. 171, 5th ed.; 2 L.Raym. 909) is now the leading case on the law of bailments, and Lord Holt, in that case, referred so much to the Civil law that it might perhaps be thought that this principle was there derived direct from the civilians, and was not generally applicable in English law except in the case of bailments; but the case of Williams v. Lloyd (W. Jones, 179), above cited, shews that the same law had been already adopted by the English law as early as The Book of Assizes. The principle seems to us to be that, in contracts in which the performance depends on the continued existence of a given person or thing, a condition is implied that the impossibility of performance arising from the perishing of the person or thing shall excuse the performance.

In none of these cases is the promise in words other than positive, nor is there any express stipulation that the destruction of the person or thing shall excuse the performance; but that excuse is by law implied, because from the nature of the contract it is apparent that the parties contracted on the basis of the continued existence of the particular person or chattel. In the present case, looking at the whole contract, we find that the parties contracted on the basis of the continued existence of the Music Hall at the

[handwritten margin note: delivery becomes impossible seller is not punished if he had no relation to incident]

time when the concerts were to be given; that being essential to their performance.

We think, therefore, that the Music Hall having ceased to exist, without fault of either party, both parties are excused, the plaintiffs from taking the gardens and paying the money, the defendants from performing their promise to give the use of the Hall and Gardens and other things. Consequently the rule must be absolute to enter the verdict for the defendants.

Rule absolute.

NOTES

(1) Upon what theory does the court excuse the defendant? Does "implied condition" mean that the court is seeking the intention of the parties or providing a term regardless of that intention? See Edwin W. Patterson, *Constructive Conditions in Contracts*, 42 Colum.L.Rev. 903, 943–954 (1942). As Lord Wright put it eighty years later: "[T]he court has to decide not what the parties actually intended, but what as reasonable men they should have intended. The court personifies for this purpose the reasonable man." Joseph Constantine S.S. Line v. Imperial Smelting Corp. (1942) A.C. 154, 185. See Kinzer Construction Co. v. State, 125 N.Y.S. 46, 54 (1910) (reviewing American cases and concluding that provisions are implied in contract by force of law and not because parties had them in mind).

(2) How is it determined that the "parties contracted on the basis of the continued existence of the Music Hall?" Suppose the defendant had another hall of similar quality and offered it to the plaintiff without additional cost. Would the plaintiff be required to accept it? Suppose the fire destroyed part of the hall but, in the judgment of the plaintiff, would not substantially affect the suitability of the hall for the proposed concerts and fetes. Is the defendant excused from the contract? If the fire destroyed the concert stage but the defendant, at a cost of 10,000, could effect repairs in time for the concert, would he be obligated to do so? If the particular hall was necessary for performance, the probable answers to the last three questions are "no", "no", and "no". See Restatement (Second) § 263, which provides:

> If the existence of a specific thing is necessary for the performance of a duty, its failure to come into existence, destruction, or such deterioration as makes performance impracticable is an event the non-occurrence of which was a basic assumption on which the contract was made.

(3) *Death or Incapacity of an Essential Person.* Restatement (Second) § 262 provides:

> If the existence of a particular person is necessary for the performance of a duty, his death or such incapacity as makes performance impracticable is an event the non-occurrence of which was a basic assumption on which the contract was made.

As with Restatement (Second) § 263, the "basic assumption" question is answered by determining whether the "particular person is necessary for the performance of a duty." The question of who is "necessary" may be determined by the agreement or, if the agreement is silent, an assessment of whether the performance was a "personal matter requiring personal experience, ability, skill and judgment...." Kelley v. Thompson Land Co., 112 W.Va. 454, 164 S.E. 667 (1932) (formation of a going corporation deemed personal on facts of case). Under this test, the death of an artist employed to paint a portrait would discharge the contract but the death of the subject of the portrait would not discharge a duty to pay the agreed price.

Another way to determine who is necessary is to ask whether the person who dies or was incapacitated could have delegated his or her duty to a third party without the other party's consent. The question is whether the other party has a "substantial interest" in having the contract performed by the particular person. See UCC 2–210(1). If so, the contract is discharged. Compare Seitz v. Mark–O–Lite Sign Contractors, Inc., 210 N.J.Super. 646, 510 A.2d 319 (1986) (death of contractor does not excuse contract to do sheet metal work) with Cazares v. Saenz, 208 Cal.App.3d 279, 256 Cal.Rptr. 209 (1989) (death of attorney discharges contract with law firm). But since people rather than corporations die or become incapacitated, the question remains whether the performance to be rendered was "so personal in nature, calling for a peculiar skill or special exercise of discretion, as to make it nondelegable." *Seitz,* supra, 510 A.2d at 313.

Canadian Industrial Alcohol Co. v. Dunbar Molasses Co.

Court of Appeals of New York, 1932.
258 N.Y. 194, 179 N.E. 383.

■ CARDOZO, C.J. A buyer sues a seller for breach of an executory contract of purchase and sale.

The subject-matter of the contract was "approximately 1,500,000 wine gallons Refined Blackstrap [molasses] of the usual run from the National Sugar Refinery, Yonkers, N.Y., to test around 60% sugars."

The order was given and accepted December 27, 1927, but shipments of the molasses were to begin after April 1, 1928, and were to be spread out during the warm weather.

After April 1, 1928, the defendant made delivery from time to time of 344,083 gallons. Upon its failure to deliver more, the plaintiff brought this action for the recovery of damages. The defendant takes the ground that, by an implied term of the contract, the duty to deliver was conditioned upon the production by the National Sugar Refinery at Yonkers of molasses sufficient in quantity to fill the plaintiff's order. The fact is that the output of the refinery, while the contract was in force, was 485,848 gallons, much less than its capacity, of which amount 344,083 gallons were allotted to the defendant and shipped to the defendant's customer. The argument for the defendant is that its own duty to deliver was proportionate to the refinery's willingness to supply, and that the duty was discharged when the output was reduced.

The contract, read in the light of the circumstances existing at its making, or more accurately in the light of any such circumstances apparent from this record, does not keep the defendant's duty within boundaries so narrow. We may assume, in the defendant's favor, that there would have been a discharge of its duty to deliver if the refinery had been destroyed ... or if the output had been curtailed by the failure of the sugar crop ... or by the ravages of war ... or conceivably in some circumstances by unavoidable strikes ..... We may even assume that a like result would have followed if the plaintiff had bargained not merely for a quantity of molasses to be supplied from a particular refinery, but for molasses to be supplied in accordance with a particular contract between the defendant and the refiner, and if thereafter such contract had been broken without fault on the defendant's part. ... The inquiry is merely this, whether the continuance of a special group of circumstances appears from the terms of the contract, interpreted in the setting of the occasion, to have been a tacit or implied presupposition in the minds of the contracting parties, conditioning their belief in a continued obligation. ...

Accepting that test, we ask ourselves the question what special group of circumstances does the defendant lay before us as one of the presuppositions immanent in its bargain with the plaintiff? The defendant asks us to assume that a manufacturer, having made a contract with a middleman for a stock of molasses to be procured from a particular refinery, would expect the contract to lapse whenever the refiner chose to diminish his production, and this in the face of the middleman's omission to do anything to charge the refiner with a duty to continue. Business could not be transacted with security or smoothness if a presumption so unreasonable were at the root of its engagements. There is nothing to show that the defendant would have been unable by a timely contract with the refinery to have assured itself of a supply sufficient for its needs. There is nothing to show that the plaintiff, in giving the order for the molasses, was informed by the defendant that such a contract had not been made, or that performance would be contingent upon obtaining one thereafter. If the plaintiff had been so informed, it would very likely have preferred to deal with the refinery directly, instead of dealing with a middleman. The defendant does not even show that it tried to get a contract from the refinery during the months that intervened between the acceptance of the plaintiff's order and the time when shipments were begun. It has wholly failed to relieve itself of the imputation of contributory fault (3 Williston on Contracts, § 1959). So far as the record shows, it put its faith in the mere chance that the output of the refinery would be the same from year to year, and finding its faith vain, it tells us that its customer must have expected to take a chance as great. We see no reason for importing into the bargain this aleatory element. The defendant is in no better position than a factor who undertakes in his own name to sell for future delivery a special grade of merchandise to be manufactured by a special mill. The duty will be discharged if the mill is destroyed before delivery is due. The duty will subsist if the output is reduced because times turn out to be hard and labor charges high. ...

* * *

The judgment should be affirmed with costs.

NOTES

(1) "A party may not, by its own conduct, create the event causing the impracticability of performance, . . . ; in fact it must make all reasonable efforts to avoid the 'impossibility,' . . . ; and, once the event occurs, it must employ any practicable means of fulfilling the contract, even if it had originally expected to meet its obligation in a particular way, . . . " Chemetron Corp. v. McLouth Steel Corp., 381 F.Supp. 245, 257 (N.D.Ill.1974), affirmed 522 F.2d 469 (7th Cir.1975).

(2) Suppose, in the *Dunbar Molasses* case, that the contract between the plaintiff and the defendant contained the following clause:

> If the failure to perform is caused by the default of a supplier, and if such default arises out of causes beyond the control of both the seller and the supplier, and without the fault or negligence of either of them, the seller shall not be liable for any excess costs for failure to perform, unless the supplies or services to be furnished by the supplier were obtainable from other sources in sufficient time to permit the seller to meet the delivery schedule.

Would this clause alter the result in *Dunbar?*

(3) Under UCC 2–615(a), if the parties specify a particular source of supply in the contract and that source fails, the seller will be excused if (1) both parties assumed that the source was exclusive, (2) the seller employed all due measures to assure that the source would perform, and (3) the seller turned over to the buyer any rights against the supplier corresponding to the seller's claim of excuse. UCC 2–615, Comment 5. See Zidell Explorations, Inc. v. Conval International, Ltd., 719 F.2d 1465 (9th Cir.1983). On the other hand, if excuse is predicated upon a *force majeure* clause in the contract for sale rather than UCC 2–615(a), the seller need not turn over its rights against the supplier to the buyer. See InterPetrol Bermuda Ltd. v. Kaiser Aluminum International Corp., 719 F.2d 992 (9th Cir.1983). Finally, as Judge Cardozo indicated in *Dunbar Molasses*, the seller's responsibility, both before and after the exclusive source failure, to avoid or mitigate the loss, exists as a condition to excuse. See InterPetrol Bermuda Ltd. v. Kaiser Aluminum Intern., Corp., Occidental Crude Sales, Inc., 719 F.2d 992 (9th Cir.1983).

PROBLEMS: CASUALTY TO IDENTIFIED GOODS

(1) F, a farmer, has 100 acres of bottom land in which he regularly plants corn. On May 1, F contracted to sell 20,000 bushels of #1 yellow corn to B, a grain dealer, for $2.40 per bushel. Delivery was expected after harvest. At the time of contracting, 50% of the land had been planted and the balance was completed within 10 days. In early July, a severe drought began and it intensified until after the usual harvest date. The crop was so bad that F ground it up for fodder. At that time, #1 yellow corn was selling at $5 per bushel. B demanded delivery of 20,000 bushels and F refused, claiming excuse under UCC 2–613 through 2–616. B claims damages of $2.60 per bushel. Should he collect them? See Alimenta (U.S.A.), Inc. v. Gibbs, Nathaniel (Canada) Ltd., 802 F.2d 1362 (11th Cir.1986) (regional drought excuses supplier of peanuts); David C. Bugg, *Crop Destruction and Forward Grain Contracts: Why Don't*

Sections 2–613 & 2–615 of the U.C.C. Provide More Relief?, 12 Hamline L.Rev. 669 (1989).

(2) B contracted to sell 11,000 combat boots of a stated quality to a country in Africa. The price was $158,000. On July 1, B contracted with S to procure those boots from a Korean manufacturer for $95,000, with delivery no later than November 1. S immediately placed the order with the manufacturer and the boots arrived in San Francisco on October 15. The boots conformed to the contract requirements, but contained no markings identifying their origin. S immediately shipped the boots to B in New York by rail under the shipment term "FOB point of Destination." The goods were totally destroyed by fire while in the carrier's possession, and S was unable to obtain substitutes in time to meet the November 1 delivery date. B then canceled the contract for breach, and sued S for damages. S claims that performance was excused under Sections 2–612 through 2–616 of the UCC. What result? You may assume that the goods were first identified to the contract between S and B when they were shipped to B from San Francisco, see UCC 2–501(1), and that the risk of loss was on S at the time of the fire. See UCC 2–319(1)(b) & 2–509(1)(b).

(3) What result if the risk of loss was on B at the time of the fire? See *Windows, Inc. v. Jordan Panel Systems Corp.*, 177 F.3d 114 (2d Cir.1999), holding that where the risk of loss is on the buyer in a "shipment" contract, the seller has performed its obligations under the contract. Under UCC 2–709(1), the buyer would owe the price (if not previously paid) and would have to seek indemnity for loss of the goods from either its insurance company or the carrier.

Dills v. Town of Enfield

Supreme Court of Connecticut, 1989.
210 Conn. 705, 557 A.2d 517.

■ Peters, Chief Justice.

The principal issue in this appeal is whether the doctrine of commercial impracticability excuses a developer from submitting construction plans when he discovers that necessary financing has become unavailable. The plaintiffs, Timothy E. Dills and the Neecon Corporation, sued the defendants, the town of Enfield (town) and the Enfield development agency (agency), to recover a $100,000 deposit Dills had paid the agency under an option and contract for sale. The trial court referred the case to Attorney J. Read Murphy, a state trial referee appointed pursuant to General Statutes § 52–434(a)(4). Following a hearing and the parties' submission of briefs, the referee reported his findings of fact and recommended that judgment enter for the plaintiffs. The trial court rejected the referee's recommendation, instead rendering judgment for the defendants. The plaintiff Neecon Corporation appealed to the Appellate Court and we transferred the case here pursuant to Practice Book § 4023. We find no error.

The relevant facts reported by the referee, accepted by the trial court and supported by the record, are as follows. The town of Enfield instructed its development agency to solicit private developers for the Enfield Memorial Industrial Park to be constructed on town property. Pursuant to an earlier option agreement, on May 1, 1974, the plaintiff Dills and the development agency entered into a contract for the sale of the land to be developed. Dills at that time paid a $100,000 deposit toward the contract price of $985,900. The plaintiff Neecon Corporation, owned by Dills, was to perform the necessary work, and has become, by virtue of an assignment from Dills, the only remaining plaintiff in this appeal.

Under the terms of the contract, the development agency agreed to convey the property to the developer sixty days after the fulfillment of two conditions: (1) the submission and approval of construction plans in accordance with section 301 of the contract; and (2) the submission of evidence of financial capacity in accordance with section 304 of the contract. The contract also included provisions for its termination by either party. Section 702(b) of the contract allowed the developer to withdraw and to reclaim his deposit if, after the preparation of construction plans satisfactory to the agency, the developer could not obtain the necessary mortgage financing. Section 703(b) of the contract allowed the agency to terminate the contract, retaining the deposit as liquidated damages, if the developer failed to submit acceptable construction plans.

Dills never submitted construction plans that were acceptable to the agency. A set of plans denominated "preliminary" was rejected by the agency on June 24, 1974. The agency accepted a revised set of "preliminary plans" and drawings three months later, but demanded the submission of full construction plans and specifications by early December. The referee found that the preliminary sets of plans did not themselves meet the definition of "construction plans" in section 301. The referee agreed with the agency's interpretation of section 301 of the contract as requiring the developer to submit full construction plans within 210 days of the agency's approval of preliminary plans.

The reason Dills failed to submit construction plans was that, despite diligent efforts, he was unable to obtain mortgage financing. Thereafter, both parties attempted, with proper notification, to invoke the contract's termination clauses. On December 19, 1974, the agency, having been informed by Dills of his financial difficulties, voted to terminate the agreement pursuant to section 703(b) of the contract of sale and to retain the $100,000 deposit as liquidated damages. On December 22, 1974, Dills' attorney notified the agency that, because of Dills' inability to obtain financing within the time specified in the contract, Dills was terminating the agreement pursuant to section 702(b) of the contract of sale.

* * *

[The referee found, among other things, that Dills' duty to provide full construction plans by December, 1974 was discharged by supervening impracticability. The trial court, however, rejected the referee's recommendation that judgment be entered for Dills, concluding that unless there was impracticability in preparing and submitting construction plans rather than obtaining financing for them there was no basis for excuse.]

B

Finally we must decide whether the trial court erred as a matter of law in rejecting the referee's determination, endorsed by the plaintiff on appeal, that the impracticability doctrine excused Dills' failure to deliver construction plans to the agency. The plaintiff contends that Dills' inability to obtain such financing made submitting the construction plans a "futile" and "useless act," and therefore the doctrine of supervening impracticability discharged his duty to submit the plans. We hold, as did the trial court, that "[t]he doctrine of impracticability and impossibility . . . [is] not relevant to this case."

The impracticability[16] doctrine represents an exception to the accepted maxim of *pacta sunt servanda,* in recognition of the fact that certain conditions cannot be met because of unforeseen occurrences. Cf. Aetna Casualty & Surety Co. v. Murphy, 206 Conn. 409, 413, 538 A.2d 219 (1988). A party claiming that a supervening event or contingency has prevented, and thus excused, a promised performance must demonstrate that: (1) the event made the performance impracticable; (2) the nonoccurrence of the event was a basic assumption on which the contract was made; (3) the impracticability resulted without the fault of the party seeking to be excused; and (4) the party has not assumed a greater obligation than the law imposes. 2 Restatement (Second), Contracts § 261; E. Farnsworth, Contracts (1982) § 9.6, p. 678. We discuss only the first two prongs of this test in disposing of the plaintiff's argument.

Although courts in recent years have liberalized the requirements for such an excuse . . . only in the most exceptional circumstances have courts concluded that a duty is discharged because additional financial burdens make performance less practical than initially contemplated. . . . Thus, the fact that preparing the construction plans would have cost Dills a great deal of money (more than the deposit he sought to recover) did not excuse him from submitting them as the contract provided.

Furthermore, the event upon which the obligor relies to excuse his performance cannot be an event that the parties foresaw at the time of the contract. We have previously held that "[t]he regular enforcement of conditions is . . . subject to the competing but equally well established principle that the occurrence of a condition may be excused in the event of impracticability *if the occurrence of the condition is not a material part of the agreed exchange* and forfeiture would otherwise result." . . . Thus, the "central inquiry" is whether the nonoccurrence of the alleged impracticable condition "was a basic assumption on which the contract was made." General Statutes § 42a–2–615(a);[17] 2 Restatement (Second), Contracts

---

16. The doctrine of "impossibility" has come to include "physical impossibility," "frustration of purpose" and "impracticability" because of contingencies rendering performance more costly. See 6 A. Corbin, Contracts (1962) § 1325; 16 S. Williston, Contracts (3d Ed. Jaeger 1978) § 1932; G. Gilmore, The Death of Contract (1972) pp. 80–82. This case concerns only the last of these.

17. General Statutes § 42a–2–615(a) provides in pertinent part: "Delay in delivery or nondelivery in whole or in part by a seller

§ 261;[18] . . . .

In this case the contingency upon which fulfilling the contract allegedly depended was Dills' obtaining the requisite financing. We cannot conclude, however, that Dills' failure to obtain financing was "an event the non-occurrence of which was a basic assumption on which the contract was made." Indeed, section 702(b) of the contract of sale demonstrates that the parties expressly contemplated that Dills might encounter financial difficulties. The contract allowed Dills to terminate for this reason "after preparation of Construction Plans satisfactory to the Agency." If "an event is foreseeable, a party who makes an unqualified promise to perform necessarily assumes an obligation to perform, even if the occurrence of the event makes performance impracticable." E. Farnsworth, supra, p. 686.[19]

This case, like virtually every case involving discharge from an obligation to perform, concerns the issue of which party bears the loss resulting from an event that renders performance by one party uneconomical. . . . "Determining whether the non-occurrence of a particular event was or was not a basic assumption involves a judgment as to which party assumed the risk of its occurrence. . . . In making such determinations, a court will look at all circumstances, including the terms of the contract." 2 Restatement (Second), Contracts, c. 11, introductory note. "Since impossibility and related doctrines are devices for shifting risk in accordance with the parties' presumed intentions, which are to minimize the costs of contract performance, one of which is the disutility created by risk, they have no place when the contract explicitly assigns a particular risk to one party or the other." Northern Indiana Public Service Co. v. Carbon County Coal Co., 799 F.2d 265, 278 (7th Cir.1986). . . . Where, as in this case, sophisticated contracting parties have negotiated termination provisions, courts should be slow to invent additional ways to excuse performance. We exercise such caution in this case.

There is no error.

In this opinion the other Justices concurred.

... is not a breach of his duty under a contract for sale if performance as agreed has been made impracticable by the occurrence of a contingency *the nonoccurrence of which was a basic assumption on which the contract was made* or by compliance in good faith with any applicable foreign or domestic governmental regulation or order whether or not it later proves to be invalid." (Emphasis added.) While the instant case does not concern the sale of goods, and therefore the Uniform Commercial Code does not apply, § 2–615 has been adopted by the Restatement and "promises to have a substantial influence on the law of contract generally. . . ." E. Farnsworth, Contracts (1982) § 9.6, p. 677.

18. The Restatement (Second) of Contracts § 261 provides: "Where, after a contract is made, a party's performance is made impracticable without his fault by the occurrence of an event *the non-occurrence of which was a basic assumption on which the contract was made,* his duty to render that performance is discharged, unless the language or the circumstances indicate the contrary." (Emphasis added.)

19. Significantly, the defendants never conceded that the promised plans would have been of no use to them. Thus, it is far from certain that submitting the plans would have been a "futile act" from the defendants' point of view.

NOTES

(1) For exactly what reason did the court conclude that Dills was not excused from the contract: (a) The parties assigned the risk to Dills in the contract; or (b) Obtaining financing was *not* a basic assumption of the contract; or (c) The extra cost of performance did not make performance impracticable? Is the conclusion sound if the court relies on *all three* reasons?

(2) Can you develop a scenario (hypothetical) where Justice Peters would grant excuse?

(3) *The Basic Assumption Test.* UCC 2–615(a) provides that a seller in a contract for the sale of goods is excused for "delay in delivery or non-delivery * * * if performance as agreed has been made impracticable by the occurrence of a contingency the non-occurrence of which was a basic assumption on which the contract was made * * *."

Without question, Restatement (Second) has jumped upon the "basic assumption" bandwagon. Whether an existing or supervening event makes performance impracticable or "frustrates" the purpose of one party to the contract, the "*non-occurrence*" of that event or fact must have been "a basic assumption on which the contract was made." See, e.g., Sections 261–66. If it was not, the promisor bears the risk of any impracticability unless the risk was otherwise allocated by agreement. How, then, does one come to grips with this crucial risk allocation test?

The Reporter of Restatement (Second), Professor E. Alan Farnsworth, has offered the following guide:

> Determining whether the non-occurrence of a particular event was or was not a basic assumption involves a judgment as to which party assumed the risk of its occurrence. In contracting for the manufacture and delivery of goods at a price fixed in the contract, for example, the seller assumes the risk of increased costs within the normal range. If, however, a disaster results in an abrupt tenfold increase in cost to the seller, a court might determine that the seller did not assume this risk by concluding that the non-occurrence of the disaster was a "basic assumption" on which the contract was made. In making such determinations, a court will look at all circumstances, including the terms of the contract. The fact that the event was unforeseeable is significant as suggesting that its non-occurrence was a basic assumption. However, the fact that it was foreseeable, or even foreseen, does not, of itself, argue for a contrary conclusion, since the parties may not have thought it sufficiently important a risk to have made it a subject of their bargaining. Another significant factor may be the relative bargaining positions of the parties and the relative ease with which either party could have included a clause. Another may be the effectiveness of the market in spreading such risks as, for example, where the obligor is a middleman who has an opportunity to adjust his prices to cover them.

Restatement (Second), Ch. 11, p. 311.

(4) *The Foreseeability Test.* The court, in *Dills,* states that the "event upon which the obligor relies to excuse his performance cannot be an event that the parties foresaw at the time of the contract." Later, the court states that the "central inquiry" is whether the nonoccurrence of the event was a "basic

assumption on which the contract was made." 557 A.2d at 524. What is the relationship between foreseeability and the "basic assumption?" Can an event be foreseeable at the time of contracting and still be an event that both parties assume will not occur?

The answer, we think, is yes. Most modern courts concede that the foreseeability of some risk and its impact on performance does not necessarily prove its allocation to the promisor. As Judge Friendly recognized, the parties cannot provide for all the possibilities of which they are aware, "sometimes because they cannot agree, often simply because they are too busy." Transatlantic Financing Corp. v. United States, 363 F.2d 312, 319 (D.C.Cir.1966). Moreover, if the occurrence of the foreseen event is improbable, it is less likely that the parties intended to allocate its risk to one or the other. See Restatement (Second) § 261, Comment c. In short, there are limitations upon human cognition. See Melvin A. Eisenberg, *The Limits of Cognition and the Limits of Contract*, 47 Stan. L. Rev. 211 (1995), for an analysis of the behavioral science literature and application to selected issues.

Thus, the key to the analysis of "basic assumption" or "foreseeabiity" is the probability that the foreseen event will occur or, if it does occur, certain consequences will follow. As one court put it, "was the contingency which developed one which the parties could reasonably be thought to have foreseen as a *real possibility* which could affect performance?" Mishara Construction Co., Inc. v. Transit–Mixed Concrete Corp., 365 Mass. 122, 310 N.E.2d 363, 367 (1974). If so, the court is unlikely to conclude that both parties assumed that the event would not occur. See also Specialty Tires of America, Inc. v. CIT Group Equipment Financing, Inc., 82 F.Supp.2d 434 (W.D.Pa.2000) (some foreseeable risks not deemed worthy of bargaining over); Aluminum Co. of America v. Essex Group, Inc., 499 F.Supp. 53, 70 (W.D.Pa.1980) ("The proper question is not simply whether the parties to a contract were conscious of uncertainty with respect to a vital fact, but whether they believed that uncertainty was effectively limited within a designated range so that they would deem outcomes beyond that range to be highly unlikely"); Paul Joskow, *Commercial Impossibility, the Uranium Market and the Westinghouse Case*, 6 J.Legal Stud. 119, 153–162 (1977) (foreseeability test should be used to delineate the boundary between those contingencies that are reasonably part of the decision-making process and those that are not).

(5) *The "Superior Risk Bearer" Test.* Professor (now Judge) Richard Posner has argued that in all cases of impracticability, the key question is "who should bear the loss resulting from an event that has rendered performance uneconomical" and that the answer, provided by economic analysis, is the party who is the "most efficient bearer of the particular risk in the particular circumstances." Richard Posner and Andrew Rosenfield, *Impossibility and Related Doctrines in Contract Law: An Economic Analysis*, 6 J.Leg.Stud. 83, 86, 90 (1977).

> The discharge question arises only in those cases where the contract does not assign the risk in question and the event giving rise to the discharge claim was not avoidable by any cost justified precautions. When these threshold conditions have been satisfied, economic analysis suggests that the loss should be placed on the party who is the superior (that is, lower-cost) risk bearer. To determine which party is the superior risk bearer

three factors are relevant—knowledge of the magnitude of the loss, knowledge of the probability that it will occur, and (other) costs of self- or market-insurance.

Id. at 117. Risk appraisal costs are incurred in acquiring knowledge of the probability that the event will occur and the magnitude of the loss if it does occur. These costs must be known "in order for the insurer to know how much to ask for from the other party to the contract as compensation for bearing the risk in question." Transaction costs are the "costs involved in eliminating or minimizing the risk through pooling it with other uncertain events * * * either through self-insurance or through the purchase of an insurance policy (market insurance)." Id. at 91–92. Thus, the promisee may be the superior risk bearer when the promisor could not "reasonably have prevented" the event and the promisee could have "insured against the occurrence of the event at a lower cost than the promisor" because it was in the best position to appraise the probability and magnitude of the loss. Id. at 92. Presumably, if the promisor is found to be the superior risk bearer, enforcement of the contract will be both efficient and fair—there is no undue hardship for a superior risk bearer to absorb the extra costs since it was in the best position ex ante to minimize or to avoid them. For an argument that it is less costly to identify and protect against existing rather than supervening risk events, see Anthony Kronman, *Mistake, Disclosure, Information, and the Law of Contracts*, 7 J.Leg.Stud. 1, 2–9 (1978) (information is the antidote to mistake). See also, Alan Sykes, *The Doctrine of Commercial Impracticability in a Second–Best World*, 19 J.Legal Stud. 43 (1990).

United States v. Winstar

Supreme Court of the United States, 1996.
518 U.S. 839, 116 S.Ct. 2432, 135 L.Ed.2d 964.

[In response to a crisis in the regulated savings and loan industry, the Federal Home Loan Bank Board (FHLBB) induced Winstar and other "healthy" savings and loan thrifts (S & Ls) to take over and operate failed S & Ls by a "supervisory merger," the primary purpose of which was to reduce the potential insurance liability of the Federal Savings and Loan Insurance Corporation (FSLIC). The inducement was an agreement to treat the excess of the liabilities of the failed thrifts over their assets ("supervisory goodwill") as capital to meet reserve requirements and to amortize it over a period of forty years. In short, the agreement promised to give Winstar favorable regulatory treatment, presumably until the goodwill was amortized. There were no explicit terms in the agreement about whether the United States could or would change the law or who bore the risk if the law were changed. Put differently, although FHLBB promised to give the S & Ls favorable accounting treatment, it did not expressly promise that the United States would not subsequently change the law or agree who would bear the risk if a law with retrospective effects was enacted.

Subsequently, Congress, in the Financial Institutions Reform, Recovery, and Enforcement Act of 1989 (FIRREA), totally revamped the surrounding legal structure and created a successor agency to FHLBB—the

Office of Thrift Supervision in the Department of the Treasury (OTS)—which issued implementing regulations that retrospectively terminated the favorable accounting treatment. Winstar (and other S & Ls), now required to meet reserve requirements from other assets or be liquidated, sued the United States for damages for breach of contract. In the lower court, the United States raised several defenses based, in part, upon its power as sovereign to legislate in the public interest without liability for breach of existing contracts. The Federal Circuit ruled for the plaintiffs. The Supreme Court affirmed and, in a plurality opinion, rejected the Government's public law defenses and purported to decide the case under ordinary principles of private contract law.]

* * *

It is important to be clear about what these contracts did and did not require of the Government. Nothing in the documentation or the circumstances of these transactions purported to bar the Government from changing the way in which it regulated the thrift industry. Rather, what the Federal Circuit said of the Glendale transaction is true of the Winstar and Statesman deals as well: "the Bank Board and the FSLIC were contractually bound to recognize the supervisory goodwill and the amortization periods reflected" in the agreements between the parties. 64 F.3d, at 1541–1542. We read this promise as the law of contracts has always treated promises to provide something beyond the promisor's absolute control, that is, as a promise to insure the promisee against loss arising from the promised condition's nonoccurrence. Holmes's example is famous: "[i]n the case of a binding promise that it shall rain tomorrow, the immediate legal effect of what the promisor does is, that he takes the risk of the event, within certain defined limits, as between himself and the promisee." Holmes, The Common Law (1881), in 3 The Collected Works of Justice Holmes 268 (S. Novick ed.1995).* Contracts like this are especially appropriate in the world of regulated industries, where the risk that legal change will prevent the bargained-for performance is always lurking in the shadows. The drafters of the Restatement attested to this when they explained that, "[w]ith the trend toward greater governmental regulation ... parties are increasingly aware of such risks, and a party may undertake a duty that is not discharged by such supervening governmental actions...." Restatement (Second) of Contracts § 264, Comment *a*. "Such an agreement," according to the Restatement, "is usually interpreted as one to pay damages if performance is prevented rather than one to render a performance in violation of law." *Ibid.*

When the law as to capital requirements changed in the present instance, the Government was unable to perform its promise and, therefore, became liable for breach. We accept the Federal Circuit's conclusion that the Government breached these contracts when, pursuant to the new

---

* See also *Day v. United States*, 245 U.S. 159, 161 (1917) (Holmes, J.) ("One who makes a contract never can be absolutely certain that he will be able to perform it when the time comes, and the very essence of it is that he takes the risk within the limits of his undertaking").

regulatory capital requirements imposed by FIRREA, 12 U.S.C. § 1464(t), the federal regulatory agencies limited the use of supervisory goodwill and capital credits in calculating respondents' net worth. 64 F.3d, at 1545. In the case of Winstar and Statesman, the Government exacerbated its breach when it seized and liquidated respondents' thrifts for regulatory noncompliance. *Ibid.*

In evaluating the relevant documents and circumstances, we have, of course, followed the Federal Circuit in applying ordinary principles of contract construction and breach that would be applicable to any contract action between private parties. * * *

[T]he Government, like any other defending party in a contract action, must show that the passage of the statute rendering its performance impossible was an event contrary to the basic assumptions on which the parties agreed, and must ultimately show that the language or circumstances do not indicate that the Government should be liable in any case. While we do not say that these conditions can never be satisfied when the Government contracts with participants in a regulated industry for particular regulatory treatment, we find that the Government as such a contractor has not satisfied the conditions for discharge in the present case.

1

For a successful impossibility defense the Government would have to show that the nonoccurrence of regulatory amendment was a basic assumption of these contracts. See, *e.g.,* Restatement (Second) of Contracts § 261; ... The premise of this requirement is that the parties will have bargained with respect to any risks that are both within their contemplation and central to the substance of the contract; as Justice Traynor said, "[i]f [the risk] was foreseeable there should have been provision for it in the contract, and the absence of such a provision gives rise to the inference that the risk was assumed." *Lloyd v. Murphy,* 25 Cal.2d 48, 54 (1944). That inference is particularly compelling, where, as here, the contract provides for particular regulatory treatment (and, *a fortiori,* allocates the risk of regulatory change). Such an agreement reflects the inescapable recognition that regulated industries in the modern world do not live under the law of the Medes and the Persians, and the very fact that such a contract is made at all is at odds with any assumption of regulatory stasis. In this particular case, whether or not the reach of the FIRREA reforms was anticipated by the parties, there is no doubt that some changes in the regulatory structure governing thrift capital reserves were both foreseeable and likely when these parties contracted with the Government, as even the Government agrees. It says in its brief to this Court that "in light of the frequency with which federal capital requirements had changed in the past ... , it would have been unreasonable for Glendale, FSLIC, or the Bank Board to expect or rely upon the fact that those requirements would remain unchanged." Brief for United States 26; see also *id.,* at 3, n. 1 (listing the changes). The Federal Circuit panel in this case likewise found that the regulatory capital requirements "have been the subject of numerous statutory and regulatory changes over the years," and "changed three times in 1982 alone." 994 F.2d, at 801. Given these fluctuations, and given the fact that a single modification of the applicable regulations could, and ultimately did, eliminate virtually all of the consideration provided by the Government in these transactions, it would be absurd to say that the nonoccurrence of a change in the regulatory capital rules was a basic assumption upon which these contracts were made. . . .

Finally, any governmental contract that not only deals with regulatory change but allocates the risk of its occurrence will, by definition, fail the further condition of a successful impossibility defense, for it will indeed indicate that the parties' agreement was not meant to be rendered nugatory by a change in the regulatory law. See Restatement (Second) of Contracts § 261 (no impossibility defense where the "language or the circumstances" indicate allocation of the risk to the party seeking discharge). The mere fact that the Government's contracting agencies (like the Bank Board and FSLIC) could not themselves preclude Congress from changing the regulatory rules does not, of course, stand in the way of concluding that those agencies assumed the risk of such change, for determining the consequences of legal change was the point of the agreements. It is, after all, not uncommon for a contracting party to assume the risk of an event he cannot control, even when that party is an agent of the Government. As the Federal Circuit has recognized, "[Government] contracts routinely include provisions shifting financial responsibility to the Government for events which might occur in the future.* That some of these events may be triggered by sovereign government action does not render the relevant contractual provisions any less binding than those which contemplate third party acts, inclement weather and other *force majeure.*" *Hughes Communications Galaxy, Inc. v. United States,* 998 F.2d 953, 958–959 (C.A.Fed.1993).

As to each of the contracts before us, our agreement with the conclusions of the Court of Federal Claims and the Federal Circuit forecloses any defense of legal impossibility, for those courts found that the Bank Board resolutions, Forbearance Letters, and other documents setting forth the accounting treatment to be accorded supervisory goodwill generated by the transactions were not mere statements of then-current regulatory policy, but in each instance were terms in an allocation of risk of regulatory change that was essential to the contract between the parties. . . . Given that the parties went to considerable lengths in procuring necessary docu-

---

* See, *e.g., Chicago, M. & St. P. R. Co. v. Hoyt,* 149 U.S. 1, 14–15 (1893) ("There can be no question that a party may by an absolute contract bind himself or itself to perform things which subsequently become impossible, or to pay damages for the nonperformance"). This is no less true where the event that renders performance impossible is a change in the governing law. See, *e.g.,* 4 R. Anderson, Anderson on the Uniform Commercial Code § 2–615:34, p. 286 (3d ed. 1983) ("Often in regard to impossibility due to change of law . . . there would be no difficulty in a promisor's assuming the risk of the legal possibility of his promise"); 6 A. Corbin, Corbin on Contracts § 1346, p. 432 (1962) ("Just as in other cases of alleged impossibility, the risk of prevention by courts and administrative officers can be thrown upon a contractor by a provision in the contract itself or by reason of established custom and general understanding").

ments and drafting broad integration clauses to incorporate their terms into the contract itself, the Government's suggestion that the parties meant to say only that the regulatory treatment laid out in these documents would apply as an initial matter, subject to later change at the Government's election, is unconvincing. See *ibid.* It would, indeed, have been madness for respondents to have engaged in these transactions with no more protection than the Government's reading would have given them, for the very existence of their institutions would then have been in jeopardy from the moment their agreements were signed.

* * *

We affirm the Federal Circuit's ruling that the United States is liable to respondents for breach of contract. Because the Court of Federal Claims has not yet determined the appropriate measure or amount of damages in this case, we remand for further proceedings.

NOTES

(1) *Some history.* An important category where, historically, excuse has been granted involves subsequent acts of government that prevent performance of existing contracts or make such performance illegal. Even before *Taylor v. Caldwell,* supra at 813, an excuse where supervening changes in domestic law made performance illegal was recognized. See A.W.B. Simpson, A History of the Common Law of Contract: The Rise of the Action of Assumpsit, 525–526 (1975). In a well known dictum, Lord Ellenborough in 1809 recognized the effect of both existing and supervening illegality:

> That no contract can properly be carried into effect, which was originally made contrary to the provisions of law; or, which being made consistently with the rules of law at the time, has become illegal in virtue of some subsequent law; are propositions which admit no doubt.

Atkinson v. Ritchie, 10 East 530, 103 Eng. Rep. 877, 878 (K.B.1809) (charter party frustrated by outbreak of war).

The effect of government action that prevented performance rather than made it illegal was raised in *Baily v. De Crespigny,* L.R. 4 Q.B. 180 (Q.B.1869). Under a long term lease of land, the defendant covenanted that neither he nor his assigns would permit any building on a paddock fronting the property. In 1862, however, Parliament conferred power on a railroad company to take the paddock for purposes of the railroad and defendant, faced with the fact that the railroad would take the paddock, conveyed it to them for value. When the railroad built a structure, the plaintiff sued the defendant for breach of the lease.

The court denied the claim on the ground that, under the circumstances, it was not possible for the defendant to perform the covenant without violating the law. The assignment was made in compliance with the requirements of the Act. It was compelled whether the defendant made the conveyance or waited until the paddock was taken by the railroad. Moreover, the defendant did not assume the risk of this governmental action under the lease. The court reasoned that the parties must be assumed to contract with reference to the state of law existing at the time of the contract. Although parties can agree to allocate the risk of a change in law, the presumption that the current law will continue ought to be rebutted by clear language showing a contrary intention.

According to the court, the general language of unconditional liability did not allocate risk to the defendant:

> [W]here the event is of such a character that it cannot reasonably be supposed to have been in the contemplation of the contracting parties when the contract was made, they will not be held bound by general words which, though large enough to include, were not used with reference to the possibility of the particular contingency which afterwards happens.... To hold a man liable by words, in a sense affixed to them by legislation subsequent to the contract, is to impose on him a contract he never made.

In essence, the defendant was "discharged from his covenant by the subsequent act of Parliament which put it out of his power to perform it."*

Again, the court, in excusing performance of the covenant, stressed that the event was not "contemplated" by the parties at the time of contracting and, in the absence of clear language to the contrary, they presumed the continued existence of the current state of law. Nevertheless, one can see in the opinion the presence of a regulatory context wherein the government was interested in fostering the development of railroads during the industrial revolution. This, however, did not affect the presumption that the current state of law would continue, at least in the absence of evidence of instability in the regulatory context at the time the lease was made.

(2) The Supreme Court, in *Winstar*, purported to apply the "ordinary" law of private contracts to a government contract. Did the Supreme Court correctly state the law? What difference would it make? Consider the following statement of the "modern" law:

> For retrospective changes in the law, however, a somewhat different risk allocation test [than that stated in Restatement, Second, Section 261] has evolved.

> For example, Restatement (Second) of Contracts, section 264 provides:

>> If the performance of a duty is made impracticable by having to comply with a domestic or foreign governmental regulation or order, that regulation or order is an event the non-occurrence of which was a basic assumption on which the contract was made.

> Similarly, U.C.C. § 2–615(a) bypasses the "basic assumption" test and provides that relief is granted "if performance as agreed has been made impracticable by ... compliance in good faith with any applicable foreign or domestic governmental regulation or order whether or not it later proves to be invalid."

---

* If, however, performance was prevented or made illegal by a change of foreign law at the place of performance, the defendant was not excused. See John D. Wladis, Common Law and Uncommon Events: The Development of the Doctrine of Impossibility of Performance in English Contract Law, 75 G.T.L.J. 1575, 1601, n. 126 (1987). Note that the railroad had power to "take" the property for compensation. Although the defendant was not liable for damages for failing to honor the covenant, the plaintiff might still have some recourse for the value of the compensation received.

Thus, the Restatement and the U.C.C. both give the party seeking relief a presumption that both parties assumed that the law would not change. The presumption does not apply if, according to the Restatement, the "language or circumstances indicate the contrary," or, according to the U.C.C. comments, unless the governmental interference "truly 'supervenes' in such a manner as to be beyond the seller's assumption of risk." If the agreement does not allocate the risk of subsequent retrospective legal change, the party seeking relief is entitled to a presumption that the other party must rebut, presumably by evidence that both parties at the time of contracting foresaw that the legal change was likely to occur. If, however, the party seeking relief acted in bad faith or caused the subsequent impairment, relief will be denied.

Legal change that prevents or makes performance illegal usually satisfies the impracticability requirement. It is more difficult to establish impracticability, however, where subsequent legal change makes performance more expensive or frustrates the purpose of one party.

Richard E. Speidel, *Contract Excuse Doctrine and Retrospective Legislation: The Winstar Case,* 2001 Wis. L. Rev. 795, 802–03.

Bolin Farms v. American Cotton Shippers Ass'n

United States District Court, Western District of Louisiana, 1974.
Reprinted, supra at 18.

NOTES

(1) *Post-Contract Changes in Market Price or Cost of Performance.* In contracts with a fixed price, the question is when, if ever, a dramatic rise or fall in the market price for the goods will provide the basis for an excuse. As *Bolin Farms* indicates, the answer is rarely if at all. See, e.g., R.N. Kelly Cotton Merchant, Inc. v. York, 494 F.2d 41 (5th Cir.1974) (market 300% higher than contract price); Hancock Paper Co. v. Champion Intern. Corp., 424 F.Supp. 285 (E.D.Pa.1976) (market price drops). As Comment 4 to UCC 2–615 states, this is "exactly the type of risk which business contracts made at a fixed price are intended to cover." See Allan Schwartz, *Sales Law and Inflations,* 50 S.Cal. L.Rev. 1 (1976). Thus, if because of the pricing mechanism, both parties did not assume that market prices would remain stable, there is no excuse.

A similar result—no excuse—is usually reached when promisor's cost of performance dramatically exceeds the contract price due to supervening market shifts beyond its control and without its fault or negligence that affect the price of performance inputs. For example, in Louisiana Power & Light v. Allegheny Ludlum Industries, 517 F.Supp. 1319 (E.D.La., 1981), a seller refused to perform contract for nuclear condenser tubing after increase in metal price would have caused seller to lose $428,500 on a $1.3 million contract. The court found that seller's non-performance was not excused by impracticability. Commercial impracticability requires an "especially severe and unreasonable loss" and seller's plant even after loss on contract would have still cleared $589,000.

In cases involving increased costs of performance however, the risk event, whether it be an Act of God, war, extreme inflation, or an oil embargo, can, unlike market price fluctuations, be viewed as a "contingency the non-occurrence of which was a basic assumption on which the contract was made." UCC 2–615(a). In these cases, the court should consider whether "performance as agreed has been made impracticable" by the risk event. In other words, the party seeking relief must prove that there was an extraordinary circumstance (both parties assumed it would not happen) that made performance so vitally different from what was reasonably to be expected as to alter the essential nature of that performance (impracticable). See Restatement (Second), Chapter 11, page 309; UCC 2–615, Comment 4 (increased cost alone does not excuse performance unless the rise in cost is due to some unforeseen contingency which alters the essential nature of the performance). Accord: Bernina Distributors, Inc. v. Bernina Sewing Machine Co., 646 F.2d 434, 438–39 (10th Cir.1981) (cost increase must cause "especially severe and unreasonable" loss). But see Florida Power & Light Co. v. Westinghouse Elec. Corp., 826 F.2d 239 (4th Cir.1987), cert. denied 485 U.S. 1021, 108 S.Ct. 1574, 99 L.Ed.2d 890 (1988) (defendant excused from obligation to remove and dispose of spent nuclear waste after government unexpectedly discontinued waste processing and use of alternative source would increase cost by $80,000,000).

Comment: Alcoa Can't Wait!

In Aluminum Company of America v. Essex Group, Inc., 499 F.Supp. 53 (W.D.Pa.1980), a case whose length and complexity belie simple analysis, the parties signed in 1967 a 17–year contract under which ALCOA was to process alumina supplied by Essex into molten aluminum to be used by Essex in the manufacture of aluminum wire products. The long-term contract, called a "toll conversion service contract," was to be performed at a plant owned by ALCOA in Indiana. As part of the pricing mechanism, the parties agreed upon an escalation clause, prepared by the noted economist, Alan Greenspan, which varied with production costs at the plant. The clause was developed in light of past cost patterns and reflected a projected variation of costs that would give ALCOA a high of $.07 and a low of $.01 profit per pound. ALCOA's target profit was $.04 per pound.

In 1973, at the time of the energy crisis, electricity costs at the Indiana plant began to escalate well beyond the projections of the contract clause. Although ALCOA had earned a profit of $27.6 million by the end of 1974 (the profit was down to $9 million at the time of trial), it was now projected that ALCOA would lose $60 million over the balance of the contract because of a 500% variation of actual to indexed energy costs. At the same time, Essex was reaping a so-called "windfall" gain by reselling converted aluminum for which it paid ALCOA $.364 per pound on the open market for $.733 per pound. When efforts by ALCOA to obtain an agreed adjustment of the contract price failed, ALCOA sued to obtain relief from the escalation clause and a reformation of the contract so that Essex would have to pay the actual costs incurred at the plant. When Essex counterclaimed for breach damages, the issue was joined.

The court concluded that ALCOA was, on the facts, entitled to "some relief" but that the remedy should be "equitable reformation" of the price term rather than discharge of the contract. The court devised a complicated adjustment formula without the agreement of the parties, who, subsequently, reached an agreement on an adjustment and settled the dispute before an appeal to the United States Court of Appeals for the Third Circuit could be decided. The district court's unique reasoning and result on the question of liability and remedy took the following path.

First, the court seemed to conclude that the case was not governed by UCC 2–615. Rather, the court discussed the law of Indiana which governed, the common law doctrines of mistake, impracticability and frustration and Tentative Drafts of the Restatement (Second), as well as Section 2–615.

Second, the court concluded that both parties assumed at the time of contracting that the production cost index was realistic, but they were wrong due to changed circumstances which were not foreseeable as likely to occur. The court stressed that the parties had undertaken a closely calculated rather than a limitless risk and concluded that neither party had assumed the risk of events which caused such a severe imbalance in the exchange.

Third, without discounting ALCOA's profit up to the time of trial, the court concluded that the projected $60 million loss over the balance of the commercial contract made continued performance under the contract "commercially senseless." The point was bolstered by the so-called "windfall" profits enjoyed by Essex. In short, the case had gone beyond the point where the community interest in predictable contract enforcement should prevail and, because continued performance would be "commercially senseless and unjust," the contractor was entitled to "some relief."[1]

Fourth, although the court's conclusions were consistent with relief under the "basic assumption—impracticability" test, the court made a

---

1. In 1975, Westinghouse repudiated its promise to deliver some 70 million tons of uranium under long-term supply contracts with 27 utility companies. The claim was that dramatic, unprecedented and unforeseen events had occurred which increased the price of uranium to Westinghouse from between $6.50 to $9.00 per pound at the times of contracting to $40 per pound at the time of repudiation. Assuming that Westinghouse could actually obtain uranium to perform the contracts, the projected loss under the contracts with the utilities was in excess of $2 billion. The legal effect of all of this was, according to Westinghouse, that the agreed performance had become impracticable under UCC 2–615(a) and that the contracts should be discharged. Suits by thirteen utilities for breach of contract were consolidated for trial in the Eastern District of Virginia, see In re Westinghouse Elec. Corp. Uranium Contracts Lit., 405 F.Supp. 316 (J.P.M.L.1975), and the breach claims were ultimately settled without a published decision on the merits. See N.Y. Times, § 3, p. 1 (March 15, 1981). Before the settlements were reached, however, the district court judge decided that Westinghouse was not excused under UCC 2–615(a) and was liable for damages. For a brief summary of the Bench Opinion of Judge Mehrige, see Richard E. Speidel, *Court-Imposed Price Adjustments Under Long–Term Supply Contracts*, 76 NwU .L.Rev. 369, 413, n. 181 (1981). For the decision in a related case, see Matter of Westinghouse Elec. Corp., Etc., 517 F.Supp. 440 (E.D.Va.1981). More detailed analyses of the issues in context can be found in Victor Goldberg, *Price Adjustment in Long–Term Contracts, 1985 Wis.L.Rev. 527.*

finding that the parties had made a "mistake * * * of fact rather than one of simple prediction of future events." 499 F.Supp. at 63. Thus, the court seemed to view the basis for relief as "existing" rather than "supervening" impracticability.

Plainly the mistake is not wholly isolated from predictions of the future or from the searching illuminations of painful hindsight. But this is not the legal test. At the time the contract was made both parties were aware that the future was unknown, and their agreed contract was intended to bind them for many years to come. Both knew that Essex sought an objective pricing formula and that ALCOA sought a formula which would cover its out of pocket costs over the years and which would yield it a return of around four cents a pound. Both parties to the contract carefully examined the past performance * * * (of production costs indices) * * * before agreeing to its use. The testimony was clear that each assumed the Index was adequate to fulfill its purpose. This mistaken assumption was essentially a present actuarial error. 499 F.Supp. at 63.

Fifth, the remedy of "equitable" reformation adjusted the price for future performance under the contract rather than for past performance. In short, the court deleted the existing cost index and imposed a new term in the "gap." The usual remedy of discharge was rejected in the interest of avoiding hardship and preserving expectations and the court-imposed adjustment was justified by what the court called a "new spirit" of contract. This "new spirit" reflected the "need for a body of law compatible with responsible practices and understandings" and the obligation of courts to give "close attention to the legitimate business aims of the parties, to their purpose of avoiding the risks of great losses, and to the need to frame a remedy to preserve the essence of the agreement." 499 F.Supp. at 91–92.

Kaiser–Francis Oil Co. v. Producer's Gas Co.

United States Court of Appeals, Tenth Circuit, 1989.
870 F.2d 563.

■ BALDOCK, CIRCUIT JUDGE.

Appellee and seller, Kaiser–Francis Oil Co. (Kaiser–Francis), sought to enforce the provisions of two similar gas purchase contracts (the "Ellis" and "Cronin" contracts) against appellant and buyer, Producer's Gas Co. (PGC). Under the contracts, PGC was required to take or pay for certain minimum quantities of gas from wells in which Kaiser–Francis had a percentage interest. When the resale price for natural gas declined, PGC did not pay Kaiser–Francis for gas taken on the theory that it was purchasing the gas from Kaiser–Francis' co-owners at reduced prices. PGC also declined to pay for the minimum contract quantities of the gas which were not taken. PGC's actions were based on various defenses to the contracts. The district court granted summary judgment on the issue of liability in favor of Kaiser–Francis, thereby rejecting all of PGC's defenses. The parties thereafter stipulated as to the appropriate damages, interest and attorney's fees that would accrue upon the liability determination. Thus, we consider only issues of liability under the contracts, whether the district court improperly rejected any or all of PGC's defenses to the contract.

On appeal, PGC contends that the district court erred in granting partial summary judgment in favor of Kaiser–Francis because 1) the force majeure provision in the contracts extends to a partial lack of demand caused by market forces, 2) the gas to be supplied by Kaiser–Francis failed to meet the quality specifications of the contract, 3) PGC was not purchasing gas from Kaiser–Francis, but rather from Kaiser–Francis' co-owners in various wells, and 4) any take-or-pay payments required under the contract would violate ceiling prices set by the Natural Gas Policy Act [NGPA]. We find each of these contentions without merit and affirm. Our jurisdiction to review this diversity case arises under 28 U.S.C. § 1291. Consistent with the choice of law provision in each contract, we apply Oklahoma substantive law. * * *

I.

PGC first contends that the force majeure provision[1] in each contract extends to a lack of demand for gas, thereby providing relief in this case from the take-or-pay obligation[2] contained in each contract. PGC suggests

---

1. *14.1* Except for Buyer's obligations to make payment due for gas delivered hereunder, neither party shall be liable for failure to perform this agreement when such failure is due to "force majeure." "Force majeure" shall mean acts of God, strikes, lockouts, or industrial disputes or disturbances, civil disturbances, arrests and restraints, interruptions by government or court orders, present and future valid order of any regulatory body having proper jurisdiction, acts of the public enemy, wars, riots, insurrections, inability to secure labor or inability to secure materials, including inability to secure materials by reason of allocations promulgated by authorized governmental agencies, epidemics, fires, explosions, breakage or accident to machinery or lines of pipe, freezing of wells or pipelines, inability to obtain easements, right-of-way or other interests in realty, the making of repairs, replacements or alterations to lines of pipe or plants, partial or entire failure of gas supply or demand over which neither Seller nor Buyer have [sic] control or any other cause, whether of the kind herein enumerated or otherwise, not reasonably within the control of the party claiming "force majeure." Events of "force majeure" shall, so far as possible, be remedied with all reasonable dispatch. The settlement of industrial difficulties shall be within the discretion of the

party having the difficulty, and the requirement that "force majeure" be remedied with all reasonable dispatch shall not require the settlement of industrial difficulties by acceding to the demands of any opposing party when such course is inadvisable in the discretion of the party having the difficulty.

Rec. vol. II (Attachment to Brief In Support of Kaiser–Francis Oil Company's Motion for Partial Summary Judgment—1980 Ellis & 1982 Cronin contracts) (emphasis added).

2. *4.1* Subject to all terms and conditions of this Agreement, Seller shall sell and deliver during each Accounting Year from the lands and leases covered hereby, and Buyer shall purchase and receive from Seller or pay for if available but not taken, a quantity of gas equal to the Daily Contract Quantities herein specified.

4.7 If at the end of any Accounting Year, Buyer shall have failed to purchase during such Year the sum the applicable Daily Contract Quantities, after credit is allowed for (i) deficiency existing by *force majeure*, ... , Buyer shall pay for the remaining deficiency as if taken.

Rec. vol. II (Attachment to Brief in Support of Kaiser–Francis Oil Company's Motion for Partial Summary Judgment—1980 Ellis and 1982 Cronin contracts).

that there is an issue of fact concerning the extent of the failure of demand for gas. Essentially, PGC contends that a force majeure event occurred because the demand for gas sharply decreased, with a corresponding decrease in the resale price of gas that PGC was obligated to take or pay for under the contracts. Unfortunately for PGC, however, the Oklahoma Supreme Court, in interpreting a similar force majeure provision, has determined that neither a decline in demand, nor an inability to sell gas at or above the contract price, constitutes a force majeure event. Golsen v. Ong Western, Inc., 756 P.2d 1209, 1213 (Okla.1988) (interpreting force majeure provision extending to "failure of gas supply or markets"). That decision applies to this case.

PGC's interpretation of the force majeure provision is antithetical to the take-or-pay provision. Under its interpretation, PGC could be expected to take only when the demand for gas resulted in a resale price at or above the contract price. PGC could never be expected to take or pay when the demand for gas resulted in a resale price below the contract price. Rather than taking or paying under the take-or-pay provision, PGC would rely on the force majeure provision. Thus, Kaiser–Francis would be shut in during any drop in demand, for up to twenty years, without any ability to sell in other markets. Such a one-sided interpretation is suspect.

The purpose of the take-or-pay clause is to apportion the risks of natural gas production and sales between the buyer and seller. The seller bears the risk of production. To compensate the seller for that risk, the buyer agrees to take, or pay for if not taken, a minimum quantity of gas. The buyer bears the risk of market demand.

Universal Resources Corp. v. Panhandle E. Pipe Line Co., 813 F.2d 77, 80 (5th Cir.1987); see also Golsen, 756 P.2d at 1213; 4 H. Williams & C. Meyers, Oil & Gas Law § 724.5 (1988) (take-or-pay provision assures the seller "of a minimum annual return and that his premises will be permitted to produce in paying quantities"). Should the resale price decline below the contract price, PGC could still take the gas and sell it, albeit at a loss, or pay for the gas without taking it, also at a loss. The change in the general or relative resale price of gas does not constitute a "partial failure of gas demand" which would relieve PGC of its obligation to take or pay. The force majeure provision cannot substitute for a price redetermination or market-out provision which would allow PGC to reduce the price paid to Kaiser–Francis for gas, thereby ameliorating PGC's take-or-pay obligation when the resale price of natural gas declined.

* * *

NOTES

(1) Are you persuaded by the court's reasoning on why the *force majeure* clause should not excuse the defendant? Suppose the clause, as in *Golsen*, had included "failure of gas supply or markets" as a ground for excuse? What contract provision would best protect the defendant from the particular events that occurred? See, generally, Lewis, *Allocating Risk in Take-or-Pay Contracts:*

Are Force Majeure and Commercial Impracticability the Same Defense?, 42 Sw.L.J. 1047 (1989).

(2) *Judge Posner on Force Majeure Clauses.* "A *force majeure* clause is not intended to buffer a party against the normal risks of a contract. The normal risk of a fixed-price contract is that the market price will change. If it rises, the buyer gains at the expense of the seller (except insofar as escalator provisions give the seller some protection); if it falls * * * the seller gains at the expense of the buyer. The whole purpose of a fixed-price contract is to allocate risk in this way. A *force majeure* clause interpreted to excuse the buyer from the consequences of the risk he expressly assumed would nullify a central term of the contract." Northern Indiana Public Service Co. v. Carbon County Coal Co., 799 F.2d 265, 275 (7th Cir.1986) (the *NIPSCO* case).

(3) *Judge Posner on Fixed Price Contracts.* The essence of the outcome in take-or-pay contracts, to be discussed below, was expressed in the *NIPSCO* case, supra, 799 F.2d at 278, where the court, speaking through Judge Posner, stated:

> Since impossibility and related doctrines are devices for shifting risk in accordance with the parties' presumed intentions, which are to minimize the costs of contract performance, one of which is the disutility created by risk, they have no place when the contract explicitly assigns a particular risk to one party or the other. [A] fixed-price contract is an explicit assignment of the risk of market price increases to the seller and the risk of market price decreases to the buyer, and the assignment of the latter risk to the buyer is even clearer where * * * the contract places a floor under price but allows for escalation. If * * * the buyer forecasts the market incorrectly and therefore finds himself locked into a disadvantageous contract, he has only himself to blame and so cannot shift the risk back to the seller by invoking impossibility or related doctrines. * * * Since "the very purpose of a fixed price agreement is to place the risk of increased costs on the promisor (and the risk of decreased costs on the promisee)," the fact that costs decrease steeply * * * cannot allow the buyer to walk away from the contract.

(4) *"A Stunning Challenge to the Sanctity of Contracts."* Contractual commitments are tested and strained when adverse conditions make performance much more difficult and costly than anticipated. An example was the widespread repudiation by major gas pipeline companies a decade ago of contracts with gas producers. *Business Week* magazine characterized the companies' conduct as "a stunning challenge to the sanctity of contracts." *Business Week*, August 22, 1983, pp. 76–77.

Companies found themselves contractually bound to buy huge quantities of natural gas they could not possibly sell. "Most of the unfavorable contracts were hastily signed after the cold winters of 1977 and 1978, when the gas shortage assumed crisis proportions. The pipeline industry faced the prospect of billions of dollars in lawsuits over its inability to supply contracted-for fuel. Massive litigation was averted only by federal regulators, who set rules that allowed the pipelines immunity. Pipeline managers, stung by public wrath, vowed never again to be caught short of gas." (Id. at 77)

Noting that the implications of the legal struggle over the repudiated contracts go far beyond the natural gas industry, the article quotes one lawyer as follows: "The gas pipelines are making one of the most substantial challenges ever to the reliability of contractual obligations." "The pipelines' case may be especially worrisome to business because it comes on the heels of other challenges to the sanctity of contract. Last spring, for example, Wilson Foods Corp. abrogated its labor agreement and filed bankruptcy even though it was not broke. More recently, the Washington State Supreme Court let a group of Northwest utilities out of pacts obligating them to pay the failing Washington Power Supply System." (Id. at 76)

The litigation raises, among other issues, the question of whether excuse can be predicated upon "commercial impracticability." In any event, "[o]bservers both within and outside the industry are worried that the complexities of the natural gas business may end up twisting contract law out of shape." (Id. at 77) One lawyer involved in the litigation put it this way: "On the one side you've got the sanctity of contract, and on the other you've got very difficult business and policy questions. Courts are going to have to do a lot of balancing." Knowing which result he preferred, this lawyer commented: "A good contract should be enforceable. It will be a sad day when a knowledgeable seller and buyer can't make a contract that will stand up." (Id. at 77)

Comment: Take-or-Pay Contracts

In the 1970's, producers entered long-term contracts with pipelines for the sale of natural gas. The pipelines agreed to "take or pay" for a portion of the producer's output at an agreed price, subject to escalation. The base price was set at an agreed dollar amount per unit, called MMBTU. In essence, the pipeline could either "take" the gas when produced and pay for it or pay without taking and expect the producer to "make up" deliveries in the future. Under this arrangement, the pipeline secured a long-term source of supply at a predictable price and the producer obtained a reliable source of cash with which to finance production and the development of reserves. In addition, the contract might contain a *force majeure* clause or other provisions allocating risk, such as a "market out" or a "matching price" clause. Under these clauses, the pipeline could terminate the contract if a lower long-term price for gas could be found from another source and the producer was unwilling or unable to match it. See Caggiano, *Understanding Natural Gas Contracts*, 38 Oil & Gas Q. 267, 267–278 (1989).

By 1983, the price of most gas at the "wellhead" had been deregulated under the Natural Gas Policy Act of 1978. At the same time, a depressed economy and lower demand for natural gas at the retail level put the pipelines in a bind. They did not need the gas they had agreed to "take" and the contract price that they had agreed to "pay" was substantially above that now available under either new long-term contracts or on the "spot" market. With large volumes of gas at stake, the dollar amount involved in a single contract could exceed $500,000,000. To no one's surprise, the pipelines began to search for ways to adjust or to terminate the contracts.

Without attempting here to exhaust the possibilities for agreed settlement, a survey of litigation under the UCC suggests that the pipelines have been singularly unsuccessful in avoiding these contracts. A summary of the judicial outcomes appears below.

(1) A long-term contract for the sale of natural gas is subject to Article 2 of the UCC if the gas is to be "severed by the seller." UCC 2–107(1);

(2) Take-or-Pay provisions are not unconscionable at the time the contract is made;

(3) Take-or-Pay provisions do not provide for liquidated damages. Rather, they give the buyer a choice between alternative performances under the contract;

(4) *Force majeure* clauses are not intended to excuse the buyer from changes in the market, no matter how dramatic;

(5) UCC 2–615 will not be applied to excuse the buyer from the contract, even though government action in deregulating natural gas prices played an important role in the market decline.

In addition to *Kaiser–Francis Oil Co.*, supra, the following decisions support the brief summary above: Universal Resources Corp. v. Panhandle Eastern Pipe Line Co., 813 F.2d 77 (5th Cir.1987); Sabine Corp. v. ONG Western, Inc., 725 F.Supp. 1157 (W.D.Okl.1989); Resources Investment Corp. v. Enron Corp., 669 F.Supp. 1038 (D.Colo.1987); Golsen v. ONG Western, Inc., 756 P.2d 1209 (Okl.1988). See also, Medina, *The Take-or-Pay Wars: A Further Status Report,* 41 Okl.L.Rev. 381 (1988); Note, *Deregulation and Natural Gas Purchase Contracts–Neoclassical and Relational Contract Theories,* 25 Washburn L.Rev. 43 (1986).

In an interesting essay on the scholarship of the late Professor John P. Dawson, the *Alcoa* case is analyzed and a search for post-*Alcoa* cases undertaken. The results indicate that *Alcoa* remains the high point (or the low point, if you prefer) in judicial efforts to adjust contracts after determining that some relief from changed circumstances was justified. There is also an interesting discussion of the "take or pay" problem—a problem that faded away with changes in contracting practices in the oil and gas industry but still lurks behind any long-term contract for the supply of energy, whether that be oil, gas, or electricity. See James J. White & David A. Peters, *Essay, A Footnote for Jack Dawson,* 100 Mich. L. Rev. 1954 (2002). See also Larry A. DiMatteo, Equity's Modification of Contract: An Analysis of the Twentieth Century's Equitable Reformation of Contract, 33 New Eng. L. Rev. 265 (1999).

Comment: Reopener Clauses in Long–Term Supply Contracts

The uncertainties involved when a court develops and imposes a price adjustment, see, e.g., Comment, 47 Mo.L.Rev. 79, 102–110 (1982), could be partially resolved if the parties included a "gross inequities" or a "reopener" clause in the contract. These clauses operate in three stages: *first,* a "gross inequity" under the existing contract resulting from "unusual economic conditions not contemplated by the parties at the time of contracting" must exist; *second,* the parties agree to negotiate in good faith to correct or to adjust the inequity by agreement and to cooperate with each other in the process; *third,* if negotiations fail to produce an agreed adjustment, the dispute is submitted to arbitration, where the decision of the arbitrator is final and conclusive. These clauses, when included, preserve both the relative equities of the parties over time and the contract. Normally, the parties agree to continue performance under the original terms while the dispute is being resolved. See, e.g., Georgia Power Co. v. Cimarron Coal Corp., 526 F.2d 101, 103–04 (6th Cir.1975), cert. denied 425 U.S. 952, 96 S.Ct. 1727, 48 L.Ed.2d 195 (1976) (dispute under "gross inequities" clause subject to arbitration); Scott, *Coal Supply Agreements,* 23 Rky.Mtn.Min.L.Inst. 107, 131–39 (1977). These clauses will vary in scope and detail with the particular industry. As one commentator has noted, contract solutions "are not self-operative and depend, in large measure, upon the good faith of both the purchaser and the seller." Snyder, *Geothermal Sales Contracts,* 13 Land & Water L.Rev. 259, 288 (1977).

Here is an edited example of a "Fair Clause" which has been used in long-term international sales contracts in the copper industry:

Fair Clause

§ 15.1   In entering into this long-term Agreement the parties hereto recognize that it is impracticable to make provision for every contingency which may arise during the term of this Agreement and the parties declare it to be their intention that this Agreement shall operate between them with fairness.

§ 15.2   Based on the foregoing principle the provisions of this Article 15 shall apply if during the term of this Agreement a new situation arises which is beyond the reasonable control of either party and which is not covered by any of the provisions of this Agreement and if such situation results in (a) a material disadvantage to one party and a corresponding material advantage to the other or (b) severe hardship to one party without an advantage to the other party.

* * *

§ 15.4   (a) In situations described under § 15.2(a) a solution shall be found in order to restore a fair balance of advantages and disadvantages as between the parties.

(b) In situations described under § 15.2(b) a solution shall be found in order to remove the severe hardship for the party affected; provided, however, that the provisions of this Agreement, as changed or modified by such solution and considered as a whole, shall remain commensurate with those of other international contracts between copper mines and independent smelters/refineries at the time of such change or modification and

(i) in case [buyer] invokes the Fair Clause, shall be no less favorable to [seller] than the provisions of any other comparable international contract between [buyer] and any independent copper mine other than [seller]; and

(ii) in case [seller] invokes the Fair Clause, shall be no less favorable to [buyer] than the provisions of any other comparable international contract between [seller] and any independent copper smelter/refinery other than [buyer].

The comparison of provisions as aforesaid shall serve as a valuation basis for the adjustment of the particular provisions of this Agreement which are involved, for instance the smelting/refining charge, but shall not result in replacing the provisions of this Agreement by the provisions of any compared contract, unless agreed upon between [seller] and [buyer].

(c) In arriving at solutions for either of the situations described in § 15.2, due consideration shall be given to such benefits as may have been obtained by each party as a result of a prior invocation of this Article 15.

§ 15.5 If either party hereto shall believe that a new situation described in § 15.2 shall have arisen, then, at the request of either party hereto, the parties shall promptly consult with a view toward reaching a mutually acceptable agreement dealing with such situation. In the event that within six months after the date of such request the parties shall not reach agreement with respect to such situation, either party shall have the right, exercisable within three months after the expiration of such six-month period, to refer the matter to arbitration pursuant to § 19.1. The arbitrator or arbitrators shall determine whether the particular situation is a "new situation" described in § 15.2(a) or in § 15.2(b) and, if so, shall, in any award entered, specify the section involved and unless the parties come to a prompt solution themselves, thereafter on the request of either party also establish a solution in conformity with § 15.4. Such arbitrator or arbitrators may obtain, for the purpose of establishing such solution, the opinion of an impartial expert of recognized standing in the international copper business, who shall not be domiciled in either the United States or Germany unless the parties hereto shall otherwise consent. Promptly after the entering of such award the parties hereto shall enter into a written agreement incorporating the terms of such award and making such changes or modifications in this Agreement as may be required in order to give effect to such award.

Practice in international trade has influenced the UNIDROIT Principles of International Commercial Contracts, which recognize that events subsequent to the contract may cause hardship and require that upon request of the disadvantaged party the other party must, at a minimum, negotiate in good faith toward an equilibrium. Articles 6.2.2 and 6.2.3, Comment 5. If the parties fail to reach agreement within a reasonable time, a court, if it finds hardship, "may, if reasonable, (a) terminate the contract at a date and on terms to be fixed, or (b) adapt the contract with a view to restoring its equilibrium." Article 6.2.3(4). See Joseph Perillo, *UNIDROIT Principles of International Commercial Contracts: The Black Letter Text and Review,* 63 Fordham L. Rev. 281 (1994).

(C) FRUSTRATION OF PURPOSE

Paradine v. Jane

King's Bench, 1647.
Aleyn, 26, 82 Eng.Rep. 897.

In debt the plaintiff declares upon a lease for years rendering rent at the four usual feasts; and for rent behind for three years, ending at the Feast of the Annunciation, 21 Car. brings his action; the defendant pleads, that a certain German prince, by name Prince Rupert, an alien born, enemy to the King and kingdom,* had invaded the realm with an hostile army of men; and with the same force did enter upon the defendant's possession, and him expelled, and held out of possession from the 19 of July 18 Car. till the Feast of the Annunciation, 21 Car. whereby he could not take the profits; whereupon the plaintiff demurred, and the plea was resolved insufficient.

1. Because the defendant hath not answered to one quarters rent.

2. He hath not averred that the army were all aliens, which shall not be intended, and then he hath his remedy against them; and Bacon cited 33 H. 61 1. e. where the gaoler in bar of an escape pleaded, that alien enemies broke the prison & c. and exception take to it, for that he ought to shew of what countrey they were, viz. Scots, & c.

3. It was resolved, that the matter of the plea was insufficient; for though the whole army had been alien enemies, yet he ought to pay his rent. And this difference was taken, that where the law creates a duty or charge, and the party is disabled to perform it without any default in him, and hath no remedy over, there the law will excuse him. As in the case of waste, if a house be destroyed by tempest, or by enemies, the lessee is excused. Dyer, 33. a. Inst. 53. d. 283. a. 12 H. 4. 6. so of an escape. Co. 4. 84. b. 33 H. 6. 1. So in 9 E. 3. 16. a supersedeas was awarded to the justices, that they should not proceed in a cessavit upon a cesser during the war, but when the party by his own contract creates a duty or charge upon himself, he is bound to make it good, if he may, notwithstanding any accident by inevitable necessity, because he might have provided against it by his contract. And therefore if the lessee covenant to repair a house, though it be burnt by lightning, or thrown down by enemies, yet he ought to repair it. Dyer 33. a. 40 E. 3. 6. h. Now the rent is a duty created by the parties upon the reservation, and had there been a covenant to pay it, there had

* Prince Rupert, son of Elizabeth, Queen of Bohemia, grandson of James I, nephew of Charles I, and first cousin to Charles II, was born in Germany in 1619. He arrived in England in 1641 to serve Charles I, and from 1641–45, he was "the toast of the Royalists, the terror of the Roundheads, and the mainstay of the King's war effort." After being defeated at the battles of Marston Moor and Naseby and surrendering the Royalists troops at Bristol in June, 1645, he fell into disfavor with the King (who still had his head) and left the country in July, 1646. After the Restoration, he returned in good standing to the court of Charles II and, upon his death in 1682, was buried in Westminster Abbey. In all things, he was loyal to the Stuart cause. The Oxford Companion to British History 827–828 (1997).

been no question but the lessee must have made it good, notwithstanding the interruption by enemies, for the law would not protect him beyond his own agreement, no more than in the case of reparations; this reservation then being a covenant in law, and whereupon an action of covenant hath been maintained (as Roll said) it is all one as if there had been an actual covenant. Another reason was added, that as the lessee is to have the advantage of casual profits, so he must run the hazard of casual losses, and not lay the whole burthen of them upon his lessor; and Dyer 56. 6. was cited for this purpose, that though the land be surrounded, or gained by the sea, or made barren by wildfire, yet the lessor shall have his whole rent: and judgment was given for the plaintiff.

Krell v. Henry

Court of Appeal, 1903.
[1903] 2 K.B. 740.

Appeal from a decision of DARLING, J. The plaintiff, Paul Krell, sued the defendant, C.S. Henry, for 50*l.*, being the balance of a sum of 75*l.*, for which the defendant had agreed to hire a flat at 56A, Pall Mall on the days of June 26 and 27, for the purpose of viewing the processions to be held in connection with the coronation of His Majesty. The defendant denied his liability, and counterclaimed for the return of the sum of 25*l.*, which had been paid as a deposit, on the ground that, the processions not having taken place owing to the serious illness of the King, there had been a total failure of consideration for the contract entered into by him.

[The defendant was induced to contract by an announcement in the window of plaintiff's flat renting windows to view the coronation, but the contract itself contained no express reference to the coronation.]

Darling J., held, upon the authority of *Taylor v. Caldwell* ... that there was an implied condition in the contract that the procession should take place, and gave judgment for the defendant on the claim and counter-claim. The plaintiff appealed.

■ VAUGHAN WILLIAMS L.J. read the following written judgment:—The real question in this case is the extent of the application in English law of the principle of the Roman law which has been adopted and acted on in many English decisions, and notably in the case of *Taylor v. Caldwell*. That case at least makes it clear that

> where, from the nature of the contract, it appears that the parties must from the beginning have known that it could not be fulfilled unless, when the time for the fulfilment of the contract arrived, some particular specified thing continued to exist, so that when entering into the contract they must have contemplated such continued existence as the foundation of what was to be done; there, in the absence of any express or implied warranty that the thing shall exist, the contract is not to be considered a positive contract, but as subject to an implied condition that the parties shall be excused in case, before breach,

performance becomes impossible from the perishing of the thing without default of the contractor.

Thus far it is clear that the principle of the Roman law has been introduced into the English law. The doubt in the present case arises as to how far this principle extends. * * *

I do not think that the principle of the civil law as introduced into the English law is limited to cases in which the event causing the impossibility of performance is the destruction or non-existence of some thing which is the subject-matter of the contract or of some condition or state of things expressly specified as a condition of it. I think that you first have to ascertain, not necessarily from the terms of the contract, but, if required, from necessary inferences, drawn from surrounding circumstances recognised by both contracting parties, what is the substance of the contract, and then to ask the question whether that substantial contract needs for its foundation the assumption of the existence of a particular state of things. If it does, this will limit the operation of the general words, and in such case, if the contract becomes impossible of performance by reason of the nonexistence of the state of things assumed by both contracting parties as the foundation of the contract, there will be no breach of the contract thus limited. . . .

In my judgment the use of the rooms was let and taken for the purpose of seeing the Royal procession. It was not a demise of the rooms, or even an agreement to let and take the rooms. It is a license to use rooms for a particular purpose and none other. And in my judgment the taking place of those processions on the days proclaimed along the proclaimed route, which passed 56A, Pall Mall, was regarded by both contracting parties as the foundation of the contract; and I think that it cannot reasonably be supposed to have been in the contemplation of the contracting parties, when the contract was made, that the coronation would not be held on the proclaimed days, or the processions not take place on those days along the proclaimed route; and I think that the words imposing on the defendant the obligation to accept and pay for the use of the rooms for the named days, although general and unconditional, were not used with reference to the possibility of the particular contingency which afterwards occurred. It was suggested in the course of the argument that if the occurrence, on the proclaimed days, of the coronation and the procession in this case were the foundation of the contract, and if the general words are thereby limited or qualified, so that in the event of the non-occurrence of the coronation and procession along the proclaimed route they would discharge both parties from further performance of the contract, it would follow that if a cabman was engaged to take some one to Epsom on Derby Day at a suitable enhanced price for such a journey, say 10*l.*, both parties to the contract would be discharged in the contingency of the race at Epsom for some reason becoming impossible; but I do not think this follows, for I do not think that in the cab case the happening of the race would be the foundation of the contract. No doubt the purpose of the engager would be to go to see the Derby, and the price would be proportionately high; but the cab had no special qualifications for the purpose which led to the selection of the cab for this particular occasion. Any other cab would have done as well. Moreover, I think that, under the cab contract, the hirer, even if the race went off, could have said, "Drive me to Epsom; I will pay you the agreed sum; you have nothing to do with the purpose for which I hired the cab," and that if the cabman refused he would have been guilty of a breach of contract, there being nothing to qualify his promise to drive the hirer to Epsom on a particular day. Whereas in the case of the coronation, there is not merely the purpose of the hirer to see the coronation procession, but it is the coronation procession and the relative position of the rooms which is the basis of the contract as much for the lessor as the hirer; and I think that if the King, before the coronation day and after the contract, had died, the hirer could not have insisted on having the rooms on the days named. It could not in the cab case be reasonably said that seeing the Derby race was the foundation of the contract, as it was of the license in this case. Whereas in the present case, where the rooms were offered and taken, by reason of their peculiar suitability from the position of the rooms for a view of the coronation procession, surely the view of the coronation procession was the foundation of the contract, which is a very different thing from the purpose of the man who engaged the cab—namely, to see the race—being held to be the foundation of the contract. Each case must be judged by its own circumstances. In each case one must ask oneself, first, what, having regard to all the circumstances, was the foundation of the contract? Secondly, was the performance of the contract prevented? Thirdly, was the event which prevented the performance of the contract of such a character that it cannot reasonably be said to have been in the contemplation of the parties at the date of the contract? If all these questions are answered in the affirmative (as I think they should be in this case), I think both parties are discharged from further performance of the contract. I think that the coronation procession was the foundation of this contract, and that the non-happening of it prevented the performance of the contract; and, secondly, I think that the non-happening of the procession . . . was an event "of such a character that it cannot reasonably be supposed to have been in the contemplation of the contracting parties when the contract was made, and that they are not to be held bound by general words which, though large enough to include, were not used with reference to the possibility of the particular contingency which afterwards happened." The test seems to be whether the event which causes the impossibility was or might have been anticipated and guarded against. * * *

I myself am clearly of opinion that in this case, where we have to ask ourselves whether the object of the contract was frustrated by the non-happening of the coronation and its procession on the days proclaimed, parol evidence is admissible to shew that the subject of the contract was rooms to view the coronation procession, and was so to the knowledge of both parties. . . .

This disposes of the plaintiff's claim for 50*l*. unpaid balance of the price agreed to be paid for the use of the rooms. The defendant at one time set up a cross-claim for the return of the 25*l*. he paid at the date of the contract. As that claim is now withdrawn it is unnecessary to say anything about it.

Appeal dismissed.

NOTES

(1) *The Development of Frustration under English Law.* After tracing the development of frustration in English law, G. H. Treitel concludes:

"From a practical point of view, the doctrine of frustration gives rise to two related difficulties. The first is that it may scarcely be more satisfactory to hold that the contract is totally discharged than to hold that it remains in force; often some compromise may be a more reasonable solution. * * * In the absence of * * * express provisions, this kind of solution is not open to the courts; they have no power to *modify* contracts in the light of supervening events. The second difficulty is that the allocation of risks produced at common law by the doctrine of frustration is not always entirely satisfactory. In a case like *Taylor v. Caldwell* it may be reasonable that neither party should be liable for loss of the benefit that the other expected to derive from performance * * * [b]ut it does not follow that loss suffered by one party as a result in acting in reliance on the contract should equally lie where it falls. In *Taylor v. Caldwell* the plaintiffs did not in fact make any claim for lost profits, but only one for expenses thrown away in advertising the concerts. It is by no means self-evident that the owners of the hall (who had presumably insured it) should escape all liability for this loss; and it might be more satisfactory if loss of this kind could be apportioned. At common law this was only possible where the contract expressly so provided; * * *. A more general, but nevertheless limited power of apportionment now exists by statute, but it does not cover all cases in which some form of apportionment would seem to be desirable. * * * (citing the Frustrated Contracts Act.)" G.H. Treitel, The Law of Contract 651–52 (6th ed. 1983). [See G.H. Treitel, The Law of Contract 807–808 (10th ed. 1999), where this passage is retained with slight modifications.] See also, Price, *The Doctrine of Frustration and Leases,* 10 J.Legal Hist. 90, 92–101 (1989).

(2) In Krell v. Henry, Henry had paid 25 pounds in advance but withdrew a cross-claim for restitution of that amount. In other "coronation" cases, the plaintiffs sought and were denied restitution of the down payment: the gains and losses were left where they lay at the time of frustration. See e.g., Chandler v. Webster, 1 K.B. 493 (1904). This dubious result was ultimately reversed in Fibrosa Spolka Akcyjna v. Fairbairn Lawson Combe Barbour, Ltd, 2 All. Eng. 122 (H.L.1942). See R.G. McElroy & Glanville Williams, The Coronation Cases–II, 5 Mod. L. Rev. 1 (1941) (discussing Chandler and related cases).

(3) *Frustration of Purpose in Early Twentieth Century American Law: The Prohibition Cases.* In the late 19th and early 20th centuries (before National Prohibition), many states passed legislation either prohibiting the manufacture and sale of alcoholic beverages or giving to local government the option to enact such prohibitions. State legislation prohibiting the manufacture and sale of alcoholic beverages was upheld against attack under the 14th Amendment by the owner of a brewery in *Mugler v. Kansas*, 123 U.S. 623, 8 S.Ct. 273, 31 L.Ed. 205 (1887), decided by the Supreme Court in 1887.

After the turn of the century, the absolute liability theory of *Paradine v. Jane*, as modified by *Krell v. Henry*, appeared but was not explicitly identified in state decisions on the effect of legislative prohibitions against the sale of alcohol that had retrospective effect on existing leases. In a typical case, an owner had leased premises for a fixed term to a lessee for the purpose of operating a bar or a saloon. After state or local legislation prohibiting the sale of alcoholic beverages was enacted, the lessee defaulted on the rent obligation on the grounds of supervening illegality. The lessee's obligation to pay rent, however, was not made illegal. Rather, a main purpose for which the property was leased was prohibited. It would now be a crime to use the premises for the sale of alcoholic beverages.

In some cases, relief was denied under a *Paradine*-like absolutist principal. For example, in *Houston Ice & Brewing Co. v. Keenan,* 99 Tex. 79, 88 S.W. 197 (1905), relief was denied even though there was a stipulation in the lease that the premises should be used for "saloon business." The Texas Supreme Court held that even if use was so restricted, the adoption of the local option did not make the contract of lease illegal or absolve the defendant from the rent. The court embraced the hard line reasoning of the Court of Civil Appeals which, while recognizing the principle of excuse from supervening illegality of performance, held that this case was not within the exception to the general rule that "where the performance becomes impossible subsequent to the making of the contract, the promisor is not thereby discharged." Key to the case, however, was the fact that the local option statute had been enacted but not implemented at the time the lease was signed: The "appellant must have known that [implementation] was likely to occur, and, if it did, the performance of the stipulation under discussion would be prohibited." Further, this was a "probable contingency which an ordinarily prudent man should have foreseen and provided for in his contract, and, having failed to so do, he took the risk upon himself, and must abide the consequences."* To put the matter in the words of the English courts, even if the Texas court had recognized and embraced the "frustration of purpose" principal, it concluded that the subsequent government act was "contemplated" at the time of contracting and unless the risk was allocated by the agreement it would be assumed by the lessee. In a modern parlance, the legal context at the time the lease was signed was unstable and the subsequent prohibition, which had retrospective effect, was foreseeable as likely to occur.

In other cases, relief was granted under the general principle of subsequent illegality. This was done either by construing the lease to limit use to a particular purpose, operating of a saloon,** or by finding that the

---

* The court cited and discussed the English case of Newby v. Sharpe, 8 Ch. Div. 39 but not *Krell v. Henry*.

** Greil Bros. Co. v. Mabson, 179 Ala. 444, 60 So. 876 (1912). The lease said the premises should be used "as a bar, and not otherwise" rather than permitting use as a saloon, a broader term. *Id*. at 878. After conducting a thorough review of the American case law on subsequent illegality, the court was careful to distinguish cases where the lease permitted use for purposes other than just a bar, and distinguished the *Houston Ice* case on the grounds that there the local option had been enacted at the time of the lease and the lessee should have protected himself "against a contingency then authorized by law." *Id.* at 879. *Accord*: The Stratford, Inc. v. Seattle Brewing & Malting Co., 94 Wash. 125, 162 Pac. 31 (1916) (primary purpose of lease to operate saloon);

purpose of both parties, as clearly expressed by the lease, was that the premises should be used as a saloon.*** Under either approach, the subsequent legislation made that common purpose illegal and discharged the contract. On the other hand, if use on the premises was not restricted or assumed to be limited to a bar or saloon (in the strict sense) and other commercial uses were possible, excuse was likely to be denied. In these cases, *Krell v. Henry* was not cited and the doctrine of "frustration of purpose" was neither identified nor discussed. But in leases at least the frustration doctrine had arrived in the United States as a possible exception to *Paradine v. Jane*, provided that the risk of subsequent, retrospective law was not foreseeable as likely to occur.

By the time of the First Restatement (1933), the doctrine of "Frustration of the Object or Effect of the Contract" was restated in Section 288, which, curiously, was placed in Chapter 10 on "Conditions" rather than in Chapter 14 on "Impossibility." Section 288 provided:

> Where the assumed possibility of a desired object or effect to be attained by either party to a contract forms the basis on which both parties enter into it, and this object or effect is or surely will be frustrated, a promisor who is without fault in causing the frustration, and who is harmed thereby, is discharged from the duty of performing his promises unless a contrary intention appears.

Comment (a) stated that the "object or effect to be gained must be so completely the basis of the contract that, as both parties know, without it the contract would have little meaning."

Washington State Hop Producers, Inc. v. Goschie Farms, Inc.

Supreme Court of Washington, 1989.
112 Wash.2d 694, 773 P.2d 70.

[From 1965 until 1985, the U.S. Department of Agriculture required hop growers to obtain federal allotments in order to market their hops. This was called "hop base." Growers could transfer excess allotments to other growers. Over time, "hop base" became a scarce, expensive commodity and a secondary market developed for trading. Plaintiff, the Trust, was organized in 1979 to acquire, lease and sell federal hop base.

Because the system restricted market entry, legal efforts to change the marketing order were commenced in 1981. The USDA considered various changes, but as late as June, 1985, substantial changes in the marketing order were not anticipated. On May 31, 1985, the Trust mailed invitations to bid on two pools of "hop base" for sale. Pool A of 633,500 pounds was available for use in 1985 and Pool B of 432,639 pounds was available for use in 1986. On June 16, 1985, bids were received ranging from $0.05 per

Kahn v. Wilhelm, 118 Ark. 239, 177 S.W. 403 (1915) (reviewing authorities).

*** Heart v. East Tennessee Brewing Co., 121 Tenn. 69, 113 S.W. 364 (1908) (common purpose made illegal).

pound to $0.76 per pound. On June 21, 1985, the Trust mailed notices of award to bids in the $0.50 to $0.76 range, including Gochie and other respondents in this case. On June 27, 1985, however, the USDA terminated the marketing order, effective December 31, 1985. All of the respondents refused to perform the contracts for sale. The Trust was able to sell nearly 50% of the "hop base" in Pool B for an average price of $0.07 per pound, compared with earlier successful bids of $0.60 per pound.

In an action by the Trust to enforce the contracts, the trial court granted summary judgment to the respondents. This was affirmed in the court of appeals which, in essence, held that the respondent's contracts were excused by the rule of supervening frustration. The Trust appealed.]

* * *

Perhaps the earliest case clearly recognizing frustration of purpose as a defense in a breach of contract action is Krell v. Henry, 2 K.B. 740 (C.A.1903). There, a lease was made to rent use of a window overlooking the route for the coronation parade of Albert Edward when he succeeded his mother, Queen Victoria. After the agreement, Edward became ill, the parade was canceled, and the purpose of renting the window was frustrated. The lessee refused to pay the agreed rent. The court held that his duty was discharged and that he was therefore not liable for breach. Both parties were capable of performing the terms of their contracts, and there was arguably still some market value in the vendor's performance. But the lessee's ultimate purpose was frustrated and he was released from his contract nonetheless.

The doctrine of "Discharge by Supervening Frustration" is recited in Restatement (Second) of Contracts § 265 (1979):

> Where, after a contract is made, a party's principal purpose is substantially frustrated without his fault by the occurrence of an event the non-occurrence of which was a basic assumption on which the contract was made, his remaining duties to render performance are discharged, unless the language or the circumstances indicate the contrary.

Comment (A) to the Section Further Explains:

> This Section deals with the problem that arises when a change in circumstances makes one party's performance virtually worthless to the other, frustrating his purpose in making the contract ... First, the purpose that is frustrated must have been a principal purpose of that party in making the contract ... The object must be so completely the basis of the contract that, as both parties understand, without it the transaction would make little sense. Second, the frustration must be substantial. It is not enough that the transaction has become less profitable for the affected party or even that he will sustain a loss. The frustration must be so severe that it is not fairly to be regarded as within the risks that he assumed under the contract. Third, the non-occurrence of the frustrating event must have been a basic assumption

on which the contract was made ... The foreseeability of the event is ... a factor in that determination, but the mere fact that the event was foreseeable does not compel the conclusion that its non-occurrence was not such a basic assumption.

This is the rule and test recited and applied by the Court of Appeals. ... However, Washington has not before now adopted the doctrine of supervening frustration as recited in Restatement (Second) of Contracts § 265 (1979).

Under the restatement formula, "the purpose that is frustrated must have been a principal purpose of that party in making the contract ... without [which] the transaction would make little sense." Restatement (Second) of Contracts § 265, comment (a) (1979). The Court of Appeals found "the principal purpose of this contract was to purchase a hop allotment base provided and created pursuant to a hop marketing agreement." Washington State Hop Producers, Inc. Liquidation Trust v. Goschie Farms, Inc., 51 Wash.App. 484, 754 P.2d 139 (1988). We agree.

Under the conditions prevailing for nearly 20 years before the termination order, ownership of hop base provided permanent access to the hop market otherwise unavailable. After the termination, what was available to "purchase" was at most access to the 1985 crop year market. The Trust had formerly been in the business of renting 1–year access to the hop market. The Growers did not seek single-year market access, nor did they bid prices in the range of the 1–year rental (6 cents ($0.06) per pound). Without the federal requirement of hop base, there would have been no subject matter for the contracts nor any consideration from the Trust to support the transactions. Because the Growers sought to *purchase* hop base instead of renting it, the inference is that *future* market access was their principal purpose in entering the transactions. This purpose was understood by both parties. Purchase, as opposed to rental, of the hop base made little sense without future market access. The record provides sufficient undisputed facts to sustain the Court of Appeals' determination on this point.

The Court of Appeals relied upon the decline in value of hop allotments in determining that the purpose of the contracts had been frustrated by termination of the hop marketing order. The pertinent language from the appellate opinion is:

> Here, we find the principal purpose of this contract was to purchase a hop allotment base provided and created pursuant to a hop marketing agreement. As is evident when the marketing order was terminated, effective December 31, 1985, the value of that allotment decreased [in June 1985 when the termination was announced], assuming a bid of $.50 fell to $.05, i.e., one-tenth the bid price. We consider that a substantial frustration falling within the rule.

Washington State Hop Producers, Inc. Liquidation Trust v. Goschie Farms, Inc., 51 Wash.App. 484, 489, 754 P.2d 139 (1988). It is not clear from the language employed whether the "frustration" is the 90 percent decline in market price, or whether the decline in value is merely evidence of the substantiality of the frustration.

The decline in price was great. Before the Termination Order, hop base was a prerequisite to the sale of hops. The annual *rental* price of hop base for 1985 was 6 cents per pound before the Termination Order. Successful bids to *purchase* Pool "A" hop base before termination ranged up to 76 cents per pound. After termination, hop base would be unnecessary following the 1985 crop year. Pool "B" hop base that had commanded a pre-termination price of not less than 50 cents (when it could be sold at all after the termination was announced) commanded an average price of just $\frac{7}{10}$ of one cent ($0.007)—a 98 percent decrease in value.

[A] rational market should have valued post-termination Pool "A" base at about 6 and $\frac{7}{10}$ cents ($0.067) per pound.... [T]he post-termination decrease remains in the range of 92 percent....

If the decline in price alone is considered to be substantial frustration, then the decision of the Court of Appeals cannot be affirmed without doing violence to established principles of contract law. See, e.g., Restatement (Second) of Contracts § 265, comment (a) (1979) ("It is not enough that the transaction has become less profitable for the affected party or even that he will sustain a loss."). The decision may be affirmed on other grounds, however. * * *

If the decline in price is regarded merely as evidence of substantiality of frustration of the purpose of the contract, then the Court of Appeals' reasoning, as well as its decision, may stand.... [I]t is not the decline in market price, but the irrelevance of control of hop base after the 1985 crop year that supplies the frustration justifying rescission.

Application of the doctrine of frustration is a question of law and not a question of fact.... Whether, as appellant states, "the value of the [Trust's] performance is ... totally or nearly totally destroyed by supervening events," as evidenced by the decline in price, seems a matter well within the sound judgment of the trial court. We will not disturb that court's determination.

In this case appellant Trust makes repeated references to "foreseeability" of the market order termination as invalidating the rescission granted by the trial court. However, as the Court of Appeals noted, "[w]hile the Trust seeks to hold the growers to knowledge that the order could be terminated at any time, it takes no responsibility for the same knowledge." Washington State Hop Producers, Inc. Liquidation Trust v. Goschie Farms, Inc., 51 Wash.App. 484, 488, 754 P.2d 139 (1988). The court noted that the Trust had incorporated no language in its bid form allocating the risk to the growers. The court also noted that the growers had not included any allocating language in their "acceptance." This latter reference seems not to be made to any particular document. All documents and exhibits in the record comprising the transactions between the parties consist of forms provided by the Trust. The growers simply filled in blanks on bid forms provided by the Trust. There is no indication that any restrictive language could have been added by the growers. By contrast, the Trust had every opportunity to draft the language to its own advantage. It did not do so.

Moreover, the inference is that, even to the Trust, the termination was unforeseeable or at least not foreseen.... In its own brief, the Trust states, "[a]s late as June, 1985 ... it was not anticipated that any substantial change in the Marketing Order would be proposed by the Secretary of Agriculture." In its introduction to Chapter 11, the Restatement notes the significance of the "relative ease with which either party could have inserted a clause" 2 Restatement (Second) of Contracts 311 (1979). In context, this factor is equivalent to foreseeability in affecting the application of the doctrine.

Under the Restatement formula, foreseeability is merely a relevant factor in determining whether nonoccurrence of the frustrating event was a basic assumption of the frustrated party in entering the transaction. If that basic assumption is found, as it was here, the "issue" of foreseeability becomes irrelevant.... The trial court, implicitly, and the Court of Appeals, explicitly, found that continued need to own or control hop base in order to sell hops was an assumption central to the subject matter of the contract. The Court of Appeals concluded that "[w]e find without this basic assumption there would neither have been an offer nor an acceptance." 51 Wash.App. 484, 490, 754 P.2d 139.

By repeating its position, the Restatement is emphatic on the role of foreseeability. The introductory note to Chapter 11 reads:

> The fact that the [frustrating] event was unforeseeable is significant as suggesting that its non-occurrence was a basic assumption. However, the fact that it was foreseeable, or even foreseen, does not, of itself, argue for a contrary conclusion, since the parties may not have thought it sufficiently important a risk to have made it a subject of their bargaining. Another significant factor may be the relative bargaining positions of the parties and the relative ease with which either party could have included a clause.

2 Restatement (Second) of Contracts 311 (1979).

Appellant refers to the Restatement (Second) of Contracts § 261 in support of its contention that foreseeability avoids the defense of commercial frustration. The section is inapposite because it concerns the defense of supervening impracticability. Frustration is covered in § 265. However, even if the reference did apply, the language does not advance appellant's argument.

> A commercial practice under which a party might be expected to insure or otherwise secure himself against a risk also militates against shifting it to the other party. If the supervening event was not reasonably foreseeable when the contract was made, the party claiming discharge can hardly be expected to have provided against its occurrence. However, if it was reasonably foreseeable, or even foreseen, the opposite conclusion [i.e., that the party should not be discharged] does not necessarily follow.

Restatement (Second) of Contracts § 261 at comment (c), p. 315. Cross reference is made to § 265, comment (a), quoted above, and § 261, comment (c). Pertinent language from this latter reference includes the following: "The fact that the event was foreseeable *or even foreseen,* does not necessarily compel a conclusion that its non-occurrence was not a basic assumption." (Italics ours.) Restatement (Second) of Contracts § 261, comment (b), p. 314.

* * *

Although language suggesting that unforeseeability is a prerequisite of supervening frustration has found its way into the case law of this state, . . . the basis for this rule does not apply to this case. The Growers did not receive an estate in land, such as would be provided by a commercial lease, see Lloyd v. Murphy, 25 Cal.2d 48, 153 P.2d 47 (1944), nor did they ever have the beneficial use of the subject matter of the contracts for which they request rescission. The Restatement (Second) of Contracts repeatedly refers to foreseeability as only a factor in determining whether the non-occurrence of the frustrating event was an assumption basic to the contract. Moreover, foreseeability of a possible frustrating event is meaningful only where the party seeking relief could have controlled the language of the contract to the extent of allocating the risk. Here, exclusive control of the contract language was in the hands of the Trust and the Trust did not include disclaimers in its contracts until after the termination order.

NOTES

(1) *Goschie Farms* is one of the rare American decisions granting relief under the doctrine of "frustration of purpose." For some other examples, see Chase Precast Corp. v. John J. Paonessa Co., 409 Mass. 371, 566 N.E.2d 603 (1991) (both parties assumed key items in project would continue to be used by government); Aluminum Company of America v. Essex Group, Inc., 499 F.Supp. 53, 76–77 (W.D.Pa.1980) (supplier's "principal purpose" to make a profit substantially frustrated by changed economic conditions); Western Properties v. Southern Utah Aviation, Inc., 776 P.2d 656, 659 (Utah App.1989) (sublessee's duty to pay rent and improve premises frustrated by government act which left property without value); Matter of Fontana D'Oro Foods, Inc., 122 Misc.2d 1091, 472 N.Y.S.2d 528 (1983) (purpose of one party to settlement frustrated by unforeseen conduct of insurance company which rendered assets valueless); Molnar v. Molnar, 110 Mich.App. 622, 313 N.W.2d 171 (1981) (death of child frustrates purpose in divorce property settlement). But see Arabian Score v. Lasma Arabian, Ltd., 814 F.2d 529 (8th Cir.1987) (death of stallion shortly after delivery to buyer did not discharge seller's duty to pay a fixed price for advertising and promotion over a five year period).

(2) *Judge Posner on Frustration of Purpose.* In the NIPSCO case, supra at 839, the buyer, an Indiana electric utility, entered into a 20 year contract to purchase a fixed quantity of coal, some 1.5 million tons per year, at a fixed price of $24 per ton, subject only to upward escalation, from a producer in Wyoming. When the market for energy turned down, the Indiana Public Service Commission directed NIPSCO to make a good faith effort to buy electricity from other

utilities at prices lower than the cost of producing it and warned that, because the coal contract was imprudent, permission to pass its high costs through to consumers might be disallowed. Later, NIPSCO stopped taking deliveries of coal and sought a declaratory judgment that it was excused from the contract. The producer, claiming breach, counterclaimed for damages and obtained a verdict in the amount of $181,000,000. On appeal, the verdict was affirmed.

One of the issues on appeal was whether the contract was unenforceable by virtue of the doctrines of "frustration or impracticability." After reviewing the excuse standards under UCC 2–615 and the Restatement, the court stated:

> The leading case on frustration remains *Krell v. Henry* ... Krell rented Henry a suite of rooms for watching the coronation of Edward VII, but Edward came down with appendicitis and the coronation had to be postponed. Henry refused to pay the balance of the rent and the court held that he was excused from doing so because his purpose in renting had been frustrated by the postponement, a contingency outside the knowledge, or power to influence, of either party. The question was, to which party did the contract (implicitly) allocate the risk? Surely Henry had not intended to insure Krell against the possibility of the coronation's being postponed, since Krell could always relet the room, at the premium rental, for the coronation's new date. So Henry was excused.

The court noted that since NIPSCO "is a buyer in the present case ... its defense is more properly frustration than impracticability." The court, however, avoided having to decide whether Indiana recognized the doctrine of frustration by concluding that "the facts of the present case do not bring it within the scope of the frustration doctrine...." 799 F.2d at 277.

Do you agree with (1) Judge Posner's analysis of *Krell v. Henry* and (2) the court's result on the frustration question? If so, must you then disagree with the Supreme Court of Washington's decision in *Gochie Farms?* See Comment, *NIPSCO: Risk Assumption, Claims or Impossibility, Impracticability, and Frustration of Purpose,* 50 Ohio St.L.J. 163 (1989).

(3) *Frustration in Leases.* In England until 1981, *Paradine v. Jane,* supra, was still thought to be good law. Lessees to whom an interest in land was conveyed were thought to have an absolute duty to pay the rent regardless of alleged frustrating events. In 1981, the House of Lords, in National Carriers Ltd. v. Panal Pina (Northern) Ltd., [1981] A.C. 675, [1981] 2 W.L.R. 45, [1981] 1 All E.R. 161, held that a lease could be discharged by frustration, but concluded that relief was not justified on the facts of the particular case and suggested that such relief would be very rare. In *National Carriers,* the tenant, under a 10–year lease of a warehouse, was denied relief even though the only access road was closed by local authority four and one-half years before the end of the term and remained closed for 20 months. The interruption was not deemed sufficiently serious to justify discharge. See G. Treitel, The Law of Contract 832–834 (10th ed. 1999); Price, *The Doctrine of Frustration and Leases,* 10 J.Legal Hist. 90 (1989).

Courts in the United States have frequently noted the possibility that a lessee might be discharged due to frustration, (see discussion of the Prohibition Cases, supra) but have rarely granted relief. In the well known case of Lloyd v. Murphy, 25 Cal.2d 48, 153 P.2d 47 (1944), Justice Traynor recognized that a lease might be frustrated in a proper case. Nevertheless, the court refused to discharge the lessee of prime commercial property when a governmental wartime order prevented use of the property for the sole purpose of the lease, the sale of new cars. The lessor, however, had modified the restriction to permit other uses and, although there were still restrictions, the lease was still valuable to the lessee. In short, in the absence of proof that the value of the lease was "totally destroyed," relief was denied. Accord: Mel Frank Tool & Supply Co. v. Di–Chem Co., 580 N.W.2d 802 (Iowa 1998) (subsequent government regulation must prohibit tenant from legally using premises for originally intended purpose).

More recently, a court discharged the duty of a sub-lessee to pay rent on the following facts: Cedar City leased undeveloped land near the municipal airport to Western Properties for a 15 year term. Western, with Cedar City approval, subleased the land for part of that term to Southern Utah Aviation. Southern agreed to pay rent and to construct a maintenance building on the land, which would revert to Western at the end of the lease. Cedar City, however, had not developed a master plan for the airport and, because of this, failed to approve Southern's application for a site plan to construct the building. Southern abandoned the site without constructing the building or paying the rent due. Western sued for damages for failure to construct and for rent due. Concluding that both parties assumed that the City would approve the site plan, the court excused the duty to construct on grounds of impracticability and excused the duty to pay rent on grounds of frustration. Without confronting the common law rule restricting discharge of a duty to pay rent, the court discharged the lessee and stated: "Without a way of productively using the land, the purpose of the leasehold was effectively frustrated. * * * There was no point in leasing this land once its development became impossible." Western Properties v. Southern Utah Aviation, Inc., 776 P.2d 656, 659 (Utah App.1989).

(4) *ALCOA Revisited.* The court in *ALCOA*, supra at 834, held, as an alternative ground for granting relief, that a principal purpose of a contract which could be frustrated was to "earn money." The court reviewed the American cases, the Restatement, Second, various treatises and foreign authorities.

> Happily some American cases and the law of many foreign countries take a different view of the problem. The problem of serious, sustained inflation is not unique to modern America. During the Revolution and the Civil War, America witnessed serious inflation. And several other nations have recently experienced more severe inflation than America has. When the problem has arisen, here and abroad, courts and legislatures have repeatedly acted to relieve parties from great and unexpected losses. See Mann, The Legal Aspect of Money (1938); . . . The exact character of the relief granted is not important here. Neither is the exact explanation of the decisions found in the cases, because even the Civil War cases antedate the evolution of the distinct doctrine of frustration. What is important is this: first, the results of those decisions would be readily explained today in terms of frustration of purpose. * * * And second, the frustration which they involved was a frustration of the purpose to earn money or to avoid losses. Thus it appears that there is no legitimate doctrinal problem which prevents relief for

frustration of this sort. There remain the customary strictures concerning risk allocation and gravity of injury. Those have been addressed above and need not be considered again here. The Court holds ALCOA is entitled to relief on its claim of frustration of purpose. [499 F.Supp. at 76–77.]

Comment: Forms of Relief After Impracticability

If a claim of "existing" or "supervening" impracticability is raised during performance, the parties may agree upon an appropriate modification or adjustment of the contract and complete performance without knowing whether the promisor was entitled to "some relief" as a matter of law. The enforceability of these agreed adjustments will be considered in Chapter Six, Section 5. The courts are unanimous that in the absence of an agreement a promisee has no duty to negotiate with the promisor in good faith over any proposed adjustment. We will also consider the soundness of this position in the next section.

If the court determines that the promisor is not entitled to relief (and there is no agreed adjustment), the legal situation is reasonably clear. If the promisor has failed to complete performance, it has breached the contract and is liable for damages to the promisee. If the promisor has completed performance despite the difficulty it must bear the burden of any costs incurred in excess of the contract price. See, e.g., Transatlantic Financing Corp. v. United States, 363 F.2d 312 (D.C.Cir.1966).

If the court determines that the promisor is entitled to "some relief" from impracticability, exactly what form should that relief take? First, let us assume that despite the existing or supervening difficulty, the promisor has completed performance at additional costs but without any default. This is risky business. Even if the promisee has requested the continued performance in light of the difficulty, some courts have denied recovery for any costs incurred after the promisor knew or had reason to know that performance was impracticable. See, e.g., the "Chugach Trilogy," Northern Corp. v. Chugach Electric Ass'n, 518 P.2d 76 (Alaska 1974), modified 523 P.2d 1243 (1974), judgment of the trial court affirmed, Chugach Elec. Ass'n v. Northern Corp., 562 P.2d 1053 (1977). For the final word, see 563 P.2d 883 (1977). A unique exception is National Presto Indus., Inc. v. United States, 338 F.2d 99 (Ct.Cl.1964), cert. denied 380 U.S. 962, 85 S.Ct. 1105, 14 L.Ed.2d 153 (1965), where the Court of Claims granted one-half of the contractor's claim for extra costs incurred in overcoming difficulties inhering in a new, experimental manufacturing process. In holding that the United States must share the excess costs, the court stressed that (1) both parties assumed that an essential step in the process would not be required but understood that time and expense would be needed to determine this with certainty, (2) the government was anxious to perfect the new process, (3) the government benefited from the perfected process and (4) if asked, the government would have agreed at the beginning of performance to share some but not all of the extra costs. As Judge Davis put it:

> For such a case it is equitable to reform the contract so that each side bears a share of the unexpected costs, instead of permitting the whole

loss to remain with the party on whom it chanced to light. ... Reformation, as the child of equity, can mold its relief to attain any fair result within the broadest perimeter of the charter the parties have established for themselves. Where that arrangement has allocated the risk to neither side, a judicial division is fair and equitable.

338 F.2d at 112. Despite the potential, reformation in this context has not been embraced in disputes in private contracts and has been limited in government contracts to a "joint enterprise" experiment where the government is more concerned with process than end product and also benefits from the contractor's trial and error. Even without loss sharing, however, a contractor whose performance is delayed by impracticability will be excused. See UCC 2–615(a).

Second, suppose the promisor, upon encountering claimed impracticability, refuses to continue performance. If the court determines that performance was excused, a traditional statement of the form of relief goes something like this. The promisor is discharged from the unexecuted portion of the contract. Neither party can recover damages for breach of contract. If there has been some part performance prior to discharge, either party can recover at the contract rate for a divisible or severable part of that performance. If part performance is not divisible, either party can recover in restitution for any benefit conferred on the other. But expenditures incurred in reliance on the contract, whether in preparation or part performance, are not recoverable unless they have met the "divisibility" or "benefit" tests.

The limited scope of this traditional position prompted parliament to enact the "Frustrated Contracts" Act in 1944. This statute, which is reprinted below,* gave limited protection to the pre-discharge reliance

* The Law Reform (Frustrated Contracts), Act 1943 (6 & 7 Geo. 6 c. 40)

1.   Adjustment of rights and liabilities of parties to frustrated contracts

(1) Where a contract governed by English law has become impossible of performance or been otherwise frustrated, and the parties thereto have for that reason been discharged from the further performance of the contract, the following provisions of this section shall, subject to the provisions of section two of this Act, have effect in relation thereto.

(2) All sums paid or payable to any party in pursuance of the contract before the time when the parties were so discharged (in this Act referred to as "the time of discharge") shall, in the case of sums so paid, be recoverable from him as money received by him for the use of the party by whom the sums were paid, and, in the case of sums so payable, cease to be so payable:

Provided that, if the party to whom the sums were so paid or payable incurred expenses before the time of discharge in, or for the purpose of, the performance of the contract, the court may, if it considers it just to do so having regard to all the circumstances of the case, allow him to retain or, as the case may be, recover the whole or any part of the sums so paid or payable, not being an amount in excess of the expenses so incurred.

(3) Where any party to the contract has, by reason of anything done by any other party thereto in, or for the purpose of, the performance of the contract, obtained a valuable benefit (other than a payment of money to which the last foregoing subsection applies) before the time of discharge, there shall be recoverable from him by the said other party such sum (if any), not exceeding the value of the said benefit to the party obtaining it, as the court considers just, having regard to all the circumstances of the case and, in particular,—

See Comment, *Restitutionary Principles and the Frustrated Con-* of 1944, 4 Auckland L.Rev. 56 (1980).

der solution is proposed in Section 272 of Restatement (Second). (1) states the classic view. Paraphrasing, in "any case" where impracticability or frustration of purpose is justified, "either have a claim for relief including restitution" under the rules Section 240, dealing with "divisible" contracts, and Section 377, with restitution in cases of impracticability. There is not much change here. Subsection (2), however, provides:

> In any case governed by the rules stated in this Chapter, if those rules together with the rules stated in Chapter 16 will not avoid injustice, the court may grant relief on such terms as justice requires including protection of the parties' reliance interests.

Thus, if the contract is discharged because of impracticability, the court, in the interest of justice, may supply a term to protect the reliance interest regardless of whether the contract was properly divisible or whether the other party has benefited from the part-performance. An American court following the Restatement (Second), therefore, would have far more flexibility than an English court under the Frustrated Contracts Act to "mop up" after the discharge.

In *ALCOA*, however, the court imposed a price adjustment as a form of "equitable" reformation rather than to discharge the contract as a response to the conclusion that ALCOA was entitled to "some relief" from commercial impracticability. The court, in effect, deleted the original cost escalation clause and filled the "gap" with a new clause intended to respond to the changed circumstances. The parties did not agree to this move and there was no "equitable adjustment" clause in the contract beyond the escalation provision which had failed its intended purpose. The criticisms of this remedy have ranged from the pious assertion that it is an unprecedented and improper exercise of judicial power to "make" a contract for the parties to the more practical concern about the feasibility of a court undertaking to provide a realistic pricing mechanism in a complex case where the parties have been unable or unwilling to agree. See Dawson, *Judicial Revision of Frustrated Contracts,* 1982 Jurid.Rev. 86, 101–05. On the other hand, the case has been applauded as a recognition of the realities of long-term contracts and as responsive to the dilemmas posed by

(a) the amount of any expenses incurred before the time of discharge by the benefited party in, or for the purpose of, the performance of the contract, including any sums paid or payable by him to any other party in pursuance of the contract and retained or recoverable by that party under the last foregoing subsection, and

(b) the effect, in relation to the said benefit, of the circumstances giving rise to the frustration of the contract.

(4) In estimating, for the purposes of the foregoing provisions of this section, the amount of any expenses incurred by any party to the contract, the court may, without prejudice to the generality of the said provisions, include such sum as appears to be reasonable in respect of overhead expenses and in respect of any work or services performed personally by the said party.

the either-or approach of the common law—either the contract is discharged or it is not. In addition, the case is seen as a healthy move toward the legal requirement of cooperation rather than competition where unanticipated events produce gains and losses that have not been "paid for" in the bargaining process. See, e.g., Richard E. Speidel, *Court-Imposed Price Adjustments Under Long-Term Supply Contracts,* 76 Nw.L.Rev. 369 (1981). Depending on your point of view, *ALCOA* is either the golden herald of the "new spirit of contract" see McGinnis v. Cayton, 173 W.Va. 102, 312 S.E.2d 765, 770 (1984) (concurring opinion of Harshbarger, J.) or another dark cloud confirming the "death" of contract.

Could a court find support for the imposed price adjustment in Restatement (Second) § 272(2)? The seeds may be there. Comment c states that in "some instances" the "just solution is to 'sever' the agreement and require that some unexecuted part of it be performed on both sides, rather than to relieve both parties of all of their duties." So far, this is ALCOA. The Comment also states that the question is "whether the court can salvage a part of the agreement that is still executory on both sides" and to supply a term which is "reasonable in the circumstances." Again, this is ALCOA. But Section 272(2) was drafted before ALCOA was decided and the illustrations do not clearly support the excision by the court of an existing contract term and the substitution of a more reasonable one.* But, as Professor Young has observed, Section 272 may be one of the most important changes in Restatement (Second). See William Young, *Half–Measures,* 81 Colum.L.Rev. 19 (1981). See also, Jeffrey L. Harrison, *A Case for Loss Sharing,* 56 S.Cal.L.Rev. 573 (1983).

---

* See Freidco of Wilmington, Del., Ltd. v. Farmers Bank, etc., 529 F.Supp. 822, 830, n. 9 (D.Del.1981), where the court conceded that if commercial impracticability were established, the reformation remedy would be proper. Citing ALCOA and Restatement (Second) § 272, the court stated that "reformation serves the purpose of filling a gap in the parties' agreement." But see Helms Const. & Development Co. v. State, etc., 97 Nev. 500, 634 P.2d 1224, 1225–26 (1981), where the court concluded that reformation for mutual mistake was limited to a party "seeking to alter a written instrument which, because of mutual mistake of fact, fails to conform to the parties' previous understanding or agreement."

CHAPTER SEVEN

BREACH OF CONTRACT AND PERMISSIBLE REMEDIAL RESPONSES

SECTION 1. RIGHT TO SUSPEND PERFORMANCE OR CANCEL UPON PROSPECTIVE INABILITY OR BREACH

A promisor commits a "breach" of contract when he or she fails without justification to perform when a promised performance is due. This breach includes the failure to perform when due and the tender of a non-conforming performance.

If the promisee has fully performed the agreed exchange, the remedy for breach is limited to an action for damages or specific performance. If the promisee still has duties to perform under the agreed exchange, the breach, if material, may also discharge those remaining duties. Thus, for a "material" breach by the promisor, the promisee has both affirmative (sue for damages for total breach) and defensive (cancel the contract) remedies. These general principles are elaborated in Sections 235–249 of Restatement (Second) and form a backdrop for our extended discussion of risk allocation in contract performance in Chapter Six. See also Farnsworth, Contracts Ch. 8.

Another type of breach occurs when a promisor, by words or conduct, repudiates a performance not yet due under the agreed exchange. If both parties still have obligations under the contract and the promisor's repudiation is of a material part of the agreed exchange and the repudiation has not been effectively nullified by a retraction or otherwise, the promisee, again, has both affirmative and defensive remedies and these remedies can be invoked *before* the time set for performance. See, in general, Restatement (Second) §§ 250–57, dealing with the effect of "Prospective Non-Performance." See Eric Andersen, *A New Look at Material Breach in the Law of Contracts*, 21 U.C. Davis L. Rev. 1073 (1988).

A final type of breach occurs when a promisor violates the "duty" of good faith and fair dealing by preventing or hindering the performance of the other party or by failing to cooperate in performing the agreed exchange. See Chapter Six, Section Two, supra.

Note that it is recognized that when the circumstances or the promisor's words or conduct create doubt whether the performance will be forthcoming as agreed but do not amount to a breach, the promisee may still have some protection. In the proper circumstances, the promisee may suspend performance and "demand adequate assurance" from the promisor. If assurance of due performance is not forthcoming, the promisee may treat it as a repudiation and resort to the usual affirmative and defensive remedies. See UCC 2–609. Even if the promisor has breached, the promisee may decide just to suspend performance, reserving any claims for damages, and seek to resolve the dispute by agreement. If so, this action is justified and increases the chance that the dispute can be resolved and the bargain preserved.

In this section, we will look more closely at the content of breach of contract, particularly "prospective non-performance." The right to suspend performance or cancel might be called the promisee's defensive remedies. A promisee's right to a promisor's performance is protected by the offensive right to seek monetary damages (or specific performance), but, as discussed in Chapter 6(2), is also protected by the defensive right of the promisee to withhold her own performance. Subsequent sections will examine the promisee's offensive remedies, damages and specific performance. But here we explore the contours of the defensive right of a promisee when a promissor breaches or anticipatorially repudiates an agreement.

The promisee's duty to perform her side of the contract is normally conditioned on the promissor not committing a material breach. So that if a promissor materially breaches, the promisee is entitled to withhold her own performance.

But a major theme of this section is that exercising your defensive rights is often fraught with uncertainty. If a promisee suspends her performance and a court subsequently determines that the other side did not materially breach the contract, then the promisee's suspension of performance would itself be deemed to be a breach—subjecting the promisee to liability for monetary damages. See generally Celia R. Taylor, *Self-Help in Contract Law: An Exploration and Proposal*, 33 Wake F. L. Rev. 839 (1998).

Hochster v. De La Tour

Queen's Bench, 1853.
2 E. & B. 678, 118 Eng.Rep. 922.

* * * On the trial, before Erle, J., at the London sittings in last Easter Term, it appeared that plaintiff was a courier, who, in April, 1852, was engaged by defendant to accompany him on a tour, to commence on June 1st, 1852, on the terms mentioned in the declaration. On May 11th, 1852, defendant wrote to plaintiff that he had changed his mind, and declined his services. He refused to make him any compensation. The action was commenced on May 22d. The plaintiff, between the commencement of the action and June 1st, obtained an engagement with Lord Ashburton, on equally good terms, but not commencing till July 4th. The defendant's counsel objected that there could be no breach of the contract before June 1st. The learned judge was of a contrary opinion, but reserved leave to enter a non-suit on this objection. The other questions were left to the jury, who found for plaintiff.

* * *

■ LORD CAMPBELL, C.J. On this motion in arrest of judgment, the question arises, whether if there be an agreement between A and B whereby B engages to employ A on and from a future day for a given period of time, to travel with him into a foreign country as a courier, and to start with him in that capacity on that day, A being to receive a monthly salary during the continuance of such service, B may, before the day, refuse to perform the agreement and break and renounce it, so as to entitle A before the day to commence an action against B to recover damages for breach of the agreement; A having been ready and willing to perform it, till it was broken and renounced by B. The defendant's counsel very powerfully contended that, if the plaintiff was not contented to dissolve the contract, and to abandon all remedy upon it, he was bound to remain ready and willing to perform it till the day when the actual employment as courier in the service of the defendant was to begin; and that there could be no breach of the agreement, before that day, to give a right of action. But it cannot be laid down as a universal rule that, where by agreement an act is to be done on a future day, no action can be brought for a breach of the agreement till the day for doing the act has arrived. If a man promises to marry a woman on a future day, and before that day marries another woman, he is instantly liable to an action for breach of promise of marriage; Short v. Stone, 8 Q.B. 358. If a man contracts to execute a lease on and from a future day for a certain term, and, before that day, executes a lease to another for the same term, he may be immediately sued for breaking the contract. Ford v. Tiley, 6 B. & C. 325. So, if a man contracts to sell and deliver specific goods on a future day, and before the day he sells and delivers them to another, he is immediately liable to an action at the suit of the person with whom he first contracted to sell and deliver them. Bowdell v. Parsons, 10 East, 359. One reason alleged in support of such an action is, that the defendant has, before the day, rendered it impossible for him to perform the contract at the day; but this does not necessarily follow; for, prior to the day fixed for doing the act, the first wife may have died, a surrender of the lease executed might be obtained, and the defendant might have repurchased the goods so as to be in a situation to sell and deliver them to the plaintiff. Another reason may be that, where there is a contract to do an act on a future day, there is a relation constituted between the parties in the meantime by the contract, and that they impliedly promise that in the meantime neither will do anything to the prejudice of the other inconsistent with that relation. As an example, a man and woman engaged to marry are affianced to one another during the period between the time of the engagement and the celebration of the marriage. In this very case, of traveller and courier, from the day of the hiring till the day when the employment was to begin, they were engaged to each other; and it seems to be a breach of an implied contract if either of them renounces the engagement. This reasoning seems in accordance with the unanimous decisions of the Exchequer Chamber in Elderton v. Emmens, 6 C.B. 160, which we have followed in subsequent cases in this court. The declaration in the present case, in alleging a breach, states a great deal more than a passing intention on the part of the defendant which he may repent of, and could only be proved by evidence that he had utterly renounced the contract, or done some act which rendered it impossible for him to perform it. If the plaintiff has no remedy for breach of contract unless he treats the contract as in force, and acts upon it down to the 1st June, 1852, it follows that, till then, he must enter into no employment which will interfere with his promise "to start with the defendant on such travels on the day and year," and that he must then be properly equipped in all respects as a courier for a three months' tour on the continent of Europe. But it is surely much more rational, and more for the benefit of both parties, that, after the renunciation of the agreement by the defendant, the plaintiff should be at liberty to consider himself absolved from any future performance of it, retaining his right to sue for any damage he has suffered from the breach of it. Thus, instead of remaining idle and laying out money in preparations which must be useless, he is at liberty to seek service under another employer, which would go in mitigation of the damages to which he would otherwise be entitled for a breach of the contract. It seems strange that the defendant, after renouncing the contract, and absolutely declaring that he will never act under it, should be permitted to object that faith is given to his assertion, and that an opportunity is not left to him of changing his mind. If the plaintiff is barred of any remedy by entering into an engagement inconsistent with starting as a courier with the defendant on the 1st June, he is prejudiced by putting faith in the defendant's assertion: and it would be more consistent with principle, if the defendant were precluded from saying that he had not broken the contract when he declared that he entirely renounced it. Suppose that the defendant, at the time of his renunciation, had embarked on a voyage for Australia, so as to render it physically impossible for him to employ the plaintiff as a courier on the continent of Europe in the months of June, July and August 1852: according to decided cases, the action might have been brought before the 1st June; but the renunciation may have been founded on other facts, to be given in evidence, which would equally have rendered the defendant's performance of the contract impossible. The man who wrongfully renounces a contract into which he has deliberately entered cannot justly complain if he is immediately sued for a compensation in damages by the man whom he has injured: and it seems reasonable to allow an option to the injured party, either to sue immediately, or to wait till the time when the act was to be done, still holding it as prospectively binding for the exercise of this option, which may be advantageous to the innocent party, and cannot be prejudicial to the wrongdoer. An argument against the action before the 1st of June is urged from the difficulty of calculating the damages: but this argument is equally strong against an action before the 1st of September, when the three months would expire. In either case, the jury in assessing the damages would be justified in looking to all that had happened, or was likely to happen, to increase or mitigate the loss of the plaintiff down to the day of trial. We do not find any decision contrary to the view we are taking of this case. * * *

If it should be held that, upon a contract to do an act on a future day, a renunciation of the contract by one party dispenses with a condition to be performed in the meantime by the other, there seems no reason for requiring that other to wait till the day arrives before seeking his remedy by action: and the only ground on which the condition can be dispensed with seems to be, that the renunciation may be treated as a breach of the contract.

Upon the whole, we think that the declaration in this case is sufficient. It gives us great satisfaction to reflect that, the question being on the record, our opinion may be reviewed in a Court of Error. In the meantime we must give judgment for the plaintiff.

Judgment for plaintiff.

NOTES

(1) What was the underlying theory of the court in *Hochster v. De La Tour?* Accepting that theory, was it necessary to give the plaintiff both an excuse for non-performance and an immediate cause of action for damages? Professor Williston, writing over a century ago, thought not. See Samuel Williston, *Repudiation of Contracts,* 14 Harv.L.Rev. 421, 432–441 (1901).

Contemporary courts, however, follow the reasoning of the "seminal case" of Hochster v. De la Tour:

> The principle of anticipatory breach of contract is supported by sound policy considerations. Once a party has indicated an unequivocal intent to forego performance of his obligations under a contract, there is little to be gained by requiring a party who will be injured to await the actual breach before commencing suit, with the attendant risk of faded memories and unavailable witnesses. However, it is clear that there must be a definite and final communication of the intention to forego performance before the anticipated breach may be the subject of legal action. . . . Mere expression of difficulty in tendering the required performance, for example, is not tantamount to renunciation of the contract.

Rachmani Corp. v. 9 East 96th Street Apartment Corp., 211 A.D.2d 262, 629 N.Y.S.2d 382, 385 (N.Y.A.D.1995). See also Keith A. Rowley, *A Brief History of Anticipatory Repudiation in American Common Law*, 69 U. Cin. L. Rev. 505 (2001).

(2) *When a Statement or an Act is a Repudiation.* Section 250 of Restatement (Second) provides:

> A repudiation is (a) a statement by the obligor to the obligee indicating that the obligor will commit a breach that would of itself give the obligee a claim for damages for total breach under § 243, or (b) a voluntary affirmative act which renders the obligor unable or apparently unable to perform without such a breach.

Comment a recites the consequences of repudiation:

"A statement by a party to the other that he will not or cannot perform without a breach, or a voluntary affirmative act which renders him unable or apparently unable to perform without a breach may impair the value of the contract to the other party. It may have several consequences under this Restatement. If it accompanies a breach by non-performance that would otherwise give rise to only a claim for damages for partial breach, it may give rise to a claim for damages for total breach instead. . . . Even if it occurs before any breach by non-performance, it may give rise to a claim for damages for total breach . . . , discharge the other party's duties . . ., or excuse the non-occurrence of a condition. . . ."

(3) *Repudiation in the Uniform Commercial Code.* The 2002 Official Text of Article 2 of the UCC contains no comprehensive definition of repudiation. Rather, it carefully sets out the options available to the aggrieved party when the other "repudiates the contract with respect to a performance not yet due the loss of which will substantially impair the value of the contract to the other. . . ." UCC 2–610. One option is to "suspend his own performance" and "for a commercially reasonable time await performance by the repudiating party." UCC 2–610(a) & (c). This has the advantage of preserving the contract for a possible settlement and the disadvantage that the repudiating party may retract the repudiation before "the aggrieved party has * * * canceled or materially changed his position or otherwise indicated that he considers the repudiation final." UCC 2–611(1). Another option, consistent with *Hochster v. De La Tour,* is to suspend performance and "resort to any remedy for breach" under UCC 2–703 or 2–711.

To illustrate, suppose that the seller has repudiated a promise to deliver goods on December 1. The date of the repudiation was November 18. The buyer had, under the contract, paid one-half of the price on November 15 and agreed to pay the balance upon delivery. Under UCC 2–711, the buyer may "where the seller * * * repudiates * * * with respect to any goods involved * * * cancel and whether or not he has done so may in addition to recovering so much of the price as has been paid" seek damages under UCC 2–712 or 2–713. Under UCC 2–106(4), cancellation occurs "when either party puts an end to the contract for breach by the other." The effect of cancellation is to discharge "all obligations which are still executory on both sides" except that the cancelling party retains "any right based on prior breach or performance" and "any remedy for breach of the whole contract or any unperformed balance." UCC 2–106(3) & (4). See UCC 1–107 and 2–720. The decision to cancel may be manifested either by notice to the breaching party or conduct inconsistent with continuing the contract. See National Cash Register Co. v. UNARCO Industries, Inc., 490 F.2d 285 (7th Cir.1974) (written notice); Goldstein v. Stainless Processing Co., 465 F.2d 392 (7th Cir.1972).

Revised UCC 2–610(2) provides: "Repudiation includes language that a reasonable party would interpret to mean that the other party will not or cannot make a performance still due under the contract or voluntary affirmative conduct that would appear to a reasonable party to make a future performance by the other party impossible." Does this help?

(4) *Retraction of Repudiation.* Under a contract with Plaintiff to supply natural gas, Defendant agreed to purchase its requirements and a specified minimum amount at $.30 per unit. Plaintiff repudiated the contract but

Defendant insisted the contract was in effect and demanded performance. Thereafter, Plaintiff offered to supply some gas at $.35 per unit. Defendant, still insisting that the original contract was in effect, accepted gas but refused to pay more than $.30 per unit. Finally, Plaintiff stopped all deliveries of gas.

At this time, Defendant was 181,982 units short on the minimum amount of gas to be purchased under the original agreement. Plaintiff dropped its claim for $.05 per unit for gas supplied after the repudiation and sued for damages for breach of the agreement to purchase a minimum amount of gas. Defendant, for the first time, asserted that the contract was cancelled when Plaintiff repudiated.

Held, the district court's judgment for Plaintiff is affirmed. At all times subsequent to the repudiation and before the trial, Defendant took the position that the contract was in effect and insisted that the Plaintiff perform under it. Thus, the parties agreed neither to rescind nor to modify the repudiated contract. Even though Plaintiff did not, in light of Defendant's election to treat the contract in force, alter its position in reliance, the court held that Defendant's election to preserve the contract was final and that "the party who has made such declaration can not alter his position even though the party who was in default has not acted in reliance thereon." Neither party was misled and Plaintiff, in effect, retracted the repudiation when at the trial it withdrew its demand for the higher price and limited the claim to damages for breach of the minimum obligation.

"Inasmuch as defendant had not prior to that time brought action for nonperformance but had insisted upon performance and had not materially changed its position in reliance on the attempted cancellation, the act of plaintiff in attempting to repudiate was 'nullified.'" Kentucky Natural Gas Corp. v. Indiana Gas & Chemical Corp., 129 F.2d 17 (7th Cir.1942). See Lowe v. Beaty, 145 Vt. 215, 485 A.2d 1255 (1984) (retraction effective); UCC 2–611 (1990); Restatement (Second) § 256 (effect of retraction).

Taylor v. Johnston

Supreme Court of California, 1975.
15 Cal.3d 130, 123 Cal.Rptr. 641, 539 P.2d 425.

■ Sullivan, Justice. In this action for damages for breach of contract defendants Elizabeth and Ellwood Johnston, individually and as copartners doing business as Old English Rancho, appeal from a judgment entered after a non-jury trial in favor of plaintiff H.B. Taylor and against them in the amount of $132,778.05 and costs.

Plaintiff was engaged in the business of owning, breeding, raising and racing thoroughbred horses in Los Angeles County. Defendants were engaged in a similar business, and operated a horse farm in Ontario, California, where they furnished stallion stud services. In January 1965 plaintiff sought to breed his two thoroughbred mares, Sunday Slippers and Sandy Fork to defendants' stallion Fleet Nasrullah. To that end, on January 19 plaintiff and defendants entered into two separate written contracts—one pertaining to Sunday Slippers and the other to Sandy Fork. Except for the mare involved the contracts were identical. We set forth in the margin the contract covering Sunday Slippers.[1]

The contract provided that Fleet Nasrullah was to perform breeding services upon the respective mares in the year 1966 for a fee of $3,500, payable on or before September 1, 1966. If the stud fee was paid in full and the mares failed to produce a live foal (one that stands and nurses without assistance) from the breeding a return breeding would be provided the following year without additional fee.

On October 4, 1965, defendants sold Fleet Nasrullah to Dr. A.G. Pessin and Leslie Combs II for $1,000,000 cash and shipped the stallion to Kentucky. Subsequently Combs and Pessin syndicated the sire by selling various individuals 36 or 38 shares, each share entitling the holder to breed one mare each season to Fleet Nasrullah. Combs and Pessin each reserved three shares.

On the same day defendants wrote to plaintiff advising the latter of the sale and that he was "released" from his "reservations" for Fleet Nasrullah. Unable to reach defendants by telephone, plaintiff had his attorney write to them on October 8, 1965, insisting on performance of the contracts. Receiving no answer, plaintiff's attorney on October 19, wrote a second letter threatening suit. On October 27, defendants advised plaintiff by letter that arrangements had been made to breed the two mares to Fleet Nasrullah in Kentucky. However, plaintiff later learned that the mares could not be boarded at Spendthrift Farm where Fleet Nasrullah was standing stud and accordingly arranged with Clinton Frazier of Elmhurst Farm to board the mares and take care of the breeding.

In January 1966 plaintiff shipped Sunday Slippers and Sandy Fork to Elmhurst Farm. At that time, however, both mares were in foal and could not be bred, since this can occur only during the five-day period in which

---

1. "Original

IMPORTANT

<u>PLEASE SIGN ORIGINAL AND RETURN AS QUICKLY AS POSSIBLE RETAINING DUPLICATE FOR YOUR OWN FILE.</u>

January 8, 1965

"OLD ENGLISH RANCHO
Route 1, Box 224–A
Ontario, California 91761

"Gentlemen:
   I hereby confirm my reservation for one services to the stallion FLEET NASRULLAH for the year 1966.
"TERMS: $3,500.00—GUARANTEE LIVE FOAL.
"FEE is due and payable on or before Sept. 1, 1966.
"IF stud fee is paid in full, and mare fails to produce a live foal (one that stands and nurses without assistance) from this breeding, a

return breeding the following year to said mare will be granted at no additional stallion fee.
"FEE is due and payable prior to sale of mare or prior to her departure from the state. If mare is sold or leaves the state, no return breeding will be granted.
"STUD CERTIFICATE to be given in exchange for fees paid.
"VETERINARIAN CERTIFICATE due in lieu of payment if mare is barren.
"I hereby agree that OLD ENGLISH RANCHO shall in no way be held responsible for accident of any kind or disease.
"Mare: SUNDAY SLIP-   Mr. H.B. Taylor
   PERS   112 North Evergreen
                                                  Street
Roan filly 1959

MOOLAH BUX-MAOLI-   Burbank, California
   ORMESBY   91505

"(Veterinary certificate must accompany all barren mares.)

"Stakes winner of $64,000.00
   last raced in 1962   /s/Mr. H.B. Taylor"

[Margin notes:]
If they didn't get pregnant + have live Foal → breed next year w/ no Fee

Fleet Sold but Δ Claimed they Could still breed

TT shipped both Mares but they Couldn't get pregnant (not in heat) they are in heat. The first heat period normally occurs nine days, and the second heat period thirty days, after foaling. Succeeding heat periods occur every 21 days.

On April 17, 1966, Sunday Slippers foaled and Frazier immediately notified Dr. Pessin. The latter assured Frazier that he would make the necessary arrangements to breed the mare to Fleet Nasrullah. On April 26, the ninth day after the foaling, Frazier, upon further inquiry, was told by Dr. Pessin to contact Mrs. Judy who had charge of booking the breedings and had handled these matters with Frazier in the past. Mrs. Judy, however, informed Frazier that the stallion was booked for that day but would be available on any day not booked by a shareholder. She indicated that she was acting under instructions but suggested that he keep in touch with her while the mare was in heat.

Sunday Slippers came into heat on May 13, 1966. Frazier telephoned Mrs. Judy and attempted to book the breeding for May 16. She informed him that Fleet Nasrullah had been reserved by one of the shareholders for that day, but that Frazier should keep in touch with her in the event the reservation was cancelled. On May 14 and May 15 Frazier tried again but without success; on the latter date, Sunday Slippers went out of heat.

On June 4, the mare went into heat again. Frazier again tried to book a reservation with Fleet Nasrullah but was told that all dates during the heat period had been already booked. He made no further efforts but on June 7, on plaintiff's instructions, bred Sunday Slippers to a Kentucky Derby winner named Chateaugay for a stud fee of $10,000.

Sandy Fork, plaintiff's other mare awaiting the stud services of Fleet Nasrullah, foaled on June 5, 1966. Frazier telephoned Mrs. Judy the next day and received a booking to breed the mare on June 14, the ninth day after foaling. On June 13, 1966, however, she cancelled the reservation because of the prior claim of a shareholder. Frazier made no further attempts and on June 14 bred Sandy Fork to Chateaugay.

Shortly after their breeding, it was discovered that both mares were pregnant with twins. In thoroughbred racing twins are considered undesirable since they endanger the mare and are themselves seldom valuable for racing. Both mares were therefore aborted. However, plaintiff was not required to pay the $20,000 stud fees for Chateaugay's services because neither mare delivered a live foal.

The instant action for breach of contract proceeded to trial on plaintiff's fourth amended complaint, which alleged two causes of action, the first for breach of the two written contracts, the second for breach of an oral agreement. Defendants cross-complained for the stud fees. The court found the facts to be substantially as stated above and further found and concluded that by selling Fleet Nasrullah defendants had "put it out of their power to perform properly their contracts," that the conduct of defendants and their agents Dr. Pessin and Mrs. Judy up to and including June 13, 1966, constituted a breach and plaintiff "was then justified in treating it as a breach and repudiation of their contractual obligations to him," and that defendants unjustifiably breached the contracts but plaintiff did not. The court awarded plaintiff damages for defendants' breach in the sum of $103,122.50 ($99,800 net damage directly sustained plus $3,322.50 for reasonable costs and expenses for mitigation of damages). "Because of defendants' wholly unwarranted, high-handed, and oppressive breach of their contractual obligation to plaintiff, the plaintiff is entitled to recover from the defendants pre-judgment interest at the rate of 7% per annum on the sum of $99,800.00 from August 1, 1968. . . ." It was concluded that defendants should take nothing on their cross-complaint. Judgment was entered accordingly. This appeal followed.

Appeal by Δ

Defendants' main attack on the judgment is two-pronged. They contend: First, that they did not at any time repudiate the contracts; and second, that they did not otherwise breach the contracts because performance was made impossible by plaintiff's own actions. To put it another way, defendants argue in effect that the finding that they breached the contracts is without any support in the evidence. Essentially they take the position that on the uncontradicted evidence in the record, as a matter of law there was neither anticipatory nor actual breach. As will appear, we conclude that the trial court's decision was based solely on findings of anticipatory breach and that we must determine whether such decision is supported by the evidence.

Δ Argues
- no time to repudiate
- π made perf. imposs.

Nevertheless both aspects of defendants' argument require us at the outset to examine the specifications for performance contained in the contracts. (See fn. 1, ante). We note that the reservation for "one services" for Fleet Nasrullah was "for the year 1966." As the evidence showed, a breeding is biologically possible throughout the calendar year, since mares regularly come into heat every 21 days, unless they are pregnant. The contracts therefore appear to contemplate breeding with Fleet Nasrullah at any time during the calendar year 1966. The trial court made no finding as to the time of performance called for by the contracts. There was testimony to the effect that by custom in the thoroughbred racing business the breeding is consummated in a "breeding season" which normally extends from January until early July, although some breeding continues through August. It is possible that the parties intended that the mares be bred to Fleet Nasrullah during the 1966 breeding season rather than the calendar year 1966.

Breeding could occur any time in 1966
OR
Breeding Season 1/66 - 7/66

However, in our view, it is immaterial whether the contract phrase "for the year 1966" is taken to mean the above breeding season or the full calendar year since in either event the contract period had not expired by June 7 and June 14, 1966, the dates on which Sunday Slippers and Sandy Fork respectively were bred to Chateaugay and by which time, according to the findings . . . defendants had repudiated the contracts. There can be no *actual* breach of a contract until the time specified therein for performance has arrived. . . . Although there may be a *breach by anticipatory repudiation*; "[b]y its very name an essential element of a true anticipatory breach of a contract is that the repudiation by the promisor occur before his performance is due under the contract." . . . In the instant case, because under either of the above interpretations the time for performance had not yet arrived, defendants' breach as found by the trial court was of necessity an anticipatory breach and must be analyzed in accordance with the principles governing such type of breach. To these principles we now direct our attention.

Anticipatory breach occurs when one of the parties to a bilateral contract repudiates the contract. The repudiation may be express or implied. An express repudiation is a clear, positive, unequivocal refusal to perform ... ; an implied repudiation results from conduct where the promisor puts it out of his power to perform so as to make substantial performance of his promise impossible ...

When a promisor repudiates a contract, the injured party faces an election of remedies: he can treat the repudiation as an anticipatory breach and immediately seek damages for breach of contract, thereby terminating the contractual relation between the parties, or he can treat the repudiation as an empty threat, wait until the time for performance arrives and exercise his remedies for actual breach if a breach does in fact occur at such time. ... However, if the injured party disregards the repudiation and treats the contract as still in force, and the repudiation is retracted prior to the time of performance, then the repudiation is nullified and the injured party is left with his remedies, if any, invocable at the time of performance. ...

As we have pointed out, the trial court found that the whole course of conduct of defendants and their agents Dr. Pessin and Mrs. Judy from the time of the sale of Fleet Nasrullah up to and including June 13, 1966, amounted to a repudiation which plaintiff was justified in treating as an anticipatory breach. ... However, when the principles of law governing repudiation just described are applied to the facts constituting this course of conduct as found by the trial court, it is manifest that such conduct cannot be treated as an undifferentiated continuum amounting to a single repudiation but must be divided into two separate repudiations.

First, defendants clearly repudiated the contracts when, after selling Fleet Nasrullah and shipping him to Kentucky, they informed plaintiff "[y]ou are, therefore, released from your reservations made to the stallion." However, the trial court additionally found that "[p]laintiff did not wish to be 'released' from his 'reservations' ... insist[ed] on performance of the stud service agreements ... [and] threaten[ed] litigation if the contracts were not honored by defendants ... " Accordingly defendants arranged for performance of the contracts by making Fleet Nasrullah available for stud service to plaintiff in Kentucky through their agents Dr. Pessin and Mrs. Judy. Plaintiff elected to treat the contracts as in force and shipped the mares to Kentucky to effect the desired performance. The foregoing facts lead us to conclude that the subsequent arrangements by defendants to make Fleet Nasrullah available to service plaintiff's mares in Kentucky constituted a retraction of the repudiation. Since at this time plaintiff had not elected to treat the repudiation as an anticipatory breach and in fact had shipped the mares to Kentucky in reliance on defendants' arrangements, this retraction nullified the repudiation. Thus, plaintiff was then left with his remedies that might arise at the time of performance.

The trial court found that after the mares had arrived in Kentucky, had delivered the foals they were then carrying and were ready for servicing by Fleet Nasrullah, plaintiff was justified in concluding from the conduct of defendants, their agent Dr. Pessin, and their subagent Mrs. Judy, that "defendants were just giving him the runaround and had no intention of performing their contract in the manner required by its terms" and in treating such conduct "as a breach and repudiation of their contractual obligation to him." . . . Since, as we have explained, defendants retracted their original repudiation, this subsequent conduct amounts to a finding of a second repudiation.

There is no evidence in the record that defendants or their agents Dr. Pessin and Mrs. Judy ever stated that Sunday Slippers and Sandy Fork would not be serviced by Fleet Nasrullah during the 1966 breeding season or that they ever refused to perform. Frazier, plaintiff's agent who made arrangements for the breeding of the mares admitted that they had never made such a statement to him. Accordingly, there was no *express* repudiation or unequivocal refusal to perform. . . .

The trial court's finding of repudiation, expressly based on the "conduct of the defendants" and their agents suggests that the court found an implied repudiation. However, there is no implied repudiation, i.e., by conduct equivalent to an unequivocal refusal to perform, unless "the promisor *puts it out of his power to perform*." . . . Once the mares arrived in Kentucky, defendants had the power to perform the contracts; Fleet Nasrullah could breed with the mares. No subsequent conduct occurred to render this performance impossible. Although plaintiff was subordinated to the shareholders with respect to the priority of reserving a breeding time with Fleet Nasrullah, there is no evidence in the record that this subordination of reservation rights rendered performance impossible. Rather it acted to postpone the time of performance, which still remained within the limits prescribed by the contracts. It rendered performance more difficult to achieve; it may even have cast doubt upon the eventual accomplishment of performance; it did not render performance impossible.[2]

Because there was no repudiation, express or implied, there was no anticipatory breach. Plaintiff contends that defendants' conduct, as found by the trial court, indicated that "defendants were just giving him the

---

2. Plaintiff suggests that this conduct, namely delaying plaintiff's breeding until a day not reserved by a shareholder, amounted to an anticipatory breach because Mrs. Judy inserted a condition to defendants' performance, which as the trial court found was not contemplated by the contracts. Assuming arguendo that this conduct might have amounted to a breach of contract by improperly delaying performance, at most it would have constituted only a partial breach—insufficiently material to terminate the contracts (see Rest.2d Contracts (Tent.Draft No. 8, 1973) §§ 262, 266, 268, 274). It did not constitute a repudiation of the contracts which was the sole basis of the trial court's decision since "[t]o justify the adverse party in treating the renunciation as a breach, the refusal to perform must be of the whole contract or of a covenant going to the whole consideration. . . ." (Atkinson v. District Bond Co., supra, 5 Cal.App.2d 738, 743.)

runaround and had no intention of performing their contract" and therefore that this conduct was the equivalent of an express and unequivocal refusal to perform. Plaintiff has not presented to the court any authority in California in support of his proposition that conduct which has not met the test for an implied repudiation, i.e. conduct which removed the power to perform, may nonetheless be held to amount to the equivalent of an express repudiation and thus constitute an anticipatory breach. Without addressing ourselves to the question whether some conduct could ever be found equal to an express repudiation, we hold that defendants' conduct in this case as a matter of law did not constitute an anticipatory breach.

To constitute an express repudiation, the promisor's statement, or in this case conduct, must amount to an unequivocal refusal to perform: "A mere declaration, however, of a party of an intention not to be bound will not of itself amount to a breach, so as to create an effectual renunciation of the contract; for one party cannot by any act or declaration destroy the binding force and efficacy of the contract. To justify the adverse party in treating the renunciation as a breach, the refusal to perform must be of the whole contract ... and must be distinct, unequivocal, and absolute." ...

To recapitulate, Sandy Fork was in foal in January 1966, the commencement of the 1966 breeding season, and remained so until June 5, 1966. Throughout this period Fleet Nasrullah could not perform his services as contracted due solely to the conduct of plaintiff in breeding Sandy Fork in 1965. Biologically the first opportunity to breed Sandy Fork was on June 14, 1966, nine days after foaling. Frazier telephoned Mrs. Judy on June 6, 1966, and received a booking with Fleet Nasrullah for June 14, 1966. On June 13 Mrs. Judy telephoned Frazier and informed him she would have to cancel Sandy Fork's reservation for the following day because one of the shareholders insisted on using that day. Mrs. Judy gave no indication whatsoever that she could not or would not breed Sandy Fork on any of the following days in that heat period or subsequent heat periods. Frazier made no further attempts to breed Sandy Fork with Fleet Nasrullah. Thus, plaintiff, who delayed the possibility of performance for five months, asserts that the delay of performance occasioned by defendants' cancellation of a reservation on the first day during the six-month period that plaintiff made performance possible amounts to an unequivocal refusal to perform, even though there was adequate opportunity for Fleet Nasrullah to perform within the period for performance specified in the contract and even though defendants never stated any intention not to perform. We conclude that as a matter of law this conduct did not amount to an unequivocal refusal to perform and therefore did not constitute an anticipatory breach of the contract covering Sandy Fork.

Sunday Slippers foaled on April 17, 1966, first came into heat on April 26 and then successively on May 13 and June 4, 1966. Mrs. Judy informed Frazier that she would breed Sunday Slippers on any day that one of the shareholders did not want to use the stallion. Frazier unsuccessfully sought to breed the mare on April 26, May 14, May 15 and June 4, 1966, Fleet Nasrullah being reserved on those dates. Mrs. Judy continued to assure

Frazier that the breeding would occur. Sunday Slippers was due to come into heat again twice during the breeding season: June 25 and July 16, 1966. At most this conduct amounts to delay of performance and a warning that performance might altogether be precluded if a shareholder were to desire Fleet Nasrullah's services on all the remaining days within the period specified for performance in which Sunday Slippers was in heat. We conclude that as a matter of law this conduct did not amount to an unequivocal refusal to perform and therefore did not constitute an anticipatory breach of the contract covering Sunday Slippers.

In sum, we hold that there is no evidence in the record supportive of the trial court's finding and conclusion that defendants repudiated and therefore committed an anticipatory breach of the contracts.

In view of the foregoing conclusion we need not consider defendants' remaining contentions.

The judgment is reversed.

NOTES

(1) In *Taylor,* the defendants never made a "statement" to the plaintiff "indicating that * * * (they) * * * will commit a breach that would of itself give the obligee a claim for damages for total breach. . . ." Restatement (Second) § 250(1). But were there "voluntary affirmative" acts which rendered the defendant "unable or apparently unable to perform" without a material breach? Section 250(2).

(2) Restatement (Second) § 251(1) provides that "where reasonable grounds arise to believe that the obligor will commit" a material breach, the "obligee may demand adequate assurance of due performance and may, if reasonable, suspend any performance for which he has not already received the agreed exchange until he receives such assurance." Section 251(2) then provides that the "obligee may treat as a repudiation the obligor's failure to provide within a reasonable time such assurance of due performance as is adequate in the circumstances of the particular case." Should the plaintiff have pursued this strategy in *Taylor?* See Arthur Rosett, *Partial, Qualified, and Equivocal Repudiation of Contract,* 81 Colum.L.Rev. 93, 106–107 (1981), who argues that § 251 should be available where equivocal behavior is not the equivalent of a refusal to perform.

Suppose the plaintiff had demanded adequate assurance and the defendant had replied "There is a chance that the stud will be available before the contract expires, but if a member claims that time you will not be entitled to those services." Would that be sufficient?

Suppose, upon a demand of adequate assurance, Ms. Taylor had said: "OK, we agree to breed Sandy Slippers the next time she is in heat regardless of claims by syndicated members but we cannot breed Sandy Forks." What should the plaintiff do now?

(3) *Use of Declaratory Judgment.* What options are available to parties who have honest but substantial disagreements about the meaning of their contract? Between the extremes of a negotiated settlement and a unilateral

termination with all of its risks, lies the possibility of a declaratory judgment. The Federal Declaratory Judgment Act, 28 U.S.C.A. § 2201 provides:

> In a case of actual controversy within its jurisdiction * * * any court of the United States, upon the filing of an appropriate pleading, may declare the rights and other legal relations of any interested party seeking such declaration, whether or not further relief is or could be sought. Any such declaration shall have the force and effect of a final judgment or decree and shall be reviewable as such.

If there is a genuine controversy, this form of relief is available to clarify and stabilize and to eliminate uncertainty as to the scope and content of existing or prospective rights. This includes the interpretation of contract rights so that a party need not risk liability for breach if he or she is wrong. The court has discretion to deny this remedy where, for example, the decree "would not terminate the uncertainty or controversy giving rise to the proceeding," Uniform Declaratory Judgment Act § 6, or where relief depends upon future hypothetical events.

PROBLEM: THE "SAFE HARBOR" DEFENSE

In the *Kaiser–Francis Oil* case, supra at 836, after deregulation and the market collapse, the pipeline (PGC) claimed that its performance was excused (1) under the *force majeure* clause and (2) because the gas produced did not meet the quality specification provision concerning allowable water vapor in the gas. The pipeline also proposed a contract amendment that would replace the take-or-pay arrangement with a system of flexible well-head prices that responded to changing market conditions. See 870 F.2d at 567. Consider the following questions:

(1) Suppose that after some discussion, Kaiser rejected PGC's offer to modify the contract and insisted upon performance under the take-or-pay provision. PGC came back with a counterproposal, more favorable to Kaiser, and stated: "We will not make the next payment unless you negotiate with us in good faith over this proposal." What is Kaiser's legal position? What would you advise Kaiser to do?

(2) Suppose, instead, that PGC filed a declaratory judgment action to have the court determine whether PGC was excused under either the *force majeure* clause or because the gas had too much water. Kaiser demanded that PGC continue to make payments during the course of the litigation, estimated to take twelve months. PGC responded that there was a "good faith" dispute over the interpretation of the contract, and that PGC would not make another payment until the dispute was finally resolved by the court. At that time, PGC would perform the contract under the court's interpretation. What is Kaiser's legal position? What would you advise Kaiser to do?

AMF, Inc. v. McDonald's Corp.

United States Court of Appeals, Seventh Circuit, 1976.
536 F.2d 1167.

■ CUMMINGS, CIRCUIT JUDGE. AMF, Incorporated, filed this case in the Southern District of New York in April 1972. It was transferred to the

Northern District of Illinois in May 1973. AMF seeks damages for the alleged wrongful cancellation and repudiation of McDonald's Corporation's ("McDonald's") orders for sixteen computerized cash registers for installation in restaurants owned by wholly-owned subsidiaries of McDonald's and for seven such registers ordered by licensees of McDonald's for their restaurants. In July 1972, McDonald's of Elk Grove, Inc. sued AMF to recover the $20,385.28 purchase price paid for a prototype computerized cash register and losses sustained as a result of failure of the equipment to function satisfactorily. Both cases were tried together during a fortnight in December 1974. A few months after the completion of the bench trial, the district court rendered a memorandum opinion and order in both cases in favor of each defendant. The only appeal is from the eight judgment orders dismissing AMF's complaints against McDonald's and the seven licensees. We affirm.

The district court's memorandum opinion and order are unreported. Our statement of the pertinent facts is culled from the 124 findings of fact contained therein or from the record itself.

In 1966, AMF began to market individual components of a completely automated restaurant system, including its model 72C computerized cash register involved here. The 72C cash register then consisted of a central computer, one to four input stations, each with a keyboard and cathode ray tube display, plus the necessary cables and controls.

In 1967, McDonald's representatives visited AMF's plant in Springdale, Connecticut, to view a working "breadboard" model 72C to decide whether to use it in McDonald's restaurant system. Later that year, it was agreed that a 72C should be placed in a McDonald restaurant for evaluation purposes.

In April 1968, a 72C unit accommodating six input stations was installed in McDonald's restaurant in Elk Grove, Illinois. This restaurant was a wholly-owned subsidiary of McDonald's and was its busiest restaurant. Besides functioning as a cash register, the 72C was intended to enable counter personnel to work faster and to assist in providing data for accounting reports and bookkeeping. McDonald's of Elk Grove, Inc. paid some $20,000 for this prototype register on January 3, 1969. AMF never gave McDonald's warranties governing reliability or performance standards for the prototype.

At a meeting in Chicago on August 29, 1968, McDonald's concluded to order sixteen 72C's for its company-owned restaurants and to cooperate with AMF to obtain additional orders from its licensees. In December 1968, AMF accepted McDonald's purchase orders for those sixteen 72C's. In late January 1969, AMF accepted seven additional orders for 72C's from McDonald's licensees for their restaurants. Under the contract for the sale of all the units, there was a warranty for parts and service. AMF proposed to deliver the first unit in February 1969, with installation of the remaining twenty-two units in the first half of 1969. However, AMF established a new delivery schedule in February 1969, providing for deliveries to commence at the end of July 1969 and to be completed in January 1970, assuming that the first test unit being built at AMF's Vandalia, Ohio, plant was built and satisfactorily tested by the end of July 1969. This was never accomplished.

During the operation of the prototype 72C at McDonald's Elk Grove restaurant, many problems resulted, requiring frequent service calls by AMF and others. Because of its poor performance, McDonald's had AMF remove the prototype unit from its Elk Grove restaurant in late April 1969.

At a March 18, 1969, meeting, McDonald's and AMF personnel met to discuss the performance of the Elk Grove prototype. AMF agreed to formulate a set of performance and reliability standards for the future 72C's including "the number of failures permitted at various degrees of seriousness, total permitted downtime, maximum service hours and cost." Pending mutual agreement on such standards, McDonald's personnel asked that production of the twenty-three units be held up and AMF agreed.

On May 1, 1969, AMF met with McDonald's personnel to provide them with performance and reliability standards. However, the parties never agreed upon such standards. At that time, AMF did not have a working machine and could not produce one within a reasonable time because its Vandalia, Ohio, personnel were too inexperienced. After the May 1st meeting, AMF concluded that McDonald's had cancelled all 72C orders. The reasons for the cancellation were the poor performance of the prototype, the lack of assurances that a workable machine was available and the unsatisfactory conditions at AMF's Vandalia, Ohio, plant where the twenty-three 72C's were to be built.

On July 29, 1969, McDonald's and AMF representatives met in New York. At this meeting it was mutually understood that the 72C orders were cancelled and that none would be delivered.

In its conclusions of law, the district court held that McDonald's and its licensees had entered into contracts for twenty-three 72C cash registers but that AMF was not able to perform its obligations under the contracts. ... Citing Section 2–610 of the Uniform Commercial Code ... and Comment 1 thereunder, the court concluded that on July 29, McDonald's justifiably repudiated the contracts to purchase all twenty-three 72C's.

Relying on Sections 2–609 and 2–610 of the Uniform Commercial Code ... §§ 2–609 and 2–610), the court decided that McDonald's was warranted in repudiating the contracts and therefore had a right to cancel the orders by virtue of Section 2–711 of the Uniform Commercial Code ...). Accordingly, judgment was entered for McDonald's.

The findings of fact adopted by the district court were a mixture of the court's own findings and findings proposed by the parties, some of them modified by the court. AMF has assailed ten of the 124 findings of fact, but our examination of the record satisfies us that all have adequate support in the record and support the conclusions of law.

Whether in a specific case a buyer has reasonable grounds for insecurity is a question of fact. Comment 3 to UCC § 2–609; Anderson, Uniform Commercial Code, § 2–609 (2d Ed.1971). On this record, McDonald's clearly had "reasonable grounds for insecurity" with respect to AMF's performance. At the time of the March 18, 1969, meeting, the prototype unit had performed unsatisfactorily ever since its April 1968 installation. Although AMF had projected delivery of all twenty-three units by the first half of 1969, AMF later scheduled delivery from the end of July 1969 until January 1970. When McDonald's personnel visited AMF's Vandalia, Ohio, plant on March 4, 1969, they saw that none of the 72C systems was being assembled and learned that a pilot unit would not be ready until the end of July that year. They were informed that the engineer assigned to the project was not to commence work until March 17th. AMF's own personnel were also troubled about the design of the 72C, causing them to attempt to reduce McDonald's order to five units. Therefore, under Section 2–609 McDonald's was entitled to demand adequate assurance of performance by AMF.*

However, AMF urges that Section 2–609 of the UCC . . . is inapplicable because McDonald's did not make a written demand of adequate assurance of due performance. In Pittsburgh–Des Moines Steel Co. v. Brookhaven Manor Water Co., 532 F.2d 572, 581 (7th Cir.1976), we noted that the Code should be liberally construed and therefore rejected such "a formalistic approach" to Section 2–609. McDonald's failure to make a written demand was excusable because AMF's Mr. Dubosque's testimony and his April 2 and 18, 1969, memoranda about the March 18th meeting showed AMF's clear understanding that McDonald's had suspended performance until it should receive adequate assurance of due performance from AMF (Tr. 395; AMF Exhibit 79; McD. Exhibit 232).

After the March 18th demand, AMF never repaired the Elk Grove unit satisfactorily nor replaced it. Similarly, it was unable to satisfy McDonald's that the twenty-three machines on order would work. At the May 1st meeting, AMF offered unsatisfactory assurances for only five units instead of twenty-three. The performance standards AMF tendered to McDonald's were unacceptable because they would have permitted the 72C's not to function properly for 90 hours per year, permitting as much as one failure in every fifteen days in a busy McDonald's restaurant. Also, as the district court found, AMF's Vandalia, Ohio, personnel were too inexperienced to produce a proper machine. Since AMF did not provide adequate assurance of performance after McDonald's March 18th demand, UCC Section 2–609(1) permitted McDonald's to suspend performance. When AMF did not furnish adequate assurance of due performance at the May 1st meeting, it

---

* McDonald's was justified in seeking assurances about performance standards at the March 18th meeting. The parts and service warranty in the contracts for the twenty-three 72C's was essentially a limitation of remedy provision. Under UCC § 2–719(2) (Ill.Rev.Stats. (1975) ch. 26, § 2–719(2)) if the 72C cash registers failed to work or could not be repaired within a reasonable time, the limitation of remedy provision would be invalid, and McDonald's would be entitled to pursue all other remedies provided in Article

2. See Riley v. Ford Motor Co., 442 F.2d 670, 673 (5th Cir.1971); Earl M. Jorgensen Co. v. Mark Construction Co., 540 P.2d 978, 985–987 (Hawaii 1975). Because McDonald's would have a right to reject the machines if they proved faulty after delivery and then to cancel the contract, it was consistent with the purposes of § 2–609 for McDonald's to require assurances that such eventuality would not occur. See Comment 1 to UCC § 2–719.

thereby repudiated the contract under Section 2–609(4). At that point, Section 2–610(b) ... permitted McDonald's to cancel the orders pursuant to Section 2–711 ... as it finally did on July 29, 1969.

In seeking reversal, AMF relies on Pittsburgh–Des Moines Steel Co. v. Brookhaven Manor Water Co., supra, 532 F.2d at 581. There we held a party to a contract could not resort to UCC Section 2–609 since there was no demonstration that reasonable grounds for insecurity were present. That case is inapt where, as here, McDonald's submitted sufficient proof in that respect. But that case does teach that McDonald's could cancel the orders under Sections 2–610 and 2–711 because of AMF's failure to give adequate assurance of due performance under Section 2–609.

* * *

Judgment affirmed.

NOTES

(1) *Right to Adequate Assurance of Performance under Article 2 of the UCC.* Read UCC 2–609 carefully. Do you agree with the court's analysis and application to the facts? As a buyer of goods, McDonald's route to victory in the *AMF* case involved the following steps: UCC 2–609(1); UCC 2–609(4); UCC 2–610(b); and UCC 2–711(1).

According to Professor James J. White, the *AMF* case is not a conventional application of UCC 2–609:

> First, the court brushed aside section 2–609's explicit requirement that the demand be written. Second, nothing in the opinion indicates that there was even a formal oral demand. In effect, the court applied section 2–609 to one party's routine negotiating behavior and gave it significant legal consequence—namely, repudiation by the other.

White, *Eight Cases and Section 251,* 67 Cornell L.Rev. 841, 846 (1982). White's study of eight cases where either UCC 2–609 or Restatement (Second) § 251 were involved leads to the conclusion that the adequate assurance strategy was less a weapon in the hands of lawyers and more a discrete, subtle tool in the hands of courts to "give legal consequences to acts taken in the course of negotiations by parties who never considered those consequences." 67 Cornell L.Rev. at 859.

> My eight cases tell me that one who acts in bad faith, appears incapable of performing, or breaches his contract in even a limited way commits a repudiation or a material breach by much more equivocal and less egregious behavior than the black letter would lead one to believe. If the courts continue down this path, it is possible that Restatement Third will read:
>
>> One has committed a material breach or a repudiation when his acts or other circumstances make it appear likely that he is either incapable of performing or unwilling to do so.

67 Cornell L.Rev. at 860.

(2) Professor Larry Garvin has expressed concern that UCC 2–609, although consistently praised, gives the party demanding assurance the opportu-

nity to demand a forced modification. To meet the demand, the other party may be compelled to "grant ex post rights which the bargain ex ante had not provided" and thus provide the insecure party with a windfall. Drawing upon a growing body of literature on cognitive psychology, however, he suggests that cognitive limitations on the assessment of risk at the time of contracting may support efforts to adjust risk after the contract is made and that, in the final analysis, the resulting modification is less troubling. Larry T. Garvin, *Adequate Assurance of Due Performance: Of Risk, Duress, and Cognition*, 69 U. Colo. L. Rev. 71 (1998).

(3) *Right to demand adequate assurance at common law*. Section 251 of the Restatement (Second), supra at 875, note 2, purports to state the common law rule on adequate assurance. The matter is a bit more complicated, however, in New York.

In Norcon Power Partners, L.P. v. Niagara Mohawk Power Corp., 92 N.Y.2d 458, 682 N.Y.S.2d 664, 705 N.E.2d 656 (1998), the following question was certified to the New York Court of Appeals by the United States Court of Appeals for the Second Circuit:

> Does a party have the right to demand adequate assurance of future performance when reasonable grounds arise to believe that the other party will commit a breach by non-performance of a contract governed by New York law, where the other party is solvent and the contract is not governed by the U.C.C.?

The court answered the question in the affirmative, but hedged its bets. It agreed that the contract (a long-term contract for the sale of electricity) was not a contract for the sale of goods to which Article 2 applied. It also noted that New York had not embraced the adequate assurance doctrine outside of the statutory framework of Article 2. What to do? The court extended UCC 2–609 to the contract by analogy, concluding that the sale of electricity was similar to a sale of goods and that parties to a "long-term commercial contract" which is "complex and not reasonably susceptible of all security features being anticipated, bargained for, and incorporated in the original contract" should have the protection of UCC 2–609. 705 N.E.2d at 662.

The court, in a self-congratulatory opinion, refused to overrule cases rejecting the adequate assurance doctrine in other contracts. This restraint was both consistent with its "customary incremental common-law development process" and with the trail blazing work of Holmes and Cardozo in "making interstitial law, filling gaps in the statutory and decisional rules, and at a snail-like pace giving some forward movement to the developing law."

(4) *A risky strategy*. While a promisee's right to demand adequate assurance at first seems to importantly enhance the promisee's defensive right to assure the promisor's performance, the use of this right carries considerable risk. The promisee who wants to suspend under UCC 2–609 must (i) have "reasonable grounds for insecurity"; (ii) demand in writing adequate assurance; and (iii) have not received "adequate assurance" from the promisor. If a promisee suspends and a court subsequently finds that one of these requirements was not present, the promisee's attempted defensive action will constitute a breach of contract by the promisee herself. What starts off as a

legitimate concern about whether the other side will perform can ultimately become a finding that you yourself breached in exercising your defensive rights.

(5) *Government Contracts*. In government contracts, a "failure to make progress" clause, protecting the government's interest, is included in the standard Default Clause for fixed-price supply contracts. See 41 C.F.R. § 1–16.901–32 cl. 11(19). Paragraph (a) provides:

> The Government may, subject to the provisions of paragraph (c) below, by written notice of default to the Contractor, terminate the whole or any part of this contract in any one of the following circumstances: (i) if the Contractor fails to make delivery of the supplies or to perform the services within the time specified herein or any extension thereof; or (ii) if the Contractor fails to perform any of the other provisions of this contract, or so fails to make progress as to endanger performance of this contract in accordance with its terms, and in either of these two circumstances does not cure such failure within a period of 10 days (or such longer period as the Contracting Officer may authorize in writing) after receipt of notice from the Contracting Officer specifying such failure.

If a termination under paragraph (a) is proper and the default is not excused under paragraph (c) because it arose "out of causes beyond the control and without the fault or negligence of the Contractor," the government's remedies are spelled out in paragraph (b): "The Government may procure, upon such terms and in such manner as the Contracting Officer may deem appropriate, supplies or services similar to those so terminated, and the Contractor shall be liable to the Government for any excess costs for such similar supplies or services." On the other hand, if the termination under paragraph (a) is premature or a default termination is excused under paragraph (c), the contractor's remedies are limited under paragraph (e) to costs incurred plus profit on work done up to the time of termination. One may not recover profits prevented by the improper termination. See John W. Whelan & James F. Nagle, Federal Government Contracts: Cases and Materials 462–470(2d ed. 2002 (discussing clause and applicable decisions).

Plotnick v. Pennsylvania Smelting & Refining Co.

United States Court of Appeals, Third Circuit, 1952.
194 F.2d 859.

■ HASTIE, CIRCUIT JUDGE. This litigation arises out of an installment contract for the sale of quantities of battery lead by a Canadian seller to a Pennsylvania buyer. The seller sued for the price of a carload of lead delivered but not paid for. The buyer counterclaimed for damages caused by the seller's failure to deliver the remaining installments covered by the contract. The district court sitting without a jury allowed recovery on both claim and counterclaim. This is an appeal by the seller from the judgment against him on the counterclaim. The ultimate question is whether the buyer had committed such a breach of contract as constituted a repudiation justifying rescission by the seller.

Suit was brought in the District Court for the Eastern District of Pennsylvania. Federal jurisdiction is based on diversity of citizenship.

[handwritten margin notes: "π - seller   Δ - Buyer   Δ wins   Recission was not proper"]

Consequently, the conflict of laws rules of the forum, Pennsylvania, are invoked to solve the choice of law problem.... This involves no difficulty since familiar conflict of laws doctrine accepted generally and in Pennsylvania tells us that legal excuse for the non-performance or avoidance of a contract is to be determined in accordance with the law of the place of performance. Restatement, Conflict of Laws, Pa.Annot. § 358 (1936). Beyond this, the parties agree, and correctly so, that Pennsylvania is the place of performance in this case. Therefore, we apply the substantive law of Pennsylvania, particularly the Uniform Sales Act, to determine the legal consequences of the operative facts.

Uncontested findings of fact show that the contract in question was the last of a series of agreements, several of them installment contracts, entered into by the parties between June and October, 1947. Under these contracts, numerous shipments of lead were made by the seller in Canada to the buyer in Philadelphia. The seller frequently complained, and with justification, that payments were too long delayed. On the other hand, several shipments were not made at the time required by the contracts. However, by the end of March 1948, all contracts other than the one in suit had been fully performed by both parties. In this connection, it was the unchallenged finding of the district court that both parties waived the delays which preceded the buyer's breach involved in this suit. The earlier delays are relevant only insofar as they may reasonably have influenced either party in its interpretation of subsequent conduct of the other party.

The contract in suit was executed October 23, 1947 and called for deliveries aggregating 200 tons of battery lead to be completed not later than December 25, 1947. The agreed price was 8.1 cents per pound, or better if quality warranted. The court found that it was the understanding of the parties that at least 63 percent of the price should be paid shortly after each shipment was delivered and the balance within four weeks after that delivery. This finding is not contested.

Under this contract a first carload was delivered November 7, 1947. About 75 percent of the price was paid six days later. A second carload was received January 8, and about 75 percent of the price was paid 10 days later. Final adjustments and payments of small balances due on these two carloads were completed March 30, and these shipments are not now in dispute. The earliest shipment immediately involved in this litigation, the third under the contract, was a carload of lead received by the buyer on March 23, 1948. This delivery followed a March 12 conference of the parties. They disagree on what transpired at that conference. However, about 290,000 pounds of lead were then still to be delivered under the contract which stated December 25, 1947 as the agreed time for the completion of performance. And shortly after the conference, one carload of 43,000 pounds was delivered. No part of the price of this third carload has been paid. It is not disputed that plaintiff is entitled to the price of this shipment and his recovery on his claim in this suit vindicates that right.

On April 7, the buyer, who had been prodding the seller for more lead for some time, notified the seller that unless the balance of the lead should be delivered within thirty days he would buy in the open market and charge the seller any cost in excess of 8.1 cents per pound. On April 10, the seller replied refusing to ship unless the recently delivered third carload should be paid for. On May 12, buyer's attorney threatened suit unless the undelivered lead should be shipped promptly and at the same time promised to pay on delivery 75 percent of the price of this prospective shipment together with the full price of the third installment already received. Seller's solicitor replied on May 22 that seller regarded the contract as "cancelled" as a result of buyer's failure to pay for lead already delivered. At the same time the letter stated the seller's willingness to deliver at the originally agreed price if the overdue payment should be made by return mail and a letter of credit established to cover the price of the lead not yet shipped. Buyer's attorney replied on May 25 that buyer had withheld the price of the third carload "only as a set-off by reason of the failure of your client to deliver" and that buyer would place the overdue payment in escrow and would accept the remaining lead if shipped to Philadelphia "sight draft attached for the full invoice price of each car." On May 27, seller's solicitors reiterated the position stated in their March 22 letter and on June 2 seller notified buyer that the Canadian government had imposed export control on lead. The district court found, and it is here admitted, that between October 1947 and May 1948 the market price of battery lead increased from 8.1 cents to 11½ cents per pound.

The court concluded that the failure of defendant to make a down payment of at least 63 percent of the price of the third carload constituted a breach of contract but "not such a material breach of the contract as to justify plaintiff in refusing to ship the balance due under the contract within the meaning of section 45 of The Sales Act." This was the decisive conclusion of law which the seller has challenged.

Section 45 of the Sales Act as in force in Pennsylvania provides in relevant part as follows: "Where there is a contract to sell goods to be delivered by stated instalments, which are to be separately paid for, and * * * the buyer neglects or refuses to * * * pay for one or more instalments, it depends in each case on the terms of the contract, and the circumstances of the case, whether the breach of contract is so material as to justify the injured party in refusing to proceed further * * * or whether the breach is severable, giving rise to a claim for compensation, but not to a right to treat the whole contract as broken." Pa.Stat.Ann.Tit. 69, § 255 (Purdon, 1931).

We are dealing, therefore, with a situation in which the controlling statute explicitly makes the circumstances of the particular case determine whether failure to pay the price of one shipment delivered under an installment contract justifies the seller in treating his own obligation with reference to future installments as ended. Our problem is how to determine the legal effect of non-payment in a particular case.

We think the key is to be found in the rational basis of the statute itself. The flexibility of the statute reflects the impossibility of generalization about the consequences of failure to pay promptly for installments as delivered. Yet, the commercial sense of the statute yields two guiding considerations. First, nonpayment for a delivered shipment may make it impossible or unreasonably burdensome from a financial point of view for the seller to supply future installments as promised. Second, buyer's breach of his promise to pay for one installment may create such reasonable apprehension in the seller's mind concerning payment for future installments that the seller should not be required to take the risk involved in continuing deliveries. If any such consequence is proved, the seller may rescind. Moreover, the Pennsylvania decisions indicate that these embarrassments and apprehensions are normal consequences of non-payment; but the cases also make it clear that they are not necessary consequences. . . .

In this case there is no evidence that the delay in payment for one carload made it difficult to provide additional lead. To the contrary, seller admits that throughout the period in controversy he had sufficient lead on hand for the full performance of this contract. He could have delivered had he chosen to do so. His excuse, if any, must be found in reasonable apprehension as to the future of the contract engendered by buyer's behavior.

The district court's finding number 16, with which seller takes issue, is a direct negation of the claim of reasonable apprehension upon which seller seeks to establish under Section 45 of the Sales Act his asserted "right to treat the whole contract as broken." It reads as follows: "Plaintiff's claim of fear that the defendant would not pay for the balance of battery lead due under Contract No. 5794 at the contract price was without foundation and unreasonable."

In considering the propriety of this finding, it is to be borne in mind that the point here is not the absence of legal justification for the withholding of an overdue payment but rather whether, under the circumstances, that withholding gave the seller reason to believe that there was likelihood of continuing or additional default when and after he should deliver the rest of the lead in accordance with his promise. The substantiality of this alleged apprehension must be judged in the light of the uncontroverted finding that no impairment of buyer's credit had been shown. Moreover, the market was rising and all of the evidence indicates that buyer needed and urgently requested the undelivered lead. Indeed, as early as March 1, before the delivery of the carload for which payment was withheld, the buyer had complained quite urgently of the non-delivery of the entire balance of some 290,000 pounds overdue since December. Thereafter, when the seller shipped 43,000 pounds, about one-seventh of what was due, the buyer insisted that he was withholding payment because of the delay in delivery of the overdue balance. The court's finding that buyer had waived any claim for damages for delay up to that time does not alter this factual picture or its rational implications. In these circumstances, the trial court was justified in concluding that buyer's explanation of his conduct merited belief and that seller had no valid reason to be fearful that payment would not be forthcoming upon full delivery.

If you're unsure use Sight Draft

The clincher here is provided by the additional evidence concerning the possibility of delivery with sight draft attached. While there is no specific finding on the point, the evidence, including testimony tendered on behalf of seller, shows without dispute that at the beginning of this series of contracts, the seller had the privilege of shipping on sight draft but elected not to do so. And just before the collapse of the efforts of the parties to work out their difficulties amicably, the buyer specifically proposed that the seller assure himself of prompt payment by the use of sight drafts accompanying shipments. It is again important that at this time the market was substantially higher than the contract price and that seller was advised of buyer's urgent need for lead to meet his own commitments. In such circumstances it is incredible that the buyer would refuse to honor sight drafts for the contract price. These facts considered together leave no basis for reasonable apprehension concerning payment.

There is one other relevant and important fact. Throughout the controversial period the seller, with a stock of lead on hand adequate for the full performance of this contract, was using this lead in a rising market for sales to other purchasers at prices higher than agreed in the present contract. The inference was not only allowable but almost inescapable that desire to avoid a bad bargain rather than apprehension that the buyer would not carry out that bargain caused the seller to renounce the agreement and charge the buyer with repudiation. Rescission for such cause is not permissible. . . .

It follows that the seller has failed to establish justification for rescission under Section 45 of the Sales Act and that judgment for the buyer on the counterclaim was proper.

The judgment will be affirmed.

NOTES

(1) In *Plotnick,* the seller canceled an installment contract because the buyer had failed to pay one installment and the court held that the cancellation was improper because the breach was not material under Section 45 of the Uniform Sales Act. According to the court, what factors are relevant to the materiality question? Compare Section 241 of the Restatement (Second), which lists five relevant "circumstances." See also materials covered in Chapter Six, Section 3(B), *supra.*

(2) *"Substantial impairment" under the UCC.* Section 45 is now superseded by UCC 2–612, the substance of which was not changed in Revised Article 2. Under the Code, the seller may cancel where the buyer "fails to make a payment due on or before delivery * * * if the breach is of the whole contract (Section 2–612) * * *." UCC 2–703(f). Section 2–612(1) defines an installment contract and, in subsection (2) states when the buyer (but not the seller) may reject a non-conforming installment. Subsection (3) then provides: "Whenever non-conformity or default with respect to one or more installments substantially impairs the value of the whole contract there is a breach of the whole." "Substantial impairment" is not defined.

In Midwest Mobile Diagnostic Imaging v. Dynamics Corp. Of America, 965 F.Supp. 1003 (W.D.Mich.1997), aff'd, 165 F.3d 27 (6th Cir.1998), the court attempted to explain "substantial impairment" of the "whole" contract:

> Whether a breach constitutes "substantial impairment" of the entire contract is a question of fact. * * * To make such a determination, the Court should consider the cumulative effect of [the breaching party's] performance under the contract, based upon the totality of the circumstances. * * * Ultimately, whether the non-conformity in any given installment justifies cancellation as to the future depends not on whether such non-conformity indicates an intent or likelihood that future deliveries will also be defective, but whether the non-conformity substantially impairs the value of the whole contract. [quoting Section 2–616, comment 6]. Thus, the question is one of present breach which focuses on the importance of the nonconforming installment relative to the contracts as a whole. If the nonconformity only impairs the aggrieved party's security with regard to future installments, s/he has the right to demand adequate assurances but ... not an immediate right to cancel the entire contract ... The right to cancel will be triggered only if material inconvenience or injustice will result if the aggrieved party is forced to wait and receive an ultimate tender minus the part or aspect repudiated. [Internal quotation marks omitted.]

Is this helpful? Would the reasoning and result of *Plotnick* be the same under UCC 2–703(f) and 2–612(3)? See also Eric Andersen, *A New Look at Material Breach in the Law of Contracts*, 21 U.C.Davis L.Rev. 1073, 1139–40 (1988), who argues that materiality should be measured by the impact on the plaintiff rather than the likelihood of the defendant's future performance.

(3) A "partial" breach coupled with a repudiation of the "whole" contract justifies cancellation of the entire contract. See, e.g., Kirkwood Agri–Trade v. Frosty Land Foods International, Inc., 650 F.2d 602 (5th Cir.1981).

(4) *CISG*. Both Canada and the United States have ratified the United Nations Convention on Contracts for the International Sale of Goods. The *Plotnick* case, if it arose today, would be subject to CISG because it involved a contract of sale of goods between private parties whose places of business were in different countries and both countries had ratified CISG. Art. 1(1)(a). Like UCC Article 2, CISG has articles on adequate assurance, Art. 71, repudiation, Art. 72, and installment contracts, Art. 73. On the facts in *Plotnick* (an installment contract), the question would be whether the buyer's failure to pay one installment gave the seller "good grounds to conclude that a fundamental breach of contract will occur with respect to future instalments." If so, the seller may avoid the contract for the future. "Fundamental breach" is defined in Article 25 and the grounds and procedure for the seller to avoid the contract are set out in Article 64. Read these Articles, please. How might *Plotnick* come out under CISG? Could the seller "avoid" the contract for "fundamental breach?"

Comment: Post–Breach Conduct Affecting the Cancellation Remedy

In Chapter Six, Section 2(A)(2), we saw that a promisor could "waive" a condition included in the bargain for his or her benefit. In this section, we

have assumed that a promisor's duty to render a performance was expressly or "constructively" conditioned upon performance by the other party.
See Chapter Six, Section 2(B). Thus, if the other party repudiated or failed
to perform a material part of the agreed exchange, the promisor's duty to
perform is, at a minimum, suspended and, at a maximum, discharged. In
short, the promisor can "cancel" the contract because of the other party's
material breach. Under what circumstances can the promisor, by action or
inaction, "waive" or alter the effect of the other's breach and thereby lose
the cancellation remedy?

First, it is important to distinguish a claim for damages arising from
breach from the cancellation remedy. In point of law, it is harder to waive
the former than the latter. The damage claim can be discharged by an
agreement supported by consideration or by a "written waiver or renunciation" when "signed and delivered by the aggrieved party." UCC 1–107. See
Restatement (Second) §§ 273 & 277. A renunciation may also be effective
without consideration or a formality if it has "induced such action or
forbearance as would make a promise enforceable." Restatement (Second)
§ 273(c). In the absence of consideration, reliance or a formality, therefore,
one would expect the damage claim to survive even though the aggrieved
party has lost the cancellation remedy through inaction or election.

Second, there are a number of situations, difficult to classify, where the
aggrieved party's action or inaction will foreclose a subsequent cancellation.
In each case, assume that the cancellation remedy would have been
available but for the aggrieved party's conduct.

1.   A repudiates the whole contract on October 1. B decides to wait a
reasonable time before cancelling the contract. A then retracts the repudiation before B has canceled or "materially changed its position or otherwise
indicated that it considers the repudiation final." The retraction nullifies
the breach and, of course, forecloses any remedy for breach of contract.
UCC 2–611(1); Restatement (Second) § 256.

2.   S tenders goods to B on October 1. B inspects them on that date
and finds a non-conformity. On November 1, B notifies S that it is rejecting
the goods, UCC 2–601, and canceling the contract. UCC 2–711(1). On these
facts, B has lost the cancellation remedy by failing to reject the goods
within a reasonable time. UCC 2–602(1). Cancellation is available for a
"rightful" rejection. Under the UCC, B has accepted the goods by failing to
make an "effective rejection," UCC 2–606(1)(b), but still could cancel if it
justifiably revokes acceptance under UCC 2–608. See UCC 2–711(1) Revocation of acceptance, however, requires action within a reasonable time, and
it is probable that this remedy is also foreclosed. Thus, B is left with a
claim for damages to accepted goods. UCC 2–714. See UCC 2–607(3)(a).
Has B, through inaction, lost its damages claim as well?

3.   C completes a construction project and O finds two breaches, one
material and one not. O rejects the work and gives only the non-material
breach as a reason. C "cures" the defect and O then attempts to avoid
payment by citing the material breach. If C has relied to its detriment on
the stated objection without reason to know about the unstated objection,

O may not assert the material breach as a basis for cancellation. See New England Structures, Inc. v. Loranger, 354 Mass. 62, 234 N.E.2d 888 (1968); UCC 2–605(1); Restatement (Second) § 248.

4. S agrees to deliver goods to B in installments over a two year period. At the end of the first year, S was substantially behind in deliveries and this substantially impaired the value of the whole contract. UCC 2–612(3). Although B could cancel the contract for breach, that remedy would be lost in the following situations: (a) B sues S "with respect only to past installments or demands performance as to future installments," UCC 2–612(3); (b) B continues to perform its part of the exchange without objecting to S's breach, see Dangerfield v. Markel, 252 N.W.2d 184 (N.D. 1977); or (c) B "accepts a non-conforming installment without seasonably notifying of cancellation." UCC 2–612(3); Restatement (Second) §§ 246 & 247. This conduct "reinstates" the contract.

As one court put it:

> Waiver of strict performance may be inferred from the circumstances or course of dealings between the parties. ... A waiver may result from one party's express or implied assent to the continued performance of the other party without objection to the delay. ... In addition, express representations by one party that strict compliance with a deadline will not be required, or other actions that reasonably lead the other party to believe such, will also cause an effective waiver of a time provision in a contract. Finally, a party may effectively waive a breach of agreement by the other party by continuing to insist on performance by the other party even after the breach. ... In our case, Seismic waived the contract provision as to time of performance through its failure to object to the delay, its failure to reject the software programs when delivered, and its subsequent conduct in both assenting to the delay and requesting additional word from Digital on the completed programs.

Seismic & Digital Concepts, Inc. v. Digital Resources Corp., 590 S.W.2d 718, 721 (Tex.Civ.App.1979).

For a more systematic treatment of situations where claims, defenses, and other rights can be lost by relinquishment or preclusion, see E. Allan Farnsworth, Changing Your Mind: The Law of Regretted Decisions 127–202 (Yale 1998).

SECTION 2. COMPENSATORY DAMAGES

(A) AN INTRODUCTION TO CONTRACT REMEDIES

The remainder of Chapter Seven amplifies and builds upon Chapter Three, An Introduction to Contract Remedies.

(B) BREACH OR REPUDIATION BY PAYOR

In most bargains, one party has agreed to render a performance, e.g., transfer and sell goods or land, construct a home, perform professional services, in exchange for an agreed price, usually the payment of money. As we saw in Chapter Six, Section 2(B), unless the parties have agreed upon a time for payment(either before or after performance) the duty to pay, whether in a lump sum or in installments, does not arise until the performer has tendered or completed all or part of its portion of the exchange. If this is done without a breach, the performer, with one exception noted in the next case, is entitled to enforce the contract for the full amount promised plus interest. This remedy offers full protection to the plaintiff's expectation interest. See, for example, UCC 1–106(1), 2–709(1)(a). Even if the performer has breached, the duty to pay is enforceable with an adjustment if there has been substantial performance.

If, however, a non-breaching performer has not completed its part of the exchange before the payor repudiates the contract or fails to make a payment due, the remedial problems become more complex. If the performer cannot recover the agreed price (arguably the best remedy), what are the alternatives?

We have already explored the performer's defensive remedies in this situation, see supra Chapter Seven, Section 1. We will now explore the distinct problems confronting the performer in achieving affirmative protection upon breach or repudiation by the payor. Look carefully for the interaction between remedial objectives and policy and the position of the performer. In the next subsection, we will reverse the coin to consider the remedial posture of the payor upon breach or repudiation by the performer.

John Hancock Mutual Life Insurance Co. v. Cohen

United States Court of Appeals, Ninth Circuit, 1958.
254 F.2d 417.

[The insured, who died in February, 1945, was protected by a life insurance policy issued by the defendant. The policy contained a provision for "family income benefit" under which, in lieu of a lump sum payment, the plaintiff-beneficiary was to receive monthly payments for 20 years from the date that the policy was issued, 1939, and a final lump sum of $5,000. The defendant made monthly payments for 15 years and at the end of that time tendered the final lump sum payment. The defendant refused to make any further monthly payments on the ground that the policy was issued for 20 years by mistake and that both parties intended protection for 15 years. The lower court found for the plaintiff on the mistake issue and held that the defendant had breached the contract by anticipatory repudiation. Accordingly, an $8,000 judgment was entered for the plaintiff which included the installments due and to become due under the policy and the final payment. On appeal, the court of appeals, speaking through Judge Barnes, affirmed the lower court on the mistake issue and then treated the anticipatory breach question.]

■ BARNES, CIRCUIT JUDGE.

* * *

Appellant's sixth alleged error is the finding that the appellant committed an anticipatory breach of said contract on or about May 13th 1954.[1]

Appellant cites ... for the proposition that " * * * notwithstanding the failure or refusal to pay the installment, the other party cannot treat the contract as repudiated and demand payment in full, contrary to the terms of the contract providing for payment in installments."

Appellee here urges that there yet remains a condition to be performed by the plaintiff—the surrender of the policy to the defendant in Boston. This being so, and relying on Corbin on Contracts § 967, he states that the plaintiff can maintain an action at once for anticipatory repudiation. Corbin divided his discussion of repudiation of unilateral insurance contracts into two classes: First, "those in which the insurer undertakes to pay a definite sum of money at a specified future time or on the happening of a future event that is certain to occur, but the time of which is uncertain. * * * A second class consists of disability and annuity policies. * * * ("Annuity" here is used, we presume, in its usual sense and not as an "annuity certain" in length of time as it was in the instant case.) In reference to the first class of cases, Corbin states:

"It is well settled by ample authority that an action lies at once for anticipatory repudiation by an insurer, either for the recovery of premiums paid or for damages." Corbin, § 968.

We need not go into Corbin's "ample authority," nor determine if this action falls within the limited type of actions which Corbin states can be filed,—for recovery of premiums or damages.

The contract here under consideration is a "payment certain" insurance contract. It has become, in effect, an unconditional unilateral contract for the payment of money in future installments. There were no contingencies which might occur to give the company a right to refuse payment. Even should the beneficiary have died, the "payment certain" would have been payable to her heirs. Particularly, after the insured's death and the company's endorsement on July 26, 1945 is this true. The insurer then undertook to pay certain sums each month and a larger certain sum at a later date.

This contract falls neither into Corbin's first class—a definite sum or sums payable on a future event certain to occur, but uncertain as to the time of occurrence—nor into his second class—"the disability and annuity policies providing for periodic payments for an indefinite time." It is a contract wherein the time for payment is certain and there remains no condition or covenant for performance by the plaintiff.

Corbin does not like the "dicta" to the effect that there can be no anticipatory breach of a unilateral contract because in the *first* class of

---

1. Finding 14: "On or about May 13, 1954 defendant notified plaintiff in writing that it 'does not consider it is liable for any further monthly payments under the family income provision,' and that it would pay a final payment of $4,993.59 but only upon surrender of the policy. Thereby defendant committed an anticipatory breach of the said contract entered into between it and said Troutfelt." [Tr. p. 104].

cases the doctrine is in fact applied. (See cases cited at Corbin, § 968, n. 35.) Nor does he care for the rule that the doctrine of anticipatory breach is inapplicable to a case of an unconditional unilateral contract for the payment of money in installments, but he cites no authority to the contrary. (Corbin, §§ 965, 969.)

We are in essence here asked to hold that the doctrine of anticipatory breach applies to an unconditional unilateral insurance contract in a case where the insurer has promised to pay definite sums of money at specified future dates and that this should be declared by the Federal Court to be the law of New Mexico because an eminent writer and authority on contracts disagrees with the more recent New York cases and the Massachusetts rule and two Supreme Court cases. (Corbin, § 968, n. 34.)

We are asked to so rule in a case where the "present value" of future payments was not raised below, nor apparently considered by the trial court. Corbin states:

"Some of the courts denying that the insurer has committed a total breach of anticipation base their decision upon the ground that the contract is a unilateral contract for the payment of money. That this is not a good reason has already been argued in a previous section. The decision of the Supreme Court does not rest upon it; indeed, in the opinion rendered it is in part, at least, rejected. We differ with the court in holding that there was no total breach by anticipatory repudiation; but its reasoning and analysis may be otherwise approved. The decision itself need not be regretted, if it leads to the granting of the truly 'appropriate relief' in all such cases. This is a single decree that money already overdue shall be paid, with interest, and that future instalments shall be paid as they fall due. * * * " Corbin, § 969, pp. 893–4.

Williston on Contracts states the general rule to be "that no unilateral promise for an executed agreed exchange to pay money at a future time can be enforced until that day arrives." (Williston, § 1328; accord, Restatement, Contracts § 318). With respect to the applicability of the doctrine of anticipatory breach to future disability payments, . . .

Williston goes on:

"The only argument for allowing immediate recovery of a future payment due under such a (disability) policy is the hardship supposedly imposed on the insured of bringing successive suits." (§ 1330A.) He then points out how this can be avoided by the courts' "full exercise of equitable powers." He quotes from Mobley v. New York Life Ins. Co., supra, to the effect that if the insured is

" * * * allowed a present recovery for all future benefits, the calculations on which insurance business is done would be upset, and the purposes for which the benefits were made payable only in installments would often be defeated." (Ibid.)

Williston then criticizes as "extreme" the application of the doctrine to a non-insurance case in Texas,[2] although "the present value" was therein determined, after use of expectancy tables—a value not herein considered by the trial court.

We conclude the general rule to be that the doctrine of anticipatory breach has no application to suits to enforce contracts for future payment of money only, in installments or otherwise. ...

* * *

It is our conclusion that the theory of anticipatory breach is not here applicable—to make it so where the defendant insurer has disputed liability in good faith would change the terms of the contract executed by the insurer and force him to pay now what he contracted to pay later; that the court should decree that money already overdue shall be paid now with interest; and that future installments shall be paid as they fall due, including the final payment.

What we have said with respect to the alleged error in holding an anticipatory breach controls the seventh specification of error, and requires us to hold the judgment as given to be error.

* * *

The cause is remanded, with directions to award plaintiff an amount equal to payments due to the date of judgment, plus interest; decreeing that future installments shall be paid when they fall due, together with the final lump sum payment; and, that appellee be awarded her costs, both below and on this appeal.

Remanded with directions.

NOTES

(1) *Repudiation of Promise to Pay Money When Other Party Has Fully Performed.* A has fully performed his obligations under the contract. All express and implied conditions have been satisfied except that the agreed time for payment, whether in installments or a lump sum, has not yet arrived. B unequivocally repudiates her obligation to pay. May A bring suit for damages and obtain a judgment *before* the time for payment has arrived?

Professor Corbin's answer was an emphatic yes. His argument was: 1) It is wrong to limit the doctrine of anticipatory repudiation, as announced in *Hochster v. De La Tour,* supra at 863, to cases where the plaintiff still has part of the exchange to perform, because the plaintiff's need for affirmative protection against repudiation is no less just because full performance has occurred; 2) The amount to be paid is certain and time is the only contingency involved; 3) Judgment for the plaintiff will neither "accelerate" the obligation nor grant specific performance. Rather, the plaintiff will recover damages for breach of a promise to pay money measured by the present value of that promise. In other

---

2. Pollack v. Pollack, Tex.Civ.App., 23 S.W.2d 890. [Texas law still rejects the distinction between executory and fully executed contracts in connection with the doctrine of anticipatory breach. Pitts v. Wetzel, 498 S.W.2d 27 (Tex.Civ.App.1973) Ed.]

words, the full amount promised must be "discounted" to reflect the defendant's loss of use. The fact that the damage amount resembles specific performance is fortuitous since, when full performance by the plaintiff has occurred, there are no savings to deduct from the total recovery. See Corbin §§ 962–70.

With regard to the *Cohen* case, Professor Corbin stated that justice would also have been achieved "if the beneficiary had been given judgment for the full amount of the future installments properly discounted to 'present value.'" "These were definite in number and amount and could be adequately discounted. This would be a judgment for 'damages' and not accelerated specific performance." 4 Corbin § 968 (1964 Pocket Part). Do you agree? Other than the possibility of multiple litigation when installments are involved, what special hardship is involved in requiring the plaintiff to wait for the money?

(2) Would the problem posed in the *Cohen* case be alleviated by a contract clause authorizing "acceleration" of the obligation in the event of default, defined to include "repudiation"? Acceleration clauses, which are standard in most loan and credit transactions, are drafted to permit the remedy denied in *Cohen*. The lump sum payment, however, must be discounted to present value, see note 5, infra.

(3) Despite criticism, see, e.g., Wiesner, *Anticipatory Breach and the Unilateral Contract: A Decade of the Status Quo*, 8 U. Dayton L.Rev. 61 (1982), the "unilateral" contract exception to the doctrine of anticipatory breach or repudiation persists. Section 253(1) of Restatement (Second) states that where an "obligor repudiates a duty before he has committed a breach by non-performance and before he has received all of the agreed exchange for it, his repudiation alone gives rise to a claim for damages for total breach." In Comment c, it is noted that "one of the established limits on the doctrine of 'anticipatory breach' is that the obligor's 'repudiation alone * * * gives rise to no claim for damages at all if he has already received all of the agreed exchange for it.' In Comment d, however, it is conceded that the "degree to which the limitation might yield on a showing of manifest injustice, as where the refusal to pay is not in good faith, is unclear." Suppose the obligor is in default on one installment and then repudiates the balance of the contract? The Restatement (Second) answer is found in Section 243(3):

> Where at the time of the breach the only remaining duties of performance are those of the party in breach and are for the payment of money in installments not related to one another, his breach by non-performance as to less than the whole, whether or not accompanied or followed by a repudiation, does not give rise to a claim for damages for total breach.

(4) One of the recurring objections to permitting an immediate suit upon repudiation is the supposed difficulty of putting a present value on a promise to pay to be performed in future installments. This uncertainty is eliminated, however, where the promise is to pay a fixed sum of money and the duty to pay is not hedged with contingencies. In these cases, the plaintiff may be relying upon installment payments for support and be put to great expense and frustration if required separately to enforce each installment. How did the *Cohen* case deal with this problem? What is the effect of its decree that "future installments shall be paid when they fall due?" Is it tantamount to a declaratory judgment that the policy is still in effect and a decree reinstating the policy? See Federal Declaratory Judgment Act, 28 U.S.C.A. §§ 2201–02. What about a judgment that the defendant shall pay in installments so long as the conditions for liability last? What about equitable relief? With the exception of one or two isolated cases, courts have been reluctant to grant conditional installment

judgments or equitable relief where the plaintiff seeks to recover money.

(5) *Discounting to Present Value; Adjusting Damage Award For Inflation.* Suppose that P has fully performed his side of the bargain in exchange for D's promise to pay $10,000 per year for the next 10 years, a total of $100,000. D then commits a material breach and the court is willing to give P a lump sum judgment for the total amount due over the ten year period. At least two things are clear: (1) D will be relieved from paying any agreed interest on the principal, and (2) the lump sum of $100,000 must be discounted to present value. The discount rate is the interest rate which is assumed to be available for future investments of the capital sum awarded as damages. Assume a rate of 10%. Thus, a $100,000 award is subject to a discount rate of 10% when it is reduced to a sum which, if invested for 10 years at an interest rate of 10%, would produce a total of principal and interest equal to $100,000. On these facts, that discounted amount is about $61,446.* D is not penalized by paying interest on principal he cannot use and P is not overcompensated by having an opportunity to invest principal that would not otherwise have been available. See Comment, *Adjusting Damage Awards for Future Inflation,* 1982 Wis.L.Rev. 397, 397–98. See UCC 2A–102(1)(u) (defining present value).

But if P's lump sum must be discounted downward, is he entitled to an upward adjustment for inflation or projected price increases over the 10 year period? If, over time, the $100,000 award would buy less and less, isn't P under-compensated unless inflation or deflation factors are employed for an adjustment? Most courts have held yes, but there is considerable disagreement over the fairest and most efficient way to accomplish the adjustment. One line of cases requires a total offset of the discount rate by the inflation rate as a matter of law, e.g., Beaulieu v. Elliott, 434 P.2d 665 (Alaska 1967), see Comment, 49 U.Chi.L.Rev. 1003 (1982), while other courts apply more flexible offsets. See Note, 57 St. Johns L.Rev. 316 (1983). The issue is of considerable importance in tort law, where judgments are frequently for injuries which extend into the future and are frequently "structured" into periodic payments.

(6) *Consequential Damages for Breach of Contract to Pay or Lend Money.* Increasingly, banks and other financial institutions have been sued for breach of a contract to lend money or to finance a particular venture. What is the lender's liability in these cases? The courts, relying upon Restatement, Second, § 351, comment e, agree that the presumptive measure is the difference between the interest rate plaintiffs contracted to pay and the actual rate plaintiffs were compelled to pay to secure substitute financing. Thus, if the bank agreed to finance at 9% and the substitute rate was 10%, the 1% spread would be the base rate for damages.

---

* The present discounted value of a series of future cashflows (where "C_i" is the cash received in the "i"th period) discounted at a periodic interest rate of "r" is equal to:

$$\sum_i \frac{c_i}{(1+r)^i}$$

But suppose the borrower is unable to obtain substitute financing and suffers other consequential damages. For example, the venture to be financed may fall through. Again, most courts agree that where it is foreseeable to the lender that substitute financing will be unavailable, the lender may be liable for the foreseeable actual damages resulting from the breach. Whether the foreseeability requirement is satisfied and the amount of loss resulting from the breach are questions of fact to be resolved in each case. See, e.g., Hill v. Ben Franklin Sav. & Loan Ass'n, 177 Ill.App.3d 51, 126 Ill.Dec. 462, 531 N.E.2d 1089 (1988) (foreseeability for the jury); Doyle v. Oregon Bank, 94 Or.App. 230, 764 P.2d 1379 (1988) (failure to allege damages were foreseeable precludes recovery).

Some courts, however, have denied consequential damage recovery to sellers under the UCC. See e.g. Afram Export Corp. v. Metallurgiki Halyps, S.A., 772 F.2d 1358 (7th Cir.1985). The reasoning is that since UCC 1–106(1) prohibits the recovery of consequential damages "except as specifically provided in this Act or by other rule of law" and there is no specific provision for the seller [there is for a buyer, see UCC 2–715(2)], the drafter's must have intended to deny that remedy to sellers. This result has been sharply criticized, and Revised UCC 2–710(2) now gives the seller the same claim to consequential damages as is given to the buyer. The seller's claim for consequential damages, however, is not available in consumer contracts.

PROBLEM: SELLER'S RESALE REMEDY UNDER THE UCC

Review the Problem of the Recalcitrant Manufacturer, supra, Chapter Three at 210, especially part (a) dealing with Seller's remedies under Article 2.

Suppose Smirgo entered into a contract with Brent's Outlet Store for the sale of 200 electric toaster ovens. The ovens were popular because of a new computer chip that monitored performance. The agreed price was $60 per oven, a total of $12,000.

Under the contract, Smirgo was to ship the goods to Brent "fob destination" (which meant that Smirgo was to pay the transportation costs) as follows: 100 ovens in three months, June 1, and the balance on September 1. Brent agreed to pay the full price for each installment within 30 days after delivery. In establishing a price of $60 per oven, Smirgo took the following costs into account:

1. coils, stainless steel, computer chips, and other materials for manufacturing		$30.00
2. labor		10.00
3. fixed costs, e.g., overhead, etc.		10.00
4. transportation to buyer		4.00
Total variable and fixed costs		54.00
Expected net profit per oven		6.00
		$60.00

Smirgo shipped and Brent accepted the first installment of ovens. On June 15, Brent telephoned and repudiated the contract. Apparently a new toaster oven with an even better computer chip had come on the market at $50 per oven. At the time of the repudiation, Smirgo had completed goods for the

MP = 50 @ time of — $40
Breach

second installment and had identified them as intended for Brent. Also, it is stipulated that at all relevant times the market price for the "contract" ovens was $30.00 per oven at the point of shipment and $25.00 per oven at the point of delivery. Brent refused to retract the repudiation. Smirgo then canceled the contract and consulted an attorney. The questions posed are as follows (please consult your UCC):

1. Will there be any problems because I (Smirgo) canceled the contract before consulting with you? See UCC 2–610, 2–703 & 2–612. [Rev. 2–610(1).]

2. If I sue *before* July 1, can I recover the full price for those goods delivered? See UCC 2–607(1), 2–709 & 2–723. In any event, can I recover the full price for the completed ovens sitting in my warehouse?

3. If I can't recover the price on the second installment, I have found a local "second hand" retail outlet which is willing to buy them for $28 per oven. Nobody else in this area is interested. If I sell them now for $28, how much can I recover from Brent? The buyer says that he will pick them up at my plant. See UCC 2–706. Suppose I can resell for $30 per oven?

4. It will cost me $100 to arrange this resale. Can I recover this from Brent? See UCC 2–710. [Rev. 2–710(1).]

5. Suppose I decide to hold rather than to resell the second installment of ovens. What can I recover from Brent? See UCC 2–708. If I recover damages under 2–708, and later the market for these ovens improves and I sell them for $10 each, do I have any duty to account to Brent?

American Mechanical Corp. v. Union Machine Co. of Lynn, Inc.

Appeals Court of Massachusetts, 1985.
21 Mass.App.Ct. 97, 485 N.E.2d 680.

[On October 16, 1976, American contracted with Union to sell its real estate and business equipment for $135,000. Union knew that American was in financial difficulty, that it was in arrears on mortgage payments to Saugus Bank and that Saugus was pressing American to sell. Union issued a $5,000 check as a down payment, to be held in escrow until closing. On November 1, 1976, Union repudiated the contract. Saugus bank took possession of the property and, after American was unable to find another purchaser, the equipment was sold by Saugus for $35,000. On June 1, 1977, Saugus conducted a foreclosure sale and purchased the real estate for $55,000. American sued Union for breach of contract. After trial, the superior court concluded that although there was a breach of contract, American had not proved the "right to recover damages beyond nominal damages." Upon appeal, the judgment was vacated and a final judgment was entered in favor of American in the amount of $46,000 with interest.]

■ FINE, JUSTICE.

* * *

Damages for Breach of Contract.

The judge ruled that the contract was one for the sale of the real estate for $100,000 and for the sale of the personal property for $35,000. Since

American owed
35k to the
bank anyway

a foreclosure
price would
not be fair
Market price

Even if it was
done in GF →
not Market
Value

Aim of Damages =
Inj. party same
position as had
been performed

$35,000 was obtained by the Saugus Bank & Trust Company when it sold the equipment and machinery, and that amount presumably was credited to American's account with the bank, the judge ruled that American had sustained no loss unless it did so with respect to the real estate. We need not decide whether a breakdown of the contract price between the real estate and the personalty was called for, or whether the price should be viewed as a lump sum for the entire sale. In our view, the result is not affected by any such determination. The judge ruled that the measure of damages for the breach of the agreement to purchase the real estate was the difference between the contract price and the fair market value on the date of the breach. Because he did not believe that the price obtained at the foreclosure sale, seven months after the breach, represented the fair market value of the property on the date of the breach, and because the plaintiff had produced no other evidence of the market value of the real estate on the date of the breach, the judge ruled that American had failed to prove actual damages.

The judge correctly stated the traditional rule generally applicable in measuring damages for breach of an agreement to purchase real estate . . . He was also correct in his conclusion that the foreclosure sale price, even if some evidence of the market value, was not binding on him as establishing the market value of the property on the date of the breach. The actual sale of a piece of property normally provides strong evidence of market value, although the "evidentiary value of such sales in less than arms-length transactions is diminished." New Boston Garden Corp. v. Assessors of Boston, 383 Mass. 456, 469, 420 N.E.2d 298 (1981) . . . We assume that the bank in conducting the sale complied with its duty of due diligence, observing the procedural requirements of both the mortgage and the statute (G.L. c. 244, § 14), and acted in good faith . . . It does not follow, however, that a sale so conducted will necessarily yield a price reflecting the full market value . . .

Based upon his view of the applicable rule for measuring damages, and his disbelief of American's evidence of market value, the judge awarded American nominal damages only. The rule relied upon by the judge for measuring damages for breach of an agreement to purchase real estate, however, does not apply in all cases.

Consistent with general principles of contract law, the aim in measuring damages in the event of a breach is to place the injured party in as good a position as he would have been in had the contract been performed . . . An important aspect of this principle is that if a party suing for breach of contract has sustained a loss as a result of a breach, and the loss is of such a nature that it was reasonably foreseeable by the parties or actually within their contemplation at the time the contract was entered into, then that loss may be recovered in an action for damages . . .

There is no logical basis for treating real estate purchase and sale agreements differently from other purchase and sale agreements, or from contracts generally, for purposes of measuring damages. See 11 Williston, Contracts § 1399 (3d ed. 1968). The usual formula for measuring damages for breach of a real estate purchase and sale agreement—the difference between the contract price and the market value on the date of the breach—is merely a different formulation of the general rule for measuring contract damages. In the usual case, the contract price less the market value represents the seller's actual loss, and the formula, therefore, affords the injured seller an adequate remedy. In some cases, however, the actual loss suffered as a result of a breach exceeds the amount yielded by that formula. The question is whether, because the contract involves the sale of real estate, we may not, in such cases, refer to that aspect of the general rule of contract damages which gives recognition to actual losses sustained as a result of a breach when the losses are reasonably foreseeable or within the contemplation of the parties. That principle has been applied to contracts which are exclusively for the sale of real estate when the particular circumstances are such that the usual rule produces an inadequate remedy....

American proved that it sustained a loss in the amount of $45,000, the difference between the contract price of $135,000 and the $90,000 received from the mortgagee bank's sale of the real estate, machinery, and equipment. The judge's findings make it clear that at the time the contract was entered into, Union knew that, if the sale of the property did not go through, the result would be that the bank would enforce its rights under the mortgage and that a foreclosure sale was likely. On almost identical facts, an Ohio court recently ruled that the correct measure of damages, on traditional contract principles, was the full amount of the actual loss, the contract price less the amount received for the property at the foreclosure sale.... We do not hesitate to reach the same result on the facts of this case. It does not seem to us to be a departure from established principles.

Union would, of course, be entitled to have American's damages reduced to the extent that American could reasonably have avoided the loss. Restatement (Second) of Contracts § 350 (1979). Thus, if, once it knew of the breach, American could reasonably have sold the property to someone else, it would be entitled to damages in an amount no greater than the difference between the contract price and the price for which it could have sold the property. Union established through cross-examination of Beckett that, following notification of the breach, no attempt was made by American to put the property back on the market. The judge found as a fact, however, that "American was unable to secure another purchaser for the realty and equipment." There is evidence in the record to support that finding. The evidentiary support consists principally of Beckett's recitation of what transpired between him and the Saugus Bank & Trust Company during the period immediately following notice of the breach. The bank moved relatively quickly to take possession, and the property was not of the kind for which one could assume there would be a ready market. Thus, it is not clear, as a practical matter, that American could have done anything to avoid the foreclosure. In any event, the burden of proving that losses could have been avoided by reasonable effort rests with the party in breach ... Farnsworth, Contracts § 12.12 (1982); Restatement (Second) of Contracts § 350, comment c (1979). Union's showing on this point was insufficient to establish that American failed to act reasonably to avoid the loss. Accordingly, there is no basis for reducing the damages to which American would otherwise be entitled because of any failure on its part to act reasonably to avoid the loss.

* * *

NOTES

(1) At what time was the market value of the real estate relevant? Suppose there was evidence that the market value was $75,000 at the date of breach and $70,000 at the date set for closing. What result under the court's reasoning? Are you persuaded that the price produced in a foreclosure sale some seven months later at which the mortgagee, Saugus, was the purchaser reflects a "fair" market value?

Problems of proof aside, the contract price/market price standard used by the court is common in contracts for the sale of improved real estate, e.g., Frank v. Jansen, 303 Minn. 86, 226 N.W.2d 739 (1975) and contracts for the lease of realty, improved or unimproved. See F. Enterprises, Inc. v. Kentucky Fried Chicken Corp., 47 Ohio St.2d 154, 351 N.E.2d 121 (1976) (measure of damages for breach by lessee is difference between the fair market rental of the property proposed to be leased and the agreed rental to be paid in the proposed lease, such sum discounted to present value, together with any special damages arising from the breach.)

A similar approach is taken under UCC 2–708(1), especially where the seller has completed goods on hand. See Kenco Homes, Inc. v. Williams, 94 Wash.App. 219, 972 P.2d 125 (1999) (UCC 2–708(1) inadequate where seller does not have completed goods on hand).

(2) Note that the real estate in the *American Mechanical* case was sold at a foreclosure sale by the mortgagee, Saugus Bank, rather than by the vendor, American. From the proceeds, Saugus is entitled to satisfy its claim against American, including expenses incurred in enforcement. If there is a surplus, it must be paid to American. If there is a deficit, American still owes that amount to Saugus, who becomes an unsecured creditor. Similar principles are employed where a creditor with a security interest in goods repossesses them and conducts a public or private resale. See UCC 9–504; Rev. UCC 9–610, 615.

(3) *Mitigation and Leases.* If an estate in land has "vested" in the lessee by a lease, the lessor's remedy upon breach by the lessee is no different than that of a vendor of land after title has passed to the vendee or a seller of goods after the buyer has accepted them: an action for the agreed rent is proper. See *Kentucky Fried Chicken Corp.,* supra. But suppose the lessee has vacated the premises. Does the lessor have any "duty" to mitigate damages by reletting the premises to another? At common law the answer was no, on the theory that an interest in land had been sold. If the lessor in fact relet the premises, the lessee's obligation would be credited by the amount obtained, but the lessor had no duty to make a reasonable effort to relet. More recently, some cases have treated the problem as if it were a contract to lease and required the lessor to made reasonable efforts to relet. The effect of this is that if the lessor fails to make these efforts, the lessee's obligation will be credited with the amount of rent that the lessor reasonably could have obtained. Restatement (Second) § 350, Comment b. See also Farmers and Bankers Life Insurance Co. v. St. Regis Paper Co., 456 F.2d 347 (5th Cir.1972), holding that the lessor may elect to treat failure to pay rent under a lease as a contract to lease and seek

damages based upon the difference between the lease price and the market price.

Article 2A of the UCC, dealing with leases of goods, gives the lessor some choices where the lessee fails to pay rent on accepted goods. See UCC 2A–523. The lessor can recover the agreed rent for the balance of the lease and leave the goods with the lessee until the end of the lease term, UCC 2A–529(1)(a), or the lessor can take possession of the leased goods, UCC 2A–525, and either re-lease them to a third party, UCC 2A–527, or claim damages under UCC 2A–528. Although the lessor is not required to take possession of the goods or re-lease them, if possession is retaken, mitigation features are built into the damage remedies. See e.g. UCC 2A–527(2) and UCC 2A–528(1).

(4) *Mitigation in Sale of Goods*. In contracts for the sale of goods, the seller who delivers goods to the buyer in exchange for a promise to pay the price cannot (normally) recover the goods if the buyer fails to pay. The buyer, however, is liable for the price of the goods accepted. UCC 2–709(1)(a). If the seller has possession of the goods at the time when the buyer breaches, the seller may either resell the goods to a third party, UCC 2–706(1), or sue for damages, UCC 2–708(1). If the seller unreasonably fails to resell goods still in its possession and identified to the contract, the buyer has some protection in the "market" damage formula in UCC 2–708(1). The seller gets no more than the difference between the contract price and the market price at the time and place for tender. See Restatement (Second) § 350, Comment c. Thus, a mitigation principle is built into the damage formula for both leases and contracts for sale of goods.

Article 77 of CISG provides:

A party who relies on a breach of contract must take such measures as are reasonable in the circumstances to mitigate the loss, including loss of profit, resulting from the breach. If he fails to take such measures, the party in breach may claim a reduction in the damages by which the loss should have been mitigated.

This would be a good provision for Revised Article 2, right?

(5) *Nominal Damages*. The trial court in the principal case awarded nominal damages. Courts agree that nominal damages can be awarded for breach of contract but limit the award to $1 or other smaller amount. See e.g. Graves v. Iowa Lakes Community College, 639 N.W.2d 22, 28 (Iowa 2002) (nominal damages are only a trivial or trifling amount).

Lowy v. United Pacific Insurance Co.

Supreme Court of California, 1967.
Supra at 790.

New Era Homes Corp. v. Forster

Court of Appeals of New York, 1949.
299 N.Y. 303, 86 N.E.2d 757.

■ DESMOND, JUDGE. Plaintiff entered into a written agreement with defendants, to make extensive alterations to defendants' home, the reference therein to price and payment being as follows:

"All above material, and labor to erect and install same to be supplied for $3,075.00 to be paid as follows:

$150.00 on signing of contract,

$1,000.00 upon delivery of materials and starting of work,

$1,500.00 on completion of rough carpentry and rough plumbing,

$425.00 upon job being completed."

The work was commenced and partly finished, and the first two stipulated payments were made. Then, when the "rough work" was done, plaintiff asked for the third installment of $1,500 but defendants would not pay it, so plaintiff stopped work and brought suit for the whole of the balance, that is, for the two last payments of $1,500 and $425. On the trial plaintiff stipulated to reduce its demand to $1,500, its theory being that, since all the necessary "rough carpentry and rough plumbing" had been done, the time had arrived for it to collect $1,500. It offered no other proof as to its damages. Defendants conceded their default but argued at the trial, and argue here, that plaintiff was entitled not to the $1,500 third payment, but to such amount as it could establish by way of actual loss sustained from defendants' breach. In other words, defendants say the correct measure of damage was the value of the work actually done, less payments made, plus lost profits. The jury, however, by its verdict gave plaintiff its $1,500. The Appellate Division, Second Department, affirmed the judgment, and we granted defendants leave to appeal to this court.

The whole question is as to the meaning of so much of the agreement as we have quoted above. Did that language make it an entire contract, with one consideration for the doing of the whole work, and payments on account at fixed points in the progress of the job, or was the bargain a severable or divisible one in the sense that, of the total consideration, $1,150 was to be the full and fixed payment for "delivery of materials and starting of work", $1,500 the full and fixed payment for work done up to and including "completion of rough carpentry and rough plumbing", and $425 for the rest. We hold that the total price of $3,075 was the single consideration for the whole of the work, and that the separately listed payments were not allocated absolutely to certain parts of the undertaking, but were scheduled part payments, mutually convenient to the builder and the owner. That conclusion, we think, is a necessary one from the very words of the writing, since the arrangement there stated was not that separate items of work be done for separate amounts of money, but that the whole alteration project, including material and labor, was "to be supplied for $3,075". There is nothing in the record to suggest that the parties had intended to group, in this contract, several separate engagements, each with its own separate consideration. They did not say, for instance, that the price for all the work up to the completion of rough carpentry and plumbing was to be $1,500. They did agree that at that point $1,500 would be due, but as a part payment on the whole price. To illustrate: it is hardly conceivable that the amount of $150, payable "on signing of contract" was a reward to plaintiff for the act of affixing its corporate name and seal.

We would, in short, be writing a new contract for these people if we broke this single promise up into separate deals; and the new contract so written by us might be, for all we know, most unjust to one or the other party.

We find no controlling New York case, but the trend of authority in this State, and elsewhere, is that such agreements express an intent that payment be conditioned and dependent upon completion of all the agreed work.... We think that is the reasonable rule—after all, a householder who remodels his home is, usually, committing himself to one plan and one result, not a series of unrelated projects. The parties to a construction or alteration contract may, of course, make it divisible and stipulate the value of each divisible part. But there is no sign that these people so intended, see Integrity Flooring v. Zandon, supra. It follows that plaintiff, on defendants' default, could collect either in quantum meruit for what had been finished, . . . or in contract for the value of what plaintiff had lost—that is, the contract price, less payments made and less the cost of completion....

The judgments should be reversed, and a new trial granted, with costs to abide the event.

■ LEWIS, JUDGE (dissenting).

A contract is entire or divisible depending upon the intention of the parties to be gathered from the agreement itself and the circumstances surrounding its execution....

The parties to the written agreement here in suit were careful to provide that the contract price was to be paid in specified installments which, after the initial payment, were in varying amounts payable upon completion of designated stages of the work. The contracting parties thus indicated their intent to be that the part to be performed by the plaintiff was to consist of several distinct and separate items and that the price to be paid by the defendants was to be apportioned accordingly to fall due when each specified stage of the work should be completed . . .

Concluding, as I do, that such a contract is divisible in character, . . . I would affirm the judgment.

NOTES

(1) *Progress payments in government contracts.* In government supply and construction contracts, there is often a long "lead time" between the beginning of work and final delivery or completion where the contractor is uncompensated for partial performance expenditures. To alleviate the impact of this on the contractor's financial position, the government will make progress payments based upon costs incurred. In construction contracts the contractor will be paid 80% of its costs incurred at various stages of performance (compare *New Era Homes*), and in supply contracts the payments are made "as work progresses,

from time to time upon request." The payments are liquidated from amounts due as construction is completed or the supplies are delivered.

(2) Suppose, in *New Era Homes,* the owner had agreed to pay 80% of the contractor's total cost at each stage of completion rather than a fixed amount. Would the contract have been divisible? Should the contractor be satisfied by an action "on the contract" to recover just 80% of his cost incurred?

Comment: Breach of Construction Contract and the "Components" Approach

New Era Homes presents a classic case of breach by the Owner while a Contractor is in the midst of performing a construction contract. Unless the contract is divisible or Contractor has "substantially" performed, an action for the agreed price for the job will not lie. Furthermore, any performance by Contractor after the breach is normally out of the question (the work is being done on Owner's land) and, in any event, would probably run afoul of the mitigation principle. See, e.g., Rockingham County v. Luten Bridge Co., 35 F.2d 301 (4th Cir.1929)(unreasonable expenditures in performance incurred after the breach not recoverable). Put another way, Contractor would probably be ousted from the project and unable to recover for any work done after the breach. What damages can Contractor recover?

A Useful Formula. New Era Homes stated that the plaintiff "could collect either in quantum meruit for what had been finished ... or in contract for what plaintiff had lost—that is, the contract price, less payments made and less the cost of completion." Leaving quantum meruit or "restitution" recovery aside for the moment, the damage recovery can be illustrated as follows. If the contract price was $3,075 and, at the time of the breach, the estimated cost to complete the project was $425 (savings realized by breach, SR), and Contractor had been paid $2,000 in progress payments (PP), the damages for breach would be $3,075 (KP) less $425 (SR) less $2,000 (PP) = $650. This figure will be enhanced if Contractor can prove other losses, including incidental or consequential damages, and, of course, Owner can always attack Contractor's attempt to prove the savings realized by the breach, here $425. See, generally, Edwin W. Patterson, *Builder's Measure of Recovery for Breach of Contract,* 31 Colum.L.Rev. 1286 (1931).

Note that the remainder above, $650, covers both the gain prevented by the breach and performance expenditures incurred up to the breach not covered by the progress payments. Assume, in our example, that Owner had made no payments under the contract and that the cost to complete (SR) was $425. The remainder, after subtracting $425 from $3,075, $2,650, should be broken down into components for a more through analysis, i.e., what part of the $2,650 represents net profit prevented, what part represents costs incurred up to the breach and, of those costs incurred, what part is variable and what part is fixed (overhead) costs? Suppose, then, that the value of the total costs incurred (TCI) at the time of breach was $2,500. The net profit prevented should be determined by subtracting from $3,075 (KP) the sum of $425 (SR) and $2,500 (TCI) for a profit figure of $150.

When this is added to the TCI figure of $2,500, the total recovery for breach of contract is still $2,650. A more thorough breakdown might try to distinguish between fixed and variable costs in the $2,500 TCI figure, especially since Owner may claim that Contractor did not exercise reasonable efforts to salvage materials purchased or to reallocate labor after the breach. If Owner is correct, the TCI figure might be reduced in the amount that would have been realized if a reasonable salvage had been effected. For a fuller exploration of these complexities, see Colorado Environments, Inc. v. Valley Grading Corp., 105 Nev. 464, 779 P.2d 80 (1989).

In the example above, the damages, whether expressed in a lump sum or components, protect both the expectation and the reliance interests. Put more directly, Contractor cannot be put in the place Owner's full performance would have put it unless it recovers both net gains prevented and unreimbursed expenses in part performance. In addition, Contractor should have the opportunity to plead and prove consequential damages resulting from the breach which were foreseeable to the defendant at the time of contracting. See Independent Mechanical Contractors, Inc. v. Gordon T. Burke & Sons, Inc., 138 N.H. 110, 635 A.2d 487 (1993)(profits lost in other ventures).

Burden of proof. Who has the burden of proving what the cost of completion would have been, the plaintiff or the defendant? In a case where the plaintiff was a terminated contractor who left a construction job that was later completed by others, it was held that the initial burden of coming forward with evidence (and, perhaps, the ultimate risk of non-persuasion) was on the defendant. United States v. Merritt–Meridian Constr. Corp., 2000 WL 272177 (S.D.N.Y.2000). The court analogized the cost to complete to a set-off, which is traditionally treated as an affirmative defense. In addition, the court concluded that the burden should be on the party with superior access to information about completion costs and who seeks to take advantage of them. In both cases, it was the defendant.

Comment: Reliance Damages or Restitution in Losing Contracts.

Reliance Damages Alternative. Because of difficulties of proof or otherwise, a contractor or other performer may prove expenditures in part performance up to the breach but not try to prove lost profits. In this situation, the evidence will include the total cost incurred (TCI) but not savings realized (SR). Without more, Contractor can, as an alternative, recover reliance expenditures. See, e.g., United States v. Behan, 110 U.S. 338, 4 S.Ct. 81, 28 L.Ed. 168 (1884); Restatement (Second) § 349 (includes reliance expenses in preparation or part-performance); Lon L. Fuller & William Perdue, *The Reliance Interest in Contract Damages*, 46 Yale L.J. 52, 76–80 (1936).

Losing Contracts. The defendant, however, may prove that if Contractor had completed performance there would have been a loss. For example, in the construction hypo above Owner may prove that Contractor's savings realized by the breach were $2,000 and that the total costs of performing a $3,075 contract would have been $4,500. In that case, there would have been a losing contract. Contractor is obviously foreclosed from recovering any profit and the reliance expenditures should be adjusted downward in proportion to the projected loss. See Bausch & Lomb Inc. v. Bressler, 977 F.2d 720, 729 (2d Cir.1992), where the court stated: "If the breaching party establishes that the plaintiff's losses upon full performance would have equaled or exceeded its reliance expenditures, the plaintiff will recover nothing under a reliance theory." See also L. Albert & Son v. Armstrong Rubber Co., 178 F.2d 182 (2d Cir.1949) (buyer can recover reliance expenditures subject to seller proof that buyer would have lost money on full performance).

Restitution Alternative. It is at this point that the "quantum meruit" or restitution alternative becomes relevant. If the plaintiff can cancel the contract for material breach and prove that the defendant has been benefited by part performance, can the plaintiff recover the value of that part performance without limitation by the contract price?

In a provocative article, Professor Robert Childres argued that use of the term "restitution" obscures the fact that the plaintiff is frequently seeking to recover for reliance in part performance of the breached contract rather than to disgorge benefits unjustly retained by the defendant. If the latter were true, such as the case where money was paid or property delivered, no one suggests that the plaintiff ought to receive less than the full amount retained. The same is generally true where the defendant has benefited from services actually rendered and retained; restitution here is in the form of a quantum meruit. But when the plaintiff seeks the reasonable value of reliance expenditures and that value exceeds the contract price, there is no apparent reason why the contract price should not control the outer limits of that recovery. Childres said:

> There is no justification for the position that the terms of the promise do not regulate the recovery of reliance damages in some cases which may be twisted into an "action in *quantum meruit*." A promise excites expectations and causes reliance, for both of which the law should justly give protection. The crucial question * * * is whether or not the promise which was relied upon, being the *provocateur* of the reliance, will regulate the damages recoverable in event of a breach. * * * By way of example, a firm agrees to manufacture X number of rifles for the government at Y unit price. After the government requires that performance cease, the firm seeks five times Y for each rifle delivered, saying that this was the reasonable value of what it did. The argument is an attempt to entirely upset the parties' original business arrangement. If freedom of contract means freedom to deviate from the standards of reasonable men, fully informed, and enjoying levels of knowledge and intelligence to be expected in the situation, it can have no more fertile field than that of allocating market and other relevant risks in a business transaction. Specifically, the parties' own allocation of the market and other risks should be upset, if at all, by substantive doctrine and not by whether one chooses the label "quantum meruit" * * * on the one hand, or "reliance damages" on the other.

On the relevant "substantive doctrine," Professor Childres states:

> There is no reason why "aggrieved" persons should, by the contract law of damages, be put in a better position than they would have occupied had they performed; secondly, the agreed market and risk allocations should not be upset by the often unclear question of who was in breach; and thirdly, the law should not encourage those who misspeculate to escape obligation by claiming that the other person is, for some contrived reason, in breach.

Childres & Garmella, *The Law of Restitution and the Reliance Interest in Contract,* 64 Nw.L.Rev. 433, 439–441, 445–446 (1969). See also Mather, *Restitution as a Remedy for Breach of Contract: The Case of the Partially Performing Seller,* 92 Yale L.J. 14 (1982), who argues that the partially performing "seller's" recovery should be "limited" to expectancy damages, a conclusion which is "derived from liberal principles of justice, which usually impel courts to protect personal liberty and minimize coercion * * *." 92 Yale L.J. at 48.

Restatement (Second) Under the Restatement, Second, one of the interests protected upon breach is called the "restitution" interest, which is the aggrieved party's interest "in having restored to him any benefit that he has conferred on the other party." Restatement (Second) § 344(c). In protecting this interest, a court might enter a judgment or order "requiring restoration of a specific thing to prevent unjust enrichment" or "awarding a sum of money to prevent unjust enrichment." Restatement (Second) § 345(c) & (d). But the plaintiff is entitled to restitution "only to the extent that he has conferred a benefit on the other party · by way of part performance or reliance." Section 370. This is in sharp contrast to the measure of damages designed to protect the expectation interest, e.g., the "loss in the value to him of the other party's performance caused by its failure or deficiency." Section 347(a). See David Simon, *A Critique of the Treatment of Market Damages in the Restatement (Second) of Contracts,* 81 Colum.L.Rev. 80 (1981). Compare Robert A. Hudec, *Restating the Reliance Interest,* 67 Cornell L.Rev. 704 (1982). When, then, is a contractor or seller of goods and services entitled to restitution as a remedy for breach by the other? Section 373(1) provides that "on a breach by nonperformance that gives rise to a claim for damages for total breach or on a repudiation, the injured party is entitled to restitution for any benefit that he has conferred on the other party by way of part performance or reliance."

Are there any limitations? Here is one: "The injured party has no right to restitution if he has performed all of his duties under the contract and no performance by the other party remains due other than payment of a definite sum of money for that performance." See John T. Brady & Co. v. City of Stamford, 220 Conn. 432, 599 A.2d 370, 376–379 (1991). The contract price is not otherwise a limitation, however, and, in theory at least, the plaintiff can recover the full amount of the benefit conferred even though it would have been a losing contract had there been no breach. See Section 373, Comment d. A possible limitation, however, lies in the measure of the restitution interest. Section 371 provides:

If a sum of money is awarded to protect a party's restitution interest, it may as justice requires be measured by either (a) the reasonable value to the other party of what he received in terms of what it would have cost him to obtain it from a person in the claimant's position, or (b) the extent to which the other party's property has been increased in value or his other interests advanced.

How is a court to exercise this choice when, say, the market price to have similar work done is $2,000 and the increase in value to the property is $1,500? One suggestion is that the court should award the smaller amount when the plaintiff is in breach. See Section 374 and Illustration 1 to Section 371. Another suggestion is that in making the choice in a losing contract, the court should "take account of standards of good faith and fair dealing during any negotiations leading up to the rupture of contractual relations." Restatement (Second) § 373, Comment d. The question is whether the plaintiff provoked a breach in a losing contract "in order to avoid having to perform." For a concise summary, see Joseph Perillo, *Restitution in the Second Restatement of Contracts*, 81 Colum.L.Rev. 37 (1982).

Bernstein v. Nemeyer

Supreme Court of Connecticut, 1990.
213 Conn. 665, 570 A.2d 164.

[Plaintiffs invested $1,050,000 as limited partners in a partnership formed to purchase and renovate two apartment complexes in Houston, Texas. The plaintiffs' objectives were capital appreciation and a tax shelter for assets previously acquired. As an inducement to invest, the defendants made a negative cash flow guaranty: They promised to lend to the partnership the amount by which defined operating and financing expenses exceeded the cash receipts from normal business operations. The guaranty was limited in time and provisions were made for the defendants to recover loans made from income or the proceeds of any sale of the complexes. The plaintiffs were informed of the risk of foreclosure in a weak real estate market.

Despite good faith efforts and after loans to the partnership of $3,000,000 under the guaranty, the defendants defaulted on their obligations to the financiers of the project. No further loans to the partnership were made. The mortgages were ultimately foreclosed and both the plaintiffs and defendants lost their entire investment.

The plaintiffs sued for rescission of the contract and restitution of their investment. The trial court denied relief, concluding inter alia that the defendant's breach of the negative cash flow guaranty was not material. The trial court also found that the plaintiff's losses resulted from a bad market rather than the defendant's breach and that, despite the breach, the plaintiffs had fully realized their tax advantages.

On appeal, the decision was affirmed. The court, speaking through Chief Justice Peters, first held that the defendant's breach was material. In short, the trial court had not given sufficient consideration to the fact that the plaintiffs had lost the substantial benefit of the bargain and that the defendant's breach was not curable.] * * *

II

The conclusion that the defendants' nonperformance of the negative cash flow guaranty was a material breach of the partnership agreement does not, however, end our inquiry. It follows from an uncured material failure of performance that the other party to the contract is discharged from any further duty to render performances yet to be exchanged ... It does not follow that the party so discharged is automatically entitled to restitution rather than to a claim for damages. We must still determine whether, in the circumstances of this case, the trial court correctly rendered judgment in favor of the defendants because the plaintiffs have failed to prove a right to restitution of the payments that they made to the partnership. We conclude that the record sustains the judgment of the trial court on this alternate ground.

"When a court grants [the remedy of restitution] for breach, the party in breach is required to account for a benefit that has been conferred on him by the injured party.... In contrast to cases in which the court grants specific performance or awards damages as a remedy for breach, the effort is not to enforce the promise by protecting the injured party's expectation or reliance interest, but to prevent unjust enrichment of the party in breach by protecting the injured party's restitution interest. The objective is not to put the *injured* party in as good a position as he would have been in if the contract had been performed, nor even to put the injured party back in the position he would have been in if the contract had not been made; it is, rather, to put the party in breach back in the position he would have been in if the contract had not been made." (Emphasis in original.) E.A. Farnsworth, Contracts (1982) § 12.19, p. 905; 1 G. Palmer, The Law of Restitution (1978) § 4.1, p. 369; 3 Restatement (Second), Contracts §§ 344(c) and 370 (1981); ...[11] When an injured party seeks an award of money to protect his restitutionary interest, any award "may as justice requires be measured by either (a) the reasonable value to the other party of what he received ... or (b) the extent to which the other party's property has been increased in value or his other interests advanced." 3 Restatement (Second), Contracts § 371 (1981).[12]

---

11. Section 344 of the Restatement (Second) of Contracts provides in relevant part: "Judicial remedies under the rules stated in this Restatement serve to protect one or more of the following interests of a promissee....

"(c) his 'restitution interest,' which is his interest in having restored to him any benefit that he has conferred a benefit on the other party."

Section 370 provides: "A party is entitled to restitution under the rules stated in this Restatement only to the extent that he has conferred a benefit on the other party by way of part performance or reliance."

12. Section 371 of the Restatement (Second) of Contracts provides: "If a sum of

The principles of the law of restitution demonstrate that the defendants' non-performance of the negative cash loan guaranty, although a material breach of the partnership agreement, does not automatically and unconditionally entitle the plaintiffs to recover their investment in the partnership. The award of a restitutionary remedy for breach of contract depends upon a showing of what justice requires in the particular circumstances. . . . The decision to award a particular restitutionary remedy thus necessarily rests in the discretion of the court.

In the present litigation, the trial court could reasonably have concluded that the plaintiffs had failed to establish their right to the return of their investments. We have regularly held that it is a condition of rescission and restitution that the plaintiff offer, as nearly as possible, to place the other party in the same situation that existed prior to the execution of the contract. . . . The record in this case is entirely unclear about what efforts the plaintiffs made to tender back their partnership interests to the defendants before bringing this law suit. The record likewise contains no finding that the financial condition of the partnership, at the time the plaintiffs learned of the defendants' breach, was already so impoverished that a restitutionary tender would have been pointless.

Even more damaging to the plaintiffs' claim for restitution is the trial court's affirmative finding that the defendants "suffered a great loss of their own, about three million dollars, in attempting to satisfy their obligations under the contract and, specifically, the guaranty provision." This unchallenged finding of fact supports the conclusion that the plaintiffs could not have restored the defendants to their position prior to their execution of the partnership agreement. Further, it demonstrates that, despite the defendants' material breach of the partnership agreement, the defendants' property interests have not been "increased in value or [their] other interests advanced." 3 Restatement (Second), Contracts § 371(b) (1981). In short, the plaintiffs have not proven that the defendants have been unjustly enriched.

There is no error.

NOTES

(1) *Restitution and reliance damages after United States v. Winstar.*

In response to a crisis in the savings and loan industry, the Federal Home Loan Bank Board (FHLBB) induced a number of healthy savings and loan companies to take over and operate failed or insolvent S & Ls under a so-called "supervisory merger." The purpose of the contracts was to reduce the potential liability of the Federal Savings and loan Insurance Corporation (FSLIC), which had insured thrift deposits, and the inducement was the government's agree-

money is awarded to protect a party's restitution interest, it may as justice requires be measured by either

"(a) the reasonable value to the other party of what he received in terms of what it would have cost him to obtain it from a person in the claimant's position, or

"(b) the extent to which the other party's property has been increased in value or his other interests advanced."

ment to treat the excess of the liabilities of the failed thrifts over their capital assets ("supervisory goodwill") to meet the takeover thrift's reserve requirements and to amortize it over a period of 40 years. Subsequently, Congress totally revamped the legal structure and created a successor agency to FHLBB, the Office of Thrift Supervision (OTS). OTS then issued regulations that effectively terminated the favorable accounting treatment given in the supervisory mergers. The "take over" S & Ls were then required to meet reserve requirements from other sources or be liquidated. Many law suits followed.

In *United States v. Winstar*, 518 U.S. 839 (1996), the Supreme Court held that the United States had breached its contracts with the plaintiff "take over" thrifts and remanded the case for a determination of damages. [A portion of this case is reprinted supra at 827.] See Richard E. Speidel, *Contract Excuse Doctrine and Retrospective Legislation: The Winstar Case*, 2001 Wis. L. Rev.795 (2001) (discussing issues of liability and breach).

At one time there were more than 120 suits by "take-over" S & Ls claiming damages against the United States. They are far from resolved. A leading example of the approach taken to remedies is Glendale Federal Bank, FSB v. United States, 239 F.3d 1374 (Fed.Cir.2001), which reversed a judgment awarding the plaintiffs $908,948,000 in restitution and non-overlapping (post-breach) reliance damages.

In *Glendale*, the court first reviewed the general approach to remedies for breach of contract (compensation not punishment), stated the expectation measure of damages, and affirmed the trial court's conclusion that the plaintiff had failed to prove expectation losses with reasonable certainty. This is a common failure in the S & L cases. But see California Federal Bank, FSB v. United States, 245 F.3d 1342 (Fed.Cir.2001) (trial court erred in granting summary judgment against plaintiff's claim for lost profits).

The court next conceded that a fall-back remedy was restitution, the purposes of which is to "restore—that is, to restore the non-breaching party to the position he would have been in had there never been a contract to breach...." According to the court, this was "not as good as lost profits, from the viewpoint of the non-breacher, but [is] a lot better than nothing."

This being said, the court reversed the trial court's award of restitution damages and remanded the case for a determination of Glendale's reliance damages, incurred before and after the breach. At the risk of over-simplification, the plaintiffs argued (and the trial court agreed) that they were entitled to the market value of their net liabilities because the take over "relieved the Government of its imminent responsibility for those liabilities." After agreeing that the government's breached promise had "substantial value," the court concluded that the acquisition of the failed thrift "did not result in the Government, specifically the FSLIC, saving the dollar value of the net obligations of the thrift." A number of variables were at play. First, it was not clear that but for the take over the government would be required to make up the deficit. There were many options in reducing this risk and a supervisory merger was just one of them. Second, the government was not free of potential liability after the take over. If interest rates had not gone down and eased the crisis, the government's contingent liability for the very losses that the plaintiff claims were benefits would mature. Third, the real benefit to the government was time—time to deal with other failed thrifts and to assess the market. Although the "value of time was more than zero, there is no proof of what in fact it was worth." In short,

> [T]he supposed gains ... are both speculative and indeterminate. We do not see how the restitution award granted by the trial court, measured in terms of a liability that never came to pass, and based on a speculative assessment of what might have been, can be upheld.

What about reliance damages? Here's what the court had to say:

> This does not mean that Glendale is without a remedy. Glendale recognized the problems in the restitution award, and cross-appealed, arguing that, should the court reject that award, Glendale nevertheless would be entitled to damages on a reliance theory. Indeed, the trial court recognized this third category of damages, known as reliance damages, and added specified reliance damages to the total award it granted plaintiff.

> The underlying principle in reliance damages is that a party who relies on another party's promise made binding through contract is entitled to damages for any losses actually sustained as a result of the breach of that promise. *See Restatement (Second) of Contracts* § 344(b) ("[Judicial remedies serve to protect the promisee's] reliance interest, which is his interest in being reimbursed for loss caused by reliance on the contract by being put in as good a position as he would have been in had the contract not been made."); 3 Dan B. Dobbs, *Law of Remedies* § 12.3(1) (2d ed. 1993) ("The reliance recovery is a reimbursement for losses the plaintiff suffers in reliance on the defendant's contractual promise."). As a general proposition, these damages are available for injuries resulting from activities that occurred either before or after the breach ...

> In the case at bar, the trial court awarded reliance damages for post-breach events, which the court denominated non-overlapping reliance damages. More specifically, it awarded Glendale damages for the following: [The court listed several types of post-breach reliance losses totaling over $370,000,000.]

> Note that, unlike restitution in which the critical event that fixes the damages is when the contract was entered into, in reliance damages the critical event is the breach itself. Damages consequent to that breach may be the result of actions before or after the breach. Though the trial court limited Glendale's reliance damages to post-breach damages, since otherwise there would be a problem with duplication of the restitution elements, there is nothing inherent in the concept to prevent a court from awarding reliance damages for pre-breach activities from which ascertainable losses as a result of the breach can be shown.

> In a case like the one before us, for all the reasons we have explained, we conclude that, for purposes of measuring the losses sustained by

Glendale as a result of the Government's breach, reliance damages provide a firmer and more rational basis than the alternative theories argued by the parties. We recognize the appeal in the restitution approach, but we find that keying an award to a liability that was at most a paper calculation, and which ignores the reality of subsequent events as they impacted on the parties, and particularly the plaintiff, is not justifiable. Reliance damages will permit a more finely tuned calculation of the actual losses sustained by plaintiff as a result of the Government's breach.

(2) *Professor Kull's Assessment*

Professor Andrew Kull, [the ALI Reporter for the revised Restatement of Restitution] writing before the decision in *Glendale Federal Bank*, *supra*, had this to say about restitution as a remedy for breach of contract. In retrospect, would he approve of Judge Plager's opinion in *Glendale*?

The confusing role played by restitution among the remedies for breach of contract can be clarified if we distinguish remedies that serve the plaintiff's restoration interest from remedies that address the defendant's unjust enrichment. The latter are more easily recognized if we call them "disgorgement," but the term is overbroad, because the significant instances of disgorgement are limited to cases in which the plaintiff recovers more than he lost. If the law requires the maker of a promissory note to pay the holder on default, there has been a breach of contract. Absent a remedy, the defendant would be unjustly enriched at the plaintiff's expense. A judgment for the amount of the debt achieves a kind of restitution and a kind of disgorgement. But it would be a complete waste of time to classify this liability within the law of restitution, or to observe that the holder of the note was seeking disgorgement for breach.

Disgorgement awarding the plaintiff more than he lost is justified in a narrow class of cases in which the defendant's election to breach imposes harms that a potential liability for provable damages will not adequately deter. It is much easier to see the analogy between the restitutionary liability in such cases and the standard instances of restitution for wrongs than it is to identify the kind of breach that justifies disgorgement. I propose, by way of hypothesis, that the necessary breach of contract be both profitable and opportunistic. The requirement that the breach be profitable immediately excludes the vast majority of contractual defaults (including ... the "losing contract" cases). Where breach is unprofitable, a liability for damages will adequately deter, and there is no profit to disgorge in any event. The further requirement that the breach be opportunistic limits this set of cases still further, because it excludes a breach in which the defendant renders a substitute performance that fulfills the plaintiff's expectation interest.

The propriety of a disgorgement remedy along more or less these lines has been a familiar topic of academic speculation. Some notable recent decisions apply a purported rule of contract law that is altogether different. [Professor Kull discusses and disapproves some Winstar related cases decided before *Glendale Federal Bank*.]

There are good reasons why breach has always had different consequences from fraudulent inducement, but they are among the elementary propositions of private law that receive less professional attention than formerly. The less confidence a court feels in its independent analysis of such a question, the more likely it is to look for the answer in a source like the Restatement. Read carefully, the Restatement (Second) of Contracts authorizes a form of disgorgement for breach only in circumstances where the remedy is well established, and never in an amount that exceeds the plaintiff's restoration interest. As the Winstar cases show, however, the second Restatement is subject to misinterpretation on this point.

Twenty years after the publication of the Restatement (Second) of Contracts, we must try once more to sort out the role of restitution in a contractual context. More than any other single factor, it is the existing vocabulary of the topic that has made this task so difficult. Ideally, we should henceforth exclude the word "restitution" from any account of the remedies for breach of an enforceable contract. We would be left with remedies that protect the plaintiff's expectation interest; remedies that protect the plaintiff's restoration interest; and the "limited extension of the disgorgement principle," whatever its ultimate contours, that Professor Farnsworth has long recommended.

Andrew Kull, *Disgorgement for Breach, The "Restitution Interest," and the Restatement of Contracts*, 79 Tex. L. Rev. 2021 (2001)

PROBLEM: RESTITUTION AS A REMEDY FOR BREACH

C contracted with O to construct a three-foot stone wall around three sides of O's residential lot for $30,000. It is stipulated that the contract was "entire" rather than divisible and that C was to be paid the full amount upon completion. When the wall was completed on one side of the lot, O, without warning, repudiated the contract. O claimed that C's work had increased the value of the lot by $5,000 and offered C that amount to discharge the contract. C, who had encountered unexpected problems in construction, the risk of which he assumed, had incurred costs of $25,000 up to the breach. Given the unexpected difficulties, these costs were reasonable. Experts will testify, however, that O would have had to pay $20,000 to obtain the same work from a contractor who was aware of the difficulties. C estimates that it will cost at least $25,000 to complete the project. On these facts, C should:

(a) Take the $5,000 and run;

(b) Sue "on the contract" for $25,000, his "reliance" interest;

(c) Sue in "restitution" for $20,000, the value to O of the work done in market terms;

(d) None of the above.

PROBLEM: SELLER'S REMEDIES UNDER UCC 2–708(2)

Return with us now to the controversy between Smirgo, those "oven guys" and Brent's Outlet. Suppose that Brent repudiated the whole contract for 200 toaster ovens before any of the ovens had been manufactured. Keeping in mind that the total contract price was $12,000, which included the cost of shipment to Brent, you, as Smirgo's attorney, have ascertained that the following situation existed at the time Smirgo learned of the repudiation:

a.   Smirgo operated in a highly competitive market. Smirgo manufactured several "lines" of ovens and possessed an expandable and highly flexible production capacity. Even though the ovens for Brent were a relatively new "line," Smirgo's production capacity could easily respond to increased demand. On the other hand, if demand slacked off, Smirgo could, with minimum disruption, discontinue a particular "line" and reallocate production resources to other contracts.

b.   Of the total fixed costs or overhead of operating the plant, Smirgo had, using generally accepted accounting principles, allocated $2,000 to Brent's contract, or, $10 per oven. These costs would have been incurred regardless of whether a contract had been entered into with Brent.

c.   The coil, steel, chips and other materials needed for production had been purchased for $6,000 and were being processed. Using reasonable efforts to reallocate the materials to other jobs or to sell for scrap, it appears that the materials could be salvaged for $3,500.

d.   If work is stopped, Smirgo will "save" $8.00 per oven in variable costs, mostly direct labor, or $1,600, and $4.00 per oven, or $800, in not having to incur any costs in shipping the goods to Brent.

e.   If Smirgo completed performance under the repudiated contract, the ovens could be sold to a local buyer for $35.00 per oven, excluding transportation costs and costs incurred in arranging a resale. At no time will the general market price for these goods exceed $30 per oven.

f.   There will be no costs of "arranging" either the salvage sale (for $3,500) or the completion sale (for $7,000).

Based upon these facts, consider the following questions:

(a) Suppose Smirgo wanted to complete the manufacturing process and resell the ovens to the local buyer for $35.00 per oven. Would this action be a failure to mitigate damages? Could Smirgo recover under UCC 2–706? See UCC 2–704.

(b) Suppose that Smirgo completed the manufacturing and, due to a shift in demand, the ovens were now worth $60 per oven on the market. Smirgo then resold them for $60 and sued Brent for $16.00 per oven, the "profit (including reasonable overhead) which the seller would have made from full performance by the buyer." UCC 2–708(2). Brent argues that since Smirgo had already sold the 200 ovens for $12,000, the claimed $3,200 would amount to a double recovery. On these facts, how would you counter this argument? See infra at 920. The question is whether a court would treat Smirgo as a "lost volume" seller.

Locks v. Wade

Superior Court of New Jersey, Appellate Division, 1955.
36 N.J.Super. 128, 114 A.2d 875.

■ CLAPP, S.J.A.D. Defendant appeals from a county district court judgment taken against him for breach of contract. Contract and breach are admitted or assumed on appeal; the only issue is damages.

Under the contract plaintiff leased to defendant an automatic phonograph, a juke box, for two years and agreed to supply records and replace parts wearing out. Proceeds of the operation were to be shared on a specified basis, but with a minimum of $20 per week to be paid plaintiff by defendant. Defendant, it is claimed, repudiated the contract; and plaintiff never installed the machine.

The court gave plaintiff judgment for $836—that is, the sum of $20 per week for two years, less apparently the costs plaintiff would have been put to, had he performed the contract, less also depreciation on the machine.

Defendant makes two points. The first rests on plaintiff's testimony that the component parts of the very machine he had intended to lease defendant were, after the breach, rented to others. Defendant argues that the amount plaintiff thus realized should have been credited on the claim sued upon.

Defendant would have us apply here the rule obtaining on the breach of an agreement to lease realty; that is, he claims the measure of the lessor's damages here is the difference between the agreed rental and the rental value of the property. His contention further is that even though under the agreement before us, the lessor is obliged to perform some personal services, he, in order to establish the rental value, has the burden of proving what he received on a reletting. . . .

Plaintiff, passing the questions (or most of them), meets the argument by referring to his testimony, not contradicted, that:

"The equipment called for by this agreement was readily available in the market. But locations were very hard to get."

We think the position plaintiff takes on the matter is sound. Where, as here, a plaintiff lessor agrees to lease an article of which the supply in the market is for practical purposes not limited, then the law would be depriving him of the benefit of his bargain if on the breach of the agreement, it required his claim against the lessee to be reduced by the amount he actually did or reasonably could realize on a reletting of the article. For if there had been no breach and another customer had appeared, the lessor could as well have secured another such article and entered into a second lease. In case of the breach of the first lease, he should have the benefit of both bargains and not—in a situation where the profit on both would be the same—be limited to the profit on the second of them.

An illustration with figures may make this more graphic. If the agreed rental under the lease amounts to $2,040, the cost of installation and of furnishing records and parts to $500, and the depreciation on the juke box over the period of the lease to $700, the lessor stands to make $840 on the deal. If another customer presents himself, the lessor will buy another juke box, which he is entitled to enter on his books at cost and depreciate in the same way as he does with the first. Thus, if he makes the same agreement with the second customer, he will make another $840 on the second lease. If the first lessee repudiates his agreement, the purchase of an additional machine will, of course, be unnecessary, because the first machine can be leased to the second customer. In such a situation, under defendant's theory, the lessor would receive as damages for this repudiation only the $2,040 rental agreed on under the first lease, less the $2,040 rental for the same machine under the second lease, or nothing. This would leave the lessee only the $840 profit he will make under the second lease; whereas had the first lessee lived up to his bargain, the lessor's profits would have been $840 on each of two leases, or $1,680.

We conclude that the proper measure of damages here is the difference between the contract price and the cost of performing the first contract, as the court apparently held below. In the case of realty which (unlike the juke box) is specific and not to be duplicated on the market, the lessor could not properly lease it to another for the same period unless the first lease were broken or terminated. In such a case the lessor should not be awarded two profits merely because of the first lessee's default.

So in general we may say that gains made by a lessor on a lease entered into after the breach are not to be deducted from his damages unless the breach enabled him to make the gains. The recoverable damages in the case of a contract are such as may reasonably be within the contemplation of the parties at the time of the contract, . . . ; and with that in view, we should not in the present case deny lessor the benefit of his bargain. * * *

Restatement of Contracts § 336(c) and Illustrations 6 and 7, and 5 Corbin, Contracts, § 1041 (1951) support these propositions. . . . The principles, however, seem not to be widely recognized, but there are cases dealing with various sorts of contracts, which can be said to sustain them. . . .

These principles lead us logically into questions with which we have no concern here—in particular, the question as to a seller's remedy on a sale of goods where he (like the plaintiff here) has for practical purposes the capacity to supply all probable customers—a matter as to which the law may perhaps be governed by statute. . . . Note, too, the change in the Sales Act proposed by the Uniform Commercial Code—Sales § 2–708 (1952), also Comment 2 thereon—a matter apparently overlooked in the 1955 amendment to the section. We limit our opinion to the situation at hand.

* * *

NOTES

(1) UCC Article 2A, covering leases of goods, has been enacted in every state but Connecticut and Louisiana. Section 2A–528(2), which purports to deal

with the problem in *Locks v. Wade*, provides that if the measure of damages provided in subsection (1) of 2A–528 is "inadequate to put a lessor in as good a position as performance would have, the measure of damages is the present value of the profit, including reasonable overhead, the lessor would have made from full performance by the lessee, together with incidental damages . . . , due allowance for costs reasonably incurred and due credit for payment or proceeds of disposition." Comment 5 provides in part: "Because this subsection is intended to give the lessor the benefit of the bargain, a court should consider any reasonable benefit or profit expected by the lessor from the performance of the lease agreement. *See . . . Locks v. Wade. . . .*"

(2) In Neri v. Retail Marine Corp., 30 N.Y.2d 393, 334 N.Y.S.2d 165, 285 N.E.2d 311 (1972), the seller, a retailer, and the buyer, a consumer, entered into a contract for the sale of a pleasure boat at an agreed price of $12,587.40. After the seller had ordered the boat from the manufacturer, the buyer repudiated the contract. Shortly thereafter, the seller, upon taking delivery of the boat from the manufacturer, resold it to a third party for $12,587.40. In the meantime, the buyer sued to recover the initial deposit of $4,250. The seller counterclaimed to recover the profit that would have been made on the sale to the buyer, some $2,579, and incidental damages in the amount of $674. The lower courts, among other things, rejected the lost profits claim as "untenable" since the boat was later sold for the same price that the buyer had contracted to pay. On appeal, this part of the decision was reversed by the New York Court of Appeals. The retail dealer had an unlimited supply of "fixed-price" goods, i.e., goods where the price is essentially fixed by the manufacturer. In this setting, the buyer's breach "costs the dealer a sale" even though the same goods are resold to a third party without any apparent loss. Had the buyer performed the contract, the seller would have made two sales instead of one. Since the breach depletes the dealer's sales to the extent of one, he should recover the lost profit from the buyer under UCC 2–708(2).

Comment: The Lost Volume Seller Under UCC Article 2

Who is a lost volume seller? Suppose that Seller contracts to manufacture and sell a specified piece of medical diagnosis equipment to Buyer for $500,000. After the goods were finished and identified to the contract, Buyer breached by refusing to accept delivery. What are Seller's remedial options under the Official Text of Article 2?

First, since Buyer did not accept the goods, Seller cannot recover the price unless a reasonable resale is not available. Seller must prove that it is "unable after reasonable effort to resell them at a reasonable price or the circumstances reasonably indicate that such effort will be unavailing." UCC 2–709(1)(b).

Second, Seller could resell the goods under UCC 2–706. Assuming that the resale conditions are satisfied, Seller "may recover the difference between the resale price and the contract price together with any incidental damages . . . but less expenses saved in consequence of the buyer's breach."

Third, whether or not the goods are resold, Seller can claim damages under UCC 2–708(1) measured by the "difference between the market price at the time and place for tender and the unpaid contract price, together with any incidental damages ... but less expenses saved in consequence of the buyer's breach."

Fourth, Seller can claim that damages under UCC 2–708(1) are "inadequate" to put it "in as good a position as performance would have done" and that it is entitled to damages measured by the "profit (including reasonable overhead) which the seller would have made from full performance by the buyer, together with any incidental damages ... , due allowance for costs reasonably incurred and due credit for payments or proceeds of resale" under UCC 2–708(2).

As suggested by the *Neri* case, supra, the lost volume problem arises when Seller resells the goods for roughly the contract price. There is, in fact, no difference between the resale price or its surrogate the relevant market price. Invoking the lost volume principle, Seller claims that neither the resale nor the "market price minus contract price" measure are adequate to protect the expectation interest and that damages for Buyer's breach should be measured under UCC 2–708(2). Under this measure, the seller can keep the proceeds of the resale *and* recover the profit that would have been made on the first sale.

This argument has been accepted by the courts. See *R.E. Davis Chemical Corp. v. Diasonics, Inc.*, 826 F.2d 678 (7th Cir.1987), a leading case which reviews the authorities. *Davis,* however, is less strict than some in determining when there is a lost volume seller. For example, Professor Robert Harris argued that a "Resale results in loss of volume only if three conditions are met: (1) the person who bought the resold entity would have been solicited by plaintiff had there been no breach and resale; (2) the solicitation would have been successful; and (3) the plaintiff could have performed that additional contract." Robert Harris, *A Radical Restatement of the Laws of Seller's Damages: Sales Act and Commercial Code Results Compared,* 18 Stan.L.Rev. 66, 80–83 (1965). The court, however, stated "[A] lost volume seller ... has a predictable and finite number of customers and ... has the capacity either to sell to all new buyers or to make the one additional sale represented by the resale the breach." If the seller "would have made the sale represented by the resale whether or not the breach occurred, damages measured by the difference between the contract price and the market price cannot put the lost volume seller in as good a position as it would have been in had the buyer performed."

On the other hand, Davis adds a restriction found in the law and economics literature but not in the other cases. In addition to whether Seller could have produced the additional item is the question "whether it would have been profitable for the seller to produce both units." Thus, the case was remanded for Seller to establish "not only that it had the capacity to produce the breached unit in addition to the unit resold, but also that it would have been profitable for it to have produced and sold both." See R.E. Davis Chemical Corp. v. Diasonics, Inc., 924 F.2d 709 (7th Cir.1991).

One court attempted to restate the lost volume principle:

In passing, we observe that this lost volume situation can be described in several ways. Focusing on the breached unit, one can say that due to a market in which supply exceeds demand, the lost volume seller cannot resell the breached unit without sacrificing the additional sale. Focusing on the additional unit, one can say that but for the buyer's breach, the lost volume seller would have made an additional sale. Focusing on both units, one can say that but for the buyer's breach, the lost volume seller would have sold both units. Each statement is equivalent to the others.

Kenco Homes, Inc. v. Williams, 94 Wash.App. 219, 972 P.2d 125, 129 (1999). Does this help?

Measuring lost profits under UCC 2–708(2). How does one measure the profit on the breached contract under UCC 2–708(2) and whether it would have been profitable to produce and sell both units? Here is a suggestion. First, determine the profit from the breached contract by subtracting the total variable costs of performance (TCI) from the contract price. The resulting "profit (including reasonable overhead) from full performance" is not adjusted by deducting any "proceeds of resale." As the cases, including *Davis*, have held, the "proceeds of resale" language in UCC 2–708(2) does not apply to the lost volume calculation. Next, subtract the total variable costs that would have been incurred in producing the next unit from the contract price of that unit. This measures the profit including overhead from the second sale. Finally, if the profit on the second sale is less than the profit on the first, make an appropriate adjustment in the first sale profit. For example, an appropriate adjustment is made if the contract prices for both sales are added together and the total variable costs from producing two units are subtracted. If variable costs for the second unit are higher, they will reduce the profit figure.

Against this backdrop, Rev.UCC 2–708(2) provides:

If the measure of damages provided in subsection (1) or in Section 2–706 is inadequate to put the seller in as good a position as performance would have done then the measure of damages is the profit (including reasonable overhead) which the seller would have made from full performance by the buyer, together with any incidental or consequential damages provided in this Article (Section 2–710).

Is this a change for the better?

For some commentators, however, the interpretation of Article 2 by the courts is flawed and the award of lost volume profits overcompensates the seller. See John M. Breen, *The Lost Volume Seller and Lost Profits Under UCC 2–708(2): A Conceptual, Linguistic Critique*, 50 U. Miami L. Rev. 779 (1996).

PROBLEM: SELLER'S REMEDIES UNDER UCC 2–708(2) CONTINUED

In the case of Brent's Outlet, suppose that Brent repudiated while Smirgo was in the middle of performing the $12,000 contract to manufacture ovens.

The resale market was very bad and Smirgo, in the exercise of commercial judgment under UCC 2–704, stopped work. At this point, the following facts are clear:

1.   Smirgo's accountant had allocated $2,000 in fixed costs or overhead ($10 per oven) to the contract.

2.   Smirgo will save $800 in not having to ship the goods to Brent.

3.   Smirgo had incurred $6,000 in expenses at the time of the breach, all in steel, chips, and materials needed for production. Smirgo can sell most of the materials on hand to a third party for $3,500, but the chips are now obsolete and have to be junked.

4.   Smirgo estimated that he would have spent $2,000 more to perform the contract, most of it on labor.

5.   The market price for the ovens, if completed, at the time and place for tender was $6,000.

(a) Do you need any more information? If so, what?

(b) Would Brent be successful in a claim that Smirgo's damages were determined by UCC 2–708(1)? Why not?

(c) How much should Smirgo recover under UCC 2–708(2)? Professor John Sebert argued that the formula in this case (no lost volume) should be: "Unpaid contract price less total variable costs, plus incidental damages, plus costs reasonably incurred, less proceeds of resale, and less the market value of goods retained." John A. Sebert, Jr, *Remedies Under Article Two of the Uniform Commercial Code: An Agenda for Review*, 130 U.Pa.L.Rev. 360, 412 (1981). Doesn't this make sense? Did Revised UCC 2–708(2) follow Professor Sebert's advice?

PROBLEM: THE SCOPE OF UCC 2–708(1)

Seller, a middleman or jobber, agrees on January 2, 2001 to supply 9,000 units of goods to Buyer in six semi-annual installments over a three year period. The parties agree on a fixed price of $100 per unit and the first delivery was scheduled for July 1, 2001. At the time of contracting, Seller had neither units on hand nor forward contracts to purchase them from manufacturers. Seller delivered and Buyer paid for 1,500 units on July 1, 2001. At that time, the retail market price at the place of tender was $95 per unit. Shortly thereafter, the market started a steep decline and, by December 1, 2001, the retail price per unit was $45. On that date, Buyer repudiated the contract. At that time, Seller had a forward contract with a manufacturer to purchase 1,500 units for the next installment at $75 per unit. Seller had no other goods on hand or forward contracts. On January 2, 2002, when the retail market price per unit was $40, Seller tendered but Buyer rejected the second installment. Buyer reiterated that it would take no more deliveries under the contract. Seller sued Buyer for damages in March, 2002. On July 1, 2002, the relevant retail market price per unit was $50, but economists were hopeful that it would gradually recover over the next two years. The case came to trial in September, 2002. Seller's attorney insisted that it was entitled to use UCC 2–708(1) as a basis for recovery.

A. You are Buyer's attorney and are persuaded that UCC 2–708(1) will overcompensate Seller. Prepare a memo for the court that defends that position and presents an alternative approach. See UCC 1–106(1), 2–711 through 2–723. See also Kenco Homes, Inc. v. Williams, 94 Wash.App. 219, 972 P.2d 125 (1999), holding that UCC 2–708(1) is not adequate to put the seller in the same position as full performance would have when the seller does not have completed goods on hand.

B. If UCC 2–708(1) applies, how are damages for the buyer's repudiation measured? Compare Rev. 2–708(1)(b).

Comment: Employee's Remedies for Breach of Employment Contract

If, in a contract for personal services, the employee has done the work and the employer fails to pay, the remedy is clear: the employee may sue for the agreed price. But suppose the employer repudiates the contract before work commences or terminates employment while work is underway. In the absence of a divisible contract, what damages may be recovered here? In all probability, the employee will stop work after the termination and consider or make some effort to find substitute employment. Does this mean that the employee's claim for damages will be treated like that in a construction contract or a contract for the sale of goods?

The answer is "not quite." Most courts have rejected the "constructive" service doctrine, which stated that a wrongfully discharged employee who remained ready and able to perform could recover the full amount of the agreed wage without any "duty" to mitigate damages. See Howard v. Daly, 61 N.Y. 362 (1875); Murray § 12.12. But a vestige of this rule remains.

> The general rule is that the measure of recovery by a wrongfully discharged employee is the amount of salary agreed upon for the period of service, less the amount which the employer affirmatively proves the employee has earned or with reasonable effort might have earned from other employment.

Parker v. Twentieth Century–Fox Film Corp., 3 Cal.3d 176, 89 Cal.Rptr. 737, 474 P.2d 689, 692 (1970). This varies from the usual rule, which allows damages based upon the "loss in the value to him of the other party's performance ... less ... any cost or other loss that he has avoided by not having to perform." Restatement (Second) § 347. In short, the discharged employee is not required to prove what savings were realized by the breach in order to establish damages. The employer, on the other hand, has the burden of proving that the employee failed to mitigate damages. Assuming that the employee will be paid for any work done, the amount that he or she reasonably could have obtained from other employment will be the measure of any savings realized over the balance of the contract.

There are a number of interesting problems around the fringes of this rule.

First, under what circumstances will the employee's failure to look for or refusal to take substitute employment constitute a failure to mitigate damages? According to the *Parker* case:

> However, before projected earnings from other employment opportunities not sought or accepted by the discharged employee can be applied in mitigation, the employer must show that the other employment was comparable, or substantially similar, to that of which the employee has been deprived; the employee's rejection of or failure to seek other available employment of a different or inferior kind may not be resorted to in order to mitigate damages. 474 P.2d at 692.

Whether the possible substitute employment was "different or inferior" or the employee's efforts to find it were reasonable are, in the main, questions of fact for each case. See, e.g., Ryan v. Superintendent of Schools of Quincy, 374 Mass. 670, 373 N.E.2d 1178 (1978) (failure of discharged art teacher to find work justified on facts).

Second, suppose, after the discharge, the employee actually finds and takes another job. Is the employer automatically entitled to deduct that income from the damages? Although the answers are not entirely clear, if "but for" the breach the employee would not have had the time, capacity or energy to take the second job, the answer is yes. This will turn on the nature and demands of the job from which the employee was discharged and whether the second job could have been undertaken without interfering with the employment promised by the defaulting employer. It goes without saying that if the employee is already "moonlighting" or engaged in some business at the time of discharge, the income from those existing activities should not be deducted.

Third, suppose the employee is not able to find suitable employment and is paid unemployment or similar benefits. Should those payments, which are a form of employment substitute, be deducted from damages? Restatement (Second) § 347, Comment e properly identifies this as a problem of collateral source, suggests that deducting the benefits from "collateral sources is less compelling in the case of a breach of contract than in the case of tort" and concludes that the answer "will turn on the court's perception of legislative policy rather than on the rule stated" in Section 347. Professor Fleming, however, has argued that legislative policy will invariably be inconclusive and that tort policies argue against deduction even for breach of contract:

> Wrongful dismissal is simply not a breach of contract which courts will view with the detachment advocated by apologists of the 'efficient' breach; its potentially devastating effect on the employee is attested by the pejorative use of the term 'wrongful' from the tort vocabulary; and the collateral source rule is justified both by the need for deterrence and by the feeling that mere indemnity for his net economic loss does not compensate the employee for all his injury, emotional as well as pecuniary.

John Fleming, *The Collateral Source Rule and Contract Damages,* 71 Cal.L.Rev. 56, 81 (1983). For a well-reasoned case refusing to deduct from damages the disability payments made to a wrongfully discharged employee, see Seibel v. Liberty Homes, Inc., 305 Or. 362, 752 P.2d 291 (1988).

Inchaustegui v. 666 5th Avenue Limited Partnership

Supreme Court of New York, Appellate Division, 2000.
268 A.D.2d 121, 706 N.Y.S.2d 396, *aff'd*, 749 N.E.2d 196 (N.Y.2001).

■ SAXE, J.

[In a commercial lease, the sub-tenant was required to "maintain comprehensive general public liability insurance in respect to the subleased premises and the conduct and operation of business therein, with sublessor and the landlord as additional insureds as set forth in the underlying lease." The sub-tenant obtained comprehensive general liability insurance for the subleased space, but failed to comply with the insurance procurement provisions of the sublease agreement by naming the landlord as the additional insured under the purchased policy. The plaintiff suffered personal injuries on the premises and sued the landlord for those injuries. The landlord, in turn, brought a third-party claim against the sub-tenant [Petrofin], alleging a violation of the lease's insurance procurement provision. The landlord moved for summary judgment, contending that Petrofin's failure to procure the requisite insurance coverage constituted a breach of the sublease agreement, entitling them to indemnity as well as money damages, including the costs incurred in the defense of the action. The lower court granted the motion but limited damages to the cost of maintaining and securing an independent policy of insurance. The appellate court affirmed, with certain modifications.] * * *

Generally, when a tenant breaches a contract with a landlord with respect to the procurement of insurance to cover the risk of liability to third parties, "[t]he usual penalty ... is to be liable for all the resulting damages ... However, case law limits the extent of damages available to a landlord when it procures its own insurance upon learning that the tenant has violated the lease by failing to procure insurance. These cases hold that under such circumstances the landlord's damages "are limited to the cost of such insurance" ...

The landlord contends that (1) these cases are contrary to settled law, ... that they are not controlling because they apply only where the contract requires or gives the landlord the option to procure its own insurance should the tenant fail to do so. [The court reviewed evolving New York cases and "fundamental" principles of contract damages.] * * *

Applying these fundamental contract law principles to a tenant's breach of the insurance procurement provision of a lease reflects two possible categories of damages. First, if the tenant fails to obtain the contemplated insurance coverage on behalf of the landlord (whether because it procured no coverage at all, or because it neglected to have the landlord included as a named insured) in the absence of the contemplated insurance coverage, any ultimate liability judgment against the landlord would fall within the category of consequential damages, and the landlord would be entitled to recoup that amount, as well as any litigation expenses, from the tenant, since the tenant's failure to purchase insurance on behalf of the landlord could reasonably be expected to result in such economic injury to the landlord.

However, if the landlord itself purchased insurance equivalent to that which the tenant was contractually obligated to procure, regardless of whether or not its purchase was motivated by the knowledge that the tenant had breached the insurance procurement provision of the lease, the landlord's only damages arising from the tenant's breach of the lease are contract damages, equivalent to the costs of procuring the insurance policy.

The dissent takes the position that our conclusion contravenes the collateral source rule. We disagree. The purpose of that rule, which evolved in the context of tort law, is to ensure that the wrongdoer is required to pay for all damages his conduct caused to the injured party, without setoff from payments the injured party receives from other, collateral sources.... While the collateral source rule has been applied in some contract cases, as the dissent notes ... we should keep in mind that the nature of contract damages is quite distinct from that of tort damages (*see generally,* Fleming, *The Collateral Source Rule and Contract Damages,* 71 Calif. L. Rev. 56, 60). While tort damages are expansive, focusing on the full spectrum of the harm caused by the tortfeasor, damages for a breach of contract are restrictive, limited to the economic injury actually caused to the claimant as a consequence of the other party's breach (*id.*).

An analysis of the application of the collateral source rule begins by determining the total extent of the damages to the injured party (here, the landlord) caused by the wrongdoer (here, the tenant). It then determines if the defendant is entitled to claim that this sum must be reduced by the amount available to the injured party from another source. Because the claim at issue here arises out of a breach of contract, the first step requires determination of the consequential economic damage caused to the landlord by the tenant's breach of the insurance procurement provision. As we discussed previously, because of the landlord's procurement of substitute insurance, the extent of damages to which it is entitled for this breach of contract is limited to the cost of its purchase of substitute coverage, and potentially, any other expenses not covered by the policy it procured. The collateral source rule is inapplicable. We are not setting off the damages to which the landlord is entitled from the tenant by the amount covered by the insurance; any insurance company's payment to the injured plaintiff is simply irrelevant to the analysis.

If this holding leaves the landlord's insurer without the right to recoup its expenses from the tenant by means of a subrogation claim, we perceive no prejudice. The premium was paid for the risk to be underwritten. Had it been the tenant, rather than the landlord, who applied to the same insurer for the coverage, the same premium would presumably have been paid and the same risk underwritten, and no subrogation claim would have been available to the insurer against the tenant.

Moreover, as the dissent recognizes, the concept of subrogation focuses on permitting the insurer to recoup its payment from "the party who has caused the damage" ... A tenant who failed to procure insurance has breached a lease provision, but did not cause the damage underlying the liability determination. This situation is distinguishable from one where a right of subrogation is clearly appropriate, for instance, where a tenant negligently causes a fire that ultimately destroys other tenants' property. In such circumstances there is a wrongdoer against whom the landlord's insurer must have a subrogation right to seek to recoup payments it made to others, such as other building occupants.

Lastly, because we recognize that despite the coverage it obtained, there is a possibility the landlord may ultimately suffer certain other economic consequential damages as a result of the tenant's breach, besides the cost of the premiums, we modify the order of the IAS court in one relatively minor respect. Although the * * * cases seem to strictly limit the landlord's damages to the cost of the premiums, we believe the proper extent of damage recovery is slightly broader. In the cases limiting the landlord's damages to the cost of the premiums, the courts have drawn a distinction between two categories of damages. On one hand, there is the "cost of insurance", generally thought of as the premiums paid, which falls under the category of expenses the landlord has had to pay as a direct result of the breach, and for which it has no source of reimbursement; these costs are therefore recoverable by the landlord in an action against the tenant. On the other hand, the amount of any eventual liability determination against the landlord, and the costs of the defense, are not recoverable damages, inasmuch as both would be covered by the insurance procured by the landlord. . . .

The same reasoning that authorizes a damages award for premiums paid by the landlord in these circumstances would also permit recovery for certain other out-of-pocket costs suffered by the landlord and not covered by the procured insurance. For instance, if the policy procured by the landlord required some sort of co-payment, deductible, or other out-of-pocket payment by the landlord, such payments should, like the premiums, be recoverable as against the tenant who breached the procurement provision. Similarly, should the landlord's insurance rate be increased as a result of the liability claim, the increase in its future insurance premiums would be recoverable as breach of contract damages.

Accordingly, the order of the Supreme Court, New York County * * * should be modified, on the law, to the extent of adding the right of third-party plaintiffs to seek damages for any other expense arising out of the liability claim and not covered by the substitute insurance procured by the landlord, and as so modified, affirmed, without costs, and the matter remanded for determination of third-party plaintiffs' damages. * * *

[The dissenting opinion of Judge Sullivan is omitted.]

(C) BREACH OF CONTRACT BY SUPPLIER OF GOODS, SERVICES, OR CONSTRUCTION

We now turn to the "flip" side, i.e., where the breach is of a promise to sell and deliver goods or land, construct a home or perform personal or professional services rather than a promise to accept and pay for the performance. Here the statement of remedial policy remains constant, but its application may vary in the different context. For example, the plaintiff may have a greater opportunity to obtain specific performance of the defendant's promise to perform. See Section 3, infra. Furthermore, the recovery of consequential losses becomes more important where the failure to deliver goods or to perform services prevents or disrupts a planned profitable use of the performance. See Section 2(D), infra. Thus, if a seller has failed to deliver goods that the buyer had planned to use in an operating business, the damages may include both the extra costs incurred in obtaining substitute goods from a third party ("direct" damages) and any profits lost because of the delay in obtaining the substitute ("consequential" damages). These issues lurked in *The Case of the Recalcitrant Manufacturer,* supra at 210. At this point, please review your analysis and conclusions in that problem, paying particular attention to the buyer's remedies. We will use the problem as a model throughout this subsection.

Reliance Cooperage Corp. v. Treat

United States Court of Appeals, Eighth Circuit, 1952.
195 F.2d 977.

[On July 12, 1950, Reliance and Treat entered a written contract under which Treat agreed to produce and deliver 300,000 "white oak bourbon staves" not later than December 31, 1950. The price was $450 per thousand, f.o.b. freight cars "nearest millsite where staves were produced." Between the middle and the end of August, 1950, Treat, by letter* and over the telephone, apparently repudiated the contract. On October 6, 1950,

---

* It was admitted that the defendant had on August 12, 1950, sent to Ralph Ettlinger, an officer of the plaintiff, the following letter:

"Marshall, Arkansas

August 12, 1950

"Dear Mr. Ralph Ettlinger:

"I have been trying to get a letter to you for some time but they return to me. I went to Harrison yesterday and got Tom Burns Co. address trying to get in touch with you. We got a mill at Hallaster, Mo. trying to get started. Have a few Bolts will have a time getting any more. I can't make these staves up there or any where else at the price I haft to pay for Bolts. Every one else are paying $475.00 to $500.00 per M. You see I can't compete with them so if you want those staves I will haft to get around what ever the market is from time to time. You can see you seff that I can get bolts say 70a price when others paying $100.00 per foot. I think the boys can make a lot of staves fast up there if they can pay as much as others are paying if not they will haft to quit. Now you can see where I am at. The other to co. that I am making for with my other 3 mills have raised from $75.00 to $100.00 on the 1000 4½" staves and said they would cancel out as the market raises. So you do just what you want to. I can't make them unless I can buy the timber so let me hear at once. I will have a car before long.

"Yours as ever,

A.R. Treat."

Reliance informed Treat by letter that they were not "confident" that Treat would perform and that they would hold him to "strict compliance" with the contract." Treat never replied and, in fact, delivered no staves to Reliance under the contract.

Reliance sued Treat for damages. At the trial, Treat, over Reliance's objection, testified that the price of bourbon staves began to advance beyond $450 a thousand around the last of August. On cross-examination, however, Treat conceded that a more accurate August price for staves was $525 per thousand. Treat also testified that he got $625 per thousand for staves toward the end of December. The evidence, however, would sustain a finding that the market price for staves on December 31, 1950 was "more than the contract price but not in excess of $750 a thousand.]

■ SANBORN, CIRCUIT JUDGE.

* * *

At the close of the evidence, the court was requested by the plaintiff to instruct the jury that the plaintiff was entitled to recover the difference between the contract price of the staves the defendant had promised to deliver on or before December 31, 1950, and the market price of similar staves on that date. The court denied the request.

The jury was instructed substantially as follows: That the undisputed facts made a prima facie case of liability against the defendant for damages based upon the difference, if any, between the contract price of $450.00 per thousand staves and the market price as of December 31, 1950. That the defendant contended that he had repudiated the contract prior to that date and that it was the plaintiff's duty to mitigate its damages by purchasing the staves elsewhere. That the burden of proving his contentions was upon the defendant. That the jury was to determine whether the defendant did in fact repudiate his contract prior to December 31, 1950, and, if so, when the repudiation occurred, and whether, after such repudiation, the plaintiff by a reasonable effort could have mitigated its damages by the purchase of the staves on the open market, and whether the damages could have been completely or partially mitigated. That if, on a date prior to December 31, 1950, the defendant definitely and unequivocally advised the plaintiff that he would not deliver any staves under the contract, this would be a breach of the contract by him as of that date; and that if, after the repudiation, the plaintiff, by a reasonable effort and without undue risk or expense, could have purchased the staves on the open market at a price equal to the contract price, it was the plaintiff's duty to do so, and that the plaintiff would, in that event, be entitled to nominal damages only. That if the plaintiff by a reasonable effort and without undue risk or expense, after the repudiation, if any, by the defendant of the contract prior to December 31, 1950, could have purchased the staves on the open market at a price in excess of the contract price, then it was the plaintiff's duty to do that and mitigate its damages so far as possible, and the plaintiff would then be entitled to damages only for the difference between the market price of the staves at that time and the contract price. That if the jury failed to find that there was a breach of the contract by the defendant prior to December 31, 1950, the plaintiff was entitled to the difference between the market price of the staves on that date and the contract price.

The plaintiff objected to the instructions relating to the duty of the plaintiff to mitigate damages, and to the right of the defendant to repudiate the contract prior to December 31, 1950.

The jury returned a verdict for the plaintiff and assessed its damages at $500.00. The plaintiff appealed from the judgment entered on the verdict.

We gather from the court's instructions that its opinion was that if the defendant had definitely notified the plaintiff prior to December 31, 1950, that he would not produce and deliver staves under the contract, and that if the plaintiff, notwithstanding its insistence that the contract be fulfilled, by a reasonable effort and without undue risk or expense could then have bought similar staves on the market, the measure of its damages would be the difference between what the plaintiff would have had to pay for staves at the time the defendant announced his refusal of performance and the contract price of such staves.

* * *

There is no doubt that a party to an executory contract such as that in suit may refuse to accede to an anticipatory repudiation of it and insist upon performance, and, if he does so, the contract remains in existence and is binding on both parties, and no actionable claim for damages arises until the time for performance expires. . . .

It is our opinion that, under the undisputed facts in this case, the unaccepted anticipatory renunciation by the defendant of his obligation to produce and deliver staves under the contract did not impair that obligation or affect his liability for damages for the nonperformance of the contract, and that the measure of those damages was no different than it would have been had no notice of renunciation been given by the defendant to the plaintiff. If there had been no anticipatory repudiation of the contract, the measure of damages for nonperformance by the seller would have been the difference between the contract price and the market price of the staves on the date when delivery was due, and that is the measure which should have been applied in assessing damages in this case.

Moreover, the measure of damages would have been the same had the plaintiff accepted the anticipatory repudiation as an actionable breach of the contract. The plaintiff would still have been entitled to recover what it had lost by reason of the defendant's failure to produce and deliver by December 31, 1950, the staves contracted for, namely, the difference between the market price and the contract price of the staves on that date. The Comment in Restatement of the Law of Contracts, § 338, Measure of Damages for Anticipatory Breach, contains the following statement (page 549): "The fact that an anticipatory repudiation is a breach of contract (see § 318) does not cause the repudiated promise to be treated as if it were a promise to render performance at the date of the repudiation. Repudiation does not accelerate the time fixed for performance; nor does it change the damages to be awarded as the equivalent of the promised performance." See, also, Williston on Contracts, Rev.Ed. Vol. 5, § 1397; 46 Am.Jur., Sales, § 688.

It seems safe to say that ordinarily no obligation to mitigate damages arises until there are damages to mitigate. No damages for the nonperformance of the contract in suit accrued before December 31, 1950. Until that time the defendant, notwithstanding his anticipatory repudiation of the contract, was obligated and was at liberty to produce and deliver the staves, and had he done so the plaintiff would have been required to take and to pay for them. There is no justification for ruling that, after the plaintiff was advised that the defendant did not intend to perform, it must hold itself in readiness to accept performance from him and at the same time, at its own risk and expense, buy the staves contracted for upon the open market in the hope of reducing the defendant's liability for damages in case he persisted in his refusal to fulfill his obligations. The plaintiff did nothing to enhance its damages and seeks no special damages.

This same question as to mitigation of damages by a purchaser who insisted upon performance of a contract after a seller's anticipatory repudiation, arose in Continental Grain Co. v. Simpson Feed Co., D.C.E.D.Ark., 102 F.Supp. 354 (tried in the Eastern District of Arkansas). In that case Judge Lemley, we think, correctly decided that the purchaser was not required to attempt to mitigate his damages by buying the commodity contracted for upon the open market. Judge Lemley said, page 363 of 102 F.Supp.:

" * * * There are two reasons for this rule. First, to require the innocent party to make an immediate purchase or sale upon receipt of notice of the other's repudiation would encourage such repudiation on the part of the seller or of the buyer as the market rose or fell. . . . Second, the immediate action of the innocent party might not have the effect of mitigating his damages, but might, on the other hand, enhance them. . . .

The doctrine of anticipatory breach by repudiation is intended to aid a party injured as a result of the other party's refusal to perform his contractual obligations, by giving to the injured party an election to accept or to reject the refusal of performance without impairing his rights or increasing his burdens. Any effort to convert the doctrine into one for the benefit of the party who, without legal excuse, has renounced his agreement should be resisted.

The plaintiff is entitled to recover as damages the amount by which on December 31, 1950, the market price of the staves contracted for exceeded their contract price. What the market price of such staves was on that date is a question of fact which has not as yet been determined.

The judgment is reversed and the case is remanded with directions to grant a new trial limited to the issue of the amount of damages.

NOTES

(1)(a) Suppose Reliance, on September 1, 1950, had canceled the contract for breach and purchased 300,000 barrel staves at $525 per thousand from another producer. On December 31, 1950, the market price had dropped back to $450 per thousand. What damages? See UCC 2–712. Note that the cost of "cover" rather than the relevant market price determines the damages. If the buyer does not cover in fact, should damages be limited to the market price when the buyer should have covered? See UCC 2–712(3). What policies support this result?

(b) Suppose, above, that the market price had risen to $750 per thousand on December 31, 1950. Instead of suing for damages under UCC 2–712, Reliance sued under UCC 2–713(1). What result? What is the strongest argument for Treat? Is it persuasive that Reliance, by electing the "cover" remedy under UCC 2–712, is precluded from proving damages under UCC 2–713(1)?

(2) Evaluate the following analysis of the *Treat* case, which was decided under pre-code law, from the standpoint of Article 2 of the UCC:

(a) The UCC does not define what a repudiation is. This is presumably left to other principles of contract law in the state. UCC 1–103. But see UCC 2–609(4). The UCC does, however, prescribe the remedial alternatives available to the buyer upon a repudiation by the seller. UCC 2–610 & 2–711(1).

Rev. UCC 2–610 does provide a definition of repudiation.

(b) The seller did not retract his repudiation before the time for performance arrived. Cf. UCC 2–611(1). Since the buyer is seeking direct rather than consequential damages, there is no affirmative UCC requirement that it seek to mitigate damages by "covering" on the open market. Even so, "covering" in an unstable market might not be a reasonable responsibility to impose because of the risk involved. Cf. UCC 2–715(2)(a). However, after repudiation by the seller, the buyer is privileged to await performance by the seller for only "a commercially reasonable time." UCC 2–610(a). What does this mean?

(c) The answer to this question depends upon how you read UCC 2–713, dealing with buyer's damages for repudiation. First, the special rule for measuring repudiation damages set out in UCC 2–723(1) does not apply here. The action did not come to trial before the time for performance arose. Thus, the measure must be determined from UCC 2–713(1). Second, the measure for repudiation by the seller is "the difference between the market price at the time when the buyer learned of the breach and the contract price * * *." The use of the phrase "learned of the breach" rather than "learned of the repudiation" is critical. Given the policy of UCC 2–610(a) and the language of UCC 2–723(1), choice of the word "breach" suggests a time for measurement *later* than the time when the buyer first heard of the repudiation. Third, without more, since the buyer elected not to treat the repudiation as a breach, it first "learned of the breach" when the seller failed to deliver the goods in December. Market price, therefore, should be measured as of the December delivery date at the "place for tender." UCC 2–713(2). This result is consistent with the *Treat* case. See J. White & R. Summers, Uniform Commercial Code § 6–7 [(4th ed. 1995).]

(d) This analysis, however, flies in the face of the language in UCC 2–610(a). Permitting a buyer to wait a commercially reasonable time affords time to assess the seriousness of the seller's repudiation and legitimate business needs of the aggrieved party. Once that time has expired, the buyer's losses should be measured at the time when it *should* have covered on the open market. While not required actually to risk covering, the buyer should not be permitted to profit or to lose on a shifting market between the time that the commercially reasonable time expired and the agreed time for performance. Otherwise, speculation and unrealistic measurement of loss would be encouraged and the objective of efficient loss avoidance would be undercut. Accord: Cosden Oil v. Karl O. Helm Aktiengesellschaft, 736 F.2d 1064 (5th Cir.1984); Thomas Jackson, *"Anticipatory Repudiation" and the Temporal Element of Contract Law: An Economic Inquiry into Contract Damages in Cases of Prospective Nonperformance*, 31 Stan.L.Rev. 69 (1978) (damages should be measured at or near time the buyer "learned" of repudiation).

(e) On the other hand, if the buyer decides to "cover" before a commercially reasonable time expires, damages will be measured under UCC 2–712(1).

(f) Revised Article 2: UCC 2–713(1)(b):

The measure of damages for repudiation by the seller is the difference between the market price at the expiration of a commercially reasonable time after the buyer learned of the repudiation, but not later than the time stated in paragraph (a) ["time for tender under the contract:] and the contract price together with any incidental or consequential damages provided in this Article … but less expenses saved in consequences of the seller's breach.

PROBLEM: THE CASE OF THE RECALCITRANT MANUFACTURER REVISITED

1. Review your analysis and conclusions on the buyer's remedies in *The Case of the Recalcitrant Manufacturer,* supra at 210, a case where the seller failed to deliver. The buyer, as you recall, is Bisko.

2. To what extent is there a doctrine of "substantial" performance under Article 2 of the UCC? What are the buyer's non-judicial remedies? Consider the following variations in the case of *Smirgo v. Bisko*:

(a) Smirgo tendered delivery of the two ovens three days late. In addition, one of the ovens failed to conform to the specifications (a minor deviation which could be corrected for $100). Bisko wants to reject the goods, cancel the contract and sue Smirgo for damages. Would you recommend this course of action? See UCC 2–601, 2–602, 2–711(1) & 2–713. Or, should Bisko accept the goods and seek damages for breach of warranty? See UCC 2–606 & 2–714(2).

(b) Would your analysis in (a), above, be altered by the following factual changes:

(1) Bisko in fact has suffered no damage and has found another manufacturer who can supply the same ovens at 20% less. See UCC 1–103, 1–203, & 2–103(1)(b). Is the buyer's remedy of rejection subject to a duty of good faith?

(2) Smirgo delivered the defective oven on October 15 rather than November 4. See UCC 2–508(1).

(3) The delay of three days was caused by Smirgo's failure promptly to notify Bisko of the shipment. See UCC 2–504.

(4) Smirgo was to deliver the ovens in two installments, the first of which was defective. See UCC 2–612.

(5) Bisko accepted delivery of both ovens, subsequently discovered the defect and now seeks to revoke acceptance and cancel the contract. See UCC 2–608.

(6) If Bisko rightfully rejects the tender of delivery, Smirgo might have a right to cure the non-conformity under UCC 2–508. Would that right exist on these facts?

3.   Suppose Bisko had paid Smirgo $15,000 upon signing the contract and agreed to pay the balance upon delivery. Consider the following questions:

(a) If Smirgo repudiated the contract before any deliveries were made, would Bisko be entitled to cancel the contract, recover the down payment *and* seek compensatory damages for breach of contract? See UCC 2–711.

(b) Suppose Bisko repudiated the contract before delivery and it is clear that Smirgo suffered no damage from the breach. May Bisko recover the $15,000 down payment? (Assume there has been no effort to liquidate damages.) See UCC 2–718(2) & (3).

4.   If Bisko rightfully rejects the tender of delivery, Smirgo might have a right to cure the non-conformity under UCC 2–508. Would that right exist on these facts?

Jacob & Youngs v. Kent

Court of Appeals of New York, 1921.
Supra at 780.

Rivers v. Deane

Supreme Court of New York, Appellate Division, 1994.
209 A.D.2d 936, 619 N.Y.S.2d 419.

MEMORANDUM.

Defendant appeals from a judgment of Supreme Court awarding plaintiffs damages for defendant's breach of contract for the construction of an addition to plaintiffs' home. Defendant in his brief challenges only that aspect of the judgment that awarded damages to plaintiffs for the difference between the market value of the structure had it been completed pursuant to the terms of the contract and the market value of the structure as actually completed. We agree with defendant's assertion that the record does not support the court's award for diminution in value, because no such proof was presented.

At trial plaintiffs produced two experts who testified that defendant failed to construct the addition in a good and workmanlike manner. They further testified that the inadequate structural support of the addition rendered unusable the third floor of the addition, which plaintiffs had intended to use as a master bedroom and bathroom. The appeal by defendant, as limited by his brief ... , does not contest those findings of fact.

The general rule in cases of faulty construction is that the measure of damages is the market value of the cost to repair the faulty construction.... The court erred in applying the "difference in value rule," as initially set forth by Justice Cardozo in Jacob & Youngs v. Kent, 230 N.Y. 239, 241, which is limited to instances where the builder's failure to perform under a construction contract is "both trivial and innocent", such that damages may be measured by the diminution in value of the building rather than the cost of tearing apart the structure and properly completing the project. Where, as here, the defect arising from the breach of the contract "is so substantial as to render the finished building partially unusable and unsafe, the measure of damage is 'the market price of completing or correcting the performance' " (Bellizzi v. Huntley Estates, 3 N.Y.2d 112, 115, quoting 5 Williston, Contracts § 1363, at 3825 [rev. ed.]). Thus, on the facts found by the court, plaintiffs are entitled to the market value of the cost of correcting the deficiencies in the addition arising from defendant's breach.

The trier of fact is in the best position to evaluate the credibility of the witnesses, who gave conflicting testimony concerning the cost of repair to the addition. Therefore, we modify the judgment appealed from by vacating the court's award of $10,000 for diminution in value due to inadequate structural support, and we remit the matter to Supreme Court for further findings of fact on the actual cost of repair for inadequate structural support and direct that judgment be entered accordingly.

Judgment unanimously modified on the law and as modified affirmed without costs and matter remitted to Supreme Court for further proceedings.

NOTES

(1) Section 346 of the First Restatement of Contracts provided that for "defective or unfinished construction" the plaintiff can get judgment for "the reasonable cost of construction and completion in accordance with the contract, if this is possible and does not involve unreasonable economic waste." In Prier v. Refrigeration Engineering Co., 74 Wash.2d 25, 442 P.2d 621 (1968) the court relied upon this section and the following excerpt from Corbin on Contracts in holding that the cost to repair deficiencies in a new ice skating rink, which were around 30% of the original contract price, were not unreasonable: "The modifications were necessary, not only to provide a usable ice sheet, but also to protect the very foundations of the building."

This treatise supports the rule that the damages should be measured in the same way whether the breach be large or small; it should be determined by the cost of completion (the cost of curing the defects) except in a case in which actual completion (the actual curing of the defects) would cause unreasonable economic waste. In the latter case the damages should be the difference between the value of full performance as promised and the value of the defective performance actually rendered. Any reasonable doubt as to whether curing defects would cause such economic waste should be resolved against the contractor guilty of the breach; and on him should be put the burden of proof if there is dispute on the issue. It is true that the phrase "unreasonable economic waste" is no more definite and certain in its meaning and application than is the phrase "substantial performance." It too raises a question of fact. Whether the "economic waste" involved in any specific tearing down and rebuilding is "unreasonable" cannot be resolved by the application of any rule of law; prevailing practices and opinions (the mores) of men, involving their emotions as well as reason and logic, must be taken into account.

5 A. Corbin, Contracts § 1089 (1964) at 491. See also § 1090.

(2) Restatement (Second) adopts a partially subjective test for the measurement of damages based upon the expectation interest. Section 347 provides, in part, that the damages are the "loss in the value to him of the other party's performance caused by the failure or deficiency" plus incidental and consequential damages less "any cost or other loss that he has avoided by not having to perform." This approach contrasts with the more objective contract price "market" price or "cover" price comparison adopted by UCC 2–712 & 2–713, and its illusory character has been criticized. See Simon, *A Critique of the Treatment of Market Damages in the Restatement (Second) of Contracts*, 82 Colum.L.Rev. 80 (1982).

Section 348, however, provides an alternative measure where the breach "results in defective or unfinished construction and the loss in value to the injured party is not proved with sufficient certainty." Here the plaintiff "may recover damages based on (a) the diminution in the market price of the property caused by the breach, or (b) the reasonable cost of completing performance or of remedying the defects if that cost is not clearly disproportionate to the probable loss in the value to him." Section 348(2). How should *Jacob & Youngs v. Kent* and the *Rivers* case be decided under this test?

(3) In discussing Sections 347 and 348 of the Restatement (Second), the court in Douglass v. Licciardi Const. Co., Inc., 386 Pa.Super. 292, 296–97, 562 A.2d 913 (1989), in affirming a jury verdict for cost-to-complete damages in the defective construction of a home, stated:

Sometimes, especially if the performance is defective as distinguished from incomplete, it may not be possible to prove the loss in value to the injured party with reasonable certainty. In that case he can usually recover damages based on the cost to remedy the defect.... Sometimes, however, such a large part of the cost to remedy the defects consists of the cost to undo what has been improperly done that the cost to remedy the defects will be clearly disproportionate to the probable loss in value to the injured party. Damages based on the cost to remedy the defects would then give the injured party a recovery greatly in excess of the loss in value to him and result in a substantial windfall. Such an award will not be made. It is sometimes said that the award would involve "economic waste," but this is a misleading expression since the injured party will not, even if awarded an excessive amount of damages, usually pay to have the defects remedied if to do so will cost him more than the resulting increase in value to him. If an award based on the cost to remedy the defects would clearly be excessive and the injured party does not prove the actual loss in value to him, damages will be based instead on the difference between the market price that the property would have had without the defects and the market price of the property with the defects. This diminution in market price is the least possible loss in value to the injured party, since he could always sell the property on the market even if it had no special value to him.... It is only where the cost of completing performance or of remedying the defects is clearly disproportionate to the probable loss in value to the injured party that damages will be measured by the difference between the market price that the property would have had without the defects and the market price of the property with the defects.

See also, Anuszewski v. Jurevic, 566 A.2d 742 (Me.1989), where the court approved an award that included both the cost to complete defective construction and a reasonable markup or profit for the general contractor. Otherwise, the plaintiff's expectation interest would not have been fully protected.

Peevyhouse v. Garland Coal & Mining Company

Supreme Court of Oklahoma, 1962.
1962 OK 267, 382 P.2d 109.

■ JACKSON, JUSTICE.

In the trial court, plaintiffs Willie and Lucille Peevyhouse sued the defendant, Garland Coal and Mining Company, for damages for breach of contract. Judgment was for plaintiffs in an amount considerably less than was sued for. Plaintiffs appeal and defendant cross-appeals. * * *

Briefly stated, the facts are as follows: plaintiffs owned a farm containing coal deposits, and in November, 1954, leased the premises to defendant for a period of five years for coal mining purposes. A 'stripmining' operation was contemplated in which the coal would be taken from pits on the surface of the ground, instead of from underground mine shafts. In addition to the usual covenants found in a coal mining lease, defendant specifically agreed to perform certain restorative and remedial work at the end of the lease period. It is unnecessary to set out the details of the work to be done, other than to say that it would involve the moving of many thousands of cubic yards of dirt, at a cost estimated by expert witnesses at about $29,000.00. However, plaintiffs sued for only $25,000.00.

During the trial, it was stipulated that all covenants and agreements in the lease contract had been fully carried out by both parties, except the remedial work mentioned above; defendant conceded that this work had not been done.

Plaintiffs introduced expert testimony as to the amount and nature of the work to be done, and its estimated cost. Over plaintiffs' objections, defendant thereafter introduced expert testimony as to the 'diminution in value' of plaintiffs' farm resulting from the failure of defendant to render performance as agreed in the contract—that is, the difference between the present value of the farm, and what its value would have been if defendant had done what it agreed to do.

At the conclusion of the trial, the court instructed the jury that it must return a verdict for plaintiffs, and left the amount of damages for jury determination. On the measure of damages, the court instructed the jury that it might consider the cost of performance of the work defendant agreed to do, 'together with all of the evidence offered on behalf of either party'.

It thus appears that the jury was at liberty to consider the 'diminution in value' of plaintiffs' farm as well as the cost of 'repair work' in determining the amount of damages.

It returned a verdict for plaintiffs for $5000.00—only a fraction of the 'cost of performance', *but more than the total value of the farm even after the remedial work is done*.

On appeal, the issue is sharply drawn. Plaintiffs contend that the true measure of damages in this case is what it will cost plaintiffs to obtain performance of the work that was not done because of defendant's default. Defendant argues that the measure of damages is the cost of performance 'limited, however, to the total difference in the market value before and after the work was performed'.

It appears that this precise question has not heretofore been presented to this court. In Ardizonne v. Archer, 72 Okl. 70, this court held that the measure of damages for breach of a contract to drill an oil well was the reasonable cost of drilling the well, but here a slightly different factual situation exists. The drilling of an oil well will yield valuable geological information, even if no oil or gas is found, and of course if the well is a producer, the value of the premises increases. In the case before us, it is argued by defendant with some force that the performance of the remedial work defendant agreed to do will add at the most only a few hundred dollars to the value of plaintiffs' farm, and that the damages should be limited to that amount because that is all plaintiffs have lost. * * * [The court finds that if the remedial work were done, the market value of the Peevyhouse's farm would increase by only $300.]

It is highly unlikely that the ordinary property owner would agree to pay $29,000 (or its equivalent) for the construction of 'improvements' upon his property that would increase its value only about ($300) three hundred dollars. The result is that we are called upon to apply principles of law theoretically based upon reason and reality to a situation which is basically unreasonable and unrealistic.

* * * Even in the case of contracts that are unquestionably building and construction contracts, the authorities are not in agreement as to the

factors to be considered in determining whether the cost of performance rule or the value rule should be applied. The American Law Institute's Restatement of the Law, Contracts, Volume 1, Sections 346(1)(a)(i) and (ii) submits the proposition that the cost of performance is the proper measure of damages 'if this is possible and does not involve *unreasonable economic waste';* and that the diminution in value caused by the breach is the proper measure 'if construction and completion in accordance with the contract would involve *unreasonable economic waste'*. (Emphasis supplied.) In an explanatory comment immediately following the text, the Restatement makes it clear that the 'economic waste' referred to consists of the destruction of a substantially completed building or other structure. Of course no such destruction is involved in the case now before us.

On the other hand, in McCormick, Damages, Section 168, it is said with regard to building and construction contracts that ' * * * in cases where the defect is one that can be repaired or cured without *undue expense'* the cost of performance is the proper measure of damages, but where ' * * * the defect in material or construction is one that cannot be remedied without *an expenditure for reconstruction disproportionate to the end to be attained'* (emphasis supplied) the value rule should be followed. The same idea was expressed in Jacob & Youngs, Inc. v. Kent, 230 N.Y. 239, as follows:

> 'The owner is entitled to the money which will permit him to complete, unless the cost of completion is grossly and unfairly out of proportion to the good to be attained. When that is true, the measure is the difference in value.'

It thus appears that the prime consideration in the Restatement was 'economic waste'; and that the prime consideration in McCormick, Damages, and in Jacob & Youngs, Inc. v. Kent, supra, was the relationship between the expense involved and the 'end to be attained'—in other words, the 'relative economic benefit'. * * *

23 O.S.1961 §§ 96 and 97 provide as follows:

'§ 96. * * * Notwithstanding the provisions of this chapter, no person can recover a greater amount in damages for the breach of an obligation, than he would have gained by the full performance thereof on both sides * * *.

'§ 97. * * * Damages must, in all cases, be reasonable, and where an obligation of any kind appears to create a right to unconscionable and grossly oppressive damages, contrary to substantial justice no more than reasonable damages can be recovered.'

* * *In spite of the agreement of the parties, these sections limit the damages recoverable to a reasonable amount not 'contrary to substantial justice'; they prevent plaintiffs from recovering a 'greater amount in damages for the breach of an obligation' than they would have 'gained by the full performance thereof'.

We therefore hold that where, in a coal mining lease, lessee agrees to perform certain remedial work on the premises concerned at the end of the lease period, and thereafter the contract is fully performed by both parties except that the remedial work is not done, the measure of damages in an action by lessor against lessee for damages for breach of contract is ordinarily the reasonable cost of performance of the work; however, where the contract provision breached was merely incidental to the main purpose in view, and where the economic benefit which would result to lessor by full performance of the work is grossly disproportionate to the cost of performance, the damages which lessor may recover are limited to the diminution in value resulting to the premises because of the non-performance.

* * * Under the most liberal view of the evidence herein, the diminution in value resulting to the premises because of non-performance of the remedial work was $300.00. After a careful search of the record, we have found no evidence of a higher figure, and plaintiffs do not argue in their briefs that a greater diminution in value was sustained. It thus appears that the judgment was clearly excessive, and that the amount for which judgment should have been rendered is definitely and satisfactorily shown by the record.

■ IRWIN, JUSTICE (dissenting).

* * * Although the contract speaks for itself, there were several negotiations between the plaintiffs and defendant before the contract was executed. Defendant admitted in the trial of the action, that plaintiffs insisted that the above provisions be included in the contract and that they would not agree to the coal mining lease unless the above provisions were included.

* * * The cost for performing the contract in question could have been reasonably approximated when the contract was negotiated and executed and there are no conditions now existing which could not have been reasonably anticipated by the parties. Therefore, defendant had knowledge, when it prevailed upon the plaintiffs to execute the lease, that the cost of performance might be disproportionate to the value or benefits received by plaintiff for the performance.

* * * In the instant action defendant has made no attempt to even substantially perform. The contract in question is not immoral, is not tainted with fraud, and was not entered into through mistake or accident and is not contrary to public policy. It is clear and unambiguous and the parties understood the terms thereof, and the approximate cost of fulfilling the obligations could have been approximately ascertained. There are no conditions existing now which could not have been reasonably anticipated when the contract was negotiated and executed. The defendant could have performed the contract if it desired. It has accepted and reaped the benefits of its contract and now urges that plaintiffs' benefits under the contract be denied. If plaintiffs' benefits are denied, such benefits would inure to the direct benefit of the defendant.

Therefore, in my opinion, the plaintiffs were entitled to specific performance of the contract and since defendant has failed to perform, the proper measure of damages should be the cost of performance. Any other measure of damage would be holding for naught the express provisions of the contract; would be taking from the plaintiffs the benefits of the contract and placing those benefits in defendant which has failed to perform its obligations; would be granting benefits to defendant without a resulting obligation; and would be completely rescinding the solemn obligation of the contract for the benefit of the defendant to the detriment of the plaintiffs by making an entirely new contract for the parties.

I therefore respectfully dissent to the opinion promulgated by a majority of my associates.

NOTES

(1) The *Peevyhouse* case has been criticized on the ground that the diminished value award undercut both the landowner's "subjective" value in having his land reclaimed and a broader "public interest" in achieving the same results. See, e.g., Note, 49 Iowa L.Rev. 597 (1964). In 1967, the Oklahoma legislature imposed a duty upon mine operators to reclaim the land after work was done and authorized the State to contract for the work to be done if the operator defaulted. The operator must, at the start of work, post a bond covering the estimated cost of reclamation and there is no exception for cases where the cost of reclamation is disproportionate to any resulting increase in the value of the land. See 45 Okl.Stat.Ann. §§ 721–92. Section 722 provides in part:

> It is hereby declared to be the policy of this State to provide, after mining operations are completed, for the reclamation and conservation of land subjected to surface disturbance by open cut mining and thereby to preserve natural resources, to aid in the protection of wildlife and aquatic resources, to establish recreational, home and industrial sites, to protect and perpetuate the taxable value of property, and to protect and promote the health, safety, and general welfare of the people of this State.

The United States Court of Appeals for the Tenth Circuit has concluded that, in light of subsequent legislative changes, the Oklahoma Supreme Court would probably no longer follow *Peevyhouse*. Rock Island Improvement Co. v. Helmerich & Payne, Inc., 698 F.2d 1075 (10th Cir.1983). Not so, at least where the breach results in damages to real property: The plaintiffs may recover the reasonable costs of repairing the damage to property so long as the recovery does not "exceed the depreciated value of the land itself." Schneberger v. Apache Corp., 890 P.2d 847, 849 (Okl.1994)(breach of settlement agreement requiring reduction in level of water pollution caused by oil and gas drilling).

(2) *"We picked a fine time to strip mine, Lucille."* Judith Maute unearthed a wealth of information about the *Peevyhouse* dispute:

> To obtain Garland's promises of remediation, the Peevyhouses waived the right to receive $3000 cash upon executing the lease. This amount equals $50 per acre and represents the amount coal operators customarily paid landowners for any surface damages caused by the mining. Upon executing the contract, the Peevyhouses received $2000 for advance royalties, and they later received an additional $500 royalty calculated on the total quantity of coal removed. Within days, Garland diverted a bothersome creek onto the Peevyhouse land so that it could continue mining elsewhere,

unimpeded by water flow. Eventually Garland mined a small portion of the leased Peevyhouse land, but left the property earlier than expected, claiming the coal ran too deep. Heavy spring rains saturated the low-lying worksite, making it dangerously unstable. Garland made little effort to complete the promised remedial work. A bulldozer spent one day knocking off sharp peaks from the highwall and constructing a makeshift dirt fill to prevent the diverted creek from running into the pit, causing further damage.

Judith L. Maute, *Peevyhouse v. Garland Coal & Mining Co. Revisited: The Ballad of Willie and Lucille*, 89 Nw. U. L. Rev. 1341 (1995).

American Standard, Inc. v. Schectman

Supreme Court of New York, Appellate Division, 1981.
80 A.D.2d 318, 439 N.Y.S.2d 529, motion for leave to appeal denied 54 N.Y.2d 604, 443 N.Y.S.2d 1027, 427 N.E.2d 512.

■ HANCOCK, JUSTICE.

Plaintiffs have recovered a judgment on a jury verdict of $90,000 against defendant for his failure to complete grading and to take down certain foundations and other subsurface structures to one foot below the grade line as promised. Whether the court should have charged the jury, as defendant Schectman requested, that the difference in value of plaintiffs' property with and without the promised performance was the measure of the damage is the main point in his appeal. We hold that the request was properly denied and that the cost of completion—not the difference in value—was the proper measure. Finding no other basis for reversal, we affirm.

Until 1972, plaintiffs operated a pig iron manufacturing plant on land abutting the Niagara River in Tonawanda. On the 26-acre parcel were, in addition to various industrial and office buildings, a 60-ton blast furnace, large lifts, hoists and other equipment for transporting and storing ore, railroad tracks, cranes, diesel locomotives and sundry implements and devices used in the business. Since the 1870's plaintiffs' property, under several different owners, had been the site of various industrial operations. Having decided to close the plant, plaintiffs on August 3, 1973 made a contract in which they agreed to convey the buildings and other structures and most of the equipment to defendant, a demolition and excavating contractor, in return for defendant's payment of $275,000 and his promise to remove the equipment, demolish the structures and grade the property as specified.

We agree with Trial Term's interpretation of the contract as requiring defendant to remove all foundations, piers, headwalls, and other structures, including those under the surface and not visible and whether or not shown on the map attached to the contract, to a depth of approximately one foot below the specified grade lines.[2] The proof from plaintiffs' witnesses and the exhibits, showing a substantial deviation from the required grade lines and the existence above grade of walls, foundations and other structures, support the finding, implicit in the jury's verdict, that defendant failed to perform as agreed. Indeed, the testimony of defendant's witnesses and the position he has taken during his performance of the contract and throughout this litigation (which the trial court properly rejected), viz., that the contract did not require him to remove all subsurface foundations, allow no other conclusion.

We turn to defendant's argument that the court erred in rejecting his proof that plaintiffs suffered no loss by reason of the breach because it makes no difference in the value of the property whether the old foundations are at grade or one foot below grade and in denying his offer to show that plaintiffs succeeded in selling the property for $183,000—only $3,000 less than its full fair market value. By refusing this testimony and charging the jury that the cost of completion (estimated at $110,500 by plaintiffs' expert), not diminution in value of the property, was the measure of damage the court, defendant contends, has unjustly permitted plaintiffs to reap a windfall at his expense. Citing the definitive opinions of Chief Judge Cardozo in Jacob & Youngs, Inc. v. Kent, 230 N.Y. 239, he maintains that the facts present a case "of substantial performance" of the contract with omissions of "trivial or inappreciable importance" (p. 245), and that because the cost of completion was "grossly and unfairly out of proportion to the good to be attained", (p. 244), the proper measure of damage is diminution in value.

The general rule of damages for breach of a construction contract is that the injured party may recover those damages which are the direct, natural and immediate consequence of the breach and which can reasonably be said to have been in the contemplation of the parties when the contract was made. . . .In the usual case where the contractor's performance has been defective or incomplete, the reasonable cost of replacement or completion is the measure. . . . When, however, there has been a substantial performance of the contract made in good faith but defects exist, the correction of which would result in economic waste, courts have measured the damages as the difference between the value of the property as constructed and the value if performance had been properly completed. . . . Jacob & Youngs is illustrative. There, plaintiff, a contractor, had

---

2. Paragraph 7 of the Agreement states in pertinent part:

> 7. After the Closing Date, Purchaser shall demolish all of the Improvements on the North Tonawanda Property included in the sale to Purchaser, cap the water intake at the pumphouse end, and grade and level the property, all in accordance with the provisions of Exhibit "C" and "C1" attached hereto.

Exhibit "C" (Notes on demolition and grading) contains specifications for the grade levels for four separate areas shown on Map "C1" and the following instruction:

> Except as otherwise excepted all structures and equipment including foundations, piers, headwalls, etc. shall be removed to a depth approximately one foot below grade lines as set forth above. Area common to more than one area will be faired to provide reasonable transitions, it being intended to provide a reasonably attractive vacant plot for resale.

constructed a house for the defendant which was satisfactory in all respects save one: the wrought iron pipe installed for the plumbing was not of Reading manufacture, as specified in the contract, but of other brands of the same quality. Noting that the breach was unintentional and the consequences of the omission trivial, and that the cost of replacing the pipe would be "grievously out of proportion" (Jacob & Youngs, Inc. v. Kent, supra, 230 N.Y. p. 244) to the significance of the default, the court held the breach to be immaterial and the proper measure of damage to the owner to be not the cost of replacing the pipe but the nominal difference in value of the house with and without the Reading pipe.

Not in all cases of claimed "economic waste" where the cost of completing performance of the contract would be large and out of proportion to the resultant benefit to the property have the courts adopted diminution in value as the measure of damage. Under the Restatement rule, the completion of the contract must involve "unreasonable economic waste" and the illustrative example given is that of a house built with pipe different in name from but equal in quality to the brand stipulated in the contract as in *Jacob & Youngs, Inc. v. Kent* (supra) (Restatement, Contracts, § 346, subd. [1], par. [a], cl. [ii], p. 573; Illustration 2, p. 576). In Groves v. John Wunder Co., 205 Minn. 163, plaintiff had leased property and conveyed a gravel plant to defendant in exchange for a sum of money and for defendant's commitment to return the property to plaintiff at the end of the term at a specified grade—a promise defendant failed to perform. Although the cost of the fill to complete the grading was $60,000 and the total value of the property, graded as specified in the contract, only $12,160 the court rejected the "diminution in value" rule, stating:

> The owner's right to improve his property is not trammeled by its small value. It is his right to erect thereon structures which will reduce its value. If that be the result, it can be of no aid to any contractor who declines performance. As said long ago in Chamberlain v. Parker, 45 N.Y. 569, 572: "A man may do what he will with his own, * * * and if he chooses to erect a monument to his caprice or folly on his premises, and employs and pays another to do it, it does not lie with a defendant who has been so employed and paid for building it, to say that his own performance would not be beneficial to the plaintiff."

(Groves v. John Wunder Co., supra, 205 Minn., p. 168).

The "economic waste" of the type which calls for application of the "diminution in value" rule generally entails defects in construction which are irremediable or which may not be repaired without a substantial tearing down of the structure as in *Jacob & Youngs* . . . .

Where, however, the breach is of a covenant which is only incidental to the main purpose of the contract and completion would be disproportionately costly, courts have applied the diminution in value measure even where no destruction of the work is entailed (see, e.g., Peevyhouse v. Garland Coal & Min. Co., 382 P.2d 109 [Okla.], cert. den. 375 U.S. 906, holding [contrary to *Groves v. John Wunder Co.*, supra] that diminution in value is the proper measure where defendant, the lessee of plaintiff's lands under a coal mining lease, failed to perform costly remedial and restorative work on the land at the termination of the lease. The court distinguished the "building and construction" cases and noted that the breach was of a covenant incidental to the main purpose of the contract which was the recovery of coal from the premises to the benefit of both parties; ...

It is also a general rule in building and construction cases, at least under *Jacob & Youngs* in New York (see *Groves v. John Wunder Co.,* supra; ... , that a contractor who would ask the court to apply the diminution of value measure "as an instrument of justice" must not have breached the contract intentionally and must show substantial performance made in good faith (Jacob & Youngs, Inc. v. Kent, supra, 230 N.Y. pp. 244, 245).

Must Prove GF

In the case before us, plaintiffs chose to accept as part of the consideration for the promised conveyance of their valuable plant and machines to defendant his agreement to grade the property as specified and to remove the foundations, piers and other structures to a depth of one foot below grade to prepare the property for sale. It cannot be said that the grading and the removal of the structures were incidental to plaintiffs' purpose of "achieving a reasonably attractive vacant plot for resale" (compare *Peevyhouse v. Garland Coal & Min. Co.,* supra). Nor can defendant maintain that the damages which would naturally flow from his failure to do the grading and removal work and which could reasonably be said to have been in the contemplation of the parties when the contract was made would not be the reasonable cost of completion.... That the fulfillment of defendant's promise would (contrary to plaintiffs' apparent expectations) add little or nothing to the sale value of the property does not excuse the default. As in the hypothetical case posed in Chamberlain v. Parker, 45 N.Y. 569, supra (cited in *Groves v. John Wunder Co.,* supra), of the man who "chooses to erect a monument to his caprice or folly on his premises, and employs and pays another to do it", it does not lie with defendant here who has received consideration for his promise to do the work "to say that his own performance would not be beneficial to the plaintiff[s]" (*Chamberlain v. Parker,* supra, p. 572).

Grading was clear + in K + Consideration

Defendant's completed performance would not have involved undoing what in good faith was done improperly but only doing what was promised and left undone (compare *Jacob & Youngs, Inc. v. Kent,* supra; Restatement, Contracts, § 346, Illustration 2, p. 576). That the burdens of performance were heavier than anticipated and the cost of completion disproportionate to the end to be obtained does not, without more, alter the rule that the measure of plaintiffs' damage is the cost of completion. Disparity in relative economic benefits is not the equivalent of "economic waste" which will invoke the rule in *Jacob & Youngs, Inc. v. Kent* (supra) (see *Groves v. John Wunder Co.,* supra). Moreover, faced with the jury's finding that the reasonable cost of removing the large concrete and stone walls and other structures extending above grade was $90,000, defendant can hardly assert that he has rendered substantial performance of the contract or that what he left unfinished was "of trivial or inappreciable importance" (Jacob & Youngs, Inc. v. Kent, supra, 230 N.Y. p. 245). Finally, defendant, instead of

Disparity ≠ economic waste

attempting in good faith to complete the removal of the underground structures, contended that he was not obliged by the contract to do so and, thus, cannot claim to be a "transgressor whose default is unintentional and trivial [and who] may hope for mercy if he will offer atonement for his wrong" (Jacob & Youngs, Inc. v. Kent, supra, p. 244). We conclude, then, that the proof pertaining to the value of plaintiffs' property was properly rejected and the jury correctly charged on damages.

The judgment and order should be affirmed.

Judgment and Order unanimously affirmed with costs.

■ SIMONS, J.P., and DOERR, DENMAN and SCHNEPP, JJ., concur.

NOTES

(1) Note, in *American Standard,* that the plaintiff's purpose was to obtain a clear, graded industrial lot for resale and that the plaintiff actually sold the lot as cleared and graded by the defendant for $183,000, "only $3,000 less than its full market value." The outcome of the case was that the plaintiff had a judgment for $90,000 *after* the property had been sold and that the difference in market value of the property in the condition at the time of sale and the property if defendant had fully performed the contract was only $3,000. How does the court justify this result? Has the plaintiff been awarded a "windfall" in a case where the value of the bargain to it can easily be measured in market terms? Or, would the award of diminished value rather than the cost of completion improperly reallocate a performance risk assumed by the defendant, especially since defendant intentionally refused to conform to the contract requirements?

These and other problems are well discussed in Timothy Muris, *Cost of Completion or Diminution in Market Value: The Relevance of Subjective Value,* 12 J.Leg.Stud. 379 (1983). Muris suggests that an award of "cost to complete" damages protects the plaintiff's "subjective" value and should be made in cases where diminution is too difficult or costly to calculate and where "subjective" value is relevant and the cost to complete does not "grossly exceed" the "subjective" value. These conditions are most likely to be met when the plaintiff is a government agency or a consumer and the property is retained for use after the breach. See also Patricia Marschall, *Willfulness: A Crucial Factor in Choosing Remedies for Breach of Contract,* 24 Ariz.L.Rev. 733 (1982), who argues that the key factor is whether the breach was willful or non-willful. If the breach was willful and not excused, the objective of deterring breaches justifies granting the plaintiff either specific performance or the "highest possible measure of expectation damages." 24 Ariz.L.Rev. at 760. For a more general study, see Polinsky, *Risk Sharing Through Breach of Contract Remedies,* 12 J.Leg.Stud. 427 (1983).

For evidence that the contractor's willful breach tipped the balance in favor of a cost-to-complete remedy protecting the plaintiff's "subjective" value, see Laurin v. De Carolis Const. Co., Inc., 372 Mass. 688, 363 N.E.2d 675, 678–79 (1977) (plaintiff entitled to reasonable value of gravel taken from land rather than diminished value of land); Kaiser v. Fishman, 138 A.D.2d 456, 525 N.Y.S.2d 870 (1988) (cost-to-complete in defective construction of residence);

Kangas v. Trust, 110 Ill.App.3d 876, 65 Ill.Dec. 757, 441 N.E.2d 1271 (1982) (nonconforming construction of residence).

Comment: Buyer's Remedies for Seller's Breach of Warranty Under the UCC

A frequent source of disputes in contracts for the sale of goods is whether the seller has met the obligation of quality under the contract. The buyer may claim, either before or after the goods have been accepted, that the goods do not conform to the contract description, or that they do not conform to expectations about basic attributes or that they are not suitable for general or particular purposes that the buyer had in mind. Since the agreement rarely details all of these aspects of quality, the UCC provides three types of warranty that may help to fill the "gap," an express warranty, UCC 2–313, an implied warranty of merchantability, UCC 2–314, and an implied warranty of fitness for particular purpose, UCC 2–315. Based upon what the agreement contains, what the seller has said, what the buyer has communicated as to needs, the commercial or consumer setting and the relative knowledge of the parties, to name a few factors, the court will try to determine from a mix of agreement, inference and policy what in fact the seller agreed to sell. See Chapter Six, Section 2(C).

Suppose, then, that the seller has described the goods as a RXB 450 Disc Computer System and stated in the agreement that the system will perform six basic functions. This description and the affirmations are express warranties under UCC 2–313. When the goods are tendered, the buyer has a right to inspect them to determine whether they conform to the express warranty. UCC 2–513(1). A certain amount of testing may be required. If a non-conformity is discovered, the buyer may reject the goods under UCC 2–601 and 2–602(2). After a "rightful" rejection, the seller has a limited "right" to cure the defects, see UCC 2–508, and, beyond this, the buyer may encourage the cure effort. If the defects are not remedied, the buyer may pursue remedies for "rightful" rejection, which include cancellation, "cover" or damages, including consequential damages. See UCC 2–711 and 2–715(2).

Suppose, however, that the buyer has accepted the goods before the defects are discovered. See UCC 2–606 for what constitutes an acceptance. Acceptance of the goods precludes the remedy of rejection, makes the buyer liable for the price and puts the burden of proving a breach of warranty on the buyer. See UCC 2–607. But UCC 2–608 provides a special remedy called "revocation" of acceptance which, if properly exercised, gives the buyer the same remedial options as if the goods had been rejected. UCC 2–608(3). "Revocation" of acceptance, however, is a complicated remedy and will be denied if the defect was insubstantial, or the buyer should have discovered it before acceptance or notice is given after an unreasonable time has elapsed since the defect was or should have been discovered. Again, if the revocation is "justifiable," the buyer can cancel the contract, obtain a substitute system through "cover" and seek any consequential damages resulting from the breach.

Finally, suppose the buyer, for one reason or another, can neither "rightfully" reject the goods nor "justifiably" revoke acceptance. Is that the end of the remedial road? The answer is no. If timely notice of the breach has been given, see UCC 2–607(3)(a), the buyer may recover damages for "breach in regard to accepted goods" under UCC 2–714 and, where appropriate, for incidental and consequential damages under UCC 2–715. In this situation, the buyer must keep the goods and pay the agreed price, but the price will be adjusted downward to reflect the loss of bargain from the breach. UCC 2–717.

One last note. All of this may change if the parties have agreed to remedies which are in addition to or differ from the usual Code scheme. For example, the buyer may give up the right to reject in exchange for the seller's promise to "cure" certain defects after acceptance. Or, the seller may attempt to "disclaim" certain warranties or exclude liability for consequential damages. We will look at the effectiveness of these efforts in the next subsection. See, e.g., UCC 2–316 and 2–719.

PROBLEM: SELLER'S POST–ACCEPTANCE LIABILITY FOR NON–CONFORMING GOODS

1. Suppose, in *Bisko v. Smirgo,* supra at 210, that Smirgo tendered delivery of the ovens on November 1 and that Bisko, after a reasonable inspection, accepted and put them into operation. Bisko paid the full contract price 90 days later. Thereafter, Bisko discovered a defect in the ovens which impaired their overall capacity to bake bread. This defect constituted a breach of warranty by Smirgo. Smirgo, however, refused either to correct the defect or to replace the ovens. Assume that at the time of delivery the value of the ovens as warranted was $29,500 and the value of the ovens as actually delivered was $25,000. Assume, also, that the reasonable cost to correct the defect would have been $8,000. Bisko has rejected the option of "revoking" the acceptance under UCC 2–608 and pursuing remedies under UCC 2–711 in favor of correcting the defect and keeping the goods. If Bisko does so, how much may Bisko recover from Smirgo for breach of warranty? See UCC 2–714, 2–717, 2–715.

    a. $5,000

    b. $8,000

    c. $4,500

    d. None of the above.

2. Suppose that Smirgo had expressly warranted that the ovens were fit for Bisko's particular needs and purposes. In fact, the ovens were fine for ordinary baking but did not satisfy Bisko's particular needs. It is clear that an oven of that design could not conform to the express warranty and that a different type of oven which cost $75,000 would be required. Bisko would like to recover $50,000, the difference in value between the oven that would have conformed to the warranty and the oven actually delivered. Smirgo argues that this recovery is not permitted under UCC 2–714(2), which limits recovery to the "value of the goods accepted" not some hypothetical oven. Otherwise, Bisko would be put in a better position than promised by Smirgo. What argument should Bisko make? Should it be accepted?

Comment: Restitution of Down Payment by Payor as Remedy for Breach by Performer

Under what circumstances can a buyer or vendee choose restitution of a down payment as a remedy for the seller's or vendor's breach?

Contracts for sale of goods. Under UCC 2–711(1), a buyer who cancels after a seller's breach may recover "so much of the price as has been paid...." More importantly, the non-breaching buyer can have restitution of the price paid in addition to damages measured by the expectation interest. To illustrate, suppose that the buyer paid $50 down on a contract to purchase goods for $100. If the seller failed to deliver and the buyer "covered" for $120, the total recovery would be $50 (restitution under UCC 2–711(1) plus $20 (expectation under UCC 2–712(2), adjusted for savings realized and incidental damages).

On the other hand, UCC 2–711(1) does not say that the price recovery should be adjusted for a losing contract. Thus, if the market price at the time and place of delivery was $80, the buyer could recover $50 in restitution without any downward adjustment for the losing contract. See Bausch & Lomb Inc. v. Bressler, 977 F.2d 720, 729–730 (2d Cir.1992)(down payment to seller adjusted for value of benefit to buyer from part performance). Other than this, Article 2 is relatively silent on the restitution interest. But see UCC 2–718(2) (permitting a breaching buyer to recover in restitution the amount that payments made exceed the seller's damages); Barco Auto Leasing Corp. v. House, 202 Conn. 106, 520 A.2d 162 (1987) (dictum that the formula in UCC 2–718(3)(b) should be extended to cover restitution by a breaching seller as well).

Contracts for sale of realty. The scope of restitution by a vendee of realty upon breach by the vendor is illustrated by Potter v. Oster, 426 N.W.2d 148 (Iowa 1988). After the vendee was in possession of a farm for six years under a contract to sell, the vendor, who had financial reverses, was unable to convey good title. The land involved, along with related tracts, had been mortgaged and, because of declining land values, the vendor had defaulted and lost his equitable title to all of the land. The vendee, who had paid a total of $65,169 in principal, interest, improvements, taxes, insurance and other reliance, was unable to pay the $27,900 still due under the contract to save his property from foreclosure. The vendee then brought a suit against the vendor to rescind the contract and to recover $65,169 in restitution. The trial court endorsed the restitution theory and, after deducting $10,800 for the value of six years' rental, awarded the vendee $54,369.

On appeal, the judgment was affirmed. The court first stated that in order to obtain rescission and restitution, the vendee must establish that (1) he was not in default, (2) the breach was material, and (3) legal remedies were inadequate. There was little dispute that the first two conditions were satisfied. Oster, however, argued that Potter should be limited in damages to the difference between the market value of the land at the time of forfeiture, $35,000, and the contract balance of $27,900.

Oster claimed that the risk of declining land values should be shared by Potter and that restitution would give Potter a windfall.

The court rejected this argument, stating that Oster had tried to limit damages by an "expectation" theory even though Potter sued only for restitution. Even if declining land values motivated Potter's selection of remedies, restitution was still proper where the first two conditions were satisfied and the legal remedies were inadequate.

> [L]egal remedies are considered inadequate when the damages cannot be measured with sufficient certainty ... [E]xpectation damages are correctly calculated as the difference between the contract price and market value at the time for performance ... Since the time of performance in this case would have been March 1990, the market value of the homestead and acreage cannot be predicted with any certainty, thus rendering such a formulation inadequate. More importantly, the fair market value of the homestead at the time of forfeiture is an incorrect measure of the benefit Potters lost. It fails to account for the special value Potters placed on the property's location and residential features that uniquely suited their family. For precisely this reason, remedies at law are presumed inadequate for breach of a real estate contract ... His characterization of the transaction as a mere market loss for Potters, compensable by a sum which would enable them to make a nominal down payment on an equivalent homestead, has no legal or factual support in this record.

426 N.W.2d at 152. Accord: Kim v. Conway & Forty, Inc., 772 S.W.2d 723 (Mo.App.1989) (vendees get restitution of earnest money when vendors fail to convey good title to condominium).

(D) CONSEQUENTIAL DAMAGES: FORESEEABILITY; MITIGATION; CERTAINTY; INCIDENTAL RELIANCE

Up to now we have considered remedies which measure the direct or immediate loss to the plaintiff-payor upon breach by the defendant. To employ a few weasel words, the courts are trying to determine the "natural and usual value of the contract under ordinary circumstances." This is normally determined by the difference in either the contract price and the cost which was or would have been incurred in purchasing substitutes on the open market at the time of breach or the value of what was promised and what was received. See UCC 2–714(1); Hawkins v. McGee, 84 N.H. 114, 146 A. 641 (1929). When the plaintiff's lost bargain is measured in this way, no consequential damages are involved, problems of certainty are minimized, and mitigation of damage policies are often built into standardized formulas for measuring loss. Cf. UCC 2–712(1).

More complex problems, however, are posed by variations of the now familiar *Case of the Recalcitrant Manufacturer.* Imagine that Bisko purchased the ovens for the purpose of expanding a well established business. And imagine that the ovens were to be used in the production process (i.e., they were not purchased for resale). Finally, assume that Bisko expended

$7,500 in preparation for using the ovens upon delivery. While this expenditure was in reliance upon Smirgo's promise to deliver, it was not part of or in preparation for Bisko's performance of its part of the bargain, i.e., to accept and pay for the goods. Expenditures of this sort have been called "incidental" reliance since they are not necessary to the perfection of Bisko's rights under the contract. Nor will they be fully reimbursed if Smirgo performs the contract. See Fuller & Perdue, *The Reliance Interest in Contract Damages,* 46 Yale L.J. 52, 78 (1936). They are, however, "necessary" if Bisko is to use the ovens to expand the business and would be reimbursed from the gross return, if any, from that expansion. Upon breach by Smirgo, therefore, possible items of additional damage to Bisko include loss of profits that might have been earned in the expanded business or the $7,500 reliance expenditure, or both.

There are four basic problems involved in compensating Bisko for these additional losses: (1) Were the losses a foreseeable consequence of the breach at the time of contracting? (2) Could Bisko have reasonably "mitigated" damages by purchasing substitute goods on the open market or continuing to deal with Smirgo? (3) Could Bisko prove what profits were lost with reasonable certainty? (4) If profits are too speculative, could Bisko recover the reliance expenditures as an alternative? Could Bisko recover both lost profits and reliance expenditures? The following materials are organized around these questions and should provide plenty of ammunition for discussion. In addition, we will examine the enforceability of clauses "excluding" consequential damages caused by a breach.

Hadley v. Baxendale

Court of Exchequer, 1854.
9 Exch. 341, 156 Eng.Rep. 145.

See supra at 206.

[Re-read the case of Hadley v. Baxendale and Notes following.]

Spang Industries, Inc., Fort Pitt Bridge Division v. Aetna Casualty & Surety Co.

United States Court of Appeals, Second Circuit, 1975.
512 F.2d 365.

■ MULLIGAN, CIRCUIT JUDGE: Torrington Construction Co., Inc. (Torrington), a Connecticut corporation, was the successful bidder with the New York State Department of Transportation for a highway reconstruction contract covering 4.47 miles of road in Washington County, New York. Before submitting its bid Torrington received an oral quotation from Spang Industries, Inc., Fort Pitt Bridge Division (Fort Pitt), a Pennsylvania corporation, for the fabrication, furnishing and erection of some 240 tons of structural steel at a unit price of 27.5 cents per pound; the steel was to be utilized to construct a 270 foot long, double span bridge over the Battenkill

River as part of the highway reconstruction. The quotation was confirmed in a letter from Fort Pitt to Torrington dated September 5, 1969, which stated in part: "Delivery to be mutually agreed upon." On November 3, 1969, Torrington, in response to a request from Fort Pitt, advised that its requirements for delivery and erection of the steel would be late June, 1970. On November 12, 1969, Fort Pitt notified Torrington that it was tentatively scheduling delivery in accordance with these requirements. On January 7, 1970, Fort Pitt wrote to Torrington asking if the June, 1970 erection date was still valid; Torrington responded affirmatively on January 13, 1970. However, on January 29, 1970, Fort Pitt advised that it was engaged in an extensive expansion program and that "[d]ue to unforeseen delays caused by weather, deliveries from suppliers, etc., it is our opinion that the June date cannot be met." On February 2, 1970, Torrington sent a letter requesting that Fort Pitt give a delivery date and, receiving no response, wrote again on May 12, 1970 requesting a written confirmation of the date of delivery and threatening to cancel out if the date was not reasonably close to the originally scheduled date. On May 20, 1970, Fort Pitt responded and promised that the structural steel would be shipped early in August, 1970.

Although some 25 tons of small steel parts were shipped on August 21, 1970, the first girders and other heavy structural steel were not shipped until August 24, 26, 27, 31 and September 2 and 4, 1970. Fort Pitt had subcontracted the unloading and erection of the steel to Syracuse Rigging Co. but neglected to advise it of the August 21st shipment. The steel began to arrive at the railhead in Shushan, New York about September 1st and the railroad demanded immediate unloading. Torrington was therefore compelled to do the unloading itself until Syracuse Rigging arrived on September 8, 1970. Not until September 16 was there enough steel delivered to the job site to permit Syracuse to commence erection. The work was completed on October 8, 1970 and the bridge was ready to receive its concrete deck on October 28, 1970. Because of contract specifications set by the State requiring that concrete be poured at temperatures of 40° Fahrenheit and above, Torrington had to get special permission from the State's supervising engineer to pour the concrete on October 28, 1970, when the temperature was at 32°.

Since the job site was in northern New York near the Vermont border and danger of freezing temperatures was imminent, the pouring of the concrete was performed on a crash basis in one day, until 1 a.m. the following morning, which entailed extra costs for Torrington in the form of overtime pay, extra equipment and the protection of the concrete during the pouring process.

[In July, 1971, Fort Pitt sued Torrington and its surety for the balance due on the subcontract, $72,247.37 with interest. Thereafter in 1972 Torrington made two further payments totaling $48,983.92 and sued Fort Pitt in another court for damages in the sum of $23,290.81 alleged to be caused by Fort Pitt's delay in furnishing the steel. The cases were removed to and consolidated for trial in the United States District Court for the

*TC =
FP breached
7,653.57
So
to TORR but
TORR still
Owed 23,290.12
→ 15,636.55
for FP*

Northern District of New York and were tried without a jury. On September 12, 1973, the court filed findings of fact and conclusions of law holding that Fort Pitt had breached its contract by its delayed delivery and that Torrington was entitled to damages in the amount of $7,653.57 but that Fort Pitt was entitled to recover $23,290.12, which was the balance due on its contract price plus interest, less the $7,653.57 damages sustained by Torrington. The Court directed that judgment be entered for Fort Pitt against Torrington and it's surety on their joint and several liability for $15,636.55 with interest from November 12, 1970.]

Fort Pitt on this appeal does not take issue with any of the findings of fact of the court below but contends that the recovery by Torrington of its increased expenses constitutes special damages which were not reasonably within the contemplation of the parties when they entered into the contract.

*FP - Claims Damages
not Contemplated*

I

While the damages awarded Torrington are relatively modest ($7,653.57) in comparison with the subcontract price ($132,274.37), Fort Pitt urges that an affirmance of the award will do violence to the rule of Hadley v. Baxendale, 156 Eng.Rep. 145 (Ex.1854), and create a precedent which will have a severe impact on the business of all subcontractors and suppliers.

While it is evident that the function of the award of damages for a breach of contract is to put the plaintiff in the same position he would have been in had there been no breach, Hadley v. Baxendale limits the recovery to those injuries which the parties could reasonably have anticipated at the time the contract was entered into. If the damages suffered do not usually flow from the breach, then it must be established that the special circumstances giving rise to them should reasonably have been anticipated at the time the contract was made.[2]

There can be no question but that Hadley v. Baxendale represents the law in New York and in the United States generally. . . . There is no dispute between the parties on this appeal as to the continuing viability of Hadley v. Baxendale and its formulation of the rule respecting special damages, and this court has no intention of challenging or questioning its principles, which Chief Judge Cardozo characterized to be, at least in some applications, "tantamount to a rule of property," Kerr S.S. Co. v. Radio Corporation of America, 245 N.Y. 284, 291, 157 N.E. 140, 142 (1927).

The gist of Fort Pitt's argument is that, when it entered into the subcontract to fabricate, furnish and erect the steel in September, 1969, it had received a copy of the specifications which indicated that the total work was to be completed by December 15, 1971. It could not reasonably have anticipated that Torrington would so expedite the work (which was accepted by the State on January 21, 1971) that steel delivery would be called for in 1970 rather than in 1971. Whatever knowledge Fort Pitt received after

---

2. [The court quoted the rule of Hadley v. Baxendale, supra.]

the contract was entered into, it argues, cannot expand its liability, since it is essential under Hadley v. Baxendale and its Yankee progeny that the notice of the facts which would give rise to special damages in case of breach be given at or before the time the contract was made. The principle urged cannot be disputed. . . . We do not, however, agree that any violence to the doctrine was done here.

Fort Pitt also knew from the same specifications that Torrington was to commence the work on October 1, 1969. The Fort Pitt letter of September 5, 1969, which constitutes the agreement between the parties, specifically provides: "Delivery to be mutually agreed upon." On November 3, 1969, Torrington, responding to Fort Pitt's inquiry, gave "late June 1970" as its required delivery date and, on November 12, 1969, Fort Pitt stated that it was tentatively scheduling delivery for that time. Thus, at the time when the parties, pursuant to their initial agreement, fixed the date for performance which is crucial here, Fort Pitt knew that a June, 1970 delivery was required. It would be a strained and unpalatable interpretation of Hadley v. Baxendale to now hold that, although the parties left to further agreement the time for delivery, the supplier could reasonably rely upon a 1971 delivery date rather than one the parties later fixed. The behavior of Fort Pitt was totally inconsistent with the posture it now assumes. In November, 1969, it did not quarrel with the date set or seek to avoid the contract. It was not until late January, 1970 that Fort Pitt advised Torrington that, due to unforeseen delays and its expansion program, it could not meet the June date. None of its reasons for late delivery was deemed excusable according to the findings below, and this conclusion is not challenged here. It was not until five months later, on May 20, 1970, after Torrington had threatened to cancel, that Fort Pitt set another date for delivery (early August, 1970) which it again failed to meet, as was found below and not disputed on this appeal.

We conclude that, when the parties enter into a contract which, by its terms, provides that the time of performance is to be fixed at a later date, the knowledge of the consequences of a failure to perform is to be imputed to the defaulting party as of the time the parties agreed upon the date of performance. This comports, in our view, with both the logic and the spirit of Hadley v. Baxendale. Whether the agreement was initially valid despite its indefiniteness or only became valid when a material term was agreed upon is not relevant. At the time Fort Pitt did become committed to a delivery date, it was aware that a June, 1970 performance was required by virtue of its own acceptance. There was no unilateral distortion of the agreement rendering Fort Pitt liable to an extent not theretofore contemplated.

Having proceeded thus far, we do not think it follows automatically that Torrington is entitled to recover the damages it seeks here; further consideration of the facts before us is warranted. Fort Pitt maintains that, under the Hadley v. Baxendale rubric, the damages flowing from its conceded breach are "special" or "consequential" and were not reasonably to be contemplated by the parties. Since Torrington has not proved any "general" or "direct" damages, Fort Pitt urges that the contractor is entitled to nothing. We cannot agree. It is common place that parties to a contract normally address themselves to its performance and not to its breach or the consequences that will ensue if there is a default.... As the New York Court of Appeals long ago stated:

> [A] more precise statement of this rule is, that a party is liable for all the direct damages which both parties to the contract would have contemplated as flowing from its breach, if at the time they entered into it they had bestowed proper attention upon the subject, and had been fully informed of the facts. [This] may properly be called the fiction of law ...

Leonard v. New York, Albany & Buffalo Electro–Magnetic Telegraph Co., 41 N.Y. 544, 567 (1870).[3]

It is also pertinent to note that the rule does not require that the direct damages must necessarily follow, but only that they are likely to follow; as Lord Justice Asquith commented in Victoria Laundry, Ltd. v. Newman Industries, Ltd., [1949] 2 K.B. 528, 540, are they "on the cards"? We believe here that the damages sought to be recovered were also "in the cards."

It must be taken as a reasonable assumption that, when the delivery date of June 1970 was set, Torrington planned the bridge erection within a reasonable time thereafter. It is normal construction procedure that the erection of the steel girders would be followed by the installation of a poured concrete platform and whatever railings of superstructure the platform would require. Fort Pitt was an experienced bridge fabricator supplying contractors and the sequence of the work is hardly arcane. Moreover, any delay beyond June or August would assuredly have jeopardized the pouring of the concrete and have forced the postponement of the work until the spring. The work here, as was well known to Fort Pitt, was to be performed in northern New York near the Vermont border. The court below found that continuing freezing weather would have forced the pouring to be delayed until June, 1971. Had Torrington refused delivery or had it been compelled to delay the completion of the work until the spring of 1971, the potential damage claim would have been substantial. Instead, in a good faith effort to mitigate damages, Torrington embarked upon the crash program we have described. It appears to us that this eventuality should have reasonably been anticipated by Fort Pitt as it was experienced in the trade and was supplying bridge steel in northern climes on a project requiring a concrete roadway.

Torrington's recovery under the circumstances is not substantial or cataclysmic from Fort Pitt's point of view. It represents the expenses of

---

3. A second fiction, added as an embellishment to Hadley v. Baxendale by Mr. Justice Holmes as federal common law in Globe Ref. Co. v. Landa Cotton Oil Co., 190 U.S. 540 (1903), would require not only knowledge of the special circumstances but a tacit agreement on the part of the party sought to be charged to accept the liability imposed by the notice. This second test has generally been rejected by the courts and commentators. Krauss v. Greenbarg, 137 F.2d 569, 571 (3d Cir.), cert. denied 320 U.S. 791 (1943).

unloading steel from the gondola due to Fort Pitt's admitted failure to notify its erection subcontractor, Syracuse Rigging, that the steel had been shipped, plus the costs of premium time, extra equipment and the cost of protecting the work, all occasioned by the realities Torrington faced in the wake of Fort Pitt's breach. In fact, Torrington's original claim of $23,290.81 was whittled down by the court below because of Torrington's failure to establish that its supervisory costs, overhead and certain equipment costs were directly attributable to the delay in delivery of the steel.

Professor Williston has commented:

> The true reason why notice to the defendant of the plaintiff's special circumstances is important is because, just as a court of equity under circumstances of hardship arising after the formation of a contract may deny specific performance, so a court of law may deny damages for unusual consequences where the defendant was not aware when he entered into the contract *how serious an injury would result from its breach.*

11 S. Williston, supra, at 295(emphasis added).

In this case, serious or catastrophic injury was avoided by prompt, effective and reasonable mitigation at modest cost.[7] Had Torrington not acted, had it been forced to wait until the following spring to complete the entire job and then sued to recover the profits it would have made had there been performance by Fort Pitt according to the terms of its agreement, then we might well have an appropriate setting for a classical Hadley v. Baxendale controversy.[8] As this case comes to us, it hardly presents that situation. We therefore affirm the judgment below permitting Torrington to offset its damages against the contract price.

Δ WINS

* * *

7. It is well understood that expenses incurred in a reasonable effort, whether successful or not, to avoid harm that the defendant had reason to foresee as a probable result of the breach when the contract was made may be recovered as an item of damage flowing from the breach. Elias v. Wright, 276 F. 908, 910 (2d Cir.1921); C. McCormick, supra, § 42; Restatement, supra, § 336(2).

8. In Hadley v. Baxendale a miller sought to recover the profits lost from the closing of the mill as a result of a carrier's failure to make timely delivery of a broken crank shaft to an engineering firm where it was to be used as a model for a replacement. A recovery of those profits was disallowed on the ground that it was not reasonably foreseeable that profits would be lost as a result of the breach of the contract of carriage. Lord Justice Asquith pointed out in Victoria Laundry, Ltd. v. Newman Indus., Ltd., supra, that the headnote in Hadley v. Baxendale is mis-

leading in stating that the clerk of the defendant carrier knew that the mill was stopped and that the broken shaft had to be delivered immediately. The *Victoria* court stated that the Court of Exchequer must have rejected this statement and decided to deny the loss of profits from the closing of the mill because the only knowledge possessed by the defendant was that the mill shaft was broken and that the plaintiffs were the millers. Otherwise, "the court must, one would suppose, have decided the case the other way round...." [1949] 2 K.B. at 537. The misleading headnote, however, was considered to reflect the actual facts by at least two scholarly articles on the famous case. Bauer, Consequential Damages in Contract, 80 U.Penn. L.Rev. 687, 689 (1932); McCormick, Damages for Breach of Contract, 19 Minn.L.Rev. 497, 500 (1935).

NOTES

(1) To what extent is the *Spang Industries* case consistent with the "logic and spirit" of *Hadley v. Baxendale,* as amplified in Note (1) at ___. Are the policy bases for this limitation upon damages any clearer in the "Yankee progeny?"

(2) *Hadley v. Baxendale and the UCC.* UCC 2–715(2)(a) provides that "consequential damages resulting from the seller's breach include any loss resulting from general or particular requirements and needs of which the seller at the time of contracting had reason to know and which could not reasonably be prevented by cover or otherwise." Comment 2 states that the "tacit agreement" test for the recovery of consequential damages is rejected and the "older rule at common law which made the seller liable for all consequential damages of which he had 'reason to know' in advance is followed." This rather expansive approach was ignored in an "early" Code case, Keystone Diesel Engine Co. v. Irwin, 411 Pa. 222, 191 A.2d 376 (1963), but the oversight was later corrected. R.I. Lampus Co. v. Neville Cement Products Corp., 474 Pa. 199, 378 A.2d 288 (1977). Most decisions have followed the spirit of UCC 2–715(2)(a). Thus, in Lewis v. Mobil Oil Corp., 438 F.2d 500, 510 (8th Cir.1971), the court rejected the restrictive "tacit agreement" test and stated:

> Where a seller provides goods to a manufacturing enterprise with knowledge that they are to be used in the manufacturing process, it is reasonable to assume that he should know that defective goods will cause a disruption of production, and loss of profits is a natural consequence of such disruption. Hence, loss of profits should be recoverable under those circumstances.

See also J. White & R. Summers, Uniform Commercial Code § 10–4(c) (5th ed. 2000).

But Comment 2 also provides that the "liberality" of the foreseeable consequences rule is "modified by refusing to permit recovery unless the buyer could not reasonably have prevented the loss by cover or otherwise." In other words, the "duty" to mitigate damages rather than the "tacit agreement" test provides the primary control upon the scope of liability.

(3) Under Restatement (2d) Section 351, the discretion given to a court to further limit the recovery of otherwise proven consequential damages has received some treatment in the courts.

In Alaska Tae Woong Venture, Inc. v. Westward Seafoods, 963 P.2d 1055 (Alaska 1998), the defendant breached a contract to take and process defined quantities of seafood over a several year period when it was unable to complete and open the processing plant on time. After suffering severe financial losses in the 1991 fishing season, the plaintiff sold the fishing boat to a third party and did not try to fish again. The plaintiff sued for lost profits during the 1991 season and for subsequent years. The court upheld the jury's determination of lost profits for 1991 and affirmed the decision not to award lost profits beyond 1993 even though it was foreseeable to the defendant that the breach would cause the plaintiff serious financial losses that would probably cause it to sell the vessel and, thus, lose profit opportunities for the balance of the contract. After brushing aside various distinctions and arguments, the court said:

But these distinctions are not determinative. We have previously adopted section 351 of the Restatement (Second) of Contracts. . . . The Restatement empowers trial courts to limit damages for foreseeable loss when "justice so requires in order to avoid disproportionate compensation." Restatement (Second) of Contracts § 351(3) (1981).[This subsection provides: A court may limit damages for foreseeable loss by excluding recovery for loss of profits, by allowing recovery only for loss incurred in reliance, or otherwise if it concludes that in the circumstances justice so requires in order to avoid disproportionate compensation.] The comment to section 351 notes that "[t]ypical examples of limitations imposed on damages under this discretionary power involve the denial of recovery for loss of profits." *Id.* at cmt. f; . . .

Our review of the record convinces us that section 351 authorized the trial court to impose a reasonable legal limit on ATWV's claim of lost future profits. ATWV did not assert that Westward's breach of contract destroyed AJVS; selling the Allegiance did not put AJVS out of business. Soon after the sale, Phillips wound down the company's business. But his action appears to have been voluntary, not dictated by AJVS's economic failure; the company evidently was not insolvent at the time. And, to the extent that Phillips acted for financial reasons, the record indicates that his actions stemmed in part from problems unrelated to Westward's breach.

By electing to stop actively engaging in business, AJVS effectively chose to make no further effort to earn *any* profits—including profits it might have earned through reinvestment of the consideration it received for selling the Allegiance. Had the company continued in business and reinvested the proceeds from the Allegiance's sale, its profits on that investment would presumably have reduced losses it suffered as a result of the vessel's absence. In light of this election, it seems anomalous for ATWV now to claim entitlement to seemingly endless years of profits that AJVS might have earned.

ATWV does not explain how such compensation would be just. AJVS's inability to replace the Allegiance cannot alone support a finding of long-term losses . . . Moreover, because ATWV does not claim that Westward caused AJVS's destruction, the causal nexus between Westward's breach and AJVS's loss of future earnings is necessarily uncertain . . . Finally, no matter how predictable it was that Westward's breach would cause AJVS to lose the Allegiance, it strains credulity to think that Westward could reasonably have anticipated perpetual liability for profits AJVS might lose in future years.

Given these circumstances, we conclude that an extended award of lost profits would be disproportionate to Westward's breach; justice does not require such compensation. *See* Restatement § 351(3). Accordingly, we hold that the trial court did not err in its alternative decision to preclude ATWV from claiming lost profits beyond June 30, 1993. * * *

(4) *Foreseeability in Tort.* The foreseeable consequences test has been used to limit the scope of liability in tort as well as contract. The critical point is the time of the alleged negligent conduct. If, given the nature of the conduct and the circumstances, the defendant could not reasonably foresee the risk of any harm to the plaintiff or a class of persons similarly situated, there is no duty of

care owed to the plaintiff. Palsgraf v. Long Island Railroad, 248 N.Y. 339, 162 N.E. 99 (1928). See Semler v. Psychiatric Institute of Washington, D.C., 538 F.2d 121 (4th Cir.1976), cert. denied 429 U.S. 827, 97 S.Ct. 83, 50 L.Ed.2d 90. If, however, the defendant has breached a duty of care owed to the plaintiff and the negligence has been the cause in fact of varied and extensive damage to person and property, the unforeseeability of that damage does not necessarily insulate the defendant from full liability. The test, according to Judge Friendly, is whether the "very risks" that made the conduct negligent produced "other and more serious consequences to such persons that were fairly foreseeable when he fell short of what the law demanded." If so, there is full liability. If, however, the "injury sprang from a hazard different from that which was improperly risked" the defendant might not be liable for the full consequences caused. Petition of Kinsman Transit Co., 338 F.2d 708, 724 (2d Cir.1964), cert. denied 380 U.S. 944, 85 S.Ct. 1026, 13 L.Ed.2d 963 (1965).

For a decision applying both foreseeability and mitigation ideas borrowed from contracts to protect a bank from economic loss caused by the negligent failure to transfer funds, see Evra Corp. v. Swiss Bank Corp., 673 F.2d 951 (7th Cir.1982). In *Evra,* Judge Posner stated that the "rule" in *Hadley v. Baxendale* is that "consequential damages will not be awarded unless the defendant was put on notice of the special circumstances giving rise to them" and that its "animating principle" is that the "costs of the untoward consequence of a course of dealings should be borne by that party who was able to avert the consequence at least cost and failed to do so." 673 F.2d 951 at 955–56, 957. In *Evra,* which was litigated on a negligence theory, the "animating principle" borrowed from contracts required conduct in avoidance by the injured party both before and after the tort. See also Rardin v. T & D Mach. Handling, Inc., 890 F.2d 24, 26–27 (7th Cir.1989) (Posner, J.).

(5) *Smirgo v. Bisko Visited Again.* Assuming that Smirgo's breach by non-delivery "caused" the losses and that all damages can be proved with reasonable certainty, has Bisko satisfied the "foreseeability" test of UCC 2–715(2)(a)? Put another way, did Bisko communicate enough information to Smirgo so as to enable it to take precautions or to insure against the harm? If so, has Bisko, after the breach, mitigated damages by taking reasonable action to "prevent" the consequential losses "by cover or otherwise?" UCC 2–715(2)(a).

(6) *Does Mitigation Duty Include A Duty to Deal With Breaching Promisor?* If Smirgo breached, would Bisko have any "duty"* to deal with Smirgo, the breaching party, if that effort would avoid a six month delay in repurchasing from a third party? The Restatement answer is yes, unless the breaching-party's offer was conditioned on the non-breaching party waiving any right for damages for breach. Restatement (Second) § 350(1) generally ordains that "damages are not recoverable for loss that the injured party could have avoided without undue risk, burden or humiliation." And the associated Comment explains:

> If the party in breach offers to perform the contract for a different price, this may amount to a suitable alternative. . . . But this is not the case if the

---

* "It is sometimes said that it is the 'duty' of the aggrieved party to mitigate damages, but this is misleading because he incurs no liability for his failure to act." Restatement (Second) § 350, Cmt.

offer is conditioned on surrender by the injured party of his claim for breach.

Id., cmt. As one court put it, the "rule" of mitigation "has never been regarded as requiring one to yield to a wrongful demand that he may thereby save the wrongdoer from the legal consequences of his own error." Lurton, J. in Hirsch v. Georgia Iron & Coal Co., 169 Fed. 578, 581 (6th Cir.1909). See, Gunn Infiniti, Inc. v. O'Byrne, 996 S.W.2d 854, 858–59 (Tex.1999); Schatz Distributing Co., Inc. v. Olivetti Corp. of America, 7 Kan.App.2d 676, 647 P.2d 820 (1982) (buyer of defective computer did not fail to mitigate by refusing seller's offer to resell the goods on buyer's behalf and to substitute new goods).

(7) *What is a "substitute."* Courts also have struggled determining whether an alternative transaction offered by either a third or the breaching party "is a suitable substitute." Id. For example, in the famous case of Shirley Maclaine Parker v. Twentieth Century–Fox Film Corp., 3 Cal.3d 176, 89 Cal.Rptr. 737, 474 P.2d 689 (1970), Twentieth Century–Fox contracted to pay film star Shirley Maclaine $750,000 to star in its musical motion picture, Bloomer Girl. The studio decided not to make that movie and instead offered Maclaine a starring role in a Western, Big Country, Big Man, for the same money. Maclaine declined the second movie and sued for the money she had not been paid for the first. The Supreme Court of California concluded that the Big Country was "different or inferior" to Bloomer Girl, and rejected the studio's mitigation defense. Mary Jo Frug emphasized the feminist politics of Amelia Bloomer in her rereading of the case. See Mary Jo Frug, Re-reading Contracts: A Feminist Analysis of a Contracts Casebook, 34 Am. U. L. Rev. 1065, 1114–22 (1985). Victor Goldberg emphasizes that the original agreement was merely a form of "option" agreement:

> The contract had a "pay-or-play" provision, common in the motion picture industry. The studio had, in effect, purchased an option on her time; they would pay her to be ready to make a particular film, but they made no promise to actually use her in making the film. When Fox canceled the project, they did not breach; they merely chose not to exercise their option. There was no breach and, therefore, there was no need to mitigate.

Victor P. Goldberg, Bloomer Girl Revisited or How to Frame an Unmade Picture, 1998 Wis. L. Rev. 1051.

PROBLEM: RECOVERY OF LOST RESALE PROFITS

(1) Bob, a retailer, entered into a contract with Sam, a manufacturer, for the purchase of goods at $100 per unit. Before the goods were delivered, Bob contracted to sell the goods to Carl, located 1,000 miles away, for $125 a unit. Sam knew at the time of contracting that Bob resold goods of this kind in the ordinary course of business but knew nothing about the prospective contract with Carl. Sam failed to deliver the goods. Bob, after considerable effort, was unable to "cover" on the open market and so informed Carl. Carl released Bob from any liability on the resale contract. Bob, however, sued Sam for lost profits, to be measured by the difference between the contract price and the resale price, some $25 per unit. Sam denied liability on the ground that he had no reason to foresee the particular resale contract with Carl or that Bob would

be unable to cover on the open market. Therefore, there was no liability for consequential damages. What result?

(2) Suppose that Bob could have "covered" at $110 per unit but failed to do so. What are Bob's damages here? Do you have enough information? Consider UCC 2–711, 2–712, 2–713, & 2–715.

Hydraform Products Corp. v. American Steel & Aluminum Corp.

Supreme Court of New Hampshire, 1985.
127 N.H. 187, 498 A.2d 339.

■ SOUTER, JUSTICE.

The defendant, American Steel & Aluminum Corporation, appeals from the judgment entered on a jury verdict against it. The plaintiff, Hydraform Products Corporation, brought this action for direct and consequential damages based on claims of negligent misrepresentation and breach of a contract to supply steel to be used in manufacturing woodstoves. American claims that prior to trial, the Superior Court (Nadeau, J.) erroneously held that a limitation of damages clause was ineffective to bar the claim for consequential damages. American further claims, inter alia, that the Trial Court (Dalianis, J.) erred (a) in allowing the jury to calculate lost profits on the basis of a volume of business in excess of what the contract disclosed and for a period beyond the year in which the steel was to be supplied; (b) in allowing the jury to award damages for the diminished value of the woodstove division of Hydraform's business; (c) in failing to direct a verdict for the defendant on the misrepresentation claim; and (d) in allowing Hydraform's president to testify as an expert witness. We hold that the trial court properly refused to enforce the limitation of damages clause, but we sustain the other claims of error and reverse the judgment.

Hydraform was incorporated in 1975 and began manufacturing and selling woodstoves in 1976. During the sales season of 1977–78 it sold 640 stoves. It purchased steel from a number of suppliers until July 1978, when it entered into a "trial run" contract with American for enough steel to manufacture 40 stoves. Upon delivery of the steel, certain of Hydraform's agents and employees signed a delivery receipt prepared by American, containing the following language:

"Seller will replace or refund the purchase price for any goods which at the time of delivery to buyer were damaged, defective or not in conformance with the buyer's written purchase order, provided that the buyer gives seller written notice by mail of such damage, defect or deviation within 10 days following its receipt of the goods. In no event shall seller be liable for labor costs expended on such goods or other consequential damages."

When some of the deliveries under this contract were late, Hydraform's president, J.R. Choate, explained to an agent of American that late deliveries of steel during the peak season for manufacturing and selling stoves could ruin Hydraform's business for a year. In response, American's agent stated that if Hydraform placed a further order, American would sheer and stockpile in advance, at its own plant, enough steel for 400 stoves, and would supply further steel on demand. Thereafter Hydraform did submit a purchase order for steel sufficient to manufacture 400 stoves, to be delivered in four equal installments on the first days of September, October, November and December of 1978.

American's acceptance of this offer took the form of deliveries accompanied by receipt forms. The forms included the same language limiting American's liability for damages that had appeared on the receipts used during the trial run agreement. Hydraform's employees signed these receipts as the steel was delivered from time to time, and no one representing Hydraform ever objected to that language.

Other aspects of American's performance under the trial run contract reoccurred as well. Deliveries were late, some of the steel delivered was defective, and replacements of defective steel were tardy. Throughout the fall of 1978 Mr. Choate protested the slow and defective shipments, while American's agent continually reassured him that the deficient performance would be corrected. Late in the fall, Mr. Choate finally concluded that American would never perform as agreed, and attempted to obtain steel from other suppliers. He found, however, that none could supply the steel he required in time to manufacture stoves for the 1978–79 sales season. In the meantime, the delays in manufacturing had led to cancelled orders, and by the end of the season Hydraform had manufactured and sold only 250 stoves. In September, 1979, Hydraform sold its woodstove manufacturing division for $150,000 plus royalties.

In December, 1979, Hydraform brought an action for breach of contract, which provoked a countersuit by American. In January, 1983, American moved to dismiss Hydraform's claims for consequential damages to compensate for lost profits and for loss on the sale of the business. American based the motion on the limitation of damages clause and upon its defense that Hydraform had failed to mitigate its damages by cover or otherwise. In February, 1983, Hydraform's pretrial statement filed under Superior Court Rule 62 disclosed that it claimed $100,000 as damages for lost profits generally and $220,000 as a loss on the sale of the business. Later in February, 1983, the superior court permitted Hydraform to amend its writ by adding further counts, which included claims for fraudulent and negligent misrepresentation. Hydraform did not, however, proceed to trial on the claim of fraud.

In April, 1983, Nadeau, J., denied American's motion to dismiss the claims for consequential damages. He relied on the Uniform Commercial Code as adopted in New Hampshire, RSA chapter 382–A, in ruling that the limitation of damages clause was unenforceable on the alternative grounds that the clause would have been a material alteration of the contract, see RSA 382–A:2207(2)(b), or was unconscionable or was a term that had failed of its essential purpose, see RSA 382–A:2–719(2) and (3). He further concluded that, under the circumstances of the case, the failure to cover, if proven, would not bar consequential damages.

The case was tried to a jury before Dalianis, J. American's exceptions at trial are discussed in detail below. At the close of the evidence, American objected to the use of a verdict form with provision for special findings, and the case was submitted for a general verdict, which the jury returned for Hydraform in the amount of $80,245.12.

American's first assignment of error for our consideration challenges the trial court's refusal to recognize the provision insulating American from liability for consequential damages caused by defective goods. We hold that the trial court was correct.

* * *

Since the clause was not enforceable, the trial court allowed the jury to consider Hydraform's claims for lost profits in the year of the contract, 1978, and for the two years thereafter, as well as its claim for loss in the value of the stove manufacturing business resulting in a lower sales price for the business in 1979. American argues that the court erred in submitting such claims to the jury, and rests its position on three requirements governing the recovery of consequential damages.

First, under RSA 382–A:2–715(2)(a) consequential damages are limited to compensation for "loss resulting from general or particular requirements and needs of which the seller at the time of contracting had reason to know ... " This reflection of Hadley v. Baxendale, 156 Eng.Rep. 145 (1854) thus limits damages to those reasonably foreseeable at the time of the contract.... To satisfy the foreseeability requirement, the injury for which damages are sought "must follow the breach in the natural course of events, or the evidence must specifically show that the breaching party had reason to foresee the injury." Salem Engineering & Const. Corp. v. Londonderry School Dist., 122 N.H. 379, 384, 445 A.2d 1091, 1094 (1982). Thus, peculiar circumstances and particular needs must be made known to the seller if they are to be considered in determining the foreseeability of damages....

Second, the damages sought must be limited to recompense for the reasonably ascertainable consequences of the breach. See RSA 382–A:2–715, comment 4. While proof of damages to the degree of mathematical certainty is not necessary, ... a claim for lost profits must rest on evidence demonstrating that the profits claimed were "reasonably certain" in the absence of the breach.... Speculative losses are not recoverable.

Third, consequential damages such as lost profits are recoverable only if the loss "could not reasonably be prevented by cover or otherwise." § 2–715(2)(a). See § 2–712(1) (i.e., by purchase or contract to purchase goods in substitution for those due from seller). In summary, consequential damages must be reasonably foreseeable, ascertainable and unavoidable.

Applying these standards, we look first at the claim for lost profits for the manufacturing season beginning in September, 1978. There is no serious question that loss of profit on sales was foreseeable up to the number of 400 stoves referred to in the contract, and there is a clear evidentiary basis for a finding that Hydraform would have sold at least that number. There was also an evidentiary basis for the trial court's ruling that Hydraform acted reasonably even though it did not attempt to cover until the season was underway and it turned out to be too late. American had led Hydraform on by repeatedly promising to take steps to remedy its failures, and the court could find that Hydraform's reliance on these promises was reasonable up to the time when it finally and unsuccessfully tried to cover.

Lost profits on sales beyond the 400 stoves presents a foreseeability issue, however. Although American's agent had stated that American would supply steel beyond the 400 stove level on demand, there is no evidence that Hydraform indicated that it would be likely to make such a demand to the extent of any reasonably foreseeable amount. Rather, the evidence was that Mr. Choate had told American's agent that the business was seasonal with a busy period of about four months. The contract referred to delivery dates on the first of four separate months and spoke of only 400 stoves. Thus, there appears to be no basis on which American should have foreseen a volume in excess of 400 for the season beginning in 1978. Lost profits for sales beyond that amount therefore were not recoverable, and it was error to allow the jury to consider them.

Nor should the claims for profits lost on sales projected for the two subsequent years have been submitted to the jury. The impediment to recovery of these profits was not total unforeseeability that the breach could have effects in a subsequent year or years, but the inability to calculate any such loss with reasonable certainty. In arguing that a reasonably certain calculation was possible, Hydraform relies heavily on Van Hooijdonk v. Langley, 111 N.H. 32 (1971), a case that arose from a landlord's cancellation of a business lease. The court held that the jury could award damages for profits that a seasonal restaurant anticipated for the three years that lease should have run. It reasoned that the experience of one two-month season provided sufficient data for a reasonably certain opinion about the extent of future profits. The court thus found sufficient certainty where damages were estimated on the basis of one year of operation and profit, as compared with no operation and hence no profit in the later years.

Hydraform's situation, however, presents a variable that distinguishes it from Van Hooijdonk. In our case the evidence did not indicate that American's breach had forced Hydraform's stove manufacturing enterprise out of business, and therefore the jury could not assume that there would be no profits in later years. Without that assumption the jury could not come to any reasonably certain conclusion about the anticipated level of sales absent a breach by American. The jury could predict that Hydraform would obtain steel from another source and would be able to manufacture stoves; but it did not have the evidence from which to infer the future volume of manufacturing and sales. Thus, it could not calculate anticipated lost profits with a reasonable degree of certainty.

There is, moreover, a further reason to deny recovery for profits said to have been lost in the later years. Although Hydraform's pretrial statement disclosed that Hydraform claimed $100,000 in lost profits, it did not indicate that the claim related to the seasons beginning in 1979 and 1980. Since the pretrial statement also listed a claim for loss of the value of the business at the time of its sale in 1979, we believe that the statement could reasonably be read as claiming lost profit only for the one year before the business was sold. Therefore the claim for profits in 1979 and 1980 should have been disallowed for failure to disclose the claim as required by Superior Court Rule 62.

We consider next the claim for loss in the value of the business as realized at the time of its sale in 1979. As a general rule, loss in the value of a business as a going concern, or loss in the value of its good will, may be recovered as an element of consequential damages. . . .

In this case, however, it was error to submit the claim for diminished value to the jury, for three reasons. First, to the extent that diminished value was thought to reflect anticipated loss of profits in future years, as a capitalization of the loss, it could not be calculated with reasonable certainty for the reasons we have just discussed. Second, even if such profits could have been calculated in this case, allowing the jury to consider both a claim for diminished value resting on lost profits and a claim for the lost profits themselves would have allowed a double recovery. . . . Third, to the extent that diminished value was thought to rest on any other theory, there was no evidence on which it could have been calculated. There was nothing more than Mr. Choate's testimony that he had sold the business in September of 1979 for $150,000 plus minimum royalties, together with his opinion that the sales price was less than the business was worth. This testimony provided the jury with no basis for determining what the business was worth or for calculating the claimed loss, and any award on this theory rested on sheer speculation.

In summary, we hold that the jury should not have been allowed to consider any contract claim for consequential damages for lost profits beyond those lost on the sale of 150 stoves, the difference between the 400 mentioned in the contract and the 250 actually sold. Nor should the trial court have allowed the jury to consider the claim for loss in the value of the business.

* * *

Reversed.

NOTES

(1) *Lost Profits Under CISG.* In Delchi Carrier SpA v. Rotorex Corp., 71 F.3d 1024 (2d Cir.1995), an American seller agreed to supply an Italian buyer 10,800 compressors in three installments for use in portable room air conditioners. The compressors did not conform to the contract and the seller was unable to cure the defect. The buyer properly avoided the contract for fundamental

breach under CISG Articles 25 and 49 and bought compressors in replacement from a third party. See Article 75. The buyer, relying on Article 74, then sued for, among other things, (1) profits lost between the time of the breach and the replacement contract, (2) expense incurred before the breach in preparing for delivery and use of the compressors, and (3) expenses incurred after the breach in effecting a repurchase contract and storing the seller's goods.

Article 74 provides:

Damages for breach of contract by one party consist of a sum equal to the loss, including loss of profit, suffered by other party as a consequence of the breach. Such damages may not exceed the loss which the party in breach foresaw or ought to have foreseen, at the time of the conclusion of the contract, in the light of the facts and matters of which he then knew or ought to have known, as a possible consequence of the breach of contract.

The court concluded that the foreseeability requirement had been satisfied and that there was no failure to mitigate damages under Article 77. Thus, the buyer was entitled to the following recovery.

First, the buyer could recover the profits lost in being unable to sell air conditioners during the period between breach and the replacement contract. Assuming that the number of units that could have been sold was proven and that the buyer could have sold all of them, these profits were measured by subtracting the total variable costs, actual and hypothetical, that would have been expended from the estimated gross proceeds of the units sold. The variable costs do not include fixed costs or overhead. Thus, the so-called profit figure would include overhead if those fixed costs had been allocated to the contracts.

Second, the buyer could recover pre-breach reliance costs (those incurred to prepare for performance) even though they were not counted as variable costs in computing lost profits. There is no double recovery if the buyer recovers profits (plus overhead) and reasonable reliance on the contract.

Third, the buyer could also recover reasonable costs incurred after the breach in an effort to effect a cure or to obtain a replacement contract. The court called then incidental costs, a phrase not used in CISG.

The court found that Article 74 did not directly support all of this, but took consolation in that fact that although the UCC did not apply per se, it could be applied by analogy.

Do you agree? See UCC 2–715.

(2) *"New Business" Rule.* The ease with which lost profits can be proved may depend upon whether the plaintiff is a new or an established business. Where did the plaintiff fit in *Hydraform*? What limitations did the court impose upon recovery of the claim lost profits.

Here is a traditional statement of the so-called "new business" or *per se* rule:

When the business that is interfered with as a result of a breach of contract is a new business or venture, or one merely in contemplation, the anticipated profits from such business cannot be recovered as an item of damages because it cannot be rendered reasonably certain that there would have been any profits at all from the conduct of the business.

Coastland Corporation v. Third National Mortgage Co., 611 F.2d 969, 978 (4th Cir.1979) (Virginia law). For a collection of the authorities and arguments for and against the *per se* rule, see Note, 67 Va.L.Rev. 431 (1981) (for); Comment, 56 N.Car.L.Rev. 693 (1978) (against). See, generally, Schaefer, *Uncertainty and the Law of Damages,* 19 Wm. & Mary L.Rev. 719 (1979). Most decisions under the UCC, however, have rejected the *per se* rule. The crucial issue is not whether the plaintiff is a new business but whether the lost profits are proven with reasonable certainty. See, e.g., Hawthorne Industries, Inc. v. Balfour Maclaine International, Limited, 676 F.2d 1385 (11th Cir.1982); Deaton, Inc. v. Aeroglide Corp., 99 N.M. 253, 657 P.2d 109 (1982) (B fails to prove damages with reasonable certainty in new business). See also Note, *The New Business Rule and the Denial of Lost Profits,* 48 Ohio St.L.J. 855 (1987).

(3) *Causation Issue.* Proof issues are frequently mixed with the question of whether the breach "caused" the lost consequential profits. Thus, a buyer was denied lost profits when a delay was attributable to a tactical business decision by the buyer rather than to a defect in the seller's product. Duracote Corp. v. Goodyear Tire & Rubber Co., 2 Ohio St.3d 160, 443 N.E.2d 184 (1983). Similarly, reduced profits attributable to the plaintiff's capital structure rather than to defendant's breach of warranty were also denied. Lewis v. Mobil Oil Corp., 438 F.2d 500 (8th Cir.1971). See also Dura–Wood Treating Co. v. Century Forest Industries, Inc., 675 F.2d 745 (5th Cir.1982) (P ties up production facilities by decision to manufacture product which D had failed to deliver rather than by covering); Overstreet v. Norden Laboratories, Inc., 669 F.2d 1286 (6th Cir.1982) (breach of warranty regarding vaccine did not cause brood mares to abort foals). As one court has put it, the "rule preventing recovery of 'speculative' damages referred more especially to the uncertainty as to the cause rather than uncertainty as to the measure or extent of damages.' " Hawthorne Industries, Inc. v. Balfour Maclaine International, Limited, 676 F.2d 1385, 1387 (11th Cir.1982). See also Redgrave v. Boston Symphony Orchestra, Inc., 855 F.2d 888, 891–94 (1st Cir.1988) (claim that reputation damaged by breach is unduly speculative and too remote).

(4) *Consequential reliance losses.* Suppose B agrees to buy machinery from S to be delivered and installed in B's factory. The machinery will replace existing factory equipment. In anticipation of delivery, B spends $5,000 in preparing a platform for the machinery to sit. S, however, fail to deliver the machinery and B makes no effort to replace it. The platform is not usable and must be removed. B sues S for $5,000 only, the amount invested in preparation and which was wasted by the breach. Can B recover?

In L. Albert & Son v. Armstrong Rubber Co., 178 F.2d 182 (2d Cir.1949), a pre-code case, the court had a similar question. Speaking through Chief Judge Learned Hand, the court concluded that the plaintiff (B) could choose to recover costs expended in reliance on the defendant's (S) performance rather than profits lost, but if the defendant proved that the contract if performed would have lost money the reliance costs should have been reduced accordingly.

As the *Delchi* case, supra, suggests, however, there may be a foreseeability problem if the reliance was necessary for the buyer to use the goods rather than necessary for the buyer to perform the contract with the seller. Put differently, if the reliance is incidental to performing the contract, it is more likely to be an expense that the seller at the time of contracting could not reasonably foresee.

PROBLEM: SMIRGO AND BISKO—ONE MORE TIME!

Assume that after Smirgo's breach, Bisko elected not to expand the bakery. After salvage, Bisko had $5,000 in unreimbursed expenses in preparing to receive the ovens. In addition, Bisko can prove with reasonable certainty that it would have grossed $150,000 in new business between the time that Smirgo promised to deliver and the time that the ovens could have been replaced by an effective cover. Bisko can also prove that the costs saved by Smirgo's breach were $100,000. Bisko claims $55,000 in consequential damages, including $50,000 in lost profits ($150,000 gross less $100,000 in costs saved) and $5,000 in reasonable reliance. Evaluate the arguments of Smirgo in response:

1. $55,000 puts Bisko in a better position than full performance would have because Bisko elected after the breach to discontinue the expansion. You can't recover lost profits on a project that was discontinued.

2. $55,000 gives Bisko a double recovery for reliance expenditures. At best, Bisko should recover the "net" profit prevented by the breach plus any unreimbursed reliance. "Net" profit is determined by subtracting costs saved ($100,000) plus reliance incurred ($5,000) from the gross prevented ($150,000), for a figure of $45,000. When reliance is added in, the amount of recovery should be $50,000, not $55,000.

3.   The substantial cause of the lost revenues, if Bisko had continued, would have been the competition from Caraway rather than the breach by Smirgo. Thus, Bisko's recovery is limited to $5,000.

4.   In any event, the cumulative effect of these factors plus the relatively small contract price, justify the application by a court of Restatement (Second) § 351(3), supra.

To what extent will a court enforce an agreement excluding consequential damages for breach of contract? For the long answer, see Chapter Seven, Section 5. For a quick answer, consult UCC 2–719(3).

SECTION 3.   EQUITABLE REMEDIES FOR BREACH OF CONTRACT: PROHIBITORY INJUNCTION AND SPECIFIC PERFORMANCE

In the materials just considered, a primary objective has been to determine the amount of compensatory damages due to the plaintiff because of the defendant's breach, whether that breach be of a contract to pay money or render some other performance, such as the sale of goods or stock, the conveyance of interests in land, construction or personal or professional services. If the court decides that the defendant is liable for damages and enters a money judgment against the defendant, that judgment is enforced against the defendant's property, that is, *in rem*. If the property is insufficient, the enforcement process may be renewed until the judgment is satisfied or the obligation is discharged. See Comment, Enforcement of Money Judgments, supra.

The defendant, however, will not be imprisoned for failure to pay the obligation represented by the judgment. See Note, *Imprisonment for Debt: In the Military Tradition*, 80 Yale L.J. 1679 (1971).* For all practical purposes, the defendant has a choice whether to perform the contract or "pay damages," that is, run the risk that the plaintiff will sue and ultimately recover the full amount of the claim from the defendant's personal assets. This, then, is the plaintiff's remedy "at law" for breach of contract. Subject to the possibility of declaratory relief for an anticipatory breach, it remains remarkably consistent with Holmes' view that the "only universal consequence of a legally binding promise is, that the law makes the promisor pay damages if the promised event does not come to pass * * * [and] * * * leaves him free from interference until the time for fulfillment has gone by, and therefore free to break his contract if he chooses." O.W. Holmes, The Common Law 235–36 (Howe ed. 1963).

Equitable remedies make it possible for the plaintiff to obtain the actual performance promised by the defendant rather than damages. The court has power to issue a personal order to the defendant, directing conduct of a specified sort, and to punish noncompliance by either a fine or imprisonment for contempt. An injunction is the main form of this personal, coercive order issued by the court. In a breach of contract action, the injunction may prohibit the defendant from taking a specified course of action or compel specific performance of the contract or both. See Kaiser Trading Co. v. Associated Metals & Minerals Corp., 321 F.Supp. 923 (N.D.Cal.1970), appeal dismissed 443 F.2d 1364 (9th Cir.1971) (seller ordered to deliver goods sold and enjoined from selling them to others). Here, then, the order is directed to the person, that is, *in personam*, and denies the defendant the choice to perform the contract or pay damages. Although the contempt power appears to punish the defendant's refusal to comply, the real purpose is to coerce performance. In the words of some immortal bard, the defendant has "the keys to the jailhouse in his own pocket."

When is the plaintiff entitled to an equitable remedy for breach of contract? Professor A.W.B. Simpson informs us that although the origin of the principle "equity treats as done that which ought to be done" remains uninvestigated, specific performance was granted by the English Court of Chancery in land cases by the mid-fifteenth century. A.W.B. Simpson, A History of the Common Law of Contract 595–598 (1975). Since that time, specific enforcement of contracts for the sale of land has been the rule

---

* Most state constitutions prohibit imprisonment for at least certain types of debt. See, e.g., S.D. Const. art. VI, § 15 ("[n]o person shall be imprisoned for debt arising out of or founded upon a contract."). But there has been a growing tendency for courts to uphold the constitutionality for non-payment of judgements in certain contexts (such as child support) where the debtor is found to have the means to pay or surprisingly even if the court finds that the defendant had an ability to earn income but willfully chose not to work. See, e.g., Moss v. Superior Ct., 17 Cal.4th 396, 71 Cal.Rptr.2d 215, 950 P.2d 59 (1998).

rather than the exception, the reason being "that land is assumed to have a peculiar value, so as to give an equity for a specific performance, without reference to its quality or quantity." Simpson also states that before the development of the writ of assumpsit in the seventeenth century, the Chancery Court regularly issued *in personam* orders in a wide range of contract disputes. What happened next is too long and complicated to relate here in full. But as the adequacy and availability of contract remedies improved, the scope of the common law expanded and England's market system developed and diversified, it became more difficult for plaintiffs to demonstrate that contract remedies in the law courts were so inadequate that invocation of the power of the Chancery Court was justified. So in matters other than land contracts, it became customary to say that specific performance was the exception rather than the rule or that equitable remedies were "extraordinary." Compare John P. Dawson, *Specific Performance in France and Germany,* 57 Mich.L.Rev. 495 (1959), where a preference for specific performance is noted in the civil law tradition. As an American court put the traditional principle, specific performance is "largely a discretionary remedy to prevent substantial injury where no adequate remedy at law obtains. . . ." Stokes v. Moore, 262 Ala. 59, 77 So.2d 331 (1955). What, more specifically, must the plaintiff show to persuade the court to exercise that discretion and grant equitable relief?

The following materials are designed to provide some insight into this important question. As you read them, keep the following questions in mind:

1.   What was the inadequacy in the legal remedy asserted by the plaintiff to justify equitable relief? The focus here should be upon the ease with which the plaintiff can obtain a substitute performance from the available market and the impact upon the plaintiff if that substitute is costly or not readily available.

2.   What, if any, are the practical problems involved in enforcing an *in personam* order in the particular case? Can and should the court order an artist to paint, a singer to sing or a builder to build? How is the court to supervise the mandated performance when the standards are aesthetic or, perhaps, the agreement is indefinite? As you will see, courts have found it easier to order the defendant in a personal service contract to refrain from doing rather than to perform.

3.   Are there any questions of fairness associated with enforcing the contract or problems of morality associated with the plaintiff's conduct? For example, would specific enforcement of the contract be unconscionable because of disproportion in the exchange? Or, to quote some choice maxims, must the plaintiff "do equity to receive equity" or "come into equity with clean hands?"

4.   May the plaintiff recover damages in addition to equitable relief? Suppose the requested equitable remedy is not available—may the court award damages in lieu of specific performance or must it remand the case for further consideration?

Although the plaintiff must struggle uphill to obtain equitable remedies for breach of contract, the test applied by the courts is flexible and, presumably, expansible as market conditions and attitudes change. With the merger in most states of the previously separate systems of law and equity and a condition of increasing scarcity in some relevant markets, one should not be surprised to find that equitable relief is increasingly available for breach of contract.

References:

Allan Farnsworth, *Legal Remedies for Breach of Contract,* 70 Colum.L.Rev. 1145, 1149–56 (1970). For a developing debate on when specific performance should be granted, see, Louis Kornhauser, *An Introduction to the Economic Analysis of Contract Remedies,* 57 U. Colo.L.Rev. 683, 711–717 (1986); Thomas Ulen, *The Efficiency of Specific Performance: Toward a Unified Theory of Contract Remedies,* 83 Mich.L.Rev. 341 (1984); Anthony Kronman, *Specific Performance,* 45 U.Chi.L.Rev. 351 (1978); Alan Schwartz, *The Case for Specific Performance,* 89 Yale L.J. 271 (1979). See also Narasimhan, *Modification: The Self–Help Specific Performance Remedy,* 97 Yale L.J. 61 (1987).

Curtice Brothers Co. v. Catts

Court of Chancery of New Jersey, 1907.
72 N.J.Eq. 831, 66 A. 935.

Reprinted supra at 200.

Laclede Gas Co. v. Amoco Oil Co.

United States Court of Appeals, Eighth Circuit, 1975.
522 F.2d 33.

■ ROSS, CIRCUIT JUDGE. The Laclede Gas Company (Laclede), a Missouri corporation, brought this diversity action alleging breach of contract against the Amoco Oil Company (Amoco), a Delaware corporation. It sought relief in the form of a mandatory injunction prohibiting the continuing breach or, in the alternative, damages. The district court held a bench trial on the issues of whether there was a valid, binding contract between the parties and whether, if there was such a contract, Amoco should be enjoined from breaching it. It then ruled that the "contract is invalid due to lack of mutuality" and denied the prayer for injunctive relief. The court made no decision regarding the requested damages.... This appeal followed, and we reverse the district court's judgment.

On September 21, 1970, Midwest Missouri Gas Company (now Laclede), and American Oil (now Amoco), the predecessors of the parties to this litigation, entered into a written agreement which was designed to provide central propane gas distribution systems to various residential developments in Jefferson County, Missouri, until such time as natural gas mains were extended into these areas. The agreement contemplated that as individual developments were planned the owners or developers would apply to Laclede for central propane gas systems. If Laclede determined that such a system was appropriate in any given development, it could request Amoco to supply the propane to that specific development. This request was made in the form of a supplemental form letter, as provided in the September 21 agreement; and if Amoco decided to supply the propane, it bound itself to do so by signing this supplemental form.

Once this supplemental form was signed the agreement placed certain duties on both Laclede and Amoco. Basically, Amoco was to "[i]nstall, own, maintain and operate ... storage and vaporization facilities and any other facilities necessary to provide [it] with the capability of delivering to [Laclede] commercial propane gas suitable ... for delivery by [Laclede] to its customers' facilities." Amoco's facilities were to be "adequate to provide a continuous supply of commercial propane gas at such times and in such volumes commensurate with [Laclede's] requirements for meeting the demands reasonably to be anticipated in each Development while this Agreement is in force." Amoco was deemed to be "the supplier," while Laclede was "the distributing utility."

For its part Laclede agreed to "[i]nstall, own, maintain and operate all distribution facilities" from a "point of delivery" which was defined to be "the outlet of [Amoco] header piping." Laclede also promised to pay Amoco "the Wood River Area Posted Price for propane plus four cents per gallon for all amounts of commercial propane gas delivered" to it under the agreement.

Since it was contemplated that the individual propane systems would eventually be converted to be natural gas, one paragraph of the agreement provided that Laclede should give Amoco 30 days written notice of this event, after which the agreement would no longer be binding for the converted development.

Another paragraph gave Laclede the right to cancel the agreement. However, this right was expressed in the following language:

> This Agreement shall remain in effect for one (1) year following the first delivery of gas by [Amoco] to [Laclede] hereunder. Subject to termination as provided in Paragraph 11 hereof [dealing with conversions to natural gas], this Agreement shall automatically continue in effect for additional periods of one (1) year each unless [Laclede] shall, not less than 30 days prior to the expiration of the initial one (1) year period or any subsequent one (1) year period, give [Amoco] written notice of termination.

There was no provision under which Amoco could cancel the agreement.

For a time the parties operated satisfactorily under this agreement, and some 17 residential subdivisions were brought within it by supplemental letters. However, for various reasons, including conversion to natural gas, the number of developments under the agreement had shrunk to eight by the time of trial. These were all mobile home parks.

During the winter of 1972–73 Amoco experienced a shortage of propane and voluntarily placed all of its customers, including Laclede, on an 80% allocation basis, meaning that Laclede would receive only up to 80% of its previous requirements. Laclede objected to this and pushed Amoco to give it 100% of what the developments needed. Some conflict arose over this before the temporary shortage was alleviated.

Then, on April 3, 1973, Amoco notified Laclede that its Wood River Area Posted Price of propane had been increased by three cents per gallon. Laclede objected to this increase also and demanded a full explanation. None was forthcoming. Instead Amoco merely sent a letter dated May 14, 1973, informing Laclede that it was "terminating" the September 21, 1970, agreement effective May 31, 1973. It claimed it had the right to do this because "the Agreement lacks 'mutuality.' "[1]

The district court felt that the entire controversy turned on whether or not Laclede's right to "arbitrarily cancel the Agreement" without Amoco having a similar right rendered the contract void "for lack of mutuality" and it resolved this question in the affirmative. We disagree with this conclusion and hold that settled principles of contract law require a reversal.

[The court held that Laclede's restricted right to terminate did not make the agreement unenforceable for lack of "mutuality," i.e., consideration. Further, the agreement, fairly construed, was nothing more than a requirements contract under which Laclede agreed to order all of its requirements for the subdivision from Amoco. The district court, therefore, erred in holding that there was no enforceable contract.]

* * *

II.

Since he found that there was no binding contract, the district judge did not have to deal with the question of whether or not to grant the injunction prayed for by Laclede. He simply denied this relief because there was no contract . . .

Generally the determination of whether or not to order specific performance of a contract lies within the sound discretion of the trial court. . . . However, this discretion is, in fact, quite limited; and it is said that when certain equitable rules have been met and the contract is fair and plain "specific performance goes as a matter of right." Miller v. Coffeen, 280 S.W.2d 100, 102 (Mo.1955), quoting, Berberet v. Myers, 240 Mo. 58, 77,(1912).

With this in mind we have carefully reviewed the very complete record on appeal and conclude that the trial court should grant the injunctive

---

1. While Amoco sought to repudiate the agreement, it resumed supplying propane to the subdivisions on February 1, 1974, under the mandatory allocation guidelines promulgated by the Federal Energy Administration under the Federal Mandatory Allocation Program for propane. It is agreed that this is now being done under the contract.

relief prayed. We are satisfied that this case falls within that category in which specific performance should be ordered as a matter of right. ...

Amoco contends that four of the requirements for specific performance have not been met. Its claims are: (1) there is no mutuality of remedy in the contract; (2) the remedy of specific performance would be difficult for the court to administer without constant and long-continued supervision; (3) the contract is indefinite and uncertain; and (4) the remedy at law available to Laclede is adequate. The first three contentions have little or no merit and do not detain us for long.

There is simply no requirement in the law that both parties be mutually entitled to the remedy of specific performance in order that one of them be given that remedy by the court....

While a court may refuse to grant specific performance where such a decree would require constant and long-continued court supervision, this is merely a discretionary rule of decision which is frequently ignored when the public interest is involved. See, e.g., Joy v. St. Louis, 138 U.S. 1, 47 (1891); ...

Here the public interest in providing propane to the retail customers is manifest, while any supervision required will be far from onerous.

Section 370 of the Restatement of Contracts (1932) provides:

Specific enforcement will not be decreed unless the terms of the contract are so expressed that the court can determine with reasonable certainty what is the duty of each party and the conditions under which performance is due.

We believe these criteria have been satisfied here. As discussed in part I of this opinion, as to all developments for which a supplemental agreement has been signed, Amoco is to supply all the propane which is reasonably foreseeably required, while Laclede is to purchase the required propane from Amoco and pay the contract price therefor. The parties have disagreed over what is meant by "Wood River Area Posted Price" in the agreement, but the district court can and should determine with reasonable certainty what the parties intended by this term and should mold its decree, if necessary accordingly. Likewise, the fact that the agreement does not have a definite time of duration is not fatal since the evidence established that the last subdivision should be converted to natural gas in 10 to 15 years. This sets a reasonable time limit on performance and the district court can and should mold the final decree to reflect this testimony.

It is axiomatic that specific performance will not be ordered when the party claiming breach of contract has an adequate remedy at law.... This is especially true when the contract involves personal property as distinguished from real estate.

However, in Missouri, as elsewhere, specific performance may be ordered even though personalty is involved in the "proper circumstances." Mo.Rev.Stat. § 400.2–716(1); Restatement of Contracts, supra, § 361. And a remedy at law adequate to defeat the grant of specific performance "must be as certain, prompt, complete, and efficient to attain the ends of justice as a decree of specific performance." National Marking Mach. Co. v. Triumph Mfg. Co., 13 F.2d 6, 9 (8th Cir.1926). . . .

One of the leading Missouri cases allowing specific performance of a contract relating to personalty because the remedy at law was inadequate is Boeving v. Vandover, 240 Mo.App. 117 (1949). In that case the plaintiff sought specific performance of a contract in which the defendant had promised to sell him an automobile. At that time (near the end of and shortly after World War II) new cars were hard to come by, and the court held that specific performance was a proper remedy since a new car "could not be obtained elsewhere except at considerable expense, trouble or loss, which cannot be estimated in advance."

We are satisfied that Laclede has brought itself within this practical approach taken by the Missouri courts. As Amoco points out, Laclede has propane immediately available to it under other contracts with other suppliers. And the evidence indicates that at the present time propane is readily available on the open market. However, this analysis ignores the fact that the contract involved in this lawsuit is for a long-term supply of propane to these subdivisions. The other two contracts under which Laclede obtains the gas will remain in force only until March 31, 1977, and April 1, 1981, respectively; and there is no assurance that Laclede will be able to receive any propane under them after that time. Also it is unclear as to whether or not Laclede can use the propane obtained under these contracts to supply the Jefferson County subdivisions, since they were originally entered into to provide Laclede with propane with which to "shave" its natural gas supply during peak demand periods.[4] Additionally, there was uncontradicted expert testimony that Laclede probably could not find another supplier of propane willing to enter into a long-term contract such as the Amoco agreement, given the uncertain future of worldwide energy supplies. And, even if Laclede could obtain supplies of propane for the affected developments through its present contracts or newly negotiated ones, it would still face considerable expense and trouble which cannot be estimated in advance in making arrangements for its distribution to the subdivisions.

Specific performance is the proper remedy in this situation, and it should be granted by the district court.[**]

CONCLUSION

For the foregoing reasons the judgment of the district court is reversed and the cause is remanded for the fashioning of appropriate injunctive relief in the form of a decree of specific performance as to those develop-

---

4. During periods of cold weather, when demand is high, Laclede does not receive enough natural gas to meet all this demand. It, therefore, adds propane to the natural gas it places in its distribution system. This practice is called "peak shaving."

[**] In fashioning its decree the district court must take into account any relevant rules and regulations promulgated under the Federal Mandatory Allocation Program.

ments for which a supplemental agreement form has been signed by the parties.

NOTES

(1) *Buyer's Right to Specific Performance or Replevin.* UCC 2–716 provides:

(1) Specific performance may be decreed where the goods are unique or in other proper circumstances.

(2) The decree for specific performance may include such terms and conditions as to payment of the price, damages, or other relief as the court may deem just.

(3) The buyer has a right of replevin for goods identified to the contract if after reasonable effort he is unable to effect cover for such goods or the circumstances reasonably indicate that such effort will be unavailing * * *.

The Comments state that UCC 2–716 furthers a "more liberal attitude than some courts have shown in connection with the specific performance of contracts of sale" through emphasis upon the "commercial feasibility of replacement." Specific performance is "no longer limited to goods which are already specific or ascertained at the time of contracting." Further:

> The test of uniqueness under this section must be made in terms of the total situation which characterizes the contract. Output and requirements contracts involving a particular or peculiarly available source or market present today the typical commercial specific performance situation, as contrasted with contracts for the sale of heirlooms or priceless works of art which were usually involved in the older cases. However, uniqueness is not the sole basis of the remedy under this section for the relief may also be granted "in other proper circumstances" and inability to cover is strong evidence of "other proper circumstances."

Some questions:

1.   Do you think that the *Laclede* case takes the "liberal" attitude of UCC 2–716 a bit too far? See Harold Greenberg, *Specific Performance Under Section 2–716 of the Uniform Commercial Code: "A More Liberal Attitude" in the "Grand Style,"* 17 N.Eng.L.Rev. 321, 344–52 (1982). See also, King Aircraft Sales, Inc. v. Lane, 68 Wash.App. 706, 846 P.2d 550, 556–557 (1993)(specific performance proper even though legal remedy not absent and goods not "absolutely" unique).

2.   In *Laclede*, would replevin under UCC 2–716(3) have been successful? See Putnam Ranches, Inc. v. Corkle, 189 Neb. 533, 203 N.W.2d 502 (1973) (replevin denied where no evidence that goods were ever identified to the contract).

3.   Can a seller get specific performance under Article 2? UCC 2–716 appears to be limited to buyers and there is no section authorizing specific performance for sellers. Revised Article 2, however, clarifies this omission in favor of the seller. See Rev. UCC 2–703(2)(j), stating that a seller can "obtain specific performance under Section 2–716." But when is such a remedy appropriate? For example, suppose the buyer has accepted the goods and refused to pay the price. Can the seller get an in personam order directing the buyer to

pay (or go to jail for contempt) or must the seller try to recover the price in rem under UCC 2–709(1)?

(2) *"Unique" or in "Other Proper Circumstances."* When are goods "unique" within the meaning of UCC 2–716(1)? In the now famous cotton fiasco in 1973, growers of cotton made contracts to sell cotton to be planted on their land to middlemen for roughly $.30 per pound. Delivery was to be made after the cotton was harvested, ginned and bailed. Between the time of contracting and the time of delivery, the price of cotton rose to roughly $.90 per pound. Cotton was available on the market, but in uncertain quantities. When the growers refused to deliver, the buyers brought suit for specific performance. In R.L. Kimsey Cotton Co., Inc. v. Ferguson, 233 Ga. 962, 214 S.E.2d 360 (1975), the parties stipulated in the contract that the cotton was "unique." The court, without extended discussion, granted specific performance. But in Duval & Co. v. Malcom, 233 Ga. 784, 214 S.E.2d 356 (1975), the same court held that, in the absence of a stipulation of uniqueness, a dramatic price rise not accompanied by an inability to cover in the open market did not constitute "other proper circumstances" under UCC 2–716(1). The court stated that "other proper circumstances" was not a "license to afford specific performance for all commercial goods and turn the courts into referees in commerce." Presumably the court was swayed by the fungibility of cotton. But if a blight had ruined the cotton to be grown by the seller, presumably he would have been excused under UCC 2–613, because the cotton involved was "required" by the contract. If the cotton was "required" by the contract, should not that mean that the goods were unique? What about replevin in the cotton cases?

(3) *Irreparable Harm?* The uniqueness requirement is related to the more general "irreparable harm" idea that equitable remedies are unavailable if legal remedies will adequately repair the harm. But Douglas Laycock, after reviewing how courts actually apply the irreparable harm rule found:

> Courts have escaped the rule by defining adequacy in such a way that damages are never an adequate substitute for plaintiff's loss. Thus, our law embodies a preference for specific relief if plaintiff wants it. The principal doctrinal expression of this preference is the rule that damages are inadequate unless they can be used to replace the specific thing that plaintiff lost. Damages can be used in this way for only one category of losses: to replace fungible goods or routine services in an orderly market. In that context, damages and specific relief are substantially equivalent. Either way, plaintiff winds up with the very thing he wanted, and the preference for specific relief becomes irrelevant. In all other contexts, there is ample basis in precedent and principle for holding that damages are inadequate.

See Douglas Laycock, The Death of the Irreparable Injury Rule 12–13 (1991)

(4) *Injunction Against Breach.* In an action for specific performance, when may the plaintiff, in order to preserve the *status quo,* obtain a temporary or permanent injunction restraining the defendant from breaching the contract? Traditionally, the courts have considered four flexible and interdependent factors: 1) Without such relief, will the plaintiff suffer irreparable harm; 2) Is there a substantial probability of success on the merits; 3) Will others be injured by the injunction; and 4) Will the injunction be inconsistent with or further the public interest? In addition, the injunction may be denied unless the facts as stated justify a specific performance decree. Thus, in Kaiser

Trading Co. v. Associated Metals & Minerals Corp., 321 F.Supp. 923 (N.D.Cal. 1970), appeal dismissed 443 F.2d 1364 (9th Cir.1971), the court first determined that California courts would grant specific performance under UCC 2–716(1) "when goods cannot be covered or replaced" and then determined on the particular facts that a failure to enjoin the seller from disposing of the goods in litigation would cause irreparable harm to the buyer. The court stressed that the supply of goods on the open market was "very scarce" in relation to what the seller had promised to deliver, the price of the goods had more than doubled in the past year and the goods were "indispensable" in the buyer's manufacturing process. See also Petereit v. S.B. Thomas, Inc., 63 F.3d 1169 (2d Cir.1995)(injunction inappropriate where expectancy damages can be computed); Simpson v. Lee, 499 A.2d 889, 892–93 (D.C.App.1985).

(5) *Mutuality of Remedy.* The *Laclede* court rejects summarily the contention that the buyer cannot have specific performance against the seller unless the seller could have specific performance against the buyer. Accord Pallas v. Black, 226 Neb. 728, 414 N.W.2d 805 (1987). The alleged remedial inequality is balanced by the court's power in equity to condition the decree to insure that the defendant receives the agreed exchange. The issue is both illuminated and resolved in Section 3386 of the California Civil Code, as amended in 1969:

> Notwithstanding that the agreed counter performance is not or would not have been specifically enforceable, specific performance may be compelled if:
>
> (a) Specific performance would otherwise be an appropriate remedy, and
>
> (b) The agreed counter performance has been substantially performed or its concurrent or future performance is assured or, if the court deems necessary, can be secured to the satisfaction of the court.

Accord: Restatement (Second) § 363.

(6) *Specific Performance in Restatement (Second).* Under Restatement (Second), specific performance of a contract or an order enjoining its nonperformance are remedies available for breach. See §§ 345(b), 357. The relief may be granted at the discretion of the court, the order "will be drawn as best to effectuate the purposes for which the contract was made and on such terms as justice requires," § 358(1), and "damages or other relief may be awarded in the same proceeding" in addition to specific performance or an injunction. § 358(3). But "specific performance or an injunction will not be ordered if damages would be adequate to protect the expectation interest of the injured party," § 359(1). Section 360 provides the "factors" affecting the adequacy of damages, viz., "(a) the difficulty of proving damages with reasonable certainty, (b) the difficulty of procuring a suitable substitute performance by means of money awarded as damages, and (c) the likelihood that an award of damages could not be collected." Comment a to Section 359, however, notes the "tendency to liberalize the granting of equitable relief by enlarging the classes of cases in which damages are not regarded as an adequate remedy" and concludes:

> Adequacy is to some extent relative, and the modern approach is to compare remedies to determine which is more effective in serving the ends of justice. Such a comparison will often lead to the granting of equitable

relief. Doubts should be resolved in favor of the granting of specific performance or injunction.

Professor Linzer has stated that this comment is "vague" and that Restatement (Second) adopts an "equivocal approach to the availability of specific performance." Linzer, *On the Amorality of Contract Remedies—Efficiency, Equity and the Second Restatement,* 81 Colum.L.Rev. 111, 120 (1981). Linzer argues for the general use of specific performance on grounds of both efficiency and fairness. Id. at 138–39.

(7) *Unconscionable Bargains.* Specific performance may be denied for reasons other than the adequacy of the legal remedy. See, e.g., DaSilva v. Musso, 53 N.Y.2d 543, 444 N.Y.S.2d 50, 428 N.E.2d 382 (1981) (mutual mistake). One such control is that the plaintiff must come into equity with "clean hands." But the conduct that sullies the hands must relate to the subject matter of the litigation and affect the "equitable" relations between the litigants. See, e.g., New York Football Giants, Inc. v. Los Angeles Chargers Football Club, Inc., 291 F.2d 471 (5th Cir.1961).

Another general limitation is that equity will not specifically enforce an inequitable or unconscionable bargain, see Campbell Soup Co. v. Wentz, 172 F.2d 80 (3d Cir.1948), and that a "shockingly" inadequate consideration may be sufficient to deny relief. But whether the consideration is inadequate or the bargain otherwise unfair "must be viewed prospectively, not retrospectively." Tuckwiller v. Tuckwiller, 413 S.W.2d 274, 278 (Mo.1967). See Arthur Leff, *Unconscionability and the Code: The Emperor's New Clause,* 115 U.Pa.L.Rev. 485, 528–41 (1967). Thus, where agreed prices for the purchase of cotton were fair at the time of contracting, a subsequent and dramatic price increase the risk of which the seller was held to assume did not foreclose specific performance. R.L. Kimsey Cotton Co., Inc. v. Ferguson, 233 Ga. 962, 214 S.E.2d 360 (1975). See also Restatement (Second) § 364(1)(c)(specific performance or an injunction "will be refused if such relief would be unfair because * * * the exchange is grossly inadequate or the terms of the contract are otherwise unfair."

Comment: Specific Performance Under the United Nations Convention on Contracts for the International Sale of Goods

CISG gives the buyer and the seller a right to require the breaching party to perform its obligations without regard to the adequacy of alternative remedies. Thus, if the seller fails to deliver the buyer may "require performance by the seller of his obligation," CISG Art. 45(1)(a), 46(1), and if the buyer fails to pay the price or take delivery as agreed the seller "may require the buyer to pay the price, take delivery, or perform his other obligations." CISG Art. 61(1)(a), 62. See also Article 46(2) & (3), where the buyer has a limited right to require the seller to deliver substitute goods or to "remedy the lack of conformity by repair."

CISG, however, does not state how the order requiring performance is to be enforced. This is left to procedures at the place where enforcement is sought. Moreover, Article 28 provides:

If, in accordance with the provisions of this Convention, one party is entitled to require performance of any obligation by the other party, a court is not bound to enter a judgment for specific performance unless the court would do so under its own law in respect of similar contracts of sale not governed by this Convention.

This Article seems to tell a judge in a state or federal court in the United States that he or she need not order specific performance under the Convention unless the seller or buyer could get such a remedy under the UCC. For an overview, see Steven Walt, *For Specific Performance under the United Nations Sales Convention*, 26 Texas Int'l L. J. 211 (1991).

Northern Indiana Public Service Co. v. Carbon County Coal Co.

United States Court of Appeals, Seventh Circuit, 1986.
799 F.2d 265.

[In 1978, NIPSCO and Carbon County entered a 20–year contract under which Carbon County, the owner and operator of a coal mine in Wyoming, agreed to sell and NIPSCO agreed to buy approximately 1.5 million tons of coal every year for 20 years, at a price of $24 a ton, subject to upward escalation. By 1985, the contract price had escalated to $44 per ton, but, because of changed economic circumstances, NIPSCO was able to buy electricity at prices below the cost of generation. Under pressure from the Indiana Public Service Commission, NIPSCO sought a declaratory judgment that it was excused from the contract. Carbon County counterclaimed for breach of contract and moved for a preliminary injunction and specific performance. The district court granted the preliminary injunction but, after a jury verdict for Carbon County in the amount of $181 million, the court denied specific performance. NIPSCO, inter alia, appealed from the verdict and Carbon County appealed from the denial of specific performance. The court, speaking through Judge Posner, first affirmed the verdict against NIPSCO.]

* * *

This completes our consideration of NIPSCO's attack on the damages judgment and we turn to Carbon County's cross-appeal, which seeks specific performance in lieu of the damages it got. Carbon County's counsel virtually abandoned the cross-appeal at oral argument, noting that the mine was closed and could not be reopened immediately—so that if specific performance (i.e., NIPSCO's resuming taking the coal) was ordered, Carbon County would not be able to resume its obligations under the contract without some grace period. In any event the request for specific performance has no merit. Like other equitable remedies, specific performance is available only if damages are not an adequate remedy, Farnsworth, supra, § 12.6, and there is no reason to suppose them inadequate here. The loss to Carbon County from the breach of contract is simply the difference between (1) the contract price (as escalated over the life of the contract in accordance with the contract's escalator provisions) times quantity, and (2) the cost of mining the coal over the life of the contract. Carbon County does not even argue that $181 million is not a reasonable estimate of the present value of the difference. Its complaint is that although the money will make the owners of Carbon County whole it will do nothing for the miners who have lost their jobs because the mine is closed and the satellite businesses that have closed for the same reason. Only specific performance will help them.

But since they are not parties to the contract their losses are irrelevant. Indeed, specific performance would be improper as well as unnecessary here, because it would force the continuation of production that has become uneconomical. Cf. *Farnsworth,* supra, at 817–18. No one wants coal from Carbon County's mine. With the collapse of oil prices, which has depressed the price of substitute fuels as well, this coal costs far more to get out of the ground than it is worth in the market. Continuing to produce it, under compulsion of an order for specific performance, would impose costs on society greater than the benefits. NIPSCO's breach, though it gave Carbon County a right to damages, was an efficient breach in the sense that it brought to a halt a production process that was no longer cost-justified. . . . The reason why NIPSCO must pay Carbon County's loss is not that it should have continued buying coal it didn't need but that the contract assigned to NIPSCO the risk of market changes that made continued deliveries uneconomical. The judgment for damages is the method by which that risk is being fixed on NIPSCO in accordance with its undertakings.

With continued production uneconomical, it is unlikely that an order of specific performance, if made, would ever actually be implemented. If, as a finding that the breach was efficient implies, the cost of a substitute supply (whether of coal, or of electricity) to NIPSCO is less than the cost of producing coal from Carbon County's mine, NIPSCO and Carbon County can both be made better off by negotiating a cancellation of the contract and with it a dissolution of the order of specific performance. Suppose, by way of example, that Carbon County's coal costs $20 a ton to produce, that the contract price is $40, and that NIPSCO can buy coal elsewhere for $10. Then Carbon County would be making a profit of only $20 on each ton it sold to NIPSCO ($40 − $20), while NIPSCO would be losing $30 on each ton it bought from Carbon County ($40 − $10). Hence by offering Carbon County more than contract damages (i.e., more than Carbon County's lost profits), NIPSCO could induce Carbon County to discharge the contract and release NIPSCO to buy cheaper coal. For example, at $25, both parties would be better off than under specific performance, where Carbon County gains only $20 but NIPSCO loses $30. Probably, therefore, Carbon County is seeking specific performance in order to have bargaining leverage with NIPSCO, and we can think of no reason why the law should give it such leverage. We add that if Carbon County obtained and enforced an order for specific performance this would mean that society was spending $20 (in our hypothetical example) to produce coal that could be gotten elsewhere for $10—a waste of scarce resources.

As for possible hardships to workers and merchants in Hanna, Wyoming, where Carbon County's coal mine is located, we point out that none of these people were parties to the contract with NIPSCO or third-party beneficiaries. They have no legal interest in the contract. Cf. Local 1330, United Steel Workers of America v. United States Steel Corp., 631 F.2d 1264, 1279–82 (6th Cir.1980); Serrano v. Jones & Laughlin Steel Co., 790 F.2d 1279, 1289 (6th Cir.1986). Of course the consequences to third parties of granting an injunctive remedy, such as specific performance, must be considered, and in some cases may require that the remedy be withheld.... The frequent references to "public interest" as a factor in the grant or denial of a preliminary injunction invariably are references to third-party effects.... But even though the formal statement of the judicial obligation to consider such effects extends to orders denying as well as granting injunctive relief, ... the actuality is somewhat different: when the question is whether third parties would be injured by an order denying an injunction, always they are persons having a legally recognized interest in the lawsuit, so that the issue really is the adequacy of relief if the injunction is denied. In Mississippi Power & Light Co. v. United Gas Pipe Line Co., 760 F.2d 618 (5th Cir.1985), for example, a public utility sought a preliminary injunction against alleged overcharges by a supplier. If the injunction was denied and later the utility got damages, its customers would be entitled to refunds; but for a variety of reasons explained in the opinion, refunds would not fully protect the customers' interests. The customers were the real parties in interest on the plaintiff side of the case, and their interests had therefore to be taken into account in deciding whether there would be irreparable harm (and how much) if the preliminary injunction was denied. See id. at 623–26. Carbon County does not stand in a representative relation to the workers and businesses of Hanna, Wyoming. Treating them as real parties in interest would evade the limitations on the concept of a third-party beneficiary and would place the promisor under obligations potentially far heavier than it had thought it was accepting when it signed the contract. Indeed, if we are right that an order of specific performance would probably not be carried out—that instead NIPSCO would pay an additional sum of money to Carbon County for an agreement not to enforce the order—it becomes transparent that granting specific performance would make NIPSCO liable in money damages for harms to nonparties to the contract, and it did not assume such liability by signing the contract....

Moreover, the workers and merchants in Hanna assumed the risk that the coal mine would have to close down if it turned out to be uneconomical. The contract with NIPSCO did not guarantee that the mine would operate throughout the life of the contract but only protected the owners of Carbon County against the financial consequences to them of a breach. As Carbon County itself emphasizes in its brief, the contract was a product of the international oil cartel, which by forcing up the price of substitute fuels such as coal made costly coal-mining operations economically attractive. The OPEC cartel is not a source of vested rights to produce substitute fuels at inflated prices. * * *

Walgreen Co. v. Sara Creek Property Co.

United States Court of Appeals, Seventh Circuit, 1992.
966 F.2d 273.

■ POSNER, CIRCUIT JUDGE.

This appeal from the grant of a permanent injunction raises fundamental issues concerning the propriety of injunctive relief.... The essential facts are simple. Walgreen has operated a pharmacy in the Southgate Mall in Milwaukee since its opening in 1951. Its current lease, signed in 1971 and carrying a 30–year, 6–month term, contains, as had the only previous lease, a clause in which the landlord, Sara Creek, promises not to lease space in the mall to anyone else who wants to operate a pharmacy or a store containing a pharmacy....

In 1990, fearful that its largest tenant—what in real estate parlance is called the "anchor tenant"—having gone broke was about to close its store, Sara Creek informed Walgreen that it intended to buy out the anchor tenant and install in its place a discount store operated by Phar–Mor Corporation, a "deep discount" chain, rather than, like Walgreen, just a "discount" chain. Phar–Mor's store would occupy 100,000 square feet, of which 12,000 would be occupied by a pharmacy the same size as Walgreen's. The entrances to the two stores would be within a couple of hundred feet of each other.

Walgreen filed this diversity suit for breach of contract against Sara Creek and Phar–Mor and asked for an injunction against Sara Creek's letting the anchor premises to Phar–Mor. After an evidentiary hearing, the judge found a breach of Walgreen's lease and entered a permanent injunction against Sara Creek's letting the anchor tenant premises to Phar–Mor until the expiration of Walgreen's lease. He did this over the defendants' objection that Walgreen had failed to show that its remedy at law—damages—for the breach of the exclusivity clause was inadequate. Sara Creek had put on an expert witness who testified that Walgreen's damages could be readily estimated, and Walgreen had countered with evidence from its employees that its damages would be very difficult to compute, among other reasons because they included intangibles such as loss of goodwill.

Sara Creek reminds us that damages are the norm in breach of contract as in other cases. Many breaches, it points out, are "efficient" in the sense that they allow resources to be moved into a more valuable use.... Perhaps this is one—the value of Phar–Mor's occupancy of the anchor premises may exceed the cost to Walgreen of facing increased competition. If so, society will be better off if Walgreen is paid its damages, equal to that cost, and Phar–Mor is allowed to move in rather than being kept out by an injunction. That is why injunctions are not granted as a matter of course, but only when the plaintiff's damages remedy is inadequate. Northern Indiana Public Service Co. v. Carbon County Coal Co., 799 F.2d 265, 279 (7th Cir.1986). Walgreen's is not, Sara Creek argues; the projection of business losses due to increased competition is a routine exercise in calculation. Damages representing either the present value of lost future profits or (what should be the equivalent, Carusos v. Briarcliff, Inc., 76 Ga.App. 346, 351–52,(1947)) the diminution in the value of the leasehold have either been awarded or deemed the proper remedy in a number of reported cases for breach of an exclusivity clause in a shopping-center lease.... Why, Sara Creek asks, should they not be adequate here?

Sara Creek makes a beguiling argument that contains much truth, but we do not think it should carry the day. For if, as just noted, damages have been awarded in some cases of breach of an exclusivity clause in a shopping-center lease, injunctions have been issued in others.... The choice between remedies requires a balancing of the costs and benefits of the alternatives.... The task of striking the balance is for the trial judge, subject to deferential appellate review in recognition of its particularistic, judgmental, fact-bound character....

The plaintiff who seeks an injunction has the burden of persuasion—damages are the norm, so the plaintiff must show why his case is abnormal. But when, as in this case, the issue is whether to grant a permanent injunction, not whether to grant a temporary one, the burden is to show that damages are inadequate, not that the denial of the injunction will work irreparable harm. "Irreparable" in the injunction context means not rectifiable by the entry of a final judgment....

The benefits of substituting an injunction for damages are twofold. First, it shifts the burden of determining the cost of the defendant's conduct from the court to the parties. If it is true that Walgreen's damages are smaller than the gain to Sara Creek from allowing a second pharmacy into the shopping mall, then there must be a price for dissolving the injunction that will make both parties better off. Thus, the effect of upholding the injunction would be to substitute for the costly processes of forensic fact determination the less costly processes of private negotiation. Second, a premise of our free-market system, and the lesson of experience here and abroad as well, is that prices and costs are more accurately determined by the market than by government. A battle of experts is a less reliable method of determining the actual cost to Walgreen of facing new competition than negotiations between Walgreen and Sara Creek over the price at which Walgreen would feel adequately compensated for having to face that competition.

That is the benefit side of injunctive relief but there is a cost side as well. Many injunctions require continuing supervision by the court, and that is costly.... A more subtle cost of injunctive relief arises from the situation that economists call "bilateral monopoly," in which two parties can deal only with each other: the situation that an injunction creates.... The sole seller of widgets selling to the sole buyer of that product would be an example. But so will be the situation confronting Walgreen and Sara Creek if the injunction is upheld. Walgreen can "sell" its injunctive right only to Sara Creek, and Sara Creek can "buy" Walgreen's surrender of its right to enjoin the leasing of the anchor tenant's space to Phar–Mor only from Walgreen. The lack of alternatives in bilateral monopoly creates a bargaining range, and the costs of negotiating to a point within that range may be high. Suppose the cost to Walgreen of facing the competition of Phar–Mor at the Southgate Mall would be $1 million, and the benefit to Sara Creek of leasing to Phar–Mor would be $2 million. Then at any price between those figures for a waiver of Walgreen's injunctive right both parties would be better off, and we expect parties to bargain around a judicial assignment of legal rights if the assignment is inefficient. R.H. Coase, "The Problem of Social Cost," 3 J. Law & Econ. 1 (1960). But each of the parties would like to engross as much of the bargaining range as possible—Walgreen to press the price toward $2 million, Sara Creek to depress it toward $1 million. With so much at stake, both parties will have an incentive to devote substantial resources of time and money to the negotiation process. The process may even break down, if one or both parties want to create for future use a reputation as a hard bargainer; and if it does break down, the injunction will have brought about an inefficient result. All these are in one form or another costs of the injunctive process that can be avoided by substituting damages.

The costs and benefits of the damages remedy are the mirror of those of the injunctive remedy. The damages remedy avoids the cost of continuing supervision and third-party effects, and the cost of bilateral monopoly as well. It imposes costs of its own, however, in the form of diminished accuracy in the determination of value, on the one hand, and of the parties' expenditures on preparing and presenting evidence of damages, and the time of the court in evaluating the evidence, on the other.

The weighing up of all these costs and benefits is the analytical procedure that is or at least should be employed by a judge asked to enter a permanent injunction, with the understanding that if the balance is even the injunction should be withheld. The judge is not required to explicate every detail of the analysis and he did not do so here, but as long we are satisfied that his approach is broadly consistent with a proper analysis we shall affirm; and we are satisfied here. The determination of Walgreen's damages would have been costly in forensic resources and inescapably inaccurate. . . . The lease had ten years to run. So Walgreen would have had to project its sales revenues and costs over the next ten years, and then project the impact on those figures of Phar–Mor's competition, and then discount that impact to present value. All but the last step would have been fraught with uncertainty.

* * *

Damages are not always costly to compute, or difficult to compute accurately. In the standard case of a seller's breach of a contract for the sale of goods where the buyer covers by purchasing the same product in the market, damages are readily calculable by subtracting the contract price from the market price and multiplying by the quantity specified in the contract. But this is not such a case and here damages would be a costly and inaccurate remedy; and on the other side of the balance some of the costs of an injunction are absent and the cost that is present seems low. The injunction here, like one enforcing a covenant not to compete . . . is a simple negative injunction—Sara Creek is not to lease space in the Southgate Mall to Phar–Mor during the term of Walgreen's lease—and the costs of judicial supervision and enforcement should be negligible. There is no contention that the injunction will harm an unrepresented third party. It may harm Phar–Mor but that harm will be reflected in Sara Creek's offer to Walgreen to dissolve the injunction. (Anyway Phar–Mor is a party.) The injunction may also, it is true, harm potential customers of Phar–Mor—people who would prefer to shop at a deep-discount store than an ordinary discount store—but their preferences, too, are registered indirectly. The more business Phar–Mor would have, the more rent it will be willing to pay Sara Creek, and therefore the more Sara Creek will be willing to pay Walgreen to dissolve the injunction.

The only substantial cost of the injunction in this case is that it may set off a round of negotiations between the parties. In some cases, illustrated by Boomer v. Atlantic Cement Co., 26 N.Y.2d 219, 309 N.Y.S.2d 312, 257 N.E.2d 870 (1970), this consideration alone would be enough to warrant the denial of injunctive relief. The defendant's factory was emitting cement dust that caused the plaintiffs harm monetized at less than $200,000, and the only way to abate the harm would have been to close down the factory, which had cost $45 million to build. An injunction against the nuisance could therefore have created a huge bargaining range (could, not would, because it is unclear what the current value of the factory was), and the costs of negotiating to a point within it might have been immense. If the market value of the factory was actually $45 million, the plaintiffs would be tempted to hold out for a price to dissolve the injunction in the tens of millions and the factory would be tempted to refuse to pay anything more than a few hundred thousand dollars. Negotiations would be unlikely to break down completely, given such a bargaining range, but they might well be protracted and costly. There is nothing so dramatic here. Sara Creek does not argue that it will have to close the mall if enjoined from leasing to Phar–Mor. Phar–Mor is not the only potential anchor tenant. Liza Danielle, Inc. v. Jamko, Inc., 408 So.2d 735, 740 (Fla.App.1982), on which Sara Creek relies, presented the converse case where the grant of the injunction would have forced an existing tenant to close its store. The size of the bargaining range was also a factor in the denial of injunctive relief in Gitlitz v. Plankinton Building Properties, Inc., 228 Wis. 334, 339–40 (1938).

To summarize, the judge did not exceed the bounds of reasonable judgment in concluding that the costs (including forgone benefits) of the damages remedy would exceed the costs (including forgone benefits) of an injunction. We need not consider whether, as intimated by Walgreen, exclusivity clauses in shopping-center leases should be considered presumptively enforceable by injunctions. Although we have described the choice between legal and equitable remedies as one for case-by-case determination, the courts have sometimes picked out categories of case in which injunctive relief is made the norm. The best-known example is specific performance of contracts for the sale of real property. . . . The rule that specific performance will be ordered in such cases as a matter of course is a generalization of the considerations discussed above. Because of the absence of a fully liquid market in real property and the frequent presence of subjective values (many a homeowner, for example, would not sell his house for its market value), the calculation of damages is difficult; and since an order of specific performance to convey a piece of property does not create a continuing relation between the parties, the costs of supervision and enforcement if specific performance is ordered are slight. The exclusivity clause in Walgreen's lease relates to real estate, but we hesitate to suggest that every contract involving real estate should be enforceable as a matter of course by injunctions. Suppose Sara Creek had covenanted to keep the entrance to Walgreen's store free of ice and snow, and breached the covenant. An injunction would require continuing supervision, and it would be easy enough if the injunction were denied for Walgreen to hire its own ice and snow remover and charge the cost to Sara Creek . . . . . On the other hand, injunctions to enforce exclusivity clauses are quite likely to be justifiable by just the considerations present here—damages are difficult to estimate with any accuracy and the injunction is a one-shot remedy requiring no continuing judicial involvement. So there is an argument for making injunctive relief presumptively appropriate in such cases, but we need not decide in this case how strong an argument.

 AFFIRMED.

NOTES

 (1) In City Stores Co. v. Ammerman, 266 F.Supp. 766 (D.D.C.1967), aff'd, 394 F.2d 950 (D.C.Cir.1968), the plaintiff obtained specific performance of defendant's agreement to grant a lease as a major tenant in a shopping center under construction despite the fact that numerous complex details were still to be agreed and that a great deal of supervision by the court would be required. The district court concluded that since "money damages would in no way compensate the plaintiff for loss of the right to participate in the shopping center enterprise and for the almost incalculable future advantages that might accrue to it as a result of extending its operations into the suburbs" equity required specific performance even though some supervision of both future construction and the terms of the lease would be required. In a *per curiam* affirmance, the Court of Appeals for the District of Columbia narrowed somewhat the district court's grounds for decision. The court stressed that specific performance was available because the obligation involved a commitment to lease in addition to construction and that the work was to be done on the defendant's land, making it impossible for the plaintiff to have the job done.

 (2) "We do not imply that in all cases where a landlord has contracted to construct a building on its property, the landlord will be required to perform on the ground that interests in land are always specifically enforceable. If the record shows that at the time the landlord breached its contract, other properties were available to the tenant that offered business advantages comparable to those offered by the landlord's property—except for differences in rent and overhead costs for which an adequate remedy at law exists—a Chancellor might properly deny the tenant's prayer for specific performance. Such a denial might be particularly appropriate in a case where the tenant has failed to lease comparable property that he knew or should have known was available, and where the costs arising from the delay in construction are such that the

landlord will no longer get his part of the bargain if the lease is specifically enforced. A plaintiff seeking equitable relief must have acted in good faith; and if the court of equity finds that a tenant could have reasonably protected his interests but failed to do so, relief may be withheld. In the present case, however, the Chancellor made no such findings, and on appeal, Wells Fargo has not raised the issue of Easton's good faith." Easton Theatres v. Wells Fargo Land & Mortg., 265 Pa.Super. 334, 401 A.2d 1333, 1345 (1979).

(3) "It is not unusual for parties involved in complicated business transactions to allow subsidiary details to remain unspecified until such time as the need for agreement actually arises. Indeed, it would be impossible to foresee in advance and presently agree upon all the details of a project as far-reaching as the development and construction of a P.U.D. [Planned Unit Development] Therefore, we do not believe that the fact that some terms pertaining to the future performance of this joint venture contract remain unspecified at this time is alone sufficient to prevent the specific enforcement of the agreement. We are no more ready to assume that the parties will breach their obligation to negotiate in good faith than we are to assume that they will breach any other contractual obligation. . . .

"Finally, plaintiffs have already expended considerable time and money in performing their obligations under the joint venture agreement. These efforts have inured to the benefit of defendants by enhancing the value of the property of which they are now the legal owners. At this stage, defendants can hardly expect an equity court to be too favorably disposed toward the argument that the instrument which they themselves drafted should not be specifically enforced—in order to allow plaintiffs to continue with their own performance—solely because it is somewhat incomplete and indefinite:

> * * * [W]hen a *contract has been partly performed* by the plaintiff, and the defendant has received and enjoys the benefits thereof, and the plaintiff would be virtually without remedy unless the contract were enforced, the court, from the plainest considerations of equity and common justice, does not regard with favor any objections raised by the defendant merely on the ground of the incompleteness or uncertainty of the agreement. Even if the agreement be incomplete, the court will then, in furtherance of justice and to prevent a most inequitable result, decree a performance of its terms as far as possible, although, perhaps, with compensation or allowance. In fact * * * one ground of the equitable jurisdiction to decree a specific performance is the incompleteness of the contract, which would prevent an action at law, but which exists to such a limited extent and under such circumstances that a refusal to grant any relief would be plainly inequitable.

Van v. Fox, 278 Or. 439, 564 P.2d 695, 701–02 (1977). See Restatement (Second) § 362.

American Broadcasting Companies v. Wolf

Court of Appeals of New York, 1981.
52 N.Y.2d 394, 438 N.Y.S.2d 482, 420 N.E.2d 363.

■ COOKE, CHIEF JUDGE.

* * *

Warner Wolf, a sportscaster who has developed a rather colorful and unique on-the-air personality, had been employed by ABC since 1976. In

February, 1978, ABC and Wolf entered into an employment agreement which, following exercise of renewal option, was to terminate on March 5, 1980. The contract contained a clause, known as a good-faith negotiation and first-refusal provision, that is at the crux of this litigation: "You agree, if we so elect, during the last ninety (90) days prior to the expiration of the extended term of this agreement, to enter into good faith negotiations with us for the extension of this agreement on mutually agreeable terms. You further agree that for the first forty-five (45) days of this renegotiation period, you will not negotiate for your services with any other person or company other than WABC–TV or ABC. In the event we are unable to reach an agreement for an extension by the expiration of the extended term hereof, you agree that you will not accept, in any market for a period of three (3) months following expiration of the extended term of this agreement, any offer of employment as a sportscaster, sports news reporter, commentator, program host, or analyst in broadcasting (including television, cable television, pay television and radio) without first giving us, in writing, an opportunity to employ you on substantially similar terms and you agree to enter into an agreement with us on such terms." Under this provision, Wolf was bound to negotiate in good faith with ABC for the 90–day period from December 6, 1979 through March 4, 1980. For the first 45 days, December 6 through January 19, the negotiation with ABC was to be exclusive. Following expiration of the 90–day negotiating period and the contract on March 5, 1980, Wolf was required, before *accepting* any other offer, to afford ABC a right of first refusal; he could comply with this provision either by refraining from accepting another offer or by first tendering the offer to ABC. The first-refusal period expired on June 3, 1980 and on June 4 Wolf was free to accept any job opportunity, without obligation to ABC.

Wolf first met with ABC executives in September, 1979 to discuss the terms of a renewal contract. Counterproposal were exchanged, and the parties agreed to finalize the matter by October 15. Meanwhile, unbeknownst to ABC, Wolf met with representatives of CBS in early October. Wolf related his employment requirements and also discussed the first refusal—good faith negotiation clause of his ABC contract. Wolf furnished CBS a copy of that portion of the ABC agreement. On October 12, ABC officials and Wolf met, but were unable to reach agreement on a renewal contract. A few days later, on October 16 Wolf again discussed employment possibilities with CBS.

Not until January 2, 1980 did ABC again contact Wolf. At that time, ABC expressed its willingness to meet substantially all of his demands. Wolf rejected the offer, however, citing ABC's delay in communicating with him and his desire to explore his options in light of the impending expiration of the 45–day exclusive negotiation period.

On February 1, 1980, after termination of that exclusive period, Wolf and CBS orally agreed on the terms of Wolf's employment as sportscaster for WCBS–TV, a CBS-owned affiliate in New York. During the next two days, CBS informed Wolf that it had prepared two agreements and divided his annual compensation between the two: one covered his services as an on-the-air sportscaster, and the other was an off-the-air production agreement for sports specials Wolf was to produce. The production agreement contained an exclusivity clause which barred Wolf from performing "services of any nature for" or permitting the use of his "name, likeness, voice or endorsement by, any person, firm or corporation" during the term of the agreement, unless CBS consented. The contract had an effective date of March 6, 1980.

Wolf signed the CBS production agreement on February 4, 1980. At the same time, CBS agreed in writing, in consideration of $100 received from Wolf, to hold open an offer of employment to Wolf as sportscaster until June 4, 1980, the date on which Wolf became free from ABC's right of first refusal. The next day, February 5, Wolf submitted a letter of resignation to ABC.

Representatives of ABC met with Wolf on February 6 and made various offers and promises that Wolf rejected. Wolf informed ABC that they had delayed negotiations with him and downgraded his worth. He stated he had no future with the company. He told the officials he had made a "gentlemen's agreement" and would leave ABC on March 5. Later in February, Wolf and ABC agreed that Wolf would continue to appear on the air during a portion of the first-refusal period, from March 6 until May 28.[1]

ABC commenced this action on May 6, 1980, by which time Wolf's move to CBS had become public knowledge. The complaint alleged that Wolf, induced by CBS breached both the good-faith negotiation and first-refusal provisions of his contract with ABC. ABC sought specific enforcement of its right of first refusal and an injunction against Wolf's employment as a sportscaster with CBS.

After a trial, Supreme Court found no breach of the contract, and went on to note that, in any event, equitable relief would be inappropriate. A divided Appellate Division, while concluding that Wolf had breached both the good-faith negotiation and first-refusal provisions, nonetheless affirmed on the ground that equitable intervention was unwarranted. There should be an affirmance.

II.

Initially, we agree with the Appellate Division that defendant Wolf breached his obligation to negotiate in good faith with ABC from December, 1979 through March 1980. When Wolf signed the production agreement with CBS on February 4, 1980, he obligated himself not to render services

---

1. The agreement also provided that on or after June 4, 1980, Wolf was free to "accept an offer of employment with anyone of [his] choosing and immediately begin performing on-air services." The parties agreed that their rights and obligations under the original employment contract were in no way affected by the extension of employment.

"of any nature" to any person, firm or corporation on and after March 6, 1980. Quite simply, then, beginning on February 4 Wolf was unable to extend his contract with ABC; his contract with CBS precluded him from legally serving ABC in any capacity after March 5. Given Wolf's existing obligation to CBS any negotiations he engaged in with ABC, without the consent of CBS, after February 4 were meaningless and could not have been in good faith.

At the same time, there is no basis in the record for the Appellate Division's conclusion that Wolf violated the first-refusal provision by entering into an oral sports casting contract with CBS on February 4. The first-refusal provision required Wolf, for a period of 90 days after termination of the ABC agreement, either to refrain from accepting an offer of employment or to first submit the offer to ABC for its consideration. By its own terms, the right of first refusal did not apply to offers accepted by Wolf prior to the March 5 termination of the ABC employment contract. It is apparent, therefore, that Wolf could not have breached the right of first refusal by accepting an offer during the term of his employment with ABC.[2] Rather, his conduct violates only the good-faith negotiation clause of the contract. The question is whether this breach entitled ABC to injunctive relief that would bar Wolf from continued employment at CBS. To resolve this issue, it is necessary to trace the principles of specific performance applicable to personal service contracts.

III.

Courts of equity historically have refused to order an individual to perform a contract for personal services.... Originally this rule evolved because of the inherent difficulties courts would encounter in supervising the performance of uniquely personal efforts....[4] During the Civil War era, there emerged a more compelling reason for not directing the performance of personal services: the Thirteenth Amendment's prohibition of involuntary servitude. It has been strongly suggested that judicial compulsion of

2. In any event, the carefully tailored written agreement between Wolf and CBS consisted only of an option prior to June 4, 1979. Acceptance of CBS's offer of employment as a sportscaster did not occur until after the expiration of the first-refusal period on June 4, 1979.

4. The New York Court of Chancery in De Rivafinoli v. Corsetti (4 Paige Chs. 264, 270) eloquently articulated the traditional rationale for refusing affirmative enforcement of personal service contracts: "I am not aware that any officer of this court has that perfect knowledge of the Italian language, or possesses that exquisite sensibility in the auricular nerve which is necessary to understand, and to enjoy with a proper zest, the peculiar beauties of the Italian opera, so fas-

cinating to the fashionable world. There might be some difficulty, therefore, even if the defendant was compelled to sing under the direction and in the presence of a master in chancery, in ascertaining whether he performed his engagement according to its spirit and intent. It would also be very difficult for the master to determine what effect coercion might produce upon the defendant's singing, especially in the livelier airs; although the fear of imprisonment would unquestionably deepen his seriousness in the graver parts of the drama. But one thing at least is certain; his songs will be neither comic, or even semi-serious, while he remains confined in that dismal cage, the debtor's prison of New York."

services would violate the express command of that amendment....[5] For practical policy and constitutional reasons, therefore, courts continue to decline to affirmatively enforce employment contracts.

Over the years, however, in certain narrowly tailored situations, the law fashioned other remedies for failure to perform an employment agreement. Thus, where an employee refuses to render services to an employer in violation of an existing contract, and the services are unique or extraordinary, an injunction may issue to prevent the employee from furnishing those services to another person for the duration of the contract.... Such "negative enforcement" was initially available only when the employee had expressly stipulated not to compete with the employer for the term of the engagement (see, e.g., Lumley v. Wagner, 1 De G.M. & G. 604, 42 Eng.Rep. 687; Schubert Theatrical Co. v. Rath, 271 F. 827, 830–833; ... Later cases permitted injunctive relief where the circumstances justified implication of a negative covenant.... In these situations, an injunction is warranted because the employee either expressly or by clear implication agreed not to work elsewhere for the period of his contract. And, since the services must be unique before negative enforcement will be granted, irreparable harm will befall the employer should the employee be permitted to labor for a competitor....

–B–

After a personal service contract terminates, the availability of equitable relief against the former employee diminishes appreciably. Since the period of service has expired, it is impossible to decree affirmative or negative specific performance. Only if the employee has expressly agreed not to compete with the employer following the term of the contract, or is threatening to disclose trade secrets or commit another tortious act, is injunctive relief generally available at the behest of the employer. ... Even where there is an express anticompetitive covenant, however, it will be rigorously examined and specifically enforced only if it satisfies certain established requirements. ... Indeed, a court normally will not decree specific enforcement of an employee's anticompetitive covenant unless necessary to protect the trade secrets, customer lists or good will of the employer's business, or perhaps when the employer is exposed to special harm because of the unique nature of the employee's services....[6] And, an otherwise valid covenant will not be enforced if it is unreasonable in time, space or scope or would operate in a harsh or oppressive manner. ... There is, in short, general judicial disfavor of anticompetitive covenants contained in employment contracts....

[margin note: Jud. Disfavor of non-comp. Clauses]

5. It is well established that legislative enactments may not coerce performance of services by penalizing nonperformance (e.g., People v. Lavender, 48 N.Y.2d 334, 338–339).

6. Although an employee's anticompetitive covenant may be enforceable where the employee's services were special or unique

(Reed, Roberts Assoc. v. Strauman, 40 N.Y.2d 303, 308, supra; Purchasing Assoc. v. Weitz, 13 N.Y.2d 267, 272–273 ... no New York case has been found where enforcement has been granted, following termination of the employment contract, solely on the basis of the uniqueness of the services.

Underlying the strict approach to enforcement of these covenants is the notion that, once the term of an employment agreement has expired, the general public policy favoring robust and uninhibited competition should not give way merely because a particular employer wishes to insulate himself from competition.... Important, too, are the "powerful considerations of public policy which militate against sanctioning the loss of a man's livelihood" (Purchasing Assoc. v. Weitz, 13 N.Y.2d at p. 272, supra). At the same time, the employer is entitled to protection from unfair or illegal conduct that causes economic injury. The rules governing enforcement of anticompetitive covenants and the availability of equitable relief after termination of employment are designed to foster these interests of the employer without impairing the employee's ability to earn a living or the general competitive mold of society.

–C–

Specific enforcement of personal service contracts thus turns initially upon whether the term of employment has expired. If the employee refuses to perform during the period of employment, was furnishing unique services, has expressly or by clear implication agreed not to compete for the duration of the contract and the employer is exposed to irreparable injury, it may be appropriate to restrain the employee from competing until the agreement expires. Once the employment contract has terminated, by contrast, equitable relief is potentially available only to prevent injury from unfair competition or similar tortious behavior or to enforce an express and valid anticompetitive covenant. In the absence of such circumstances, the general policy of unfettered competition should prevail.

IV.

Applying these principles, it is apparent that ABC's request for injunctive relief must fail. There is no existing employment agreement between the parties; the original contract terminated in March, 1980. Thus, the negative enforcement that might be appropriate during the term of employment is unwarranted here. Nor is there an express anticompetitive covenant that defendant Wolf is violating, or any claim of special injury from tortious conduct such as exploitation of trade secrets. In short, ABC seeks to premise equitable relief after termination of the employment upon a simple, albeit serious, breach of a general contract negotiation clause.[7] To grant an injunction in that situation would be to unduly interfere with an individual's livelihood and to inhibit free competition where there is no corresponding injury to the employer other than the loss of a competitive edge. Indeed, if relief were granted here, any breach of an employment

---

7. Even if Wolf had breached the first-refusal provision, it does not necessarily follow that injunctive relief would be available. Outside the personal service area, the usual equitable remedy for breach of a first-refusal clause is to order the breaching party to perform the contract with the person possess-ing the first-refusal right (e.g., 5A Corbin, Contracts, § 1197, at pp. 377–378). When personal services are involved, this would result in an affirmative injunction ordering the employee to perform services for plaintiff. Such relief, as discussed, cannot be granted.

contract provision relating to renewal negotiations logically would serve as the basis for an open-ended restraint upon the employee's ability to earn a living should he ultimately choose not to extend his employment.[8] Our public policy, which favors the free exchange of goods and services through established market mechanisms, dictates otherwise.

Equally unavailing is ABC's request that the court create a noncompetitive covenant by implication. Although in a proper case an implied-in-fact covenant not to compete for the term of employment may be found to exist, anticompetitive covenants covering the postemployment period will not be implied. Indeed, even an express covenant will be scrutinized and enforced only in accordance with established principles.

This is not to say that ABC has not been damaged in some fashion or that Wolf should escape responsibility for the breach of his good-faith negotiation obligation. Rather, we merely conclude that ABC is not entitled to equitable relief. Because of the unique circumstances presented, however, this decision is without prejudice to ABC's right to pursue relief in the form of monetary damages, if it be so advised.

Accordingly, the order of the Appellate Division should be affirmed.

■ FUCHSBERG, JUDGE (dissenting).

I agree with all the members of this court, as had all the Justices at the Appellate Division, that the defendant Wolf breached his undisputed obligation to negotiate in good faith for renewal of his contract with ABC. Where we part company is in the majority's unwillingness to mold an equitable decree, even one more limited than the harsh one the plaintiff proposed, to right the wrong.

Central to the disposition of this case is the first-refusal provision. Its terms are worth recounting. They plainly provided that, in the 90-day period immediately succeeding the termination of his ABC contract, before Wolf could accept a position as sportscaster with another company, he first had to afford ABC the opportunity to engage him on like terms. True, he was not required to entertain offers, whether from ABC or anyone else, during that period. In that event he, of course, would be off the air for that 90 days, during which ABC could attempt to orient its listeners from Wolf to his successor. On the other hand, if Wolf wished to continue to broadcast actively during the 90 days, ABC's right of first refusal put it in a position to make sure that Wolf was not doing so for a competitor. One way or the other, however labeled, the total effect of the first refusal agreement was that of an express conditional covenant under which Wolf could be restrict-

---

8. Interestingly, the negative enforcement ABC seeks—an injunction barring Wolf from broadcasting for CBS—is for a two-year period. ABC's request is premised upon the fact that Wolf and CBS entered into a two-year agreement. Had the agreement been for 10 years, presumably ABC would have requested a 10-year restraint. In short, since it lacks an express anticompetitive clause to enforce, plaintiff seeks to measure its relief in a manner unrelated to the breach or the injury. This well illustrates one of the reasons why the law requires an express anticompetitive clause before it will restrain an employee from competing after termination of the employment.

ed from appearing on the air other than for ABC for the 90–day posttermination period.

One need not be in the broadcasting business to understand that the restriction ABC bargained for, and Wolf granted, when they entered into the original employment contract was not inconsequential. The earnings of broadcasting companies are directly related to the "ratings" they receive. This, in turn, is at least in part dependent on the popularity of personalities like Wolf. It therefore was to ABC's advantage, once Wolf came into its employ, especially since he was new to the New York market, that it enhance his popularity by featuring, advertising and otherwise promoting him. This meant that the loyalty of at least part of the station's listening audience would become identified with Wolf, thus enhancing his potential value to competitors, as witness the fact that, in place of the $250,000 he was receiving during his last year with ABC, he was able to command $400,000 to $450,000 per annum in his CBS "deal". A reasonable opportunity during which ABC could cope with such an assault on its good will had to be behind the clause in question.

Moreover, it is undisputed that, when in late February Wolf executed the contract for an extension of employment during the 90–day hiatus for which the parties had bargained, ABC had every right to expect that Wolf had not already committed himself to an exclusivity provision in a producer's contract with CBS in violation of the good-faith negotiation clause.... Surely, had ABC been aware of this gross breach, had it not been duped into giving an uninformed consent, it would not have agreed to serve as a self-destructive vehicle for the further enhancement of Wolf's potential for taking his ABC-earned following with him.

In the face of these considerations, the majority rationalizes its position of powerlessness to grant equitable relief by choosing to interpret the contract as though there were no restrictive covenant, express or implied. However, as demonstrated, there is, in fact, an express three-month negative covenant which, because of Wolf's misconduct, ABC was effectively denied the opportunity to exercise. Enforcement of this covenant, by enjoining Wolf from broadcasting for a three-month period, would depart from no entrenched legal precedent. Rather, it would accord with equity's boasted....

That said, a few words are in order regarding the majority's insistence that Wolf did not breach the first-refusal clause. It is remarkable that, to this end, it has to ignore its own crediting of the Appellate Division's express finding that, as far back as February 1, 1980, fully a month before the ABC contract was to terminate, "Wolf and CBS orally agreed on the terms of Wolf's employment as sportscaster for WCBS–TV" ... It follows that the overt written CBS–Wolf option contract, which permitted Wolf to formally accept the CBS sports casting offer at the end of the first-refusal period, was nothing but a charade.

Further, on this score, the majority's premise that Wolf could not have breached the first-refusal clause when he accepted the producer's agreement, exclusivity provision and all, *during* the term of his ABC contract, does not withstand analysis. So precious a reading of the arrangement with ABC frustrates the very purpose for which it had to have been made. Such a classical exaltation of form over substance is hardly to be countenanced by equity. . . .

For all these reasons, in my view, literal as well as proverbial justice should have brought a modification of the order of the Appellate Division to include a 90–day injunction—no more and no less than the relatively short and certainly not unreasonable transitional period for which ABC and Wolf struck their bargain.

Order affirmed, with costs.

NOTES

(1) *Specific Performance of Personal Service Contract.* Suppose that ABC and Wolf had, in 1978, signed a five-year contract under which Wolf was to render "exclusive" sportscasting services. In 1980, Wolf repudiated and signed a five-year contract with CBS. ABC can prove that because of Wolf's unique style and ability he will be "difficult if not impossible" to replace. Further, ABC can prove that damages to it in the New York area from Wolf's competition at CBS will be "substantial and extremely difficult to measure." ABC sues in 1980, seeking specific performance of the contract. Should it be granted?

The traditional answer is no. See Restatement (Second) § 367(2). What justifications are there for this result? According to Comment a, the reasons fall into three overlapping categories: (1) It is undesirable to compel the continuation of a personal relationship after a dispute has undercut confidence and loyalty; (2) The difficulties inherent in passing judgment on the quality of what frequently is a subjective performance are too great; and (3) An award requiring performance may impose a form of involuntary servitude that is prohibited by the 13th Amendment to the Constitution. See In re A.P. Johnson, 178 B.R. 216, 221–222 (BAP 9th Cir.1995); Read v. Wilmington Sneior Center, Inc., 1992 WL 296870 (Del.Ch.1992). See also Restatement (Second) §§ 365, 366.

(2) *Availability of Injunctive Relief.* If specific performance is not available, could ABC enjoin Wolf from sports casting with CBS or anyone else for the balance of the five-year contract? The answer is probably yes, and the "probably" relates to the question whether the injunction will, in effect, compel a performance "involving personal relations the enforced continuance of which is undesirable or will be to leave the employee without other reasonable means of making a living." Restatement (Second) § 367(2). The starting point for the analysis is Lumley v. Wagner, 42 Eng.Rep. 687 (Ch.1852), where a famous opera singer agreed to a three-month engagement at the plaintiff's theater and promised not to appear in any other theater or concert during that period without the plaintiff's written approval. The defendant was induced by a third person to breach the negative covenant and, at the plaintiff's request, the English Court of Chancery, among other things, enjoined the defendant from appearing at the third party's theater. The Lord Chancellor was of the opinion that the total agreement necessarily excluded the defendant from singing elsewhere and that a denial of the injunction would leave the plaintiff "to the mere chance of any damages which a jury may give." Conceding that the court

had no power to compel the defendant to sing, the Lord Chancellor stated that the defendant had "no cause of complaint, if I compel her to abstain from the commission of an act which she has bound herself not to do, and thus possibly cause her to fulfill her engagement." He disclaimed "doing indirectly what I cannot do directly." According to Professor Treitel, English courts will enforce an express covenant not to work elsewhere, but only if the breaching party has some other reasonable means of earning a living. G. Treitel, The Law of Contract 970–974 (10th ed. 1999). The defendant must not be given a choice between starving and working for the plaintiff. Accord: Restatement (Second) § 362(2).

The *Lumley* principle was adopted in America, see McCaull v. Braham, 16 Fed. 37 (S.D.N.Y.1883), and expanded equity jurisdiction in two ways: first, by enforcing the negative covenant where the direct promise was not specifically enforceable, and second, by granting the plaintiff an injunction where comparable relief was not available to the defendant. See, e.g., Philadelphia Ball Club v. Lajoie, 202 Pa. 210, 51 A. 973 (1902) (absence of mutual remedy not fatal to injunction). And the injunction, whose primary purpose is to protect the plaintiff from unfair competition from a contract breacher whose unique services cannot easily be replaced, is available whether or not an express negative covenant has been made. As Professor Corbin put it, an injunction against competition is proper if the competition "will do additional irreparable injury to the plaintiff, and if the injunction may induce proper performance of the entire contract by economic pressure without at the same time creating harmful personal relations." 5A Corbin § 1206, p. 412.

Comment: The Gendered Origins of the Lumley Doctrine

Professor Lea S. VanderVelde has this to say about the gender implications of Lumley v. Wagner:

In the familiar case of Lumley v. Wagner, [42 Eng. Rep. 687, 693 (Ch. 1852,] the English Court of Equity held that although opera singer Johanna Wagner could not be ordered to perform her contract, she would be enjoined from singing at any competing music hall for the term of the contract. Lumley is usually lauded in first year contracts courses as a just and fair decision, one that illustrates the proper distinction between equitable orders that force performance (unworkable and unjust) and equitable orders that prevent performance (sometimes workable, usually practical, and not necessarily unjust).

Contracts classes, however, rarely consider the central labor issue: whether an injunction preventing an employee from quitting and working elsewhere violates the American tradition of free labor and the right to quit employment. In American employment law, the Lumley rule was a regressive development. The beneficial side of the rule, that the opera singer would not be ordered to perform, was already secured by the Thirteenth Amendment. Before Lumley took hold in American courts, employers had considerably less leverage to compel the continued service of employees under contact. With the Lumley rule in effect, employers could shut employees out of work unless they returned to work for them for the remainder of the employment contract, a term which sometimes lasted several years. An employer holding the power of an injunction over an employee could dictate the terms on which that employee would be free to work elsewhere.

The Lumley rule's regressive effect was expressly denounced by a leading American jurist at its first introduction in the labor emancipatory era following the Civil War; yet it quiescently attained the status of the dominant common law rule in American courts by the 1890's. How did the rule of Lumley v. Wagner come to be incorporated into the canon of rules pertaining to equitable intervention in cases of departing employees?

The answer appears to be related to the gendered context in which the rule was examined at the time that American courts constructed the canon. Suits involving the services of women constituted the core of cases and provided the central contextual focus in which the rule was examined. Many more actresses than actors were sued under this cause of action. Indeed, in the nineteenth century, all of the prominent cases in this line involved the services of women, and only women performers were subjected to permanent injunctions against performing elsewhere for the duration of the contract.*

The fact that suits over women dominate this line of cases appears to be more than a coincidence. On no other topic of employment litigation, save the tort of seduction, do women figure so prominently in the leading cases. This concentration of women litigants is anomalous in the nineteenth century, an era when women were unlikely to be parties to any employment litigation. Both legal and cultural constraints discouraged women from working for wages. If they were married, the doctrine of coverture submerged women's legal identity under their husbands'. Thus, it is indeed unusual to find that on a gender-neutral legal issue like an employee's right to quit, women's cases would so considerable outnumber men's cases in a profession where women worked alongside men. Moreover, it is unusual that these women's cases would be raised to establish the standard.

[I] offer a tentative explanation of this phenomenon: that the Lumley rule's reception in the United States was facilitated by the fact that the majority of cases that employers won were cases involving women. I have chosen the term "gendered" to describe this phenomenon because the term covers a broad range of gender-specific elements that recur in this line of cases.... The phenomenon was not a simple one of misogyny or sexism, and it did not appear uniformly in every case involving a woman employee. Deeper cultural constructions of the role of women in the public workplace, particularly the very public workplace of the stage, explain the phenomenon better than would attributions of sexism to the few key individuals involved. A woman appearing in public on the stage posed a particular challenge to the dominant

---

* In the corpus of reported cases, no male performer was ever permanently enjoined from quitting and performing elsewhere during the entire nineteenth century.

norm of the Victorian Era that women were supposed to remain in the privacy of the home.

I maintain that, unlike male actors, nineteenth-century women performers were less likely to be viewed as free and independent employees. Nineteenth-century women were generally perceived as relationally bound to men. In this line of cases, that perception of women manifested itself in the need to bind actresses to their male theater managers. Moreover, in the view of the dominant culture, women performers were more likely to be perceived as subordinate than were their male counterparts. The decisions in this line of cases reflect larger "belief systems out of which knowledge is constructed, [belief systems that] place constraints on thought [and] that have real consequences for the behavior of individuals who live within them." This conceptualization of women in the nineteenth century paved the way for the adoption of the Lumley rule in America.

The story that emerges is one of reversal of a legal rule due in large part to the increasing presence of women in the acting profession. When Lumley first appeared in the United States, the cultural repulsion to anything that even hinted of slavery led to its unequivocal rejection. But later in the century, the cultural aversion to mastery had lessened and no longer seemed to apply to men's domination of women in particular. In the later cases, courts were harsher upon women defendants who attempted to leave their employment than they were in the few parallel cases involving men. And, in the later cases, courts were harsher upon women than they had been earlier in the century. By the end of the century, the courts' subjugation of actresses to the control of theater managers surpassed even the language of their contracts and became an incident of a status classification constructed largely by the courts, rather than the consequence of any voluntary agreement between the parties.

Although no court articulated gender as a factor influencing its decision, the tone of the opinions as well as the pattern of results demonstrates that the courts of New York, where the core cases were litigated, were unable to ignore differential cultural constructions of women's proper behavior as reflected in the larger society and in other legal rules. Women's attempts to control their work lives and to assert their agency and independence by terminating employment that they no longer found desirable was no more to be tolerated than the emerging trend of women's attempts to divorce their husbands. Although courts deciding employment cases spoke of "binding men's consciences," they rarely did so when presented with male defendants. The courts appeared more willing and even eager to sanction what they perceived as women's infidelity to their male employers.

Lea S. VanderVelde, The Gendered Origins of the Lumley Doctrine: Binding Men's Consciences and Women's Fidelity, 101 Yale L. J. 775, 775–780 (1992).

Although there are many variables to consider, the *Lumley* principle has survived in the United States and found its home in the domain of professional sports and entertainment. At times the papers have been full of reports about players and coaches of exceptional and not so exceptional talent who have joined other teams in violation of contracts or "reserve" clauses and have been enjoined from competing until the period of commitment to the plaintiff team has expired. For a typical example, see Nassau Sports v. Peters, 352 F.Supp. 870 (E.D.N.Y.1972) (hockey). See also, Note, *Professional Athletic Contracts and the Injunctive Dilemma,* 8 J. Marshall J. of Prac. & Proc. 437 (1975), where the author asserts that injunctive relief has become the ordinary rather than the extraordinary relief and that this is based upon a misguided assumption that such relief is necessary to protect the plaintiff's large investment in acquiring and developing talented players. Be this as it may, professional sports is big business and such restraints on player mobility raise important questions concerning the scope of federal antitrust and labor policy. See, e.g., Flood v. Kuhn, 407 U.S. 258, 92 S.Ct. 2099, 32 L.Ed.2d 728 (1972).

Comment: Remedies for Breach of Valid Restrictive Covenant in Employment Contracts

It is common in many industries for employment contracts to contain a restrictive covenant. The covenant, in essence, states that if the employee leaves the company for any reason, the employee agrees not to compete with the employer for a stated time in a defined area. Although one purpose of the restriction is to protect the employer against harmful competition, other objectives are to protect the employer's confidential information and the investment in the employee's training. See Comment, *Post–Employment Restraint Agreements: A Reassessment,* 50 U.Chi.L.Rev. 703 (1985). The employee's freedom and the public's interest in competition, however, must be weighed in the balance. Thus, a court will not enforce the restriction unless it is "reasonable," which in turn depends upon such factors as whether the employee's services are "special, unique or extraordinary," or there is a risk that the employee will disclose trade secrets or solicit the employer's customers. The duration and scope of the restraint are also relevant to the inquiry. See, e.g., Purchasing Associates, Inc. v. Weitz, 13 N.Y.2d 267, 246 N.Y.S.2d 600, 196 N.E.2d 245 (1963) (restraint unreasonable). See also, Handler & Lazerof, *Restraint of Trade and the Restatement (Second) of Contracts,* 57 N.Y.U.L.Rev. 669 (1982); Kniffen, *Employee Noncompetition Covenants: The Perils of Performing Unique Services,* 10 Rut.Cam.L.J. 25 (1978); Note, *Economic and Critical Analyses of the Law of Covenants Not to Compete,* 72 Geo.L.J. 1425 (1984). See also, Christopher T. Wonnell, The Contractual Disempowerment of Employees, 46 Stan. L. Rev. 687, 92–95 (1993); Stewart E. Sterk, Restraints on Alienation of Human Capital, 79 Va. L. Rev. 383, 401–403 (1993).

If the restriction passes the test of reasonableness, in whole or in part, the probabilities are that normal damage remedies will be inadequate. There is a risk of irreparable harm that cannot be measured with reasonable certainty. Without more, a court should enforce the employee's promise not to compete through an injunction. In some contracts, however, there may be a clause attempting to liquidate the probable damages in the event of breach. For example, the contract may provide that in the event of breach the employee will pay the employer $100,000 as "liquidated damages and not a penalty" for the breach.

We will consider when liquidated damage provisions are enforceable in the next section. For now, remember this: If the liquidated damage provision is valid and the contract provides that is the *exclusive* remedy, the employer is not entitled to injunctive relief. It must take the money and run. In the absence of an exclusive remedy clause, however, the employer has a choice: Enforce the liquidated damage clause or seek an injunction. The employer cannot have both (do you see why?) If the employer obtains an injunction, however, the employer may recover any actual damages caused between the time of the breach and the date the injunction issues. See Karpinski v. Ingrasci, 28 N.Y.2d 45, 320 N.Y.S.2d 1, 268 N.E.2d 751 (1971); Restatement (Second) § 361 (provision for liquidated damages will not bar injunctive relief).

SECTION 4.   EFFECT OF AGREEMENT LIQUIDATING DAMAGES OR ALTERING THE SCOPE OF LIABILITY OR REMEDY

(A) LIQUIDATED DAMAGES

As we have seen, punitive damages are not recoverable in the ordinary action for breach of contract. This is true, generally, even though the defendant's breach is willful, malicious or in bad faith. Courts insist that the remedial objective is to compensate the plaintiff, not to punish the defendant.

But what if the parties provide in their contract what the damages are to be in the event of breach, and they set a figure which is greatly in excess of probable harm? Suppose, for example, in a building contract (to cost $100,000) it is agreed that for every day's delay in completion the builder is to pay the owner $5,000. Is such a provision, from the standpoint of fairness and justice, objectionable? Would it likely be upheld in court? Consider the following statements of Judge Irving Kaufman and Professor Lewis Kornhauser:

> [Judge Kaufman.] More than three centuries ago, in *The Merchant of Venice*, Shakespeare tellingly illustrated the evil of agreements which exact a "pound of flesh." Since that time, courts have grappled with the problem of oppressive contracts through the doctrine of unconscionability. Originating in Equity as a form of relief against the harshness of penal bonds, this doctrine has been employed by courts to deny enforcement to harsh and unreasonable contract terms. Today we are asked to determine whether the liquidated damages provisions of several commercial leasing agreements are unconscionable as a matter of law. In reaching our decision, we must resolve a significant tension

between two important goals served by rules governing the enforceability of liquidated damages clauses: rejecting clauses which operate as a penalty or forfeiture while upholding provisions which are reasonable attempts by parties to estimate the probable damages which would flow from a breach. This tension is an example of a more general conflict between contract law as a system of private ordering and contract law as an expression of the public interest. * * *

Determining the enforceability of a liquidated damages clause or other contractual provision governing a lessor's remedies upon default reveals a tension between two often conflicting goals. On the one hand, courts will not enforce such a provision if it operates as a penalty or forfeiture clause. ... The law is clear that contractual terms providing for the payment of a sum disproportionate to the amount of actual damages exact a penalty and are unenforceable. ... The rationale for this principle is that contractual terms fixing damages in an amount clearly disproportionate to actual loss seek to deter breach through compulsion and have an *in terrorem* effect: fearing severe economic loss, the promisor is compelled to continue performance, while the promisee may reap a windfall well in excess of his just compensation. ...

On the other hand, courts uphold contractual provisions fixing damages for breach when the terms constitute a reasonable mechanism for estimating the compensation which should be paid to satisfy any loss flowing from the breach. ... These provisions have value in situations where it is difficult to estimate the amount of actual damages. From these principles, the standards for evaluating appellants' claim that the challenged lease terms are unconscionable are easily discernible. Contractual provisions fixing liquidated damages in the event of breach will not be voided as unconscionable or contrary to public policy if the amount liquidated bears a reasonable proportion to the probable loss and the amount of actual loss is incapable or difficult of precise estimation. ... If the amount fixed by contract is plainly or grossly disproportionate to the probable loss, the contractual provisions exact a penalty and will not be enforced. ...

Leasing Service Corp. v. Justice, 673 F.2d 70, 73 (2d Cir.1982).

[Professor Kornhauser.] *Liquidated Damages Clause.*" The judicial attitude towards contract clauses that specify the amount to be paid in the event of breach is one of the few areas of contract law that has received generally adverse criticism from economic analysts. The traditional rule against the enforcement of "penalty" clauses runs strongly counter to the elaboration of the efficiency criterion, particularly in commercial contexts.

Several reasons account for the economists' antagonism. First, the assumption of rationality entails that a party will not accept a clause for which he is inadequately compensated. When the promisee demands a "penalty clause," the promisor will agree only if the price is increased sufficiently to cover any increase in the cost of performance.

Thus, if parties are "rational", no contract should require performance when the (expected) costs to party A of performing exceed the (expected) benefits to party B of receiving it. Of course, the parties may have different expectations as to the likelihood of some contingency occurring, and one may be more accurate than the other. Moreover, the occurrence of the contingency may impose some inequality of costs and benefits between the parties. But, since it seems plausible that commercial contractors act largely in their "rational" self-interest, it is likely that both parties initially saw a benefit even in a clause which a court later terms a penalty. This benefit might simply be to trade a risk that one party perceives as high to a second party who perceives it as low. Such trades may be "efficient" because trading the risk may be cheaper for the first party than correcting or improving his estimate of the risk to which he was exposed. In that event, judicial intervention after the fact would only serve to induce excessively costly gathering of information. Alternatively, the benefits to the parties may be more "substantial" than those arising from different perceptions. For instance, a new entrant into a market may be willing to accept a clause imposing a penalty in the event his product fails to meet some quality standard precisely because he has no other means of credibly assuring quality and thereby successfully entering the market.

A second reason economists criticize limitations on liquidated damage clauses lies in the informational advantage that the parties themselves are presumed to have; at the time of contracting the parties are likely to have better information about any idiosyncratic damages that might be incurred than a court will have at or after the time of breach. Particularly in markets where substitute performance is difficult to obtain, this informational advantage argues strongly for liberal enforcement of liquidated damage clauses. An analogous argument derives from the widespread belief that expectation damages are in fact undercompensatory. If the law seeks to promote efficient decisions to perform or not, then allowing parties to estimate damages in advance will induce more appropriate decisions in this respect than court-imposed rules.

A third problem with the current proscription of "penalty" clauses lies in its implicit distributional bias; it forces the parties to allocate some risks in a particular way. Suppose the breach is caused by the appearance of a third party willing to pay more for the good than the first buyer agreed to pay. The ban on penalties (together with a rule of expectation damages) effectively allocates the entire gain from the appearance of the third party to the seller, while the parties might rationally have wished to divide this risk differently. On the other hand, if the breach is prompted by an uneconomic increase in costs, expectation damages allocates all of the loss to the breaching party, while contractors, negotiating before the breach, might knowingly have chosen to share this risk differently.

These arguments suggest that the current rules governing liquidated damage clauses are too restrictive. They do not necessarily contend that every liquidation clause, whether it appears to be a "penalty" or not, should be permitted. Most commentators would make exceptions for clauses that resulted from defective bargaining procedures (akin to those covered by unconscionability). These defects, however, seem unlikely to occur in commercial contexts, where one can presume that the parties are sophisticated and rational in their negotiations. Other commentators suggest that liquidated damage clauses be policed for more than fraud or oppression in bargaining. In some circumstances, a clause which unduly benefitted one party might stimulate it to induce a breach by the other; in that case, these commentators suggest the clause should not be enforced.

Kornhauser, *An Introduction to the Economic Analysis of Contract Remedies,* 57 U.Colo.L.Rev. 683, 720–21 (1986)[Reprinted with permission].

Southwest Engineering Co. v. United States

United States Court of Appeals, Eighth Circuit, 1965.
341 F.2d 998, cert. denied 382 U.S. 819, 86 S.Ct. 45, 15 L.Ed.2d 66.

■ VAN OOSTERHOUT, CIRCUIT JUDGE. Plaintiff Southwest Engineering Company, hereinafter called Southwest, has appealed from summary judgment dismissing its complaint against the United States for recovery of $8,300 withheld as liquidated damages for delay in performance on four construction contracts entered into between Southwest and the United States.

This appeal is before us upon an agreed statement of the record. Four contracts entered into between Southwest and the Government called for the construction by Southwest of three V.O.R. radio facilities at Readsville, Blackwater, and Maryland Heights, Missouri, and for a high intensity approach light lane at Lambert Field, Missouri. Each of the contracts fixed a completion date and provided for liquidated damages on a per diem basis for each day's delay beyond the agreed completion date. The agreed liquidated damage on the Lambert Field project was $100 per day, and $50 per day on each of the other projects. Each contract contained the general provisions set forth in Standard Form 23–A (March 1953) prescribed by the General Services Administration, including, among others, a provision that plaintiff was not to be charged with delays "due to unforeseeable causes beyond the control and without the fault or negligence of the Contractor, including, but not restricted to, acts of God or of the public enemy, acts of the Government, in either its sovereign or contractual capacity, acts of another contractor in the performance of a contract with the Government, fires, floods, epidemics, quarantine restrictions, strikes, freight embargoes, and unusually severe weather, or delays of subcontractors or suppliers due to such causes." Within ten days from the beginning of any such delay, plaintiff was to notify the contracting officer in writing of the causes of delay. The contracting officer was to ascertain the facts and extent of the delay, and extend the time for completing the work when "in his judgment the findings of fact justify such an extension." His findings of fact were to be final, subject only to appeal to the "head of the department."

The Blackwater project was completed 97 days late. Plaintiff requested time extensions, alleging the delay resulted from causes for which it was not responsible, including acts and omissions of defendant. Administrative appeals resulted in extensions by the C.A.A. because of delays by the Government, and, later on, a remission of an additional $4,200 liquidated damages by the Comptroller General under the authority of 41 U.S.C. § 256a, because of late delivery of Government-furnished material. This left $550 (11 days) withheld as liquidated damages on the Blackwater project.

The Readsville project was completed 84 days late. Administrative appeals resulted in a three-days extension, leaving liquidated damages for 81 days totalling $4,050.

The Maryland Heights project was completed 48 days late. On administrative appeal, a fourteen-days extension was allowed resulting in liquidated damages of $1,700 for 34 days delay.

The Lambert Field project was completed 54 days late, 34 days extension was granted, leaving $2,000 as liquidated damages for 20 days delay.

The parties stipulated "although each project was not completed until after the date prescribed in its contract, defendant suffered no actual damage on any project." The Government withheld the liquidated damages for delays provided in the contracts after giving credit for the extensions of time administratively allowed. This suit by Southwest is for recovery of the $8,300 so withheld as liquidated damages. The Government counterclaimed for the liquidated damages here involved. Plaintiff by reply admitted the projects were not completed within the time limits as administratively extended but denied the Government was entitled to liquidated damages because the Government caused and contributed to the delays and because the Government suffered no actual damages.

The trial court determined that the Government was entitled to liquidated damages in the amount claimed, offset such damages which equaled the amount of payments withheld, sustained the motion for summary judgment, and dismissed the complaint.

Southwest as a basis for reversal urges the trial court's decision was induced by two erroneous views of the law, either of which requires reversal. The points relied upon for reversal are thus stated:

* * *

2. "The court erred in awarding the Government liquidated damages because a contract provision for liquidated damages is clearly a penalty and not enforceable where the party seeking to enforce it formally admits he sustained no actual damage."

At the outset, we observe that the contracts here involved were entered into pursuant to federal law by an authorized federal agency. Federal law controls in the construction and determination of rights under federal contracts. Priebe & Sons, Inc. v. United States, 332 U.S. 407, 411, 68 S.Ct. 123, 92 L.Ed.2d 32; ...

In the Priebe case, the Supreme Court states:

"It is customary, where Congress has not adopted a different standard, to apply to the construction of government contracts the principles of general contract law. United States v. Standard Rice Co., 323 U.S. 106, 111, and cases cited. That has been done in other cases where the Court has considered the enforceability of 'liquidated damages' provisions in government contracts." 332 U.S. 407.

* * *

Southwest's second point in substance is that the parties' stipulation that the Government suffered no actual damage bars any recovery of liquidated damages. Such stipulation was made. It relates to the situation as it existed at the time of the completion of the work. The stipulation does not go to the extent of agreeing that the parties at the time of contracting did not reasonably contemplate that damages would flow from a delay in performance.

The contracts prescribe the payments to be made for delays as liquidated damages. Southwest urges that such provision is a penalty provision. The agreed record is highly condensed and does not show the contract price for the various projects, but such projects appear to be substantial. There is no showing that the liquidated damages for delay provided for are beyond damages reasonably contemplated by the parties at the time of the contract.

Two requirements must be considered to determine whether the provision included in the contract fixing the amount of damages payable on breach will be interpreted as an enforceable liquidated damage clause rather than an unenforceable penalty clause: First, the amount so fixed must be a reasonable forecast of just compensation for the harm that is caused by the breach, and second, the harm that is caused by the breach must be one that is incapable or very difficult of accurate estimation. ...

Whether these requirements have been complied with must be viewed as of the time the contract was executed rather than when the contract was breached or at some other subsequent time. Courts presently look with candor upon provisions that are deliberately entered into between parties and therefore do not look with disfavor upon liquidated damage stipulations. ...

In the Bethlehem Steel case, the Court sets out the standard to be applied for determining whether a liquidated damage provision can be upheld as follows: "The question always is, What did the parties intend by the language used? When such intention is ascertained it is ordinarily the duty of the court to carry it out." 205 U.S. 105, 119.

Here Southwest has failed to establish that the intention of the parties was to do anything other than execute a valid liquidated damage provision.

Priebe & Sons, Inc. v. United States, supra, involved a Government contract for purchase of dried eggs for foreign shipment. The Court observes the contract contains two provisions for liquidated damages. The one involved in the case related to failure to have eggs inspected and ready for delivery for the date specified in the order. The court construed the contract to mean that performance was not due until demand for delivery and held that since inspection was made before such demand, the provision for liquidated damages could not possibly be a reasonable forecast of just compensation for breach of contract. The Court further observes that the contract contains a provision for liquidated damages for delay in delivery upon demand and with respect to such provision, breach of which was not involved, states: "It likewise is apparent that the only thing which could possibly injure the Government would be failure to get prompt performance when delivery was due. We have no doubt of the validity of the provision for 'liquidated damages' when applied under those circumstances." 332 U.S. 407, 412.

The Court also speaks of standards applicable to allowance of liquidated damages, stating:

"Today the law does not look with disfavor upon 'liquidated damages' provisions in contracts. When they are fair and reasonable attempts to fix just compensation for anticipated loss caused by breach of contract, they are enforced. * * * They serve a particularly useful function when damages are uncertain in nature or amount or are unmeasurable, as is the case in many government contracts. * * * And the fact that the damages suffered are shown to be less than the damages contracted for is not fatal. These provisions are to be judged as of the time of making the contract." 332 U.S. 407, 411–412.

* * *

We recognize that there are cases . . . which reach a contrary result. We believe that the cases holding that the situation existing at the time of the contract is controlling in determining the reasonableness of liquidated damages are based upon sound reasoning and represent the weight of authority. Where parties have by their contract agreed upon a liquidated damage provision as a reasonable forecast of just compensation for breach of contract and damages are difficult to estimate accurately, such provision should be enforced. If in the course of subsequent developments, damages prove to be greater than those stipulated, the party entitled to damages is bound by the liquidated damage agreement. It is not unfair to hold the contractor performing the work to such agreement if by reason of later developments damages prove to be less or nonexistent. Each party by entering into such contractual provision took a calculated risk and is bound by reasonable contractual provisions pertaining to liquidated damages.

Southwest has completely failed to demonstrate that the court committed an error of law in determining that absence of actual damages at the time of breach of the contract or thereafter does not bar recovery of liquidated damages. The court at least impliedly found that the liquidated damage provisions of the contracts here involved were reasonable when viewed in the light of circumstances existing at the time the contract was entered into. We find nothing in the record which would compel a contrary conclusion. The court committed no error in allowing liquidated damages.

The judgment appealed from is affirmed.

NOTES

(1) *"Time of Contracting" Test.* Most jurisdictions follow the "time of contracting" test. See Watson v. Ingram, 124 Wash.2d 845, 881 P.2d 247 (1994). This approach makes the most sense when both parties, in negotiations, have addressed themselves to the inability of standard damages to provide adequate compensation under the peculiar facts of their case. On the other hand, liquidated damage clauses usually serve the interest of one party more than the other and may be the product of superior bargaining power. Put another way, the ability of one party—the plaintiff—to overstate remedies may raise the same problems posed when a defendant has attempted to limit liability through disclaimer clauses or other "agreed" remedies. See Melodee Lane Lingerie Co. v. American District Telephone Co., 18 N.Y.2d 57, 271 N.Y.S.2d 937, 218 N.E.2d 661 (1966); Fritz, *"Underliquidated" Damages as a Limitation of Liability,* 33 Tex.L.Rev. 196 (1954).

Arguably, the "hindsight" rule, i.e., the power of a court to assess the liquidation in light of actual damage caused by the breach, becomes more appealing when the plaintiff has been able to impose the clause on the defendant with little or no actual bargaining. See UCC 2–718(1)[UCC 2–809 (1997)]. In view of this, how well does *Southwest Engineering* fit the realities of most government contracting? Do you suppose the contractor had any say about inclusion of the liquidated damage clause or its amount? Did the contractor fail to satisfy its burden of proof in attacking the clause? See, generally, Gantt & Breslauer, *Liquidated Damages in Federal Government Contracts,* 47 Boston U.L.Rev. 71 (1967). For an economic argument supporting the enforcement of reasonable *ex ante* forecasts of damages, see Rea, *Efficiency Implications of Penalties and Liquidated Damages,* 13 J.Legal Stud. 147 (1984).

(2) Might one be able to disguise an impermissible penalty by phrasing it in terms of an "alternative performance" or as a "premium" for timely performance? See Blank v. Borden, 11 Cal.3d 963, 115 Cal.Rptr. 31, 524 P.2d 127 (1974). For example, how would you classify a "take-or-pay" commitment, as an alternative performance or a liquidated damage clause? See Universal Resources Corp. v. Panhandle Eastern Pipe Line Co., 813 F.2d 77 (5th Cir. 1987) (alternative performance).

(3) Eric Talley has suggested that the limitation on liquidated damages may reduce "both parties' incentives and abilities to engage in deceptive behavior during renegotiation, and it thereby mitigates the inefficiencies that usually accompany bilateral monopoly" Eric L. Talley, Note, Contract Renegotiation, Mechanism Design, and the Liquidated Damages Rule, 46 Stan. L. Rev. 1195, 1218–42 (1994); but see Lars A. Stole, The Economics of Liquidated

Damage Clauses in Contractual Environments with Private Information, 8 J. L. ECON. & ORG. 582 (1992).

(4) Where, at the time of the breach, the plaintiff has fully performed and the defendant has failed to pay money due, efforts to liquidate damages are more difficult to sustain. As one court put it: "In this context [breach by lessee of a covenant to pay rent] it is a relevant general rule that a failure to pay a sum of money due will rarely, if ever, justify a further sum, in excess of interest, to be paid by way of liquidated damages. On the contrary, such a requirement is likely to be condemned as a penal forfeiture which the law will not recognize." Breitel, J. in Manhattan Syndicate, Inc. v. Ryan, 14 A.D.2d 323, 220 N.Y.S.2d 337, 340–41 (1961). But see United Merchants and Manufacturers, Inc. v. Equitable Life Assurance Society, 674 F.2d 134 (2d Cir.1982) (Applying New York law, Court upheld provision in loan agreement that upon default the principal of the note plus interest would be due, together with an amount equal to the pre-payment charges that would be payable if the borrower were pre-paying the note.) See also Garrett v. Coast & Southern Federal Savings & Loan Association, 9 Cal.3d 731, 108 Cal.Rptr. 845, 511 P.2d 1197 (1973) (late charge assessed at 2% of unpaid balance of due notes is void because parties "failed to make a reasonable endeavor to estimate a fair compensation which would be sustained on the default").

(5) *Liquidated Damages under the UCC and Restatement (Second).* UCC 2–718(1) provides:

> Damages for breach by either party may be liquidated in the agreement but only at an amount which is reasonable in the light of the anticipated or actual harm caused by the breach, the difficulties of proof of loss, and the inconvenience or nonfeasibility of otherwise obtaining an adequate remedy. A term fixing unreasonably large liquidated damages is void as a penalty.

How does this approach differ from that adopted in *Southwest Engineering*? Does the Code appear to be more supportive or less supportive of the power of contracting parties to fix the amount of damage in advance of breach?

Revised UCC 2–718(1) provides:

> Damages for breach by either party may be liquidated in the agreement but only at the amount which is reasonable in the light of the anticipated or actual harm caused by the breach, and in a consumer contract, in addition the difficulties of proof of loss and the inconvenience or nonfeasibility of otherwise obtaining an adequate remedy.

What changes were made?

Restatement (Second) § 356(1), drafted so as to harmonize with pre-revision UCC 2–718, reads: "Damages for breach by either party may be liquidated in the agreement but only at an amount that is reasonable in the light of the anticipated or actual loss caused by the breach and the difficulties of proof of loss. A term fixing unreasonably large liquidated damages is unenforceable on grounds of public policy as a penalty." See Note, 67 Cornell L.Rev. 862 (1982).

The focus upon the time of breach as well as the time of contracting raises a number of questions. For example, what if the agreed upon figure is unreasonable in the light of anticipated loss but reasonable in the light of actual loss? Or what if it is reasonable in the light of anticipated harm, but not reasonable in terms of actual harm caused by the breach? See Roy R. Anderson, *Liquidated Damages Under the Uniform Commercial Code*, 41 Sw.L.J. 1083 (1988). See also, Irving Tire Co., Inc. v. Stage II Apparel Corp., 230 A.D.2d 772, 646 N.Y.S.2d 528, 530 (N.Y.A.D.1996), where the court refused to enforce a purported liquidated damage clause where the damages actually arising from the breach were readily ascertainable and the "sum fixed is disproportionate to the landlord's loss."

United Air Lines, Inc. v. Austin Travel Corp.

United States Court of Appeals, Second Circuit, 1989.
867 F.2d 737.

■ MINER, CIRCUIT JUDGE:

Defendant-appellant Austin Travel Corp. ("Austin") appeals from a summary judgment entered in the United States District Court for the Southern District of New York (Pollack, J.) awarding plaintiff-appellee United Air Lines, Inc. ("United") $408,375 in liquidated damages and unpaid debt plus interest and costs. United sued Austin to recover (i) damages for breach of leases obligating Austin to use a United computerized reservation system ("CRS") called Apollo and a United business and accounting system known as Apollo Business System ("ABS"), and (ii) unpaid accrued rentals. Austin claimed that the liquidated damages clauses of its Apollo contracts with United were unreasonable and unenforceable. * * *

The district court held that the liquidated damages clauses were reasonable and enforceable. * * * 681 F.Supp. 176 (S.D.N.Y.1988). On appeal, Austin reasserts its liquidated damages [claim]. Because we hold that the liquidated damages provisions of the United–Austin contracts were at the time of execution a reasonable forecast of damages in case of breach * * *, we affirm the entry of summary judgment in United's favor.

BACKGROUND

United owns and markets to travel agents and others the Apollo CRS. A CRS provides subscribers access to a vast data bank through which they may make airline reservations, issue tickets, reserve car rentals and hotel rooms and perform other travel-related functions. By licensing this system, United earns income in two ways: First, the travel agent pays United a monthly subscription fee, either fixed or based on use, and second, each time the travel agent uses Apollo to book a flight on an airline other than United, United charges that airline a booking fee. United flights booked through Apollo do not generate booking fees. United's Apollo contracts require an agent to book a minimum of 50% of that agent's average monthly bookings through Apollo. United also markets its ABS, a back-office accounting and management system for travel agents.

Competing nationwide with Apollo are four other CRS systems, SystemOne, PARS, DATAS II and SABRE, each owned by separate air carriers. SABRE, owned by American Airlines, is used as a principal CRS by approximately 28% of the more than 28,000 travel agency locations across the country. SABRE also holds the largest share of CRS transactions nationally, more than 45% in the years 1983–1985. Nationally, Apollo is the second largest CRS, used by approximately 25% of travel agency locations in the United States, and, according to Austin, accounting for 31% of all CRS transactions in this country. On Long Island, New York, Apollo ranks fourth, used by 3% of Long Island travel agency locations and earning 8% of all Long Island CRS revenues.

Austin is a travel agency with thirteen offices on Long Island. Prior to mid–1985, Austin used a variety of CRSs, but it never used Apollo. In 1985, Austin acquired two smaller Long Island agencies, Karson Travel and Fantasy Adventures, both of which subscribed to Apollo. By separate agreements with United, Austin assumed Karson's ABS contract and Fantasy's Apollo contract. Austin then executed a five-year Apollo contract covering two of its other locations in Oceanside and Mitchell Field.

Each of the Apollo contracts that Austin signed provided for payment of liquidated damages upon premature termination of the contract. In the contract for the Oceanside and Mitchell Field locations, the liquidated damages consist of: (i) 80% of the remaining monthly fees due under the contract, (ii) 80% of variable charges, accrued by generation of tickets and itineraries, for the month preceding termination, multiplied by the number of months remaining in the contract term and (iii) 50% of the average monthly booking fee revenues, using the first six months of the contract as a basis for calculation, multiplied by the number of months remaining in the contract term. In the contract assuming Fantasy's Apollo obligation, only the first two elements are used to define liquidated damages. The contracts specify that Illinois law governs disputes; for the contract issues raised by this case, the law of Illinois is the same as that of New York, the state where the claim arose, and virtually all other states.

Austin then moved the SABRE CRS into its three locations covered by Apollo, using the two systems side by side at each location. Austin later notified United that it wished to discontinue use of the ABS system at the Karson Travel location. United agreed to the discontinuance and to forego the $90,511.43 in liquidated damages Austin owed under the Karson ABS agreement provided that Austin continue to use Apollo until November 30, 1989. Austin accepted the condition and discontinued use of ABS.

Thereafter, representatives of the rival SystemOne CRS, owned and operated by Texas Air Corp., offered Austin indemnity against any damages incurred for breach of the existing Apollo agreements if Austin would contract for use of SystemOne. In June 1986, Austin adopted the System-One CRS at Mitchell Field, its principal Apollo location, and abandoned all of its Apollo obligations before the expiration of the term of the contracts. At Austin's request, United removed all Apollo equipment from Austin premises. Austin had never paid United for the use of Apollo equipment and services provided by the contracts.

United brought this breach of contract action on the two Apollo contracts and the ABS agreement. Austin defended and counterclaimed on two grounds relevant to this appeal: first, that the liquidated damages clauses included in the Apollo contracts were unenforceable penalties; * * *

The district court rejected Austin's defenses and counterclaims. It held that the liquidated damages clauses were reasonable and enforceable. * * *

On appeal, Austin argues that the district court erred by enforcing liquidated damages that are penalties, * * * and abused summary judgment standards by deciding in plaintiff's favor issues of fact that should have been submitted to a jury.

DISCUSSION

A.   Liquidated Damages

It is commonplace for contracting parties to determine in advance the amount of compensation due in case of a breach of contract.... A liquidated damages clause generally will be upheld by a court, unless the liquidated amount is a penalty because it is plainly or grossly disproportionate to the probable loss anticipated when the contract was executed.... Liquidated damages are not penalties if they bear a "reasonable proportion to the probable loss and the amount of actual loss is incapable or difficult of precise estimation." Leasing Service Corp. v. Justice, 673 F.2d 70, 73 (2d Cir.1982).

The liquidated damages fixed in the Apollo contracts[1] were, as the district court found, reasonable at the time the contracts were executed. Most of United's costs when providing Apollo service are either fixed or determined in the early stages of the contractual relationship. The few costs that United would avoid by an early termination of an Apollo contract are estimated to be "less than 20 percent of the amount of revenue from the monthly fixed usage fees and variable charges." 681 F.Supp. at 187.' The Apollo contracts' liquidated damages clauses provide for recovery by

---

1. The Apollo Subscriber Lease Agreement between United and Austin for the Oceanside and Mitchell Field locations includes the following paragraphs:

12.   TERMINATION FOR CAUSE

If either party (the "Defaulting Party") shall refuse, neglect, or fail to perform, observe or keep any of the covenants, agreements, terms or conditions contained herein on its part to be performed, observed and kept, and such refusal, neglect or failure shall continue for a period of thirty (30) days after written notice (except in the case of any payments due where the period to cause such nonpayment shall be five (5) days

after notice) to the Defaulting Party thereof, then without prejudice to any other rights or remedies of the other party, this Agreement shall terminate at the expiration of the notice period.

21.   LIQUIDATED DAMAGES

In the event that prior to the expiration of the term of this Agreement, as specified in Article 11 ... , this Agreement is terminated by Subscriber, except pursuant to Article 12, or by United pursuant to the provisions of this Agreement, then Subscriber will pay to United liquidated damages....

The other contract at issue contains substantially the same language.

United of only 80% of the fixed and variable charges. Austin is thus provided with better than adequate credit for the costs United is able to avoid by the early removal of the Apollo CRSs from Austin premises.

* * *

Austin complains that the 20% discount incorporated by the liquidated damages provisions underestimates the savings realized by United in the event of early contract termination. Austin points to testimony by a representative of a competing CRS vendor that United's avoidable costs likely equal 40% to 50% of United's total costs. The testimony of a competitor about United's costs and savings is inherently suspect, and United presented sufficient evidence to justify the 20% figure. The appropriate analysis is not whether a better quantification of damages could have been drafted by the contracting parties, but whether the amount of liquidated damages actually inserted in the contract is reasonable. "[T]he disputable analysis of presumed costs savings belatedly submitted by Austin does not discredit the reasonableness of United's anticipatory estimate in light of anticipated or actual loss caused by the breach and the difficulties of proof." 681 F.Supp. at 188. We note as well, as the district court did, that CRS contracts of United's competitors often call for 100% of rent due on the unexpired term of the contract; United obligated Austin for only 80%. There is no indication that the estimate of probable loss, identified in the contracts as liquidated damages, is either unfair or unreasonable. Indeed, the liquidated damages provisions edge closer toward over-generousness to Austin than they do toward unreasonableness.

Austin complains that in the disputed contract covering its Oceanside and Mitchell Field locations the liquidated damages formula, which envisions repayment for all potential booking fees, fails to account for the fact that United does not receive booking fees for United flights booked on the Apollo CRS. The booking fees reimbursement, however, is based on a lenient minimum usage level of Apollo—future monthly bookings are estimated as 50% of the average level of all bookings Austin made on Apollo in the early months of the contract. Any unfairness suggested by a failure to exclude United bookings from the liquidated damages formula is negated by the low level of Apollo usage employed for estimation of future bookings.

Austin further depicts the liquidated damages clauses as imposing penalties because they provide the same amount of damages for each possible breach of the contract, no matter how insignificant. Austin argues that establishing a single liquidated damages amount for any breach indicates that a fair estimation of probable loss for each breach was not conceived when the contract was drafted and executed.

Austin, however, ignores basic tenets of contract law. "A party may terminate a contract only because of substantial nonperformance by the other party so fundamental 'as to defeat the objects of the parties in making the agreement.'" Maywood Sportservice, Inc. v. Maywood Park Trotting Ass'n, Inc., 14 Ill.App.3d 141 (1973) ... Neither United nor Austin can terminate the contracts because of a non-material breach. Thus, liquidated damages can only be owed to United in the event of a material breach by Austin.

Furthermore, the presumed intent of the parties is that a liquidated damages provision will apply only to material breaches. . . . Additionally, for a non-material breach to allow an aggrieved party to abrogate the contract, it must be explicitly stated in the agreement of the parties. . . .

We are not persuaded that the liquidated damages outlined in the Apollo contracts were meant to apply to trivial breaches. Article 12 of the Lease Agreement states in unexceptional language that liquidated damages are to be awarded for a failure of "any of the covenants, agreements, terms or conditions." We take this language to refer to material breach. Absent a more explicit demonstration of intent to apply the termination provisions to trivial breaches, the liquidated damages clauses must be enforced.[2]

The parties to the contracts negotiated at arms length and without misinformation. Since summary judgment is rendered appropriately when there exists no genuine issue as to any material fact, Fed.R.Civ.P. 56(c), the district court was correct to enforce the liquidated damages clauses by summary judgment. See Katz v. Goodyear Tire & Rubber Co., 737 F.2d 238, 244 (2d Cir.1984). * * *

Leeber v. Deltona Corp.

Supreme Judicial Court of Maine, 1988.
546 A.2d 452.

■ CLIFFORD, JUSTICE.

Defendants, The Deltona Corporation and Marco Surfside, Inc., appeal from a judgment for the plaintiffs, Donald A. Leeber, Jeremy Morton and Jan Drewry, on Count I of their complaint entered in the Superior Court, Cumberland County, following a jury-waived trial. The plaintiffs cross-appeal from a judgment against them on the remaining two counts in their complaint.

This case arises out of a dispute involving a Florida real estate transaction. Defendant Marco Surfside, Inc., a wholly owned subsidiary of defendant The Deltona Corporation,[1] was the developer of a condominium real estate development on Marco Island in Florida. The plaintiffs, Portland area residents, decided to invest as a group in one of the condominium units being constructed by Deltona. On May 14, 1980, the plaintiffs, dealing with defendant Maine–Florida Properties, the exclusive sales agent in

2. Professor Corbin writes that in a case where the liquidated damages specified in the contract are a reasonable estimate of the injury actually caused, but would not have been so for injuries caused by other possible breaches, and the extent of the injury is difficult to estimate, the liquidated damages clause should be enforced. 5 Corbin on Contracts § 1066, at 383–84.

1. Because Marco Surfside and Deltona have acted as one entity during this litigation and at all other relevant times, they will frequently be treated as one entity in this opinion and will be referred to collectively as "Deltona."

Maine for Deltona, signed a Subscription and Purchase Agreement ("the Agreement") to buy a condominium unit in the Marco Island project, designated as unit 711. The price for the unit was $150,200, with 15% of this amount, $22,530, paid at the time the Agreement was signed and the balance due at the closing date, to be specified by Deltona within four years from the time of the Agreement. Under the express terms of the Agreement, the $22,530 was to be retained by Deltona as liquidated damages in the event of a breach by the plaintiffs.

Beginning in May 1982, Deltona notified the plaintiffs several times that they would be required to close on the condominium on certain dates or the liquidated damages deposit would be retained by Deltona. After each notice, the plaintiffs were able to obtain an extension from Deltona. Deltona sent the plaintiffs a final closing notice on July 8, 1982, which set a closing date of July 20, 1982. The July 8 letter advised the plaintiffs that the Agreement would be canceled if they did not close on unit 711. The plaintiffs did not close on the July 20 date. On July 27, 1982, Deltona informed the plaintiffs in writing that the Agreement had been canceled and the liquidated damages deposit would be retained by Deltona. Deltona then sold unit 711 to another party on July 31, 1982, for what the trial court found to be $167,500.[2] That party paid a 15% deposit of $25,125.

Deltona refused to return the plaintiffs' deposit, and this suit was initiated in the Superior Court. Plaintiffs' complaint contained three counts: Count I, directed against Deltona and Marco Surfside, alleged that the liquidated damages provision was unenforceable. * * *

At the close of the plaintiffs' evidence in the nonjury trial in this case, the trial justice granted the defendants' motion for dismissal with respect to Counts II and III * * *. As to Count I, the trial justice determined that the enforcement of the liquidated damages provision was unconscionable. The trial justice found that Deltona had proved it incurred actual damages consisting of some administrative costs and a $5,704 commission paid to Maine–Florida from the deposit and awarded plaintiffs $15,020—the balance of the deposit. * * * Defendants Deltona and Marco Surfside then appealed on Count I to this court in timely fashion. The plaintiffs cross-appealed on Counts II and III. We vacate the judgment as to Count I of the complaint, and affirm as to Counts II and III.

I.

The defendants contend that the liquidated damages provision in the Agreement was valid and enforceable under Florida law.[3] The Agreement provided for the retention by Deltona of the 15% deposit in the event of a breach of the Agreement on the part of the plaintiffs. The validity of a liquidated damages clause is assessed in the following way under Florida law:

2. The Superior Court rejected the contention of defendants that the actual resale price was $150,000.

3. All parties agree with the determination of the trial justice that Florida law controls the substantive issue of liquidated damages.

> If the damages are ascertainable on the date of the contract, the clause is a penalty and unenforceable; if they are not so ascertainable, the clause is truly one for liquidated damages and enforceable; however, if subsequent circumstances demonstrate it would be unconscionable to allow the seller to retain the sum in question as liquidated damages, equity may relieve against the forfeiture.

Bruce Builders, Inc. v. Goodwin, 317 So.2d 868, 869–70 (Fla.Dist.Ct. App.1975); . . .

The plaintiffs do not dispute that damages were not ascertainable at the time the Agreement was entered into. Thus, the issue placed before us in this case is whether the Superior Court erred in its determination that retention of money by the sellers under an otherwise valid liquidated damage provision was unconscionable under the standard set out in *Bruce Builders.*

A determination of unconscionability cannot be made unless the circumstances of the case truly "shock the conscience" of the court. . . . The factual findings upon which the conclusion of unconscionability is based are reviewed on a clearly erroneous basis. . . .

Under Florida law, if the liquidated damages provision is not a penalty, it is enforceable unless the plaintiff proves the existence of one or more of the following factors:

> (1) an intimation of fraud on the seller's part; (2) misfortune beyond his control accounting for the buyer's failure to fulfill the contract; (3) a mutual rescission of the contract; or (4) a benefit to the seller "the retention of which [when compared to the total contract price would be] shocking to the conscience of the court."

Johnson v. Wortzel, 517 So.2d 42, 43 (Fla.Dist.Ct.App.1987) (per curiam) (alteration by court in *Johnson* opinion) (quoting Beatty, 49 So.2d at 82).[4] Here, there was no showing of fraud on Deltona's part, nor evidence that plaintiffs' failure to buy was caused by misfortune beyond their control, nor evidence of mutual rescission. Only Deltona's retention of $22,530, 15% of the purchase price, examined under a "shocking to the conscience" standard, is properly considered by the court. Id.

---

4. Plaintiffs cite Multitech Corp. v. St. Johns Bluff Inv. Corp., 518 So.2d 427, 433 (Fla.Dist.Ct.App.1988), for the proposition that another factor to be considered in an unconscionability analysis under Florida law is "whether or not the sellers actually suffered any damage as a result of the breach." We are reluctant to accept this as a valid factor for assessing unconscionability under Florida law. The *Multitech* court, only one of several District Courts of Appeal in Florida, failed to cite any precedent for that holding and we can find no case decided by Florida's highest court, the Florida Supreme Court, that incorporates this factor. Moreover, to routinely allow such a consideration in determining unconscionability would unduly undermine one of the purposes of liquidated damages, namely to avoid the difficulties and uncertainties of proof of actual damages. Restatement (Second) of Contracts § 356 comment a (1981); 5 A. Corbin, Corbin on Contracts §§ 1054, 1062 (1964). See Dairy Farm Leasing Co., Inc. v. Hartley, 395 A.2d 1135, 1139 (Me.1978). In any event, *Multitech* is distinguishable from the instant case because the court found unconscionability in a case where the liquidated damage amount was $120,000 and the seller suffered no damage.

Liquidated damages are favored under Florida law, Hutchison, 259 So.2d at 132, and Florida courts have uniformly viewed liquidated damage sums in the range of 15% as reasonable. Wortzel, 517 So.2d at 43 (18.2% not unconscionable); . . .

The Superior Court, despite its recitation that it found defendants' retention of the liquidated damages to be unconscionable, did not apply a true "shock the conscience" standard in overriding the liquidated damage provision in this case. The court considered the fact of the resale of the condominium unit by Deltona several days after the default but several months after the originally designated closing date, and allowed the plaintiff buyers to recover from Deltona all of the previously paid deposit except what Deltona convinced the court were its actual out of pocket losses resulting from plaintiffs' breach.[5] Such an approach nullified the effect of the liquidated damages provision and made this case indistinguishable from one of ordinary breach of contract. This result undercut the traditional role of liquidated damages provisions, which have always served as an economical alternative to the costly and lengthy litigation involved in a conventional breach of contract action. Restatement (Second) of Contracts § 356 comment a (1981); 5 A. Corbin, Corbin on Contracts §§ 1054, 1062 (1964). See Dairy Farm Leasing Co., Inc. v. Hartley, 395 A.2d 1135, 1139 (Me. 1978).

Efforts by contracting parties to avoid litigation and to equitably resolve potential conflicts through the mechanism of liquidated damages should be encouraged. . . . Prompt resale of real estate units by sellers upon breach of contract by buyers likewise should be encouraged. However, the Superior Court ruling in this case, if allowed to stand, would have the opposite effect.

Florida law provides that, under a real estate contract containing a liquidated damages clause similar in language to the instant contract, sellers are denied the remedy of specific performance. . . . Moreover, their damage recovery is limited to the liquidated damage amount. . . . Buyers breaching such contracts, not being subject to specific performance nor to liability for excess damages should the sellers' losses exceed the amount of liquidated damages, would have nothing to lose in challenging the amount of liquidated damages retained or sought to be recovered by the sellers in every case where the buyers suspected the actual losses of the sellers to be less than the liquidated damage amount.

Under Florida law, the determination of the unconscionability of allowing a seller to retain liquidated damages under an otherwise valid liquidated damage provision should be based on the circumstances existent "at the time of breach." Hutchinson, 259 So.2d at 132.[6] A case of liquidated

---

5. The court was unpersuaded by evidence presented by defendants that plaintiffs' delays in closing the transaction resulted in substantial losses to defendants.

6. Some states, including Maine, measure the soundness of a liquidated damage provision as of the time the contract is made and not at the time of the breach. Dairy Farm Leasing, 395 A.2d at 1137; Walter F.

damages, when the liquidated damage amount is not unreasonable on its face, is not converted as a matter of course to one of ordinary breach of contract by the seller's fortuitous resale of the contract real estate subsequent to the buyer's breach. Sellers are inescapably bound by the liquidated damage provisions in such contracts. Buyers should be bound as well unless the plaintiff proves that the circumstances are so extraordinary that the sellers' retention of the liquidated damage amount would truly shock the conscience of the court. Beatty, 49 So.2d at 82.

It is undisputed that this liquidated damage amount of $22,530, 15% of the total contract price of the Florida real estate, was reasonable on its face and not a penalty. The retention of that sum by the sellers in this case, when plaintiff buyers delayed closing on the project for several months before breaching the contract, and sellers subsequently were able to resell the real estate through their own efforts and in doing so reduced their actual losses flowing from plaintiffs' breach, is not so extraordinary or unfair as to shock the conscience of the court. Id. The plaintiffs having failed to demonstrate circumstances sufficiently extraordinary to meet the shock the conscience test of Beatty, defendants must be allowed to retain the liquidated damage amount.

* * *

NOTES

(1) In Lake Ridge Academy v. Carney, 66 Ohio St.3d 376, 613 N.E.2d 183 (Ohio 1993), the court, in upholding a clause in a school "reservation agreement" that imposed liability for full tuition if the reservation were not canceled before a stated date, used a three point step to determine whether the parties had agreed upon liquidated damages or a penalty: "Where the parties have agreed on the amount of damages, ascertained by estimation and adjustment, and have expressed this agreement in clear and unambiguous terms, the amount so fixed should be treated as liquidated damages and not as a penalty, if the damages would be (1) uncertain as to amount and difficult of proof, and if (2) the contract as a whole is not so manifestly unconscionable, unreasonable, and disproportionate in amount as to justify the conclusion that it does not express the true intention of the parties, and if (3) the contract is consistent with the conclusion that it was the intention of the parties that damages in the amount stated should follow the breach thereof." 613 N.E.2d at 188. Is this helpful?

(2) For recent cases enforcing liquidated damage clauses, see Metlife Capital Fin. Corp. v. Washington Ave. Associates, L. P., 159 N.J. 484, 732 A.2d 493 (1999) (in commercial loan, 5.5% late charge and 12.5% default rate reasonable liquidated damages); Wallace Real Estate Investment, Inc. v.

Heller & Co. v. American Flyers Airline Corp., 459 F.2d 896, 898 (2d Cir.1972) (N.Y. law); Pembroke v. Gulf Oil Corp., 454 F.2d 606, 611 (5th Cir.1971) (La. law); Babbitt Ford, Inc. v. Navajo Indian Tribe, 519 F.Supp. 418, 432 (D.Ariz.1981); Monsen Eng'g Co. v. Tami–Githens, Inc., 219 N.J.Super. 241, 530 A.2d 313 318–19 (App.Div. 1987).

Groves, 124 Wash.2d 881, 881 P.2d 1010 (1994)(payment of $15,000 for each 30 day delay); Reliance Insurance Co. v. Utah Department of Transportation, 858 P.2d 1363 (Utah 1993)(liquidated damages for delay in construction contract).

Comment: Disclaimer, Exculpation and Under-Liquidated Damage Clauses

A careful distinction must be drawn between clauses that disclaim or exculpate liability from specified conduct, such as an alleged breach or warranty or negligence, and clauses that vary or limit remedies for that conduct.

A good example of the former are clauses in contracts for the sale of goods where the seller attempts to disclaim liability if the goods are not merchantable, see UCC 2–314, or are unfit for the buyer's particular purposes, see UCC 2–315. These implied warranty disclaimers are enforceable if the disclosure requirements of UCC 2–316 (i.e., conspicuous language) are satisfied and, in effect, put the risk of product quality on the buyer. Another example is contract clauses purporting to exculpate one party from the consequences of negligence. These clauses are enforceable in commercial contracts if they clearly and conspicuously set out the purpose of the drafter. See, e.g., Neville Chemical Co. v. Union Carbide Corp., 422 F.2d 1205 (3d Cir.1970); Mayfair Fabrics v. Henley, 48 N.J. 483, 226 A.2d 602 (1967); Goldman v. Ecco–Phoenix Electric Corp., 62 Cal.2d 40, 41 Cal.Rptr. 73, 396 P.2d 377 (1964) (indemnification clause). See Gates Rubber Co. v. USM Corp., 508 F.2d 603 (7th Cir.1975) (valid exculpation need not mention negligence). The exculpation effort may, however, be against public policy when attempted by a party who is "under a public duty entailing the exercise of care," such as common carriers or public utilities, or is in a position of superior bargaining power, such as a hospital exacting a release from an entering patient, Mayfair Fabrics v. Henley, supra, 226 A.2d at 605, or a landlord exculpating itself from the duty of care in an apartment lease.

An example of the latter are clauses that provide an exclusive, limited remedy upon breach or attempt to exclude or limit liability for consequential damages resulting from a breach. See UCC 2–719. A subtle form of exculpation or exclusion takes the form of a liquidated damage clause which, in effect, states a limit almost always under the amount of actual damage caused by negligence or breach of contract. A classic example is the case where one party agrees to install and maintain, in connection with the telephone company, a system designed promptly to detect and report fires or burglary. If there is defective equipment or negligent maintenance, the delay in reporting the critical event can contribute to substantial loss of life, property and economic opportunity. These contracts invariably contain a clause providing some limitation, such as if the contractor "should be found liable for loss or damage due to a failure of service in any respect, its liability shall be limited to a sum equal to ten percent of the annual service charge or $250, whichever is the greater." If the contractor is negligent and this negligence causes losses of, say, $50,000, will the limitation clause be enforced?

The answer appears to be yes. In California, the issue has been treated as involving liquidated damages and the limitation has been enforced under Cal.Civ.Code §§ 1670 & 1671. In New York, the clause is treated as an effort to limit liability rather than to liquidate damages and is enforced where the limitation is conspicuous and the other party could have obtained "more coverage ... for a negotiable fee." See Melodee Lane Lingerie Co. v. American District Telephone Co., 18 N.Y.2d 57, 271 N.Y.S.2d 937, 218 N.E.2d 661 (1966). If the other party has a choice to pay more for greater protection and selects less, it would be "unfair to hold the defendant liable for the grossly disproportionate losses sustained by the plaintiff." Rinaldi & Sons v. Wells Fargo Alarm Service, 47 A.D.2d 462, 367 N.Y.S.2d 518, 522 (1975). In New Jersey, such limitations are not *per se* against public policy and will be enforced if conscionable at the time of contracting. Abel Holding Co., Inc. v. American District Telephone Co., 138 N.J.Super. 137, 350 A.2d 292 (Law Div.1975). When all is said and done, which approach do you prefer? Does it matter whether insurance against the risk is available at a reasonable cost?

Note that Revised UCC 2–718(1) attempts a clarification by stating: "Section 2–719 determines the enforceability of a term that limits but does not liquidate damages." Thus, UCC 2–718(1) would govern where the parties attempted to liquidate damages that turned out to be less than actual damages and UCC 2–719(3) would govern where the parties, without any effort to liquidate, agreed that consequential damages shall not exceed $100.

PROBLEM: THE CASE OF THE "BIG SHIP" DEAL

Big Sugar Company, owner of a sugar plantation in Hawaii, was in need of a ship to transport "raw sugar," the crushed cane in the form of coarse brown crystal, from the islands to the mainland. Sugar is a seasonal crop, and Big Sugar had storage capacity in Hawaii for no more than a quarter of the crop. It was, therefore, imperative to have assured transportation. To this end, Big Sugar entered into extensive negotiations with Tall Ships, Inc. for the construction and sale of a ship specially designed for this purpose. Eventually, the parties executed a written contract for a sale of such a ship for $24,000,000. The agreed delivery date was April 30, with a provision for payment by Tall Ships of $17,000 for each day's unexcused delay in delivery.

The ship was not delivered until October 30, some 150 days late. Fortunately for Big Sugar, it was able to avoid catastrophic losses by utilizing older equipment and renting from others. A fair estimate of the loss actually caused by Tall Ship's breach is $250,000.

(A) What, if anything, should Big Sugar recover from Tall Ships? Cf. California and Hawaiian Sugar Co. v. Sun Ship, Inc., 794 F.2d 1433 (9th Cir.1986).

(B) Suppose that Big Sugar's actual losses, after reasonable efforts to mitigate damages, was $7,500,000. What, if anything, should Big Sugar recover from Tall Ships?

(C) Suppose that at the time of contracting, Tall Ships had stated, "We don't care about estimating actual damages if we breach. We won't pay more than $5,000 per day under any circumstances." Big Sugar agreed to a clause limiting the per diem liability to $5,000. If Big Sugar's actual loss was $17,000, what if anything can be recovered?

(B) AGREED REMEDIES

Through proper use of a liquidated damage clause the parties may fashion their own remedy. UCC 2–718(1) prescribes the Code standards. There are, in addition, other ways in which the parties may attempt to settle in advance what the remedy is to be in the event of breach. They might, for example, provide that in the event of breach the seller's obligation is to repair or replace the goods. The applicable Code provision is Section 2–719, which provides as follows:

(1) Subject to the provisions of subsection (2) and (3) of this section and of the preceding section on liquidation and limitation of damages,

(a) the agreement may provide for remedies in addition to or in substitution for those provided in this Article and may limit or alter the measure of damages recoverable under this Article, as by limiting the buyer's remedies to return of the goods and repayment of the price or to repair and replacement of non-conforming goods or parts; and

(b) resort to a remedy as provided is optional unless the remedy is expressly agreed to be exclusive, in which case it is the sole remedy.

(2) Where circumstances cause an exclusive or limited remedy to fail of its essential purpose, remedy may be had as provided in this Act.

(3) Consequential damages may be limited or excluded unless the limitation or exclusion is unconscionable. Limitation of consequential damages for injury to the person in the case of consumer goods is prima facie unconscionable but limitation of damages where the loss is commercial is not.

The materials which follow deal with aspects of this "agreed remedy" problem. See also, Chapter Five, Section 2(C)(2). There are no revisions in UCC 2–719 in Revised Article 2.

Lewis Refrigeration Co. v. Sawyer Fruit, Vegetable And Cold Storage Co.

United States Court of Appeals, Sixth Circuit, 1983.
709 F.2d 427.

■ NEWBLATT, DISTRICT JUDGE.

I FACTS

This is an appeal in a diversity action originally brought on March 18, 1974 by Lewis Refrigeration Co. (hereinafter Lewis) against Sawyer Fruit,

Vegetable and Cold Storage Cooperative Co. (hereinafter Sawyer). Lewis sued Sawyer to collect a balance allegedly due under an agreement in which Lewis sold Sawyer a freezer. Sawyer counterclaimed against Lewis asserting counts of breach of contract, breach of warranty and misrepresentation.

The case arose out of a 1970 contract between Sawyer and Lewis. The contract provided for Lewis to sell Sawyer an individually quick-frozen freezer. The typed portion of the contract covered contract pages 2–7; the printed portion covered contract pages 7–12.

The typed portion of the contract contained warranties that the freezer was capable of processing six thousand pounds of various fruits per hour and that the freezer would use no more than 1.8 liquid pounds of Freon per one hundred pounds of frozen products. Paragraph 6A of the typewritten portion of the contract contained a clause setting out a guarantee obligating Lewis to supply, for a given period of time, the Freon that the freezer consumed over the warranted rate. Paragraph B3 of the printed portion of the agreement provided that, in the event the machine failed to perform at the warranted rates, Lewis would have the right to repair or replace promptly the malfunctioning part of the machine. Paragraph B3 provided that rescission was the only other available remedy.

Terms

In addition to paragraph B3, the contract contained another remedy limitation. This limitation, found at paragraph B4 of the handwritten portion of the contract, excluded consequential damages.

CD excluded

A consent judgment eventually was entered in favor of Lewis for the claim for the balance due on the contract. Trial on Sawyer's counterclaim began on April 4, 1978. After denying Lewis's motions for a directed verdict and for judgment notwithstanding the verdict, the district court instructed and then sent the case to the jury. A verdict was returned for Sawyer in the amount of $25,823 in lost profits and $27,080 in excess Freon costs.

initial dec. for π → but Dc found for Δ

In this appeal, Lewis advances four arguments: (1) the district court erroneously allowed the jury to consider whether, under the state of Washington version of UCC § 2–719(2), the paragraph B3 repair and rescission limitation failed its essential purpose; (2) the district court erred by not generally disallowing consequential damages in favor of benefit of the bargain damages under Washington's version of UCC § 2–714(2); (3) the district court should have granted a new trial on the ground that Sawyer failed to amend and supplement discovery responses as required by Rule 26(e)(2) of the Federal Rules of Civil Procedure; (4) the district court erroneously omitted making a judicial determination of whether the B3 consequential damages exclusion was unconscionable—in the absence of such a determination the consequential damages exclusion should have blocked the jury from awarding consequential damages.

π's Appeal

1) Dc erred on UCC – 2-719 2

2) should have used 2-714(2)

3) New Trial

4) CD should have been excluded b/c it wasn't UN-c

We shall now consider each of the four arguments advanced by Lewis. For the reasons to follow, we affirm the district court as to the first three arguments and vacate and remand as to the fourth argument.

II LEGAL ANALYSIS

A.   Failure of Repair and Rescission Remedy to Achieve its Essential Purpose.

The first argument raised by Lewis involves the district court's treatment of RCW § 62A.2–719(2), the state of Washington's statutory version of UCC § 2–719(2). The statute provides:

"Where circumstances cause an exclusive or limited remedy to fail of its essential purpose, remedy may be had as provided in this Title."

Lewis argues that the district court erroneously allowed the jury to reach the issue of whether the paragraph B3 repair and rescission exclusive remedy failed its essential purpose as described in section 2–719(2). Lewis contends that its motions for directed verdict and judgment notwithstanding the verdict should have been granted as to the issue of the repair and rescission remedy barring the award of any other damages. Lewis thus urges us to vacate the jury's verdict to the extent that it includes $25,823 in lost profit consequential damages.

In opposing this argument, Sawyer contends that it presented enough evidence to permit a reasonable fact finder to determine that the exclusive remedy contractual provision failed its essential purpose. In deciding this issue, we shall separately consider the repair and rescission portions of the exclusive remedy.

Lewis appears to concede that the repair remedy failed its essential purpose. . . . We agree. In any event, there can be no doubt but that the record contains trial evidence adequate to support the conclusion that Lewis was unable to repair promptly the freezer to meet performance warranties. . . .

Furthermore, we note that Washington appellate decisions clearly hold that a seller's inability to repair fully a product causes the repair and rescission remedy to fail of its essential purpose under RCW 62A.2–719(2). . . . We thus conclude that a jury could reasonably have determined that the repair remedy failed its essential purpose under section 2–719(2).

A much closer question obtains with respect to the rescission remedy. Sawyer contends that the jury could reasonably have determined that the rescission remedy failed its essential purpose because of either of the following two reasons: (1) Lewis would have been extremely reluctant to rescind the transaction or (2) Sawyer would have experienced severe financial loss in the event the contract was rescinded.

Sawyer's first contention must be rejected outright. The section 2–719(2) "essential purpose" language refers to circumstances that make it exceedingly impractical to carry out the essence of an agreed-upon remedy. Given that Lewis had categorically refused to rescind the transaction, the rescission provision could have been enforced in a court action, and thus the essence of the remedy could have been carried out.

As to the rescission remedy, Sawyer contends that there was enough evidence in the record to permit a reasonable jury to conclude that Lewis deliberately concealed the machine's inability to meet cherry processing warranties until sometime in 1972. By this time, Sawyer contends, it had made significant commitments with respect to frozen products. Sawyer further asserts that rescission and the concomitant removal of the freezer in 1972 would have been financially destructive in that it would have caused Sawyer to lose revenues and breach important commitments.

Having studied the record below, we believe that there was adequate evidence to support Sawyer's version as set out above. Letters and trial testimony indicate that Lewis was either unable or reluctant to promptly and effectively administer performance tests on the cherries. This well could have prevented Sawyer from making an intelligent decision on rescission until 1972, by which time Sawyer had made numerous frozen product commitments. . . .

We believe it was appropriate for the jury to consider these circumstances in connection with the issue of whether the rescission remedy failed of its essential purpose. Washington cases hold that an exclusive remedy fails its essential purpose where a conceded defect is not detectable until it is impractical to effectuate the exclusive remedy. While the latent defect theory is most often applied in cases involving the repair remedy, and while the facts of this case are not nearly as strong as Sawyer seems to believe, we find that it was not erroneous for the district court to allow the jury to consider whether Lewis concealed the facts until such time as a rescission would have caused severe financial damages to Sawyer. And given that this factual version was true, it was within the ambit of section 2–719(2) for the jury to find that the rescission remedy failed of its essential purpose. Thus, we reject appellant's contention that the district court erred by allowing the jury to consider the evidence in this case as applied to the issue of whether the repair and rescission remedy failed its essential purpose under RCW 62A.2–719(2).

B. Lewis's General Argument Against Consequential Damages.

Lewis next contends that, assuming arguendo that the repair and rescission remedy failed of its essential purpose, the district court should generally have prohibited the jury from awarding consequential damages. This argument is bottomed on Lewis's apparent belief that damages in breach of warranty actions are confined to the benefit of the bargain measure of damages set out in RCW 62A.2–714(2).

This contention is patently incorrect. RCW 62A.2–714(3) authorizes consequential damages in appropriate cases. RCW 62A.2–715(2) then provides that consequential damages from a seller's breach include losses reasonably foreseeable that cannot be mitigated by cover.

Cover is not an issue in this appeal. And since there is a good deal of evidence in the record indicating that the freezer was to be an important part of Lewis's production, we conclude that a reasonable jury easily could have determined that Lewis should have foreseen that its breach of warranty would cause consequential damages. ... Thus, it certainly was not erroneous for the district court to not generally preclude damages for lost profits.

C.   Sawyer's Failure to Supplement Discovery Responses.

[The Court rejected Lewis' argument for a new trial based on alleged discovery abuses of Sawyer.]

D.   District Court's Failure to Make a Separate Determination of Unconscionability Under RCW § 62A.2–719(3).

Lewis's final argument centers on the district court's treatment of the paragraph B4 exclusion of consequential damages. This paragraph excludes consequential damages apparently under the authority of RCW 62A.2–719(3), the Washington version of UCC § 2–719(3). RCW 62A.2–719(3) provides in pertinent part:

> Limitation of consequential damages for injury to the person in the case of goods purchased primarily for personal, family or household use or of any services related thereto is invalid unless it is proved that the limitation is not unconscionable ... Limitation of other consequential damages is valid unless it is established that the limitation is unconscionable."

The district court did not give a separate instruction on the paragraph B4 consequential damages exclusion. Instead, the district court merely instructed that lost profits could be awarded.

> "if you find that circumstances not caused by Sawyer Fruit ... caused the exclusion of lost profits to deprive Sawyer Fruit of the substantial value of its bargain under the Agreement." ...

Apparently, the district court believed that if the jury determined that the exclusive repair and rescission remedy failed of its essential purpose, the exclusion of consequential damages provision automatically became unconscionable under section 2–719(3). Alternatively, the district court may have believed that the "remedy may be had as provided in the act" phrase of RCW 62A.2–719(2) authorizes all UCC damages—including consequential damages—upon a finding of unconscionability.

While a number of courts have taken the general approach of the district court, a larger number of courts—including the Courts of Appeals of the Third and Ninth Circuits—have construed subsection (3) of UCC 2–719 as the governing provision on the issue of consequential damages. We believe that this is the correct approach.

In arriving at this conclusion, we are mindful that Washington law governs this case. And while the Washington appellate courts have not squarely decided this issue, it is notable that in 1955 the Washington

Supreme Court indicated that analogous provisions in the Uniform Sales Act should be dealt with separately and distinctly. See Ketel v. Hovich, 47 Wash.2d 368, 287 P.2d 739 (1955). Furthermore, for several reasons, we believe that sound statutory construction leads to the conclusion that subsection (3) of RCW 62A.2–719 must be viewed as the governing provision on the issue of consequential damages exclusion.

In this respect it should first be noted that, absent the specific language of subsection (3), the general language of subsection (2) would seem to cover the issue of consequential damages. Since it is a basic principle of statutory construction that the particular governs over the general, we believe that the section 2–719 drafters intended subsection (3) to deal with the issue of consequential damages.

Second, the distinctly different substantive content of subsections (2) and (3) must be considered. Subsection (2) turns on the failure of essential purpose; subsection (3) turns on a judicial determination of unconscionability. Unconscionability deals with grossly unequal bargaining power at the time of the contracts formation. As numerous decisions have pointed out, unconscionability rarely exists unless the buyer is a consumer. Indeed, the consumer orientation of subsection (3) is reflected in the subsection's different allocations of proof. Where the transaction involves a consumer buyer, the limitation is prima facie unconscionable. Where the transaction does not involve a consumer, however, the exclusion of consequential damages is not prima facie unconscionable.

Thus, subsection (3) is a powerful provision designed to protect against abuse of consumers in contract formation. The Official UCC comment to UCC 2–719(3) indicates, however, that another basic purpose of subsection (3) is to allow merchants to allocate business risks. This purpose is consonant with the general UCC philosophy of freedom in commercial transactions. Taking these two statutory policies together, we believe that section 2–719(3) is meant to allow freedom in excluding consequential damages unless a consumer is involved in the contract. This freedom would be abridged by the sweeping interpretation of subsection (2) applied by the district court.

We thus hold that the district court had an obligation to take evidence and then determine whether the consequential damages exclusion clause was unconscionable. In the absence of an unconscionability determination, the district court should have allowed the paragraph B2 consequential damages exclusion to stand. Accordingly, we must vacate the portion of the judgment reflecting the jury's award of $25,283 in lost profits and remand this case to the district court for a judicial determination of whether the consequential damages exclusion clause was unconscionable. In the event the district court determines that the consequential damages clause was not unconscionable, the jury's award of $25,823 in lost profits must be voided."*

---

* The jury's award of $27,080 in Freon costs should not be disturbed even if the consequential damages limitation is upheld. This is because the Freon costs are incidental

III CONCLUSION AND ORDER

We hereby affirm the district court as to the issues discussed in Parts IIA–IIC of the foregoing Opinion. We hereby Vacate the jury's award of $25,823 in lost profits and Remand to the district court for the reasons stated in Part IID of this Opinion. On remand, the district court is to conduct the proceedings specified in part IID of this Opinion.

NOTES

(1) *Integral Part of Commercial Warranty Package.* A clause attempting to exclude liability for consequential damages is an integral part of a commercial warranty package which (1) *gives* the buyer an express warranty that the goods are free from defects in material and workmanship, (2) *disclaims* all other warranties, express or implied, (3) *limits* the remedy for breach of the express warranty to repair or replacement of the defective part or workmanship, and (4) *excludes* consequential damages from the scope of liability. This "package" is supported by the UCC, see UCC 2–313(1), 2–316, 2–719(1) & 2–719(3).

The recurring question (dozens of cases have tried to resolve it) is the fate of the excluder clause in the package when the limited remedy fails of its essential purpose. Unless the contract clearly states that the excluder depends upon the availability of the limited remedy (i.e., you don't get your excluder unless I get my limited remedy), most courts have interpreted UCC 2–719 to separate the excluder from the package. Thus, the buyer might get damages from the seller under UCC 2–714 but not consequential damages unless the excluder was unconscionable under UCC 2–719(3). This is rare in commercial cases. See e.g. Rheem Mfg. Co. v. Phelps Heating & Air Conditioning, Inc., 746 N.E.2d 941 (Ind.2001); James J. White & Robert S. Summers, Uniform Commercial Code 449–466 (5th ed.2000)

(2) "NCR repeatedly attempted to correct the deficiencies in the system, but nevertheless still had not provided the product warranted a year and a half after Chatlos had reasonably expected a fully operational computer. In these circumstances, the delay made the correction remedy ineffective, and it therefore failed of its essential purpose. Consequently, the contractual limitation was unenforceable and did not preclude recovery of damages for the breach of warranty.

"This conclusion, however, does not dispose of the contractual clause excluding consequential damages. * * *

"Several cases have held that when a limited remedy fails of its purpose, an exclusion of consequential damages also fails, but approximately the same number of decisions have treated that preclusion as a separate matter. * * *

"It appears to us that the better reasoned approach is to treat the consequential damage disclaimer as an independent provision, valid unless unconscionable. This poses no logical difficulties. A contract may well contain no limitation on breach of warranty damages but specifically exclude conse-

damages rather than consequential damages. See Lewis v. Mobil Oil Corp., 438 F.2d 500 (C.A.8, 1971). See generally White & Sum-mers, *Uniform Commercial Code,* pp. 312–314.

quential damages. Conversely, it is quite conceivable that some limitation might be placed on a breach of warranty award, but consequential damages would expressly be permitted.

"The limited remedy of repair and a consequential damages exclusion are two discrete ways of attempting to limit recovery for breach of warranty. . . . The Code, moreover, tests each by a different standard. The former survives unless it fails of its essential purpose, while the latter is valid unless it is unconscionable. We therefore see no reason to hold, as a general proposition, that the failure of the limited remedy provided in the contract, without more, invalidates a wholly distinct term in the agreement excluding consequential damages. The two are not mutually exclusive.

"Whether the preclusion of consequential damages should be effective in this case depends upon the circumstances involved. The repair remedy's failure of essential purpose, while a discrete question, is not completely irrelevant to the issue of the conscionability of enforcing the consequential damages exclusion. The latter term is 'merely an allocation of unknown or undeterminable risks.' U.C.C. § 2–719, Official Comment 3, N.J.Stat.Ann. § 12A:2–719, at 537 (West 1962). Recognizing this, the question here narrows to the unconscionability of the buyer retaining the risk of consequential damages upon the failure of the essential purpose of the exclusive repair remedy.

"One fact in this case that becomes significant under the Code is that the claim is not for personal injury but for property damage. Limitations on damages for personal injuries are not favored, but no such prejudice applies to property losses. It is also important that the claim is for commercial loss and the adversaries are substantial business concerns. We find no great disparity in the parties' bargaining power or sophistication. Apparently, Chatlos, a manufacturer of complex electronic equipment, had some appreciation of the problems that might be encountered with a computer system. Nor is there a 'surprise' element present here. The limitation was clearly expressed in a short, easily understandable sales contract. This is not an instance of an ordinary consumer being misled by a disclaimer hidden in a 'linguistic maze. . . .'

"Thus, at the time the contract was signed there was no reason to conclude that the parties could not competently agree upon the allocation of risk involved in the installation of the computer system."

Chatlos Systems v. National Cash Register Corp., 635 F.2d 1081, 1086–87 (3d Cir.1980).

(3) Section 2–810(b) of the 1999 Draft of revised Article 2 proposed the following solution to the problems posed above:

(b) If, because of a breach of contract or other circumstances, an exclusive, agreed remedy fails substantially to achieve the intended purposes of the parties, the following rules apply:

(1) In a contract other than a consumer contract, the aggrieved party may resort to all remedies provided in this article, but an agreement expressly providing that consequential damages, including those resulting from the failure to provide the limited remedy, are excluded is enforceable to the extent permitted under subsection (c)

(2) In a consumer contract, an aggrieved party may reject the goods or revoke acceptance and, to the extent of the failure, may resort to all remedies provided in this article.

This revision does not appear in Revised UCC 2–719. Would the 1999 revision have clarified the confusion?

(4) Here is an example of a well drafted limited remedy package with an exclusion of consequential damages:

WARRANTY/LIMITATION OF LIABILITY

1. WARRANTY—The Corporation warrants that the equipment to be delivered will be of the kind and quality described in the order or contract [and] will be free of defects in workmanship or material. Should any failure to conform to this warranty appear within one year after the initial date of synchronization, the Corporation shall, upon notification thereof and substantiation that the equipment has been stored, installed, maintained and operated in accordance with the Corporation's recommendations and standard industry practice, correct such nonconformities, including nonconformance with the specifications, at its option, by suitable repair or replacement at the Corporation's expense. This warranty is in lieu of all warranties of merchantability, fitness for purpose, or other warranties, express or implied, except of title and against patent infringement. Correction of nonconformities, in the manner and for the period of time provided above, shall constitute fulfillment of all liabilities of the Corporation to the Purchaser, whether based on contract, negligence or otherwise with respect to, or arising out of such equipment.

2. LIMITATION OF LIABILITY—The Corporation shall not be liable for special, or consequential damages, such as, but not limited to, damage or loss of other property or equipment, loss of profits or revenue, loss of use of power system, cost of capital, cost of purchased or replacement power, or claims of customers of Purchaser for service interruption. The remedies of the Purchaser set forth herein are exclusive, and the liability of the Corporation with respect to any contract, or anything done in connection therewith such as the performance or breach thereof, or from the manufacture, sale, delivery, resale, installation or use of any equipment covered by or furnished under this contract whether in contract, in tort, under any warranty, or otherwise, shall not, except as expressly provided herein, exceed the price of the equipment or part on which such liability is based.

PROBLEM: THE CASE OF THE DISAPPOINTED FANS

A fervent group of Chicago Bears football fans, living in Chicago, decided to charter a bus to an NFL game between the Bears and the Packers, played that year at Champaign–Urbana, Illinois while Soldier Field was under renovation. "Rabid" Ron was authorized by the group to negotiate the charter. In negotiating the matter with Mr. Smith, president of the Reliable Transit Co. (and a "Cheese Head"), Ron stressed how important it was to his "fans" that they arrive in plenty of time for the game, that it would not be televised this year, this group was exceptionally "interested" in the rivalry and would be terribly disappointed if anything went wrong. In short, Ron stated that his group would want damages if a charter were arranged and the bus did not go. Mr. Smith stated that he would be glad to arrange the charter (there were six weeks to go) for a flat fee of $750, round trip, but that the usual practice was to expressly limit liability of the Company for failure "to go" to a return of any amount paid on the charter. This was unsatisfactory to Ron. After more negotiations and consultation with the other "fans," Ron made the following proposition to Smith: "Look, I've talked with my group and here's the way it is. We will pay you $1,500 for the charter if you will agree to pay us $15,000 as liquidated damages if, for any reason, the bus fails to go and we miss the game. We are willing to pay $750 extra to know that our disappointment will be well compensated if we don't go. Take it or leave it." Smith "took it" and an appropriate written contract was prepared which included the "liquidated damage" clause. The "group" paid $750 on the charter and were told to assemble at a specified point in Davis no later than 7:30 AM on game day. As by now you have suspected, the bus did not show at 7:30 AM or at anytime on game day. In fact, Smith chartered the bus to a group of Packers fans in the Chicago suburbs who paid $3,000 for the charter. By the time it was clear what had happened, it was not possible for Ron to arrange another method of transportation and none of the Bears fans saw the game (which turned out to be a blessing in disguise).

Ron has demanded $15,000 from Smith and been politely refused. Smith, however, did tender back to Ron the $750, which Ron, so far, has refused. Ron and a few of his fans are in your law office and have asked your assessment of their chances. What would you advise? See Charles Goetz and Robert Scott, *Liquidated Damages: Penalties and the Just Compensation Principle: Some Notes on an Enforcement Model and a Theory of Efficient Breach,* 77 Colum.L.Rev. 554 (1977).

CHAPTER EIGHT

CONTRACT DISPUTE RESOLUTION: SOME ALTERNATIVES TO COURTS

SECTION 1. THE LEGAL FRAMEWORK FOR SETTLEMENT

A variety of disputes may arise during the course of contract performance. Most involve one of more of the following: (1) the meaning of contract language; (2) the existence and effect of conditions; (3) the order and extent of the agreed exchange; (4) whether the contractor's performance conformed to the contract and promisee's permissible responses; (5) prospective inability to perform; (6) the responsibility for conduct by one party which prevents or hinders performance by the other or alters the character of the agreed exchange; and (7) the effect of unforeseen conditions or events which materially alter the ability or incentives of one party to perform.

In some cases, the aggrieved party may elect promptly to treat conduct by the other as a breach of contract, cancel the contract and seek affirmative remedies in the court. See Chapter Seven, Section 1. In other cases, some effort may be made by both parties to modify the contract by agreement. See Chapter Six, Section 4(C). In still others, a form of modification or adjustment from action or inaction by one party rather than a bilateral modification may occur. This conduct often answers to the name of "waiver" or "estoppel." In general, contract law both permits the parties considerable latitude for settlement and readily supports *bona fide* efforts to resolve disputes and complete the exchange.

Yet contract law, as such, has no direct contact with the dispute until settlement efforts break down and one party seeks judicial assistance by filing a lawsuit. One can only speculate how much the presence of contract law and courts actually influences behavior in the countless disputes which are settled, in one way or another, without formal adjudication or intervention by the legal system.*

---

* A few examples from Article 2 of the UCC illustrate how modern contract law supports and facilitates the process of private dispute settlement. First, as we have seen, a seller and buyer of goods have considerable latitude to fashion their own remedies by agreement, and this includes consent to commercial arbitration. See UCC 2–718 & 2–719. Second, it is fairly easy to achieve a binding modification by agreement. UCC 2–209(1) & 2–208(1). Third, uncertainty over whether cancellation requires a "material" breach and a lack of precision on the content of "materiality" tend to restrain precipitous cancellation and induce discussion. Fourth, in a number of situations an aggrieved party may properly suspend his or her own performance or elect to ignore a repudiation in the hope that uncertainty will be allayed, breach cured or repudiation retracted. See UCC 2–609(1); 2–612, comment 7; 2–610(a); 2–611(1). Fifth, in some cases a seller may

It is important, of course, to understand the extent to which efforts to adjust or settle contract disputes by agreement or otherwise will "stand up" in court. However, a vital function of the commercial lawyer may well be in the area of "preventive law." Put another way, the lawyer who by creative planning and drafting can avoid contract disputes and who by skillful negotiation can settle once they have arisen may perform a more valuable service for his client than the victorious litigator. See Louis Brown, *The Law Office—A Preventive Law Laboratory*, 104 U.Pa.L.Rev. 940 (1956).** Without question, modern lawyers will have more rather than less opportunity to put the skills of planner, negotiator and drafter to work. Litigation is costly, time consuming and often delays justice. It is a last-ditch recourse after a variety of nonlegal options and sanctions have broken down. See Harold Havighurst, The Nature of Private Contract 45–92 (1961).

In a similar vein, an influential study by Professor Stewart Macaulay reveals that business people and, to a lesser extent, their attorneys, pay little attention in planning and dispute settlement to the supposed sanctions for breach of contract imposed by courts. Often contract law is not needed because its functions are performed by other devices, e.g., both sides understand primary obligations, little room exists for honest misunderstanding, trade usage fills gaps, and sophisticated product testing can be accomplished. Similarly, informal sanctions or values in the trade substitute for those imposed by courts, e.g., commitments are to be honored, one "ought" to produce a good product and stand behind it, business is organized to perform not litigate and one desiring to remain in business will avoid conduct which might interfere with attaining this goal. Stewart Macaulay, *Non-Contractual Relations in Business: A Preliminary Study*, 28 Am.Soc.Rev. 55 (1963). See also James J. White, *Contract Law in Modern Commercial Transactions, An Artifact of Twentieth Century Business Life*, 22 Wash.L.J. 1 (1982).

But when careful planning and good faith settlement efforts fail,*** must the parties always go to court to obtain a final resolution of their

---

"cure" a breach of contract whether the buyer likes it or not. UCC 2–508(1). Finally, if contract rights or remedial claims have not been "waived" under UCC 2–209(5), they can be "discharged in whole or in part without consideration by a written waiver or renunciation signed and delivered by the aggrieved party." UCC 1–107. In short, these illustrations reflect a pervasive policy which supports and sometimes requires private efforts to settle disputes and complete the agreed exchange. As Chief Justice Peters put it: "[A]rticle 2 urges the contracting parties to engage in a continuing dialogue about what will constitute acceptable performance of their sales contract.... It is entirely consistent with this article 2 policy to provide, as

does [1–207], a statutory methodology for the effective communication of objections." County Fire Door Cop. v. C.F. Wooding Co., 202 Conn. 277, 520 A.2d 1028, 1035 (1987). See, generally, Robert Hillman, *Keeping the Deal Together After Material Breach—Common Law Mitigation Rules, the UCC and the Restatement (Second) of Contracts*, 47 U.Colo. L.Rev. 553 (1976).

** See also Macneil, *A Primer of Contract Planning*, 48 S.Cal.L.Rev. 627 (1975).

*** See Melvin Eisenberg, *Private Ordering through Negotiation: Dispute–Settlement and Rulemaking*, 89 Harv.L.Rev. 637 (1976); Lon L. Fuller, *Mediation—Its Forms and Functions*, 44 S.Cal.L.Rev. 305 (1971). See dispute? And if a lawsuit is filed, must every dispute proceed to a final judgment?

The answer to both questions, of course, is no. Increasingly, the parties to disputes are taking advantage of alternative practices and techniques for dispute resolution. A good working definition of alternative dispute resolution (ADR) has been suggested: "ADR is a set of practices and techniques that aim (1) to permit legal disputes to be resolved outside the courts for the benefit of all disputants; (2) to reduce the cost of conventional litigation and the delays to which it is ordinarily subject; or (3) to prevent legal disputes that would otherwise likely be brought to the courts." Lieberman & Henry, *Lessons From the Alternative Dispute Resolution Movement*, 53 U.Chi.L.Rev. 424, 425–26 (1986). But see Edward Brunet, *Questioning the Quality of Alternate Dispute Resolution*, 62 Tul.L.Rev. 1 (1987).

According to Eric Green, there are "primary" and "hybrid" dispute resolution processes. "Primary" processes include adjudication, arbitration, mediation and conciliation, and traditional negotiation. "Hybrid" processes include private judging, neutral expert fact finding, minitrial, and settlement conferences. Green, *A Comprehensive Approach to the Theory and Practice of Disputes Resolution*, 34 J.Legal Ed. 245 (1984). Except for adjudication in court, all other processes are, in large part, voluntary. Thus, consent is necessary and careful planning for dispute resolution is well advised.

In order to highlight the similarities and differences between "primary" and "hybrid" dispute resolution processes, we have reprinted with permission a chart prepared by Eric Green. See Green, supra, 34 J.Legal Ed. at 257–58.

"PRIMARY" DISPUTE RESOLUTION PROCESSES

ADJUDICATION	ARBITRATION	MEDIATION/ CONCILIATION	TRADITIONAL NEGOTIATION
Nonvoluntary	Voluntary unless contractual or court centered	Voluntary	Voluntary
Binding, subject to appeal	Binding (usually), no appeal	Nonbinding	Nonbinding (except through use of adjudication to enforce agreement)
Imposed, third-party neutral decision maker, with no specialized expertise in dispute subject	Party-selected third-party decision maker, usually with specialized subject expertise	Party-selected outside facilitator, often with specialized subject expertise	No third-party facilitator
Highly procedural; formalized and highly structured by predetermined, rigid rules	Procedurally less formal; procedural rules and substantive law may be set by parties	Usually informal, unstructured	Usually informal, unstructured

also, Robert Cover, *Foreward: Dispute Resolution*, 88 Yale L.J. 905, 910 (1979); Frank Sander, *Varieties of Dispute Processing*, 70 F.R.D. 111 (1976).

ADJUDICATION	ARBITRATION	MEDIATION/ CONCILIATION	TRADITIONAL NEGOTIATION
Opportunity for each party to present proofs supporting decision in its favor	Opportunity for each party to present proofs supporting decision in its favor	Presentation of proofs less important than attitudes of each party; may include principled argument	Presentation of proofs usually indirect or nonexistent; may include principled argument
Win/Lose result	Compromise result possible (probable?)	Mutually acceptable agreement sought	Mutually acceptable agreement sought
Expectation of reasoned statement	Reason for result not usually required	Agreement usually embodied in contract or release	Agreement usually embodied in contract or release
Process emphasizes attaining substantive consistency and predictability of results	Consistency and predictability balanced against concern for disputants' relationship	Emphasis on disputants' relationship, not on adherence to or development of consistent rules	Emphasis on disputants' relationship, not on adherence to or development of consistent rules
Public process: lack of privacy of submissions	Private process unless judicial enforcement sought	Private process	Highly private process

"HYBRID" DISPUTE RESOLUTION PROCESSES

PRIVATE JUDGING	NEUTRAL EXPERT FACT FINDING	MINITRIAL	SETTLEMENT CONFERENCE
Voluntary	Voluntary or nonvoluntary under FRE 706	Voluntary	Voluntary or mandatory
Binding but subject to appeal and possibly review by trial court	Nonbinding but results may be admissible	Nonbinding (except through use of adjudication to enforce agreement)	Binding or nonbinding
Party-selected third-party decision maker; may have to be former judge or lawyer	Third-party neutral with specialized subject matter expertise may be selected by the parties	Third-party neutral advisor with specialized subject expertise	Judge, other judge, or third-party neutral selected by parties
Statutory procedure (see, e.g., Cal.Code Civ. Proc. § 638 et seq.) but highly flexible as to timing, place and procedures	Informal	Less formal than adjudication and arbitration but procedural rules and scope of issues may be set by the parties and implemented by neutral advisor	Informal, off-the-record
Opportunity for each party to present proofs supporting decision in its favor	Investigatory	Opportunity and responsibility to present proofs supporting result in its favor	Presentation of proofs may or may not be allowed
Win/lose result (judgment of court)	Report or testimony	Mutually acceptable agreement sought	Mutually acceptable agreement sought; binding conference is similar to arbitration
Findings of fact and conclusions of law possible but not required	May influence result or settlement	Agreement usually embodied in contract or release	Agreement usually embodied in contract or release
Adherence to norms, laws and precedent	Emphasis on reliable fact determination	Emphasis on sound, cost-effective and fair resolution satisfactory to both parties	Emphasis on resolving the dispute
Private process unless judicial enforcement sought	May be highly private or discussed in court	Highly private process	Private process but may be discovered

SECTION 2.   AGREED SETTLEMENT OR DISCHARGE

(A) TWO PARTY AGREEMENTS

Douthwright v. Northeast Corridor Foundations

Appellate Court of Connecticut, 2002.
72 Conn.App. 319, 805 A.2d 157.

■ PETERS, J.

This case concerns the applicability of the doctrine of accord and satisfaction, a common-law doctrine that, for negotiable instruments such as checks, has now been codified in article three of the Uniform Commercial Code, General Statutes § 42a–3–311.* Invoking this doctrine, a debtor maintains that its belated payment of the principal amount of a debt discharged it of any obligation to pay interest on the debt because its payment check was accompanied by a letter stating that the check was tendered as an accord and satisfaction.

A precondition of an enforceable accord and satisfaction is that the tender of payment occur in the context of a good faith dispute about the amount of an unpaid debt. This was the rule at common law and, for checks, it is now the rule of § 42a–3–311 (a) . . . The trial court found that the debtor did not prove that it had satisfied this precondition because, at the time when the check was sent, the amount of the debt, both as to principal and as to interest, was liquidated and therefore not subject to a good faith dispute.

In its appeal, the debtor contests the validity of the court's refusal to apply the doctrine of accord and satisfaction. We, however, are persuaded that the court's decision is amply supported by the facts of record at trial. Accordingly, we affirm the judgment of the court ordering the payment of interest for the time between the accrual of the debt and the acceptance of the check.

On February 13, 2001, the plaintiff Vincent Douthwright filed a motion pursuant to General Statutes § 52–195c for a default judgment arising out of the failure of the named defendant et al. to pay their full share of an oral

---

* General Statutes § 42a–3–311 provides in relevant part: "Accord and satisfaction by use of instrument. (a) If a person against whom a claim is asserted proves that (i) that person in good faith tendered an instrument to the claimant as full satisfaction of the claim, (ii) the amount of the claim was unliquidated or subject to a bona fide dispute, and (iii) the claimant obtained payment of the instrument, the following subsections apply.

"(b) Unless subsection (c) applies, the claim is discharged if the person against whom the claim is asserted proves that the instrument or an accompanying written communication contained a conspicuous statement to the effect that the instrument was tendered as full satisfaction of the claim. . . .

"(d) A claim is discharged if the person against whom the claim is asserted proves that within a reasonable time before collection of the instrument was initiated, the claimant, or an agent of the claimant having direct responsibility with respect to the disputed obligation, knew that the instrument was tendered in full satisfaction of the claim."

settlement agreement. The agreement entitled the plaintiff to recover $3.2 million as settlement of his tort action to recover damages for serious injuries that he received when concrete pylons rolled off a truck and crushed his leg. Pursuant to the agreement, the defendants were obligated to pay $2.5 million of that sum. Although the defendants' primary insurer had paid $1 million, the defendants' excess insurance carrier had refused to pay the remaining $1.5 million.

The plaintiff sought a default judgment in the amount of $1.5 million plus interest. In response, on March 13, 2001, the defendants denied that the settlement agreement imposed upon them an obligation to pay the plaintiff immediately.

On March 26, 2001, the parties appeared before the court for an initial hearing on the motion for default.* Subsequent to that hearing, the defendants sent the plaintiff a check in the amount of $1.5 million, accompanied by a cover letter. The amount of the check represented the principal sum then due. It did not include any payment of interest.

On May 8, 2001, after an evidentiary hearing, the trial court rendered judgment in favor of the plaintiff in the amount of $40,931.45. That amount represented interest at the rate of 12 percent per year as specified in § 52–195c (d) for the period between February 2, 2001, when the defendants' payment became due, and April 25, 2001, when the defendants paid $1.5 million.

As the basis for its judgment, the court made two central findings of fact. One concerned the terms of the settlement agreement and the other concerned the date when the defendants' obligation to pay became due. The defendants' appeal challenges the propriety of these findings as they relate to their claim of accord and satisfaction.

Our review of the defendants' appeal is governed by the well established principle that an appellate court will overturn the factual findings of a trial court only if these findings are clearly erroneous. . . . * * *

To support their claim of accord and satisfaction, the defendants maintain that the trial court improperly determined the terms of an oral settlement agreement to which the parties had agreed on December 15, 2000. The court found that the agreement unconditionally entitled the plaintiff to receive $3.2 million in full settlement of his claims against the defendants and New England Pipe Corporation. On an interim basis, the agreement allocated $2.5 million of this payment to the defendants. Further, the agreement provided that the ultimate allocation of payments between the defendants and New England Pipe Corporation would be decided by a subsequent arbitration. The court's final and most significant finding was that the settlement agreement entitled the plaintiff to immediate payment and that this payment was *not* conditioned on the execution of the contemplated arbitration agreement. The defendants disagree with the finding that the plaintiff should have been paid immediately.

---

* At that time, the defendants indicated that they would issue a check to the plaintiff for $1.5 million. The plaintiff reasserted his right to interest on the delayed payment.

The court based its finding on the testimony of all the participants in the settlement proceedings. The defendants' counsel testified that, at the time of the settlement negotiations, he had made it clear that the settlement was contingent upon the execution of the contemplated arbitration agreement between the defendants and New England Pipe Corporation. This testimony was flatly contradicted by the testimony of the other four attorneys who participated in the mediation that led to the settlement agreement. One of these attorneys was the mediator. The court expressly found that, even though the defendants' counsel believed his testimony to be accurate, the testimony was not credible. * * *

Having determined that the settlement agreement entitled the plaintiff to immediate payment, the trial court found that the defendants' debt matured upon the plaintiff's delivery of the appropriate releases and the withdrawal of his complaint. See General Statutes § 52–195c (a). The plaintiff fulfilled his responsibilities on January 2, 2001. Accordingly, the defendants' debt became due and payable on February 2, 2001. The defendants' only challenge to this finding is their aforementioned contention that the settlement agreement was not unconditional. That claim we have already rejected.

The court's finding that the plaintiff was unconditionally entitled to payment on February 2, 2001, knocked out the underpinnings of the defendants' claim that their obligation to pay interest was discharged by their tender and payment of a check in the principal amount of their indebtedness.* In order to obtain such a discharge, the defendants bore the burden of proving not only that there was "a dispute" between the parties, but also that the amount of the plaintiff's claim was "unliquidated or subject to a bona fide dispute...." General Statutes § 42a–3–311 (a)(ii).

After February 2, 2001, there was no basis for a *good faith* dispute about the defendants' indebtedness to the plaintiff. Likewise, there was no basis for a *good faith* dispute about the amount of the defendants' indebtedness for interest. Section 52–195c unequivocally required the defendants to pay interest at the rate of 12 percent per year after February 2, 2001. Under these circumstances, the court found that the defendants' letter

---

* The check was accompanied by a letter, dated April 24, 2001, stating: "As you know, it is our position that any settlement of the above-referenced matter [*Vincent Douthwright Et Al. v. Northeast Corridor Foundations Et Al.*, Docket No. X04–CV–98–0119322S] was expressly contingent upon the defendants reaching an agreement with respect to arbitration. We understand you disagree with that position and, as a result, seek interest on the settlement amount to be paid by my clients. We dispute that any interest is owing.

"Despite our dispute, we hereby enclose American Alternative Insurance Corporation's check #0018404361 on behalf of defendants Northeast Corridor Foundations, Balfour Beatty Construction, Inc., Mass Electric Construction, Inc., J.F. White Corporation and David Gilman in the amount of $1.5 million made payable to 'Matthew Shafner, Esq. Attorney for Vincent & Sandra Douthwright' in full and final settlement of the referenced matter." The plaintiff's counsel responded on May 1, 2001, in a letter stating: "I received the check for Mr. and Mrs. Douthwright in the amount of $1,500,000 on Wednesday, April 25, 2001 by Federal Express delivery. While I cannot agree that this is a full and final settlement in view of the pending motion, I do thank you for sending the check at this time."

stating that the check was tendered as full satisfaction of its indebtedness had no legal effect.*

We are persuaded that the court's findings must be sustained. The defendants did not satisfy the burden of proof assigned to them by § 42a–3–311 (a) or by the common law. We conclude, therefore, that the defendants have not provided any sustainable basis for their argument that the trial court's judgment should be set aside. None of the court's findings of fact was clearly erroneous. * * *

The judgment is affirmed.

NOTES

(1) In County Fire Door Corp. v. C. F. Wooding Co., 202 Conn. 277, 520 A.2d 1028 (1987), Justice Ellen Peters found:

> When there is a good faith dispute about the existence of a debt or about the amount that is owed, the common law authorizes the debtor and the creditor to negotiate a contract of accord and satisfaction to settle the outstanding claim. Such a contract is often initiated by the debtor, who offers an accord by tendering a check as "payment in full" or "in full satisfaction." If the creditor knowingly cashes such a check, or otherwise exercises full dominion over it, the creditor is deemed to have assented to the offer of accord. Upon acceptance of the offer of accord, the creditor's receipt of the promised payment discharges the underlying debt and bars any further claim relating thereto, if the contract of accord is supported by consideration. * * * A contract of accord and satisfaction is sufficiently supported by consideration if it settles a monetary claim that is unliquidated in amount.* * * [A] claim is unliquidated when the debtor tenders payment in an amount that does not exceed that to which the creditor is concededly entitled.* * * Where the claim is unliquidated any sum, given and received in settlement of the dispute, is sufficient consideration.

The court also noted that if the debtor offers "in good faith to settle an unliquidated debt by tendering, in full satisfaction, the payment of an amount less than demanded" by the creditor, the creditor cannot "simultaneously cash such a check and disown the condition on which it had been tendered." In short, the tender is an offer to settle which the offeree must accept in full or not at all.

(2) *Law Reform*.

Before 1990, UCC 1–207 provided:

> A party who, with explicit reservation of rights performs or promises performance or assents to performance in a manner demanded or offered

---

* General Statutes § 42a–3–311 (b) further conditions a discharge on the debtor's proof of "a conspicuous statement to the effect that the instrument was tendered as full satisfaction" of the disputed debt. The court found that the letter sent by the defen- dant did not communicate its intent to seek discharge of its principal obligation as well as of its indebtedness for interest. Presumably, this failure of communication means that the requirements of subsection (b) were also not met.

by the other party does not thereby prejudice the rights reserved. Such words as "without prejudice", "under protest" or the like are sufficient.

Some courts and commentators read this language as a modification of the common law rule. In essence, the reading was that the tender of a full payment check was an offer of "performance" by the debtor to which the creditor could assent without prejudice to any rights explicitly reserved. Thus, in the case of an unliquidated debt, if the debtor tendered a check for $10,000 in "full settlement" of the amount and the creditor cashed the check with an explicit reservation of rights to sue for the claimed excess, there was no accord and satisfaction. Mixed with an interpretation of the UCC was a judicial concern for small creditors dealing with strong debtors who might be forced to take a lesser amount because the money was needed and litigation was expensive. See AFC Interiors v. DiCello, 46 Ohio St.3d 1, 544 N.E.2d 869 (Ohio 1989); Horn Waterproofing Corp. v. Bushwick Iron & Steel Co., Inc., 66 N.Y.2d 321, 497 N.Y.S.2d 310, 488 N.E.2d 56 (1985).

Other commentators and courts disagreed, including Chief Justice Peters, who in the *County Fire Door* decision interpreted UCC 1–207 in a way that preserved the common law rule.

In 1990, the American Law Institute and the National Conference of Commissioners on Uniform State Law approved amendments of the UCC designed to resolve the disagreement over UCC 1–207. First, UCC 1–207 was amended to state that it did not apply to an accord and satisfaction. Second, a new section, UCC 3–311, was placed in Article 3, to deal with an accord and satisfaction when a negotiable instrument was involved. Please read that section, which is quoted by Judge Peters in the instant case.

Some questions: (1) How does UCC 3–311 differ from the common law of accord and satisfaction? (2) Under what circumstances would a full payment check cashed by the creditor not be an accord and satisfaction? See James J. White & Robert S. Summers, Uniform Commercial Code 501–504 (5th ed. 2000).

PROBLEM: MODIFICATION OR DISCHARGE OF DUTY TO PAY MONEY

(1) LE leased a store from LR for 36 months at $2,000 per month to operate a small deli. After 18 months, a general recession had set in and LE's business had dropped by 50%. LE came to LR and stated that due to the business drop off she could not continue to lease the premises at the agreed rent. There was a risk that she would have to vacate the premises and declare bankruptcy. LR said "Oh, don't do that. Surely we can work something out." LE then stated that she would pay LR $20,000 cash today in full settlement of the balance of the rent and would remain in the premises until the lease terminated. LR agreed and took the cash. The economy improved and LE's business began to flourish. At the end of the lease, LR refused to renew and sued LE for $16,000, the alleged balance due on the rent. May LR recover?

(2) Suppose, instead, that the lease terminated after the third year with LE owing $10,000 back rent. LE proposed to pay LR $5,000 cash in full settlement of the back rent and LR took the money. Later LR sued LE for

$5,000. What result? Would it make any difference if LE had tendered and LR had cashed a check for $5,000 "in full payment of all of my indebtedness"?

(3) If you represented LE in the two transactions above, how would you structure the deals to maximize the chances of enforcement?

(B) SETTLEMENTS INVOLVING A THIRD PARTY: MEDIATION

Comment: Lon L. Fuller on Mediation—Its Forms and Functions

"[C]asual treatments of the subject in the literature of sociology tend to assume that the object of mediation is to make the parties aware of the 'social norms' applicable to their relationship and to persuade them to accommodate themselves to the 'structure' imposed by these norms. From this point of view the difference between a judge and a mediator is simply that the judge orders the parties to conform themselves to the rules, while the mediator persuades them to do so. But mediation is commonly directed, not toward achieving conformity to norms, but toward the creation of the relevant norms themselves. This is true, for example, in the very common case where the mediator assists the parties in working out the terms of a contract defining their rights and duties toward one another. In such a case there is no pre-existing structure that can guide mediation; it is the mediational process that produces the structure. * * *

"It may be suggested that mediation is always, in any event, directed toward bringing about a more harmonious relationship between the parties, whether this be achieved through explicit agreement, through a reciprocal acceptance of the 'social norms' relevant to their relationship, or simply because the parties have been helped to a new and more perceptive understanding of one another's problems. The fact that in ordinary usage the terms 'mediation' and 'conciliation' are largely interchangeable tends to reinforce this view of the matter.

"But at this point we encounter the inconvenient fact that mediation can be directed, not toward cementing a relationship, but toward terminating it. * * * [O]ne of the most dramatically successful uses of mediation I ever witnessed involved a case in which an astute mediator helped the parties rescind a business contract. Two corporations were entrapped by a long-term supply contract that had become burdensome and disadvantageous to both. Canceling it, however, was a complicated matter, requiring a period of 'phasing out' and various financial adjustments back and forth. For some time the parties had been chiefly engaged in reciprocal threats of a law suit. On the advice of an attorney for one of the parties, a mediator (whose previous experience had been almost entirely in the field of labor relations) was brought in. Within no time at all a severance of relations was accomplished and the two firms parted company happily.

"Thus we find that mediation may be directed toward, and result in discrepant and even diametrically opposed results. This circumstance argues against our being able to derive any general structure of the mediational process from some identifiable goal shared by all mediational efforts. * * * [T]he central quality of mediation [is] its capacity to reorient the parties toward each other, not by imposing rules on them, but by helping them to achieve a new and shared perception of their relationship, a perception that will redirect their attitudes and dispositions toward one another. * * * This suggests a certain antithesis between mediational processes, on the one hand, and the standard procedures of law, on the other, for surely central to the very notion of law is the concept of *rules*.

" * * * It is not difficult to see why, under a system of state-made law, the standard instrument of dispute settlement should be adjudication and not mediation. If the question is whether A drove through a red light, or has paid his grocery bill, or has properly reported his earnings to Internal Revenue, even the most ardent advocate of conciliative procedures would hardly recommend mediation as the standard way of dealing with such problems. A pervasive use of mediation could here obliterate the essential guideposts and boundary markers men need in orienting their actions toward one another and could end by producing a situation in which no one could know precisely where he stood or how he might get where he wanted to be. As between black and white, gray may sometimes seem an acceptable compromise, but there are circumstances in which it is essential to work hard toward keeping things black and white. Maintaining a legal system in functioning order is one of those occasions.

"It is, then, not in the making of legal rules, but in their enforcement and administration that a certain incompatibility may be perceived between mediative procedures and 'the rule of law.' We may express something of the nature of this incompatibility by saying that, whereas mediation is directed toward *persons*, judgments of law are directed toward *acts*; it is acts, not people, that are declared proper or improper under the relevant provisions of law. This distinction is not quite so simple as it seems on the surface, for there are routine occasions within the operations of a legal system when judgment must be passed on persons. This necessity arises, for example, when a court must decide whether a convicted criminal should be admitted to probation or when a judge must determine which of two contesting parents should be given custody of a child. But in its core operations, in deciding, for example, whether a man has committed a crime or broken a contract, the standards of legal judgment are derived from rules defining the consequences of specific acts or failures to act; these rules do not attempt or invite any general appraisal of the qualities or dispositions of the person, exception being made, of course, for cases where the problem of legal accountability is raised, as when the defense of insanity is pleaded.

"The distinction just taken has been blurred in modern sociology by the indiscriminate use of the term 'social norm.' This expression seems to be so used as to embrace indifferently, on the one hand, rules attributing legal or social consequences to overt and specifically defined acts, and, on the other, precepts eliciting dispositions of the person, including a willingness to respond to somewhat shifting and indefinite 'role expectations.' The stance that it lifts from the user the responsibility for making any such distinction. Complex and difficult as making this distinction may in some contexts become, it is vitally important to keep it in mind in any inquiry directed toward discerning the limits of the effectiveness of 'law,' or toward defining the proper place and function of the various forms of social ordering, including mediation. . . .

"[I]n seeking now to delineate, within the processes of society as a whole, the proper domain of mediation, I suggest that we may usefully apply two tests; the first of these tells us when mediation *should not* be used, the second tells us when it *cannot* be used. The two tests are as follows: *First*, is the underlying relationship such that it is best organized by impersonal act-oriented rules? If so, then mediation will generally be out of place except as it is employed to create or modify rules. *Second*, is the problem presented amenable to solution through mediational processes? Mediation is itself subject to intrinsic limitation; I have discerned two of these; (1) it cannot generally be employed when more than two parties are involved; (2) it presupposes an intermeshing of interests of an intensity sufficient to make the parties willing to collaborate in the mediational effort."

Lon L. Fuller, *Mediation—Its Forms and Functions*, 44 S. Cal. L. Rev. 305 (1971).

DeValk Lincoln Mercury, Inc. v. Ford Motor Company

United States Court of Appeals, Seventh Circuit, 1987.
811 F.2d 326.

■ HARLINGTON WOOD, JR. CIRCUIT JUDGE.

Plaintiffs Harold DeValk, John Fitzgerald, and DeValk Lincoln Mercury, Inc. ("DLM"), appeal a grant of summary judgment in favor of defendants Ford Motor Company and Ford Leasing Development Company (collectively "Ford"). Plaintiffs DeValk and Fitzgerald were owners and managers of an automobile dealership, DeValk Lincoln Mercury, in Chicago, Illinois. In August 1979, after several months of poor performance, DLM submitted its resignation as a Lincoln–Mercury dealership to Ford. DLM and Ford then entered into negotiations to wind up the dealership's affairs and to transfer DLM's inventory back to Ford pursuant to contractual agreements. Disputes arose during these negotiations. The disputes went unresolved and plaintiffs eventually brought this lawsuit against Ford alleging violations of the Automobile Dealers Day in Court Act, 15 U.S.C. §§ 1221 et seq. (1982), breach of contract, breach of fiduciary duty, and fraud. After some of plaintiffs' claims were dismissed, defendants moved for summary judgment on the remaining claims. The district court granted defendants' motion for summary judgment on all the remaining claims. We affirm.

I.   FACTUAL BACKGROUND

In 1976 three Lincoln–Mercury dealerships served the near northwest side of Chicago, Illinois. In the spring of that year, Ford conducted a marketing study of the area and concluded that, in light of a declining market trend, consideration should be given to eliminating one of the three dealerships at the time ownership changed hands at any one of them. At the time this study was completed, and unaware of its existence, plaintiff DeValk was negotiating with Czarnowski Lincoln–Mercury, one of the three dealerships, to purchase its assets and also was approaching Ford to seek approval to operate a dealership at Czarnowski's geographic location. DeValk also worked at this time as general manager of Czarnowski. In March 1977 Ford approved DLM as a Lincoln–Mercury dealership and executed with DLM standard Lincoln and Mercury Sales and Service Agreements ("Sales Agreements") by which DLM could purchase automobiles, parts, signs, tools, and other items from Ford.

At the time control of the dealership changed hands, Czarnowski Lincoln–Mercury was struggling. It did not have floor plan financing to purchase new automobiles. It could only get parts from Ford on a C.O.D. basis. Czarnowski did not have adequate resources to perform warranty work and its reputation in the community suffered as a result. Moreover, employee morale was low.

In spite of DeValk's efforts as the new owner, the dealership continued to suffer. Throughout 1977 and into 1978, DLM experienced losses. In July 1978, based in part on the amended market study completed in the spring of 1976, Ford informed DeValk it had placed DLM on "delete status." That delete status meant that Ford would not continue a Lincoln–Mercury dealership at DLM's location once DeValk ceased to be the majority owner of the dealership. In late September or early October, DLM hired plaintiff Fitzgerald as the general sales manager. Five months later, in February 1979, Fitzgerald purchased a 45% interest in DLM. In February, March, and April, DLM managed to turn a profit. By August, however, DeValk and Fitzgerald decided to terminate the dealership. DLM submitted its resignation to Ford on August 23rd to become effective in October. DLM's resignation letter made no claims against Ford and reserved no rights to pursue any action against Ford. DLM's resignation letter also requested Ford to repurchase DLM's current inventory of automobiles. Ford accepted the resignation on October 1st, and DLM ceased operations on October 11th. In late October Ford took back DLM's inventory of parts and current model automobiles and credited DLM's account for those repurchases. Negotiations ensured over the inventory repurchases and other items, which engendered the disputes eventually giving rise to this lawsuit. * * *

Plaintiffs' contentions for purposes of this appeal can be divided into two categories. One set of claims relates to paragraph 23 of the Sales Agreements between Ford and DLM and the other set relates to paragraphs 21(b) & 21(c). * * *

B. Paragraph 23 Claims

Among other things, the Sales Agreements between Ford and DLM provide that when Ford or the dealer terminates or fails to renew the dealership, the dealer is entitled to receive certain benefits. These benefits include Ford's willingness to buy back the current inventory of automobiles and parts from the dealer. But in consideration of agreeing to buy back the inventory, the Sales Agreements provide in relevant part of paragraph 23 that the dealer will release Ford from liability except with respect to claims arising under paragraphs 19(f), 21, and 22 of the Sales Agreements:

> *[U]pon the Dealer's demand of any such benefits upon any termination or nonrenewal by the Dealer, the Company shall be released from any and all other liability to the Dealer* with respect to all relationships and actions between the Dealer and the Company, however claimed to arise, except any liability that the Company may have under subparagraph 19(f) and said paragraphs 21 and 22, and except for such amounts as the Company may have agreed in writing to pay to the Dealer. *Simultaneously with the receipt of any benefits so elected or demanded, the Dealer shall execute and deliver to the Company a general release* with exceptions, as above described, satisfactory to the Company. (emphasis added)

[The court considered and rejected the plaintiff's arguments that the release was invalid on the grounds of ambiguity, unconscionability, or waiver.]

C.   Paragraph 21(b) & 21(c) Claims

Aside from the claims arising under paragraph 23, a second set of claims arises under paragraphs 21(b) & 21(c). This second set of claims is not subject to paragraph 23's release of liability. Rather, these claims are specifically exempted from the release. Paragraph 23 releases all liability, "except any liability that the Company may have under subparagraph 19(f) and said paragraphs 21 and 22."

Although the paragraph 21(b) & 21(c) claims are not subject to paragraph 23's release, they are subject to a mediation clause. The mediation clause, found in paragraph 18(b) of the Sales Agreements, provides:

> *Any protest, controversy or claim by the Dealer* (whether for damages, stay of action or otherwise) with respect to any termination or nonrenewal of this agreement by the Company or the settlement of the accounts of the Dealer with the Company after any termination or nonrenewal of this agreement by the Company or the Dealer has become effective, *shall be appealed by the Dealer to the Policy Board* within fifteen (15) days after the Dealer's receipt of notice of termination or nonrenewal, or, as to settlement of accounts after termination or nonrenewal, within one year after the termination or nonrenewal has become effective. *Appeal to the Policy Board shall be a condition precedent to the dealer's right to pursue any other remedy available under this agreement or otherwise available under law.* The Company, but not the Dealer, shall be bound by the decision of the Policy Board. (emphasis added)

The mediation clause is straightforward. It requires DLM to appeal any "protest, controversy or claim" it has with Ford to the Dealer Policy Board. The mediation clause further specifies that the "[a]ppeal to the Policy Board shall be a condition precedent to the Dealer's right to pursue any other remedy ... available under law."

1. Substantial Performance

Plaintiffs concede they did not appeal their dispute with Ford to the Dealer Policy Board. But plaintiffs contend their failure to take the appeal is not fatal to their claims under paragraphs 21(b) & 21(c) because they "substantially complied" with the mediation clauses's requirements.* Plaintiffs base this contention on their view of the underlying purpose of the mediation clause: "It must be inferred that the purpose of requiring an appeal to the Dealer Policy Board is to give Ford Motor notice of any potential claim the dealer may have with respect to matters covered under paragraph 18(b) and to allow Ford Motor an opportunity to attempt to settle the claim prior to litigation." Plaintiffs argue that their post-resignation actions fulfill this two-pronged purpose of the mediation clause, and thus represent substantial compliance with its requirements, even though an appeal was not taken to the Dealer Policy Board.

Plaintiffs believe they fulfilled the first alleged purpose of the mediation clause by writing four letters to Ford detailing DLM's grievances. Plaintiffs argue these letters gave Ford all the notice it needed of the claims with which plaintiffs were concerned. As for the second alleged purpose of the mediation clause, plaintiffs contend they presented Ford with ample opportunity to settle their claims prior to litigation. The negotiations between plaintiffs and Ford's representatives spanned over eight months. Both Ford and plaintiffs effectively articulated their respective positions during these negotiations. Plaintiffs argue this negotiation process fulfilled the purpose of allowing Ford to attempt to settle its claims with DLM.

Although it is true that "Michigan follows the substantial performance rule," P & M Construction Co. v. Hammond Ventures, Inc., 142 N.W.2d 468, 473 (1966), and that in Michigan "the extent of nonperformance [is] viewed in relation to the full performance promised," Gordon v. Great Lakes Bowling Corp., 171 N.W.2d 225, 228–29 (1969), we cannot agree with plaintiffs' contention.

As an initial matter, we hesitate to apply the substantial performance rule outside the realm of cases in which that rule is applied in Michigan. The substantial performance rule in Michigan allows contractors, engineers, builders, and other construction professionals to recover a proportionate share of a contractual sum when they have substantially performed their construction obligations. Outside of those construction-type cases, however, we are unable to find any evidence that Michigan's courts are willing to more broadly apply the substantial performance rule. Cf. Gordon v. Great Lakes Bowling Corp., 18 Mich.App. 358, 171 N.W.2d 225, 228–29 (1979) (applying substantial performance rule to lease dispute, but in addition to rent, parties argued over construction costs and construction delay).

Even if we were confident that Michigan's courts would apply the substantial performance rule to a wider variety of contractual disputes, we

---

* Based on this language of the mediation clause, Ford contends it is released from any liability that may have arisen under paragraphs 21(b) a & 21 (c).

would not apply the rule here. Although the substantial performance rule in Michigan seems to derive in part from the maxim, "The law abhors a forfeiture," we are convinced it applies only in the absence of conditions precedent. E.g., Knox v. Knox, 337 Mich. 109, 59 N.W.2d 108, 112 (1953) ("While parties to a contract may by specific provision, or by necessary implication, make performance by one party a condition precedent to liability on the part of the other, courts are not disposed, in the absence of specific provisions or reasonable implications, to give such construction to an agreement, especially if so doing brings about an unfair result."); Kachanowski v. Cohen, 305 Mich. 438, 9 N.W.2d 667, 668 (1943) ("The law is well settled that one who executes a contract may protect himself from liability by a distinct agreement that it shall not become operative until there has been compliance with certain conditions thereof.")

The mediation clause here states that it is a condition precedent to any litigation. As a result, the clause takes itself outside the sphere of influence of the substantial performance rule. Because the mediation clause demands strict compliance with its requirement of appeal to the Dealer Policy Board before the parties can litigate, plaintiffs' substantial performance arguments must fail.

2.   Waiver of Mediation Clause

Undaunted, plaintiffs argue that even if the mediation clause operates as a condition precedent to litigation, Ford waived the requirements of that clause by its conduct following the final date on which an appeal could be taken to the Dealer Policy Board. The mediation clause requires the dissatisfied dealer to appeal its claims to the Dealer Policy Board "within one year after the termination or nonrenewal has become effective." Ford accepted DLM's resignation and DLM ceased operations in October 1979. Therefore, any continuing negotiations between DLM and Ford after October 1980, plaintiffs argue, constitute a waiver by Ford of the requirements of the mediation clause. As evidence of such continuing negotiations, plaintiffs point to a letter from Ford dated December 1980, an unpaid credit reflected in June 1981, and a claimed reduction in unpaid credit in October 1985; all three items addressing credits to DLM's parts account with respect to the repurchasing of parts by Ford.

Initially, we note that "a waiver of a breach of contract must be a 'voluntary intentional relinquishment of a known right.'" Bissell v. L.W. Edison Co., 9 Mich.App. 276 (1967). We then ask, under Michigan law, what evidence is necessary to show the relinquishment of the right? The Supreme Court of Michigan has explained that "[a] waiver may be shown by proof of express language of agreement or inferably established by such declarations, acts, and conduct of the party against whom it is claimed as are inconsistent with a purpose to exact strict performance." Strom–Johnson Construction Co. v. Riverview Furniture Co., 227 Mich. 55 (1924). So the waiver can be express, or it may be inferred from the conduct of the nonbreaching party. * * *

In this regard, plaintiffs point us to the law of arbitration clauses as a closely analogous area of contractual agreement by which we should be guided. The Supreme Court of Michigan has held that an insurer "may waive the compulsory arbitration provision of its insurance policy by its conduct." Bielski v. Wolverine Insurance Co., 150 N.W.2d 788, 790 (1967). That court also explained:

> "A clause in an insurance policy providing for arbitration or appraisal of the loss or damage as a condition precedent to a suit by the policyholder to recover insurance is inserted wholly for the protection of the insurer and may be waived by it. Such waivers need not be expressed in terms, but may be implied by the acts, omissions, or conduct of the insurer or its agents authorized in such respect."

Superficially, it appears that Ford's conduct after the time expired for an appeal to the Dealer Policy Board possibly constitutes a waiver. And we might find persuasive plaintiffs' arguments in this regard were it not for Ford's response, with which we agree, that Michigan's courts uphold anti-waiver clauses. Because DLM agreed in paragraph 27 of the Sales Agreements that implied waivers of Sales Agreements' provisions would not be permitted, plaintiffs' waiver argument cannot stand.

[The court then considered the plaintiff's arguments that Ford's alleged material breaches of the Sales Agreements relieved DLM of any duty to appeal its grievances to the Dealer Policy Board. It concluded that because the plaintiffs had not raised this repudiation argument in the district court, they had waived it on appeal.]

IV.   CONCLUSION

Even after drawing all the reasonable inferences in favor of plaintiffs' positions on this appeal from an adverse grant of summary judgment, we cannot find any genuine issues of material fact. Because there are no such issues, the judgment granted to defendants by the district judge as a matter of law is

AFFIRMED.

NOTES

One of your co-authors is Chair of the Ford Motor Company Arbitration Panel. Under procedures noted in the instant case, a terminated dealer is required to take the dispute to the Ford Motor Company Policy Board for mediation. An effort to settle the dispute is made at that stage. If settlement cannot be reached, the dealer has a choice to file a lawsuit against Ford or to initiate arbitration under balanced procedures drafted by Ford. The arbitration is conducted before a permanent three-person panel, one arbitrator appointed by the Dealer Association, a second arbitrator appointed by Ford, and the Chair, a neutral arbitrator appointed by the other two arbitrators. The arbitration is subject to the Federal Arbitration Act.

Comment: The Mediator's Privilege

"California law confers on mediators a privilege that is independent of the privilege conferred on parties to a mediation. By declaring that, subject to exceptions not applicable here, mediators are incompetent to testify "as to any statement, conduct, decision, or ruling, occurring at or in conjunction with [the mediation]," section 703.5 of the Evidence Code has the effect of making a mediator the holder of an independent privilege. Section 1119 of the Evidence Code appears to have the same effect—as it prohibits courts from compelling disclosure of evidence about mediation communications and directs that all such communications "shall remain confidential." As the California Court of Appeal recently pointed out, "the Legislature intended that the confidentiality provision of section 1119 may be asserted by the mediator as well as by the participants in the mediation." *Rinaker v. Superior Court,* 62 Cal.App.4th 155, n. 2 at 163, 74 Cal.Rptr.2d 464 (3d Dist.1998). It follows that, under California law, a waiver of the mediation privilege by the parties is not a sufficient basis for a court to permit or order a mediator to testify. Rather, an independent determination must be made before testimony from a mediator should be permitted or ordered.

"In the case at bar, the mediator (Mr. Herman) was and is an employee of the federal court (a 'staff neutral'). He hosted the mediation at the behest of the court and under this court's ADR rules. These facts are not sufficient to justify ordering him to testify about what occurred during the mediation—even when the parties have waived their mediation privilege and want the mediator to testify. Mr. Herman is a member of the California bar—and no doubt feels bound to honor the directives of California law. He also is a professional in mediation—and feels a moral obligation to preserve the essential integrity of the mediation process—an integrity to which he believes the promise of confidentiality is fundamental.

"Out of respect for these feelings, the court chose not to put Mr. Herman in an awkward position where he might have felt he had to choose between being a loyal employee of the court, on the one hand, and, on the other, asserting the mediator's privilege under California law. Instead, the court announced that it would proceed on the assumption that Mr. Herman was respectfully and appropriately asserting the mediator's privilege and was formally objecting to being called to testify about anything said or done during the mediation.

"Regardless of whether Mr. Herman invoked the mediator's privilege, the wording of section 703.5 can be understood as imposing an independent duty on the courts to determine whether testimony from a mediator should be accepted. Unlike some other privilege statutes, which expressly confer a right on the holder of the privilege to refuse to disclose protected communications, as well as the power to prevent others from disclosing such communications, section 703.5 is framed in terms of competence to testify. In its pertinent part, it declares that (subject to exceptions not applicable here) a mediator is not competent to testify "in any subsequent civil proceeding" about words uttered or conduct occurring during a mediation. This wording appears to have two consequences: it would not empower a mediator to prevent others from disclosing mediation communications, but it would require courts, on their own initiative, to determine whether it would be lawful to compel or permit a mediator to testify about matters occurring within a mediation.

" * * * The most important opinion by a California court in this arena is *Rinaker v. Superior Court,* 62 Cal.App.4th 155 (3d Dist.1998). In that case the Court of Appeal held that there may be circumstances in which a trial court, over vigorous objection by a party and by the mediator, could compel testimony from the mediator in a juvenile delinquency proceeding (deemed a "civil" matter under California law). The defendant in the delinquency proceeding wanted to call the mediator to try to impeach testimony that was expected from a prosecution witness. That witness and the delinquency defendant had earlier participated in a mediation—and the delinquency defendant believed that the complaining witness had made admissions to the mediator that would substantially undermine the credibility of the complaining witnesses testimony—and thus would materially strengthen the defense. In these circumstances, the *Rinaker* court held that the mediator could be compelled to testify if, after *in camera* consideration of what her testimony would be, the trial judge determined that her testimony might well promote significantly the public interest in preventing perjury and the defendant's fundamental right to a fair judicial process.

"In essence, the *Rinaker* court instructs California trial judges to conduct a two-stage balancing analysis. The goal of the first stage balancing is to determine whether to compel the mediator to appear at an *in camera* proceeding to determine precisely what her testimony would be. In this first stage, the judge considers all the circumstances and weighs all the competing rights and interests, including the values that would be threatened not by public disclosure of mediation communications, but by ordering the mediator to appear at an *in camera* proceeding to disclose only to the court and counsel, out of public view, what she would say the parties said during the mediation. At this juncture the goal is to determine whether the harm that would be done to the values that underlie the mediation privileges simply by ordering the mediator to participate in the *in camera* proceedings can be justified—by the prospect that her testimony might well make a singular and substantial contribution to protecting or advancing competing interests of comparable or greater magnitude.

"The trial judge reaches the second stage of balancing analysis only if the product of the first stage is a decision to order the mediator to detail, *in camera,* what her testimony would be. A court that orders the *in camera* disclosure gains precise and reliable knowledge of what the mediator's testimony would be—and only with that knowledge is the court positioned to launch its second balancing analysis. In this second stage the court is to weigh and comparatively assess (1) the importance of the values and interests that would be harmed if the mediator was compelled to testify (perhaps subject to a sealing or protective order, if appropriate), (2) the magnitude of the harm that compelling the testimony would cause to those values and interests, (3) the importance of the rights or interests that would be jeopardized if the mediator's testimony was not accessible in the specific proceedings in question, and (4) how much the testimony would contribute toward protecting those rights or advancing those interests—an inquiry that includes, among other things, an assessment of whether there are alternative sources of evidence of comparable probative value."

Olam v. Congress Mortgage Company, 68 F.Supp.2d 1110 (N.D.Cal.1999).

NOTES

(1) The Uniform Mediation Act (which was adopted by the National Conference of Commissioners on Uniform State Laws in 2001) establishes:

(a) A mediation communication is confidential and, if privileged, is not subject to discovery or admissible in evidence in a proceeding.

(b) In a proceeding, the following privileges apply:

(1) A party may refuse to disclose, and may prevent any other person from disclosing, a mediation communication.

(2) A mediator may refuse to disclose a mediation communication.

(3) A mediator may refuse to disclose, and may prevent any other person from disclosing, a mediation communication of the mediator.

(4) A nonparty participant may refuse to disclose, and may prevent any other person from disclosing, a mediation communication of the nonparty participant.

Uniform Mediation Act § 5 (2001)

(2) *Disclosures in "Caucus" Mediation*:

"Sequential caucusing is uniquely mediative: arbitrators generally do not conduct ex parte meetings with the parties and negotiation necessarily requires the parties to meet together. By shuttling back and forth between meetings with individual disputants, mediators can collect and distribute private information. An economic rationale for mediation centers on caucusing because it is here that the mediator most clearly controls the flow of information between the disputants. * * *

"ADR theory, however, has been particularly unhelpful in explaining how caucusing creates value. Although psychological explanations are offered for caucusing, no one has ventured an economic or strategic justification for the practice. Why, for instance, would rational disputants disclose private information to a mediator that they would not disclose directly to the other side? And what should mediators do with this information? Mediators and analysts often claim that the mediator should maintain the confidentiality of all private communications learned in the caucus. If confidentiality is scrupulously maintained, however, the mediator is doing nothing more than what an advisor individually retained by each party could do. This extreme form of "Chinese wall" caucusing thus seems not only a poor example of mediation, but also an activity that could be more cheaply accomplished by independent advisors concerned only with one side of the dispute.

"In practice, however, mediators often do make disclosures of private information, if only indirectly. By caucusing, for example, the mediator might 'determine whether a zone of agreement exists' or 'figure out a set of trades that will bring the participants as close to agreement as they can possibly get.'

Revealing that there are gains from trade or that a particular set of trades might be acceptable to the other side has the effect of indirectly disclosing to each party some of the mediator's private discussions with the other side. The ADR literature has often failed to acknowledge the tension between the mediator's duty of confidentiality and the need for indirect disclosure. Indeed, generally when ADR scholars have written about confidentiality, the focus has been on whether the mediation will be privileged from discovery by outsiders, rather than on the extent to which one party's caucus information can be disclosed to the other side. Knowing, however, how a mediator is allowed to transmit caucus information is not only important in assessing the ethics of a particular mediator's behavior, but also determines whether private parties will disclose information and whether that disclosure will be truthful. * * *

"[Caucus mediation] can create value by controlling the flow of private information (variously eliminating, translating, or even creating it) . . .

Jennifer Gerarda Brown & Ian Ayres, *Economic Rationales for Mediation*, 80 Va. L. Rev. 323, 326 (1994). See also Ian Ayres & Barry J. Nalebuff, Common Knowledge as a Barrier to Negotiation, 44 UCLA L. Rev. 1631, 1640 (1997).

SECTION 3.   PRIVATE ADJUDICATION; ARBITRATION

By private adjudication, we mean situations where the parties to a dispute delegate to a third person who is not a judge the power to decide the dispute on the merits. In most cases, this delegation will be agreed as an alternative to a judicial determination and the agreement to delegate may occur before any dispute arises. The purpose of this subsection is to explore the legal standing of these alternatives, which depend upon agreement between the parties and frequently involve disputes arising out of a contract between the parties.

Comment: Dispute Resolution in Construction Contracts.

Role of Architect or Engineer. In most construction contracts, Owner will appoint an architect or engineer (an independent professional) to insure that Prime Contractor's performance conforms to the plans and specifications and is rendered on time. Decisions by Architect that Prime has complied are typically conditions precedent to Owner's duty to pay.

Without more, Architect is not an arbitrator and the procedure by which decisions on conformity are made is not arbitration unless both parties have agreed to that procedure. Architect's decisions, however, are presumptively final. As one court put it:

> An authority on construction law posits that when a contract assigns the project architect or engineer responsibility to make decisions on all claims of contractors, as in this case, the architect's decision on responsibility for delay should control unless it is shown to be dishonestly made or to be clearly wrong. J. Sweet, Legal Aspects of Architecture, Engineering, and the Construction Process § 33.09 (3rd edition 1985). The rule is adopted from cases concerned with conditions

precedent to payment. . . . See Restatement 2nd Contracts § 227 comment c.

In Laurel, [Laurel Race Course, Inc. v. Regal Construction Co., 333 A.2d 319 (Md. 1975)] the contractor sued the owner for amounts allegedly due under the contract. Owner defended that contractor had failed to produce the certification of the project engineer which would entitle it to payment under the terms of the contract. Id. Finding for the owner, the court stated:

"By this contract, which is perfectly lawful, the parties expressly agreed to submit the question . . . to the judgment of [a] third party, . . . [whose] judgment, no matter how erroneous or mistaken it may be, or how unreasonable it may appear to others, is conclusive between the parties, unless it be tainted with fraud or bad faith. To substitute for it the opinions and judgments of other persons, whether judge, jury or witnesses, would be to annul the contract, and make another in its place."

Id. at 151, 333 A.2d at 325 (quoting Lynn v. B. & O.R.R. Co., 60 Md. 404, 415 (1883)).

* * *

The Architect or Engineer is charged with the responsibility of interpretation of the contract documents and general directions of the work. He shall make decisions on all claims of the Contractor or the Owner, or on any matter dealing with the execution of the work. His decisions relating to artistic effect and technical matters shall be final, provided such decisions are within the limitations of the contract terms.

The architect interprets the contract which governs the relationship of the parties, and makes decisions on all claims of contractors "on any matter dealing with the execution of the work." Finality is accorded only to decisions relating to artistic effect and technical matters.

As in any construction project, contractors in a multiple-prime situation co-exist in a delicate state of symbiosis. Each prime's ability to maintain timely progress is as much a part of their work, and is as important to the other primes, as their ability to perform more tangible tasks. We hold that judgment of the quality of a prime's ability to perform its jobs and to maintain timely progress in those jobs is delegated to the architect by the contract. The architect's determination is "*prima facie* correct, and the burden is upon the other parties to show fraud or mistake." *Barnes,* 134 Ind.App. at 466, 184 N.E.2d at 764–65. * * *

Loving's argument that the Uniform Arbitration Act, N.C.G.S. § 1–567.1 et seq., somehow lessens the power of the architect to settle disputes concerning cause for delay is also without merit. Loving correctly observes that the architect is not specifically made an arbitrator. The contract does not contemplate arbitration, and the parties are in no way bound to that procedure by the contract. However, the parties have agreed to be bound by the architect's judgments made under the powers given the architect in Articles 18, 31, and 35, and the correct forum to introduce such evidence is in a court of law. * * *

Bolton Corp. v. T. A. Loving Co., 94 N.C.App. 392, 380 S.E.2d 796 (1989)

As the court in *Bolton Corp.* correctly states, unless the parties have agreed to arbitration, the legal effect of a contract conferring some decision-making authority on the architect is not affected by any arbitration legislation enacted in the state. Put differently, the decision process is not arbitration, the architect is not an arbitrator, and the finality of the architect's decisions will be determined by the court under contract and common law standards. See, e.g., Thomas Crimmins Contracting Co. v. City of New York, 74 N.Y.2d 166, 544 N.Y.S.2d 580, 542 N.E.2d 1097 (1989) (contract did not clearly give chief engineer power to make final legal determinations).

The construction contract, however, may contain an arbitration clause. An example of a typical provision is found in Article 10 of Document A107 of the American Institute of Architects (1987):

§ 10.5   The Architect will interpret and decide matters concerning performance under and requirements of the Contract Documents on written request of either the Owner or Contractor. The Architect will make initial decisions on all claims, disputes or other matters in question between the Owner and Contractor, but will not be liable for results of any interpretations or decisions rendered in good faith. The Architect's decision in matters relating to aesthetic effect will be final if consistent with the intent expressed in the Contract Documents. All other decisions of the Architect, except those which have been waived by making or acceptance of final payment, shall be subject to arbitration upon the written demand of either party. * * *

§ 10.8   All claims or disputes between the Contractor and the Owner arising out or relating to the Contract, or the breach thereof, shall be decided by arbitration in accordance with the Construction Industry Arbitration Rules of the American Arbitration Association currently in effect unless the parties mutually agree otherwise and subject to an initial presentation of the claim or dispute to the Architect as required under Paragraph 10.5. Notice of the demand for arbitration shall be filed in writing with the other party to this Agreement and with the American Arbitration Association and shall be made within a reasonable time after the dispute has arisen. The award rendered by the arbitrator shall be final and judgment may be entered upon it in accordance with applicable law in any court having jurisdiction thereof. * * *

Under the dispute resolution system noted above, the architect's decision is final on "matters relating to aesthetic effect" and is not subject to arbitration. All other disputes, however, whether relating to the architect or not are subject to arbitration. Obviously, the contract must be interpreted to determine which decisions of the architect are final unless overturned by a court and which decisions are subject to arbitration. For useful discussion see Fabyanske & Halverson, *Arbitration: Is It an Acceptable Method of Resolving Construction Contract Disputes?*, 16 Forum 281 (1980); Trapasso, *The Lawyer's Use of AIA Construction Contracts*, 19 Prac.Law 37 (#5, 1973). See also McCormick, *Representing the Owner in Contracting with the Architect and Contractor*, 8 The Forum 435 (1973). See also, Thomas J. Stipanowich, *Beyond Arbitration: Innovation and Evolution in the United States Construction Industry, 31 Wake Forest L. Rev. 65 (1996).*

Excuse of Conditions Precedent to Payment. In construction contracts, the interwoven doctrines of "constructive" conditions of exchange, express conditions precedent and contract interpretation frequently converge around payment and coordination decisions by the architect, who, as has been noted, acts as the owner's representative during the construction period. As one might expect, an important aspect of this authority relates to payments.

Assume that the contract authorizes progress payments. The owner's obligation to pay depends upon an application for payment submitted to the architect by the contractor and a certificate for payment issued by the architect. Based upon observation of the work and the application for payment, the architect, who is a party to the contract, agrees to issue the certificates for payment unless he or she finds the following: 1) defective work not remedied, 2) claims filed, 3) failure of the contractor to make payments properly to subcontractors or for labor, materials, or equipment, 4) damage to another contractor, or 5) unsatisfactory prosecution of the work by the contractor. Final payment shall not be made until these conditions have occurred and the contractor has delivered a complete release of liens arising out of the contract, or receipts in full covering work for which a lien could be filed, or a satisfactory indemnity bond.

Recall that in *Jacob & Youngs v. Kent,* supra at 780, the court, after concluding that the defendant's duty to make the final payment was constructively conditioned upon the plaintiff substantially completing the work under the contract, held that the constructive condition was satisfied by substantial performance. But an architect was involved in the project, and it is clear from the opinion that the architect refused to issue the certificate of payment when the plaintiff refused to "do the work anew." Except for noting that the architect failed to notice the discrepancy in the pipe until after the house was completed, the court did not consider the effect of substantial performance upon the express condition that issuance of the certificate was to precede the duty to pay.

One reason for this may be the case of Nolan v. Whitney, 88 N.Y. 648 (1882), where the court held that when a contractor has substantially performed the contract the architect is "bound" to issue the certificate. An unreasonable and wrongful refusal excuses the necessity that the certificate be issued. This is evidently still the law in New York. Arc Electrical Construction Co. v. George A. Fuller Co., 24 N.Y.2d 99, 104–105, 299

N.Y.S.2d 129, 131–33, 247 N.E.2d 111, 113 (1969). See Van Iderstine Co. v. Barnet Leather Co., 242 N.Y. 425, 433, 152 N.E. 250, 252 (1926).

Most states, however, have followed the principle of review set forth in Section 303 of the first Restatement: "Where a certificate of an architect, surveyor or engineer is a condition precedent to a duty of immediate payment for work, the condition is excused if the architect, surveyor or engineer (a) dies or becomes incapacitated, or (b) refuses to give a certificate because of collusion with the promisor, or (c) refuses to give a certificate after making examination of the work and finding it adequate, or (d) fails to make proper examination of the work, or (e) fails to exercise an honest judgment, or (f) makes a gross mistake with reference to facts on which a refusal to give a certificate is based."

An assumption here is that the architect, as a professional, should have more room for the exercise of honest judgment than that permitted if the decision were reviewable under standards of reasonableness. Other policies are also involved:

> Agreements to submit specific determinations of controversies and disputes arising under a contract to a third party chosen by the contracting parties are valid. * * * The decision of the third party as to matters entrusted to him, like the award of an arbitrator, is final and binding upon the parties unless the decision is impeached for fraud, accident, or gross mistake of such a nature that fraud may be inferred. * * * Parties competent to enter into this construction contract are competent to agree that the architect, even though he is the agent of one of the contracting parties, shall determine the question of claimed losses and damages. They are also competent to agree that said designated person's determination shall be final and binding on them. * * * Anticipatory provisions for settlements of disputes are favored and have the approval of the courts. United States v. Moorman, 338 U.S. 457, 70 S.Ct. 288, 94 L.Ed. 256 (1950).

E.H. Marhoefer, Jr., Co. v. Mount Sinai, Inc., 190 F.Supp. 355, 359–60 (E.D.Wis.1961). See Laurel Race Course, Inc. v. Regal Construction Co., Inc., 274 Md. 142, 333 A.2d 319, 325–28 (1975); Restatement (Second) § 227, Illus. 5–8.

But even an honest judgment may collide with the policy against forfeiture. Restatement (Second) § 229 provides:

> To the extent that the non-occurrence of a condition would cause extreme forfeiture, a court may excuse the non-occurrence of a condition unless its occurrence was a material part of the agreed exchange.

Could *Jacob & Youngs v. Kent* also be explained under the anti-forfeiture policy? Should the same approach be followed where the question is the binding effect on the owner of an issued certificate? Suppose, for example, that the architect in *Kent* had issued a certificate approving pipe that was substantially inferior to that specified. Although the answer is not free from doubt, the certificate can be set aside if there was a gross mistake of fact or a failure to exercise honest judgment on the part of the architect or engineer. See *James I. Barnes Construction Co. v. Washington Township*, 134 Ind.App. 461, 184 N.E.2d 763 (1962).

Parisi v. Netlearning, Inc.

United States District Court, Eastern District of Virginia, 2001.
139 F.Supp.2d 745.

■ BRINKEMA, DISTRICT JUDGE.

MEMORANDUM OPINION

Before the Court is defendant Netlearning, Inc.'s Motion to Dismiss, in which defendant argues that plaintiff Dan Parisi's declaratory judgment action constitutes an improper motion to vacate an arbitration award. This motion raises the question of whether the "mandatory administrative proceedings" conducted under the Uniform Domain–Name Dispute Resolution Policy ("UDRP")* of the Internet Corporation for Assigned Names and Numbers ("ICANN") constitute an arbitration subject to the Federal Arbitration Act ("FAA"), 9 U.S.C. § 1 *et seq.*** Because we find that the FAA's restrictions on judicial review of arbitration awards do not apply to civil actions challenging UDRP panel decisions, the defendant's motion will be DENIED.

BACKGROUND

This action arises from a dispute concerning Parisi's registration and use of the Internet domain name "netlearning.com."*** Such disputes

---

* *See* ICANN, *Uniform Domain–Name Dispute–Resolution Policy* (August 26, 1999) www.icann.org/udrp/udrp-policy–24oct99.htm ("UDRP"); ICANN, *Rules for Uniform Domain Name Dispute Resolution Policy* (October 24, 1999) www.icann.org/udrp/udrp-rules–24oct99.htm ("UDRP Rules").

** ICANN, a non-profit California corporation, governs the assignment of Internet domain names, the allocation of Internet Protocol (IP) address space, and management of the Domain Name System (DNS) and Internet "root" server under the auspices of the Department of Commerce. *See* ICANN, *About ICANN* (last modified March 23, 2001) www.icann.org/general/abouticann.htm.

*** Previous decisions have amply discussed the technical and commercial importance of "domain names" as well as the allocation of responsibilities for their administration and registration between ICANN and various "top-level" domain registrars. *See e.g., America Online v. Huang*, 106 F.Supp.2d 848, 848–53 (E.D.Va.2000) ... Briefly, each "host" computer or network connected to the Internet is principally identified by an Inter-

net Protocol ("IP") address consisting of four sets of digits separated by periods. Under the Domain Name System (DNS), each host is also identified by a corresponding alphanumeric domain name, such as "vaed.uscourts.gov." A domain name indicates a specific host's relative position within the hierarchical structure of the DNS. The Internet is anchored to a nameless "root" file. Sprouting from the root file are numerous "Top Level Domains" (TLDs), which are denoted by the alphanumeric segment at the extreme right within any domain name. TLDs include both "generic" TLDs, such as the familiar ".com" and ".net," and country-code TLDs such as the United Kingdom's ".uk". Each TLD encompasses numerous Second Level Domains (SLDs), denoted by the alphanumeric segment to the immediate left of the TLD segment. Each SLD may be divided into subdomains, which may in turn be further divided into subdomains. Thus, the domain name "lawclerks.ao.uscourts.gov" indicates the "lawclerks" subdomain of the "ao" subdomain of the "uscourts" SLD of the ".gov" TLD.

have spread with the Internet's emergence as a primary channel for worldwide commercial, recreational, and educational communications. In response to widespread dissatisfaction with extant mechanisms for resolving disputes between domain name registrants and holders of trademark and other intellectual property rights, ICANN adopted the UDRP in 1999.

1. The UDRP

Although ICANN exerts quasi-governmental sway over the growth and administration of the Internet, the UDRP is enforced through contract rather than regulation. Every domain name registrar accredited by ICANN must incorporate the UDRP into each individual domain name registration agreement. *See* UDRP, ¶ 1. In effect, the UDRP binds registrants by virtue of their contracts with registrars, such as Network Solutions, Inc., "to submit" to "mandatory administrative proceedings" initiated by third-party "complainants." UDRP, ¶ 4. The scope of such UDRP proceedings is limited to claims of "abusive" registrations of Internet domain names. The UDRP covers no other disputes. UDRP, ¶ 5. Complainants in UDRP proceedings must prove that the disputed "domain name is identical or confusingly similar to a trademark or service mark in which the complainant has rights," that the registrant has "no rights or legitimate interests in respect of the domain name," and that the domain name "has been registered and is being used in bad faith." UDRP, ¶ 4(a). The UDRP identifies badges of "bad faith" and grounds for demonstrating a registrant's "rights and legitimate interests" in a domain name. UDRP, ¶ 4(b)–(c). * * *

Complainants initiate UDRP proceedings directly with a dispute resolution service "provider" designated by ICANN. *See* UDRP Rules, ¶ 3. The UDRP and the UDRP Rules prescribe detailed procedures for appointing either a solo arbitrator or a three-member panel to conduct the inquiry. The UDRP is fashioned as an "online" procedure administered via the Internet. Although a panel may opt in exceptional cases to hold live or telephonic hearings, it is expected to base its decision on "the statements and documents submitted" in accordance with the UDRP, the UDRP Rules, and any "rules and principles of law that it deems applicable." UDRP Rules, ¶ ¶ 13, 15(a). In the absence of "exceptional circumstances," a panel is expected to issue its decision within fourteen days of its appointment. UDRP Rules, ¶ 15(b).

If the panel rules in the complainant's favor, the only available remedy is for the registrar to cancel the domain name registration or transfer it to the complainant. UDRP, ¶ 4(i). A registrar may automatically implement a UDRP panel decision after ten days unless the aggrieved registrant notifies the registrar within this ten day period that it has "commenced a lawsuit against the complainant in a jurisdiction to which the complainant has

---

ICANN accredits institutions and corporations to serve as domain name "registrars." Registrars assign specific SLDs within a TLD to "registrants," ensure that each registered SLD is unique within the TLD, and maintain and distribute information correlating SLDs with the appropriate IP addresses. Network Solutions, Inc. is a principal registrar of the second-level domain names within the popular ".com" TLD.

submitted" as required by the UDRP Rules. *See* UDRP, ¶ 4(k); UDRP Rules, ¶ 5(e). Upon such notification, the registrar "will take no further action" until it receives "satisfactory" evidence of the resolution of the dispute, the dismissal or withdrawal of the lawsuit, or a court order that the registrant does "not have the right to continue using" the domain name. UDRP, ¶ 4(k).

To date, 3,622 separate proceedings concerning 6,410 separate domain names have been initiated under the UDRP. *See* ICANN, *Summary of Status of Proceedings,* (last modified May 7, 2001) www.icann.org/udrp/proceedings-stat.htm. One of these administrative proceedings concerned the "netlearning.com" dispute now before us.

2. *The "netlearning.com" Dispute*

According to the complaint, Parisi filed a trademark application for the "NETLEARNING" mark on April 1, 1996. On April 5, 1996, he registered the second-level domain name "netlearning.com" with Network Solutions, Inc. The Patent and Trademark Office (USPTO) subsequently denied the trademark application on grounds of descriptiveness and likelihood of confusion with the existing "LEARN NET" mark (not held by any party to this action). Parisi abandoned the application as of October 15, 1997. Parisi alleges that he nevertheless continued to use the domain name to operate a website with "links" to university websites, and he claims to be developing "netlearning.com" as a component of his "Megasearch.com" search engine.

Meanwhile, Netlearning, Inc. began using the mark "NET LEARNING THE ULTIMATE LEARNING SYSTEM" on June 1, 1997. Netlearning registered and began operating its "Net–Learning.com" website on May 12, 1997, and filed a trademark application for "NET LEARNING THE ULTIMATE LEARNING SYSTEM" on April 3, 2000. Parisi alleges that Netlearning offered to purchase his "netlearning.com" domain name for as much as $22,500 in early 2000, but he refused to transfer the registration. Netlearning subsequently initiated UDRP administrative proceedings challenging Parisi's registration and use of the "netlearning.com" domain name.

On October 16, 2000, a three-member UDRP administrative panel issued a split decision in Netlearning's favor, with one panelist dissenting. *See Netlearning, Inc. v. Dan Parisi,* FA 95471 (Nat.Arb.Forum, October 16, 2000). The panel directed Network Solutions to transfer the registration for "netlearning.com" to the defendant.

On October 30, 2000, Parisi filed this declaratory judgment action seeking a declaration of lawful use under the Anti–Cybersquatting Consumer Protection Act ("ACPA"), 15 U.S.C. § 1114(2)(D), and the Federal Declaratory Judgment Act, 28 U.S.C. § 2201, as well as a declaration of non-infringement under the Lanham Act, 15 U.S.C. § 1125(a). Parisi also seeks an order directing the USPTO to refuse defendant's pending trademark application for the "NETLEARNING THE ULTIMATE LEARNING SYSTEM" mark, an award of fees and costs, and further relief as the Court deems "just and proper." (Compl. at ¶ 81).

DISCUSSION

Netlearning moves for dismissal on the sole ground that the complaint constitutes an improper motion to vacate an arbitration award. Specifically, defendant alleges that Parisi fails to assert any grounds cognizable under the FAA for setting aside an arbitration award and that, in any event, Parisi's action is time-barred under the FAA because it was not served on the defendant within three months of the panel's ruling.

The FAA evinces the "liberal federal policy favoring arbitration," *Moses H. Cone Memorial Hosp. v. Mercury Constr. Corp.,* 460 U.S. 1, 24 (1983). Congress enacted the FAA in 1925 to counteract the "hostility of American courts to the enforcement of arbitration agreements." *Circuit City Stores, Inc. v. Adams,* 121 S.Ct. 1302, 1307 (2001). The FAA "compels judicial enforcement of a wide range of written arbitration agreements." *Id.*

Federal courts apply the FAA, first and foremost, to effectuate contracting parties' expectations for resolving disputes. This is fundamentally a matter of contract interpretation. "Arbitration is a creature of contract, a device of the parties rather than the judicial process." *AMF Inc. v. Brunswick Corp.,* 621 F.Supp. 456, 460 (E.D.N.Y.1985)(Weinstein, J.).... Because the FAA does not define "arbitration," courts have liberally construed that term to encompass various diverse dispute-settlement mechanisms. "If the parties have agreed to submit a dispute for a decision by a third party, they have agreed to arbitration." *See AMF Inc.,* 621 F.Supp. at 460. An arbitration agreement may, by its own terms, be amenable to enforcement through some provisions of the FAA, but not others. The Fourth Circuit recently distinguished "mandatory arbitration, as a prerequisite to initiation of litigation" from "binding arbitration, where the parties must accept an award or decision of the arbitrator." *Bankers Insurance Co.,* 245 F.3d 315. Commitments to participate in such "mandatory" proceedings are regularly enforced by compelling arbitration,* or staying litigation pending arbitration.** *See Harrison v. Nissan Motor Corp.,* 111 F.3d 343, 350 (3d Cir.1997) ("[I]f one party seeks an order compelling arbitration and it is granted, the parties must then arbitrate their dispute to an arbitrators' [sic] decision, and cannot seek recourse to the courts before that time."). * * *

* Section 4 of the FAA provides, in relevant part:

A party aggrieved by the alleged failure, neglect, or refusal of another to arbitrate under a written agreement for arbitration may petition [an appropriate U.S. District Court] for an order directing that such arbitration proceed in the manner provided for in such agreement. 9 U.S.C. § 4.

** Section 3 of the FAA provides:

If any suit or proceeding be brought in any of the courts of the United States upon any issue referable to arbitration under an agreement in writing for such arbitration, the court in which such suit is pending, upon being satisfied that the issue involved in such suit or proceeding is referable to arbitration under such an agreement, shall on application of one of the parties stay the trial of the action until such arbitration has been had in accordance with the terms of the agreement, providing the applicant for the stay is not in default in proceeding with such arbitration. 9 U.S.C. § 3.

Binding arbitration awards may be confirmed through entry of judgment pursuant to the arbitration agreement. *See* 9 U.S.C. § 9. Binding awards may, however, be vacated in narrow circumstances of arbitrator misconduct, serious procedural flaws, or "manifest disregard of the law." *See* 9 U.S.C. §§ 10*–11**; ... A motion to vacate an arbitration award under § 10 constitutes the "sole method to challenge" a binding award.... A party seeking to vacate such an award must file a § 10 motion and serve notice of the motion "upon the adverse party or his attorney within three months after the award is filed or delivered." 9 U.S.C. § 12. A motion to vacate served more than three months after the award is time-barred.... Aggrieved parties may not circumvent the FAA by packaging a motion to vacate as a fresh complaint....

Netlearning argues that the UDRP "administrative proceedings" should be deemed an "arbitration" as envisioned by the FAA and that Parisi's declaratory judgment complaint should be treated as a motion to vacate an arbitration panel's award which must comport with the requirements of § 10 and § 12 of the FAA. Netlearning argues that because it was served with Parisi's complaint over three months after the UDRP panel issued its decision, any motion to vacate is time-barred under 9 U.S.C. § 12. Netlearning further argues that the complaint articulates no cognizable ground for vacating an arbitration award under the FAA. Parisi counters that the FAA does not apply to the UDRP and that his complaint raises issues far beyond the scope of the UDRP panel ruling.

We begin our analysis of the FAA's applicability by examining the specific arbitration agreement at issue, that is, the UDRP. Clearly, the UDRP creates a contract-based scheme for addressing disputes between domain name registrants and third parties challenging the registration and use of their domain names. However, in our view, the UDRP's unique contractual arrangement renders the FAA's provisions for judicial review of arbitration awards inapplicable.

* Under 9 U.S.C. § 10(a), a court may vacate an award:

(1) Where the award was procured by corruption, fraud, or undue means.

(2) Where there was evident partiality or corruption in the arbitrators, or either of them.

(3) Where the arbitrators were guilty of misconduct in refusing to postpone the hearing, upon sufficient cause shown, or in refusing to hear evidence pertinent and material to the controversy; or of any other misbehavior by which the rights of any party have been prejudiced.

(4) Where the arbitrators exceeded their powers, or so imperfectly executed them that a mutual, final, and definite award upon the subject matter submitted was not made. 9 U.S.C. § 10(a).

** Pursuant to 9 U.S.C. § 11, a court may modify an award:

(a) Where there was an evident material miscalculation of figures or an evident material mistake in the description of any person, thing, or property referred to in the award.

(b) Where the arbitrators have awarded upon a matter not submitted to them, unless it is a matter not affecting the merits of the decision upon the matter submitted.

(c) Where the award is imperfect in matter of form not affecting the merits of the controversy. 9 U.S.C. § 11.

First, there is no reason to "stay" litigation under § 3 because, quite simply, the UDRP contemplates parallel litigation. Nothing in the UDRP restrains either party from filing suit before, after, or during the administrative proceedings. *See* UDRP, ¶ 4(k). If litigation commences during the course of a proceeding, the panel has "the discretion to decide whether to suspend or terminate the administrative proceeding, or to proceed to a decision." UDRP Rules, ¶ 8(a) . . .

Second, it would not be appropriate to "compel" participation in UDRP proceedings under § 4 as a prerequisite to litigation because UDRP complainants, as strangers to the registration agreement, are under no obligation to avail themselves of the UDRP. . . . Only the registrant is obligated to participate in a UDRP proceeding if a complaint is filed. If a registrant declines to participate in the panel process, the panel may simply "decide the dispute based on the complaint." UDRP Rules, ¶ 5(e). Although the UDRP describes the process as "mandatory" in the sense that a registrant's refusal to participate may lead to an uncontested loss of the domain name, the process is not "mandatory" in the sense that either disputant's legal claims accrue only after a panel's decision. . . .

Third, because the remedies available through the UDRP are so narrow and specific, we find no basis for confirming and enforcing a UDRP panel decision through § 9. Moreover, the FAA only permits entry of judgment "if the parties in their agreement have agreed that a judgment of the court shall be entered upon the award made pursuant to the arbitration." 9 U.S.C. § 9. The UDRP nowhere suggests such agreement. It not only countenances parallel litigation; it mandates a judicial forum for challenges to UDRP decisions. To initiate UDRP proceedings, a complainant must first agree to litigate any challenges to the panel's ruling in either the jurisdiction encompassing the registrar's principal place of business or the jurisdiction encompassing the registrant's record address. *See* UDRP Rules ¶ 3(xiii). An aggrieved registrant can effectively suspend the panel's decision by filing a lawsuit in the specified jurisdiction and notifying the registrar in accordance with ¶ 4(k) of the UDRP.* From these provisions, it is clear that ICANN intended to provide "parity of appeal," ensuring a "clear mechanism" for "seeking judicial review of a decision of an administrative panel canceling or transferring the domain name." ICANN, *Staff Report on Implementation Documents for the Uniform Dispute Resolution Policy* (September 29, 1999).

Finally, we specifically hold that judicial review of UDRP decisions is not confined to a motion to vacate an arbitration award under § 10 of the FAA. To begin with, the FAA's structure and basic tenets of contract interpretation limit the extreme deference of §§ 10 and 12 to proceedings

---

* However, the UDRP only requires the registrar to suspend implementation of the panel decision when the registrant files a lawsuit in the same jurisdiction to which the complainant consented when initiating the UDRP process. If the registrant were to bring a lawsuit against the complainant in any other jurisdiction, the UDRP would not, as a matter of contract, restrain the registrar from transferring or cancelling the domain name.

intended by the contracting parties to be binding. The UDRP's contemplation of parallel litigation and abbreviated proceedings does not invite such deference.

More importantly, the UDRP itself calls for comprehensive, *de novo* adjudication of the disputants' rights. Registrars will move forward with a panel's decision only after a competent court or arbitration panel determines that the original registrant does "not have the right to continue to use" the disputed domain name. This implies more than a review of the procedural soundness of the UDRP decision under § 10 of the FAA; it implies resolution of the parties' overarching trademark, contract, and other claims and defenses. WIPO's Final Report specifically recommended that

> the availability of the administrative procedure should not preclude resort to court litigation by a party. In particular, a party should be free to initiate litigation by filing a claim in a competent national court instead of initiating the administrative procedure, if this is the preferred course of action, and should be able to seek a *de novo* review of a dispute that has been the subject of the administrative procedure.

WIPO Final Report, ¶ 150(iv). . . .

Based on this analysis, we conclude that the Federal Arbitration Act's limitations on judicial review of arbitration awards do not apply to civil actions seeking review of UDRP panel decisions concerning domain names. * * * For these reasons, the defendant's Motion to Dismiss will be DENIED by an appropriate order.

NOTES

According to the Supreme Court, "in the classic sense, arbitration occurs when parties in dispute choose a judge to render a final and binding decision on the merits of the controversy and on the basis of proofs presented by the parties." Rush Prudential HMO, Inc. v. Moran, 536 U.S. 355, 122 S.Ct. 2151, 2168, 153 L.Ed.2d 375 (2002). What was missing in the UDRP procedures? If arbitration law does not determine the scope of judicial review, by what standard will the court review the award? Can it ignore it and conduct a de novo proceeding?

Comment: The Nature and Characteristics of Arbitration

[The following is reprinted from the Ohio State Journal of Dispute Resolution.]

Arbitration: The Classic Model

Let us start with the basics. Arbitration is a form of Alternative Dispute Resolution (ADR). Unlike other methods of ADR, however, arbitration is a private adjudicatory process invoked as an alternative to filing a law suit. The classic model of arbitration can be reduced to three essential elements. First, arbitration depends upon consent. The parties must agree, either before or after the dispute arises, to arbitrate the dispute. In most cases, that agreement will be evidenced by mutual assent to a commercial or consumer contract which contains a written arbitration term.

Second, arbitration is a less formal adjudicatory process that has assumed advantages over litigation in courts or other forms of ADR. The parties expect that an unbiased and competent private arbitrator will conduct a relatively expeditious, informal, inexpensive, and private hearing and decide the merits of the dispute fairly between them.

Third, the arbitrator is empowered by the agreement and applicable arbitration rules to make a final decision on the merits of the dispute, i.e., to decide both questions of fact and of law and to provide appropriate remedies.

Unlike the judicial process, there is no review of the merits of this primary decision by the arbitrator. In the absence of fraud, bias, or process defects, the court is empowered to confirm and enforce the award as if it were a final judgment. There are, of course, incentives for negotiated settlement within the arbitral process and the arbitrator's decision will frequently contain an element of compromise. Nevertheless, in whatever contexts arbitration is invoked, the parties participate in the decisional process by presenting evidence and reasoned arguments to an arbitrator whose final decision should be responsive to the dispute as presented. As a practical matter, finality is achieved when both parties acquiesce in the arbitrator's decision with or without seeking limited judicial review.

Characteristics of Arbitration

Although an objective of arbitration is to achieve justice between the parties through less formal adjudication, the quality of justice may be different (if not less) than that achieved in civil litigation. As one court warned, arbitration is "not the most perfect alternative to adjudication" in the courts. It is "an inferior system of justice, structured without due process, rules of evidence, accountability of judgment or rules of law." In short, "parties should be aware that they get what they bargain for and that arbitration is far different from adjudication."*

What do the parties get when they bargain for arbitration? The characteristics of the classic model of arbitration, along with its potential strengths and limitations, emerge when it is contrasted with the judicial process. For emphasis, the differences will be stated in the extreme.

1. *Control Over Scope, Content and Arbitrator Selection.* As a voluntary dispute resolution technique, one party can avoid arbitration by refusing to agree to arbitrate an existing or future dispute. But if a decision to arbitrate is made, the parties have an opportunity to define the scope and content of the process as well as to control its procedures in the agreement. The same cannot be said for civil litigation. Similarly, the

* Stroh Container Co. v. Delphi Indus., 783 F.2d 743, 751, n. 12 (8th Cir.), cert. denied, 476 U.S. 1141, 106 S.Ct. 2249, 90 L.Ed.2d 695 (1986).

arbitrator is selected by or through procedures agreed to by the parties while the judge is imposed upon them by law and local allocation practices.

2. *Less Formality and Complexity.* Arbitration procedures and fact finding processes are not clearly defined or required by arbitration statutes. They depend upon the agreement, relevant arbitration practice or institutional procedures, such as the American Arbitration Association (AAA) Arbitration Rules, and are usually less formal than those in court. The arbitrator has less authority than a judge to order discovery or to compel the attendance of witnesses or the production of evidence. The parties have less power to engage in pretrial discovery. The parties, however, may define by agreement the procedures and the powers of and even the substantive law and remedies to be applied by the arbitrator. In the absence of such agreement, arbitration procedures may be attended with a great deal of uncertainty.

3. *Duration of Proceedings.* In arbitration, the arbitrator and the parties control the timing, duration, and complexity of the hearings. In judicial proceedings, these matters may be beyond the parties' control. The potential for savings in time and cost, therefore, differs. In short, arbitration is expected (and assumed) to be quicker, less formal and less expensive than litigation in court.

4. *Arbitrator Expertise.* In arbitration, the arbitrator is expected to be an expert in or familiar with the context within which the dispute arose while a judge will, normally, have no special expertise. Furthermore, an arbitrator is not required to produce a written opinion with reasons for the decision. Presumably, this reduces the risk of disagreement over reasons by parties otherwise satisfied with the result. In court, a reasoned opinion by a judge is required.

5. *Confidentiality.* Arbitration is touted as a private process where confidence is normally maintained while the opposite is true in court.

6. *Justice Between the Parties.* A primary objective in arbitration is to achieve a just result between the parties. But arbitration seeks particularized justice rather than to foster substantive consistency and predictable results for the future. Courts, on the other hand, are concerned both about just results and announced precedent and the effect of the decision on third persons who are not parties to the litigation.

Furthermore, in arbitration, a compromise decision is possible while judicial decisions tend to be either win all or lose all. According to some observers: "The arbitration process frequently resembles three-party negotiation or mediation, with many arbitrators consciously or unconsciously identifying outside parameters of possible settlement and endeavoring to reach a decision that will at least be minimally acceptable to both parties."*

* E. Johnson, V. Kantor & E. Schwartz, Alternatives in Civil Cases 55 (1977). Outside the Courts; A Survey of Diversion

In sum, arbitration is a form of consensual, relatively informal, personalized adjudication where the primary objective is to obtain less expensive justice between the parties. The challenge is to obtain particularized justice in an extra-legal adjudicatory process which has potential strengths and weakness when compared to civil litigation.

[Reprinted with permission from Richard E. Speidel, *Arbitration of Statutory Rights Under the Federal Arbitration Act: The Case for Reform,* 4 Ohio St. J. Disp. Res. 157, 158–61 (1989).]

Michael–Curry Co. v. Knutson Shareholders

Supreme Court of Minnesota, 1989.
449 N.W.2d 139.

■ KEITH, JUSTICE.

The central issue in this case is whether an arbitration clause which provides for arbitration of, *inter alia,* "[a]ny controversy or claim arising out of or relating to * * * the making" of a contract, compels arbitration of a claim that an amendment to the contract was fraudulently induced. The trial court held in the negative. The court of appeals reversed, holding that the clause was sufficiently broad to comprehend that the issue of fraud in the inducement be submitted to arbitration. We affirm.

* * *

1.   The issue of arbitrability is to be determined by ascertaining the intention of the parties through examination of the language of the arbitration agreement.... A reviewing court is not bound by the trial court's interpretation of the arbitration agreement and independently determines whether the trial court correctly interpreted the clause ...

The purchase and sale agreement in this case provided that "this Agreement shall be construed in accordance with, and governed by, the laws of the State of Minnesota." Both parties agree that Minnesota law governs the agreement and the amendment, which incorporates the terms of the agreement.

Minn.Stat. § 572.08 (1988) provides that written agreements or contract provisions to arbitrate are valid, enforceable, and irrevocable absent grounds for revocation of the contract. Under the procedural rules of Minn.Stat. § 572.09, if one party refuses to arbitrate, the court must order arbitration. A party wishing to stay arbitration must show that there is no agreement to arbitrate. "Such an issue, when in substantial bona fide dispute, shall be forthwith and summarily tried and the stay ordered if found for the moving party." Minn.Stat. § 572.09(b) (1988). Otherwise the court must order arbitration. Id.

A claim of fraud in the inducement puts the "making" of the contract itself in issue. This court has said that "that issue is more properly determined by those trained in the law." Atcas v. Credit Clearing Corp., 292 Minn. 334, 350 (1972). Minnesota has ruled that fraud which vitiates a contract also vitiates an arbitration clause within the contract. Atcas v. Credit Clearing Corp., 292 Minn. at 349 (1972); Minn.Stat. § 572.08. By claiming fraud in the inducement, the Trust is asserting that no valid agreement to arbitrate exists under Minn.Stat. § 572.09. The court must therefore determine whether the parties agreed to arbitrate the issue of fraud in the inducement.

Parties may validly choose to arbitrate all controversies, including fraud in the inducement. . . . To determine intent to arbitrate fraud in the inducement, the court must look to the language of the arbitration clause. The language in the clause must either (1) specifically show that the parties intended to arbitrate fraud in the inducement, or (2) be "sufficiently broad to comprehend that the issue of fraudulent inducement be arbitrated. . . ." If the clause does not specifically include fraud in the inducement and is not sufficiently broad to comprehend it, then a trial must be had on the issue of fraud in the inducement. . . .

The arbitration clause in the instant case states:

> 13.01 *Arbitration.* Any controversy or claim arising out of, or relating to, this Agreement, or the making, performance, or interpretation thereof, shall be settled by arbitration * * *. (Emphasis supplied).

The clause does not specifically mention fraud. We find, however, that it meets the second prong of the Atcas test.

The clause in this case is broader than the clauses in previous cases this court has considered. First, it provides for arbitration of controversies relating to "the making" of the contract, which clauses Atcas and later cases did not contain. The word "making" refers to circumstances surrounding formation of the contract. See Atcas, 292 Minn. at 350 (a claim of fraudulent inducement puts "the making of the agreement itself * * * in issue"). See also . . . Prima Paint v. Flood & Conklin Mfg., 388 U.S. 395, 403–04 (1967) (under the FAA, a fraud in the inducement claim "goes to the 'making' of the agreement"). It is difficult to see how the parties in this case could have drafted a "broader" agreement.

The Trust attempts to circumvent the Atcas "broadly worded" option by arguing that specificity is always required. The Trust argues that the word "fraud" must appear in the arbitration clause. The Minnesota Uniform Arbitration Act changed "the common law policy of judicial hostility toward arbitration to one favoring arbitration." Layne–Minnesota Co. v. Regents of Univ. of Mn., 266 Minn. 284, 288 (1963). This policy requires the court to give effect to parties' arbitration agreements, and weighs against the Trust's assertion. The Trust's suggested standard would render meaningless the second alternative of the Atcas test. Requiring a specific list of all possible claims constituting grounds for rescission would be impractical, defeating the policy favoring arbitration. Further, given the realities of commercial dealings, parties would hesitate to enter into a contract when fraud is mentioned at the outset. . . .*

---

* In a related area, this court has held that parties who fashion a "broad" arbitration clause must enumerate specifically whatever they wish to exclude from the powers of the arbitrators.

2. We are also concerned that parties often allege fraud in the inducement as a final attempt to avoid arbitration. We therefore emphasize that, where a party applies for a stay of arbitration, "circumstances constituting fraud * * * shall be stated with particularity." See Atcas, 292 Minn. at 348. Minn.Stat. §§ 572.09(a) and (b) should not be invoked without such particularity.

For the reasons stated above, we affirm the judgment of the court of appeals and remand to the district court for an order compelling arbitration pursuant to the arbitration clause in the parties' purchase agreement.

NOTES

(1) *Revised Uniform Arbitration Act.* Minnesota, like many states, has enacted legislation based upon the Uniform Arbitration Act. That legislation has recently been revised (in 2000) by the National Conference of Commissioners on Uniform State Law and the revision has been proposed to the states for adoption. Section 6 of the Revision, entitled "Validity of Agreement to Arbitrate" provides:

(a) An agreement contained in a record to submit to arbitration any existing or subsequent controversy arising between the parties to the agreement is valid, enforceable, and irrevocable except upon a ground that exists at law or in equity for the revocation of a contract.

(b) The court shall decide whether an agreement to arbitrate exists or a controversy is subject to an agreement to arbitrate.

(c) An arbitrator shall decide whether a condition precedent to arbitration has been fulfilled and whether a contract containing a valid agreement to arbitrate is enforceable.

(d) If a party to a judicial proceeding challenges the existence of, or claims that a controversy is not subject to, an agreement to arbitrate, the arbitration proceeding may continue pending final resolution of the issue by the court, unless the court otherwise orders.

Revised Section 7 deals with motions to compel arbitration and to stay litigation pending arbitration. It is clear that the court, when these motions are made, has authority to determine whether there was an enforceable agreement to arbitrate and, if there is, to both order arbitration and "stay any judicial proceeding that involves a claim alleged to be subject to the arbitration. . . ."

In David Co. v. Jim W. Miller Constr., Inc., 444 N.W.2d 836 (Minn.1989), this court upheld an "innovative and unique" award fashioned by arbitrators as authorized by a broad arbitration clause, even though "it may be correct to surmise that initially neither party specifically contemplated" that such an award could be made. Id. at 840, 842. The parties were experienced in construction; therefore they should have been aware of the extent of the liability and possible awards involved. Thus, if the parties had desired to limit the powers of the arbitrators, they should have specifically expressed this in the broadly-worded arbitration clause. Supporting this conclusion is the "long-established policy favoring expansion of the arbitration remedy." Id. at 842.

Section 7(f), (g). Under Section 28(a)(1), an appeal may not be taken from an order compelling arbitration.

If enacted in Minnesota, how would these revisions affect the analysis in the *Curry* case?

(2) *Preemptive Effect of Federal Arbitration Act.* The Federal Arbitration Act, 9 U.S.C.A. §§ 1–15, was enacted by Congress in 1925. The FAA, with some exceptions, applies to "[A] written provision in any maritime transaction or a contract evidencing a transaction involving commerce to settle by arbitration a controversy thereafter arising out of such contract or transaction, or the refusal to perform the whole or any part thereof, or an agreement in writing to submit to arbitration an existing controversy arising out of such a contract, transaction, or refusal." FAA § 2. Thus, under both the FAA and the Uniform Arbitration Act [see Revised UAA 6(a)], written agreements to arbitrate existing and future disputes are enforceable.

Suppose, however, that state arbitration law denied enforcement to agreements to arbitrate future disputes and, allegedly, the "contract evidenced a transaction involving commerce" under FAA sec. 2. In Allied–Bruce Terminix Companies, Inc. v. Dobson, 513 U.S. 265, 115 S.Ct. 834, 130 L.Ed.2d 753 (1995), the Court held that the FAA's scope extended to the limits of Congress's power to regulate interstate commerce and that state law conflicting with the enforceability of the federal contract to arbitrate was preempted. Thus, Alabama law, which (then) did not enforce agreements to arbitrate future disputes, could not preclude the enforcement of such an agreement within the scope of the FAA.

The *Allied–Bruce* test for the scope of interstate activity, however, was narrowed by the Court in a non-arbitration case, United State v. Lopez, 514 U.S. 549, 115 S.Ct. 1624, 131 L.Ed.2d 626 (1995), and disagreements over the impact of *Lopez* on arbitration issues are evident in recent cases. See Sisters of the Visitation v. Cochran Plastering Co., 775 So.2d 759 (Ala.2000).

Similarly, state law that imposes conditions on the enforcement of the federal contract to arbitrate that are not found in the FAA itself and are not applicable to other state contracts is preempted. For example, in Doctor's Associates, Inc. v. Casarotto, 517 U.S. 681, 116 S.Ct. 1652, 134 L.Ed.2d 902 (1996), the Court struck down a Montana statute that required that "notice that a contract is subject to arbitration ... shall be typed in underlined capital letters on the first page of the contract, and unless such notice is displayed thereon, the contract may not be subject to arbitration." The vice was that the statute did not apply generally to all contracts. To pass muster under the FAA, the law, (whether it be a required notice or principles of fraud, capacity, or unconscionability), must have general application and not just apply to arbitration provisions. According to the Court, Congress in enacting the FAA "precluded states from singling out arbitration provisions for suspect status" and required, instead, that arbitration terms be put on the "same footing as other contracts." 517 U.S. at 686–87. See Stephen J. Ware, *Arbitration and Unconscionability After Doctor's Associates, Inc. v. Casarotto*, 31 Wake Forest L. Rev. 1001 (1996).

Suppose, however, that the parties choose in clear language state arbitration law that differs from the FAA or state substantive law that singles out federal arbitration agreements for special treatment. This raises the difficult question of whether the parties can through a choice of law clause contract out of the FAA or vary the effect of its provisions by agreement. In most cases, however, the power to contract out or vary will be recognized if clearly expressed. See Volt Information Sciences, Inc. v. Board of Trustees of Leland Stanford Junior University, 489 U.S. 468, 109 S.Ct. 1248, 103 L.Ed.2d 488 (1989)(choice of California law). See also Mastrobuono v. Shearson Lehman Hutton, Inc., 514 U.S. 52, 115 S.Ct. 1212, 131 L.Ed.2d 76 (1995) (dictum); Stone & Webster, Inc. v. Baker Process, Inc., 210 F.Supp.2d 1177 (S.D.Cal. 2002) (agreement construed against choice of California procedural rule).

For more discussion of these and other cases interpreting the FAA, see Stephen L. Hayford, *Commercial Arbitration in the Supreme Court, 1983–1995: A Sea Change*, 31 Wake Forest L. Rev. 1 (1996).

(3) *Separability and competence to decide arbitrability?* In most commercial contracts, the parties will agree to a "broad" arbitration clause, that covers all disputes arising under or relating to the contract in which the clause is contained. Two questions recur: who has authority, court or arbitrators, to decide (1) attacks on the enforceability of the agreement to arbitrate (competence issues), and (2) attacks on the enforceability of the contract in which the arbitration term is contained (separability issues)?

Competence to decide arbitrability. Taking the first question, under the FAA, arbitrability issues (i.e., was there a written agreement to arbitrate, was the dispute within the scope of the agreement, was the arbitration agreement induced by fraud) are for the court unless the parties have "clearly agreed" to have the arbitrator decide them. First Options of Chicago, Inc. v. Kaplan, 514 U.S. 938, 115 S.Ct. 1920, 131 L.Ed.2d 985 (1995). This is not the case under the usual broad agreement to arbitrate, but the language used is always open to interpretation. See Bell v. Cendant Corp., 293 F.3d 563 (2d Cir.2002) (finding clear agreement in an exceptionally broad clause). This result is significant. If, for example, the arbitral tribunal has been selected and a challenge to their jurisdiction is then made on the grounds that the agreement to arbitrate was not enforceable, the challenging party could seek an injunction against arbitration and argue the issue to the court.

The opposite result is reached in international arbitration. For example, Section 16(1) of the UNCITRAL Model Law on International Commercial Arbitration provides that the "arbitral tribunal may rule on its own jurisdiction, including any objections with respect to the existence or validity of the arbitration agreement." This principle is also found in the arbitration rules of the leading international arbitration institutions, such as the American Arbitration Association, the International Chamber of Commerce, and the London Court of International Arbitration. See e.g. ICC Rules of Arbitration Art. 6(4). Section 30 of the English Arbitration Act (1996) is in accord.

Separability. In *Michael–Curry*, the claim was that an amendment to the contract containing the arbitration clause was induced by fraud. There was no claim that the arbitration clause itself was induced by fraud. The court, however, suggested that fraud that vitiates the underlying contract "also vitiates an arbitration clause within the contract" and held that a court should first decide whether the fraud issue was within the scope of the agreement to arbitrate. Why? According to the court, the scope issue was "more properly determined by those trained in law." Once the scope issue is decided, however, whether there was fraud in fact is for the arbitrators.

Is this result changed by Section 6(c) of the Revised UAA, which states that an "arbitrator shall decide whether * * * a contract containing a valid agreement to arbitrate is enforceable."

Under the FAA, a claim that the underlying contract or an amendment was induced by fraud does not constitute a direct attack on the arbitration clause, even though the vitiation of the underlying contract might vitiate the arbitration clause. Under Prima Paint Corp. v. Flood & Conklin Mfg. Co., 388 U.S. 395, 87 S.Ct. 1801, 18 L.Ed.2d 1270 (1967) and its better reasoned progeny, a fraud attack on the underlying contract is for the arbitrator to decide unless the claim was beyond the scope of the agreement to arbitrate. This approach expands the scope of the arbitrator's power and, of course, assumes that the arbitrators are capable of resolving fraud and similar claims.

Suppose, however, that the party opposing arbitration claims that the underlying contract was void (never came into existence) rather than voidable? Should that make any difference? There is some authority for the proposition that a challenge to the "very existence" of a contract is an attack on the enforceability of the arbitration clause and should not be submitted to arbitration (unless the parties have clearly agreed). See Primerica Life Ins. Co. v. Brown, 304 F.3d 469, 473 (5th Cir.2002) (concurring opinion).

This is a non-issue in international commercial arbitration, however, where relevant legislation and arbitration rules give the tribunal power to decide the validity of the underlying contract in all cases. For example, Section 16(1) of the UNCITRAL Model law states that the arbitration clause that "forms part of a contract shall be treated as an agreement independent of the other terms of the contract" and that a decision by the "arbitral tribunal that the contract is null and void shall not entail ipso jure the invalidity of the arbitration clause." Section 7 of the English Arbitration Act is in accord.

Brook v. Peak International, Ltd.

United States Court of Appeals, Fifth Circuit, 2002.
294 F.3d 668.

■ EDITH H. JONES, CIRCUIT JUDGE:

Brook and Peak International, Ltd., Brook's former employer, arbitrated their contractual dispute before an arbitrator selected by the American Arbitration Association ("AAA"). The arbitrator's award favored Peak. Brook filed a motion to vacate the arbitration award in the district court. The district court held that the arbitrator selected by the AAA was without power to decide the dispute because the AAA did not follow the selection procedure outlined in Brook's Employment Agreement. The district court vacated the arbitration award pursuant to 9 U.S.C. § 10(a)(4). Peak has appealed. Although we agree that AAA seriously erred by deviating from the parties' contractual selection process, we conclude that Brook never timely objected to the selection process on the ground he now espouses, hence, the objection was waived.

BACKGROUND

On January 1, 1998, Richard Brook entered into an employment agreement (the "Employment Agreement") with Peak International to become its president and chief operating officer. Less than a year later, he was terminated. A dispute arose regarding Brook's severance benefits. On May 7, 1999, pursuant to the terms of the Agreement, Brook filed a demand for arbitration with the AAA alleging breach of his Employment Agreement.*

This appeal concerns the arbitrator selection process. The process began on May 18, 1999, when the AAA submitted a list of nine prospective arbitrators and instructed the parties to follow the procedure outlined in the Employment Agreement to select the arbitrator. On May 28, Brook struck one individual from the list. Brook's counsel also stated:

> [Peak's] counsel [] has agreed to Austin as the site of the arbitration hearing and hence it strikes us that perhaps an arbitrator from Austin would be more efficient and economical for all concerned. To that end, [Peak's counsel] and I will try to come up with a mutually acceptable Austin-based arbitrator from your AAA–Austin list, if this is acceptable to the association.

Peak, citing its understanding that a new list of arbitrators from Austin was to be provided by the AAA, did not submit a strike to the AAA's first list of arbitrators.

On June 9, the AAA informed the parties that "there were no mutual choices [from the previously provided list of arbitrators] who were able to accept the appointment." The AAA then advised: "[the AAA is] enclosing a second list of names from our panel. We ask that this list be considered supplemental to the list previously provided and every consideration be given to releasing names struck from that list." The AAA's June 9 letter did not refer to Brook's May 28 letter or Brook's request for selection of an arbitrator from the AAA's Austin list, and it did not direct the parties to employ the selection process outlined in the Employment Agreement. Rather, the letter instructed the parties to strike the names of unacceptable arbitrators and indicate their order of preference by number. The letter also provided that "[i]f this list is not received by the [AAA] on or before

---

* The dispute resolution clause of the Employment Agreement provided as follows:

4. Resolution of Disputes; Arbitration. Should a dispute arise concerning this Agreement, its interpretation or termination, either party may request a conference with the other party to this Agreement and the parties shall meet to attempt to resolve the dispute. Failing such resolution within thirty (30) days of either party's request for conference, the Company and the Employee shall endeavor to select an arbitrator who shall hear the dispute. In the event the parties

are unable to agree on an arbitrator, the Employee and the Company shall request the American Arbitration Association to submit a list of nine (9) names of persons who could serve as an arbitrator. The Company and Employee shall alternately remove names from this list (beginning with the party which wins a flip of a coin) until one person remains and this person shall serve as the impartial arbitrator. The decision of the arbitrator is final and binding on both parties. Each party shall bear equally all the costs of the arbitrator.

Monday, June 21, 1999, or if there are no mutual choices, the appointment will be made per Section 12 of the [AAA] Rules." If the parties failed to submit their strikes by June 21, the letter warned, "all names submitted may be deemed acceptable."

Complying with the June 9 letter, Brook submitted his strike list and ranked the remaining arbitrators in order of preference.* Peak did not submit a list of strikes before June 21.

On July 14, Peak's counsel informed the AAA that he was withdrawing and that Peak intended to substitute John McCamish as counsel. Peak also advised the AAA of ongoing discussions with Brook's counsel regarding the possible mutual selection of Judge Joe Hart as arbitrator. On July 16, Mr. McCamish requested a seven-day extension of time from Brook's counsel to review the file before advising whether his client would agree to the selection of Judge Joe Hart. Brook's counsel rejected the request for extension of time.

On July 26, the AAA notified the parties that Professor David Sokolow had been selected as arbitrator. Peak immediately protested the appointment of Professor Sokolow, citing concerns regarding Professor Sokolow's potential conflicts with counsel and his inexperience with employment-related disputes. Peak also submitted its strikes to the list of arbitrators. On August 5, Peak sent a second letter of objection to the AAA, arguing that "the entire appointment process violates the parties' written agreement." Peak requested that the AAA comply with the terms of the Employment Agreement by providing a list of nine, rather than seven, potential arbitrators and by allowing the parties to alternately remove names from the list until only one remained. Brook filed no objection to the selection of Professor Sokolow or the process used by the AAA and did not respond to Peak's objections.

On August 11, the AAA withdrew the appointment of Professor Sokolow and appointed Judge Chuck Miller as arbitrator. The AAA's letter appointing Judge Miller refers neither to Peak's objections to the selection process nor to its demand for compliance with the selection process outlined in the Employment Agreement.

On August 13, Brook registered "his protest to the process used by the [AAA] in the selection of the arbitrator." In a letter to the AAA and opposing counsel, Brook objected to the appointment of Judge Miller "because the appointment [was] not made in compliance with AAA rules and procedures." Brook also requested that the AAA reinstate "the properly appointed individual, Professor David Sokolow," as arbitrator. However, Brook's August 13 letter does not mention the Employment Agreement or the AAA's failure to follow the contractual selection process.

On August 26, Peak notified the AAA that it was "willing to forego its complaints of procedural irregularities that have occurred and proceed forward if Brook agrees to Mr. Miller as arbitrator." Peak also stated that

---

* Although Brook now challenges the selection of Judge Miller as arbitrator, he did not strike Judge Miller from the AAA's second list.

"if Brook is unwilling to agree to [the appointment of Judge Miller] . . . then Peak would continue to assert its complaint, outlined in [its] letter of August 4, 1999, that the entire appointment process to date has violated the terms of Brook's employment agreement. . . ." The record contains no response from Brook, and no further objection by Brook to the appointment of Judge Miller. The parties proceeded to arbitrate their dispute before Judge Miller.

After months of discovery and related disputes, the parties participated in an eight-day arbitration hearing before Judge Miller. In his opening remarks to the parties on the first day of arbitration, Judge Miller stated: "I have executed the oath of arbitrator . . . [s]o unless there are any other objections, we'll go ahead and convene the arbitration." Brook raised no objections, and the arbitration convened. After considerable expense to the parties and a lengthy arbitration process,* Judge Miller entered an arbitration award favorable to Peak.

Brook filed a federal lawsuit in which he moved to vacate the arbitration award, arguing that (1) the arbitration award was arbitrary and capricious and/or based on a manifest disregard for the law, (2) the arbitrator exceeded his authority by addressing issues not raised by the parties, and (3) "the arbitrators were guilty of misconduct . . . or other misbehavior" that warranted vacatur pursuant to 9 U.S.C. § 10(a)(3) because the AAA violated its own arbitrator selection rules. Brook's motion to vacate does not refer to the Employment Agreement, does not raise the AAA's failure to follow the selection process outlined in the Employment Agreement as grounds for vacatur, and does not cite 9 U.S.C. § 10(a)(4).

On January 17, 2001, a magistrate judge heard oral argument regarding Brook's motion to vacate and raised, *sua sponte,* the AAA's failure to follow the selection process outlined in the Employment Agreement as a possible ground for vacating the arbitration award. Several days later, Brook filed his "Supplement to Motion to Vacate Arbitration Award," asserting for the first time that the AAA's failure to select the arbitrator in the manner provided by the Employment Agreement rendered Judge Miller powerless to arbitrate the dispute. Based on this argument, the magistrate judge recommended that the district court vacate the arbitration award pursuant to 9 U.S.C. § 10(a)(4). The district court agreed with the magistrate judge's recommendation, vacated the award, and precipitated Peak's appeal.

DISCUSSION

A. In light of the strong federal policy favoring arbitration, "[j]udicial review of an arbitration award is extraordinarily narrow." *Gulf Coast Indus. Worker's Union v. Exxon Co.,* 70 F.3d 847, 850 (5th Cir.1995). This court reviews an order vacating an arbitration award *de novo,* a standard that is "intended to reinforce the strong deference due an arbitrative tribunal." *McIlroy v. PaineWebber, Inc.,* 989 F.2d 817, 820 (5th Cir.1993).

---

* The record before us indicates that the parties spent over $650,000 in fees and costs related to the arbitration of their dispute before Judge Miller.

Section 10 of the Federal Arbitration Act, 9 U.S.C. §§ 1–16 ("FAA"), provides "the only grounds upon which a reviewing court may vacate an arbitrative award." *McIlroy*, 989 F.2d at 820. Section 10 allows vacatur, *inter alia*, "[w]here the arbitrators exceeded their powers...." 9 U.S.C. § 10(a)(4). A reviewing court examining whether arbitrators exceeded their powers must resolve all doubts in favor of arbitration....

B. Arbitration is a matter of contract.... Thus, "[t]he power and authority of arbitrators in an arbitration proceeding is dependent on the provisions under which the arbitrators were appointed." *Szuts v. Dean Witter Reynolds, Inc.*, 931 F.2d 830, 831 (11th Cir.1991). Parties to an arbitration agreement may determine by contract the method for appointment of arbitrators. The FAA expressly provides that where a method for appointment is set out in the arbitration agreement, the agreed upon method of appointment "shall be followed." 9 U.S.C. § 5.

Several courts, relying on § 5, have determined that "[a]rbitration awards made by arbitrators not appointed under the method provided in the parties' contract must be vacated." *Cargill Rice, Inc. v. Empresa Nicaraguense Dealimentos Basicos*, 25 F.3d 223, 226 (4th Cir.1994); ... However, "a 'trivial departure' from the parties' agreement [ ] may not bar enforcement of an award." *R.J. O'Brien*, 64 F.3d at 263. Brook relies on these cases and argues that the arbitration award must be vacated because Judge Miller was not appointed according to the process outlined in the Employment Agreement.

To state that the AAA failed to follow the simple selection procedure outlined in Brook's Employment Agreement is insufficient: the AAA flouted the prescribed procedures and ignored complaints from both sides about the irregular selection process. Rather than submitting a list of nine names and instructing the parties alternately to strike names from the list until only one remained, the AAA submitted two lists containing the names of fifteen potential arbitrators. The AAA instructed the parties to strike all unacceptable arbitrators and rank the remaining candidates in order of preference. The AAA's departure from the selection procedure outlined in the Employment Agreement was utterly unwarranted. Because arbitration is a creature of contract, the AAA's departure from the contractual selection process fundamentally contradicts its role in voluntary dispute resolution. The AAA must follow the selection procedures outlined in the arbitration agreement. 9 U.S.C. § 5.

Nevertheless, despite its asserted efficiencies over judicial proceedings, arbitration remains an adversarial event, and parties must insist upon the enforcement of their contractual rights before the arbitrators as they do in court. This is especially true if any case is to be made, under the exceedingly narrow statutory standards, for a later judicial review of the arbitration.

In the cases cited above, where federal courts vacated arbitration awards because of irregularities in the process for selecting arbitrators, the complaining party preserved its objection during the arbitration proceeding. Here, however, Brook never objected to the AAA's failure to follow the selection process in the Employment Agreement (until prompted by the federal magistrate judge long after the arbitration had run its course). It is true that Brook filed a written objection to the AAA's failure to follow its own selection rules,but he also condoned the AAA's ignoring the Employment Agreement when he urged the AAA to reinstate the "properly appointed" arbitrator, Professor Sokolow, although Sokolow had not been appointed according to the terms of the Employment Agreement. The failure to file a clear written objection to a defect in the selection process constitutes waiver....

Brook compounded his inaction by failing to object to the error in the selection process before Judge Miller during the arbitration proceedings. In particular, at the outset of the arbitration hearing, Judge Miller invited the parties to state their objections to the arbitration on the record, and Brook did nothing. This court has previously held that objections to the composition of arbitration panels must be raised "at the time of the hearing." *Bernstein Seawell & Kove v. Bosarge*, 813 F.2d 726, 732 (5th Cir.1987). Brook's failure to object at the hearing constitutes waiver. *Id.*

Alternatively, before proceeding to arbitration, Brook could have sought an order from the district court compelling arbitration before a properly selected arbitrator pursuant to sections 4 and 5 of the FAA. But Brook did not timely go to court. In sum, Brook did not state clearly his objection to the AAA's failure to follow the Employment Agreement when an arbitrator was selected; Brook made no effort to preserve his objection to arbitrating while the dispute was pending before Judge Miller; and Brook finally raised the crucial objection after the magistrate judge conceived it. "It is well settled that a party may not sit idle through an arbitration procedure and then collaterally attack the procedure on grounds not raised before the arbitrators when the result turns out to be adverse." *Marino v. Writers Guild of America, East, Inc.*, 992 F.2d 1480, 1484 (9th Cir.1993).

We do not hold that Brook had to exhaust all of the described avenues of objecting to the arbitrator selection process, but as was done in the cases on which he relies, he had to make plain and timely his exact objection so that a responsible party—whether the AAA or the arbitrator or a federal court—could have enforced the Employment Agreement.

CONCLUSION

For the reasons stated above, we REVERSE the judgment of the district court and REMAND for further proceedings consistent with this opinion.

NOTES

(1) *Attacking arbitral awards under the FAA.* The primary focus of the FAA is upon enforcing the agreement to arbitrate, Sections 1–4, and confirming and enforcing the arbitral award, Sections 9–12. The statute says little if anything about such problems as how the arbitral tribunal is appointed, duties of disclosure by the arbitrators, conduct of the hearing, or immunity of

arbitrators. By default, these matters are left to the arbitration rules (if any) adopted by the parties and to the courts.

When the winner seeks to confirm an award under Section 9 of the FAA, however, the loser has a limited chance under Section 10 to review the propriety of what went on before. For example, an award can be vacated if the loser establishes any of the following statutory grounds.

(1) The award was procured by corruption, fraud, or undue means. Here the conduct of the parties or their lawyers rather than the arbitrators is on trial.

(2) There was "evident partiality or corruption" in the arbitrators. Here the focus is on the arbitrators, particularly on their independence and impartiality.

(3) The arbitrators were guilty of misconduct in refusing to postpone the hearing, or refusing to hear evidence relevant and material to the controversy, or "any other misbehavior by which the rights of any party have been prejudiced."

(4) The arbitrators have exceeded their powers or so imperfectly executed them that a "mutual, final, and definite award upon the subject matter was not made."

What was the ground relied upon by the plaintiff in *Brook v. Peak International*? If the selection of arbitrators did not follow the contract requirements, why wasn't the award vacated?

(2) *Judicial review of law questions decided by the arbitrators*. The grounds for vacating arbitral awards under Section 10 of the FAA, Section 23 of the Revised UAA, and Article V of the New York Convention (dealing with international arbitration) do not include erroneous decisions of law or fact by the tribunal. Without more, these decisions are final and are not subject to judicial review.

In the United States, at least, a non-statutory ground for vacating an award has emerged; an arbitrator's award may be vacated for "manifest disregard" of the law. According to the Second Circuit, "a party seeking vacatur must ... demonstrate that the arbitrator knew of the relevant principle, appreciated that this principle controlled the outcome of the disputed issue, and nonetheless willfully flouted [decided to ignore or pay no attention to] the governing law by refusing to apply it." Westerbeke Corp. v. Daihatsu Motor Co., Ltd., 304 F.3d 200, 217 (2d Cir.2002) (stating principle and reviewing cases). Arguably, this non-statutory ground is part of the ground stated in FAA Section 10(4) that the arbitrator may not exceed his or her powers. Thus, if the parties chose the law of a state that had Rule X and the arbitrator disregarded it, the arbitrator exceeded his or her authority. But as the cases reveal, it is not this simple. Even though there are very few cases actually vacating an award for manifest disregard, one can safely conclude that a doctrine of dubious origin frequently invoked by losers has caused more delay and expense in the final enforcement of awards.

A more recent issue involves the enforceability of agreements between the parties to an arbitration to expand the grounds in FAA Section 10 to include review for errors of law. At this time, there is a split among the circuits, with the 9th Circuit willing to enforce the agreement, Lapine Technology Corp. v. Kyocera Corp., 130 F.3d 884 (9th Cir.1997), and the 5th Circuit denying enforcement, Bowen v. Amoco Pipeline Co., 254 F.3d 925 (10th Cir.2001). Which position do you prefer? If arbitration is a creature of contract and the parties have power to chose state arbitration law that differs from the FAA, shouldn't they also have power to vary the effect of the FAA for their particular arbitration?

Finally, the position of the English Arbitration Act of 1996, which applies to almost all arbitrations where the "seat" of arbitration is in the UK, is worth noting. First, Section 45(1) permits a court, upon application of a party, to "determine any question of law arising in the course of the proceedings which the court is satisfied substantially affects the rights of one or more of the parties." The process, however, is hedged with conditions and can be blocked if one party to the proceeding does not agree. More to the point, in addition to the grounds for challenge stated in Section 68 (serious irregularity affecting the tribunal, the proceedings or the award), a party to an arbitration proceeding may appeal to the court on a question of law arising out of the award. Section 69(1). Once again, all parties must agree to the appeal, which will be granted only if the determination will substantially affect the rights of one or more parties and the decision of the tribunal was obviously wrong or the question is one of "general public importance and the decision of the tribunal is at least open to serious doubt." Section 69(3).

(3) *Scope of the Revised Uniform Arbitration Act.* The Revised UAA, like its predecessor, is far more comprehensive than the FAA. It has sections on provisional remedies (8), the initiation of arbitration (9), consolidation of separate arbitration proceedings (10), the appointment of and disclosure by arbitrators (11–12), the immunity of arbitrators (14), the arbitration process (15), discovery and witnesses (17), the award (19–20), and remedies (21). Most but not all of these rules are variable by agreement of the parties. See Section 4.

Section 23, which tracks FAA Section 10, states a bit more elaborately the grounds for vacating an award. The revision, however, is silent on two pesky questions, whether an award can be vacated for manifest disregard of the law and whether the parties have power to expand the scope of judicial review by agreement.

For a discussion of this impressive revision by the Reporter, see Timothy J. Heinsz, *The Revised Uniform Arbitration Act: An Overview*, 56 Disp. Res. J. 28 (May/June 2001). For a comparison of the Revised UAA and the ICANN Uniform Domain Name Dispute Resolution Policy, see Richard E. Speidel, *ICANN Domain Name Dispute Resolution, The Revised Uniform Arbitration Act, and the Limitations of Modern Arbitration Law*, 6 J. of Small & Emerging Bus. L. 167, 177–188 (2002).

CHAPTER NINE

THIRD PARTY INTERESTS

We turn now to two issues that are often given short shrift in first-year courses: (i) a contractor's ability subsequent to an initial contract to assign the rights or delegate the duties of performance to third-persons (not in privity with the initial contractors) and (ii) a contractor's ability as part of the initial contract to confer rights on so-called "third-party beneficiaries" (who do not themselves provide any consideration for these benefits).

SECTION 1. ASSIGNMENT AND DELEGATION

Once a contract right exists, can it be sold or given to another? Can one assign rights and delegate duties or performance to someone else?

Basic transactions. There are two common transactions that produce assignments. First, A sells and delivers goods to or performs services for B who promises to pay the price at some future time. A's right against B is commonly called an account receivable. Second, C agrees to construct a home for D who promises to pay as work progresses. Since C, unlike A, has not yet earned payment by performance under the contract, the right against D is commonly called a contract right, although it is now swept under the definition of "account" in Revised Article 9. UCC Rev. 9–102(a)(2). Note that both A and C have extended credit. If they need cash before B's and D's duties mature, they may try to assign or sell the account or contract right to a third party for an immediate but discounted cash payment. If there is a willing third party and contract law will permit enforcement of A's and C's contract rights against B and D, A and C can convert a promise of future payment into present cash. This ability is the hallmark of a credit economy, for it permits the third party immediately to finance A and C on the strength of B's and D's promises.

Occasionally, a contractor in the position of C will attempt to transfer the contract to the third party, i.e., assign the rights and delegate the duties. More frequently a construction contractor will assign rights to a bank for immediate financing and delegate some performance duties to subcontractors. As you might imagine, the risks involved to the third party who pays value for rights or assumes the responsibility for performance are considerable and vary from transaction to transaction. See Grant Gilmore, *The Assignee of Contract Rights and His Precarious Security,* 74 Yale L.J. 216 (1964). For example, the rights of an assignee are, in general, subject to all the terms of the contract between the assignor and the account debtor and any claim or defense arising therefrom. See Rev. 9–404(a); Restatement, (Second) §§ 334–339.

Since assignments are commonplace today—indeed one cannot imagine our complex credit structure existing without them—it may come as a surprise to learn that at one time common law courts refused to recognize the assignability of a "chose in action," including a right arising *ex contractu*.* The emphasis upon the personal relationship of the contracting parties, discernible also in the development of third party beneficiary contracts, tended to make the lack of privity an insurmountable obstacle to the third party's right of action. However, at a time when common law courts steadfastly refused to recognize assignments, the law merchant, presumably in response to commercial demand, developed a considerable body of assignment doctrine. As the economy expanded, the common law courts, spurred on by courts of equity, came to fashion legal doctrine which, in effect, permitted the assignment of a contract right.**

Effect of UCC Article 9. The widespread adoption of UCC Article 9, the secured transactions article, however, has preempted a considerable chunk of assignments law. Pre-revision Article 9 applied to "any transaction (regardless of its form) which is intended to create a security interest in personal property * * * including * * * general intangibles * * * or accounts; and also * * * to any sale of accounts." UCC 9–102(1). Expressly excluded from Article 9, however, was a "sale of accounts * * * which is for the purpose of collection only, or a transfer of a right to payment under a contract to an assignee who is also to do the performance under the contract * * *." UCC 9–104(f). This preemption is continued and enhanced in Revised Article 9. See Rev. 9–109 on the scope of Article 9.

With one exception, the emphasis here is on assignment law which is not preempted by Article 9.***

* The severe proscription of maintenance and champerty, the unlawful interference in or purchase of an interest in another's lawsuit, helped create a climate of judicial disfavor to the notion of one suing to enforce a right arising out of a transaction to which one was not privy.

** This was accomplished ostensibly within the framework of settled law, but actually amounted to a sharp departure from precedent. The "owner" of the right could appoint another as agent for collection and agree that the latter would keep the proceeds. As time went on, even if the transaction was formally denominated an assignment, courts would say the effect was to create a power of attorney, enabling the "assignee" to sue in the name of the "assignor." There were serious drawbacks to this agency evasion, however. The "assignor" could revoke the agency, and revocation was effected automatically by death or bankruptcy. To overcome this defect in the process, litigants appealed, characteristically, to the Chancery court. And, again characteristically, equity responded. If the "assignee" gave value, he or she would be treated as "owner" of the claim, which ownership could not be divested by the "assignor's" attempted revocation or by death or bankruptcy. At this point the future of assignment doctrine was assured. While there persisted for years a language which described choses in action as assignable in equity but not at law, the subsequent merger of law and equity caused even this terminology to all but disappear. The result is that the power of assignment is firmly embedded in the law, and judicial attention has been given to the implications and ramifications of this power. See Lon L. Fuller, Basic Contract Law 585–92 (1947).

*** For collateral reading, see Farnsworth §§ 11.1–11.11; Calamari and Perillo §§ 18.1–18.32; Murray §§ 135–142.

Sale of goods. For the sale of goods, the assignment of contractual rights is presumptively valid "unless otherwise agreed" or unless "the assignment would materially change the duty of the other party or increase materially the burden or risk imposed on him by his contract." UCC 2–210(2). Accord Restatement (Second) § 317(2). This subsection, however, is subject to Rev. 9–406. See Rev. 2–210.

There are relatively few cases where the assignment of a contract right alone has been held to materially increase the obligor's risk, especially where the right is to the payment of money. For a few examples, see Crane Ice Cream Co. v. Terminal Freezing & Heating Co., 147 Md. 588, 128 A. 280 (1925); Kingston v. Markward & Karafilis, Inc., 134 Mich.App. 164, 350 N.W.2d 842 (1984) (assignment of right to indemnification materially increases risk). But see Collins Co., Ltd. v. Carboline Co., 125 Ill.2d 498, 127 Ill.Dec. 5, 532 N.E.2d 834 (1988) (assignment by buyer of right to express warranty does not materially increase seller's risk); Evening News Association v. Peterson, 477 F.Supp. 77 (D.D.C.1979) (assignment of right to services of newscaster does not materially increase risk); Tennell v. Esteve Cotton Co., 546 S.W.2d 346 (Tex.Civ.App.1976) (buyer's assignment of cotton contract does not materially increase seller's risk).

Once a right to payment is due, the UCC also allows promisees to assign their rights even if the initial contract prohibits assignment—thus giving promisees an immutable option to assign rights which are no longer executory, including a right to damages for breach or a right to payment of an "account." See UCC 2–210(2) and Rev. 9–406(d).

(A) ASSIGNMENT OF RIGHTS

Fitzroy v. Cave

Court of Appeal, 1905.
2 K.B. 364.

■ COZENS-HARDY L.J. read the following judgment:—This is an appeal from the judgment of Lawrance J. in favour of the defendant. The plaintiff is the assignee of five debts amounting together to over 50*l.* due from the defendant to five creditors resident in Ireland. The assignment is effected by a deed dated October 13, 1904.

[The deed provided: "And the assignee hereby covenants with the assignors, and with each of them, that, in case he shall be able to recover and realize the amount of the said debts from the said Arthur Oriel Singer Cave, he will immediately thereupon pay over to them, the assignors, their executors, administrators, and assigns, the said respective amounts, or so much thereof as he may be able to recover or realize, after payment of all costs necessarily incurred by him." Notice in writing of this assignment had been given to the defendant.

It appeared in evidence that the plaintiff was interested in, and a director of, a company called the Cork Mineral Development Company. The defendant was a co-director and the local manager of the company. The plaintiff, being dissatisfied with the action of the defendant as a director of the company, had, acting under the advice of a solicitor, taken the assignment of the before-mentioned debts with the view of procuring an adjudication in bankruptcy against the defendant, and so getting him removed from the directorate of the company.]

It is desirable to consider the limits of the doctrine of maintenance as applied to choses in action. There are undoubtedly many choses in action which are not and never were assignable either at law or in equity. * * *

There are, however, other choses in action which, though not assignable at common law, were always regarded as assignable in equity. A debt presently due and payable is an instance. At common law such a debt was looked upon as a strictly personal obligation, and an assignment of it was regarded as a mere assignment of a right to bring an action at law against the debtor. Hence the assignment was, with some exceptions which need not be referred to . . . looked upon as open to the objection of maintenance. After a time the Common Law Courts recognized the right of any one who had a pecuniary interest in the debt to sue in the name of the creditor. This, however, was the limit of their departure from the old strict rule, so far as I have been able to discover. But the Courts of Equity took a different view: . . . They admitted the title of an assignee of a debt, regarding it as a piece of property, an asset capable of being dealt with like any other asset, and treating the necessity of an action at law to get it in as a mere incident. They declined to hold such a transaction open to the charge of maintenance. * * *

A Court of Equity recognized not merely transactions which amounted to sales or mortgages of debts, under which the assignee took a beneficial interest in the debt, but also the creation of trusts, under which the trustee took no interest. Thus A., the creditor, might assign the debt to B., with or without a power of attorney, upon trust for C. Or A. might simply declare himself a trustee of the debt for C. In either case the trustee would take no beneficial interest, and would, by virtue of his position as trustee, be entitled to be indemnified out of the moneys recovered against all costs of the action brought in the name of A. against the debtor. If the debt were secured by a promissory note or bill or other negotiable instrument, A. might deliver the instrument to B. upon trust for C., and B. could sue at law on it. Or A. might create a trust in favour of himself by delivering the instrument to B. upon trust for himself. It would, I apprehend, in this case be no objection to say that B. had no interest in the debt. It has never, so far as I am aware, been suggested that a trustee to whom a debt is assigned is exposed to a charge of maintenance. Mortgages are every day dealt with in this fashion, including an assignment of the debt. From time to time particular classes of obligation have by statute been rendered assignable at law, and by the Judicature Act, 1873, s. 25, sub-s. 6, any debt is made assignable at law by an absolute assignment in writing, of which notice is given to the debtor. Henceforth in all Courts a debt must be regarded as a piece of property capable of legal assignment in the same sense as a bale of goods. And on principle I think it is not possible to deny the right of the owner of any property capable of legal assignment to vest that property in a trustee for himself, and thereby to confer upon such trustee a right of indemnity. It is not easy to see how the doctrine of maintenance can be applied to a case like the present. * * * It is said that the plaintiff does not really desire to be paid and can take nothing for his own benefit under the judgment. For the reasons above stated I think this is of no moment. It is further urged that his only object is to obtain a judgment which may serve as the foundation of bankruptcy proceedings, the ultimate result of which will be the removal of the defendant from his position as director of a company in which the plaintiff is largely interested. But I fail to see that we have anything to do with the motives which actuate the plaintiff, who is simply asserting a legal right consequential upon the possession of property which has been validly assigned to him. If the defendant pays, no bankruptcy proceedings will follow. If he does not pay, bankruptcy is a possible result. In my opinion this appeal must be allowed.

Appeal allowed.

NOTES

(1) Is not the effect of the decision, in *Fitzroy,* to obligate the defendant to do something which he had not agreed to do; *viz.,* pay the plaintiff rather than the "five tradesmen in Ireland"? Does this holding improperly impinge freedom of contract? For a treatment of assignment in English law, see G. Treitel, The Law of Contract, ch. 16 (10th ed. 1999).

(2) What policy justification is there for the recognition of a power to assign a contract right? Cozens–Hardy, L.J., states that "a debt must be regarded as a piece of property capable of legal assignment in the same sense as a bale of goods." Do you agree? With what qualification(s), if any?

(3) Does the fact that the assignee is *persona non grata* with the debtor bar an action? Should it? Suppose, for example, that you have leased an apartment from your favorite cousin and "cousin" assigns her right to payment of the rent to Skinflint, a collection agent who is known as a "hard nose."

(4) *Irrevocable Gratuitous Assignments.* Restatement (Second) Contracts § 332(1) provides: "(1) Unless a contrary intention is manifested, a gratuitous assignment is irrevocable if (a) the assignment is in a writing either signed or under seal that is delivered by the assignor; or (b) the assignment is accompanied by delivery of a writing of a type customarily accepted as a symbol or as evidence of the right assigned." In both parts, one expressly and the other impliedly, the pattern adopted is consistent with the requirement respecting gifts of chattels that a symbolic or constructive "delivery" is required. See Brown, The Law of Personal Property § 7.2 (3d ed. 1975).

(5) *Assignment of "Future Accounts" under Article 9.* If one "owns" something—a tract of land, an automobile, a chose in action—one has a legal and practical advantage, an "asset." With this asset one can, for example, obtain money, either by transferring ownership (as in a sale) or by using the asset as security for a loan (as in a mortgage or pledge). But what if this something has no present existence in the ordinary sense, such as fish to be caught, gears to be manufactured, crops to be grown, accounts receivable from

future sales? Can there be a present sale or assignment of whatever there is—the "expectancy," or "hope"? Why should not one be able to sell "anything" which another is willing to buy, providing of course the transaction is not violative of public policy?

It became particularly useful for sellers to assign their expected accounts receivable for future sales as security to help the seller receive credit. The financing of accounts receivable has developed into a major industry. Indeed, the transfer of these rights may be the most notable contemporary implementation of the power of assignment. A serious difficulty encountered in the operation of receivables financing was the problem of handling future accounts. Early in the twentieth century courts were hostile to the assignment of future accounts. See, e.g., Taylor v. Barton–Child Co., 228 Mass. 126, 117 N.E. 43 (1917). To circumvent such precedents, it was deemed necessary for the debtor/seller to execute supplementary assignments as the accounts came into existence.

Restatement (Second) § 321, however, reflects a much more congenial attitude toward the assignment of future accounts: "(1) Except as otherwise provided by statute, an assignment of a right to payment expected to arise out of an existing employment or other continuing business relationship is effective in the same way as an assignment of an existing right. (2) Except as otherwise provided by statute and as stated in Subsection (1), a purported assignment of a right expected to arise under a contract not in existence operates only as a promise to assign the right when it arises and as a power to enforce it."

Article 9 of the UCC goes even further in facilitating the sale or assignment of future accounts. Pre-revision UCC 9–204(1) provided:

> [A] security agreement may provide that any or all obligations covered by the security agreement are to be secured by after-acquired collateral.

Under this provision, the secured party may include in the security agreement an "after-acquired property" clause, file a financing statement with the proper officer, give value to the debtor and be assured of a perfected security interest at the time when the debtor obtains rights in the described collateral—including any "accounts receivable" subsequently acquired. No further agreement or filing is required. This policy is continued in Revised Article 9. See Rev. 9–204.

(6) *Future Wages.* Modern legislation has limited the assignability of "future wages." A few states prohibit all such assignments; most regulate the practice, as by restricting the amount of wages subject to assignment, etc. See Statutory Note, Restatement (Second) Ch. 15.

Allhusen v. Caristo Construction Corp.

Court of Appeals of New York, 1952.
303 N.Y. 446, 103 N.E.2d 891.

■ FROESSEL, JUDGE. Defendant, a general contractor, subcontracted with the Kroo Painting Company (hereinafter called Kroo) for the performance by the latter of certain painting work in New York City public schools. Their contracts contained the following prohibitory provision: "The assignment by the second party [Kroo] of this contract or any interest therein, or of any money due or to become due by reason of the terms hereof without the written consent of the first party [defendant] shall be void." Kroo subsequently assigned certain rights under the contracts to Marine Midland Trust Company of New York, which in turn assigned said rights to plaintiff. These rights included the "moneys due and to become due" to Kroo. The *contracts* were not assigned, and no question of improper delegation of contractual duties is involved. No written consent to the assignments was procured from defendant.

Plaintiff as assignee seeks to recover, in six causes of action, $11,650 allegedly due and owing for work done by Kroo. Defendant answered with denials, and by way of defense set up the aforementioned prohibitory clause, in addition to certain setoffs and counterclaims, alleged to have existed at the time of the assignments. It thereupon moved for summary judgment under rule 113 of the Rules of Civil Practice, and demanded dismissal of plaintiff's several causes of action on the sole ground that the prohibitory clause constituted a defense sufficient as a matter of law to defeat each cause of action. Special Term dismissed the complaint, holding that the prohibition against assignments "must be given effect." The Appellate Division affirmed, one Justice dissenting on the ground that the "account receivable was assignable by nature, and could not be rendered otherwise without imposing an unlawful restraint upon the power of alienation of property." 278 App.Div. 817, 104 N.Y.S.2d 565, 566.

Whether an anti-assignment clause is effective is a question that has troubled the courts not only of this State but in other jurisdictions as well.
. . .

Our courts have not construed a contractual provision against assignments framed in the language of the clause now before us. Such kindred clauses as have been subject to interpretation usually have been held to be either (1) personal covenants limiting the covenantee to a claim for damages in the event of a breach ... or (2) ineffectual because of the use of uncertain language ... But these decisions are not to be read as meaning that there can be no enforceable prohibition against the assignment of a claim; indeed, they are authority only for the proposition that, in the absence of language clearly indicating that a contractual right thereunder shall be nonassignable, a prohibitory clause will be interpreted as a personal covenant not to assign. * * *

[The court reviewed relevant New York cases.]

In the light of the foregoing, we think it is reasonably clear that, while the courts have striven to uphold freedom of assignability, they have not failed to recognize the concept of freedom to contract. In large measure they agree that, where appropriate language is used, assignments of money due under contracts may be prohibited. When "clear language" is used, and the "plainest words * * * have been chosen", parties may "limit the freedom of alienation of rights and prohibit the assignment." [Citing authority.] ... We have now before us a clause embodying clear, definite and appropriate language, which may be construed in no other way but that any attempted assignment of either the contract or any rights created thereunder shall be "void" as against the obligor. One would have to do violence to the language here employed to hold that it is merely an agreement by the subcontractor not to assign. The objectivity of the language precludes such a construction. We are therefore compelled to conclude that this prohibitory clause is a valid and effective restriction of the right to assign.

Such a holding is not violative of public policy. * * * Plaintiff's claimed rights arise out of the very contract embodying the provision now sought to be invalidated. The right to moneys under the contracts is but a companion to other jural relations forming an aggregation of actual and potential interrelated rights and obligations. No sound reason appears why an assignee should remain unaffected by a provision in the very contract which gave life to the claim he asserts.

Nor is there any merit in plaintiff's contention that section 41 of the Personal Property Law, Consol.Laws, c. 41, requires that the prohibitory clause be denied effect. Because the statute provides that a person may transfer a claim, it does not follow that he may not contract otherwise. Countless rights granted by statutes are voluntarily surrendered in the everyday affairs of individuals. In Rosenthal Paper Co. v. National Folding Box & Paper Co., 226 N.Y. 313, 325–326, we noted: "The general rule now prevailing * * * that any property right, not necessarily personal, is assignable, *is overcome only by agreement of the contracting parties* or a principal of law or public policy. In this jurisdiction the statute, in effect, so provides [referring to the predecessor of section 41 of the Personal Property Law]."

The judgment should be affirmed, with costs.

NOTES

(1) In terms of legal consequence, what is the difference between saying the prohibition deprived Kroo of the power to assign rather than merely created a duty on his part not to do so? What policy conflicts are discernible in a case of this type?

(2) *Assignment of Claims Against the United States.* There has been legislation prohibiting the assignment of executory contract claims against the United States since 1792. See 41 U.S.C.A. § 15 and 31 U.S.C.A. § 203. As a noted practitioner of government contract law once put it, the basic purposes of this prohibition are to "protect the government against harassment caused by a multiplication of the firms with which it has to deal; prevent collusive bidding; prevent persons of influence from buying up claims against the government which then might be used against government officials; preserve for the government any defense it might have against the assignor by way of set-off or counterclaim; and secure for the government the performance of the firm with which it contracts." Gilbert Cuneo, Government Contracts Handbook 7 (1962). In 1940, however, an amendment was approved by Congress permitting contractors to assign money due or to become due from the United States under a contract providing for payments aggregating $1,000 or more to a "bank, trust company, or other financing institution." The purpose of this amendment was

to assist government contractors in obtaining private financing on the security of the government's promise to pay for work done or to be done.

Owen v. CNA Insurance/Continental Casualty Company

Supreme Court of New Jersey, 2001.
167 N.J. 450, 771 A.2d 1208.

■ STEIN, J.

This appeal involves a tort victim who brought an action against a liability insurer for a declaratory judgment that the non-assignment clause in a structured settlement agreement was unenforceable. The trial court granted summary judgment in favor of the tort victim, holding that under current law the non-assignment clause was unenforceable. The Appellate Division reversed, concluding that the enforceability of the non-assignment clause depended on its materiality to the primary purposes of the settlement agreement and remanding the matter for further fact finding on that question. One member of the appellate panel dissented, stating that "a holding that the assignment in this case was ineffective has no current legitimate provenance in law." The tort victim appealed as of right based on the dissent below. . . . The specific issue is whether the non-assignment clause in the structured settlement agreement at issue is enforceable.

I

In September 1983, plaintiff Carol Owen (Owen) signed a release in favor of parties she had sued in a personal-injury action arising out of a slip-and-fall accident at a Bamberger's Store in East Brunswick, New Jersey. . . . In connection with that release, Owen entered into a settlement agreement with the tortfeasor's insurer, Continental Casualty Corporation (Continental). . . . Under the terms of the settlement agreement, Owen was entitled to receive an initial lump sum payment of $10,000, attorney's fees of $15,000, and five deferred periodic payments totaling $81,067.24. *Ibid.* The periodic payments were scheduled as follows: December 21, 1986—$6,505.48; December 21, 1991—$9,558.68; December 21, 1996—$14,044.84; December 21, 2001—$20,636.48; December 21, 2006—$30,321.76. The non-assignment provision of the settlement agreement stated:

> The claimant shall have the right to change the Contingent Payee at any time during the term of this Agreement by filing written notice with the Company, such change to be effective when accepted by the Company in writing as of the date such notice was signed, except as to any payments made by the Company before such change was accepted. To the extent provided by law, the aforesaid deferred lump sum payments shall not be subject to assignment, transfer, commutation, or encumbrance, except as provided herein.

Because of mounting medical bills due to illness unrelated to her lawsuit, in December 1997 Owen entered into a "Purchase and Sale Agreement" with Metropolitan Mortgage and Securities Company (Metropolitan) pursuant to which she agreed to " 'sell, convey, transfer and assign' to Metropolitan all her 'rights and benefits' under the settlement agreement with [Continental] for $8,520.20." ... At the time of the assignment to Metropolitan, Owen was entitled to receive the 2001 ($20,636.48) and 2006 ($30,321.76) payments under the structured settlements.... However, the parties dispute whether Owen sold both remaining payments or only the 2001 payment to Metropolitan.... Under the assignment agreement, Owen also agreed (1) to defend, indemnify, and hold Metropolitan harmless for any claim that her periodic payments were not assignable and (2) to "order and conduct [her] affairs [so] as to prevent the assertion of any claim that the Benefits were not assignable." ...

In January 1998, in furtherance of the assignment, Owen sent Continental a notarized letter directing it to send "all future payments and other mail" to a new address in Syracuse, New York. Continental responded by sending Owen a copy of the settlement agreement and noting that the deferred periodic payments were not subject to assignment. After Owen's attorney wrote three letters to Continental seeking confirmation that Continental had changed the address, Continental in turn requested confirmation that Owen resided at the Syracuse address. Owen's counsel responded by enclosing a draft letter of complaint to the New Jersey Department of Banking and Insurance (Department of Insurance) and indicated that she would file the complaint in the absence of immediate written acknowledgment that Continental had changed Owen's address. In another letter, Owen's counsel indicated that Owen's place of residence was "irrelevant" and demanded again that Continental change the address to which future payments were to be sent. In response, Continental then advised Owen's counsel that

> Continental Casualty Company is required to make payments to the claimant. The payments are not assignable by the claimant. Accordingly, the payments are always sent to the claimant's actual address. The Company does not send payments to a street address at which the claimant does not reside.

Subsequently, Owen filed a complaint with the Department of Insurance, but the Department took no action. * * *

[The court reviewed the decisions of the trial court and the court of appeals.]

II

Although our statutes do not contain specific provisions regulating the transfer of structured settlement rights,* effective January 1, 1963, the

---

* We note that in February 2000, Senate Bill S–944 and its companion Assembly Bill A–2146 were introduced in the New Jersey Senate and Assembly. On December 4, 2000, the Senate adopted its substitute for S–944. On May 24, 2001 the General Assembly passed its substitute for A–2146. Further action on those bills is pending. Relevant language in those bills prohibits transfer of structured settlement rights except under certain circumstances:

4. No direct or indirect transfer of structured settlement payment rights shall be effective and no structured settlement obligor or annuity issuer shall be required to make

Uniform Commercial Code (U.C.C.) became the governing statutory law in New Jersey regulating commercial transactions throughout the State. *N.J.S.A.* 12A:10–106. A threshold issue is whether Article 9 of the U.C.C. affects the validity of Continental's non-assignment clause. *N.J.S.A.* 12A:9–318(4) provides:

> A term in any contract between an account debtor and an assignor is ineffective if it prohibits assignment of an account or prohibits creation of a security interest in chattel paper or a security interest in a general intangible for money due or to become due or requires the account debtor's consent to the assignment or security interest.

Although that provision invalidates contractual non-assignment provisions, *N.J.S.A.* 12A:9–104(k) provides that Article 9 does not apply "[t]o a transfer in whole or in part of any claim arising out of tort." Because the meaning of "any claim arising out of tort" is not explicitly defined in the statute, whether or not section 9–104(k)'s exclusion applies to the proceeds of tort claims has become a highly controversial issue. The Appellate Division determined that the exclusion in *N.J.S.A.* 12A:9–104(k) also applied to the proceeds of tort claims.... However, no clear majority rule exists concerning the application of Article 9 to tort claim proceeds. *Barclays Bus. Credit, Inc. v. Four Winds Plaza Partnership*, 938 *F.Supp.* 304, 308 (D.Vi.1996). * * *

[The court reviewed the arguments for and against applying Article 9 to assignments of proceeds of tort claims.]

Putting to one side the Article 9 debate and focusing instead on New Jersey assignment law, we note that *N.J.S.A.* 2A:25–1 provides that "all judgments and decrees recoverable in any of the courts" in New Jersey are assignable. Thus, New Jersey law generally permits the assignment of settlement proceeds unless the parties have expressly agreed otherwise. *Chelsea–Wheeler Coal Co. v. Marvin*, 134 *N.J. Eq.* 432, 35 A.2d 874 (E. & A.1944), established the common-law doctrine that a contractual provision that prohibits the assignment of rights under a contract may be disregarded when it is not the main purpose of the contract. * * *

[The court discussed the case, which held that the main purpose of the assignment of proceeds under a life insurance contract was to provide a

any payment directly or indirectly to any transferee of structured settlement payment rights unless the transfer has been approved in advance in a final court order or order of a responsible administrative authority based on express findings by the court or responsible administrative authority that:

a. the transfer is in the best interest of the payee, taking into account the welfare and support of the payee's dependents; b. the payee has been advised in writing by the transferee to seek independent professional advice regarding the transfer and has either received the advice or knowingly waived the right to seek that advice in writing; and c. the transfer does not contravene any applicable statute or the order of any court or other government authority.

[Senate Substitute for Senate Committee Substitute for S. 944, 209th Legis. (Dec. 4, 2000); Assembly Committee Substitute for A. 2146, 209th Legis. (final passage on May 24, 2001).]

modest, regular income to the assignee and that, therefore, the clause prohibiting the assignment was not effective.]

Since the 1944 decision in *Chelsea–Wheeler*, we have not again considered the effect of contractual provisions limiting or prohibiting assignments. However, in *Garden State Buildings L.P. v. First Fidelity Bank, N.A.*, 305 *N.J.Super.* 510 (App.Div.1997), the Appellate Division addressed the issue, relying primarily on Section 322 of the Restatement of Contracts, which states in pertinent part:

> (2) A contract term prohibiting assignment of rights under the contract, unless a different intention is manifested, (a) does not forbid assignment of a right to damages for breach of the whole contract or a right arising out of the assignor's due performance of his entire obligation; (b) gives the obligor a right to damages for breach of the terms forbidding assignment but does not render the assignment ineffective; (c) is for the benefit of the obligor, and does not prevent the assignee from acquiring rights against the assignor or the obligor from discharging his duty as if there were no such prohibition.

[*Restatement (Second) of Contracts* § 322 (1981).]

The crucial phrase in section 322 is "unless a different intention is manifested." Courts diverge, however, regarding the standard for determining when parties to a contract have sufficiently manifested an intention to prohibit the power of assignment. * * *

To resolve the issue, the Appellate Division looked to Restatement section 322(2) as well as to out-of-state case law.... The court adopted the following test as the standard for determining whether non-assignment language in a contract invalidates an assignment made in violation of the contractual provisions:

> [T]o reveal the intent necessary to preclude the power to assign, or cause an assignment violative of contractual provisions to be wholly void, such clause must contain express provisions that any assignment shall be void or invalid if not made in a certain specified way ...

The Appellate Division held that, absent such express provisions, the assignment is valid, and that the obligor simply has the right to damages.

In adopting the standard advocated by Restatement section 322, the Appellate Division joined other jurisdictions that follow the general rule that contractual provisions limiting or prohibiting assignments operate only to limit a party's *right* to assign the contract, but not their *power* to do so, unless the parties manifest an intent to the contrary with specificity. *Bel–Ray Co. v. Chemrite (Pty) Ltd.*, 181 *F.*3d 435, 442 (3d Cir.1999) ...
* * *

In other jurisdictions, courts generally uphold non-assignment provisions of structured-settlement agreements when they include language stating that a plaintiff or payee shall not "have the power to sell, mortgage, encumber, or anticipate the Periodic Payments." *Liberty Life Assurance Co. v. Stone Street Capital, Inc.*, 93 *F.Supp.*2d 630, 637 (D.Md.2000); ...

In another relevant section, the Restatement of Contracts recognizes the validity of assignments of contractual rights, but with three important exceptions:

(2) A contractual right can be assigned unless

(a) the substitution of a right of the assignee for the right of the assignor would materially change the duty of the obligor, or materially increase the burden or risk imposed on him by his contract, or materially impair his chance of obtaining return performance, or materially reduce its value to him, or

(b) the assignment is forbidden by statute or is otherwise inoperative on grounds of public policy, or

(c) assignment is validly precluded by contract.

[*Restatement (Second) of Contracts* § 317 (1981).]

Comment d to section 317 indicates that exception (a) involves a fact-sensitive inquiry in which "[w]hat is a material variation, an increase in burden or risk, or an impairment of the obligor's expectation of counter-performance ... depends on the nature of the contract and on the circumstances."

In [*Grieve, supra,* 58 *F.Supp.*2d 319,] the court found that all three exceptions to the general assignability of rights under a contract recognized by section 317(2) applied to a structured settlement. After setting out the tax treatment of structured settlements in sections 104(a) and 130 of the Internal Revenue Code, that court determined that an assignment might cause the company funding the structured settlement to lose its eligibility for favorable tax treatment. *Id.* at 323. The court also was satisfied, however, that the assignment of settlement proceeds materially increased the risks to the company funding the structured settlement, which resulted in a material reduction of the value of the contract for that company. *Ibid.;* ... * * *

[The court reviewed other cases to the same effect and the treatment of structured settlements under the Internal Revenue Code.]

Based on those Code provisions, the typical personal-injury structured settlement operates in the following manner. The tortfeasor's insurance company assigns to another company, a structured-settlement company (typically a subsidiary of the insurance company), its liability to make the periodic payments to the plaintiff. In exchange for assuming its liability, the insurance company pays the structured-settlement company a lump sum that the insurance company immediately can deduct from its gross income. The structured settlement company then uses the lump sum to purchase an annuity to fund the periodic payments to the plaintiff. If the transaction meets the requirements of section 130, the structured-settlement company would not have to report the lump sum as income until it received the annuity payments, at which time it would be entitled to an offsetting deduction for periodic payments made to the plaintiff. And if the plaintiff meets the requirements of section 104(a)(2), he or she could exclude the periodic payments from his or her gross income, including only any portion of the periodic payment that represents interest income generated by the annuity.

III

A preliminary issue before us is whether the application of Article 9 of the U.C.C. is controlling. The Appellate Division concluded that Article 9 did not prohibit the non-assignment provision of the structured-settlement agreement because the express exclusion of tort claims from Article 9 includes tort-settlement proceeds.... Specifically, the Appellate Division concluded that "Article 9's express exclusion of tort claims includes the proceeds of a tort claim, and therefore ... Article 9 does not prohibit the non-assignment provision of plaintiff's contract with defendant." However, because we reach the same conclusion regarding the enforceability of the non-assignment clause irrespective of whether Article 9 applies to the proceeds of tort claims, and in view of the likely enactment of a statute specifically regulating assignments of structured settlements, we focus on whether the non-assignment provision is otherwise enforceable under New Jersey law and decline to decide whether tort-settlement proceeds are included in the express exclusion of tort claims of Article 9. * * *

Sections 322 and 317 are the relevant sections in the Restatement of Contracts dealing with assignments of contractual rights. Section 322 addresses the effect of contract terms that prohibit assignment of rights under a contract. Section 317 recognizes the validity of assignments, but specifically identifies important exceptions that limit the assignability of contractual rights. We are persuaded that the combined application of those two sections provides the best analytical framework to assess the validity of non-assignment provisions in a contract.

With regard to whether the non-assignment provision in Owen's structured-settlement agreement contains the explicit language necessary to void the assignment, we analyze the non-assignment provision under Restatement section 322, which embodies the general, now-majority rule that contractual provisions prohibiting or limiting assignments operate only to limit the parties' right to assign the contract, but not their power to assign, unless the parties manifest with specificity an intent to the contrary. In the absence of such a manifestation, a non-assignment provision is interpreted merely as a covenant not to assign, the breach of which renders the assigning party liable in damages. The assignment, however, remains valid and enforceable.

The non-assignment provision contained in Owen's structured settlement agreement stated: "To the extent provided by law, the aforesaid deferred lump sum payments shall not be subject to assignment, transfer, commutation, or encumbrance, except as provided herein." In our view, that language merely constitutes a covenant not to assign. It contains no specific prohibition on the power to make an assignment, and it does not specifically state that the assignments are "void," "invalid" or "that the assignee shall acquire no rights or the nonassigning party shall not recognize any such assignment." ... Therefore, the non-assignment provision does not "reveal the intent necessary to preclude the power to assign, or cause an assignment violative of contractual provisions to be wholly void." ... Thus, because the language does not specifically restrict Owen's power of assignment, the assignment is not void under section 322(2) of the Restatement.

With regard to section 317 of the Restatement, we address Continental's argument that the assignment of Owen's rights under the settlement agreement could cause it to face tax-reporting issues it allegedly bargained to avoid. We note that Owen's structured settlement agreement with Continental is not the typical personal-injury structured settlement in which a tortfeasor's insurance company assigns to a structured-settlement company its liability to make the periodic payments to the plaintiff. This record reveals that there is no structured-settlement company to which Continental paid a lump sum to purchase an annuity with the purpose of making periodic payments to Owen. As we understand the transaction, Continental itself undertook to make periodic payments to Owen. Because there is no structured-settlement company involved, section 130 of the Internal Revenue Code does not appear to entitle Continental to an offsetting deduction for periodic payments made to Owen.

Moreover, because Owen's structured settlement agreement was signed in 1983, the same year that Congress established the tax-incentive scheme favoring structured settlements, this settlement agreement apparently was not designed to take advantage of that favorable tax treatment. Accordingly, we reject Continental's contention that the assignment would cause it to lose tax benefits that it never anticipated receiving. * * * [T]he assignment would not cause Continental to "lose its eligibility for favorable tax treatment."

* * *

Accordingly, because the language in the non-assignment provision in Owen's structured settlement agreement does not specifically restrict Owen's power of assignment, and because the assignment would not "materially increase the burden or risk" imposed on Continental, we hold that in the context of this record Continental's non-assignment clause is unenforceable. We emphasize that because our holding is based on the record before us, it should not be understood to indicate that non-assignment provisions in structured settlement agreements generally are unenforceable.

We express our concern about the exceptionally high interest charge imposed by Metropolitan as compensation for its lump sum payment to Owen, and we anticipate that the Legislature will take cognizance of such interest charges in its statutory regulation of structured settlement assignments.

IV

We acknowledge that the terms of the original assignment agreement between Owen and Metropolitan may not be possible to implement because of the time that has elapsed between the agreement and our determination that the assignment is enforceable. We reverse the judgment of the Appellate Division and remand the matter to the Law Division to resolve any open issues relating to the terms and scope of the assignment that are susceptible to resolution by the court.

NOTES

(1) The *Owen* case is one of several recent decisions dealing with the enforceability of assignments of the right to payment created by structured settlements of tort and other claims. See e.g. Liberty Life Assur. Co. of Boston v. Stone Street Capital, Inc., 93 F.Supp.2d 630 (D.Md.2000) (anti-assignment clause valid and enforceable). Frequently, the stream of payments is created by an annuity established to implement the structured settlement. As the court notes, New Jersey, NJSA sec. 2A: 16–63 et seq. (and now 26 other states, including California and New York) have enacted legislation regulating these transactions. Review the statute, quoted in the court's note 1, *supra*. Would it change the result in this case? What is the purpose of this statute? See In re Transfer of Structured Settlement Rights by Spinelli, 353 N.J.Super. 459, 803 A.2d 172 (2002) (interpreting New Jersey's new legislation). See also Gregory Scott Crespi, Selling Structured Settlements: The Uncertain Effect of Anti-assignment Clauses, 28 Pepp. L. Rev. 787 (2001).

(2) In the absence of regulatory legislation, the assignee's strategy is to claim that the assignment of the right to payment is a secured transaction subject to Article 9 of the UCC. Why? The quick answer is that clauses prohibiting such assignments are, with some limitations, not effective. UCC 9–318(4); Rev. 9–406(d). The problem is that Revised Article 9 (as well as its predecessor) does not apply to the assignment of a claim "arising in tort", Rev. 9–109(c)(12), or the transfer of a claim "under a policy of insurance." Rev. 9–109(c)(8). What is not clear, however, is whether the assignment of rights under an annuity set up to implement the structured settlement of a tort claim is a claim arising in tort or under a policy of insurance. Revised Article 9 is not clear on this, and the cases have disagreed. Compare West Loop Sav. Ass'n v. Knostman, 1992 WL 511854 (S.D.Tex.1992), aff'd, 993 F.2d 90 (5th Cir.1993) (claims under annuities not excluded) with Wonsey v. Life Ins. Co. of North America, 32 F.Supp.2d 939, 942 (E.D.Mich.1998) (annuity is a policy of insurance).

(3) The *Owen* court ducks the Article 9 issue because it could achieve the same result, enforcement of the assignment, under the common law and the Restatement. Do you agree? If you were the company promising to pay, how would you redraft the contract to insure that assignments were prohibited?

(4) *The Feds Step In.* The service of paying money today in exchange for the assignment of future structured-settlement payments is referred to as "factoring." Congress in 2002 imposed a tax equal to 40 percent of the amount paid by the factoring company "on any person who acquires directly or indirectly structured settlement-payment rights" unless approval is first obtained from a state court that has determined the transaction is in the best interests of the person who wants to sell. See 26 U.S.C. 5891 (2002).

Continental Purchasing Co. v. Van Raalte Co.

Supreme Court of New York, Appellate Division, 1937.
251 App.Div. 151, 295 N.Y.S. 867.

■ EDGCOMB, JUSTICE. This action is brought by the plaintiff, as assignee of Ethel L. Potter, to recover from the Van Raalte Company, Inc., the employer of Mrs. Potter, the sum of $19.20, wages earned by her while employed by the company. The defendant claims exoneration from liability by reason of having paid the amount involved direct to the assignor.

It is conceded that on April 21, 1934, Mrs. Potter assigned to the plaintiff all wages, or claims for wages, salary, or commission earned, or to be earned, and all claims or demands due her from any person, firm, or corporation by whom she was employed, or who might owe her money, as security for the payment of an account which the Steckler Sporting Goods Store had against her, and which account had been purchased by and assigned to the plaintiff.

This assignment, having been made prior to July 1, 1934, when section 46 was added to the Personal Property Law by chapter 738 of the Laws of that year (section 1), is not void by reason of any statutory prohibition relating to wage assignments. Neither is such transfer contrary to public policy. . . .

While the assignee of a chose in action succeeds to all the rights of the assignor, a debtor is not affected by the assignment until he has notice thereof. If he pays his indebtedness to the assignor in ignorance of the assignment, he is relieved from all liability to the assignee. He may set up against the claim of the assignee any defense acquired prior to notice which would have been available against the assignor had there been no assignment. . . .

After notice of the transfer, however, the debtor is put on his guard, and if he pays the assignor any money which, under the assignment, belongs to the assignee, or if he does anything prejudicial to the rights of the latter, he is liable for the resulting damage. . . .

No set form of notice is required. It is sufficient if such information is given the debtor as will fully inform him that the alleged assignee is the owner of the chose in action, or as will serve to put him on inquiry. . . .

Here the plaintiff protected itself against any bona fide payments made by the debtor to its employee by giving the defendant a written notice of this assignment on September 12, 1934. Seven days later defendant acknowledged receipt of the notice, and suggested that, inasmuch as Mrs. Potter had no other income except her weekly earnings, it would be a great accommodation if a deduction of $2 per week could be made until the total amount of plaintiff's claim was paid. Plaintiff consented to this adjustment, and withdrew its formal notice. But defendant still knew of the assignment, and on six occasions during the following two months deducted $1.50 from Mrs. Potter's wages, and forwarded the same to the plaintiff. This arrangement was discontinued after November 20th. Plaintiff then gave defendant another formal notice of the assignment, and demanded payment direct to it of the wages due Mrs. Potter, and called attention to the fact that any sums paid to the employee would not relieve the defendant from its obligation to the plaintiff. With full knowledge that the plaintiff was entitled to receive Mrs. Potter's wages, defendant has chosen to pay them to Mrs. Potter. In so doing, defendant acted at its peril.

Defendant claims immunity from liability in this action because of the fact that neither the original assignment, nor a copy thereof, was ever filed with or exhibited to it. This defense has found favor in the courts below. Such a requirement is not necessary to render a debtor liable to the assignee of a chose in action for the failure to pay him a debt owed to the assignor. Especially is that so where, as here, no such demand or request has ever been made. . . . The cases relied upon by the respondent do not lay down any different rule.

Here a full and complete notice of the assignment was given to the defendant, and a demand was made that the assignor's wages be paid to the plaintiff. Defendant never questioned the existence or validity of the transfer, nor asked for any additional proof thereof. On the contrary, it acknowledged its validity, and made six separate payments to the assignee, totaling $9, in reliance thereon. Later it utterly ignored plaintiff's rights in the premises, and paid the assignor her wages as they became due, notwithstanding the fact that it knew this money belonged to the plaintiff. Its only excuse for so doing was the fact that Mrs. Potter was receiving aid from a local charitable organization, and that the matter had been referred to that organization for a decision. Under these circumstances, defendant cannot escape its liability to the plaintiff because it paid Mrs. Potter's wages to her.

For the reasons stated, we think that the judgments of the City Court of Dunkirk, and of the County Court of Chautauqua county, should be reversed with costs, and that judgment should be ordered in favor of the plaintiff for the sum of $19.20, with interest thereon from the 21st day of November, 1934. * * *

NOTES

(1) If, after April 21, 1934, the defendant, without notice of the assignment, had paid Ethel Potter, would the plaintiff here have been successful against the defendant? Does the answer depend upon whether the assignment was operative at that time or when notification was given to the obligor?

(2) *Modification of Contract After Notification of Assignment.* Since the obligor, after notice of the assignment, cannot secure a discharge by payment thereafter to the assignor, it would seem to follow as well that one cannot thereafter be discharged by obtaining a release from the assignor, or by executing an accord and satisfaction or a novation. One must get a discharge from the assignee. See Corbin § 894. It also follows that the original parties could not then modify the contract. The consent of the assignee would be essential to a modification. It has been argued that this may be commercially

inconvenient, especially where a prime contractor must make adjustments with subcontractors as the work progresses.

This policy is continued and elaborated in Rev. 9–406(a),(b). What if an account debtor continues to make payments to the assignor after receiving a proper notice? Unless the assignee knows and does not object, the obligation is not discharged. Rev. 9–406(a), last sentence.

(3) *Counterclaims and Set–Offs.* Clearly the assignee must be concerned about defenses available to the obligor, such as fraud, failure of consideration and the like. But account must also be taken of possible counterclaims and set-offs which the obligor might assert against the assignor, whether growing out of the original transaction or collateral transactions. Pre-revision 9–318(1) provided: "Unless an account debtor has made an enforceable agreement not to assert defenses or claims arising out of a sale as provided in Section 9–206 the rights of an assignee are subject to (a) all the terms of the contract between the account debtor and assignor and any defense or claim arising therefrom; and (b) any other defense or claim of the account debtor against the assignor which accrues before the account debtor receives notification of the assignment." This policy is continued and expanded in Rev. 9–404. See Restatement (Second) § 336.

(4) *Assignor's Liability to Assignee.* If the assignee, when suing the obligor, is met with a valid defense, he or she must then consider the possibility of recourse against the assignor. Even absent the assignor's promise or representation that no defense was available, thereby furnishing the basis for an express warranty, the assignee may still be successful. "[T]he assignor of a chose in action, for a valuable consideration, impliedly warrants to the assignee that the chose assigned is a valid, subsisting obligation in his favor against the debtor to the extent to which it purports to be such, and as a general rule the assignor of a claim impliedly warrants that it is valid and that the debtor or obligator is liable to pay it, and if in fact the claim is invalid, the assignor is liable to the assignee for the amount paid for the assignment." Friedman v. Schneider, 238 Mo.App. 778, 186 S.W.2d 204, 206 (1945). See Corbin § 904; Williston § 445. It will be noted that an assignor does not warrant that the obligor is solvent or will perform the obligation. Restatement (Second) § 333(2).

This points out a significant difference between assignment and negotiation. Unless otherwise specified in the instrument, the indorser of a negotiable note dishonored by the maker is obliged to pay the amount due on the instrument to a person "entitled on the instrument." UCC 3–415(a). In addition to this liability, the indorser, if a transferor of the instrument, gives the warranties stated in UCC 3–416. For more differences between assignment and negotiation, see the Comment infra at 1096.

(5) *Priority of Successive Assignees of the Same Right.* Suppose that AR assigned a contract right against D to AE#1 for value. Later, AR assigned the same contract right to AE#2, who takes for value and without notice. AE#2 notified D of the assignment but AE#1 did not. When the debt is due, both AE#1 and AE#2 demand full payment from D. Who should D pay? Put differently, which assignee should have priority?

American courts have rejected the English rule that priority goes to the assignee who first notified the debtor. See, e.g., Salem Trust Co. v. Manufacturers' Finance Co., 264 U.S. 182, 44 S.Ct. 266, 68 L.Ed. 628 (1924). Unless modified by statute, priority goes to the assignee whose enforceable assignment is first in time unless the second assignee, in good faith and without reason to know of the prior assignment, "gives value and obtains (i) payment or satisfaction of the obligation, (ii) judgement against the obligor, (iii) a new contract with the obligor by novation, or (iv) possession of a writing of a type customarily accepted as a symbol or as evidence of the right assigned." Restatement (Second) § 342. See Murray § 142. See, generally, Axelrod, *Successive Assignments—Conflicting Priorities,* 14 U.Dayton L. Rev. 295 (1989).

Under UCC Article 9, however, priority usually goes to the first assignee or purchaser of accounts to perfect a security interest in the accounts by filing a financing statement. See Pre-revision 9–312; Rev. 9–322. The first to file has priority even though he or she knows that there is an assignment earlier in time.

Comment: A Comparison of the Assignment Process and the Negotiation Process

In the assignment process the assignor transfers a contract right to the assignee. The assignor's right of performance from the obligor is thereby extinguished, in whole or in part depending upon whether it is a total or partial assignment, and the assignee acquires a right to such performance. Restatement (Second) § 317(1). A corollary is that the right is not somehow transformed in the process; it is subject to the same imperfections as before. Thus, if the obligor, when sued by the assignor, could have successfully asserted a defense (e.g., lack of consideration), this defense is also available against the assignee. Restatement (Second) § 336. If, however, the obligor has entered into an enforceable agreement with the obligee not to assert defenses against an assignee, the assignee takes the assignment free of those defenses. See Rev. 9–403(b), stating the conditions for enforceability.

By contrast, a holder in due course of a negotiable instrument may obtain in the negotiation process a right superior to that of the one from whom he or she receives the instrument. One does not simply "step into the shoes" of the other. The extraordinary legal effect given to a negotiable instrument derives from the law merchant and is carefully delineated by statute. The writing must meet certain formal requirements, UCC 3–104, and must be transferred in prescribed ways. UCC 3–202. If the one to whom the instrument is transferred qualifies as a holder in due course, UCC 3–304, he or she takes the instrument free of many defenses. UCC 3–305. For example, in exchange for merchandise, the maker executes and delivers to the payee a negotiable promissory note for the purchase price. The payee indorses the note and delivers it to a third person, the holder, in repayment of an outstanding loan. Even though the maker is able to assert against the payee a number of ordinary defenses, such as lack or failure of consideration, the maker is not able to so defend against one who is a holder in due course.

The emergence in our legal system of the concept of negotiability has been of inestimable value in facilitating commercial transactions. It is an important part of "the triumph of the good faith purchaser," aptly characterized as "one of the most dramatic episodes in our legal history." Grant Gilmore, *The Commercial Doctrine of Good Faith Purchase,* 63 Yale L.J. 1057 (1954). A high-energy economic system is dependent upon the free flow of commerce; accordingly, impediments to voluntary exchange should be kept to a minimum. Allowing purchaser of a right evidenced by a negotiable note to prevail, despite the availability of so-called "personal defenses" of the maker, enhances the value of negotiable paper.

It is now, however, an "unfair or deceptive act or practice" under Section 5 of the Federal Trade Commission Act for a seller who ordinarily sells or leases goods or services to consumers to enter into a consumer credit contract which does not contain the following provision in at least ten point, bold face type:

ANY HOLDER OF THIS CONSUMER CREDIT CONTRACT IS SUBJECT TO ALL CLAIMS AND DEFENSES WHICH THE DEBTOR COULD ASSERT AGAINST THE SELLER OF GOODS OR SERVICES OBTAINED PURSUANT HERETO OR WITH THE PROCEEDS HEREOF. RECOVERY HEREUNDER BY THE DEBTOR SHALL NOT EXCEED AMOUNTS PAID BY THE DEBTOR HEREUNDER.

16 C.F.R. § 433.2. See Sturley, *The Legal Impact of the Federal Trade Commission's Holder in Due Course Notice on a Negotiable Instrument: How Clever Are the Rascals at the FTC?,* 68 N.C.L.Rev. 953 (1990).

(B) DELEGATION OF DUTIES

To what extent can one party delegate the duty of performance created by a contract to a third party without the consent of the other party? For example, can an artist delegate a contractual duty to paint a portrait to another artist without consent of the client? If so (and this is highly dubious), suppose the other artist fails to paint. What, if anything, is the liability of the delegator?

The test for delegation under Restatement (Second) § 318 and UCC 2–210(1) turns crucially on the phrase "substantial interest":

Restatement (Second) § 318: "(1) An obligor can properly delegate the performance of his duty to another unless the delegation is contrary to public policy or the terms of his promise. (2) Unless otherwise agreed, a promise requires performance by a particular person only to the extent that the obligee has a substantial interest in having that person perform or control the acts promised. (3) Unless the obligee agrees otherwise, neither delegation of performance nor a contract to assume the duty made with the obligor by the person delegated discharges any duty or liability of the delegating obligor."

UCC 2–210(1): "A party may perform his duty through a delegate unless otherwise agreed or unless the other party has a substantial interest in having his original promisor perform or control the acts required by the

contract. No delegation of performance relieves the party delegating of any
duty to perform or any liability for breach." See Rev. 2–210(2) preserving
and elaborating this principle.

Sally Beauty Co. v. Nexxus Products Co., Inc.

United States Court of Appeals, Seventh Circuit, 1986.
801 F.2d 1001.

■ CUDAHY, CIRCUIT JUDGE.

Nexxus Products Company ("Nexxus") entered into a contract with
Best Barber & Beauty Supply Company, Inc. ("Best"), under which Best
would be the exclusive distributor of Nexxus hair care products to barbers
and hair stylists throughout most of Texas. When Best was acquired by and
merged into Sally Beauty Company, Inc. ("Sally Beauty"), Nexxus cancelled the agreement. Sally Beauty is a wholly-owned subsidiary of Alberto–
Culver Company ("Alberto–Culver"), a major manufacturer of hair care
products and a competitor of Nexxus. Sally Beauty claims that Nexxus
breached the contract by cancelling; Nexxus asserts by way of defense that
the contract was not assignable or, in the alternative, not assignable to
Sally Beauty. The district court granted Nexxus' motion for summary
judgment, ruling that the contract was one for personal services and
therefore not assignable. We affirm on a different theory—that this contract could not be assigned to the wholly-owned subsidiary of a direct
competitor under section 2–210 of the Uniform Commercial Code. * * *

[The court held that the sales aspect of the distributorship dominated and
that the transaction was governed by Article 2 of the UCC.]

The fact that this contract is considered a contract for the sale of goods
and not for the provision of a service does not, as Sally Beauty suggests,
mean that it is freely assignable in all circumstances. The delegation of
performance under a sales contract (whether in conjunction with an
assignment of rights, as here, or not) is governed by UCC section 2–210(1),
Tex.Bus. & Com.Code § 2–210(a) (Vernon 1968). The UCC recognizes that
in many cases an obligor will find it convenient or even necessary to relieve
himself of the duty of performance under a contract, see Official Comment
1, UCC § 2–210 ("[T]his section recognizes both delegation of performance
and assignability as normal and permissible incidents of a contract for the
sale of goods."). The Code therefore sanctions delegation except where the
delegated performance would be unsatisfactory to the obligee: "A party
may perform his duty through a delegate unless otherwise agreed to or
unless the other party has a substantial interest in having his original
promisor perform or control the acts required by the contract." UCC § 2–
210(1), Tex.Bus. & Com.Code Ann. § 2–210(a) (Vernon 1968). Consideration is given to balancing the policies of free alienability of commercial
contracts and protecting the obligee from having to accept a bargain he did
not contract for.

We are concerned here with the delegation of Best's duty of performance under the distribution agreement, as Nexxus terminated the agreement because it did not wish to accept Sally Beauty's substituted performance."* Only one Texas case has construed section 2–210 in the context of a party's delegation of performance under an executory contract. In *McKinnie v. Milford*, 597 S.W.2d 953 (Tex.Civ.App.1980, writ ref'd, n.r.e.), the court held that nothing in the Texas Business and Commercial Code prevented the seller of a horse from delegating to the buyer a pre-existing contractual duty to make the horse available to a third party for breeding. '[I]t is clear that Milford [the third party] had no particular interest in not allowing Stewart [the seller] to delegate the duties required by the contract. Milford was only interested in getting his two breedings per year, and such performance could only be obtained from McKinnie [the buyer] after he bought the horse from Stewart.' Id. at 957. In *McKinnie*, the Texas court recognized and applied the UCC rule that bars delegation of duties if there is some reason why the non-assigning party would find performance by a delegate a substantially different thing than what he had bargained for.

In the exclusive distribution agreement before us, Nexxus had contracted for Best's "best efforts" in promoting the sale of Nexxus products in Texas. UCC § 2–306(2), Tex.Bus. & Com.Code Ann. § 2–306(b) (Vernon 1968), states that "[a] lawful agreement by either buyer or seller for exclusive dealing in the kind of goods concerned imposes unless otherwise agreed an obligation by the seller to use best efforts to supply the goods and by the buyer to use best efforts to promote their sale." This implied promise on Best's part was the consideration for Nexxus' promise to refrain from supplying any other distributors within Best's exclusive area. See Official Comment 5, UCC § 2–306. It was this contractual undertaking which Nexxus refused to see performed by Sally.

In ruling on Nexxus' motion for summary judgment, the district court noted: "Unlike Best, Sally Beauty is a subsidiary of one of Nexxus' direct competitors. This is a significant distinction and in the court's view, it raises serious questions regarding Sally Beauty's ability to perform the distribution agreement in the same manner as Best." Memorandum Opinion and Order at 7. In Berliner Foods Corp. v. Pillsbury Co., 633 F.Supp. 557 (D.Md.1986), the court stated the same reservation more strongly on similar facts. Berliner was an exclusive distributor of Haagen–Dazs ice cream when it was sold to Breyer's, manufacturer of a competing ice cream line. Pillsbury Co., manufacturer of Haagen–Dazs, terminated the distributorship and Berliner sued. The court noted, while weighing the factors for

---

* If this contract is assignable, Sally Beauty would also, of course, succeed to Best's rights under the distribution agreement. But the fact situation before us must be distinguished from the assignment of contract rights that are no longer executory (e.g., the right to damages for breach or the right to payment of an account), which is considered in UCC section 2–210(2), Tex.Bus. & Com.Code Ann. § 2–210(b) (Vernon 1968), and in several of the authorities relied on by appellants. The policies underlying these two situations are different and, generally, the UCC favors assignment more strongly in the latter. See UCC § 2–210(2) (non-executory rights assignable even if agreement states otherwise).

and against a preliminary injunction, that "it defies common sense to require a manufacturer to leave the distribution of its products to a distributor under the control of a competitor or potential competitor." Id. at 559–60.* We agree with these assessments and hold that Sally Beauty's position as a wholly-owned subsidiary of Alberto–Culver is sufficient to bar the delegation of Best's duties under the agreement. * * *

At oral argument, Sally Beauty argued that the case should go to trial to allow it to demonstrate that it could and would perform the contract as impartially as Best. It stressed that Sally Beauty is a "multi-line" distributor, which means that it distributes many brands and is not just a conduit for Alberto–Culver products. But we do not think that this creates a material question of fact in this case.** When performance of personal services is delegated, the trier merely determines that it is a personal services contract. If so, the duty is *per se* nondelegable. There is no inquiry into whether the delegate is as skilled or worthy of trust and confidence as the original obligor: the delegate was not bargained for and the obligee need not consent to the substitution. * * * The judgment of the district court is AFFIRMED.

■ POSNER, CIRCUIT JUDGE, dissenting.

[Judge Posner could find no support for the Majority's *per se* rule in either the UCC or the case law.]

My brethren find this a simple case—as simple (it seems) as if a lawyer had undertaken to represent the party opposing his client. But notions of conflict of interest are not the same in law and in business, and judges can go astray by assuming that the legal-services industry is the pattern for the entire economy. The lawyerization of America has not reached that point. Sally Beauty, though a wholly owned subsidiary of Alberto–Culver, distributes "hair care" supplies made by many different companies, which so far as appears compete with Alberto–Culver as vigorously as Nexxus does. * * *

Selling your competitor's products, or supplying inputs to your competitor, sometimes creates problems under antitrust or regulatory law—but only when the supplier or distributor has monopoly or market power and uses it to restrict a competitor's access to an essential input or to the market for the competitor's output. . . . There is no suggestion that Alberto–Culver has a monopoly of "hair care" products or Sally Beauty a monopoly of distributing such products, or that Alberto–Culver would ever have ordered Sally Beauty to stop carrying Nexxus products. Far from

* The effort by the dissent to distinguish *Berliner* merely because the court there apparently assumed in passing that distributorship agreements were a species of personal service contracts must fail. The *Berliner* court emphasizes that the sale of a distributorship to a competitor of the supplier is by itself a wholly sufficient reason to terminate the distributorship.

** We do not address here the situation in which the assignee is not completely under the control of a competitor. If the assignee were only a partially-owned subsidiary, there presumably would have to be fact-finding about the degree of control the competitor-parent had over the subsidiary's business decisions.

complaining about being squeezed out of the market by the acquisition, Nexxus is complaining in effect about Sally Beauty's refusal to boycott it!

How likely is it that the acquisition of Best could hurt Nexxus? Not very. Suppose Alberto–Culver had ordered Sally Beauty to go slow in pushing Nexxus products, in the hope that sales of Alberto–Culver "hair care" products would rise. Even if they did, since the market is competitive Alberto–Culver would not reap monopoly profits. Moreover, what guarantee has Alberto–Culver that consumers would be diverted from Nexxus to it, rather than to products closer in price and quality to Nexxus products? In any event, any trivial gain in profits to Alberto–Culver would be offset by the loss of goodwill to Sally Beauty; and a cost to Sally Beauty is a cost to Alberto–Culver, its parent. Remember that Sally Beauty carries beauty supplies made by other competitors of Alberto–Culver; Best alone carries "hair care" products manufactured by Revlon, Clairol, Bristol–Myers, and L'Oreal, as well as Alberto–Culver. Will these powerful competitors continue to distribute their products through Sally Beauty if Sally Beauty displays favoritism for Alberto–Culver products? Would not such a display be a commercial disaster for Sally Beauty, and hence for its parent, Alberto–Culver? * * *

Another relevant consideration is that the contract between Nexxus and Best was for a short term. Could Alberto–Culver destroy Nexxus by failing to push its products with maximum vigor in Texas for a year? In the unlikely event that it could and did, it would be liable in damages to Nexxus for breach of the implied best-efforts term of the distribution contract. Finally, it is obvious that Sally Beauty does not have a bottleneck position in the distribution of "hair care" products, such that by refusing to promote Nexxus products vigorously it could stifle the distribution of those products in Texas; for Nexxus has found alternative distribution that it prefers—otherwise it wouldn't have repudiated the contract with Best when Best was acquired by Sally Beauty.

Not all businessmen are consistent and successful profit maximizers, so the probability that Alberto–Culver would instruct Sally Beauty to cease to push Nexxus products vigorously in Texas cannot be reckoned at zero. On this record, however, it is slight. And there is no principle of law that if something happens that trivially reduces the probability that a dealer will use his best efforts, the supplier can cancel the contract. * * * At most, so far as the record shows, Nexxus may have had grounds for "insecurity" regarding the performance by Sally Beauty of its obligation to use its best efforts to promote Nexxus products, but if so its remedy was not to cancel the contract but to demand assurances of due performance. See UCC § 2–609; Official Comment 5 to § 2–306. No such demand was made.

NOTES

(1) In the assignment of an executory bilateral contract, is the "probable intention of the assignee" to assume duties as well as rights?

(2) UCC 2–210(4): "An assignment of 'the contract' or of 'all my rights under the contract' or an assignment in similar general terms is an assignment of rights and unless the language or the circumstances (as in an assignment for security) indicate the contrary, it is a delegation of performance of the duties of the assignor and its acceptance by the assignee constitutes a promise by him to perform those duties. This promise is enforceable by either the assignor or the other party to the original contract." See Continental Can Co. v. Poultry Processing, Inc., 649 F.Supp. 570, 573 (D.Me.1986) (phrase is "term of art"); Restatement (Second) § 328(1).

(3) *The Case of "All in the Family."* Tandem Productions, Inc., producer of "All in the Family," and Columbia Broadcasting System, Inc. entered into a contract covering the distribution and syndication of the series. In a "Memorandum of Agreement," it was provided that "CBS may assign its rights hereunder in full or in part to any person, firm or corporation provided, however, that no such assignment shall relieve CBS of its obligations hereunder." Later CBS purported to assign to Viacom International, Inc. the rights it possessed to distribute and syndicate television programs, including "All in the Family." Tandem maintained that this transcended the power of assignment granted by the written agreement, insisting that CBS could only assign the right to receive distribution and syndication fees called for by the contract but not relinquish or delegate obligations. Do you agree? See Viacom International, Inc. v. Tandem Productions, Inc., 526 F.2d 593 (2d Cir.1975).

SECTION 2.   THIRD PARTY BENEFICIARIES

For a consideration furnished by B (e.g., delivery of merchandise), A promises to render a performance (e.g., payment of $1,000) to T. If A refuses to abide by the commitment, may T successfully sue A for breach of contract? Have A and B conferred a contract right upon T, who was not privy to the transaction? Stated another way, is T a protected third party beneficiary of the A–B contract?

It may first be wondered why A and B would ever so agree. A's apparent purpose is the receipt of the merchandise, but what of B's? B may in this way pay a debt owed to T or may simply wish to give T the $1,000. In either situation, what objections would you expect to be asserted as a bar to recovery? That T did not pay for A's promise; i.e., did not furnish the consideration? That T was a stranger to the transaction; i.e., was not the promisee? Are these sound objections? In short, ought A and B be recognized as having the power to confer a contract right upon T?

Assuming a general willingness to recognize third party beneficiary contracts, how is a court in a particular case to determine when the third party acquires a right against the promisor? Surely one ought not be able to sue in every case where performance of the contract would somehow inure to his or her benefit. But where is the line to be drawn? What are properly to be regarded as elements of judgment?

Granted the right of a beneficiary to sue in a particular case, what is the nature of that right? What defenses can A assert against T? Moreover, after execution of the contract may A and B so act as to deprive T of any rights in the transaction?

(A) CREATION OF RIGHTS

KMART Corporation v. Balfour Beatty, Inc.

District Court of the Virgin Islands, 1998.
994 F.Supp. 634.

■ MOORE, CHIEF JUDGE.

This matter is before the Court on motion of defendant Balfour Beatty Incorporated ["BBI"] to dismiss on the basis that plaintiff, KMART Corporation ["KMART"] is not an intended third-party beneficiary of a construction contract ["contract"] between BBI and the plaintiff's landlord, Tutu Park Ltd. ["TPL"]. In the event this Court denies the motion and holds that plaintiff is a third-party beneficiary of the contract, BBI has requested that the action be stayed pending enforcement of the contract's arbitration clause. The Court has diversity jurisdiction in this case. . . .

I. FACTS

In January of 1992, BBI entered into a contract with TPL for the design and construction of a shopping center in St. Thomas. In September of 1995, the roof of the shopping center was damaged by the winds accompanying Hurricane Marilyn.

KMART Corporation was one of the tenants of the shopping center. Contending that it is a third-party beneficiary of the construction contract, plaintiff instituted this action in August, 1997, alleging breach of contract and negligence.

For its part, KMART points out that a number of provisions in the relevant documents indicate that the parties intended to convey a benefit to KMART. The specifications for the construction as described in defendant Bentley Engineers & Architects documentation ["Bentley Specifications"] call for the construction schedules to comply with KMART's requirements. (*Bentley Specifications,* ¶ 1.04A3). The drawings made in the design phase of performance were to be submitted to KMART. (*Id.* ¶ 1.04A4.) Warranties of work performed by defendant and its subcontractors were to be executed in KMART's favor and submitted directly to KMART. (*Id.* ¶ 2.01B.)

II. APPLICATION OF LAW AND FACT

BBI asserts that, because it is not a party to the construction contract, KMART may not claim relief under the agreement and moves to dismiss for failure to state a claim under Fed.R.Civ.P. 12(b)(6). In considering such a motion, the Court is constrained to view all factual allegations in KMART's amended complaint as true and to give it the benefit of every reasonable inference. . . . BBI further prays that, if the Court should find KMART to be a party to the contract, the instant litigation should be stayed pending arbitration as mandated in the contract. The Court will address each of defendant's motions in turn.

In sum, the Court finds that KMART is indeed a third-party beneficiary to the contract and that, as such, KMART is bound by the contract's terms to submit its claims to arbitration.

A. KMART's Standing As A Third–Party Beneficiary

Section 302 of the Restatement (Second) of Contracts ["Restatement"] provides a blueprint for determining whether or not a party is an intended third-party beneficiary.*

(1) Unless otherwise agreed between promisor and promisee, a beneficiary of a promise is an intended beneficiary if recognition of a right to performance in the beneficiary is appropriate to effectuate the intention of the parties** and either:

(a) the performance of the promise will satisfy an obligation of the promisee to pay money to the beneficiary; or

(b) the circumstances indicate that the promisee intends to give the beneficiary the benefit of the promised performance.

(2) An incidental beneficiary is a beneficiary who is not an intended beneficiary.

An intended beneficiary acquires a right under the contract. *Id.* § 304 ("A promise in a contract creates a duty in the promisor to any intended beneficiary to perform the promise, and the intended beneficiary may enforce the duty."). An incidental beneficiary does not. *Id.* § 315 ("An incidental beneficiary acquires by virtue of the promise no right against the promisor or the promisee."). Promises to render performances other than the payment of money require some expression of an intent by the parties to give the benefit of performance to the beneficiary. *Id.* § 304 cmt. c.***

In a 1985 case construing the Restatement (First) of Contracts, a Maryland court found that "one is a[n] [intended] beneficiary when 'performance of the promise will satisfy an actual or supposed or asserted duty of the promisee to the beneficiary.' " *District Moving & Storage Co., Inc. v. Gardiner & Gardiner, Inc.,* 63 Md.App. 96 (1985). In *District Moving,* the landlord owed a contractual duty under a lease to provide the putative third-party beneficiary with a building.

---

* Absent local law to the contrary, the Restatements of Law will control. V.I.Code Ann. tit. 1 § 4 (1994).

** The Restatement (Second) abandons the familiar dichotomy of donee and creditor beneficiary used in the earlier Restatement because, according to the commentary the terms, "carry overtones of obsolete doctrinal difficulties." *Restatement (Second) of Contracts,* ch. 14 Introductory Note (1981). Any beneficiary that acquires rights under a contract, whether a donee or creditor beneficiary according to the first Restatement, is an intended beneficiary according to the Restatement (Second).

*** In the older cases involving construction contracts, courts generally denied recovery. *See,* E. Allen Farnsworth, *Contracts* § 10.4 at 756–57 (2d ed.1990). However, the modern trend seems to countenance expanded recognition of third-party beneficiary status. *Id.* Such appears to be the case in this circuit. *See, e.g., Pierce Assoc. v. Nemours Foundation,* 865 F.2d 530 (3d Cir.1988) (applying Delaware law).

Just as the Maryland court had no difficulty finding the tenant was a third-party beneficiary to the construction contract, so does this Court find that KMART was a third-party beneficiary of the construction contract between BBI and TPL. The contractual duty of performance owed by BBI to its promisee, TPL, would satisfied TPL's duty to it's beneficiary, KMART. KMART, then, is a third party beneficiary to the construction contract between BBI and TPL.

Continuing to bear in mind the requirement to construe factual issues in favor of the non-movant, the language of the contract at issue here also conveys an intent among the contracting parties to bestow a benefit upon KMART. The contract's specifications call for construction schedules to comport with KMART's requirements. The drawings to be used were to be submitted to KMART and all warranties were to be executed in KMART's favor. All of these facts support a conclusion that BBI and TPL entered into the construction contract to erect a building for the benefit of KMART.

BBI asserts that the following contract provision specifically excludes KMART as a third-party beneficiary:

> 2.2.9 The Design/Builder warrants **to the Owner** ... that the Work will be of good quality, free from faults and defects, and in conformance with the Contract Documents. (emphasis added).

The contract defines "owner" as TPL. Even if this paragraph could be read as BBI urges, the inclusion of provisions in the contract specifications contemplating KMART's active participation in design and construction of the building creates an ambiguity which, at this stage of the litigation, must be resolved in the plaintiff's favor.

Other common law courts have applied different standards, principally two, to determine whether or not the parties to a contract intended to benefit one claiming third-party beneficiary status. Some attempt to determine if the performance of the contract runs to the putative third-party beneficiary. (*See,* John D. Calamari and Joseph M. Perillo, *Contracts,* § 17.3 at 695 (3d ed.1987).) Others, and the increasingly more modern view, hold that it is enough that the promisor (here, BBI) understood that the promisee had an intent to benefit the third party (here, KMART). (*See, id.* at 696, citing *Lucas v. Hamm,* 56 Cal.2d 583 (1961).)

Under either formulation, the result is the same. Given the lease plaintiff had with TPL, and the extensive involvement of KMART in the specifications for the construction of the space, there is little question but that the performance in this case, construction of the building, ran directly to the benefit of the plaintiff. The promisor, BBI, clearly had notice that its promisee, TPL, had an intent to benefit KMART.

For all these reasons the Court concludes that KMART is an intended third-party beneficiary to the BBI–TPL contract. KMART can enforce such rights as it may have under that contract per Restatement § 304.

B.   BBI's Motion For Stay To Enforce Arbitration

The Court can quickly dispense with the defendant's motion for stay to enforce arbitration. Here, BBI is on solid ground.

As BBI points out in its reply memorandum, the very case KMART, and ultimately, this Court, relies upon as authority that it is entitled to third party beneficiary status held that the third-party beneficiary was bound by the contract's arbitration clause. Then too, defendant reminds the Court of its dictum that a "third-party beneficiary cannot accept the benefits and avoid the burdens or limitations of a contract; the third-party beneficiary assumes the legal obligations as well as the rights of its promisee." *American Fidelity Fire Insurance Co. v. Construcciones Werl, Inc.,* 407 F.Supp. 164, 182 (D.Vi.1975). * * *

The Court holds that the contract at issue in this motion contains an arbitration clause sufficient to require the submission of the plaintiff's dispute to arbitration.

NOTES

(1) *Restatement Categories.* The first Restatement defined contract beneficiaries as follows in § 133(1): "Where performance of a promise in a contract will benefit a person other than the promisee that person is * * * (a) a donee beneficiary if it appears from the terms of the promise in view of the accompanying circumstances that the purpose of the promisee in obtaining the promise of all or part of the performance thereof is to make a gift to the beneficiary or to confer upon him a right against the promisor to some performance neither due nor supposed or asserted to be due from the promisee to the beneficiary; (b) a creditor beneficiary if no purpose to make a gift appears from the terms of the promise in view of the accompanying circumstances and performance of the promise will satisfy an actual or supposed or asserted duty of the promisee to the beneficiary, * * * (c) an incidental beneficiary if neither the facts stated in Clause (a) nor those stated in Clause (b) exist."

(2) *The Concept of Privity and the Third Party Beneficiary Contract.* The third party beneficiary contract involves judicial recognition of the power of contracting parties to vest rights in others. The recognition of the power to assign a contract right both paves the way for validation of third party beneficiary contracts and enables one to properly analyze the so-called lack of privity objection. "Privity, in the law of contracts, is merely the name for a legal relation arising from right and obligation. For example, A, by contract, secures a promise from B. A may transfer his right of enforcement to C. C thereby succeeds to A's right of action, and, in consequence, comes into the relationship with A and B which we call privity of contract. Instead of waiting to do it by assignment, A may, at the outset, extract from B the same promise in favor of C." *La Mourea v. Rhude,* 209 Minn. 53, 56, 295 N.W. 304, 307 (1940).

(3) *Weakening Resistance.* For over a century Massachusetts resisted the movement in this country recognizing third party beneficiary contracts. In 1979, however, the Supreme Judicial Court of Massachusetts joined ranks with the other jurisdictions in a forthright opinion that acknowledged "the hand-

writing has long been on the wall." Choate, Hall & Stewart v. SCA Services, Inc., 378 Mass. 535, 546, 392 N.E.2d 1045, 1051 (1979).

Third party claimants have not fared as well in other common law jurisdictions. For example, despite the initiative in some early cases, the English courts, since at least the middle of the nineteenth century, have rejected third party recovery. Tweddle v. Atkinson (1861) 1.B. & S. 393. The courts have, however, managed to fashion various "exceptions," so as to allow recovery in certain situations. See G. H. Treitel, The Law of Contract 594–618 (10th ed. 1999) (discussing inter alia the Contracts (Rights of Third Parties) Bill of 1998). For a discussion of Canadian resistance, see Comment, 59 Can.B.Rev. 549 (1981).

Johnson v. Holmes Tuttle Lincoln–Mercury, Inc.

Court of Appeals of California, 1958.
160 Cal.App.2d 290, 325 P.2d 193.

■ VALLÉE, JUSTICE. Appeal from a judgment for plaintiffs as third party beneficiaries of an oral agreement to procure public liability and property damage insurance.

The agreement is alleged to have been entered into between Holmes Tuttle Lincoln–Mercury, Inc., called defendant, and Phillip R. Caldera and his wife, Ruth, in connection with the purchase by the Calderas of a new Mercury automobile from defendant on November 23, 1953.

On December 11, 1953, about three weeks after the Calderas purchased the car, Phillip Caldera was involved in an accident with the Mercury. Plaintiffs, Willie Mae Johnson and Fletcher Jones, a passenger, were injured and Johnson's car was damaged.

Separate actions were filed by plaintiffs against Phillip Caldera. Judgments were entered May 23, 1955 in favor of plaintiff Johnson for $4,413.89, and in favor of plaintiff Jones for $2,070. These judgments remain unsatisfied.

Plaintiffs allege defendant, by its salesman Harry Rozany, had agreed with Caldera at the time the Mercury was purchased to procure "full coverage" insurance for Caldera, including public liability and property damage, for the operation of the Mercury; both Caldera and defendant understood the insurance was to be obtained for the usual term and for no less than the minimum legal limits; defendant failed to obtain the public liability and property damage insurance after Caldera had performed all of the terms of the agreement on his part. The prayer is for the amounts of the judgments obtained against Caldera with interest. In a jury trial the verdict was for plaintiffs as prayed. Defendant appeals from the judgment which followed.

On November 23, 1953 Caldera appeared with his wife, Ruth, at the showroom of defendant for the purpose of purchasing a new Mercury. One of defendant's salesmen, Harry Rozany, approached the Calderas and discussed with them the prospective purchase of a new Mercury like the one then in the showroom. After about five minutes Rozany took them to a "closing room" where terms were discussed for about an hour and the purchase consummated. The Calderas told Rozany they had a 1948 Chevrolet as a trade-in and $900 cash as a down payment. They indicated they could not afford to make payments of over $80 a month on the balance. During the discussion Caldera told Rozany he wanted "full coverage insurance," and Rozany replied, "Oh, yes you are getting it." Rozany made out the papers and sold them "another insurance," a policy by which the insurer engaged to pay the balance of the purchase price of the car in the event of the death or disability of Caldera. The premium of $2.50 to $3.00 a month was to be included in the installment payments. Rozany computed the figures in the transaction on "scratch paper." He had Caldera sign the car order and the conditional sale contract in blank. Rozany took the papers "upstairs," saying he was going to complete filling them out.

About December 2, 1953, Mrs. Caldera received by mail a copy of the conditional sale contract dated December 1, 1953, which showed fire, theft, comprehensive, and $50 deductible collision insurance thereon, but which made no reference to public liability and property damage insurance. Mrs. Caldera read only the figures. * * * Caldera first learned he had no public liability and property damage insurance after his wife went to the office of Olympic Insurance Company "to find out about the insurance." * * *

Defendant first asserts the evidence does not support the implied finding of the jury that there was a contract to procure public liability and property damage insurance between Caldera and defendant; nor does the evidence support the implied finding that plaintiffs were third party beneficiaries of a contract between Caldera and defendant. It is argued there was no consideration paid by Caldera for defendant's agreement to procure full coverage insurance, including public liability and property damage. The agreement alleged and proved was that in consideration of Caldera's purchasing the Mercury defendant would procure full coverage insurance, including public liability and property damage.

[The court found "contrary to defendant's claim" sufficient evidence of "a meeting of minds" that "full coverage" insurance meant insurance against damage cause by insured's car.]

Defendant contends plaintiffs were not third party beneficiaries. "A contract, made expressly for the benefit of a third person, may be enforced by him at any time before the parties thereto rescind it." Civ.Code, § 1559. Where one person for a valuable consideration engages with another to do some act for the benefit of a third person, and the agreement thus made has not been rescinded, the party for whose benefit the contract or promise was made, or who would enjoy the benefit of the act, may maintain an action against the promisor for the breach of his engagement. While the contract remains unrescinded, the relations of the parties are the same as though the promise had been made directly to the third party. Although the party for whose benefit the promise was made was not cognizant of it when made, it is, if adopted by him, deemed to have been made to him. He may sue on the promise. Where a promise is made to benefit a third party on the happening of a certain contingency, the third party may enforce the contract on the occurrence of that contingency.... The action by a third party beneficiary for the breach of the promisor's engagement does not rest on the ground of any actual or supposed relationship between the parties but on the broad and more satisfactory basis that the law, operating on the acts of the parties, creates the duty, establishes a privity, and implies the promise and obligation on which the action is founded....

It is not necessary that the beneficiary be named and identified as an individual; a third party may enforce a contract if he can show he is a member of a class for whose benefit it was made. ... It is no objection to the maintenance of an action by a third party that a suit might be brought also against the one to whom the promise was made....

The test for determining whether a contract was made for the benefit of a third person is whether an intent to benefit a third person appears from the terms of the contract. ... If the terms of the contract necessarily require the promisor to confer a benefit on a third person, then the contract, and hence the parties thereto, contemplate a benefit to the third person. The parties are presumed to intend the consequences of a performance of the contract. It is held that a person injured may sue on a contract for the benefit of all members of the public who are so injured since the happening of the injury sufficiently determines his identity and right of action ... * * *

There is no escape from the conclusion that the agreement between defendant and Caldera was not for the sole benefit of the latter but that it was intended to inure to the benefit of third persons who might be protected by a full coverage policy. The intent to confer a benefit on anyone to whom Caldera might become liable as a result of a hazard incident to ownership and operation of the Mercury is obvious. This is precisely what Caldera wanted as a means of obtaining a benefit to himself. It must have been in the contemplation of the parties when Rozany agreed to procure public liability and property damage insurance that injury to third persons might result from ownership and operation of the Mercury. It was reasonable for the jury to infer that Caldera, in making the agreement with defendant, desired and intended that such persons be protected in the event of an accident with the Mercury. The jury's finding that there was a third party beneficiary contract breached by defendant to plaintiffs' damage is amply supported by the record. * * *

Affirmed.

NOTES

(1) *"Donee" and "Creditor" Beneficiaries: Categorical Imperatives?* The first Restatement distinction between "creditor" and "donee" beneficiaries is not preserved in the revised Restatement. Definition of donees as recipients of a "gift promise" and creditors as recipients of "a promise to discharge the promisee's duty" arguably compels courts to restrict recovery to cases in which a "gift" or "debt" moving from promisee to third party exists in a legal or

quasi-legal sense. The creditor category is on its face limited, since it includes only third parties who either possess a legal "right ... against the promisee" presently barred by technicalities or to whom the promisee owes an "actual or supposed or asserted duty." Although the donee category is more open-ended, use of the terms "donee" and "gift" at least provides opportunities for courts to restrict recovery to cases where traditional "donative intent" is clear. See, e.g., United States v. Inorganics, Inc., 109 F.Supp. 576, 579–80 (E.D.Tenn. 1952), where the court denied relief because no "beneficial impulse" existed.

Restatement (Second) § 302 provides: "(1) Unless otherwise agreed between promisor and promisee, a beneficiary of a promise is an intended beneficiary if recognition of a right to performance in the beneficiary is appropriate to effectuate the intention of the parties and either (a) the performance of the promise will satisfy an obligation of the promisee to pay money to the beneficiary; or (b) the circumstances indicate that the promisee intends to give the beneficiary the benefit of the promised performance. (2) An incidental beneficiary is a beneficiary who is not an intended beneficiary." See, generally, Note, *Third Party Beneficiaries and the Restatement (Second) of Contracts*, 67 Cornell L.Rev. 880 (1982).

Was the desired avoidance of the old categories complete? It seems the drafters did not come up with an entirely "new" test; many courts have long employed variations on the intent theme to resolve third party beneficiary problems.

(2) *The Use, Misuse and Limitations of the "Intention to Benefit" Standard.* The "travail" experienced during the emergence of the third party beneficiary contract is mild compared to that accompanying the efforts at delineation. The task of differentiating the protected and the unprotected (or incidental) beneficiary has proven to be extraordinarily difficult.

Ostensibly the courts seek to ascertain the manifested "intention" of the contracting parties. But in the litigated cases there is rarely any clear manifestation of intention; no explicit provision is made, one way or the other, relative to rights of third persons who may in some way benefit from performance of the contract. Moreover, the emphasis upon an elusive "intention" criterion, often to the exclusion of all other considerations, precludes an analysis that is responsive to what might otherwise be regarded as appropriate policy considerations. Because of the imprecision of the intent to benefit approach, one writer maintains that "[t]he major need of third party beneficiary law is to expand the scope of inquiry and thereby bring decisions in line with both the commercial needs and policies of the market in which the parties are functioning and more general concepts of equity and justice." Note, *Third Party Beneficiaries and the Intention Standard: A Search for Rational Contract Decision–Making*, 54 Va. L.Rev. 1166, 1172 (1968).

Hale v. Groce

Supreme Court of Oregon, 1987.
304 Or. 281, 744 P.2d 1289.

■ LINDE, JUSTICE.

Defendant, who is an attorney, was directed by a client to prepare testamentary instruments and to include a bequest of a specified sum to plaintiff. After the client's death, it was discovered that the gift was not included either in the will or in a related trust instrument. After an unsuccessful attempt to obtain judicial reformation of the will and trust, plaintiff brought the present action for damages against the attorney.

The complaint alleged as two separate claims, first, that defendant was negligent in a number of particulars and, second, that he failed to carry out a contractual promise to his client, the decedent, which the decedent had intended specifically for the benefit of plaintiff. In other states plaintiffs in such cases have sometimes been allowed to recover on one or both of these theories, as negligently injured parties or as third-party beneficiaries under a contract. It is a new question in this court. * * *

We agree that the beneficiary in [this type of case] is not only a plausible but a classic "intended" third-party beneficiary of the lawyer's promise to his client within the rule of Restatement section 302(1)(b) and may enforce the duty so created, as stated id. section 304. See, e.g., Johnson v. Doughty, 236 Or. 78, 83, 385 P.2d 760 (1963), Parker v. Jeffery, 26 Or. 186, 189, 37 P. 712 (1894) (stating rule that a contract may be enforced by one for whose benefit it was intended). The promise, of course, was not that the lawyer would pay plaintiff the stipulated sum, and it is too late for the lawyer to perform the promise that he did make, but this does not preclude an action for damages for the nonperformance. In principle, such an action is available to one in plaintiff's position. * * *

[W]e reverse so much of the decision of the Court of Appeals as affirmed the dismissal of the contract claim.

NOTES

(1) *"The Assault Upon the Citadel of Privity is Proceeding in These Days Apace."* One of the most dramatic legal developments in recent decades has involved the enlargement of the rights of third parties not in "privity" with the defendant. One facet is the growing enlargement of the category of protected beneficiaries of third party beneficiary contracts. Even more spectacular has been the expansion of tort recovery by third persons. See, e.g., Prosser, *The Assault on the Citadel (Strict Liability to the Consumers)*, 69 Yale L.J. 1099 (1960); Prosser, *The Fall of the Citadel (Strict Liability to the Consumer)*, 50 Minn.L.Rev. 791 (1966). In the area of contracted-for services there has been scant recognition of strict liability to third persons, but there has been a pronounced extension of liability predicated upon the contractor's negligence in performing promised service. For example, in an attorney malpractice case, the court emphasized the special status of an attorney: "Public policy requires that the attorney exercise his position of trust and superior knowledge responsibly so as not to affect adversely persons whose rights and interests are certain and foreseeable." Heyer v. Flaig, 70 Cal.2d 223, 227, 74 Cal.Rptr. 225, 449 P.2d 161 (1969) (intended beneficiaries recovered where attorney failed to revise will in accordance with decedent's instructions). Moreover, the court pointed out that if the third parties could not recover, no one could do so.

What are the competing policy considerations? California courts have balanced the following factors: (1) the extent to which the transaction was intended to affect the plaintiff; (2) the foreseeability of harm to plaintiff; (3) the degree of certainty that plaintiff suffered injury; (4) the closeness of connection between the defendant's conduct and injuries suffered; (5) the moral blame attached to the defendant's conduct; (6) the policy of preventing future harm. Biakanja v. Irving, 49 Cal.2d 647, 650, 320 P.2d 16 (1958).

(2) *The Case of Alleged Referee Malpractice.* In a basketball game between Purdue and Iowa on March 6, 1982, James C. Bain, a referee, called a foul on an Iowa player, which resulted in free throws that gave Purdue a last-minute victory. John and Karen Gillispie operated a store, known as Hawkeye John's Trading Post, that specialized in University of Iowa sports memorabilia. Alleging that Bain's performance was below the standard of competence required of a professional referee, they sought damages for malpractice (asserting that the Iowa loss eliminated it from the Big Ten championship and destroyed a potential market for Gillispies' memorabilia touting Iowa as a Big Ten champion) and as beneficiaries of a contract between Bain and the Big 10. In rejecting both tort and contract claims, the trial judge observed: "Heaven knows what uncharted morass a court would find itself in if it were to hold that an athletic official subjects himself to liability every time he might make a questionable call. The possibilities are mind boggling." The Court of Appeals affirmed. Bain v. Gillispie, 357 N.W.2d 47 (Iowa App.1984).

(3) *The Privity Barrier and Economic Loss.* In J'Aire Corp. v. Gregory, 24 Cal.3d 799, 157 Cal.Rptr. 407, 598 P.2d 60 (1979), a contractor agreed with Owner to renovate a building. Tenant, operator of a restaurant in the building, sued Contractor, based upon alleged negligence of Contractor in delaying completion of the work and resulting in loss of business by Tenant. Applying the "special relationship" factors referred to in note 1, the court concluded: "Where the risk of harm is foreseeable, as it was in the present case, an injury to the plaintiff's economic interests should not go uncompensated merely because it was unaccompanied by any injury to his person or property." 24 Cal.3d at 805, 157 Cal.Rptr. at 411. Tenant chose to sue Contractor rather than Owner, because it "did not wish to upset its friendly relations with the building owner and thereby jeopardize the continuation of the lease arrangement." Gary Schwartz, *Economic Loss in American Tort Law: The Examples of J'Aire and of Products Liability,* 23 San Diego L.Rev. 37, 41 (1986).

The privity barrier has been lowered for tort actions, whether negligence or strict liability, where the plaintiff seeks compensation for personal injury or property damage, but, by and large, the citadel still stands where the plaintiff seeks recovery of economic loss. See, e.g., East River S.S. Corp. v. Transamerica Delaval, Inc., 476 U.S. 858, 106 S.Ct. 2295, 90 L.Ed.2d 865 (1986); For an argument that the privity defenses should be abolished in economic loss cases, see Richard E. Speidel, *Warranty Theory, Economic Loss, and the Privity Requirement: Once More Into the Void,* 67 B.U.L.Rev. 9 (1987).

(4) *Interrelationship of Third Party Beneficiary and Promissory Estoppel.* The law pertaining to promissory estoppel and to the rights of third persons to sue on contracts made for their benefit when combined has the potential for dramatic growth. Two types of situations come to mind. First, the promisor makes a promise in a contract that would not normally be regarded as being for

the third party's benefit, but the latter nonetheless relies on the promise. See Restatement § 90 (covering reliance "on the part of the promisee *or a third person*"). Second, a gratuitous promise causes the promisee to rely, and a third party claims as beneficiary of the legal relationship thereby created.

Zigas v. Superior Court

California Court of Appeal, 1981.
120 Cal.App.3d 827, 174 Cal.Rptr. 806.

■ FEINBERG, ASSOCIATE JUSTICE.

Petitioners are tenants of an apartment building at 2000 Broadway in San Francisco, which was financed with a federally insured mortgage in excess of $5 million, pursuant to the National Housing Act (12 U.S.C. § 1701 et seq.) (the Act) and the regulations promulgated thereunder (24 C.F.R. § 207 et seq.). They seek in a class action, inter alia, damages for the landlords' (real parties in interest) violation of a provision of the financing agreement which requires that the landlords charge no more than the Department of Housing and Urban Development (HUD) approved schedule of rents. The trial court has sustained demurrers without leave to amend to 5 causes of action of 15 alleged, apparently on the ground that there is no right in the tenants to enforce the provisions of an agreement between their landlords and the federal government.

Petitioners allege that their landlords were required under their contract with HUD to file a maximum rental schedule with HUD and to refrain from charging more than those rents without the prior approval of the Secretary of HUD. Petitioners further allege that real parties are, and have been, charging rent in excess of the maximums set out in the rental schedule; the complaint avers that real parties have collected excessive rents and fees in an amount exceeding $2 million.

In addition to sustaining demurrers as to the third-party causes of action, the trial court granted real parties' motion to strike all references to the Act, the regulations promulgated thereunder, and the terms of the agreement between HUD and real parties. It is these orders sustaining the demurrers and granting the motion to strike that petitioners seek to have set aside. * * *

At this juncture, we conclude as follows: Granted that the National Housing Act does not create a *federal* statutory right of action in petitioners, nevertheless, they may have standing to sue based on a cause of action under applicable state law.

We turn now to the question of whether petitioners have a cause of action under California law. * * *

California law clearly allows third-party suits for breaches of contract where no government agency is a party to the contract. (Civ.Code, § 1559.) Whether such suits are allowed when the government contracts with a private party depends upon analysis of the decisions in Shell v. Schmidt

(1954) 126 Cal.App.2d 279, and Martinez v. Socoma Companies, Inc., supra, 11 Cal.3d 394.

In *Shell*, plaintiffs sued as third-party beneficiaries to defendant's contract with the Federal Housing Authority (FHA). The contract entailed an agreement by the defendant to build homes for sale to veterans according to plans and specifications submitted by the defendant to FHA in return for which FHA gave priorities to the defendant to secure the materials necessary for the building.

In deciding that plaintiffs had standing to enforce the terms of the contract between the defendant and the FHA, the *Shell* court relied on common law principles as embodied in Civil Code section 1559, which states: "A contract, made expressly for the benefit of a third person, may be enforced by him at any time before the parties thereto rescind it." Applying this provision to the facts before it, the *Shell* court observed: "Once it is established that the relationship between the contractor and the government is contractual, it follows that veterans purchasing homes, that is, the class intended to be protected by that contract, are third party beneficiaries of that contract. As already pointed out, the statute and the regulations passed thereunder resulting in the contract were passed to aid and assist veterans and for their benefit. Purchasing veterans constitute the class intended to be benefitted, and the contract must therefore be for their benefit. (Id., 126 Cal.App.2d at p. 290.)

It is evident that petitioners are entitled to maintain a third-party cause of action under the *Shell* rationale. Real parties do not dispute the contractual nature of their relationship with HUD. And it is clear that a requirement of HUD approval of rent increases could *only* benefit the tenants.

Furthermore, even the most cursory review of the statutes and regulations which resulted in the contract in the present case leads to the conclusion that the tenants constitute the class which Congress intended to benefit. As stated in 12 United States Code section 1701t: "The Congress affirms the national goal, as set forth in section 1441 of Title 42, of 'a decent home under a suitable living environment for every American family.' " (Section 1713(b) of Title 12, United States Code, also provides, in part: *"The insurance of mortgages under this section is intended to facilitate particularly the production of rental accommodations, at reasonable rents,* ... The Secretary is, therefore, authorized ... to take action, by regulation or otherwise, which will direct the benefits of mortgage insurance hereunder primarily to those projects which make adequate provision for families with children, and *in which every effort has been made to achieve moderate rental charges."* (Emphasis added, see also 24 C.F.R. § 207.19(e)). * * *

In the subsequent case of Martinez v. Socoma Companies, Inc., supra, 11 Cal.3d 394, the court approved of the result in *Shell* but, at the same time, applied a different standard.* Plaintiffs in *Martinez* sought to enforce

---

* The *Martinez* court approved of the result in *Shell*, based upon a finding that the legislation under which the homes in *Shell* were built included a provision empowering

the terms of a contract between Socoma Companies, Inc. and the Secretary of Labor. Under this agreement, defendants received government funds in exchange for a promise to hire and train "hard core unemployed" residents of a "Special Impact Area" in East Los Angeles. Defendants failed to perform, and plaintiffs, who were residents of East Los Angeles and members of the class which the government intended to benefit, sought to recover under the contract.

In holding that the plaintiffs had no standing to sue as third-party beneficiaries, the *Martinez* court adopted a more restrictive standard than that embodied in Civil Code section 1559, choosing instead to be guided by the principles set forth in section 145 of the Restatement of Contracts: " 'A promisor bound to the United States or to a State or municipality by contract to do an act or render a service to some or all of the members of the public, is subject to no duty under the contract to such members to give compensation for the injurious consequences of performing or attempting to perform it, or of failing to do so, unless, ... *an intention is manifested in the contract,* as interpreted in the light of the circumstances surrounding its formation, *that the promisor shall compensate members of the public for such injurious consequences....*' " (Martinez v. Socoma Companies, Inc., *supra,* at pp. 401–402; Contracts, *supra,* § 145.)*

Thus, under *Martinez,* standing to sue as a third-party beneficiary to a government contract depends on the intent of the parties as manifested by the contract and the circumstances surrounding its formation. "Insofar as intent to benefit a third person is important in determining his right to bring an action under a contract, it is sufficient that the promisor must have understood that the promisee had such intent. No specific manifestation by the promisor of an intent to benefit the third person is required." (Lucas v. Hamm (1961) 56 Cal.2d 583, 591.) We therefore must determine, from the terms of the contract between HUD and real parties and the attendant circumstances, whether there was manifested an intention that petitioners be compensated in the event of real parties' nonperformance. Mindful of the rule that "[w]hen a complaint is based on a written contract which it sets out in full, a general demurrer to the complaint admits not only the contents of the instrument but also any pleaded meaning to which the instrument is reasonably susceptible." (Martinez v. Socoma Companies, Inc., supra, 11 Cal.3d at p. 400) and focusing upon the precepts of *Martinez*

---

the government to obtain payment by the contractor to the veteran purchasers for deficiencies resulting from failure to comply with specifications. (*Martinez, supra,* at p. 403, 113 Cal.Rptr. 585, 521 P.2d 841.) Thus, the intent to compensate which Restatement, Contracts, section 145 requires was present. However, the *Shell* court made no mention of section 145.

   * It has been suggested that section 145 was meant only to preclude lawsuits for *consequential* damages arising out of government contracts, because the resulting potential liability may be disproportionately burdensome in relation to the value of the promised performance. (See Rest., Contracts, *supra,* § 145, illus. 1 and 2.) Thus, the underlying rationale of section 145 is inapplicable where, as here, the money sought is not a *consequence* of the breach, it is the breach. In such a situation, standard third-party beneficiary doctrines should apply.

as to standing, we are of the view that the case falls within *Shell;* that is to say, appellants were direct beneficiaries of the contract and have standing, and not, as in *Martinez,* incidental beneficiaries without standing.

We explicate:

1.   In *Martinez,* the contract between the government and Socoma provided that if Socoma breached the agreement, Socoma would refund to the government that which the government had paid Socoma pursuant to the contract between them. Thus, it is clear in *Martinez* that it was the government that was out of pocket as a consequence of the breach and should be reimbursed therefor, not the people to be trained and given jobs. In the case at bench, as in *Shell,* the government suffered no loss as a consequence of the breach, it was the renter here and the veteran purchaser in *Shell* that suffered the direct pecuniary loss.

2.   Unlike *Martinez,* too, in the case at bench, no governmental administrative procedure was provided for the resolution of disputes arising under the agreement. Thus, to permit this litigation would in no way affect the "efficiency and uniformity of interpretation fostered by these administrative procedures." (Martinez v. Socoma Companies, Inc., supra, 11 Cal.3d at p. 402.) On the contrary, as we earlier noted, lawsuits such as this promote the federal interest by inducing compliance with HUD agreements.

3.   In *Martinez,* the court held that "To allow plaintiffs' claim would nullify the limited liability for which defendants bargained and which the Government may well have held out as an inducement in negotiating the contracts." (At p. 403.) Here, there is no "limited liability." As we shall point out, real parties are liable under the agreement, *without limitation,* for breach of the agreement.

4.   Further, in *Martinez,* the contracts "were designed not to benefit individuals as such but to utilize the training and employment of disadvantaged persons as a means of improving the East Los Angeles neighborhood." (At p. 406.) Moreover, the training and employment programs were but one aspect of a "broad, long-range objective" (*id.*) contemplated by the agreement and designed to benefit not only those to be trained and employed but also "other local enterprises and the government itself through reduction of law enforcement and welfare costs." (*Id.*) * * *

5.   Finally, we believe the agreement itself manifests an intent to make tenants direct beneficiaries, *not* incidental beneficiaries, of real parties' promise to charge no more than the HUD approved rent schedule.

Section 4(a) and 4(c) of the agreement, providing that there can be no increase in rental fees, over the approved rent schedule, without the prior approval in writing of HUD, were obviously designed to protect the tenant against arbitrary increases in rents, precisely that which is alleged to have occurred here. Certainly, it was not intended to benefit the Government as a guarantor of the mortgage.

Furthermore, the provision in section 11(d) of the agreement, authorizing the Secretary of HUD to "[a]pply to any court ... for specific performance ... , for an injunction against any violation ... or *for such other relief as may be appropriate* "(emphasis added) would entitle the secretary to seek restitution on behalf of the tenants overcharged, for such relief would surely be "appropriate." (See Porter v. Warner Co. (1946) 328 U.S. 395.) Thus, there was an intent upon the part of the government in executing the agreement with real parties, to secure the return of any rents exacted in excess of the rent schedule.

We are supported in our view by section 17 of the Agreement which specifically provides that real parties are personally liable, "(a) for funds ... of the project coming into their hands which, by the provisions [of the Agreement] *they are not entitled to retain*; and (b) for their own acts and deeds or acts and deeds of other [sic] which they have authorized in violation of the provisions [of the Agreement]." (Emphasis added.)

By the allegations of the complaint, real parties have "retained" in excess of two million ($2,000,000) dollars in violation of the Agreement. Therefore, they are liable for that sum. To whom should they be liable? To ask the question is to answer it. It is not the government from whom the money was exacted; it was taken from the tenants. Therefore, it should be returned to the tenants.

In the face of this evidence of intent to direct the benefits of mortgage insurance to the tenants of the facilities involved, real parties argue that petitioners have no standing to sue because enforcement of the agreement is vested solely in the Secretary. They point to 12 United States Code section 1731a, which empowers the Secretary to refuse the benefits of participation to any mortgagor who violates the terms of the agreement. However, section 1731a's authorization does not constitute the exclusive remedy for enforcement of the agreement by the Secretary or by third parties. As stated by the court in Shell v. Schmidt, supra, 126 Cal.App.2d at p. 287: "This fundamental purpose would, in many cases, be defeated if the statute were interpreted so as to deprive the veterans of their normal remedies to the benefit of defaulting contractors—the very class it was the purpose of the statute to protect the veterans against. It must be held, therefore, that the enumeration of remedies in the statute merely created new enumerated remedies and was not intended to and did not deprive the veterans of any action for fraud or breach of contract that they might have under general contract principles." * * *

Thus, for reasons we have set forth, appellants are entitled to maintain a third-party beneficiary action against real parties.

NOTES

(1) One writer, in commenting upon *Martinez,* underscores a particular difficulty in utilizing the "intention to benefit" standard when the Federal government is one of the contracting parties: "The relevant intent to be divined is no longer that of a single individual or entity, but rather that of an amalgam of legislative bodies, administrative agencies, and government officials—each of whom may have differing expectations and objectives with regard to the contract." Recent Cases, 88 Harv.L.Rev. 646, 651–2 (1975). Since the govern-

ment's decision to benefit a certain group through a contract is usually based on broad policy objectives, it is urged that these objectives be taken into account in determining the rights of the various beneficiaries. The author draws an analogy to the question of whether a court should imply a private right of action from a statute: "When implying a private right of action, courts have carefully considered the impact of an additional remedy in the hands of private parties on the legislative policy underlying the statute. Courts tend to imply a right of action when there is evidence that existing remedies are inadequate and that additional remedies would increase the likelihood of compliance and afford direct relief to a class which the legislature wished to protect. Strong arguments against allowing such a right arise when it would interfere with the policy goals of the legislature by imposing disproportionate liability or impinging excessively on administrative discretion." Id. at 653.

(2) *Problems: Varieties of Third Party Beneficiary Controversy.* (a) *The Case of the Ingested Birds.* A jet crashed because of the ingestion of a large number of birds swarming over the airport and an adjacent garbage dump. Are injured passengers entitled to sue as third party beneficiaries of a contract between the Federal Aviation Administration and the County under which the latter agreed "to restrict the use of land adjacent to or in the vicinity of the airport to activities and purposes compatible with normal airport operations including landing and take-off of aircraft"? See Miree v. United States, 538 F.2d 643 (5th Cir.1976).

(b) *The Case of the Striking Ferry Workers.* Union ferry workers went out on strike in violation of a collective bargaining agreement with a State agency, thereby causing a cessation of normal ferry service during a holiday weekend. Could a resort owner, who lost bookings, sue as third party beneficiary of this contract? See Burke & Thomas, Inc. v. International Organization of Masters, Mates & Pilots, 92 Wash.2d 762, 600 P.2d 1282 (1979).

(c) *The Case of the Unimproved Roads.* Developer, in order to obtain approval of subdivision plat, agreed with County to construct certain road improvements. Developer failed to keep its commitment. Can lot owners in the subdivision sue as third party beneficiaries of the Developer/County contract? See Vale Dean Canyon Homeowners Association v. Dean, 100 Or.App. 158, 785 P.2d 772 (1990).

(d) *The Case of the Parking Meter Contract.* City entered into a contract with Company for the maintenance of parking meters, the contract specifying certain minimum wages and working conditions. Employees of Company seek to persuade the court that they are third party beneficiaries of this contract. Will they succeed? See Alicea v. City of New York, 145 A.D.2d 315, 534 N.Y.S.2d 983 (1988).

(e) *The Case of the Ungrateful Medical Student.* A scholarship fund agreed to pay a medical student $200 monthly during his time in medical school, in exchange for his promise to practice upon graduation in a specified area. Are the residents of the area third party beneficiaries of this contract? See Suthers v. Booker Hospital District, 543 S.W.2d 723 (Tex.Civ.App.1976).

(f) *The Case of the Cable Television Subscribers.* City granted franchise to television cable company, prescribing a rate schedule. Could subscribers bring an action as third party beneficiaries to recover damages for violation of the schedule? See Bush v. Upper Valley Telecable Co., 96 Idaho 83, 524 P.2d 1055 (1973).

(g) *The Case of the Bank's Loan Commitment.* Vendor contracts to sell land to Purchaser, conditional upon Purchaser securing loan. Bank makes the loan commitment to Purchaser and then reneges. Is Vendor an intended beneficiary of the Bank–Purchaser contract? See Khabbaz v. Swartz, 319 N.W.2d 279 (Iowa 1982).

(h) *The Case of the Undelivered Machine.* Company A, in need of a particular type of machine, contacts Company B. B learns that yet another company, Company C, owns such a machine. B asks A to examine the machine on C's premises. A does so and thereafter enters into a contract with B to buy the machine. B then contracts with C for the purchase of the machine, the contract providing that shipment is to be direct to A and the latter is to pay the freight. Later A, B and C enter into negotiations whereby the delivery date specified in the contracts is extended. Thereafter, A and B get into a dispute (on an unrelated matter) and B directs C to ship the machine to yet another party. C does so. Is A a protected beneficiary of the B/C contract? See Corrugated Paper Products, Inc. v. Longview Fibre Co., 868 F.2d 908 (7th Cir.1989).

(i) *The Case of the Federal Tax Lien.* Taxpayer underpaid federal income taxes, and the United States secured a tax lien. Thereafter, Taxpayer and his wife executed a property settlement in contemplation of their impending divorce. The agreement required the taxpayer to convey certain property to his wife, who was required, in turn, to sell the property and was authorized to retain any proceeds of sale after existing liens and mortgages were paid off. Was the United States a third party beneficiary of this agreement? See United States v. Wood, 877 F.2d 453 (6th Cir.1989).

(j) *The Case of the Pre–Paid Legal Plan.* The Fraternal Order of Police made available to "a member and his eligible dependents" a pre-paid legal plan. One of the services under the plan was described as "[d]omestic problems— including divorce, legal separation, adoption of children, change of name." A law firm servicing the plan represented a member in a divorce action. His wife also requested representation by the firm, but was refused on grounds of conflict of interest. She then retained other counsel and later claimed reimbursement from the plan for her lawyer's fees as a third party beneficiary of the contract. What result? See Baltimore City Lodge No. 3 of Fraternal Order of Police, Inc. v. Mantegna, 61 Md.App. 694, 487 A.2d 1252 (1985).

(k) *The Case of the Injured Tenant.* Was a tenant, who was injured during an electrical blackout, an intended beneficiary of contract between electric company and landlord? See Shubitz v. Consolidated Edison Co., 59 Misc.2d 732, 301 N.Y.S.2d 926 (1969). Cf. Koch v. Consolidated Edison Co., 62 N.Y.2d 548, 479 N.Y.S.2d 163, 468 N.E.2d 1 (1984) (suit by city and public benefit corporations to recover damages allegedly sustained from utility's gross negligence that caused citywide blackout).

(*l*) *The Case of the Stranded Motorist.* An oil company had a contract with the New York State Thruway Authority, under which it had the exclusive right to service cars on the thruway. The company promised to provide roadside automobile service to disabled vehicles within thirty minutes from the time called. The decedent's car had a flat tire at about 3:00 P.M. About an hour later a state trooper stopped by and radioed a request for assistance to the oil company. Not having received any assistance by 6:00 P.M., the decedent attempted to change the tire himself. In doing so he experienced difficulty and complained of chest pains. He was taken to a hospital and died 28 days later. Was the decedent, as user of the thruway, a third party beneficiary of the contract between the oil company and the thruway authority? See Kornblut v. Chevron Oil Co., 62 A.D.2d 831, 407 N.Y.S.2d 498 (1978).

(m) *The Case of the Housing Project Tenants.* The owners of a housing project entered into a contract with the Secretary of Housing and Urban Development. One of the provisions of this "Regulatory Agreement" obligated the owners to maintain the premises in good repair and condition. Citing numerous failures to properly maintain the premises, tenants asserted rights as third party beneficiaries. What result? See Little v. Union Trust Co. of Maryland, 45 Md.App. 178, 412 A.2d 1251 (1980). Cf. Holbrook v. Pitt, 643 F.2d 1261 (7th Cir.1981) (project tenants sue for housing assistance payments under contract between owner and Department of Housing and Urban Development); Ayala v. Boston Housing Authority, 404 Mass. 689, 536 N.E.2d 1082 (1989) (tenants sue city housing authority for failing to inspect for lead paint hazards and for failing to enforce elimination of those hazards).

(n) *The Case of the Defective Appraisal.* Purchaser signed a contract to purchase certain property, conditional upon his obtaining a loan. Upon applying for a loan, a bank officer informed him that there would have to be an appraisal of the property before the loan could be approved. The purchaser paid the bank $100 for the appraisal, and the bank arranged for the defendant to do the appraisal. If the defendant-appraiser negligently failed to discover, and to disclose in his report, serious structural defects in the property, what are the purchaser's prospects of recovery? Upon what theory? See Alva v. Cloninger, 51 N.C.App. 602, 277 S.E.2d 535 (1981).

(o) *The Case of the Undelivered Body.* The children of Rozena Neal, deceased, arranged with Inman Nationwide Shipping to transport their mother's body to Alabama for burial. Inman, in turn, contracted with Republic Airlines, which, through some error, delayed the shipment. Could the children claim as third party beneficiaries of the Inman/Republic contract? See Neal v. Republic Airlines, Inc., 605 F.Supp. 1145 (N.D.Ill.1985).

(p) *The Case of the Fake Diamond Ring.* Fiance buys "diamond" ring from Jeweler and gives it to his prospective bride as an engagement ring. The ring turns out to be nothing more than "cut glass or cubic zirconia." Can she maintain a suit for breach of contract as a third party beneficiary? See Warren v. Monahan Beaches Jewelry Center, Inc., 548 So.2d 870 (Fla.App.1989).

(q) *The Case of the Infringed Trademark.* Suppose that S develops a web site for Fantasy Baseball enthusiasts and registers the domain name "Speiderman" with a domain name registrar licensed by the Internet Corporation for Assigned Names and Numbers (ICANN). As a condition to registration, S must agree to "arbitrate" any claims that the domain name is "identical or confusingly similar" to a registered trademark of a third person. Sure enough, the holder of the Spiderman trademark files a claim and seeks to have the domain name Speiderman canceled. S objects, arguing that since the trademark holder did not sign a written agreement to arbitrate it cannot compel S to arbitrate.

Does the trademark holder qualify as an intended beneficiary of the contract between S and ICANN? See Collins v. International Dairy Queen, 2 F.Supp.2d 1465 (M.D.Ga.1998) (non-signatory of arbitration clause an intended beneficiary). But see E. I. DuPont de Nemours v. Rhone Poulenc Fiber, 269 F.3d 187, 195–99 (3d Cir.2001) (no intended beneficiary on facts). For an overview, see Richard E. Speidel, *ICANN Domain Name Dispute Resolution, the Revised Uniform Arbitration Act, and the Limitations of Modern Arbitration Law*, 6 J. of Small & Emerging Bus. L. 167 (2002).

(B) NATURE OF RIGHTS

Tweeddale v. Tweeddale

Supreme Court of Wisconsin, 1903.
116 Wis. 517, 93 N.W. 440.

[The defendant, Daniel Tweeddale, in exchange for consideration received from his mother, gave the latter a bond for support secured by a mortgage on certain land. The bond indebtedness was $1,350, conditioned, among other things, that in case the defendant should sell the land, $1,200 should immediately become due from him to his mother, $50 should likewise become due to his sister, and $100 to his brother, the plaintiff Edward Tweeddale. Subsequently, the defendant did sell the land, making operative the foregoing promises. The defendant made a settlement with his mother, fully discharging him of all obligation to her, and she released the mortgage. The plaintiff brought a foreclosure action, insisting that such release did not bar him from recovery. Neither the plaintiff nor his sister knew that the bond and mortgage made any provision for them until after the mortgage was discharged. The trial court held that plaintiff had no cause of action, and ordered the complaint dismissed.]

■ MARSHALL, J. * * * [T]he turning point in the case, in the mind of the circuit judge, we apprehend, was that the beneficiaries did not know of the agreement and did not accept the same or in any way become parties thereto till their mother, with the consent of Daniel Tweeddale, rescinded the transaction. * * * Whether the benefit secured to the third person is a gift, strictly so called, or one intended, when realized, to discharge some liability of such promisee to the third person does not change the situation. It is the exchange of promises between the immediate parties, and the operation of law thereon, that binds the promisor to the third person. The idea which ruled this case,—that where a person for a consideration paid to him by another agrees to pay a sum of money to a third person, a stranger to the transaction, the latter does not thereby become possessed of the absolute right to the benefit of the promise, nor until he accepts the same in some way; and that while he is ignorant of the promise, or thereafter, at any time before he assents to the transaction, it may be rescinded,—we must admit is well supported in the books. The authorities so holding, in the main, go upon the ground that privity between parties is absolutely essential to a liability of one to another of a contractual nature, and that until the third person brings himself into privity with the one who has promised to be his debtor by at least assenting thereto, he has at least no legal right to the benefit of the promise; and that, till then, the parties to the transaction may rescind it or change it as they see fit. There is also much authority to the effect that, while the element of privity between the promisor and the third person is essential to render the promise absolutely binding upon the former, no act of the latter is necessary thereto; that the law, operating upon the acts of the parties to the transaction, creates the privity immediately upon its being consummated between them, and that neither one nor both of them can thereafter, without the third person's consent, enforce the promise. * * * It is useless to endeavor to review the authorities touching the subject before us with a view of harmonizing them upon any one single theory as to the principle upon which the liability to the third person is based or as to what are the essential elements to effect it. * * *

Without further discussion of the matter we adhere to the doctrine that where one person, for a consideration moving to him from another, promises to pay to a third person a sum of money, the law immediately operates upon the acts of the parties, establishing the essential of privity between the promisor and the third person requisite to binding contractual relations between them, resulting in the immediate establishment of a new relation of debtor and creditor, regardless of the relations of the third person to the immediate promisee in the transaction; that the liability is, as binding between the promisor and the third person as it would be if the consideration for the promise moved from the latter to the former and such promisor made the promise directly to such third person, regardless of whether the latter has any knowledge of the transaction at the time of its occurrence; that the liability being once created by the acts of the immediate parties to the transaction and the operation of the law thereon, neither one nor both of such parties can thereafter change the situation as regards the third person without his consent. It is plainly illogical to hold that immediately upon the completion of the transaction between the immediate parties thereto, the law operates upon their acts and creates the element of privity between the promisor and the third person, and at the same time to hold that such third person's status as regards the promise may be changed thereafter without his consent. The idea that privity between the promisor and the third person is necessary to render the transaction between the original parties thereto beyond the reach of either of them to revoke it, or both acting together to rescind it, springs from the supposed necessity of contractual relations between the promisor and the third person, binding upon the promisor at law. The moment such essential is established, it seems clear that such third person's right accrues and becomes absolute.

NOTES

(1) *When Should the Third Party's Right "Vest"?* "Suppose A and B enter into a contract for the benefit of C. Suppose further that C never knew of the agreement between A and B, and therefore had placed no reliance on such contract, and in nowise had changed his position. Is the contract between A and

B, the moment executed, like the laws of the Medes and Persians—no longer subject to change? * * * Is the contractual status of the parties immutably fixed? Before A and B are permitted to change or abrogate their agreement must they of necessity secure consent of the third party C, who, until then, is a stranger to the contract, and at all times a mere windfall volunteer? To hold that the moment A and B enter into an agreement for the benefit of C, that such third party C has at that moment and under all circumstances acquired an interest in the contract which is indefeasibly vested, is an affront to common sense." Stanfield v. W.C. McBride, Inc., 149 Kan. 567, 88 P.2d 1002, 1005–06 (1939).

(2) *Vesting and the Restatement.* The Restatement of Contracts, § 142, recognized the right of a donee beneficiary as vesting immediately upon execution of the contract, but the Restatement did not accord the creditor beneficiary such favorable treatment. Is there a sound basis for the differentiation? Cf. Restatement (Second) § 311: "(1) Discharge or modification of a duty to an intended beneficiary by conduct of the promisee or by a subsequent agreement between promisor and promisee is ineffective if a term of the promise creating the duty so provides. (2) In the absence of such a term, the promisor and promisee retain power to discharge or modify the duty by subsequent agreement. (3) Such a power terminates when the beneficiary, before he receives notification of the discharge or modification, materially changes his position in justifiable reliance on the promise or brings suit on it or manifests assent to it at the request of the promisor or promisee. * * *" The Supreme Court of Pennsylvania recently refused to abandon its long-held adherence to Restatement § 142 which makes a contractual gift to a donee beneficiary irrevocable upon execution of the contract, in contrast with Restatement (Second) § 311 which postpones vesting until a beneficiary "materially changes his position in justifiable reliance on the promise or brings suit on it or manifests assent to it at the request of the promisor or promisee." Biggins v. Shore, 523 Pa. 148, 565 A.2d 737 (1989).

(3) *"Acceptance" by Beneficiary.* The Indiana Supreme Court has affirmed that the right to rescind or modify a third party beneficiary contract, without the assent of the beneficiary, ceases once the contract is *accepted, adopted or acted upon* by the third party. In re Estate of Fanning, 263 Ind. 414, 333 N.E.2d 80 (1975). This has been characterized as the "majority view." Detroit Bank and Trust Co. v. Chicago Flame Hardening Co., Inc., 541 F.Supp. 1278, 1283 (N.D.Ind.1982). But what is meant by "acceptance"? Is a beneficiary's knowledge of the contract, coupled with a failure to object, sufficient to "vest" the right? *Detroit Bank*, applying Indiana law, said it was not. The court did indicate that there would be such a "presumption of acceptance" in the case of an infant beneficiary, a view not supported by the drafters of the revised Restatement. See Restatement (Second) § 311, Comment d.

*

INDEX

†

1-58778-488-2

9 781587 784880

99990